UNIVERSITY CASEBOOK SERIES®

TORT LAW AND ALTERNATIVES

CASES AND MATERIALS

TENTH EDITION

MARC A. FRANKLIN
Frederick I. Richman Professor of Law, Emeritus
Stanford University

ROBERT L. RABIN
A. Calder Mackay Professor of Law
Stanford University

MICHAEL D. GREEN
Bess & Walter Williams Professor of Law
Wake Forest University

MARK A. GEISTFELD
Sheila Lubetsky Birnbaum Professor of Civil Litigation
New York University

FOUNDATION
PRESS

University Casebook Series is a trademark registered in the U.S. Patent and Trademark Office.

© 1971, 1979, 1983, 1987, 1992, 1996, 2001, 2006 FOUNDATION PRESS
© 2011 by THOMSON REUTERS/FOUNDATION PRESS
© 2016 LEG, Inc. d/b/a West Academic
    444 Cedar Street, Suite 700
    St. Paul, MN 55101
    1-877-888-1330

Printed in the United States of America

ISBN: 978-1-63459-300-7

To Ruth's memory and to Yemima, Carol, and Janette

PREFACE TO THE TENTH EDITION

We continue our practice of sifting through new developments and cases and incorporating them into this new edition. Tort law remains a dynamic area, and we enjoy the challenge of addressing emerging issues and incorporating them into the structure of this text. As in the past, we have added substantial new material, sometimes because it reflects recent developments, but in other instances because we think that the new material offers a better pedagogical approach to understanding the current state of tort law and alternative systems. In a number of respects, our revisions reflect feedback we have received from the many users who have reached out to us. We are grateful to those who have communicated these helpful suggestions to us and welcome future comments.

We have added new principal cases, dozens of recent cases and other materials to the notes, while at the same time endeavoring to keep the number of notes manageable. Long-time users will notice that we have condensed and, in some cases, eliminated notes that appeared in the Ninth Edition. Organizationally, we have divided the causation materials into separate chapters on factual causation and proximate cause (scope of liability). We have also reorganized the previous chapter on trespass and nuisance, so that nuisance (private and public) is a stand-alone chapter, and trespass to land and property appears in the chapter on intentional harm.

These are some of the highlights of the changes in the new edition. At the same time, we have attempted to integrate these new developments with the landmark cases and doctrinal principles that give torts its distinctive character. We look forward to continue hearing from users with suggestions about how we can best meet their pedagogical goals and needs in the future.

We are grateful to Kelsey Kolb, class of 2016 at Wake Forest School of Law for superb research assistance in this Tenth Edition.

MARC A. FRANKLIN
ROBERT L. RABIN
MICHAEL D. GREEN
MARK A. GEISTFELD

Stanford, California
Winston-Salem, North Carolina
New York, New York
March 2016

ACKNOWLEDGMENTS

This revision has been substantially aided by the assistance of many colleagues, who have offered helpful suggestions since the publication of the previous edition.

We would also like to thank the authors and copyright holders of the following works, who permitted their inclusion in this book:

American Law Institute. Restatement Third, Torts: Liability for Physical and Emotional Harm, copyright 2010 & 2012. Reprinted with the permission of the American Law Institute;

American Law Institute. Restatement Third, Torts: Apportionment of Liability, copyright 2000. Reprinted with permission of the American Law Institute;

American Law Institute. Restatement Third, Torts: Products Liability, copyright 1998. Reprinted with permission of the American Law Institute;

American Law Institute. Restatement of Torts, Restatement (Second) of Torts, copyright 1938, 1965, 1977, 1979. Reprinted with permission of the American Law Institute;

American Law Institute. Report to the American Law Institute, Enterprise Responsibility for Personal Injury, Volume II, pp. 187–92, copyright 1991. Reprinted with permission of the American Law Institute;

Fleming, John, The Collateral Source Rule and Loss Allocation in Tort Law, 54 California Law Review, 1478, 1546–49 (1966) copyright 1966, California Law Review, Inc. Reprinted by permission;

King, Joseph H., Jr., A Goals-Oriented Approach to Strict Liability for Abnormally Dangerous Activities, 48 Baylor Law Review 341, 349–61 (1996);

Kramer, Orin and Briffault, Richard, Workers Compensation: Strengthening the Social Compact, pp. 13–27, 73–75 (1991), reprinted by permission of Insurance Information Institute;

National Conference of Commissioners on Uniform State Laws, Uniform Comparative Fault Act, Sections 1–6, copyright 1981. Reprinted by permission;

Posner, Richard A., Economic Analysis of Law, 8th ed. 2010, pp. 226–31, reprinted with the permission of Aspen Publishers;

Rabin, Robert L., The Ideology of Enterprise Liability, 55 Maryland Law Review 1190, 1194–99 (1996);

Rabin, Robert L., The Renaissance of Accident Law Plans Revisited, 64 Maryland Law Review 698, 703–13 (2005);

Rabin, Robert L., Environmental Liability and the Tort System, 24 Houston Law Review 27, 28–32 (1987);

Ross, H. Laurence, Settled Out of Court (1980 ed.), reprinted with permission, Aldine de Gruyter, New York, copyright 1980 by H. Laurence Ross;

Schwartz, Gary, T., Tort Law and the Economy in Nineteenth Century America: A Reinterpretation, reprinted by permission of The Yale Law Journal Company and Fred B. Rothman & Company from the Yale Law Journal, Vol. 90, pp. 1717–27.

SUMMARY OF CONTENTS

TABLE OF CONTENTS

TABLE OF CASES

The principal cases are in bold type.

TORT LAW AND ALTERNATIVES

CASES AND MATERIALS

TENTH EDITION

CHAPTER I

INTRODUCTION TO TORT LIABILITY

A. PROLOGUE

This book is concerned with the array of injuries that are by-products of a complex society, and with how the legal system responds to the diverse problems raised by such injuries. We will consider a broad range of situations including automobile collisions, airplane crashes, medical mishaps, consumer product injuries, industrial accidents, toxic exposures, fist fights, false accusations of misconduct, invasions of privacy, and false statements to competitors' prospective customers. In each situation, someone claims that another has caused harm and looks to the law for relief. We will not consider how the criminal law might react, but deal only with civil redress. Among civil harms our focus will be on those that do not arise out of disputes over contractual interpretation. The primary concern of tort law has been whether one whose actions cause harm to another should be required to pay compensation for the harm done.

For several centuries tort law was the one outlet through which the legal system did provide such redress. Other sources of compensation have grown dramatically; indeed, a study by the Institute for Civil Justice found that tort liability payments comprised only 7% of the total compensation for economic loss in nonfatal accidents in the United States—11% when tort payments for intangible loss were added in. (The figures rose to 22% and 33%, respectively, in the category of motor vehicle accident victims.) See D. Hensler, et al., Compensation for Accidental Injuries in the United States 107–08 (Rand 1991). Nonetheless, as another study of the tort system underscored, the role of tort as a compensation scheme remains pivotal:

> [T]he situation in this country leaves many Americans at risk of suffering sizable uninsured medical expenses and income loss as a result of illness or injury. Perhaps one-fourth of the non-elderly population has no medical insurance and must depend on savings or charity if they need expensive care. A significant percentage of workers have little or no protection against short-term, non-employment-related disability. Again, only savings, charity, or, for some, a state welfare payment will be available if they are unable to work for a period up to six months. For long-term disability Social Security offers protection, but only if the inability to work meets a stringent standard of totality, and only for a portion of the disabled

person's lost wages. The majority of workers have no insurance for long-term disability except for the partial coverage supplied through the Social Security system or, if the disability is employment-related, the workers' compensation system.

Currently the tort system partially fills some of these gaps by compensating many persons who would not otherwise receive reimbursement for the medical expenses and wage losses occasioned by an illness or injury. Without tort damages many of these accident victims would be uncompensated or undercompensated for their out-of-pocket losses.

Report to the American Law Institute, II Enterprise Responsibility for Personal Injury 555–56 (1991). With the increased number of Americans who have health insurance due to the Affordable Care Act (the number of uninsured has been reduced by one-third) the gap on medical expenses has been narrowed.

We first consider physical harm to one's person—commonly called "personal injury"—because it raises serious legal, economic, social and political issues. Although we will discuss intentionally caused harm, we stress unintentional physical harm, which is far more common and presents great analytical and philosophical dilemmas. During that exploration we will also consider the emotional distress and economic harm that frequently accompany fatal injury, broken bones, and destroyed property. The last part of the book introduces other interests in personality and economic security that the law seeks to protect, such as reputation, privacy, and commercial fair dealing.

B. WHEN SHOULD UNINTENDED INJURY RESULT IN LIABILITY?

The fundamental issue addressed by a system of tort liability for unintended injury is when losses should be shifted from an injury victim to an injurer or some other source of compensation. Of course, no tort system would be required in the first place if losses were simply allowed to remain where they fall. (Is it clear that such a "no-liability" system would be objectionable?) On the other hand, a system of social insurance could be established that provided full compensation in every instance of harm to the individual. Again, choosing this option would obviate the need for judicial fashioning and administration of a body of tort principles.

Because considerations of injury prevention and fairness have been thought to dictate rejection of the no-liability option, and limited resources (and perhaps injury prevention and fairness, as well?) have been thought to preclude the social insurance approach, the courts have developed a complex network of liability rules for determining the allocation of losses in cases of unintended harm. These rules, located in an intermediate zone between no-liability and universal compensation, reflect not only the influence of those polar positions, but, perhaps even more importantly, a tension between two court-fashioned liability principles—strict liability and negligence—that will be a significant concern of ours in this course. The following case provides a first look at the issue. We will also use it to introduce the basic procedural aspects of tort litigation.

Hammontree v. Jenner[*]

Court of Appeal of California, 1971.
20 Cal.App.3d 528, 97 Cal.Rptr. 739.

■ LILLIE, J.

Plaintiffs Maxine Hammontree and her husband sued defendant for personal injuries and property damage arising out of an automobile accident. The cause was tried to a jury. Plaintiffs appeal from judgment entered on a jury verdict returned against them and in favor of defendant.

The evidence shows that on the afternoon of April 25, 1967, defendant was driving his 1959 Chevrolet home from work; at the same time plaintiff Maxine Hammontree was working in a bicycle shop owned and operated by her and her husband; without warning defendant's car crashed through the wall of the shop, struck Maxine and caused personal injuries and damage to the shop.

Defendant claimed he became unconscious during an epileptic seizure losing control of his car. He did not recall the accident but his last recollection before it, was leaving a stop light after his last stop, and his first recollection after the accident was being taken out of his car in plaintiffs' shop. Defendant testified he has a medical history of epilepsy and knows of no other reason for his loss of consciousness except an epileptic seizure; prior to 1952 he had been examined by several neurologists whose conclusion was that the condition could be controlled and who placed him on medication; in 1952 he suffered a seizure while fishing; several days later he went to Dr. Benson Hyatt who diagnosed his condition as petit mal seizure and kept him on the same medication; thereafter he saw Dr. Hyatt every six months and then on a yearly basis several years prior to 1967; in 1953 he had another seizure, was told he was an epileptic and continued his medication; in 1954 Dr. Kershner prescribed dilantin and in 1955 Dr. Hyatt prescribed phelantin; from 1955 until the accident occurred (1967) defendant had used phelantin on a regular basis which controlled his condition; defendant has continued to take medication as prescribed by his physician and has done everything his doctors told

---

[*]   Text omissions are indicated by three dots. Omitted citations are indicated by [ ]. There is no indication when footnotes are omitted. When they do appear, footnotes are numbered as in the material quoted.—Eds.

him to do to avoid a seizure; he had no inkling or warning that he was about to have a seizure prior to the occurrence of the accident.

In 1955 or 1956 the Department of Motor Vehicles was advised that defendant was an epileptic and placed him on probation under which every six months he had to report to the doctor who was required to advise it in writing of defendant's condition. In 1960 his probation was changed to a once-a-year report.

Dr. Hyatt testified that during the times he saw defendant, and according to his history, defendant "was doing normally" and that he continued to take phelantin; that "[t]he purpose of the [phelantin] would be to react on the nervous system in such a way that where, without the medication, I would say to raise the threshold so that he would not be as subject to these episodes without the medication, so as not to have the seizures. He would not be having the seizures with the medication as he would without the medication compared to taking medication"; in a seizure it would be impossible for a person to drive and control an automobile; he believed it was safe for defendant to drive.

Appellants' contentions that the trial court erred in refusing to grant their motion for summary judgment on the issue of liability and their motion for directed verdict on the pleadings and counsel's opening argument are answered by the disposition of their third claim that the trial court committed prejudicial error in refusing to give their jury instruction on absolute liability.[1]

Under the present state of the law found in appellate authorities beginning with Waters v. Pacific Coast Dairy, Inc., [131 P.2d 588 (Cal.App.1942)] (driver rendered unconscious from sharp pain in left arm and shoulder) through Ford v. Carew & English, [200 P.2d 828 (Cal.App.1948)] (fainting spells from strained heart muscles), Zabunoff v. Walker, [13 Cal.Rptr. 463 (App. 1961)] (sudden sneeze), and Tannyhill v. Pacific Motor Trans. Co., [38 Cal.Rptr. 774 (App. 1964)] (heart attack), the trial judge properly refused the instruction. The foregoing cases generally hold that liability of a driver, suddenly stricken by an illness rendering him unconscious, for injury resulting from an accident occurring during that time rests on principles of negligence. However, herein during the trial plaintiffs withdrew their claim of negligence and, after both parties rested and before jury argument, objected to the giving of any instructions on negligence electing to stand solely on the theory of absolute liability. The objection was overruled and the court refused plaintiffs' requested instruction

---

[1] "When the evidence shows that a driver of a motor vehicle on a public street or highway loses his ability to safely operate and control such vehicle because of some seizure or health failure, that driver is nevertheless legally liable for all injuries and property damage which an innocent person may suffer as a proximate result of the defendant's inability to so control or operate his motor vehicle.

"This is true even if you find the defendant driver had no warning of any such impending seizure or health failure." [This is the instruction plaintiffs requested.—Eds.]

after which plaintiffs waived both opening and closing jury arguments. Defendant argued the cause to the jury after which the judge read a series of negligence instructions. . . .

Appellants seek to have this court override the established law of this state which is dispositive of the issue before us as outmoded in today's social and economic structure, particularly in the light of the now recognized principles imposing liability upon the manufacturer, retailer and all distributive and vending elements and activities which bring a product to the consumer to his injury, on the basis of strict liability in tort expressed first in Justice Traynor's concurring opinion in Escola v. Coca Cola Bottling Co., [150 P.2d 436 (Cal.1944)]; and then in Greenman v. Yuba Power Products, Inc., [377 P.2d 897 (Cal.1963)]; Vandermark v. Ford Motor Co., [391 P.2d 168 (Cal.1964)]; and Elmore v. American Motors Corp., [451 P.2d 84 (Cal.1969)]. These authorities hold that "A manufacturer [or retailer] is strictly liable in tort when an article he places on the market, knowing that it is to be used without inspection for defects, proves to have a defect that causes injury to a human being." [Greenman and Vandermark]. Drawing a parallel with these products liability cases, appellants argue, with some degree of logic, that only the driver affected by a physical condition which could suddenly render him unconscious and who is aware of that condition can anticipate the hazards and foresee the dangers involved in his operation of a motor vehicle, and that the liability of those who by reason of seizure or heart failure or some other physical condition lose the ability to safely operate and control a motor vehicle resulting in injury to an innocent person should be predicated on strict liability.

We decline to superimpose the absolute liability of products liability cases upon drivers under the circumstances here. The theory on which those cases are predicated is that manufacturers, retailers and distributors of products are engaged in the business of distributing goods to the public and are an integral part of the over-all producing and marketing enterprise that should bear the cost of injuries from defective parts. [Vandermark and Greenman]. This policy hardly applies here and it is not enough to simply say, as do appellants, that the insurance carriers should be the ones to bear the cost of injuries to innocent victims on a strict liability basis. In Maloney v. Rath, [445 P.2d 513 (Cal.1968)], followed by Clark v. Dziabas, [445 P.2d 517 (Cal.1968)], appellant urged that defendant's violation of a safety provision (defective brakes) of the Vehicle Code makes the violator strictly liable for damages caused by the violation. While reversing the judgment for defendant upon another ground, the California Supreme Court refused to apply the doctrine of strict liability to automobile drivers. The situation involved two users of the highway but the problems of fixing responsibility under a system of strict liability are as complicated in the instant case as those in [Maloney v. Rath], and could only create uncertainty in the area of its concern. As stated in Maloney:

"To invoke a rule of strict liability on users of the streets and highways, however, without also establishing in substantial detail how the new rule should operate would only contribute confusion to the automobile accident problem. Settlement and claims adjustment procedures would become chaotic until the new rules were worked out on a case-by-case basis, and the hardships of delayed compensation would be seriously intensified. Only the Legislature, if it deems it wise to do so, can avoid such difficulties by enacting a comprehensive plan for the compensation of automobile accident victims in place of or in addition to the law of negligence."

The instruction tendered by appellants was properly refused for still another reason. Even assuming the merit of appellants' position under the facts of this case in which defendant knew he had a history of epilepsy, previously had suffered seizures and at the time of the accident was attempting to control the condition by medication, the instruction does not except from its ambit the driver who suddenly is stricken by an illness or physical condition which he had no reason whatever to anticipate and of which he had no prior knowledge.

The judgment is affirmed.

■ WOOD, P.J., and THOMPSON, J., concurred.

Appellants' petition for a hearing by the Supreme Court of California was denied December 16, 1971.

NOTES AND QUESTIONS

1.   In *Hammontree*, there is no indication that plaintiff was in any way to blame for her injuries. Defendant's loss of control of his automobile appears to have been the precipitating event that caused the harm to her. Why should it make any difference whether he had reason to believe that he might suffer a seizure? Why shouldn't it suffice that he caused the harm? Consider the following criticism of strict liability from Oliver Wendell Holmes, The Common Law 94–96 (1881):

> The general principle of our law is that loss from accident must lie where it falls, and this principle is not affected by the fact that a human being is the instrument of misfortune. . . . If this were not so, any act would be sufficient, however remote, which set in motion or opened the door for a series of physical sequences ending in damage; such as riding the horse, in the case of the runaway, or even coming to a place where one is seized with a fit and strikes the plaintiff in an unconscious spasm. Nay, why need the defendant have acted at all, and why is it not enough that his existence has been at the expense of the plaintiff? The requirement of an act is the requirement that the defendant should have made a choice. But the only possible purpose of introducing this moral element is to make the power of avoiding the evil complained of a condition of liability. There is no such power where the evil cannot be foreseen. . . .

A man need not, it is true, do this or that act,—the term *act* implies a choice,—but he must act somehow. Furthermore, the public generally profits by individual activity. As action cannot be avoided, and tends to the public good, there is obviously no policy in throwing the hazard of what is at once desirable and inevitable upon the actor.

The state might conceivably make itself a mutual insurance company against accidents, and distribute the burden of its citizens' mishaps among all its members. There might be a pension for paralytics, and state aid for those who suffered in person or estate from tempest or wild beasts. As between individuals it might adopt the mutual insurance principle *pro tanto,* and divide damages when both were in fault, as in the *rusticum judicium* of the admiralty, or it might throw all loss upon the actor irrespective of fault. The state does none of these things, however, and the prevailing view is that its cumbrous and expensive machinery ought not to be set in motion unless some clear benefit is to be derived from disturbing the *status quo.* State interference is an evil, where it cannot be shown to be a good. Universal insurance, if desired, can be better and more cheaply accomplished by private enterprise. The undertaking to redistribute losses simply on the ground that they resulted from the defendant's act would not only be open to these objections, but, as it is hoped the preceding discussion has shown, to the still graver one of offending the sense of justice. Unless my act is of a nature to threaten others, unless under the circumstances a prudent man would have foreseen the possibility of harm, it is no more justifiable to make me indemnify my neighbor against the consequences, than to make me do the same thing if I had fallen upon him in a fit, or to compel me to insure him against lightning.

Is Holmes persuasive?

2.   Suppose that defendant made his living as a driver and argued that the social benefits derived from his engaging in the activity outweighed the very small likelihood of injury. Would that be a reason to reject strict liability in favor of holding defendant liable only for negligent acts? Consider the following economic perspective on the issue in Posner, A Theory of Negligence, 1 J. Legal Stud. 29, 33 (1972):

Perhaps, then, the dominant function of the fault system is to generate rules of liability that if followed will bring about, at least approximately, the efficient—the cost-justified—level of accidents and safety. Under this view, damages are assessed against the defendant as a way of measuring the costs of accidents, and the damages so assessed are paid over to the plaintiff (to be divided with his lawyer) as the price of enlisting their participation in the operation of the system. Because we do not like to see resources squandered, a judgment of negligence has inescapable overtones of moral disapproval, for it implies that there was a cheaper alternative to the accident. Conversely, there is no moral indignation in the case in which the cost of prevention would have exceeded the cost of the accident. Where the measures necessary to avert the accident would have consumed excessive resources, there is no occasion to condemn the defendant for not having taken them.

3.   The grounds for rejecting strict liability in favor of negligence referred to in the two preceding notes, as well as the counter-arguments, are explored in much greater detail throughout this book. Why does the court refuse to adopt a strict liability approach in *Hammontree*?

4.   As the court states, strict liability in tort is now recognized for some aspects of defective product injuries. We examine the products liability area in great detail in Chapter IX. For now, however, consider briefly the analogy to auto accidents. On initial consideration, do you find the court's distinction between liability of an enterprise for its product-related injuries and liability of drivers for auto accidents convincing? Would you be more disposed to hold defendant strictly liable if he had been a taxi driver engaged in his business?

5.   Why is it "not enough to simply say . . . that the insurance carriers should be the ones to bear the cost of injuries to innocent victims on a strict liability basis"? The influence of insurance on tort liability will be another recurrent theme in this course. The topic of insurance is covered in Chapter XI.

6.   Consider the prospect of establishing strict liability against defendant on the basis of a statutory violation of the Vehicle Code. In the cited case of *Maloney v. Rath*, the court refused to hold defendant strictly liable for her non-negligent violation of the traffic law (brake failure due to her garage mechanic's negligence), stating that:

> In few cases, however, are the facts likely to be as simple as they are here. In the next case an accident might be caused by the combination of a brake failure and a stoplight failure under circumstances that would have permitted effective use of an emergency handbrake had the following motorist been properly alerted by the stoplight required by the Vehicle Code. (Veh.Code § 24603.) In another case, a pedestrian might stumble and fall on a dangerous and defective pavement causing a motorist having the right of way to drive across the center line of the highway and strike a speeding oncoming car. Who is to be strictly liable to whom in such cases? However imperfectly it operates, the law of negligence allocates the risks and determines who shall or shall not be compensated when persons simultaneously engaged in the common enterprise of using the streets and highways have accidents.

Would the determination of who was to be held strictly liable in such cases be markedly more difficult than deciding who would be liable for negligence?

Assume that, irrespective of negligence, the defendant in *Maloney* would be *criminally* liable for violation of Vehicle Code section 24603. (Note that Jenner had complied with a reporting requirement to the Department of Motor Vehicles.) Should that affect liability in tort? Again, this issue will be explored in greater depth in Chapter II. Potential legislative solutions to the accident problem referred to toward the end of the *Hammontree* opinion are covered in Chapter XII.

7. As to the possibility of suing the DMV, consider Waschek v. Department of Motor Vehicles, 69 Cal.Rptr.2d 296 (App.1997). An experienced DMV driving inspector gave a 96-year-old driver a driving test, on which he scored 94 out of 100. The inspector concluded that the driver was able to operate a car safely on the highway and authorized reissue of the driver's license. Twenty months later, the driver struck a pedestrian who sued the DMV for issuing the license. By statute, the DMV would be liable only if it negligently performed a "mandatory duty." The court decided that this would have occurred only if the DMV had concluded that the driver was unqualified but had nonetheless issued the license. That did not occur here, and the DMV was immune for its discretionary decision to issue the license. The subject of government liability is considered at length in Chapter III.

8. The court uses the terms "strict liability" and "absolute liability" interchangeably in the course of its opinion. Treating the two terms as synonymous is likely to cause confusion. As we will see, the various forms of strict liability that have been recognized are virtually never "absolute" even though they do not require fault. Consider a single example. In no case of product-related injuries is liability "absolute" in the sense that plaintiff need only establish that defendant's product "caused" the injury. Typically, plaintiff must also establish a defect in the product, and plaintiff's own conduct may reduce or bar her recovery. We will explore a number of other limitations on the "absolute" character of strict liability. For present purposes, we simply note that you should keep strict liability distinct from absolute liability.

C. THE LITIGATION PROCESS

1. *Procedure.* In personal injury cases, as in litigation generally, the aggrieved party must initiate the claim and pursue it until she gains redress or has exhausted her legal remedies. Why should she bear this burden? What are the alternatives? In *Hammontree*, Maxine Hammontree and her husband's first step would be to consult and then retain an attorney. The attorney initially might try to obtain a settlement from those who may be liable for causing her harm. If that fails, the claimant becomes a plaintiff before the courts by initiating a lawsuit with the filing of a "complaint" stating what occurred and the relief sought. The complaint will allege "facts" that plaintiff contends justify granting relief. The legal theory under which the plaintiff is proceeding will usually be apparent from the nature of the facts that the plaintiff contends to be material to her case. In many cases, plaintiffs assert multiple claims, as the Hammontrees did with their negligence and strict liability claims. In such cases, plaintiffs may recover if successful on any one of their claims.

You should appreciate that much of the procedure that follows is designed to determine if a jury is required to resolve the dispute or, on the other hand, if the court can resolve the case without the need for a jury. In that regard, questions about the law are for the court while factual disputes require jury determination. Thus, for example, the question of which witnesses are telling the truth is classically reserved for trial and for determination by the trier of fact, usually a jury of six to twelve persons chosen from the community.* Occasionally, we shall see cases in which the facts are determined by the trial judge who, in addition to deciding legal questions, doubles as fact-finder as well.

The person sued, the defendant, will retain an attorney who will consider several options available at this early stage of the proceedings. If the plaintiff has sued the defendant on what the attorney believes to be a novel—and unsound—legal theory, the defendant may make a motion (a request for a ruling by the court) to dismiss the complaint— also called a demurrer—on the ground that even if the allegations of fact in the complaint are true, there is no sound legal theory upon which plaintiff is entitled to relief. The defendant will support this motion with legal arguments. When the plaintiff's attorney responds by arguing that the legal theory is sound, the issue will be posed for the judge. For example, assume a complaint that alleged that the defendant failed to invite the plaintiff to a social event, knowing that such a snub would hurt the plaintiff, and that plaintiff suffered emotional distress. The defendant might move to dismiss that complaint on the ground that even if all the facts are true, there is no valid legal reason for the defendant to pay for the plaintiff's distress. This raises a legal question for the judge to decide under the relevant law.

If the judge decides for the defendant, the plaintiff's case will be dismissed, and the litigation will be at an end unless the plaintiff decides to appeal. (Sometimes the judge will grant the plaintiff permission to amend the allegations to add essential facts to invoke a sound legal theory where one was lacking before. A defendant who still believes the complaint to be inadequate will make another motion and the case will proceed as before.)

If the judge denies the defendant's motion to dismiss the complaint, the judge will be saying in effect that the plaintiff's complaint states a good legal theory and the plaintiff will be entitled to recover damages from the defendant if the plaintiff can prove that the essential facts alleged in the complaint are true. At this stage procedures diverge. In some states, a defendant may appeal the judge's ruling immediately; in most states, however, the defendant must usually wait until the trial is

---

* Uniquely among western countries, parties in civil cases in the United States are routinely entitled to have a jury trial.

completed before appealing from unfavorable rulings. Under the latter view the defendant must now contest the plaintiff's allegations of fact or admit them and be held legally liable and then appeal.

The defendant may meet the plaintiff's fact allegations by a pleading called an "answer" in which the defendant denies some or all of the plaintiff's allegations of fact and perhaps adds some new ones of his own that will defeat the plaintiff's case (known as "affirmative defenses"). Although we traditionally resolve fact disputes at a trial, that process is used only for genuine disputes of fact. Some apparent disputes can be decided without a trial because one of the parties has conclusive evidence that it is telling the truth. Thus, for example, if a merchant sues a customer for not paying a bill and the customer asserts payment we have an apparent dispute of fact. If, in addition, the customer can present a cancelled check and the merchant does not claim that the check was forged or is in some other way irrelevant to this transaction, we will not need a trial because the dispute is so one-sided that no reasonable jury could resolve it in favor of the merchant. There is no need to hold a trial because the conclusion is foreordained. The customer would make a motion for "summary judgment" and attach a sworn statement and copies of the check and bill of sale. If the plaintiff does not respond with evidence that restores a genuine fact dispute, the judge will grant customer's motion for summary judgment and enter an order dismissing the case—not on the ground that the plaintiff's legal theory was inadequate but rather on the ground that the plaintiff's facts cannot possibly be proven to be true and that a trial would be unnecessary.

It is no coincidence that the foregoing example involved contracts, in which documentary evidence is usually available. In tort cases, on the other hand, the situation is usually quite different because many of the episodes that concern us happen suddenly and rarely lend themselves to documentation. We are more likely to encounter disputes between eyewitnesses as to whether the defendant went through the intersection on a green light or on a red light, or whether a particular product was being used properly at the time plaintiff was hurt. We will often be at the mercy of recollection without being able to reconstruct or to document the actual event.

During the period before trial, the parties may engage in "discovery." Discovery rules afford the parties an opportunity to obtain evidence by, for example, requesting documents, including electronic files and e-mails, from an adversary or a third-party, questioning opponents or independent witnesses under oath in what is known as a "deposition," and sending written "interrogatories" to another party to inquire about matters relevant to the case. In complex cases, discovery can be both intensive and extensive, require considerable attorney effort, and cost a great deal.

At the trial, the plaintiff has the burden of proving the essential facts of her case. There are two components to the burden of proof. First, the plaintiff must introduce sufficient evidence that the jury could rationally find in her behalf. If, for example, the plaintiff has no evidence about what the defendant did wrong, the plaintiff will have failed to satisfy the initial requirement to provide sufficient evidence, the "burden of production," and the court will dismiss the case. The second requirement is the "burden of persuasion." After having introduced sufficient evidence, the plaintiff must still persuade the factfinder that her version is correct. That is to say, she must persuade the factfinder that her version of the facts is "more likely than not" what occurred. In other states, the burden of persuasion is articulated as convincing the jury of her version by a "preponderance of the evidence." However formulated, plaintiff's burden in a civil case is less onerous than the requirement in criminal trials that the state must prove its case "beyond a reasonable doubt." The jury will also be told that if after all of their deliberations they are in equipoise—they cannot decide which side presented the stronger case—they are to return a verdict against the party who had the burden of persuading them, generally the plaintiff.

As the parties proffer evidence in support of their theory of the facts, objection may be raised by the opponent as to the admissibility of the evidence—a witness's testimony, a document or e-mail, or a reconstruction of the accident. In such instances, the court must decide, based on rules of evidence, whether the evidence can be admitted and thereby taken into account by the fact-finder. In recent years, rules on the admissibility of expert testimony have become more rigorous. Often the admissibility of an expert's testimony, such as whether defendant's drug caused plaintiff's birth defect, will be dispositive with regard to the outcome of the claim.

As in the case when an expert's testimony on a prima facie element—such as causation—is ruled inadmissible, sometimes the trial may not reach the jury stage. If, after plaintiff has presented her evidence, the defendant believes that an essential fact has not been proven, the defendant may make a motion for a "directed verdict," today called "judgment as a matter of law." This, in effect, asks the judge to rule that the plaintiff's evidence is so lacking on at least one essential fact that no jury could reasonably find in the plaintiff's favor and thus it is pointless to continue the trial. The plaintiff will argue against the motion by trying to show that she has presented enough evidence on each essential point so that a jury could find that her version is more likely than not to have occurred. The judge again will be called upon to rule. A judge who rules in favor of the defendant will dismiss the case, and the litigation will be over unless the plaintiff appeals successfully. A judge who denies the motion is essentially saying that the plaintiff has presented sufficient facts from which a jury could reasonably find in the plaintiff's favor at this stage of the case—and the trial will continue.

If the defendant should rest without presenting any evidence, the case then proceeds to the closing arguments. Each attorney will summarize the case and will try to persuade the jury to accept a favorable version of the facts. The jury will then be "charged" by the judge. The charge or "instructions" will tell the jurors about burdens of proof and the legal rules they should apply to the facts that they find. After deliberation, the jury reports its "verdict" to the judge.

A defendant who does present evidence will proceed much as did the plaintiff—by calling witnesses and introducing documents to bolster the defendant's contentions about what happened in the case. At the end of the defendant's evidence, defendant may again move for a judgment as a matter of law (or directed verdict) on the ground that his presentation has been such a powerful refutation of the plaintiff's claims that no jury could reasonably decide for the plaintiff.* Again, the judge will grant or deny the motion. Or, the judge may "reserve decision"—delay deciding it until learning how the jury has reacted to the case. If the jury decides the same way the judge would have, the result is clear. If the jury decides for the plaintiff, but the judge thinks the defendant should have received judgment as a matter of law, the judge may now dismiss the case. The advantage of waiting for the jury is that if an appellate court thinks the jury verdict should stand, it can reverse the trial judge's decision and reinstate the jury's verdict. If the judge had granted the directed verdict without waiting for the jury's verdict, and the appellate court disagreed, the only recourse would be to order a complete new trial.

After a verdict for the plaintiff, an unresigned defendant has several choices. He may once again move for a judgment as a matter of law or, as it was formerly called, judgment notwithstanding the verdict (judgment n.o.v.—non obstante veredicto) on essentially the same grounds asserted earlier in seeking a judgment as a matter of law: that the jury has reached a verdict that no jury could reasonably have reached on the evidence in this case.

In some cases, the plaintiff's case is so lacking that no jury could reasonably find in plaintiff's favor; in other cases, the plaintiff has presented evidence that would justify a jury believing her side but the defendant has presented an overwhelming amount of conflicting evidence. In the first situation, the judge will properly grant judgment as a matter of law since there is nothing to support the plaintiff's case. In the second situation, however, some evidence supports the plaintiff's contention. This might arise, for example, when the issue is whether

---

*   After all evidence is in, the plaintiff may also move for a judgment as a matter of law if the evidence will permit only that outcome. Similarly, plaintiffs may move for summary judgment before trial on the question of the defendant's liability if no triable question of fact appears to remain in the case.

the defendant drove through a red light. The plaintiff and an admittedly intoxicated bystander swear that the light was red but ten sober disinterested bystanders swear that it was green. If the jury believes the plaintiff and her witness it could reasonably find that the light was red. This would mean that the judge could not properly grant a directed verdict for the defendant because there is evidence that a jury could reasonably believe to support the plaintiff's case. On the other hand, what about the ten disinterested bystanders who swear that the light was green? If the jury finds that the light was green that verdict would also be supported by the evidence.

Although we have said the judge could not grant judgment as a matter of law when there is a conflict between sets of witnesses, the judge may have an abiding sense that the party who prevailed before the jury did not have the stronger case, and that the jury may have been swayed by some other factor such as the severity of the plaintiff's injury. Another reason for a new trial is that the jury's award of damages is so insufficient or excessive that it also appears to be the product of improper factors, such as dislike of the defendant. Either of these grounds may lead the judge to order a new trial to see whether a second jury will respond in the same way as did the first jury.

Both of these motions are used largely by the defense, but they are also available to the plaintiff if the jury returns a verdict for the defendant. The plaintiff's most likely recourse, however, is to try to obtain a new trial by asserting that the trial judge committed errors in the admission or exclusion of evidence or the charge to the jury, and that these errors were "prejudicial," meaning that there is a likelihood that they affected the outcome of the case.

After reaching a conclusive disposition of the case, the judge will enter judgment in favor of the successful party. As we have seen, this may occur at any of several stages. It may be at the outset, if the judge grants defendant's motion to dismiss the plaintiff's complaint on the ground that it asks for relief in a situation in which the law does not provide relief. It may happen on a motion for judgment as a matter of law at the end of the plaintiff's case or following all the evidence. It may happen after the verdict, when the trial judge accepts what the jury has done, rejects the defense motions, and enters a judgment for the plaintiff for the amount awarded by the jury.

These motions all occur at the trial court level, but virtually all the cases in this book are appellate cases, and we now turn to the issues presented by an appeal. In general, "the trial judge tries the case and the appellate court tries the trial judge." The party against whom judgment has been entered will seek to persuade the appellate court that the trial judge committed prejudicial error in making rulings in the case. Note that the plaintiffs in *Hammontree* conceded that the jury could reasonably have accepted defendant's version of the facts.

They did, however, claim that the judge committed a specific legal error in failing to charge that the jury could find defendant liable irrespective of negligence on his part. This is a question of law, and the appellate court will decide whether the ruling was erroneous and, if so, whether the error was prejudicial to appellants' case.

2.   *Hammontree reconsidered.* In light of this brief look at the procedural aspects of tort litigation, consider the following questions about *Hammontree*:

a. How do you think the jury instruction on liability tendered by the judge differed from the plaintiffs' rejected instruction? A version of the negligence charge frequently used by California judges may be found at p. 47 infra.

b. According to the court, plaintiffs withdrew their claim of negligence during the trial and apparently sought to proceed exclusively on a strict liability theory. Why might plaintiffs have adopted this strategy?

c. If plaintiffs' theory of the case had been adopted, would they have been entitled to summary judgment on liability, as they requested? Summary judgments and directed verdicts in favor of plaintiffs are rare as compared to successful motions by defendants on these grounds. Why do you think this is the case?

d. In view of the trial court's rejection of plaintiffs' theory, might defendant have been entitled to a directed verdict? At what stage in the trial might defendant have tendered the motion? Might summary judgment in his favor have been warranted?

3.   *Damages.* Once a plaintiff has brought herself within the rules allowing recovery for personal injury, the traditional goal of tort law has been to restore her to the equivalent of her condition prior to the harm. Most plaintiffs seek money damages, although other remedies exist: sometimes a plaintiff would prefer an injunction to prevent conduct that threatens harm, and in a defamation case the plaintiff may prefer a retraction. In personal injury cases, money damages are viewed as the best solution. Can you think of anything better?

The categories of personal injury damages available to a plaintiff are meant to compensate for both tangible and intangible loss. Tangible losses may already have been incurred or be predictable. The former includes such easily proven items as doctors' bills, hospital bills, and other actual medical expenses. Loss of income is proven almost as easily, especially if the plaintiff is salaried. The projection of such loss, especially for self-employed victims, is speculative, but may be facilitated by effective use of expert testimony. Experts also assist in the projection of medical costs.

The common law "single judgment rule" (addressed in more detail in Chapter XI, at p. 715) provides that a plaintiff sues only once for the harm she has suffered, and statutes of limitations establish time limits within which she must do so (further details and an important exception is discussed in Chapter VII, at p. 435).

The intangible element of pain and suffering, which plays a central role in most cases of serious personal injury, presents problems of valuation as to both past and future losses. Through this item, the law recognizes that the impact of the injury is more than financial. Suppose Maxine Hammontree had suffered serious injuries that left her crippled and disfigured. It is difficult to put price tags on such consequences, but if the law seeks to restore the plaintiff to her prior condition or its equivalent, the continuing pain and embarrassment she suffers must be assessed and translated into monetary terms.

Note that plaintiffs in *Hammontree* also sued for property loss because of the damage to the shop caused by defendant's loss of control of his auto. This is another common category of damage in personal injury cases, particularly in auto accident situations. (The subject of damages is discussed in detail in Chapter XI.)

4. *Collecting on a judgment.* Once a judgment for a plaintiff becomes final—which requires that all appeals be exhausted or the time for any further appeal has expired—the matter of collecting on that judgment arises; a judgment is not self-executing. In many cases, defendants will simply pay the plaintiff the amount of the judgment, and it will then be deemed satisfied. However, some defendants do not voluntarily meet their judgment obligations, requiring the plaintiff to pursue measures designed to obtain property or funds that can be used to satisfy the judgment. Proceedings to "execute" on a judgment exist and can include seizing certain property owned by the defendant or garnishing a portion of any wages. In the end, however, these procedures are cumbersome and expensive and, unless employed against parties with substantial assets, unlikely to be worth the effort. And, of course, no amount of execution effort can obtain funds from parties who do not have assets or whose assets are protected by law from execution. For those reasons, most plaintiff's attorneys are loath to sue an uninsured individual or company, unless the individual is wealthy or the company substantial.

5. *Attorneys and fees.* The attorney's fee presents two questions: who pays and how much.

In most countries, losing litigants pay the attorney's fees and other litigation costs of their opponents, as well as their own. In the United States it was feared that such a rule would deny persons of limited means access to the courts in close cases. When the courts were used mainly to settle vast estates or large commercial disputes and poor people had few claims, it may have been appropriate for a losing party to pay for both attorneys, but with the industrial revolution, the railroad, and later the automobile, wider access to the courts was essential.

Even requiring a party to pay her own attorney presents serious problems for the poor and, frequently, the middle class. In the mid-19th century, the contingent fee developed and had an important impact on the ability of many Americans to obtain access to the court system and justice from those who had wronged them. With contingent fees, the injured plaintiff is required to pay her attorney only if her case is concluded successfully. The fee is paid from the recovery and is based on a previously set percentage of the amount recovered. Typically, contingent fees range from 20–40% of the damages award. Many other legal systems consider this system unethical or illegal, although recently there has been movement toward similar arrangements in other countries. What might be the basis for the view that contingent fees are unethical? Modern critiques focus on attorneys taking unfair advantage of naïve clients. What may be said in their defense? Do you understand why many tort reform efforts by those who are subject to suit have sought to impose limits on contingent fees? For a critique and response, see Brickman, Contingency Fee Abuses: Ethical Mandates, and the Disciplinary System: The Case Against Case-by-Case Enforcement, 53 Wash. & Lee L.Rev. 1339 (1996); Kritzer, Advocacy and Rhetoric vs. Scholarship and Evidence in the Debate Over Contingency Fees: A Reply to Professor Brickman, 82 Wash.U.L.Q. 477 (2004).

Most personal injury cases in this country are handled for the plaintiff's side by a specialized group of lawyers who accept cases on a contingent fee basis and who often advance the other costs of litigation. Lawyers for the defense are also specialized and are hired by insurance companies or represent large commercial and industrial enterprises. Some are permanent employees of their client; others work in independent law firms that are compensated according to the time devoted to a particular case.

6. *Appellate decisions.* During much of this course we will read and discuss appellate opinions. You should know from the outset that these opinions are only a small fraction of the yield of the legal process; in personal injury law, for example, only about two percent of all claims actually go to trial and far fewer are appealed. The few appellate decisions, of course, shape the evolution of the law; cases are dropped and settlements are made on the basis of predictions of how the trial and appellate courts will view the controversy. Thus our appellate focus means that instead of seeing a cross-section of typical personal injury cases, we shall consider a small group of particularly significant cases.

Notice that tort problems are more likely to reach litigation than are contract problems. Parties to a contract are seeking an agreement that will provide specific foreseeable benefits. Even if a dispute arises, they have strong incentives to reach an accord that will preserve their mutually advantageous relationship. In tort situations, however, most claims arise from unintended harms. Prior legal counseling is rare. The attorney usually enters after the harm has occurred, and with litigation in mind if settlement negotiations fail. Often, the parties initially become aware of one another when at least one of them is hurt—and probably angry. There is no continuing relationship between the parties encouraging them to settle, and tort suits are hotly disputed because the critical events—as in a car crash—may have taken place within a few seconds.

7.   *Court structure.* The California court system is fairly typical of state judicial organization—with its trial court of general jurisdiction (the superior court), a group of regional intermediate appellate courts (the court of appeal) and a single highest court (the supreme court). The major aberration in naming courts is the important state of New York. There the trial level court is called "the supreme court," the regional intermediate appellate court is the "appellate division of the supreme court," or simply the "appellate division," and the state's highest court is called the "court of appeals."

8.   Suggestions for further reading appear throughout this book. Five general books on tort law will be helpful on the doctrinal issues discussed. D. Dobbs, P. Hayden, & E. Bublick, Hornbook on Torts (2d ed.2016); K. Abraham, The Forms and Functions of Tort Law (4th ed.2012); The American Law Institute, A Concise Restatement of Torts (3d ed.2013); M. Geistfeld, Tort Law: The Essentials (2008); F. Harper, F. James, Jr. & O. Gray, The Law of Torts (2d & 3d eds.1986 and 2006) (6 vols.). The intellectual foundations of tort law are explored in J. Davies, L. Levine & E. Kionka, A Torts Anthology (2d ed.1999); R. Rabin, Perspectives on Tort Law (4th ed.1995); and S. Levmore & C. Sharkey, Foundations of Tort Law (2d ed.2009). R. Rabin & S. Sugarman (eds.), Torts Stories (2003) provides in-depth examination of a number of classic tort cases, many found in this book.

Throughout this book, cases and notes will refer to relevant sections of the Restatement of the Law of Torts (4 vols. 1934–39) and the Second Restatement (4 vols. 1965–79). A Restatement (Third) of Torts: Products Liability was completed in 1998. A Restatement (Third) of Torts: Apportionment of Liability was published in 2000. The two-volume Restatement (Third) of Torts: Liability for Physical and Emotional Harm was published in 2010 and 2012. Two further pieces of the Third Restatement, addressing intentional torts and economic harm, are underway. The Restatement is an unofficial effort to summarize the decisional law on a subject. It is prepared by the American Law Institute—a group of lawyers, judges, and scholars.

D. THE PARTIES AND VICARIOUS LIABILITY

1. *Plaintiffs. Hammontree* involved an adult plaintiff who suffered personal injury. Her age, physical condition, and occupation would have been relevant to her damage recovery. In other situations, it may be more difficult to find the proper plaintiff and to measure the recoverable loss. If a minor is hurt, suit generally will be brought on her behalf by her parent or guardian, and a damage award will be divided so that the minor will recover for any permanent physical harm (although the money will be placed in trust for her) and her parent will recover medical expenses borne on the child's behalf. It is now generally held that an infant who is born alive may sue through a legal guardian for harm suffered before birth. This problem is well discussed in Woods v. Lancet, 102 N.E.2d 691 (N.Y.1951).

Recoveries in cases of death are regulated by statute because under early common law the death of either the plaintiff or the defendant terminated the lawsuit. The death of the defendant now rarely causes the abatement of otherwise valid lawsuits. As for a deceased victim, two separate interests are involved: the victim's interest in her own bodily security and her dependents' interest in continued economic support and in other factors we shall consider later. The first is protected by "survival" statutes that allow the estate of the deceased to bring suit for any harm for which the deceased could have sued had she survived. This would include such items as medical expenses, lost wages, and pain and suffering up to her death. The second interest is generally recognized through "wrongful death" statutes. One common pattern provides that an action may be brought by and on behalf of legally designated beneficiaries, usually close family members or next of kin, to recover for the pecuniary loss that the death has caused. Generically, these statutes are called Lord Campbell's Acts, after the first such statute adopted in 1846 in England. The survival and wrongful death interests may be vindicated in a single action.

In a lawsuit on behalf of a dead victim the actual plaintiff is usually an administrator (administratrix) or executor (executrix). An administrator is named by the court to handle the affairs of one who died intestate (with no will). If the deceased has left a will, it usually names an executor to handle the settling of estate matters, including bringing and defending lawsuits. In these cases, the deceased may be referred to as the decedent, as plaintiff's intestate, or as plaintiff's testator (testatrix).

Why is Maxine Hammontree's husband a co-plaintiff? Although the property damage to their jointly owned business is one reason, it may be that his principal claim is for loss of consortium—loss of his wife's companionship—due to the injuries she suffered. The various aspects of "relational harm" in cases of death and injury are discussed in Chapters IV and XI.

2. *Defendants.* We will see throughout the course that defendants are being held vicariously liable for the torts of another person. This is certainly true when a corporation is held liable for the torts of its employees, whether they are lower, middle or upper level employees. It is also true when any person in business is held liable for the torts of his or her employees. These forms of vicarious liability, called "respondeat superior," are the most common. We briefly explore that concept here.

Christensen v. Swenson

Supreme Court of Utah, 1994.
874 P.2d 125.

■ DURHAM, JUSTICE.

[Swenson, a Burns employee, was assigned to guard Gate 4 at Geneva Steel Plant. Guards worked eight-hour continuous shifts, with no scheduled breaks. However, employees were permitted to take ten-to fifteen-minute unscheduled lunch and restroom breaks. Gate 4 guards generally ate a bag lunch but occasionally ordered take-out food from the sole restaurant within close physical proximity to Gate 4, the Frontier Cafe. The Frontier Cafe was located directly across the street from the Geneva plant, approximately 150 to 250 yards from Gate 4. The cafe's menu was posted near the telephone at Gate 4. Aside from vending machines located within a nearby Geneva office building, the Frontier Cafe provided the sole source of food accessible to Gate 4 guards within their breaks. Whether they brought their lunches or ordered from the cafe, Gate 4 guards were expected to eat at their posts.

Shortly after 11 a.m. on the day of the accident, Swenson noticed a lull in the traffic at Gate 4 and decided to get a cup of soup from the Frontier Cafe. She placed a telephone order for the soup from Gate 4 and then drove her automobile to the cafe. She intended to pick up the soup and return to Gate 4 to eat at her post. She expected the round trip to take approximately ten to fifteen minutes, as permitted by Burns' unscheduled break policy. On her return trip, however, she collided with plaintiffs' motorcycle at a public intersection just outside Geneva's property. Several people were injured.

When suit was brought against Swenson and Burns, claiming that Swenson had driven negligently, Burns moved for summary judgment on the ground that Swenson was not acting in the scope of her employment at the time of the accident. The trial court granted the motion and the court of appeals affirmed.]

Summary judgment is appropriate when the record indicates that there is no genuine issue as to any material fact and the moving party is entitled to judgment as a matter of law. . . . [W]e view all relevant facts and all inferences arising from those facts in the light most favorable to the party opposing the motion. . . .

Under the doctrine of respondeat superior, employers are vicariously liable for torts committed by employees while acting within the scope of their employment. [ ] Whether an employee is acting within the scope of her employment is ordinarily a question of fact. [ ] The question must be submitted to the jury " 'whenever reasonable minds may differ as to whether the [employee] was at a certain time involved wholly or partly in the performance of [the employer's] business or within the scope of employment.' " [ ] However, when the employee's activity is so clearly within or outside the scope of employment that reasonable minds cannot differ, the court may decide the issue as a matter of law. [ ]; Birkner v. Salt Lake County, 771 P.2d 1053, 1057 (Utah 1989).

In *Birkner*, we stated that acts falling within the scope of employment are " 'those acts which are so closely connected with what the servant is employed to do, and so fairly and reasonably incidental to it, that they may be regarded as methods, even though quite improper ones, of carrying out the objectives of employment.' " [ ] We articulated three criteria helpful in determining whether an employee is acting within or outside the scope of her employment. First, the employee's conduct must be of the general kind the employee is hired to perform, that is, "the employee must be about the employer's business and the duties assigned by the employer, as opposed to being wholly involved in a personal endeavor." [ ] Second, the employee's conduct must occur substantially within the hours and ordinary spatial boundaries of the employment. [ ] Finally, "the employee's conduct must be motivated, at least in part, by the purpose of serving the employer's interest." [ ]

The court of appeals held that Swenson was not substantially within the ordinary spatial boundaries of her employment because the accident did not occur on Geneva property. . . .

Because the court of appeals concluded that Swenson failed to satisfy the second *Birkner* criterion, it did not address the first and third criteria. [ ] However, our review of the record indicates that reasonable minds could differ on all three criteria. Thus, to avoid a second summary judgment on remand, we address all three of the *Birkner* criteria.

The first *Birkner* criterion requires that the employee's conduct be of the general kind the employee is hired to perform, that is, "the employee must be about the employer's business and the duties assigned by the employer, as opposed to being wholly involved in a personal endeavor." [ ] Reasonable minds could differ as to whether Swenson was about Burns' business when she was involved in the traffic accident between Gate 4 and the Frontier Cafe.

We base this conclusion on two disputed issues of material fact. First, Swenson claims that Burns employed her as a security guard to "see and be seen" on and around the Geneva plant. Thus, traveling the short distance to the Frontier Cafe in uniform arguably heightened the secure atmosphere that Burns sought to project. Burns, on the other hand, claims that Swenson was not hired to perform that function. Burns' position is supported by the deposition of another security guard who stated that he considered lunch trips to the Frontier Cafe to be entirely personal in nature.

A second material issue of fact remains as to whether Burns tacitly sanctioned Gate 4 guards' practice of obtaining lunch from the Frontier Cafe. Burns expected its Gate 4 guards to work eight-hour continuous shifts and to remain at their posts as much as possible. However, because Burns also recognized that the guards must at times eat meals and use the restroom, the company permitted them to take ten-to fifteen-minute paid breaks. The record indicates that Burns was aware that its employees occasionally traveled to the Frontier Cafe during these unscheduled breaks but had never disciplined them for doing so. Indeed, Swenson asserts that a menu from the Frontier Cafe was posted in plain view at Gate 4. Thus, reasonable minds could differ as to whether Burns tacitly sanctioned, or at least contemplated, that its guards would satisfy their need for nourishment by obtaining meals from the Frontier Cafe.

The second *Birkner* criterion states that the employee's conduct must occur substantially within the hours and ordinary spatial boundaries of the employment. [] It is undisputed that Swenson's action occurred within the hours of her employment. She was at her post and in uniform when she decided to take advantage of a lull in plant traffic to eat lunch.

With respect to spatial boundaries, we find that reasonable minds might differ as to whether Swenson was substantially within the ordinary spatial boundaries of her employment when traveling to and from the Frontier Cafe. . . . While it is true that Swenson was not on Geneva property when the accident occurred, she was attempting to obtain lunch from a restaurant within the geographic area accessible during her ten-to fifteen-minute break. Given the other facts of this case, reasonable minds could differ as to whether Swenson's trip to the Frontier Cafe fell substantially within the ordinary spatial boundaries of her employment.

Furthermore, Burns could not point to specific orders barring guards from leaving the facility in their own vehicles to go to the Frontier Cafe on break, although two managers opined that such behavior was prohibited. This dispute alone presents a genuine issue of material fact. If guards were expressly forbidden to drive to the Frontier Cafe to pick up lunch during their break, a jury could find that Swenson was substantially outside the ordinary spatial boundaries of her employment; if they were not so forbidden, a jury might find her to have been acting substantially within the ordinary spatial boundaries of her employment.

Under the third criterion of the *Birkner* test, "the employee's conduct must be motivated, at least in part, by the purpose of serving the employer's interest." [ ] Applying this criterion to the instant case poses the question of whether Swenson's trip to the Frontier Cafe was motivated, at least in part, by the purpose of serving Burns' interest. Reasonable minds might also differ on this question.

First, two Burns managers admitted in their depositions that employee breaks benefit both the employee and the employer. Employees must occasionally eat meals and use the restroom, and employers receive the corresponding benefit of productive, satisfied employees. Reasonable minds could differ as to whether Swenson's particular break fell into this mutual-benefit category.

Second, given the continuous-shift nature of the job and the comparatively brief breaks permitted, Burns' break policy obviously placed a premium on speed and efficiency. Swenson claimed that traveling to the Frontier Cafe enabled her to obtain lunch within the allotted period and thus maximize the time spent at her post. In this respect, reasonable minds might conclude that Swenson's conduct was motivated, at least in part, by the purpose of serving Burns' interest. Evidence indicating that Swenson tried to save time on her lunch break by phoning her order ahead, driving instead of walking, and attempting to return immediately to her post is also relevant in this regard.

In sum, we hold that reasonable minds could differ as to whether Swenson was acting within or outside the scope of her employment when she collided with plaintiffs' motorcycle. Thus, summary judgment is inappropriate. We reverse and remand for further proceedings.

■ ZIMMERMAN, C.J., STEWART, ASSOCIATE C.J., and GREENWOOD, COURT OF APPEALS JUDGE, concur.

■ HOWE, JUSTICE, concurring. . . .

NOTES AND QUESTIONS

1. The court suggests that if Burns had ordered guards not to go off the premises for food that might make a difference. What if a master orders a servant trucker not to run red lights or not to drive drunk and the servant causes an accident by doing just that? See Warner Trucking, Inc. v. Carolina Casualty Insurance Co., 686 N.E.2d 102 (Ind.1997)(master may be liable for actions of driver who violated company rule against driving after having consumed alcohol).

2. Consider how the case would be analyzed under section 7.07(2) of the Restatement (Third) of Agency (2006):

> An employee acts within the scope of employment when performing work assigned by the employer or engaging in a course of conduct subject to the employer's control. An employee's act is not within the scope of employment when it occurs within an

independent course of conduct not intended by the employee to serve any purpose of the employer.

3. Why do courts and the Restatement frame their inquiries as they do? What is the underlying justification for respondeat superior? Consider the conclusion in Lisa M. v. Henry Mayo Newhall Memorial Hospital, 907 P.2d 358 (Cal.1995), in which a hospital technician sexually assaulted a patient under his care. The court, 4–3, stated that it had "identified policy goals of the respondeat superior doctrine—preventing future injuries, assuring compensation to victims, and spreading the losses caused by an enterprise equitably—for additional guidance as to whether the doctrine should be applied in these circumstances." The majority concluded that the assault was "not a risk predictably created by or fairly attributed to the nature of the technician's employment." Is that the right question? Are these three policy goals helpful in resolving the questions raised in *Swenson*?

4. In a review article, Professor Gary Schwartz observes that "employer vicarious liability is a doctrine that is embedded in the American tort system." He then identifies justifications for the doctrine starting with "fairness" (about which he is skeptical)—quoting a prominent judge in 1968 who stated that the doctrine is based "in a deeply rooted sentiment that business enterprise cannot justly disclaim responsibility for accidents which may fairly be said to be characteristic of its activities." Turning to economic justifications, Schwartz summarizes three:

> First, vicarious liability gives employers strong incentives to shrewdly select employees and effectively supervise employees; sound and shrewd employer practices should reduce the rate of employee negligence. Secondly, vicarious liability gives employers an incentive to discipline employees who have committed negligence and thereby exposed the employer to liability. This discipline can take the form either of a demotion or an outright discharge; effective disciplinary programs can both remove employees capable of causing future harm and give employees an ongoing incentive to abstain from negligence. Third, insofar as the prospect of employee negligence cannot be fully eliminated by ambitious selection, training, supervision, and disciplining of employees, vicarious liability gives employers incentives to consider alternatives to employee efforts. One such alternative might be the mechanization of particular tasks; another might be simply the reduction in the overall scale of the employer's activities.

After further consideration, Schwartz concludes that these economically based justifications "are promising, yet incomplete." Schwartz, The Hidden and Fundamental Issue of Employer Vicarious Liability, 69 S.Cal.L.Rev. 1739 (1996). Do they seem incomplete? Despite the skepticism of some commentators, the legal doctrine is firmly established.

5. Other forms of vicarious liability exist in addition to that of employers for their employees. In some states, the owner of an automobile is vicariously liable for the negligence of those driving the automobile with the permission of the owner. Typically, this vicarious liability is prescribed by statute, e.g., RI G.L.1956 § 31–33–6, but in some states it is imposed through common law decisions. See, e.g., Christensen v. Bowen, 140 So.3d 498, 501 (Fla.2014). The purpose of imposing vicarious liability on the owner is to secure the owner's automobile liability insurance for the benefit of third-party victims who may be injured by the negligence of the permitted driver. Similar is the "family-purpose doctrine," which holds parents who own an automobile vicariously liable for the negligent use of the vehicle by one of their children.

6.   Although most issues involve negligent conduct by the employee, at times employees engage in intentional misconduct, raising the question whether a different standard for imposing vicarious liability applies to this category of more culpable conduct. In Clark v. Pangan, 998 P.2d 268 (Utah 2000), a postal supervisor allegedly struck a subordinate in a dispute that arose over "how to conduct an inspection and complete the required paperwork." The court rejected the view held by some states that intentional harm can never be within the scope of employment. Rather, it held that the three *Birkner* factors should apply. In *Birkner*, which involved a "sexual battery," the court noted that "if the employee acts 'from purely personal motives . . . in no way connected with the employer's interests' or if the conduct is 'unprovoked, highly unusual, and quite outrageous,'" it could be considered outside the scope. The case was then sent back to the trial court where the jury would have to determine the outcome in light of the standard provided by the court. Should the result depend on whether the altercation was over business matters, as in the case, or over the previous night's televised sporting event?

7.   The theory of vicarious liability includes the idea that the person held liable may recover indemnity from the person whose negligence or other tort created the liability. There is serious doubt about the frequency with which employers exercise this right. See the discussion in Alvarez v. New Haven Register, Inc., 735 A.2d 306 (Conn.1999); see also G. Schwartz, note 4, supra at 1753 & 1764–67 (discussing the paucity of indemnification claims). Do considerations about indemnity affect your conclusions about the basic doctrine?

8.   *Employer negligence.* What should happen if it were to turn out that the negligent or criminal employee had a record of such behavior in the past? In Foster v. The Loft, Inc., 526 N.E.2d 1309 (Mass.App.1988), plaintiff customer at defendant's bar was punched by a bartender in a melee that broke out after the customer's friend complained that his drink had been improperly mixed. The claim against the defendant bar owner was not that the bartender was functioning within the scope of his employment, but that the owner had hired someone to deal with the public in a hectic environment (a large complex of five bars) who had previously pleaded guilty to assault and battery with a knife and to related charges. Although refusing to hold that an employer can never hire a person with a criminal record, the court did conclude that the jury could reasonably find that the owner failed to take reasonable steps to screen the employees who

would be dealing most closely with the public in an atmosphere that was "volatile" and in which "there was a high potential for violence." How does this analysis differ from that of respondeat superior?

The Employee/Independent Contractor Distinction

Birkner was plainly an employee of Burns. Just as clearly, she was not an employee of the Geneva Steel Plant. Birkner (and Burns) were independent contractors rather than employees of Geneva. While Birkner's status was quite clear, in some cases this determination can be more difficult. (Consider whether drivers for Uber or Lyft are employees or independent contractors. See James Surowiecki, *The Financial Page: Gigs with Benefits*, The New Yorker (July 6 & 13, 2015.)) It matters for tort law because, as we saw in *Swenson*, employers are vicariously liable for the torts of their employees while acting in the scope of employment whereas hirers of independent contractors ordinarily are not vicariously liable. It matters as well for a number of other purposes not relevant to tort law, such as federal tax law, state workers' compensation, labor law, and other fields. Determination for one of these purposes is not necessarily dispositive for the others.

How do courts analyze close cases? The primary, although not exclusive, consideration is the right of the hirer to control the manner and means of how the agent performs the work. Restatement (Third) of Agency § 7.07(a). Thus, in *Swenson*, Burns controlled how Birkner performed her job while Geneva did not, save in a general way of specifying that it sought security for its plant. Note that it is the right to control, not whether it is actually exercised, that is the primary consideration. A hirer of an agent may retain broad general supervision over the job without turning the relationship into an employer-employee one. See Shaffer v. Acme Limestone Co., Inc., 524 S.E.2d 688 (W.Va.1999).

The Restatement of Agency section 7.07 comment f identifies other considerations relevant to determining the status of one hired to perform a job:

> Numerous factual indicia are relevant to whether an agent is an employee. These include: . . . whether the agent is engaged in a distinct occupation or business; whether the type of work done by the agent is customarily done under a principal's direction or without supervision; the skill required in the agent's occupation; whether the agent or the principal supplies the tools and other instrumentalities required for the work and the place in which to perform it; the length of time during which the agent is engaged by a principal; whether the agent is paid by the job or by the time worked; whether the agent's work is part of the principal's regular business; whether the principal and the agent believe that they are creating an employment relationship; and whether the principal is or is

not in business. Also relevant is the extent of control that the principal has exercised in practice over the details of the agent's work.

Roessler v. Novak

Florida District Court of Appeal, 2003.
858 So.2d 1158.

■ SALCINES, JUDGE.

[Plaintiff, Klaus Roessler, was diagnosed at a walk-in clinic as having a perforated viscus, a potentially life-threatening disease. Upon diagnosis, Roessler was referred to the emergency room at Sarasota Memorial Hospital. He was evaluated there by a surgeon and admitted to the hospital. Diagnostic scans of his abdomen were taken and read by Dr. Richard Lichtenstein, a radiologist on duty at Sarasota Memorial. After surgery, Roessler suffered serious complications that required his continued hospitalization for $2^1/_2$ months. The complications included renal failure, a heart condition, systemic sepsis, and multiple brain abscesses that had to be surgically treated. Roessler sued Sarasota Memorial.]

. . . Mr. Roessler alleged that Dr. Lichtenstein misinterpreted the scans taken in Sarasota Memorial's radiology department and was negligent in failing to include an abdominal abscess in his differential diagnosis of Mr. Roessler's abdominal scans. He further alleged that Dr. Lichtenstein did so while an agent of Sarasota Memorial, that he did so within the scope of the agency, and that the hospital was, thus, vicariously liable for Dr. Lichtenstein's alleged negligence.

In response, Sarasota Memorial asserted in its answer . . . that Dr. Lichtenstein was an independent contractor and was not an agent, servant, or employee of Sarasota Memorial. Sarasota Memorial filed a motion for summary judgment which asserted, in relevant part, that it was not liable for the acts of Dr. Lichtenstein because he was not an employee or agent of Sarasota Memorial. The trial court granted Sarasota Memorial's motion for summary judgment and entered a final judgment thereon.

In this appeal, we are asked to determine whether Sarasota Memorial satisfied its burden to establish that no genuine issues of material fact existed regarding its vicarious liability, thereby entitling it to summary judgment as a matter of law. We find that Sarasota Memorial did not satisfy that burden.

As a general rule, a principal may be held liable for the acts of its [non-employee] agent that are within the course and scope of the agency. [ ] Although some agencies are based upon an express agreement, a principal may be liable to a third party for acts of its agent which are within the agent's apparent authority. [ ] Apparent authority is authority which a principal knowingly tolerates or permits, or which the principal by its actions or words holds the agent out as possessing. [ ] The rationale for the doctrine of apparent authority is that a principal should be estopped to deny the authority of an agent when the principal permitted an appearance of authority in the agent and, in so doing, justified a third party's reliance upon that appearance of authority as if it were actually conferred upon the agent. [ ]

An apparent agency exists only if all three of the following elements are present: (a) a representation by the purported principal; (b) a reliance on that representation by a third party; and (c) a change in position by the third party in reliance on the representation.[3] [ ] Apparent authority does not arise from the subjective understanding of the person dealing with the purported agent or from appearances created by the purported agent himself. [ ] Rather, apparent authority exists only where the principal creates the appearance of an agency relationship. [ ]

While some hospitals employ their own staff of physicians, others enter into contractual arrangements with legal entities made up of an association of physicians to provide medical services as independent contractors with the expectation that vicarious liability will not attach to the hospital for the negligent acts of those physicians. [ ] Indeed, Sarasota Memorial and the professional association of radiologists with which Dr. Lichtenstein was affiliated had entered into such an independent contractor agreement.

Under certain circumstances, however, a hospital may be held vicariously liable for the acts of physicians, even if they are independent contractors, if these physicians act with the apparent authority of the hospital. [ ] The doctrine of apparent authority has been applied to physicians who rendered care and treatment to individuals treated in hospital emergency rooms, [ ], as well as in hospital departments other than emergency rooms, [ ]. The question of a physician's apparent authority to act for a hospital is often a question of fact for the jury. [ ]

In the present matter, evidence presented to the trial court for the purpose of the summary judgment proceeding demonstrated that Sarasota Memorial maintained a radiology department which was physically located within the hospital's grounds. Sarasota Memorial contracted with SMH Radiology Associates, P.A., for it to be the exclusive provider of professional radiological services at the hospital.

---

[3] In the portion of its motion for summary judgment addressing Mr. Roessler's medical malpractice claim, Sarasota Memorial did not contest Mr. Roessler's reliance or change of position based upon that reliance and, rather, asserted only that it did not represent that Dr. Lichtenstein acted as its agent. In this appeal, Sarasota Memorial suggests that Mr. Roessler's claim should fail on the latter two elements required for a showing of apparent agency. It reasons that where Mr. Roessler never spoke to Dr. Lichtenstein, there was no reliance and since there was no reliance, there was no change in position on Mr. Roessler's part.

The crucial issue as to the latter two elements, however, is not what interaction transpired between Dr. Lichtenstein (the agent) and Mr. Roessler (the third party), but rather what representations were made by Sarasota Memorial (the principal) which would have led Mr. Roessler (the third party) to rely upon it to provide radiological services.

Dr. Lichtenstein was an employee of SMH Radiology on the date he interpreted Mr. Roessler's scans. Neither Dr. Lichtenstein nor SMH Radiology had offices outside of Sarasota Memorial's hospital grounds. The radiologists employed by SMH Radiology, including Dr. Lichtenstein, worked at Sarasota Memorial to provide all professional radiological services twenty-four hours a day, seven days a week, to Sarasota Memorial's inpatients and outpatients.

Mr. Roessler sought the services offered by Sarasota Memorial when he went to Sarasota Memorial's emergency department. He was admitted to Sarasota Memorial as an inpatient through Sarasota Memorial's emergency department. Once Mr. Roessler arrived at Sarasota Memorial and was admitted as an inpatient, the hospital provided him with the health care services and providers it determined to be necessary. Such services included inpatient professional radiological services, which were provided by Sarasota Memorial through its radiology department. After abdominal scans were taken in its radiology department, Sarasota Memorial assigned Dr. Lichtenstein to interpret them. Like the plaintiff in [ ], Mr. Roessler did not attempt to secure a specialist on his own, but instead accepted the physician provided to him by the hospital.

During a trial, other facts might be developed which could negate a conclusion that Sarasota Memorial should be vicariously liable under an apparent agency theory. However, as presented to the trial court the foregoing facts created a jury question concerning whether Sarasota Memorial, through its actions, represented that Dr. Lichtenstein was its apparent agent. Therefore, the entry of the summary judgment was improper.

Reversed and remanded for further proceedings consistent herewith.

■ NORTHCUTT, J., concurs.

■ ALTENBERND, CHIEF JUDGE, concurring.

I concur because precedent requires me to do so. I believe, however, that our twenty-year experiment with the use of apparent agency as a doctrine to determine a hospital's vicarious liability for the acts of various independent contractors has been a failure. Patients, hospitals, doctors, nurses, other licensed professionals, risk managers for governmental agencies, and insurance companies all need to have predictable general rules establishing the parameters of vicarious liability in this situation. Utilizing case-specific decisions by individually selected juries to determine whether a hospital is or is not vicariously liable for the mistakes of a radiology department, an emergency room, or some other corporate entity that has been created as an independent contractor to provide necessary services within the hospital is inefficient, unpredictable and, perhaps most important, a source of avoidable litigation. Our society can undoubtedly function well and provide insurance coverage to protect the risks of malpractice if there is either broad liability upon the hospital for these services as nondelegable duties or if liability is restricted to the independent contractor. The uncertainty of the current system, however, does not work. The supreme court or the legislature needs to simplify the rules of liability in this area.

As well explained in the majority opinion, in the context of tort law, apparent agency was intended to create vicarious liability for a principal who retains an independent contractor and then represents to the world that the independent contractor is an agent whom the principal has the authority to control. When a specific plaintiff actually relies upon the misrepresentation to his or her detriment, the plaintiff is entitled to recover from the principal for the negligence of the independent contractor. [ ] To some extent, apparent agency can be viewed as a form of vicarious liability for personal injuries and property damage that is warranted because of false information negligently supplied by the principal for the guidance of others. [ ] This theory works reasonably well to create vicarious liability for isolated cases of negligence involving motor vehicles or premises liability. [ ] It has not worked well to establish responsibility for torts in the context of a complex institution like a hospital that has many interrelated independent contractors working side-by-side for the same customers.

It appears that Florida first utilized apparent agency in the context of medical malpractice in the early 1980s. [ ] I suspect that the doctrine arose at that time because that is when hospitals first began spinning off their departments into separate corporations. Over the last twenty years, the apparent agency theory has not allowed the law to establish predictable, general rules of liability because a theory that requires a representation by the principal and reliance by the plaintiff is inherently case specific. Thus, after twenty years of precedent, if a hospital were sued by two different patients for two identical acts of malpractice occurring on the same day and committed by the same doctor in the radiology department, the hospital's vicarious liability would be a fact question for resolution by two different juries. Because such liability is based on case-specific representations by the defendant and reliance by the plaintiff, the two juries would be free to decide that the hospital was vicariously liable for one act but not the other.

. . .

Two recent cases, which are admittedly distinguishable from today's case, seem to favor a theory of nondelegable duty over that of apparent agency in the context of medical negligence. [ ]. This trend suggests that hospitals should be vicariously liable as a general rule for activities within the hospital where the patient cannot and does not realistically have the ability to shop on the open market for another provider. Given modern marketing approaches in which hospitals aggressively advertise the quality and safety of the services provided within their hospitals, it is quite arguable that hospitals should have a nondelegable duty to provide adequate radiology departments, pathology laboratories, emergency rooms, and other professional services necessary to the ordinary and usual functioning of the hospital. The patient does not usually have the option to pick among several independent contractors at the hospital and has little ability to negotiate and bargain in this market to select a preferred radiology department. The hospital, on the other hand, has great ability to assure that competent radiologists work within an independent radiology department and to bargain with those radiologists to provide adequate malpractice protections for their mutual customers. I suspect that medical economics would work better if the general rule placed general vicarious liability upon the hospital for these activities. Thus, I would consider adopting a theory of nondelegable duty, similar to the approach used in [ ], if it were not for the existing precedent that employs the theory of apparent agency.

NOTES AND QUESTIONS

1.   In light of the majority opinion, what might Memorial do to minimize the possibility that it will be found vicariously liable for its independent-contractor physicians? In Baptist Memorial Hospital System v. Sampson, 969 S.W.2d 945 (Tex.1998), the hospital defendant posted signs stating that certain doctors were not employees of the hospital and also required patients to sign a form acknowledging their awareness of that fact and that the hospital did not control those physicians in their practice of medicine. The plaintiff, who was treated in the emergency room denied seeing the signs or recalling reading any such statement in the forms she signed. The court affirmed summary judgment for the hospital on the ground that nothing the hospital did could have created a reasonable belief that the physicians were hospital agents.

2.   In footnote 3 of its opinion, the court addresses the second and third elements required to establish an apparent agency—reliance and that the party relying change position. These two elements are sometimes collapsed into the phrase "detrimental reliance." How could Roessler satisfy this third element?

3.   Section 57 of the Restatement (Third) of Torts: Liability for Physical and Emotional Harm states:

> Except as stated in §§ 58–65, an actor who hires an independent contractor is not subject to vicarious liability for physical harm caused by the tortious conduct of the contractor.

One of those exceptions, section 65, provides:

> An actor who hires an independent contractor to perform services is subject to vicarious liability for physical harm if:
>
> > (a) the services are accepted in the reasonable belief that the actor or the actor's employees are rendering the services; and

> (b) the independent contractor's negligence is a factual cause of harm to one who receives the services, and such harm is within the scope of liability.

Is this different from the rule provided in *Roessler*? If so, which is preferable?

4. Some courts, however, do not require reliance on the physician's being an employee, but instead demand only that the patient rely on the hospital to provide competent medical care. See York v. Rush-Presbyterian-St. Luke's Medical Center, 854 N.E.2d 635 (Ill.2006). For a discussion of the range of approaches employed by courts on the issue of apparent agency of hospital physicians and whether reliance is required, see Ingram, Vicarious Liability of the Employer of an Apparent Servant, 41 Tort Trial & Ins. Prac.L.J. 1 (2005).

5. How persuasive is the concurrence in advocating adoption of a nondelegable duty approach? If certainty is to be provided, should it be to make a hospital vicariously liable for all of its attending physicians, regardless of employment status? Or should the hospital be exempt from vicarious liability so long as the doctor is not an employee of the hospital?

In *Maloney v. Rath*, p. 5 supra, involving the brake failure, the court concluded that the owner of the car should be held liable for the negligence of the garage mechanic who worked on the brakes, even though the owner had chosen a reputable mechanic and had no reason to suspect that the job had been badly done. The court stressed two statutory requirements that car brakes be in working order. These were said to show that the legislature recognized that improperly maintained motor vehicles threaten "a grave risk of serious bodily harm or death." Responsibility for proper maintenance of such potentially dangerous property "properly rests with the person who owns and operates the vehicle." That person "selects the contractor and is free to insist upon one who is financially responsible and to demand indemnity from him." Is it sound to require car owners to learn the solvency of their mechanics before entrusting their cars to them?

6. Another exception to the rule on independent contractors is contained in section 58 of the Third Restatement. This section makes the employer of an independent contractor vicariously liable for work that involves a peculiar risk if the contractor fails to take appropriate precautions in light of the risk. Work involving a peculiar risk has been evocatively explained by Professor Mechem:

> [T]he work [is] conspicuously, exceptionally, unusually dangerous . . . its salient characteristic is that the mention or sight of such work immediately causes the reaction "DANGER!" in the mind of the listener or witness in a way that other work, perhaps in fact equally dangerous, does not. Thus one observing a tree being cut down in a populous area or a heavy electric sign being put in place above a much-travelled street is instinctively impressed with the danger and the need for special precautions as he is not where he sees a neighbor's porch being painted, although

he may be drenched the next moment with paint from a fallen bucket.

P. Mechem, Outlines of the Law of Agency § 488, at 336–37 (4th ed.1952).

7.   Do the justifications for respondeat superior mentioned by Professor Schwartz at p. 24 supra seem consistent with the exception from liability for hospitals that employ physicians as independent contractors? From liability for a homeowner who hires a roofer to replace the roof when shingles negligently secured by the roofer fall on a visitor to the homeowner? Does it matter to your answer whether the agent has adequate resources to pay for the damage caused?

CHAPTER II

THE NEGLIGENCE PRINCIPLE

A. HISTORICAL DEVELOPMENT OF FAULT LIABILITY

The law of negligence is of relatively recent origin. As late as 1850, one finds only a handful of isolated cases that refer to liability based on negligence. In A History of American Law (3d ed.2005), Lawrence Friedman observes (at p. 350) that:

> [T]he law of torts was totally insignificant before 1800, a twig on the great tree of law. The old common law had very little to say about personal injuries caused by careless behavior. A good many basic doctrines of tort law first appeared before 1850; but it was in the late nineteenth century that this area of law (and life) experienced its greatest spurt of growth.
>
> . . .
>
> . . . The new machines [of the Industrial Revolution] had a marvelous, unprecedented capacity for smashing the human body. Factories manufactured injury and sudden death as well as their ordinary products.

Was the pre-industrial era characterized by strict liability? Some commentators have thought so. Others have argued that fault considerations always tempered the strictness of tort doctrine in cases of unintended harm. The debate is complicated by the fact that tort law, as Friedman points out, only ripened into a field during the latter part of the nineteenth century. Before the Industrial Revolution, the infrequent cases of accidental harm that occurred were filtered through the Anglo-American writ system—a procedural system requiring that tort-like wrongs be pleaded as actions in "trespass" or "trespass on the case," rather than the substantive categories we now employ. The flavor of the writ system is well captured in the classic distinction put forward by Fortescue, J., in Reynolds v. Clarke, (1725) 92 Eng.Rep. 410 (K.B.):

> [I]f a man throws a log into the highway, and in that act it hits me; I may maintain trespass, because it is an immediate wrong; but if as it lies there I tumble over it, and receive an injury, I must bring an action upon the case; because it is only prejudicial in consequence, for which originally I could have no action at all.

We begin our consideration of negligence with a closer look at the English common law approach that laid the foundations for the American treatment of unintended harm. In the following excerpt, Gary Schwartz draws upon the leading historical accounts in addressing the question of whether pre-industrial injury law was dominated by a strict liability approach.

Tort Law and the Economy in Nineteenth Century America: A Reinterpretation

Gary T. Schwartz.
90 Yale Law Journal 1717, 1722–27 (1981).

Research into pre-1800 English tort doctrine is fraught with hazards. One can look at judges' remarks ventured in the course of what amounted to oral argument. But as has been observed, "[t]o ransack the Year Books for large statements of doctrine made in irrelevant circumstances by judges barely conscious of their significance is neither a pleasing nor a profitable task." One can also study the pleadings and trial verdicts available in the mostly unpublished plea rolls and rely on them in attempting to infer the pertinent liability standards. But the process of drawing "believable inferences" from raw documents of this sort is frequently "perilous." And whether one turns to the Year Books or the plea rolls, questions of substantive law frequently are obscured or confounded by the demands of the English writ system.

Despite these inadequacies of evidence,[35] many scholars have confidently found huge portions of strict liability in traditional English law. Professor Gregory finds strict liability inherent in the English writ of trespass.[36] But this alignment of English trespass with strict liability is misleading. As developed in the late twelfth century, the early writ of trespass—far from entailing strict liability—seems to have been primarily addressed to intentional harm-causing conduct, conduct that would now be identified as basically criminal. To be sure, by a process we now may be barely able to reconstruct, trespass began to extend to conduct that involved "*vi et armis*" (the trespass formula) only in the loose sense of harm that was forcibly, even if accidentally, inflicted. The propriety of this extension was confirmed, and the standard of liability in trespass explicitly—though ambiguously—discussed, in Weaver v. Ward,[41] a 1616 case concerning the accidental discharge of firearms. Although *Weaver* did suggest that the trespass-plaintiff's proof of immediately caused harm established a prima facie case, it also indicated that the defendant could refute liability by showing that what

---

[35] Even if medieval law *had* been subject to a significant strict liability rule, that rule would require interpretation. Perhaps medieval thinking imputed a motive (whether conscious or unconscious) to every action in a way that just about eliminated the concept of unintended harm. See A. Ehrenzweig, Psychoanalytic Jurisprudence 244 (1971). Perhaps in a simple medieval world, almost every serious injury was the result of intentional or at least negligent conduct. See J. Fleming, An Introduction to the Law of Torts 3 (3d ed.1967); [ ].

[36] ... A semantic point: "strict liability" was not a phrase that courts employed during the periods under review. On those occasions when strict liability was considered, the idea was conveyed in a variety of indirect ways.

[41] Hobart 134, 80 Eng.Rep. 284 (1616). . . .

happened had been an "inevitable accident"—that the defendant had been "utterly without fault" or had "committed no negligence." While these various formulations clearly rule out the idea of unqualified strict liability, their precise meaning is far from clear.[42]

The question of the liability standard in trespass was further complicated by what was then routine trespass procedure. A trespass writ generally took the form of a "stark uninformative declaration." In answering the writ the defendant could offer a "blank plea of Not Guilty," and then present to the jury whatever extenuating evidence he thought relevant. The standard of liability in trespass thus was left to the effective discretion of the individual jury, and we simply lack information as to how juries exercised this discretion; jury verdicts of guilty and not guilty remain largely "inscrutable."

Professor Malone emphasizes the strict liability he finds in the English fire cases. Though the judicial statements in question contain certain strict liability phrases, they also avail themselves of the language of negligence. Whether these negligence references were mere rhetorical flourishes or were instead intended to posit an actual liability standard is a question that has provoked disagreement. No one contends, however, that a strict liability rule applied to fires that were accidentally set. Rather, the rule is said to have covered deliberately started fires that accidentally spread to a neighbor's property. Even these fires were subject to strict liability only to the extent that they remained "within the control" of the defendant. And since, for example, an unexpectedly strong wind tended to negate control, the control requirement can easily be regarded as a correlate or proxy for fault.

The fire cases were pleaded in trespass on the case. As a general matter, the case variation on the trespass writ provided a remedy for English victims who could not make any plausible claim of forcible injury. In the absence of such a claim, however, the case plaintiff needed to explain in his writ why the imposition of liability was appropriate in his situation. Since it appears that a number of situations were found sufficient in this respect, case possessed from the start a catch-all or "miscellaneous" quality that makes it difficult to generalize about its standard of liability. Traditionally, however, case has been affiliated with negligence, and overall this affiliation seems fair. The earliest instances of case involved suits against professionals like blacksmiths, physicians, and veterinarians who were held liable for negligence in their undertakings. In the fifteenth and sixteenth centuries, a limited number of claims were litigated in case between parties not in any preexisting contractual relation; for these claims, a liability standard approaching negligence was applied. By the late seventeenth century, collision suits began to come before the courts—

---

[42] Related to the "inevitable accident" defense was the idea that trespass would not lie if the object immediately causing the injury—a ship or a horse, for example—had escaped the defendant's control. . . .

collisions of vessels at sea, of horse-drawn carriages on highways, and of carriages with pedestrians. Since these collisions involved forceful contacts, they raised a clear trespass possibility. Yet, for several possible reasons,[61] these suits were frequently pleaded in case, with liability depending on proof of the defendant's negligence. Even when the facts of a particular collision led to its being presented in trespass, it appears that negligence was recognized as the liability pivot. Of course, collisions of one sort or another—often involving railroads—came to typify tort litigation in the nineteenth century.

One early fire opinion, in vacillating between strict liability and negligence, indicates that an employer could be held strictly liable for the within-the-employment negligence of his employee in allowing a fire to spread. In general, any claim of vicarious liability relegated a plaintiff to case, and as late as 1685 the law was willing—the fire cases apart—to hold employers liable only for torts they had actually commanded. In its sixteenth-century form, moreover, the command rule evidently required the employer to have "commanded the very act in which the wrong consisted (unless the command had been to do a thing in itself unlawful)." Gradually, however, in eighteenth-century England the modern notion developed that the employer could be held liable for any of his employee's scope-of-employment torts;[68] but in personal injury cases this notion seems to have been associated with the assumption of some negligent conduct on the employee's part.

Therefore, whatever the strict liability possibilities that may have harbored in the writ of trespass, these possibilities evidently were connected to or at least contained by a narrow rule of employer vicarious liability, a rule that, as it eventually expanded, acquired a noticeable negligence orientation. Negligence, moreover, was all along the accepted standard of liability in the malpractice and the collision cases. Indeed, if one searches traditional English tort law for clear instances of strict liability, one winds up mainly with the animal cases. Even these cases reveal an uncertain prior history. Cattle owners originally were held liable for those cattle trespasses that their owners deliberately incited; and the early suits over animals attacking humans may well have involved plain negligence on the part of the animals' custodians. To be sure, over time each of these animal doctrines inclined in the direction of strict liability. But the explanations for these evolutions remain very much in doubt; and in any event the modest animal rules posed no particular threat to nineteenth-century industrialization.

---

[61] One reason was loss of control. See note 42 supra. Another reason was vicarious liability. [ ]

[68] The account afforded here is in opposition to the common assumption that the scope-of-employment test is of "ancient" origin. [ ]

To sum up, then, the strict liability strands in traditional English law seem ambivalent and confused; the negligence strands, both more distinct and more capable of extended application.

NOTES AND QUESTIONS

1. The leading historical sources analyzed by Schwartz are J. Baker, An Introduction to English Legal History (2d ed.1979); C. Fifoot, History and Sources of the Common Law: Tort and Contract (1949); A. Harari, The Place of Negligence in the Law of Torts (1962); S. Milsom, Historical Foundations of the Common Law (2d ed.1981); T. Plucknett, A Concise History of the Common Law (5th ed.1956); M. Pritchard, *Scott v. Shepherd* (1773) and the Emergence of the Tort of Negligence (1976); Arnold, Accident, Mistake and the Rules of Liability in the Fourteenth-Century Law of Torts, 128 U.Pa.L.Rev. 361 (1979); Gregory, Trespass to Negligence to Absolute Liability, 37 Va.L.Rev. 359 (1951); and Malone, Ruminations on the Role of Fault in the History of the Common Law of Torts, 31 La.L.Rev. 1 (1970).

2. Virtually all of these sources take as their starting point the question of whether strict liability was dominant at early common law, or whether it was tempered to some extent by fault considerations. As we trace the modern development of negligence and strict liability in the materials that follow, keep in mind the possibility of another perspective: that the pre-industrial era was in fact substantially committed to a "no-liability" approach based on court-imposed immunities, limited duties, and restrictive notions of what constituted an actionable claim in the first instance. This thesis is developed in Rabin, The Historical Development of the Fault Principle: A Reinterpretation, 15 Ga.L.Rev. 925 (1981), arguing that "no-liability" thinking continued to influence tort law well into the negligence era.

See also Gilles, Inevitable Accident in Classical English Tort Law, 43 Emory L.J. 575 (1994), arguing that English precedents in the pre-industrial era established a liability regime falling between strict causal-based liability and negligence. That regime was identified as one in which "the question was not whether actors had behaved unreasonably—whether they *should* have avoided the accident—but whether they *could* have avoided it by greater practical care." Id. at 577 (emphasis added).

3. Undoubtedly, the leading English precedents played a role in shaping early American tort law. In the early nineteenth century, however, the states began to develop their own accident law. Again, there is scholarly disagreement over the role of strict liability in the early post-Revolutionary period. Compare M. Horwitz, The Transformation of American Law, 1780–1860 (1977), at 67–108, and Gregory, cited in note 1 supra, with Schwartz at 1727–34, and Schwartz, The Character of Early American Tort Law, 36 UCLA L.Rev. 641 (1989). Whatever the situation might have been before 1850, the universality of the negligence principle was an open question in this country when the following landmark case was decided.

Brown v. Kendall

Supreme Judicial Court of Massachusetts, 1850.
6 Cush. (60 Mass.) 292.

This was an action of trespass for assault and battery, originally commenced against George K. Kendall, the defendant, who died pending the suit, and his executrix was summoned in.

It appeared in evidence, on the trial . . . that two dogs, belonging to the plaintiff and the defendant, respectively, were fighting in the presence of their masters; that the defendant took a stick about four feet long, and commenced beating the dogs in order to separate them; that the plaintiff was looking on, at the distance of about a rod, and that he advanced a step or two towards the dogs. In their struggle, the dogs approached the place where the plaintiff was standing. The defendant retreated backwards from before the dogs, striking them as he retreated; and as he approached the plaintiff, with his back towards him, in raising his stick over his shoulder, in order to strike the dogs, he accidentally hit the plaintiff in the eye, inflicting upon him a severe injury.

Whether it was necessary or proper for the defendant to interfere in the fight between the dogs; whether the interference, if called for, was in a proper manner, and what degree of care was exercised by each party on the occasion; were the subject of controversy between the parties, upon all the evidence in the case, of which the foregoing is an outline.

[Under instructions from the trial judge, which are reviewed in the opinion, the jury returned a verdict for the plaintiff and the trial judge entered judgment.]

■ SHAW, C.J.

        . . .

The facts set forth in the bill of exceptions preclude the supposition, that the blow, inflicted by the hand of the defendant upon the person of the plaintiff, was intentional. The whole case proceeds on the assumption, that the damage sustained by the plaintiff, from the stick held by the defendant, was inadvertent and unintentional; and the case involves the question how far, and under what qualifications, the party by whose unconscious act the damage was done is responsible for it. We use the term "unintentional" rather than involuntary, because in some of the cases, it is stated, that the act of holding and using a weapon or instrument, the movement of which is the immediate cause of hurt to another, is a voluntary act, although its particular effect in hitting and hurting another is not within the purpose or intention of the party doing the act.

It appears to us, that some of the confusion in the cases on this subject has grown out of the long-vexed question, under the rule of the common law, whether a party's remedy, where he has one, should be sought in an action of the case, or of trespass. This is very distinguishable from the question, whether in a given case, any action will lie. The result of these cases is, that if the damage complained of is the immediate effect of the act of the defendant, trespass *vi et armis* lies; if consequential only, and not immediate, case is the proper remedy. [ ]

In these discussions, it is frequently stated by judges, that when one receives injury from the direct act of another, trespass will lie. But we think this is said in reference to the question, whether trespass and not case will lie, assuming that the facts are such, that some action will lie. These *dicta* are no authority, we think, for holding, that damage received by a direct act of force from another will be sufficient to maintain an action of trespass, whether the act was lawful or unlawful, and neither wilful, intentional, or careless. . . .

We think, as the result of all the authorities, the rule is correctly stated by Mr. Greenleaf, that the plaintiff must come prepared with evidence to show either that the *intention* was unlawful, or that the defendant was *in fault;* for if the injury was unavoidable, and the conduct of the defendant was free from blame, he will not be liable. 2 Greenl.Ev. §§ 85 to 92; [ ]. If, in the prosecution of a lawful act, a casualty purely accidental arises, no action can be supported for an injury arising therefrom. [ ] In applying these rules to the present case, we can perceive no reason why the instructions asked for by the defendant ought not to have been given; to this effect, that if both plaintiff and defendant at the time of the blow were using ordinary care, or if at that time the defendant was using ordinary care, and the plaintiff was not, or if at that time, both the plaintiff and defendant were not using ordinary care, then the plaintiff could not recover.

In using this term, ordinary care, it may be proper to state, that what constitutes ordinary care will vary with the circumstances of cases. In general, it means that kind and degree of care, which prudent and cautious men would use, such as is required by the exigency of the case, and such as is necessary to guard against probable danger. A man, who should have occasion to discharge a gun, on an open and extensive marsh, or in a forest, would be required to use less circumspection and care, than if he were to do the same thing in an inhabited town, village, or city. To make an accident, or casualty, or as the law sometimes states it, inevitable accident, it must be such an accident as the defendant could not have avoided by the use of the kind and degree of care necessary to the exigency, and in the circumstances in which he was placed.

. . . We can have no doubt that the act of the defendant in attempting to part the fighting dogs, one of which was his own, and for the injurious acts of which he might be responsible, was a lawful and proper act, which he might do by proper and safe means. If, then, in doing this act, using due care and all proper precautions necessary to the exigency of the case, to avoid hurt to others, in raising his stick for that purpose, he accidentally hit the plaintiff in his eye, and wounded him, this was the result of pure accident, or was involuntary and unavoidable, and therefore the action would not lie. . . .

The court instructed the jury, that if it was not a necessary act, and the defendant was not in duty bound to part the dogs, but might with propriety interfere or not as he chose, the defendant was responsible for the consequences of the blow, unless it appeared that he was in the exercise of extraordinary care, so that the accident was inevitable, using the word not in a strict but a popular sense. This is to be taken in connection with the charge afterwards given, that if the jury believed, that the act of interference in the fight was unnecessary, (that is, as before explained, not a duty incumbent on the defendant), then the burden of proving extraordinary care on the part of the defendant, or want of ordinary care on the part of plaintiff, was on the defendant.

The court are of opinion that these directions were not conformable to law. If the act of hitting the plaintiff was unintentional, on the part of the defendant, and done in the doing of a lawful act, then the defendant was not liable, unless it was done in the want of exercise of due care, adapted to the exigency of the case, and therefore such want of due care became part of the plaintiff's case, and the burden of proof was on the plaintiff to establish it. 2 Greenl.Ev. § 85; [ ].

Perhaps the learned judge, by the use of the term extraordinary care, in the above charge, explained as it is by the context, may have intended nothing more than that increased degree of care and diligence, which the exigency of particular circumstances might require, and which men of ordinary care and prudence would use under like circumstances, to guard against danger. If such was the meaning of this part of the charge, then it does not differ from our views, as above explained. But we are of opinion, that the other part of the charge, that the burden of proof was on the defendant, was incorrect. Those facts which are essential to enable the plaintiff to recover, he takes the burden of proving. The evidence may be offered by the plaintiff or by the defendant; the question of due care, or want of care, may be essentially connected with the main facts, and arise from the same proof; but the effect of the rule, as to the burden of proof, is this, that when the proof is all in, and before the jury, from whatever side it comes, and whether directly proved, or inferred from circumstances, if it appears that the defendant was doing a lawful act, and unintentionally hit and hurt the plaintiff, then unless it also appears to the satisfaction of the jury, that the defendant is chargeable with some fault, negligence, carelessness, or want of prudence, the plaintiff fails to sustain the burden of proof, and is not entitled to recover.

New trial ordered.

NOTES AND QUESTIONS

1. How does Chief Justice Shaw resolve the issue of whether the pre-existing common law recognized strict liability for unintended harm? Was plaintiff arguing for a strict liability standard? What might the trial court have intended by recognizing a distinct standard of care when defendant's conduct "was not a necessary act"?

2. Apart from the trial court's erroneous reference to necessary acts, how did the jury instruction misstate the law? What, precisely, were the unsettled questions before *Brown v. Kendall* that Shaw resolved in the opinion?

3. Does Shaw indicate *why* the fault principle establishes the appropriate standard of liability? We have already given brief consideration to two scholarly efforts to justify liability based on negligence. Recall the excerpts from Holmes and Posner in Chapter I. Compare their positions with the following interpretation of *Brown v. Kendall* in Gregory, Trespass to Negligence to Absolute Liability, 37 Va.L.Rev. 359, 368 (1951):

> While it is pure speculation, one of Chief Justice Shaw's motives underlying his opinion appears to have been a desire to make risk-creating enterprise less hazardous to investors and entrepreneurs than it had been previously at common law. Certainly that interpretation is consistent with his having furthered the establishment of the fellow servant doctrine and the expansion of the assumption-of-risk defense in actions arising out of industrial injuries. Judicial subsidies of this sort to youthful enterprise removed pressure from the pocket-books of investors and gave incipient industry a chance to experiment on low-cost operations without the risk of losing its reserve in actions by injured employees. Such a policy no doubt seems ruthless; but in a small way it probably helped to establish industry, which in turn was essential to the good society as Shaw envisaged it.

Gregory's mention of the fellow servant doctrine refers to Shaw's famous opinion in Farwell v. Boston & Worcester Railroad Corp., 45 Mass. (4 Metc.) 49 (1842), in which an injured worker's suit against his employer was dismissed on the grounds that a master was not vicariously liable for injuries caused by a fellow worker's negligence. More broadly, under nineteenth-century negligence law the carelessness of a fellow servant was one of many risks that an employee was taken to assume, and which prevented suit against the employer. See Friedman & Ladinsky, Social Change and the Law of Industrial Accidents, 67 Colum.L.Rev. 50 (1967).

Is Gregory's thesis distinctively different from the views of Holmes and Posner? In what sense could the fault principle be viewed as providing a "subsidy" to industry? Why should a dog-fight case involving two neighbors be regarded as relevant to protection of industrial enterprises? As you study the materials that follow, ask yourself which rationale for the fault principle seems most convincing. Is it likely that a single rationale will be applicable to every type of unintentional harm?

B. THE CENTRAL CONCEPT

1. THE STANDARD OF CARE

Until now, we have discussed fault liability without making any effort to give content to the central concept of negligence—apart from referring to it as "unreasonable" conduct. Although we have given brief consideration to moral and economic justifications for the fault principle, we have yet to examine how the system actually operates. What standard does a court utilize in deciding whether the defendant's behavior was "negligent"? We begin by exploring the concept of unreasonable risk.

Note that "negligence" is commonly used to refer to the issue examined in this section: breach of the standard of reasonable care. But it is just as commonly used more broadly to encompass negligence as a theory that permits a plaintiff to recover damages—"the law of negligence"—which includes elements of duty, causation, and defenses (explored in later chapters), along with the concept of unreasonable conduct examined in this section.

Adams v. Bullock

Court of Appeals of New York, 1919.
227 N.Y. 208, 125 N.E. 93.

■ CARDOZO, J.

The defendant runs a trolley line in the city of Dunkirk, employing the overhead wire system. At one point, the road is crossed by a bridge or culvert which carries the tracks of the Nickle Plate and Pennsylvania railroads. Pedestrians often use the bridge as a short cut between streets, and children play on it. On April 21, 1916, the plaintiff, a boy of twelve years, came across the bridge, swinging a wire about eight feet long. In swinging it, he brought it in contact with the defendant's trolley wire, which ran beneath the structure. The side of the bridge was protected by a parapet eighteen inches wide. Four feet seven and three-fourths inches below the top of the parapet, the trolley wire was strung. The plaintiff was shocked and burned when the wires came together. He had a verdict at Trial Term, which has been affirmed at the Appellate Division by a divided court.

We think the verdict cannot stand. The defendant in using an overhead trolley was in the lawful exercise of its franchise. Negligence, therefore, cannot be imputed to it because it used that system and not another [ ]. There was, of course, a duty to adopt all reasonable precautions to minimize the resulting perils. We think there is no evidence that this duty was ignored. The trolley wire was so placed that no one standing on the bridge or even bending over the parapet could reach it. Only some extraordinary casualty, not fairly within the area of ordinary prevision, could make it a thing of danger. Reasonable care in the use of a destructive agency imports a high degree of vigilance (Nelson v. Branford L. & W. Co., 75 Conn. 548, 551 [1903]; Braun v. Buffalo Gen. El. Co., 200 N.Y. 484 [1911]). But no vigilance, however alert, unless fortified by the gift of prophecy, could have predicted the point upon the route where such an accident would occur. It might with equal reason have been expected anywhere else. At any point upon the route, a mischievous or thoughtless boy might touch the wire with a metal pole, or fling another wire across it [ ]. If unable to reach it from the walk, he might stand upon a wagon or climb upon a tree. No special danger at this bridge warned the defendant that there was need of special measures of precaution. No like accident had occurred before. No custom had been disregarded. We think that ordinary caution did not involve forethought of this extraordinary peril. It has been so ruled in like circumstances by courts in other jurisdictions. [ ] Nothing to the contrary was held in [*Braun*]; [ ]. In those cases, the accidents were well within the range of prudent foresight [ ]. That was also the basis of the ruling in [*Nelson*]. There is, we may add, a distinction, not to be ignored, between electric light and trolley wires. The distinction is that the former may be insulated. Chance of harm, though remote, may betoken negligence, if needless. Facility of protection may impose a duty to protect. With trolley wires, the case is different. Insulation is impossible. Guards here and there are of little value. To avert the possibility of this accident and others like it at one point or another on the route, the defendant must have abandoned the overhead system, and put the wires underground. Neither its power nor its duty to make the change is shown. To hold it liable upon the facts exhibited in this record would be to charge it as an insurer.

The judgment should be reversed. . . .

■ HISCOCK, CH. J., CHASE, COLLIN, HOGAN, CRANE and ANDREWS, JJ., concur.

NOTES AND QUESTIONS

1.   What negligence might the jury have found? That in turn will depend on how the trial proceeded and what evidence was introduced. Consider the following observation in Grady, Untaken Precautions, 18 J. Legal Stud. 139, 144 (1989):

> Events do not define what negligence analysis will be the case, and the court does not define it either. Instead, by selecting an untaken precaution on which to rely, the plaintiff defines the analysis that everyone else will use—including the defendant, the court that will try the case, and any court that may hear an appeal. . . . The plaintiff makes his choice from among a group of possible contenders and frequently alleges several untaken precautions in the alternative. . . .

What untaken precautions might have avoided the injury in *Adams*? What about insulating the wires? Building some sort of umbrella over the wires when they pass under bridges? Posting signs on the approaches to bridges, in language that children would understand, warning of the danger of twirling long wires? Are some of these more promising than others?

2.   In *Braun*, cited by Judge Cardozo, defendant had strung electric wires some 25 feet above a vacant lot. The wires had been strung around 1890 with insulation that was expected to last three years. They were never inspected. Fifteen years later, a building was constructed on the lot. When joists reached over 20 feet from the ground, it would be "natural for one desiring to go from one side of the building to the other to raise the wires so that he could pass under or bear down on them so that he could step over." The decedent, a carpenter, came in contact with the now-exposed wires and was electrocuted. After the lower courts dismissed the complaint, the court of appeals reversed and remanded for trial. Discussing negligence, the court observed:

> Little need or can be said about the condition of the wires, for if the respondent owed any obligation whatever of making them safe it would scarcely have been more negligent if, instead of allowing them to remain uninspected and unrepaired as it did, it had strung and maintained absolutely naked wires. The only question which is at all close is whether the respondent in the exercise of the reasonable care and foresight should have apprehended that the premises over which the wires were strung might be so used as to bring people in contact with them, and whether, therefore, it should have guarded against such a contingency. As indicated, I think this was fairly a question for the jury. Here was a vacant lot in the midst of a thickly built-up section of a large city. It was no remote or country lot where no buildings could be expected. The neighboring land was covered with buildings. It was the only vacant lot in the vicinity. It fronted on a street and there was plenty of space for a building. Now, what was reasonably to be anticipated—that this lot would be allowed indefinitely to lie unimproved and unproductive, or that it, like other surrounding lots, would be improved by additions to the old building or by the erection of new and independent ones? Was it to be anticipated that its use would be an exception to the rule prevailing in the entire neighborhood or that it would be in conformity therewith? It seems to me that the answer to these questions should have been made by the jury, and that the latter would be justified in saying that the respondent was bound to anticipate what was usual rather than that which was exceptional and act accordingly. It does not appear how much this neighborhood may have changed since the wires were first strung, but assuming that it had materially changed in respect of the use of lots for buildings, such a change in a neighborhood for aught that appears in this case requires some time, and as a basis for responsibility it is not too much to charge a company stringing such wires with notice of gradual changes in the locality through which the wires pass.

Is *Braun* distinguishable from *Adams*?

3. What result in *Adams v. Bullock* if the same thing had happened twice in recent years? How important is it that "no like accident had occurred before"?

4. How is the concept of "ordinary caution" or "reasonable care" referred to in *Adams* and the note cases conveyed to the jury? Consider the following version recommended for use in California Jury Instructions Civil (BAJI) § 3.10 (April 2015):

> Negligence is the doing of something which a reasonably prudent person would not do, or the failure to do something which a reasonably prudent person would do, under circumstances similar to those shown by the evidence.
>
> It is the failure to use ordinary or reasonable care.
>
> Ordinary or reasonable care is that care which persons of ordinary prudence would use in order to avoid injury to themselves or others under circumstances similar to those shown by the evidence.

Does this formulation capture the spirit of these cases?

The formulation suggests two questions that need to be pursued in greater detail. First, is the concept too general to be used effectively by courts and juries? Second, how do the courts construct the "reasonably prudent person" referred to in the charge? We turn to these questions in order.

First, is it feasible to establish a calculus of risk—a more structured approach to the due care inquiry? Consider the approach to defining unreasonable risk suggested by Judge Learned Hand in the following case.

United States v. Carroll Towing Co.
United States Court of Appeals, Second Circuit, 1947.
159 F.2d 169.

■ Before L. HAND, CHASE and FRANK, CIRCUIT JUDGES.

■ L. HAND, CIRCUIT JUDGE.

[The harbormaster and a deckhand aboard the Carroll, a tug, readjusted the lines holding fast the Anna C, a barge owned by plaintiff Connors, in the course of their efforts to "drill out" another barge in New York Harbor. Because of their negligence in securing the Anna C, it later broke loose and rammed against a tanker. The tanker's propeller broke a hole near the bottom of the Anna C, which soon filled with water and sank, with loss of cargo (owned by the United States) as well as the vessel itself. In this part of the case, Connors was trying to recover the value of its barge from Carroll. Carroll sought to reduce damages pursuant to admiralty law because the plaintiff's bargee was absent from the Anna C. The evidence indicated that siphoning efforts by other boats present in the area would have kept the barge afloat if the bargee had been aboard to sound a warning. The trial judge, as fact finder, found no negligence on the part of the bargee, and Carroll appealed that finding among others.]

. . .

It appears from the foregoing review that there is no general rule to determine when the absence of a bargee or other attendant will make the owner of the barge liable for injuries to other vessels if she breaks away from her moorings. . . . It becomes apparent why there can be no such general rule, when we consider the grounds for such a liability. Since there are occasions when every vessel will break from her moorings, and since, if she does, she becomes a menace to those about her, the owner's duty, as in other similar situations, to provide against resulting injuries is a function of three variables: (1) The probability that she will break away; (2) the gravity of the resulting injury, if she does; (3) the burden of adequate precautions. Possibly it serves to bring this notion into relief to state it in algebraic terms: if the probability be called P; the injury, L; and the burden, B; liability depends upon whether B is less than L multiplied by P: i.e., whether $B < PL$. Applied to the situation at bar, the likelihood that a barge will break from her fasts and the damage she will do, vary with the place and time; for example, if a storm threatens, the danger is greater; so it is, if she is in a crowded harbor where moored barges are constantly being shifted about. On the other hand, the barge must not be the bargee's prison, even though he lives aboard; he must go ashore at times. We need not say whether, even in such crowded waters as New York Harbor a bargee must be aboard at night at all, it may be that the custom is otherwise . . . and that, if so, the situation is one where custom should control. We leave that question open; but we hold that it is not in all cases a sufficient answer to a bargee's absence without excuse, during working hours, that he has properly made fast his barge to a pier, when he leaves her. In the case at bar the bargee left at five o'clock in the afternoon of January 3rd, and the flotilla broke away at about two o'clock in the afternoon of the following day, twenty-one hours afterwards. The bargee had been away all the time, and we hold that his fabricated story was affirmative evidence that he had no excuse for his absence. At the locus in quo—especially during the short January days and in the full tide of war activity—barges were being constantly "drilled" in and out. Certainly it was not beyond reasonable expectation that, with the inevitable haste and bustle, the work might not be done with adequate care. In such circumstances we hold—and it is all that we do hold—that it was a fair requirement that the Conners Company should have a bargee aboard (unless he had some excuse for his absence), during the working hours of daylight.

[The court reversed and remanded for reconsideration of the allocation of damages.]

NOTES AND QUESTIONS

1. Consider the following comments by Judge (then Professor) Richard Posner on the *Carroll Towing* formula in A Theory of Negligence, 1 J. Legal Stud. 29, 32–33 (1972):

> It is time to take a fresh look at the social function of liability for negligent acts. The essential clue, I believe, is provided by Judge Learned Hand's famous formulation of the negligence standard—one of the few attempts to give content to the deceptively simple concept of ordinary care. . . . [The formulation] never purported to be original but was an attempt to make explicit the standard that the courts had long applied. In a negligence case, Hand said, the judge (or jury) should attempt to measure three things: the magnitude of the loss if an accident occurs; the probability of the accident's occurring; and the burden of taking precautions that would avert it. If the product of the first two terms exceeds the burden of precautions, the failure to take those precautions is negligence. Hand was adumbrating, perhaps unwittingly, an economic meaning of negligence. Discounting (multiplying) the cost of an accident if it occurs by the probability of occurrence yields a measure of the economic benefit to be anticipated from incurring the costs necessary to prevent the accident. The cost of prevention is what Hand meant by the burden of taking precautions against the accident. It may be the cost of installing safety equipment or otherwise making the activity safer, or the benefit forgone by curtailing or eliminating the activity. If the cost of safety measures or of curtailment—whichever cost is lower—exceeds the benefit in accident avoidance to be gained by incurring that cost, society would be better off, in economic terms, to forgo accident prevention. A rule making the enterprise liable for the accidents that occur in such cases cannot be justified on the ground that it will induce the enterprise to increase the safety of its operations. When the cost of accidents is less than the cost of prevention, a rational profit-maximizing enterprise will pay tort judgments to the accident victims rather than incur the larger cost of avoiding liability. Furthermore, overall economic value or welfare would be diminished rather than increased by incurring a higher accident-prevention cost in order to avoid a lower accident cost. If, on the other hand, the benefits in accident avoidance exceed the costs of prevention, society is better off if those costs are incurred and the accident averted, and so in this case the enterprise is made liable, in the expectation that self-interest will lead it to adopt the precautions in order to avoid a greater cost in tort judgments.

Is Posner correct in attributing a strictly economic definition of negligence to Judge Hand? For example, why should the "customary" night-time hours of bargees be relevant? The role of custom in negligence cases is considered in greater detail later in this chapter.

2.   Is the *Carroll Towing* formula useful in determining whether particular conduct is negligent? How would the formulation apply to *Adams?* To *Braun?* Does allegedly careless driving present distinct difficulties in applying the *Carroll Towing* formula because it involves a claim of careless *personal behavior*, rather than an allegation of unreasonable business judgment? Is this a meaningful distinction? Which type of case is *Carroll Towing?* Even in a "business judgment" case such as *Adams*, how would Cardozo have responded to the argument that a warning notice on the bridge would have involved a trivial expense? Should a court assess the cost of such a warning in purely economic terms? As far as the usefulness of the formula is concerned, should it make a difference that *Carroll Towing* involved property damage and all the other cases involved personal harm?

3.   In McCarty v. Pheasant Run, Inc., 826 F.2d 1554 (7th Cir.1987), plaintiff guest was assaulted in her room at defendant's resort by an intruder who entered through a sliding glass door. The door, which opened onto a walkway, had not been locked but the security chain had been fastened. The plaintiff's theories of negligence included that the defendant should have made sure the door was locked before renting the room; or should have warned her to keep the door locked; or should have equipped the door with a better lock; or should have had more security guards on duty; or should have made the walkway inaccessible to the rooms; or some combination of these things.

After a jury verdict for defendant, plaintiff moved for judgment notwithstanding the verdict. The trial court's denial of the motion was affirmed on appeal. The court, in an opinion by Judge Posner, observed that:

> Ordinarily, and here, the parties do not give the jury the information required to quantify the variables that the Hand Formula picks out as relevant. That is why the formula has greater analytic than operational significance. Conceptual as well as practical difficulties in monetizing personal injuries may continue to frustrate efforts to measure expected accident costs with the precision that is possible, in principle at least, in measuring the other side of the equation—the cost or burden of precaution. [ ] For many years to come juries may be forced to make rough judgments of reasonableness, intuiting rather than measuring the factors in the Hand Formula; and so long as their judgment is reasonable, the trial judge has no right to set it aside, let alone substitute his own judgment.

Judge Hand was even less sanguine about ever knowing or valuing the factors. In Moisan v. Loftus, 178 F.2d 148 (2d Cir.1949), he observed, in a case in which a car ran off the road, that of the three factors,

> care is the only one ever susceptible of quantitative estimate, and often that is not. The injuries are always a variable within limits, which do not admit of even approximate ascertainment; and, although probability might theoretically be estimated, if any

statistics were available, they never are; and, besides, probability varies with the severity of the injuries. It follows that all such attempts are illusory; and, if serviceable at all, are so only to center attention upon which one of the factors may be determinative in any given situation.

Is this observation sound? Is it significant that this case, unlike *Carroll Towing*, involved personal injury?

4. For consideration of the tension between the cost-benefit standard for negligence in *Carroll Towing* and community attitudes about trading off injury or death for dollars framed by the well-known "Ford Pinto" case, see Schwartz, The Myth of the Ford Pinto Case, 43 Rutgers L.Rev. 1013 (1991), which is excerpted in note 2, p. 751 infra.

5. Recall the concern with notice and foreseeability of the risk of harm in *Adams v. Bullock*, p. 44 supra. Nowhere in *Carroll Towing* does Judge Hand qualify P and L by stating that it is the foreseeable likelihood of harm and its foreseeable severity that are the relevant considerations. Yet, when these factors are considered in a negligence case, they are understood to be limited to the foreseeable probability and severity. See Restatement (Third) of Torts: Liability for Physical and Emotional Harm § 3 (2010).

6. Mark Grady has identified what he refers to as a pocket of strict liability within the negligence rule, linked to the impossibility of driving—or engaging in any high-repetition precautionary behavior—without an occasional lapse as "compliance error." Unlike the rest of us, the reasonable person never makes an inadvertent mistake. Liability in these cases does not involve personal culpability or blameworthiness and accordingly functions like a rule of strict liability. See Grady, Res Ipsa Loquitur and Compliance Error, 142 U.Pa.L.Rev. 887 (1994).

7. Another perspective on defining reasonable care is suggested in the following excerpt from the concurring opinion of Lord Reid in Bolton v. Stone, [1951] A.C. 850. A visiting team member drove the ball out of the defendant's cricket field on to a relatively untraveled road that had a few houses on the far side. Plaintiff happened to be standing in that road near her house and was injured when the ball hit her. In 28 years 6 balls had been driven over the field's fence, but no one had been hurt before. The House of Lords unanimously held that the risk was so small that the defendant club might reasonably disregard it. In his response to plaintiff's claim that at least after a ball had once gone over the fence defendants had a duty to prevent a recurrence, Lord Reid observed:

> Once a ball has been driven on to a road without there being anything extraordinary to account for the fact, there is clearly a risk that another will follow, and if it does there is clearly a chance, small though it may be, that someone may be injured. On the theory that it is foreseeability alone that matters it would be irrelevant to consider how often a ball might be expected to land in the road and it would not matter whether the road was the

busiest street, or the quietest country lane; the only difference between these cases is in the degree of risk.

It would take a good deal to make me believe that the law has departed so far from the standards which guide ordinary careful people in ordinary life. In the crowded conditions of modern life even the most careful person cannot avoid creating some risks and accepting others. What a man must not do, and what I think a careful man tries not to do, is to create a risk which is substantial. . . . In my judgment the test to be applied here is whether the risk of damage to a person on the road was so small that a reasonable man in the position of the appellants, considering the matter from the point of view of safety, would have thought it right to refrain from taking steps to prevent the danger.

In considering that matter I think that it would be right to take into account not only how remote is the chance that a person might be struck but also how serious the consequences are likely to be if a person is struck; but I do not think that it would be right to take into account the difficulty of remedial measures. If cricket cannot be played on a ground without creating a substantial risk, then it should not be played there at all.

Is Lord Reid's argument persuasive? Why isn't the risk a "needless" one as that term was used in *Adams*? On the other hand, why does he say that in cases of "substantial risk" it would not be "right to take into account the difficulty of remedial measures"? Is he suggesting that one who exposes another to a substantial risk is always negligent for doing so? Do either the Cardozo opinions or Judge Hand's formula suggest any such threshold of harm?

8.   For a close look at the background of the *Carroll Towing* case and an assessment of its significance, see Gilles, *United States v. Carroll Towing Co.*: The Hand Formula's Home Port, in R. Rabin & S. Sugarman (eds.), Torts Stories 11 (2003). Note, in particular, Gilles's discussion of "[t]wo alternatives to Hand Formula balancing [that] have been especially influential in Anglo-American negligence law: . . . the 'foreseeable-danger' approach and the 'community expectations' approach." On the former, reconsider the excerpt from Holmes, note 1, p. 6 supra, and on the latter, consider the excerpt from Holmes, note 4, p. 56 infra. Are there cases in this section in which these alternative conceptions would be likely to lead to different results?

We turn now to the second matter noted above—a parallel understanding of the concept of due care, reflected in the construction of the "reasonably prudent person."

2. THE REASONABLE PERSON

Bethel v. New York City Transit Authority

Court of Appeals of New York, 1998.
92 N.Y.2d 348, 703 N.E.2d 1214, 681 N.Y.S.2d 201.

■ LEVINE, JUDGE.

Over a century ago this Court adopted its version of the rule which came to prevail at the time in almost all state jurisdictions, imposing the duty upon common carriers of "the exercise of the *utmost* care, *so far as human skill and foresight can go*," for the safety of their passengers in transit (Kelly v. Manhattan Ry. Co., 112 N.Y. 443, 450 [1889] [emphasis supplied]). . . .

. . .

We granted leave to appeal in this case to confront directly whether a duty of highest care should continue to be applied, as a matter of law, to common carriers and conclude that it should not. We thus realign the standard of care required of common carriers with the traditional, basic negligence standard of reasonable care under the circumstances. Under that standard, there is no stratification of degrees of care as a matter of law [ ]. Rather, "there are only different amounts of care as a matter of fact" [ ].

[Plaintiff was hurt on defendant's bus when the "wheelchair accessible seat" collapsed under him. Plaintiff could not prove that defendant actually knew of the defect but relied on a theory of constructive notice "evidenced by a computer printout repair record of Bus No. 2209, containing two notations that, 11 days before the accident, repairs (adjustment and alignment) were made to a 'Lift Wheelchair.' Plaintiff contended that the repairs to the 'Lift Wheelchair' were to the seat in question, and that a proper inspection during those repairs would have revealed the defect causing the seat to collapse 11 days later."]

The court charged the jury that, as a common carrier, "[t]he bus company here . . . had a duty to use the highest degree of care that human prudence and foresight can suggest in the maintenance of its vehicles and equipment for the safety of its passengers" [ ]. On the issue of constructive notice, arising out of the earlier inspection and repair, the trial court submitted to the jury the question of whether "considering *the duty of care that is imposed on common carriers with respect to this equipment*, a reasonable inspection would have led to the discovery of the condition and its repair" before the accident (emphasis supplied).

[The jury found for plaintiff on the constructive notice theory and the Appellate Division affirmed without addressing the issue of standard of care. The court of appeals concluded that the instruction was the "dispositive issue" on appeal.]

The duty of common carriers to exercise the highest degree of care ... was widely adopted at the advent of the age of steam railroads in 19th century America. Their primitive safety features resulted in a phenomenal growth in railroad accident injuries and with them, an explosion in personal injury litigation, significantly affecting the American tort system [ ]. In this century, however, through technological advances and intense governmental regulation, "public conveyances ... have become at least as safe as private modes of travel" [ ].

Time has also disclosed the inconsistency of the carrier's duty of extraordinary care with the fundamental concept of negligence in tort doctrine.

> "The whole theory of negligence presupposes some uniform standard of behavior. Yet the infinite variety of situations which arise makes it impossible to fix definite rules in advance for all conceivable human conduct. ... The standard of conduct which the community demands must be an external and objective one, rather than the individual judgment, good or bad, of the particular actor. ... The courts have dealt with this very difficult problem by creating a fictional person ... the 'reasonable [person] of ordinary prudence'" (Prosser and Keeton, Torts § 32, at 173–174 [5th ed.]).

> . . .

The objective, reasonable person standard in basic traditional negligence theory, however, necessarily takes into account the circumstances with which the actor was actually confronted when the accident occurred, including the reasonably perceivable risk and gravity of harm to others and any special relationship of dependency between the victim and the actor.

> "The [reasonable person] standard provides sufficient flexibility, and leeway, to permit due allowance to be made ... for all of the particular circumstances of the case which may reasonably affect the conduct required" (Restatement [Second] of Torts § 283, comment c; [ ]).

[The court traced criticisms of the carrier's duty of extraordinary care through a case in 1919, a law review article in 1928, and its own decision in 1950, and concluded that the "single, reasonable person standard is sufficiently flexible by itself to permit courts and juries fully to take into account the ultrahazardous nature of a tortfeasor's activity."]

. . .

someone who commits a tort

For all of the foregoing reasons, we conclude that the rule of a common carrier's duty of extraordinary care is no longer viable. Rather, a common carrier is subject to the same duty of care as any other potential tortfeasor—reasonable care under all of the circumstances of the particular case. Here, because the jury was specifically charged that the defendant carrier was required to exercise "the highest degree of care that human prudence and foresight can suggest" in connection with the issue of its constructive notice of the defective seat, the error cannot be deemed merely harmless.

] holding
] rule

[The case was remanded for a new trial.] — *disposition*

■ KAYE, C.J., and BELLACOSA, SMITH, CIPARICK and WESLEY, JJ., concur.

NOTES AND QUESTIONS

1. What was the original justification for the carrier rule? Was it never valid or did it cease to be valid? If the history of steam railroads is the explanation, why was the same rule extended to buses? Is it relevant that passengers have contractual relationships with carriers? Is it relevant that passengers still do not know what goes on in bus repair shops? We return to this issue later in the section on proof of negligence. If you were a juror, how would the court's change in the law be likely to affect your consideration of whether the Transit Authority was negligent?

2. As *Bethel* indicates, courts traditionally have utilized a hypothetical person whose conduct is taken to measure what is reasonable under the circumstances—recall the court's use of an "external and objective" standard. Consider the following description from 3 F. Harper, F. James, Jr. & O. Gray, The Law of Torts § 16.2 at 432–34 (3d ed.2007):

General formula: Reasonable person; The external as against the subjective standard. We come next to inquire into the nature of the standard below which conduct must not fall if it is to avoid being negligence. This is ordinarily measured by what the reasonably prudent person would do in the circumstances. As everyone knows, this reasonable person is a creature of the law's imagination. He is an abstraction. . . .

Now this reasonably prudent person is not infallible or perfect. In foresight, caution, courage, judgment, self-control, altruism and the like he represents, and does not excel, the general average of the community. He is capable of making mistakes and errors of judgment, of being selfish, of being afraid—but only to the extent that any such shortcoming embodies the normal standard of community behavior. On the other hand the general practice of the community, in any given particular, does not necessarily reflect what is careful. The practice itself may be negligent. "Neglect of duty does not cease by repetition to be neglect of duty." Thus the standard represents the general level of moral judgment of the community, what it feels ought ordinarily to be done, and not necessarily what is ordinarily done, although in practice the two would very often come to the same thing.

Is "the general level of moral judgment of the community" necessarily the same as "the general average of the community"?

3. As the section heading from Harper, James, and Gray suggests, the authors subsequently discuss the question whether reasonable care should be based on an external standard or the defendant's own capacity for care. In fact, the reasonable care inquiry raises two threshold questions. The first is whether the salient measuring stick of due care is the conduct or the state of mind of the defendant. The second—if defendant's conduct is the determining factor—is whether it is to be measured against the defendant's own capacity or against an external standard. Employing a reasonable person test suggests, of course, that defendant's conduct is the critical determinant, and that the conduct is to be measured against external, "objective" norms, rather than "subjective" ability. In adopting this two-fold external standard, the legal system adheres to a definition of "fault" that is arguably at odds with our everyday usage of the term. Is the approach justifiable?

4. Might the content of the reasonable person influence views on the wisdom of the court's approach in *Bethel*? Consider the approach that Justice Holmes explored in an excerpt from The Common Law 108–10 (1881):

> The standards of the law are standards of general application. The law takes no account of the infinite varieties of temperament, intellect, and education which make the internal character of a given act so different in different men. It does not attempt to see men as God sees them, for more than one sufficient reason. In the first place, the impossibility of nicely measuring a man's powers and limitations is far clearer than that of ascertaining his knowledge of law, which has been thought to account for what is called the presumption that every man knows the law. But a more satisfactory explanation is that, when men live in society, a certain average of conduct, a sacrifice of individual peculiarities going beyond a certain point, is necessary to the general welfare. If, for instance, a man is born hasty and awkward, is always having accidents and hurting himself or his neighbors, no doubt his congenital defects will be allowed for in the courts of Heaven, but his slips are no less troublesome to his neighbors than if they sprang from guilty neglect. His neighbors accordingly require him, at his proper peril, to come up to their standard, and the courts which they establish decline to take his personal equation into account.

> The rule that the law does, in general, determine liability by blameworthiness, is subject to the limitation that minute differences of character are not allowed for. The law considers, in other words, what would be blameworthy in the average man, the

man of ordinary intelligence and prudence, and determines liability by that. If we fall below the level in those gifts, it is our misfortune; so much as that we must have at our peril, for the reasons just given. But he who is intelligent and prudent does not act at his peril, in theory of law. On the contrary, it is only when he fails to exercise the foresight of which he is capable, or exercises it with evil intent, that he is answerable for the consequences.

There are exceptions to the principle that every man is presumed to possess ordinary capacity to avoid harm to his neighbors, which illustrate the rule, and also the moral basis of liability in general. When a man has a distinct defect of such a nature that all can recognize it as making certain precautions impossible, he will not be held answerable for not taking them. A blind man is not required to see at his peril; and although he is, no doubt, bound to consider his infirmity in regulating his actions, yet if he properly finds himself in a certain situation, the neglect of precautions requiring eyesight would not prevent his recovering for an injury to himself, and, it may be presumed, would not make him liable for injuring another. So it is held that, in cases where he is the plaintiff, an infant of very tender years is only bound to take the precautions of which an infant is capable; the same principle may be cautiously applied where he is defendant. Insanity is a more difficult matter to deal with, and no general rule can be laid down about it. There is no doubt that in many cases a man may be insane, and yet perfectly capable of taking the precautions, and of being influenced by the motives, which the circumstances demand. But if insanity of a pronounced type exists, manifestly incapacitating the sufferer from complying with the rule which he has broken, good sense would require it to be admitted as an excuse.

Taking the qualification last established in connection with the general proposition previously laid down, it will now be assumed that, on the one hand, the law presumes or requires a man to possess ordinary capacity to avoid harming his neighbors, unless a clear and manifest incapacity be shown; but that, on the other, it does not in general hold him liable for unintentional injury, unless, possessing such capacity, he might and ought to have foreseen the danger, or, in other words, unless a man of ordinary intelligence and forethought would have been to blame for acting as he did. . . .

Notwithstanding the fact that the grounds of legal liability are moral to the extent above explained, it must be borne in mind that law only works within the sphere of the senses. If the external phenomena, the manifest acts and omissions, are such as it requires, it is wholly indifferent to the internal phenomena of conscience. A man may have as bad a heart as he chooses, if his conduct is within the rules. In other words, the standards of the law are external standards, and, however much it may take moral considerations into account, it does so only for the purpose of drawing a line between such bodily motions and rests as it permits, and such as it does not. What the law really forbids, and the only thing it forbids, is the act on the wrong side of the line, be that act blameworthy or otherwise. . . .

5. *Gender.* In the preceding passages from both Harper, James, and Gray and Holmes, as in tort discourse generally until recent years, gender references regarding reasonable conduct, among other issues, were pervasively male in content; indeed, the "reasonable man" standard was the established reference point. Whether this masculine orientation translated into favorable or unfavorable treatment of female litigants in tort cases is, of course, a separate question. References to the gender/tort literature can be found in Schlanger, Injured Women Before Common Law Courts, 1860–1930, 21 Harv. Women's L.J. 79 (1998), a study of the judicial treatment of female litigants in three categories of transportation injury cases. In an earlier study of fright-based claims, Chamallas & Kerber, Women, Mothers, and the Law of Fright: A History, 88 Mich.L.Rev. 814, 863 (1990), the authors remarked, "[t]hat recognizing difference may lead to marginalization, while ignoring difference may lead to inequitable results, has long been the Scylla and Charybdis of feminist theory. A major goal of feminist theory is to find a route past these monsters: first, by being skeptical of conceptual dualisms enshrined in familiar cultural and legal practice, and second, by unmasking claims of difference to reveal unstated norms against which difference is judged." See generally M. Chamallas, Introduction to Feminist Legal Theory 262–70 (3d ed.2013).

In the following notes we explore several of the themes raised by the Holmes excerpt.

6. *Mental ability.* In the leading case of Vaughan v. Menlove, (1837) 132 Eng.Rep. 490 (C.P.), the defendant landowner piled hay in a way that created a fire hazard to neighbors, including plaintiff. A fire occurred and plaintiff sued and won. Defendant's attorney sought a new trial on the ground that instead of charging the standard of ordinary prudence, the judge should have asked the jury to decide whether defendant had acted to the best of his judgment. He emphasized that since the "measure of prudence varies so with the varying faculties of men," it was impossible to say what was negligence "with reference to the standard of what is called ordinary prudence." Perhaps alluding delicately to his client's limitation, the attorney urged that if the defendant had acted to the best of his judgment "he ought not to be responsible for the misfortune of not possessing the highest order of intelligence." The court unanimously rejected the argument on the ground that "it would leave so vague a line as to afford no rule at all, the degree of judgment belonging to each individual being infinitely various."

Is the court's position persuasive? Should cases of distinctive physical handicap—such as blindness, the example used by Holmes—be measured by a standard that takes defendant's disability into account (presumably the reasonable blind person)? Is the problem of degree likely to be manageable in the physical handicap situation?

7. *Physical disability.* In Roberts v. Ramsbottom, [1980] 1 All E.R. 7 (Q.B.1979), the judge found that the 73-year-old defendant had suffered a stroke a few minutes before setting out on a drive; that he had experienced no previous warnings or symptoms; that though his consciousness was impaired he was in sufficient possession of his faculties "(i) to have some, though an impaired, awareness of his surroundings and the traffic conditions and (ii) to make a series of deliberate and voluntary though inefficient movements of his hands and legs to manipulate the controls of his car;" and that the defendant "was at no time aware of the fact that he was unfit to drive; accordingly no moral blame can be attached to him for continuing to do so." After reviewing the English case law, the judge concluded:

> The driver will escape liability if his actions at the relevant time were wholly beyond his control. The most obvious case is sudden unconsciousness. But if he retained some control, albeit imperfect control, and his driving, judged objectively, was below the required standard, he remains liable. His position is the same as a driver who is old or infirm. In my judgment unless the facts establish what the law recognizes as automatism the driver cannot avoid liability on the basis that owing to some malfunction of the brain his consciousness was impaired. Counsel for the plaintiff put the matter accurately, as I see it, when he said "One cannot accept as exculpation anything less than total loss of consciousness."

The judge also accepted the alternative ground of liability based on defendant's failure to realize, after one or two misadventures on the road, that he was unfit to continue driving that day. Had he recognized his condition, he would have stopped driving before he hit the plaintiff's car. Although not morally to blame for failing to realize his inadequacy, the defendant was nonetheless responsible for failing to "appreciate [the] proper significance" of his prior mishaps.

Does *Ramsbottom* suggest that the reasonable person standard applies without considering the deficiencies of the elderly or those with relatively minor handicaps? Should it be otherwise? Is the holding consistent with *Hammontree v. Jenner*, p. 3 supra?

8. In Bashi v. Wodarz, 53 Cal.Rptr.2d 635 (App.1996), defendant rear-ended a car, left the scene without stopping, and shortly thereafter collided with plaintiffs. Defendant claimed to have little recall of the events. The traffic report stated: ". . . Somewhere, shortly after making the turn, she stated, 'I wigged out.' She stated that all she could remember was ramming into the back of someone's vehicle and then continuing east. She had no control of her actions at that time and then she remembered being involved in a second collision at an unknown location on White Lane. She also stated, 'My family has a history of mental problems and I guess I just freaked out.'" Apparently concluding that the defendant had a "sudden,

unanticipated onset of mental illness," the trial judge granted summary judgment for defendant. The court of appeal reversed, noting that California "has approved the rule of Cohen v. Petty (D.C.Cir.1933) 65 F.2d 820, that as between an innocent passenger and an innocent fainting driver, the former must suffer. . . . Under a line of appellate authorities beginning in 1942, these cases generally hold that a driver, suddenly stricken by [a physical illness rendering the driver unconscious, is not chargeable with negligence [citing several cases, including *Hammontree* v. *Jenner*]."

The defendant argued that California should extend its rule to "sudden and unanticipated mental illness as well as to physical illness," because the public policy grounds of *Cohen* were equally applicable to disabling mental illnesses. The court declined. In addition to a statute that it thought favored plaintiff, the court noted that Restatement section 283B was in accord: "Unless the actor is a child, his insanity or other mental deficiency does not relieve the actor from liability for conduct which does not conform to the standard of a reasonable man under like circumstances." The court extracted four justifications for the position from a comment to the section:

> (1) the "difficulty of drawing any satisfactory line between mental deficiency and those variations of temperament, intellect, and emotional balance which cannot" be considered in imposing liability; (2) the "unsatisfactory character of the evidence of mental deficiency in many cases, together with the ease with which it can be feigned"; (3) "if mental defectives are to live in the world they should pay for the damage they do, and that it is better that their wealth, if any, should be used to compensate innocent victims than that it should remain in their hands"; and (4) the expectation that liability will stimulate "those who have charge of them or their estates . . . to look after them, keep them in order, and see that they do not do harm."

Section 283C of the Second Restatement provides that "[i]f the actor is ill or otherwise physically disabled, the standard of conduct to which he must conform to avoid being negligent is that of a reasonable man under like disability."

A comment notes that "a heart attack, or a temporary dizziness due to fever or nausea, as well as a transitory delirium, are regarded merely as circumstances to be taken into account in determining what the reasonable man would do. The explanation for the distinction between such physical illness and the mental illness dealt with in section 283B probably lies in the greater public familiarity with the former, and the comparative ease and certainty with which it can be proved."

On the facts of *Bashi*, which Restatement section applies: 283B or 283C?

9. *Superior attributes.* Section 12 of the Third Restatement provides that actors with "skills or knowledge that exceed those possessed by most others . . . are circumstances to be taken into account in determining whether the actor has exercised reasonable care." In Dakter v. Cavallino,

866 N.W.2d 656 (Wis.2015), the court affirmed a trial court instruction that a semi-truck driver was required to exercise the degree of care that a reasonable semi-truck driver would exercise under the circumstances. Is the Restatement section, as applied in *Dakter*, consistent with *Bethel*? Is it sound?

10. *Children.* Apart from statutes making parents vicariously liable for malicious mischief committed by their children, usually up to a modest amount, parents are rarely vicariously liable for their children. Parents may, however, be liable for their own negligence in permitting children to do something beyond their ability or in failing to exercise control over a dangerous child.

The narrow scope of vicarious liability has meant that plaintiffs must often sue the child directly. Traditionally, children have been held to a blended standard—one that recognizes their age and abilities, but also invokes an objective component: children must exercise the care that a reasonable child of their actual age, intelligence, and experience would exercise. How might such a standard be applied to a child riding a bicycle or throwing a ball? How should we analyze a case involving a child who is unusually rash? Unusually dull? Unusually forgetful? Why should children be treated differently from adults in taking into account individual characteristics?

A few states hold that children below the age of 6 or 7 are conclusively presumed to be unable to comprehend risk sufficiently to be held negligent. These states also use a rebuttable presumption for children between 7 and 14. See Price v. Kitsap Transit, 886 P.2d 556 (Wash.1994).

When children engage in adult activities, courts have applied adult standards. In Dellwo v. Pearson, 107 N.W.2d 859 (Minn.1961), involving a 12-year-old driving a motor boat, the court said:

> While minors are entitled to be judged by standards commensurate with age, experience, and wisdom when engaged in activities appropriate to their age, experience, and wisdom, it would be unfair to the public to permit a minor in the operation of a motor vehicle to observe any other standards of care and conduct than those expected of all others. A person observing children at play with toys, throwing balls, operating tricycles or velocipedes, or engaged in other childhood activities may anticipate conduct that does not reach an adult standard of care or prudence. However, one cannot know whether the operator of an approaching automobile, airplane, or powerboat is a minor or an adult, and usually cannot protect himself against youthful imprudence even if warned. Accordingly, we hold that in the operation of an automobile, airplane, or powerboat, a minor is to be held to the same standard of care as an adult.

Is this sound? *Dellwo* has been especially influential in automobile cases. There is dispute about what activities should be categorized as "adult." In Goss v. Allen, 360 A.2d 388 (N.J.1976), a 17-year-old beginning skier, while attempting to negotiate a turn, collided with plaintiff. The court held that skiing was an activity for persons of all ages and did not qualify as an activity for which minors should be held to an adult standard. The court thought that 18, the age of legal majority, was the appropriate age for holding persons to the adult standard. Although the difference between 17 and 18 was hard to define, the court recognized that no matter what age was selected for adult responsibility the line would seem arbitrary.

What about the fact that defendant was a beginner in *Goss v. Allen*? Should inexperienced persons, regardless of age, be held to a less demanding standard? Apart from other considerations, are the line-drawing problems insurmountable?

———

We turn now to a consideration of factors that sometimes circumscribe the role of juries in determining what constitutes due care. After an initial look at the interplay between judge and jury, we examine the roles of custom and statute.

C. THE ROLES OF JUDGE AND JURY

1. IN GENERAL

Baltimore & Ohio Railroad Co. v. Goodman
Supreme Court of the United States, 1927.
275 U.S. 66, 48 S.Ct. 24, 72 L.Ed. 167.

■ MR. JUSTICE HOLMES delivered the opinion of the Court.

This is a suit brought by the widow and administratrix of Nathan Goodman against the petitioner for causing his death by running him down at a grade crossing. The defense is that Goodman's own negligence caused the death. At the trial, the defendant asked the Court to direct a verdict for it, but the request, and others looking to the same direction, were refused, and the plaintiff got a verdict and a judgment which was affirmed by the Circuit Court of Appeals. 10 F.2d 58.

Goodman was driving an automobile truck in an easterly direction and was killed by a train running southwesterly across the road at a rate of not less than sixty miles an hour. The line was straight, but it is said by the respondent that Goodman "had no practical view" beyond a section house two hundred and forty-three feet north of the crossing until he was about twenty feet from the first rail, or, as the respondent argues, twelve feet from danger, and that then the engine was still obscured by the section house. He had been driving at the rate of ten or twelve miles an hour, but had cut down his rate to five or six miles at about forty feet from the crossing. It is thought that there was an emergency in which, so far as appears, Goodman did all that he could.

We do not go into further details as to Goodman's precise situation, beyond mentioning that it was daylight and that he was familiar with the crossing, for it appears to us plain that nothing is suggested by the evidence to relieve Goodman from responsibility for his own death. When a man goes upon a railroad track he knows that he goes to a place where he will be killed if a train comes upon him before he is clear of the track. He knows that he must stop for the train, not the train stop for him. In such circumstances it seems to us that if a driver cannot be sure otherwise whether a train is dangerously near he must stop and get out of his vehicle, although obviously he will not often be required to do more than to stop and look. It seems to us that if he relies upon not hearing the train or any signal and takes no further precaution he does so at his own risk. If at the last moment Goodman found himself in an emergency it was his own fault that he did not reduce his speed earlier or come to a stop. It is true as said in Flannelly v. Delaware & Hudson Co., 225 U.S. 597, 603, that the question of due care very generally is left to the jury. But we are dealing with a standard of conduct, and when the standard is clear it should be laid down once for all by the Courts. [ ]

Judgment reversed.

NOTES AND QUESTIONS

1.   Under the *Goodman* view, when would plaintiffs win grade-crossing cases?

2.   Almost a half century before *Goodman*, Holmes stated his position on the role of the jury in negligence cases in The Common Law 123–24:

> When a case arises in which the standard of conduct, pure and simple, is submitted to the jury, the explanation is plain. It is that the court, not entertaining any clear views of public policy applicable to the matter, derives the rule to be applied from daily experience, as it has been agreed that the great body of the law of tort has been derived. But the court further feels that it is not itself possessed of sufficient practical experience to lay down the rule intelligently. It conceives that twelve men taken from the practical part of the community can aid its judgment. Therefore it aids its conscience by taking the opinion of the jury.

> But supposing a state of facts often repeated in practice, is it to be imagined that the court is to go on leaving the standard to the jury forever? Is it not manifest, on the contrary, that if the jury is, on the whole, as fair a tribunal as it is represented to be, the lesson which can be got from that source will be learned? Either the court will find that the fair teaching of experience is that the conduct complained of usually is or is not blameworthy, and therefore, unless explained, is or is not a ground of liability; or it will find the jury oscillating to and fro, and will see the necessity of making up its mind for itself. . . .

> If this be the proper conclusion in plain cases, further consequences ensue. Facts do not often exactly repeat themselves in practice; but cases with comparatively small variations from

each other do. A judge who has long sat at *nisi prius* ought gradually to acquire a fund of experience which enables him to represent the common sense of the community in ordinary instances far better than an average jury. He should be able to lead and to instruct them in detail, even where he thinks it desirable, on the whole, to take their opinion. Furthermore, the sphere in which he is able to rule without taking their opinion at all should be continually growing.

Do these arguments justify his position in *Goodman*?

Pokora v. Wabash Railway Co.

Supreme Court of the United States, 1934.
292 U.S. 98, 54 S.Ct. 580, 78 L.Ed. 1149.

■ MR. JUSTICE CARDOZO delivered the opinion of the Court.

[Pokora was driving his truck west across four tracks of defendant's railroad. The easternmost track was a switch track and the one next to that was the main track. A string of boxcars standing on the switch track 5–10 feet north of the crossing cut off plaintiff's view of the track north. As he moved past that track he listened but heard no bell or whistle. As he reached the main track he was struck by a train coming from the north at 25–30 miles per hour. The distance between the western rail of the switch track and the eastern rail of the main track was 8 feet, but 2–3 feet were lost to the overhang of the boxcars. Although there was no showing how far from the front of the truck Pokora was sitting, the opinion suggests "perhaps five feet or even more." Although a view 130 feet north may have been available from a nearby point, the opinion notes that this would not protect plaintiff if the train was 150 feet away when Pokora looked. "For all that appears, he had no view of the main track northward, or none for a substantial distance, till the train was so near that escape had been cut off." Relying on *Goodman,* the court of appeals had upheld a directed verdict for the railroad.]

. . .

In such circumstances the question, we think, was for the jury whether reasonable caution forbade his going forward in reliance on the sense of hearing, unaided by that of sight. No doubt it was his duty to look along the track from his seat, if looking would avail to warn him of the danger. This does not mean, however, that if vision was cut off by obstacles, there was negligence in going on, any more than there would have been in trusting to his ears if vision had been cut off by the darkness of the night. [ ] Pokora made his crossing in the day time, but like the traveler by night he used the faculties available to one in his position. [ ] A jury, but not the court, might say that with faculties thus limited, he should have found some other means of assuring himself of safety before venturing to cross. The crossing was a frequented highway in a populous city. Behind him was a line of other cars, making ready to follow him. To some extent, at least, there was assurance in the thought that the defendant would not run its train at such a time and place without sounding bell or whistle. . . .

The argument is made, however, that our decision in [*Goodman*], is a barrier in the plaintiff's path, irrespective of the conclusion that might commend itself if the question were at large. There is no doubt that the opinion in that case is correct in its result. Goodman, the driver, traveling only five or six miles an hour, had, before reaching the track, a clear space of eighteen feet within which the train was plainly visible.[2] With that opportunity, he fell short of the legal standard of duty established for a traveler when he failed to look and see. This was decisive of the case. But the court did not stop there. It added a remark, unnecessary upon the facts before it, which has been a fertile source of controversy. "In such circumstances it seems to us that if a driver cannot be sure otherwise whether a train is dangerously near he must stop and get out of his vehicle, although obviously he will not often be required to do more than to stop and look."

. . .

Standards of prudent conduct are declared at times by courts, but they are taken over from the facts of life. To get out of a vehicle and reconnoitre is an uncommon precaution, as everyday experience informs us. Besides being uncommon, it is very likely to be futile, and sometimes even dangerous. If the driver leaves his vehicle when he nears a cut or curve, he will learn nothing by getting out about the perils that lurk beyond. By the time he regains his seat and sets his car in motion, the hidden train may be upon him. [ ] Often the added safeguard will be dubious though the track happens to be straight, as it seems that this one was, at all events as far as the station, about five blocks to the north. A train traveling at a speed of thirty miles an hour will cover a quarter of a mile in the space of thirty seconds. It may thus emerge out of obscurity as the driver turns his back to regain the waiting car, and may then descend upon him suddenly when his car is on the track. Instead of helping himself by getting out, he might do better to press forward with all his faculties alert. So a train at a neighboring station, apparently at rest and harmless, may be transformed in a few seconds into an instrument of destruction. At times the course of safety may be different. One can figure to oneself a roadbed so level and unbroken that getting out will be a gain. Even then the balance of advantage depends on many circumstances and can be easily disturbed. Where was Pokora to leave his truck after getting out to reconnoitre? If he was to leave it on the switch, there was the possibility that the box cars would be shunted down upon him before he could regain his seat. The defendant did not show whether there was a

---

[2] For a full statement of the facts, see the opinion of the Circuit Court of Appeals, 10 F.2d 58, 59.

locomotive at the forward end, or whether the cars were so few that a locomotive could be seen. If he was to leave his vehicle near the curb, there was even stronger reason to believe that the space to be covered in going back and forth would make his observations worthless. One must remember that while the traveler turns his eyes in one direction, a train or a loose engine may be approaching from the other.

Illustrations such as these bear witness to the need for caution in framing standards of behavior that amount to rules of law. The need is the more urgent when there is no background of experience out of which the standards have emerged. They are then, not the natural flowerings of behavior in its customary forms, but rules artificially developed, and imposed from without. Extraordinary situations may not wisely or fairly be subjected to tests or regulations that are fitting for the common-place or normal. In default of the guide of customary conduct, what is suitable for the traveler caught in a mesh where the ordinary safeguards fail him is for the judgment of a jury. [ ] The opinion in Goodman's case has been a source of confusion in the federal courts to the extent that it imposes a standard for application by the judge, and has had only wavering support in the courts of the states. We limit it accordingly.

The judgment should be reversed and the cause remanded for further proceedings in accordance with this opinion.

NOTES AND QUESTIONS

1.   Under the *Pokora* view, is it ever proper to take cases from the jury on the issues of negligence and contributory negligence? Is Justice Cardozo's opinion consistent with his opinion in *Adams*?

2.   Plaintiff was hit in the eye by a foul ball while watching a high school baseball game. Her suit against the school district, which owned the field, was dismissed, 4–3. Akins v. Glens Falls City School District, 424 N.E.2d 531 (N.Y.1981). The majority noted that the field was equipped with a backstop 24 feet high and 50 feet wide located 60 feet behind home plate. Seats for 120 adults and standing room for others were behind the backstop. In addition, two chain link fences, three feet high, ran from each end of the backstop along the baselines to a point 60 feet behind first and third bases. Plaintiff, who arrived while the game was in progress, stood along the third base line, 10 to 15 feet past the end of the backstop. She was hit 10 minutes after arriving.

The majority held that there was no basis for a jury to find defendant negligent. Although "what constitutes reasonable care under the circumstances ordinarily is a question for the jury," not every case is for the jury. On the record here, "the school district fulfilled its duty of reasonable care to plaintiff as a matter of law and, therefore, no question of negligence remained for the jury's consideration."

The dissenters argued that the majority had engaged in "an unfortunate exercise in judicial rulemaking in an area that should be left to the jury. This attempt to precisely prescribe what steps the proprietor of a baseball field must take to fulfill its duty of reasonable care is unwarranted and unwise." They found the majority's opinion "reminiscent" of the effort in *Goodman* to impose a specific duty on drivers at grade crossings:

> The wisdom of eschewing such blanket rules where negligence is concerned is obvious. In the present context, the majority has held as a matter of law that the proprietor of the baseball field has fulfilled his duty of reasonable care by erecting a backstop that was 24 feet high and 50 feet wide. The court issues this rule with no more expertise available to it than Justice Holmes had in 1927. . . . It has selected one of a variety of forms of protection currently in use . . . and has designated it as sufficient protection as a matter of law.

The dissent thought it "would make as much sense for the court to decree, as a matter of law, what sort of batting helmet or catcher's mask a school district should supply to its baseball team. Baseball . . . is hardly immune from technological change and shifts in public perception of what constitute reasonable safety measures. It has traditionally been the jury that reflects these shifts and changes."

Does the fact that the judges disagree necessarily indicate, in itself, that a jury question on reasonable care exists?

3. Although motions for summary judgment and for directed verdicts are usually made by defendants in negligence cases, plaintiffs occasionally make such motions. In Andre v. Pomeroy, 320 N.E.2d 853 (N.Y.1974), plaintiff daughter was a passenger in a car driven by defendant mother. Defendant, who ran into the car in front of her, admitted that she was driving in heavy traffic, that she knew a car was in front of her, but that she nonetheless took her eyes off the road to look down into her purse. When she looked back at the road, she found that she was too close to the car in front, which had either stopped or slowed significantly, and she could not avoid it.

The court approved granting plaintiff summary judgment as to liability, 4–3. The majority stated that plaintiffs are entitled to such relief "only in cases in which there is no conflict at all in the evidence [and] the defendant's conduct fell far below any permissible standard of due care. . . ."

When the negligence is so clear, why would plaintiff risk appeal and reversal of a motion for summary judgment instead of relying on the jury?

Andrews v. United Airlines, Inc.

United States Court of Appeals, Ninth Circuit, 1994.
24 F.3d 39.

■ Before: FLETCHER, KOZINSKI and TROTT, CIRCUIT JUDGES.

■ KOZINSKI, CIRCUIT JUDGE.

We are called upon to determine whether United Airlines took adequate measures to deal with that elementary notion of physics—what goes up, must come down. For, while the skies are friendly enough, the ground can be a mighty dangerous place when heavy objects tumble from overhead compartments.

I

During the mad scramble that usually follows hard upon an airplane's arrival at the gate, a briefcase fell from an overhead compartment and seriously injured plaintiff Billie Jean Andrews. No one knows who opened the compartment or what caused the briefcase to fall, and Andrews doesn't claim that airline personnel were involved in stowing the object or opening the bin. Her claim, rather, is that the injury was foreseeable and the airline didn't prevent it.

The district court dismissed the suit on summary judgment, and we review de novo. [ ] This is a diversity action brought in California, whose tort law applies.* [ ]

II

The parties agree that United Airlines is a common carrier and as such "owe[s] both a duty of utmost care and the vigilance of a very cautious person towards [its] passengers." Acosta v. Southern Cal. Rapid Transit Dist., 2 Cal. 3d 19, 27 (1970); [ ]. Though United is "responsible for any, even the slightest, negligence and [is] required to do all that human care, vigilance, and foresight reasonably can do under all the circumstances," [ ], it is not an insurer of its passengers' safety, [ ]. "[T]he degree of care and diligence which [it] must exercise is only such as can reasonably be exercised consistent with the character and mode of conveyance adopted and the practical operation of [its] business. . . ." [ ]

To show that United did not satisfy its duty of care toward its passengers, Ms. Andrews presented the testimony of two witnesses. The first was Janice Northcott, United's Manager of Inflight Safety, who disclosed that in 1987 the airline had received 135 reports of items falling from overhead bins. As a result of these incidents, Ms. Northcott testified, United decided to add a warning to its arrival announcements,

---

* In Erie Railroad Co. v. Tompkins, 304 U.S. 64 (1938), the Supreme Court held that federal courts did not have the authority to make federal common law. Hence, in the absence of federal constitutional or statutory law, state law governs. This means that, as the court in *Andrews* indicates, in cases that are in federal court because of diversity jurisdiction, state law provides the applicable substantive law.—Eds.

to wit, that items stored overhead might have shifted during flight and passengers should use caution in opening the bins. This announcement later became the industry standard.

Ms. Andrews's second witness was safety and human factors expert Dr. David Thompson, who testified that United's announcement was ineffective because passengers opening overhead bins couldn't see objects poised to fall until the bins were opened, by which time it was too late. Dr. Thompson also testified that United could have taken additional steps to prevent the hazard, such as retrofitting its overhead bins with baggage nets, as some airlines had already done, or by requiring passengers to store only lightweight items overhead [although—as the court noted in a footnote—Dr. Thompson "recognized that this was not a very practical solution from either the airlines' or the passengers' point of view"].

United argues that Andrews presented too little proof to satisfy her burden [ ]. One hundred thirty-five reported incidents, United points out, are trivial when spread over the millions of passengers travelling on its 175,000 flights every year. Even that number overstates the problem, according to United, because it includes events where passengers merely observed items falling from overhead bins but no one was struck or injured. Indeed, United sees the low incidence of injuries as incontrovertible proof that the safety measures suggested by plaintiff's expert would not merit the additional cost and inconvenience to airline passengers.

III

It is a close question, but we conclude that plaintiff has made a sufficient case to overcome summary judgment. United is hard-pressed to dispute that its passengers are subject to a hazard from objects falling out of overhead bins, considering the warning its flight crews give hundreds of times each day. The case then turns on whether the hazard is serious enough to warrant more than a warning. Given the heightened duty of a common carrier, [ ], even a small risk of serious injury to passengers may form the basis of liability if that risk could be eliminated "consistent with the character and mode of [airline travel] and the practical operation of [that] business. . . ." [ ] United has demonstrated neither that retrofitting overhead bins with netting (or other means) would be prohibitively expensive, nor that such steps would grossly interfere with the convenience of its passengers. Thus, a jury could find United has failed to do "all that human care, vigilance, and foresight reasonably can do under all the circumstances." [ ]

The reality, with which airline passengers are only too familiar, is that airline travel has changed significantly in recent years. As harried travelers try to avoid the agonizing ritual of checked baggage, they hand-carry more and larger items—computers, musical instruments, an occasional deceased relative. [ ] The airlines have coped with this trend, but perhaps not well enough. Given its awareness of the hazard, United may not have done everything technology permits and prudence dictates to eliminate it. See Treadwell v. Whittier, 80 Cal. 574, 600 (1889)("common carriers . . . must keep pace with science, art, and modern improvement"); Valente v. Sierra Ry., 151 Cal. 534, 543 (1907)(common carriers must use the best precautions in practical use "known to any company exercising the utmost care and diligence in keeping abreast with modern improvement in . . . such precautions").

Jurors, many of whom will have been airline passengers, will be well equipped to decide whether United had a duty to do more than warn passengers about the possibility of falling baggage. A reasonable jury might conclude United should have done more; it might also find that United did enough. Either decision would be rational on the record presented to the district court which, of course, means summary judgment was not appropriate.

Reversed and Remanded.

NOTES AND QUESTIONS

1. On occasion, legislatures have enacted statutes using such terms as gross negligence, recklessness, or willfulness—and courts have occasionally developed such notions themselves. One legislative example is statutes protecting physicians who provide uncompensated emergency services (good Samaritan laws) that protect doctors from negligence claims, requiring proof of recklessness or gross negligence in order to subject them to liability for damages. See, e.g., Frezzell v. City of New York, 21 N.E.3d 1028 (N.Y.2014), discussing a statute granting the driver of an authorized emergency vehicle special driving privileges when involved in an emergency operation. We consider these enhanced standards of culpability at p. 436 infra. Until then, we shall concern ourselves with the basic negligence formulation of reasonable care. In this regard, can the phrase "utmost care," used in *Andrews*, be squared with *Bethel*?

2. How would the analysis differ if an airline employee had stowed the bag in the compartment or had opened the compartment at the end of the trip? See Brosnahan v. Western Air Lines, Inc., 892 F.2d 730 (8th Cir.1989), holding that a jury might find airline personnel negligent in failing to adequately supervise the boarding process during which a passenger dropped his carry-on bag on another passenger's head while attempting to stow it in the overhead compartment. See also USAir, Inc. v. United States Department of the Navy, 14 F.3d 1410 (9th Cir.1994), holding that a passenger (and his employer) might be held liable for negligently stowing in the overhead compartment a briefcase that fell and hurt another passenger.

3. Why does the court demand that United demonstrate that "retrofitting overhead bins with netting . . . would be prohibitively expensive" or that such steps "would grossly interfere with the convenience of its passengers"? If we assume that 35 of the 135 incidents in 1987 involved no harm whatever and that the other 100 involved 60 bruised

bodies, 30 broken bones and 10 serious brain damage cases, might that affect the analysis?

4.   One quoted passage demands that carriers "must keep pace with science, art, and modern improvement." How does that obligation differ from what is expected of any reasonable company? Does the "utmost care" standard of *Andrews* require that a common carrier adopt any available safety precaution regardless of how expensive or inconvenient it might be? In Metropolitan Atlanta Rapid Transit Authority v. Rouse, 612 S.E.2d 308 (Ga.2005), the court held that Georgia's "extraordinary diligence" standard did not require a common carrier to update its previously acquired non-defective equipment with every new safety device that later becomes available.

5.   In Wood v. Groh, 7 P.3d 1163 (Kan.2000), plaintiff was accidentally shot with defendant's gun fired by his 15-year-old son. The son had used a screwdriver to open his father's locked gun cabinet and had removed the unloaded gun as well as ammunition. The claim was that defendant was responsible for the removal and injury. The trial judge gave an ordinary negligence charge, and the jury found for the defendant. Plaintiff appealed on the ground that the judge should have charged that defendant owed "the highest degree of care in safekeeping the handgun." The court agreed:

> We have concluded that the parents in this case owed the highest duty to protect the public from the misuse of the gun, a dangerous instrumentality, stored in their home. The fact that the gun was not loaded is insignificant, for the ammunition was kept in the same locked cabinet. Once access to the gun was obtained, access to the ammunition immediately followed. Storage of the ammunition in the same location as the gun in this case resulted in the gun being easily loaded and made it a dangerous instrumentality.

Although the father kept the cabinet locked, retained the key on his person at all times, and told the son not to take the gun without supervision, the court noted that the son needed only a screwdriver to obtain the gun and the ammunition. On the question of prejudice, the court stated that there was "a real possibility that the jury would have returned a different verdict had the correct standard been given." What reason is there to think that the jury would have reached a different result if given a different charge? Under the due care standard would the jury, in connection with the father's behavior, consider different factors than under the "highest degree" standard?

2. THE ROLE OF CUSTOM

Trimarco v. Klein

Court of Appeals of New York, 1982.
56 N.Y.2d 98, 436 N.E.2d 502, 451 N.Y.S.2d 52.

■ FUCHSBERG, JUDGE.

[Plaintiff tenant was very badly cut when he fell through the glass door that enclosed his tub in defendant's apartment building. The door turned out to be ordinary thin glass that looked the same as the tempered glass that plaintiff thought it was. The building had been built, and the shower installed, in 1953.

Plaintiff presented expert evidence that at least since the 1950s a practice of using shatterproof glass in bathroom enclosures had come into common use, so that by 1976, the date of the accident, "the glass door here no longer conformed to accepted safety standards." Defendant's managing agent admitted that, at least since 1965, it had been "customary for landlords who had occasion to install glass for shower enclosures, whether to replace broken glass or to comply with the request of a tenant or otherwise, to do so with 'some material such as plastic or safety glass.'"

The jury awarded plaintiff damages. A divided appellate division reversed the plaintiff's judgment. Even if there was "a custom and usage at the time to substitute shatterproof glass" and even if that was a "better way or a safer method of enclosing showers," there was no common-law duty on the defendant to replace the glass unless prior notice of the danger had come to the defendant either from the plaintiff or by reason of a similar accident in the building. Since plaintiff had made no such showing, the appellate division majority reversed and dismissed the case.

The dissenters in the appellate division observed that in the 1,000-page trial record there was ample showing that landlords generally had known of the danger of ordinary glass for more than ten years before this accident. The dissenters saw no need for specific notice to this landlord either by prior accident in the building or by personal request from the plaintiff.]

. . .

Which brings us to the well-recognized and pragmatic proposition that when "certain dangers have been removed by a customary way of doing things safely, this custom may be proved to show that [the one charged with the dereliction] has fallen below the required standard" (Garthe v. Ruppert, 264 N.Y. 290, 296 [1934]). Such proof, of course, is not admitted in the abstract. It must bear on what is reasonable conduct under all the circumstances, the quintessential test of negligence.

It follows that, when proof of an accepted practice is accompanied by evidence that the defendant conformed to it, this may establish due care [ ], and, contrariwise, when proof of a customary practice is coupled with a showing that it was ignored and that this departure was a proximate cause of the accident, it may serve to establish liability (Levine v. Russell Blaine Co., 273 N.Y. 386, 389 [1937] [custom to equip dumbwaiter with rope which does not splinter]). Put more conceptually, proof of a common practice aids in "formulat[ing] the general expectation of society as to how individuals will act in the course of their undertakings, and thus to guide the common sense or expert intuition of a jury or commission when called on to judge particular conduct under particular circumstances" [ ].

The source of the probative power of proof of custom and usage is described differently by various authorities, but all agree on its potency. Chief among the rationales offered is, of course, the fact that it reflects the judgment and experience and conduct of many [ ]. Support for its relevancy and reliability comes too from the direct bearing it has on feasibility, for its focusing is on the practicality of a precaution in actual operation and the readiness with which it can be employed (Morris, Custom and Negligence, 42 Colum.L.Rev. 1147, 1148). Following in the train of both of these boons is the custom's exemplification of the opportunities it provides to others to learn of the safe way, if that the customary one be. [ ]

From all this it is not to be assumed customary practice and usage need be universal. It suffices that it be fairly well defined and in the same calling or business so that "the actor may be charged with knowledge of it or negligent ignorance" [ ].

However, once its existence is credited, a common practice or usage is still not necessarily a conclusive or even a compelling test of negligence [ ]. Before it can be, the jury must be satisfied with its reasonableness, just as the jury must be satisfied with the reasonableness of the behavior which adhered to the custom or the unreasonableness of that which did not. [ ] After all, customs and usages run the gamut of merit like everything else. That is why the question in each instance is whether it meets the test of reasonableness. As Holmes' now classic statement on this subject expresses it, "[w]hat usually is done may be evidence of what ought to be done, but what ought to be done is fixed by a standard of reasonable prudence, whether it usually is complied with or not" [ ].

So measured, the case the plaintiff presented . . . was enough to send it to the jury and to sustain the verdict reached. The expert testimony, the admissions of the defendant's manager, the data on which the professional and governmental bulletins were based, the evidence of how replacements were handled by at least the local building industry for the better part of two decades, these in the aggregate easily filled that bill. Moreover, it was also for the jury to decide whether, at the point in time when the accident occurred, the modest cost and ready availability of safety glass and the dynamics of the growing custom to use it for shower enclosures had transformed what once may have been considered a reasonably safe part of the apartment into one which, in the light of later developments, no longer could be so regarded.

Furthermore, the charge on this subject was correct. The Trial Judge placed the evidence of custom and usage "by others engaged in the same business" in proper perspective, when, among other things, he told the jury that the issue on which it was received was "the reasonableness of the defendant's conduct under all the circumstances." He also emphasized that the testimony on this score was not conclusive, not only by saying so but by explaining that "the mere fact that another person or landlord may have used a better or safer practice does not establish a standard" and that it was for the jurors "to determine whether or not the evidence in this case does establish a general custom or practice."

[The court reversed the dismissal but ordered a new trial because the trial judge had erroneously admitted certain evidence that had hurt the defense.]

■ CHIEF JUDGE COOKE and JUDGES JASEN, GABRIELLI, JONES, WACHTLER and MEYER concur.

NOTES AND QUESTIONS

1. How did the proof of custom affect the plaintiff's case in *Trimarco*?

2. Recall that in *Carroll Towing*, p. 47 supra, Judge Hand observed that it "may be that the custom" in New York Harbor was not to have bargees on board ships at night and that, if so, it may be that "the situation is one where custom should control." Why might custom establish the standard of care? Although the court did not reach that question, Judge Hand had stated the basic proposition about the role of custom in an earlier case, The T.J. Hooper v. Northern Barge Corp., 60 F.2d 737 (2d Cir.1932). In that case, a tug plying the Atlantic coast sank in a storm, causing the loss of barges it was towing and their cargoes. If the tug had had a radio, it would have learned about the storm in time to avoid it. The tug owner sought to make the alleged lack of radios on most tugs the standard of care. Judge Hand observed that some court pronouncements might be read to say that general practice sets the standard. He continued:

Indeed in most cases reasonable prudence is in fact common prudence; but strictly it is never its measure; a whole calling may have unduly lagged in the adoption of new and available devices. It never may set its own tests, however persuasive be its usages. Courts must in the end say what is required; there are precautions so imperative that even their universal disregard will not excuse their omission. But here there was no custom at all as to receiving sets; some had them; some did not; the most that can be urged is that they had not yet become general. Certainly in such a case we need not pause; when some have thought a device necessary, at least we may say that they were right, and the others too slack.

Except in malpractice cases, courts have rejected the argument that a prevailing custom defines the standard of care. The malpractice situation is discussed at p. 108 infra.

3. Even if prevailing custom does not set the standard of care, adherence to, and deviation from, custom may be important in deciding whether the actor behaved reasonably.

A defendant who can prove that it has adhered to a prevailing custom may eliminate what might otherwise be a jury question. In a classic article, Morris, Custom and Negligence, 42 Colum.L.Rev. 1147 (1942), Professor Morris suggested that such proof alerts the trial court to three main points. First, if an industry adheres to a single way of doing something, the court may be wary of plaintiff's assertion that there are safer ways to do that thing—and may insist that plaintiff clearly demonstrate the feasibility of the asserted alternative. Second, even if the plaintiff can show a feasible alternative, the fact that it may not have been in use anywhere may suggest that it was not unreasonable for the defendant to be unaware of the possibility. Third, the existence of a custom that involves large fixed costs may warn the court of the social impact of a jury or court decision that determines the custom to be unreasonable.

4. On the other hand, as Professor Morris pointed out, a plaintiff will find it useful to prove that the defendant fell below the industry custom because it tends to show that others, usually competitors, found it feasible to do something in a safer manner than did the defendant; that the defendant had ample opportunity to learn about the alternative; and that no great social upheaval will follow a judicial determination that the defendant's failure to follow custom was negligence.

In *Levine v. Russell Blaine Co.*, cited in *Trimarco*, plaintiff cut her hand on a rough rope while operating a dumbwaiter. Infection led to amputation of her arm. She sought to show that the defendant building owner had failed to follow the custom of using smooth ropes in dumbwaiters. The court held that if plaintiff could show that the purpose of the customary use of smooth rope was to avoid such injuries, the evidence of custom was admissible.

5. Note that the plaintiff can achieve some of these goals simply by proving that others in the industry, although not establishing a custom, have developed safer techniques than did defendant. In *Garthe v. Ruppert,* cited in *Trimarco*, plaintiff slipped on a wet brewery floor. In an effort to show that it was feasible to keep the floors dry, plaintiff sought to show that, although most breweries had slippery floors, one local brewery had a technique that kept floors from getting slippery. The court held that such evidence was inadmissible because it had never "been permitted to take one or two instances as a gauge or guide in place of the custom of the trade." But this evidence might have been relevant if the defendant had tried to

argue that it had no way of learning about the techniques that plaintiff claimed it should have used. For an exploration of the difference in the rules regarding admissibility of custom and inadmissibility of non-custom practices and the implications for understanding negligence, see Abraham, Custom, Noncustomary Practice, and Negligence, 109 Colum. L. Rev. 1784 (2009).

In *Andrews*, p. 68 supra, plaintiff's evidence showed that British Airways had begun using restraining netting the year before plaintiff was hurt. What is the significance of the fact that one other airline used baggage nets? Would the plaintiff necessarily have lost if she had been hurt the month before British Airways began using the baggage nets—even if she had proven that such nets were economically and technically feasible? How might the analysis have changed if the plaintiff had proven that more than two-thirds of all American carriers used baggage nets at the time of the accident?

6.   Should evidence of deviation from custom be usable against a company that is barely profitable—and which would have been unable to continue operations had it made the expenditures necessary to bring it into conformity? If the larger members of an industry follow a custom, should evidence be admitted showing that smaller companies engaged in the same line of business deviate from that custom?

3.   THE ROLE OF STATUTES

Martin v. Herzog

Court of Appeals of New York, 1920.
228 N.Y. 164, 126 N.E. 814.

■ CARDOZO, J.

The action is one to recover damages for injuries resulting in death. Plaintiff and her husband, while driving toward Tarrytown in a buggy on the night of August 21, 1915, were struck by the defendant's automobile coming in the opposite direction. They were thrown to the ground, and the man was killed. At the point of the collision the highway makes a curve. The car was rounding the curve when suddenly it came upon the buggy, emerging, the defendant tells us, from the gloom. Negligence is charged against the defendant, the driver of the car, in that he did not keep to the right of the center of the highway (Highway Law, sec. 286, subd. 3; sec. 332; Consol.Laws, ch. 25). Negligence is charged against the plaintiff's intestate, the driver of the wagon, in that he was traveling without lights (Highway Law, sec. 329a, as amended by L.1915, ch. 367). There is no evidence that the defendant was moving at an excessive speed. There is none of any defect in the equipment of his car. The beam of light from his lamps pointed to the right as the wheels of his car turned along the curve toward the left; and looking in the direction of the plaintiff's approach, he was peering into the shadow. The case against him must stand therefore, if at all, upon the divergence of his course from the center of the highway. The jury found him delinquent and his victim blameless. The Appellate Division reversed, and ordered a new trial.] *proced. hist.*

We agree with the Appellate Division that the charge to the jury was erroneous and misleading. The case was tried on the assumption that the hour had arrived when lights were due. It was argued on the same assumption in this court. In such circumstances, it is not important whether the hour might have been made a question for the jury [ ]. A controversy put out of the case by the parties is not to be put into it by us. We say this by way of preface to our review of the contested rulings. In the body of the charge the trial judge said that the jury could consider the absence of light "in determining whether the plaintiff's intestate was guilty of contributory negligence in failing to have a light upon the buggy as provided by law. I do not mean to say that the absence of light necessarily makes him negligent, but it is a fact for your consideration." The defendant requested a ruling that the absence of a light on the plaintiff's vehicle was *prima facie* evidence of contributory negligence." This request was refused, and the jury were again instructed that they might consider the absence of lights as some evidence of negligence, but that it was not conclusive evidence. The plaintiff then requested a charge that "the fact that the plaintiff's intestate was driving without a light is not negligence in itself," and to this the court acceded. The defendant saved his rights by appropriate exceptions.

We think the unexcused omission of the statutory signals is more ✱ than some evidence of negligence. It *is* negligence in itself. Lights are intended for the guidance and protection of other travelers on the highway (Highway Law, sec. 329a). By the very terms of the hypothesis, to omit, willfully or heedlessly, the safeguards prescribed by law for the benefit of another that he may be preserved in life or limb, is to fall short of the standard of diligence to which those who live in organized society are under a duty to conform. That, we think, is now the established rule in this state. [ ] Whether the omission of an absolute duty, not willfully or heedlessly, but through unavoidable accident, is also to be characterized as negligence, is a question of nomenclature into which we need not enter, for it does not touch the case before us. There may be times, when if jural niceties are to be preserved, the two wrongs, negligence and breach of statutory duty, must be kept distinct in speech and thought [ ]. In the conditions here present they come together and coalesce . . .

In the case at hand, we have an instance of the admitted violation of a statute intended for the protection of travelers on the highway, of whom the defendant at the time was one. Yet the jurors were instructed in effect that they were at liberty in their discretion to treat the omission of lights either as innocent or as culpable. They were allowed to "consider the default as lightly or gravely" as they would (Thomas, J., in the court below). They might as well have been told that they could use a like discretion in holding a master at fault for the omission of a safety appliance prescribed by positive law for the protection of a workman [ ]. Jurors have no dispensing power by which they may relax the duty that one traveler on the highway owes under the statute to another. It is error to tell them that they have. The omission of these lights was a wrong, and being wholly unexcused was also a negligent wrong. No license should have been conceded to the triers of the facts to find it anything else.

[At this point Judge Cardozo concluded that the jury could well have found that the absence of the light was causally related to the accident.]

We are persuaded that the tendency of the charge and of all the rulings following it, was to minimize unduly, in the minds of the triers of the facts, the gravity of the decedent's fault. Errors may not be ignored as unsubstantial when they tend to such an outcome. A statute designed for the protection of human life is not to be brushed aside as a form of words, its commands reduced to the level of cautions, and the duty to obey attenuated into an option to conform.

disposition

The order of the Appellate Division should be affirmed, and judgment absolute directed on the stipulation in favor of the defendant, with costs in all courts.

■ HISCOCK, CH. J., POUND, MCLAUGHLIN, ANDREWS and ELKUS, JJ., concur with CARDOZO, J.; HOGAN, J., reads dissenting opinion [in which he viewed the record as indicating no causal relation between the plaintiff's violation and the crash.]

NOTES AND QUESTIONS

1.   On the question of the husband's negligence, what did the trial judge charge? What did the defendant ask the trial judge to charge? What does Judge Cardozo say the trial judge should have charged? What distinguishes these formulations? What are the respective roles of the judge and the jury under each view?

2.   What kind of penalties do you think the legislature provided for crossing the center line and traveling without lights after dark? Should it matter whether they linked the violation of such requirements to civil liability in personal injury cases? If the legislature failed to do so, why does the court get involved with these statutes at all?

3.   In Clinkscales v. Carver, 136 P.2d 777 (Cal.1943), defendant ran a stop sign and crashed into plaintiff. The stop sign had been erected under an ordinance that had never become effective because it had not been properly published, which meant that defendant could not be punished criminally for his action. He argued that this made it improper for the trial judge to use the ordinance in his charge. Justice Traynor, writing for the majority, upheld the charge and the plaintiff's judgment:

Whatever the effect of the irregularity on defendant's criminal liability, it cannot be assumed that the conditions that limit it also limit civil liability. The propriety of taking from the jury the determination of negligence does not turn on defendant's criminal liability. A statute that provides for a criminal proceeding only does not create a civil liability; if there is no provision for a remedy by civil action to persons injured by a breach of the statute it is because the Legislature did not contemplate one. A suit for damages is based on the theory that the conduct inflicting the injuries is a common-law tort. . . . The decision as to what the civil standard should be still rests with the court, and the standard formulated by a legislative body in a police regulation or criminal statute becomes the standard to determine civil liability only because the court accepts it. In the absence of such a standard the case goes to the jury, which must determine whether the defendant has acted as a reasonably prudent man would act in similar circumstances. The jury then has the burden of deciding not only what the facts are but what the unformulated standard is of reasonable conduct. When a legislative body has generalized a standard from the experience of the community and prohibits conduct that is likely to cause harm, the court accepts the formulated standards and applies them [ ] except where they would serve to impose liability without fault. [ ]

Is this consistent with *Martin v. Herzog*?

Tedla v. Ellman

Court of Appeals of New York, 1939.
280 N.Y. 124, 19 N.E.2d 987.

■ LEHMAN, J.

[Two junk collectors, brother and sister, were walking eastward along Sunrise Highway, a major route connecting New York City and Long Island. There were no sidewalks and they could not use the grass center strip because they were transporting junk in baby carriages that would have gotten mired in the soft ground. A 1933 statute provided:

Pedestrians walking or remaining on the paved portion, or traveled part of a roadway shall be subject to, and comply with, the rules governing vehicles, with respect to meeting and turning out, except that such pedestrians shall keep to the left of the center line thereof, and turn to their left instead of right side thereof, so as to permit all vehicles passing them in either direction to pass on their right. Such pedestrians shall not be subject to the rules governing vehicles as to giving signals.

It was Sunday night and "very heavy traffic" was heading westbound back to New York City but there were "very few cars going east." The two were walking eastward on the edge of the eastbound lane when they were hit from behind by defendant's car. The trial judge entered judgment on a plaintiffs' verdict and the appellate division affirmed. On this appeal the defendant does not contest his negligence, but argues that both pedestrians were contributorily negligent as a matter of law.]

. . .

. . . The appellants lean heavily upon [*Martin v. Herzog*] and kindred cases and the principle established by them.

The analogy is, however, incomplete. The "established rule" should not be weakened either by subtle distinctions or by extension beyond its letter or spirit into a field where "by the very terms of the hypothesis" it can have no proper application. At times the indefinite and flexible standard of care of the traditional reasonably prudent man may be, in the opinion of the Legislature, an insufficient measure of the care which should be exercised to guard against a recognized danger; at times, the duty, imposed by custom, that no man shall use what is his to the harm of others provides insufficient safeguard for the preservation of the life or limb or property of others. Then the Legislature may by statute prescribe additional safeguards and may define duty and standard of care in rigid terms; and when the Legislature has spoken, the standard of the care required is no longer what the reasonably prudent man would do under the circumstances but what the Legislature has commanded. That is the rule established by the courts and "by the very terms of the hypothesis" the rule applies where the Legislature has prescribed safeguards "for the benefit of another that he may be preserved in life or limb." In that field debate as to whether the safeguards so prescribed are reasonably necessary is ended by the legislative fiat. Obedience to that fiat cannot add to the danger, even assuming that the prescribed safeguards are not reasonably necessary and where the legislative anticipation of dangers is realized and harm results through heedless or willful omission of the prescribed safeguard, injury flows from wrong and the wrongdoer is properly held responsible for the consequent damages.

The statute upon which the defendants rely is of different character. It does not prescribe additional safeguards which pedestrians must provide for the preservation of the life or limb or property of others, or even of themselves, nor does it impose upon pedestrians a higher standard of care. What the statute does provide is rules of the road to be observed by pedestrians and by vehicles, so that all those who use the road may know how they and others should proceed, at least under usual circumstances. A general rule of conduct—and, specifically, a rule of the road—may accomplish its intended purpose under usual conditions, but, when the unusual occurs, strict observance may defeat the purpose of the rule and produce catastrophic results.

Negligence is failure to exercise the care required by law. Where a statute defines the standard of care and the safeguards required to meet a recognized danger, then, as we have said, no other measure may

ruling in Martin [

be applied in determining whether a person has carried out the duty of care imposed by law. Failure to observe the standard imposed by statute is negligence, as matter of law. On the other hand, where a statutory general rule of conduct fixes no definite standard of care which would under all circumstances tend to protect life, limb or property, but merely codifies or supplements a common-law rule which has always been subject to limitations and exceptions; or where the statutory rule of conduct regulates conflicting rights and obligations in a manner calculated to promote public convenience and safety, then the statute, in the absence of clear language to the contrary, should not be construed as intended to wipe out the limitations and exceptions which judicial decisions have attached to the common-law duty; nor should it be construed as an inflexible command that the general rule of conduct intended to prevent accidents must be followed even under conditions when observance might cause accidents. We may assume reasonably that the Legislature directed pedestrians to keep to the left of the center of the road because that would cause them to face traffic approaching in that lane and would enable them to care for their own safety better than if the traffic approached them from the rear. We cannot assume reasonably that the Legislature intended that a statute enacted for the preservation of the life and limb of pedestrians must be observed when observance would subject them to more imminent danger.

. . .

Even under that construction of the statute, a pedestrian is, of course, at fault if he fails without good reason to observe the statutory rule of conduct. The general duty is established by the statute, and deviation from it without good cause is a wrong and the wrongdoer is responsible for the damages resulting from his wrong. [ ]

. . .

In each action, the judgment should be affirmed, with costs.

■ CRANE, CH. J., HUBBS, LOUGHRAN and RIPPEY, JJ., concur; O'BRIEN and FINCH, JJ., dissent on the authority of *Martin v. Herzog* [ ].

NOTES AND QUESTIONS

1. In Bassey v. Mistrough, 450 N.Y.S.2d 604 (App.Div.1982), a vehicle "came to a stop partially on the highway, and the entire electrical system of the car failed to function." While plaintiff was standing in front of his car searching for the source of the electrical trouble, his car was hit from behind and he was hurt. The judge read the jury the statute requiring the illumination of vehicles on the highway. He refused a request to tell the jury about the possibility of an excuse. Judgment was entered on a jury verdict for the defendant. On appeal, the court reversed. The jury should have been advised that if they found plaintiff "unable to avoid temporarily

leaving his stalled, unlighted vehicle on the highway" the violation would be excused.

What if a driver testified that the car's lights failed ten minutes earlier, but that the driver continued on while looking for a store to buy a replacement switch and had not passed one? What if plaintiff testified that although the lights failed ten minutes earlier, the driver continued on and passed a store with the needed switch in order to take a child to the hospital for emergency treatment? Is there a difference between the type of excuse that Tedla offered and the excuse by the plaintiff in *Martin* that the light had just gone out?

2. Might the situation in *Tedla* be one in which, as Judge Cardozo said in *Martin v. Herzog*, "the two wrongs, negligence and breach of statutory duty, must be kept distinct in speech and thought"?

3. Tedla's brother, Bachek, was deaf. If he had been walking alone might the case have been different?

4. Section 15 of the <u>Restatement Third</u> addresses excused violations:

An actor's violation of a statute is excused and not negligent if:

(a) the violation is reasonable in light of the actor's childhood, physical disability, or physical incapacitation;

(b) the actor exercises reasonable care in attempting to comply with the statute;

(c) the actor neither knows nor should know of the factual circumstances that render the statute applicable;

(d) the actor's violation of the statute is due to the confusing way in which the requirements of the statute are presented to the public;

(e) the actor's compliance with the statute would involve a greater risk of physical harm to the actor or to others than noncompliance.

Would plaintiffs' conduct in *Tedla* be excused under the Restatement approach? Are the Restatement provisions consistent with *Martin v. Herzog*?

With these excuses to negligence per se, how different is the doctrine from the prima facie evidence of negligence proposed by the plaintiff in *Martin*?

5. Consider the potential interplay between the role of custom and statutory violations. In Robinson v. District of Columbia, 580 A.2d 1255 (D.C.1990), plaintiff, who had been hit by a police van, was held contributorily negligent for violating a traffic regulation by crossing the street outside of a marked crosswalk. She argued that her behavior was reasonable because it was "the common practice of pedestrians at the location of the accident." The court disagreed: there was no basis to "excuse violations of the law where such violations are common practice."

6. *Statutory purpose.* Courts have long been unwilling to use statutory violations in cases in which the harm that occurred was different from the harm that the legislature apparently was seeking to prevent.

In violation of the Contagious Diseases Act, defendant shipowner failed to build pens on the deck in order to keep groups of sheep separated. During the voyage, some sheep were washed overboard. A suit by the owners of the sheep failed. Gorris v. Scott, [1874] 9 L.R. Exch. 125. The court observed that "the damage is of such a nature as was not contemplated at all by the statute, and as to which it was not intended to confer any benefit on the plaintiffs."

In De Haen v. Rockwood Sprinkler Co. of Mass., 179 N.E. 764 (N.Y.1932), a radiator placed about a foot from the edge of an unprotected hoistway on a construction project fell down the shaft and killed a man below. The court, in an opinion by Judge Cardozo, first upheld the liability of defendant Rockwood because its employees had negligently struck the radiator and brought about its fall. The court next upheld liability against defendant LeBeau, whose employees negligently placed the radiator dangerously near the open shaft. The fact that it took the act of another to cause the fall did not exculpate LeBeau. "One may not place an engine of destruction in a position where a heedless touch by someone else will awaken its destructive power." At least, "a jury may so find."

The court then turned to the liability of defendant Turner, the general contractor. Turner had violated a statute by failing to erect a barrier around the hoistway. Two sides were to be rigid. The other two, "which may be used for taking off and putting on materials . . . shall be guarded by an adjustable barrier not less than three nor more than four feet from the floor and not less than two feet from the edges of such shafts or openings."

Although the statute had been violated, that violation "does not establish liability if the statute is intended to protect against a particular hazard, and a hazard of a different kind is the occasion of the injury." Why should that requirement be imposed? The court then sought the purpose of the statute:

> The chief object of this statute is to protect workmen from the hazard of falling into a shaft. We cannot say, however, that no other hazard was within the zone of apprehension. On two sides of the shaft there must be a solid or comparatively solid fence. Only on the other sides where material is taken on or off may there be a single bar. If there was no thought to give protection against falling missiles or debris, the lawmakers might well have stopped with a requirement that there be a single bar on every side. The fact that they did not stop there is evidence of a broader purpose. True, indeed, it is that on two of the four sides the security is only partial and imperfect. A barrier set in place at a height of four feet will often be of little avail in holding back material or rubbish collected on the floor. Even so, security against the hazard of falling objects will not be lacking altogether. One of the requirements of the statute is that the guard shall be placed at

least two feet from the edge. In a barrier so fixed there is warning, if no more. Workmen, who may otherwise be tempted to store material in dangerous proximity to the edge of an open shaft will be reminded of the danger and will tend to stand afar. The thoughtless will be checked, though the recklessly indifferent will be free to go their way.

The potencies of protection that reside in such a barrier have illustration in the case before us. If the hoistway had been guarded, it is unlikely that the radiators thirty-eight inches high would have been placed as they were within falling distance of the edge. It is still less likely that a worker would heedlessly have brushed against them and so brought about the fall. We do not mean to say that these considerations are decisive. Liability is not established by a showing that as chance would have it a statutory safeguard might have avoided the particular hazard out of which an accident ensued. The hazard out of which the accident ensued must have been the particular hazard or class of hazards that the statutory safeguard in the thought and purpose of the Legislature was intended to correct [ ]. Nonetheless, the sequence of events may help to fix the limits of a purpose that would be obscure if viewed alone. A safeguard has been commanded, but without distinct enumeration of the hazards to be avoided. In the revealing light of experience the hazards to be avoided are disclosed to us as the hazards that ensued.

Compare Di Ponzio v. Riordan, 679 N.E.2d 616 (N.Y.1997), in which defendant gas station—in violation of an ordinance requiring that car engines be turned off while the car is being filled with gas—permitted a customer to leave his engine running while he pumped gasoline and then went inside to pay for it. After about five minutes on a level surface, the vehicle inexplicably rolled backward and pinned plaintiff, another customer, between two cars. The court held that the violation of the ordinance, which was in the city's fire prevention code, was irrelevant because its apparent purpose was to prevent fires and not to avoid injuries from moving vehicles. The court analogized the situation to a Restatement example involving a defendant who gives a loaded pistol to a child, who then drops it on a playmate's toe—but it does not fire a bullet.

7. If the court in *De Haen* had concluded that the only purpose of the statute was to keep workers from falling into the open shaft and had refused to use the statute in the case, would Turner necessarily have won the case?

8. The statutory-purpose limitation of negligence per se is criticized in Geistfeld, Tort Law in the Age of Statutes, 99 Iowa L.Rev. 957 (2014). For the reasons provided in note 3, p. 78, the statutes in these cases do not have any obligatory tort law effects—they neither preempt nor otherwise directly modify the common-law duty—and so courts instead defer to the legislative policy determination in order to resolve the issue of reasonable care. According to Geistfeld, deference does not necessarily tether the tort claim to statutory purpose:

When the scope of the defendant's safety obligation is defined by a pre-existing common-law duty, the court can insert the statutory safety standard into the common-law tort duty. If the plaintiff's harm is encompassed by the common-law duty, then an unexcused statutory violation with respect to a more limited set of statutory risks also establishes unreasonable behavior with respect to the larger set of risks encompassed by the common-law duty. By permitting recovery for these statutory violations, courts fully defer to the legislative safety determination without being limited to the types of risks contemplated by the statutory scheme, contrary to the black-letter rule of negligence per se.

9. When defendant driver parked outside the pharmacy on the grounds of the Middletown Psychiatric Center, she left her keys in the ignition. "Moments later," a patient drove away in the vehicle and "met his death soon thereafter when it left the road and struck a tree." Plaintiff, the patient's administrator, moved for summary judgment based on violation of the state statute against leaving keys in the ignition of an unattended car. The majority concluded that the statute was enacted to "deter theft and injury from the operation of motor vehicles by unauthorized persons" and was "plainly not designed to protect such unauthorized users from the consequences of their own conduct." Two judges thought the purpose was "to protect the public generally from the consequences that foreseeably flow from unauthorized use of motor vehicles." It was "patently unfair to deny to plaintiff the evidentiary weight of such violation and leave him to the more vigorous burden of establishing common law negligence."

The court unanimously concluded that plaintiff could proceed under common law negligence. Rushink v. Gerstheimer, 440 N.Y.S.2d 738 (App.Div.1981). Why the difference?

Several state courts have concluded that the purpose of the "key-in-the-ignition" statutes is to reduce thefts, and thus reduce both the time police must spend tracking down stolen cars and the payments insurers must make to owners of such cars. In this view there is no safety purpose, and the statute is not relevant in personal injury cases. See Peck, An Exercise Based upon Empirical Data: Liability for Harm Caused by Stolen Automobiles, 1969 Wis.L.Rev. 909.

10. *Licensing.* Licensing statutes have generally not been used to set standards of care. The explanation has been that the purpose of such a statute is to protect the public from actions performed by unskilled persons. If that is the purpose, then plaintiff must prove that the defendant lacked the required skill—in effect proving negligence.

The most common example is a motor vehicle accident involving an unlicensed driver. The lack of a license is irrelevant to the tort claim—whether the unlicensed driver is the plaintiff or the defendant.

Another example occurred in Brown v. Shyne, 151 N.E. 197 (N.Y.1926), in which a chiropractor allegedly hurt plaintiff by undertaking a treatment only licensed physicians could perform. The court held the defendant to the standard of a physician but ruled that the jury should not be told about defendant's violation of the licensing statute.

Are the driving and medical cases comparable? Should a distinction be drawn between a driver who inadvertently allowed a driving license to expire and one who never took the driving test? Should it matter whether a person's medical license was revoked for income tax evasion or for performing an illegal abortion? Or if the person never had a license?

In 1971, the rule of *Brown v. Shyne* was changed by statute. CPLR section 4504(d) provides that in any action for personal injuries against a person not authorized to practice medicine "the fact that such person practiced medicine without being so authorized shall be deemed prima facie evidence of negligence."

11. *Compliance.* In *Tedla*, is it conceivable that plaintiffs might have been contributorily negligent if they had been walking in compliance with the statute and had been hit by an oncoming car? More generally, should compliance with a safety statute necessarily satisfy the standard of due care? The question often poses a federalism issue; in particular, whether compliance with federal regulations should, as a matter of judicial deference, insulate the defendant from common law tort liability. Thus, in Edwards v. Basel Pharmaceuticals, 933 P.2d 298 (Okla.1997), suit was brought on behalf of a smoker who had died of a nicotine-induced heart attack while smoking and wearing two nicotine patches. Defendant argued that its compliance with FDA warning requirements should serve as a defense to liability. Although a relatively comprehensive warning was given to prescribing physicians, the package insert cautioned only that an "overdose might cause you to faint." (We take up in Chapter IX whether a warning to the physician in itself should suffice, a question that the court in *Edwards* answered in the negative.) Regarding the defendant's compliance with the requirement of warning the user in this case, the court concluded:

> [T]he manufacturer's duty to warn the consumer is not necessarily satisfied by compliance with FDA minimum warning requirements. The required warnings must not be misleading, and must be adequate to explain to the user the possible dangers associated with the product. Whether that duty has been satisfied is governed by the common law of the state, not the regulations of the FDA.

The question can also arise in the context of compliance with a state regulatory scheme. See Alvarado v. J.C. Penney Co., 735 F.Supp. 371 (D.Kan.1990), in which the defendant claimed compliance with the Kansas Product Liability Act. Plaintiff was burned when the nightgown and the robe she wore were both ignited by an open flame gas heater. The court held that compliance with the regulatory standard was not conclusive. See generally Dueffert, The Role of Regulatory Compliance in Tort Actions, 26 Harv.J.Legis. 175 (1989).

The appropriate relation between tort law and legislative safety mandates is an important and controversial issue, to which we return—in the context of whether federal legislation preempts state tort remedies—in Chapter VII. In the meantime, evaluate this excerpt from the conclusion of Huber, Safety and the Second Best: The Hazards of Public Risk Management in the Courts, 85 Colum.L.Rev. 277, 334–35 (1985):

> [J]udicial nondeference may make some sense when the administrative regulatory regime is casual or sporadic, as with consumer products. But it is wholly unpersuasive for comprehensively regulated industries. Vaccines, pesticides, aircraft, electric power plants and the like all entail potentially enormous mass-exposure hazards. Precisely because they can create public risks of this nature, these products and services are also subject to the most searching and complete state and federal safety regulation. Administrative agencies may find it politically convenient to disclaim final responsibility for the public risk choices that inhere in such licensing decisions. But the simple fact is that an agency cannot intelligently issue a license for such public-risk activities without comparing the licensee's risks to those of the competition and determining that the new offering represents some measure of progress or, at worst, no measure of regression in the risk market in question.
>
> Once that determination has been made by an expert licensing agency, the courts should respect it. Regulatory agencies are equipped to make the risk comparisons on which all progressive transformation of the risk environment must be based. The courts are simply not qualified to second-guess such decisions; when they choose to do so they routinely make regressive risk choices. Requiring—or at least strongly encouraging—the courts to respect the comparative risk choices made by competent, expert agencies would inject a first, small measure of rationality into a judicial regulatory system that currently runs quite wild.

For a critique of this view, discussing both the claims for and against judicial deference to regulatory compliance, and concluding that there should be no general presumption in favor of deference, see Rabin, Reassessing Regulatory Compliance, 88 Geo.L.J. 2049 (2000); see also Gillette & Krier, Risk, Courts, and Agencies, 138 U.Pa.L.Rev. 1027 (1990).

D. PROVING NEGLIGENCE WITH CIRCUMSTANTIAL EVIDENCE

Problems of proof occur at virtually every stage of the negligence action. In this section, we focus on the plaintiff's burden of proving that the defendant's conduct fell below the standard of reasonable care. This, in turn, involves proving what the defendant actually did or did not do and, at times, the unreasonableness of such behavior.

The most convincing type of proof is usually documentary or "real" evidence: the broken bottle, the flight recorder in an airplane accident, the "smoking gun" document, or a videotape of an automobile crash. Such evidence, however, is available in only a few personal injury accidents. A "lucky" plaintiff will be able to present photographs of skid marks or other visible evidence that might serve almost as well as "real" evidence. The plaintiff may also use "direct" evidence: eyewitnesses may testify. Whether the witness describes skid marks or the crash itself, the party hurt by such testimony may seek to undermine it by cross-examination in an effort to show erroneous recall of the facts or to cast doubt on the witness's credibility. When documentary and photographic proof are used, accuracy and credibility are less readily challenged. In practice, however, most evidence is circumstantial.

Negri v. Stop and Shop, Inc.

Court of Appeals of New York, 1985.
65 N.Y.2d 625, 480 N.E.2d 740, 491 N.Y.S.2d 151.

■ MEMORANDUM.

[After a plaintiff's verdict, the trial court entered judgment for the plaintiff in a slip and fall case. The Appellate Division reversed and dismissed the complaint.]

The order of the Appellate Division, [ ] should be reversed, with costs, and remitted to that court for consideration of the facts and of other issues not previously addressed.

The record contains some evidence tending to show that defendant had constructive notice of a dangerous condition which allegedly caused injuries to its customer. There was testimony that the injured plaintiff, while shopping in defendant's store, fell backward, did not come into contact with the shelves, but hit her head directly on the floor where "a lot of broken jars" of baby food lay; that the baby food was "dirty and messy"; that a witness in the immediate vicinity of the accident did not hear any jars falling from the shelves or otherwise breaking during the 15 or 20 minutes prior to the accident; and that the aisle had not been cleaned or inspected for at least 50 minutes prior to the accident—indeed, some evidence was adduced that it was at least two hours.

Viewing the evidence in a light most favorable to the plaintiffs and according plaintiffs the benefit of every reasonable inference [ ], it cannot be said, as a matter of law, that the circumstantial evidence was insufficient to permit the jury to draw the necessary inference that a slippery condition was created by jars of baby food which had fallen and broken a sufficient length of time prior to the accident to permit defendant's employees to discover and remedy the condition. [ ] Plaintiffs having made out a prima facie case, it was error to dismiss the complaint. If the jury verdict be deemed by the Appellate Division to be against the weight of the evidence, that court's power is limited to ordering a new trial. [ ]

■ WACHTLER, C.J., and JASEN, MEYER, SIMONS, KAYE and ALEXANDER, JJ., concur.

Gordon v. American Museum of Natural History

Court of Appeals of New York, 1986.
67 N.Y.2d 836, 492 N.E.2d 774, 501 N.Y.S.2d 646.

■ MEMORANDUM.

The order of the Appellate Division, [ ], should be reversed, with costs, the complaint dismissed and the certified question answered in the negative.

Plaintiff was injured when he fell on defendant's front entrance steps. He testified that as he descended the upper level of steps he slipped on the third step and that while he was in midair he observed a piece of white, waxy paper next to his left foot. He alleges that this paper came from the concession stand that defendant had contracted to have present and which was located on the plaza separating the two tiers of steps and that defendant was negligent insofar as its employees failed to discover and remove the paper before he fell on it. The case was submitted to the jury on the theory that defendant had either actual or constructive notice of the dangerous condition presented by the paper on the steps. The jury found against defendant on the issue of liability. A divided Appellate Division affirmed and granted defendant leave to appeal on a certified question.

There is no evidence in the record that defendant had actual notice of the paper and the case should not have gone to the jury on that theory. To constitute constructive notice, a defect must be visible and apparent and it must exist for a sufficient length of time prior to the accident to permit defendant's employees to discover and remedy it (Negri v. Stop & Shop [ ]). The record contains no evidence that anyone, including plaintiff, observed the piece of white paper prior to the accident. Nor did he describe the paper as being dirty or worn, which would have provided some indication that it had been present for some period of time (cf. [*Negri*] (broken baby food jars were dirty)). Thus, on the evidence presented, the piece of paper that caused plaintiff's fall could have been deposited there only minutes or seconds before the accident and any other conclusion would be pure speculation.

Contrary to plaintiff's contentions, neither a general awareness that litter or some other dangerous condition may be present [ ] nor the fact that plaintiff observed other papers on another portion of the steps approximately 10 minutes before his fall is legally sufficient to charge defendant with constructive notice of the paper he fell on. [Two cited cases] are not to the contrary. In both cases constructive notice was established by other evidence and the issue was whether plaintiffs had presented sufficient evidence on the issue of causation insofar as both plaintiffs failed to specify which step they had fallen on and what condition—wear, wetness or litter—had caused them to slip. In each case, the court concluded that plaintiff had presented a prima facie case because a fall was a natural and probable consequence of the conditions present on the stairs. The defect in plaintiff's case here, however, is not an inability to prove the causation element of his fall but the lack of evidence establishing constructive notice of the particular condition that caused his fall.

■ WACHTLER, C.J., and MEYER, SIMONS, KAYE, ALEXANDER, TITONE and HANCOCK, JJ., concur in memorandum.

NOTES AND QUESTIONS

1.   Are *Negri* and *Gordon* distinguishable?

2.   What more might plaintiff have done in *Gordon*? Does the court suggest that the judgment below would have been affirmed if Gordon had testified that the paper looked dirty?

3.   Recall the difference, noted in *Negri*, between dismissing the complaint (or granting summary judgment) and ordering a new trial. What controls the appropriate appellate response?

4.   Should plaintiff be able to show that the week before she fell, a broken baby food jar had been on the floor in that aisle for more than two hours before being cleaned up? In Moody v. Haymarket Associates, 723 A.2d 874 (Me.1999), plaintiff slipped on a wet floor in an office building and sued the owner of the building for the negligence of its janitor in not drying the floor or warning about the wetness. The trial judge admitted evidence showing that defendant's premises had been free of accidents for ten years prior to trial (four before the accident and six afterward). The jury found no negligence. The supreme court reversed the defendant's judgment because the judge erred in admitting that evidence, explaining that

> even if the evidence is relevant, the court "must then consider whether the probative value of such evidence is substantially outweighed by the countervailing considerations . . ." that is, the danger of unfair prejudice, confusion of the issue, or undue delay.

The court concluded that the evidence here "was not relevant to the very narrow issue of whether the janitor acted in a particular way on the day in question. Simply put, because of the narrow issue before the jury, the absence of other accidents in the lobby did not present information about substantially similar circumstances." Might the same evidence be relevant on a different theory: that defendant had negligently hired and retained an incompetent janitor?

5.   *Business practice rule.* Plaintiff slipped and fell on "a wet, slimy piece of green lettuce" while at defendant's self-service salad bar. Concluding that she failed to establish actual or constructive notice, the trial court entered a directed verdict for defendant. On appeal, the Connecticut Supreme Court reversed, adopting the "business practice" or "mode of operation" rule. Kelly v. Stop & Shop, Inc., 918 A.2d 249 (Conn.2007). Under the rule, a customer need not establish actual or

constructive notice when the business practice of the store—in this case a self-service salad bar—provided a continuous and foreseeable risk of harm to customers. In addition to surveying a wide array of courts that had adopted the rule, the court explained its rationale:

> The rule, which evolved in response to the proliferation of self-service retail establishments, is rooted in the theory that traditional notice requirements are unfair and unnecessary in the self-service context. "The modern self-service form of retail sales encourages . . . patrons to obtain for themselves from shelves and containers the items they wish to purchase, and to move them from one part of the store to another in baskets and shopping carts as they continue to shop for other items, thus increasing the risk of droppage and spillage." [ ]; *see also* [ ] ("It is common knowledge that the modern merchandizing method of self-service poses a considerably different situation than the older method of individual clerk assistance. It is much more likely that items for sale and other foreign substances will fall to the floor."). "It is also common knowledge that modern merchandising techniques employed by self-service retail stores are specifically designed to attract a customer's attention to the merchandise on the shelves and, thus, away from any hazards that might be on the floor." [ ]

Are the "business practice" and "mode of operation" rules consistent with the negligence approach we have seen in this Chapter or are they a form of strict liability? What if a store kept a clerk at the produce counter who mopped the area every five minutes?

Byrne v. Boadle 源于英国的初始案例)
Court of Exchequer, 1863.
2 H. & C. 722, 159 Eng.Rep. 299.

At the trial before the learned Assessor of the Court of Passage at Liverpool, the evidence adduced on the part of the plaintiff was as follows:—A witness named Critchley said: "On the 18th July, I was in Scotland Road, on the right side going north, defendant's shop is on that side. When I was opposite to his shop, a barrel of flour fell from a window above in defendant's house and shop, and knocked the plaintiff down. He was carried into an adjoining shop. A horse and cart came opposite the defendant's door. Barrels of flour were in the cart. I do not think the barrel was being lowered by a rope. I cannot say: I did not see the barrel until it struck the plaintiff. It was not swinging when it struck the plaintiff. It struck him on the shoulder and knocked him towards the shop. No one called out until after the accident." The plaintiff said: "On approaching Scotland Place and defendant's shop, I lost all recollection. I felt no blow. I saw nothing to warn me of danger. I was taken home in a cab. I was helpless for a fortnight." (He then described his sufferings.) "I saw the path clear. I did not see any cart opposite defendant's shop." Another witness said: "I saw a barrel falling. I don't know how, but from defendant's." The only other witness

[handwritten margin note: Witness testimony + "facts"]

was a surgeon, who described the injury which the plaintiff had received. It was admitted that the defendant was a dealer in flour.

It was submitted, on the part of the defendant, that there was no evidence of negligence for the jury. The learned Assessor was of that opinion, and nonsuited the plaintiff, reserving leave to him to move the Court of Exchequer to enter the verdict for him with £50 damages, the amount assessed by the jury.

Littler, in the present Term, obtained a rule nisi to enter the verdict for the plaintiff, on the ground of misdirection of the learned Assessor in ruling that there was no evidence of negligence on the part of the defendant. . . .

POLLOCK, C.B. We are all of opinion that the rule must be absolute to enter the verdict for the plaintiff. The learned counsel was quite right in saying that there are many accidents from which no presumption of negligence can arise, but I think it would be wrong to lay down as a rule that in no case can presumption of negligence arise from the fact of an accident. Suppose in this case the barrel had rolled out of the warehouse and fallen on the plaintiff, how could he possibly ascertain from what cause it occurred? It is the duty of persons who keep barrels in a warehouse to take care that they do not roll out, and I think that such a case would, beyond all doubt, afford prima facie evidence of negligence. A barrel could not roll out of a warehouse without some negligence, and to say that a plaintiff who is injured by it must call witnesses from the warehouse to prove negligence seems to me preposterous. So in the building or repairing of a house, or putting pots on the chimneys, if a person passing along the road is injured by something falling upon him, I think the accident alone would be prima facie evidence of negligence. Or if an article calculated to cause damage is put in a wrong place and does mischief, I think that those whose duty it was to put it in the right place are prima facie responsible, and if there is any state of facts to rebut the presumption of negligence, they must prove them. The present case upon the evidence comes to this, a man is passing in front of the premises of a dealer in flour, and there falls down upon him a barrel of flour. I think it apparent that the barrel was in the custody of the defendant who occupied the premises, and who is responsible for the acts of his servants who had the control of it; and in my opinion the fact of its falling is prima facie evidence of negligence, and the plaintiff who was injured by it is not bound to show that it could not fall without negligence, but if there are any facts inconsistent with negligence it is for the defendant to prove them.

■ [The concurring opinion of BARON CHANNELL is omitted. BRAMWELL, B., and PIGOTT, B., concurred without opinion.]

NOTES AND QUESTIONS

1. In the midst of the defendant's argument, Pollock, C.B., interrupted to observe, "There are certain cases of which it may be said res ipsa loquitur, and this seems one of them. In some cases the Courts have held that the mere fact of the accident having occurred is evidence of negligence, as, for instance, in the case of railway collisions." This was apparently the first use of a term that was to become central to negligence litigation. Defense counsel sought to distinguish railway cases as limited to collisions involving two trains of the same railroad company. He then argued that in one case the suit was by a passenger and that there was an implicit contract of safe carriage between the passenger and the railroad. What difference would it have made, Pollock inquired, if the case cited had been brought by a bystander instead of a passenger? Defense counsel responded that because of the contract, "The fact of the accident might be evidence of negligence in the one case, though not in the other." What is the relevance of this exchange to the decision in *Byrne?*

2. Is *Kelly*, note 5, p. 90 supra, consistent with *Byrne?*

3. In Larson v. St. Francis Hotel, 188 P.2d 513 (Cal.App.1948), plaintiff pedestrian was struck by a chair thrown out of the window of one of defendant's rooms on the day when World War II formally ended. Plaintiff proved this and her injuries and then rested. Defendant's motion for a nonsuit at the end of plaintiff's case was granted.

Compare Connolly v. Nicollet Hotel, 95 N.W.2d 657 (Minn.1959), in which the hotel had been taken over by a convention of the National Junior Chamber of Commerce. In the days before plaintiff's injury, the hotel management had learned that objects were being thrown from windows and that vandalism was occurring throughout the hotel. The day before the incident, the general manager sent a memo to the hotel staff saying in part, "We have almost arrived at the end of the most harrowing experience we have had in the way of conventions, at least in my experience. . . . We had no alternative but to proceed and 'turn the other cheek.' . . ." The following night, plaintiff pedestrian lost an eye when hit by an object thrown from a room.

The majority held that the hotel could have been found to have behaved negligently after knowing of the dangers. Management decided not to try to find out who had thrown the earlier objects, because the convention was "out of control." No increased patrolling was instituted, no new guards were hired, and no appeal was made to responsible officers of the convention. Perhaps the most significant step taken was to cut holes in the corners of the hotel's laundry bags to prevent their use as water containers.

The dissenters argued that it was not reasonable to expect the management to enter every room, or make random entries, or to remain in them to prevent possible misconduct. They relied on *Larson*.

Is the majority relying on a res ipsa argument? Is negligence inferred from the accident itself?

McDougald v. Perry

Supreme Court of Florida, 1998.
716 So.2d 783.

■ WELLS, JUSTICE.

[In 1990, plaintiff was driving behind a tractor-trailer being driven by Perry. As the tractor-trailer went over some railroad tracks the 130-pound spare tire came out of its cradle underneath the trailer and fell to the ground. The trailer's rear tires then ran over the spare, causing the spare to bounce into the air and crash into the windshield of plaintiff's Jeep Wagoneer.]

The spare tire was housed in an angled cradle underneath the trailer and was held in place by its own weight. Additionally, the tire was secured by a four to six-foot long chain with one-inch links, which was wrapped around the tire. Perry testified that he believed the chain to be the original chain that came with the trailer in 1969. Perry also stated that, as originally designed, the chain was secured to the body of the trailer by a latch device. At the time of the accident, however, the chain was attached to the body of the trailer with a nut and bolt.

Perry testified that he performed a pre-trip inspection of the trailer on the day of the accident. This included an inspection of the chain, although Perry admitted that he did not check every link in the chain. After the accident, Perry noticed that the chain was dragging under the trailer. Perry opined that one of the links had stretched and slipped from the nut which secured it to the trailer. [The chain could not be located at the time of trial.] The judge instructed the jury on the doctrine of res ipsa loquitur. The jury subsequently returned a verdict in McDougald's favor.

On appeal, the district court reversed with instructions that the trial court direct a verdict in respondents' [both Perry and his employer were sued by McDougald] favor. The district court concluded that the trial court erred by: (1) not directing a verdict on the issue of negligence; (2) instructing the jury on res ipsa loquitur. . . . We granted McDougald's petition for review. . . .

This Court discussed the applicability of the doctrine of res ipsa loquitur in Marrero v. Goldsmith, 486 So.2d 530 (Fla.1986); [ ]. In *Marrero*, we stated:

Res ipsa loquitur is a Latin phrase that translates "the thing speaks for itself." Prosser and Keeton, Law of Torts § 39 (5th ed.1984). It is a rule of evidence that permits, but does not compel, an inference of negligence under certain circumstances. "[T]he doctrine of res ipsa loquitur is merely a rule of evidence. Under it an inference may arise in aid of the proof." [ ] In Goodyear Tire & Rubber Co. v. Hughes Supply, Inc., 358 So.2d 1339 (Fla.1978), we explained the doctrine as follows:

It provides an injured plaintiff with a common-sense inference of negligence where direct proof of negligence is wanting, provided certain elements consistent with negligent behavior are present. Essentially the injured plaintiff must establish that the instrumentality causing his or her injury was under the exclusive control of the defendant, and that the accident is one that would not, in the ordinary course of events, have occurred without negligence on the part of the one in control.

[ ]

In concluding that it was reversible error for the trial court to give the res ipsa loquitur instruction, the Second District determined that "McDougald failed to prove that this accident would not, in the ordinary course of events, have occurred without negligence by the defendants." . . .

The Second and Third Districts misread and interpret too narrowly what we stated in *Goodyear*. We did not say, as those courts conclude, that "the mere fact that an accident occurs does not support the application of the doctrine." Rather, we stated:

> An *injury standing alone, of course, ordinarily does not indicate negligence. The doctrine of res ipsa loquitur simply recognizes that in rare instances an injury may permit an inference of negligence if coupled with a sufficient showing of its immediate, precipitating cause.* (emphasis added).

[ ] *Goodyear* and our other cases permit latitude in the application of this common-sense inference when the facts of an accident in and of themselves establish that but for the failure of reasonable care by the person or entity in control of the injury producing object or instrumentality the accident would not have occurred. On the other hand, our present statement is not to be considered an expansion of the doctrine's applicability. We continue our prior recognition that *res ipsa loquitur* applies only in "rare instances."

The following comments in section 328D of Restatement (Second) of Torts (1965) capture the essence of a proper analysis of this issue:

> c.   *Type of event.* The first requirement for the application of the rule stated in this Section is a basis of past experience which reasonably permits the conclusion that such events do not ordinarily occur unless someone has been negligent. There are many types of accidents which commonly occur without the fault of anyone. The fact that a tire blows out, or that a man falls down stairs is not, in the absence of anything more, enough to permit the conclusion that there was negligence in inspecting the tire, or in the construction of the stairs, because it is common human experience that such events all too frequently occur without such negligence. On the other hand there are many events, such as those of objects falling from the

> defendant's premises, the fall of an elevator, the escape of gas or water from mains or of electricity from wires or appliances, the derailment of trains or the explosion of boilers, where the conclusion is at least permissible that such things do not usually happen unless someone has been negligent. To such events res ipsa loquitur may apply.
>
> *d.   Basis of conclusion.* In the usual case the basis of past experience from which this conclusion may be drawn is common to the community, and is a matter of general knowledge, which the court recognizes on much the same basis as when it takes judicial notice of facts which everyone knows. It may, however, be supplied by the evidence of the parties; and expert testimony that such an event usually does not occur without negligence may afford a sufficient basis for the inference. . . .

Restatement (Second) of Torts § 328D cmts. c–d (1965).

We conclude that the spare tire escaping from the cradle underneath the truck, resulting in the tire ultimately becoming airborne and crashing into McDougald's vehicle, is the type of accident which, on the basis of common experience and as a matter of general knowledge, would not occur but for the failure to exercise reasonable care by the person who had control of the spare tire. As the Fifth District noted, the doctrine of *res ipsa loquitur* is particularly applicable in wayward wheel cases. [Cheung v. Ryder Truck Rental, Inc., 595 So.2d 82 (Fla.App.1992)]; [ ]; Wilson v. Spencer, 127 A.2d 840, 841 (D.C.1956)("Thousands of automobiles are using our streets, but no one expects the air to be filled with flying hubcaps."). We do not agree with respondent that *Cheung* can be properly distinguished on the basis that in *Cheung* the escaped tire was attached to the axle, whereas in this case the escaped tire was a spare cradled underneath the truck. Rather, common sense dictates an inference that both a spare tire carried on a truck and a wheel on a truck's axle will stay with the truck unless there is a failure of reasonable care by the person or entity in control of the truck. Thus an inference of negligence comes from proof of the circumstances of the accident.

Furthermore, we do not agree with the Second District that McDougald failed to establish this element because "[o]ther possible explanations exist to explain the failure of the chain." [ ] Such speculation does not defeat the applicability of the doctrine in this case. As [a treatise] has noted:

> The plaintiff is not required to eliminate with certainty all other possible causes or inferences. . . . All that is required is evidence from which reasonable persons can say that on the whole it is more likely that there was negligence associated with the cause of the event than that there was not.

[ ]

Respondents also contend that the *res ipsa* instruction was inapplicable because McDougald failed to prove that direct evidence of negligence was unavailable. Respondents cite to *Goodyear* for the proposition that res ipsa is not applicable where "the facts surrounding the incident were discoverable and provable." This statement from *Goodyear* was made in a products liability tire blow-out case in which the plaintiff was in possession and control of the injury-causing device. In that case, the plaintiff, who was in possession of the product alleged to have been negligently manufactured, was in the best position to determine the alleged cause of the accident. Thus, the res ipsa inference was not applicable. Here, unlike *Goodyear*, we find that there was insufficient evidence available to McDougald. The likely cause of this accident, the chain and securing device, were in the exclusive possession of respondents and were not preserved. Moreover, this was not the basis upon which the Second District held *res ipsa loquitur* to be inapplicable.

[The district court's decision was reversed and the case remanded for consideration of remaining issues.]

■ HARDING, C.J., and OVERTON, SHAW, KOGAN and PARIENTE, JJ., concur.

[ANSTEAD, J., concurred in an opinion that quoted *Byrne* v. *Boadle* in its entirety and observed that "we can hardly improve upon this explanation for our decision today. The common law tradition is alive and well."]

NOTES AND QUESTIONS

1.   The *McDougald* court identified one element for res ipsa loquitur—that the instrumentality was in the exclusive control of the defendant. Why is exclusive control required? Is it satisfied in *McDougald*? Might any negligence have been that of the chain maker, the trailer owner, a co-employee of the driver, and not of the driver? Would res ipsa apply against the driver if the accident had occurred in 1970? What about six months after the installation of the nut and bolt by an auto repairer?

2.   The Third Restatement adopts a single element formulation for res ipsa loquitur:

> The factfinder may infer that the defendant has been negligent when the accident causing the plaintiff's harm is a type of accident that ordinarily happens as a result of the negligence of a class of actors of which the defendant is the relevant member.

Restatement (Third) of Torts: Liability for Physical and Emotional Harm § 17 (2010). Does the Third Restatement deal adequately with the issue of exclusive control?

3.   Is there a difference between a tire that falls onto the road from its restraining cradle and a tire that blows out during driving?

4.   Is the principal case as strong for the plaintiff as *Byrne v. Boadle*?

5.   At various points in *McDougald* such terms as "inference" and "presumption" are used. What weight should res ipsa loquitur have in the trial? If the judge has concluded that a jury could find that the barrel came out of the defendant's window, should the judge tell the jury (a) that it may but need not find the defendant negligent, (b) that it must find the defendant negligent unless the defendant presents plausible rebutting evidence, or (c) that it must find the defendant negligent unless persuaded that defendant was not negligent?

Most states adopt the inference view; some a stronger view. But even in a state that purports to follow the inference view, the facts may be so strong that the jury is instructed that it must find negligence in the absence of a persuasive exculpation. For example, in New York, which purports to follow the inference view, an airplane passenger was injured when the plane went off the runway while landing at Kennedy Airport. This showing was "so convincing that the inference of negligence arising therefrom is inescapable if not rebutted by other evidence." In the absence of such counter evidence the plaintiff was entitled to summary judgment on the question of liability. Farina v. Pan American World Airlines, Inc., 497 N.Y.S.2d 706 (App.Div.1986).

In some states if res ipsa applies it is treated as a "presumption affecting the burden of producing evidence." This means that if the defendant offers no plausible rebutting evidence, the plaintiff is entitled to judgment as a matter of law on liability. If, however, the defendant offers such evidence, the jury is to be informed that the plaintiff still bears the burden of persuading the jury that defendant was negligent. See, e.g., Calif. Evidence Code § 646.

6.   Can the defendant ever sufficiently rebut the plaintiff's case as to obtain judgment as a matter of law? In Leonard v. Watsonville Community Hospital, 305 P.2d 36 (Cal.1956), a Kelly clamp, about six inches long, was left inside plaintiff after an abdominal operation. The court held initially that res ipsa loquitur applied against all three participating physicians, the surgical nurse, and the hospital. One of the physicians testified that he had worked only on the lower abdomen, had left before the incision was closed, and had used only curved clamps—whereas Kelly clamps were uncurved. The testimony of the other two physicians corroborated the third physician. The court held that since this testimony increased the possibility that the other two physicians would be held liable, the "record indicates no rational ground for disbelieving their testimony." The case against the third physician "was dispelled as a matter of law."

7.   Is it appropriate to give the benefit of res ipsa loquitur to a plaintiff who also seeks to prove specific acts of negligence? In Abbott v. Page Airways, Inc., 245 N.E.2d 388 (N.Y.1969), plaintiff's husband was killed in the crash of a helicopter owned by defendant and operated by its employee. In addition to relying on res ipsa loquitur, plaintiff presented witnesses who testified that the pilot waved to someone on the ground just before the crash, had flown too low and too slowly, and had taken several drinks before the flight. The trial judge charged that the jury could properly find negligence in the specific acts charged or they "could infer negligence from the happening of the accident." The charge was upheld on appeal. A few courts disagree. See, e.g., Malloy v. Commonwealth Highland Theatres, Inc., 375 N.W.2d 631 (S.D.1985).

8.   In a state with well-developed pretrial discovery procedures, is there still a place for res ipsa loquitur? In Fowler v. Seaton, 394 P.2d 697 (Cal.1964), plaintiff was a four-year-old child who went to nursery school one morning in good health but returned that evening with a bump on her forehead, a concussion and crossed eyes. Is this enough for res ipsa loquitur? Based on these and other facts, the court thought it was. Two justices dissented on the ground that plaintiff had an obligation "to present such facts as were available to show that the accident was more probably than not the result of the alleged inadequate supervision by defendant." The dissent then listed several omissions from plaintiff's case and observed that they were "undoubtedly obtainable by discovery." Should it suffice for plaintiff to prove the minimum required to permit the critical inference? Do the facts already stated here suffice? Should all facts available by discovery but not presented be taken as adverse to plaintiff?

The court denied plaintiffs the benefit of res ipsa loquitur and upheld a summary judgment for the defense. Res ipsa was "inapplicable where the instrumentality producing the injury or damage is unknown or is not in the exclusive control of the defendant." A jury could "only speculate, surmise or guess as to how Melissa's injury occurred, and for this reason the case is one to be decided by the court as a matter of law."

Spoliation of Evidence

The *McDougald* court noted that the chain could not be located at the time of trial. The disappearance of evidence is a common phenomenon in torts cases—usually because the object has been misplaced or lost over time. But another line of cases involves claims alleging that a party destroyed important evidence to prevent its adversary from gaining access to it. Some courts that have considered the question have recognized a tort called "spoliation of evidence" with complex issues about whether the claim covers both intentional and negligent destruction. E.g., Oliver v. Stimson Lumber Co., 993 P.2d 11 (Mont.1999).

California rejected the action on the grounds that procedural sanctions may be imposed during the original trial—such as an instruction to the jury that it may draw an adverse inference against the spoliator—and because of a concern about endless litigation. See Cedars-Sinai Medical Center v. Superior Court, 954 P.2d 511 (Cal.1998)(rejecting action against party for intentional destruction). In Coprich v. Superior Court, 95 Cal.Rptr.2d 884 (App.2000), the court understood the logic of earlier cases to bar actions for negligent spoliation as well. The same concerns—endless litigation, the difficulty of telling what impact the missing evidence might have had on the original case, costs of preserving evidence after all accidents—existed in both. The court did, however, uphold an action for breach of contract to preserve evidence.

Sanctions and adverse inferences are unavailable, however, when third parties destroy or lose evidence. In Killings v. Enterprise Leasing Co., 9 So.3d 1216 (Ala.2008), the court became one of a few to recognize an independent cause of action for negligent spoliation of evidence. Plaintiff was driving a van rented from defendant when the wheel came off. Driver sued the van manufacturer and others who had maintained the vehicle. Plaintiff's lawyer called the car rental company and requested that the van, which had been totaled, be preserved and that he be notified before it was scrapped or otherwise disposed of. Despite agreeing, the rental company disposed of the wreck, and plaintiff's expert testified that he couldn't determine the cause of the wheel coming off of the car without testing the car. The court recognized a third-party negligent spoliation claim, conditioned on:

1) actual knowledge of "pending or potential litigation" on the part of the spoliator;

2) a voluntary undertaking, agreement, or specific request establishing a duty; and

3) evidence that the missing evidence was vital to the underlying claim.

How will plaintiffs in third-party spoliation suits prove their claims?

For a good overview of the area of spoliation in a case that adopts the reasoning of the California courts, see Fletcher v. Dorchester Mutual Insurance Co., 773 N.E.2d 420 (Mass.2002)(rejecting an independent cause of action for negligent or intentional spoliation in an action by tenants against a homeowner's insurer for failure to maintain evidence relevant to the cause of a fatal fire); see also Wilhoit, Spoliation of Evidence: The Viability of Four Emerging Torts, 46 UCLA L.Rev. 631 (1998).

———

In the last paragraph of the majority opinion in *McDougald* the court discusses who had access to relevant evidence. Is that issue part of the court's earlier analysis? Part of its discussion of section 328D? Should it be relevant to the applicability of res ipsa loquitur? Was this issue of accessibility relevant in *Byrne v. Boadle*? Consider these questions in connection with the following case.

Ybarra v. Spangard

Supreme Court of California, 1944.
25 Cal.2d 486, 154 P.2d 687.

■ GIBSON, C.J.

This is an action for damages for personal injuries alleged to have been inflicted on plaintiff by defendants during the course of a surgical operation. The trial court entered judgments of nonsuit as to all defendants and plaintiff appealed.

On October 28, 1939, plaintiff consulted defendant Dr. Tilley, who diagnosed his ailment as appendicitis, and made arrangements for an ʃappendectomy]to be performed by defendant Dr. Spangard at a hospital owned and managed by defendant Dr. Swift. Plaintiff entered the hospital, was given a hypodermic injection, slept, and later was awakened by Doctors Tilley and Spangard and wheeled into the operating room by a nurse whom he believed to be defendant Gisler, an employee of Dr. Swift. Defendant Dr. Reser, the anesthetist, also an employee of Dr. Swift, adjusted plaintiff for the operation, pulling his body to the head of the operating table and, according to plaintiff's testimony, laying him back against two hard objects at the top of his shoulders, about an inch below his neck. Dr. Reser then administered the anesthetic and plaintiff lost consciousness. When he awoke early the following morning he was in his hospital room attended by defendant Thompson, the special nurse, and another nurse who was not made a defendant.

Plaintiff testified that prior to the operation he had never had any pain in, or injury to, his right arm or shoulder, but that when he awakened he felt a sharp pain about half way between the neck and the point of the right shoulder. He complained to the nurse, and then to Dr. Tilley, who gave him diathermy treatments while he remained in the hospital. The pain did not cease, but spread down to the lower part of his arm, and after his release from the hospital the condition grew worse. He was unable to rotate or lift his arm, and developed paralysis and atrophy of the muscles around the shoulder. He received further treatments from Dr. Tilley until March, 1940, and then returned to work, wearing his arm in a splint on the advice of Dr. Spangard.

Plaintiff also consulted Dr. Wilfred Sterling Clark, who had X-ray pictures taken which showed an area of diminished sensation below the shoulder and atrophy and wasting away of the muscles around the shoulder. In the opinion of Dr. Clark, plaintiff's condition was due to trauma or injury by pressure or strain, applied between his right shoulder and neck.

Plaintiff was also examined by Dr. Fernando Garduno, who expressed the opinion that plaintiff's injury was a paralysis of traumatic origin, not arising from pathological causes, and not systemic, and that the injury resulted in atrophy, loss of use and restriction of motion of the right arm and shoulder.

Plaintiff's theory is that the foregoing evidence presents a proper case for the application of the doctrine of res ipsa loquitur, and that the inference of negligence arising therefrom makes the granting of a nonsuit improper. Defendants take the position that, assuming that plaintiff's condition was in fact the result of an injury, there is no showing that the act of any particular defendant, nor any particular instrumentality, was the cause thereof. They attack plaintiff's action as an attempt to fix liability "en masse" on various defendants, some of whom were not responsible for the acts of others; and they further point to the failure to show which defendants had control of the instrumentalities that may have been involved. Their main defense may be briefly stated in two propositions: (1) that where there are several defendants, and there is a division of responsibility in the use of an instrumentality causing the injury, and the injury might have resulted from the separate act of either one of two or more persons, the rule of res ipsa loquitur cannot be invoked against any one of them; and (2) that where there are several instrumentalities, and no showing is made as to which caused the injury or as to the particular defendant in control of it, the doctrine cannot apply. We are satisfied, however, that these objections are not well taken in the circumstances of this case.

The doctrine of res ipsa loquitur has three conditions: "(1) the accident must be of a kind which ordinarily does not occur in the absence of someone's negligence; (2) it must be caused by an agency or instrumentality within the exclusive control of the defendant; (3) it must not have been due to any voluntary action or contribution on the part of the plaintiff." (Prosser, Torts, p. 295.) It is applied in a wide variety of situations, including cases of medical or dental treatment and hospital care. [ ]

There is, however, some uncertainty as to the extent to which res ipsa loquitur may be invoked in cases of injury from medical treatment. This is in part due to the tendency, in some decisions, to lay undue emphasis on the limitations of the doctrine, and to give too little attention to its basic underlying purpose. The result has been that a simple, understandable rule of circumstantial evidence, with a sound background of common sense and human experience, has occasionally been transformed into a rigid legal formula, which arbitrarily precludes its application in many cases where it is most important that it should be applied. If the doctrine is to continue to serve a useful purpose, we should not forget that "the particular force and justice of the rule, regarded as a presumption throwing upon the party charged the duty of producing evidence, consists in the circumstance that the chief evidence of the true cause, whether culpable or innocent, is practically accessible to him but inaccessible to the injured person." (9 Wigmore, Evidence [3d ed.], § 2509, p. 382; [ ]; Maki v. Murray Hospital, [7 P.2d 228 (Mont.

1932)]). In the last-named case, where an unconscious patient in a hospital received injuries from a fall, the court declared that without the doctrine the maxim that for every wrong there is a remedy would be rendered nugatory, "by denying one, patently entitled to damages, satisfaction merely because he is ignorant of facts, peculiarly within the knowledge of the party who should, in all justice, pay them."

The present case is of a type which comes within the reason and spirit of the doctrine more fully perhaps than any other. The passenger sitting awake in a railroad car at the time of a collision, the pedestrian walking along the street and struck by a falling object or the debris of an explosion, are surely not more entitled to an explanation than the unconscious patient on the operating table. Viewed from this aspect, it is difficult to see how the doctrine can, with any justification, be so restricted in its statement as to become inapplicable to a patient who submits himself to the care and custody of doctors and nurses, is rendered unconscious, and receives some injury from instrumentalities used in his treatment. Without the aid of the doctrine a patient who received permanent injuries of a serious character, obviously the result of someone's negligence, would be entirely unable to recover unless the doctors and nurses in attendance voluntarily chose to disclose the identity of the negligent person and the facts establishing liability. [ ] If this were the state of the law of negligence, the courts, to avoid gross injustice, would be forced to invoke the principles of absolute liability, irrespective of negligence, in actions by persons suffering injuries during the course of treatment under anesthesia. But we think this juncture has not yet been reached, and that the doctrine of res ipsa loquitur is properly applicable to the case before us.

The condition that the injury must not have been due to the plaintiff's voluntary action is of course fully satisfied under the evidence produced herein; and the same is true of the condition that the accident must be one which ordinarily does not occur unless someone was negligent. We have here no problem of negligence in treatment, but of distinct injury to a healthy part of the body not the subject of treatment, nor within the area covered by the operation. The decisions in this state make it clear that such circumstances raise the inference of negligence, and call upon the defendant to explain the unusual result. [ ]

The argument of defendants is simply that plaintiff has not shown an injury caused by an instrumentality under a defendant's control, because he has not shown which of the several instrumentalities that he came in contact with while in the hospital caused the injury; and he has not shown that any one defendant or his servants had exclusive control over any particular instrumentality. Defendants assert that some of them were not the employees of other defendants, that some did not stand in any permanent relationship from which liability in tort would follow, and that in view of the nature of the injury, the number of defendants and the different functions performed by each, they could not all be liable for the wrong, if any.

We have no doubt that in a modern hospital a patient is quite likely to come under the care of a number of persons in different types of contractual and other relationships with each other. For example, in the present case it appears that Doctors Swift, Spangard and Tilley were physicians or surgeons commonly placed in the legal category of independent contractors; and Dr. Reser, the anesthetist, and defendant Thompson, the special nurse, were employees of Dr. Swift and not of the other doctors. But we do not believe that either the number or relationship of the defendants alone determines whether the doctrine of res ipsa loquitur applies. Every defendant in whose custody the plaintiff was placed for any period was bound to exercise ordinary care to see that no unnecessary harm came to him and each would be liable for failure in this regard. Any defendant who negligently injured him, and any defendant charged with his care who so neglected him as to allow injury to occur, would be liable. The defendant employers would be liable for the neglect of their employees; and the doctor in charge of the operation would be liable for the negligence of those who became his temporary servants for the purpose of assisting in the operation.

In this connection, it should be noted that while the assisting physicians and nurses may be employed by the hospital, or engaged by the patient, they normally become the temporary servants or agents of the surgeon in charge while the operation is in progress, and liability may be imposed upon him for their negligent acts under the doctrine of *respondeat superior*. Thus a surgeon has been held liable for the negligence of an assisting nurse who leaves a sponge or other object inside a patient, and the fact that the duty of seeing that such mistakes do not occur is delegated to others does not absolve the doctor from responsibility for their negligence.

It may appear at the trial that, consistent with the principles outlined above, one or more defendants will be found liable and others absolved, but this should not preclude the application of the rule of res ipsa loquitur. The control, at one time or another, of one or more of the various agencies or instrumentalities which might have harmed the plaintiff was in the hands of every defendant or of his employees or temporary servants. This, we think, places upon them the burden of initial explanation. Plaintiff was rendered unconscious for the purpose of undergoing surgical treatment by the defendants; it is manifestly unreasonable for them to insist that he identify any one of them as the person who did the alleged negligent act.

The other aspect of the case which defendants so strongly emphasize is that plaintiff has not identified the instrumentality any more than he has the particular guilty defendant. Here, again, there is a misconception which, if carried to the extreme for which defendants contend, would unreasonably limit the application of the res ipsa loquitur rule. It should be enough that the plaintiff can show an injury resulting from an external force applied while he lay unconscious in the hospital; this is as clear a case of identification of the instrumentality as the plaintiff may ever be able to make.

An examination of the recent cases, particularly in this state, discloses that the test of actual exclusive control of an instrumentality has not been strictly followed, but exceptions have been recognized where the purpose of the doctrine of res ipsa loquitur would otherwise be defeated. Thus, the test has become one of right of control rather than actual control. [ ] In the bursting bottle cases where the bottler has delivered the instrumentality to a retailer and thus has given up actual control, he will nevertheless be subject to the doctrine where it is shown that no change in the condition of the bottle occurred after it left the bottler's possession, and it can accordingly be said that he was in constructive control. [ ] Moreover, this court departed from the single instrumentality theory in the colliding vehicle cases, where two defendants were involved, each in control of a separate vehicle. [ ] Finally, it has been suggested that the hospital cases may properly be considered exceptional, and that the doctrine of res ipsa loquitur "should apply with equal force in cases wherein medical and nursing staffs take the place of machinery and may, through carelessness or lack of skill, inflict, or permit the infliction of injury upon a patient who is thereafter in no position to say how he received his injuries." [*Maki v. Murray Hospital*]; see, also, Whetstine v. Moravec, [291 N.W. 425, 435 (Iowa 1940)], where the court refers to the "instrumentalities" as including "the unconscious body of the plaintiff."

In the face of these examples of liberalization of the tests for res ipsa loquitur, there can be no justification for the rejection of the doctrine in the instant case. As pointed out above, if we accept the contention of defendants herein, there will rarely be any compensation for patients injured while unconscious. A hospital today conducts a highly integrated system of activities, with many persons contributing their efforts. There may be, e.g., preparation for surgery by nurses and interns who are employees of the hospital; administering of an anesthetic by a doctor who may be an employee of the hospital, an employee of the operating surgeon, or an independent contractor; performance of an operation by a surgeon and assistants who may be his employees, employees of the hospital, or independent contractors; and post surgical care by the surgeon, a hospital physician, and nurses. The number of those in whose care the patient is placed is not a good reason for denying him all reasonable opportunity to recover for negligent harm. It is rather a good reason for reexamination of the statement of legal theories which supposedly compel such a shocking result.

We do not at this time undertake to state the extent to which the reasoning of this case may be applied to other situations in which the doctrine of res ipsa loquitur is invoked. We merely hold that where a plaintiff receives unusual injuries while unconscious and in the course of medical treatment, all those defendants who had any control over his body or the instrumentalities which might have caused the injuries may properly be called upon to meet the inference of negligence by giving an explanation of their conduct.

The judgment is reversed.⌋ Disposition

■ SHENK, J., CURTIS, J., EDMONDS, J., CARTER, J., and SCHAUER, J., concurred.

NOTES AND QUESTIONS

1.   The opinion quotes Prosser's formulation of res ipsa loquitur that conditions its application upon proof of three factors. In this case how is each of them met? Is that formulation consistent with the passage quoted from Wigmore? Would the plaintiff's case have been stronger, or weaker, under the Prosser approach to res ipsa loquitur if he had sued only Drs. Swift and Spangard?

2.   On remand the trial judge as trier of fact accepted the testimony of plaintiff's experts and of an independent court-appointed expert that the injury was traumatic in origin and did not result from an infection. Except for the hospital owner, who did not personally attend plaintiff, each defendant testified that he or she "saw nothing occur which could have caused the injury." The trial judge found against all defendants and his ruling was affirmed. The court observed that "[t]here is nothing inherent in direct testimony which compels a trial court to accept it over the contrary inferences which may reasonably be drawn from circumstantial evidence," and quoted Justice Holmes to the effect that "law does not always keep step with logic." Ybarra v. Spangard, 208 P.2d 445 (Cal.Dist.Ct.App.1949). Is this result sensible? Could the trial judge have found some defendants liable and some not liable?

3.   In Inouye v. Black, 47 Cal.Rptr. 313 (App.1965), the defendant surgeon implanted stainless steel wire in plaintiff's neck to stabilize it. Although the tension was expected to break the wire, it was expected that the wire would remain in the body and cause no physical damage. The wire fragmented into unexpectedly small pieces that migrated downward toward the lower spine, necessitating further surgery to retrieve the pieces. Plaintiff sued only the surgeon. Uncontroverted medical testimony showed that he had selected the right type of wire; that if he was telling the truth, he had properly inspected it visually and manually before using it; and that the fragmentation was unexpected. The trial judge's grant of a nonsuit was affirmed on appeal. Res ipsa loquitur was inapplicable because common experience "reveals defendant's negligence as one of several available speculations, but not as a probability." It might have been that the surgeon failed to do some of the things he said he did; but it might also have been that the hospital left the wire too long in the supply room or that the wire left the manufacturer's plant with hidden flaws.

The court observed that a "group of persons and instrumentalities may combine in the performance of a medical procedure culminating in an unexpected, mysterious and disastrous result. With the sources of disaster personified in a group of defendants, the demand for evidence pointing the finger of probability at any one of them is relaxed; all may be called upon to give the jury evidence of care," citing *Ybarra* and other cases. The court then noted that because only the surgeon was before the court, that principle did not apply. If all three had been before the court, might the surgeon still have received a nonsuit?

4.   In Fireman's Fund American Insurance Cos. v. Knobbe, 562 P.2d 825 (Nev.1977), plaintiff, a hotel's fire insurer, sued four guests to recover insurance payments it had made as the result of a fire that started in the room occupied by two of the guests. That couple and another couple, who were occupying a connecting room, had all been smoking in the room shortly before the fire broke out. Plaintiff was unable to prove which defendant had been negligent and sought to invoke res ipsa loquitur. The court upheld a summary judgment motion granted for the defendants and rejected *Ybarra*. In doing so, it agreed with Justice Traynor who, dissenting in Raber v. Tumin, 226 P.2d 574 (Cal.1951), had warned of the danger of extending *Ybarra*. He asserted that under *Ybarra*, a plaintiff "who is struck on the head by a flower pot falling from a multistoried apartment building may recover judgment against all the tenants unless the innocent tenants are able to identify the guilty one."

If you are run over by a negligent hit-and-run driver as you cross the street and all you can identify is the year, make and color of the car, what analysis if you sue jointly all local owners of such cars and rest after your testimony about what happened?

5.   In Judson v. Giant Powder Co., 40 P. 1020 (Cal.1895), the defendant's nitroglycerine factory exploded, killing all who could possibly have explained why it happened. In a suit by plaintiff, whose property was damaged, the court held that evidence of the explosion sufficed to withstand a nonsuit. Is this sound in a situation in which rebuttal is impossible? Consider also Newing v. Cheatham, 540 P.2d 33 (Cal.1975), in which a private airplane crashed—killing all aboard, including the pilot— on a day when the weather was clear, visibility was unrestricted, and the pilot had sent no danger messages. A directed verdict on liability for the estate of a passenger was upheld on appeal.

6.   *Ybarra* has been widely rejected. See, e.g., Barrett v. Emanuel Hospital, 669 P.2d 835 (Or.Ct.App.1983). First, "modern discovery practice" casts doubt on the need for the *Ybarra* approach. Second, the inference of res ipsa "is permitted only when the plaintiff is able to establish . . . the probability that a particular defendant's conduct was the cause of the plaintiff's harm." Finally, special protections for unconscious patients could "be achieved in various direct ways which may warrant societal consideration, e.g., strict liability or some form of *respondeat superior* liability. However, we do not think the objective should be pursued by stretching a permissible inference beyond the point where there are underlying facts other than the result from which it can reasonably be drawn." The complaint was dismissed.

E. THE SPECIAL CASE OF MEDICAL MALPRACTICE

In this section we consider special legal and practical problems involved in medical malpractice cases. In the process we review the standard of care, the role of custom, and questions of proof. Consider the following excerpt from Robbins v. Footer, 553 F.2d 123 (D.C.Cir.1977), involving a claim against an obstetrician:

> The conduct of a defendant in a negligence suit is usually measured against the conduct of a hypothetical reasonably prudent person acting under the same or similar circumstances. [ ] In medical malpractice cases, however, courts have required that the specialized knowledge and skill of the defendant must be taken into account. [ ] Although the law had thus imposed a higher standard of care on doctors, it has tempered the impact of that rule by permitting the profession, as a group, to set its own legal standards of reasonable conduct. Whether a defendant has or has not conformed his conduct to a customary practice is generally only evidence of whether he has acted as a reasonably prudent person. [ ] In a malpractice case, however, the question of whether the defendant acted in conformity with the common practice within his profession is the heart of the suit. [ ] As part of his prima facie case a malpractice plaintiff must affirmatively prove the relevant recognized standard of medical care exercised by other physicians and that the defendant departed from that standard when treating the plaintiff. [ ] In almost all cases the plaintiff must present expert witnesses since the technical complexity of the facts and issues usually prevents the jury itself from determining both the appropriate standard of care and whether the defendant's conduct conformed to that standard. In such cases there can be no finding of negligence without expert testimony to support it. [ ]

Despite the refined standard of care, judges must still be sure to use language in their charges that conveys the objective nature of the inquiry. In DiFranco v. Klein, 657 A.2d 145 (R.I.1995), the court overturned a defense verdict in a malpractice case because the trial judge had probably prejudiced the plaintiff by stating that the defendant was not liable "if in the exercise of . . . good faith judgment she has made a mistake as to the course of treatment taken" and that a physician "is not liable for damages resulting from an honest mistake or error in judgment."

Sheeley v. Memorial Hospital

Supreme Court of Rhode Island, 1998.
710 A.2d 161.

■ GOLDBERG, JUSTICE.

[At the time plaintiff gave birth, in 1987, Dr. Ryder, a second-year family practice resident, performed an episiotomy, which involves cutting into the mother's perineum to facilitate the birth and then stitching the incision after the birth. Plaintiff developed complications at the site of this surgery and sued Dr. Ryder and the hospital.]

This case is before the court on the appeal of Joanne Sheeley (Sheeley) from the directed verdict entered against her in the underlying medical malpractice action. Specifically Sheeley asserts that the trial justice erred in excluding the testimony of her expert witness, which exclusion resulted in the entry of the directed verdict. For the reasons set forth below, we hold that the trial justice erred in excluding the testimony and reverse the judgment from which the appeal was taken. Furthermore, we take this opportunity to reexamine the proper standard of care to be applied in medical malpractice cases and, in so doing, abandon the "similar locality" rule, which previously governed the admissibility of expert testimony in such actions. . . .

. . .

At the trial on the malpractice action, Sheeley sought to introduce the expert medical testimony of Stanley D. Leslie, M.D. (Dr. Leslie), a board certified obstetrician/gynecologist (OB/GYN). Doctor Leslie planned to testify about Dr. Ryder's alleged malpractice and the applicable standard of care as it relates to the performance of an episiotomy. The defendants objected and filed a motion in limine to exclude the testimony, arguing that Dr. Leslie, as an OB/GYN, was not qualified under G.L.1956 § 9–19–41[3] to testify against a family practice resident who was performing obstetric and gynecological care. A hearing on the motion was conducted, at which time it was disclosed that Dr. Leslie had been board certified in obstetrics and gynecology since 1961 and recertified in 1979. Doctor Leslie testified that board certification represents a level of achievement of skill and knowledge as established by a national standard in which the standard of care is uniform throughout the medical specialty. Doctor Leslie is currently a clinical professor of obstetrics and gynecology at the Hill-Science Center, State University, College of Medicine in Syracuse. He is a member of the New York Statewide Professional Standards Review Council, which reviews disputes between doctors and hospitals

---

[3]   [Section 9–19–41] states:

"In any legal action based upon a cause of action arising on or after January 1, 1987, for personal injury or wrongful death filed against a licensed physician . . . only those persons who by knowledge, skill, experience, training or education qualify as experts in the field of the alleged malpractice shall be permitted to give expert testimony as to the alleged malpractice."

regarding diagnosis and management, and the Credentials and Certification Committee at the Crouse-Irving Hospital, where his responsibilities include drafting standards for family practice physicians. It was further revealed that Dr. Leslie has in the course of his career delivered approximately 4,000 babies and that even though he has been retired from the practice of obstetrics since 1975, he has maintained his familiarity with the standards and practices in the field of obstetrics through weekly conferences, active obstetric work, professorial responsibilities, and continuing education.

Nevertheless, relying on Soares v. Vestal, 632 A.2d 647 (R.I.1993), defendants maintained that § 9–19–41 requires a testifying expert to be in the same medical field as the defendant physician. In *Soares* this court upheld the trial justice's decision to exclude the testimony of the plaintiff's expert witness in a situation in which the expert was board certified in neurology and internal medicine, and the underlying malpractice action involved a family practitioner performing emergency medicine. [ ] Agreeing that *Soares* was determinative, the trial justice here granted defendants' motion. . . . Sheeley did not have any other experts prepared to testify, nor was she able to procure one within the two-day period allowed by the trial justice. Consequently defendants' motion for a directed verdict was granted. This appeal ensued.

. . .

. . . In a medical malpractice case expert testimony is an essential requirement in proving the standard of care applicable to the defendant, "unless the lack of care is so obvious as to be within the layman's common knowledge." . . .

"The determination of the competency of an expert witness to testify is within the discretion of the trial justice." [ ] This court will not disturb that decision in the absence of clear error or abuse. [ ] In fairness to the trial justice, we note that in making her determination with respect to the admissibility of the expert's testimony, she was without the benefit of our decisions in Marshall v. Medical Associates of Rhode Island, Inc., 677 A.2d 425 (R.I.1996), and more importantly Buja v. Morningstar, 688 A.2d 817 (R.I.1997), which have distinguished *Soares* and limited its holding to situations in which the physician-expert lacks knowledge, skill, experience, or education in the same medical field as the alleged malpractice. Nevertheless, after a review of these cases, we find it clear that the trial justice did in fact abuse her discretion and commit reversible error in excluding the testimony of Dr. Leslie.

In *Buja* the plaintiffs brought a medical malpractice action against their family practitioners when their child suffered severe medical complications, including cerebral palsy and mental retardation, after having been deprived of oxygen just prior to birth. [ ] At trial, the plaintiffs sought to introduce testimony of a board certified obstetrician. The trial justice, however, excluded the testimony and stated that testimony concerning the standard of care required of a family practitioner practicing obstetrics had to be introduced by an expert in family medicine, not an expert in OB/GYN. [ ] Relying on our previous holding in *Marshall*, this court reversed the trial justice and stated that even though the proposed expert did not practice in the same specialty as the defendants, he clearly had the prerequisite "knowledge, skill, experience, training or education . . . in the field of the alleged malpractice." [ ] The *Buja* court held that nothing in the language of § 9–19–41 requires the expert to practice in the same specialty as the defendant. [ ] "Such an additional requirement is unnecessary and is in contravention to the General Assembly's clear intentions, as expressed in § 9–19–41." [ ] In view of this holding and the striking factual similarities of the instant matter to *Buja*, there can be little doubt that we must reverse the decision of the trial justice and remand the case for a new trial.

Yet in spite of our holdings in *Buja* and *Marshall*, defendants continue to insist that Dr. Leslie is not qualified to testify. In essence defendants argue that Dr. Leslie is overqualified, stating that a board certified OB/GYN does not possess the same knowledge, skill, experience, training, or education as a second-year family practice resident performing obstetrics in Rhode Island. Furthermore defendants argue that because Dr. Leslie has not actually practiced obstetrics since 1975, his experience in providing obstetrical care is "clearly outdated" and he is therefore not competent to testify concerning the appropriate standard of care as it applied to the performance of an episiotomy and the repair of the same—even while they acknowledge that the standard of care relative to the procedures involved in the alleged malpractice has changed little over the last thirty years. Finally defendants assert that pursuant to the limitations of the "similar locality" rule, Dr. Leslie must be disqualified because he lacks any direct knowledge about the applicable standard of care for a family practice resident providing obstetric care in Rhode Island.

The defendants suggest that Dr. Leslie, although he has attended national conferences and studied medical journals and treatises in addition to his national certification, is not qualified to testify about the applicable local standard of care. In light of these arguments and with a view toward preventing any further confusion regarding the necessary qualifications of an expert testifying about the proper standard of care in medical malpractice actions, we take this opportunity to revisit our position on the appropriate standard of care.

For over three-quarters of a century this court has subscribed to the principle "that when a physician undertakes to treat or diagnose a patient, he or she is under a duty to exercise 'the same degree of diligence and skill which is commonly possessed by other members of the profession who are engaged in the same type of practice in similar localities having due regard for the state of scientific knowledge at the time of treatment.'" [ ] This "same or similar locality" rule is a somewhat expanded version of the "strict locality" rule, which requires that the expert testifying be from the same community as the defendant. See Shilkret v. Annapolis Emergency Hospital Association, [349 A.2d 245, 248 (Md.1975)]; [ ]. The rationale underlying the development of the "strict locality" rule was a recognition that opportunities, experience, and conditions may differ between densely and sparsely populated communities. [ ]

[handwritten margin note: this is what is used @ the time of this case]

This restrictive rule, however, soon came under attack in that it legitimized a low standard of care in certain smaller communities and that it also failed to address or to compensate for the potential so-called conspiracy of silence in a plaintiff's locality that would preclude any possibility of obtaining expert testimony. [ ] Furthermore, as this court noted in [ ], the locality rule is somewhat of an anachronism in view of "[m]odern systems of transportation and communication." [ ] Thus many jurisdictions, including our own, adopted the "same or similar locality" rule, which allows for experts from similarly situated communities to testify concerning the appropriate standard of care. [ ] Nevertheless, even with this somewhat expanded view, the medical malpractice bar has continually urged a narrow application of the rule, arguing the need for similar, if not identical, education, training, and experience. . . . This is a consequence that we have never intended.

[handwritten margin note: rule]

The appropriate standard of care to be utilized in any given procedure should not be compartmentalized by a physician's area of professional specialization or certification. On the contrary, we believe the focus in any medical malpractice case should be the procedure performed and the question of whether it was executed in conformity with the recognized standard of care, the primary concern being whether the treatment was administered in a reasonable manner. Any doctor with knowledge of or familiarity with the procedure, acquired through experience, observation, association, or education, is competent to testify concerning the requisite standard of care and whether the care in any given case deviated from that standard. The resources available to a physician, his or her specific area of practice, or the length of time he or she has been practicing are all issues that should be considered by the trial justice in making his or her decision regarding the qualification of an expert. No one issue, however, should be determinative. Furthermore, except in extreme cases, a witness who has obtained board certification in a particular specialty related to the procedure in question, especially when that board certification reflects a national standard of training and qualification, should be presumptively qualified to render an opinion. See [*Shilkret*]; [ ].

This court is of the opinion that whatever geographical impediments may previously have justified the need for a "similar locality" analysis are no longer applicable in view of the present-day realities of the medical profession. As the *Shilkret* court observed:

The modern physician bears little resemblance to his predecessors. As we have indicated at length, the medical schools of yesterday could not possibly compare with the accredited institutions of today, many of which are associated with teaching hospitals. But the contrast merely begins at that point in the medical career: vastly superior postgraduate training, the dynamic impact of modern communications and transportation, the proliferation of medical literature, frequent seminars and conferences on a variety of professional subjects, and the growing availability of modern clinical facilities are but some of the developments in the medical profession which combine to produce contemporary standards that are not only much higher than they were just a few short years ago, but are also national in scope.

In sum, the traditional locality rules no longer fit the present-day medical malpractice case. [ ]

We agree. Furthermore, we note that in enacting § 9–19–41, the Legislature failed to employ any reference to the "similar locality" rule. We conclude that this omission was deliberate and constitutes a recognition of the national approach to the delivery of medical services, especially in the urban centers of this country, of which Rhode Island is certainly one.

Accordingly we join the growing number of jurisdictions that have repudiated the "same or similar" communities test in favor of a national standard and hold that a physician is under a duty to use the degree of care and skill that is expected of a reasonably competent practitioner in the same class to which he or she belongs, acting in the same or similar circumstances. [The court cited cases from 20 states.] In this case the alleged malpractice occurred in the field of obstetrics and involved a procedure and attendant standard of care that has remained constant for over thirty years. Doctor Leslie, as a board certified OB/GYN with over thirty years of experience, a clinical professor of obstetrics and gynecology at a major New York hospital, and a member of the New York Statewide Professional Standards Review Council, is undoubtedly qualified to testify regarding the appropriate standard of care.

holding

[The case was remanded to the lower court for a new trial.] – *disposition*

NOTES AND QUESTIONS

1.   What was the trial judge's error? What are the arguments for and against "the same locality"? The "same or similar locality"? How should a court determine whether a locality is "similar" for purpose of qualifying an expert?

2.   Confronting head on an issue lurking in *Sheeley* but which is neither addressed nor resolved there is Arpin v. United States, 521 F.3d 769 (7th Cir.2008), holding residents to the same standard of care as

physicians who have completed their residency in the same field of medicine. For a thorough assessment of the range of views on this question reflected in the case law—from using a standard specific to residents of that amount of training to the standard of care for specialists—see King, The Standard of Care for Residents and Other Medical School Graduates in Training, 55 Am.U.L.Rev. 683 (2006).

3.   In some states national standards are more likely to be invoked if the defendant is "board certified." That fact was central to the resolution of *Robbins*, where the obstetrician was board certified:

> Modern medical education and postgraduate training has been nationalized. Scientific information flows freely among medical institutions throughout the country. Professional journals and numerous other networks of continuing education are all national in scope. [ ] Several courts have ... established a national standard of care for all physicians, completely abandoning any locality limitation. . . .

> Even in jurisdictions which have not adopted a national standard for all malpractice issues, if a physician holds himself out as a specialist, [as defendant had done here], he is held to the general standard of care required of all physicians in the same specialty. [ ] In order to become a certified specialist in obstetrics, a physician must meet nationally uniform educational and residency requirements. [ ] The textbooks used are national textbooks and the required examination is a national exam graded by a body of examiners selected so as to eliminate any regional peculiarities. [ ] After certification, specialists keep abreast of developments in their field through medical specialty journals available throughout the nation and medical specialty societies with national memberships. It seems clear that the medical profession itself has adopted a national standard for membership in one of its certified specialties. If the law remains tied to a locality standard it ignores the reality of modern medicine in favor of an outdated mythology.

Is there any remaining room for a locality-based standard?

4.   In Gala v. Hamilton, 715 A.2d 1108 (Pa.1998), defendants used local anesthetic while working on plaintiff's neck tumor. Plaintiff alleged that general anesthetic should have been used. The trial judge charged the jury:

> Where there are two schools of thought in the use of local anesthesia, a physician may rightfully choose to practice under either school of thought. If you the Jury find as a fact that the Defendants followed a procedure recognized by [a] reputable and respected, considerable number of medical experts in the use of local anesthesia, even if in the minority, the Defendants would not be deemed negligent or in violation of the standard of care in the use of local anesthesia in 1988 and you must find for the Defendants on this issue.

On appeal from a verdict and judgment for defendants, the court upheld the charge. It held that a "school" could exist even if it has never been described in written materials. Must the school be national in scope? Suppose at the trial plaintiff shows that the "local-anesthetic school" in fact produces a higher rate of bad outcomes than the "general-anesthetic school"—and that this would have been apparent if anyone in the local school had ever published (or tried to publish) anything on the subject?

5. How are experts retained and compensated? If witnesses to auto accidents are not paid, why should medical experts be paid? In Henning v. Thomas, 366 S.E.2d 109 (Va.1988), the court held that the trial judge committed reversible error by not permitting defendants to try to persuade the jury that the plaintiff's expert was a " 'doctor for hire' who was part of a nationwide group that offered themselves as witnesses, on behalf of medical malpractice plaintiffs. Once the jury was made aware of this information it was for the jury to decide what weight, if any, to give to [the expert's] testimony. This was a classic case of an effort to establish bias, prejudice, or relationship." Is it relevant if an expert retained by one side has never rendered an opinion on behalf of the other side? Is it relevant if an expert has testified in 20 cases during the past year—and has seen patients only 3 weeks during that period?

6. *Sheeley's* reference to the conspiracy of silence probably alluded to the assertion that the requirement of local expert testimony in malpractice cases has been difficult for some plaintiffs to meet for reasons unrelated to the merits of the case. In 1961, a survey of surgeons indicated that only 30% would be willing to testify against another surgeon who had removed the wrong kidney. Medical Economics, Aug. 28, 1961. Physicians who criticized colleagues might face expulsion from the local medical society. Bernstein v. Alameda-Contra Costa Medical Ass'n, 293 P.2d 862 (Cal.Dist.Ct.App.1956); see also L'Orange v. Medical Protective Co., 394 F.2d 57 (6th Cir.1968), in which plaintiff alleged that defendant insurer had cancelled his malpractice policy because he had testified in court against a dentist also insured by the defendant. The potential for concern has not been eliminated by the passage of time or by changes in the organization of medical services. After *Sheeley*, the same court confronted a case in which, as of 1990, all three of the state's pediatric surgeons were associated in the same office. Flanagan v. Wesselhoeft, 712 A.2d 365 (R.I.1998). The case was decided on other grounds.

These concerns undoubtedly induced courts to devise techniques for avoiding the need for experts in certain kinds of cases. One change permitted a plaintiff to call the defendant physician and try to use that testimony to fill gaps in plaintiff's case. Some courts permitted the plaintiff to read treatises to educate the jury. We return to expert testimony in Chapter V.

7. At one point, the *Sheeley* court refers to situations "within the layman's common knowledge." As that suggests, on such occasions plaintiffs in malpractice cases do not need experts. For example, it might be shown that without any need for hasty termination of a surgical procedure, a sponge or a surgical instrument was inadvertently left in the plaintiff's abdomen. Or it might be shown that the surgeon operated on the left leg when it was the right leg that needed the treatment. In such cases, it would necessarily follow that even if an expert testified for the defense that the relevant segment of the medical profession normally behaved as the defendant did, the jury would not be required to accept that as the proper standard.

8.   *Medical malpractice and res ipsa.* In Sides v. St. Anthony's Medical Center, 258 S.W.3d 811 (Mo.2008), the court addressed the question of whether a plaintiff in a medical malpractice case can proceed on a res ipsa theory when the plaintiff offers a medical expert's opinion that the injury would not have occurred in the absence of negligence by defendant. Plaintiff alleged that an infection she suffered during surgery was caused by one of various failures to take standard operative infection precautions before, during and after the operation. Her further allegation was that she was unconscious due to anesthesia given to her at the time of the surgery, that her body and the surgical site were under the exclusive and joint control of defendant surgeon and hospital, that defendants had greater knowledge of the possible causes of the infection, and that the defendants "infected plaintiff Janice F. Sides' body at the site of the surgery" with E. coli.

In allowing the case to proceed on a res ipsa theory, the Missouri court asserted that it joined 28 out of 36 other jurisdictions that had considered the question and answered in the affirmative, along with the endorsement of the Restatement Second in section 328D. Why do you suppose that some courts are unwilling to allow res ipsa in this situation—that is, where expert testimony rather than common knowledge is the basis for the inference of negligence? If experts testify that out of every 100 operations of a particular type, 5 fail, has plaintiff made out a res ipsa case? What if the testimony is that of those 5 failures on average 3 are due to malpractice?

9.   In Stein, Toward a Theory of Medical Malpractice, 97 Iowa L.Rev. 1201 (2012), the author finds that courts continue to defer to medical custom as conclusive on quality of treatment, as distinguished from issues of medical resource management (what Stein labels "setup rules"): management of staffing and credentialing, rationing of medical care, and equipment and facility management.

10.   Jena et al., Malpractice Risk According to Physician Specialty, 365 New Eng.J.Med. 629 (2011), found that during the period from 1991–2003, 7.4% of all physicians had at least one malpractice claim, with 1.6% of all having a claim leading to payment. This empirical study also found wide variability in the claims filed against physicians across specialties, with the lifetime risk of being sued faced by practitioners in some specialties being a near certainty (99% in high risk areas like neurosurgery).

11.   For comprehensive treatment of the medical malpractice area, see Stein, note 9 supra; T. Baker, The Medical Malpractice Myth (2005); P. Weiler, Medical Malpractice on Trial (1991); F. Sloan & R. Bovbjerg, Medical Malpractice: Crisis, Response and Effects (1989). In Chapter XII

we consider recent developments and proposals for changing the handling of medical malpractice litigation.

Matthies v. Mastromonaco

Supreme Court of New Jersey, 1999.
160 N.J. 26, 733 A.2d 456.

■ POLLOCK, J.

This appeal presents the question whether the doctrine of informed consent requires a physician to obtain the patient's consent before implementing a nonsurgical course of treatment. It questions also whether a physician, in addition to discussing with the patient treatment alternatives that the physician recommends, should discuss medically reasonable alternative courses of treatment that the physician does not recommend. We hold that to obtain a patient's informed consent to one of several alternative courses of treatment, the physician should explain medically reasonable invasive and noninvasive alternatives, including the risks and likely outcomes of those alternatives, even when the chosen course is noninvasive.

[In 1990, the 81-year-old plaintiff fell in her apartment and broke her right hip. When she was discovered two days later she was transported to emergency care. Defendant orthopedic surgeon prescribed bed rest rather than surgery. Further facts are reported in the opinion. The trial court refused to permit an informed consent claim to go to the jury because (1) the doctrine did not apply where the recommendation was noninvasive and (2) the claim was subsumed within the malpractice claim. The jury found that defendant had not committed malpractice by failing to perform surgery on plaintiff. The Appellate Division reversed because of the failure to charge on informed consent.]

. . . Dr. Mastromonaco reviewed Matthies's medical history, condition, and X-rays. He decided against pinning her hip, a procedure that would have involved the insertion of four steel screws, each approximately one-quarter inch thick and four inches long.

Dr. Mastromonaco reached that decision for several reasons. First, Matthies was elderly, frail, and in a weakened condition. Surgery involving the installation of screws would be risky. Second, Matthies suffered from osteoporosis, which led Dr. Mastromonaco to conclude that her bones were too porous to hold the screws. He anticipated that the screws probably would loosen, causing severe pain, and necessitating a partial or total hip replacement. Third, forty years earlier, Matthies had suffered a stroke from a mismatched blood transfusion during surgery. The stroke had left her partially paralyzed on her right side. Consequently she had worn a brace and essentially used her right leg as a post while propelling herself forward with her left leg. After considering these factors, Dr. Mastromonaco decided that with bed rest, a course of treatment that he recognized as "controversial," Matthies's fracture could heal sufficiently to restore her right leg to its limited function. . . .

facts

Before her fall, Matthies had maintained an independent lifestyle. She had done her own grocery shopping, cooking, housework, and laundry. Her dentist of many years, Dr. Arthur Massarsky, testified that he often had observed Matthies climbing unassisted the two flights of stairs to his office. Matthies is now confined to a nursing home.

Plaintiff's expert

Matthies's expert, Dr. Hervey Sicherman, a board-certified orthopedic surgeon, testified that under the circumstances, bed rest was an inappropriate treatment. He maintained that bed rest alone is not advisable for a hip fracture unless the patient does not expect to regain the ability to walk. Essentially, he rejects bed rest except when the patient is terminally ill or in a vegetative state. Dr. Sicherman explained that unless accompanied by traction, the danger of treating a hip fracture with bed rest is that the fracture could dislocate. In fact, shortly after Matthies began her bed-rest treatment, the head of her right femur displaced. Her right leg shortened, and she has never regained the ability to walk. According to Dr. Sicherman, the weakness and porosity of Matthies's bones increased the likelihood of this bad outcome. Even defendant's expert, Dr. Ira Rochelle, a board-certified orthopedic surgeon, admitted that pinning Matthies's hip would have decreased the risk of displacement. He nonetheless agreed with Dr. Mastromonaco that Matthies's bones were probably too brittle to withstand insertion of the pins.

Defendant's argument

Dr. Mastromonaco's goal in conservatively treating Matthies was to help her "get through this with the least complication as possible and to maintain a lifestyle conducive to her disability." He believed that rather than continue living on her own, Matthies should live in a long-term care facility. He explained, "I'm not going to give her that leg she wanted. She wanted to live alone, but she couldn't live alone. . . . I wanted her to be at peace with herself in the confines of professional care, somebody to care for her. She could not live alone."

Matthies asserts that she would not have consented to bed rest if Dr. Mastromonaco had told her of the probable effect of the treatment on the quality of her life. . . .

A jury question existed whether Dr. Mastromonaco consulted either with plaintiff or her family about the possibility of surgery. [There were conflicting recollections on this issue.]

. . . [Plaintiff was transferred to a residential nursing home where she received physical therapy. She] also saw psychiatrists and was treated . . . for depression because she grew increasingly despondent over her continued inability to walk.

. . .

Choosing among medically reasonable treatment alternatives is a shared responsibility of physicians and patients. To discharge their responsibilities, patients should provide their physicians with the information necessary for them to make diagnoses and determine courses of treatment. Physicians, in turn, have a duty to evaluate the relevant information and disclose all courses of treatment that are medically reasonable under the circumstances. Generally, a physician will recommend a course of treatment. As a practical matter, a patient often decides to adopt the physician's recommendation. Still, the ultimate decision is for the patient.

rule

We reject defendant's contention that informed consent applies only to invasive procedures. Historically, the failure to obtain a patient's informed consent to an invasive procedure, such as surgery, was treated as a battery. The physician's need to obtain the consent of the patient to surgery derived from the patient's right to reject a nonconsensual touching. Eventually, courts recognized that the need for the patient's consent is better understood as deriving from the right of self-determination. . . .

holding

The rationale for basing an informed consent action on negligence rather than battery principles is that the physician's failure is better viewed as a breach of a professional responsibility than as a nonconsensual touching. . . . Analysis based on the principle of battery is generally restricted to cases in which a physician has not obtained any consent or has exceeded the scope of consent. [ ] The essential difference in analyzing informed consent claims under negligence, rather than battery principles, is that the analysis focuses not on an unauthorized touching or invasion of the patient's body, but on the physician's deviation from a standard of care.

In informed consent analysis, the decisive factor is not whether a treatment alternative is invasive or noninvasive, but whether the physician adequately presents the material facts so that the patient can make an informed decision. That conclusion does not imply that a physician must explain in detail all treatment options in every case. For example, a physician need not recite all the risks and benefits of each potential appropriate antibiotic when writing a prescription for treatment of an upper respiratory infection. Conversely, a physician could be obligated, depending on the circumstances, to discuss a variety of treatment alternatives, such as chemotherapy, radiation, or surgery, with a patient diagnosed with cancer. Distinguishing the two situations are the limitations of the reasonable patient standard, which need not unduly burden the physician-patient relationship. The standard obligates the physician to disclose only that information material to a reasonable patient's informed decision. [ ] Physicians thus remain obligated to inform patients of medically reasonable treatment alternatives and their attendant probable risks and outcomes.

Otherwise, the patient, in selecting one alternative rather than another, cannot make a decision that is informed.

... In sum, physicians do not adequately discharge their responsibility by disclosing only treatment alternatives that they recommend.

To assure that the patient's consent is informed, the physician should describe, among other things, the material risks inherent in a procedure or course of treatment. [ ] The test for measuring the materiality of a risk is whether a reasonable patient in the patient's position would have considered the risk material. [ ] Although the test of materiality is objective, a "patient obviously has no complaint if he would have submitted to the therapy notwithstanding awareness that the risk was one of its perils." Canterbury v. Spence, 464 F.2d 772, 790 (D.C.Cir.), cert. denied, 409 U.S. 1064 (1972)(citation omitted). As the court stated in *Canterbury*:

> We think a technique which ties the factual conclusion on causation simply to the assessment of the patient's credibility is unsatisfactory.... [W]hen causality is explored at a postinjury trial with a professedly uninformed patient, the question whether he actually would have turned the treatment down if he had known the risks is purely hypothetical.... And the answer which the patient supplies hardly represents more than a guess, perhaps tinged by the circumstance that the uncommunicated hazard has in fact materialized. In our view, this method of dealing with the issue on causation comes in second-best.... Better it is, we believe, to resolve the causality issue on an objective basis: in terms of what a prudent person in the patient's position would have decided if suitably informed of all perils bearing significance. If adequate disclosure could reasonably be expected to have caused that person to decline the treatment because of the revelation of the kind of risk or danger that resulted in harm, causation is shown, but otherwise not. The patient's testimony is relevant on that score of course but it would not threaten to dominate the findings. And since that testimony would probably be appraised congruently with the factfinder's belief in its reasonableness, the case for a wholly objective standard for passing on causation is strengthened. [ ]

For consent to be informed, the patient must know not only of alternatives that the physician recommends, but of medically reasonable alternatives that the physician does not recommend. [The court found support for this in the regulations of the state's Department of Health and in the Code of Medical Ethics of the American Medical Association.]

[The court rejected the argument that the patient was adequately protected by the negligence charge that was given to the jury.] A physician may select a method of treatment that is medically reasonable, but not the one that the patient would have selected if informed of alternative methods. Like the deviation from a standard of care, the physician's failure to obtain informed consent is a form of medical negligence. . . . Physicians may neither impose their values on their patients nor substitute their level of risk aversion for that of their patients. One patient may prefer to undergo a potentially risky procedure, such as surgery, to enjoy a better quality of life. Another patient may choose a more conservative course of treatment to secure reduced risk at the cost of a diminished lifestyle. The choice is not for the physician, but the patient in consultation with the physician. By not telling the patient of all medically reasonable alternatives, the physician breaches the patient's right to make an informed choice.

The physician's duty to inform the patient of alternatives is especially important when the alternatives are mutually exclusive. If, as a practical matter, the choice of one alternative precludes the choice of others, or even if it increases appreciably the risks attendant on the other alternatives, the patient's need for relevant information is critical. That need intensifies when the choice turns not so much on purely medical considerations as on the choice of one lifestyle or set of values over another.

. . .

The issue of informed consent often intertwines with that of medical malpractice. [ ] Because of the interrelationship between the malpractice and informed consent issues in the present case, the jury should consider both issues at the retrial.

The judgment of the Appellate Division is affirmed.

■ CHIEF JUSTICE PORITZ and JUSTICES HANDLER, O'HERN, GARIBALDI, STEIN, and COLEMAN join in JUSTICE POLLOCK'S opinion.

NOTES AND QUESTIONS

1.   What standard does the court use for determining how much the defendant should have told the patient? Does an expert have a role in that determination? What was Dr. Sicherman's role in *Matthies*?

Some states require that plaintiff produce an expert in cases claiming a consent based on inadequate information. In New York, for example, the disclosure standard is framed as that which would be made by "a reasonable medical or dental practitioner under similar circumstances." This standard requires the introduction of expert testimony to show that the alleged conduct fell short of that standard. N.Y.Pub. Health Law § 2805–d and N.Y.C.P.L.R. § 4401–a. What would the expert testify about? Other states, such as New Jersey, use the "reasonable patient" standard under which the physician's obligation is to provide the information that a reasonable patient would want.

2.   The *Matthies* court rejected the view of states like Pennsylvania in which the essence of the claim is one of battery. Instead, the *Matthies* court reserved medical battery for cases in which there has been no consent. See, e.g., Shuler v. Garrett, 743 F.3d 170 (6th Cir.2014)(concluding that the administration of drugs over a patient's objections or despite the patient's contrary instructions is a medical battery, and providing citations to other cases reaching the same result).

3.   In most consent cases the physician or surgeon has undertaken an invasive procedure and the patient complains that the risk—which came to pass—was insufficiently explained. In McKinney v. Nash, 174 Cal.Rptr. 642 (App.1981), for example, the plaintiff underwent surgery to repair a bilateral inguinal hernia. Both his testicles atrophied—a 1 in 1000 risk of the surgery even if the surgery is carefully done. The court thought a jury question was presented on the consent issue. Does that kind of case raise different issues from those raised in *Matthies*?

4.   The patient's informed consent to a procedure does not limit a physician's liability for negligent treatment. "Put differently, there is no assumption-of-the-risk defense available to a defendant physician which would vitiate his duty to provide treatment according to the ordinary standard of care. . . . That being the case, in a trial on a malpractice complaint that only asserts negligence, and not lack of informed consent, evidence that a patient agreed to go forward with the operation in spite of the risks of which she was informed is irrelevant and should be excluded." Brady v. Urbas, 111 A.3d 1155 (Pa.2015). This rule has the potential for stifling medical innovations for reasons given by Laakmann, When Should Physicians Be Liable for Innovation?, 36 Cardozo L.Rev. 913 (2015), who points out that while a customary practice ordinarily works well, it is not necessarily best for an individual whose condition or needs are not like the average patient. An innovative departure from custom could help such a patient, but since the standard of reasonable care is defined by custom, the innovation would increase the risk that the physician will be second-guessed in a lawsuit. Because the patient's informed consent to the innovative treatment provides no protection from the threat of malpractice liability, the resultant disincentives for medical innovation are quite clear. To resolve this problem, Laakmann proposes a "medical judgment rule" that would limit malpractice liability when the physician properly determines that a departure from custom is warranted and receives the patient's informed consent for the innovative treatment. In these cases, is the standard of reasonable care properly defined in terms of custom? *Cf.* Morris, Custom and Negligence, 42 Colum.L.Rev. 1147, 1155 (1942)("When the defendant must practice his craft under conditions significantly different from others in the same business, there is no customary way of acting-under-the-circumstances.")

5.   The consent issue is also raised by assertions that health care provider D should not have done the procedure but should have referred the patient to provider T because the collected statistics show that provider D has a 15% rate of adverse outcomes, compared to provider T's rate of 10%. Note that the providers might be hospitals or surgeons. Should the duty to obtain informed consent require that D tell the patient the different statistics (and provide a reasonable and honestly believed explanation for any disparity)? See Twerski & Cohen, Comparing Medical Providers: A First Look at the New Era of Medical Statistics, 58 Brook.L.Rev. 15 (1992). The authors suggest that the patient might be awarded 5/15 of the damages sustained in the cited example. Other articles in the same symposium issue address such questions as whether comparative statistics benefit the health care delivery system and whether they should be admissible in malpractice cases. Proposals to create a national registry that would list a physician's malpractice awards, license suspensions and criminal convictions are discussed in Barringer, *Seeking Access to Data on Doctors*, N.Y.Times, Sept. 18, 2000, at C15. Although nothing in this regard has happened on the federal level, several states have enacted disclosure laws. For example, the California statute mandates that the Medical Board provide the public access to suspensions, malpractice judgments and settlements, felony convictions, and hospital disciplinary actions for all physicians. Cal.Bus. & Prof. Code § 803.1.

   6.   What must an inexperienced physician tell a patient? In Howard v. University of Medicine & Dentistry of New Jersey, 800 A.2d 73 (N.J.2002), plaintiff, suffering from back problems, went to defendant surgeon. The claim was that defendant misrepresented both his credentials and his experience in performing the proposed procedure. The procedure went badly. The court held that plaintiff may claim lack of informed consent because of the false answers allegedly given. The court left open whether there was an affirmative duty to disclose the information in question. Contra Duttry v. Patterson, 771 A.2d 1255 (Pa.2001)(holding that experience in performing a procedure—physician said he had performed 60, but had only done 9—is not relevant to informed consent).

   Must physicians volunteer information that is not directly related to the procedure? See Albany Urology Clinic, P.C. v. Cleveland, 528 S.E.2d 777 (Ga.2000), holding, 4–3, that a urologist was not obligated to tell patients of his illegal use of cocaine. The majority was concerned about requiring physicians to tell patients that they were "binge drinkers" or had just received "bad news." The dissenters argued that the cocaine use was different because it was criminal.

   7.   When must a physician disclose a financial interest in a proposed treatment? In Shapira v. Christiana Care Health Care Services, Inc., 99 A.3d 217 (Del. 2014), the court concluded that defendant physician failed to obtain informed consent to use the "On-Q procedure" by not disclosing his business relationship with the manufacturer of the catheter used for the procedure. "This is not a case where a doctor fails to disclose that she owns some stock in a publicly traded medical company. [Defendant] was making a name for himself, and earning money, by promoting the On-Q procedure. In addition, he was gathering data about the procedure's efficacy. He had a strong incentive to play down the risks of the On-Q procedure and play up the problems with alternative treatments."

   8.   Consider the physician's obligation if the patient says "Don't tell me the options or the risks. I'll get frightened. Do what you think is best."

Alternatively, consider the physician's response if the patient says "Tell me everything, even the most minimal risks." Or, "I am very nervous about my eyes. I want to know every risk—no matter how unlikely—that each option might mean for my eyes."

9. If the patient has not been given a choice or expressed one, why does it not suffice for such patients to testify that if given the necessary information, they would have made a different choice?

In Ashe v. Radiation Oncology Associates, 9 S.W.3d 119 (Tenn.1999), the court reviewed the conflict between the objective and subjective standards for determining consent. The subjective standard is consistent with the view that individuals, no matter how misguided, should be able to make their own treatment decisions. The objection to that approach is "the unfairness of allowing the issue of causation to turn on the credibility of the hindsight of a person seeking recovery after experiencing a most undesirable result." The argument for the objective standard is "that neither the plaintiff nor the fact-finder can provide a definitive answer as to what the patient would have done had the patient known of the particular risk prior to consenting to the procedure or treatment." The court chose the objective standard. How does this causation question differ from the issue of whether the physician was negligent in failing to obtain informed consent?

10. Doesn't adoption of the objective standard for determining causation frustrate the goals of informed consent for patients who have unusual or idiosyncratic views? Consider Ms. Matthies, for whom independent living was a high priority, despite her age and debilitation. Suppose a jury decides that a "reasonable patient" would have accepted bed rest? Some courts, while retaining an objective standard for determining causation, nevertheless endow the reasonable patient with relevant characteristics of the patient. See Bernard v. Char, 903 P.2d 667 (Haw.1995). Thus, in *Matthies*, the causal inquiry would proceed with a reasonable elderly patient for whom the ability to maintain independent living was an important goal.

11. Courts conceive of the "harm" in informed consent cases as the adverse physical outcome suffered by the patient. The difficult causation question would be obviated by reconceptualizing the harm as a dignitary matter—denying the patient the ability to make an informed autonomous decision about a matter of personal importance. Consider in this regard, Twerski & Cohen, Informed Decision Making and the Law of Torts: The Myth of Justiciable Causation, 1988 U.Ill.L.Rev. 607, 609, arguing for:

> a radical restructuring of the informed choice doctrine. Rather than focusing on personal injury damages flowing from the hypothetical 'but for,' which seeks to determine what the plaintiff would have decided had the defendant provided the information, we suggest that courts should identify and value the decision rights of the plaintiff which the defendant destroyed by withholding adequate information. . . . The right to participate in, and indeed, make important decisions concerning one's health is a

critical element of personal autonomy. The value of this process right is largely independent of the ultimate decision. . . . The legal system should protect these rights and provide significant recompense for their invasion, rather than continue its single-minded and ill-considered attention to personal injuries allegedly caused by the lack of information.

12. Some patients adopt an active role in their treatment, which may produce other disputes. In Shine v. Vega, 709 N.E.2d 58 (Mass.1999), a 29-year-old woman went to the hospital during a bad asthmatic attack. Over her vehement objections she was intubated. As a consequence, she developed an intense fear of hospitals such that, two years later, when she really did need emergency help, she delayed so long that she died. On the consent issue, the trial judge charged that in a life-threatening case consent was not needed—and that the jury should decide whether the situation was life-threatening. The resulting defense judgment was unanimously reversed on appeal. The defendant argued that he should be able to "override [the patient's] wishes as long as he acted 'appropriately and consistent with the standard of accepted medical practice.'" Relying in part on section 892D of the Second Restatement, the court held that a competent adult may refuse life-saving treatment. "If, and only if, the patient is unconscious or otherwise incapable of giving consent, and either time or circumstances do not permit the physician to obtain the consent of a family member, may the physician presume that the patient, if competent, would consent to life-saving medical treatment." Even that intervention was permissible only "if the actor has no reason to believe that the other, if he had the opportunity to consent, would decline."

There is a constitutional dimension to these "end of life" decisions, as well. In Cruzan v. Director, Missouri Department of Health, 497 U.S. 261 (1990), the Supreme Court articulated a constitutionally protected liberty interest in refusing unwanted medical treatment.

13. As the *Matthies* case reveals, health care professionals who rely on an oral consent for informed consent do so at considerable risk. Many states have legislation that addresses the requisites for written consent forms. For a case revolving around the use of written consents and the statutory requirements for such consents, see Allan v. Levy, 846 P.2d 274 (Nev.1993).

14. For comprehensive discussion of the informed consent issue, see Grady, Enduring and Emerging Challenges of Informed Consent, 372 New Eng.J.Med. 855 (2015); Schuck, Rethinking Informed Consent, 103 Yale L.J. 899 (1994). As new pathways open to multiple sources of health information, both health care providers and patients confront the psychological costs, as well as benefits, of super-abundant information. See Hoffman, *Awash in Information, Patients Face a Lonely, Uncertain Road*, N.Y. Times, Aug. 14, 2005, at 1. For a skeptical assessment of patients' ability to comprehend and analyze the information they receive, see Schneider, After Autonomy, 41 Wake Forest L.Rev. 411 (2006).

Strick Liability

- Duty

- Harm

- Causation

- Proximate Cause

Product Liability

- Defect.

$\downarrow$

Hospital : Don't know,
It's not intention
to harm.

CHAPTER III

THE DUTY REQUIREMENT: PHYSICAL INJURIES

A. INTRODUCTION

In Chapter II we considered a wide variety of cases involving the basic characteristics of the negligence concept. Typically, the defendant did not deny an obligation to behave reasonably toward the plaintiff. We turn now to cases in which the defendant makes precisely that contention—that there was no duty to exercise due care in the particular situation. This Chapter explores situations in which such claims are asserted and seeks to determine how they should be analyzed. The connection between the "negligence" question of Chapter II and the "duty" question of Chapter III is demonstrated by the fact that "negligence" is often referred to as "breach of duty"—a clear indication that some duty must exist before a defendant can be said to have committed actionable negligence. Although pedagogical reasons favored initial exploration of the negligence issue, it should be evident that, logically, the duty question is an antecedent issue.

An appropriate starting point is the question whether a plaintiff must show that a specific duty governs the context in which the case arose—or whether a general duty of due care exists unless the defendant can invoke an exception. As the materials in this chapter will indicate, there seems to be a clear long-term movement toward recognizing a general duty of due care. The Third Restatement reflects that trend in providing that "ordinarily . . . a duty to exercise reasonable care" exists with regard to causing physical harm but recognizes that for reasons of "principle or policy" courts may determine that an exception should be created for a given class of cases. Restatement (Third) Torts: Liability for Physical and Emotional Harm § 7 (2010). But the early historical picture is hazy. In many early cases, specific relationships appeared to be the bases for imposing duties of care. These were the classic relationships, such as innkeeper-guest, carrier-passenger, and the like. Yet, during this period, one also finds highway collision cases in which the courts appear to recognize a general obligation of care to others.

The view that duties arose in specific contexts is supported by the fact that *failure* to establish a relational setting was often fatal to the claim that defendant should be held responsible for a lack of due care. A noteworthy example of this restrictive view is the privity doctrine. Under one aspect of that doctrine, courts held that the manufacturer of a product generally owed a duty of due care in its manufacture only to the person who acquired the product from the maker. No general duty of care was owed to remote buyers or users. The survival of the privity doctrine into the twentieth century and its eventual demise are traced in MacPherson v. Buick Motor Co., 111 N.E. 1050 (N.Y.1916), reprinted at p. 557 infra. In *MacPherson*, Judge Cardozo, concluding that a car manufacturer owed a duty of due care to someone who bought a car from an intermediate dealer, asserted:

> If the nature of a thing is such that it is reasonably certain to place life and limb in peril when negligently made, it is then a thing of danger. Its nature gives warning of the consequences to be expected. If to the element of danger is added knowledge that the thing will be used by persons other than the purchaser, and used without new tests, then, irrespective of contract, the manufacturer of this thing of danger is under a duty to make it carefully. . . . We have put aside the notion that the duty to safeguard life and limb, when the consequences of negligence may be foreseen, grows out of contract and nothing else. We have put the source of the obligation where it ought to be. We have put its source in the law.

As early as 1883, Brett, M.R., in Heaven v. Pender, [1883] 11 Q.B.D. 503, offered a general approach to the existence of duty, although one that failed to convey how uneven the landscape remained:

> The proposition which these recognized cases suggest, and which is, therefore, to be deduced from them, is that whenever one person is by circumstances placed in such a position with regard to another that everyone of ordinary sense who did think would at once recognize that if he did not use ordinary care and skill in his own conduct with regard to those circumstances he would cause danger of injury to the person or property of the other, a duty arises to use ordinary care and skill to avoid such danger.

In this Chapter, we will examine a number of discrete categories of cases in which Brett's straightforward proposition has been tested by moral and economic considerations—often of long-standing acceptance—that established limitations on the duty to act reasonably. Related problems, involving the invasion of nonphysical interests, will be considered in Chapter IV.

B. AFFIRMATIVE OBLIGATIONS TO ACT

We begin with a fundamental inquiry. If an individual is in a situation of danger, should the law impose a duty on others affirmatively to assist that person? The affirmative obligations addressed in this section include not only instances in which a person is in imminent peril, but also instances in which another is subject to a

If you put risk to someone, then you have duty —

less immediate risk. Can a meaningful distinction always be drawn between harm arising from action and inaction? Consider the following case.

Negligence
— duty   *→ choice*
— unreasonable   Breach
*   fault — wrong*
— Causation.

Harper v. Herman

Supreme Court of Minnesota, 1993.
499 N.W.2d 472.

— HARM → Comparative, assumed of risk
■ PAGE, JUSTICE.   *— Proximate Cause*

Model *u care every indication it would*
— P: — I DODN'T know be safe
— U should warn me
— U know

This case arises upon a reversal by the court of appeals of summary judgment in favor of the defendant. The court of appeals held that defendant, the owner and operator of a private boat on Lake Minnetonka, had a duty to warn plaintiff, a guest on the boat, that water surrounding the boat was too shallow for diving. We reverse and reinstate judgment in favor of defendant.

— P: Didn't know

P Didn't know

The facts are undisputed for the purpose of this appeal. On Sunday, August 9, 1986, Jeffrey Harper ("Harper") was one of four guests on Theodor Herman's ("Herman") 26-foot boat, sailing on Lake Minnetonka. Harper was invited on the boat outing by Cindy Alberg Palmer, another guest on Herman's boat. Herman and Harper did not know each other prior to this boat outing. At the time Herman was 64 years old, and Harper was 20 years old. Herman was an experienced boat owner having spent hundreds of hours operating boats on Lake Minnetonka similar to the one involved in this action. As owner of the boat, Herman considered himself to be in charge of the boat and his passengers. Harper had some experience swimming in lakes and rivers, but had no formal training in diving.

facts

After a few hours of boating, the group decided to go swimming and, at Herman's suggestion, went to Big Island, a popular recreation spot. Herman was familiar with Big Island, and he was aware that the water remains shallow for a good distance away from its shore. Harper had been to Big Island on one previous occasion. Herman positioned the boat somewhere between 100 to 200 yards from the island with the bow facing away from the island in an area shallow enough for his guests to use the boat ladder to enter the water, but still deep enough so they could swim. The bottom of the lake was not visible from the boat. After positioning the boat Herman proceeded to set the anchor and lower the boat's ladder which was at its stern.

While Herman was lowering the ladder, Harper asked him if he was "going in." When Herman responded yes, Harper, without warning, stepped onto the side of the middle of the boat and dove into approximately two or three feet of water. As a result of the dive, Harper struck the bottom of the lake, severed his spinal cord, and was rendered a C6 quadriplegic.

Harper then brought suit, alleging that Herman owed him a duty of care to warn him that the water was too shallow for diving. [The trial *pro. hist.*

court granted defendant's motion for summary judgment on the ground that defendant owed plaintiff no duty to warn. The court of appeals held that defendant voluntarily assumed such a duty when he allowed Harper onto his boat.]

issue

The sole issue on appeal is whether a boat owner who is a social host owes a duty of care to warn a guest on the boat that the water is too shallow for diving.

Harper alleges that Herman owed him a duty to warn of the shallowness of the water because he was an inexperienced swimmer and diver, whereas Herman was a veteran boater. Under those circumstances, Harper argues, Herman should have realized that Harper needed his protection.

reason 1

We have previously stated that an affirmative duty to act only arises when a special relationship exists between the parties. "The fact that an actor realizes or should realize that action on his part is necessary for another's aid or protection does not of itself impose upon him a duty to take such action . . . unless a special relationship exists . . . between the actor and the other which gives the other the right to protection." Delgado v. Lohmar, 289 N.W.2d 479, 483 (Minn.1979), [ ]. Accepting, *arguendo,* that Herman should have realized that Harper needed protection, Harper must still prove that a special relationship existed between them that placed an affirmative duty to act on the part of Herman.

rule

Harper argues that a special relationship requiring Herman to act for his protection was created when Herman, as a social host, allowed an inexperienced diver on his boat. Generally, a special relationship giving rise to a duty to warn is only found on the part of common carriers, innkeepers, possessors of land who hold it open to the public, and persons who have custody of another person under circumstances in which that other person is deprived of normal opportunities of self-protection. Restatement (Second) of Torts § 314A (1965). Under this rule, a special relationship could be found to exist between the parties only if Herman had custody of Harper under circumstances in which Harper was deprived of normal opportunities to protect himself.[2] These elements are not present here.

reason

The record before this court does not establish that Harper was either particularly vulnerable or that he lacked the ability to protect himself. Further, the record does not establish that Herman held considerable power over Harper's welfare, or that Herman was

---

[2]   Prosser describes a circumstance in which one party would be liable in negligence because another party was deprived of normal opportunities for self-protection as occurring when the plaintiff is typically in some respect particularly vulnerable and dependent upon the defendant who, correspondingly, holds considerable power over the plaintiff's welfare. In addition, such relations have often involved some existing or potential economic advantage to the defendant. Fairness in such cases thus may require the defendant to use his power to help the plaintiff, based upon the plaintiff's expectation of protection, which itself may be based upon the defendant's expectation of financial gain. [ ]

receiving a financial gain by hosting Harper on his boat. Finally, there is nothing in the record which would suggest that Harper expected any protection from Herman; indeed, no such allegation has been made. *] reason*

The court of appeals found that Herman owed Harper a duty to warn him of the shallowness of the water because Herman knew that it was "dangerously shallow." We have previously stated that "[a]ctual knowledge of a dangerous condition tends to impose a special duty to do something about that condition." Andrade v. Ellefson, 391 N.W.2d 836, 841 (Minn.1986)(holding that county was not immune to charge of improper supervision of day care center where children were abused when county knew about overcrowding at the center). However, superior knowledge of a dangerous condition by itself, in the absence of a duty to provide protection, is insufficient to establish liability in negligence. Thus, Herman's knowledge that the water was "dangerously shallow" without more does not create liability. *Andrade* involved a group of plaintiffs who had little opportunity to protect themselves, children in day care, and a defendant to whom the plaintiffs looked for protection. In this case, Harper was not deprived of opportunities to protect himself, and Herman was not expected to provide protection.

"There are many dangers, such as those of fire and water, . . . which under ordinary conditions may reasonably be expected to be fully understood and appreciated by any child. . . ." Restatement (Second) of Torts § 339 cmt. *j* (1965). If a child is expected to understand the inherent dangers of water, so should a 20-year-old adult. Harper had no reasonable expectation to look to Herman for protection, and we hold that Herman had no duty to warn Harper that the water was shallow. *] holding*

Reversed and judgment in favor of defendant reinstated. *- Disposition*

NOTES AND QUESTIONS

1.   What are the arguments in favor of imposing a duty on the defendant? What are the arguments against such an imposition? When it would be virtually costless for defendant to offer assistance, should there be a distinction between moral and legal obligations? Certainly, moral and legal obligations are not *always* distinct. Is it self-evident why they should diverge in a situation involving, say, a helpless infant lying on a railroad track who could easily be rescued before a train arrives? Consider Epstein, A Theory of Strict Liability, 2 J. Legal Stud. 151, 197–98 (1973):

> The common law position on the good Samaritan question does not appeal to our highest sense of benevolence and charity, and it is not at all surprising that there have been many proposals for its alteration or abolition. Let us here examine but one of these proposals. After concluding that the then (1908) current position of the law led to intolerable results, James Barr Ames argued [in Law and Morals, 22 Harv.L.Rev. 97 (1908)], that the appropriate rule should be that:

One who fails to interfere to save another from impending death or great bodily harm, when he might do so with little or no inconvenience to himself, and the death or great bodily harm follows as a consequence of his inaction, shall be punished criminally and shall make compensation to the party injured or to his widow and children in case of death.

Even this solution, however, does not satisfy the *Carroll Towing* formula. The general use of the cost-benefit analysis required under the economic interpretation of negligence does not permit a person to act on the assumption that he may as of right attach special weight and importance to his own welfare. Under Ames' good Samaritan rule, a defendant in cases of affirmative acts would be required to take only those steps that can be done "with little or no inconvenience." But if the distinction between causing harm and not preventing harm is to be disregarded, why should the difference in standards between the two cases survive the reform of the law? The only explanation is that the two situations are regarded at bottom as raising totally different issues, even for those who insist upon the immateriality of this distinction. Even those who argue, as Ames does, that the law is utilitarian must in the end find some special place for the claims of egoism which are an inseparable byproduct of the belief that individual autonomy—individual liberty—is a good in itself not explainable in terms of its purported social worth. It is one thing to *allow* people to act as they please in the belief that the "invisible hand" will provide the happy congruence of the individual and the social good. Such a theory, however, at bottom must regard individual autonomy as but a means to some social end. It takes a great deal more to assert that men are *entitled* to act as they choose . . . even though it is certain that there will be cases where individual welfare will be in conflict with the social good. Only then is it clear that even freedom has its costs. . . .

For an article proposing a duty of "easy rescue" and providing a detailed criticism of Epstein's views, see Weinrib, The Case for a Duty to Rescue, 90 Yale L.J. 247 (1980).

2.   *Exceptions to the no-duty-to-rescue rule.* Perhaps because of the tension invoked by a rule that does not impose a duty to rescue the helpless infant, courts have fashioned a number of exceptions to this no-duty rule.

a.   *Special relationships.* As *Harper* suggests, "special relationships" have led courts to impose duties to act in these affirmative duty situations, in essence creating an exception to the no affirmative duty rule. Do the relationships listed by the court suggest a unifying principle for an affirmative obligation? What criteria did the court use to guide its decision on whether a special relationship existed?

What if defendant had met Harper at a party a week earlier and had invited him to join other guests for this trip? If one found that the boat owner owed a duty, would the rationale extend to the person who invited the plaintiff onto the boat?

The same court that decided *Harper* recognized an arguably new special relationship in Bjerke v. Johnson, 742 N.W.2d 660 (Minn.2007). Defendant owned a stable and had minor-plaintiff reside there for significant periods of time with the approval of her parents. Defendant told the parents she would look after their child. The minor, during a period when she was 14–18 years old, had a sexual relationship with the defendant's live-in boyfriend. In the minor's suit against defendant, the court found a special relationship based on the surrogate parent/custodial role to which defendant agreed when she invited plaintiff to live with her. Would *Harper* be a different case if the plaintiff had been 10-years-old when he went out on Herman's boat?

b.   *Undertakings.* This basis for an affirmative duty is addressed in *Farwell v. Keaton,* p. 135 infra and *Randi W.,* p. 141 infra.

c.   *Non-negligent injury.* At common law, one who innocently injured another had no duty to exercise due care to ensure the other's subsequent wellbeing. See, e.g., Union Pacific Railway Co. v. Cappier, 72 P. 281 (Kan.1903), in which the court held that there was no duty to do anything to help a victim who was non-tortiously run over while trespassing on defendant's railroad tracks.

That attitude has faded. In Maldonado v. Southern Pacific Transportation Co., 629 P.2d 1001 (Ariz.Ct.App.1981), plaintiff claimed that as he was attempting to board one of defendant's freight trains, it jerked or bumped and he fell off—and under the wheels, suffering a severed arm and other serious injuries. Alleging that defendant's employees knew about his plight but did nothing to help him, he sued for aggravation of his injuries. The court imposed a duty recognized by section 322 of the Second Restatement:

> If the actor knows or has reason to know that by his conduct, whether tortious or innocent, he has caused such bodily harm to another as to make him helpless and in danger of further harm, the actor is under a duty to exercise reasonable care to prevent such further harm.

d.   *Non-negligent creation of risk.* "Whoever places an obstruction in a public highway, even by an involuntary act and without negligence, is under an obligation to remove such a nuisance from the highway or is required to use ordinary care to warn the traffic on said highway of the dangers incident to said obstruction." Simonsen v. Thorin, 234 N.W. 628 (Neb.1931). In Menu v. Minor, 745 P.2d 680 (Colo.App.1987), a driver lost control of his car. It hit the median, came to rest and was disabled, blocking a lane of an interstate highway. What might the driver's duties be? A taxicab picked up the driver and drove him away. Sometime later, plaintiffs crashed into the disabled car. In a suit against the cab company, plaintiffs contended that the cab should have either stayed at the scene to warn, removed the car, or called the police. The court held that the cab driver had no affirmative duty to do any of these things. The cab driver had not "voluntarily assumed a duty to plaintiffs by acting affirmatively to induce" them to rely on him. Nor had he "created a peril or changed the nature of the existing risk" to them. Transporting the driver from the scene did not change the existing risk. The knowledge of the danger alone did not create a special relationship.

In Tresemer v. Barke, 150 Cal.Rptr. 384 (App.1978), plaintiff was seriously injured from use of the Dalkon Shield intrauterine device. She never consulted defendant physician after he inserted the device. Within two years, there was medical information about the dangers of using the device, but the plaintiff was unaware of the risk for another year afterwards and suffered injury because of the delay. The court held that she stated a cause of action against the defendant for failure to warn her about the newly discovered dangers.

e.   *Statutes.* This basis for an affirmative duty is addressed in *Uhr v. East Greenbush Central School District*, p. 159 infra.

3.   The distinction between the ordinary duty of reasonable care applicable in Chapter II and the no-duty rule addressed in *Harper* and note 1 has sometimes been expressed in terms of acts of commission as distinguished from acts of omission. See *H. R. Moch Co. v. Rensselaer Water Co.*, p. 173 infra. Yet that distinction has caused considerable confusion when, for example, a defendant fails to stop at a red light by neglecting to apply her brakes. Some have suggested that recharacterizing the defendant's actions as "running a red light" can solve this problem, but that leaves hanging the question of when recharacterization is legitimate. Does consideration of the entirety of the defendant's conduct and whether it created risks to others help in drawing the distinction? See Restatement (Third) Torts: Liability for Physical and Emotional Harm § 37 cmt. c (2010), which adopts this approach.

Adams v. Northern Illinois Gas Co., 809 N.E.2d 1248 (Ill.2004), confronted the same issue of the intersection between ordinary duties of care and affirmative duties. The court overturned old precedent and held that a gas utility has a duty to warn its customer of dangers of which it knows, even though the danger is due to fittings in the home that were not provided by the utility and not under its control.

4.   Harper *reconsidered.* Would *Harper* have been a different case if, instead of diving in "without warning," Harper had stood on the side of the boat poised in a diving position and announced in a loud voice, "watch this 1½ gainer that I'm going to do; I nearly made the Olympic diving team four years ago," and Herman heard the announcement and stood by mute? If so, then is *Harper* a case about "no duty" or about no negligence? Why might courts prefer a no-duty ruling as in *Harper* to a no-negligence ruling?

Farwell v. Keaton ←--beat up Farwell

Supreme Court of Michigan, 1976.
396 Mich. 281, 240 N.W.2d 217.

■ LEVIN, J.

There is ample evidence to support the jury determination that David Siegrist failed to exercise reasonable care after voluntarily coming to the aid of Richard Farwell and that his negligence was the proximate cause of Farwell's death. We are also of the opinion that Siegrist, who was with Farwell the evening he was fatally injured and, as the jury found, knew or should have known of his peril, had an affirmative duty to come to Farwell's aid.

I

On the evening of August 26, 1966, Siegrist and Farwell drove to a trailer rental lot to return an automobile which Siegrist had borrowed from a friend who worked there. While waiting for the friend to finish work, Siegrist and Farwell consumed some beer.

Two girls walked by the entrance to the lot. Siegrist and Farwell attempted to engage them in conversation; they left Farwell's car and followed the girls to a drive-in restaurant down the street.

The girls complained to their friends in the restaurant that they were being followed. Six boys chased Siegrist and Farwell back to the lot. Siegrist escaped unharmed, but Farwell was severely beaten. Siegrist found Farwell underneath his automobile in the lot. Ice was applied to Farwell's head. Siegrist then drove Farwell around for approximately two hours, stopping at a number of drive-in restaurants. Farwell went to sleep in the back seat of his car. Around midnight Siegrist drove the car to the home of Farwell's grandparents, parked it in the driveway, unsuccessfully attempted to rouse Farwell, and left. Farwell's grandparents discovered him in the car the next morning and took him to the hospital. He died three days later of an epidural hematoma.

At trial, plaintiff [Farwell's father, in this wrongful death action] contended that had Siegrist taken Farwell to the hospital, or had he notified someone of Farwell's condition and whereabouts, Farwell would not have died. A neurosurgeon testified that if a person in Farwell's condition is taken to a doctor before, or within half an hour after, consciousness is lost, there is an 85 to 88 percent chance of survival. Plaintiff testified that Siegrist told him that he knew Farwell was badly injured and that he should have done something.

The jury returned a verdict for plaintiff and awarded $15,000 in damages. The Court of Appeals reversed, finding that Siegrist had not assumed the duty of obtaining aid for Farwell and that he neither knew nor should have known of the need for medical treatment.

II

. . .

The existence of a duty is ordinarily a question of law. However, there are factual circumstances which give rise to a duty. The existence of those facts must be determined by a jury. . . .

. . .

Without regard to whether there is a general duty to aid a person in distress, there is a clearly recognized legal duty of every person to avoid any affirmative acts which may make a situation worse. "[I]f the defendant does attempt to aid him, and takes charge and control of the situation, he is regarded as entering voluntarily into a relation which is attended with responsibility. Such a defendant will then be liable for a failure to use reasonable care for the protection of the plaintiff's interests." [ ] "Where performance clearly has begun, there is no doubt that there is a duty of care." [ ]

In a case such as the one at bar, the jury must determine, after considering all the evidence, whether the defendant attempted to aid the victim. If he did, a duty arose which required defendant to act as a reasonable person.

. . .

There was ample evidence to show that Siegrist breached a legal duty owed Farwell. Siegrist knew that Farwell had been in a fight, and he attempted to relieve Farwell's pain by applying an ice pack to his head. While Farwell and Siegrist were riding around, Farwell crawled into the back seat and laid down. The testimony showed that Siegrist attempted to rouse Farwell after driving him home but was unable to do so.

[The court summarized the testimony of Farwell's father that when he asked Siegrist why he didn't tell someone when he knew that Farwell was badly hurt, Siegrist replied: "I know I should have, I don't know."]

. . .

III

Siegrist contends that he is not liable for failure to obtain medical assistance for Farwell because he had no duty to do so.

Courts have been slow to recognize a duty to render aid to a person in peril. Where such a duty has been found, it has been predicated upon the existence of a special relationship between the parties; in such a case, if defendant knew or should have known of the other person's peril, he is required to render reasonable care under all the circumstances.

. . .

Farwell and Siegrist were companions on a social venture. Implicit in such a common undertaking is the understanding that one will render assistance to the other when he is in peril if he can do so without endangering himself. Siegrist knew or should have known when he left Farwell, who was badly beaten and unconscious, in the back seat of his car that no one would find him before morning. Under these circumstances, to say that Siegrist had no duty to obtain medical assistance or at least to notify someone of Farwell's condition and whereabouts would be "shocking to humanitarian considerations" and fly in the face of "the commonly accepted code of social conduct." "[C]ourts will find a duty where, in general, reasonable men would recognize it and agree that it exists." [Prosser, *Torts*]

Farwell and Siegrist were companions engaged in a common undertaking; there was a special relationship between the parties. Because Siegrist knew or should have known of the peril Farwell was in and could render assistance without endangering himself he had an affirmative duty to come to Farwell's aid.

The Court of Appeals is reversed and the verdict of the jury reinstated.

- KAVANAGH, C.J., and WILLIAMS, J., concurred with LEVIN, J.

- LINDEMER and RYAN, JJ., took no part in the decision of this case.

- FITZGERALD, J. (dissenting).

. . .

The close relationship between defendant and the decedent is said to establish a legal duty upon defendant to obtain assistance for the decedent. No authority is cited for this proposition other than the public policy observation that the interest of society would be benefited if its members were required to assist one another. This is not the appropriate case to establish a standard of conduct requiring one to legally assume the duty of insuring the safety of another. . . .[4]

Plaintiff believes that a legal duty to aid others should exist where such assistance greatly benefits society and only a reasonable burden is imposed upon those in a position to help. He contends further that the determination of the existence of a duty must rest with the jury where questions of foreseeability and the relationship of the parties are primary considerations.

It is clear that defendant's nonfeasance, or the "passive inaction or a failure to take steps to protect [the decedent] from harm" is urged as being the proximate cause of Farwell's death. We must reject plaintiff's proposition which elevates a moral obligation to the level of a legal duty

---

[4] Were a special relationship to be the basis of imposing a legal duty upon one to insure the safety of another, it would most probably take the form of "co-adventurers" who embark upon a hazardous undertaking with the understanding that each is mutually dependent upon the other for his own safety. There is no evidence to support plaintiff's position that decedent relied upon defendant to provide any assistance whatsoever. . . .

where, as here, the facts within defendant's knowledge in no way indicated that immediate medical attention was necessary and the relationship between the parties imposes no affirmative duty to render assistance. . . .

The relationship of the parties and the question of foreseeability does not require that the jury, rather than the court, determine whether a legal duty exists. We are in agreement with the general principle advanced by plaintiff that the question of negligence is one of law for the court only when the facts are such that all reasonable men must draw the same conclusion. However, this principle becomes operative only after the court establishes that a legal duty is owed by one party to another. Prosser's analysis of the role of the court and jury on questions of legal duty bears repeating:

> "The existence of a duty. In other words, whether, upon the facts in evidence, such a relation exists between the parties that the community will impose a legal obligation upon one for the benefit of the other—or, more simply, whether the interest of the plaintiff which has suffered invasion was entitled to legal protection at the hands of the defendant. This is entirely a question of law, to be determined by reference to the body of statutes, rules, principles and precedents which make up the law; and it must be determined only by the court. . . . A decision by the court that, upon any version of the facts, there is no duty, must necessarily result in judgment for the defendant." Prosser, Torts (4th ed.), § 37, p. 206.

. . .

The Court of Appeals properly decided as a matter of law that defendant owed no duty to the deceased.

We would affirm.

■ COLEMAN, J., concurred with FITZGERALD, J.

NOTES AND QUESTIONS

1. As the first paragraph of the opinion indicates, the majority recognizes an obligation of due care on two independent grounds: (1) that Siegrist voluntarily came to the assistance of Farwell and (2) that Siegrist, in any event, had an affirmative duty to aid Farwell on the basis of their pre-existing relationship. We have already examined the second ground in the *Harper* case. How does that apply in *Farwell*? What if Siegrist had never returned, but knew that Farwell had been physically attacked? Would the dissent find that one member of a two-person mountain-climbing team has a duty to aid the other? Is *Farwell* different?

2. Compare Ronald M. v. White, 169 Cal.Rptr. 370 (App.1980). Plaintiff was one of a group of ten minors who had been cruising around in an auto during the day, some of whom were drinking and taking drugs. Suit was brought against the members of the group who had not been

Ron v White - kids not drinking have duty to those who are?

drinking or taking drugs—or furnished or paid for any—for their alleged failure to restrain the driver before his negligence injured others in the group. The court affirmed the granting of summary judgment for defendants. Is *Farwell* distinguishable?

3. What role should the jury play in deciding these issues? Is the threshold question of whether a special relationship exists for the jury? What about the question of whether there has been a voluntary undertaking? Or should the jury only determine whether there has been a breach of duty? See Restatement (Third) of Torts: Liability for Physical and Emotional Harm §§ 40 cmt. e & 42 cmts. d & g (2010). The Restatement makes the question of whether any relationship is sufficient to impose a duty a question for the court but leaves to the jury whether, on the facts of the case, such a relationship exists. The Restatement also leaves to the jury the matter of whether an undertaking exists and its scope.

special relationship a matter for jury to decide?

4. We return now to the court's first ground of recovery in *Farwell*—the duty Siegrist assumed by voluntarily attempting to aid Farwell. Should a voluntary actor assume the same duty of due care as an actor bound by a pre-existing relationship to the plaintiff? Suppose a passerby had discovered Farwell and "voluntarily acted" by trying to revive him, but then decided not to get further involved and left the scene. Should that passerby be held liable for failing to exercise the due care that might be expected of a close relative? Recall the *Farwell* court's statement about a "duty . . . to avoid any affirmative acts which may make a situation worse." How did Siegrist's efforts make the "situation worse" for Farwell?

passerby attempts to provide aid and leaves, liable?

Section 324 of the Second Restatement provides that one who, being under no duty to do so, takes charge of another who is helpless is subject to liability caused by "(a) the failure of the actor to exercise reasonable care to secure the safety of the other while within the actor's charge, or (b) the actor's discontinuing his aid or protection, if by so doing he leaves the other in a worse position than when the actor took charge of him." The Restatement expresses no opinion as to whether "an actor who has taken charge of a helpless person may be subject to liability for harm resulting from his discontinuance of the aid or protection, where by doing so he leaves the other in no worse position than when the actor took charge of him." The Third Restatement requires an actor to exercise reasonable care in discontinuing aid for someone who reasonably appears to be in imminent peril. Restatement (Third) Torts: Liability for Physical and Emotional Harm § 43 (2010).

Second Restatement

Third

5. Induced reliance, however reasonable it might otherwise be, does not necessarily create a duty if the defendant did not otherwise create the risk in question. In Lacognata v. Hospira, Inc., 521 Fed.Appx. 866 (11th Cir.2013), plaintiff suffered from a Vitamin A deficiency that could be treated only by a prescription form of injectable Vitamin A that was solely manufactured by defendant. Due to a change in defendant's operations, the supply of the injectable Vitamin A was disrupted. Plaintiff alleged that the defendant's conduct was negligent, but the court concluded that the defendant owed no duty: "There is no authority that supports Plaintiff's argument that a drug manufacturer . . . has a duty to continue supplying a

induced reliance - does not create duty
Lacognata v Hospira - D owed no duty who couldn't supply vitamin A to P who needed it

patient with a drug that it knows the patient relies upon for his or her medical health." The profit motive obviously gives the sole manufacturer of a drug reason to continue providing a steady supply of the drug. If doing so is not profitable, would an affirmative tort duty be justified in order to guarantee users with a continued supply?

6. Beyond the rescue context, when an actor voluntarily acts in a way designed to reduce the risk to which others may be exposed, a duty of reasonable care exists if the actor increases the risk of harm or if others rely on the actor's undertaking. In Mixon v. Dobbs Houses, Inc., 254 S.E.2d 864 (Ga.Ct.App.1979), husband informed the manager of the restaurant where he worked that his wife was pregnant and might call at any time to ask for a ride to the hospital. Since husband did not have access to a phone, the manager promised to tell him if his wife called. When the wife went into labor, she called the restaurant three times, and although the manager received the message that the wife had called, he failed to deliver the message to the husband. When husband returned home, his wife had already given birth to a baby girl, "all alone, unassisted and unmedicated, experiencing total fear and excruciating pain." The court held that the manager was obligated to exercise due care in performing his promise. The lower court's dismissal was reversed.

7. In Jansen v. Fidelity & Casualty Co. of New York, 589 N.E.2d 379 (N.Y.1992), defendant was the workers' compensation insurance carrier for plaintiff's employer. Defendant under the contract had the right to—and did—carry out regular inspections of the premises in an effort to reduce the occurrence of worker injuries. Plaintiff worker, who was injured in an accident on the premises, alleged that the defendant had "performed its inspection negligently" and that he had been hurt as a result. The court rejected a duty because it was "apparent that the safety inspections were undertaken solely for defendant's own underwriting purposes—to reduce the risks that might give rise to liability under the policy." For a critique of decisions such as *Jansen*, see Ingram, Liability of Insurers for Negligence in Inspection of Insured Premises, 50 Drake L.Rev. 623 (2002).

Conceptually similar to inspections such as those in *Jansen* are pre-employment physicals in which a physician hired by a prospective employer performs a physical examination of a non-patient prospective employee. It has been widely, although not uniformly, held that those physicians owe no duty to tell the person being examined if they find signs of trouble. The cases are reviewed in Reed v. Bojarski, 764 A.2d 433 (N.J.2001), which adopted the minority position. The court held that, during a pre-employment physical examination paid for by the prospective employer, the physician determines that the person being examined has a potentially serious medical condition, the physician has a duty to inform the patient and that obligation may not be delegated to the referring employer or other agency. See also Draper v. Westerfield, 181 S.W.3d 283 (Tenn.2005), in which a defendant radiologist hired by the state department of social services to review scans of the infant child because of suspected child abuse did not report that the tests revealed strong evidence of abuse. The child was subsequently killed by her father. The court held the defendant owed a duty based on the physician's undertaking to review the medical records and report the results to state investigators. Do these inspection and examination cases satisfy the requirement of section 324 of the Second Restatement that there be reliance or that the victim be left worse off?

Randi W. v. Muroc Joint Unified School District

Supreme Court of California, 1997.
14 Cal.4th 1066, 929 P.2d 582, 60 Cal.Rptr.2d 263.

■ CHIN, ASSOCIATE JUSTICE.

[Plaintiff, a 13-year-old student at the time, alleged that four school districts, former employers of Robert Gadams, placed unreservedly affirmative references in a placement file for Gadams despite knowing that prior charges or complaints of sexual misconduct and impropriety had been leveled against Gadams during the period he worked in each district; that plaintiff student's school district (Livingston) relied on defendants' letters in hiring Gadams as vice-principal, and that Gadams then sexually assaulted plaintiff. Although plaintiff pressed several theories, the only relevant ones before the court are negligent misrepresentation and fraud. The superior court granted demurrers on both of these claims, but the court of appeal reversed. Further facts are set forth in the opinion.]

In this case, we must decide under what circumstances courts may impose tort liability on employers who fail to use reasonable care in recommending former employees for employment without disclosing material information bearing on their fitness. . . .

. . .

Although policy considerations dictate that ordinarily a recommending employer should not be held accountable to third persons for failing to disclose negative information regarding a former employee, nonetheless liability may be imposed if, as alleged here, the recommendation letter amounts to an affirmative misrepresentation presenting a foreseeable and substantial risk of physical harm to a third person.

We also conclude, contrary to the Court of Appeal judgment in this case, that defendants' alleged failure to report the charges of Gadams's improper activities to the appropriate authorities pursuant to state statutory law fails to afford an alternate basis for tort liability in this case, and that the trial court properly sustained defendants' demurrers to the count in the complaint relying on this theory of liability.

. . .

II. DISCUSSION

A. *Fraud and Negligent Misrepresentation*

. . .

Section 311 of the Restatement Second of Torts, involving negligent conduct, provides that:

"(1) One who negligently gives *false information* to another is subject to liability for physical harm caused by action taken by the other *in reasonable reliance upon such information*, where such harm results

(a) to the other, or

(b) *to such third persons as the actor should reasonably expect to be put in peril by the action taken.*

(2) Such negligence may consist of failure to exercise reasonable care

(a) in ascertaining the accuracy of the information, or

(b) in the manner in which it is communicated." (Italics added.)

. . . [W]e consider whether plaintiff has sufficiently pleaded that defendants owed her a duty of care, that they breached that duty by making misrepresentations or giving false information, and that Livingston's reasonable reliance on their statements proximately caused plaintiff's injury. [ ] We examine each element separately.

1. *Duty to Plaintiff*

Did defendants owe plaintiff a duty of care? In defendants' view, absent some special relationship between the parties, or some specific and known threat of harm to plaintiff, defendants had no duty of care toward her, and no obligation to disclose in their letters any facts regarding the charges against Gadams. (See Rest.2d Torts, § 315 [generally no duty to warn those threatened by third person's conduct]; [ ]; *Thompson v. County of Alameda* [infra] [duty to warn "readily identifiable" victim]; *Tarasoff v. Regents of University of California* [infra] ["special relationship" creates duty to warn or control another's conduct]; [ ].)

Plaintiff does not argue that a special relationship existed between defendants and her or Gadams. Instead, she relies on [Garcia v. Superior Court, 789 P.2d 960 (Cal.1990)], where we held that, under section 311 of the Restatement Second of Torts, a parole officer had a duty to exercise reasonable care in giving the victim information regarding the parolee who ultimately killed her. We noted that although the parole officer had no duty to volunteer information regarding the released criminals he supervised, ". . . the absence of a duty to speak does not entitle one to speak falsely." [ ] We concluded that the parole officer, "having chosen to communicate information about [the parolee] to [the victim], had a duty to use reasonable care in doing so," and that the officer either knew or should have known that the victim's safety might depend on the accuracy of the information imparted. [ ]

Plaintiff acknowledges that *Garcia* is distinguishable, and that no California case has yet held that one who intentionally or negligently provides false information to another owes a duty of care to a third person who did not receive the information and who has no special relationship with the provider. Accordingly, the issue before us is one of first impression, and we apply the general analytical principles used to determine the existence of duty in particular cases.

In this state, the general rule is that all persons have a duty to use ordinary care to prevent others from being injured as the result of their conduct. [ ] As we have observed, "*Rowland* [v. Christian, 443 P.2d 561 (Cal.1968)] enumerates a number of considerations . . . that have been taken into account by courts in various contexts to determine whether a departure from the general rule is appropriate: 'the major [considerations] are *the foreseeability of harm to the plaintiff,* the degree of certainty that the plaintiff suffered injury, the closeness of the connection between the defendant's conduct and the injury suffered, the moral blame attached to the defendant's conduct, the policy of preventing future harm, the extent of the burden to the defendant and consequences to the community of imposing a duty to exercise care with resulting liability for breach, and the availability, cost, and prevalence of insurance for the risk involved.' (Italics added.) [ ] The foreseeability of a particular kind of harm plays a very significant role in this calculus [citation], but a court's task—in determining 'duty'—is not to decide whether a *particular* plaintiff's injury was reasonably foreseeable in light of a *particular* defendant's conduct, but rather to evaluate more generally whether the category of negligent conduct at issue is sufficiently likely to result in the kind of harm experienced that liability may appropriately be imposed on the negligent party." (*Ballard v. Uribe,* [715 P.2d 624 n. 6 (Cal.1986)].)

a.   *Foreseeability and causality*

Applying these factors here, we first examine whether plaintiff's injuries were a *foreseeable* result of defendants' representations regarding Gadams's qualifications and character, coupled with their failure to disclose to the Fresno Pacific College placement office information regarding charges or complaints of Gadams's sexual misconduct. Could defendants reasonably have foreseen that the representations and omissions in their reference letters would result in physical injury to someone? Although the chain of causation leading from defendants' statements and omissions to Gadams's alleged assault on plaintiff is somewhat attenuated, we think the assault was reasonably foreseeable. Based on the facts alleged in the complaint, defendants could foresee that Livingston's officers would read and rely on defendants' letters in deciding to hire Gadams. Likewise, defendants could foresee that, had they not unqualifiedly recommended Gadams, Livingston would not have hired him. And, finally, defendants could foresee that Gadams, after being hired by Livingston, might molest or injure a Livingston student such as plaintiff. We must assume, for purposes of demurrer, that plaintiff was indeed *injured* in the manner she alleges, and that a *causal connection exists between defendants' conduct and the injury suffered.* As plaintiff's complaint alleges, her injury was a "direct and proximate result" of defendants' fraud and misrepresentations.

b.   Moral blame

Whether defendants were guilty of any *moral blame* would depend on the proof adduced at trial, although it is certainly arguable that their unreserved recommendations of Gadams, together with their failure to disclose facts reasonably necessary to avoid or minimize the risk of further child molestations or abuse, could be characterized as morally blameworthy.

c.   Availability of insurance or alternative courses of conduct

Next, we may assume that standard business liability *insurance* is available to cover instances of *negligent* misrepresentation or nondisclosure as alleged in count three of the complaint, but is not available for the fraud or intentional misconduct alleged in count four. [ ] Perhaps more significantly, defendants had *alternative courses of conduct* to avoid tort liability, namely, (1) writing a "full disclosure" letter revealing all relevant facts regarding Gadams's background, or (2) writing a "no comment" letter omitting any affirmative representations regarding Gadams's qualifications, or merely verifying basic employment dates and details. The parties cite no case or Restatement provision suggesting that a former employer has an affirmative duty of disclosure that would preclude such a no comment letter. As we have previously indicated, liability may not be imposed for mere nondisclosure or other failure to act, at least in the absence of some special relationship not alleged here. [ ]

d.   Public policy considerations

As for public policy, the law certainly recognizes a *policy of preventing future harm* of the kind alleged here. One of society's highest priorities is to protect children from sexual or physical abuse. [ ]; Pen.Code, § 11166 [duty to report suspected child abuse].

Defendants urge that *competing social or economic policies* may disfavor the imposition of liability for misrepresentation or nondisclosure in employment references. They observe that a rule imposing liability in these situations could greatly inhibit the preparation and distribution of reference letters, to the general detriment of employers and employees alike.

. . .

In defendants' view, rather than prepare a recommendation letter stating all "material" facts, positive and negative, an employer would be better advised to decline to write a reference letter or, at most, merely to confirm the former employee's position, salary, and dates of employment. According to defendants, apart from the former employer's difficulty in deciding how much "negative" information to divulge, an employer who disclosed more than minimal employment data would risk a defamation, breach of privacy, or wrongful interference suit from a rejected job seeker. (See, e.g., Jensen v. Hewlett-Packard Co. [18 Cal.Rptr.2d 83 (App. 1993)] [libel action may be based on false accusations in employee evaluation form of criminal conduct, dishonesty, incompetence, or reprehensible personal characteristics or behavior]; [ ]).

. . .

In response, plaintiff asserts it is unlikely that employers will decline to write reference letters for fear of tort liability, at least in situations involving no foreseeable risks of physical injury to someone. Plaintiff observes that an employer would be protected from a defamation suit by the statutory qualified privilege for nonmalicious communications regarding a job applicant's qualifications. [ ] This provision was amended in 1994 to provide that the qualified privilege available for communications to and by "interested" persons "applies to and includes a communication concerning the job performance or qualifications of an applicant for employment, based upon credible evidence, made without malice, by a current or former employer of the applicant to, and upon request of, the prospective employer." (Civ.Code, § 47, subd. (c).) As plaintiff suggests, the existence of this privilege may encourage more open disclosure of relevant information regarding former employees. [ ] (See also [*Jensen v. Hewlett-Packard Co.,*] [acknowledging public policy disfavoring libel suits based on comments in employee evaluation forms].)

. . .

In light of these factors and policy considerations, we hold, consistent with Restatement Second of Torts sections 310 [intentional misrepresentation] and 311, that the writer of a letter of recommendation owes to third persons a duty not to misrepresent the facts in describing the qualifications and character of a former employee, if making these misrepresentations would present a substantial, foreseeable risk of physical injury to the third persons. In the absence, however, of resulting physical injury, or some special relationship between the parties, the writer of a letter of recommendation should have no duty of care extending to third persons for misrepresentations made concerning former employees. In those cases, the policy favoring free and open communication with prospective employers should prevail.

Having concluded that defendants owed plaintiff a duty not to misrepresent Gadams's qualifications or character in their letters of recommendation, we next must determine whether defendants' letters indeed contained "misrepresentations" or "false information" within the meaning of Restatement Second of Torts sections 310 or 311. If defendants made no misrepresentations, then as a matter of law they could not be found liable under those provisions.

2.   Misleading Misrepresentation or Mere Nondisclosure?

The Court of Appeal majority determined that plaintiff adequately alleged defendants committed actual misrepresentation rather than mere nondisclosure, because their letters of recommendation amounted to "misleading half-truths," containing incomplete information regarding Gadams's character and reliability. According to the Court of Appeal, defendants' unqualified recommendation of Gadams, coupled with their failure to disclose that Gadams had been in "sexual situations" with female students and had made "sexual overtures" to them, or that defendants knew complaints regarding Gadams's conduct had resulted in his resignation, amounted to affirmative misrepresentations.

Defendants join the Court of Appeal dissent in asserting that their letters of recommendation contained no misrepresentations that would invoke either Restatement Second of Torts section 310 or 311. As defendants observe, their letters neither discussed nor denied prior complaints of sexual misconduct or impropriety against Gadams.

Like the Court of Appeal majority, we view this case as a "misleading half-truths" situation in which defendants, having undertaken to provide some information regarding Gadams's teaching credentials and character, were obliged to disclose all other facts which "materially qualify" the limited facts disclosed. [ ]; Civ.Code, § 1710, subd. 3 [deceit is the suppression of a material fact by one who gives misleading information of other facts]; [ ].

As the Court of Appeal observed, defendants' letters offered general and unreserved praise for Gadams's character and personality (e.g., "dependable [and] reliable," "pleasant personality," "high standards," "relates well to the students"). According to the Court of Appeal, having volunteered this information, defendants were obliged to complete the picture by disclosing material facts regarding charges and complaints of Gadams's sexual improprieties.

Defendants suggest that a letter noting only a candidate's favorable qualities cannot reasonably be deemed misleading as to any unfavorable ones, and the recipient of such a letter cannot reasonably rely on any implication that the candidate lacks unfavorable qualities. [ ] As one commentator observes, " . . . half of the truth may obviously amount to a lie, *if it is understood to be the whole*." [ ] Prosser & Keeton, The Law of Torts [§ 106] (5th ed. 1984)(italics added.) According to defendants, no reasonable person would assume a letter of recommendation purports to state the whole truth about a candidate's background and character.

In defendants' view, we should characterize letters of recommendation stating only the favorable aspects of an applicant's background or character as a *permissible* variety of "half-truth," which misleads no one, and which, for that reason alone, should not form the basis for liability on a theory of negligent misrepresentation or fraud. ([ ] [failure of church officers to disclose pastor's history of pedophilia not actionable in absence of affirmative representation denying that history, because "[t]he tort of negligent misrepresentation requires a 'positive assertion' and does not apply to implied misrepresentations"]; [ ] [county officers' failure to notify former district attorney of threats posed by vindictive probationer not actionable despite implied representation to warn]; [ ] [auto club tourbook endorsing motel's accommodations contained no "positive assertion concerning neighborhood safety," precluding negligent misrepresentation suit]; [ ] [failure to disclose sexual misconduct charges against former employee/teacher not actionable because "[t]he mere recommendation of a person for potential employment is not a proper basis for asserting a claim of negligence where another party is responsible for the actual hiring"]; [ ]; cf. [ ] [liability of employment agency based on positive misrepresentation that job seeker's innocent explanation for his rape conviction "had been verified by military officials"].)

But plaintiff argues convincingly that, under the facts pleaded in this case, defendants indeed made "positive assertion[s]" regarding Gadams's character, assertions deceptively incomplete because defendants knowingly concealed material facts regarding Gadams's sexual misconduct with students. Thus, defendant Mendota, through its officer Rossette, allegedly extolled Gadams's "genuine concern" for and "outstanding rapport" with students, knowing that Gadams had engaged in inappropriate physical contact with them. Rossette declared in the letter that he "wouldn't hesitate to recommend Mr. Gadams for any position!"

Defendant Golden Plains, through its officer Cole, stated it would recommend Gadams for "any administrative position," despite its knowledge of Gadams's prior inappropriate conduct while an employee of Golden Plains, conduct that had allegedly led to Gadams's "resigning under pressure from Golden Plains due to sexual misconduct charges. . . ."

Finally, defendant Muroc, through its officers Rice and Malcolm, allegedly recommended Gadams "for an assistant principalship or equivalent position without reservation," describing Gadams as "an upbeat, enthusiastic administrator who relates well to the students," despite its knowledge of disciplinary actions taken against him regarding sexual harassment allegations made during his employment with Muroc, allegations that induced Muroc to force Gadams to resign.

We conclude that these letters, essentially recommending Gadams for any position without reservation or qualification, constituted affirmative representations that strongly implied Gadams was fit to interact appropriately and safely with female students. These representations were false and misleading in light of defendants' alleged knowledge of charges of Gadams's repeated sexual improprieties. We also conclude that plaintiff's complaint adequately alleged misleading half-truths that could invoke an exception to the general rule excluding liability for mere nondisclosure or other failure to act. [ ]

3.   *Reliance*

[The court concluded that the allegations of Livingston's reliance were sufficient under both sections 310 and 311. The court also concluded that sufficient causal connection was alleged between the misrepresentation and the harm.]

[The court affirmed on negligent misrepresentation and fraud, but reversed as to a third theory.]

■ GEORGE, C.J., MOSK and BROWN, JJ., concur.

■ [JUSTICES KENNARD, BAXTER and WERDEGAR dissented on a different issue.]

NOTES AND QUESTIONS

1.   Is the concept of categorical foreseeability, which *Ballard* identifies as an issue for the court, a matter that is capable of determination? That is, won't the foreseeability of harm vary, sometimes dramatically, from case to case within the category of misleading employment reference letters? Notwithstanding the California emphasis on foreseeability as a critical issue in the determination of duty, the Third Restatement criticizes the use of foreseeability in duty determinations, observing that the foreseeability of the risk is a matter for the factfinder in deciding negligence and that categorical foreseeability "cannot usefully be assessed." Restatement (Third) Torts: Liability for Physical and Emotional Harm § 7, cmt. j (2010); see also *A.W. v. Lancaster County School District 0001*, p. 209 infra. Does the *Randi W.* court employ categorical foreseeability in determining whether the defendant owed a duty?

2.   In the cited *Garcia* case, a woman was worried about a violent man with whom she had been living (but who had since moved out). He was on parole from a prior offense and defendant was his parole officer. In response to the woman's expression of concern, the officer told her, "I don't think you have anything to worry about. He's not going to come looking for you." Also, the officer assured her of her safety by emphasizing to her that "[the man] had told him that he was still in love with plaintiff, and repeatedly asking if she really wanted to end the relationship." The man killed her. Why does *Garcia* not control the outcome in *Randi W.*? Does *Garcia* differ from *Mixon v. Dobbs Houses, Inc.*, note 6, p. 140 supra?

3.   Assume that in their letters the districts had hidden the fact that Gadams was habitually unable to process important papers before the deadlines. Assume that Gadams failed to process documents for the Livingston district in time for its superintendent to get a raise that would have been automatic if the filing had been timely. Does the principal case suggest the analysis for that situation? Cases involving economic loss are discussed in greater detail in Chapter IV.

Assume that Gadams's laxity about deadlines resulted in his failure to file school transcripts before the deadline—as a result of which five students were rejected by colleges to which it was clear they would otherwise have been admitted. Although the students can show no economic harm, they are greatly distressed by this turn of events. Does the principal case suggest the analysis for this situation? Cases involving emotional distress are discussed in greater detail in Chapter IV.

4.   In several recent cases, parents who have adopted children have sued the agencies involved for failing to reveal negative information about the child before the adoption. In Jackson v. State, 956 P.2d 35 (Mont.1998), the state did not tell the plaintiffs known information, including the results of "psychological evaluations performed on [the adoptee's] biological parents." The court noted that several courts had based a duty on the adopting agencies' "voluntary dissemination of health information concerning the child to potential adopting parents," and held that defendant was subject to a duty of due care based on its providing background information to the plaintiffs. What is the harm in this type of case? Is it feasible for an adoption agency to say nothing whatsoever about the child's health?

5.   Is the court correct to minimize concern about the willingness of employers to write recommendation letters for former employees? If the court had judged that concern to be substantial, might it have relied on the policy of encouraging recommendation letters—especially when a former employee poses a risk of physical harm—to rule that no duty exists to potential third-party victims for employers who write recommendation letters? In Passmore v. Multi-Management Services, Inc., 810 N.E.2d 1022 (Ind.2004), the court refused to adopt section 311 of the Second Restatement to protect the free-flow of information between past and prospective employers. Compare Armstrong v. Thompson, 80 A.3d 177 (D.C.2013)(ruling on five different tort claims pursued against defendant former co-worker who allegedly maliciously alerted plaintiff's prospective employer about plaintiff's past work problems).

Tarasoff v. Regents of the University of California

Supreme Court of California, 1976.
17 Cal.3d 425, 551 P.2d 334, 131 Cal.Rptr. 14.

■ TOBRINER, J.

facts

[Dr. Moore, a psychologist employed by the University of California, was treating one Poddar. Poddar killed Tatiana Tarasoff. Plaintiffs, the parents of Tatiana Tarasoff, allege that Poddar had confided his intention to kill Tarasoff to Dr. Moore; that based on Moore's request that Poddar be confined, campus police briefly detained Poddar; but released him because he appeared rational; that after he was released, the chief of psychiatry, Moore's superior, ordered that Poddar not be further detained; and that no one warned Tatiana or plaintiffs of the peril posed by Poddar. The trial judge dismissed the suit that was brought against several therapists and others.]

. . .

The second cause of action can be amended to allege that Tatiana's death proximately resulted from defendants' negligent failure to warn Tatiana or others likely to apprise her of her danger. Plaintiffs contend that as amended, such allegations of negligence and proximate causation, with resulting damages, establish a cause of action. Defendants, however, contend that in the circumstances of the present case they owed no duty of care to Tatiana or her parents and that, in the absence of such duty, they were free to act in careless disregard of Tatiana's life and safety.

In analyzing this issue, we bear in mind that legal duties are not discoverable facts of nature, but merely conclusory expressions that, in cases of a particular type, liability should be imposed for damage done. . . .

In the landmark case of *Rowland v. Christian* [ ], Justice Peters recognized that liability should be imposed "for injury occasioned to another by his want of ordinary care or skill" as expressed in § 1714 of the Civil Code. Thus, Justice Peters, quoting from Heaven v. Pender (1883) 11 Q.B.D. 503, 509 stated: " 'whenever one person is by circumstances placed in such a position with regard to another . . . that if he did not use ordinary care and skill in his own conduct . . . he would cause danger of injury to the person or property of the other, a duty arises to use ordinary care and skill to avoid such danger.' "

What is considered while determining duty of care

We depart from "this fundamental principle" only upon the "balancing of a number of considerations"; major ones "are the foreseeability of harm to the plaintiff, the degree of certainty that the plaintiff suffered injury, the closeness of the connection between the defendant's conduct and the injury suffered, the moral blame attached to the defendant's conduct, the policy of preventing future harm, the extent of the burden to the defendant and consequences to the community of imposing a duty to exercise care with resulting liability for breach, and the availability, cost and prevalence of insurance for the risk involved." [citing several cases]

The most important of these considerations in establishing duty is foreseeability. As a general principle, a "defendant owes a duty of care to all persons who are foreseeably endangered by his conduct, with respect to all risks which make the conduct unreasonably dangerous." [ ] As we shall explain, however, when the avoidance of foreseeable harm requires a defendant to control the conduct of another person, or to warn of such conduct, the common law has traditionally imposed liability only if the defendant bears some special relationship to the dangerous person or to the potential victim. Since the relationship between a therapist and his patient satisfies this requirement, we need not here decide whether foreseeability alone is sufficient to create a duty to exercise reasonable care to protect a potential victim of another's conduct.

Although, as we have stated above, under the common law, as a general rule, one person owed no duty to control the conduct of another[5] [ ], nor to warn those endangered by such conduct [ ], the courts have carved out an exception to this rule in cases in which the defendant stands in some special relationship to either the person whose conduct needs to be controlled or in a relationship to the foreseeable victim of that conduct (see Restatement, Second, Torts, supra, §§ 315–320). Applying this exception to the present case, we note that a relationship of defendant therapists to either Tatiana or Poddar will suffice to establish a duty of care; as explained in section 315 of the Restatement Second of Torts, a duty of care may arise from either "(a) a special relation . . . between the actor and the third person which imposes a duty upon the actor to control the third person's conduct, or (b) a special relation . . . between the actor and the other which gives to the other a right of protection."

Although plaintiffs' pleadings assert no special relation between Tatiana and defendant therapists, they establish as between Poddar and defendant therapists the special relation that arises between a patient and his doctor or psychotherapist. Such a relationship may support affirmative duties for the benefit of third persons. Thus, for example, a hospital must exercise reasonable care to control the behavior of a patient which may endanger other persons. A doctor must also warn a patient if the patient's condition or medication renders certain conduct, such as driving a car, dangerous to others.

---

[5] This rule derives from the common law's distinction between misfeasance and nonfeasance, and its reluctance to impose liability for the latter. (See Harper & Kime, The Duty to Control the Conduct of Another (1934) 43 Yale L.J. 886, 887.) Morally questionable, the rule owes its survival to "the difficulties of setting any standards of unselfish service to fellow men, and of making any workable rule to cover possible situations where fifty people might fail to rescue. . . ." (Prosser, Torts (4th ed. 1971) § 56, p. 341.) Because of these practical difficulties, the courts have increased the number of instances in which affirmative duties are imposed not by direct rejection of the common law rule, but by expanding the list of special relationships which will justify departure from that rule. [ ]

Although the California decisions that recognize this duty have involved cases in which the defendant stood in a special relationship *both* to the victim and to the person whose conduct created the danger,[9] we do not think that the duty should logically be constricted to such situations. Decisions of other jurisdictions hold that the single relationship of a doctor to his patient is sufficient to support the duty to exercise reasonable care to protect others against dangers emanating from the patient's illness. The courts hold that a doctor is liable to persons infected by his patient if he negligently fails to diagnose a contagious disease [ ], or having diagnosed the illness, fails to warn members of the patient's family [ ].

. . .

defendants argue

Defendants contend, however, that imposition of a duty to exercise reasonable care to protect third persons is unworkable because therapists cannot accurately predict whether or not a patient will resort to violence. In support of this argument amicus representing the American Psychiatric Association and other professional societies cites numerous articles which indicate that therapists, in the present state of the art, are unable reliably to predict violent acts; their forecasts, amicus claims, tend consistently to overpredict violence, and indeed are more often wrong than right. Since predictions of violence are often erroneous, amicus concludes, the courts should not render rulings that predicate the liability of therapists upon the validity of such predictions.

support for D's argue

. . .

We recognize the difficulty that a therapist encounters in attempting to forecast whether a patient presents a serious danger of violence. . . . Within the broad range of reasonable practice and treatment in which professional opinion and judgment may differ, the therapist is free to exercise his or her own best judgment without liability; proof, aided by hindsight, that he or she judged wrongly is insufficient to establish negligence.

In the instant case, however, the pleadings do not raise any questions as to failure of defendant therapists to predict that Poddar presented a serious danger of violence. On the contrary, the present complaints allege that defendant therapists did in fact predict that Poddar would kill, but were negligent in failing to warn.

Amicus contends, however, that even when a therapist does in fact predict that a patient poses a serious danger of violence to others, the therapist should be absolved of any responsibility for failing to act to

---

[9] Ellis v. D'Angelo, [253 P.2d 675 (Cal.App.1953)], upheld a cause of action against parents who failed to warn a babysitter of the violent proclivities of their child; Johnson v. State of California, [447 P.2d 352 (Cal.1968)], upheld a suit against the state for failure to warn foster parents of the dangerous tendencies of their ward; Morgan v. County of Yuba, [41 Cal.Rptr. 508 (App.1964)], sustained a cause of action against a sheriff who had promised to warn decedent before releasing a dangerous prisoner, but failed to do so.

protect the potential victim. In our view, however, once a therapist does in fact determine, or under applicable professional standards reasonably should have determined, that a patient poses a serious danger of violence to others, he bears a duty to exercise reasonable care to protect the foreseeable victim of that danger. While the discharge of this duty of due care will necessarily vary with the facts of each case,[11] in each instance the adequacy of the therapist's conduct must be measured against the traditional negligence standard of the rendition of reasonable care under the circumstances. . . .

. . . Weighing the uncertain and conjectural character of the alleged damage done the patient by such a warning against the peril to the victim's life, we conclude that professional inaccuracy in predicting violence cannot negate the therapist's duty to protect the threatened victim.

The risk that unnecessary warnings may be given is a reasonable price to pay for the lives of possible victims that may be saved. We would hesitate to hold that the therapist who is aware that his patient expects to attempt to assassinate the President of the United States would not be obligated to warn the authorities because the therapist cannot predict with accuracy that his patient will commit the crime.

Defendants further argue that free and open communication is essential to psychotherapy. . . . The giving of a warning, defendants contend, constitutes a breach of trust which entails the revelation of confidential communications.

We recognize the public interest in supporting effective treatment of mental illness and in protecting the rights of patients to privacy [ ], and the consequent public importance of safeguarding the confidential character of psychotherapeutic communication. Against this interest, however, we must weigh the public interest in safety from violent assault. The Legislature has undertaken the difficult task of balancing the countervailing concerns. In Evidence Code section 1014, it established a broad rule of privilege to protect confidential communications between patient and psychotherapist. In Evidence Code section 1024, the Legislature created a specific and limited exception to the psychotherapist-patient privilege: "There is no privilege if the psychotherapist has reasonable cause to believe that the patient is in such mental or emotional condition as to be dangerous to himself or to the person or property of another and that disclosure of the communication is necessary to prevent the threatened danger."

---

[11] Defendant therapists and amicus also argue that warnings must be given only in those cases in which the therapist knows the identity of the victim. We recognize that in some cases it would be unreasonable to require the therapist to interrogate his patient to discover the victim's identity, or to conduct an independent investigation. But there may also be cases in which a moment's reflection will reveal the victim's identity. The matter thus is one which depends upon the circumstances of each case, and should not be governed by any hard and fast rule.

We realize that the open and confidential character of psychotherapeutic dialogue encourages patients to express threats of violence, few of which are ever executed. Certainly a therapist should not be encouraged routinely to reveal such threats; such disclosures could seriously disrupt the patient's relationship with his therapist and with the persons threatened. To the contrary, the therapist's obligations to his patient require that he not disclose a confidence unless such disclosure is necessary to avert danger to others, and even then that he do so discreetly, and in a fashion that would preserve the privacy of his patient to the fullest extent compatible with the prevention of the threatened danger. [ ]

The revelation of a communication under the above circumstances is not a breach of trust or a violation of professional ethics; as stated in the Principles of Medical Ethics of the American Medical Association (1957), section 9: "A physician may not reveal the confidence entrusted to him in the course of medical attendance . . . *unless he is required to do so by law or unless it becomes necessary in order to protect the welfare of the individual or of the community.*" (Italics added.) We conclude that the public policy favoring protection of the confidential character of patient-psychotherapist communications must yield to the extent to which disclosure is essential to avert danger to others. The protective privilege ends where the public peril begins.

Our current crowded and computerized society compels the interdependence of its members. In this risk-infested society we can hardly tolerate the further exposure to danger that would result from a concealed knowledge of the therapist that his patient was lethal. If the exercise of reasonable care to protect the threatened victim requires the therapist to warn the endangered party or those who can reasonably be expected to notify him, we see no sufficient societal interest that would protect and justify concealment. The containment of such risks lies in the public interest. . . .

. . .

For the reasons stated, we conclude that plaintiffs can amend their complaints to state a cause of action against defendant therapists by asserting that the therapists in fact determined that Poddar presented a serious danger of violence to Tatiana, or pursuant to the standards of their profession should have so determined, but nevertheless failed to exercise reasonable care to protect her from that danger.

holding

. . .

■ WRIGHT, C.J., SULLIVAN, J., and RICHARDSON, J., concurred.

■ MOSK, J., concurring and dissenting.

I concur in the result in this instance only because the complaints allege that defendant therapists did in fact predict that Poddar would kill and were therefore negligent in failing to warn of that danger. . . .

. . .

I cannot concur, however, in the majority's rule that a therapist may be held liable for failing to predict his patient's tendency to violence if other practitioners, pursuant to the "standards of the profession," would have done so. The question is, what standards? Defendants and a responsible amicus curiae, supported by an impressive body of literature discussed at length in our recent opinion in [], demonstrate that psychiatric predictions of violence are inherently unreliable.

. . .

[JUSTICE CLARK, joined by JUSTICE MCCOMB, dissented. First, he argued that certain legislation indicated an intention that therapists not disclose this information. Entirely apart from the statute, he believed that general tort principles favored nondisclosure. He considered confidentiality critical for three reasons: without such assurances those requiring treatment would be deterred; confidentiality encouraged the full disclosure necessary for effective treatment; and even with full disclosure, confidentiality is necessary to allow the patient to maintain his trust in his psychiatrist. Given the lack of precision in predicting violence, psychiatrists will be tempted either to issue excessive warnings or to commit patients—a practice already used to excess. "We should accept legislative and medical judgment, relying upon effective treatment rather than on indiscriminate warning."]

NOTES AND QUESTIONS

1.   Does the line of cases referred to in the opinion in which a physician failed to warn a patient's family or friends of the patient's contagious condition provide persuasive support for *Tarasoff*? The courts differ in their analyses.

a.   *Imposing duty to third-parties based on the physician-patient relationship.* In Reisner v. Regents of the University of California, 37 Cal.Rptr.2d 518 (App.1995), a day after a 12-year-old child received a transfusion, her doctor discovered that the blood had been contaminated with HIV antibodies. Although the same doctor continued treating the child, he never told her about the situation. Three years later, the now 15-year-old adolescent became intimate with plaintiff. Two years after that the doctor told her; she died a month later. Shortly thereafter, plaintiff was tested and learned that he was HIV infected. The court, relying largely on *Tarasoff*, held that defendant doctor owed a duty to plaintiff despite the lack of a physician-patient relationship. (Note the causal aspect of plaintiff's case—that if the adolescent had been told when she should have been told, she would have warned plaintiff, and he would not have been infected.)

In Pate v. Threlkel, 661 So.2d 278 (Fla.1995), defendant surgeon, who operated on a patient, knew or should have known of the likelihood that the patient's adult children would contract the carcinoma involved because it was genetically transferable. The court imposed a duty to the patient's child who alleged that her cancer would have been discovered sooner and been treatable if her mother had been told about the genetic situation. Since the obligation here was "obviously for the benefit of certain identified third parties and the physician knows of the existence of those third parties, then the physician's duty runs to those third parties."

Although the court in Safer v. Estate of Pack, 677 A.2d 1188 (N.J.Super.Ct.App.Div.1996), refused to dismiss the case because of *Pate*, it observed that it "may be necessary, at some stage, to resolve a conflict between the physician's broader duty to warn and his fidelity to an expressed preference of the patient that nothing be said to family members about the details of the disease."

b.   *No duty. Pate* was distinguished in Hawkins v. Pizarro, 713 So.2d 1036 (Fla.Dist.Ct.App.1998). Defendant physician incorrectly and negligently told his patient that she had tested negative for hepatitis C. Some months later, she met, and married, a man who later tested positive for hepatitis C. A physician's affidavit asserted that it was "foreseeable that a single, attractive, thirty-nine-year-old woman [such as this patient] would be dating and engaging in sexual relations." The court rejected the husband's suit because *Pate* required that the third party's existence or identity be known at the time of the negligence, and here the patient "had not yet met [her husband] at the time of the incorrect diagnosis."

How persuasive is the *Hawkins* court's distinction of *Pate*, given that, in the latter, knowledge of who was at risk was essential to taking any precautions, while in *Hawkins* that was not necessary?

Hawkins, nevertheless, presages how courts approach this matter when the third party is a stranger. The subject is explored in detail in Lester by Mavrogenis *ex rel.* Lester v. Hall, 970 P.2d 590 (N.M.1998). The court, in a suit by a motorist injured by defendant's patient, held that the physician had no duty to the motorist to warn the patient about the dangers of driving while taking lithium or to monitor his condition where the accident occurred five days after the last visit. The court distinguished a case in which it had held that a duty was owed "when the patient has just been injected with drugs known to affect judgment and driving ability." Are these cases consistent with *Tarasoff?*

c.   *Creating risk as distinguished from failing to prevent it.* In Hardee v. Bio-Medical Applications of South Carolina, Inc., 636 S.E.2d 629 (S.C.2006), plaintiff alleged that defendant provided health care to a patient that compromised the patient's ability to drive, which resulted in the accident that injured plaintiff. The court held:

> [A] medical provider who provides treatment which it knows may have detrimental effects on a patient's capacities and abilities owes a duty to prevent harm to patients and to reasonably foreseeable third parties by warning the patient of the attendant risks and effects before administering the treatment. Therefore, if Respondent knew that Patient could experience ill

> effects following dialysis treatment, Respondent owed Appellants a duty to warn Patient of the risks of driving.

Emphasizing the limited scope of its decision, the court added: "We note that this is a very narrow holding . . . [T]his duty owed to third parties is identical to the duty owed to the patient, i.e., a medical provider must warn a patient of the attendant risks and effects of any treatment. Thus, our holding does not hamper the doctor-patient relationship."

2.   The *Tarasoff* court lists a number of factors that are said to play a role in the determination whether to impose a duty, asserting that the most important of these factors is foreseeability. At the same time, the court also states that it need not decide if foreseeability alone is enough to impose a duty. If foreseeability were sufficient, what effect would it have on the no-affirmative-duty rule in instances of easy rescue, such as the infant lying on the railroad tracks, note 1, p. 131 supra?

3.   Later California cases have adhered to *Tarasoff* with caution. See Bellah v. Greenson, 146 Cal.Rptr. 535 (App.1978), in which a patient of the defendant psychiatrist committed suicide. The patient's parents claimed that defendant negligently failed to take sufficient measures to prevent the suicide; that he failed to warn plaintiffs, who were out of state, of the seriousness of their daughter's condition; and that she was consorting with heroin addicts. The court held plaintiffs had no failure-to-warn claim. *Tarasoff* does not apply where the risk is "self-inflicted harm or mere property damage." The court acknowledged that a traditional malpractice claim on behalf of the deceased might be availing. See Marshall v. Klebanov, 902 A.2d 873 (N.J.2006)(psychotherapist subject to liability for patient's suicide if he failed to exercise the customary care of psychiatrists in treating patient).

In Thompson v. County of Alameda, 614 P.2d 728 (Cal.1980), the county released James, a violent juvenile offender, into his mother's custody even though the county knew that he had threatened to kill some unidentified child in the neighborhood. Within 24 hours, James killed plaintiff's son, a boy in his neighborhood. The plaintiffs claimed that the county had been negligent in failing to warn the public, the police, and James's mother.

The trial court's dismissal of the complaint was affirmed, 5–2. There was no identified potential victim. Warnings to the general public were unlikely to do much good because the public is already conditioned to protecting itself against crime and violence and a specific warning might negate the rehabilitative purposes of the probation and parole systems. Nor was a warning to the juvenile's mother likely to be effective. She would not be likely to "inform other neighborhood parents or children that her son posed a general threat to their welfare, thereby perhaps thwarting any rehabilitative effort, and also effectively stigmatizing both the mother and son in the community."

In Hedlund v. Superior Court, 669 P.2d 41 (Cal.1983), the court held that a young child harmed during a violent assault on his mother stated a claim based on threats of violence against the mother that had been communicated to defendant psychotherapists. Injuries to a child were foreseeable in an assault upon the mother, and consequently fell within the *Tarasoff* principle.

4.   After *Tarasoff*, Cal. Civil Code section 43.92 was enacted to provide that therapists are immune from liability for failure to warn "except when the patient has communicated to the psychotherapist a serious threat of physical violence against a reasonably identifiable victim or victims." If there is a duty to warn, it "shall be discharged by the psychotherapist making reasonable efforts to communicate the threat to the victim or victims and to a law enforcement agency." How does this legislation modify the holding in *Tarasoff*?

5.   Most states have accepted and some have extended *Tarasoff*. See, e.g., Peck v. Counseling Service of Addison County, Inc., 499 A.2d 422 (Vt.1985)(extending the duty in favor of the patient's parents, whose barn was burned down). A number have adopted limitations similar to those in California detailed in note 3 supra. On the other hand, a few jurisdictions have rejected *Tarasoff*. See, e.g., Tedrick v. Community Resource Center, Inc., 920 N.E.2d 220 (Ill.2009)(declining to adopt a *Tarasoff* duty to avoid subjecting psychotherapists to divided loyalties). For a review of the case developments and an empirical study of how the cases have shaped professional behavior, see Buckner & Firestone, "Where the Public Peril Begins": 25 Years After *Tarasoff*, 21 J. Legal Med. 187 (2000); see also Herbert & Young, *Tarasoff* at Twenty-Five, 30 J.Am.Acad.Psychiatry.L. 275 (2002). For an in-depth examination of the *Tarasoff* case as well as an assessment of its impact on the mental health profession and the law, see Schuck & Givelber, *Tarasoff v. Regents of the University of California*: The Therapist's Dilemma, in R. Rabin & S. Sugarman (eds.), Torts Stories 99 (2003).

6.   What if a regular patron of Joe's Tavern tells the bartender that he has "had it" with his girlfriend's behavior and is going to her apartment to kill her? What if he told his dentist explicitly what he was going to do? Are these stronger or weaker cases for imposing a duty than the facts in *Tarasoff*?

Is harm to the girlfriend more or less foreseeable than in *Tarasoff*?

7.   In an omitted part of the *Tarasoff* opinion, Justice Tobriner concluded that no duty was owed to the plaintiffs by the campus police who detained Poddar for a short while but released him when he appeared rational, and did not warn Tatiana or her parents of any danger. No special relationship was found between the police and Tatiana or Poddar sufficient to impose a duty to warn upon the police. Neither the police nor Moore's supervisor could be liable based on a duty arising from the undertaking to confine and then release him because of a statute immunizing government employees for their confinement decisions. The affirmative duties of the police and other governmental entities are considered in section G infra.

8.   Note that these extended-duty cases arise primarily in situations in which the immediately responsible party is unlikely to be a solvent defendant. In the *Tarasoff* sequence of cases, for example, doctors and

clinics are generally more promising defendants than homicidal psychopaths.

———

In contrast to the preceding cases in this section, which confronted whether common law affirmative duties should be imposed, the following case addresses the role of legislation in this area.

Uhr v. East Greenbush Central School District

Court of Appeals of New York, 1999.
94 N.Y.2d 32, 720 N.E.2d 886, 698 N.Y.S.2d 609.

■ ROSENBLATT, J.

[Plaintiff parents sued defendant school district alleging that defendant, in violation of a state statute, had failed to test the infant plaintiff annually for scoliosis, and that this failure necessitated surgery that could have been avoided if the statute had been obeyed. Education Law § 905(1) required testing of all students between 8 and 16 years of age for scoliosis at least once in each school year. "Plaintiffs assert, in essence, that the District was negligent in failing to examine the minor plaintiff for scoliosis during the 1993–1994 school year, as a result of which her ailment was allowed to progress undetected, to her detriment. Supreme Court granted the District's motion for summary judgment, holding that Education Law § 905(1) does not create a private right of action, and that plaintiffs had otherwise failed to state a claim for common-law negligence." The Appellate Division affirmed.]

We first address plaintiffs' claim that Education Law § 905(1) may be enforced by a private right of action. Three provisions of the Education Law are relevant to our inquiry. Education Law § 905(1) states that "[m]edical inspectors or principals and teachers in charge of schools in this state shall . . . examine all . . . pupils between eight and sixteen years of age for scoliosis, at least once in each school year." Education Law § 905(2) provides that "[n]otwithstanding any other provisions of any general, special or local law, the school authorities charged with the duty of making such tests or examinations of pupils for the presence of scoliosis pursuant to this section shall not suffer any liability to any person as a result of making such test or examination, which liability would not have existed by any provision of law, statutory or otherwise, in the absence of this section." Finally, Education Law § 911 charges the Commissioner of Education with the duty of enforcing the provisions of sections 901 through 910 of the Education Law and authorizes the Commissioner to "adopt rules and regulations" for such purpose.

The Test for the Availability of a Private Right of Action

As plaintiffs point out, the District's obligation to examine for scoliosis is plain enough. A statutory command, however, does not necessarily carry with it a right of private enforcement by means of tort litigation (see, e.g., Mark G. v. Sabol, 93 N.Y.2d 710 [1999]).

The availability of a private right of action for the violation of a statutory duty—as opposed to one grounded in common-law negligence—is not a new concept. [ ] When a statute itself expressly authorizes a private right of action (e.g., Social Services Law § 420[2] [civil liability for "knowingly and willfully" failing to "report a case of suspected child abuse or maltreatment"]; General Obligations Law § 11–100[1] [civil liability for serving alcohol to a minor who gets intoxicated and then hurts others]), there is no need for further analysis. When a statute is silent, as it is here, courts have had to determine whether a private right of action may be fairly implied. In [ ], this Court articulated the standards that were synthesized into a three-part test in Sheehy v. Big Flats Community Day, 73 N.Y.2d 629 [1989]. In making the determination, we ask:

> (1) whether the plaintiff is one of the class for whose particular benefit the statute was enacted;

> (2) whether recognition of a private right of action would promote the legislative purpose; and

> (3) whether creation of such a right would be consistent with the legislative scheme [ ].

There is no doubt that the infant plaintiff is a member of the class for whose particular benefit Education Law § 905(1) was enacted. The first prong is satisfied.

The second prong is itself a two-part inquiry. We must first discern what the Legislature was seeking to accomplish when it enacted the statute, and then determine whether a private right of action would promote that objective [ ].

Here, the purpose of the statute is obvious. Scoliosis is a curvature of the spine which, if left undetected in children, can be crippling [ ]. Upon early detection, scoliosis can be treated successfully, often without the need for surgery. In 1978 the Legislature amended Education Law § 905(1) to add scoliosis screening to the then existing obligations to test children's vision and hearing [ ].

It is apparent that the Legislature was seeking to benefit the population as a whole by creating broad-based screening examinations for scoliosis, recognizing that early detection could serve the entire public in both its health and its purse. A main proponent of the legislation stated that: "The Bill will help reduce the cost of medical care to the general public as well as to the State in the case of indigent consumers. It will reduce hospital utilization as those cases which are detected in their early stage can be medically managed without hospitalization" [ ].

Early detection of the condition serves the dual legislative purpose of promoting public health and avoiding costly hospitalization.

In arguing that a private right of action would promote these objectives, plaintiffs assert that the risk of liability for failure to screen will encourage compliance with Education Law § 905(1), and thereby further the statute's purpose of providing broad-based screenings that benefit the public. In response, the District argues that the risk of liability will prompt school districts to seek waivers of the requirement to screen and thus defeat the statute's purpose.

. . .

In all, we conclude that a private right of action would promote the legislative purpose and, therefore, the second prong is satisfied.

We turn next to the third *Sheehy* prong—whether a private right of action is consistent with the legislative scheme. It is not always easy to distinguish this "consistency" prong from the second *Sheehy* prong, which centers on "promotion" of the legislative goal. The two prongs may overlap and to that extent may resist pigeon-holing. A private right of action may at times further a legislative goal and coalesce smoothly with the existing statutory scheme [ ]. Conversely, a statute's goal may not necessarily be enhanced by adding a private enforcement mechanism. In assessing the "consistency" prong, public and private avenues of enforcement do not always harmonize with one another. A private enforcement mechanism may be consistent with one statutory scheme, but in another the prospect may disserve the goal of consistency—like having two drivers at the wheel. Both may ultimately, at least in theory, promote statutory compliance, but they are born of different motivations and may produce a different allocation of benefits owing to differences in approach [ ].

Plaintiffs argue that a private right of action is not only consistent with Education Law § 905(1) but also necessary for its operation. They assert that the statute offers no other practical means of enforcement and that a private right of action is imperative, in order to give it life. We disagree and conclude that a private right of action would not be consistent with the statutory scheme. To begin with, the statute carries its own potent official enforcement mechanism. The Legislature has expressly charged the Commissioner of Education with the duty to implement Education Law § 905(1) and has equipped the Commissioner with authority to adopt rules and regulations for such purpose [ ]. Moreover, the Legislature has vested the Commissioner with power to withhold public funding from noncompliant school districts. Thus, the Legislature clearly contemplated administrative enforcement of this statute.

The question then becomes whether, in addition to administrative enforcement, an implied private right of action would be consistent with the legislative scheme. It would not. The evolution of Education Law § 905(2) is compelling evidence of the Legislature's intent to immunize the school districts from any liability that might arise out of the scoliosis screening program. By the language of Education Law § 905(2) the Legislature deemed that the school district "shall not suffer any liability to any person as a result of *making* such test or examination" (emphasis added). Plaintiffs contend that by implication, the District is denied immunity for failing to perform the examination. In effect, plaintiffs would interpret the statute as conferring immunity for misfeasance but not nonfeasance. On the other hand, the District contends that it would be incongruous for the Legislature to accord immunity for one circumstance but not the other.

[The court accepted the defendant's contention. It found "persuasive evidence" of legislative desire to immunize school districts in its overturning of one related appellate court ruling together with its failure to overrule two others that barred tort relief. The court also noted that statements antedating the legislation at issue in this case had stated that the program "would have minimal financial impact on school districts."]

In sum, we conclude that a private right of action to enforce Education Law § 905(1) is inconsistent with the statute's legislative scheme and therefore cannot be fairly implied [ ].

Common-Law Negligence

Plaintiffs contend that the lower courts erred in holding that they failed to state a claim for common-law negligence. Essentially, plaintiffs argue that the District assumed a duty to the infant plaintiff and her parents by creating a special relationship with them in connection with the Education Law § 905(1) program and that it breached its duty by failing to perform the examination during the 1993–1994 school year. We agree with the courts below that plaintiffs have failed as a matter of law to state a claim for common-law negligence (see, Cuffy v. City of New York, 69 N.Y.2d 255, 261 [1987]) [note 1c, p. 232 infra].

Accordingly, the order of the Appellate Division should be affirmed, with costs.

■ CHIEF JUDGE KAYE and JUDGES BELLACOSA, SMITH, LEVINE, CIPARICK and WESLEY concur.

NOTES AND QUESTIONS

1.   Is the court persuasive in arguing that an implied private right of action can promote the legislative purpose, but nonetheless be inconsistent with the legislative scheme?

2. Why isn't the school nurse's failure to examine plaintiff, in violation of the statute, negligence per se as that concept was used in *Martin v. Herzog*, p. 76 supra? How is the issue different here?

3. We have seen that the common law will not generally require rescue. What should happen in a state that has made it a crime not to rescue? In the mid-1960s, Vermont adopted such a statute. The statute, Vt.Stat.Ann., tit. 12, § 519, provides:

> (a) A person who knows that another is exposed to grave physical harm shall, to the extent that the same can be rendered without danger or peril to himself or without interference with important duties owed to others, give reasonable assistance to the exposed person unless that assistance or care is being provided by others.
>
> . . .
>
> (c) A person who willfully violates subsection (a) of this section shall be fined not more than $100.00.

Only a handful of states have followed Vermont's lead. See Bagby Note, Justifications for State Bystander Intervention Statutes: Why Crime Witnesses Should Be Required to Call for Help, 33 Ind.L.Rev. 571, 574–75 (2000).

Based on the statute, should a court find a civil duty to rescue? See the extended discussion in Franklin & Ploeger, Of Rescue and Report: Should Tort Law Impose a Duty to Help Endangered Persons or Abused Children?, 40 Santa Clara L.Rev. 991 (2000). See Morris The Role of Criminal Statutes in Negligence Actions, 49 Colum.L.Rev. 21 (1949), arguing that the existence of a criminal statute removes judicial concerns about lack of notice and lack of feasibility.

4. In Cuyler v. United States, 362 F.3d 949 (7th Cir.2004), a babysitter fatally abused plaintiff's child. A month previously, personnel at a federal naval hospital violated an Illinois statute by not reporting to state officials their suspicions that the babysitter had abused another child. The plaintiffs sued the United States, claiming that it owed a duty because of the statute. The court, in a wide-ranging opinion by Judge Posner, addressed the difference between negligence per se and an affirmative obligation in tort. The court held that there was no common law duty to report and concluded that no private right of action should be found in the statute. The court reasoned that imposing liability for merely negligently failing to report might put individuals on a razor's edge in deciding whether to report suspicions of abuse and thereby risk being sued for defamation (even though the statute immunized good-faith reports) or to not report and thereby risk being sued if the abuse was genuine and repeated so as to harm others. The court did not explicitly address the question of whether an affirmative duty in tort might be adopted in light of the statute, presumably because it believed that if there was no implied right of action, no common law affirmative duty should be adopted based on the statute.

5. *Child abuse reporting statutes.* Child abuse reporting statutes are prominent in providing the basis for an affirmative obligation. Every state has now adopted some form of law requiring reports by those who have knowledge of or reason to suspect child abuse. As *Uhr* indicates, some statutes explicitly impose civil liability. There may also be compelling policy reasons for courts to recognize private causes of action even when state laws do not mandate civil liability. Franklin & Ploeger, note 3 supra, suggest several distinctions between duties to rescue and duties to report, including: (a) "the need for child abuse reporting seems to be far more pressing than the need for easy rescue" since child abuse "is done in secret and is much harder to ferret out"; (b) "victims of child abuse are unable to articulate their harm or even to contact police or other officials"; (c) "a duty to report child abuse—just keeping the child away from an abusive person—may infringe less on personal freedom than a duty of easy rescue"; (d) "the harm occurs slowly and over a period of time, allowing the legal system a better chance to measure the harm done by the delay." Do these considerations justify different tort treatment for the two areas?

For differing approaches to child abuse statutes, compare Doe v. Marion, 645 S.E.2d 245 (S.C.2007) (statute requiring reporting of known or suspected child abuse did not provide implied private right of action) with Radke v. County of Freeborn, 694 N.W.2d 788 (Minn.2005)(child-abuse reporting statute created a duty that is enforceable in a tort action).

6.   Might a voluntarily adopted safety rule serve as the basis for an affirmative duty? In Morgan v. Scott, 291 S.W.3d 622 (Ky.2009), a car dealership had a rule that a salesperson was obligated to go along on any test drives by potential customers. The salesman did not, the customer was in an accident, and a third-party was injured and sued the dealership. Because the court found no other basis for a duty, it considered whether the dealership's rule created a duty and concluded it did not. Everitt v. General Electric Co., 979 A.2d 760 (N.H.2009)(citing and discussing other cases), is a similar case involving an employer with a policy of not allowing impaired employees to drive themselves home. The court, after its survey of other cases, decided the rule should not be used as basis for a duty to third parties, suggesting that to rule otherwise might impede employers from adopting rules such as these. Might such rules be relevant with regard to breach if there were otherwise a basis for a duty of reasonable care?

7.   *Duty to report crime.* Several legislatures have penalized those who fail to report crimes that they witness. The stimulus was the 1997 murder of 7-year-old Sherrice Iverson in a Las Vegas casino bathroom while David Cash, the 17-year-old murderer's friend, did not intervene. See Ziegler, Comment, Nonfeasance and the Duty to Assist: The American Seinfeld Syndrome, 104 Dick.L.Rev. 525, 527 (2000). Should courts create civil actions based on these statutes?

California's response to the Iverson murder is contained in Penal Code 152.3, adopted in 2000. The statute, known as the "Sherrice Iverson Victim Protection Act," provides that "any person who reasonably believes he or she has observed the commission" of murder, rape or other listed sex crimes "where the victim is under the age of 14 years shall notify a peace officer." That duty is satisfied if "the notification or an attempt to provide notice is made by telephone or any other means." Failure to comply is a misdemeanor punishable by a fine of up to $1,500, imprisonment for six months, or both. Three groups of people are relieved of the duty to report: (1) a relative of either the victim or the offender; (2) one who fails to report because of a "reasonable mistake of fact"; and (3) those in reasonable fear of their safety or that of their family. How does this differ from the Vermont statute?

8. *Federal statutes.* In the absence of federal common law, the federal courts cannot create civil liability independent of congressional enactments. In the absence of express statutory provisions, they must decide whether to imply private rights of action. See Cort v. Ash, 422 U.S. 66 (1975); Alexander v. Sandoval, 532 U.S. 275 (2001). Supreme Court jurisprudence has been restrictive, and implied private rights of action are infrequently found in federal legislation. For comprehensive discussion of the subject, see Stewart & Sunstein, Public Programs and Private Rights, 95 Harv.L.Rev. 1195 (1982); see also Stabile, The Role of Congressional Intent in Determining the Existence of Implied Private Rights of Action, 71 Notre Dame L.Rev. 861 (1996).

Of course, as *Uhr* noted, states may enact statutory "torts." Congress, too, may sometimes explicitly create a federal tort action. The Emergency Medical Treatment and Active Labor Act (EMTALA) requires that hospitals with emergency facilities accept patients in an "emergency medical condition" and treat them until they are stabilized and can be moved safely. Congress provided a statutory damage action for anyone injured by violations of the Act.

9. *Statutory limitations on liability.* Statutes may be enacted to encourage rescue by providing carrots rather than employing sticks. In 2009, California amended a statute to provide immunity from civil liability for any medical or emergency personnel who in good faith render emergency aid without compensation. Others who similarly provide emergency aid in good faith can be held liable only for gross negligence or wanton or willful conduct. Health & Safety Code § 1799.102(a) & (b). Provisions of this kind are customarily known as "good Samaritan" statutes. If fear that victims aided in an emergency will sue for malpractice is a major factor in the alleged reluctance of physicians to volunteer, how effective are statutes like California's? How about a statute that protects physicians against liability for negligence but not for gross negligence? How about a total bar on suits against those who try to help at the scenes of accidents? Should these statutes be limited to physicians or should all volunteers be similarly protected? Virtually every state has adopted some version of the good Samaritan statute. See Levit, The Kindness of Strangers: Interdisciplinary Foundations of a Duty to Act, 40 Washburn L.Rev. 463 (2001)(listing 44 jurisdictions with good Samaritan statutes and discussing theories supporting and opposing such statutes). The Vermont duty to rescue, discussed earlier, evolved from a lobbying effort to exempt physicians who stopped and assisted at emergency scenes from liability for negligence.

In general, do some situations lend themselves better to "carrots" and others to "sticks"?

C. POLICY BASES FOR INVOKING NO DUTY

The previous section addressed the general rule that a person does not have an affirmative duty to act—for policy reasons explained there—and the exceptions to the general rule. This section is also about policies affecting duty rules but with a different twist. In all of the cases in this section, the defendant has played a role in creating the risk that harmed the plaintiff. Nevertheless, for specific policy reasons thought to be important, courts sometimes determine that no duty exists, thereby withdrawing the possibility of the defendant being held liable for the harm, even if negligent. Courts properly do this, according to the Third Restatement, when they articulate "categorical, bright-line rules of law applicable to a general class of cases." Restatement (Third) Torts: Liability for Physical and Emotional Harm § 7(b) cmt. a (2010). For example, courts might decide that the burden on First Amendment principles of free speech would be too great if movie producers could be held liable when a movie influenced someone to commit a "copycat" assault, rape, or killing. See, e.g., James v. Meow Media, Inc., 300 F.3d 683 (6th Cir.2002).

Strauss v. Belle Realty Co.

Court of Appeals of New York, 1985.
65 N.Y.2d 399, 482 N.E.2d 34, 492 N.Y.S.2d 555.

■ KAYE, JUDGE.

On July 13, 1977, a failure of defendant Consolidated Edison's power system left most of New York City in darkness. In this action for damages allegedly resulting from the power failure, we are asked to determine whether Con Edison owed a duty of care to a tenant who suffered personal injuries in a common area of an apartment building, where his landlord—but not he—had a contractual relationship with the utility. We conclude that in the case of a blackout of a metropolis of several million residents and visitors, each in some manner necessarily affected by a 25-hour power failure, liability for injuries in a building's common areas should, as a matter of public policy, be limited by the contractual relationship.

This court has twice before confronted legal questions concerning the 1977 blackout—see, Koch v. Consolidated Edison Co., [468 N.E.2d 1 (N.Y.1984)]; Food Pageant v. Consolidated Edison Co., [429 N.E.2d 738 (N.Y.1981)].

Plaintiff, Julius Strauss, then 77 years old, resided in an apartment building in Queens. Con Edison provided electricity to his apartment pursuant to agreement with him, and to the common areas of the building under a separate agreement with his landlord, defendant Belle Realty Company. As water to the apartment was supplied by electric pump, plaintiff had no running water for the duration of the blackout. Consequently, on the second day of the power failure, he set out for the basement to obtain water, but fell on the darkened, defective basement stairs, sustaining injuries. In this action against Belle Realty and Con Edison, plaintiff alleged negligence against the landlord, in failing to maintain the stairs or warn of their dangerous condition, and negligence against the utility in the performance of its duty to provide electricity.

Plaintiff moved for partial summary judgment against Con Edison (1) to estop it from contesting the charge of gross negligence in connection with the blackout, and (2) to establish that Con Edison owed a duty of care to plaintiff. He argued that Con Edison . . . owed plaintiff a duty even though he was "not a customer of Consolidated Edison in a place where the accident occurred." Con Edison cross-moved for summary judgment dismissing the complaint, maintaining it had no duty to a noncustomer.

The court granted the motion insofar as it sought collateral estoppel regarding gross negligence,[1] and denied Con Edison's cross motion to dismiss the complaint, finding a question of fact as to whether it owed plaintiff a duty of care. The Appellate Division reversed and dismissed the complaint against Con Edison. Citing *Moch Co. v. Rensselaer Water Co.* [p. 173 infra], the plurality concluded that "Con Ed did not owe a duty to plaintiff in any compensable legal sense" [ ]. Justice Gibbons dissented, finding extension of the duty tolerable here because "[t]he tenants of the building in question constitute a defined, limited and known group of people" [ ]. On public policy grounds, we now affirm the Appellate Division order dismissing the complaint against Con Edison.

A defendant may be held liable for negligence only when it breaches a duty owed to the plaintiff—Pulka v. Edelman, [358 N.E.2d 1019 (N.Y.1976)]. The essential question here is whether Con Edison owed a duty to plaintiff, whose injuries from a fall on a darkened staircase may have conceivably been foreseeable, but with whom there was no contractual relationship for lighting in the building's common areas.

Duty in negligence cases is defined neither by foreseeability of injury [ ] nor by privity of contract. As this court has long recognized, an obligation rooted in contract may engender a duty owed to those not in privity, for "[t]here is nothing anomalous in a rule which imposes upon A, who has contracted with B, a duty to C and D and others according as he knows or does not know that the subject-matter of the contract is intended for their use" (*MacPherson v. Buick Motor Co.*, [ ]). In Fish v. Waverly Elec. Light & Power Co., [82 N.E. 150 (N.Y.1907)], for example, an electric company which had contracted with the plaintiff's employer to install ceiling lights had a duty to the plaintiff to exercise reasonable care. And in Glanzer v. Shepard, [135 N.E. 275 (N.Y.1922)], a public

---

[1]   The collateral estoppel question was decided against Con Edison in [*Koch*].

weigher, hired by a seller of beans to certify the weight of a particular shipment, was found liable in negligence to the buyer. [ ]

But while the absence of privity does not foreclose recognition of a duty, it is still the responsibility of courts, in fixing the orbit of duty, "to limit the legal consequences of wrongs to a controllable degree" [ ], and to protect against crushing exposure to liability [ ]. "In fixing the bounds of that duty, not only logic and science, but policy play an important role" [ ]. The courts' definition of an orbit of duty based on public policy may at times result in the exclusion of some who might otherwise have recovered for losses or injuries if traditional tort principles had been applied.

Considerations of privity are not entirely irrelevant in implementing policy. Indeed, in determining the liability of utilities for consequential damages for failure to provide service—a liability which could obviously be "enormous," and has been described as *sui generis*," rather than strictly governed by tort or contract law principles—see, Prosser and Keeton, Torts § 92, at 663 [5th ed.]—courts have declined to extend the duty of care to noncustomers. For example, in *Moch Co. v. Rensselaer Water Co.*, [ ], a water works company contracted with the City of Rensselaer to satisfy its water requirements. Plaintiff's warehouse burned and plaintiff brought an action against the water company in part based on its alleged negligence in failing to supply sufficient water pressure to the city's hydrants. The court denied recovery, concluding that the proposed enlargement of the zone of duty would unduly extend liability. Similarly, in Beck v. FMC Corp., [369 N.E.2d 10 (N.Y.1977)], *affg.* [385 N.Y.S.2d 956 (App.Div.1976)], an explosion interrupted a utility's electrical service, which in turn resulted in the loss of a day's pay for hourly workers at a nearby automobile plant. In an action brought by the workers, the court denied recovery on the basis of controlling the unwarranted extension of liability [ ].

Moch involved ordinary negligence, while Con Edison was guilty of gross negligence, but the cases cannot be distinguished on that basis. In reserving the question of what remedy would lie in the case of "reckless and wanton indifference to consequences measured and foreseen," the court in *Moch* contemplated a level of misconduct greater than the gross negligence involved here [ ]. The court in [*Food Pageant v. Consolidated Edison Co.*], in upholding the jury's verdict against Con Edison, noted as instances of Con Edison's misconduct its employee's failure to follow instructions to reduce voltage by "shedding load" after lightning had hit the electrical system, and its staffing decisions [ ]. Though found by the jury to constitute gross negligence, this behavior was not so consciously culpable as to fall into the category of conduct contemplated as "reckless and wanton" by the court in *Moch* [ ].

In the view of the Appellate Division dissenter, *Moch* does not control because the injuries here were foreseeable and plaintiff was a member of a specific, limited, circumscribed class with a close relationship with Con Edison. The situation was thought to be akin to White v. Guarente, [372 N.E.2d 315 (N.Y.1977)], where an accounting firm was retained by a limited partnership to perform an audit and prepare its tax returns. As the court noted there, the parties to the agreement contemplated that individual limited partners would rely on the tax returns and audit. Refusing to dismiss a negligence action brought by a limited partner against the accounting firm, the court said, "the services of the accountant were not extended to a faceless or unresolved class of persons, but rather to a known group possessed of vested rights, marked by a definable limit and made up of certain components"; see also, [*Glanzer v. Shepard*].

Central to these decisions was an ability to extend the defendant's duty to cover specifically foreseeable parties but at the same time to contain liability to manageable levels. In *White,* for instance, liability stemmed from a single isolated transaction where the parties to the agreement contemplated the protection of identified individuals. Here, insofar as revealed by the record, the arrangement between Con Edison and Belle Realty was no different from those existing between Con Edison and the millions of other customers it serves.... When plaintiff's relationship with Con Edison is viewed from this perspective, it is no answer to say that a duty is owed because, as a tenant in an apartment building, plaintiff belongs to a narrowly defined class.[2]

Additionally, we deal here with a system-wide power failure occasioned by what has already been determined to be the utility's gross negligence. If liability could be found here, then in logic and fairness the same result must follow in many similar situations. For example, a tenant's guests and invitees, as well as persons making deliveries or repairing equipment in the building, are equally persons who must use the common areas, and for whom they are maintained. Customers of a store and occupants of an office building stand in much the same position with respect to Con Edison as tenants of an apartment building. In all cases the numbers are to a certain extent limited and defined, and while identities may change, so do those of apartment dwellers (compare, *White v. Guarente*, [ ] ["situation did not involve prospective limited partners, unknown at the time"]). While limiting recovery to customers in this instance can hardly be said to confer immunity from negligence on Con Edison (see, [*Koch*]) permitting recovery to those in plaintiff's circumstances would, in our view, violate

---

[2] In deciding that public policy precludes liability to a noncustomer injured in the common areas of an apartment building, we need not decide whether recovery would necessarily also be precluded where a person injured in the home is not the family bill payer but the spouse. In another context, where this court has defined the duty of a public accounting firm for negligent financial statements, we have recognized that the duty runs both to those in contractual privity with the accountant and to those whose bond is so close as to be, in practical effect, indistinguishable from privity, and we have on public policy grounds precluded wider liability to persons damaged by the accountant's negligence. (See, Credit Alliance Corp. v. Arthur Andersen & Co., 65 N.Y.2d 536 [1985].)

the court's responsibility to define an orbit of duty that places controllable limits on liability.

. . .

In sum, Con Edison is not answerable to the tenant of an apartment building injured in a common area as a result of Con Edison's negligent failure to provide electric service as required by its agreement with the building owner. Accordingly, the order of the Appellate Division should be affirmed, with costs.

■ MEYER, JUDGE (dissenting).

My disagreement with the majority results not from its consideration of public policy as a factor in determining the scope of Con Ed's duty, but from the fact that in reaching its public policy conclusion it has considered only one side of the equation and based its conclusion on nothing more than assumption. I, therefore, respectfully dissent.

. . .

The majority's blind acceptance of the notion that Consolidated Edison will be crushed if held liable to the present plaintiff and others like him ignores the possibility that through application to the Public Service Commission Con Ed can seek such reduction of the return on stockholders' equity [ ] or increase in its rates, or both, as may be necessary to pay the judgments obtained against it. It ignores as well the burden imposed upon the persons physically injured by Con Ed's gross negligence or, as to those forced to seek welfare assistance because their savings have been wiped out by the injury, the State. Doing so in the name of public policy seems particularly perverse, for what it says, in essence, is the more persons injured through a tort-feasor's gross negligence, the less the responsibility for injuries incurred.

. . . There simply is no basis other than the majority's say so for its assumptions [ ], that the impact of a city-wide deprivation of electric power upon the utility is entitled to greater consideration than the impact upon those injured; that a rational boundary cannot be fixed that will include some (apartment tenants injured in common areas, for example), if not all of the injured; that the consequence of imposing some bystander liability will be more adverse to societal interests than will follow from blindly limiting liability for tort to those with whom the tort-feasor has a contractual relationship. Before we grant Con Ed's motion to dismiss, therefore, we should require that a rational basis for such assumptions be established.

Con Ed may well be able to do so, but before its motion is granted at the expense of an unknown number of victims who have suffered injuries the extent and effects of which are also unknown, it should be required to establish that the catastrophic probabilities are great enough to warrant the limitation of duty it seeks [ ].

I would, therefore, deny the summary judgment motions of both sides and remit to Supreme Court for determination of the preliminary fact issues involved.

■ CHIEF JUDGE WACHTLER and JUDGES SIMONS, ALEXANDER and TITONE concur with JUDGE KAYE; JUDGE MEYER dissents and votes to reverse in a separate opinion in which JUDGE JASEN concurs.

NOTES AND QUESTIONS

1.   What are the public policy grounds on which the court concludes that Consolidated Edison owed Strauss no duty?

2.   Presumably if, during the blackout, Strauss had fallen, without fault on his part, in a personal residence that he owned, he would have been able to collect as a ratepayer of Con Edison. Is the *Belle Realty* result nonetheless a substantial assurance against crushing liability?

3.   What does the court mean in its statement that "duty . . . is defined neither by foreseeability of injury nor by privity of contract?" Is the court minimizing the importance of foreseeability or instead emphasizing that foreseeability alone is not sufficient for a tort duty? Compare the discussion of foreseeability in *Randi W.*, p. 141 supra and *Tarasoff*, p. 150 supra?

4.   Public Service Commission approval of Con Edison's rate schedule included a proviso that the utility would be liable only for "willful misconduct or gross negligence." See the discussion in *Food Pageant v. Consolidated Edison Co.*, cited in the principal case, involving an action by a grocery chain for food spoilage and loss of business due to the blackout. Why was this limitation alone not a sufficient concession to the court's concern about crushing liability?

5.   Does the dissent persuasively deal with the majority's concern about crushing liability?

6.   In Palka v. Servicemaster Management Services Corp., 634 N.E.2d 189 (N.Y.1994), plaintiff nurse was hurt when a wall-mounted fan in a patient's room fell. Defendant had contracted with the hospital to perform all maintenance functions. The defendant argued that its only duty was owed to the hospital with which it had contracted. The court disagreed. The unanimous court rejected "an open-ended range of tort duty arising out of contractual breaches." To find a duty, the relationship between the defendant's contract obligation and the "injured noncontracting party's reliance and injury must be direct and demonstrable, not incidental or merely collateral [citing *Strauss* and other cases]."

Here, the functions to be performed by Servicemaster were not directed to a faceless or unlimited universe of persons. Rather, a known and identifiable group—hospital employees, patients and visitors—was to benefit and be protected by safety maintenance protocols assumed and acquired exclusively by Servicemaster. It cannot reasonably claim that it was unaware or that it was entitled to be unaware that individuals would expect some entity's

[handwritten margin note: limited group]

direct responsibility to perform maintenance services with ordinary prudence and care. [ ] In fact, the very "end and aim" of the service contract was that Servicemaster was to become the sole privatized provider for a safe and clean hospital premises [ ].

How is *Strauss* different?

7.   *"Take home" asbestos cases.* Courts have confronted "take home" asbestos cases, in which an employee who works with asbestos brings home asbestos fibers on her clothes, thereby exposing other family members to those fibers. These cases are especially tragic, as the most serious disease from asbestos exposure—mesothelioma, an almost invariably fatal form of cancer—requires only a modest dose of exposure to fibers. The cases involve a variety of defendants, including asbestos product manufacturers and property owners, and have reached different results on diverse grounds. In one case, In re New York City Asbestos Litigation, 840 N.E.2d 115 (N.Y.2005), plaintiff spouse sued her husband's employer, the Port Authority, which owned buildings where the husband was exposed to asbestos. Invoking concern about "limitless liability to an indeterminate class of persons" and observing that the experience with asbestos is that new claims, such as these secondhand exposure claims, can rarely be confined, the unanimous court held that defendant owed no duty to the plaintiff, either in its capacity as employer of plaintiff's husband or as a landowner in control of the premises at which asbestos products were used. The court stated that as employer, the defendant would be dependent on its employee's taking risk-reduction efforts, and the court found no basis for imposing a duty to control a third party. No duty existed as landowner because the Port Authority did not discharge asbestos into the environment, as in a prior case; rather it failed to warn its employee of the risk posed to his spouse.

By contrast with the New York Court of Appeals, the New Jersey Supreme Court had little difficulty finding that a refinery owed a duty to the spouse of a welder who was exposed to asbestos at the defendant's refinery between 1947 and 1984, concluding defendant "was aware by 1937 that exposure, of sufficient duration and intensity, to asbestos dust or raw asbestos was associated with asbestosis." Olivo v. Owens-Illinois, Inc., 895 A.2d 1143 (N.J.2006). Relying on the foreseeability of harm to the spouse, the court brushed aside the "limitless liability" concern that weighed heavily with the New York court. Unlike *Olivo*, in Georgia Pacific, LLC v. Farrar, 69 A.3d 1028 (Md.2013), the Maryland Court of Appeals found the risk of harm to plaintiff from her grandfather's exposure to asbestos in the mid-1960s to be unforeseeable and hence defendant owed no duty to the plaintiff. For an assessment of the conflicting state court decisions addressing duty to "take-home" plaintiffs, see Flinn, Note, Continuing War with Asbestos: The Stalemate Among State Courts on Liability for Take-Home Asbestos Exposure, 71 Wash. & Lee L.Rev. 707 (2014).

The Moch *Case*

In H.R. Moch Co. v. Rensselaer Water Co., 159 N.E. 896 (N.Y.1928), discussed in *Strauss*, defendant water works had a contract with the City of Rensselaer to supply water for various purposes, including service at fire hydrants. A building caught fire and the flames spread to plaintiff's warehouse, destroying it. Plaintiff alleged that the water company's failure to supply adequate water permitted the spread of the fire to the warehouse. The court of appeals, in an opinion by Judge Cardozo, held that the complaint should be dismissed. Among other grounds discussed, Cardozo held that there was no common law tort action available to users of the water supplied to the city:

"It is ancient learning that one who assumes to act, even though gratuitously, may thereby become subject to the duty of acting carefully, if he acts at all" (Glanzer v. Shepard, [135 N.E. 275 (N.Y.1922)]; [ ]). The plaintiff would bring its case within the orbit of that principle. The hand once set to a task may not always be withdrawn with impunity though liability would fail if it had never been applied at all. A time-honored formula often phrases the distinction as one between misfeasance and nonfeasance. Incomplete the formula is, and so at times misleading. Given a relation involving in its existence a duty of care irrespective of a contract, a tort may result as well from acts of omission as of commission in the fulfillment of the duty thus recognized by law [ ]. What we need to know is not so much the conduct to be avoided when the relation and its attendant duty are established as existing. What we need to know is the conduct that engenders the relation. It is here that the formula, however incomplete, has its value and significance. If conduct has gone forward to such a stage that inaction would commonly result, not negatively merely in withholding a benefit, but positively or actively in working an injury, there exists a relation out of which arises a duty to go forward (Bohlen, Studies in the Law of Torts, p. 87). So the surgeon who operates without pay, is liable though his negligence is in the omission to sterilize his instruments (cf. *Glanzer v. Shepard*, supra); the engineer, though his fault is in the failure to shut off steam [ ]; the maker of automobiles, at the suit of someone other than the buyer, though his negligence is merely in inadequate inspection (*MacPherson v. Buick Motor Co.*, [ ]). The query always is whether the putative wrongdoer has advanced to such a point as to have launched a force or instrument of harm, or has stopped where inaction is at most a refusal to become an instrument for good [ ].

The plaintiff would have us hold that the defendant, when once it entered upon the performance of its contract with the city, was brought into such a relation with everyone who might potentially be benefited through the supply of water at the hydrants as to give to negligent performance, without reasonable notice of a refusal to continue, the quality of a tort. . . . We are satisfied that liability would be unduly and indeed indefinitely extended by this enlargement of the zone of duty. . . . What we are dealing with at this time is a mere negligent omission, unaccompanied by malice or other aggravating elements. The failure in such circumstances to furnish an adequate supply of water is at most the denial of a benefit. It is not the commission of a wrong.

How is *Moch* different from the cited examples of the negligent surgeon and the engineer? Note Cardozo's conclusion that the defendant's behavior was "at most the denial of a benefit. It is not the commission of a wrong." How is the distinction between misfeasance and nonfeasance being used here? Is there a danger that the result in *Moch* will reduce incentives toward safety?

Your house catches on fire. Your neighbor, who has a swimming pool with a pump to allow the water to be drawn from the pool to fight fires, refuses to allow you to use any of that water to fight your fire. Is this like *Moch*?

Is there a relationship between the misfeasance-nonfeasance point and the existence of the contractual relationship with the city? Is the existence of the contract relevant to the question of whether the defendant has denied a benefit or committed a wrong? Does the existence of the contract help or hurt the plaintiff's case?

Noting that only four states then allowed recovery against water companies in fire cases, Libbey v. Hampton Water Works Co., 389 A.2d 434 (N.H.1978), adopted the majority view of *Moch*. Among other reasons, the court noted that water companies do not charge higher rates in areas of high fire risk. If they did, "water would no longer be a cheap, easily procurable commodity. In areas of high risk, water could become prohibitively expensive." Is *Moch* better explained by policy considerations under the approach of *Strauss* than the no-undertaking rationale offered by Judge Cardozo? Is it a stronger or weaker case for no duty than *Strauss*?

Moch has not fared well more recently. In Clay Electric Cooperative, Inc. v. Johnson, 873 So.2d 1182 (Fla.2003), the court held that a utility under contract to a city to maintain street lights might owe a duty to a pedestrian who was run down in an area that was darkened due to the utility's negligence in maintaining street lights. The court relied on the "undertaking" rule discussed at note 1b, p. 133 supra. *Moch* was rejected as being decided before the undertaking doctrine became established and for failing to recognize the distinction between installing a system and maintaining it. See also Louisville Gas and Electric Co. v. Roberson, 212 S.W.3d 107 (Ky.2006)(relying on the undertaking doctrine to impose a duty on utility that contracted to maintain street lights).

Reynolds v. Hicks

Supreme Court of Washington, 1998.
134 Wash.2d 491, 951 P.2d 761.

■ MADSEN, JUSTICE.

Plaintiffs appeal a trial court decision dismissing their personal injury action on summary judgment against the Defendants. At issue is whether the Defendant social hosts who furnished alcohol to a minor owe a duty of care to third persons injured by the intoxicated minor. We affirm the trial court's dismissal finding that the Defendant social hosts owed no duty to third persons injured by the intoxicated minor.

Jamie and Anna Hicks were married on September 10, 1988, at St. Bernadette Church in Seattle. Three hundred people attended the wedding, including Jamie Hicks' under-age nephew, Steven Hicks. The wedding was followed by a dinner reception where wine and champagne were served. After dinner, drinks were available at a hosted bar.

[A jury could have found that Steven Hicks consumed alcohol at the reception, despite claims that the bar was "hosted at all times." At approximately midnight, Steven Hicks left the reception in his sister Dianne's car. At 1:00 a.m. he was involved in an automobile accident with the plaintiff Reynolds. Reynolds and his family alleged that Jamie and Anna Hicks were "negligent in serving alcoholic beverages to Defendant [Steven] with knowledge and/or reason to believe that [he] was below the age of 21 years and/or became intoxicated." Plaintiffs settled with Steven and Dianne Hicks. Defendants sought summary judgment arguing, among other claims, that "Washington law does not extend social host liability for furnishing alcohol to a minor to third persons injured by the intoxicated minor." The superior court granted the motion and the court of appeals certified the case directly to the supreme court.]

Plaintiffs contend that RCW 66.44.270 creates a duty of care owed by the Defendants to the Plaintiffs. RCW 66.44.270(1) makes it unlawful for any person [except a parent] to

> give, or otherwise supply liquor to any person under the age of twenty-one years or permit any person under that age to consume liquor on his or her premises or on any premises under his or her control. [Other sections exempt medicinal and religious uses.]

. . .

In Hansen v. Friend, [824 P.2d 483 (Wash.1992)], this court recognized that a minor who is injured as a result of alcohol intoxication has a cause of action against the social host who supplied the alcohol based on RCW 66.44.270. [ ] Plaintiffs ask this court to extend the ruling of *Hansen* to allow a cause of action for third persons who are injured by an intoxicated minor against the social host. We find that such an expansion is not warranted by the statute or Washington case law.

. . .

Because of the inherent differences between social hosts and commercial vendors, we have indicated our reluctance to allow a cause of action against a social host to the same extent that we have recognized commercial vendor liability. We have explained:

> There is good reason to withhold common law liability for social hosts even though such liability already exists for commercial and quasi-commercial hosts. Social hosts are not as capable of handling the responsibilities of monitoring their guests' alcohol consumption as are their commercial and quasi-commercial counterparts. . . .
>
> [T]he commercial proprietor has a proprietary interest and profit motive, and should be expected to exercise greater supervision than in the (non-commercial) social setting. Moreover, a person in the business of selling and serving alcohol is usually better organized to control patrons, and has the financial wherewithal to do so. . . .

Additionally, the implications of social host liability are so much more wide sweeping and unpredictable in nature than are the implications of commercial host liability. While liability for commercial providers affects only a narrow slice of our populations, social host liability would touch most adults in the state on a frequent basis. Because social hosts are generally unaccustomed to the pressures involved in taking responsibility for the intoxication of their guests, we cannot predict how well social hosts would respond when the scope of their duties would be so ill defined.

Burkhart v. Harrod, [755 P.2d 759 (Wash.1988)].

Because of these important concerns, this court does not recognize a cause of action in negligence for a third person injured by an intoxicated adult against the social host that served the person while in an obviously intoxicated state, [ ], but does recognize a cause of action against a commercial vendor in the same situation, [ ]. This case dramatically highlights the concerns expressed above. To expect Jamie and Anna Hicks, on their wedding day, to monitor their minor guests' alcohol consumption in the same manner as we expect of an alcohol vendor is unrealistic and has far reaching social implications.

Recognizing an expanded duty to protect third persons raises problematic questions for social hosts in all contexts. Is the host required to card persons at social and family gatherings? Must the host hire a bartender to control and monitor the alcohol in the home so that a minor cannot obtain alcohol at a party? Must the host assure that a minor has not brought outside alcohol to the gathering? Must the host obtain a breathalyzer to check all minor guests before leaving the premises? The differences between the ability of commercial vendors and social hosts in regulating the consumption of alcohol along with the far-reaching implications of social host liability are persuasive reasons for not expanding liability in this case. As Justice Dolliver noted in his dissent in *Hansen*, the " 'judiciary is ill equipped' to impose social host liability." [ ]

[The court discussed two decisions of the court of appeals.]

We agree with the Court of Appeals that the exceptions to liability in RCW 66.44.270 lend weight to the argument that the statute was not enacted to protect third persons. . . . Because the statute allows a parent or guardian to legally give alcohol to a minor who may then injure a third person it is apparent that the statute was not enacted to protect third persons injured by intoxicated minors. . . .

. . .

In conclusion, we decline to extend social host liability to third persons injured by intoxicated minors. We have long recognized that social hosts are ill-equipped to handle the responsibilities of their guests' alcohol consumption, unlike commercial vendors who are in the business of serving and selling alcohol. Thus, we have not allowed a cause of action against social hosts to the extent that we have recognized commercial vendor liability. Washington courts have also recognized that RCW 66.44.270 does not protect third persons injured by an intoxicated minor but, rather, protects minors from their own injuries as a result of their intoxication. We agree and affirm the trial court's dismissal of the Plaintiff's cause of action.

■ GUY and ALEXANDER, JJ., concur.

■ DURHAM, CHIEF JUSTICE, concurring.

I agree with the majority that the Defendants, as social host, should not be liable for injuries to third parties caused by an intoxicated minor guest. I am not persuaded, however, by the majority's suggestion that the parental exception to the otherwise criminal prohibition against furnishing alcohol to minors somehow indicates that third parties are not within the statutory protected class. Instead, I would hold that the Defendants are not liable for the reasons expressed in the dissent in Hansen v. Friend, [824 P.2d 483 (Wash.1992)] (Dolliver, J., dissenting).

■ DOLLIVER and SANDERS, JJ., concur.

■ JOHNSON, JUSTICE, dissenting.

The majority holds a social host who furnishes alcohol to a minor, in violation of a criminal statute, does not owe a duty of care to third persons injured by that intoxicated minor. I disagree with the majority's shielding from possible civil liability persons who commit a criminal act. I also disagree with the majority's analysis, which confuses the issues of duty and ultimate liability. For these reasons, I respectfully dissent.

This court has clearly recognized where the Legislature has made it a criminal offense to furnish alcohol to a minor, that minor has a civil cause of action. [*Hansen*] This court has also clearly recognized where the Legislature has made it a criminal offense to sell alcohol to a minor, third parties foreseeably injured by that minor have a civil cause of action. [ ] The majority draws an insupportable distinction between social hosts and commercial vendors by ignoring that both are committing criminal acts when they furnish alcohol to a minor. . . .

The Legislature, in criminalizing the act of furnishing or selling alcohol to a minor, has declared that act as the point on which to focus in the causal chain of underage drunk driving. The Legislature has directed us to view the point at which a minor is furnished or sold alcohol as the significant event from which consequences flow. If the minor never obtains the alcohol, the causal chain is stopped.

The majority, however, leaves us with the rule that a person commits a crime by furnishing alcohol to a minor, and yet avoids all civil liability for the consequences of that same act. This contradicts common sense. . . . The list of concerns for social hosts expressed by the majority places more emphasis on the possible difficulties posed for social hosts than on a potential remedy for victims of underage drunk driving. However, it is the social hosts that are in the best position to know the ages of the guest they are serving and to regulate their own conduct so as to avoid committing a crime. Should social hosts have to "card" guests before serving them alcohol? Yes, if that's what it takes. Social hosts already have a responsibility to avoid criminal conduct. Nothing changes regarding the actions necessary to meet this responsibility upon imposition of a duty of care.

Under the majority, we are also left with the strained result of different standards for commercial vendors than for social hosts who furnish alcohol to minors. A vendor owes a duty to third parties, whereas a social host does not. . . . I find no justification exists for applying different standards to vendors than to social hosts who furnish alcohol to minors. Both commit crimes. . . . The source of the alcohol should not dictate whether a remedy is available.

. . .

■ SMITH and TALMADGE, JJ., concur.

NOTES AND QUESTIONS

1.   Why might the statute have exempted parents? Might there be non-safety reasons for this exemption? If so, what are the implications of

the parental exemption for cases in which a third party seeks to recover for statutory violation?

2. If a duty of due care had been imposed in *Reynolds*, how would you analyze the due care question? Would this be a different case if, after they were married, the newlyweds invited Steven and his sister, Dianne, over to their apartment for the evening and the four drank tequila into the early morning when Jamie handed the keys to Dianne's car to Steven, remarking, "I assume you're going to drive, you've only had a dozen shots to Dianne's 20"? In Marcum v. Bowden, 643 S.E.2d 85 (S.C.2007), the court adopted a duty not to knowingly and intentionally serve alcohol to someone under 21, and that those who did so would be subject to liability to all who were injured as a result. Does *Marcum* respond to the concerns that led the *Reynolds* court to a no-duty rule?

3. In a handful of states in which courts found a duty on the part of a social host to a person hurt by the drinker, the legislatures have quickly reinstated either complete immunity (plus more in California) or granted the social host very strong protection (e.g., New Jersey). Another handful of states impose social host liability for serving adults, and a few more for serving minors. See Raymond, Jr., Social Host's Liability for Injuries Incurred by Third Parties as a Result of Intoxicated Guest's Negligence, 62 A.L.R.4th 16.

4. In Gilger v. Hernandez, 997 P.2d 305 (Utah 2000), the court refused to impose a duty on a social host to protect guests from another guest who had become drunk at a party on the premises. First, the court found no social host liability because the state's dram shop act was the exclusive source of duty with regard to serving alcohol. Second, with regard to any "special relationship," the court understood that "[r]equiring a social host either to control a belligerent guest or to protect her guests from the threat of injury by another guest would impose a duty 'that is realistically incapable of performance' in the usual circumstances." There was no element of dependency and the other guests were able to protect themselves. A duty did arise, however, after the guest was injured. Does this case follow readily from the principal case?

5. Does a person who agrees to act as a designated driver have a duty to third persons? Yes, qualifiedly, concluded the court in White v. Sabatino, 415 F.Supp.2d 1163 (D.Haw.2006). The qualification is that a duty arising from the undertaking exists only if performance begins. Thus, a broken promise to serve as a designated driver cannot be the basis for a duty. (The issue of whether a bare promise, without any further action, is sufficient for an undertaking has long been a matter of controversy, although it appears the modern view is that it can be. See Restatement (Third) Torts: Liability for Physical and Emotional Harm § 42 cmt. e (2010).) Should it matter that the promise to serve as a designated driver was made to someone other than the third-party victim?

6. *Dram shop acts*. Most states have enacted dram shop acts that impose liability on commercial enterprises for harm resulting from intoxication when they serve a person to the point of intoxication or serve an already intoxicated person. There is considerable variation among those statutes on questions such as the trigger for liability and the causation requirement. See generally J. Mosher, Liquor Liability Law (1987). The Georgia statute, for example, requires not only intoxication but also knowledge by the dram shop that the "person will soon be driving a motor vehicle" Ga. Code Ann. § 51–1–40(b). Thus in Delta Airlines, Inc. v. Townsend, 614 S.E.2d 745 (Ga.2005), the court held that an airline that served a passenger until he was intoxicated was not liable under the dram shop act to a third person injured by the passenger while driving home. Although the airline knew the passenger would disembark from the plane, it did not know whether that passenger was going on to a connecting flight, taking public transportation, or driving.

Should dram shop principles apply to alcohol served at a sports stadium? A 2005 trial highlights this question. A New Jersey jury awarded a total of $110 million (including $75 million in punitive damages) to the family of a two-year-old child who was rendered a quadriplegic and required a ventilator to breathe due to an accident caused by a drunk driver. The driver had just departed a football game at Giants Stadium and had a blood alcohol level 2½ times the legal limit from consuming the equivalent of 16 beers, most of them during the game. The award was against the concessionaire who served him while he was intoxicated—the driver was sentenced to a five-year prison term—and the NFL commented that this was a "wakeup call" for NFL football teams. Tom Fitzgerald, *A Sobering Reality for NFL Concessionaires*, San Francisco Chron., Sept. 25, 2005, at D3. On appeal, the verdict was vacated and a new trial ordered because of the erroneous admission of evidence of a "culture of intoxication" at the stadium. The case subsequently settled for $25 million. Mark Mueller, *Paralyzed Girl and Mom Get $25m Settlement from Beer Vendor*, The Star-Ledger (Newark, N.J.), Dec. 4, 2008, at 13. See generally Diamantopoulos, Note, A Look at Social Host and Dram Shop Liability from Pre-Game Tailgating to Post-Game Barhopping, 4 DePaul J. Sports L. & Contemp.Probs. 201 (2008).

7.   In a variety of other contexts, courts invoke public-policy reasons for limiting duty. See, e.g., Yost v. Wabash College, 3 N.E.3d 509 (Ind.2014)(rejecting claim by plaintiff, a fraternity pledge injured in a hazing incident, that his college owed him a duty of care based on its policy against fraternity hazing in part because the court believed that "colleges and universities should be encouraged, not disincentivized, to undertake robust programs to discourage hazing and substance abuse"); MacGregor v. Walker, 322 P.3d 706 (Utah 2014)(rejecting claim by abuse victim that she was owed a duty by defendant church pursuant to its provision of a Help Line as "a service intended to assist its ecclesiastical leaders in counseling abuse victims" because to "hold that the creation of such policies and programs gives rise to a duty under tort law would discourage organizations from creating these beneficial programs"). See generally Geistfeld, Social Value as a Policy-Based Limitation of the Ordinary Duty to Exercise Reasonable Care, 44 Wake Forest L.Rev. 899 (2009)(arguing that it is appropriate for courts to reject or limit a duty if the safety benefits

of the proposed duty for the relevant category of cases are outweighed by the reduction in socially valuable conduct across these cases).

Vince v. Wilson

Supreme Court of Vermont, 1989.
151 Vt. 425, 561 A.2d 103.

■ Before ALLEN, C.J., and PECK, GIBSON, DOOLEY and MAHADY, JJ.

■ MAHADY, JUSTICE.

This personal injury action requires us to further refine our definition of the tort of negligent entrustment. Plaintiff, seriously injured in an automobile accident, brought suit against defendant Wilson, who had provided funding for her grandnephew, the driver of the car in which plaintiff was a passenger at the time of the accident, to purchase the vehicle. Subsequently Ace Auto Sales, Inc. and its president Gary Gardner were added as defendants. Ace sold the vehicle to the driver; Gardner was the salesman of the vehicle.

At the close of plaintiff's case, the trial court directed verdicts in favor of defendants Ace and Gardner. Plaintiff appeals from this ruling. The claim against Wilson, on the other hand, was submitted to the jury, which returned a substantial verdict in favor of plaintiff. Wilson appeals from the judgment entered against her on the jury verdict. For the reasons stated below, we hold that the trial court erred in directing verdicts in favor of Ace and Gardner. As to the judgment against Wilson, we affirm the court's decision to submit the question to the jury, and remand for proceedings consistent with this opinion.

I

The tort of negligent entrustment has long been recognized in Vermont. [ ] In Dicranian v. Foster, [45 A.2d 650 (Vt.1946)], we noted that such "liability . . . arises out of the combined negligence of both, the negligence of one in entrusting the automobile to an incompetent driver and of the other in its operation." [ ]

Plaintiff argues that the rule should be applied to a person who knowingly provides funding to an incompetent driver to purchase a vehicle and to a person who knowingly sells a vehicle to an incompetent driver. We have not previously had an opportunity to address this issue. In [an earlier case], the defendant negligently entrusted a firearm and ammunition to his child, who negligently discharged the firearm resulting in the death of the plaintiff's intestate. In *Dicranian,* the defendant negligently entrusted his motor vehicle to an incompetent operator whose negligent operation of the vehicle caused injury to the plaintiff.

Defendants urge us to follow those courts which have limited recovery under a claim of negligent entrustment to situations where the defendant "is the owner or has the right to control" the instrumentality entrusted. [ ] These courts have denied liability where a father sold a car to his son who was known to have a drinking problem but not a driver's license, [ ]; where a vehicle was given to an incompetent operator, [ ]; or where a bailee automobile dealer returned an automobile after repair to its obviously intoxicated owner, [ ].

Other courts have applied the rule more broadly. For example, courts have allowed recovery against an automobile dealer who sold a vehicle to an inexperienced and incompetent driver whose driving injured several people when the seller knew or should have known of the incompetency. [ ] These courts hold that the fact that a defendant had ownership and control over the instrumentality at the time it was turned over to an incompetent individual is sufficient. [ ] Thus, a father was held liable for funding the purchase of an automobile by a son whom the father knew to be an irresponsible driver, [ ], and a complaint against a father who purchased a vehicle for his epileptic son was held to state a cause of action. Golembe v. Blumberg, [27 N.Y.S.2d 692 (App.Div.1941)].

Both lines of cases derive their rule from the Restatement of Torts, which provides:

> One who supplies directly or through a third person a chattel for the use of another whom the supplier knows or has reason to know to be likely because of his youth, inexperience, or otherwise, to use it in a manner involving unreasonable risk of physical harm to himself and others whom the supplier should expect to share in or be endangered by its use, is subject to liability for physical harm resulting to them.

Restatement (Second) of Torts § 390 (1965). The comments to the Restatement support those decisions which extend the rule to individuals such as sellers:

> The rule stated applies to anyone who supplies a chattel for the use of another. It applies to sellers, lessors, donors or lenders, and to all kinds of bailors, irrespective of whether the bailment is gratuitous or for a consideration.

Id., comment *a*.

The cases noted above which restrict the rule to situations where the defendant is the owner or has the right to control the instrumentality have been severely criticized. See [law review comments].

Indeed, the leading commentators on the law of torts have said that such decisions "look definitely wrong," explaining:

> It is the negligent entrusting which creates the unreasonable risk; and this is none the less when the goods are conveyed.

Prosser and Keeton on Torts § 104, at 718 (5th ed. 1984). Seen in this light, the issue is clearly one of negligence to be determined by the jury under proper instruction; the relationship of the defendant to the particular instrumentality is but one factor to be considered. The key factor is that "[t]he negligent entrustment theory requires a showing that the entrustor knew or should have known some reason why entrusting the item to another was foolish or negligent." [ ] This approach, based upon traditional negligence analysis, is consistent with our prior decisions. . . .

II.

With regard to plaintiff's claim against defendant Wilson, we must view the evidence in the light most favorable to plaintiff because of the jury's verdict in plaintiff's favor. [ ] With regard to plaintiff's claims against defendants Ace and Gardner, the trial court directed a verdict in favor of the defendants; as such, we must view the evidence in the light most favorable to plaintiff, excluding the effect of any modifying evidence. [ ]

So viewed, the evidence indicates that Wilson knew that the operator for whom she provided funding to purchase the vehicle had no driver's license and had failed the driver's test several times. Indeed, she communicated this fact to defendant Gardner, an agent of defendant Ace, prior to the sale of the vehicle. Defendant Wilson was also aware of the fact that her grandnephew abused alcohol and other drugs. The evidence also tended to show that the operator's inexperience and lack of training contributed to the accident which caused plaintiff's injuries. The evidence was sufficient to make out a prima facie case of negligent entrustment, and the trial court properly submitted the question to the jury.

Verdicts should not have been directed in favor of defendants Ace and Gardner, however. There was evidence which, if believed by the jury, would establish that they knew the operator had no operator's license and that he had failed the driver's test several times. Viewed in the light most favorable to plaintiff, the evidence tends to demonstrate negligence on the part of Ace and Gardner, and the issue should have been determined by the jury. [ ]

. . .

Cause remanded for further proceedings not inconsistent with this opinion [which, for procedural reasons, might include a new trial for Wilson].

NOTES AND QUESTIONS

1.   Are there persuasive arguments supporting the notion that lending should produce a different result from selling? From giving? From providing funds for purchase? (Some states impose vicarious liability on car

owners who lend their cars even to the best of drivers. Why might these states do this? The subject is considered in Chapter XI.)

2.   In Peterson v. Halsted, 829 P.2d 373 (Colo.1992), defendant father co-signed a financial note so that his adult daughter could get financing for a car. She made all the payments. She caused an accident due to her drunk driving—which plaintiffs alleged defendant knew about all along. The court declined to impose a duty on a co-signer. Because of the large number of variables in financing arrangements, the court thought it "unwise and destructive of flexibility of analysis to classify suppliers of money or credit categorically as suppliers of chattels . . . even though the loan or credit may be essential to the borrower in obtaining possession of the chattel." The court then turned to the question of whether the parents had a general common law duty to refrain from helping their daughter get a car because they knew of her drinking problems. The court held that a duty in this case would not "comport with fairness under contemporary standards." The court emphasized that the accident occurred three years after the co-signing.

3.   The *Vince* court suggests that the theory requires the combined negligence of two or more persons. In the case cited by the court in which an adult had entrusted a firearm and ammunition to his child, what if the child had been too young to have behaved negligently? Or if the child was eight years old and acted reasonably for a child that age?

4.   In Osborn v. Hertz Corp., 252 Cal.Rptr. 613 (App.1988), the court rejected the claim that a car rental company had a duty to investigate the driving record of a sober customer who had a valid driver's license before entrusting a car to that customer—who later had an accident while drunk. A search would have shown two prior convictions for drunk driving and one related six-month license suspension. The court cited cases imposing liability for renting a car to a customer who did not hold a valid driver's license.

5.   If an obviously intoxicated person needs assistance in purchasing gasoline, can the seller be subject to liability for assisting in the purchase if the driver subsequently causes an accident and injures someone? In West v. East Tennessee Pioneer Oil Co., 172 S.W.3d 545 (Tenn.2005), the court rejected defendant's claim that a special relationship was required before a duty of reasonable care existed. Defendant owed a duty based on its conduct in assisting the driver in his purchase of gasoline and thereby creating a risk of harm. The court also found that plaintiff's negligent entrustment claim could go forward: it reversed a prior case that required the entruster to retain control and, citing both the Second Restatement and Prosser and Keeton, reached the same conclusion as the *Vince* court that negligent entrustment applied to sales.

6.   *Keys in the ignition.* A related issue occurs when the defendant has permitted a third party to acquire a chattel and cause harm. The most common scenario involves the "key in the ignition" case. A car owner leaves an auto unlocked with the key in the ignition, and a thief takes the opportunity to steal it. The thief negligently runs into the plaintiff causing

injuries for which a claim is brought against the only solvent party, the car owner, alleging negligence in leaving the car vulnerable to theft. In some states courts derive liability from the violation of a statute. Others reject that approach on the ground that the goal of the statute is not safety but the avoidance of time-consuming and expensive police searches for cars and payments by insurers for their loss. Recall note 9, p. 85 supra, involving key-in-the-ignition statutes.

In Palma v. U.S. Industrial Fasteners, Inc., 681 P.2d 893 (Cal.1984), defendant's driver left a truck unlocked overnight with the key in the ignition in a highly dangerous neighborhood. The court reviewed the leading California cases, which require "special circumstances" in order to find a duty owed by car owners to the general public, and then observed:

> Factors which distinguished the conduct in [Hergenrether v. East, 393 P.2d 164 (Cal. 1964)] and were held sufficient to establish a duty, are also present here. They included the area in which the truck had been parked—one frequented by persons who had little respect for the rights of others, and populated by alcoholics; the intent that the truck remain in the location for a relatively long period of time—overnight; the size of the vehicle— rendering it capable of inflicting more serious injury or damage if not properly controlled; and the fact that safe operation of a half-loaded two-ton truck was not a matter of common experience. These factors together led to a conclusion there, as similar factors may here, that a foreseeable risk of harm was posed by the truck left with its keys in the ignition or cab warranting imposition of a duty on the owner or operator to refrain from exposing third persons to the risk.

What rationale would limit the duty to "special circumstances"?

Compare Lucero v. Holbrook, 288 P.3d 1228, 1235 (Wyo.2012). Defendant left her car unattended with the motor running in her private driveway while she briefly returned to her home to retrieve her pocketbook. In the interim, a methamphetamine user stole her vehicle and later got into a high-speed chase with the police. The chase ended when the car he was driving collided with a vehicle driven by plaintiff, the mother of two other plaintiffs. Plaintiffs alleged that defendant breached a duty by leaving her car unattended with the keys in the ignition. In affirming summary judgment for the defendant, the court explained why such a duty would be unreasonably burdensome:

> The appellants argue that the appellee easily could have removed her keys from the ignition before returning to her house and that imposing a duty on the appellee to that extent would not impose a substantial burden. The burden that this factor addresses is not, however, the effortlessness in removing the keys, but rather the burden that will result from imposing a duty not to leave the motor running temporarily in a vehicle parked in one's driveway. It must be remembered that the imposition of a duty not to leave the motor running in a vehicle in one's driveway would apply

across the board, and would create potential liability for every person in Wyoming who, on a cold winter day, starts his or her car to warm it up and defrost the windshield before driving upon the public highways.

Suppose a driver left his keys in the ignition and his motor running on a beautiful spring day while he returned to his house to obtain a hairbrush?

7. Is there any reason to limit the duty to control the actions of third parties to defendants who bear a particularized relationship—such as host or parent—to the dangerous actor? Suppose, instead, that the defendant is responsible for a situation in which dangerous conduct is generally encouraged or facilitated, without reference to any specific risky individual? For a discussion of broader implications, see generally, Rabin, Enabling Torts, 49 DePaul L.Rev. 435 (1999).

In Weirum v. RKO General, Inc., 539 P.2d 36 (Cal.1975), defendant radio station, which commanded the largest teenage audience in the Los Angeles area, conducted a contest in which the driver who reached a peripatetic disk jockey first would win a prize. The disk jockey was traveling freeways of the area and stopping at various spots for short times. The station was broadcasting clues that identified specific or general destinations, such as "The Real Don Steele is back on his feet again with some money and he is headed for the Valley." In their efforts to be the first to reach him when he stopped, two minor drivers in separate vehicles were following the disc jockey on a freeway. During the course of their pursuit, one of the drivers negligently forced a car off the highway killing its driver. In a suit against the station, the court unanimously upheld a plaintiff's judgment.

See also Rice v. Paladin Enterprises, Inc., 128 F.3d 233 (4th Cir.1997), involving murders allegedly accomplished by following defendant publisher's book entitled "Hit Man: A Technical Manual for Independent Contractors." Summary judgment for defendant based on the First Amendment was reversed, and the case was remanded for trial in light of the defendant's stipulation of its knowledge and intent that the book be used to assist criminals in contract murders.

D. THE DUTIES OF LANDOWNERS AND OCCUPIERS

This section deals with duties owed to entrants by those who own, or are in possession of, land for harm arising from conditions on the land. By contrast, different rules may apply when the harm is the result of active operations of the land possessor. Significant reforms have occurred in this area, although there remains a substantial minority of courts that have adhered to traditional rules. Thus, there are two distinct approaches to landowner duties extant today. We begin with the traditional view.

Carter v. Kinney

Supreme Court of Missouri, 1995.
896 S.W.2d 926.

■ ROBERTSON, JUDGE.

. . .

Ronald and Mary Kinney hosted a Bible study at their home for members of the Northwest Bible Church. Appellant Jonathan Carter, a member of the Northwest Bible Church, attended the early morning Bible study at the Kinneys' home on February 3, 1990. Mr. Kinney had shoveled snow from his driveway the previous evening, but was not aware that ice had formed overnight. Mr. Carter arrived shortly after 7:00 a.m., slipped on a patch of ice in the Kinneys' driveway, and broke his leg. The Carters filed suit against the Kinneys.

The parties agree that the Kinneys offered their home for the Bible study as part of a series sponsored by their church; that some Bible studies took place at the church and others were held at the homes of church members; that interested church members signed up for the studies on a sheet at the church, which actively encouraged enrollment but did not solicit contributions through the classes or issue an invitation to the general public to attend the studies; that the Kinneys and the Carters had not engaged in any social interaction outside of church prior to Mr. Carter's injury, and that Mr. Carter had no social relationship with the other participants in the class. Finally, the parties agree that the Kinneys received neither a financial nor other tangible benefit from Mr. Carter in connection with the Bible study class.

They disagree, however, as to Mr. Carter's status. Mr. Carter claims he was an invitee; the Kinneys say he was a licensee. And the parties dispute certain facts bearing on the purpose of his visit, specifically, whether the parties intended a future social relationship, and whether the Kinneys held the Bible study class in order to confer some intangible benefit on themselves and others.

On the basis of these facts, the Kinneys moved for summary judgment. The trial court sustained the Kinneys' summary judgment motion on the ground that Mr. Carter was a licensee and that the Kinneys did not have a duty to a licensee with respect to a dangerous condition of which they had no knowledge. This appeal followed.

. . .

As to premises liability, "the particular standard of care that society recognizes as applicable under a given set of facts is a question of law for the courts." Harris v. Niehaus, 857 S.W.2d 222, 225 (Mo.banc 1993). Thus, whether Mr. Carter was an invitee, as he claims, or a licensee is a question of law and summary judgment is appropriate if the defendants' conduct conforms to the standard of care Mr. Carter's status imposes on them.

. . .

Historically, premises liability cases recognize three broad classes of plaintiffs: trespassers, licensees and invitees. All entrants to land are trespassers until the possessor of the land gives them permission to enter. All persons who enter a premises with permission are licensees until the possessor has an interest in the visit such that the visitor "has reason to believe that the premises have been made safe to receive him." [ ] That makes the visitor an invitee. The possessor's intention in offering the invitation determines the status of the visitor and establishes the duty of care the possessor owes the visitor. Generally, the possessor owes a trespasser no duty of care, [ ]; the possessor owes a licensee the duty to make safe dangers of which the possessor is aware, [ ]; and the possessor owes invitees the duty to exercise reasonable care to protect them against both known dangers and those that would be revealed by inspection. [ ] The exceptions to these general rules are myriad, but not germane here.

A social guest is a person who has received a social invitation. [ ] Though the parties seem to believe otherwise, Missouri does not recognize social guests as a fourth class of entrant. [ ] In Missouri, social guests are but a subclass of licensees. The fact that an invitation underlies a visit does not render the visitor an invitee for purposes of premises liability law. This is because "[t]he invitation was not tendered with any material benefit motive" . . . and "[t]he invitation was not extended to the public generally or to some undefined portion of the public from which invitation, . . . entrants might reasonably expect precautions have been taken, in the exercise of ordinary care, to protect them from danger." [ ] Thus, this Court held that there "is no reason for concluding it is unjust to the parties . . . to put a social guest in the legal category of licensee." [ ]

It does not follow from this that a person invited for purposes not strictly social is perforce an invitee. As [cited case] clearly indicates, an entrant becomes an invitee when the possessor invites with the expectation of a material benefit from the visit or extends an invitation to the public generally. See also Restatement (Second) of Torts, § 332[2] (defining an invitee for business purposes) and 65 C.J.S. Negligence, § 63(41)(A person is an invitee "if the premises are thrown open to the public and [the person] enters pursuant to the purposes for which they are thrown open."). Absent the sort of invitation from the possessor that lifts a licensee to invitee status, the visitor remains a licensee as a matter of law.

---

    [2] Section 332 [provides that an invitee is either "a public invitee or a business visitor." A public invitee is defined as a "person who is invited to enter or remain on land as a member of the public for a purpose for which the land is held open to the public." "A business visitor" is one who is invited to enter or remain on land "for a purpose directly or indirectly connected with business dealings with the possessor of the land."]

The record shows beyond cavil that Mr. Carter did not enter the Kinneys' land to afford the Kinneys any material benefit. He is therefore not an invitee under the definition of ["business visitor"] contained in Section 332 of the Restatement. The record also demonstrates that the Kinneys did not "throw open" their premises to the public in such a way as would imply a warranty of safety. The Kinneys took no steps to encourage general attendance by some undefined portion of the public; they invited only church members who signed up at church. They did nothing more than give permission to a limited class of persons—church members—to enter their property.

[handwritten margin note: reason]

Mr. Carter's response to the Kinneys' motion for summary judgment includes Mr. Carter's affidavit in which he says that he did not intend to socialize with the Kinneys and that the Kinneys would obtain an intangible benefit, albeit mutual, from Mr. Carter's participation in the class. Mr. Carter's affidavit attempts to create an issue of fact for the purpose of defeating summary judgment. But taking Mr. Carter's statement of the facts as true in all respects, he argues a factual distinction that has no meaning under Missouri law. Human intercourse and the intangible benefits of sharing one's property with others for a mutual purpose are hallmarks of a licensee's permission to enter. Mr. Carter's factual argument makes the legal point he wishes to avoid: his invitation is not of the sort that makes an invitee. He is a licensee.

[handwritten margin note: Defend. argue.]

The trial court concluded as a matter of law that Mr. Carter was a licensee, that the Kinneys had no duty to protect him from unknown dangerous conditions, and that the defendants were entitled to summary judgment as a matter of law. In that conclusion, the trial court was eminently correct.

[handwritten margin note: holding]

. . .

The judgment of the trial court is affirmed. *[handwritten margin note: disposition]*

■ COVINGTON, C.J., and HOLSTEIN, BENTON, THOMAS, and LIMBAUGH, JJ., concur.

■ PRICE, J., concurs in result.

NOTES AND QUESTIONS

1. What is the justification for treating a social guest as a licensee? Why not an invitee? Consider comment h (3) to section 330 of the Second Restatement:

> The explanation usually given by the courts for the classification of social guests as licensees is that there is a common understanding that the guest is expected to take the premises as the possessor himself uses them, and does not expect and is not entitled to expect that they will be prepared for his reception, or that precautions will be taken for his safety, in any manner in

which the possessor does not prepare or take precautions for his own safety, or that of the members of his family.

Is this persuasive?

2.   Section 332 of the Restatement Second, as the court notes, also extends invitee status to a person who is "invited to enter or remain on land as a member of the public for a purpose for which the land is held open to the public." What changes in the facts might have led the court to classify plaintiff as an invitee under section 332?

3.   It is one thing to put the plaintiff into one of the three boxes, although the court notes that there are "myriad" exceptions. It is another to determine what duty is owed to each category. For example, the duty to trespassers is stated in section 333:

> Except as stated in §§ 334–339, a possessor of land is not liable to trespassers for physical harm caused by his failure to exercise reasonable care
>
>> (a) to put the land in a condition reasonably safe for their reception, or
>>
>> (b) to carry on his activities so as not to endanger them.

The listed exceptions create obligations to warn, for example, when the possessor knows that persons "constantly intrude upon a limited area" of the land and may encounter a hidden danger, or when the possessor fails to exercise reasonable care for the safety of a known trespasser. Generally, though, the duty is simply not to willfully or wantonly harm trespassers. In Bennett v. Napolitano, 746 A.2d 138 (R.I.2000), plaintiff was walking his dogs in a city park at 2 a.m. when a tree limb fell on him. The court held him a trespasser because the park was legally closed every night at 9 p.m. Because the only duty owed plaintiff was to avoid willful or wanton conduct, defendant had not breached its duty. There was no evidence that the limb's weakness was known and disregarded. What would happen if the limb had fallen on plaintiff while taking an afternoon walk with his dog?

4.   What duty did the Kinneys owe Mr. Carter? Why does the court hold that they met that duty as a matter of law?

5.   If Mr. Carter had been categorized as an invitee, what duty would the Kinneys have owed? With regard to the condition of the premises, section 342 provides that an occupier is subject to liability to invitees if the occupier:

> (a) knows or by the exercise of reasonable care would discover the condition, and should realize that it involves an unreasonable risk of harm to such invitees, and
>
> (b) should expect that they will not discover or realize the danger, or will fail to protect themselves against it, and
>
> (c) fails to exercise reasonable care to protect them against the danger.

How does this general obligation differ from what the court found was owed to licensees? What result if Mr. Carter were an invitee?

6. *Open and obvious dangers.* One issue that has divided courts involves the duty owed invitees where the danger is "open and obvious." Some courts have concluded that no duty is owed since the danger was apparent to the invitee. Recently, courts have focused more on whether such notice was enough to make the premises reasonably safe. See Kentucky River Medical Center v. McIntosh, 319 S.W.3d 385 (Ky.2010). The court overturned its open and obvious rule, imposing a duty if there remains foreseeable risk created by the plaintiff's confronting and negotiating the obvious risk, subject to consideration of comparative fault, which is discussed in Chapter VII.

7. *Activities.* The foregoing discussion has focused on the condition of the premises. Another set of questions involves *activities* taking place on the premises. The traditional rule was that licensees and trespassers could not recover for active negligence while they were on the premises. See, e.g., Britt v. Allen County Community Junior College, 638 P.2d 914 (Kan.1982).

Britt was overruled in Bowers v. Ottenad, 729 P.2d 1103 (Kan.1986), involving a social guest who was burned during the preparation of "flaming Irish coffee":

> We hold . . . that when a licensee, whose presence is known or should be known, is injured or damaged by some affirmative activity conducted upon the property by the occupier of the property the duty owed to such person is one of reasonable care under the circumstances.

Assume that a burglar, discovered lurking outside the auditorium of a junior college, is brought into the auditorium by the police for investigation. Should the burglar have an action if the custodian carelessly loses control of a piano that he is moving nearby so that it tips over on the burglar's foot?

8. *Child trespassers.* In Holland v. Baltimore & Ohio Railroad Co., 431 A.2d 597 (D.C.1981), a nine-year-old boy was injured by a freight train. The court invoked one of the most influential sections of the Restatement, section 339:

> A possessor of land is subject to liability for physical harm to children trespassing thereon caused by an artificial condition upon the land if
>
> (a) the place where the condition exists is one upon which the possessor knows or has reason to know that children are likely to trespass, and
>
> (b) the condition is one of which the possessor knows or has reason to know and which he realizes or should realize will involve an unreasonable risk of death or serious bodily harm to such children, and
>
> (c) the children because of their youth do not discover the condition or realize the risk involved in intermeddling with it or in coming within the area made dangerous by it, and

(d) the utility to the possessor of maintaining the condition and the burden of eliminating the danger are slight as compared with the risk to children involved, and

(e) the possessor fails to exercise reasonable care to eliminate the danger or otherwise to protect the children.

The judge found the section inapplicable because "a moving train is a danger so obvious that any nine-year-old child allowed at large would readily discover it and realize the risk involved in coming within the area made dangerous by it."

The special treatment of children dates to the "turntable" cases, involving injuries to children tampering with railroad track-switching devices. These cases evolved into a broader "attractive nuisance" doctrine that covered injuries to children who were unaware, because of their immaturity, of risks associated with a land occupier's property. Most courts did not require that the child have been enticed onto the land by the sight of the danger. The evolution of the doctrine is discussed in Prosser, Trespassing Children, 47 Cal.L.Rev. 427 (1959).

9. *Recreational use of land.* Almost all states have enacted statutes that limit the liability of owners of land used for recreational purposes. One goal is to encourage landowners to permit others to use the land for recreational purposes rather than fencing in their property to avoid liability. Another is to prevent persons injured on open land from suing for natural dangers on such land or demanding that warnings be posted of such dangers. Willful misconduct is generally required for liability. See generally Ford, Comment, Wisconsin's Recreational Use Statute: Towards Sharpening the Picture at the Edges, 1991 Wis.L.Rev. 491. For a summary of the considerations behind this type of legislation, see Bragg v. Genesee County Agricultural Society, 644 N.E.2d 1013 (N.Y.1994).

Heins v. Webster County

Supreme Court of Nebraska, 1996.
250 Neb. 750, 552 N.W.2d 51.

■ WHITE, C.J., and CAPORALE, FAHRNBRUCH, LANPHIER, WRIGHT, CONNOLLY, and GERRARD, JJ.

■ CONNOLLY, JUSTICE.

The question presented is whether this court should abolish the common-law classifications of licensee and invitee and require a duty of reasonable care to all nontrespassers.

. . .

[After a heavy snowfall, plaintiff Roger Heins, accompanied by his wife, visited the defendant's hospital.] The evidence is disputed concerning the nature of this trip. Webster County claims that Heins was merely paying a social visit to his daughter Julie Heins, who was the director of nursing for the hospital. Heins claims that his visit was not only social, but also to coordinate plans for him to play Santa Claus for the hospital staff during the upcoming Christmas season. During their visit with Julie, [Heins] made plans to have lunch with Julie and a friend at a local restaurant.

While . . . exiting the hospital through the main entrance, Roger fell. At trial, Roger testified that [after he held the front door open for his wife and started to exit, he slipped and fell to the ground, allegedly because of the accumulation of ice and snow, and injured his hip.]

facts

Heins [claimed] that Webster County was negligent (1) in failing to properly inspect the above-described entrance prior to inviting the public to use the entrance, (2) in failing to warn Heins of the existence of a dangerous condition, (3) in allowing the ice and snow to accumulate, and (4) in failing to remove the ice and snow.

allegations

Following a bench trial, the district court found that Heins "went to the Webster County Hospital to visit his daughter who was an employee of the hospital." Furthermore, the court concluded that Heins was a licensee at the time of his fall and that the county did not act willfully or wantonly or negligently fail to warn of known hidden dangers unobservable by Heins. Thus, the court entered judgment in favor of Webster County. Heins appeals.

procedural history

Summarized, Heins assigns that the district court erred in not generally holding the hospital to a duty of reasonable care to Heins. In the alternative, he argues the hospital should be held to a duty of reasonable care for one of the following reasons: (1) he was a public invitee, (2) he was a social guest on the hospital premises, or (3) hospital personnel knew he was on the premises.

. . .

[Plaintiff] calls into question the continued usefulness of the licensee and invitee classifications. In fact, a number of jurisdictions have decided that the common-law classifications have outlived their usefulness, and have either partially or completely abandoned the common-law classifications.

issue

In 1957, England statutorily abolished the common-law distinction between licensees and invitees and imposed upon the occupier a "common duty of care" toward all persons who lawfully enter the premises. [ ] Shortly thereafter, in 1959, the U.S. Supreme Court decided that the classifications would not apply in admiralty law, stating that the classifications created a "semantic morass." See, Kermarec v. Compagnie Generale, 358 U.S. 625, 631 (1959); [ ]. In 1968, the Supreme Court of California decided the landmark case Rowland v. Christian, 443 P.2d 561 (Cal.1968), which abolished the traditional duty classification scheme for licensees, invitees, and trespassers and replaced it with ordinary negligence principles.

. . .

Policy Reasons for and Against Abolishing Classifications

A number of policy reasons have been asserted for either abandoning or retaining the common-law classifications. Among the jurisdictions retaining the categories, most find value in the predictability of the common law. Some courts rejecting change have reasoned that replacement of a stable and established system of loss allocation results in the establishment of a system devoid of standards for liability. [ ] It also has been suggested that the harshness of the common-law rules has been ameliorated by the judicial grafting of exceptions and that creation of sub-classifications ameliorated the distinctions between active and passive negligence. [ ] These states have concluded that abandoning the established system of liability in favor of a standard of reasonable care would decrease predictability and ensure that each case would be decided on its facts. Therefore, these states claim that landowners would be less able to guard against risks. . . .

The most common reason asserted for abandoning the categories is that an entrant's status should not determine the duty that the landowner owes to him or her. As the California Supreme Court stated in *Rowland v. Christian*, [ ]:

> A man's life or limb does not become less worthy of protection by the law nor a loss less worthy of compensation under the law because he has come upon the land of another without permission or with permission but without a business purpose. Reasonable people do not ordinarily vary their conduct depending upon such matters, and to focus upon the status of the injured party as a trespasser, licensee, or invitee in order to determine the question whether the landowner has a duty of care, is contrary to our modern social mores and humanitarian values. The common law rules obscure rather than illuminate the proper considerations which should govern determination of the question of duty.

In abolishing the invitee-licensee distinction, the Massachusetts Supreme Judicial Court recognized:

> It no longer makes any sense to predicate the landowner's duty solely on the status of the injured party as either a licensee or invitee. Perhaps, in a rural society with sparse land settlements and large estates, it would have been unduly burdensome to obligate the owner to inspect and maintain distant holdings for a class of entrants who were using the property "for their own convenience" . . . but the special immunity which the licensee rule affords landowners cannot be justified in an urban industrial society.

Mounsey v. Ellard, 297 N.E.2d 43, 51 (Mass.1973).

Another justification for abandoning the classifications is to eliminate the complex and unpredictable state of the law necessitated by the harsh nature of the common-law rules. [ ] As the U.S. Supreme Court proclaimed,

> courts have found it necessary to formulate increasingly subtle verbal refinements, to create subclassifications among traditional common-law categories, and to delineate fine gradations in the standards of care which the landowner owes to each. Yet even within a single jurisdiction, the classifications and subclassifications bred by the common law have produced confusion and conflict.

Kermarec v. Compagnie Generale, [ ]. The Court recognized that the "distinctions which the common law draws between licensee and invitee were inherited from a culture deeply rooted to the land, a culture which traced many of its standards to a heritage of feudalism." [ ] Referring to the judicial interpretation of the common-law distinctions as a "semantic morass," the Court declined to adopt them into admiralty law. [ ]

Those states abandoning the distinctions argue that instead of the entrant's status, the foreseeability of the injury should be the controlling factor in determining the liability of the landowner. [ ] Many jurisdictions that have abandoned the common-law classifications as determinants of liability have found that they remain relevant in determining the foreseeability of the harm under ordinary negligence principles. [ ]

Application of the Law to Heins

The present case illustrates the frustration inherent in the classification scheme. In many instances, recovery by an entrant has become largely a matter of chance, dependent upon the pigeonhole in which the law has put him, e.g., "trespasser," "licensee," or "invitee." [ ] When he was injured, Heins was exiting a county hospital, using the main entrance to the hospital, over the lunch hour. If Heins had been on the hospital premises to visit a patient or purchase a soft drink from a vending machine, he could have been classified as an invitee. [ ] However, he came to visit his daughter and was denied recovery as a matter of law.

Thus, Heins was denied the possibility of recovering under present law, merely because on this trip to the hospital he happened to be a licensee rather than an invitee. In the instant case, the hospital would undergo no additional burden in exercising reasonable care for a social visitor such as Heins, because it had the duty to exercise reasonable care for its invitees. A patient visitor could have used the same front entrance at which Heins fell and would have been able to maintain a negligence action; however, Heins has been denied the opportunity to recover merely because of his status at the time of the fall.

Modern commercial society creates relationships between persons not contemplated by the traditional classifications. [ ] Yet we have continued to pigeonhole individuals as licensees or invitees as a convenient way to ascertain the duty owed by the landowner. For instance, in Presho v. J.M. McDonald Co., 151 N.W.2d 451 (Neb.1967), a customer of a retail store was injured when she entered a back room of the store with the permission of the store manager, in order to retrieve an empty box. We held the customer to be a licensee rather than an invitee because "[s]he was on an errand personal to herself, not in any way connected with the business of the defendant." We recognized that while she was in the store proper, she was an invitee. However, we found her to be a licensee when she entered the back room, despite the fact that the ladies' restroom was located in this back room area and was used by customers to the store.

The common-law status classifications should not be able to shield those who would otherwise be held to a standard of reasonable care but for the arbitrary classification of the visitor as a licensee. We find no merit in the argument that the duty of reasonable care is difficult for a fact finder to understand or apply, because it has been used successfully with regard to invitees and is the standard used in almost all other tort actions.

holding

We conclude that we should eliminate the distinction between licensees and invitees by requiring a standard of reasonable care for all lawful visitors. We retain a separate classification for trespassers because we conclude that one should not owe a duty to exercise reasonable care to those not lawfully on one's property. Adopting this rule places the focus where it should be, on the foreseeability of the injury, rather than on allowing the duty in a particular case to be determined by the status of the person who enters upon the property.

rule

Our holding does not mean that owners and occupiers of land are now insurers of their premises, nor do we intend for them to undergo burdens in maintaining such premises. We impose upon owners and occupiers only the duty to exercise reasonable care in the maintenance of their premises for the protection of lawful visitors. Among the factors to be considered in evaluating whether a landowner or occupier has exercised reasonable care for the protection of lawful visitors will be (1) the foreseeability or possibility of harm; (2) the purpose for which the entrant entered the premises; (3) the time, manner, and circumstances under which the entrant entered the premises; (4) the use to which the premises are put or are expected to be put; (5) the reasonableness of the inspection, repair, or warning; (6) the opportunity and ease of repair or correction or giving of the warning; and (7) the burden on the land occupier and/or community in terms of inconvenience or cost in providing adequate protection.

Factors of reasonable care

Although we have set forth some of the factors to be considered in determining whether a landowner or occupier has exercised reasonable care for the protection of lawful visitors, it is for the fact finder to determine, on the facts of each individual case, whether or not such factors establish a breach of the duty of reasonable care.

Conclusion

We determine that the invitee-licensee distinction should be abandoned and the new rule applied in the instant case. Considering that other litigants may have relied on our previous rule and incurred time and expense in prosecuting or defending their claims, we conclude, with the exception of the instant case, that the rule announced today shall be applied only to all causes of action arising after this date. We reverse, and remand for a new trial. — *disposition*

holding

■ FAHRNBRUCH, JUSTICE, dissenting.

. . .

The majority opinion dismantles longstanding common law by eliminating the concept of licensee, thereby forcing a landowner to treat a person who is allowed to enter or remain upon premises with the same standard of care as a person who is invited onto the premises for the mutual benefit of both landowner and invitee.

Under the majority opinion, a landowner owes a duty of reasonable care to an individual who becomes injured by conducting activities on the premises without the landowner's express permission or knowledge. From this moment on, public and private institutions, as well as residential homeowners, must be especially aware of unknown, uninvited individuals who take advantage of their land and facilities.

In McCurry v. Young Men's Christian Assn., 313 N.W.2d 689 (Neb.1981), an individual brought an action against a Young Men's Christian Association (YMCA) as a result of an injury which arose from a fall while the individual was playing basketball on an outdoor asphalt playground owned by the YMCA. The plaintiff was not a member of the YMCA and had not obtained any express permission to use the playground. This court held that the plaintiff was a licensee and affirmed the trial court's directed verdict in favor of the YMCA. Under the majority's opinion, the YMCA and similar institutions will be subject to lawsuits which hold them to a duty to treat such uninvited users of their facilities with the same standard of care as the paying members of the institution.

This court should not enact public policy which, in effect, socializes the use of privately owned property to the extent that the landowner owes the same duty to all, except trespassers, who enter the owner's land. It is not the function of the court to create a liability where the law creates none. [ ]

Under the majority's opinion, a homeowner would have potential liability for any number of not only uninvited but unwanted solicitors or visitors coming to the homeowner's door.

■ CAPORALE, J., joins in this dissent.

NOTES AND QUESTIONS

1.   Under the traditional categories why does Mr. Heins lose? How might playing Santa Claus have been relevant?

2.   In rejecting the use of the categories, why does the court exclude trespassers? Suppose that Mr. Heins were entering the hospital to visit a patient after visiting hours were over and slipped and fell? Recall the *Bennett* case involving the dog walker who was hit by a falling tree limb after the park closed, note 3, p. 190 supra.

3.   What if a shoplifter, who had just stolen something from the hospital gift shop, slipped while carefully leaving the hospital and fell for the same reasons that Mr. Heins fell? Would the court's factors help in analyzing this case? How would the factors work in deciding the cited *Presho* case involving the woman who went into the back of the store? How would they work in the case of the basketball player raised by the dissent? Under the *Heins* approach would the judge or jury decide the shoplifter, *Presho*, and basketball player cases?

4.   Although *Rowland* abolished separate treatment of trespassers, trespassers rarely brought cases. In the early 1980s, however, concern about potential liability to trespassers and burglars induced the California legislature to adopt a provision that protected landowners against liability to persons hurt on premises while committing or attempting to commit one of 25 enumerated criminal offenses. The bar applies only upon a charge of a felony and the conviction for that felony or a lesser included felony or misdemeanor. The civil action is to be delayed until the conclusion of the criminal action. Calif. Civil Code § 847. The Third Restatement is modeled on this approach, distinguishing between "flagrant" trespassers and other trespassers. The former are those whose presence on the land "is so antithetical to the right of the land possessor" that it would be unfair to subject the possessor to liability for negligence. An illustration uses burglars as flagrant trespassers, while trespassers such as the plaintiff in *Bennett*, note 3, p. 190 supra are ordinary trespassers. Restatement (Third) Torts: Liability for Physical and Emotional Harm § 52 (2010).

5.   The dissent is concerned about liability to licensees. How might the majority analyze the case of an uninvited solicitor coming to the front door who slips on a defective stair? Is the case different if the solicitor was hurt while going down the stairs after talking with the occupier?

6.   The court concludes that its decision should operate prospectively, applying only to claims arising after the court's decision—except for this case. What are the arguments for and against prospective overruling generally? What are the arguments for and against making only the decision in the case before the court retroactive? Would making the new rule applicable to all cases filed thereafter have better served the court's purpose? Why have we not previously encountered prospective rulings in this course?

7. For a time after *Rowland*, it appeared that the case would signal a massive shift among the states. After a handful of states quickly followed California, the movement lost momentum, but appeared to gain strength in the late 1990s, and apparently now is followed in a majority of states (although far fewer states extend the *Rowland* approach to trespassers). See Demag v. Better Power Equipment, Inc., 102 A.3d 1101 (Vt.2014)(adopting a duty to invitees and licensees).

In *Carter v. Kinney*, p. 187 supra, after failing to persuade the court to categorize Mr. Carter as an invitee, the Carters asked the court to overturn the categorical approach and follow California's lead. The court refused to abandon the categories:

> [T]he maintenance of the distinction between licensee and invitee creates fairly predictable rules within which entrants and possessors can determine appropriate conduct and juries can assess liability. To abandon the careful work of generations for an amorphous "reasonable care under the circumstances" standard seems—to put it kindly—improvident.

The court quoted a passage from Prosser and Keeton that speculated that the failure of more states to join the "trend"

> may reflect a more fundamental dissatisfaction with certain developments in accident law that accelerated during the 1960's— reduction of whole systems of legal principles to a single, perhaps simplistic, standard of reasonable care, the sometimes blind subordination of other legitimate social objectives to the goals of accident prevention and compensation, and the commensurate shifting of the balance of power to the jury from the judge.

The *Carter* court concluded that the "experience of the states that have abolished the distinction between licensee and invitee does not convince us that their idea is a better one. Indeed, we are convinced that they have chosen wrongly."

The Third Restatement reflects the *Rowland* movement, adopting a duty of reasonable care to all entrants, save for flagrant trespassers described in note 4 supra. Restatement (Third) of Torts: Liability for Physical and Emotional Harm § 51. Although these provisions supersede the Second Restatement's treatment of land possessors' duties, relied on by the court in *Carter*, courts that continue to adhere to the status-based duty rules will likely continue to rely on the Second Restatement.

For comprehensive treatment of *Rowland*, see Rabin, *Rowland v. Christian*: Hallmark of an Expansionary Era, in R. Rabin & S. Sugarman (eds.), Torts Stories 73 (2003).

8. In Louis v. Louis, 636 N.W.2d 314 (Minn.2001), defendant argued that he owed plaintiff, his brother who was attending a family gathering and who was injured on a pool slide in defendant's backyard, no duty based on *Harper v. Herman*, p. 129 supra and the absence of a special relationship between the parties. (Previously, the court had adopted the *Rowland* rule that a duty of reasonable care was owed to all invited persons.) The court held that in landowner cases plaintiff need not establish a special relationship: "We have consistently recognized that a duty based on a special relationship theory is separate and distinct from a duty based on a [landowner] theory." Why are landowner cases different with regard to the existence of a duty?

9. The issue of whether a land possessor owes a duty of care for natural conditions on the property that threaten others off the property is addressed in Pesaturo v. Kinne, 20 A.3d 284 (N.H.2011). Defendant's trees overhung plaintiff's property, limiting plaintiff's use of her driveway and damaging a fence. Since the harm occurred on the neighbor's property, this case is not about possessors' duties to entrants. It is interesting, nevertheless, because the risk of natural conditions on one's property does not implicate misfeasance by the possessor. The court, invoking foreseeability, held that a land possessor who knows or should know of a dangerous natural condition on his or her property must act reasonably to eliminate or ameliorate the risk posed by such a condition.

Do land possessors owe a duty to those on the land with regard to risks that exist off their land? In Collins v. Marriott International, Inc., 749 F.3d 951 (11th Cir.2014), plaintiff went from a resort owned by defendant in the Bahamas to an adjacent promontory point from which he fell and died. In response to defendant's claim that it had no duty with regard to risks on adjacent property, the court responded:

> As part of the duty to maintain the premises in a reasonably safe condition, a property owner also has a duty to maintain the property to prevent foreseeable risks that exist on adjacent property. This is true because the "duty element of a negligence action focuses on whether the defendant's conduct foreseeably created a broader 'zone of risk' that poses a general threat of harm to others."

Compare Galindo v. Town of Clarkstown, 814 N.E.2d 419 (N.Y.2004)(holding, 4–3, "a person who lacks ownership or control of property cannot fairly be held accountable for injuries resulting from a hazard on the property").

Landlord and Tenant

What affirmative obligations, if any, does a landlord owe a tenant to protect the latter from harm? The traditional rules of liability for defective conditions have insulated landlords from liability except in a few situations. As summarized in Sargent v. Ross, 308 A.2d 528 (N.H.1973), a landlord was liable in tort only "if the injury is attributable to (1) a hidden danger in the premises of which the landlord but not the tenant is aware, (2) premises leased for public use, (3) premises retained under the landlord's control, such as common stairways, or (4) premises negligently repaired by the landlord."

Liability was much less likely if the landlord had promised to repair but had failed to take any steps to do so. The distinction between bad repairs and no repairs at all is disappearing. In Putnam v. Stout,

345 N.E.2d 319 (N.Y.1976), the court overturned its earlier view and imposed a duty where a promise had been made.

In the cited *Sargent v. Ross*, the court took a much more dramatic step to increase the liability of landlords. A child visiting a tenant in defendant's residential building fell to her death from a stairway. The claim was that the stairway was too steep and the railing inadequate. (The stairway was not common premises because it went only to the tenant's apartment.) On appeal, the court adopted the following position:

> [A] landlord must act as a reasonable person under all of the circumstances, including the likelihood of injury to others, the probable seriousness of such injuries, and the burden of reducing or avoiding the risk. . . . The questions of control, hidden defects and common or public use, which formerly had to be established as a prerequisite to even considering the negligence of a landlord, will now be relevant only inasmuch as they bear on the basic tort issues such as the foreseeability and unreasonableness of the particular risk of harm.

How does this new approach differ from the *Sargent* court's summary of earlier law?

Another source of expanded tort duties for landlords, beyond common law decisions such as *Sargent*, are housing codes, especially the Uniform Residential Landlord and Tenant Act, enacted in some form in about 20 states. The Act requires landlords to maintain the premises in habitable and safe condition. In addition, specific state and local provisions are employed to impose a duty on landlords. Thus, in Childs v. Purll, 882 A.2d 227 (D.C.2005), the court relied on a District of Columbia ordinance requiring lead-free apartments when minors are occupants. If the Act were violated, the court held, the defendant was negligent per se, unless he showed he "did everything a reasonably prudent person would have done to comply with" the Act.

Criminal Activity

During the long development of the category-based approach, most cases involved physical conditions of the premises or the negligent conduct of others. Later, plaintiffs began to sue for harms resulting from criminal conduct occurring on the premises. Most commonly, tenants began suing landlords for providing inadequate protection against criminal activity. The major early case was Kline v. 1500 Massachusetts Avenue Apartment Corp., 439 F.2d 477 (D.C.Cir.1970), in which the court imposed a duty of care on the landlord of a large apartment building toward a tenant who had been assaulted in a common hallway of the building. Crime had been occurring on the premises with mounting frequency. Although the owner could take some steps, such as extra heavy locks or guards, "no individual tenant had it within his power to take measures to guard" against these same perils:

> Not only as between landlord and tenant is the landlord best equipped to guard against the predictable risk of intruders, but even as between landlord and the police power of government, the landlord is in the best position to take the necessary protective measures. Municipal police cannot patrol the entryways and the hallways, the garages and the basements of private multiple unit apartment dwellings. They are neither equipped, manned, nor empowered to do so. In the area of the predictable risk which materialized in this case, only the landlord could have taken measures which might have prevented the injuries suffered by appellant.
>
> . . .
>
> . . . We do not hold that the landlord is an insurer of the safety of his tenants. His duty is to take those measures of protection which are within his power and capacity to take, and which can reasonably be expected to mitigate the risk of intruders assaulting and robbing tenants. The landlord is not expected to provide protection commonly owed by a municipal police department; but as illustrated in this case, he is obligated to protect those parts of his premises which are not usually subject to periodic patrol and inspection by the municipal police.

Id. at 487.

The court recognized that the discharge of this duty might often cause "the expenditure of large sums" and that these costs "will be ultimately passed on to the tenant in the form of increased rents. This prospect, in itself, however, is no deterrent to our acknowledging and giving force to the duty, since without protection the tenant already pays in losses from theft, physical assault and increased insurance premiums." The landlord "is entirely justified in passing on the cost of increased protective measures to his tenant, but the rationale of compelling the landlord to do it in the first place is that he is the only one who is in a position to take the necessary protective measures for overall protection of the premises."

Posecai v. Wal-Mart Stores, Inc.

Supreme Court of Louisiana, 1999.
752 So.2d 762.

■ MARCUS, JUSTICE.

Shirley Posecai brought suit against Sam's Wholesale Club ("Sam's") in Kenner after she was robbed at gunpoint in the store's parking lot. On July 20, 1995, Mrs. Posecai went to Sam's to make an exchange and to do some shopping. She exited the store and returned to her parked car at approximately 7:20 p.m. It was not dark at the time. As Mrs. Posecai was placing her purchases in the trunk, a man who was hiding under her car grabbed her ankle and pointed a gun at her. The unknown assailant instructed her to hand over her jewelry and her wallet. While begging the robber to spare her life, she gave him her purse and all her jewelry. Mrs. Posecai was wearing her most valuable jewelry at the time of the robbery because she had attended a downtown luncheon earlier in the day. She lost a two and a half carat diamond ring given to her by her husband for their twenty-fifth wedding anniversary, a diamond and ruby bracelet and a diamond and gold watch, all valued at close to $19,000.

facts

When the robber released Mrs. Posecai, she ran back to the store for help. The Kenner Police Department was called and two officers came out to investigate the incident. The perpetrator was never apprehended and Mrs. Posecai never recovered her jewelry despite searching several pawn shops.

At the time of this armed robbery, a security guard was stationed inside the store to protect the cash office from 5:00 p.m. until the store closed at 8:00 p.m. He could not see outside and Sam's did not have security guards patrolling the parking lot. At trial, the security guard on duty, Kenner Police Officer Emile Sanchez, testified that he had worked security detail at Sam's since 1986 and was not aware of any similar criminal incidents occurring in Sam's parking lot during the nine years prior to the robbery of Mrs. Posecai. He further testified that he did not consider Sam's parking lot to be a high crime area, but admitted that he had not conducted a study on the issue.

The plaintiff presented the testimony of two other Kenner police officers. Officer Russell Moran testified that he had patrolled the area around Sam's from 1993 to 1995. He stated that the subdivision behind Sam's, Lincoln Manor, is generally known as a high crime area, but that the Kenner Police were rarely called out to Sam's. Officer George Ansardi, the investigating officer, similarly testified that Lincoln Manor is a high crime area but explained that Sam's is not considered a high crime location. He further stated that to his knowledge none of the other businesses in the area employed security guards at the time of this robbery.

trial testimony

An expert on crime risk assessment and premises security, David Kent, was qualified and testified on behalf of the plaintiff. It was his opinion that the robbery of Mrs. Posecai could have been prevented by an exterior security presence. He presented crime data from the Kenner Police Department indicating that between 1989 and June of 1995 there were three robberies or "predatory offenses" [defined by the court as crimes against the person] on Sam's premises, and provided details from the police reports on each of these crimes. The first offense occurred at 12:45 a.m. on March 20, 1989, when a delivery man sleeping in his truck parked in back of the store was robbed. In May of 1992, a person was mugged in the store's parking lot. Finally, on February 7, 1994, an employee of the store was the victim of a purse snatching, but she indicated to the police that the crime was related to a domestic dispute.

In order to broaden the geographic scope of his crime data analysis, Mr. Kent looked at the crime statistics at thirteen businesses on the same block as Sam's, all of which were either fast food restaurants, convenience stores or gas stations. He found a total of eighty-three predatory offenses in the six and a half years before Mrs. Posecai was robbed. Mr. Kent concluded that the area around Sam's was "heavily crime impacted," although he did not compare the crime statistics he found around Sam's to any other area in Kenner or the New Orleans metro area.

Mrs. Posecai contends that Sam's was negligent in failing to provide adequate security in the parking lot considering the high level of crime in the surrounding area. Seeking to recover for mental anguish as well as for her property loss, she alleged that after this incident she had trouble sleeping and was afraid to go out by herself at night. After a bench trial, the trial judge held that Sam's owed a duty to provide security in the parking lot because the robbery of the plaintiff was foreseeable and could have been prevented by the use of security. A judgment was rendered in favor of Mrs. Posecai, awarding $18,968 for her lost jewelry and $10,000 in general damages for her mental anguish. [The court of appeals affirmed the defendant's liability but modified the allocation of damages.]

The sole issue presented for our review is whether Sam's owed a duty to protect Mrs. Posecai from the criminal acts of third parties under the facts and circumstances of this case.

. . .

This court has never squarely decided whether business owners owe a duty to protect their patrons from crimes perpetrated by third parties. It is therefore helpful to look to the way in which other jurisdictions have resolved this question. Most state supreme courts that have considered the issue agree that business owners do have a duty to take reasonable precautions to protect invitees from foreseeable criminal attacks.

We now join other states in adopting the rule that although business owners are not the insurers of their patrons' safety, they do have a duty to implement reasonable measures to protect their patrons from criminal acts when those acts are foreseeable. We emphasize, however, that there is generally no duty to protect others from the criminal activities of third persons. [] This duty only arises under limited circumstances, when the criminal act in question was reasonably foreseeable to the owner of the business. Determining when a crime is foreseeable is therefore a critical inquiry.

Other jurisdictions have resolved the foreseeability issue in a variety of ways, but four basic approaches have emerged. [ ] The first approach, although somewhat outdated, is known as the specific harm rule. [ ] According to this rule, a landowner does not owe a duty to protect patrons from the violent acts of third parties unless he is aware of specific, imminent harm about to befall them. [ ] Courts have generally agreed that this rule is too restrictive in limiting the duty of protection that business owners owe their invitees. [ ]

More recently, some courts have adopted a prior similar incidents test. [ ] Under this test, foreseeability is established by evidence of previous crimes on or near the premises. [ ] The idea is that a past history of criminal conduct will put the landowner on notice of a future risk. Therefore, courts consider the nature and extent of the previous crimes, as well as their recency, frequency, and similarity to the crime in question. [ ] This approach can lead to arbitrary results because it is applied with different standards regarding the number of previous crimes and the degree of similarity required to give rise to a duty. [ ]

The third and most common approach used in other jurisdictions is known as the totality of the circumstances test. [ ] This test takes additional factors into account, such as the nature, condition, and location of the land, as well as any other relevant factual circumstances bearing on foreseeability. [ ] As the Indiana Supreme Court explained, "[a] substantial factor in the determination of duty is the number, nature, and location of prior similar incidents, but the lack of prior similar incidents will not preclude a claim where the landowner knew or should have known that the criminal act was foreseeable." [ ] The application of this test often focuses on the level of crime in the surrounding area and courts that apply this test are more willing to see property crimes or minor offenses as precursors to more violent crimes. [ ] In general, the totality of the circumstances test tends to place a greater duty on business owners to foresee the risk of criminal attacks on their property and has been criticized "as being too broad a standard, effectively imposing an unqualified duty to protect customers in areas experiencing any significant level of criminal activity." [ ]

The final standard that has been used to determine foreseeability is a balancing test, an approach which has been adopted in California [in Ann M. v. Pacific Plaza Shopping Center, 863 P.2d 207 (Cal.1993)] and Tennessee. . . . The balancing test seeks to address the interests of both business proprietors and their customers by balancing the foreseeability of harm against the burden of imposing a duty to protect against the criminal acts of third persons. [ ] The Tennessee Supreme Court formulated the test as follows: "In determining the duty that exists, the foreseeability of harm and the gravity of harm must be balanced against the commensurate burden imposed on the business to

[margin handwritten note: Types of foreseeability tests]

protect against that harm. In cases in which there is a high degree of foreseeability of harm and the probable harm is great, the burden imposed upon defendant may be substantial. Alternatively, in cases in which a lesser degree of foreseeability is present or the potential harm is slight, less onerous burdens may be imposed." McClung v. Delta Square Ltd. Partnership, 937 S.W.2d 891, 902 [Tenn.1996]. Under this test, the high degree of foreseeability necessary to impose a duty to provide security, will rarely, if ever, be proven in the absence of prior similar incidents of crime on the property. [ ]

We agree that a balancing test is the best method for determining when business owners owe a duty to provide security for their patrons. The economic and social impact of requiring businesses to provide security on their premises is an important factor. Security is a significant monetary expense for any business and further increases the cost of doing business in high crime areas that are already economically depressed. Moreover, businesses are generally not responsible for the endemic crime that plagues our communities, a societal problem that even our law enforcement and other government agencies have been unable to solve. At the same time, business owners are in the best position to appreciate the crime risks that are posed on their premises and to take reasonable precautions to counteract those risks.

With the foregoing considerations in mind, we adopt the following balancing test to be used in deciding whether a business owes a duty of care to protect its customers from the criminal acts of third parties. The foreseeability of the crime risk on the defendant's property and the gravity of the risk determine the existence and the extent of the defendant's duty. The greater the foreseeability and gravity of the harm, the greater the duty of care that will be imposed on the business. A very high degree of foreseeability is required to give rise to a duty to post security guards, but a lower degree of foreseeability may support a duty to implement lesser security measures such as using surveillance cameras, installing improved lighting or fencing, or trimming shrubbery. The plaintiff has the burden of establishing the duty the defendant owed under the circumstances.

The foreseeability and gravity of the harm are to be determined by the facts and circumstances of the case. The most important factor to be considered is the existence, frequency and similarity of prior incidents of crime on the premises, but the location, nature and condition of the property should also be taken into account. It is highly unlikely that a crime risk will be sufficiently foreseeable for the imposition of a duty to provide security guards if there have not been previous instances of crime on the business' premises.

In the instant case, there were only three predatory offenses on Sam's premises in the six and a half years prior to the robbery of Mrs. Posecai. The first of these offenses occurred well after store hours, at almost one o'clock in the morning, and involved the robbery of a delivery man who was caught unaware as he slept near Sam's loading dock behind the store. In 1992, a person was mugged while walking through the parking lot. Two years later, an employee of the store was attacked in the parking lot and her purse was taken, apparently by her husband. A careful consideration of the previous incidents of predatory offenses on the property reveals that there was only one other crime in Sam's parking lot, the mugging in 1992, that was perpetrated against a Sam's customer and that bears any similarity to the crime that occurred in this case. Given the large number of customers that used Sam's parking lot, the previous robbery of only one customer in all those years indicates a very low crime risk. It is also relevant that Sam's only operates during daylight hours and must provide an accessible parking lot to the multitude of customers that shop at its store each year. Although the neighborhood bordering Sam's is considered a high crime area by local law enforcement, the foreseeability and gravity of harm in Sam's parking lot remained slight.

We conclude that Sam's did not possess the requisite degree of foreseeability for the imposition of a duty to provide security patrols in its parking lot. Nor was the degree of foreseeability sufficient to support a duty to implement lesser security measures. [At this point, in a footnote, the court rejected a lower court conclusion that defendant had assumed a duty to protect its patrons from crime when it hired security guards.] Accordingly, Sam's owed no duty to protect Mrs. Posecai from the criminal acts of third parties under the facts and circumstances of this case. . . .

■ LEMMON, J., concurring.

    . . .

■ JOHNSON, J., concurring.

[The concurrer noted that the majority discusses "four approaches to determine the duty owed by a business owner to an invitee, then selects the more narrow balancing test because of the economic and social impact of requiring business owners to provide security in high crime areas. Only California and Tennessee have adopted the balancing test."]

The totality of circumstances test is best suited for resolving this question. The totality of the circumstances test takes all factors of an incident into account when evaluating the issue of duty. [] It incorporates the specific harm and prior similar incidents tests as factors to consider when determining whether a business owes a duty to an invitee without arbitrarily limiting the inquiry to a limited set of factors. [] It additionally takes into account the physical characteristics of the premises (i.e. lighting, fencing), other security measures, the location of the premises, the nature of the operation of business, and the owner's observations regarding criminal activity. [] While this approach does not require a business to ensure an invitee's safety, it does require that reasonable measures be taken to prevent foreseeable criminal acts against an invitee.

While I agree with the majority's conclusion that the defendant, Sam's Wholesale Club, did not have a duty to provide security patrols in its parking lot under the facts of this case, the majority's analysis, using the balancing test to arrive at this conclusion, is flawed. I would adopt the totality of circumstances test to determine defendant's duty.

NOTES AND QUESTIONS

1.   What is the difference between the "totality of the circumstances" test and the "balancing" test? In what kinds of cases will the two tests lead to different results?

2.   In *Posecai* is it crucial what type of security the plaintiff sought? Recall the discussion of "untaken precautions" at note 1, p. 45 supra.

3.   Under the approach in *Posecai* what issue is left for the jury in determining breach that has not already been decided by the court under duty? In Williams v. Cunningham Drug Stores, Inc., 418 N.W.2d 381 (Mich.1988), the court held that defendant drug store owed no duty of care to a customer who was hurt during a robbery. Although juries normally decide what constitutes reasonable care, "in cases in which overriding public policy concerns arise, the court determines what constitutes reasonable care." Is that what happened in *Posecai*?

4.   Is the *Posecai* court suggesting that it would apply its analysis to cases of residential harm, as in *Kline*, p. 201 supra? Are the two situations different?

5.   *Resisting the robbery and apprehending perpetrators.* The foregoing cases dealt with the duty to anticipate and try to avert robberies and other criminal conduct. In a case where the proprietor is present, might there be liability for trying to thwart the robbers once the robbery has begun?

In Kentucky Fried Chicken of California, Inc. v. Superior Court, 927 P.2d 1260 (Cal.1997), defendant restaurant cashier did not comply immediately with a robber's demand. A customer who was taken hostage feared being killed—but was not physically harmed. In denying summary judgment, the lower court stressed that it was foreseeable that if the cashier did not comply the robber would hurt the patron and that this created a duty to comply. It also cited police pamphlets that urged citizens to comply with robbers' demands. On appeal, the court, 4–3, reversed the denial of summary judgment. The majority framed the issue as "whether a shopkeeper owes a duty to a patron to comply with an armed robber's demand for money in order to avoid increasing the risk of harm to patrons." The answer was that the shopkeeper "never" owed such a duty.

The majority, finding few cases on point, concluded that compliance was not required because of other provisions of state law, including a statute that recognized the right to defend property with reasonable force. Moreover, the majority doubted the benefits of compliance because "robbers are unpredictable and often injure victims and others even though there has been no resistance." A duty to comply would only encourage hostage-taking without assured benefit. (The court declined to consider cases involving "active resistance" to the robber.)

One dissenter objected to the absolute nature of the holding: "a harsh and unjust rule that a business proprietor is never under a duty to accede to the demands of a robber when his customers are present," so that the proprietor "is never required to subordinate any of his own property interests—no matter how insignificant the object and no matter how slightly it is jeopardized—to his customers' safety—no matter how many there are and no matter how gravely they are threatened."

The other two dissenters argued at length that the reasonableness of the proprietor's response to the attack was a jury question, asserting three arguments for not foreclosing the jury's role in this type of case. The first arose "from the irreducible variety of circumstances which may surround an event that causes harm to someone." The "greater accuracy" that results from fact-based decisions "advances the economic function of tort law." An "individualized determination of reasonableness increases efficiency because it allows for the optimal level of care to be determined under the circumstances of each case; it asks not whether in general the cost of additional precautions would be greater than the cost of additional injuries but whether, under the specific circumstances of the case at hand, additional precautions would have been cost effective."

Second, the use of juries allows "successive juries to reassess what precautions are reasonable as social, economic, and technological conditions change over time. . . . By contrast, locking defendants forever into a straitjacket of prescribed conduct removes the incentive for them to lower the costs and increase the level of precautions they provide."

Third, in deciding reasonableness, jurors "bring a wider array of practical experience and knowledge to that task than could a single individual such as a judge."

E. A REPRISE OF DUTY

A.W. v. Lancaster County School District 0001

Supreme Court of Nebraska, 2010.
784 N.W.2d 907.

■ GERRARD, J.

C.B., a kindergarten student at Arnold Elementary School in northwest Lincoln, Nebraska, was sexually assaulted in a school restroom during the school day. C.B.'s mother, A.W., sued the Lincoln Public Schools (LPS) on C.B.'s behalf, alleging that LPS' negligence permitted the assault to occur. The district court, however, entered summary judgment for LPS, reasoning that the assault was not foreseeable.

The fundamental issue in this appeal, as framed by the parties, is whether LPS had a legal duty to C.B. to protect him from the assault. But we conclude that our case law has, in the past, placed factual questions of foreseeability in the context of a legal duty when they are more appropriately decided by the finder of fact in the context of determining whether an alleged tort-feasor's duty to take reasonable care has been breached. As a result, we find that the questions of foreseeability presented in this appeal are matters of fact, not of law, and that there is a genuine issue of material fact regarding whether LPS' conduct met its duty of reasonable care. We reverse, and remand for further proceedings.

BACKGROUND

[Joseph Siems entered Arnold Elementary School through the main entrance during lunchtime. He walked past the main office without signing in, as visitors were requested to do, and without being noticed by those staffing the office. Siems was first observed by a teacher, Kathi Olson. "Siems had a cigarette behind his ear, . . . was carrying a backpack, . . . looked out of place," and ignored Olson's inquiry about whether she could help him; she proceeded to the office to see whether he had signed in.]

Two other teachers, Kelly Long and Connie Peters, were monitoring some first graders when they also saw Siems in the hallway. They decided that Long would talk to Siems while Peters stayed with the students. Long saw the contact between Siems and Olson, and when Siems came near, Long asked Siems if she could help him. Siems did not respond, but after the question was repeated, Siems said he needed to use the restroom. Long pointed out a nearby restroom and told Siems that he needed to return to the main office after using the restroom. Siems went toward the restroom, and Long went to her classroom and used the telephone to report the incident to the main office. Long knew that there were no students in that restroom at the time. But Long did not watch Siems to see where he went. Peters saw Siems go into the restroom that Long had indicated, then saw him come out and go back down the hallway. Then she lost sight of him. Although no one saw him, it is apparent that Siems went back down the hallway and into another restroom closer to the main entrance.

. . . After hearing from Olson and Long, the [school] secretary went to the cafeteria to inform Shannon Mitchell, the administrator in charge of the school at the time. In the meantime, C.B., who was 5 years old, had returned from a trip to the restroom and told his teacher, Susan Mulvaney, that "there was a bad man in the restroom." C.B. later reported that Siems had pulled down C.B.'s pants and briefly performed oral sex on him. Mulvaney stayed at the door of her classroom, next to C.B., and watched the restroom door.

After speaking to the secretary in the cafeteria, Mitchell went to the restroom and saw Siems sitting in a stall. When Mitchell arrived, there were no children in the restroom. Mitchell also saw some children in the hallway approaching the restroom; she prevented them from entering. While doing so, she encountered Mulvaney, who told her what C.B. had said. Mitchell used Mulvaney's telephone to call the office and initiate a "Code Red" lockdown of the school, then went to the office and called the 911 emergency dispatch service.

[Both the Code Red and 911 call were pursuant to a safety and emergency plan for the school and school district.]

After initiating the Code Red and calling 911, Mitchell went to some benches in the hallway near the restroom and watched the restroom door, along with an assistant principal who was in the building and a school custodian. After being contacted by the assistant principal, Siems left the restroom and then the building, followed by the assistant principal and custodian. The custodian detained Siems as police arrived, and Siems was taken into police custody.

ASSIGNMENTS OF ERROR

A.W. assigns . . . that the district court erred in finding that (1) LPS did not owe a duty to protect C.B. from the danger of sexual assault by Siems, (2) the sexual assault of C.B. was not reasonably foreseeable, (3) LPS took reasonable steps to protect against foreseeable acts of violence on its premises. . . .

. . .

ANALYSIS
FORESEEABILITY AND DUTY UNDER
RESTATEMENT (THIRD) OF TORTS

In order to recover in a negligence action, a plaintiff must show a legal duty owed by the defendant to the plaintiff, a breach of such duty, causation, and damages. The duty in a negligence case is to conform to the legal standard of reasonable conduct in the light of the apparent risk. The question whether a legal duty exists for actionable negligence is a question of law dependent on the facts in a particular situation. But it is for the fact finder to determine, on the facts of each individual case, whether or not the evidence establishes a breach of that duty.

A.W. first argues that LPS had a duty to protect C.B. from the danger of sexual assault, that the sexual assault of C.B. was reasonably foreseeable, and that LPS' response was inadequate to that foreseeable danger. . . .

But LPS does not dispute that it would owe C.B. a duty to protect him against any reasonably foreseeable acts of violence on its premises. So A.W.'s first three arguments are really three different ways of framing the same question: Was Siems' assault of C.B. reasonably foreseeable? A.W.'s arguments with respect to foreseeability boil down to two primary contentions: first, that the LPS employees who saw Siems on the day of the assault should have foreseen the danger that he represented and, second, that the neighborhood in which Arnold Elementary School is located was sufficiently dangerous to place LPS on notice of a danger that a student could be sexually assaulted.

In previous cases, because the existence of a legal duty is a question of law, we have also treated the foreseeability of a particular injury as a question of law. This places us in the peculiar position, however, of deciding questions, as a matter of law, that are uniquely rooted in the facts and circumstances of a particular case and in the reasonability of the defendant's response to those facts and circumstances.

For that reason, the use of foreseeability as a determinant of duty has been criticized, most pertinently in the recently adopted Restatement (Third) of Torts. The Restatement (Third) explains that because the extent of foreseeable risk depends on the specific facts of the case, courts should leave such determinations to the trier of fact unless no reasonable person could differ on the matter. Indeed, foreseeability determinations are particularly fact dependent and case specific, representing "a [factual] judgment about a course of events . . . that one often makes outside any legal context." So, by incorporating foreseeability into the analysis of duty, a court transforms a factual question into a legal issue and expands the authority of judges at the expense of juries or triers of fact.

That is especially peculiar because decisions of foreseeability are not particularly "legal," in the sense that they do not require special training, expertise, or instruction, nor do they require considering far-reaching policy concerns. Rather, deciding what is reasonably foreseeable involves common sense, common experience, and application of the standards and behavioral norms of the community— matters that have long been understood to be uniquely the province of the finder of fact.

In addition, we have defined a "duty" as an obligation, to which the law gives recognition and effect, to conform to a particular standard of conduct toward another. Duty rules are meant to serve as broadly applicable guidelines for public behavior, i.e., rules of law applicable to a category of cases. But foreseeability determinations are fact specific, so they are not categorically applicable, and are incapable of serving as useful behavioral guides. And, as the Arizona Supreme Court explained, "[r]eliance by courts on notions of 'foreseeability' also may obscure the factors that actually guide courts in recognizing duties for purposes of negligence liability." [Gipson v. Kasey, 150 P.3d 228, 231 (Ariz.2007).]

Instead, as the Restatement (Third) explains, an actor ordinarily has a duty to exercise reasonable care when the actor's conduct creates a risk of physical harm. But, in exceptional cases, when an articulated countervailing principle or policy warrants denying or limiting liability in a particular class of cases, a court may decide that a defendant has no duty or that the ordinary duty of reasonable care requires modification. A no-duty determination, then, is grounded in public policy and based upon legislative facts, not adjudicative facts arising out of the particular circumstances of the case. And such ruling should be explained and justified based on articulated policies or principles that justify exempting these actors from liability or modifying the ordinary duty of reasonable care.

[The court discussed other recent decisions, including Thompson v. Kaczinski, 774 N.W.2d 829 (Iowa 2009), adopting the reasoning of the Restatement (Third), contrasting them with the confusion in some of the court's earlier opinions on the relationship between foreseeability and duty-breach analysis.]

The ensuing complications are illustrated by our reasoning in *Sharkey v. Board of Regents,* in which we relied upon foreseeability in determining a university's legal duty to protect students on its campus from criminal activity. . . . [W]e reasoned, in the end, that because the evidence showed that violent altercations were not unknown at the location on campus where the plaintiff was attacked, the attack was foreseeable; thus, we held that the university owed a duty "to its students to take reasonable steps to protect against foreseeable acts of violence on its campus and the harm that naturally flows therefrom."

In other words, we reasoned that because the attack at issue in that case was foreseeable, the defendant had a duty to protect against foreseeable acts of violence. Our reasoning was tautological. It is evident that the university had a landowner-invitee duty to protect against *foreseeable* acts even had the attack in that case *not* been foreseeable. While we purported to be discussing duty, we were in fact assuming the conclusion we claimed to be proving, and we were actually evaluating the sufficiency of the evidence to sustain a conclusion that the university had breached its duty to take reasonable care.

Our mistake was a common one. As the Restatement notes, in a number of cases, courts have rendered judgments under the rubric of duty that are better understood as applications of the negligence standard to a particular category of recurring facts. . . . As the Wisconsin Supreme Court explained, in a negligence case, a defendant's conduct should be examined "not . . . in terms of whether . . . there is a duty to [perform] a specific act, but rather whether the conduct satisfied the duty placed upon individuals to exercise that degree of care as would be exercised by a reasonable person under the circumstances."

To summarize: Under the Restatement (Third), foreseeable risk is an element in the determination of negligence, not legal duty. In order to determine whether appropriate care was exercised, the fact finder must assess the foreseeable risk at the time of the defendant's alleged negligence. The extent of foreseeable risk depends on the specific facts of the case and cannot be usefully assessed for a category of cases; small changes in the facts may make a dramatic change in how much risk is foreseeable. Thus, courts should leave such determinations to the trier of fact unless no reasonable person could differ on the matter. And if the court takes the question of negligence away from the trier of fact because reasonable minds could not differ about whether an actor exercised reasonable care (for example, because the injury was not reasonably foreseeable), then the court's decision merely reflects the one-sidedness of the facts bearing on negligence and should not be misrepresented or misunderstood as involving exemption from the ordinary duty of reasonable care.

We find the reasoning of the Restatement (Third), and our fellow courts that have endorsed it, to be persuasive. The circumstances of this case illustrate how incorporating foreseeability into a duty analysis can confuse the issues. Here, it is not disputed that LPS owed C.B. a duty of reasonable care. The duty of instructors to supervise and protect students is well established under the Restatement (Second) of Torts, the Restatement (Third) of Torts, and our current case law. Instead, the question is whether Siems' assault of C.B. was reasonably foreseeable. That determination involves a fact-specific inquiry into the circumstances that might have placed LPS on notice of the possibility of the assault. Stated another way, it requires us to ask what LPS employees knew, when they knew it, and whether a reasonable person would infer from those facts that there was a danger. Those are *factual* inquiries that should not be reframed as questions of law.

    . . .

FORESEEABILITY IN PRESENT CASE

[The court next applied the Restatement (Third) principles to the facts of the case "to provide the parties and the district court clearer guidance of how the case should proceed on remand." The court was not persuaded by A.W.'s evidence of past criminal behavior in the vicinity of the school, finding it inadequate to present a jury question that the security plan at the school was inadequate.]

After Siems entered the building, however, reasonable minds could differ as to whether LPS' initial failure to note his presence, and response to his presence, satisfied its duty of reasonable care. The sequence of events presented by the evidence is essentially undisputed. Siems was spotted by a number of LPS employees, more than one of whom observed that Siems seemed out of place. While each of them responded to the threat that they recognized Siems represented, none of them effectively made sure that Siems did not make contact with a student. Specifically, they did not keep track of Siems' location and permitted him to evade them. Nor did they prevent C.B. from entering the restroom, alone, while Siems' whereabouts were unknown. And reasonable minds could differ as to whether Siems' assault of C.B. was a foreseeable result of those failures. These facts, taken in the light most favorable to A.W., establish a genuine issue of material fact as to whether LPS breached the duty of reasonable care it owed C.B. For that reason, A.W.'s first three assignments of error have merit and A.W. is entitled to a full trial to resolve these respective issues.

. . .

Reversed and remanded for further proceedings.

NOTES AND QUESTIONS

1. What, precisely, is the role of foreseeability in the court's determination of whether reasonable care was exercised? Is a lack of reasonable foreseeability sufficient by itself to justify a determination that there was no negligence as a matter of law, as the court suggests? Conversely, does the presence of reasonable foreseeability, in itself, warrant a finding of negligence? More specifically, how should the court's discussion of foreseeability bear on its earlier (and continued) adherence to a risk-utility test of due care?

Compare Cabral v. Ralphs Grocery Co., 248 P.3d 1170 (Cal.2011), which clarified the California Supreme Court's approach to duty, at least for cases in which the defendant created the risk that caused physical harm. Defendant truck driver pulled over to the side of the road to have a snack. Plaintiff's decedent, in a pickup, veered out of his lane and crashed into the rear of the tractor-trailer, causing decedent's death. Plaintiff claimed that defendant was negligent by parking in the breakdown lane of the freeway. The jury found both decedent and defendant negligent and allocated fault to the two. On appeal, the court of appeals concluded defendant owed no duty to others in parking on the side of the road.

The Supreme Court reversed. First, California recognizes a general duty of reasonable care in carrying out one's affairs. Second, "categorical" exceptions in special cases are possible, the court emphasized, but none are applicable here. Third, the factors involved in *Rowland v. Christian*, reiterated in *Tarasoff*, p. 150 supra, should be employed at an appropriate level of generality (for the category being considered) to determine whether those exceptions exist. Fourth, the court distinguished a determination, made as a matter of law based on the specific facts of the case, that *no breach had occurred*.

Applying these principles, the court reasoned that cars going off the road are a foreseeable circumstance for which drivers must account in exercising reasonable care. In doing so, the court employed an "ethics of particularism" approach as in *Pokora*, p. 64 supra, to conclude that cases of vehicles parked on the road should, like other traffic cases, be decided by a jury as a matter of breach. Or, "[o]n the facts of a particular case, a trial or appellate court may hold that no reasonable jury could find the defendant failed to act with reasonable prudence under the circumstances. Such a holding is simply to say that as a matter of law the defendant did not breach his or her duty of care, i.e., was not negligent toward the plaintiff under the circumstances shown by the evidence." Such a holding, however, would not imply that drivers never owe any duty to others parking on the side of the road, the categorical conclusion reached by the court of appeals that the Supreme Court reversed.

2. Does the *A.W.* court treat this case as involving misfeasance or nonfeasance? Is it correct? If this case is viewed as one of nonfeasance, is there nevertheless a basis for imposing a duty on the Lincoln Public Schools? If a case does involve nonfeasance, is that fact relevant to determining whether reasonable care was exercised?

3. Professor Jonathan Cardi authored an article, cited by the court, advocating the change in treatment of foreseeability adopted by the *A.W.* court. In that article, Professor Cardi explained why, in his view, adoption of the Restatement framework will have "little significant change in the outcome of negligence cases." Cardi, Purging Foreseeability: The New Vision of Duty and Judicial Power in the Proposed Restatement, 58 Vand.L.Rev. 739, 804–08 (2005). Is Professor Cardi right? How would the *Posecai* court have decided *A.W.*?

F. INTRAFAMILY DUTIES

In this section we consider the impact on duty when the plaintiff and the defendant are part of the same family unit.

Spousal suits. At common law, courts quite commonly barred spouses from suing one another for personal injury. The common law view was that husband and wife were a unity for legal purposes—and suits between them were a logical impossibility. But in the 19th century, legislatures began adopting so-called "Married Women's Acts" that gave wives the right to own property and to sue over property and contract disputes. With this destruction of the "unity," state courts slowly began eliminating the immunity from tort liability that spouses had enjoyed against being sued by one another.

Initially, abrogation occurred in suits for intentional torts because these claims showed that any spousal harmony sought to be preserved had probably already dissipated. It was harder to abrogate the immunity in suits for negligence because the courts feared not marital disharmony, but rather fraud and collusion against insurers as one spouse readily admitted negligence in hurting the other spouse. Virtually all remnants of spousal immunity have disappeared as to both intentional and negligent harms.

Parent-child suits. The parent-child relationship was never treated as a unity. The origin of the immunity of parents to suits by their children can be traced to the late nineteenth century. The ban was very widely adopted, and has recently been an active area of litigation. We have already considered suits within the family, although they did not address the ability of the child to sue.

Claims by children against parents for intentional harm are almost universally permitted today. For an extended discussion of an "issue of first impression," concluding that a child should be permitted to sue her father for sexual abuse, see Henderson v. Woolley, 644 A.2d 1303

(Conn.1994). The major battleground in parent-child injuries has involved negligently inflicted harms.

Broadbent v. Broadbent
Supreme Court of Arizona, 1995.
184 Ariz. 74, 907 P.2d 43.

■ CORCORAN, JUSTICE.

We must determine whether the doctrine of parental immunity bars Christopher Broadbent's action against his mother for negligence. . . .

[While defendant mother was watching her 2½-year-old son swimming at the family residence, the phone rang. Defendant went inside to answer it. When she looked out and could not see her son she ran out and found him at the bottom of the pool. Although he was ultimately revived, he "suffered severe brain damage because of lack of oxygen. He has lost his motor skills and has no voluntary movement." The action was brought by the father as conservator of his son. The trial court dismissed the case based on state precedents and the court of appeals affirmed, 2–1. The parties have "stipulated that: (1) the real party in interest was Northbrook Indemnity Company, who provided personal umbrella liability insurance coverage* for Laura Broadbent on the date of the accident; (2) Laura may be entitled to indemnity from Northbrook if Laura is liable for the injuries to Christopher; (3) Laura did not want to defend the action but agreed that Northbrook should be permitted to defend; and (4) the only issue in the case was whether the doctrine of parental immunity applied. The court of appeals ordered that Northbrook be permitted to appear and defend the case."]

I.   History and Purpose of the Parental Immunity Doctrine

A.   The Origins of Parental Immunity

We begin by stating a few basic facts about the treatment of children under the law and family immunities. Under common law, a child has traditionally been considered a separate legal entity from his or her parent. [ ] Children have generally been allowed to sue their parents in property and contract actions. Goller v. White, [122 N.W.2d 193, 197 (Wis.1963)]; [ ]. In contrast, at common law the courts merged the identity of husband and wife; therefore, spousal immunity prohibited any action by a wife against her husband because to do so would have been to sue herself. [ ] The doctrine of spousal immunity has been abolished and there has not been a prohibition against siblings suing each other [in Arizona].

---

*   An umbrella policy protects the insured for sums greater than those afforded by other more common insurance coverages, such as automobile liability or homeowner's liability insurance. The umbrella insurer was involved in this case because the homeowners' policy, the first layer of coverage, had an exclusion for intrafamily suits. See note 7 infra.—Eds.

The doctrine of parental immunity is an American phenomenon unknown in the English common law. See Gibson v. Gibson, [479 P.2d 648, 649 (Cal.1971)]; [ ]. Courts in Canada and Scotland have held that children may sue their parents in tort. [ ]

In early American history, children were viewed as "evil and in need of strict discipline," and the courts recognized wide parental discretion. [ ] See, e.g., S.C.Code Ann. § 16–3–40 (Law.Co-op. 1976)(statute originating from 1712 that provided a defense to "[k]illing by stabbing or thrusting" if done while chastising or correcting your child). Only recently has the state intervened to protect children. [ ] Viewed against this backdrop, it is not surprising that no American child had sought recovery against a parent for tortious conduct until the late nineteenth century.

[The court reviewed three famous early cases. In Hewellette v. George, 9 So. 885, 887 (Miss.1891), the court held "without citation to legal authority, that a child could not sue her parent for being falsely imprisoned in an insane asylum because of parental immunity, a doctrine which that court created from whole cloth." The basic ground was that the "peace of society, and of the families composing society, and a sound public policy, designed to subserve the repose of families and the best interests of society, forbid to the minor child a right to appear in court in the assertion of a claim to civil redress for personal injuries suffered at the hands of the parent."

In McKelvey v. McKelvey, 77 S.W. 664 (Tenn.1903), the court held that a minor child could not sue her father for "cruel and inhuman treatment" allegedly inflicted by her stepmother with the consent of her father. In Roller v. Roller, 79 P. 788 (Wash.1905), the court "held that a minor child could not sue her father for rape, even though he had been convicted of the criminal violation, because of the doctrine of parental immunity."]

This "great trilogy" was the inauspicious beginning of the doctrine of parental immunity, which was soon embraced by almost every state. [ ] However, the courts soon began fashioning several exceptions to the doctrine, and in several states the doctrine has been abolished. See [Gibson]; Glaskox v. Glaskox, 614 So.2d 906, 909–11 (Miss.1992)(abolishing parental immunity where minor injured as result of parents' negligence in car accident). In several situations, parental immunity does not apply: if the parent is acting outside his parental role and within the scope of his employment; if the parent acts willfully, wantonly, or recklessly; if the child is emancipated; if the child or parent dies; if a third party is liable for the tort, then the immunity of the parent does not protect that third party; and if the tortfeasor is standing in loco parentis, such as a grandparent, foster parent, or teacher, then the immunity does not apply [ ].

B.   Parental Immunity in Arizona

[The state first recognized parental immunity in 1967. In 1970, an unemancipated minor was allowed to sue her parents for injuries resulting from a car accident. Streenz v. Streenz, 471 P.2d 282 (Ariz.1970).] In *Streenz*, this court adopted [*Goller*]. Under the *Goller* standard, parental immunity is abrogated except:

> "(1) where the alleged negligent act involves an exercise of parental authority over the child; and
>
> (2) where the alleged negligent act involves an exercise of ordinary parental discretion with respect to the provision of food, clothing, housing, medical and dental services, and other care."

original parental immunity (handwritten)

[ ] The cases following *Streenz* show the difficulty in applying this ambiguous standard.

[In 1981, a child sued his father for leaving the front yard gate open so that the child could ride his tricycle into traffic. The court held that "the parent would not be immune if the parent had a duty to the world at large." Sandoval v. Sandoval, 623 P.2d 800, 802 (Ariz.1981). If the parent's duty was "owed to the child alone and a part of the parental 'care and control' or 'other care' to be provided by the parents," then the parent was immune from liability. The suit failed. In Schleier v. Alter, 767 P.2d 1187 (Ariz.App.1989), the family dog, which had a history of attacking children, bit the Alters' 11-month-old child. The court "held that the parents had a duty to the world at large and therefore were not immune from liability." In Sandbak v. Sandbak, 800 P.2d 8 (Ariz.App.1990), the child wandered onto the next door neighbors' property where the neighbors' pit bull terrier severely mauled her. Her parents "knew that the next door neighbors owned pit bull terriers and that their daughter had a habit of wandering onto the neighbors' property." The court barred the child's claim.]

C.   Analysis of the Policy Reasons Advanced in Support of Parental Immunity

Courts and commentators have postulated many policy reasons for the parental immunity doctrine. The primary justifications for this immunity are:

(1) Suing one's parents would disturb domestic tranquility;

(2) Suing one's parents would create a danger of fraud and collusion;

(3) Awarding damages to the child would deplete family resources;

(4) Awarding damages to the child could benefit the parent if the child predeceases the parent and the parent inherits the child's damages; and

why parental immunity exists (handwritten)

(5) Suing one's parents would interfere with parental care, discipline, and control.

[ ] We believe that all of these justifications provide weak support for the parental immunity doctrine.

The injury to the child, more than the lawsuit, disrupts the family tranquility. In fact, if the child is not compensated for the tortious injury, then peace in the family is even less likely. In the seminal Arizona case on parental immunity, the court recognized that family tranquility would not be disturbed if the parents had liability insurance. [ ]

This fear of upsetting the family tranquility also seems unrealistic when we consider how such a lawsuit is initiated. The parent most often makes the decision to sue himself, and the parent is in effect prepared to say that he was negligent. [ ]

The danger of fraud and collusion is present in all lawsuits. We should not deny recovery to an entire class of litigants because some litigants might try to deceive the judicial system. The system can ferret out fraudulent and collusive behavior in suits brought by children against their parents just as the system detects such behavior in other contexts.

. . .

A damage award for the child will not deplete, or unfairly redistribute, the family's financial resources. These cases will generally not be brought if no insurance coverage is available, and therefore the worry that the family's resources will be depleted for the benefit of one child is illusory. The opposite is true. If a child has been seriously injured and needs expensive medical care, then a successful lawsuit against the parent and subsequent recovery from the insurance company could ease the financial burden on the family. It would not be a viable rule to say that liability only exists where insurance exists, but we recognize that lawsuits generally will be brought when there is potential insurance coverage.

The possibility that the parent might inherit money recovered by the child is remote. This becomes a concern only if the parent inherits as a beneficiary under intestate succession laws. This is a concern for the probate courts and the laws of intestate succession, not tort law. The remedy would be to prohibit inheritance by the parent—not to deny recovery to the injured child. [ ]

The Arizona courts have embraced the rationale that allowing a child to sue a parent would interfere with parental care, discipline, and control. See [Streenz]. We have [in Sandoval] cited with approval the Wisconsin Supreme Court's statement that:

[a] new and heavy burden would be added to the responsibility and privilege of parenthood, if within the wide scope of daily

experiences common to the upbringing of children a parent could be subjected to a suit for damages for each failure to exercise care and judgment commensurate with the risk.

The justification that allowing children to sue their parents would undercut parental authority and discretion has more appeal than the other rationales. However, if a child were seriously injured as a result of the exercise of parental authority, such as by a beating, then it would constitute an injury willfully inflicted, and parents are generally not immune for willful, wanton, or malicious conduct. [ ] Furthermore, such a willful beating would probably constitute child abuse and could be criminally prosecuted. [ ]

We want to protect the right of parents to raise their children by their own methods and in accordance with their own attitudes and beliefs. The New York Court of Appeals aptly stated this concern:

> Considering the different economic, educational, cultural, ethnic and religious backgrounds which must prevail, there are so many combinations and permutations of parent-child relationships that may result that the search for a standard would necessarily be in vain. . . . For this reason parents have always had the right to determine how much independence, supervision and control a child should have, and to best judge the character and extent of development of their child.

Holodook v. Spencer, [324 N.E.2d 338, 346 (N.Y.1974)]. Though we recognize the importance of allowing parental discretion, we disagree that our searching for a standard would be "in vain." Parents do not possess unfettered discretion in raising their children.

II.   The Abolishment of Parental Immunity and Adoption of the "Reasonable Parent" Standard for Parent-Child Suits

Although the above concerns make it difficult to draft a proper standard for the type of action a child may maintain against a parent, we will attempt to do so. We need to "fashion an objective standard that does not result in second-guessing parents in the management of their family affairs." [ ] First, we should make clear what the standard is not. We reject and hereby overrule *Sandoval*, which created the "duty to the world at large versus duty to the child alone" distinction. [ ] This distinction is not capable of uniform application and has no connection with the rationale for parental immunity. This is especially evident when we compare the facts of *Schleier* and *Sandbak*.

In *Schleier*, the negligent act was failure to restrain a dog, and the court found that this was a duty to the world; therefore, parental immunity did not apply. [ ] In *Sandbak*, the negligent act was failure to supervise a child who was bitten by a neighbor's dog, and the court found this was a duty to the child alone; therefore, parental immunity applied. [ ] The children in *Schleier* and *Sandbak* suffered similar injuries; neither case involved parental discipline, and neither case involved the "provision of food, clothing, housing, medical and dental services, and other care," unless "other care" is broadly defined. Both cases involved the negligent supervision of children. If we were to hold that parents are immune for negligent supervision of children, then the issue of liability would revolve around whether an activity could be described as "supervision" and whether lack of supervision was the cause of the injury. This would not involve a consideration of whether the activity infringed on the parents' discretionary decisions regarding care, custody, and control. Almost everything a parent does in relation to his child involves "care, custody, and control."

We add that parents always owe a parental duty to their minor child. The issue of liability should revolve around whether the parents have breached this duty and, if so, whether the breach of duty caused the injury.

In accord with the California Supreme Court, "we reject the implication of *Goller* [which this court approved in *Streenz*] that within certain aspects of the parent-child relationship, the parent has carte blanche to act negligently toward his child. . . . [A]lthough a parent has the prerogative and the duty to exercise authority over his minor child, this prerogative must be exercised within reasonable limits." [*Gibson*]. We hereby reject the *Goller* test as set forth in *Streenz*, and we approve of the "reasonable parent test," in which a parent's conduct is judged by whether that parent's conduct comported with that of a reasonable and prudent parent in a similar situation. [ ]

A parent is not immune from liability for tortious conduct directed toward his child solely by reason of that relationship. [ ] And, a parent is not liable for an act or omission that injured his child if the parent acted as a reasonable and prudent parent in the situation would.

III. Application to the Present Case

In this case, the trier of fact may find that the mother, Laura Broadbent, did not act as a reasonable and prudent parent would have in this situation. The finder of fact must determine whether leaving a two-and-a-half year old child unattended next to a swimming pool is reasonable or prudent. . . .

The paradox of parental immunity can be seen if we assume that a neighbor child from across the street was a guest and was injured at the same time and under the same circumstances as Christopher. Should the neighbor child be permitted to sue and recover damages from Laura but Christopher be denied the same opportunity?

A parent may avoid liability because there is no negligence, but not merely because of the status as parent. Children are certainly accident prone, and oftentimes those accidents are not due to the negligence of any party. The same rules of summary judgment apply to these cases as to others, and trial courts should feel free to dismiss frivolous cases on the ground that the parent has acted as a reasonable and prudent parent in a similar situation would. [ ]

[The court vacated the decision below and remanded to the trial court for further proceedings.]] disposition

■ MOELLER, V.C.J., and ZLAKET and MARTONE, JJ., concur.

■ FELDMAN, CHIEF JUSTICE, specially concurring.

I join in the abrogation of parental immunity and the court's adoption of the reasonable and prudent parent test but write separately to sound a note of caution. Although we abolish a rule of tort immunity, we must bear in mind that "difficult problems" remain in "determining when a physical harm should be regarded as actionable." Restatement (Second) of Torts § 895G cmt. *k*. If the alleged tortious conduct does not grow out of the family relationship, the question of negligence "may be determined as if the parties were not related." [ ] However, there are areas of broad discretion in which only parents have authority to make decisions. In these areas, I agree with the Restatement's view that "the standard of a reasonable prudent parent . . . recognize[s] the existence of that discretion and thus . . . require[s] that the [parent's] conduct be palpably unreasonable in order to impose liability." . . .

[Here the opinion distinguishes between enrolling "a two-year-old child in swimming lessons at a neighborhood pool"—where the standard would be "palpably unreasonable"—and "leaving an unsupervised two-year-old child, who was unable to swim, at the side of a swimming pool."]

NOTES AND QUESTIONS

1. Evaluate the five reasons the court offers for the immunity. Can you think of any others that the court omits? The majority asserts that "virtually everything a parent does in relation to his child involves 'care, custody and control.'" Is that correct? What about automobile driving?

2. How does the concurrer disagree with the majority? How different is the standard of "palpably unreasonable" from the majority's standard of a "reasonably prudent parent in a similar situation"? Suppose that two parents, both former Marine drill sergeants, believe that toughness and stoicism are the keys to success in life, and so require their nine-year-old son to do demanding physical tasks routinely and as punishment. During one particularly extended and strenuous session, the child suffers an aneurysm with consequent long-term deficits.

3. The implications of the New York view, which bars suits against parents for negligent supervision of their children, were spelled out in *Zikely v. Zikely*, 470 N.Y.S.2d 33, 34 (App.Div.1983), *aff'd* on the opinion below, 467 N.E.2d 892 (N.Y.1984). The "infant plaintiff was injured when the defendant parent turned on a hot water faucet in a tub to prepare a bath and then left the room. The child, left unsupervised, wandered into the bathroom and fell into or otherwise entered the tub, suffering severe

burns." The majority understood *Holodook* to protect parents who created dangers as well as those who failed to protect children against dangers:

> [T]o at least some degree the parents in *Holodook* took some affirmative action in creating a danger. Bringing a young child to a neighbor and letting the child loose in a yard where an eight-year old is playing with a power mower or bringing a child to a playground containing an 11-foot-high slide involves some affirmative behavior on the part of the parent in creating a danger that the child, if left unsupervised, will suffer injury. [To read *Holodook* to allow suits in such cases would mean that] [e]very time a parent plugged in an iron, started a toaster, or boiled a pot of water on the stove, he would be subjected to potential liability if an unsupervised child came in contact with these common, daily household hazards in a manner which resulted in injury. To accept such a position would be to strip *Holodook* of a significant part of its meaning.

How would the facts of *Broadbent* be analyzed in New York?

4. Does the *Broadbent* approach permit taking into account the various kinds of diversity that the New York court deems necessary?

5. Was the limitation of parental liability justifiable at the time it was developed at the end of the nineteenth century? If so, what has changed? Would it be defensible to impose a duty of care and eliminate the immunity only in automobile accident cases? Is it defensible to allow a child's friends to sue the child's mother for negligent driving but bar the child from such a suit?

6. *Harm to the fetus.* In Bonte v. Bonte, 616 A.2d 464 (N.H.1992), a child born alive was allowed to sue her mother for "catastrophic" injuries sustained when her mother failed "to use reasonable care in crossing the street and fail[ed] to use a designated crosswalk." The court, 3–2, held that because a fetus born alive could sue a third party for harm sustained before birth, and because the court had abolished parental immunity, "it follows" that this action should lie. The majority rejected the notion that fetal injury warranted different treatment from claims brought by a child already born. One of the three justices, urging case-by-case development in this area, concluded that the negligence alleged here was actionable "because a breach of the duty owed to [the] fetus could foreseeably cause serious harm to an unborn child." (The majority noted in passing that the defendant mother was "represented by counsel provided by her insurance company," but made nothing of that fact in its decision.)

Remy v. MacDonald, 801 N.E.2d 260 (Mass.2004) is contrary. The pregnant defendant drove negligently and hurt her fetus. After birth, the baby sued. The court unanimously held that the mother did not owe a duty of care to her fetus. The court rejected *Bonte* and two similar cases on the ground that they undertook

> no serious analysis of the unique relationship between a pregnant woman and the fetus she carries. The courts also failed to address the collateral social and other impacts of the imposition of a legal

(as opposed to a moral) obligation that would hold a pregnant woman to a standard of care towards her unborn child. . . . We conclude that there are inherent and important differences between a fetus, *in utero*, and a child already born, that permits a bright line to be drawn around the zone of potential tort liability of one who is still biologically joined to an injured plaintiff.

Should a child be permitted to sue a parent for smoking-related harm suffered prior to birth? What about a suit for respiratory harm caused to a child by a smoking parent after birth? Suppose a mother uses crack cocaine during her pregnancy?

7. *The impact of insurance. Broadbent* appears influenced by the institution of insurance. Yet, the court asserts that it "would not be a viable rule to say that liability only exists where insurance exists." Why not? See Ard v. Ard, 414 So.2d 1066 (Fla.1982), allowing intrafamily suits up to the limit of any insurance coverage. (Of course, this may be so attractive to the family that it creates concerns about collusion that must be addressed.)

A few courts have decided that immunity should remain in the face of insurance. See the discussion in Renko v. McLean, 697 A.2d 468 (Md.1997), an automobile accident case in which the court unanimously rejected any liability. The court noted that it had permitted some exceptions, such as a suit against a father's business partner for the negligence of the partnership, and one where "within the span of one week, the father both murdered the child's mother and committed suicide in the child's presence." But an exception for automobile accidents "would effectively negate the rule and open courthouse doors to every conceivable dispute between parent and child."

The court saw several "infirmities" in the limited abrogation, including the concern that insurers were placed in the "unenviable position of attempting to defend a suit that its insured has every incentive to lose." Moreover, the court was concerned that "a jury's generosity is proportionate to the amount of available insurance." Maryland and most states bar telling the jury that insurance is involved in a case. Is this type of case more likely to lead to jury speculation about insurance than the typical auto accident? Finally, the court was concerned about judgments that exceeded the available liability insurance. In such a case the feared intrafamily rancor would reappear. If the court were to try to limit the child's recovery to the amount of available insurance, "the argument that his or her recovery should be no different than that of any person negligently injured once again takes center stage." Further, "many families carry medical insurance that would necessarily compensate the injured child, and therefore, his or her family, for injury-related expenses." How might *Broadbent* answer each of these concerns? *Renko* was superseded by statute. See Allstate Insur. Co. v. Kim, 829 A.2d 611 (Md.2003).

When states have permitted intrafamily suits for auto accidents or other types of harm, insurers have frequently responded by excluding that coverage from the policy. Some courts permit insurers to exclude coverage of intrafamily claims in non-auto suits but refuse to allow it in auto suits especially where such insurance is compulsory or strongly encouraged. We return to insurance in more detail in Chapter XI.

G. GOVERNMENTAL ENTITIES

Sovereign immunity, based on the precept that "the King can do no wrong," was a part of the English common law heritage. Despite the absence of a monarch in this country, governmental immunity to tort liability was imported and became firmly established here. In Kawananakoa v. Polyblank, 205 U.S. 349 (1907), Justice Holmes summed up the received wisdom in his characteristically concise fashion: "A sovereign is exempt from suit, not because of any formal conception or obsolete theory, but on the logical and practical ground that there can be no legal right as against the authority that makes the law on which the right depends." See generally D. Dobbs et al., Hornbook on Torts § 22.1 (2d ed. 2016).

If the Holmes position sounds suspiciously conclusory, so too did the public policy rationale stating that tax funds ought not to be diverted from the public purposes for which they were collected.* Nonetheless, the protective embrace of governmental immunity to suit encompassed federal, state and municipal entities until the end of World War II.

In the two succeeding decades, judicial abrogation and legislative refinement went hand-in-hand in reversing the earlier state of affairs: immunity became the exception rather than the rule.

The abrogation of blanket immunity, however, did not lead to uniform treatment of public and private acts causing unintentional harm. Two themes pervade the different treatment of tort liability for public entities: 1) governmental officials make many policy choices, balancing costs and benefits for public or political gain; and 2) much of governmental activity is in the affirmative duty sphere: protecting the public from risk created by others. This section explores the ramifications of governmental liability from a duty perspective, because duty limitations have in fact been the principal technique for continued recognition of the special character of certain public functions.

---

* For hundreds of years courts protected charities by giving them immunity from liability for the negligent actions of their employees. This limit on respondeat superior was justified on the ground that benefactors gave money to these organizations to further their charitable work and not to be given to those harmed by the work. This protection has virtually disappeared at common law. See, e.g., Albritton v. Neighborhood Centers Ass'n for Child Development, 466 N.E.2d 867 (Ohio 1984). But see Picher v. Roman Catholic Bishop of Portland, 974 A.2d 286 (Me. 2009)(charity immune from negligence but not intentional tort claims in suit alleging priest sexually abused plaintiff and bishop failed to supervise properly). In some states legislative limits have been placed on the amount for which a charity might be held liable and some states condition liability on whether the charity carries liability insurance to cover the risk. See, e.g., Schultz v. Roman Catholic Archdiocese of Newark, 472 A.2d 531 (N.J.1984).

1. MUNICIPAL AND STATE LIABILITY

Riss v. City of New York
Court of Appeals of New York, 1968.
22 N.Y.2d 579, 240 N.E.2d 860, 293 N.Y.S.2d 897.

■ BREITEL, J.

[The facts are taken from the dissenting opinion, which the majority opinion adopted by reference. Linda Riss was terrorized for six months by Pugach who had formerly dated her. He warned that if he could not have her, "no one else will have you, and when I get through with you, no one else will want you." She sought police protection unsuccessfully. She then became engaged to another man and at a celebration party she received a call saying that this was her last chance. She again sought police help but was refused. The next day a thug hired by Pugach threw lye in plaintiff's face, leaving her permanently scarred, blind in one eye, and with little vision in the other.]

This appeal presents, in a very sympathetic framework, the issue of the liability of a municipality for failure to provide special protection to a member of the public who was repeatedly threatened with personal harm and eventually suffered dire personal injuries for lack of such protection. . . . The issue arises upon the affirmance by a divided Appellate Division of a dismissal of the complaint, after both sides had rested but before submission to the jury.

It is necessary immediately to distinguish those liabilities attendant upon governmental activities which have displaced or supplemented traditionally private enterprises, such as are involved in the operation of rapid transit systems, hospitals, and places of public assembly. Once sovereign immunity was abolished by statute the extension of liability on ordinary principles of tort law logically followed. To be equally distinguished are certain activities of government which provide services and facilities for the use of the public, such as highways, public buildings and the like, in the performance of which the municipality or the State may be liable under ordinary principles of tort law. The ground for liability is the provision of the services or facilities for the direct use by members of the public.

In contrast, this case involves the provision of a governmental service to protect the public generally from external hazards and particularly to control the activities of criminal wrongdoers. [ ] The amount of protection that may be provided is limited by the resources of the community and by a considered legislative-executive decision as to how those resources may be deployed. For the courts to proclaim a new and general duty of protection in the law of tort, even to those who may be the particular seekers of protection based on specific hazards, could and would inevitably determine how the limited police resources of the community should be allocated and without predictable limits. This is quite different from the predictable allocation of resources and liabilities when public hospitals, rapid transit systems, or even highways are provided.

Before such extension of responsibilities should be dictated by the indirect imposition of tort liabilities, there should be a legislative determination that that should be the scope of public responsibility [ ].

It is notable that the removal of sovereign immunity for tort liability was accomplished after legislative enactment and not by any judicial arrogation of power (Court of Claims Act, § 8). It is equally notable that for many years, since as far back as 1909 in this State, there was by statute municipal liability for losses sustained as a result of riot (General Municipal Law, § 71). Yet even this class of liability has for some years been suspended by legislative action [ ], a factor of considerable significance.

When one considers the greatly increased amount of crime committed throughout the cities, but especially in certain portions of them, with a repetitive and predictable pattern, it is easy to see the consequences of fixing municipal liability upon a showing of probable need for and request for protection. To be sure these are grave problems at the present time, exciting high priority activity on the part of the national, State and local governments, to which the answers are neither simple, known, or presently within reasonable controls. To foist a presumed cure for these problems by judicial innovation of a new kind of liability in tort would be foolhardy indeed and an assumption of judicial wisdom and power not possessed by the courts.

Nor is the analysis progressed by the analogy to compensation for losses sustained. It is instructive that the Crime Victims Compensation and "good Samaritan" statutes, compensating limited classes of victims of crime, were enacted only after the most careful study of conditions and the impact of such a scheme upon governmental operations and the public fisc [ ]. And then the limitations were particular and narrow.

For all of these reasons, there is no warrant in judicial tradition or in the proper allocation of the powers of government for the courts, in the absence of legislation, to carve out an area of tort liability for police protection to members of the public. Quite distinguishable, of course, is the situation where the police authorities undertake responsibilities to particular members of the public and expose them, without adequate protection, to the risks which then materialize into actual losses (Schuster v. City of New York, 5 N.Y.2d 75 [1958]).

Accordingly, the order of the Appellate Division affirming the judgment of dismissal should be affirmed.

■ CHIEF JUDGE FULD and JUDGES BURKE, SCILEPPI, BERGAN and JASEN concur with JUDGE BREITEL.

■ KEATING, J., dissents and votes to reverse in a separate opinion.

. . .

It is not a distortion to summarize the essence of the city's case here in the following language: "Because we owe a duty to everybody, we owe it to nobody." Were it not for the fact that this position has been hallowed by much ancient and revered precedent, we would surely dismiss it as preposterous. To say that there is no duty is, of course, to start with the conclusion. The question is whether or not there should be liability for the negligent failure to provide adequate police protection.

. . .

The fear of financial disaster is a myth. The same argument was made a generation ago in opposition to proposals that the State waive its defense of "sovereign immunity." The prophecy proved false then, and it would now. The supposed astronomical financial burden does not and would not exist. No municipality has gone bankrupt because it has had to respond in damages when a policeman causes injury through carelessly driving a police car or in the thousands of other situations where, by judicial fiat or legislative enactment, the State and its subdivisions have been held liable for the tortious conduct of their employees. . . . [Judge Keating then observed that less than two-tenths of one percent of the city's annual budget was being allocated to payment of tort claims.] That Linda Riss should be asked to bear the loss, which should properly fall on the city if we assume, as we must, in the present posture of the case, that her injuries resulted from the city's failure to provide sufficient police to protect Linda is contrary to the most elementary notions of justice.

The statement in the majority opinion that there are no predictable limits to the potential liability for failure to provide adequate police protection as compared to other areas of municipal liability is, of course, untenable. When immunity in other areas of governmental activity was removed, the same lack of predictable limits existed. Yet, disaster did not ensue.

Another variation of the "crushing burden" argument is the contention that, every time a crime is committed, the city will be sued and the claim will be made that it resulted from inadequate police protection. . . . The argument is . . . made as if there were no such legal principles as fault, proximate cause or foreseeability, all of which operate to keep liability within reasonable bounds. No one is contending that the police must be at the scene of every potential crime or must provide a personal bodyguard to every person who walks into a police station and claims to have been threatened. They need only act as a reasonable man would under the circumstances. At first there would be a duty to inquire. If the inquiry indicates nothing to substantiate the alleged threat, the matter may be put aside and other matters attended to. If, however, the claims prove to have some basis, appropriate steps would be necessary.

. . .

More significant, however, is the fundamental flaw in the reasoning behind the argument alleging judicial interference. It is a complete oversimplification of the problem of municipal tort liability. What it ignores is the fact that indirectly courts are reviewing administrative practices in almost every tort case against the State or a municipality, including even decisions of the Police Commissioner. Every time a municipal hospital is held liable for malpractice resulting from inadequate record-keeping, the courts are in effect making a determination that the municipality should have hired or assigned more clerical help or more competent help to medical records or should have done something to improve its record-keeping procedures so that the particular injury would not have occurred. Every time a municipality is held liable for a defective sidewalk, it is as if the courts are saying that more money and resources should have been allocated to sidewalk repair, instead of to other public services.

. . .

The truth of the matter, however, is that the courts are not making policy decisions for public officials. In all these municipal negligence cases, the courts are doing two things. First, they apply the principles of vicarious liability to the operations of government. Courts would not insulate the city from liability for the ordinary negligence of members of the highway department. There is no basis for treating the members of the police department differently.

Second, and most important, to the extent that the injury results from the failure to allocate sufficient funds and resources to meet a minimum standard of public administration, public officials are presented with two alternatives: either improve public administration or accept the cost of compensating injured persons. Thus, if we were to hold the city liable here for the negligence of the police, courts would no more be interfering with the operations of the police department than they "meddle" in the affairs of the highway department when they hold the municipality liable for personal injuries resulting from defective sidewalks, or a private employer for the negligence of his employees. In other words, all the courts do in these municipal negligence cases is require officials to weigh the consequences of their decisions. If Linda Riss' injury resulted from the failure of the city to pay sufficient salaries to attract qualified and sufficient personnel, the full cost of that choice should become acknowledged in the same way as it has in other areas of municipal tort liability. Perhaps officials will find it less costly to choose the alternative of paying damages than changing their existing practices. That may be well and good, but the price for the refusal to provide for an adequate police force should not be borne by Linda Riss and all the other innocent victims of such decisions.

. . .

No doubt in the future we shall have to draw limitations just as we have done in the area of private litigation, and no doubt some of these limitations will be unique to municipal liability because the problems will not have any counterpart in private tort law. But if the lines are to be drawn, let them be delineated on candid considerations of policy and fairness and not on the fictions or relics of the doctrine of "sovereign immunity." Before reaching such questions, however, we must resolve the fundamental issue raised here and recognize that, having undertaken to provide professional police and fire protection, municipalities cannot escape liability for damages caused by their failure to do even a minimally adequate job of it.

. . .

NOTES AND QUESTIONS

1.   Safeguarding the personal security of the community is, of course, one of the traditional functions of government. *Riss* has been a pivotal case because it raises fundamental issues about police responsibility to the public at large. Consider the following cases that arguably pose more focused questions of government responsibility for personal security:

a.   In the earlier case of *Schuster v. City of New York*, cited by Judge Breitel, Schuster provided information to the police that led to the capture of a noted criminal, Willie Sutton. Schuster recognized Sutton from an FBI flyer that had been posted in his father's store. Shortly after he supplied the information to the police his life was threatened, and three weeks later he was killed. The court, 4–3, sustained plaintiff's claim that the police were under a legal duty to respond reasonably to Schuster's request for protection. The court remarked:

> In a situation like the present, government is not merely passive; it is active in calling upon persons "in possession of any information regarding the whereabouts of" Sutton, quoting from the FBI flyer, to communicate such information in aid of law enforcement. Where that has happened, as here, or where the public authorities have made active use of a private citizen in some other capacity in the arrest or prosecution of a criminal, it would be a misuse of language to say that the law enforcement authorities are merely passive. They are active in calling upon the citizen for help, and in utilizing his help when it is rendered.

Is there a satisfying distinction between *Schuster* and *Riss*?

b.   Sorichetti v. City of New York, 482 N.E.2d 70 (N.Y.1985), involved a suit on behalf of a young child who was badly mutilated by her father while he was exercising his visitation rights. The father had a long history of violent and abusive behavior towards his ex-wife, the child's mother, which had led the Family Court to issue a series of protective orders (which, by statute, gave the police broad discretion to take the father into custody at the petition of his ex-wife). On the weekend in question, when the father picked up his daughter, he threatened to kill his wife and shouted to the child, "You see Dina; you better do the sign of the cross before this weekend is up." His ex-wife made repeated efforts to initiate police intervention to get the child, but the officers refused to take action on the basis of the father's verbal threats, and told her to go home. An hour after the father was to have returned the child on Sunday evening, he severely injured her in a drunken rage.

In imposing a duty based on the police inaction, the court distinguished *Riss* on the basis of the protective orders, the father's history of violent behavior, and the front-desk officer's assurance that at some point the police would take action. Is *Riss* distinguishable?

c.   In Cuffy v. City of New York, 505 N.E.2d 937 (N.Y.1987), the court attempted to establish guidelines for its continuing line of police protection cases. On a number of occasions, the Cuffys sought police protection from their downstairs neighbors (and tenants) the Aitkins, with whom they had had a number of skirmishes. After Mr. Aitkins physically attacked Ms. Cuffy, Mr. Cuffy finally received assurance from the police that something would be done—possibly an arrest—"first thing in the morning." The next evening, when Ralston Cuffy (a son) came to visit, Mr. Aitkins attacked him with a baseball bat, and Ms. Aitkins slashed Ms. Cuffy and Cyril Cuffy (another son who lived at home) with a knife. In the interim, the police had done nothing, and the three Cuffys subsequently sued the city for their injuries.

The court stated the general rule to be no tort duty to provide police protection, but recognized an exception in cases of "special relationship"— the elements of which were stated to be: "1) an assumption by the municipality through promises or action, of an affirmative duty to act on behalf of the party who was injured; 2) knowledge on the part of the municipality's agents that inaction could lead to harm; 3) some form of direct contact between the municipality's agents and the injured party; and 4) that party's justifiable reliance on the municipality's undertaking."

Under these principles, Ralston Cuffy was denied recovery because he could establish neither direct contact nor reliance on the police promise— indeed he apparently didn't even know about the promise when he came to visit—and the other Cuffys were denied recovery because by the evening, when the harm occurred, they were no longer relying on a police promise to respond that morning.

Do the four "elements" seem a fair summary of the standards used in deciding the affirmative duty cases in this section? Are they sound? Do they seem to have been properly applied in *Cuffy*? In Mastroianni v. County of Suffolk, 691 N.E.2d 613 (N.Y.1997), a husband fatally stabbed his wife shortly after police officers, who had been called to investigate his presence at her residence and allegedly disorderly conduct in violation of a protective order, left without making an arrest although the husband was still there. The court held that under these circumstances the first two *Cuffy* elements were satisfied by the protective order itself, and that the latter two elements were satisfied by the officers' direct contact with the decedent and their promise to "do whatever they could" if she had any further problems with her husband.

d.   A more recent New York case involving municipal liability for failure to provide police protection is Valdez v. City of New York, 960 N.E.2d 356 (N.Y.2011). Plaintiff, after her boyfriend had threatened to kill her, contacted the police. The police told her to return to her apartment with her two children and that the former boyfriend would be arrested immediately. She returned with her children but had no further communication with the police. The former boyfriend shot her outside her apartment 28 hours after the phone conversation. Relying on the fourth *Cuffy* factor of justifiable reliance, the court held that she failed to establish a special relationship imposing a duty on the City. It was not reasonable for the plaintiff to conclude that she could relax her vigilance indefinitely and exit her apartment some 28 hours later without further contact with the police.

2.   *The 911 call*. In De Long v. County of Erie, 457 N.E.2d 717 (N.Y.1983), a woman called 911 to report a burglar outside. The court treated a 911 operator's assurance that help was being sent "right away" as the assumption of a duty to respond with due care to the victim's call for help.

But both direct communication and reliance by the caller are needed to create the special relationship that New York requires for that duty. In Merced v. City of New York, 551 N.E.2d 589 (N.Y.1990), a 911 case in which the caller apparently was not the victim, the court held that the required relationship "cannot be established without proof that the injured party had direct contact with the municipality's agents and justifiably relied to his or her detriment on the municipality's assurances that it would act on that party's behalf."

In Muthukumarana v. Montgomery County, 805 A.2d 372 (Md.2002), an adolescent who became severely intoxicated was sexually abused at a party. Afterwards, she was dragged, semi-conscious, out of the house and into a wooded area while lightly dressed and with a winter storm forecast. Someone present called 911 and related her condition and location to the dispatcher who promised the caller that an officer would be dispatched. The dispatcher provided an incorrect address to the officer who never located the victim; she died of hypothermia. Although the dispatcher had promised the anonymous caller that an officer would be dispatched, no duty existed because the person at risk must have a special relationship with the government—a third party was insufficient.

In contrast, to *Cuffy* and *Muthukumarana* is Reis v. Delaware River Port Authority, 2008 WL 425522 (N.J.Super.Ct.App.Div.2008). Plaintiff's decedent was abducted, and a witness called 911, relaying information about the abductors, their car, and direction of travel. The 911 dispatcher inadvertently failed to enter the information and consequently no officers were dispatched to the location. Decedent was brutally beaten before being murdered. The court interpreted the state governmental immunity statute to not preclude liability based on the dispatcher's negligence.

3. *Educational malpractice.* A graduate of a San Francisco public high school sued the school district for, among other things, its negligent failure to teach him to read above fifth-grade level. Peter W. v. San Francisco Unified School District, 131 Cal.Rptr. 854 (App.1976). After noting that the district had no governmental immunity, the court stated that while the problem was one of duty, cases involving the duty of a school to exercise due care for the physical safety of the students did not control this situation:

> On occasions when the Supreme Court has opened or sanctioned new areas of tort liability, it has noted that the wrongs and injuries involved were both comprehensible and assessable within the existing judicial framework. [ ] This is simply not true of wrongful conduct and injuries allegedly involved in educational malfeasance. Unlike the activity of the highway or the market place, classroom methodology affords no readily acceptable standards of care, or cause, or injury. The science of pedagogy itself is fraught with different and conflicting theories of how or what a child should be taught, and any layman might—and commonly does—have his own emphatic views on the subject. The "injury" claimed here is plaintiff's inability to read and write. Substantial professional authority attests that the achievement of literacy in the schools, or its failure, are influenced by a host of factors which affect the pupil subjectively, from outside the formal teaching process, and beyond the control of its ministers. They may be physical, neurological, emotional, cultural, environmental; they may be present but not perceived, recognized but not identified.

> We find in this situation no conceivable "workability of a rule of care" against which defendants' alleged conduct may be measured, [ ], no reasonable "degree of certainty that . . . plaintiff suffered injury" within the meaning of the law of negligence (see Rest.2d Torts, § 281), and no such perceptible "connection between the defendant's conduct and the injury suffered," as alleged, which would establish a causal link between them within the same meaning. [ ]

> These recognized policy considerations alone negate an actionable "duty of care" in persons and agencies who administer the academic phases of the public educational process. Others, which are even more important in practical terms, command the same result. Few of our institutions, if any, have aroused the controversies, or incurred the public dissatisfaction, which have attended the operation of the public schools during the last few decades. Rightly or wrongly, but widely, they are charged with outright failure in the achievement of their educational objectives; according to some critics, they bear responsibility for many of the social and moral problems of our society at large. Their public plight in these respects is attested in the daily media, in bitter governing board elections, in wholesale rejections of school bond

proposals, and in survey upon survey. To hold them to an actionable "duty of care," in the discharge of their academic functions, would expose them to the tort claims—real or imagined—of disaffected students and parents in countless numbers. They are already beset by social and financial problems which have gone to major litigation, but for which no permanent solution has yet appeared. [ ] The ultimate consequences, in terms of public time and money, would burden them—and society— beyond calculation.

How might the damages be measured?

4. *Other custodial relationships.* In addition to educational malpractice claims, the school setting has given rise to a variety of other duty claims based on a custodial relationship. For example, in Hoyem v. Manhattan Beach City School District, 585 P.2d 851 (Cal.1978), a ten-year-old student slipped away from school during the day and was run over by a motorcyclist four blocks from the school. The court, 4–3, reversed dismissal of the complaint and held that the defendant school district owed a duty of due care in supervising the plaintiff.

Justice Tobriner's opinion for the majority stressed that the alleged negligence occurred on the school premises even though the injury occurred elsewhere. The decision did not require "truant-proof" schools: "We require ordinary care, not fortresses; schools must be reasonably supervised, not truant-proof."

The dissenters in *Hoyem* thought it odd that a truant had a lawsuit when a student who had attended all day and was run over after school did not. They wanted to limit the district's liability to students injured on school property or in school-related activities off the premises.

Do the school cases raise the issue of concern about interfering with "the discretionary nature of the functions of planning and allocation of resources" in governmental activities? On this score, reconsider *Schuster* and *Riss*.

Lauer v. City of New York

Court of Appeals of New York, 2000.
95 N.Y.2d 95, 733 N.E.2d 184, 711 N.Y.S.2d 112.

■ KAYE, CHIEF JUDGE.

On this appeal we revisit a familiar subject: whether a member of the public can recover damages against a municipality for its employee's negligence. Here we answer that question in the negative.

The Facts

Three-year-old Andrew Lauer died on August 7, 1993. That same day, Dr. Eddy Lilavois, a New York City Medical Examiner, performed an autopsy and prepared a report stating that the child's death was a homicide caused by "blunt injuries" to the neck and brain. Although the report indicated that the brain was being preserved for further examination, the following day a death certificate was issued stating that Andrew's death was a homicide. Based on the Medical Examiner's conclusion, the police began investigating what they thought was a homicide, focusing primarily on plaintiff, Andrew's father. Weeks later, on August 31, 1993, the Medical Examiner and a neuropathologist conducted a more detailed study of Andrew's brain. The report, prepared in October 1993, indicated that a ruptured brain aneurysm caused the child's death, thus contradicting the earlier conclusion. The Medical Examiner, however, failed to correct the autopsy report or death certificate, and failed to notify law enforcement authorities.

Meanwhile, the police department's investigation into Andrew's death continued. Some 17 months later, in March 1995, after a newspaper exposé the autopsy findings were revised, the police investigation ceased and an amended death certificate was prepared. As a result of this incident, the City Medical Examiner who had conducted the examination resigned.

[Plaintiff brought a number of claims against the City of New York all of which were dismissed by the trial court. On appeal, the Appellate Division affirmed the dismissals, except for the claim of negligent infliction of emotional distress, which it reinstated by a divided court. "Viability of that single remaining claim is the issue now before us on this appeal." It should be noted that only emotional distress, and not physical injury formed the basis for the plaintiff's claims, but the opinions in the case do not rely on this fact—focusing instead on the municipal liability issue. We consider the topic of claims for emotional distress absent physical injury in detail in the next Chapter.]

The Law as Applied to the Facts

Analysis begins with several undisputed propositions. Municipalities long ago surrendered common law tort immunity for the negligence of their employees. A distinction is drawn, however, between "discretionary" and "ministerial" governmental acts. A public employee's discretionary acts—meaning conduct involving the exercise of reasoned judgment—may not result in the municipality's liability even when the conduct is negligent. By contrast, ministerial acts—meaning conduct requiring adherence to a governing rule, with a compulsory result—may subject the municipal employer to liability for negligence [ ]. No one disputes that the Medical Examiner's misconduct here in failing to correct the record and deliver it to the authorities was ministerial.

There agreement ends. Plaintiff contends that the City should be liable for the Medical Examiner's "ministerial negligence," while defendant urges that the complaint be dismissed.

We do not agree with plaintiff that a ministerial breach by a governmental employee necessarily gives rise to municipal liability. Rather, a ministerial wrong "merely removes the issue of governmental immunity from a given case" [ ]. Ministerial negligence may not be immunized, but it is not necessarily tortious [ ]. There must still be a basis to hold the municipality liable for negligence (see, *Florence v. Goldberg*, [ ] ["Absent the existence and breach of . . . a duty, the abrogation of governmental immunity, in itself, affords little aid to a plaintiff seeking to cast a municipality in damages"]; see also, *De Long v. County of Erie*, [note 2, p. 233 supra] [liability for ministerial failure to process "911" call rested on County employee's affirmative assurances of assistance made to victim]; [ ]).

This brings us directly to an essential element of any negligence case: duty. Without a duty running directly to the injured person there can be no liability in damages, however careless the conduct or foreseeable the harm (see, *Pulka v. Edelman* [ ]). . . While the Legislature can create a duty by statute, in most cases duty is defined by the courts, as a matter of policy.

Fixing the orbit of duty may be a difficult task. Despite often sympathetic facts in a particular case before them, courts must be mindful of the precedential, and consequential, future effects of their rulings, and "limit the legal consequences of wrongs to a controllable degree" ([ ]; *Strauss v. Belle Realty Co.*, [p. 166 supra]). Time and again we have required "that the equation be balanced; that the damaged plaintiff be able to point the finger of responsibility at a defendant owing, not a general duty to society, but a specific duty to him" ([ ]).

This is especially so where an individual seeks recovery out of the public purse. To sustain liability against a municipality, the duty breached must be more than that owed the public generally (see, *Florence v. Goldberg*, [ ]). Indeed, we have consistently refused to impose liability for a municipality in performing a public function absent "a duty to use due care for the benefit of particular persons or classes of persons" [ ]. Here, because plaintiff cannot point to a duty owed to him by the Office of the Chief Medical Examiner, his negligence claim must fail.

Pointing to New York City Charter § 557, plaintiff argues that the Office of the Chief Medical Examiner owed him a duty to communicate accurate information to authorities pertaining to his son's death. Section 557 charges the Chief Medical Examiner with examining "bodies of persons dying from criminal violence" or other suspicious circumstances, keeping "full and complete records in such form as may be provided by law," and promptly delivering "to the appropriate district attorney copies of all records relating to every death as to which there is, in the judgment of the medical examiner in charge, any indication of criminality."

Violation of a statute resulting in injury gives rise to a tort action only if the intent of the statute is to protect an individual against an invasion of a property or personal interest [ ].

In [ ], for example, plaintiff sought to recover damages suffered as a result of a fire, relying on a City Charter provision requiring maintenance of a fire department. We concluded that liability could not be predicated on the Charter provision, which was not designed to protect the personal interest of any individual, but rather was "designed to secure the benefits of well ordered municipal government enjoyed by all as members of the community" [ ]. We explained that:

> An intention to impose upon the city the crushing burden
> of such an obligation should not be imputed to the Legislature
> in the absence of language clearly designed to have that effect.
>
> . . .
>
> Such [City Charter] enactments do not import intention to protect the interests of any individual except as they secure to all members of the community the enjoyment of rights and privileges to which they are entitled only as members of the public. Neglect in the performance of such requirements creates no civil liability to individuals [ ].

New York City Charter § 557 similarly defines one of the municipality's governmental functions. It establishes the Office of the Chief Medical Examiner as part of the City's Department of Health, and requires performance of autopsies and preparation of reports for the benefit of the public at large. Significantly, the only individual to whom the Medical Examiner must by statute report is "the appropriate district attorney" (see, New York City Charter § 557[g]). Neither plaintiff, nor other members of the general public who may become criminal suspects upon the death of a person, are persons "for whose especial benefit the statute was enacted" [ ]. Permitting recovery here would rewrite section 557, radically enlarging both the responsibility of the Office of the Chief Medical Examiner and the potential liability of the City.

Nor do we find any duty to plaintiff derived from a "special relationship" with him. [The court then recited the *Cuffy* factors, note 1c, p. 232 supra.]

Those requirements are not met here. The Medical Examiner never undertook to act on plaintiff's behalf. He made no promises or assurances to plaintiff, and assumed no affirmative duty upon which plaintiff might have justifiably relied. Plaintiff alleges no personal contact with the Medical Examiner, and therefore also fails to satisfy the "direct contact" requirement of the test. There is, moreover, no indication that the Medical Examiner knew that plaintiff, or anyone else, had become a suspect in the case. Nor do Medical Examiners generally owe a "special duty" to potential homicide suspects. Their function in this context is not as a law enforcement agency but solely to impart objective information to the appropriate authorities for the benefit of the public at large [ ].

As we explained in De Angelis v. Lutheran Med. Ctr., [449 N.E.2d 406 (N.Y.1983)]:

> A line must be drawn between the competing policy considerations of providing a remedy to everyone who is injured and of extending exposure to tort liability almost without limit. It is always tempting, especially when symmetry and sympathy would so seem to be best served, to impose new duties, and, concomitantly, liabilities, regardless of the economic and social burden. But, absent legislative intervention, the fixing of the "orbit" of duty, as here, in the end is the responsibility of the courts.

Here, in order for plaintiff's claim for negligent infliction of emotional distress to be successful, we would have to impose a new duty on the Office of the Chief Medical Examiner, which for the future would run to members of the public who may become subjects of a criminal investigation into a death. This we refuse to do.

. . .

In the end, plaintiff's claim is not supported by existing law, and we cannot agree that the proposed enlargement of the orbit of duty, resting largely on the foreseeability of harm, is a sound one.

Accordingly, the order of the Appellate Division should be reversed, without costs, the complaint dismissed and the certified question answered in the negative.

■ SMITH, J., dissenting.

Because I believe that plaintiff Edward G. Lauer has adequately pleaded a prima facie case for negligent infliction of emotional distress, I dissent.

. . .

■ BELLACOSA, J., dissenting.

I agree with Judge Smith's lead dissenting opinion, and add this expression to augment my vote for affirmance of the Appellate Division order.

. . .

The ruling I propose is especially warranted when the public servant, who precipitated the investigation of plaintiff as the suspect in the wrongfully certified homicide of his three-year-old son, fails to remove or at least mitigate the risk and harm that enveloped the life of that one knowable person. Time, circumstance, and place make the Medical Examiner's matter-of-course intervention a reasonable and feasible obligation. The care would, in balanced and controllable theory, extend only to this plaintiff. Indeed, the theoretical, foreseeable class would be a relatively self-defined, small circle of potential suspects, in any event, . . . Moreover, a mathematical process of elimination naturally reduces the operational reach of this rule, and would not result in some open-ended potential drain on the public purse.

Next, the juridical norm I proffer is particularly appropriate—arguably, at an *a fortiori* level—when the culpable employee unilaterally possesses the exclusive knowledge and singular power to right the wrong. He should be legally accountable for failing to act reasonably at the time when complete innocence became medically known and certain to him. It should not be overlooked that the public at large was never potentially a suspect in the infant's death; as it turned out and from the outset, only plaintiff was a beleaguered suspect from the moment the mistaken notice of a "homicide" by "blunt injuries to the neck and brain" was reported by the Medical Examiner to the District Attorney of Queens County. Death actually occurred from a natural cause—a ruptured aneurysm within the youngster's brain.

. . .

To immunize the kind of alleged misconduct described by the pleading of this case would reward government agents who hide the truth and sweep wrongdoings under a rug of tort impunity. In such instances, truly responsible public employees have little to no incentive to own up to wrongdoings, since their official information is usually their secret (especially so in this case), and aggrieved parties will be barred from even entering a courthouse, no less reaching a trial airing of the truth.

The danger to the public purse and public tort policy is not sufficient or proportionate enough to block any chance of accountability and redress here. The zone of the proposed duty, as paradigmed through this case for future guidance, would be prudently limited by the exceptional quality and quantum of factors in this hard, and yes sympathetic, case. The sympathy feature, I must emphasize, does not drive my analysis; nor should it, on the other hand, disqualify the plaintiff and his case from common law evolvement. . . .

. . .

Plaintiff has sought only a day in court that is now foreclosed, thus immunizing the government's alleged wrongdoing against a concededly innocent citizen.

■ Opinion by CHIEF JUDGE KAYE. JUDGES LEVINE, CIPARIK, WESLEY and ROSENBLATT concur. JUDGES BELLACOSA and SMITH dissent and vote to affirm in separate opinions in which each concurs.

NOTES AND QUESTIONS

1.   According to the majority, what is the connection between the duty and immunity analyses?

2. How does the court distinguish between discretionary and ministerial functions? Why does the determination that the Medical Examiner's failure was ministerial not control the outcome of the case?

3. Would *Lauer* have been any different with regard to the existence of a duty if the medical examiner had, while traveling between city offices, run a red light and killed a child-pedestrian? If so, what distinguishes the two cases?

4. Relying on *Cuffy*, note 1c, p. 232 supra, the court suggests the special relationship doctrine could impose a duty here but is inapplicable on the facts. Are the concerns animating protecting the police from tort liability the same as the concerns the court employs in *Lauer* to conclude that there is no duty?

5. Is the majority's fear of unlimited liability justifiable? How would it affect the criminal justice system if the court's judgment had been different? Is the Judge Bellacosa's dissent persuasive on these points?

6. *"Public duty."* The "special relationship" requirement that the *Lauer* majority adopts from the *Cuffy* factors, see note 1c, p. 232 supra, is not universally followed. See, e.g., Cope v. Utah Valley State College, 342 P.3d 243 (Utah 2014). Plaintiff was injured while performing a dance routine for a college team at the direction of the team's coach. She was injured allegedly due to negligent direction by the coach. The court addressed the liability of the college, a state entity, through the public duty doctrine. The lower court dismissed on the ground that there was no special relationship. The court reversed, limiting the public duty doctrine to cases in which the state has not created the risk. Because plaintiff's claim arose out of risk-creating conduct by the state, no special relationship was required.

7. *Governmental v. proprietary.* Consider In re World Trade Center Bombing Litigation, 957 N.E.2d 733 (N.Y.2011). Among other issues in this litigation arising from the 1993 bombing of the World Trade Center (WTC) garage, which was owned and operated by a governmental authority, are the questions of: 1) whether plaintiffs' claims involved governmental or proprietary matters; and if the former 2) whether the claims implicated discretionary matters over police resources similar to *Riss*, or instead involved ministerial matters such as in *Lauer*. The Court of Appeals (4–3) concluded that although both governmental and proprietary actions were involved, the claims in this case involved predominantly the governmental function of providing adequate security against terrorist attacks of the WTC. The court also concluded that not only was this a governmental function but one that was discretionary: "[U]nlike the safety precautions required of every reasonable landowner, the Port Authority's security operations featured policy-based decisionmaking involving due consideration of pertinent factors such as the risk of harm, and the costs and benefits of pursuing a particular allocation of resources." The three dissenters responded that the Port Authority was acting in the same role as a commercial landlord (balancing costs and benefits) in providing adequate security in its garage and building.

8. *Official immunities*. What considerations, if any, identified by the court apply specifically to the Medical Examiner? Traditionally, special immunities have been granted to judges and prosecutors. In Falls v. Superior Court, 49 Cal.Rptr.2d 908 (App.1996), plaintiffs were parents of Eduardo Samaniego, a 14-year-old youth who witnessed the gang murder of his friend and gave evidence at the preliminary hearing. Although the gang had threatened another witness, a deputy district attorney told the witnesses that he had never heard of non-gang-member witnesses to a gang crime being injured or killed in retaliation for testifying. Before trial, however, the gang killed Samaniego. Plaintiffs brought a wrongful death claim against, among others, the prosecutors.

In its opinion, the court distinguished judicial immunity from police immunity, analogizing prosecutorial immunity to the former rather than the latter. Explaining that judicial immunity was entrenched in the common law tradition, the court asserted that "[j]udicial immunity is absolute, not qualified"; therefore, even if the judge has acted maliciously or corruptly, or in excess of his jurisdiction, he will remain immune. According to the court, "when exercising judicial functions, a judge who has a duty, breaches that duty, and causes injury—however intentionally, maliciously, and corruptly—is immune from civil suit."

By contrast, police did not, at common law, have immunity from civil suit, but simply a "good-faith defense." Thus, the court acknowledged that police might be liable if a special relationship exists. It then contrasted the nature of prosecutorial immunity to police immunity. The court explained that because prosecutors perform a quasi-judicial function, they have been granted absolute immunity in both federal and state contexts. This immunity shields a prosecutor only when he "acts within his official capacity," or, in other words, "when his conduct is an 'integral part of the judicial process' or 'intimately associated with the judicial phase of the criminal process.'" In this case, interviewing Samaniego and persuading him to testify were essential to the prosecutors' role—and, therefore, the prosecutors were immune from civil suit.

How would the *Falls* court analyze *Lauer*?

Friedman v. State of New York

Court of Appeals of New York, 1986.
67 N.Y.2d 271, 493 N.E.2d 893, 502 N.Y.S.2d 669.

■ ALEXANDER, J.

[Three personal injury actions involving crossover collisions were consolidated in this appeal. All were brought under the Court of Claims Act, which provides for court hearing without a jury in a case against the state. In *Friedman v. State of New York*, plaintiff's car was sideswiped on a viaduct causing her to swerve into the oncoming traffic where she was hit head-on. She claimed that the state was negligent in failing to construct a median barrier. The state Department of Transportation (DOT) had studied the question five years earlier and decided that a median barrier should be constructed. But at the time of the accident no action had been taken. Although the state attempted to justify its non-action by pointing to funding priorities and project revisions, it did not offer concrete evidence in support of its claims. The Appellate Division affirmed a judgment for plaintiff.

Both *Cataldo v. New York State Thruway Authority* and *Muller v. State of New York* involved accidents on the Tappan Zee bridge. Once again, the plaintiffs claimed negligence in failing to construct a median barrier that would have prevented the crossover accidents. In these cases, however, departmental studies between 1962 and 1972 had determined that the risks of rear-end collisions from "bounce-back" occurrences and stranded autos if a barrier were constructed exceeded the dangers of crossover collisions without a barrier. Cataldo's accident occurred shortly after the last of these studies. Her claim that the studies reached the wrong conclusion was rejected by the Appellate Division on the ground that the agency decision "was premised on a reasonable public safety plan." By the time Muller was injured, however, the department had changed its mind and decided to construct a barrier. More than three years had passed with no further action taken. Nonetheless, the Appellate Division held that the delay was not unreasonable and dismissed Muller's claim.]

. . .

We now affirm the orders of the Appellate Division in *Friedman* and *Cataldo,* and reverse the order appealed from in *Muller.*

It has long been held that a municipality " 'owe[s] to the public the absolute duty of keeping its streets in a reasonably safe condition' " (Weiss v. Fote, 7 N.Y.2d 579, 584 [1960]). While this duty is nondelegable, it is measured by the courts with consideration given to the proper limits on intrusion into the municipality's planning and decision-making functions. Thus, in the field of traffic design engineering, the State is accorded a qualified immunity from liability arising out of a highway planning decision [ ]. In the seminal *Weiss* case, we recognized that "[t]o accept a jury's verdict as to the reasonableness and safety of a plan of governmental services and prefer it over the judgment of the governmental body which originally considered and passed on the matter would be to obstruct normal governmental operations and to place in inexpert hands what the Legislature has seen fit to entrust to experts" [ ]. The *Weiss* court examined a municipality's decision to design a traffic light with a four-second interval between changing signals, and concluded that there was no indication that "due care was not exercised in the preparation of the design or that no reasonable official could have adopted it" [ ]. We went on to note that "something more than a mere choice between conflicting opinions of experts is required before the State or one of its subdivisions may be charged with a failure to discharge its duty to plan highways for the safety of the traveling public" [ ].

Under this doctrine of qualified immunity, a governmental body may be held liable when its study of a traffic condition is plainly inadequate or there is no reasonable basis for its traffic plan (Alexander v. Eldred, 63 N.Y.2d 460, 466 [1984] [municipality's traffic engineer's mistaken belief that the city had no authority to place a stop sign on a private road]). Once the State is made aware of a dangerous traffic condition it must undertake reasonable study thereof with an eye toward alleviating the danger [ ]. Moreover, after the State implements a traffic plan it is "under a continuing duty to review its plan in the light of its actual operation" [ ].

Before analyzing the cases before us in light of these principles, it is pertinent to discuss the procedural posture in which they are presented. In *Friedman v. State of New York*, there is an affirmed finding of fact that the State breached its duty by its unreasonable delay in acting to remedy a known dangerous highway condition once the decision to do so had been made. This finding must be upheld if supported by evidence in the record [ ]. In both *Cataldo v. New York State Thruway Auth.* and *Muller v. State of New York*, however, the intermediate appellate courts reached the factual conclusion, contrary to the respective trial courts, that the duty to the claimants was not breached. Thus, the scope of our review is limited to determining whether the evidence of record in each of these cases more nearly comports with the trial court's findings or with those of the Appellate Division [ ].

In *Cataldo* and *Muller* it is clear that no liability can flow from the Authority's initial decision in 1962 not to construct median barriers on the tangent section of the bridge. This decision was consistent with the opinions that were expressed by experts in the Authority's employ and was a rational response to valid safety concerns. The claimants argue, however, that by failing to reevaluate the barrier issue between 1962 and 1972 the Authority breached its "continuing duty to review its plan in the light of its actual operation" (*Weiss v. Fote*, [ ]). They contend that this inactivity was inexcusable given the changes in the state of the art of highway design occurring during that time. While this position might have some force if urged with respect to an accident occurring during the 10-year period of inactivity, such is not the case at bar. Here, both accidents occurred after the Authority reviewed its plan in 1972 and again reached the conclusion that the public's safety would be better served by not installing median barriers.

Claimants argue, however, that the 1972 engineer's reports upon which the Authority's decision was made were the product of inadequate study of the issue [see *Alexander*]. The gravamen of this assertion is that the reports failed to consider the history of the west curve barrier since its installation in 1962 and attached inordinate importance to operational difficulties that would be incurred while downplaying safety concerns to an inappropriate degree.

Strong policy considerations underpin the qualified immunity doctrine set forth in *Weiss* (*supra*), and, in cases such as these where a governmental body has invoked the expertise of qualified employees, the *Weiss* directive should not be lightly discounted. Appellants would have us examine the criteria that were considered by the State's professional staff, emphasize factors allegedly overlooked, and, with the benefit of hindsight, rule that the studies were inadequate as a matter of law. We decline this invitation, for to do so, as the Appellate Division correctly concluded, "would constitute the type of judgment substitution that *Weiss v. Fote* (*supra*) prohibits" [ ].

Because the Authority's decisions prior to the *Cataldo* accident in 1973 not to install median barriers were based on reasonable public safety considerations the Appellate Division properly dismissed the claim in that case. The Authority fulfilled its duty under *Weiss* by studying the dangerous condition, determining that design changes were not advisable and later reaching the same conclusion upon reevaluation of its decision.

In *Friedman* and *Muller,* however, a further basis upon which the defendants may be held liable is tendered: that once a decision has been reached to go forward with a plan intended to remedy a dangerous condition, liability may result from a failure to effectuate the plan within a reasonable period of time. Although this precise question has not been specifically addressed by this court, several Appellate Division decisions have held that when the State is made aware of a dangerous highway condition and does not take action to remedy it, the State can be held liable for resulting injuries [ ]. This conclusion flows logically from the premise that the State has a nondelegable duty to maintain its roads in a reasonably safe condition [ ], and it applies even if the design in question complied with reasonable safety standards at the time of construction. Of course as we have said, when a municipality studies a dangerous condition and determines as part of a reasonable plan of governmental services that certain steps need not be taken, that decision may not form the basis of liability [ ]. When, however, as in *Friedman* and *Muller,* analysis of a hazardous condition by the municipality results in the formulation of a remedial plan, an unjustifiable delay in implementing the plan constitutes a breach of the municipality's duty to the public just as surely as if it had totally failed to study the known condition in the first instance.

In *Friedman,* there is evidence to support the affirmed finding that the State unreasonably delayed its remedial action. The State failed to demonstrate at trial either that the five-year delay between DOT's recognition of the hazardous condition on the viaduct and its project proposal and the Friedman accident was necessary in order to study and formulate a reasonable safety plan, that the delay was itself part of a considered plan of action taken on the advice of experts, or that the delay stemmed from a legitimate ordering of priorities with other projects based on the availability of funding [ ].

Similarly, in *Muller,* we conclude that the record evidence more nearly comports with the trial court's finding that the three-year delay between the Authority's decision in 1974 to construct median barriers and the Muller accident in 1977 was unreasonable. This is not to say that the study and resolution of issues surrounding the concurrent installation of a traffic control system and the optimum location of the barrier, the ostensible cause of the delay, was not warranted. Indeed, a reasonable delay justified by design considerations, as with one resulting from a legitimate claim of funding priorities, would not be actionable. Our review of the evidence, however, reveals that the period of consideration in this case was marked by only intermittent spurts of study and evaluation and long gaps of inactivity, wholly inconsistent with the project's designation in an Authority press release as one having a "high priority" for which "[n]o significant delay [wa]s expected."

. . .

We conclude, therefore, that the order of the Appellate Division in *Cataldo* should be affirmed, with costs. The order appealed from in *Muller* should be reversed, with costs, and the judgment of the Court of Claims reinstated. In *Friedman,* the order of the Appellate Division should be affirmed. . . .

■ CHIEF JUDGE WACHTLER and JUDGES MEYER, SIMONS, KAYE, TITONE and HANCOCK, JJ., concur.

NOTES AND QUESTIONS

1.   The court quotes the leading case of *Weiss v. Fote* for the proposition that government liability turns on whether "due care was not exercised in the preparation of the design or that no reasonable official could have adopted it." How does this standard, or the court's more detailed discussion of governmental immunity, differ from the ordinary test of negligence applicable to private parties? In what sense does the state transportation agency have a "qualified immunity"?

2.   Can *Lauer,* which protects negligent ministerial acts, and *Friedman,* which does not, be reconciled?

3.   Suppose the plaintiff's injury resulted from a large pothole in the road that was known to the highway department but which had been designated for repair six months later because of funding shortages. Does the nature of the risk bear on the legal obligation to repair?

4.   The *Friedman* case consolidates two distinct types of claims. Should a court exercise a different degree of oversight when an agency has allegedly delayed action inordinately as opposed to a situation in which the agency has purportedly made the wrong decision?

5.   Do these planning and maintenance cases raise different issues, so far as government immunity is concerned, from the police protection and custodial cases considered in conjunction with *Riss*?

6.   Should it matter that municipal negligence cases are ordinarily tried to a jury? Consider the following passage from *Weiss v. Fote*:

> To accept a jury's verdict as to the reasonableness and safety of a plan of governmental services and prefer it over the judgment of the governmental body which originally considered and passed on the matter would be to obstruct normal governmental operations and to place in inexpert hands what the Legislature has seen fit to entrust to experts. Acceptance of this conclusion, far from effecting revival of the ancient shibboleth that "the king can do no wrong," serves only to give expression to the important and continuing need to preserve the pattern of distribution of governmental functions prescribed by constitution and statute.

Reconsider *Riss*, p. 227 supra. Does this separation of powers argument provide additional support for the no-duty ruling by the court in that police protection case?

What rationale might support a qualified immunity in cases such as *Friedman,* brought against the state and heard by a court of claims without the right to a jury?

2.   THE FEDERAL TORT CLAIMS ACT

The federal government waived its general tort immunity in 1946 in the Federal Tort Claims Act, 28 U.S.C. §§ 1346(b), 2402, 2671 et seq. The most significant sections follow:

§ 1346(b). [T]he district courts . . . shall have exclusive jurisdiction of civil actions on claims against the United States, for money damages, accruing on and after January 1, 1945, for injury or loss of property, or personal injury or death caused by the negligent or wrongful act or omission of any employee of the Government while acting within the scope of his office or employment, under circumstances where the United States, if a private person, would be liable to the claimant in accordance with the law of the place where the act or omission occurred.

§ 2402. Any action against the United States under section 1346 shall be tried by the court without a jury. . . .

§ 2674. The United States shall be liable, respecting the provisions of this title relating to tort claims, in the same manner and to the same extent as a private individual under like circumstances, but shall not be liable for interest prior to judgment or for punitive damages.

§ 2678. No attorney shall charge, demand, receive, or collect for services rendered, fees in excess of 25 per centum of any judgment rendered [under § 1346(b)]. . . .

§ 2679(b). The remedy against the United States . . . for injury or loss of property, or personal injury or death, arising or resulting from the negligent or wrongful act or omission of any employee of the Government while acting within the scope of his office or employment is exclusive of any other civil action or proceeding for money damages by reason of the same subject matter against the employee whose act or omission gave rise to the claim or against the estate of such employee. Any other civil action or proceeding for money damages arising out of or relating to the same subject matter against the employee or the employee's estate is precluded without regard to when the act or omission occurred.

§ 2680. The provisions of this chapter and section 1346(b) of this title shall not apply to—

(a) Any claim based upon an act or omission of an employee of the Government, exercising due care, in the execution of a statute or regulation, whether or not such statute or regulation be valid, or based upon the exercise or performance or the failure to exercise or perform a discretionary function or duty on the part of a federal agency or an employee of the Government, whether or not the discretion involved be abused.

(b) Any claim arising out of the loss, miscarriage, or negligent transmission of letters or postal matter.

. . .

(h) [a list of exceptions for intentional torts, discussed at p. 994 infra].

(i) Any claim for damages caused by the fiscal operations of the Treasury or by the regulation of the monetary system.

(j) Any claim arising out of the combatant activities of the military or naval forces, or the Coast Guard, during time of war.

(k) Any claim arising in a foreign country.

What might justify each of the exceptions listed?

The "discretionary function" exception was read broadly in Dalehite v. United States, 346 U.S. 15 (1953), which involved hundreds of cases resulting from an explosion in the loading of a shipment of fertilizer. In denying liability, the Court drew a distinction between "planning decisions," which are policy oriented, and "operational decisions," which are of a nondiscretionary nature. Unfortunately, the distinction between the categories, as used in the cases, has often been less than clear. The following case discusses and applies the framework of analysis developed by the Supreme Court in later cases revisiting the discretionary functions exception.

Cope v. Scott

United States Court of Appeals, District of Columbia Circuit, 1995.
45 F.3d 445.

■ Before WALD, GINSBURG, and TATEL, CIRCUIT JUDGES.

■ TATEL, J.

In this negligence case, John R. Cope appeals a grant of summary judgment against him in favor of the government. The District Court concluded that the government's allegedly negligent actions were "discretionary functions" immune from suit under the Federal Tort Claims Act ("FTCA"). 28 U.S.C. §§ 1346(b), 2671–2680 (1988 & Supp. V 1993). With respect to Cope's allegations of negligent road maintenance, we affirm the District Court's decision. We find, however, that any discretion exercised by the government with respect to where and how to post signs warning of dangerous road conditions did not implicate "political, social, or economic" policy choices of the sort that Congress intended to protect from suits under the FTCA. We therefore affirm in part, reverse in part, and remand so that the case may proceed to trial on the allegations of improper warnings.

I

Beach Drive, a two-way, two-lane road, is the main north-south route through Rock Creek Park, an urban park in Washington, D.C. that is maintained by the National Park Service. The road was "originally designed for pleasure driving," [ ], as seems evident given what an engineering study described as its "poor alignment"—which we understand to refer to its many sharp curves. The Park Service alleges that the road is not "intended to provide fast and convenient transportation," but to "enhance visitor experience" in the park. [ ] Commuters in Washington appear to believe otherwise, however, and the Park Service has allowed Beach Drive to become an important commuter route connecting downtown Washington with its northern suburbs. As a result, the road carries heavy traffic throughout the day. National Park Service road standards recommend that a road like Beach Drive carry a maximum of 8,000 vehicles daily, but recent estimates indicate that the average daily traffic on the stretch of road involved in this case was between two and three times that load.

On a rainy spring evening in 1987, Cope was driving north along Beach Drive. As a southbound vehicle driven by Roland Scott rounded a curve, it slid into the northbound lane and hit Cope's car. Cope alleges he suffered neck and back injuries. The Park Service officer who responded to the scene classified the pavement in his accident report as a "worn polished surface" that was "slick when wet." [ ] Cope sued Scott and the Park Service, alleging that the latter was negligent "in failing to appropriately and adequately maintain the roadway of Beach Drive . . . and failing to place and maintain appropriate and adequate warning signs along the roadway." [ ]

While preparing for trial, Cope discovered an engineering study of roads in Rock Creek Park that was conducted between 1986 and 1988. The study identified this stretch of Beach Drive as one of nine "high accident areas" in the park, and noted that sections of Beach Drive, including, apparently, the location of the accident, fell below "acceptable skid-resistance levels" in a test conducted five months after the accident. [ ] The study recommended that future repaving use "polish-resistant coarse aggregate" as an overlay in the most dangerous curves. [ ] As for the stretch of road in question here, the study noted that "[t]he curves should be adequately signed and the skid resistance maintained with an opened graded friction course." [ ] Cope also offers an affidavit from a traffic engineer to the effect that over 50% of the accidents that occurred on that stretch of road over the last five years occurred during wet weather, while only 18% of accidents nationwide occur in wet conditions.

Despite the less-than-perfect road surface, the 1988 study listed this stretch of Beach Drive as 33rd on a maintenance priority list of 80 sections of park road. [ ] Maintenance work on this section of road was preceded on the list by at least 15 other projects estimated to be of equal or less cost.

As for the presence of relevant warning signs, the record does not reflect precisely where such signs were located as of the date of the accident. A 1981 road sign inventory indicated that "slippery when wet" signs were located in two places on the half-mile stretch of road bracketing the curve where the accident occurred, and the Assistant Chief of Maintenance of the park stated that in 1990, a slippery road sign was posted in each direction on the same stretch of road, although there is no indication of how close such signs were to the curve where the accident occurred.

In the District Court, the government moved for summary judgment, arguing that its action (or inaction) with respect to the road was discretionary and therefore exempt from suit under the FTCA. [ ] The District Court agreed, ruling that it had no jurisdiction to hear the case. [ ] Cope settled with Scott and now appeals the District Court's immunity ruling.

II

. . .

[The "discretionary function" exception in § 2680(a)] lies at the heart of the dispute in this case. When an individual is injured by an act of the government or a government employee, section 1346(b) allows him or her to bring suit unless the action that allegedly caused the injuries is a discretionary function as defined under the FTCA. This exception was designed to prevent the courts from "second guessing," through decisions in tort actions, the way that government officials choose to balance economic, social, and political factors as they carry out their official duties. See United States v. Varig Airlines, 467 U.S. 797 (1984).

Discretionary function determinations are jurisdictional in nature. While we must review the complaint to determine what actions allegedly caused the injuries, we do so only to determine whether the district court has jurisdiction over those actions, not to prejudge the merits of the case. If the district court has jurisdiction over the suit, the plaintiff must still prove that the government's actions were negligent in order for him to prevail.

The Supreme Court has established a two-step test that we use to determine whether an action is exempt from suit under the discretionary function exemption. See United States v. Gaubert, 499 U.S. 315 (1991); Berkovitz v. United States, 486 U.S. 531 (1988). [The first step asks] whether any "federal statute, regulation, or policy specifically prescribes a course of action for an employee to follow." *Gaubert* (citing *Berkovitz*). If a specific directive exists, then the employee had no "choice." The only issue is whether the employee followed the directive, and is thus exempt under the first clause, or whether the employee did not follow the directive, thus opening the government to suit. See 28 U.S.C. § 2680(a). Because no choice is involved where a "specific prescription" exists, the discretionary function exception . . . is not applicable.

The discretionary function exception *may* be applicable where there is no specific prescription and the government employee has a "choice" regarding how to act in a particular circumstance. This is true more often than one might expect. Despite the pervasiveness of regulation, government policies will almost always leave some room for individual choice. If the choice led to the events being litigated, the exception may apply. But not all actions that require choice—actions that are, in one sense, "discretionary"—are protected as "discretionary functions" under the FTCA.

This brings us to the second step of the test, where the "basic inquiry" is whether the challenged discretionary acts of a government employee "are of the nature and quality that Congress intended to shield from tort liability." [*Varig*] Decisions that require choice are exempt from suit under the FTCA only if they are "susceptible to policy judgment" and involve an exercise of "political, social, [or] economic judgment." [*Gaubert*; *Varig*]; see [*Berkovitz*] (focusing the analysis on whether a decision is "based on considerations of public policy"). The Court recognized in *Gaubert*, for example, that daily decisions regarding the management of a troubled savings and loan "implicate[d] social, economic, or political policies," and were therefore exempt. [*Gaubert*] In contrast, the Court noted that a government employee may cause an automobile accident through the exercise of poor discretion, but that this type of "garden-variety" discretion is not protected. See id., [ ]. Only discretionary actions of greater significance—those grounded in "social, economic, or political goals"—fall within the protection of the statute. See [*Gaubert*].

Determining whether a decision is "essentially political, social, or economic," [ ], is admittedly difficult, since nearly every government action is, at least to some extent, subject to "policy analysis." See, e.g., [*Gaubert*] (Scalia, J., concurring) (noting that even the decisions of a government driver may implicate policy choices). "Budgetary constraints," for example, "underlie virtually all government activity." [ ]. At oral argument, counsel for the government asserted that these underlying fiscal constraints should therefore exempt "virtually all government activity." With the exception of discretion exercised by bad drivers, the government appears to argue that decisions that involve choice and the faintest hint of policy concerns are discretionary and subject to the exception. This approach, however, would not only eviscerate the second step of the analysis set out in *Berkovitz* and *Gaubert*, but it would allow the exception to swallow the FTCA's sweeping waiver of sovereign immunity. [ ] It was thus not surprising that, when pressed at oral argument, government counsel was unable to provide, under its theory, even one example of a discretionary decision that would not be exempt for failure to implicate policy concerns.

The government reads the exception far too broadly. The question is not whether there is any discretion at all, but whether the discretion is "*grounded* in the policy of the regulatory regime." [*Gaubert*] (emphasis added). The mere association of a decision with regulatory concerns is not enough; exempt decisions are those "fraught with . . . public policy considerations." [ ] The mere presence of choice—even if that choice involves whether money should be spent—does not trigger the exception.

Just as we reject the government's effort to expand the exception too far, we also reject Cope's efforts to restrict its application. Cope argues, first, that the government cannot claim the exemption unless it is able to demonstrate that there was an "actual, specific decision involving the balancing of competing policy considerations." [ ] The Supreme Court has emphasized, however, that the issue is not the decision as such, but whether the "nature" of the decision implicates policy analysis [ ] What matters is not what the decisionmaker was thinking, but whether the type of decision being challenged is grounded in social, economic, or political policy. *See* [*Gaubert*.] Evidence of the actual decision may be helpful in understanding whether the "nature" of the decision implicated policy judgments, but the applicability of the exemption does not turn on whether the challenged decision involved such judgments.

For the same reasons, we reject Cope's argument that the government's acts are not discretionary since they involve the "implementation" of government policy. [ ] Cope draws this argument from Indian Towing v. United States, 350 U.S. 61 (1955), in which the

Supreme Court allowed the plaintiffs to sue the government for negligent failure to maintain a lighthouse. Cope argues that *Indian Towing* means that the "implementation" or "execution" of policy decisions—particularly with respect to warning the public about hazards resulting from negligence—is never protected under the exception. Cope's argument, however, is merely an effort to establish yet another in a long series of "analytical frameworks" that the Supreme Court has rejected as an inappropriate means of addressing the discretionary function exemption. [ ] The mechanistic application of these frameworks encourages courts to avoid the proper analysis: Whether the nature of the decision involved the exercise of policy judgment. *Gaubert* cautioned against this sort of shortcut when it rejected a lower court decision that relied upon a distinction between exempt "planning" decisions and non-exempt "operational" decisions. [ ]; *see also* [*Indian Towing*] (rejecting, in a similar context, a "governmental"/"nongovernmental" distinction). Recognizing that the focus is on the nature of the decision, not on the semantic pigeonhole into which the action can be put, we decline to follow Cope's reading of the case law, focusing instead, as we are required, on whether the decision is "fraught with" economic, political, or social judgments. No matter the level at which the decision was made, the nature of the decision, or the impact it had on others, we have consistently held that the discretionary function exception applies "only where 'the question is not negligence but social wisdom, not due care but political practicability, not reasonableness but economic expediency.'" [ ] Using this approach as our touchstone, we proceed to an analysis of this case.

III

Both because the District Court granted a motion for summary judgment, and because the question before us relates to a purely legal issue—the jurisdiction of the District Court—we review the decision below *de novo*. [ ] As long as the District Court's legal conclusion was correct, its grant of summary judgment was appropriate, for we perceive in the record no genuine issues of fact material to the jurisdictional issue.

In his complaint, Cope makes two allegations regarding the conduct of the United States. He argues, first, that the government failed "to appropriately and adequately maintain the roadway of Beach Drive," and second, that the government failed "to place and maintain appropriate and adequate warning signs along the roadway." [ ] We address each of his points in turn, again emphasizing that we do not decide the merits of the case, but only whether Cope is entitled to an opportunity to prove his case at trial.

With respect to his allegation regarding the state of the road surface, Cope points to a manual entitled "Park Road Standards," and, applying step one of the analysis, argues that it sets forth "specific prescriptions" regarding skid resistance and surface type. We do not read the manual to set forth such requirements. . . .

. . .

We turn, then, to the second step of the analysis, in which we ask whether the discretion exercised over the maintenance and reconstruction of Beach Drive is "subject to policy analysis" and thus discretionary in the sense of the FTCA. . . .

As we understand the record and the facts as presented by the parties, no regular maintenance would have prevented the road from deteriorating in the way Cope alleges. This case is therefore different from a case involving mundane decisions to fill or not fill potholes, or even the cumulative effect of such decisions. . . . The state of Beach Drive alleged by Cope could have been prevented only by reducing the traffic load, initially paving it with a different surface, resurfacing the curve entirely, or at least milling the curve to create grooves in the surface. [ ] Determining the appropriate course of action would require balancing factors such as Beach Drive's overall purpose, the allocation of funds among significant project demands, the safety of drivers and other park visitors, and the inconvenience of repairs as compared to the risk of safety hazards. These balances are apparent throughout the 1988 study that placed maintenance on this section of Beach Drive in the middle of a priority list of work that needed to be done on eighty different sections of park roads. Park Service decisions regarding the management of Beach Drive are therefore much like the decisions exempted by the Supreme Court in *Varig* [involving the FAA's spot check system for determining the safety of airplanes]: "[S]uch decisions require the agency to establish priorities for the accomplishment of its policy objectives by balancing the objectives sought to be obtained against such practical considerations as staffing and funding." [ ] And, as in *Varig*, we decline to "second guess" those judgments here. [ ]

IV

We reach a different conclusion with respect to Cope's allegation that the government failed to post adequate warning signs about the nature of the road surface. His case rests on the argument that given the "very specific slippery road problem" on Beach Drive, a "permanently displayed static 'slippery when wet' road sign is inadequate to warn" of the hazard. [ ] Cope hints that the failure to post an adequate sign is nondiscretionary, but relies mostly on the second step argument that any discretion does not implicate policy concerns. The government argues that no specific prescriptions regarding the posting of signs exist, that the resulting discretion involves the exercise of "engineering and aesthetic factors" as well as economic considerations, and that the presence of those concerns in the decision making means that the decisions are exempt from suit under the FTCA.

The government admits that it "is the policy of the National Park Service to follow" the Manual on Uniform Traffic Control Devices when posting signs, but argues that the final decision depends on a variety of engineering and aesthetic considerations. [ ] Our own review of this manual reveals that it is more of a guidebook for the installation of signs than a "specific prescription" relied on by the Park Service. As the manual points out, it is "not a substitute for engineering judgment," [ ], and warning signs should be posted only "when it is deemed necessary." [ ] We conclude, then, that the posting of signs in Rock Creek Park involves the exercise of discretion.

In contrast to our decision regarding the road surface, however, we find that the discretion regarding where and what type of signs to post is not the kind of discretion protected by the discretionary function exception. While it may be true, as the government claims, that the placement of signs involves judgments because engineering and aesthetic concerns determine where they are placed, such judgments are not necessarily protected from suit; only if they are "fraught with public policy considerations" do they fall within the exception, and we do not think that is the case here. The "engineering judgment" the government relies on is no more a matter of policy than were the "objective scientific principles" that the *Berkovitz* court distinguished from exempt exercises of policy judgment. [ ]

With respect to the aesthetic considerations, while we acknowledge the Park Service's desire to maintain the park in as pristine a state as possible, the government has failed to demonstrate how such a desire affects the placement of traffic signs on Beach Drive. Indeed, the government's argument is difficult for us to accept in view of the fact that, including the "slippery when wet" signs, no less than "twenty-three traffic control, warning, and informational signs" already exist on the half-mile stretch of road bracketing the curve on which the accident occurred—a stretch of road that carries 20,000 vehicles daily. [ ] We agree that in certain circumstances, decisions will be exempt under the FTCA because they involve difficult policy judgments balancing the preservation of the environment against the blight of excess signs. But this is not one of those circumstances. Beach Drive is not the Grand Canyon's Rim Drive, nor Shenandoah's Skyline Drive. Here, the Park Service has chosen to manage the road in a manner more amenable to commuting through nature than communing with it. Having done so, and having taken steps to warn users of dangers inherent in that use, the Park Service cannot argue that its failure to ensure that those steps are effective involves protected "discretionary" decisions.

. . .

. . . Beach Drive is a commuter route through an urban park. The Park Service has already posted signs in an effort to alert drivers to safety hazards on the road. In light of these factors, the Park Service has understandably been unable to articulate how the placement of additional or different signs on Beach Drive implicates the type of economic, social, or political concerns that the discretionary function exception protects from suit under the FTCA.

We affirm the District Court's dismissal of Cope's claim regarding negligent maintenance of the road surface. We conclude, however, that the District Court had jurisdiction over the allegations that the Park Service failed adequately to warn of dangers on Beach Drive. To the extent the Court ruled to the contrary, we vacate its order and remand for further proceedings. Cope is entitled to try to persuade a factfinder that the government acted negligently by failing adequately to sign the curve on Beach Drive.

So ordered.

NOTES AND QUESTIONS

1. According to *Cope*, what differentiates situations involving "garden-variety" discretion (which does not implicate "social, economic, or political goals") from those covered by the discretionary function exception? At what point does "regular maintenance" become major roadwork? What if the park service had deliberately allowed the road to decay—by forgoing regular maintenance—to the point at which only a policy decision could renovate it?

2. The court rejects the government's claim that whenever the public fisc is implicated, the discretionary function exception is applicable. Recall the role that limited resources played in *Friedman*, p. 242 supra. In Whisnant v. United States, 400 F.3d 1177 (9th Cir.2005), toxic mold was allowed to accumulate at a military commissary. The government argued that safety always involves a trade-off with cost and that making those judgments involves discretion. The court responded:

> Every slip and fall, every failure to warn, every inspection and maintenance decision can be couched in terms of policy choices based on allocation of limited resources. As we have noted before in the discretionary function exception context, '[b]udgetary constraints underlie virtually all governmental activity.'

3. Why does the court emphasize that there need not be—as Cope argued—an "actual, specific decision involving the balancing of competing policy considerations" for the discretionary function exception to apply? How would it analyze a case in which there was no evidence whatsoever that the action plaintiff argued should be taken had even been considered? Suppose, for example, that Congress enacts a statute requiring the National Park Service to conduct a study on the best way to improve safety at a national park where there had been an especially large number of serious accidents. The relevant officials neglect to do anything and, as a result, several hikers are injured. Can the government invoke the discretionary function exception?

4. Why does the difference between policy decisions and their "implementation"—or between "planning" and "operational" decisions—not determine the outcome in this case? Does the *Cope* court replace these dichotomies with another? Are there any guidelines for case-by-case decisions about whether the exception applies?

5. What is the relationship between the discretionary function analysis that the court calls "jurisdictional" and the negligence analysis?

6. Does the discretionary function exception, as interpreted by the court in *Cope*, express a different set of policy concerns from those just considered in municipal and state liability cases?

7. The range of cases testing the breadth of the discretionary function exception is suggested by Macharia v. United States, 334 F.3d 61 (D.C.Cir.2003)(level of security provided at a foreign embassy that was subject to bomb attack in 1998 is discretionary); Dykstra v. United States Bureau of Prisons, 140 F.3d 791 (8th Cir.1998)(prison counselor's decision not to explain that a youthful-looking prisoner might be at risk in the general prison population and corrections officer's subsequent failure to transfer him to protective custody both fell under the discretionary function exception and precluded government liability for prisoner's rape by another inmate); Fisher Bros. Sales, Inc. v. United States, 46 F.3d 279 (3d Cir.1995)(Chilean fruit growers' and others' claims against the United States for damages arising from the FDA's alleged negligence in finding fruit to be contaminated dismissed).

In re Katrina Canal Breaches Litigation, 696 F.3d 436 (5th Cir.2012), involved numerous suits by victims of flooding during Hurricane Katrina alleging that the Army Corp of Engineers was negligent. A prior Fifth Circuit panel had found the discretionary function exception inapplicable because, although room for the exercise of policy existed, the record evidence revealed that rather than being based on policy, it was based on a flawed scientific judgment. Such proof, the court said, is sufficient to overcome the presumption that the exception applies when discretionary room exists. On rehearing, the same panel (and author) reversed itself in this opinion, omitting any mention that a plaintiff can overcome the existence of the availability of a policy-based judgment by showing that the actual decision was made for other reasons. In both opinions, the court cited and quoted from *Cope* but included the emphasized language below only in its rehearing opinion: "Evidence of the actual decision may be helpful in understanding whether the 'nature' of the decision implicated policy judgments, *but the applicability of the exemption does not turn on whether the challenged decision involved such judgments* (emphasis in part in original and in part added)." The rehearing opinion also omitted mention of a presumption and overcoming it with evidence that the actual decision was made for non-policy reasons.

8. *The* Feres *doctrine*. The Court broadened the armed services exception beyond claims "arising out of the combatant services of the military" in Feres v. United States, 340 U.S. 135, 138 (1950), to encompass all injuries that arise out of or in the course of military service. The Court adhered to the doctrine, explained its rationale (including a restatement of the traditional concern about maintaining military discipline and effectiveness), and expanded its reach in United States v. Johnson, 481 U.S. 681 (1987), a case in which *Feres* was invoked to bar a surviving wife's claim against the Federal Aviation Administration for negligence in providing guidance to a military helicopter pilot who died in a rescue mission. For analysis of the history and evolution of the *Feres* doctrine, see Taber v. Maine, 67 F.3d 1029 (2d Cir.1995).

In Stencel Aero Engineering Corp. v. United States, 431 U.S. 666 (1977), the Court decided that a government contractor who was held liable to military personnel for a defective product could not obtain indemnity from the government. The point was to avoid an end run around *Feres*.

9. *Intentional torts.* Exceptions for a variety of intentional torts, including assault and battery, are contained in section 2680(h) of the FTCA. In Matsko v. United States, 372 F.3d 556 (3d Cir.2004), plaintiff managed an interesting detour around that exception. Plaintiff attended a business meeting at an office of the Federal Mine Safety and Health Administration. Without provocation, one of the federal inspectors working at MSHA assaulted plaintiff, slamming his face into a briefcase lying on the desk in front of him. Plaintiff sued, claiming that the inspector's actions should be imputed to the United States as his employer and also that the United States owed plaintiff a duty as a business invitee and failed to protect him from injury. The court held that the FTCA does not waive sovereign immunity for intentional assaults by government workers who are acting outside the scope of their employment. The government does, however, have an affirmative duty to protect business invitees from risks posed by third parties and can be held liable under the FTCA if it is found that government employees negligently failed to prevent the assault.

10. Actions against federal officials for violations of constitutional rights generally involve claims of intentional wrongdoing. Although most intentional harms are exempted under the FTCA, a constitutional tort, independent of the Act, was recognized in Bivens v. Six Unknown Named Agents of Federal Bureau of Narcotics, 403 U.S. 388 (1971), discussed in Chapter XIII.

11. Similar claims of constitutional protection against state and municipal officials, under the Civil Rights Act of 1871, 42 U.S.C. § 1983, are discussed in Chapter XIII. The interplay between the issues arising in section 1983 cases and issues considered in this section, as well as the earlier section in this Chapter on duties of affirmative action, is illustrated by Town of Castle Rock, Colorado v. Gonzales, 545 U.S. 748 (2005). Three children were murdered by their father who took them from their mother in violation of a restraining order. The mother claimed a section 1983 violation, alleging that the police refused to respond to numerous requests over several hours to enforce the decree. To be successful in her claim, plaintiff had to establish that she was deprived of a "property" interest grounded in the Fourteenth Amendment that she had by virtue of the restraining order and state statutes mandating its enforcement. The Court denied that the mother had such a property interest in the enforcement of the order, thereby effectively eliminating any federally imposed obligation on state or local officials to intervene to enforce a restraining order and protect an individual from others. The Court characterized its decision as reflecting its "continuing reluctance to treat the Fourteenth Amendment as 'a font of tort law.' "

Castle Rock follows DeShaney v. Winnebago County Department of Social Services, 489 U.S. 189 (1989), in which plaintiff, a young boy, suffered serious permanent brain damage from beatings administered by his father. The section 1983 claim against defendant social services agency was based on a failure to intervene and remove plaintiff from his father's custody despite notice from concerned parties on various occasions. The Court denied the claim of constitutional denial of liberty under the Due Process Clause, holding that there is no affirmative duty on the part of the state to protect individuals against invasion by other private parties.

CHAPTER IV

THE DUTY REQUIREMENT: NONPHYSICAL HARM

All of the cases we have read to this point involve "physical harms" —bodily injury or damage to real or tangible property. In this Chapter we deal with protection against nonphysical harms. The focus, therefore, is on the *type* of harm that plaintiff suffers. The common law has distinguished situations in which the only (or "stand-alone") harm suffered was emotional or economic from the classic physical harm, and has developed limited or no-duty rules for reasons that we will explore. Damages for economic and emotional harm are routinely recoverable, however, when they occur as a result of physical harm for which the plaintiff establishes liability. Thus, if a business owner is injured in an automobile accident and suffers lost profits as a result, that loss is routinely recoverable as consequential to the physical injury. By contrast, the owner's employees who suffer only lost wages as a result of the owner's injury would be subject to the limited-duty rules addressed in this Chapter.

We begin with a type of harm generically referred to as "emotional harm." Historically, this type of harm has been far less widely protected than the interest in being free from physical harm. Here, we consider when the courts protect nonphysical interests against unintended interference.

A. EMOTIONAL HARM

1. DIRECTLY INFLICTED EMOTIONAL HARM

This section is organized by distinguishing "directly" inflicted emotional harm from harm suffered by "bystanders"—those who suffer emotional harm as the result of observing serious injury to another in close proximity, such as a mother who observes her child being hit by a car. By contrast, those, like the plaintiff in the next case, who are at risk of physical injury, but do not suffer it constitute one group of "direct" victims. Another class of direct victims is comprised of those who are not at risk of physical harm but suffer their emotional distress as a result of the defendant's negligent conduct and not as a bystander. Thus, one such case would be a parent who is negligently and erroneously informed of the death of his daughter.

These categories are not conceptually pure, and, as we will see, there can be cases that overlap more than one category as well as cases that are difficult to classify. Nevertheless, this organization is the one adopted by the Third Restatement of Torts and assists in understanding what would otherwise be an unruly body of case law.

a.   RISK OF PHYSICAL INJURY TO PLAINTIFF

Falzone v. Busch

Supreme Court of New Jersey, 1965.
45 N.J. 559, 214 A.2d 12.

■ PROCTOR, J.

The question before us on this appeal is whether the plaintiff may recover for bodily injury or sickness resulting from fear for her safety caused by a negligent defendant, where the plaintiff was placed in danger by such negligence, although there was no physical impact.

The complaint alleges in the first count that the plaintiff, Charles Falzone, was standing in a field adjacent to the roadway when he was struck and injured by defendant's negligently driven automobile. The second count alleges that the plaintiff, Mabel Falzone, wife of Charles, was seated in his lawfully parked automobile close to the place where her husband was struck and that the defendant's negligently driven automobile "veered across the highway and headed in the direction of this plaintiff," coming "so close to plaintiff as to put her in fear for her safety." As a direct result she became ill and required medical attention. . . .

[The trial court granted summary judgment for defendant on the second count,] holding that it was constrained to follow the existing New Jersey rule that where there is no physical impact upon the plaintiff, there can be no recovery for the bodily injury or sickness resulting from negligently induced fright. We certified the plaintiffs' appeal before it was considered by the Appellate Division.

Neither this Court nor the former Court of Errors and Appeals has considered a case directly presenting this question. However, since a decision of our former Supreme Court in 1900, Ward v. West Jersey & Seashore R.R. Co., [ ], it has been considered settled that a physical impact upon the plaintiff is necessary to sustain a negligence action. [ ]

. . . Three reasons for denying recovery were set forth in [Ward]. The first was that physical injury was not the natural and proximate result of the negligent act:

> The doctrine of non-liability . . . rests upon the principle that a person is legally responsible only for the natural and proximate results of his negligent act. Physical suffering is not the probable or natural consequences of fright, in the case of a person of ordinary physical and mental vigor; and in the general conduct of business, and the ordinary affairs of life, although we are bound to anticipate and guard against consequences, which may be injurious to persons who are

liable to be affected thereby, we have a right, in doing so, to assume, in the absence of knowledge to the contrary, that such persons are of average strength both of body and of mind. [ ]

Second, the court concluded that since this was the first action of its kind in New Jersey, the consensus of the bar must have been that no liability exists in the absence of impact. [ ] The third reason was "public policy" which the court explained by quoting with approval from Mitchell v. Rochester Ry. Co., [45 N.E. 354 (N.Y.1896)]:

> If the right of recovery in this class of cases should be once established, it would naturally result in a flood of litigations in cases where the injury complained of may be easily feigned without detection, and where the damages must rest upon mere conjecture and speculation. The difficulty which often exists in cases of alleged physical injuries, in determining whether they exist, and, if so, whether they were caused by the negligent act of the defendant, would not only be greatly increased, but a wide field would be opened for [fictitious] or speculative claims. [*Ward*]

We think that the reasons assigned in *Ward* for denying liability are no longer tenable, and it is questionable if they ever were. The court there first stated that it is not "probable or natural" for persons of normal health to suffer physical injuries, when subjected to fright, and that since a person whose acts cause fright alone could not reasonably anticipate that physical harm would follow, such acts cannot constitute negligence as to the frightened party. It appears that the court decided as a matter of law an issue which we believe is properly determinable by medical evidence. . . .

And even in Spade v. Lynn & B.R. Co., [47 N.E. 88, 89 (Mass.1897)] (relied upon in *Ward*), where recovery was denied for the physical consequences of fright, the court recognized that:

> Great emotion, may, and sometimes does, produce physical effects . . . A physical injury may be directly traceable to fright, and so may be caused by it. We cannot say, therefore, that such consequences may not flow proximately from unintentional negligence; . . .

Moreover, medical knowledge on the relationship between emotional disturbance and physical injury has steadily expanded, and such relationship seems no longer open to serious challenge. [ ]

    . . .

The second reason given in *Ward* for denying recovery was that the absence of suits of this nature in New Jersey demonstrated the concurrence of the bar with the rule of no liability. We do not believe the court meant to imply that it would deny recovery because of opinions held by lawyers on the legal question presented. And if the court intended to bar the cause of action because of a lack of precedent in this State, a sufficient answer is that the common law would have atrophied hundreds of years ago if it had continued to deny relief in cases of first impression. [ ]

Public policy was the final reason given in *Ward* for denying liability. The court was of the opinion that proof or disproof of fear-induced physical suffering would be so difficult that recovery would often be based on mere conjecture and speculation, and that the door would be opened to extensive litigation in a class of cases where injury is easily feigned. We realize that there may be difficulties in determining the existence of a causal connection between fright and subsequent physical injury and in measuring the extent of such injury. However, the problem of tracing a causal connection from negligence to injury is not peculiar to cases without impact and occurs in all types of personal injury litigation. [ ] As Judge Burke said for the New York Court of Appeals in dealing with the same problem:

> In many instances, just as in impact cases, there will be no doubt as to the presence and extent of the damage and the fact that it was proximately caused by defendant's negligence. In the difficult cases, we must look to the quality and genuineness of proof, and rely to an extent on the contemporary sophistication of the medical profession and the ability of the court and jury to weed out the dishonest claims. Battalla v. State, [176 N.E.2d 729 (N.Y.1961)].

In any event, difficulty of proof should not bar the plaintiff from the opportunity of attempting to convince the trier of fact of the truth of her claim.

As to the possibility of actions based on fictitious injuries, a court should not deny recovery for a type of wrong which may result in serious harm because some people may institute fraudulent actions. Our trial courts retain sufficient control, through the rules of evidence and the requirements as to the sufficiency of evidence, to safeguard against the danger that juries will find facts without legally adequate proof. [ ] Moreover, the allowance of recovery in cases where there has been an impact, however slight, negates the effectiveness of the no impact rule as a method of preventing fraudulent claims. . . .

Ward also asserts that public policy demands denial of recovery in no impact cases to prevent a "flood of litigations." However, there is no indication of an excessive number of actions of this type in other states which do not require an impact as a basis for recovery. And, of more importance, the fear of an expansion of litigation should not deter courts from granting relief in meritorious cases; the proper remedy is an expansion of the judicial machinery, not a decrease in the availability of justice.

The many eminent legal scholars who have considered the rule denying recovery in the absence of impact are virtually unanimous in condemning it as unjust and contrary to experience and logic. [The court cites several law review articles and also notes that both England and New York have repudiated the requirement of "impact."] A great majority of jurisdictions now hold that where physical injury results from wrongfully caused emotional stress, the injured person may recover for such consequences notwithstanding the absence of any physical impact upon him at the time of the mental shock. [ ] Indeed, Dean Prosser has recently written that the impact requirement "is almost certainly destined for ultimate extinction." Prosser, Torts § 55, p. 351 (3d ed. 1964).

Our conclusion is that *Ward* should no longer be followed in New Jersey. We are not dealing with property law, contract law or other fields where stability and predictability may be crucial. We are dealing with torts where there can be little, if any, justifiable reliance and where the rule of *stare decisis* is admittedly limited. [ ] We hold, therefore, that where negligence causes fright from a reasonable fear of immediate personal injury, which fright is adequately demonstrated to have resulted in substantial bodily injury or sickness, the injured person may recover if such bodily injury or sickness would be regarded as proper elements of damage had they occurred as a consequence of direct physical injury rather than fright. Of course, where fright does not cause substantial bodily injury or sickness, it is to be regarded as too lacking in seriousness and too speculative to warrant the imposition of liability.

We recognize that where there is no impact a defendant may be unaware of the alleged incident and thus not forewarned to preserve evidence upon which he might base his defense. However, this consideration should not be sufficient to bar a meritorious claim. Rather, it is appropriate that the trial judge charge the jury that an undue delay in notifying the defendant of the incident and the resulting injury may weigh heavily in determining the truth of the plaintiff's claim. It is unnecessary to decide here whether an undue delay short of the statute of limitations would justify a dismissal by the trial court.

The plaintiffs should be given the opportunity of submitting proof that Mrs. Falzone suffered substantial bodily injury or sickness and that such bodily injury or sickness was the proximate result of the defendant's negligence.

■ For reversal: CHIEF JUSTICE WEINTRAUB and JUSTICES JACOBS, FRANCIS, PROCTOR, HALL, SCHETTINO and HANEMAN—7.

■ For affirmance: None.

NOTES AND QUESTIONS

1.   The court here rejects the requirement of impact, but how would it have ruled if the plaintiff suffered only emotional distress and no "bodily injury or sickness"? The distinction between bodily injury or sickness and

emotional distress is uncertain, and courts have tended to expand the former category so as to grant recovery for serious mental distress that is accompanied by physical symptomology. See, e.g., Petition of United States, 418 F.2d 264 (1st Cir.1969)("The term 'physical' is not used in its ordinary sense for purposes of applying the 'physical consequences' rule. Rather, the word is used to indicate that the condition or illness for which recovery is sought must be one susceptible of objective determination. Hence, a definite nervous disorder is a 'physical injury' sufficient to support an action for damages for negligence.").

2. In the cited *Mitchell* case, a team of horses ran out of control and was brought to a halt so that plaintiff pregnant woman was situated between the two horses—but apparently untouched by either of them. She soon had a miscarriage. The New York Court of Appeals denied recovery. In the cited *Battalla* case, defendant negligently failed to secure plaintiff in her ski chair lift. In allowing an action for her fright engendered by such a situation, the court overruled *Mitchell* on the requirement of impact, which has virtually disappeared today.

3. Although the *Falzone* court noted that plaintiff's husband was hit by the same car, this event plays no apparent part in the analysis of the wife's claim. As we shall see shortly, at the time of *Falzone* a plaintiff in New Jersey could not recover damages for suffering emotional distress from witnessing an injury to a family member. How might the wife here meet the defendant's argument that at least a large part of her emotional distress was brought about by concern for her husband's safety and not for her own safety?

4. *The distinction between physical and emotional harm.* In Wooden v. Raveling, 71 Cal.Rptr.2d 891 (App.1998), the court allowed plaintiff property owner to recover for her emotional distress when defendant's negligently driven car came up onto her property and nearly hit her. In Lawson v. Management Activities, Inc., 81 Cal.Rptr.2d 745 (App.1999), the plaintiffs were employees of a Honda dealership who feared that a falling plane would crash into them. In fact, the plane crashed nearby. The *Lawson* court "decline[d] to follow the *Wooden* decision to the degree that its facts—a car crash in which a literal bystander feared for her own safety—might be extrapolated to the airplane crash before us." Can you think of a persuasive distinction between airplane and auto crashes? The court, 2–1, noting that the fear had existed "for a brief moment," concluded that California rejected the "independent tort of negligent infliction of emotional distress":

> Indeed, civilized life would not be possible if there were such a tort. To borrow a phrase from Blake, if tort damages were available for anything which would foreseeably cause our fellow human beings emotional distress, then "who can stand?" No one, saint or sinner, can go through life without "negligently" inflicting emotional distress on others.

The majority then concluded that there was no good reason for recognizing a duty in the emotional distress context:

[It takes] no imagination to realize that people on the ground who are close to an airplane crash are going to be very scared. By the same token, while it is foreseeable that the fright will be intense, it is also foreseeable that the actual fright itself will be short lived. What is not foreseeable is the severity of people's psychological reactions to the crash. Emotional distress is a murky cauldron of actuarial imprecision, inherently limitless. It is also an area of remarkable individual idiosyncrasy, with great extremes at either end.

The dissenter in *Lawson* rejected the majority's approach and concluded that the majority justices were simply uncomfortable with the concept of emotional distress; they "are just unimpressed with 'weak' people. . . . If they had their way, we would all be certified war heroes. We certainly would not reward those who succumb to fear as a result of someone else's negligence." The two opinions also disagreed about whether "tort law could countenance" an "eggshell psyche." That term alludes to the "eggshell plaintiff"—one who suffers from an abnormally sensitive physical condition, such as hemophilia or brittle bones. We will explore this issue in Chapter VI. The California Supreme Court did not review either *Wooden* or *Lawson*.

Is the interest in emotional tranquility inherently less important than the interest in bodily integrity? Or are other concerns at work that explain more restrictive rules for the recovery of the former?

5. *Airplane passengers. Falzone* involved fear of imminent physical harm that did not occur. Other examples occur in airplane crises that do not result in crashes. In Quill v. Trans World Airlines, Inc., 361 N.W.2d 438 (Minn.Ct.App.1985), the court upheld an award of $50,000 to a passenger in an airplane that plunged 34,000 feet in an uncontrolled tailspin before pilots regained control. The plane then continued to shake and shudder for 40 minutes until it could be brought to a safe emergency landing. The plaintiff's claim for negligent infliction of emotional distress ("NIED")was grounded in the severe anxiety he experienced whenever he took an airplane flight after the accident. The court held that the plaintiff had made out a prima facie case:

[T]he unusually disturbing experience plaintiff endured combined with his physical symptoms assure that his claim is real. There can be few experiences as terrifying as being pinned to a seat by gravity forces as an airplane twists and screams towards earth at just under the speed of sound.

6. *Emotional distress of victims who realize they are doomed.* By contrast with the frightened passenger in an airplane that did not crash, many die or are seriously injured in a crash. Their pre-impact distress is not a result of bodily injury that they have suffered, so once again courts are faced with whether their stand-alone distress is recoverable.

Most courts have allowed recovery where plaintiff was aware of impending death or injury, even if the period of awareness was very short. These cases are quite fact-specific. Compare Shatkin v. McDonnell Douglas

Corp., 727 F.2d 202 (2d Cir.1984)(insufficient evidence to show that passenger on right side of plane was even aware of impending disaster until just before the crash) with Shu-Tao Lin v. McDonnell Douglas Corp., 742 F.2d 45 (2d Cir.1984)(upholding judgment of $10,000 for pre-impact fright for passenger in seat over left wing on same flight where jury might reasonably have found that the passenger saw "the left engine and a portion of the wing break away at the beginning of the flight, which lasted some thirty seconds between takeoff and crash").

The phenomenon of pre-impact fright is not limited to airplane cases. For an extended consideration of the issue, see Beynon v. Montgomery Cablevision Ltd. Partnership, 718 A.2d 1161 (Md.1998), in which the court, 4–3, upheld an award for decedent's "pre-impact fright" which was shown to exist by 71.5 feet of skid marks. Affirming, the majority noted that had decedent survived, he would have had an action under state law (why?). Given that fact, it "would be illogical" to deny the item where the feared harm came to pass.

7.   After the abrogation of the physical impact rule, what new criteria should be developed for limiting liability for emotional harm? Should a new rule allow recovery in certain types of factual situations and not in others? What are the parameters adopted in *Falzone*? Are they well-designed to ensure proof of injury and prevent a flood of litigation? These issues are addressed in the next case and later in the Chapter.

Metro-North Commuter Railroad Company v. Buckley

Supreme Court of the United States, 1997.
521 U.S. 424, 117 S.Ct. 2113, 138 L.Ed.2d 560.

■ JUSTICE BREYER delivered the opinion of the Court.

The basic question in this case is whether a railroad worker negligently exposed to a carcinogen (here, asbestos) but without symptoms of any disease can recover under the Federal Employers' Liability Act (FELA or Act), for negligently inflicted emotional distress. We conclude that the worker before us here cannot recover unless, and until, he manifests symptoms of a disease. [In an omitted part, the Court also considered a claim for medical monitoring costs, which we explore in Chapter V.]

I

Respondent, Michael Buckley, works as a pipefitter for Metro-North, a railroad. For three years (1985–1988) his job exposed him to asbestos for about one hour per working day. During that time Buckley would remove insulation from pipes, often covering himself with insulation dust that contained asbestos. Since 1987, when he attended an "asbestos awareness" class, Buckley has feared that he would develop cancer—and with some cause, for his two expert witnesses testified that, even after taking account of his now-discarded 15-year habit of smoking up to a pack of cigarettes per day, the exposure created an added risk of death due to cancer, or to other asbestos-related diseases, of either 1% to 5% (in the view of one of plaintiff's experts), or 1% to 3% (in the view of another). Since 1989, Buckley has received periodic medical checkups for cancer and asbestosis. So far, those check-ups have not revealed any evidence of cancer or any other asbestos-related disease.

Buckley sued Metro-North under the FELA, a statute that permits a railroad worker to recover for an "injury . . . resulting . . . from" his employer's "negligence." 45 U.S.C. § 51. He sought damages for his emotional distress and to cover the cost of future medical checkups. His employer conceded negligence, but it did not concede that Buckley had actually suffered emotional distress, and it argued that the FELA did not permit a worker like Buckley, who had suffered no physical harm, to recover for injuries of either sort. After hearing Buckley's case, the District Court dismissed the action. The court found that Buckley did not "offer sufficient evidence to allow a jury to find that he suffered a real emotional injury." [ ] And, in any event, Buckley suffered no "physical impact"; hence any emotional injury fell outside the limited set of circumstances in which, according to this Court, the FELA permits recovery. [ ]; see Consolidated Rail Corporation v. Gottshall, 512 U.S. 532 (1994). . . . [The Second Circuit reversed.]

II

The critical question before us in respect to Buckley's "emotional distress" claim is whether the physical contact with insulation dust that accompanied his emotional distress amounts to a "physical impact" as this Court used that term in *Gottshall*. In *Gottshall*, an emotional distress case, the Court interpreted the word "injury" in FELA § 1, a provision that makes "[e]very common carrier by railroad . . . liable in damages to any person suffering injury while . . . employed" by the carrier if the "injury" results from carrier "negligence." [ ] In doing so, it initially set forth several general legal principles applicable here. . . . It pointed out that the Act expressly abolishes or modifies a host of common-law doctrines that previously had limited recovery. [ ] It added that this Court has interpreted the Act's language "liberally" in light of its humanitarian purposes. [ ] But, at the same time, the Court noted that liability under the Act rests upon "negligence" and that the Act does not make the railroad "the insurer" for all employee injuries. [ ] The Court stated that "common-law principles," where not rejected in the text of the statute, "are entitled to great weight" in interpreting the Act, and that those principles "play a significant role" in determining whether, or when, an employee can recover damages for "negligent infliction of emotional distress." [ ]

The Court also set forth several more specific legal propositions. It recognized that the common law of torts does not permit recovery for negligently inflicted emotional distress unless the distress falls within certain specific categories that amount to recovery-permitting exceptions. The law, for example, does permit recovery for emotional distress where that distress accompanies a physical injury, see, e.g., Simmons v. Pacor, Inc., [674 A.2d 232, 239 (Pa.1996)]; Restatement (Second) of Torts § 924(a)(1977), and it often permits recovery for distress suffered by a close relative who witnesses the physical injury of a negligence victim, e.g., Dillon v. Legg, [441 P.2d 912 (Cal.1968)—to be discussed shortly]; [ ]. The Court then held that FELA § 1, mirroring the law of many States, sometimes permitted recovery "for damages for negligent infliction of emotional distress," [ ], and, in particular, it does so where a plaintiff seeking such damages satisfies the common law's "zone of danger" test. It defined that test by stating that the law permits "recovery for emotional injury" by

> "those plaintiffs who *sustain a physical impact* as a result of a defendant's negligent conduct, or who are placed in immediate risk of physical harm by that conduct." [ ](emphasis added).

The case before us, as we have said, focuses on the italicized words "physical impact." The Second Circuit interpreted those words as including a simple physical contact with a substance that might cause a disease at a future time, so long as the contact was of a kind that would "cause fear in a reasonable person." [ ] In our view, however, the "physical impact" to which *Gottshall* referred does not include a simple physical contact with a substance that might cause a disease at a substantially later time—where that substance, or related circumstance, threatens no harm other than that disease-related risk.

First, *Gottshall* cited many state cases in support of its adoption of the "zone of danger" test quoted above. And in each case where recovery for emotional distress was permitted, the case involved a threatened physical contact that caused, or might have caused, immediate traumatic harm [citing cases that involved a car accident, a gas explosion, a train striking a car, clothing caught in an escalator and choking victim, and an intruder assaulting plaintiff's husband].

Second, *Gottshall's* language, read in light of this precedent, seems similarly limited. [ ]; id., at 547–548 (quoting Pearson, Liability to Bystanders for Negligently Inflicted Emotional Harm—A Comment on the Nature of Arbitrary Rules, 34 U. Fla. L.Rev. 477, 488–489 (1982))("[T]hose within the zone of danger of physical impact" should be able to "recover for fright" because "a near miss may be as frightening as a direct hit").

Taken together, language and cited precedent indicate that the words "physical impact" do not encompass every form of "physical contact." And, in particular, they do not include a contact that amounts to no more than an exposure—an exposure, such as that before us, to a substance that poses some future risk of disease and which contact causes emotional distress only because the worker learns that he may become ill after a substantial period of time.

Third, common-law precedent does not favor the plaintiff. Common-law courts do permit a plaintiff who suffers from a disease to recover for related negligently caused emotional distress, [ ], and some courts permit a plaintiff who exhibits a physical symptom of exposure to recover [ ]. But with only a few exceptions, common-law courts have denied recovery to those who, like Buckley, are disease and symptom free. [ ]; [*Simmons v. Pacor, Inc.*]; [ ]; see also Potter v. Firestone Tire & Rubber Co., [863 P.2d 795 (Cal.1993)] (no recovery for fear of cancer in a negligence action unless plaintiff is "more likely than not" to develop cancer).

Fourth, the general policy reasons to which *Gottshall* referred—in its explanation of why common-law courts have restricted recovery for emotional harm to cases falling within rather narrowly defined categories—militate against an expansive definition of "physical impact" here. Those reasons include: (a) special "difficult[y] for judges and juries" in separating valid, important claims from those that are invalid or "trivial," [ ]; (b) a threat of "unlimited and unpredictable liability," [ ]; and (c) the "potential for a flood" of comparatively unimportant, or "trivial," claims, [ ].

To separate meritorious and important claims from invalid or trivial claims does not seem easier here than in other cases in which a plaintiff might seek recovery for typical negligently caused emotional distress. The facts before us illustrate the problem. The District Court, when concluding that Buckley had failed to present "sufficient evidence to allow a jury to find ... a real emotional injury," pointed out that, apart from Buckley's own testimony, there was virtually no evidence of distress. [ ] Indeed, Buckley continued to work with insulating material "even though ... he could have transferred" elsewhere, he "continued to smoke cigarettes" despite doctors' warnings, and his doctor did not refer him "either to a psychologist or to a social worker." [ ] The Court of Appeals reversed because it found certain objective corroborating evidence, namely, "workers' complaints to supervisors and investigative bodies." [ ] Both kinds of "objective" evidence—the confirming and disconfirming evidence—seem only indirectly related to the question at issue, the existence and seriousness of Buckley's claimed emotional distress. Yet, given the difficulty of separating valid from invalid emotional injury claims, the evidence before us may typify the kind of evidence to which parties and the courts would have to look.

. . .

More important, the physical contact at issue here—a simple (though extensive) contact with a carcinogenic substance—does not seem to offer much help in separating valid from invalid emotional distress claims. That is because contacts, even extensive contacts, with serious carcinogens are common. [ ] (estimating that 21 million Americans have been exposed to work-related asbestos); [ ] (3 million workers exposed to benzene, a majority of Americans exposed outside the workplace); [ ] (reporting that 43% of American children lived in a home with at least one smoker, and 37% of adult nonsmokers lived in a home with at least one smoker or reported environmental tobacco smoke at work). They may occur without causing serious emotional distress, but sometimes they do cause distress, and reasonably so, for cancer is both an unusually threatening and unusually frightening disease. See [ ] (23.5% of Americans who died in 1994 died of cancer); [ ] (half of all men and one-third of all women will develop cancer). The relevant problem, however, remains one of evaluating a claimed emotional reaction to an increased risk of dying. An external circumstance—exposure—makes some emotional distress more likely. But how can one determine from the external circumstance of exposure whether, or when, a claimed strong emotional reaction to an increased mortality risk (say, from 23% to 28%) is reasonable and genuine, rather than overstated—particularly when the relevant statistics themselves are controversial and uncertain (as is usually the case), and particularly since neither those exposed nor judges or juries are experts in statistics? The evaluation problem seems a serious one.

The large number of those exposed and the uncertainties that may surround recovery also suggest what *Gottshall* called the problem of "unlimited and unpredictable liability." Does such liability mean, for example, that the costs associated with a rule of liability would become so great that, given the nature of the harm, it would seem unreasonable to require the public to pay the higher prices that may result? [ ] The same characteristics further suggest what *Gottshall* called the problem of a "flood" of cases that, if not "trivial," are comparatively less important. In a world of limited resources, would a rule permitting immediate large-scale recoveries for widespread emotional distress caused by fear of future disease diminish the likelihood of recovery by those who later suffer from the disease? [ ]

We do not raise these questions to answer them (for we do not have the answers), but rather to show that general policy concerns of a kind that have led common-law courts to deny recovery for certain classes of negligently caused harms are present in this case as well. That being so, we cannot find in *Gottshall*'s underlying rationale any basis for departing from *Gottshall*'s language and precedent or from the current common-law consensus. That is to say, we cannot find in *Gottshall*'s language, cited precedent, other common-law precedent, or related concerns of policy a legal basis for adopting the emotional distress recovery rule adopted by the Court of Appeals.

Buckley raises several important arguments in reply. He points out, for example, that common-law courts do permit recovery for emotional distress where a plaintiff has physical symptoms; and he argues that his evidence of exposure and enhanced mortality risk is as strong a proof as an accompanying physical symptom that his emotional distress is genuine.

This argument, however, while important, overlooks the fact that the common law in this area does not examine the genuineness of emotional harm case by case. Rather, it has developed recovery-permitting categories the contours of which more distantly reflect this, and other, abstract general policy concerns. The point of such categorization is to deny courts the authority to undertake a case-by-case examination. The common law permits emotional distress recovery for that category of plaintiffs who suffer from a disease (or exhibit a physical symptom), for example, thereby finding a special effort to evaluate emotional symptoms warranted in that category of cases—perhaps from a desire to make a physically injured victim whole or because the parties are likely to be in court in any event. In other cases, however, falling outside the special recovery-permitting categories, it has reached a different conclusion. The relevant question here concerns the validity of a rule that seeks to redefine such a category. It would not be easy to redefine "physical impact" in terms of a rule that turned on, say, the "massive, lengthy, [or] tangible" nature of a contact that amounted to an exposure, whether to contaminated water, or to germ-laden air, or to carcinogen-containing substances, such as insulation dust containing asbestos. But, in any event, for the reasons we have stated, we cannot find that the common law has done so.

. . .

[The opinion turned to claims for recovery of medical monitoring costs, discussed in Chapter V. It then reversed the decision of the Second Circuit and remanded the case on that claim.]

■ CHIEF JUSTICE REHNQUIST, and JUSTICES O'CONNOR, KENNEDY, SCALIA, SOUTER and THOMAS concurred.

■ JUSTICE GINSBURG, with whom JUSTICE STEVENS joins, concurring in the judgment in part and dissenting in part.

. . .

Buckley's extensive contact with asbestos particles in Grand Central's tunnels, as I comprehend his situation, constituted "physical impact" as that term was used in *Gottshall*. Nevertheless, I concur in the Court's judgment with respect to Buckley's emotional distress claim. In my view, that claim fails because Buckley did not present objective evidence of severe emotional distress. [ ] Buckley testified at trial that he was angry at Metro-North and fearful of developing an asbestos-related disease. However, he sought no professional help to ease his distress, and presented no medical testimony concerning his mental health. [ ] Under these circumstances, Buckley's emotional distress claim fails as a matter of law. Cf. [*Gottshall*] (Ginsburg, J., dissenting)(describing as "unquestionably genuine and severe" emotional distress suffered by one respondent who had a nervous breakdown, and another who was hospitalized, lost weight, and had, inter alia, suicidal preoccupations, anxiety, insomnia, cold sweats, and nausea).

[Justices Ginsburg and Stevens dissented on the monitoring question.]

NOTES AND QUESTIONS

1. Although the Supreme Court applies the FELA in this case, it draws principles from the common law into the Act, and engages in a lengthy discussion of common law precedent. What does the majority mean by saying that courts must develop categorical liability rules rather than decide on recovery case by case? How does the majority's attitude toward the development of the common law compare with that of the *Falzone* court?

2. The Court enumerates several categories of cases where recovery would be permitted. Among these, it included the situation in which the plaintiff was placed in a "zone of danger." The *Gottshall* court explained one prong of the "zone of danger" test by stating that it involved "immediate risk of physical harm," but which did not require physical impact.

Why should *immediate* risk be required? Plaintiff was put at an increased risk of physical harm, but because of the latency period for the diseases risked, many years or decades would pass before he might suffer harm.

Might it matter if the exposure was sudden rather than gradual? Would this be a different case if the exposure risked an acute response, say a serious asthma attack? Did *Falzone* implicitly adopt a "zone of danger" rule?

3. Another common law category the Court identifies is comprised of those who have suffered physical harm and seek to "recover for [future] related negligently caused emotional distress." In Norfolk & Western Railway Co. v. Ayers, 538 U.S. 135 (2003), workers suffering from asbestosis, a non-malignant respiratory disease, asserted FELA claims for emotional distress at the prospect that they might contract cancer in the future. Splitting 5–4, the majority permitted recovery for emotional distress if plaintiffs proved it was "genuine and serious." The dissent in *Ayers* argued that plaintiffs' emotional harm was not a result of their physical harm, but instead caused by the prospect of future disease and therefore not sufficiently related to the asbestosis to permit recovery.

To what extent are *Buckley* and *Ayers* affected by the unique nature of asbestos litigation, which has involved hundreds of thousands of claims and been involved in the bankruptcies of over 100 companies, while estimates are that almost 30 million Americans have been occupationally exposed to asbestos?

How serious is the concern that a flood of emotional distress litigation might prevent recovery by later plaintiffs who had actually contracted a disease? For more discussion of this issue, see the treatment of increased risk of future harm at p. 343 infra.

4. In *Potter v. Firestone Tire and Rubber Co.*, cited in the majority opinion, defendant's dumping of toxic wastes into a landfill near its plant site exposed plaintiffs to carcinogens over a prolonged period. Although none of the plaintiffs suffered from any current condition, they faced "an enhanced but unquantified risk of developing cancer in the future due to the exposure." The court held that:

> [I]n the absence of a present physical injury or illness, damages for fear of cancer may be recovered only if the plaintiff pleads and proves that 1) as a result of the defendant's negligent breach of a duty owed to the plaintiff, the plaintiff is exposed to a toxic substance which threatens cancer, *and* 2) the plaintiff's fear stems from a knowledge, corroborated by reliable medical or scientific opinion, that it is more likely than not that the plaintiff will develop the cancer in the future due to the toxic exposure.

The court went on to add that the plaintiff must further show "a serious fear that the toxic ingestion or exposure was of such magnitude and proportion as to likely result in the feared cancer." Since the claim in these cases is based on emotional distress, not the likelihood of actually contracting cancer, why shouldn't a "serious fear" requirement be the exclusive test for liability?

The *Potter* court also held that if plaintiff could establish "oppression, fraud or malice"—the California standard for punitive damages—then a showing that the plaintiff's fear is "serious, genuine and reasonable," would suffice.

5. *HIV cases.* Litigation over fear of contracting HIV has arisen in many state courts. Where the plaintiff is concerned because he or she was given an injection with a dirty needle, or was pricked by a needle that should have been sheathed in trash, the courts have tended to require the plaintiff to show that the needle in question actually contained the virus. Most have adopted an actual "zone of danger" analysis that requires that the needle be shown to have been infected.

A few courts in HIV cases allow recovery for the "window" between the event that creates the concern and the results of tests showing that infection did not occur. See Faya v. Almaraz, 620 A.2d 327 (Md.1993). But should recovery be limited to the "window"? See Chizmar v. Mackie, 896 P.2d 196 (Alaska 1995)(permitting an action for negligently misdiagnosing a patient as being HIV positive, and concluding that damages might be recovered for distress suffered after the date on which the patient learns that she is not HIV positive). The negligent diagnosis scenario is discussed further at p. 279 infra.

Another "window" situation involves fears induced by negligent acts affecting pregnant women. See Jones v. Howard University, Inc., 589 A.2d 419 (D.C.1991), upholding a mother's claim for the mental distress she suffered as a result of defendant hospital's negligence in giving her an X-ray exam while she was pregnant. The mother alleged that she suffered emotional distress during her pregnancy term due to the possibility that the radiation had harmed her unborn twins and the chance that she might experience severe pregnancy complications.

6. On the variety of issues discussed in the preceding notes, see generally, Rabin, Emotional Distress in Tort Law: Themes of Constraint, 44 Wake Forest L.Rev. 1197 (2009); Goldberg & Zipursky, Unrealized Torts, 88 Va.L.Rev. 1625 (2002); Wells, The Grin Without the Cat: Claims for Damages from Toxic Exposure Without Present Injury, 18 Wm. & Mary J.Envtl.L. 285 (1994).)

b.   NO RISK OF PHYSICAL HARM TO PLAINTIFF

In the last half century, courts have tended to expand the scope of liability for stand-alone emotional harm. *Falzone* is one such example. Beginning with *Dillon v. Legg*, 441 P.2d 912 (Cal.1968), courts have allowed bystanders to recover for their emotional distress under certain conditions addressed p. 285 infra. In addition, courts have permitted recovery of emotional harm in a limited number of circumscribed circumstances where the risk of causing serious emotional harm is particularly acute. These are situations that do not involve a risk of physical harm to the plaintiff (as in *Falzone*) and are not bystander cases (ones in which the distress is suffered from observing physical harm suffered by another). The Third Restatement, in section 47(b) provides for liability when negligently inflicted serious emotional harm "occurs in the course of specified categories of activities, undertakings, or relationships in which negligent conduct is especially likely to cause serious emotional harm." When reading the next two cases, consider whether that standard helpfully defines the conditions under which courts permit recovery for emotional harm.

Gammon v. Osteopathic Hospital of Maine, Inc.

Supreme Judicial Court of Maine, 1987.
534 A.2d 1282.

■ Before MCKUSICK, C.J., and NICHOLS, ROBERTS, WATHEN, SCOLNIK and CLIFFORD, JJ.

■ ROBERTS, JUSTICE.

[Plaintiff's father, Linwood, died in defendant hospital. Plaintiff asked defendant funeral home to make the arrangements. He alleged that the defendants negligently conducted their operations so that he received a bag that was supposedly personal effects, but which in fact contained "a bloodied leg, severed below the knee, and bluish in color." He yelled "Oh my God, they have taken my father's leg off." He ran into the kitchen where an aunt testified that he "was as white as a ghost." In fact the leg was a pathology specimen removed from another person. Thereafter, plaintiff "began having nightmares for the first time in his life, his personality was affected and his relationship with his wife and children deteriorated." After several months Gammon's emotional state began to improve, although he still had occasional nightmares. He sought no medical or psychiatric attention and offered no medical evidence at trial.

The trial court granted a directed verdict on count I—plaintiff's negligence claim for severe emotional distress. On other counts, not directly relevant here, the judge had charged the jury that "severe emotional distress" was distress "such that no reasonable man should be expected to endure it."]

The issue is whether, in these circumstances Gammon has established a claim, in tort, for negligent infliction of severe emotional distress. A person's psychic well-being is as much entitled to legal protection as is his physical well-being. We recognize as much and provide compensation when the emotional distress is intentionally or recklessly inflicted, when the emotional distress results from physical injury negligently inflicted, or when negligently inflicted emotional distress results in physical injury. In order to ensure that a claim for emotional distress without physical injury is not spurious, we have previously required a showing of physical impact, objective manifestation, underlying or accompanying tort, or special circumstances. In the case before us, we conclude that these more or less arbitrary requirements should not bar Gammon's claim for compensation for severe emotional distress.

[At this point the court reviewed eight emotional distress cases that it had decided over a period of 100 years.]

No useful purpose would be served by more detailed analyses of our prior decisions or by consideration of whether the holdings of these cases follow a consistent trend. They demonstrate in a variety of ways the difficulty courts have had dealing with psychic injury.[5] They also demonstrate the frailty of supposed lines of demarcation when they are subjected to judicial scrutiny in the context of varying fact patterns. Moreover, these cases disclose our awareness of the extensive criticism aimed at the artificial devices used by courts to protect against fraudulent claims and against undue burden on the conduct of defendants.

The analyses of commentators and the developing trend in case law encourage us to abandon these artificial devices in this and future tort actions and to rely upon the trial process for protection against fraudulent claims. In addition, the traditional tort principle of foreseeability relied upon in [two earlier cases] provides adequate protection against unduly burdensome liability claims for emotional distress. Jurors or trial judges will be able to evaluate the impact of psychic trauma with no greater difficulty than pertains to assessment of

---

[5]   When discussing this type of injury, the courts of other jurisdictions and the commentators have used as the adjective either "emotional, mental, nervous or psychic" together with the noun "distress, pain, injury, harm, trauma, disturbance or shock." These phrases have not become words of art although each, with varying degrees of accuracy, seems to refer to non-tactile trauma resulting in injury to the psyche.

damages for any intangible injury. We do not foresee any great extension of tort liability by our ruling today. We do not provide compensation for the hurt feelings of the supersensitive plaintiff—the eggshell psyche. A defendant is bound to foresee psychic harm only when such harm reasonably could be expected to befall the ordinarily sensitive person.[8]

We have previously recognized that courts in other jurisdictions have allowed recovery for mental distress alone for negligent mishandling of corpses. [ ] In recognizing that Gammon has made out a claim in the instant case, we do not find it necessary to rely on an extension of this exception. Instead, we look to the rationale supporting the exception. Courts have concluded that the exceptional vulnerability of the family of recent decedents makes it highly probable that emotional distress will result from mishandling the body. [ ] That high probability is said to provide sufficient trustworthiness to allay the court's fear of fraudulent claims. [ ] This rationale, it seems, is but another way of determining that the defendant reasonably should have foreseen that mental distress would result from his negligence. By the same token, on the record before us, a jury could conclude that the hospital and the mortician reasonably should have foreseen that members of Linwood Gammon's family would be vulnerable to emotional shock at finding a severed leg in what was supposed to be the decedent's personal effects. Despite the defendants' argument to the contrary, we hold that the evidence in this case would support a jury finding that either or both defendants failed to exercise reasonable care to prevent such an occurrence.

Although the analysis in the instant case may impact upon the rationale of our recent cases, we do not find it necessary to overrule those cases. We do not hold that any prior case was wrongly decided. Rather, we recognize that the elimination of some barriers to recovery for negligent infliction of severe emotional distress may compel further evaluation of other policy considerations. . . .

On the facts and circumstances of the case before us, however, we find no sound basis to preclude potential compensation to Gammon. We hold, therefore, that the trial court erred in directing a verdict on Gammon's claim for negligent infliction of severe emotional distress.[9] Accordingly, we vacate the judgment in favor of the defendants on Count I.

Remanded for further proceedings consistent with the opinion herein.

---

[8] We described serious mental distress in *Culbert* as being "where a reasonable person, normally constituted, would be unable to adequately cope with the mental stress engendered by the circumstances of the event." [ ]

[9] By virtue of the pleadings and the jury finding in the case before us, our holding necessarily is limited to negligently inflicted *severe* emotional distress. We do not decide whether a defendant shall be liable for negligently inflicted emotional distress of any lesser degree.

NOTES AND QUESTIONS

1. Is the obligation recognized here limited to situations involving death and the special sensitivity of families after a death? If not, are there any limits to the types of situations that may give rise to a claim for emotional distress from a defendant's negligent conduct? Suppose that the package arrived during a 30th birthday party for plaintiff attended by several dozen friends and family and during the party the package is opened to the horror of all guests? Could the guests recover?

2. Twelve years after *Gammon*, the Maine Supreme Court confronted another emotional distress case, Bryan R. v. Watchtower Bible & Tract Society of New York Inc., 738 A.2d 839 (Me.1999). Plaintiff sued the church for abuse alleged to have been inflicted by an adult member of the church, claiming that the church had an affirmative duty to protect members from sexual abuse by other church members when the church was aware of prior incidents of abuse. In the course of denying a claim against the church based on "pure foreseeability," the court stated, "[o]nly where a particular duty based upon the unique relationship of the parties has been established may a defendant be held responsible, absent some other wrongdoing, for harming the emotional wellbeing of another. See, e.g., [ ]; [*Gammon*] (holding that a hospital's relationship to the family of deceased gives rise to a duty to avoid emotional harm from handling of remains)." Is the "unique relationship" limitation a fair reading of the holding in *Gammon*?

3. In addressing the concern with fraudulent claims, *Gammon* states, "jurors or trial judges will be able to evaluate the impact of psychic trauma with no greater difficulty than pertains to assessment of damages for any intangible injury." Is that persuasive? Responsive?

Taking on this issue, Professor Grey argues that neuroscience has reached the point where concern about false or exaggerated claims is no longer valid and that it is time to put emotional harm on the same basis as physical injury for purposes of tort recovery. The author is critical of the limited-duty rules for negligent infliction of emotional distress adopted in the Third Restatement. Grey, The Future of Emotional Harm, 83 Fordham L.Rev. 2605 (2015).

4. In Hedgepeth v. Whitman Walker Clinic, 22 A.3d 789 (D.C.2011), plaintiff was misdiagnosed as being HIV-positive, resulting in depression over a five-year period before he discovered the error. The trial court dismissed because plaintiff was never in the zone of danger, and the court of appeals affirmed. On rehearing en banc, the court, relying on section 47(b) of the Third Restatement, changed its law on stand-alone emotional harm to reject any zone of danger requirement for otherwise valid emotional harm claims. The court also held that the doctor-patient relationship in the context of HIV made it one of those cases in which a duty to protect against emotional harm exists:

> We hold that a duty to avoid negligent infliction of serious emotional distress will be recognized only where the defendant has an obligation to care for the plaintiff's emotional well-being or

the plaintiff's emotional well-being is necessarily implicated by the nature of the defendant's undertaking to or relationship with the plaintiff, and serious emotional distress is especially likely to be caused by the defendant's negligence.

How might the court in *Gammon* analyze *Hedgepeth*?

5. Two other contexts in which courts have recognized a claim for NIED are reflected in Bylsma v. Burger King Corp., 293 P.3d 1168 (Wash.2013) and Miranda v. Said, 836 N.W.2d 8 (Iowa 2013). In *Bylsma*, a sheriff ordered a Whopper that was delivered with a glob of phlegm (later confirmed by DNA to be from an employee) on the hamburger. The court responded to a certified question: "We answer that the [Washington Product Liability Act] permits relief in such circumstances, but only if the emotional distress is a reasonable reaction and manifest by objective symptomatology."

Miranda provides a very different context for emotional distress damages. An immigration attorney grossly erred in suggesting a plan for two undocumented Ecuadorian immigrants whose son was about to become a U.S. citizen. Under the plan, the couple would voluntarily return to Ecuador and then have their son sponsor them to return based on a program to alleviate extreme hardship. However, the program relied on by the defendant attorney was limited to children and spouses of the sponsor, and the parents were thus ineligible for a hardship waiver. In addition, because they had returned to Ecuador voluntarily, they were barred from returning to the United States for ten years, separating them from their two children. The district court had granted a directed verdict for defendant on the emotional harm claim, which the court of appeals reversed.

The Iowa Supreme Court, recognizing the trend toward more permissive recognition of NIED claims, stated: "We recognize 'a duty to exercise ordinary care to avoid causing emotional harm' " in categories of cases when the relationship between the parties and the acts engaged in by the defendant create a likelihood that victims will suffer emotional distress. Applying that standard to this case, the court concluded that plaintiffs could recover for their emotional harm.

6. *Falzone* required "reasonable" fear of immediate injury. *Gammon* refers to the "ordinarily sensitive person" as supplemented in footnote 8. Do these formulations help provide adequate control for the expansion of this type of liability?

7. *Physical manifestations.* Recall note 1, p. 265 supra, which addressed the distinction between bodily injury or sickness and emotional distress in the context of direct claims. Throughout this section, there has been the underlying question of whether plaintiffs must prove that their emotional distress led to physical manifestations. The *Chizmar* court, p. 275 supra, noted that "examples of serious emotional distress may include 'neuroses, psychoses, chronic depression, phobia, and shock.' [ ] However, temporary fright, disappointment or regret does not suffice. . . ." Although "some jurisdictions have required claims of emotional distress to be 'medically diagnosable or objectifiable,' we do not believe that such a limitation is necessary or desirable." The existence of the required distress was a matter of proof for the trier of fact.

In Sullivan v. Boston Gas Co., 605 N.E.2d 805 (Mass.1993), two plaintiffs stood across the street as their house burned to the ground. In an earlier case the court had said that in emotional distress cases the plaintiff must generally show, in addition to other items, "physical harm manifested by objective symptomology." The court, paraphrasing the Second Restatement of Torts section 436, rejecting the line between physical and mental harm in this area, concluded that "repeated hysterical attacks" are illnesses sufficient to corroborate the existence of the claimed distress; that "headaches or nausea" could qualify if they "lasted for a substantial period of time;" but that "transient symptoms such as vomiting" did not qualify "even though they clearly involve physical functions of the body."

Plaintiff McDonald alleged that she suffered from post-traumatic stress disorder that sometimes occurred as often as once or twice a week, the symptoms of which were diarrhea and heart palpitation. In addition, she asserted that she had experienced "sleeplessness, weeping, depression, and feelings of despair." Sullivan alleged that he had experienced tension headaches, muscle tenderness in the back of his head, and problems with concentration and reading, as well as "sleeplessness, gastrointestinal distress, upset stomach, nightmares, depression, feelings of despair, difficulty in driving and working, and an overall 'lousy' feeling" from the explosion. Both were held to meet the required standard, which was seen as an attempt to strike a balance between "our desire to ferret out fraudulent claims and our duty to grant deserving plaintiffs a chance to present their case to a fact finder."

Is a requirement of physical manifestation likely to serve as a meaningful limitation against fraud in these cases?

8. In Chapter XIII, we take up situations in which there is intentionally inflicted emotional distress.

Johnson v. Jamaica Hospital

Court of Appeals of New York, 1984.
62 N.Y.2d 523, 467 N.E.2d 502, 478 N.Y.S.2d 838.

■ KAYE, JUDGE.

[Plaintiffs' daughter, Kawana, was born in defendant hospital. After the plaintiff mother was discharged, Kawana was kept for further treatment. When the mother visited a week later, Kawana was discovered missing. She apparently had been abducted that day—a day on which the hospital received two bomb threats. While she was missing, plaintiffs brought suit for the emotional distress brought about by defendant's negligence. Kawana was recovered by the police and returned to plaintiffs after four and one-half months. A separate suit was brought on Kawana's behalf, which is not part of this appeal. The trial court denied defendant's motion to dismiss the parents' action for *proced. history*

failure to state a cause of action. The Appellate Division affirmed by a divided vote and certified the question whether it had acted properly.]

Assuming the allegations of plaintiffs' complaint to be true [ ], no cause of action is stated. . . . Plaintiffs contend, and the courts below concluded, that their complaint states a cause of action because the defendant hospital owed a duty directly to them, as parents, to care properly for their child, and that it was or should have been foreseeable to defendant that any injury to Kawana, such as abduction, would cause them mental distress. There is no basis for establishing such a direct duty. This court has refused to recognize such a duty on the part of a hospital to the parents of hospitalized children (Kalina v. General Hosp., [195 N.E.2d 309 (N.Y. 1963)]), and there is no reason to depart from that rule here.

rule

In *Kalina,* the plaintiffs, an observant Jewish couple, gave express instructions to the defendant hospital that their newborn son was to be ritualistically circumcised on his eighth day by a mohel in accordance with the tenets of their religion. Instead, due to the alleged negligence and malpractice of the hospital, the baby was circumcised on his fourth day by a physician. The plaintiff parents sought recovery for their mental pain and suffering caused by the assault and battery upon their son. Special Term granted defendants' motion to dismiss the complaint [ ], and we ultimately affirmed on Special Term's opinion. In that opinion, the parents of the hospitalized child were held to be "interested bystanders" to whom no direct duty was owed.

Both of the pleadings are insufficient because the plaintiffs as individuals, apart from their status as representatives of their son, do not have a legally protected interest under these circumstances [ ]. To paraphrase the language of [*Palsgraf v. Long Island R. Co.*, reprinted in Chapter VI], the conduct of the defendants, if a wrong in relation to the son, was not a wrong in its relation to the plaintiffs, remote from the event. Rights are not abstractions but exist only correlatively with duties. Everyone who has been damaged by an interruption in the expected tenor of his life does not have a cause of action. The law demands that the equation be balanced; that the damaged plaintiff be able to point the finger of responsibility at a defendant owing, not a general duty to society, but a specific duty to him.

The defendants here in accepting a relationship with the son assumed the risk of liability for a tortious performance to him. They did not assume any risk of liability that their acts might violate the personal sensibilities of others, be they the son's parents, his coreligionists or the community at large. [ ]

Jamaica Hospital owed no more of a direct duty to the plaintiff parents to refrain from causing them psychic injury than did the defendants in *Kalina* [and three other cases]. The direct injury allegedly caused by defendant's negligence—abduction—was sustained by the infant, and plaintiffs' grief and mental torment which resulted from her disappearance are not actionable. The foreseeability that such psychic injuries would result from the injury to Kawana does not serve to establish a duty running from defendant to plaintiffs (*Albala v. City of New York*, [ ]; *Pulka v. Edelman*, [ ]), and in the absence of such a duty, as a matter of law there can be no liability [ ]. That sound policy reasons support these decisions is evident here, for to permit recovery by the infant's parents for emotional distress would be to invite open-ended liability for indirect emotional injury suffered by families in every instance where the very young, or very elderly, or incapacitated persons experience negligent care or treatment.

. . .

Finally, our prior holdings in *Johnson v. State of New York*, [ ], and *Lando v. State of New York*, [ ], provide no basis for recovery. In neither case was liability based upon a hospital's breach of care to its patient causing direct injury to the patient resulting in emotional injury to relatives of the patient. In *Johnson* the defendant hospital negligently sent a telegram to plaintiff notifying her of her mother's death when in fact her mother had not died, and in *Lando* the defendant hospital negligently failed to locate a deceased patient's body for 11 days, when it was found in an advanced state of decomposition. Each case presented exceptional circumstances in which courts long ago recognized liability for resultant emotional injuries: a duty to transmit truthfully information concerning a relative's death or funeral [ ] which the hospital assumed by sending the message [ ], and the mishandling of or failure to deliver a dead body with the consequent denial of access to the family [ ]. Neither exception is applicable here.

In summary, Jamaica Hospital, even if negligent in caring for Kawana and directly liable to her, is not liable for emotional distress suffered by plaintiffs as a consequence of the abduction. This is in accord with the majority rule in this country. [ ] There is no duty owing from defendant to plaintiffs to refrain from negligently causing such injury. To hold otherwise would be to invite the very sort of boundless liability for indirect emotional injury that we have consistently rejected.

[The court rejected a dissent argument that liability here can be circumscribed by limiting any duty owed to those parents whose custodial rights have been interfered with because this was not a common occurrence. The majority responded that "any right to recover for emotional injury sustained by plaintiffs because of defendant's negligence in the 'care, custody and management' of their child cannot rationally be refused to other parents, relatives or custodians of persons to whom caretakers of various types, such as schools and day care centers, are alleged to have breached a similar duty."] Accordingly, the order of the Appellate Division should be reversed, the certified question answered in the negative, and the complaint dismissed.

■ COOKE, C.J., and JONES, WACHTLER and SIMONS, JJ., concur with KAYE, J.

■ MEYER, J., dissents and votes to affirm in a separate opinion in which JASEN, J., concurs.

NOTES AND QUESTIONS

1. As the court notes, Kawana's own action is not involved at this time. Does she have a claim if she is returned in good health? Is the court overlooking the deterrence function? Are there other sources of incentives for hospitals to prevent kidnappings that overlap any deterrence that tort law might provide?

2. Suppose that Kawana died shortly after she was born, but the hospital lost her corpse before it was to be turned over to the funeral home. Would the *Johnson* plaintiffs have had a valid claim for emotional harm? If so, can the outcome of this hypothetical and the *Johnson* case be reconciled?

3. Is *Johnson* a stronger or weaker category to permit recovery for emotional distress than *Gammon*? If you think it is stronger or strong enough to permit recovery, would that mean that a parent could recover for any negligent treatment of a child by a medical care provider?

4. Is there a meaningful distinction between "direct" and "indirect" harms in these emotional distress cases?

In other contexts, courts have viewed emotional distress suffered by a mother resulting from harm to her child during labor and delivery as a special case. She is not seen as a direct victim since the alleged malpractice was addressed to the fetus. The mother has an action whether conscious at the time or not. (There was concern that the use of anesthetic might become more common in deliveries if the courts barred suits when the mother was not aware of the negligence at the time it occurred.)

5. Contrast with *Johnson*, Larsen v. Banner Health System, 81 P.3d 196 (Wyo.2003). Defendant hospital switched babies, and plaintiffs, mother and daughter, were separated for 43 years during which time mother was suspected of adultery because the switched child did not resemble father in coloring. The court allowed recovery in this case "in the limited circumstances where a contractual relationship exists for services that carry with them deeply emotional responses in the event of breach." Is *Larsen* distinguishable from *Johnson*?

6. *Damage to property*. In Lubner v. City of Los Angeles, 53 Cal.Rptr.2d 24 (App.1996), the plaintiff artists sued for property damage and emotional distress when the city's trash truck crashed into their house, damaging the house, two cars and much of their artwork. The court denied recovery for the distress, refusing categorically to allow recovery for emotional distress caused by loss of property:

> The policy of preventing future harm is served by the sanction of compensation for the economic loss, which also meets the factor of the burden on the defendant to avoid runaway trash trucks in the

future. The principal consequences to the community of imposing an incremental liability for these damages are the additional taxes to citizens of the City in exchange for city services. . . . On balance, the factors do not favor permitting the emotional distress damages.

How would the court in *Falzone* analyze *Lubner*? Would it matter whether the Lubners were at home when the truck hit the house?

By contrast with *Lubner*, Rodrigues v. State, 472 P.2d 509 (Haw. 1970), involved a house that plaintiffs had built with their own hands. Due to the state's negligence, water flooded the house to a depth of six inches causing damage. In addition to recovery for property damage, the court, 3–2, held that plaintiffs could recover damages for their emotional distress upon a showing that "a reasonable man normally constituted, would be unable adequately to cope with the mental stress engendered by the circumstances of the case." Two of the five justices dissented on the ground that it was inappropriate to award such damages as a result of harm to property. Is *Rodrigues* inconsistent with *Lubner*?

7.   *Pets.* In Campbell v. Animal Quarantine Station, 632 P.2d 1066 (Haw.1981), plaintiffs learned over the telephone that their dog had died because of the negligence of defendant, which had occurred on the same island in Hawaii. Recovery of $200 for each of five plaintiffs was upheld after a finding that they had each suffered "severe" emotional distress. Is the amount awarded inconsistent with the description of the severity of harm suffered? But see Roman v. Carroll, 621 P.2d 307 (Ariz.App.1980), in which plaintiff alleged that she sustained emotional distress from "watching defendants' St. Bernard dismember plaintiff's poodle while she was walking the dog near her home." The poodle died two days later. The court rejected plaintiff's effort to use the bystander analysis because a dog "is personal property" and "distress from witnessing injury to property" did not give rise to an action. See also Kondaurov v. Kerdasha, 629 S.E.2d 181 (Va.2006), similarly rejecting a cause of action and discussing the line of cases to which it adheres. Several states have enacted statutes reversing the common law antipathy to owners recovering for distress resulting from abuse or neglect of their pets.

2.   BYSTANDERS

This section, by contrast with the earlier cases in this Chapter, is concerned with the situation in which the plaintiff's emotional harm occurs because she is a bystander who witnesses an accident in which another suffers serious bodily injury or death.

Portee v. Jaffee

Supreme Court of New Jersey, 1980.
84 N.J. 88, 417 A.2d 521.

■ PASHMAN, J.

We are asked to determine whether a parent can recover damages for the emotional anguish of watching her young child suffer and die in an accident caused by defendant's negligence. In Falzone v. Busch, [214 A.2d 12 (N.J.1965)], this Court imposed liability for such infliction of mental or emotional distress when negligence created the potential, but not the occurrence, for physical harm to the traumatized individual. The question presented here is whether liability should exist where there was no potential for personal injury, but distress resulted from perceiving the negligently inflicted injuries of another.

. . .

Since plaintiff had concededly not been subjected to any risk of physical harm caused by defendants' alleged negligence, the trial court found that plaintiff's claims for psychological injury did not meet the requirements of Falzone. Because the trial court considered this Court's decision in Falzone dispositive, we begin our discussion with that case. [The court discussed *Falzone* at length.]

[Plaintiff and her seven-year-old son, Guy, lived in an apartment building owned by Jaffee. One afternoon Guy became trapped in the building's elevator between its outer door and the wall of the elevator shaft. The elevator was activated and the boy was dragged up to the third floor. Another child ran to seek help. Plaintiff and police arrived and the police worked for four and one-half hours to free the child. While their efforts continued, plaintiff "watched as her son moaned, cried out and flailed his arms. Much of the time she was restrained from touching him, apparently to prevent interference with the attempted rescue." Guy suffered multiple bone fractures and internal injuries. He died while still trapped, "his mother a helpless observer." Companies involved in designing and maintaining the elevator were also sued.

After Guy's death, plaintiff became severely depressed and self-destructive. She slashed her wrist in a suicide attempt and required physical therapy for her wrist and extensive counseling and psychotherapy. The trial court granted summary judgment for defendants on claims by plaintiff for mental and emotional distress. The dismissal was reviewed directly by the supreme court.]

. . .

On many occasions, the law of negligence needs no other formulation besides the duty of reasonable care. Other cases, however, present circumstances rendering application of that general standard difficult, if not impossible. Without adequate guidance, juries may impose liability that is not commensurate with the culpability of defendant's conduct.

This difficulty has been recognized when courts considered liability for mental and emotional distress. We have noted the traditional argument, rejected by this Court in *Falzone,* that the imposition of such liability unoccasioned by any physical impact would lead to "mere conjecture and speculation." [ ] Even where the causal relationship between conduct and emotional harm was clear, courts would deny liability unless the fault of defendant's conduct could be demonstrated by the occurrence of physical harm to the plaintiff. [ ] Under *Falzone,* it became clear that the creation of a risk of physical harm would be a sufficient indication that defendant's conduct was unreasonable. Without such an indication, it might be argued that a jury could not form a reliable judgment regarding negligence. The question now before us is whether we are left to "mere conjecture and speculation" in assessing the culpability of conduct that creates neither the risk nor the occurrence of physical harm.

The task in the present case involves the refinement of principles of liability to remedy violations of reasonable care while avoiding speculative results or punitive liability. The solution is close scrutiny of the specific personal interests assertedly injured. By this approach, we can determine whether a defendant's freedom of action should be burdened by the imposition of liability. In the present case, the interest assertedly injured is more than a general interest in emotional tranquility. It is the profound and abiding sentiment of parental love. The knowledge that loved ones are safe and whole is the deepest wellspring of emotional welfare. Against that reassuring background, the flashes of anxiety and disappointment that mar our lives take on softer hues. No loss is greater than the loss of a loved one, and no tragedy is more wrenching than the helpless apprehension of the death or serious injury of one whose very existence is a precious treasure. The law should find more than pity for one who is stricken by seeing that a loved one has been critically injured or killed.

Courts in other jurisdictions which have found liability in the circumstances before us have placed limits on this type of negligence liability consistent with their view of the individual interest being injured. In Dillon v. Legg, [441 P.2d 912 (Cal.1968)], the California Supreme Court identified three factors which would determine whether an emotional injury would be compensable because "foreseeable":

(1) Whether plaintiff was located near the scene of the accident as contrasted with one who was a distance away from it. (2) Whether the shock resulted from a direct emotional impact upon plaintiff from the sensory and contemporaneous observance of the accident, as contrasted with learning of the accident from others after its occurrence. (3) Whether plaintiff and the victim were closely related, as contrasted with an

absence of any relationship or the presence of only a distant relationship. [ ]

. . .

We agree that the three factors described in *Dillon* together create a strong case for negligence liability. In any given case, as physical proximity between plaintiff and the scene of the accident becomes closer, the foreseeable likelihood that plaintiff will suffer emotional distress from apprehending the physical harm of another increases. The second requirement of "direct . . . sensory and contemporaneous observance" appears to reflect a limitation of the liability rule to traumatic distress occasioned by immediate perception. The final criterion, that the plaintiff be "closely related" to the injured person, also embodies the judgment that only the most profound emotional interests should receive vindication for their negligent injury.

Our analysis of the specific emotional interest injured in this case—a fundamental interest in emotional tranquility founded on parental love—reveals where the limits of liability would lie. Addressing the *Dillon* criteria in reverse order, we find the last—the existence of a close relationship—to be the most crucial. It is the presence of deep, intimate, familial ties between the plaintiff and the physically injured person that makes the harm to emotional tranquility so serious and compelling. The genuine suffering which flows from such harm stands in stark contrast to the setbacks and sorrows of everyday life, or even to the apprehension of harm to another, less intimate person. The existence of a marital or intimate familial relationship is therefore an essential element of a cause of action for negligent infliction of emotional distress. In the present case, the instinctive affection of a mother for her seven-year-old son would be a sufficiently intimate bond on which to predicate liability.

The second requirement—that the plaintiff witness the incident which resulted in death or serious injury—is equally essential. We recognize that to deny recovery solely because the plaintiff was not subjected to a risk of physical harm would impose an arbitrary barrier that bears no relation to the injury to his basic emotional stability. [ ] Yet avoiding arbitrary distinctions does not entail that a cause of action should exist for all emotional injuries to all the close relatives of the victim. This expansive view would extend judicial redress far beyond the bounds of the emotional interest entitled to protection. To avoid imposing liability in excess of culpability, the scope of recovery must be circumscribed to negligent conduct which strikes at the plaintiff's basic emotional security.

Discovering the death or serious injury of an intimate family member will always be expected to threaten one's emotional welfare. Ordinarily, however, only a witness at the scene of the accident causing death or serious injury will suffer a traumatic sense of loss that may destroy his sense of security and cause severe emotional distress. . . .

Such a risk of severe emotional distress is present when the plaintiff observes the accident at the scene. Without such perception, the threat of emotional injury is lessened and the justification for liability is fatally weakened. The law of negligence, while it redresses suffering wrongfully caused by others, must not itself inflict undue harm by imposing an unreasonably excessive measure of liability. Accordingly, we hold that observing the death or serious injury of another while it occurs is an essential element of a cause of action for the negligent infliction of emotional distress.

The first factor discussed in *Dillon*—that the plaintiff be near the injured person—embodies the same observations made concerning the other requirements of direct perception and close familial relationship. Physical proximity may be of some relevance in demonstrating the closeness of the emotional bond between plaintiff and the injured family member. For example, one would generally suppose that the risk of emotional distress to a brother who is halfway across the country is not as great as to a mother who is at the scene of the accident. The proximity of the plaintiff to the accident scene increases the likelihood that he will witness the event causing the death or serious injury of a loved one. Yet it appears that if the plaintiff must observe the accident that causes death or serious injury, a requirement of proximity is necessarily satisfied. The risk of emotional injury exists by virtue of the plaintiff's perception of the accident, not his proximity to it.

An additional factor yet undiscussed is the severity of the physical injury causing emotional distress. The harm we have determined to be worthy of judicial redress is the trauma accompanying the observation of the death or serious physical injury of a loved one. While any harm to a spouse or a family member causes sorrow, we are here concerned with a more narrowly confined interest in mental and emotional stability. When confronted with accidental death, "the reaction to be expected of normal persons," [ ], is shock and fright. We hold that the observation of either death or this type of serious injury is necessary to permit recovery. Since the sense of loss attendant to death or serious injury is typically not present following lesser accidental harm, perception of less serious harm would not ordinarily result in severe emotional distress. Thus, the risk of an extraordinary reaction to less serious injury is not sufficient to result in liability. To impose liability for any emotional consequence of negligent conduct would be unreasonable; it would also be unnecessary to protect a plaintiff's basic emotional stability. Therefore, a cause of action for emotional distress would require the perception of death or serious physical injury.

The cause of action we approve today for the negligent infliction of emotional distress requires proof of the following elements: (1) the death or serious physical injury of another caused by defendant's negligence; (2) a marital or intimate familial relationship between plaintiff and the injured person; (3) observation of the death or injury at

test

the scene of the accident; and (4) resulting severe emotional distress. We find that a defendant's duty of reasonable care to avoid physical harm to others extends to the avoidance of this type of mental and emotional harm. . . .

. . .

[The trial court judgment was reversed.]

■ For *reversal*—CHIEF JUSTICE WILENTZ, and JUSTICES SULLIVAN, PASHMAN, CLIFFORD, SCHREIBER, HANDLER and POLLOCK—7.

■ For *affirmance*—none.

NOTES AND QUESTIONS

1.   At several points, the *Portee* court expresses concern that "juries may impose liability that is not commensurate with the culpability of defendant's conduct." Is this more of a concern in cases producing non-physical harm than in those involving broken bones and death? Didn't the defendants here, like the defendant in *Falzone*, create a risk of physical harm?

2.   Indeed, given that plaintiff cut her wrists as a result of her son's being trapped, why wasn't this a bodily injury case? And emotional distress consequent to physical injury?

3.   The *Dillon-Portee* elements of proximity to the scene and sensory impact are closely related to each other, but are not overlapping. In Scherr v. Las Vegas Hilton, 214 Cal.Rptr. 393 (App.1985), plaintiff wife, in California, saw live television coverage of a fire then taking place at the Las Vegas Hilton Hotel. She knew that her husband was attending a meeting at that hotel and that he was supposed to be in the hotel at that time. She never saw him on camera and did not discover until later that he had in fact been hurt in the fire. The court found that plaintiff had failed to come within the sensory perception requirement. Her perception "of endangerment, while potentially stressful, is insufficient to cause legally cognizable harm, for the stress has not yet ripened into disabling shock." The court did not reach the television aspect of the case. What if the plaintiff had watched her husband, about to be enveloped by flames, jump from a balcony on a high floor and hit the ground?

4.   The *Portee* court adds another element—the death or serious injury to the victim. In Barnhill v. Davis, 300 N.W.2d 104 (Iowa 1981), the plaintiff and his mother were driving one behind the other to the same destination. After plaintiff cleared an intersection, he looked in the rear view mirror and saw his mother's car hit on the driver's side by the defendant's car. In fact, the mother was only slightly injured. Plaintiff alleged serious emotional and physical harm from his concern before he learned how slight the injury was. The court said the proper test was whether a reasonable person would believe, and the plaintiff did believe, that his mother would be seriously injured in the type of accident that occurred.

5.   After a period of expansion, California narrowed its decisions in this area. Contrast Ochoa v. Superior Court, 703 P.2d 1 (Cal.1985) (upholding claim, despite no "contemporaneous observance of [an] accident," as per the *Dillon* factors, where a mother watched child in juvenile hall deteriorate from apparently serious illness when medical staff would not respond to the emergency; he died after she left for the night) with the denial of recovery in Thing v. La Chusa, 771 P.2d 814 (Cal.1989) (mother, who was nearby, neither heard nor saw accident injuring her child, but was told about it and rushed to the scene to see the child's bloody and unconscious body lying in the roadway). The court in *Thing* concluded that the three factors set forth in *Dillon* were defining elements and not simply guidelines: "Experience has shown that, contrary to the expectation of the *Dillon* majority, . . . there are clear judicial days on which a court can foresee forever and thus determine liability but none on which that foresight alone provides a socially and judicially acceptable limit on recovery of damages for that injury."

In elaborating on the three elements, the *Thing* court stated that "absent exceptional circumstances, recovery should be limited to relatives residing in the same household, or parents, siblings, children, and grandparents of the victim." As to the second element, the viewing of "consequences" of an accident was insufficient—even if they were, as the dissent had argued, "immediate consequences." As to the third element, the court identified the requisite distress as "a reaction beyond that which would be anticipated in a disinterested witness and which is not an abnormal response to the circumstances." Is it superfluous to require that plaintiff be in a close relationship with the victim and then to require a reaction beyond "that which would be anticipated in a disinterested witness"?

6.   Illustrating the impact of the movement from the *Dillon* factor approach to the *Thing* rule-based treatment of bystander NIED is Entergy Mississippi, Inc. v. Acey, 153 So.3d 670, 671 (Miss.2014). The plaintiff's daughter was playing on a farm and, after climbing on an agricultural machine, made contact with a sagging power line and was badly burned. As the court described the scene:

> At the time of the accident, A.A.'s mother, Mary Bethanne Acey, was en route to Moon Lake, in Coahoma County, Mississippi, with her son and Charles Graves. A Tunica County 911 dispatcher called Graves to inform him of the accident. Graves immediately turned the car around to proceed to the [farm where the accident took place]. Acey then spoke with the dispatcher, who explained the gravity of the situation to Acey and informed her that A.A. had been "shocked." Acey arrived at the accident scene and saw her daughter in [the arms of a farm employee]. Acey's affidavit explains that she observed smoke coming from her daughter's skin, skin flaking and turning gray, fingers missing and bones exposed, and she could smell the odor of burning flesh.

The 5–4 majority explains the adoption of *Dillon* in Mississippi and its subsequent adoption of requirements rather than factors. Here, both contemporaneous observance and proximity are missing, and the court reverses the denial of summary judgment. What is there to be said for the *Acey* court's ruling? Against it?

On the other hand, some states are going beyond *Dillon* and *Portee* in some respects. In Marzolf v. Stone, 960 P.2d 424 (Wash.1998), close relatives came by the scene of an accident shortly after it happened. The court said their claims for emotional distress should be upheld if the distress is "caused by observing an injured relative at the scene of an accident shortly after its occurrence and before there is a substantial change in the relative's condition or location." The "challenge is to create a rule that acknowledges the shock of seeing a victim shortly after an accident, without extending a defendant's liability to every relative who grieves for the victim." A bright line had simplicity but was said to be arbitrary. Does the likelihood of serious emotional harm depend on how soon after the accident the plaintiff learns of the consequences? See also Wages v. First National Insurance Co. of America, 79 P.3d 1095 (Mont. 2003)(parent who was not present and did not witness accident may nevertheless recover for emotional distress provided court finds parent was a foreseeable plaintiff). On balance, would you prefer the rule-based approach of *Thing* and *Acey* or the flexible standard employed in *Marzolf*?

7.   Some states are even more restrictive than *Thing* and *Acey*. One of those is New York. Early on, Tobin v. Grossman, 249 N.E.2d 419 (N.Y.1969), rejected *Dillon*, concluding that it would be difficult if not impossible to draw lines limiting the action. No recovery for emotional distress was to be permitted in such cases. In Bovsun v. Sanperi, 461 N.E.2d 843 (N.Y.1984), the court, 4–3, overruled *Tobin*'s total refusal to allow an action, and extended a duty to members of the "immediate family" who were themselves in the zone of physical danger:

> The zone-of-danger rule, which allows one who is himself or herself threatened with bodily harm in consequence of the defendant's negligence to recover for emotional distress resulting from viewing the death or serious physical injury of a member of his or her immediate family, is . . . premised on the traditional negligence concept that by unreasonably endangering the plaintiff's physical safety the defendant has breached a duty owed to him or her for which he or she should recover all damages sustained including those occasioned by witnessing the suffering of an immediate family member who is also injured by the defendant's conduct. Recognition of this right to recover for emotional distress attributable to observation of injuries suffered by a member of the immediate family involves a broadening of the duty concept but—unlike the *Dillon* approach—not the creation of a duty to a plaintiff to whom the defendant is not already recognized as owing a duty to avoid bodily harm. In so doing it permits recovery for an element of damages not heretofore allowed. Use of the zone-of-danger rule thus mitigates the possibility of unlimited recovery, an overriding apprehension expressed in *Tobin*, by restricting liability in a much narrower

fashion than does the *Dillon* rule. Additionally, the circumstances in which a plaintiff who is within the zone of danger suffers serious emotional distress from observing severe physical injury or death of a member of the immediate family may not be altogether common.

In addition, the emotional distress had to be "serious and verifiable."

8. *Child sexual abuse.* Another area in which it is plain that bystanders will be unable to satisfy the conventional bystander rules involves sexual abuse of children. In Doe Parents No. 1 v. State Department of Education, 58 P.3d 545 (Haw.2002), the court held that the plaintiff parents of children who had been fondled and otherwise molested by a schoolteacher could recover for their emotional distress without proof that their children had suffered physical injury. (The court did not address the fact that the parents did not contemporaneously perceive the abuse.) The court found the circumstances sufficient to assure that the parents' emotional distress was severe and genuine.

9. The standard for categorizing a plaintiff as either direct or bystander remains in flux. In Huggins v. Longs Drug Stores California, Inc., 862 P.2d 148 (Cal.1993), plaintiff parents followed an incorrect label and gave their infant an excessive dose of medicine. The child was not permanently injured. The parents' claim against the pharmacist was rejected, 5–2. The goal of the transaction was to provide medication for the baby: "Because plaintiffs were not the patients for whom defendant dispensed the prescribed medication, they cannot recover as direct victims of defendant's negligence." One dissenter thought plaintiffs were "direct victims," since they were "necessary parties to the administration" of the medicine. The other dissenter emphasized the guilt that parents feel when they are the—even innocent—instruments of harm to their children: "It is this additional injury that renders the parent a direct victim." Might the plaintiffs in *Huggins* be categorized as direct victims because they were the consumers who purchased the mislabeled product? Might *Johnson* more appropriately be considered a bystander case?

See also Jarrett v. Jones, 258 S.W.3d 442 (Mo.2008). Plaintiff suffered minor physical injuries in an automobile accident resulting from defendant's negligence. Plaintiff went to check on the occupants of defendant's car, where he found defendant's two-year-old child dead. Plaintiff sought to recover for his physical injury, consequential emotional harm, and emotional harm from observing the child. The court categorized plaintiff as a direct victim and, as such, the restrictive rules on bystander recovery did not apply. The court relied on the fact that direct victims in automobile accidents are a limited class, so concerns about floodgates are relieved. The court also remarked that the administrative difficulty of distinguishing between distress consequential to his own harm and distress from observing the deceased child could be avoided by its result.

10. *Unmarried couples and emotional distress.* In Elden v. Sheldon, 758 P.2d 582 (Cal.1988), Richard was hurt in an auto accident allegedly caused by the defendant's negligence. This case involved claims for his emotional distress from witnessing the death of Linda, who was in Richard's car and with whom Richard alleged he had an "unmarried cohabitation relationship . . . which was both stable and significant and parallel to a marital relationship." The court, 6–1, relying on three "policy reasons," affirmed dismissal of claims for emotional distress.

The first was that "the state has a strong interest in the marriage relationship; to the extent unmarried cohabitants are granted the same rights as married persons, the state's interest in promoting marriage is inhibited. . . ." The policy favoring marriage is 'rooted in the necessity of providing an institutional basis for defining the fundamental relational rights and responsibilities of persons in organized society.' [ ] Formally married couples are granted significant rights and bear important responsibilities toward one another which are not shared by those who cohabit without marriage." The court cited property rights and support obligations, among others. The second justification involved the administrative expense and difficulty of determining if the relationship was "stable and significant." The final justification was to limit the scope of liability "to a controllable degree." A bright-line rule limiting recovery to those in close family relationships would serve these purposes.

The *Elden* approach was rejected in Dunphy v. Gregor, 642 A.2d 372 (N.J.1994), involving a claim by a woman who witnessed the death of her fiancé. They had been engaged two years earlier and had set the wedding for four years hence. Plaintiff alleged that at the time of the death they had been living together for two years; had taken out life-insurance policies making each other beneficiaries; maintained a joint checking account from which they paid their bills; and had jointly purchased an automobile. In addition, she alleged that the decedent "had asked her several times to elope with him, and he had introduced her in public as his wife." The court, 5–1, after reviewing *Portee v. Jaffee* and its progeny at length, was "convinced that the solution to the posed question lies not in a hastily-drawn 'bright line' distinction between married and unmarried persons but in the 'sedulous application' of the principles of tort law."

In 2001, the California legislature also rejected *Elden*, in an interesting twist on tort reform: "Domestic partners shall be entitled to recover damages for negligent infliction of emotional distress to the same extent that spouses are entitled to do so under California law." Cal.Civ. Code § 1714.01. "Domestic partners" is defined by several criteria in the Code. One of those requires that, in the case of partners of opposite sex, one of the partners is at least 62 years old. No such requirement exists for gay or lesbian couples.

Negligent Interference with Consortium

A very important aspect of family relationships is the harm to one spouse when the other is seriously injured. The history of a third party's liability to one spouse for seriously injuring the other is traced in the following extended excerpt from the opinion of Justice Kaplan in Diaz v. Eli Lilly & Co., 302 N.E.2d 555 (Mass.1973):

In olden days, when married women were under legal disabilities corresponding to their inferior social status, any action for personal or other injuries to the wife was brought in the names of the husband and wife, and the husband was ordinarily entitled to the avails of the action as of his own property. The husband had, in addition, his own recourse by action without even nominal joinder of the wife against those who invaded the conjugal relationship, for example, by criminal conversation with or abduction of his wife. At one time the gravamen of the latter claims for loss of consortium was the deprivation of the wife's services conceived to be owing by the wife to the husband; the action was similar to that of a master for enticement of his servant. Later the grounds of the consortium action included loss of the society of the wife and impairment of relations with her as a sexual partner, and emphasis shifted away from loss of her services or earning capacity. The defendant, moreover, need not have infringed upon the marital relation by an act of adultery or the like, for he could inflict similar injuries upon the husband in the way of loss of consortium by an assault upon the wife or even a negligent injury. Meanwhile, what of the wife's rights? She had none analogous to the husband's. The husband was of course perfectly competent to sue without joinder of the wife for injuries to himself, and there was no thought that the wife had any legal claim to the husband's services or his sexual or other companionship—any claim, at any rate, in the form of a cause of action for third-party damage to the relationship.

With the coming in of the married women's acts in the mid-nineteenth century, the wife became competent to sue in her own name for injuries to herself and could retain the proceeds of those actions. . . . It was held very widely that husbands still retained their consortium rights, the element of loss of wives' services and earnings, however, being excluded from the husbands' recoveries as belonging to the wives themselves. And it was generally held that the new status of married women implied at least some rights of consortium on their part. If adultery with or alienation of the affections of a wife was a wrong to the husband, similar traffic of another woman with the husband should be actionable by the wife. Wives were readily accorded these rights of action.

However, there was difficulty about wives' recovery for acts of third parties not so plainly attacking the marriage relation, say acts of negligence toward the husband injuring him in such a way as to deprive the wife of his society and sexual comfort. The difficulty was perhaps traceable in the end to the reluctance of judges to accept the women's emancipation acts as introducing a broad general premise for fresh decision. . . .

[After reviewing the course of decisions in Massachusetts, Justice Kaplan turned to the situation in the rest of the country. He noted that the wife's right to an action for lost consortium was recognized in the 1950s, and had been adopted in about half the states as of 1973.]

To a few critics the idea of a right of consortium seems no more than an anachronism harking back to the days when a married woman was a chattel slave, and in a formulation such as that of the new Restatement they would find a potential for indefinite expansion of a questionable liability. But that formulation, reflecting a strong current of recent decisions, is a natural expression of a dominant (and commonplace) theme of our modern law of torts, namely, that presumptively there should be recourse for a definite injury to a legitimate interest due to a lack of the prudence or care appropriate to the occasion. That it would be very difficult to put bounds on an interest and value it is a possible reason for leaving it without protection at least in the form of money damages. But the law is moderately confident about the ability of the trier (subject to the usual checks at the trial and appellate levels) to apply common sense to the question. The marital interest is quite recognizable and its impairment may be definite, serious, and enduring, more so than the pain and suffering or mental or psychic distress for which recovery is now almost routinely allowed in various tort actions. The valuation problem here may be difficult but is not less manageable. Nor does it follow that if the husband-wife relationship is protected as here envisaged, identical protection must be afforded by analogy to other relationships from that of parent-child in a lengthy regress to that of master-servant; courts will rather proceed from case to case with discerning caution. . . .

————

In the years since Justice Kaplan's opinion, virtually all states have come to recognize the loss of consortium action for both spouses. In this regard, there is the question whether loss of consortium claims will be recognized in cases of same-sex relationships. See Charron v. Amaral, 889 N.E.2d 946 (Mass.2008)(categorically denying such claims in a case arising prior to the court's recognition of same-sex marriages). Other questions today are those raised by Justice Kaplan at the end of the passage—the extension of similar actions to other relationships and the measurement of damages.

In some lost consortium cases courts have upheld jury awards of substantial sums. In Ossenfort v. Associated Milk Producers, Inc., 254

N.W.2d 672 (Minn.1977), the court upheld an award of $500,000 to a wife whose 34-year-old husband suffered severe brain damage and was rendered "a spastic quadriplegic." The award was assumed to be almost all for lost consortium. The court noted proof that the marital relationship had been "one of exceptional harmony and happiness. . . . The jury could find that the companionship that would have been [the wife's] for years to come would have provided her with a life more meaningful than the great majority of people could anticipate or would experience." See also Spaur v. Owens-Corning Fiberglas Corp., 510 N.W.2d 854 (Iowa 1994), upholding an award of $800,000 for lost past and future consortium where the couple had been married 34 years, had three grown children, the husband had been a "devoted" husband, and the husband's life expectancy (he died after suit was brought) was 16 years. To what extent is the interest protected in consortium claims distinct from the interest protected in the emotional distress cases considered earlier? To what extent do you think juries can compartmentalize those interests?

Some courts have extended the consortium action to cover nonphysical injuries to the first spouse. In Barnes v. Outlaw, 964 P.2d 484 (Ariz.1998), defendant minister revealed to others information he had learned about plaintiff during confidential counseling sessions. The court held that damages for loss of consortium are not barred solely because the spouse's injury is purely emotional. The court would rely

> on the factfinder to determine the legitimacy, nature, and extent of any alleged damages. . . . Fact-finders, usually jurors, can . . . and are frequently called upon to do so. . . . Clearly, a marriage may be damaged by emotional trauma. Since loss of consortium is no longer exclusively based on the deprivation of services theory, we see no reason to require physical injury in one spouse before the other may bring a claim. . . . Whether the marital relationship has been harmed enough to warrant damages in any given case is a matter for the jury to decide.

Should damages be measured the same way as in a case in which the spouse has suffered serious physical harm?

Loss of companionship involving injured parents and children. Building on the economic history that Justice Kaplan reviewed, most courts began giving the husband, and then both parents, an action for the loss of the companionship of their seriously injured child. Countering this trend, the court in Roberts v. Williamson, 111 S.W.3d 113 (Tex.2003), articulated a strong need to hold consortium rules tightly in check. The court, 6–3, rejected a cause of action for parents for the lost consortium of their injured (but not dead) child. Siblings were also barred from suing for lost consortium of other injured siblings. The dissent argued that there was no good reason to distinguish the death of a child (for which consortium was available) from injury to a child.

The extension of such an action to the child has encountered substantial resistance. In Borer v. American Airlines, Inc., 563 P.2d 858 (Cal.1977), the court refused to allow a suit for the benefit of nine young children whose mother had been injured to such an extent that she was unable to provide the usual parental care. The financial aspects of this loss were recoverable in the mother's action. The mother could also recover the emotional aspects of this loss of ability to care for her children if she were conscious of that loss. The denial of the child's claim was reached after taking into account "all considerations which bear on the question, including the inadequacy of monetary compensation to alleviate the tragedy, the difficulty of measuring damages, and the danger of imposing extended and disproportionate liability."

A few states have accepted the action. In Ferriter v. Daniel O'Connell's Sons, Inc., 413 N.E.2d 690 (Mass.1980), the children of a paralyzed accident victim asserted a claim for parental consortium. The court was "skeptical" of any suggestion that the children's interests were any less intense than the wife's. The court reviewed and rejected the reasons offered by the majority in *Borer* and held that the children "have a viable claim for loss of parental society if they can show that they are minors dependent on the parent, Michael Ferriter. This dependence must be rooted not only in economic requirements, but also in filial needs for closeness, guidance, and nurture."

The refusal of the alleged "direct" victim to go along with the suit may persuade the court to deny an action. In Jacoby v. Brinckerhoff, 735 A.2d 347 (Conn.1999), plaintiff husband sought to sue defendant psychiatrist for treatment of plaintiff's wife that hurt the marriage and caused his children to lose maternal care. The wife would not cooperate. The court had already decided that lost consortium was a derivative action, in the sense that the consortium claim could succeed only if the direct victim's claims succeeded. In that part of the case, it was "not prepared to hold that a derivative cause of action may proceed upon the mere possibility that the plaintiff's spouse may have sustained an injury that resulted from negligent or intentional misconduct on the part of a psychiatrist." (On the husband's direct claims in the case, "sound public policy counsels that a psychiatrist's treatment of a troubled spouse should not be burdened by accountability to the other spouse.")

A similar result was reached in a case in which a minor child, through his father, sought damages against mental health care providers for loss of his mother's companionship by causing her to develop false memories. The patient objected to the suit. The court rejected a duty running to nonpatients in this type of case. Plaintiff argued that the patient may be too "emotionally altered to recognize the harm that has taken place." The court rejected "this paternalistic approach." Eliminating "the potential for divided loyalties and maintaining confidentiality will in the end preserve the relationship," and this end will outweigh "any threat of foreseeable harm to nonpatient family members." The court explicitly observed that it was not passing on a "provider's duty to protect an identifiable potential victim from a dangerous patient." J.A.H. v. Wadle & Associates, P.C., 589 N.W.2d 256 (Iowa 1999).

B. ECONOMIC HARM

In this section, we consider cases in which the defendant has caused plaintiff only economic harm without any related personal injury or damage to real or personal property. As with emotional distress, the courts have not protected economic interests as extensively as those involving physical security of person and property—even when the harm was inflicted intentionally, by fraud. We consider fraud or intentional misrepresentation at length in Chapter XVI. In addressing unintentionally caused economic harm in this section, we continue our focus on identifying the situations in which courts do, or should, impose duties of due care—in this instance, the obligation to use reasonable care to avoid causing stand-alone economic harm.

Initially, we will look at cases in which no personal injury or property damage is threatened to anyone—situations such as a creditor who makes a loan in reliance on negligently prepared financial statements or a beneficiary who fails to receive an inheritance because of a defectively drawn will. After considering cases that threaten only pure economic harm, we examine a variety of situations in which the defendant's negligence threatened to cause or actually caused personal injury or property damage to a third party, but the plaintiff only suffered economic loss (for example, when a negligently caused explosion in the vicinity of plaintiff's business causes a loss of profits because customers can no longer reach the shop).

Nycal Corporation v. KPMG Peat Marwick LLP.

Supreme Judicial Court of Massachusetts, 1998.
426 Mass. 491, 688 N.E.2d 1368.

■ Before WILKINS, C.J., LYNCH, GREANEY, FRIED and IRELAND, JJ.

■ GREANEY, JUSTICE.

On May 24, 1991, the plaintiff, allegedly in reliance on an auditors' report of the 1990 financial statements of Gulf Resources & Chemical Corporation (Gulf) prepared by the defendant, entered into a stock purchase agreement with the controlling shareholders of Gulf and, on July 12, 1991, the sale was completed. Gulf filed for bankruptcy protection in October, 1993, rendering the plaintiff's investment worthless. The plaintiff filed a civil complaint against the defendant seeking damages and costs incurred as a result of its alleged reliance on the auditors' report. The plaintiff claimed that the report materially misrepresented the financial condition of Gulf.[1] . . . After applying the liability standard embodied in § 552 of the Restatement (Second) of Torts (1977), a judge in the Superior Court granted summary judgment for the defendant. We granted the parties' applications for direct appellate review of the final judgment. We conclude that the defendant did not breach any legal duty owed to the plaintiff and, accordingly, we affirm the judgment.

1.   The following material facts are undisputed. Gulf retained the defendant to audit its 1990 financial statements. At that time, Gulf was listed on the New York Stock Exchange, and was controlled by several of its officers and directors who held their Gulf shares through two other entities (Inoco P.L.C. and Downshire N.V.). The financial statements were prepared by, and were the responsibility of, Gulf's management.

. . .

The defendant's completed auditors' report was included in Gulf's 1990 annual report, which became publicly available on February 22, 1991. In March, 1991, the plaintiff entered into discussions with Gulf concerning the possible purchase of a large block of Gulf shares, and during the course of those discussions, Gulf provided the plaintiff with a copy of its 1990 annual report. Thereafter, the plaintiff purchased 3,626,775 shares of Gulf (approximately 35% of the outstanding shares) in exchange for $16,000,000 in cash and $18,000,000 in the plaintiff's stock. The acquisition gave the plaintiff operating control of Gulf.

The defendant first learned of the transaction between the plaintiff and Gulf a few days prior to the July 12, 1991, closing. Until that time, the defendant did not know that any transaction between the plaintiff and Gulf had been contemplated.

2.   We have not addressed the scope of liability of an accountant to persons with whom the accountant is not in privity. Three tests have generally been applied in other jurisdictions, either by common law or by statute, to determine the duty of care owed by accountants to nonclients. These include the foreseeability test, the near-privity test, and the test contained in § 552 of the Restatement.

The plaintiff urges our adoption of the broad standard of liability encompassed in the foreseeability test. Pursuant to this test, which is derived from traditional tort law concepts as first enunciated in Palsgraf v. Long Island R.R., [162 N.E. 99 (N.Y.1928)] [reprinted in Chapter VI], an accountant may be held liable to any person whom the accountant could reasonably have foreseen would obtain and rely on the accountant's opinion, including known and unknown investors. See,

---

[1]   The plaintiff asserted that the report failed to take into account recurring substantial losses from operations, the extent of liability for environmental clean-up costs, inadequate accruals of pension and retirement obligations, and restrictions on transfers in certain bank covenants.

e.g., H. Rosenblum, Inc. v. Adler, [461 A.2d 138 (N.J.1983)]. This test is generally disfavored, having been adopted by courts in only two jurisdictions. [ ]

Our cases draw a distinction between the duty owed by a professional to a third party for personal injuries and that owed to a third party for pecuniary loss due to a professional's negligence. While we apply traditional tort law principles in cases involving the former, we have not done so in cases concerning the latter. Such principles are particularly unsuitable for application to accountants where, "regardless of the efforts of the auditor, the client retains effective primary control of the financial reporting process." Bily v. Arthur Young & Co., [834 P.2d 745 (Cal.1992)]. The auditor prepares its report from statements and information supplied by the client, and once the report is completed and provided to the client, the client controls its dissemination. If we were to apply a foreseeability standard in these circumstances, "a thoughtless slip or blunder, the failure to detect a theft or forgery beneath the cover of deceptive entries, may expose accountants to a liability in an indeterminate amount for an indeterminate time to an indeterminate class." Ultramares Corp. v. Touche, [174 N.E. 441 (N.Y.1931)]. We refuse to hold accountants susceptible to such expansive liability, and conclude that Massachusetts law does not protect every reasonably foreseeable user of an inaccurate audit report.

The near-privity test, which originated in Chief Judge Cardozo's decision in [*Ultramares*], and was modified by Credit Alliance Corp. v. Arthur Andersen & Co., [483 N.E.2d 110 (N.Y.1985)], limits an accountant's liability exposure to those with whom the accountant is in privity or in a relationship "sufficiently approaching privity." Under this test, an accountant may be held liable to noncontractual third parties who rely to their detriment on an inaccurate financial report if the accountant was aware that the report was to be used for a particular purpose, in the furtherance of which a known party (or parties) was intended to rely, and if there was some conduct on the part of the accountant creating a link to that party, which evinces the accountant's understanding of the party's reliance. [ ]

The defendant professes that the near-privity test is consistent with the standard we have previously applied to other professionals in the absence of privity. We disagree. A review of the relevant cases demonstrates that the first two elements of the near-privity test— reliance by the third party and knowledge that the party intended to rely—have analogs in our case law, but the third element—conduct by the accountant providing a direct linkage to the third party—does not.

. . .

We believe that the third test, taken from § 552 of the Restatement (Second) of Torts (1977), comports most closely with the liability standard we have applied in other professional contexts. Section 552 describes the tort of negligent misrepresentation committed in the process of supplying information for the guidance of others as follows:

(1) One who, in the course of his business, profession or employment, or in any other transaction in which he has a pecuniary interest, supplies false information for the guidance of others in their business transactions, is subject to liability for pecuniary loss caused to them by their justifiable reliance upon the information, if he fails to exercise reasonable care or competence in obtaining or communicating the information.

That liability is limited [under § 552(2)] to

loss suffered (a) by the person or one of a limited group of persons for whose benefit and guidance he intends to supply the information or knows that the recipient intends to supply it; and (b) through reliance upon it in a transaction that he intends the information to influence or knows that the recipient so intends or in a substantially similar transaction.

. . .

The comments explain with regard to the requirement that the plaintiff be a member of a "limited group of persons for whose benefit and guidance" the information is supplied as follows:

[I]t is not required that the person who is to become the plaintiff be identified or known to the defendant as an individual when the information is supplied. It is enough that the maker of the representation intends it to reach and influence either a particular person or persons, known to him, or a group or class of persons, distinct from the much larger class who might reasonably be expected sooner or later to have access to the information and foreseeably to take some action in reliance upon it. . . . It is sufficient, in other words, insofar as the plaintiff's identity is concerned, that the maker supplies the information for repetition to a certain group or class of persons and that the plaintiff proves to be one of them, even though the maker never had heard of him by name when the information was given. It is not enough that the maker merely knows of the ever-present possibility of repetition to anyone, and the possibility of action in reliance upon it, on the part of anyone to whom it may be repeated. [Comment *h*]

We concur with the California Supreme Court's conclusion in [*Bily*] that the Restatement test properly balances the indeterminate liability of the foreseeability test and the restrictiveness of the near-privity rule. Section 552 "recognizes commercial realities by avoiding both unlimited and uncertain liability for economic losses in cases of professional mistake and exoneration of the auditor in situations where it clearly intended to undertake the responsibility of influencing particular business transactions involving third persons." [ ]

Although the Restatement standard has been widely adopted by other jurisdictions, courts differ in their interpretations of the standard. The better reasoned decisions interpret § 552 as limiting the potential liability of an accountant to noncontractual third parties who can demonstrate "actual knowledge on the part of accountants of the limited—though unnamed—group of potential [third parties] that will rely upon the [report], as well as actual knowledge of the particular financial transaction that such information is designed to influence." [ ] The accountant's knowledge is to be measured "at the moment the audit [report] is published, not by the foreseeable path of harm envisioned by [litigants] years following an unfortunate business decision." [ ]

The plaintiff argues that, by limiting § 552 to allow recovery only by those persons, or limited group of persons, that an accountant actually knows will receive and rely on an audit report, we will be rewarding an accountant's efforts to "remain blissfully unaware" of the report's proposed distribution and uses. We are unpersuaded by this argument. The axiom we have applied in other contexts applies to accountants as well: the Restatement standard will not excuse an accountant's "wilful ignorance" of information of which the accountant would have been aware had the accountant not consciously disregarded that information. [ ]

The judge correctly concluded under § 552, that the undisputed facts failed to show that the defendant knew (or intended) that the plaintiff, or any limited group of which the plaintiff was a member, would rely on the audit report in connection with an investment in Gulf. To the contrary, the record suggests that the defendant did not prepare the audit report for the plaintiff's benefit and that the plaintiff was not a member of any "limited group of persons" for whose benefit the report was prepared. At the time the audit was being prepared, the plaintiff was an unknown, unidentified potential future investor in Gulf. The defendant was not aware of the existence of the transaction between the plaintiff and Gulf until after the stock purchase agreement had been signed and only a few days before the sale was completed.

The summary judgment record further indicates that the defendant neither intended to influence the transaction entered into by the plaintiff and Gulf nor knew that Gulf intended to influence the transaction by use of the audit report. . . .

Moreover, the record suggests that the defendant's audit report was prepared for inclusion in Gulf's annual report and not for the purpose of assisting Gulf's controlling shareholders in any particular transaction. The record does not exhibit that the defendant knew of any particular use that would be made of its audit report. Cf. Guenther v. Cooper Life Sciences, Inc., 759 F.Supp. 1437, 1443 (N.D.Cal.1990) (accountants knew that audit report would be placed in prospectus for public offering and had expressly consented to its inclusion). "Under the Restatement rule, an auditor retained to conduct an annual audit and to furnish an opinion for no particular purpose generally undertakes no duty to third parties." [*Bily*].[6]

The rule we adopt today will preclude accountants from having to ensure the commercial decisions of nonclients where, as here, the accountants did not know that their work product would be relied on by the plaintiff in making its investment decision.

Judgment affirmed.

NOTES AND QUESTIONS

1.   As the court notes, *Palsgraf*, which is reprinted in Chapter VI, involved personal injury. Why does the court here reject foreseeability as the standard in cases of pecuniary harm? As noted, in *Ultramares,* Judge Cardozo was concerned that "a thoughtless slip or blunder, the failure to detect a theft or forgery beneath the cover of deceptive entries, may expose accountants to a liability in an indeterminate amount for an indeterminate time to an indeterminate class." Are these indeterminacies of equal concern? Are they unique to this type of case?

2.   What is gained by protecting professionals, such as accountants, from liability to foreseeable users for their negligence? How would the court analyze a case in which the client tells the accountant in advance that it plans to show the results to John Smith?

3.   Can you rewrite the facts in *Nycal* so that liability would be imposed under section 552?

4.   *Approaches to accountants' liability.* As noted, states have developed four basic approaches to the question of the duty owed by accountants to those not in privity with them. This topic is surveyed in Feinman, Liability of Accountants for Negligent Auditing: Doctrine, Policy, and Ideology, 31 Fla. St. U. L. Rev. 17 (2003).

a.   *Actual privity.* A very small group of states still requires actual privity.

b.   *Near-privity.* The New York approach restricts liability by demanding a "linking" between the accountant and the relying party that requires more than notice from the relying party to the accountant. Credit Alliance Corp. v. Arthur Andersen & Co., cited in *Nycal*, is the leading case. How *much* more is the question. In Security Pacific Business Credit, Inc. v. Peat Marwick Main & Co., 597 N.E.2d 1080 (N.Y.1992), plaintiff lender claimed that it was owed a duty of due care by defendant auditor based essentially on a "single unsolicited phone call" that plaintiff's vice-president had made to defendant. That call had been made after the defendant had completed the field audit of the client but before the final report had been prepared. The defendant responded to the call by saying, at most, that

---

[6]   We also note that the plaintiff had had the opportunity to conduct more detailed due diligence prior to its purchase of the Gulf shares, although it apparently did not do so. In addition, although the plaintiff asserts reliance on the defendant's report as the basis for making its investment in Gulf, such decisions typically involve other factors. See [*Bily*, p. 301, supra].

"nothing untoward had been uncovered in the course of the audit." The court held that a lender could not meet the state's requirements and impose "negligence liability of significant commercial dimension and consequences by merely interposing and announcing its reliance in this fashion." If this single call could suffice,

> . . . then every lender's due diligence list will in the future mandate such a telephone call. For the small price of a phone call, [the lender's lawyer] would in effect acquire additional loan protection by placing the auditor in the role of an insurer or guarantor of loans extended to its clients." The facile acquisition of deep pocket surety coverage, with no opportunity for actuarial assessment and self-protection, by the party sought to be charged, at the mere cost of a telephone call by the lender, is a bargain premium rate indeed.

What if the plaintiff had made the phone call after the client had requested the audit, but before the defendant had agreed to do the work? Is there properly a concern about "blissful ignorance" in states that do not use foreseeability? Could a plaintiff who has had no contact with the defendant ever prevail? See Anschutz Corp. v. Merrill Lynch & Co., 690 F.3d 98, 115 (2d Cir.2012)("[T]here are no allegations of any direct contact between Anschutz and the Rating Agencies. We therefore conclude that Anschutz has failed to state a claim for negligent misrepresentation under New York law.").

c.   *Modified foreseeability*. A few states, exemplified by New Jersey, have adopted an approach close to general foreseeability thereby allowing more expansive liability. Would you expect accountants in New Jersey to exercise greater care in their work than those in New York? If so, would the higher degree of care exercised be desirable? Would it affect fees? In 1995, New Jersey enacted legislation that brought itself closer to the New York position. A few states still follow the cited *Rosenblum* case.

d.   *The Restatement view*. Almost half the states follow the approach developed in section 552 and discussed in *Nycal*. Consider the following examples suggested by comments and illustrations to that section:

> 1.   The client asks D to prepare an audit so that the client can show it to Bank B to get a loan of $50,000. D prepares the requested statements. Bank B fails and, without telling D, the client shows the statements to Bank A, which lends $50,000 in reliance and loses the money when the client goes bankrupt. D is said to owe no duty to Bank A. Why not?

> 2.   If the client had told D that it intended to seek a loan of $50,000 from an unidentified bank, D would owe a duty to any bank that lends the money—even if the client had Bank X in mind at the time but later goes to Bank Y. Why? What if the loan is for $250,000?

> 3.   The client tells D that the documents are to help get a loan of $50,000 from B. Instead, B decides to buy an interest in

the client for $250,000. The client soon collapses and B loses everything. D does not owe a duty to B.

How would each of these examples be analyzed in New York?

e.   *Federal securities law.* Some professional liability is controlled by federal securities law—the Securities Act of 1933 and the Securities Exchange Act of 1934. This regulatory scheme is discussed in *Bily* and applied in O'Melveny & Myers v. Federal Deposit Insurance Corp., 512 U.S. 79 (1994). This subject is pursued in upper class courses.

5.   *Beyond accountants.*

a.   In Mohr v. Commonwealth, 653 N.E.2d 1104 (Mass.1995), adoptive parents alleged that the defendant social service agency, after learning that the child's mother had suffered from schizophrenia and that the child had cerebral atrophy, made negligent misrepresentations to plaintiffs regarding the child's emotional and medical history. The court, after tracing the development of this type of claim, upheld a "wrongful adoption" action for the adoptive parents. An adoption agency, whether public or private, has "an affirmative duty to disclose to adoptive parents information about a child that will enable them to make a knowledgeable decision about whether to accept the child for adoption." The award was for economic harm that would be sustained in providing "the structured, residential placement that Elizabeth will need throughout her lifetime." See also Gibbs v. Ernst, 647 A.2d 882 (Pa.1994)(imposing a duty of disclosure in adoption cases but rejecting an affirmative duty on the agency to investigate the child's background). Should damages for emotional distress be recoverable in this type of case?

b.   In Sain v. Cedar Rapids Community School District, 626 N.W.2d 115 (Iowa 2001), a high school college counselor mistakenly told plaintiff student that a senior course would meet NCAA requirements for college sports eligibility. Because the course did not meet that requirement the plaintiff lost a full tuition scholarship to college. The court, 5–2, imposed a duty of due care under section 552 similar to that imposed on other professionals who give advice. The defendant need not be in a professional relationship with the person relying if the defendant's profession involves providing that kind of information and defendant realizes that the plaintiff is likely to rely on the information provided. This guidance function was distinguished from the type of information conveyed as part of negotiating a deal—where Iowa follows the rule that there is no duty of due care between parties to an arm's-length transaction. Additionally, the counselor is paid by the school district and is not providing gratuitous information. There was no reason to confine this tort "to traditional commercial transactions when the rationale for the tort allows it to be applied beyond those factual circumstances which originally gave rise to the tort."

Attorneys and Clients

After accountants, the second largest group involved in these cases is the legal profession. Before analyzing the due care obligations that an attorney may owe to third parties, we consider the duty of due care the attorney owes to the client.

a.　*Meeting filing deadlines.* Questions of legal malpractice tend to arise in two contexts. One involves cases in which attorneys fail to file complaints within the statute of limitations or in some other way fail to perform a non-judgmental task. In such cases, the client may have a good legal claim for malpractice if it is possible to show that the action, if filed, would have been successful. Do you see why this can require a "trial within a trial"?

b.　*Making strategic choices.* The second type of claim arises from judgmental strategic decisions that usually occur during litigation which later turn out badly. Here, the courts are not likely to permit second-guessing the attorney's decision unless it lacked any plausible justification. As in the medical situation, attorneys are not expected to "be perfect or infallible," nor "must they always secure optimum outcomes for their clients." In both situations, an expert is usually needed to explain to the jury the standard of care and the deviation.

c.　*Settlements.* The strategy question extends beyond how to conduct litigation—to whether and on what terms to settle pending litigation. Advice to settle a claim for too little may lead to liability for malpractice. See Grayson v. Wofsey, Rosen, Kweskin & Kuriansky, 646 A.2d 195 (Conn.1994)(upholding an action where the attorney was alleged to have negligently valued the marital estate so as to induce his client to settle for too little). In addition, attorneys have an absolute ethical obligation to convey settlement offers to their clients; failure to do so can be the basis for a malpractice claim. See First Nat'l Bank of LaGrange v. Lowrey, 872 N.E.2d 447 (Ill.App.Ct.2007)(affirming judgment against attorney who failed to transmit a $1 million settlement offer in a medical malpractice case, after which plaintiffs were unsuccessful at trial).

d.　*Criminal cases.* Clients in criminal cases may face the requirement that they demonstrate their innocence. In Wiley v. County of San Diego, 966 P.2d 983 (Cal.1998), the court held that a plaintiff who had been convicted of a crime could not sue his defense attorney for malpractice without proving that he was innocent of the underlying crime. "Regardless of the attorney's negligence, a guilty defendant's conviction and sentence are the direct consequence of his own perfidy." Then, quoting another case:

> Tort law provides damages only for harms to the plaintiff's legally protected interests, [ ], and the liberty of a guilty criminal is not one of them. The guilty criminal may be able to obtain an acquittal if he is skillfully represented, but he has no right to that result (just as he has no right to have the jury nullify the law, though juries sometimes do that), and the law provides no relief if the "right" is denied him.

Wiley also offered pragmatic reasons for treating criminal and civil malpractice differently. All malpractice cases necessitate a "trial within a trial" to determine if the outcome would have been different if the attorney had behaved differently. But retrying a criminal case in a civil damage action presents especially complex problems. "[Plaintiff] must prove by a preponderance of the evidence that, but for the negligence of his attorney, the jury could not have found him guilty beyond a reasonable doubt. . . . Moreover, while the plaintiff would be limited to evidence admissible in the criminal trial, the defendant attorney could introduce additional evidence, including 'any and all confidential communications, as well as otherwise suppressible evidence of factual guilt.' "

e.   *Emotional distress.* In these cases, it is unusual for the awards to include recovery for the client's emotional distress due to the attorney's negligence. In Pleasant v. Celli, 22 Cal.Rptr.2d 663 (App.1993), an attorney missed the statute of limitations on what the jury could have found to have been a successful medical malpractice case. The claim against the attorney properly included economic harm (which could have included damages for emotional harm in the underlying medical malpractice case), but an award of $500,000 for emotional distress was reversed. The plaintiff in such a case must show that she sustained "highly foreseeable shock stemming from an abnormal event." Missing the statute of limitations did not suffice.

Other courts have suggested that when the attorney is retained for non-economic purposes, such as criminal defense, adoption proceedings, or marital dissolution, damages for emotional distress may be foreseeable and may be recovered as one item of damages. See, e.g., Holliday v. Jones, 264 Cal.Rptr. 448 (App.1989)(incompetent counsel permits client to be convicted of involuntary manslaughter); Kohn v. Schiappa, 656 A.2d 1322 (N.J.Super.Ct. Law Div.1995) (lawyer representing clients seeking to adopt a child improperly reveals their names to the natural mother); Wagenmann v. Adams, 829 F.2d 196 (1st Cir.1987) (malpractice led to client's involuntary incarceration in psychiatric hospital). Is this consistent with the general treatment of negligent infliction of emotional distress that we considered earlier?

Attorneys and Third Parties

In Biakanja v. Irving, 320 P.2d 16 (Cal.1958), the defendant notary public drew up plaintiff's brother's will giving plaintiff the entire estate. Because of the notary's negligent failure to have the will properly witnessed, the will failed and the brother's property passed by law to other relatives, so that plaintiff received only one-eighth of the estate. Her recovery against the notary, despite the lack of privity between plaintiff and the notary, for the difference was affirmed:

> Here, the "end and aim" of the transaction was to provide for the passing of Maroevich's estate to plaintiff. (See [*Glanzer v.*

Shepard]). Defendant must have been aware from the terms of the will itself that, if faulty solemnization caused the will to be invalid, plaintiff would suffer the very loss which occurred.

In Lucas v. Hamm, 364 P.2d 685 (Cal.1961), a will was invalid because it violated the rule against perpetuities. In a malpractice action, the court denied that liability "would impose an undue burden" on the legal profession because "although in some situations liability could be large and unpredictable in amount, this is also true of an attorney's liability to his client." Also, as *Lucas* recognized, "unless the beneficiary could recover against the attorney in such a case, no one could do so and the social policy of preventing future harm would be frustrated." The *Lucas* court ultimately concluded, however, that the legal error did not demonstrate negligence because—if you are taking or have taken property you will appreciate this—the rule was so difficult to understand and apply.

In these cases, the beneficiary of the will is an intended third-party beneficiary of the contract between the client and the attorney. The concept of third-party beneficiaries may help to understand other cases in which courts have extended duties to non-clients when the client has asked the attorney to provide information or prepare documents for a third party. Thus, in Petrillo v. Bachenberg, 655 A.2d 1354 (N.J.1995), the court imposed a duty of due care on a seller's attorney in connection with an arguably misleading percolation-test report given to the prospective buyer. The court extended the opinion-letter line of cases to other kinds of information that the attorney knows or should know will influence a non-client because the "objective purpose of documents such as opinion letters, title reports, or offering statements" is to induce others to rely on them.

A small but firm group of states requires privity in will cases. In Barcelo v. Elliott, 923 S.W.2d 575 (Tex.1996), grandchildren who lost their inheritance because of an invalid will were denied recovery. Recognizing that the majority rule extended liability in this situation, the court, 5–3, preferred the minority view that an attorney owed a duty solely to the client. The court feared cases in which the claim was not invalidity but that the will did not reflect the actual instructions of the testator or in which the testator never signed the will. The court was concerned that it would not be able to tell whether that was because of attorney malpractice or because of the testator's change of mind. Do these concerns exist where the will is invalid? The court was "unable to craft a bright-line rule" that would exclude cases that raised doubt about the testator's intentions.

———————

Courts often invoke the "economic loss rule" to deny recovery for stand-alone economic loss. Although many trace this rule to the advent of strict products liability in the mid-20th century, which we cover at p.

672 infra, the idea has a longer vintage as the next case explains. In the products liability context, recovery in tort is barred when the product fails to perform as it should but does not cause personal injury or damage to other property. Instead, disappointed consumers are left to their contractual remedies under the Uniform Commercial Code. The key idea is that tort law should not interfere with contractual agreements that address this matter unless the loss concerns personal security or property damage, the core interests protected by tort law. Many different versions of the economic loss doctrine exist, ranging from a narrow version that only bars economic loss recovery in products liability claims to the broad form that bars any tort claim for pure economic loss. See Tiara Condominium Ass'n v. Marsh & McLennan Cos., 110 So.3d 399 (Fla.2013)(limiting economic loss rule to products liability cases). The question in the next case concerns the application of the economic loss rule to contracts for services.

LAN/STV v. Martin K. Eby Construction Co., Inc.

Supreme Court of Texas, 2014.
435 S.W.3d 234.

■ CHIEF JUSTICE HECHT delivered the opinion of the Court.

In actions for unintentional torts, the common law has long restricted recovery of purely economic damages unaccompanied by injury to the plaintiff or his property [ ]—a doctrine we have referred to as the economic loss rule. [ ] The rule serves to provide a more definite limitation on liability than foreseeability can and reflects a preference for allocating some economic risks by contract rather than by law. [ ] But the rule is not generally applicable in every situation; it allows recovery of economic damages in tort, or not, according to its underlying principles.[4] The issue in this case is whether the rule permits a general contractor to recover the increased costs of performing its construction contract with the owner in a tort action against the project architect for negligent misrepresentations—errors—in the plans and specifications. We conclude that the economic loss rule does not allow recovery and accordingly reverse the judgment of the court of appeals and render judgment for the architect.

I

The Dallas Area Rapid Transportation Authority ("DART") contracted with LAN/STV to prepare plans, drawings, and specifications for the construction of a light rail transit line from

---

[4] *Sharyland*, 354 S.W.3d at 415 (" '[T]here is not one economic loss rule broadly applicable throughout the field of torts, but rather several more limited rules that govern recovery of economic losses in selected areas of the law.'") (quoting Vincent R. Johnson, *The Boundary-Line Function of the Economic Loss Rule*, 66 WASH. & LEE L.REV. 523, 534–535 (2009)); *see* [Restatement (Third) of Torts: Liability for Economic Harm § 1 cmt. b (Tent. Draft No. 1, 2012)] ("[D]uties of care with respect to economic loss are not general in character; they are recognized in specific circumstances according to the principles stated in Comment c.").

Dallas's downtown West End to the American Airlines Center about a mile away. LAN/STV agreed to "be responsible for the professional quality, technical accuracy, and . . . coordination of all designs, drawings, specifications, and other services furnished", and to be "liable to the Authority . . . for all damages to the Authority caused by [LAN/STV's] negligent performance of any of the services furnished". DART incorporated LAN/STV's plans into a solicitation for competitive bids to construct the project. Martin K. Eby Construction Company . . . was awarded the contract. The contract provided an administrative procedure for Eby to assert contract disputes with DART, including complaints about design problems. Eby and LAN/STV had no contract with each other. Thus, LAN/STV was contractually responsible to DART for the accuracy of the plans, as was DART to Eby, but LAN/STV owed Eby no contractual obligation.

Days after beginning construction, Eby discovered that LAN/STV's plans were full of errors—about bridge structures, manhole and utility line locations, subsurface soil conditions, an existing retaining wall, and many other aspects of the proposed construction, [requiring that 80% of LAN/STV's drawings be changed]. This disrupted Eby's construction schedule and required additional labor and materials. In all, Eby now calculates it lost nearly $14 million on the project.

. . . [Eby pursued Dart for breach of contract and settled with Dart for $4.7 million that the court concluded did not overlap with the damages that Eby subsequently sought from LAN/STV.]

Meanwhile, Eby filed this tort suit against LAN/STV, asserting causes of action for negligence and negligent misrepresentation. . . . [T]his case proceeded to trial . . . on Eby's claim that LAN/STV negligently misrepresented the work to be done in its error-ridden plans. The jury agreed and assessed Eby's damages for its losses on the project at $5 million. . . .

Both LAN/STV and Eby appealed, and following the court of appeals' affirmance, both petitioned for review. We granted both petitions, but as we view the case, we need only address LAN/STV's argument that Eby's recovery for negligent misrepresentation is barred by the economic loss rule. We begin by surveying the development of the rule in American law and its status in Texas. We then turn to its application in this case.

II

A

The law has long limited the recovery of purely economic damages in an action for negligence. An early example, oft-cited, is Justice Holmes's opinion in *Robins Dry Dock & Repair Co. v. Flint,* [275 U.S. 303 (1927)], a suit by the charterers of a steamship against a dry dock for damages for loss of the use of the vessel from a delay in repairs due to the dry dock's negligence. The Supreme Court held that the charterers could not recover their economic damages from the dry dock, either as third-party beneficiaries of the contract between the owners and the dry dock, or for the dry dock's negligence. Justice Holmes explained:

> Of course the contract of the [dry dock] with the owners imposed no immediate obligation upon the [dry dock] to third persons [the charterers] as we already have said, and whether the [dry dock] performed it promptly or with negligent delay was the business of the owners and of nobody else. . . . [The charterers'] loss arose only through their contract with the owners. . . . [N]o authority need be cited to show that, as a general rule, at least, a tort to the person or property of one man does not make the tort-feasor liable to another merely because the injured person was under a contract with that other unknown to the doer of the wrong. . . . The law does not spread its protection so far. [ ]

Nearly sixty years later, Judge Higginbotham observed in *State of Louisiana v. M/V Testbank* that "*Robins* broke no new ground. . . . [T]he prevailing rule [in the United States and England] denied a plaintiff recovery for economic loss if that loss resulted from physical damage to property in which he had no proprietary interest." . . .

> . . .

. . . As one commentator has explained:

> If there is a convincing rationale for the economic loss rule, it is that the rule performs a critical boundary-line function, separating the law of torts from the law of contracts. More specifically, "[t]he underlying purpose of the economic loss rule is to preserve the distinction between contract and tort theories in circumstances where both theories could apply." [ ]

. . . From our review of the cases and commentary on the subject, we think the principal rationales for the rule are well-summarized by Dean Farnsworth in the recently approved *Restatement (Third) of Torts: Liability for Economic Harm,* which we quote at length:

> Economic injuries may be no less important than injuries of other kinds; a pure but severe economic loss might well be worse for a plaintiff than a more modest personal injury, and the difference between economic loss in itself and economic loss resulting from property damage may be negligible from the victim's standpoint. For several reasons, however, courts impose tort liability for economic loss more selectively than liability for other types of harms.
>
> (1). *Indeterminate and disproportionate liability.* Economic losses proliferate more easily than losses of other kinds. Physical forces that cause injury ordinarily spend themselves in predictable ways; their exact courses

may be hard to predict, but their lifespan and power to harm are limited. A badly driven car threatens physical harm only to others nearby. Economic harm is not self-limiting in this way. A single negligent utterance can cause economic loss to thousands of people who rely on it, those losses may produce additional losses to those who were relying on the first round of victims, and so on. Consequences of this sort may be at least generally foreseeable to the person who commits the negligent act. Defendants in such cases thus might face liabilities that are indeterminate and out of proportion to their culpability. Those liabilities may in turn create an exaggerated pressure to avoid an activity altogether.

(2). *Deference to contract.* Risks of economic loss tend to be especially well suited to allocation by contract. First, economic injuries caused by negligence often result from a decision by the victim to rely on a defendant's words or acts when entering some sort of transaction—an investment in a company, the purchase of a house, and so forth. A potential plaintiff making such a decision has a full chance to consider how to manage the risks involved, whether by inspecting the item or investment, obtaining insurance against the risk of disappointment, or making a contract that assigns the risk of loss to someone else. Second, money is a complete remedy for an economic injury. Insurance benefits, indemnification by agreement, or other replacements of money payments are just as good as the money lost in a transaction that turns out badly. This fungibility makes those other ways of managing risk—insurance, indemnity, and the like—more attractive than they might be to a party facing a prospect of personal injury.

Those same points often will make it hard for a court to know what allocation of responsibility for economic loss would best serve the interests of the parties to a risky situation. A contract that settles responsibility for such a risk will therefore be preferable in most cases to a judicial assignment of liability after harm is done. The contract will better reflect the preferences of the parties and help prevent the need for speculation and litigation later. Contracts also are governed by a body of commercial law that has been developed to address economic loss, and thus will often be better suited for that task than the law of torts. In short, contracts to manage the risk of economic loss are more often possible, and more often desirable, than contracts to manage risks of other types of injury. As a result, courts generally do not recognize tort liability for economic losses caused by the breach of a contract between the parties, and often restrict the role of tort law in other circumstances in which protection by contract is available. [ ]

Thus, the *Restatement* concludes, while there is "no general duty to avoid the unintentional infliction of economic loss," the duty may exist when the rationales just stated for limiting recovery are "weak or absent". . . .

B

The absence of a bright-line rule, and the failure to analyze whether denying tort recovery for an economic loss in a particular kind of situation is justified by the rationales for limiting recovery of such losses, has led to some confusion. . . .

. . .

. . . Texas courts of appeals have uniformly applied the economic loss rule to deny recovery of purely economic losses in actions for negligent performance of services. [ ] Professional malpractice cases are an exception. A client can recover purely economic losses from a negligent lawyer, regardless of whether the lawyer and client have a contract. [ ] Lawyer malpractice is actionable as negligence no doubt because agreements regarding legal representation are not required in Texas, except for contingent fees, [ ] and until relatively recently have not been the norm. Also, the standards governing legal representation are deeply developed and their application uniform and well-settled. These factors also support negligence actions against other professionals. [ ]

Although Texas courts have repeatedly invoked the economic loss rule to disallow recovery of purely economic losses in actions for negligent services not involving professionals, this Court, without citing the rule, has allowed recovery of such losses in an action for negligent misrepresentation, the cause of action in the present case. [The court reviewed several Texas cases permitting such claims based on section 552 of the Second Restatement.]

These cases should not be read to suggest that recovery of economic loss is broader for negligent misrepresentation than for negligent performance of services. We agree with the [Third] *Restatement* that "[t]he general theory of liability is the same" for both torts, which is that

> [a] plaintiff's reliance alone, even if foreseeable, is not a sufficient basis for recovery; under either [tort] a defendant generally must act with the apparent purpose of providing a basis for the reliance. It may be useful to say that a defendant held liable under either [tort] must "invite reliance" by the plaintiff, so long as the expression is understood to refer to the

defendant's apparent purpose and not to a temptation incidentally created by the defendant's words or acts. [ ]

And for both torts, whether and how to apply the economic loss rule "does not lend itself to easy answers or broad pronouncements." [ ] Rather, as we have already observed, the application of the rule depends on an analysis of its rationales in a particular situation.

III

Eby argues that the economic rule should not apply in this case when it did not bar recovery in our other negligent misrepresentation cases. . . . LAN/STV counters that to allow such recovery on construction projects, where relationships are contractual and certainty and predictability in risk allocation are crucial, would be disruptive.

Construction projects operate by agreements among the participants. Typically, those agreements are vertical: the owner contracts with an architect and with a general contractor, the general contractor contracts with subcontractors, a subcontractor may contract with a sub-subcontractor, and so on. The architect does not contract with the general contractor, and the subcontractors do not contract with the architect, the owner, or each other.

We think it beyond argument that one participant on a construction project cannot recover from another—setting aside the architect for the moment—for economic loss caused by negligence. If the roofing subcontractor could recover from the foundation subcontractor damages for extra costs incurred or business lost due to the latter's negligent delay of construction, the risk of liability to everyone on the project would be magnified and indeterminate—the same result Justice Holmes rejected in *Robins*. As the [Third] *Restatement* explains:

> There is no liability in tort . . . when the owner of a construction project sues a subcontractor for negligence resulting in economic loss; nor is liability found when one subcontractor is sued by another because the negligence of the first drives up the costs of the second. A subcontractor's negligence in either case is viewed just as a failure in the performance of its obligations to its contractual partner, not as the breach of a duty in tort to other subcontractors on the same job, or to the owner of the project. . . .

The issues are whether to treat the architect differently and whether to distinguish between an action for negligent performance of services and an action for negligent misrepresentations. On the latter issue, we agree with the *Restatement*: "[b]oth [torts] are based on the [same] logic" and "[t]he general theory of liability is the same." [ ] The economic loss rule should not apply differently to these two tort theories in the same situation.

On the former issue, we diverge from the *Restatement* [which permits tort claims against the architect]. We agree that

[t]he plans drawn by the architect are intended to serve as a basis for reliance by the contractor who forms a bid on the basis of them and is then hired to carry them out. The architect's plans are analogous to the audit report that an accountant supplies to a client for distribution to potential investors—a standard case of liability [for negligent misrepresentation]. [ ]

But we think the contractor's principal reliance must be on the presentation of the plans by the owner, with whom the contractor is to reach an agreement, not the architect, a contractual stranger. The contractor does not choose the architect, or instruct it, or pay it. Under, [a prior Texas case], the contractor could not recover economic damages from the owner's lawyer's negligent drafting of the construction contract. And while there is some analogy between the architect's plans and an accountant's audit report, under [another prior case], the latter is not an invitation to all investors to rely, but only those to whom it is more specifically directed. Here, the architect's plans are no more an invitation to all potential bidders to rely.

The *Restatement* adds that if allowing recovery against the architect in negligence "is not congenial to the parties, they are free to change it in the contracts that link them." [ ] But the parties are just as free to provide for liability by contract that the law does not allow in tort. The *Restatement* acknowledges this, noting that if the architect is contractually liable to the owner for defects in the plans, and the owner in turn has the same liability to the contractor, the contractor is protected. But the *Restatement* concludes that while this assignment of risk by contract should be encouraged, it jeopardizes unsophisticated parties:

> Forbidding tort claims between parties who are indirectly linked by contract would put pressure on them to specify their rights carefully in advance, thus sparing courts the need to inquire into them later. But that incentive is most likely to be noticed by sophisticated parties negotiating large projects, and for them the rule is unlikely to be of great importance. They will negotiate allocations of risk that look similar in the end notwithstanding the rule of tort law in the background. Meanwhile, less sophisticated parties would stand a good chance of being tripped up by a broad rule, as when they fail to provide for indemnification in some direction and inadvertently leave a party who has been wronged with no remedy. [ ]

We think it more probable that a contractor will assume it must look to its agreement with the owner for damages if the project is not as represented or for any other breach.

Though there remains the possibility that a contractor may not do so, we think the availability of contractual remedies must preclude tort recovery in the situation generally because, as stated above, "clarity allows parties to do business on a surer footing". "Where contracts might readily have been used to allocate the risk of a loss," the *Restatement* observes, "a duty to avoid the loss is unlikely to be recognized in tort—not because the economic loss rule applies, but simply because courts prefer, in general, that economic losses be allocated by contract where feasible." [ ] We see no reason not to apply the economic loss rule to achieve this end.

Analyzing the economics of the construction site, Professor Powers proposed this result more than twenty years ago, and we quote his analysis at length:

> In fact, construction disputes . . . are good candidates for precluding recovery under the "economic loss" rule, because the parties are in a position to protect themselves through bargaining. Though the parties do not necessarily have contracts with each other, they typically all have contracts with the owner, or subcontracts with someone who does have a contract with the owner. If contractors want to be protected, they can insist on that protection from the owner who will get protection from the architect. The contractors can take less compensation from the owner, so that the owner can in turn compensate the architect for the added risk.

> The issue is who will buy business protection insurance. It makes sense to let the parties bargain about this rather than impose a "legal" solution. . . .

> . . .

Finally, the courts are fairly evenly divided over whether to apply the economic loss rule in this situation. [ ] We side with those who do.

DART was contractually responsible to Eby for providing accurate plans for the job. Eby agreed to specified remedies for disputes, pursued those remedies (when the federal court would not allow it to sue), and settled its claims for $4.7 million. Had DART chosen to do so, it could have sued LAN/STV for breach of their contract to provide accurate plans. But Eby had no agreement with LAN/STV and was not party to LAN/STV's agreement with DART. . . . We think Eby should not be treated differently.

* * *

The reasons for the economic loss rule support its application in this case to preclude a general contractor from recovering delay damages from the owner's architect. Accordingly, we reverse the judgment of the court of appeals and render judgment that Eby take nothing from LAN/STV.

NOTES AND QUESTIONS

1.   The court in *LAN/STV* analogizes the contractor in that case with the investors such as the plaintiffs in *Nycal*. How strong is that analogy?

2.   In a case two months after *LAN/STV*, Chapman Custom Homes, Inc. v. Dallas Plumbing Co., 445 S.W.3d 716 (Tex.2014), a homeowner sued a plumber (a subcontractor of the contractor) for negligence that resulted in water damage to the home. The trial court granted summary judgment for the plumber, and the court of appeals affirmed. The Supreme Court reversed. The economic loss rule invoked in *LAN/STV* does not bar all tort claims arising out of negligent performance of a contract obligation. It doesn't bar this tort claim because the plumber's negligence caused property damage rather than pure economic loss. Id. at 718.

3.   As the court in *LAN/STV* stated, many courts do permit tort claims for economic loss when the parties are not in a contractual relationship. Thus, in Sullivan v. Pulte Home Corp., 306 P.3d 1 (Ariz.2013), the court permitted a subsequent home buyer who purchased the home from the initial purchaser to sue the builder for negligent construction of the house. The court limited the Arizona economic loss rule to circumstances in which the parties were in a contractual relationship.

4.   By contrast with the *Sullivan* approach permitting tort claims, some European countries have expanded contract actions by those such as subsequent buyers or contractors like Eby through the concept of a "chain of contracts," which creates a special relationship between these non-contracting parties and accordingly, permits a contract claim by subsequent purchasers or contractors. Does the chain-of-contracts concept provide clarity or is the critical distinction one between construction contracts and subsequent sales of homes?

5.   As the court notes and as described at p. 306 supra, attorneys and other professionals can be sued in tort for stand-alone economic harm. This is true of physicians as well. Thus, in Aufrichtig v. Lowell, 650 N.E.2d 401 (N.Y.1995), the court decided that a physician could be sued for understating the severity of plaintiff patient's medical condition in an affidavit, resulting in the patient settling her claim for too low an amount. The *LAN/STV* court explains that clients (or patients) can sue in tort "whether the lawyer and client have a contract." Don't lawyers and their clients always have a contract? How persuasive are the grounds the court explains for this exception?

The Third Restatement explains that professional contracts typically only provide a promise to make careful efforts on behalf of the client or patient, rather than promising a particular result. Thus, the contractual and tort standards are quite similar. Moreover, customers of professionals have informational difficulties that prevent their ability to negotiate terms of the contract on equal footing to reach an optimal allocation of risk. They also ordinarily do not have the means to monitor the professional's work to determine if it meets the contractual standards. See Restatement (Third) of Torts: Liability for Economic Harm § 4, cmt. a (Tent. Draft No. 1, 2012).

6. Should there be a distinction between cases involving consumers and those involving commercial transactions? Consider the relative ease of modifying the default rule with regard to whether tort law is available, as discussed by the *LAN/STV* court. How about the distinction between professional services and other types of transactions? The underlying question is when the nature of the relationship warrants limiting parties in a chain of contracts to their contractual remedies.

532 Madison Avenue Gourmet Foods, Inc. v. Finlandia Center, Inc.

Court of Appeals of New York, 2001.
96 N.Y.2d 280, 750 N.E.2d 1097, 727 N.Y.S.2d 49.

■ KAYE, CHIEF J.

The novel issues raised by these appeals—arising from construction-related disasters in midtown Manhattan—concern first, a landholder's duty in negligence where plaintiffs' sole injury is lost income and second, the viability of claims for public nuisance.

Two of the three appeals involve the same event. On December 7, 1997, a section of the south wall of 540 Madison Avenue, a 39-story office tower, partially collapsed and bricks, mortar and other material fell onto Madison Avenue at 55th Street, a prime commercial location crammed with stores and skyscrapers. The collapse occurred after a construction project, which included putting 94 holes for windows into the building's south wall, aggravated existing structural defects. New York City officials directed the closure of 15 heavily trafficked blocks on Madison Avenue—from 42nd to 57th Street—as well as adjacent side streets between Fifth and Park Avenues. The closure lasted for approximately two weeks, but some businesses nearest to 540 Madison remained closed for a longer period.

In *532 Madison Ave. Gourmet Foods v. Finlandia Ctr.,* plaintiff operates a 24-hour delicatessen one-half block south of 540 Madison, and was closed for five weeks. The two named plaintiffs in the companion case, *5th Ave. Chocolatiere v. 540 Acquisition Co.,* are retailers at 510 Madison Avenue, two blocks from the building, suing on behalf of themselves and a putative class of "all other business entities, in whatever form, including but not limited to corporations, partnerships and sole proprietorships, located in the Borough of Manhattan and bounded geographically on the west by Fifth Avenue, on the east by Park Avenue, on the north by 57th Street and on the South by 42nd Street." Plaintiffs allege that shoppers and others were unable to gain access to their stores during the time Madison Avenue was closed to traffic. Defendants in both cases are Finlandia Center (the building owner), 540 Acquisition Company (the ground lessee) and Manhattan Pacific Management (the managing agent).

On defendants' motions in both cases, [the trial court] dismissed plaintiffs' negligence claims on the ground that they could not establish that defendants owed a duty of care for purely economic loss in the absence of personal injury or property damage, and dismissed the public nuisance claims on the ground that the injuries were the same in kind as those suffered by all of the businesses in the community. In *5th Ave. Chocolatiere,* plaintiffs' additional claims for gross negligence and negligence per se were dismissed on the ground that plaintiffs could not establish a duty owed by defendants, and their private nuisance cause of action was dismissed on the ground that they could not establish either intentional or negligent wrongdoing.

Goldberg Weprin & Ustin v. Tishman Constr. involves the July 21, 1998 collapse of a 48-story construction elevator tower on West 43rd Street between Sixth and Seventh Avenues—the heart of bustling Times Square. Immediately after the accident, the City prohibited all traffic in a wide area of midtown Manhattan and also evacuated nearby buildings for varying time periods. Three actions were consolidated— one by a law firm, a second by a public relations firm and a third by a clothing manufacturer, all situated within the affected area. Plaintiff law firm sought damages for economic loss on behalf of itself and a proposed class "of all persons in the vicinity of Broadway and 42nd Street, New York, New York, whose businesses were affected and/or caused to be closed" as well as a subclass of area residents who were evacuated from their homes. Plaintiff alleged gross negligence, strict liability, and public and private nuisance.

Noting the enormity of the liability sought, including recovery by putative plaintiffs as diverse as hot dog vendors, taxi drivers and Broadway productions, [the trial court] concluded that the failure to allege personal injury or property damage barred recovery in negligence. The court further rejected recovery for strict liability, and dismissed both the public nuisance claim (because plaintiff was unable to show special damages) and the private nuisance claim (because plaintiff could not show that the harm threatened only one person or relatively few).

The Appellate Division affirmed dismissal of the *Goldberg Weprin* complaint, concluding that, absent property damage, the connection between defendants' activities and the economic losses of the purported class of plaintiffs was "too tenuous and remote to permit recovery on any tort theory." [ ] The court, however, reinstated the negligence and public nuisance claims of plaintiffs [in the other two cases], holding that defendants' duty to keep their premises in reasonably safe condition extended to "those businesses in such close proximity that their negligent acts could be reasonably foreseen to cause injury" (which included the named merchant plaintiffs) [ ], and that, as such, they established a special injury distinct from the general inconvenience to the community at large. Two [of the five] Justices dissented, urging application of the "economic loss" rule, which bars recovery in negligence for economic damage absent personal injury or property damage. The dissenters further concluded that the public nuisance claims were properly dismissed because plaintiffs could not establish special injury.

We now reverse in *532 Madison* and *5th Ave. Chocolatiere* and affirm in *Goldberg Weprin & Ustin*.

Plaintiffs' Negligence Claims

Plaintiffs contend that defendants owe them a duty to keep their premises in reasonably safe condition, and that this duty extends to protection against economic loss even in the absence of personal injury or property damage. Defendants counter that the absence of any personal injury or property damage precludes plaintiffs' claims for economic injury.

The existence and scope of a tortfeasor's duty is, of course, a legal question for the courts, which "fix the duty point by balancing factors, including the reasonable expectations of parties and society generally, the proliferation of claims, the likelihood of unlimited or insurer-like liability, disproportionate risk and reparation allocation, and public policies affecting the expansion or limitation of new channels of liability" (Hamilton v. Beretta U.S.A. Corp., [750 N.E.2d 1055 (N.Y.2001) (quoting *Palka v. Servicemaster Mgt. Servs. Corp.*, [p. 171 supra])]). At its foundation, the common law of torts is a means of apportioning risks and allocating the burden of loss. In drawing lines defining actionable duty, courts must therefore always be mindful of the consequential, and precedential, effects of their decisions.

As we have many times noted, foreseeability of harm does not define duty [ ]. Absent a duty running directly to the injured person there can be no liability in damages, however careless the conduct or foreseeable the harm. This restriction is necessary to avoid exposing defendants to unlimited liability to an indeterminate class of persons conceivably injured by any negligence in a defendant's act.

. . .

In *Strauss v. Belle Realty Co.*, [p. 166 supra] we considered whether a utility owed a duty to a plaintiff injured in a fall on a darkened staircase during a citywide blackout. While the injuries were logically foreseeable, there was no contractual relationship between the plaintiff and the utility for lighting in the building's common areas. As a matter of policy, we restricted liability for damages in negligence to direct customers of the utility in order to avoid crushing exposure to the suits of millions of electricity consumers in New York City and Westchester.

Even closer to the mark is *Milliken & Co. v. Consolidated Edison Co.*, [644 N.E.2d 268 (N.Y.1994)] in which an underground water main burst near 38th Street and 7th Avenue in Manhattan. The waters flooded a subbasement where Consolidated Edison maintained an electricity supply substation, and then a fire broke out, causing extensive damage that disrupted the flow of electricity to the Manhattan Garment Center and interrupting the biannual Buyers Week. Approximately 200 Garment Center businesses brought more than 50 lawsuits against Con Edison, including plaintiffs who had no contractual relationship with the utility and who sought damages solely for economic loss. Relying on *Strauss,* we again held that only those persons contracting with the utility could state a cause of action. We circumscribed the ambit of duty to avoid limitless exposure to the potential suits of every tenant in the skyscrapers embodying the urban skyline.

A landowner who engages in activities that may cause injury to persons on adjoining premises surely owes those persons a duty to take reasonable precautions to avoid injuring them. [ ] We have never held, however, that a landowner owes a duty to protect an entire urban neighborhood against purely economic losses. A comparison of Beck v. FMC Corp. (385 N.Y.S.2d 956, *affd.,* 369 N.E.2d 10 [N.Y.1977]) and Dunlop Tire & Rubber Corp. v. FMC Corp. (385 N.Y.S.2d 971 [App.Div.1976]) is instructive. Those cases arose out of the same incident: an explosion at defendant FMC's chemical manufacturing plant caused physical vibrations, and rained stones and debris onto plaintiff Dunlop Tire's nearby factory. The blast also caused a loss of electrical power—by destroying towers and distribution lines owned by a utility—to both Dunlop Tire and a Chevrolet plant located one and one-half miles away. Both establishments suffered temporary closure after the accident. Plaintiffs in *Beck* were employees of the Chevrolet plant who sought damages for lost wages caused by the plant closure. Plaintiff Dunlop Tire sought recovery for property damage emanating from the blast and the loss of energy, and lost profits sustained during the shutdown.

In *Dunlop Tire,* the Appellate Division observed that, although part of the damage occurred from the loss of electricity and part from direct physical contact, defendant's duty to plaintiffs was undiminished. The court permitted plaintiffs to seek damages for economic loss, subject to the general rule requiring proof of the extent of the damage and the causal relationship between the negligence and the damage. The *Beck* plaintiffs, by contrast, could not state a cause of action, because, to extend a duty to defendant FMC would, "like the rippling of the waters, [go] far beyond the zone of danger of the explosion," to everyone who suffered purely economic loss. [ ]

Plaintiffs' reliance on *People Express Airlines v. Consolidated Rail Corp.*, [495 A.2d 107 (N.J.1985)] is misplaced. There, a fire started at defendant's commercial freight yard located across the street from plaintiff's airport offices. A tank containing volatile chemicals located in the yard was punctured, emitting the chemicals and requiring closure of the terminal because of fear of an explosion. Allowing the plaintiff to seek damages for purely economic loss, the New Jersey court reasoned that the extent of liability and degree of foreseeability stand in direct proportion to one another: the more particular the foreseeability that economic loss would be suffered as a result of the defendant's negligence, the more just that liability be imposed and recovery permitted. The New Jersey court acknowledged, however, that the presence of members of the public, or invitees at a particular plaintiff's business, or persons traveling nearby, while foreseeable, is nevertheless fortuitous, and the particular type of economic injury that they might suffer would be hopelessly unpredictable. Such plaintiffs, the court recognized, would present circumstances defying any appropriately circumscribed orbit of duty. We see a like danger in the urban disasters at issue here, and decline to follow *People Express.*

Policy-driven line-drawing is to an extent arbitrary because, wherever the line is drawn, invariably it cuts off liability to persons who foreseeably might be plaintiffs. The *Goldberg Weprin* class, for example, would include all persons in the vicinity of Times Square whose businesses had to be closed and a subclass of area residents evacuated from their homes; the *5th Ave. Chocolatiere* class would include all business entities between 42nd and 57th Streets and Fifth and Park Avenues. While the Appellate Division attempted to draw a careful boundary at storefront merchant-neighbors who suffered lost income, that line excludes others similarly affected by the closures—such as the law firm, public relations firm, clothing manufacturer and other displaced plaintiffs in *Goldberg Weprin,* the thousands of professional, commercial and residential tenants situated in the towers surrounding the named plaintiffs, and suppliers and service providers unable to reach the densely populated New York City blocks at issue in each case.

As is readily apparent, an indeterminate group in the affected areas thus may have provable financial losses directly traceable to the two construction-related collapses, with no satisfactory way geographically to distinguish among those who have suffered purely economic losses (*see also, Matter of Kinsman Tr. Co., (II)*) [p. 421 infra]). In such circumstances, limiting the scope of defendants' duty to those who have, as a result of these events, suffered personal injury or property damage—as historically courts have done—affords a principled basis for reasonably apportioning liability.

We therefore conclude that plaintiffs' negligence claims based on economic loss alone fall beyond the scope of the duty owed them by defendants and should be dismissed.

[The court then addressed and rejected claims based on public nuisance.]

[The court concluded by reversing *532 Madison* and *5th Ave. Chocolatiere,* and affirming *Goldberg Weprin & Ustin.*]

■ JUDGES SMITH, LEVINE, CIPARICK, WESLEY, ROSENBLATT and GRAFFEO concur.

NOTES AND QUESTIONS

1. Note that the court assumes (and the cited *Dunlop Tire* case holds) that recovery for economic loss would be allowed as a matter of course if it resulted from property damage that was also caused by defendant's negligence. Does the same set of concerns lead courts to invoke no-duty rules for certain stand-alone emotional distress claims and for economic loss of the sort occurring in *532 Madison Ave.*?

2. In declining to follow *People Express*, the court rejects the notion that a requirement of "particular foreseeability" can adequately serve as a baseline for recognizing recovery for stand-alone economic loss. Do you agree? As the court notes, *People Express* illustrated the limits of the "particular foreseeability" principle by rejecting extension of recovery to members of the public, passersby, shoppers—generally to those whose presence in the closed-off area was "fortuitous." Why doesn't this limitation satisfy the court in *532 Madison Avenue*? *People Express* has not been followed elsewhere.

3. Recall that, as explained in note 3, p. 318 supra, *Sullivan v. Pulte Home Corp.*, limited the economic loss rule to claims where the parties were in privity of contract, thereby permitting suits for economic loss by those not in a contractual relationship. How would the *Sullivan* court decide *532 Madison*?

4. In Koch v. Consolidated Edison Co. of New York, Inc., 468 N.E.2d 1 (N.Y.1984), the City of New York attempted to recover damages for various economic losses suffered as a result of the 1977 blackout discussed in *Strauss v. Belle Realty*, p. 166 supra. The court held that the city stated a cause of action for damages caused by looting and vandalism of its property, but dismissed plaintiff's claims for recovery of emergency wages paid to city personnel, such as police and fire officers and municipal revenues lost as a consequence of the blackout. What considerations might have led the New York court to its conclusions about recovery? What recovery might have been allowed under the *People Express* test?

5. In mid-April 2010, a massive oil spill occurred at the BP Deepwater Horizon rig in the Gulf of Mexico. Two months later, BP agreed to set up a $20 billion fund to compensate state, local and private losses, the vast bulk of which were for stand-alone economic harm. Two class actions were filed, one asserting economic and property harm and the other medical claims and, following their settlement, a court-supervised administrator accepted, reviewed, and paid claims. BP reports that, as of July 31, 2015, it had paid individuals and businesses $14.5 billion. See http://www.bp.com/en_us/bp-us/commitment-to-the-gulf-of-mexico/gulf-economic-restoration.html. Claims ranged from lost hotel and restaurant business in Florida (outside the area of the actual oil slick) to lost profits by directly affected commercial enterprises—many associated with the fishing industry—in Louisiana and Alabama. What relief would be available, if any, under tort law for these claimants?

Aside from those who suffered damage to their land or personal property from the oil spill and workers on the Deepwater Horizon who were injured or killed, virtually all of the claims are for economic loss and fall squarely into the duty limitation of *532 Madison Avenue*. Prior oil spills had established a limited exception for commercial fisherman. See Union Oil Co. v. Oppen, 501 F.2d 558 (9th Cir.1974)(permitting recovery for commercial fishermen for "loss of a resource of the sea, viz. its fish in the ordinary course of their business," arising from an oil spill off the Santa Barbara coast in 1969). The district court, presiding over lawsuits for losses from the oil spill by the Exxon Valdez ruled similarly, permitting commercial fishermen to recover their losses. In re Exxon Valdez, 1994 WL 182856, at *6 (D. Alaska 1994); see also Lloyd's Leasing Ltd. v. Conoco, 868 F.2d 1447 (5th Cir.1989)(denying claims by businesses suffering lost profits due to an oil spill in Galveston, Texas). The Third Restatement of Torts explains these cases as instances of private recovery for public nuisance, see Chapter X, p. 712 infra, rather than negligence. Public nuisance permits certain private parties who suffer different injuries from the remainder of the public due to the nuisance to recover their economic losses. See Restatement (Third) of Torts: Liability for Economic Loss § 7, cmt. e (Tent. Draft No. 2, 2014).

In the aftermath of the Exxon Valdez spill, Congress enacted the Oil Pollution Act of 1990, 33 U.S.C. §§ 2701 et seq., ("OPA"), which imposes liability for certain losses arising from an oil spill into navigable waters on a strict liability basis. Covered losses include the costs of governmental efforts to clean the spill and other public losses, including lost tax revenues, as well as for an array of private claims for economic loss, so long as they are "due to" an oil spill. However, the statute caps liability for private losses at $75 million, with an exception for "gross negligence," "willful misconduct," or violation of an applicable safety statute. After a finding that BP had been grossly negligent, it settled all federal, state and local claims under the OPA for $18.7 billion. Total cost to BP of stemming the leak and paying private and governmental claims is $54 billion. Campbell Robertson et al., *BP to Pay $18.7 Billion for Deepwater Horizon Oil Spill*, N.Y. Times July 2, 2015, at A1.

For discussion of the Deepwater Horizon oil spill, summaries of investigations into its causes, and description of the Gulf Coast Claims Facility ("GCCF") initially administered by Kenneth Feinberg, its procedures for addressing claims, and a memorandum prepared for the GCCF on the law applicable to those claims, see *Times Topics, Gulf of Mexico Oil Spill* (2010), http://topics.nytimes.com/top/reference/timestopics/subjects/o/oil_spills/gulf_of_mexico_2010/index.html?scp=4&sq=bp%20oil%20spill %20claims&st=cse.

For overall discussion of stand-alone economic loss, see Rabin, Respecting Boundaries and the Economic Loss Rule in Tort, 48 Ariz.L.Rev. 857 (2006).

C. WRONGFUL BIRTH AND WRONGFUL LIFE

Spurred by legal and technological developments in contraception, abortion, and genetic counseling, courts have confronted a cluster of tort questions concerning the nature and extent of the legal obligations doctors incur when they assist in procreation decisions. The claims may involve genetic counseling prior to or during pregnancy, medical diagnoses during pregnancy, or surgery aimed at avoiding conception or terminating a pregnancy. Suits by parents are sometimes designated "wrongful conception," "wrongful pregnancy," or "wrongful birth" claims, and those by children are labeled "wrongful life" claims. This terminology is disputed, however, and not central to analyzing the underlying legal issues. For surveys of these and related issues, see Strasser, Misconceptions and Wrongful Births: A Call for a Principled Jurisprudence, 31 Ariz.St.L.J. 161 (1999); Strasser, Wrongful Life, Wrongful Birth, Wrongful Death, and the Right to Refuse Treatment: Can Reasonable Jurisdictions Recognize All But One?, 64 Mo.L.Rev. 29 (1999); and Murtaugh, Wrongful Birth: The Courts' Dilemma in Determining a Remedy for a "Blessed Event," 27 Pace L.Rev. 241 (2007)(addressing variations existing among states that recognize such claims in the damages that can be recovered).

As you read this section, ask yourself whether it makes a difference if these suits are categorized according to the types of harms involved, as opposed to being analyzed along traditional medical malpractice lines. Professor Strasser claims that the multiplication of terms in the procreation area needlessly obfuscates the real issues and causes confusion. In any event, many state courts have addressed the various issues that arise when errors are made that interfere with procreative decisions. Although we will further explore these issues in the notes and questions, no attempt will be made to indicate the varying state positions in this fluid area beyond the analysis in the following case. As you work through these materials, also consider the interplay between constitutional law and tort law.

Emerson v. Magendantz

Supreme Court of Rhode Island, 1997.
689 A.2d 409.

■ WEISBERGER, CHIEF JUSTICE.

[A trial judge certified two questions to the state supreme court:

1. Is there a cause of action under Rhode Island law when a physician negligently performs a sterilization procedure and the patient subsequently becomes pregnant and delivers a child from that pregnancy?

2. If so, what is the measure of damages?]

The facts giving rise to these certified questions may be summarized as follows from the pleadings and the documents filed by the parties in the Superior Court and in this court. Following the birth of their first child, the Emersons decided for financial reasons to limit their family to one child. Having made this decision, Diane consulted defendant, who was a gynecological specialist, concerning sterilization procedures. The defendant agreed to perform a surgical tubal ligation and did so upon Diane on January 10, 1991. Subsequently, on or about May 31, 1991, Diane was seen by an obstetrician, who determined that she was pregnant in spite of the preceding tubal ligation. Diane gave birth to a child on January 11, 1992. The child, who was named Kirsten, is alleged to have congenital problems that are only generally described in the complaint. Following Kirsten's birth, Diane underwent a second tubal ligation.

[Plaintiffs husband and wife sued, alleging that the birth "was proximately caused by defendant's negligent performance of the tubal ligation procedure." The tubal ligation, however, was not responsible for Kirsten's birth defects.]

The Emersons also allege that as a result of defendant's negligence Diane suffered severe physical pain and required additional invasive medical treatment. The Emersons further allege that they have suffered mental anguish and distress and that they have lost wages and earning capacity as a result of Diane's unanticipated pregnancy. The Emersons further complain that as a proximate result of defendant's negligence, they have incurred an obligation to expend monetary resources for the medical care and maintenance of Kirsten and that they will continue to be so obligated for many years to come.

I

Is There a Cause of Action under Rhode Island Law When a
Physician Negligently Performs a Sterilization Procedure
and the Patient Subsequently Becomes
Pregnant and Delivers a Child?

This question poses an issue of first impression in this state. Of the numerous courts that have considered this question, only one state court of last resort has declined to recognize a cause of action in tort arising out of the negligent performance of a sterilization procedure. [citing a Nevada case]. Even Nevada has suggested there may be an action for breach of warranty. [ ] All other jurisdictions that have considered this question have determined that the negligent performance of a sterilization procedure is a tort for which recovery would be allowed under state law. [ ] In all, approximately thirty-five jurisdictions recognize a cause of action for negligent performance of sterilization procedures whether performed on the wife or on the husband.

We are persuaded by the overwhelming majority of opinions that recognize negligent performance of a sterilization procedure as a tort for which recovery may be allowed. Therefore, we answer the first question in the affirmative.

II

What Is the Measure of Damages?

Courts that have recognized the cause of action arising out of the negligent performance of sterilization or comparable procedures have adopted three general types of remedies as compensation for negligent procedures resulting in unwanted pregnancies. Thirty jurisdictions have adopted a remedy of limited recovery. [ ]

Under the limited-recovery rule the foregoing jurisdictions frequently grant compensation to the plaintiffs for the medical expenses of the ineffective sterilization procedure, for the medical and hospital costs of the pregnancy, for the expense of a subsequent sterilization procedure, for loss of wages, and sometimes for emotional distress arising out of the unwanted pregnancy and loss of consortium to the spouse arising out of the unwanted pregnancy. They also generally include medical expenses for prenatal care, delivery, and postnatal care.

A number of jurisdictions allow for recovery of the cost of child rearing as an element of damages. These jurisdictions may be divided into two groups. One group allows the cost of child rearing but balances against this cost the benefits derived by the parents, either economic or emotional, from having a healthy child. [citing cases from three states]

Two jurisdictions have adopted a full-recovery rule without offsetting either the economic or the emotional benefits to be derived from having a healthy child. Lovelace Medical Center v. Mendez, [805 P.2d 603 (N.M.1991)]; Marciniak v. Lundborg, [450 N.W.2d 243 (Wis.1990)]. These two courts apply traditional tort principles in allowing for recovery of all damages that are reasonably foreseeable and that would result from the negligent performance of the sterilization procedure. In analyzing § 920 of the Restatement (Second) Torts (1979), which recommends consideration of benefits conferred in mitigation of damages, the New Mexico Supreme Court concluded that applying emotional benefits to economic loss did not apply similar benefits to similar losses. Lovelace, [ ]. Consequently that court denied recovery for emotional distress and also denied any offset of emotional benefits derived from having a healthy child. [ ]

Similarly the Supreme Court of Wisconsin declined to offset emotional benefits against economic loss. Marciniak, [ ]. The court also declined to offset economic benefits because the court deemed them to be insignificant. [ ]

After considering with great care the opinions in support of limited recovery, of full recovery with benefit offsets, and of full recovery without benefit offsets, we have decided to adopt the limited-recovery rule as described above, save for the element of emotional distress arising out of an unwanted pregnancy that results in the birth of a healthy child.

The Supreme Court of Washington in *McKernan v. Aasheim*, [687 P.2d 850 (Wash.1984)], has made some pertinent comments:

> "We believe that it is impossible to establish with reasonable certainty whether the birth of a particular healthy, normal child damaged its parents. Perhaps the costs of rearing and educating the child could be determined through use of actuarial tables or similar economic information. But whether these costs are outweighed by the emotional benefits which will be conferred by that child cannot be calculated. The child may turn out to be loving, obedient and attentive, or hostile, unruly and callous. The child may grow up to be President of the United States, or to be an infamous criminal. In short, it is impossible to tell, at an early stage in the child's life, whether its parents have sustained a net loss or net gain." [ ]

Similarly, the Delaware Supreme Court, in denying recovery of child-rearing costs, suggested that determining damage from the birth of a child was an "exercise in prophecy." [ ] Such a weighing process might be applied at the end of a life but not at the beginning. Such an undertaking was not felt to be within the specialty of factfinders. . . .

. . .

We are of the opinion that the public policy of this state would preclude the granting of rearing costs for a healthy child whose parents have decided to forgo the option of adoption and have decided to retain the child as their own with all the joys and benefits that are derived from parenthood. Their decision to forgo the option of releasing the child for adoption constitutes most persuasive evidence that the parents consider the benefit of retaining the child to outweigh the economic costs of child rearing. [ ]

In implementing the limited-benefit rule, such parents would be entitled to recover the costs that the overwhelming majority of jurisdictions have allowed. Under this rule, plaintiffs would be entitled to recover the medical expenses of the ineffective sterilization procedure, the medical and hospital costs of the pregnancy, the expense of a subsequent sterilization procedure, loss of wages, loss of consortium to the spouse arising out of the unwanted pregnancy, and medical expenses for prenatal care, delivery, and postnatal care. However, no recovery would be allowable for emotional distress arising out of the birth of a healthy child.

In the event of the birth of a child who suffers from congenital defects, which birth is a result of an unwanted pregnancy arising out of a negligently performed sterilization procedure, we would follow the reasoning of the Supreme Court of Florida [in Fassoulas v. Ramey, 450

So.2d 822 (Fla.1984)]. In [*Fassoulas*], the prospective parents, having had two children both of whom had been born with severe congenital abnormalities, sought to prevent the birth of further children through a vasectomy performed upon the husband. The vasectomy was unsuccessful . . . The court [answering a certified question denied] child-rearing damages for a normal, healthy child, [ ], but observed that in the case of a physically or a mentally handicapped child, special medical and educational expenses [that went] beyond normal rearing costs should be allowed. [ ] The court recognized that the " 'financial and emotional drain associated with raising such a child is often overwhelming to the affected parents.' " [ ] Therefore, the court held that special costs associated with bringing up a handicapped child would be recoverable. We believe that the reasoning of the Florida court is sound but would add that when a physician is placed on notice, in performing a sterilization procedure, that the parents have a reasonable expectation of giving birth to a physically or a mentally handicapped child or if the physician should be placed on notice, by reason of statistical information of which he/she is or should be aware in the practice of his/her profession, then the entire cost of raising such a child would be within the ambit of recoverable damages. It should also be noted that the extraordinary costs of maintaining a handicapped child would not end when the child reached majority. Nor would the physician's liability necessarily end at that point. Offset against such liability would be any economic benefits derived by the parents from governmental or other agencies that might contribute to defraying the costs of caring for the child or its support in adult life. Also in the event of the birth of a physically—or a mentally—handicapped child, the parents should be entitled to compensation for emotional distress.

The foregoing determinations are made by this court in answer to the second certified question submitted by the Superior Court. The papers in the case may be remanded to the Superior Court for further proceedings.

[Two of the five justices wrote separately.]

■ BOURCIER, J., with whom FLANDERS, J., joins, concurring in part and dissenting in part.

I concur with my colleagues' response to the first certified question. . . . I dissent, however, from their response to the second certified question regarding the measure of damages available to the unfortunate patient upon whom the doctor's negligence has been visited.

I believe that the true legal nature of the cause of action that we all recognize and acknowledge in this certification proceeding is nothing more and nothing less than a medical malpractice cause of action. . . .

. . .

I acknowledge, as do my colleagues, that appellate courts throughout this country that have considered this damage question have been sharply divided with regard to what should be proper compensation for the victim of medical negligence malpractice in the course of a sterilization procedure.

... The most balanced ... cases, however, follow the Massachusetts and Connecticut rule and the Restatement (Second) Torts § 920 (1979) which both permit full recovery for all damages proximately resulting from the physician's negligence while also permitting the trial jury to mitigate or reduce any damage award by what may be proven to be the value of the benefit that is conferred upon the plaintiff parent or parents by the birth of the child.

. . .

That "abort, give away, and get no emotional trauma and child support damages" rule announced by [*McKernan v. Aasheim*] appears, in my opinion, to deny a woman's constitutional right not to have children recognized in [decisions of the United States Supreme Court]. ... I perceive of no justification for courts to force a Hobson's choice upon the unfortunate victim of a physician's negligence by ordering her to abort her unplanned pregnancy, or to give up her unplanned baby for adoption when born, or to accept in lieu of doing either, the judicially created concept that the "joy" of the unplanned birth will serve as full recompense for the doctor's negligence and for the victim's denial of her constitutional right to choose whether to become pregnant and give birth to a child. That "joy" reasoning concept is in my humble opinion nothing more than delusive reasoning employed to justify conclusion-oriented judicial decisions by certain appellate courts. In addition, it either ignores or refuses to recognize what is considered to be one of life's basic human realities, namely, that any normal woman will be hard-pressed to abort her pregnancy or later to give away her unplanned-for baby for adoption without thereafter incurring some form of resulting emotional trauma.

. . .

The reasoning advanced by my colleagues in support of insulating and absolving the negligent physician from all but minuscule responsibility for his or her patient's unplanned-for-child costs and expenses is that "[w]e are of the opinion that the public policy of this state would preclude the granting of rearing costs for a healthy child whose parents have decided to forgo the option of adoption and have decided to retain the child as their own with all the joys and benefits that are derived from parenthood." I respectfully disagree with that assumed public policy view expressed by my colleagues. I agree instead with the view regarding damage recovery and public policy as expressed by the Connecticut Supreme Court [in Ochs v. Borrelli, 445 A.2d 883 (Conn.1982)]:

"In our view, the better rule is to allow parents to recover for the expense of rearing an unplanned child to majority when the child's birth results from negligent medical care. The defendants ask us to carve out an exception, grounded in public policy, to the normal duty of a tortfeasor to assume liability for all the damages that he has proximately caused. . . . But public policy cannot support an exception to tort liability when the impact of such an exception would impair the exercise of a constitutionally protected right. It is now clearly established that parents have a constitutionally protected interest located 'within the zone of privacy created by several fundamental constitutional guarantees' . . . to employ contraceptive techniques to limit the size of their family." [ ]

. . .

I respectfully suggest that the so-called unwanted pregnancy that my colleagues believe transforms itself into a total joy or blessing that then serves to absolve the negligent physician from practically all liability to his victim patient is indeed a total joy or blessing, but only for the errant physician and not for the unfortunate victim. The joy or blessing concept emerging from the unplanned birth perhaps superficially, at first blush, would appear reasonable in the case of the happily married couple yearning for a child or children. But that is not what is before us in this certification, and that is not the nature of any of the medical-malpractice claims that are usually made against the errant physician who negligently performs a sterilization procedure. The factual reality in the usual medical malpractice case that is brought not only by women but also by males against the errant physicians who have negligently performed sterilization procedures is that the plaintiffs in those cases have decided for various reasons, economic or otherwise, not to have children. In those case situations I do not believe that the joy or blessing concept should automatically apply and restrict the tort recovery allowable to the married couple who had elected not to have children or to limit their family size for health or economic reasons. Neither should it so apply to the detriment of the unmarried young male or female college student or the professional career man or woman, married or single, who did not want to have a child or did not have the time to care for a child without first giving up his or her college, business, or professional career. To adopt a simple joy or blessing rule and then have it apply automatically to all litigants in those fact situations for purposes of limiting, to the point of practically eliminating, the liability of a negligent physician is neither fair nor in compliance with the age-old general tort-recovery damages rule. The joy or blessing rule in those situations is in my humble opinion nothing more than a judicial mirage, invisible to most ordinary mortals.

. . .

NOTES AND QUESTIONS

1.   How does the result in Part I of the court's opinion differ from what would occur in an ordinary medical malpractice claim against the defendant?

If a healthy fetus is harmed by a doctor's negligence, liability is clear. In the situations we are considering here, however, plaintiffs are not claiming that defendant physician's negligence *caused* the relevant defect in the child, just that it allowed the child to be conceived or born.

In the cases that follow, the issue is no longer whether plaintiff may recover the items that the *Emerson* majority recognized—those connected with the birth and the need for another sterilization. These are almost universally awarded.

2.   *The role of the Constitution.* Toward the end of its opinion, the majority suggests that, in awarding damages, it would distinguish quite sharply between cases in which the baby that resulted from a physician's negligence was healthy and those in which the baby was disabled. The dissent instead places priority upon the parents' ability to make autonomous decisions about their family, citing Supreme Court decisions on contraception and abortion. Which approach to the area seems more appropriate? Since most courts tend to differentiate along the lines of whether the child is healthy or unhealthy, the following notes will adhere to that division, but keep in mind the problems it may entail. In Misconceptions and Wrongful Births, supra, Professor Strasser argues that the healthy/unhealthy distinction is unhelpful, and contends that the relevant issue should be procreative autonomy. He then suggests that there is no reason the decision not to have an unhealthy child should be valued more than the decision not to have a child at all—as courts that agree with the *Emerson* majority seem to do. According to each approach, how would you justify compensating the harm of having a disabled child and not that of having a healthy one when the parents' decision was simply not to procreate?

3.   *The reasons for the choice.* A person or couple could decide that they do not want a child (or any more children) for several reasons. In *Emerson* it was "financial." Does that mean that they fear falling into serious poverty? Might it mean instead that they wish to preserve a life style to which they have become accustomed or to which they aspire? Or that with already-born children the parents consider their family complete? In other cases they may believe that they would not make good parents. In still other cases, there is concern about the mother's physical and mental well-being during a pregnancy. If the concern is about having a child with a congenital defect, as we have already seen, separate issues arise that are discussed later in these notes.

4.   *The nature of the negligence.* When the parties wanted no children or no more children the claims are usually brought against surgeons whose sterilization surgeries have failed, or against physicians who have negligently failed to diagnose a pregnancy in time for an abortion. In the case of those who wish to avoid an unhealthy child, the claim is usually

brought for incorrect medical advice that encouraged a pregnancy—from a physician or a genetic counselor. It may also be brought for conduct during a pregnancy—such as misreading of amniocentesis tests or sonograms. See, e.g., Schirmer v. Mt. Auburn Obstetrics & Gynecologic Associates, Inc., 844 N.E.2d 1160 (Ohio 2006)(parents of child born with profound mental and physical defects, asserting claim of negligent genetic testing, could recover only for costs incurred in pregnancy and child birth, and could not recover any damages for providing extraordinary care required by disabled child).

In all of these cases, there is the lurking causation question of what the parents would have done if they had been informed of the risks of defect. Should they have to prove that they would have availed themselves of the opportunity to terminate the pregnancy?

5. For a thought-provoking article on the legal and ethical challenges created by new technology that permits prenatal genetic testing for a variety of diseases and birth defects, set in the context of a story about a family that had a child with a non-hereditary genetic defect that resulted in severe mental retardation and their malpractice suit against their obstetrician, see Elizabeth Weil, *A Wrongful Birth?*, N.Y. Times Mag., March 12, 2006, at 1.

6. *Healthy baby.* Although some have challenged the value of the distinction between healthy and unhealthy babies, *Emerson* shows that courts do tend to analyze cases that way. We follow that pattern in the following notes.

When the plaintiffs have sought to avoid having any more children, the dispute over what damages are recoverable has centered on the parents' emotional distress and on the economic burden of the new child. The *Emerson* court denies damages for the costs of raising a healthy child, reasoning that the parents' decision not to put the child up for adoption suggests they consider the benefits of raising the child to be greater than the burden. Is that reasoning satisfactory? What about similar reasoning that the decision not to have an abortion means the parents value the child to a greater extent than the rearing costs? If the parents had opted for an abortion, should they be entitled to damages for emotional distress? Suppose instead they put their child up for adoption?

7. If the costs of raising a healthy baby are to be awarded, should emotional benefits be offset against economic damages? Section 920 of Second Restatement provides:

> When the defendant's tortious conduct has caused harm to the plaintiff or to his property and in so doing has conferred a special benefit to the interest of the plaintiff that was harmed, the value of the benefit conferred is considered in mitigation of damages, to the extent that this is equitable.

Comment b states that damages resulting from "an invasion of one interest are not diminished by showing that another interest has been benefited." Why not? One example offered is that "damages for pain and suffering are not diminished by showing that the earning capacity of the plaintiff has been increased by the defendant's act."

Does that suggest how setoffs should be treated in the *Emerson* case? How do the *Emerson* majority and dissent answer this question?

8.   As to damages for emotional distress, what are the damages that parents might suffer upon becoming parents of an unwanted healthy child? Are any or all of these items avoidable by giving the child up for adoption? What are the emotional benefits for parents of unwanted healthy babies? Should emotional distress damages be offset by emotional benefits?

9.   *The unwanted baby that is unhealthy. Emerson* involves the unusual situation of plaintiffs who wanted no children for financial reasons but instead became parents of an unwanted and unhealthy child. In that scenario what, if any, economic costs should be awarded? Note that here there are two kinds of economic costs—normal rearing expenses and extraordinary medical expenses.

The *Emerson* court relies on a Florida case, *Fassoulas v. Ramey*, to conclude that the plaintiffs can recover for the excess costs associated with their daughter's birth defects. How good a precedent for the *Emerson* case was *Fassoulas*, in which the parents sought sterilization because they had previously had two children born with birth defects? In Simmerer v. Dabbas, 733 N.E.2d 1169 (Ohio 2000), the parents sought damages for the extraordinary costs of raising their child who was born with a heart defect and died at the age of 15 months. The mother had undergone sterilization after her second child was born. The court denied recovery, stating that although the birth of the child was a proximate cause of the negligent procedure, a defective child was not proximately caused by defendants' negligence. The court relied on an earlier case that distinguished the situation where, as in *Fassoulas*, the sterilization was undertaken because of concern for having a child with birth defects, a fact of which the defendant was aware.

10.   *Wrongful life.* If the child's condition is one that will shorten life, or cause great pain, and the child's case seems to be based on the proposition that it would have been better off not being born, the courts have declined to recognize her "wrongful life" claim. The most commonly offered explanation in these cases is that it would be impossible to compare life with the disability to nonexistence. Is the problem an inability to measure one or both of the two items or is it the inability to compare the two even if both were measurable? See Strasser, in Wrongful Life, Wrongful Birth, Wrongful Death, p. 326 supra.

Some courts have recognized an action when the condition is not life-shortening and the child is likely to incur extraordinary medical expenses as an adult, but they limit the damages to economic ones. See, e.g., Harbeson v. Parke-Davis, Inc., 656 P.2d 483 (Wash.1983); Turpin v. Sortini, 643 P.2d 954 (Cal.1982)(congenital deafness). Why might courts distinguish along these lines? Does it matter whether economic damages are recovered by the child or by the parent? Are these cases really "wrongful life" cases? Consider the Florida Supreme Court's reasons for permitting the same damages as part of a "wrongful birth" cause of action when the child suffered from a variety of genetic defects:

> [S]ome jurisdictions have at least suggested that the tort of
> "wrongful life" can address two separate concerns: (1) the
> extraordinary expenses associated with caring for the impaired
> child until its death; and (2) liability for "suffering" caused by the
> impairment. . . . A lawsuit aimed at recovering the second type of
> "damages" necessarily would require the finder of fact to weigh
> the value of impaired life against the value of nonexistence. . . .
> [The same] does not hold true, however, for the extraordinary
> expenses that will arise from the impairment of a wrongfully born
> child. These expenses are not properly an aspect of a wrongful life
> claim at all, but an aspect of wrongful birth. Such damages are
> quantifiable with reasonable certainty. . . .

Kush v. Lloyd, 616 So.2d 415, 423–24 (Fla.1992). Does allowing wrongful
life suits for economic damages alone solve all logical problems with the
cause of action? Why haven't courts recognized "wrongful life" suits when
the child is afflicted with a life-shortening problem?

Should the unhealthy child be able to sue the parents for her
conception and birth despite genetic contraindications? In Curlender v. Bio-
Science Laboratories, 165 Cal.Rptr. 477 (App.1980), the court suggested in
dictum that parents who conceive with knowledge of a high risk of birth
defects might be liable to a child born with such defects. The legislature
responded with Calif. Civil Code § 43.6(a), providing that "No cause of
action arises against a parent of a child based upon the claim that the child
should not have been conceived or, if conceived, should not have been
allowed to have been born alive."

CHAPTER V

FACTUAL CAUSATION

In earlier chapters we asked whether the defendant owed a duty of due care to the plaintiff and whether defendant had violated that duty. In this chapter we ask whether the defendant's negligence (or other tortious conduct) "caused" the harm for which the plaintiff is suing. This inquiry seeks to tie the defendant's tortious conduct to the plaintiff's harm in an almost physical or scientific way, by inquiring whether defendant's negligence made a difference with regard to the harm suffered by plaintiff.

Another, but different, issue is sometimes referred to with similar language. "Proximate" or "legal" causation is not about factual causation but rather whether defendant should be held liable for unexpected consequences notwithstanding that her negligence was a factual cause of plaintiff's harm. We defer consideration of this subject to Chapter VI.

A. BASIC DOCTRINE

From the outset of the book, we have implicitly accepted the notion that a defendant who behaves negligently should not have to compensate an injured plaintiff unless the plaintiff's injury is causally connected to the defendant's negligent conduct. Judicial decisions have accepted the need for some connection between the plaintiff's harm and the defendant's negligent conduct before imposing tort liability on the defendant. Courts have traditionally denied liability when it is clear that the connection was missing. Consider a situation in which a motorist should have sounded the car's horn when going around a dangerous bend that had a sign requiring that the horn be sounded. The negligence is clear. But the causal connection is missing if the lone motorist coming the other way was deaf and thus would not have heard the horn even if it had been sounded.

What do we mean when we say that "X caused Y"? The core of causation is that if X had not occurred, Y would not have occurred. This requirement is frequently referred to as "but for" or sine qua non. It means that X must have been necessary for the outcome Y (with a qualification addressed later at p. 346 infra), but does not require that it be sufficient by itself. There are always multiple causes of any event, stemming back to the origins of the universe, and we do not require that X be "the" (only) cause; so long as X is "a" cause it is sufficient. As is revealed from the causal inquiry above, before causation can be assessed, X and Y must be identified. For our purposes at this point, X is the tortious conduct of the defendant and Y is the physical harm suffered by the plaintiff. Once the causal inquiry is framed, answering the question requires the counterfactual inquiry: what would have happened (in terms of Y) if X had never occurred?

In Rinaldo v. McGovern, 587 N.E.2d 264 (N.Y.1991), involving an errant golf drive, one claim was that the golfer negligently failed to shout "fore" before hitting the ball. On this point, the court concluded that a warning "would have been all but futile." Even if the defendant had shouted, "it is unlikely that plaintiffs, who were driving in a vehicle on a nearby roadway, would have heard, much less had the opportunity to act upon, the shouted warning." The chance was "too 'remote' to justify submission of the case to the jury." What might the court have meant by characterizing the chance as "too remote"?

Sometimes the lack of actual cause is shown in a different way. Defendant may be negligent for not maintaining a dam so that it could withstand an ordinary rainfall. If such a normal rain had fallen, the dam would have given way and the defendant's liability for the downstream flooding would have been clear. In fact, however, the next rainfall is not of the ordinary variety; it is an unprecedented deluge beyond anything that the courts would require dam keepers to anticipate. The dam bursts under conditions that would have caused even a well-constructed dam to burst—and downstream flooding occurs that does roughly the same type and amount of harm to the same plaintiffs as would have been done if the dam had burst under the anticipated rain. What arguments support liability on the dam owner? What arguments cut the other way?

In many situations in which actual cause is an issue, drawing an inference of causation is quite straightforward: think about a pedestrian hit by a car who emerges with a broken arm. Sometimes, however, inferring the cause of plaintiff's harm is more difficult because there are a number of different potential explanations.

Stubbs v. City of Rochester

Court of Appeals of New York, 1919.
226 N.Y. 516, 124 N.E. 137.

■ HOGAN, J.

[Defendant supplied Hemlock system water for drinking and Holly system water for firefighting. The evidence indicated that through the city's negligence in May 1910, the systems had become intermingled near the Brown Street Bridge. The Hemlock water became contaminated by sewage known to be present in the Holly water, but this was not discovered until October. Plaintiff contracted typhoid fever in September and attributed it to the city's negligence. By a 3–2 vote, without opinion, the Appellate Division affirmed a nonsuit granted by the trial judge at the close of plaintiff's case. Other facts are stated in the opinion.]

facts

procedural history

The important question in this case is—did the plaintiff produce evidence from which inference might reasonably be drawn that the cause of his illness was due to the use of contaminated water furnished by defendant. Counsel for respondent argues that even assuming that the city may be held liable to plaintiff for damages caused by its negligence in furnishing contaminated water for drinking purposes, (a) that the evidence adduced by plaintiff fails to disclose that he contracted typhoid fever by drinking contaminated water; (b) that it was incumbent upon the plaintiff to establish that his illness was not due to any other cause to which typhoid fever may be attributed for which defendant is not liable. The evidence does disclose several causes of typhoid fever which is a germ disease, the germ being known as the typhoid bacillus, which causes may be classified as follows:

First. Drinking of polluted water. *Second.* Raw fruits and vegetables in certain named localities where human excrement is used to fertilize the soil are sometimes sources of typhoid infection. *Third.* The consumption of shell fish, though not a frequent cause. *Fourth.* The consumption of infected milk and vegetables. *Fifth.* The house fly in certain localities. *Sixth.* Personal contact with an infected person by one who has a predilection for typhoid infection and is not objectively sick with the disease. *Seventh.* Ice if affected with typhoid bacilli. *Eighth.* Fruits, vegetables, etc., washed in infected water. *Ninth.* The medical authorities recognize that there are still other causes and means unknown. This fact was developed on cross-examination of physicians called by plaintiff.

[Counsel argues first] that the evidence fails to disclose that plaintiff contracted typhoid fever by drinking contaminated water. The plaintiff having been nonsuited at the close of his case is entitled to the most favorable inference deducible from the evidence. That plaintiff on or about September 6th, 1910, was taken ill and very soon thereafter typhoid fever developed is not disputed. That he was employed in a factory located one block distant from the Brown street bridge in which Hemlock lake water was the only supply of water for potable and other purposes, and that the water drawn from faucets in that neighborhood disclosed that the water was roily and of unusual appearance is not questioned. And no doubt prevails that the Holly system water was confined to the main business part of the city for use for fire purposes and sprinkling streets and is not furnished for domestic or drinking purposes.

The evidence of the superintendent of water works of the city is to the effect that Hemlock lake water is a pure wholesome water free from contamination of any sort at the lake and examinations of the same are made weekly; that the Holly water is not fit for drinking purposes taken as it is from the Genesee river. Further evidence was offered by plaintiff by several witnesses, residents in the locality of Brown street bridge, who discovered the condition of the water at various times during July,

August and September and made complaint to the water department of the condition of the same. Dr. Goler, a physician and health officer of the city, was called by plaintiff and testified that in September when complaint was made to him by a resident of the district he went to the locality, visited houses in the immediate neighborhood, found that the water drawn from the faucet of the Hemlock supply looked badly and smelled badly. He took a sample of the water to the laboratory and had it examined by a chemist who found that it contained an increase in solids and very many times, that is twenty to thirty times as much chlorine or common salt as is found in the domestic water supply—the presence of chlorine in excessive quantities indicates contamination in that quantity, bad contamination and usually sewage contamination. Further examination followed in the district. Water was collected from various houses and a large number of samples, perhaps less than one hundred, but over twenty-five. . . . About the following day, the source of contamination having been discovered, the doctor made an investigation as to the reported cases of typhoid fever in the city in the months of August, September and October for the purpose of determining the number of cases, where the cases came from, what gave rise to it, and he stated that in his opinion the outbreak of typhoid was due to polluted water, contaminated as he discovered afterwards by sewage. In answer to a hypothetical question embracing generally the facts asserted by plaintiff the witness testified that he had an opinion as to the cause of the infection of plaintiff and such opinion was that it was due to contaminated water.

Doctor Dodge, of the faculty of the University of Rochester, a professor of biology, also bacteriologist of the city of Rochester, about October first made an analysis of samples of water. . . . While his examination did not disclose any colon bacillus, it did disclose some evidence of the same. Dr. Brady, the physician who attended the plaintiff, and Dr. Culkin both testified that in their opinion the plaintiff contracted typhoid fever from drinking polluted water.

Plaintiff called a witness who resided on Brown street about two minutes' walk from the bridge and proved by her that she drank water from the Hemlock mains in the fall of 1910 and was ill with typhoid fever. Thereupon counsel for defendant stipulated that fifty-seven witnesses which the plaintiff proposed to call will testify that they drank water from the Hemlock taps in the vicinity of the district west of the Genesee river and north of Allen street in the summer and fall of 1910 and during said summer and fall suffered from typhoid fever, that in view of the stipulation such witnesses need not be called by plaintiff and the stipulation shall have the same force and effect as though the witnesses had been called and testified to the facts.

The plaintiff resided with his wife some three miles distant from the factory where he was employed. The water consumed by him at his house outside the infected district was Hemlock water. The only water in the factory was Hemlock water and he had there an individual cup from which he drank. He was not outside of the city during the summer of 1910. Therefore, the only water he drank was in the city of Rochester.

A table of statistics as to typhoid fever in the city of Rochester for the years 1901–1910, inclusive, was produced by the health officer and received in evidence. . . . The statistics disclose that the number of typhoid cases in the city in 1910 was 223, an excess of 50 cases of any year of the nine years preceding. Recalling that complaints as to water commenced in the summer of 1910 and as shown by the evidence that typhoid fever does not develop until two or three weeks after the bacilli have been taken into the system, in connection with the fact that the source of contamination was not discovered until October, the statistics disclose that of the 223 cases of typhoid in the city in the year 1910, 180 cases appear during the months of August, September, October and November as against forty-three cases during the remaining eight months; thirty-five of which were prior to August and eight in the month of December, two months after the source of contamination of the water was discovered.

The evidence on the trial discloses that at least fifty-eight witnesses, residents of the district, drank the contaminated water and suffered from typhoid fever in addition to plaintiff; thus one-third of the 180 cases during the months stated were shown to exist in that district.

Counsel for respondent asserts that there was a failure of proof on the part of plaintiff in that he did not establish that he contracted disease by drinking contaminated water and in support of his argument cites a rule of law, that when there are several possible causes of injury for one or more of which a defendant is not responsible, plaintiff cannot recover without proving that the injury was sustained wholly or in part by a cause for which defendant was responsible. He submits that it was essential for plaintiff to eliminate all other of seven causes from which the disease might have been contracted. If the argument should prevail and the rule of law stated is not subject to any limitation the present case illustrates the impossibility of a recovery in any case based upon like facts. One cause of the disease is stated by counsel to be "personal contact with typhoid carriers or other persons suffering with the disease, whereby bacilli are received and accidentally transferred by the hands or some other portion of the person or clothes to the mouth." Concededly a person is affected with typhoid some weeks before the disease develops. The plaintiff here resided three miles distant from his place of employment and traveled to and from his work upon the street car. To prove the time when he was attacked with typhoid, then find every individual who traveled on the same car with him and establish by each one of them that he or she was free from the disease even to his or her clothing is impossible. Again the evidence disclosed that typhoid fever was caused by sources unknown to medical science. If the word of the rule stated is to prevail plaintiff would be required to eliminate sources which had not yet been determined or ascertained. I do not believe the rule stated to be as inflexible as claimed for. If two or more possible causes exist, for only one of which a defendant may be liable, and a party injured establishes facts from which it can be said with reasonable certainty that the direct cause of the injury was the one for which the defendant was liable the party has complied with the spirit of the rule.

rule

The plaintiff was employed in the immediate locality where the water was contaminated. He drank the water daily. The consumption of contaminated water is a very frequent cause of typhoid fever. In the locality there were a large number of cases of typhoid fever and near to sixty individuals who drank the water and had suffered from typhoid fever in that neighborhood appeared as witnesses on behalf of plaintiff. The plaintiff gave evidence of his habits, his home surroundings and his method of living, and the medical testimony indicated that his illness was caused by drinking contaminated water. Without reiteration of the facts disclosed on the trial I do not believe that the case on the part of plaintiff was so lacking in proof as matter of law that his complaint should be dismissed. On the contrary the most favorable inferences deducible from the plaintiff were such as would justify a submission of the facts to a jury as to the reasonable inferences to be drawn therefrom, and a verdict rendered thereon for either party would rest not in conjecture but upon reasonable possibilities.

disposition

The judgment should be reversed and a new trial granted, costs to abide the event.

■ CARDOZO, POUND and ANDREWS, JJ., concur; HISCOCK, CH. J., CHASE and MCLAUGHLIN, JJ., dissent [without opinion].

NOTES AND QUESTIONS

1.   Why is it the plaintiff's burden to show the causal relationship or, indeed, any of the prima facie elements of his claim? Recall that the party with the burden of proof must establish each element by a "preponderance of the evidence," p. 12 supra, or alternatively that the element is "more likely than not." Consider how that standard of proof affects plaintiff's efforts to establish causation throughout the remainder of this Chapter.

2.   Each party pays for its expert witnesses and the preparation of its statistics. Who should pay for these expenses? Is it permissible in asking whether a plaintiff has met the burden of showing causation to ask what more the plaintiff might have done? Should the practical and financial impediments to doing more be taken into account in deciding whether the plaintiff has satisfied her burden?

3.   Note that the aspect of causation at issue in *Stubbs* (and in the next case, *Zuchowicz,* as well) is whether the suspected agent— contaminated water—was a cause of plaintiff's disease. What makes this inquiry difficult is the existence of competing potential causes—the other causes that might alternatively be responsible for his disease. Note also the

additional difficulty posed when some of the competing potential causes are unknown. Consider one piece of evidence employed by plaintiff:

Why is it relevant that 58 persons who drank the water got typhoid? Didn't they also sleep and get typhoid, or drink milk and get typhoid? Might they all have been bitten by houseflies and gotten typhoid? What further data would be helpful? Epidemiology is the discipline that attempts to identify the causes of disease based on statistical evidence. Understanding epidemiologic principles has become a necessity for attorneys working in the toxic substances arena. An excellent resource on scientific methods, including epidemiology, written for judges and lawyers, is Federal Judicial Center & National Research Council, Reference Manual on Scientific Evidence (3d ed.2011).

4. If each of the other 57 victims sued one at a time, would it be possible for 35 juries to hold for the plaintiffs and 22 juries for the defendant if the evidence was essentially the same in each case?

5. Suppose all 58 residents of the district who contracted typhoid fever sued. Suppose historical studies—from earlier years when there was no intermixing of the water supplies—further suggest that ten residents of the district would have contracted typhoid fever from one of the other causes. All 58 residents might well collect full damages, even though it seems clear that ten should not recover. Liability exceeding its responsibility is thus being assigned to the City of Rochester, creating overdeterrence and unfairness. Is this an insoluble dilemma?

One solution to this problem that has been suggested in recent years as toxic tort cases have become more prevalent is "proportional liability." In Rosenberg, The Causal Connection in Mass Exposure Cases: A "Public Law" Vision of the Tort System, 97 Harv.L.Rev. 851 (1984), Professor David Rosenberg included proportional liability in a broader proposal for a "public law tort model" that would include class action treatment of claims, scheduled damages, probabilistic determination of causation, and proportional liability based on the probability of causation. Under proportional liability, defendant in the circumstances above would compensate each of the 58 victims for 48/58 of the damages. Are there problems with this approach? For references to the many proposals for proportional liability and a critique of them, see Green, The Future of Proportional Liability: The Lessons of Toxic Substance Causation, in S. Madden (ed.), Exploring Tort Law (2005).

6. *Probabilistic recovery for harm in the future.* Might a proportionate recovery scheme be employed at the time of exposure, even before actual harm was experienced? Or at the time of suit when plaintiff has suffered harm but is at risk of a new disease developing? This has been a common aspect of asbestos litigation where the initial harm may be relatively minor but the future dangers are great.

a. *Existing disease cases.* Recall that the single judgment rule, p. 16 supra, requires that the plaintiff sue only once for all harm arising from the tort. When plaintiff has suffered a disease, but is at risk of another disease in the future, may or must she seek recovery for the risk of the future disease? The most common response has been to create an exception to the single judgment rule, and require the plaintiff to sue for the second disease when it develops. See Simmons v. Pacor, Inc., 674 A.2d 232 (Pa.1996), adopting a two-disease rule, whereby the plaintiff with, for example, asbestosis recovers (if at all) only for that present disease and recovers for consequent lung cancer or mesothelioma only when the more serious disease occurs. The court also held that plaintiff could only obtain recovery for emotional distress related to the prospect of developing the more serious condition at the time of the suit for the second disease.

Several reasons argue against giving someone with a 75% chance of future harm 100% recovery now. One is the possibility that plaintiff will not get the second disease and will receive money for nonexistent damages. Apart from the unfairness of such an award, it may also deplete the defendant's coffers in a mass tort context so that there will be no money left for those who ultimately do get the disease. At the same time, there is concern about giving a large sum to someone who does not yet need it—and who may spend it now and not have it when the disease does strike. To allow for future recovery when the disease does in fact strike, the rules on statutes of limitation and on splitting causes of action are altered to target "discovery" rather than (or in addition to) "exposure." If a disease may not develop for 20 years, how can a plaintiff prove now a sufficient likelihood of getting it—and what the likely severity will be?

Several arguments cut in favor of permitting those who can show a better-than-even chance of future disease to sue now. These include the difficulty of proof if one must wait 20 or more years to sue. This goes to any fault requirement and also to causation since many more events have intervened (but, consider, that better scientific information about causation may also emerge). Also, the deterrent aspect of tort law is being delayed and diminished.

If arguments for current suit are sound, do they also extend to those who can prove a less-than-even chance of contracting the future disease? Various positions are discussed in Mauro v. Raymark Industries, Inc., 561 A.2d 257 (N.J.1989), in which the majority allowed those with better-than-even claims to sue for full future damages, and the dissenter wanted to permit those with less-than-even chances to recover that percentage of their damages.

In Dillon v. Evanston Hospital, 771 N.E.2d 357 (Ill.2002) a piece of a catheter was left in plaintiff's body. Because of its location, removal was thought to entail greater risks than leaving it in place, which entailed several small risks, estimated at 0–20%, of adverse future consequences. She sued for past and future pain and suffering for which the jury awarded $3 million. The jury also awarded her $500,000 for the risk of adverse future consequences. Retreating from prior decisions requiring reasonable certainty for recovery for future harm, the court permitted plaintiff to recover for an increased risk of future injuries: "A plaintiff can obtain compensation for a future injury that is not reasonably certain to occur, but the compensation would reflect the low probability." See also Petriello v. Kalman, 576 A.2d 474 (Conn.1990)(similar holding to *Dillon*).

b.   *Pure risk cases.* Suppose the plaintiff does not suffer from any disease, but seeks to accelerate resolution of her claim by suing for the *risk* that she will contract the disease in the future? How do the concerns, addressed just above, apply to this situation? Are pure risk cases stronger or weaker than existing disease cases for employing probabilistic liability? Does *Dillon* support probabilistic recovery for pure risk?

Our major concern here is the actual enhanced risk of physical harm. Although the enhanced risk also raises questions of emotional distress, as in *Simmons*, based on the fear of contracting the disease, that issue was addressed in depth at p. 268 supra. Nor do we deal here with claims for current recovery for medical monitoring to facilitate an early diagnosis of disease should it occur. That issue is discussed at p. 392 infra.

c.   *Legally compensable harm threshold.* Up to this point in the course, the physical injuries suffered by plaintiffs (and even the emotional and economic harm in Chapter IV) constituted legally compensable harm, in the sense that if plaintiffs could make out the other elements of a tort case, they could recover for that type of harm. But not all harms are legally compensable, as Paz v. Brush Engineered Materials, Inc., 555 F.3d 383 (5th Cir.2009), demonstrates. Plaintiffs were exposed to beryllium and claimed that they suffered from chronic beryllium disease ("CBD") and beryllium sensitization ("BeS"). The court found insufficient proof of CBD and that plaintiffs only suffered from BeS, an immune system response to beryllium exposure that is real in the sense that there are physiologic changes but that causes no impairment. Such a harm is not compensable, the court decided, as a result of which plaintiffs have no present injury and therefore are asserting only a pure risk case. In asbestos litigation, a number of courts decided similarly that pleural plaque, a small fibrous deposit on the lungs that causes no clinical symptoms, is not a compensable injury. See *Simmons v. Pacor,* supra.

7.   *Proof of causation in conventional traumatic injury cases.* In Mitchell v. Pearson Enterprises, 697 P.2d 240 (Utah 1985), a guest in defendant's hotel was murdered in his room by an unknown person. The motive appeared to be robbery. There were no signs of a forced entry. Local police had several hypotheses. Some centered on a person entering the room with a passkey and then being surprised by the guest. Another suggested a gangland killing in which the guest was accosted in the hallway or elevator. The suit claimed inadequate security measures.

Accepting that the plaintiff had made a sufficient showing of negligence, the court affirmed summary judgment for the defendant on the ground that proof of causation was lacking. It was not known how the murderer first encountered the guest or whether they had a prior relationship. The lack of forced entry "could be probative of entrance by a person using an unauthorized master or room key. However, it could also be probative of entrance, at [the deceased's] invitation, by a friend or colleague. Any supposition, therefore, as to the manner of entrance to [the deceased's] room or the identity of the assailant would be totally speculative. A jury cannot be permitted to engage in such speculation."

Contrast Burgos v. Aqueduct Realty Corp., 706 N.E.2d 1163 (N.Y.1998), in which a tenant sued her landlord for an assault committed in the building and sought to prove that the assault was by an intruder rather than another tenant. The court thought it unreasonable to require the tenant to identify the perpetrator. It was enough if the jury could, through "logical inferences to be drawn from the evidence," conclude that it was "more likely or more reasonable than not that the assailant was an intruder who gained access to the premises through a negligently maintained entrance." The two cases before the court met the standard: in one, involving a building of 25 apartments, the plaintiff testified that she was familiar with all the tenants and did not recognize her assailant; in the second, a large apartment building, the plaintiff and eyewitness tenants testified that they did not recognize the assailant who entered and left through a broken rear door.

How can courts distinguish between the speculation found impermissible in *Mitchell* and the inference deemed acceptable in *Burgos*?

Multiple Sufficient Causes

Suppose that two parties, acting independently, each negligently start a fire. The two fires burn separately but then arrive simultaneously at the plaintiff's home and burn it down. Either fire alone would have been sufficient to destroy the house. In the classic case of Anderson v. Minneapolis, St. P. & S.S.M. Ry. Co., 179 N.W. 45 (Minn.1920), the court employed the "substantial factor" test to determine whether the defendant's fire was a cause of the harm. Do you see why the but-for test does not work appropriately with multiple sufficient causes? As explained in note 5, p. 356 infra, the Second Restatement adopted the substantial factor language as the black letter standard for causation.

In Basko v. Sterling Drug, Inc., 416 F.2d 417 (2d Cir.1969), the plaintiff was allegedly blinded after taking three drugs manufactured by the defendant. Under one view of the case, the defendant would have been liable if the blinding had been caused by its Triquin but not if caused by its Aralen (the third drug was exonerated as a potential cause). The blinding was caused either by one drug, the other, a combination of the two, or could have been produced by each independently. The court recognized the problem with employing the but-for test if each one independently could have produced the harm and held that causation would be satisfied if the defendant's negligence was a substantial factor in producing the harm. How is *Basko* different from the two fires hypothetical? The *Basko* court explained its rationale:

> The reason for imposing liability in such a situation, as Harper and James explain, is that the "defendant has committed a wrong and this has been a cause of the injury; further, such negligent conduct will be more effectively

deterred by imposing liability than by giving the wrongdoer a windfall in cases where an all sufficient innocent cause happens to concur with his wrong in producing the harm." [ ] Similarly, in Navigazione Libera T. S. A. v. Newtown Creek Towing Co., 98 F.2d 694, 697 (2d Cir.1938), Judge Learned Hand stated that "the single tortfeasor cannot be allowed to escape through the meshes of a logical net. He is a wrongdoer; let him unravel the casuistries resulting from his wrong." See also Malone, Ruminations on Cause In Fact, 9 Stan. L. Rev. 60, 88–94 (1956). The contrary arguments have been rejected by the Restatement, and there is good reason to believe that the Connecticut courts would follow the Restatement approach. [ ]

Is the court's resolution persuasive? Would *Basko* apply if there were two separate manufacturers of two drugs, each of which would have caused the harm but only one manufacturer had been negligent and sued? Compare the two classic articles that take opposing positions on this question, Peaslee, Multiple Causation and Damage, 47 Harv.L.Rev. 1127 (1934)(negligent defendant should not be liable because no damage caused by defendant's act) with Carpenter, Concurrent Causation, 83 U.Pa.L.Rev. 941 (1935)(negligent defendant should be held liable in this type of case). See also Green, The Intersection of Factual Causation and Damages, 55 DePaul L.Rev. 671 (2006).

Zuchowicz v. United States

United States Court of Appeals, Second Circuit, 1998.
140 F.3d 381.

■ Before: NEWMAN, ALTIMARI, and CALABRESI, CIRCUIT JUDGES.

■ CALABRESI, CIRCUIT JUDGE.

[This is an action under the Federal Tort Claims Act, based on Connecticut law. Defendant admitted that its doctors and/or pharmacists at the naval hospital had been negligent in directing Mrs. Zuchowicz to ingest 1600 milligrams of Danocrine—double the maximum authorized dosage. She took the excessive doses for one month, after which her dosage was reduced to the maximum amount for a little over two months. She was then told to discontinue Danocrine. About four months after stopping, she was diagnosed with primary pulmonary hypertension (PPH), "a rare and fatal disease in which increased pressure in an individual's pulmonary artery causes severe strain on the right side of the heart." Treatments include "calcium channel blockers and heart and lung transplants." While Mrs. Zuchowicz was on the waiting list for a lung transplant she became pregnant, which made her ineligible for a transplant and also "exacerbates PPH." One month after giving birth, Mrs. Zuchowicz died and her husband continued the pending case on behalf of her estate. After a bench trial, the court awarded damages. Further facts are stated in the opinion.]

Did the action for which the defendant is responsible cause, in a legal sense, the harm which the plaintiff suffered?—a question easily put and often very hard to answer. . . .

Over the centuries the courts have struggled to give meaning to this requirement—in the simplest of situations, who hit whom, and in the most complex ones, which polluter's emissions, if any, hurt which plaintiff. It is the question that we must seek to answer today in the context of modern medicine and a very rare disease.

[The court summarized the treatment sequence and then turned to the nature of PPH.]

2.   Primary Pulmonary Hypertension

Pulmonary hypertension is categorized as "primary" when it occurs in the absence of other heart or lung diseases. "Secondary" pulmonary hypertension is diagnosed when the hypertension results from another heart or lung disease, such as emphysema or blood clots. PPH is very rare. A National Institute of Health registry recorded only 197 cases of PPH from the mid-1980s until 1992. It occurs predominantly in young women. Exogenous agents known to be capable of causing PPH include birth control pills, some appetite suppressants, chemotherapy drugs, rapeseed oil, and L-Tryptophan.

According to the district court's findings of fact, the disease involves the interplay of the inner layers of the pulmonary blood vessels known as the endothelium and the vascular smooth muscle. The endothelium releases substances called vasodilators and vasoconstrictors, which dilate and constrict the blood vessels. These substances can also cause growth of the vascular smooth muscle. Experts currently believe that an imbalance in vasodilators and vasoconstrictors plays a part in the development of pulmonary hypertension. If too many vasoconstrictors are released, the blood vessels contract, the endothelial cells die, and the vascular smooth muscle cells proliferate. These actions create increased pulmonary vascular resistance.

[The court reported that much of the original research on Danocrine, which was used to treat endometriosis, was done by Dr. W. Paul D'Mowski, one of plaintiff's witnesses, who testified that it is safe and effective when properly used. He also testified that there had been no formal studies of excess doses and that "very, very, few women have received doses this high in any setting."]

B.   The Expert Testimony

The rarity of PPH, combined with the fact that so few human beings have ever received such a high dose of Danocrine, obviously impacted on the manner in which the plaintiff could prove causation. The number of persons who received this type of overdose was simply too small for the plaintiff to be able to provide epidemiological, or even anecdotal, evidence linking PPH to Danocrine overdoses. [Plaintiff], therefore, based his case primarily on the testimony of two expert witnesses, Dr. Richard Matthay, a physician and expert in pulmonary diseases, and Dr. Randall Tackett, a professor of pharmacology who has published widely in the field of the effects of drugs on vascular tissues. In rendering a judgment for the plaintiff, the district court relied heavily on the evidence submitted by these two experts. The defendant challenges both the admissibility and the sufficiency of their testimony.

1. Dr. Matthay

Dr. Richard Matthay is a full professor of medicine at Yale and Associate Director and Training Director of Yale's Pulmonary and Critical Care Section. He is a nationally recognized expert in the field of pulmonary medicine, with extensive experience in the area of drug-induced pulmonary diseases. Dr. Matthay examined and treated Mrs. Zuchowicz. His examination included taking a detailed history of the progression of her disease, her medical history, and the timing of her Danocrine overdose and the onset of her symptoms.

Dr. Matthay testified that he was confident to a reasonable medical certainty that the Danocrine caused Mrs. Zuchowicz's PPH. When pressed, he added that he believed the overdose of Danocrine to have been responsible for the disease. His conclusion was based on the temporal relationship between the overdose and the start of the disease and the differential etiology method of excluding other possible causes. While Dr. Matthay did not rule out all other possible causes of pulmonary hypertension, he did exclude all the causes of secondary pulmonary hypertension. On the basis of Mrs. Zuchowicz's history, he also ruled out all previously known drug-related causes of primary pulmonary hypertension.

Dr. Matthay further testified that the progression and timing of Mrs. Zuchowicz's disease in relation to her overdose supported a finding of drug-induced PPH. Dr. Matthay emphasized that, prior to the overdose, Mrs. Zuchowicz was a healthy, active young woman with no history of cardiovascular problems, and that, shortly after the overdose, she began experiencing symptoms of PPH such as weight gain, swelling of hands and feet, fatigue, and shortness of breath. He described the similarities between the course of Mrs. Zuchowicz's illness and that of accepted cases of drug-induced PPH, and he went on to discuss cases involving classes of drugs that are known to cause other pulmonary diseases (mainly anti-cancer drugs). He noted that the onset of these diseases, which are recognized to be caused by the particular drugs, was very similar in timing and course to the development of Mrs. Zuchowicz's illness.

2. Dr. Tackett

Dr. Randall Tackett is a tenured, full professor of pharmacology and former department chair from the University of Georgia. He has published widely in the field of the effects of drugs on vascular tissues. Dr. Tackett testified that, to a reasonable degree of scientific certainty, he believed that the overdose of Danocrine, more likely than not, caused PPH in the plaintiff by producing: 1) a decrease in estrogen; 2) hyperinsulinemia, in which abnormally high levels of insulin circulate in the body; and 3) increases in free testosterone and progesterone. Dr. Tackett testified that these hormonal factors, taken together, likely caused a dysfunction of the endothelium leading to PPH. Dr. Tackett relied on a variety of published and unpublished studies that indicated that these hormones could cause endothelial dysfunction and an imbalance of vasoconstrictor effects.

II. Discussion

A. Was the Admission of the Plaintiff's Experts' Testimony Manifestly Erroneous?

The defendant's first argument is that the district court erred in admitting the testimony of Dr. Tackett and Dr. Matthay. We review the district court's decision to admit or exclude expert testimony under a highly deferential abuse of discretion standard. See General Elec. Co. v. Joiner, [522 U.S. 136 (1997)]; McCullock v. H.B. Fuller Co., 61 F.3d 1038, 1042 (2d Cir.1995)("The decision to admit expert testimony is left to the broad discretion of the trial judge and will be overturned only when manifestly erroneous.").

The Federal Rules of Evidence permit opinion testimony by experts when the witness is "qualified as an expert by knowledge, skill, experience, training, or education," and "[i]f scientific, technical, or other specialized knowledge will assist the trier of fact to understand the evidence or to determine a fact in issue." Fed.R.Evid. 702. And though in Daubert v. Merrell Dow Pharmaceuticals, Inc., 509 U.S. 579, 588–89 (1993), the Supreme Court altered the traditional test for the admissibility of expert testimony, it did not change the standard of appellate review of these decisions, see [Joiner].[5]

Under Daubert, trial judges are charged with ensuring that expert testimony "both rests on a reliable foundation and is relevant to the task at hand." [ ] Thus, while Daubert and the Federal Rules of Evidence "allow district courts to admit a somewhat broader range of scientific testimony than would have been admissible under Frye, they leave in place the 'gatekeeper' role of the trial judge in screening such evidence." [Joiner]. Indeed Daubert strengthens this role, for it requires

---

[5] In Daubert, the Supreme Court rejected the traditional Frye rule (which had required that a scientific theory be generally accepted by the scientific community to be admissible, see Frye v. United States, 293 F. 1013, 1014 (D.C. Cir.1923)), concluding that adherence to Frye's "rigid 'general acceptance' requirement would be at odds with the 'liberal thrust' of the Federal Rules [of Evidence]."

that judges make a "preliminary assessment of whether the reasoning or methodology underlying the testimony is scientifically valid and of whether that reasoning or methodology properly can be applied to the facts in issue." [ ]

The factors identified by the Supreme Court as relevant to this inquiry are: (1) whether the theory can be (and has been) tested according to the scientific method; (2) whether the theory or technique has been subjected to peer review and publication; (3) in the case of a particular scientific technique, the known or potential rate of error; and (4) whether the theory is generally accepted. [ ] The Court emphasized, however, that these factors were not an exclusive or dispositive list of what should be considered, and that the trial court's inquiry should be a "flexible one." [ ]

The question in this case is whether, in light of these factors, the district court's decision to admit the testimony of Dr. Matthay and Dr. Tackett was an abuse of discretion. We addressed a similar question in [*McCullock*, supra]. In *McCullock*, we upheld the district court's decision to admit the testimony of an engineer and a medical doctor in a case involving a worker's exposure to glue fumes and her subsequent development of throat polyps. Applying the "manifestly erroneous" standard, we rejected the defendant's argument that the district court had not properly performed its gatekeeping function as required by *Daubert*. . . .

McCullock provides strong support for the instant plaintiff's position. In the case before us, as in *McCullock*, the district court carefully undertook and fulfilled its role in making the evaluation required by *Daubert*—a "preliminary assessment of whether the reasoning or methodology underlying the testimony is scientifically valid and of whether that reasoning or methodology properly can be applied to the facts in issue." . . .

The district court rejected [attacks on the validity of the experts' methods] stating that the plaintiff's experts "based their opinions on methods reasonably relied on by experts in their particular fields." We do not believe that the district court's decision in this regard was erroneous, let alone manifestly so.

B. Were the District Court's Factual Findings with Respect to Causation Clearly Erroneous?

We review the district court's factual findings for clear error. [ ]. The defendant argues that, even assuming that the testimony of the plaintiff's experts was admissible, the district court's finding that the Danocrine overdose more likely than not caused Mrs. Zuchowicz's illness was clearly erroneous. The defendant contends that, since Danocrine has never been previously linked to PPH, the district court's conclusion that the drug caused Mrs. Zuchowicz's illness was impermissible. For the reasons stated below, we reject the defendant's arguments.

. . .

[The court accepted that Connecticut law applied.] In addition to proving fault, "the plaintiff must establish a causal relationship between the physician's negligent actions or failure to act and the resulting injury by showing that the action or omission constituted a substantial factor in producing the injury." [ ] This "substantial factor" causation requirement is the crux of the case before us.

2.   *The Connecticut Law of Causation*

To meet the requirement that defendant's behavior was a substantial factor in bringing about the plaintiff's injury, the plaintiff must generally show: (a) that the defendant's negligent act or omission was a *but for* cause of the injury, (b) that the negligence was causally linked to the harm, and (c) that the defendant's negligent act or omission was proximate to the resulting injury. [We will consider proximate cause in the next Chapter—Eds.]

. . .

[The case before us] turns only on the difficulty of showing a *but for* cause. On whether, in other words, the plaintiff has sufficiently demonstrated: (a) that defendant's act in giving Mrs. Zuchowicz Danocrine was the source of her illness and death, and (b) that it was not just the Danocrine, but its negligent overdose that led to Mrs. Zuchowicz's demise.

. . .

4.   *Was Danocrine a But For Cause of Mrs. Zuchowicz's Illness and Death?*

[The court held that the finding that the PPH "was, more likely than not, caused by Danocrine" was not clearly erroneous. The finding was justified exclusively on the testimony of Dr. Matthay that he had excluded all causes of secondary pulmonary hypertension and all the previously known drug-related causes of PPH. In addition, he had testified that the "progression and timing of Mrs. Zuchowicz's illness in relationship to the timing of her overdose [led him to] a finding of *drug-induced* PPH to a reasonable medical certainty."]

5.   *Was the Overdose a But For Cause of Mrs. Zuchowicz's Illness and Death?*

To say that Danocrine caused Mrs. Zuchowicz's injuries is only half the story, however. In order for the causation requirement to be met, a trier of fact must be able to determine, by a preponderance of the evidence, that the defendant's *negligence* was responsible for the injury. In this case, defendant's negligence consisted in prescribing an overdose of Danocrine to Mrs. Zuchowicz. For liability to exist, therefore, it is necessary that the fact finder be able to conclude, more probably than not, that the *overdose* was the cause of Mrs. Zuchowicz's illness and ultimate death. The mere fact that the exposure to Danocrine was likely responsible for the disease does not suffice.

The problem of linking defendant's negligence to the harm that occurred is one that many courts have addressed in the past. A car is speeding and an accident occurs. That the car was involved and was a cause of the crash is readily shown. The accident, moreover, is of the sort that rules prohibiting speeding are designed to prevent. But is this enough to support a finding of fact, in the individual case, that *speeding* was, in fact, more probably than not, the cause of the accident? The same question can be asked when a car that was driving in violation of a minimum speed requirement on a super-highway is rear-ended. . . .

At one time, courts were reluctant to say in such circumstances that the wrong could be deemed to be the cause. They emphasized the logical fallacy of *post hoc, ergo propter hoc*, and demanded some direct evidence connecting the defendant's wrongdoing to the harm. See, e.g., Wolf v. Kaufmann, 237 N.Y.S. 550, 551 (App. Div. 1929)(denying recovery for death of plaintiff's decedent, who was found unconscious at foot of stairway which, in violation of a statute, was unlighted, because the plaintiff had offered no proof of "any causal connection between the accident and the absence of light").

All that has changed, however. And, as is so frequently the case in tort law, Chief Judge Cardozo in New York and Chief Justice Traynor in California led the way. In various opinions, they stated that: if (a) a negligent act was deemed wrongful because that act increased the chances that a particular type of accident would occur, and (b) a mishap of that very sort did happen, this was enough to support a finding by the trier of fact that the negligent behavior caused the harm. Where such a strong causal link exists, it is up to the negligent party to bring in evidence denying *but for* cause and suggesting that in the actual case the wrongful conduct had not been a substantial factor.

Thus, in a case involving a nighttime collision between vehicles, one of which did not have the required lights, Judge Cardozo stated that lights were mandated precisely to reduce the risk of such accidents occurring and that this fact sufficed to show causation unless the negligent party demonstrated, for example, that in the particular instance the presence of very bright street lights or of a full moon rendered the lack of lights on the vehicle an unlikely cause. See Martin v. Herzog, [reprinted at p. 76, supra]; see also Clark v. Gibbons, 426 P.2d 525, 542 (Cal. 1967)(Traynor, C.J., concurring in part and dissenting in part on other grounds).

. . .

The case before us is a good example of the above-mentioned principles in their classic form. The reason the FDA does not approve the prescription of new drugs at above the dosages as to which extensive tests have been performed is because all drugs involve risks of untoward side effects in those who take them. Moreover, it is often true that the higher the dosage the greater is the likelihood of such negative effects. At the approved dosages, the benefits of the particular drug have presumably been deemed worth the risks it entails. At greater than approved dosages, not only do the risks of tragic side effects (known and unknown) increase, but there is no basis on the testing that has been performed for supposing that the drug's benefits outweigh these increased risks. See generally 21 U.S.C. § 355(d)(indicating that the FDA should refuse to approve a new drug unless the clinical tests show that the drug is safe and effective for use under the conditions "prescribed, recommended, or suggested in the proposed labeling"). It follows that when a negative side effect is demonstrated to be the result of a drug, and the drug was wrongly prescribed in an unapproved and excessive dosage (i.e. a strong causal link has been shown), the plaintiff who is injured has generally shown enough to permit the finder of fact to conclude that the excessive dosage was a substantial factor in producing the harm.

In fact, plaintiff's showing in the case before us, while relying on the above stated principles, is stronger. For plaintiff introduced some direct evidence of causation as well. On the basis of his long experience with drug-induced pulmonary diseases, one of plaintiff's experts, Dr. Matthay, testified that the timing of Mrs. Zuchowicz's illness led him to conclude that the overdose (and not merely Danocrine) was responsible for her catastrophic reaction.

Under the circumstances, we hold that defendant's attack on the district court's finding of causation is meritless.

[The court rejected challenges to the damage award and affirmed.]

NOTES AND QUESTIONS

1.   How does the court support the conclusion that there was sufficient evidence that Danocrine was a "but for" cause in the death? Would your analysis be affected if it turned out that the "exogenous agents" cited in the opinion taken as a group accounted for only 50 of the 197 reported cases—with the cause "unknown" in the remaining 147 cases? Why does the plaintiff have to show that it was the overdose that was causally related to the death? What argument might the plaintiff make that causation is satisfied if the appropriate dose was sufficient to cause the decedent's PPH?

2.   The court states at one point that when a negligent act increases the risk that a particular type of accident would occur and such an accident does occur, the defendant must come forward with evidence negating causation, in effect adopting a rebuttable presumption of causation. In what negligence cases would this presumption of causation not be invoked?

In Williams v. Utica College of Syracuse University, 453 F.3d 112 (2d Cir.2006), plaintiff, a college student, was sexually assaulted in her dorm room. She sued the college, alleging it should have had better security to keep intruders from entering the building. The causal issue was whether better security would have prevented the attack. The difficulty is that the individual who committed the assault could have been either an outsider or someone who lived within the dormitory. One might have thought that the "increasing the risk" language of *Zuchowicz* would save the day for the plaintiff who had no evidence about the assaulter. But that is not the case, the court, per Calabresi, J., held. Summary judgment was properly granted against the plaintiff based on her inability to prove causation. The court retreated from the burden shifting in *Zuchowicz*. Three factors bear on whether a plaintiff can satisfy the burden of proof on causation based only on the negligent act and inference: 1) circumstantial evidence; 2) the relative ability of the parties to obtain evidence about what happened; and 3) whether the case is one in which there is reason to have different concerns about errors favoring plaintiffs as opposed to defendants. Does this case provide a significant restriction on the presumption rule adopted in *Zuchowicz*? Do the three factors identified by the *Williams* court provide a convincing basis for distinguishing *Williams* from *Zuchowicz*?

In Abraham, Self-Proving Causation, 99 Va.L.Rev. 1811 (2013), the author assesses the use of increased risk as the basis for an inference of causation, concluding that it may be appropriate in those instances when the negligence substantially increases the risk of harm. How substantial an increase in risk should be required? Recall the preponderance standard of proof set out in note 1, p. 342 supra.

3. What is the court suggesting when it discusses "the logical fallacy of *post hoc, ergo propter hoc*"? If a person falls down in a darkened hallway, who should bear the burden of proving whether darkness was the actual cause of the fall? Compare the cited case of *Wolf v. Kaufmann* with Hinman v. Sobocienski, 808 P.2d 820 (Alaska 1991), in which a tenant who was found injured at the foot of a flight of stairs proved only that the stairs were "unreasonably dangerous and that she was found injured at its bottom. She introduced no further evidence, however, tending to show that the condition of the stairway contributed to her injuries." The trial court granted a directed verdict for the defendant landlord because there was no showing that she had fallen due to the condition rather than that she was thrown down the stairs or had jumped—though nothing in the record suggested these possibilities. The Alaska supreme court, 4–1, reversed:

> Common experience . . . suggests that the presence in a bar/apartment building of a dangerous, dimly lighted staircase greatly increases the chances that a patron or resident will accidentally fall and suffer injury. When a resident is then found injured at the bottom of those stairs, a reasonable inference is that the dangerous condition more likely than not played a substantial part in the mishap. "The court can scarcely overlook the fact that the injury which has in fact occurred is precisely the sort of thing that proper care on the part of the defendant would be intended to prevent." [ ] The absence of evidence that the

plaintiff fell—rather than jumped or was pushed—does not negate the reasonableness of the inference.

Assume a fall down a flight of negligently unlighted interior stairs with no further evidence. Compare two analyses: (a) the proof is sufficient because, although we know that individuals fall down lighted stairways, falls occur more frequently due to unlighted stairways; and (b) since individuals often fall down lighted stairs, we would have to engage in impermissible speculation as to whether the lack of light or other potential causes were responsible for the fall. In what way is the problem in *Wolf* and *Hinman* like the problem confronted in the section on res ipsa loquitur, p. 91 supra? In what way are these different problems?

4. The *Zuchowicz* court suggests that epidemiology would be preferable proof of causation if it were available. Why? Why don't courts seek epidemiology when an individual such as the plaintiffs in *Wolf* or *Hinman* falls down a flight of stairs and suffers, say, broken bones? Consider another difference between toxic and traumatic injury cases: Plaintiff in *Zuchowicz* called two expert witnesses to testify on causation. Would an expert on causation be required in an auto accident case in which the plaintiff suffers a fractured skull?

In Estate of Joshua T. v. State, 840 A.2d 768 (N.H.2003), suit was brought against the state social services department for negligence in placement on behalf of a foster child who committed suicide. The court required expert testimony about the causal connection and generalized: "In particular, expert testimony is necessary to establish causation 'if any inference of the requisite causal link must depend [upon] observation and analysis outside the common experience of jurors.' . . . Lay testimony suffices, however, 'only if the cause and effect are so immediate, direct and natural to common experience as to obviate any need for an expert medical opinion.' "

5. *Substantial factor.* The *Zuchowicz* court, like many others, employs the "substantial factor" test for causation. (Often, as in *Zuchowicz*, courts employ that rule to encompass both factual cause and proximate cause; we limit discussion here to the former.) As the court notes, but-for causation is required before a substantial factor exists. The latter test, rather than the but-for standard, was first adopted in the Restatement of Torts for two reasons. One is to supplement the but-for test when there are multiple sufficient causes, recall note at p. 346 supra following *Stubbs*. The other reason for its adoption was that some causes are so insignificant that they should not "count" and subject the sources responsible for them to liability. See Restatement of Torts (Second) §§ 431–32. But isn't any cause at least a necessary condition, without which the harm would not have occurred? To put the point differently, isn't the straw that breaks a camel's back a factual cause of the broken back?

In June v. Union Carbide Corp., 577 F.3d 1234 (10th Cir.2009), a hazardous waste case arising from the disposal of uranium from mining and milling operations that allegedly caused radiation injuries, plaintiffs argued that a substantial factor test was appropriate. The court rejected that argument, and in the process, employed the Third Restatement, returning to the basics of causation. The court explained the differences among multiple necessary conditions (no need for substantial factor), multiple sufficient conditions (where substantial factor was used in the Second Restatement), and multiple competing potential causes (i.e., the *Stubbs* case). This case, however, does not involve multiple sufficient causes, so even the Second Restatement's substantial factor test is inapplicable. The court also concurred with the Third Restatement's assessment that a substantial factor test is a poor means to deal with multiple sufficient causes. See Restatement (Third) of Torts: Liability for Physical and Emotional Harm § 26, cmt. j (2010); see also Stapleton, Legal Cause: Cause-in-Fact and the Scope of Liability for Consequences, 54 Vand.L.Rev. 941 (2001)("obfuscating terminology of . . . substantial factor should be replaced"). The Third Restatement, in section 27, provides that where there are multiple independent and sufficient causes, each is a factual cause notwithstanding the failure to satisfy the but-for standard.

The admissibility of expert testimony about causation: The Daubert *case.*

In virtually every case involving a toxic exposure claim, plaintiffs rely on scientific or medical experts to establish that the exposure was in fact the cause of the plaintiff's harm. As toxic tort litigation has proliferated, there has been great controversy over threshold questions of standards of reliability and relevance that are to guide the trial court in determining expert qualifications. For sharp criticism of the courts, see P. Huber, Galileo's Revenge: Junk Science in the Courtroom (1991); see also M. Angell, Science on Trial: The Clash of Medical Evidence and the Law in the Breast Implant Case (1996).

Traditionally, the dominant approach to admissibility, as the court notes, had been the *Frye* test, requiring that scientific evidence be based on techniques generally regarded as reliable in the scientific community. But in *Daubert*, one of the many cases in which Bendectin, a morning-sickness drug, was alleged to have caused birth defects, the Court held that Federal Rule of Evidence 702 set a more easily satisfied standard of qualification. As the Court notes, the rule provides:

> If scientific, technical, or other specialized knowledge will assist the trier of fact to understand the evidence or to determine a fact in issue, a witness qualified as an expert by knowledge, skill, experience, training, or education, may testify thereto. . . .

The Court concluded that Rule 702 entailed "a preliminary assessment of whether the reasoning or methodology underlying the testimony is scientifically valid and of whether that reasoning or methodology properly can be applied to the facts in issue." This created a judicial "gatekeeping role" that might take general scientific acceptability into account, but that dictated an inquiry beyond scientific orthodoxy in the search for relevance and reliability.

Note the *Daubert* four-factor test for determining relevance and reliability of proposed expert witnesses, mentioned in *Zuchowicz*. What are the underlying suppositions of the test about the kinds of evidence that experts will rely upon? Can the testimony of Drs. Matthay and Tackett be analyzed under the *Daubert* criteria?

In the cited *General Electric Co. v. Joiner*, the Supreme Court held that the standard for review of trial court decisions to admit or reject expert testimony under *Daubert* should be "abuse of discretion."

Then, in Kumho Tire Co. v. Carmichael, 526 U.S. 137 (1999), the Court elaborated further on *Daubert*. Here the trial judge had excluded an expert's testimony about why a tire blew out. On appeal from a defense verdict and judgment, the court of appeals reversed. In turn, the Supreme Court reversed. For the majority, Justice Breyer situated the case as follows:

> This case requires us to decide how *Daubert* applies to the testimony of engineers and other experts who are not scientists. We conclude that *Daubert*'s general holding—setting forth the trial judge's general "gatekeeping" obligation— applies not only to testimony based on "scientific" knowledge, but also to testimony based on "technical" and "other specialized" knowledge. [ ] We also conclude that a trial court may consider one or more of the more specific factors that *Daubert* mentioned when doing so will help determine that testimony's reliability. But, as the Court stated in *Daubert*, the test of reliability is "flexible," and *Daubert*'s list of specific factors neither necessarily nor exclusively applies to all experts or in every case. Rather, the law grants a district court the same broad latitude when it decides how to determine reliability as it enjoys in respect to its ultimate reliability determination. See [*Joiner*] (courts of appeals are to apply "abuse of discretion" standard when reviewing district court's reliability determination). Applying these standards, we determine that the District Court's decision in this case—not to admit certain expert testimony—was within its discretion and therefore lawful.

The expert sought to identify a set of factors that one must consider in deciding why a tire blew out. If a certain number of those factors are present, the expert would conclude a defect in the tire caused the blowout. In the actual case, this process led him to attribute the blowout to defective manufacturing even though the tire in question had been worn down to the point that it had no tread at all along parts of it and at least two prior punctures had been inadequately repaired. Justice Breyer noted:

The particular issue in this case concerned the use of [expert witness] Carlson's two-factor test and his related use of visual/tactile inspection to draw conclusions on the basis of what seemed small observational differences. We have found no indication in the record that other experts in the industry use Carlson's two-factor test or that tire experts such as Carlson normally make the very fine distinctions about, say, the symmetry of comparatively greater shoulder tread wear that were necessary, on Carlson's own theory, to support his conclusions. Nor, despite the prevalence of tire testing, does anyone refer to any articles or papers that validate Carlson's approach. [ ] Indeed, no one has argued that Carlson himself, were he still working for Michelin, would have concluded in a report to his employer that a similar tire was similarly defective on grounds identical to those upon which he rested his conclusion here. Of course, Carlson himself claimed that his method was accurate, but, as we pointed out in *Joiner* "nothing in either *Daubert* or the Federal Rules of Evidence requires a district court to admit opinion evidence that is connected to existing data only by the *ipse dixit* of the expert." [ ]

Three justices concurred in a short opinion by Justice Scalia:

I join the opinion of the Court, which makes clear that the discretion it endorses—trial-court discretion in choosing the manner of testing expert reliability—is not discretion to abandon the gatekeeping function. I think it worth adding that it is not discretion to perform the function inadequately. Rather, it is discretion to choose among reasonable means of excluding expertise that is *fausse* and science that is junky. Though, as the Court makes clear today, the *Daubert* factors are not holy writ, in a particular case the failure to apply one or another of them may be unreasonable, and hence an abuse of discretion.

Does the *Daubert* test, as articulated in these cases, appear to establish a more or less liberal standard than *Frye* for qualifying experts? See L. Dixon & B. Gill, Changes in the Standards for Admitting Expert Evidence in Federal Civil Cases Since the *Daubert* Decision (2001)(examining federal trial court civil case opinions and finding that after *Daubert* more expert opinions were found unreliable and excluded; however, whether that increased screening improved outcomes "has not been determined"). The *Daubert* decision has spawned an extensive literature. For a flavor of some of that work, see, e.g., Flores et al., Examining the Effects of the *Daubert* Trilogy on Expert Evidence Practices in Federal Civil Court: An Empirical Analysis, 34 S.Ill.U.L.J. 533 (2010)(surveying prior empirical work on the effect of *Daubert* and extending that work by examining broader set of one state's cases); Cheng & Yoon, Does *Frye* or *Daubert* Matter? A Study of Scientific Admissibility Standards, 91 Va.L.Rev. 471 (2005)(suggesting "the real contribution of the *Daubert* decision was not in creating a new doctrinal test, but rather in raising the overall awareness of judges . . . to the problem of unreliable or 'junk' science"); Risinger, Navigating Expert Reliability: Are Criminal Standards of Certainty Being Left on the Dock?, 64 Alb.L.Rev. 99 (2000)(concluding *Daubert* has had much greater impact in screening experts in civil cases as opposed to criminal cases).

Since *Daubert* is interpreting a federal rule, state courts may adopt it, continue to adhere to *Frye,* or employ some other standard. See, e.g., Howerton v. Arai Helmet, Ltd., 597 S.E.2d 674 (N.C.2004)(rejecting *Daubert* and instead using a "flexible system" to assess the foundational reliability of expert testimony). See also Cheng & Yoon, supra (concluding, tentatively, that based on an empirical analysis of decisions, whether a state uses *Frye* or *Daubert* does not make a practical difference in decisions on the admissibility of expert opinions).

————

By contrast with *Zuchowicz* and the difficulties of proof of causation with toxic substances, the next case presents a different problem. Plaintiff in these "lost chance" or "lost opportunity" cases is attempting to show that the defendant's negligence failed to prevent an unfavorable outcome. The plaintiff, however, cannot meet the traditional burden of demonstrating by a preponderance of the evidence that, had the defendant acted non-negligently, the harm would not have occurred.

Matsuyama v. Birnbaum

Supreme Judicial Court of Massachusetts, 2008.
890 N.E.2d 819.

■ MARSHALL, C.J.

We are asked to determine whether Massachusetts law permits recovery for a "loss of chance" in a medical malpractice wrongful death action, where a jury found that the defendant physician's negligence deprived the plaintiff's decedent of a less than even chance of surviving cancer. We answer in the affirmative. As we later explain more fully, the loss of chance doctrine views a person's prospects for surviving a serious medical condition as something of value, even if the possibility of recovery was less than even prior to the physician's tortious conduct. Where a physician's negligence reduces or eliminates the patient's prospects for achieving a more favorable medical outcome, the physician has harmed the patient and is liable for damages. Permitting recovery for loss of chance is particularly appropriate in the area of medical negligence. Our decision today is limited to such claims.

The case before us was tried before a jury ... that found the defendant physician negligent in misdiagnosing the condition of the decedent over a period of approximately three years. They found as well that the physician's negligence was a "substantial contributing factor" to the decedent's death. They awarded $160,000 to the decedent's estate for the pain and suffering caused by the physician's negligence, and $328,125 to the decedent's widow and son for the decedent's loss of chance. The defendants appealed, asserting, among other things, that loss of chance was not cognizable under the Massachusetts wrongful death statute, [ ] or otherwise.

. . .

1. *Background.* [Because the plaintiff won before the jury, the court related the facts in a light most favorable to the plaintiff. Defendant, Dr. Birnbaum, was the primary-care physician of the decedent, Matsuyama from July 1995 until his death, in 1999. Matsuyama had complained about gastric distress dating back to 1988 and reiterated his problem at his first appointment with Birnbaum. Birnbaum knew that Matsuyama, a person of Asian ancestry who had lived there for 24 years and was a smoker, had a risk of gastric cancer 10 to 20 times the risk of the average American. Nevertheless, Birnbaum only conducted a physical examination and did not order any tests to determine the cause of Matsuyama's complaints. Birnbaum diagnosed Matsuyama with reflux and recommended over-the-counter medications to relieve Matsuyama's symptoms. Birnbaum did the same again when Matsuyama returned complaining of even more severe heartburn.

Matsuyama also went to Birnbaum to inquire about moles that had developed on his body. Birnbaum concluded that they were benign, common, and "not something that I would [have] overly been that fearful of." Later, Matsuyama presented with a mole over his left eye and related an urgent care facility visit he had had the month before for severe stomach pain. Birnbaum then ordered a test for a bacteria, H. pylori, associated with several diseases, including gastric cancer. The test came back positive, but Birnbaum still did not order tests that would confirm Birnbaum's then working diagnosis of gastritis, a non-malignant irritation of the stomach lining.]

[O]n May 3, 1999, . . . Matsuyama went to Birnbaum complaining of epigastric pain, vomiting, sudden weight loss, and premature feelings of fullness after eating. Birnbaum ordered a gastrointestinal series and an abdominal ultrasound, which revealed a two-centimeter mass in Matsuyama's stomach. Subsequent medical procedures confirmed the presence of [gastric cancer] from which Matsuyama died in October 1999.

In June, 2000, the plaintiff filed suit against Birnbaum. . . . Trial began in the Superior Court in July, 2004. The jury heard testimony from, among others, the plaintiff's expert witness, Dr. Stuart Ira Finkel, a gastroenterologist. Finkel testified that, in his opinion, Birnbaum breached the applicable standard of care in evaluating and treating Matsuyama, resulting in Matsuyama's death. Specifically, Finkel opined that, in light of Matsuyama's complaints, symptoms, and risk factors, including the presence of H. pylori, his Japanese ancestry, his having lived in Japan or Korea for extended periods, his smoking history, and other well-known risk factors, an internist exercising the expected standard of care would have ordered an upper gastrointestinal series X-ray or an endoscopy, or referred Matsuyama to a specialist for endoscopy, beginning in 1995. The expert also testified that the appearance of Matsuyama's [moles] in September, 1997, "could have and should have" triggered a suspicion of stomach cancer "right then and there." Finkel told the jury that if Birnbaum had ordered the appropriate testing on Matsuyama in 1995, the cancer "would have been diagnosed" and "treated in a timely fashion when it might still have been curable." As a result of Birnbaum's failure to make a timely diagnosis, Finkel opined, the cancer metastasized to an advanced, inoperable phase, resulting in Matsuyama's premature death.

[Gastric cancer is classified in stages, ranging from 0 to 4. The higher the stage the less likely a victim will survive and remain cancer free for five years. Survival rates range from 90% for stage 0 to between 30% and 50% for stage 2 and less than 4% for stage 4.] Finkel opined that, as a result of Birnbaum's breach of the standard of care, Matsuyama lost the opportunity of having gastric cancer "diagnosed and treated in a timely fashion when it might still have been curable."

. . .

After a six-day trial, the case went to the jury. [T]he jury found Birnbaum negligent in Matsuyama's treatment . . . They also found that Birnbaum's negligence was a "substantial contributing factor" to Matsuyama's death,[20] and awarded Matsuyama's estate $160,000 for pain and suffering caused by the negligence. Then, in response to a special jury question, [ ], the jury awarded damages for loss of chance, which they calculated as follows: they awarded $875,000 as "full" wrongful death damages [based on the loss of 18 additional years of work and 28 years of life], and found that Matsuyama was suffering from stage 2 adenocarcinoma at the time of Birnbaum's initial negligence and had a 37.5% chance of survival at that time. They awarded the plaintiff "final" loss of chance damages of $328,125 ($875,000 multiplied by .375) [along with the $160,000 for pain and suffering].

2.   *Loss of chance.* Although we address the issue for the first time today, a substantial and growing majority of the States that have

---

[20]   The judge instructed the jury that "substantial" "doesn't mean that Mr. Matsuyama's chance of survival was [50%] or greater, only that there was a fair chance of survival or cure had Dr. Birnbaum not been negligent and had he conformed to the applicable standard of care."

considered the question have indorsed the loss of chance doctrine, in one form or another, in medical malpractice actions [the court listed 20 states in which the highest court had adopted lost chance and 10 in which the highest court had refused to do so]. We join that majority to ensure that the fundamental aims and principles of our tort law remain fully applicable to the modern world of sophisticated medical diagnosis and treatment.

The development of the loss of chance doctrine offers a window into why it is needed. The doctrine originated in dissatisfaction with the prevailing "all or nothing" rule of tort recovery. See generally King, Jr., Causation, Valuation, and Chance in Personal Injury Torts Involving Preexisting Conditions and Future Consequences, 90 Yale L.J. 1353, 1365–1366 (1981)(King I). Under the all or nothing rule, a plaintiff may recover damages only by showing that the defendant's negligence more likely than not caused the ultimate outcome, in this case the patient's death; if the plaintiff meets this burden, the plaintiff then recovers 100% of her damages. Thus, if a patient had a 51% chance of survival, and the negligent misdiagnosis or treatment caused that chance to drop to zero, the estate is awarded *full* wrongful death damages. On the other hand, if a patient had a 49% chance of survival, and the negligent misdiagnosis or treatment caused that chance to drop to zero, the plaintiff receives nothing. So long as the patient's chance of survival before the physician's negligence was less than even, it is logically impossible for her to show that the physician's negligence was the but-for cause of her death, so she can recover nothing. Thus, the all or nothing rule provides a "blanket release from liability for doctors and hospitals any time there was less than a 50 percent chance of survival, regardless of how flagrant the negligence." [ ]

As many courts and commentators have noted, the all or nothing rule is inadequate to advance the fundamental aims of tort law. [ ] Fundamentally, the all or nothing approach does not serve the basic aim of "fairly allocating the costs and risks of human injuries," [ ]. The all or nothing rule "fails to deter" medical negligence because it immunizes "whole areas of medical practice from liability." [ ] It fails to provide the proper incentives to ensure that the care patients receive does not slip below the "standard of care and skill of the average member of the profession practicing the specialty." [ ] And the all or nothing rule fails to ensure that victims, who incur the real harm of losing their opportunity for a better outcome, are fairly compensated for their loss. [ ]

[Handwritten margin note: Why the all or nothing case is not great]

. . .

Courts adopting the loss of chance doctrine also have noted that, because a defendant's negligence effectively made it impossible to know whether the person would have achieved a more favorable outcome had he received the appropriate standard of care, it is particularly unjust to deny the person recovery for being unable "to demonstrate to an absolute certainty what would have happened in circumstances that the wrongdoer did not allow to come to pass." [ ]

. . .

Addressing the specific arguments advanced by the defendants is useful for delineating the proper shape of the doctrine. The defendants argue that the loss of chance doctrine "lowers the threshold of proof of causation" by diluting the preponderance of the evidence standard that "has been the bedrock of the Massachusetts civil justice system." Some courts have indeed approached the issue of how to recognize loss of chance by carving out an exception to the rule that the plaintiff must prove by a preponderance of the evidence that the defendant "caused" his injuries. See, e.g., [ ] (adopting rule that "permits the case to go to the jury on the issue of causation with less definite evidence of probability than the ordinary tort case," and requiring jury to "find for the defendant unless they find a *probability* that defendant's negligence was a cause of plaintiff's injury" [emphasis in original]). We reject this approach. "It is fundamental that the plaintiff bears the burden of establishing causation by a preponderance of the evidence." [ ] Therefore, in a case involving loss of chance, as in any other negligence context, a plaintiff must establish by a preponderance of the evidence that the defendant caused his injury.

However, "injury" need not mean a patient's death. Although there are few certainties in medicine or in life, progress in medical science now makes it possible, at least with regard to certain medical conditions, to estimate a patient's probability of survival to a reasonable degree of medical certainty. [ ] That probability of survival is part of the patient's condition. When a physician's negligence diminishes or destroys a patient's chance of survival, the patient has suffered real injury. The patient has lost something of great value: a chance to survive, to be cured, or otherwise to achieve a more favorable medical outcome. [ ] Thus we recognize loss of chance not as a theory of causation, but as a theory of injury. [ ] Recognizing loss of chance as a theory of injury is consistent with our law of causation, which requires that plaintiffs establish causation by a preponderance of the evidence. [ ] In order to prove loss of chance, a plaintiff must prove by a preponderance of the evidence that the physician's negligence caused the plaintiff's likelihood of achieving a more favorable outcome to be diminished. That is, the plaintiff must prove by a preponderance of the evidence that the physician's negligence caused the plaintiff's injury, where the injury consists of the diminished likelihood of achieving a more favorable medical outcome. . . .

We reject the defendants' contention that a statistical likelihood of survival is a "mere possibility" and therefore "speculative." The magnitude of a probability is distinct from the degree of confidence with which it can be estimated. A statistical survival rate cannot conclusively determine whether a particular patient will survive a medical condition. But survival rates are not random guesses. They are estimates based on data obtained and analyzed scientifically and accepted by the relevant medical community as part of the repertoire of diagnosis and treatment, as applied to the specific facts of the plaintiff's case. [ ] Where credible evidence establishes that the plaintiff's or decedent's probability of survival is 49%, that conclusion is no more speculative than a conclusion, based on similarly credible evidence, that the probability of survival is 51%.

The defendants also point out that "[t]he cause, treatment, cure and survivability related to cancer is tremendously uncertain and complex," and argue that loss of chance is "rife with practical complexities and problems." Such difficulties are not confined to loss of chance claims. A wide range of medical malpractice cases, as well as numerous other tort actions, are complex and involve actuarial or other probabilistic estimates. Wrongful death claims, for example, often require, as part of the damages calculation, an estimate of how long the decedent might have lived absent the defendant's conduct. . . .

The key is the reliability of the evidence available to the fact finder. As we noted above, at least for certain conditions, medical science has progressed to the point that physicians can gauge a patient's chances of survival to a reasonable degree of medical certainty, and indeed routinely use such statistics as a tool of medicine. [ ] Reliable modern techniques of gathering and analyzing medical data have made it possible for fact finders to determine based on expert testimony—rather than speculate based on insufficient evidence—whether a negligent failure to diagnose a disease injured a patient by preventing the disease from being treated at an earlier stage, when prospects were more favorable. . . . Through appropriate expert evidence, a plaintiff in a medical malpractice case may be able to sustain her burden of showing that, as a result of defendant's negligence, a decedent suffered a diminished likelihood of achieving a more favorable medical outcome.

We are unmoved by the defendants' argument that "the ramifications of adoption of loss of chance are immense" across "all areas of tort." We emphasize that our decision today is limited to loss of chance in medical malpractice actions. Such cases are particularly well suited to application of the loss of chance doctrine.[33] See Restatement (Third) of Torts: Liability for Physical Harm § 26 comment n (Proposed Final Draft No. 1, 2005)(Draft Restatement). First, as we noted above, reliable expert evidence establishing loss of chance is more likely to be available in a medical malpractice case than in some other domains of tort law. *Id.* Second, medical negligence that harms the patient's chances of a more favorable outcome contravenes the expectation at the heart of the doctor-patient relationship that "the physician will take every reasonable measure to obtain an optimal outcome for the patient."

---

[33] We do not decide today whether a plaintiff may recover on a loss of chance theory when the ultimate harm (such as death) has not yet come to pass. [ ]

Id. See K.S. Abraham, Forms and Functions of Tort Law 117–118 (3d ed. 2007)(discussing argument that "health care providers undertake to maximize a patient's chances of survival, [and so] their failure to do so should be actionable. Ordinary actors who negligently risk causing harm have not undertaken such a duty"). Third, it is not uncommon for patients to have a less than even chance of survival or of achieving a better outcome when they present themselves for diagnosis, so the shortcomings of the all or nothing rule are particularly widespread. Finally, failure to recognize loss of chance in medical malpractice actions forces the party who is the least capable of preventing the harm to bear the consequences of the more capable party's negligence. [ ]

In sum, whatever difficulties may attend recognizing loss of chance as an item of damages in a medical malpractice action, these difficulties are far outweighed by the strong reasons to adopt the doctrine. . . .

. . .

4. *Damages.* Our conclusion that loss of chance is a separate, compensable item of damages in an action for medical malpractice does not fully resolve the issues on appeal. We must consider, among other things, how the loss of the likelihood of a more favorable outcome is to be valued. The first question is *what* is being valued. In this case, the patient's prospects for achieving a more favorable outcome were measured in terms of the patient's likelihood of surviving for a number of years specified by the relevant medical standard: for gastric cancer, the five-year survival rate. There is no single measure that will apply uniformly to all medical malpractice cases. [ ] Precisely what yardstick to use to measure the reduction in the decedent's prospects for survival—life expectancy, five-year survival, ten-year survival, and so on—is a question on which the law must inevitably bow to some extent to the shape of the available medical evidence in each particular case. [ ]

A second, more challenging issue is how to calculate the monetary value for the lost chance. . . . Under the proportional damages approach, loss of chance damages are measured as "the percentage probability by which the defendant's tortious conduct diminished the likelihood of achieving some more favorable outcome." [ ] The formula aims to ensure that a defendant is liable in damages only for the monetary value of the *portion* of the decedent's prospects that the defendant's negligence destroyed. In applying the proportional damages method, the court must first measure the monetary value of the patient's full life expectancy and, if relevant, work life expectancy as it would in any wrongful death case. But the defendant must then be held liable only for the portion of that value that the defendant's negligence destroyed. [ ]

Deriving the damages for which the physician is liable will require the fact finder to undertake the following calculations:[41]

(1) The fact finder must first calculate the total amount of damages allowable for the death under the wrongful death statute, [ ], or, in the case of medical malpractice not resulting in death, the full amount of damages allowable for the injury. This is the amount to which the decedent would be entitled if the case were *not* a loss of chance case: the full amount of compensation for the decedent's death or injury.

(2) The fact finder must next calculate the patient's chance of survival or cure immediately preceding ... the medical malpractice.

(3) The fact finder must then calculate the chance of survival or cure that the patient had as a result of the medical malpractice.

(4) The fact finder must then subtract the amount derived in step 3 from the amount derived in step 2.

(5) The fact finder must then multiply the amount determined in step 1 by the percentage calculated in step 4 to derive the proportional damages award for loss of chance.

how to calculate damages

To illustrate, suppose in a wrongful death case that a jury found, based on expert testimony and the facts of the case, that full wrongful death damages would be $600,000 (step 1), that the patient had a 45% chance of survival prior to the medical malpractice (step 2), and that the physician's tortious acts reduced the chances of survival to 15% (step 3). The patient's chances of survival were reduced 30% (i.e., 45% minus 15%) due to the physician's malpractice (step 4), and the patient's loss of chance damages would be $600,000 multiplied by 30%, for a total of $180,000 (step 5). [ ]

. . .

5. *Evidence of causation. . . .*

The defendants claim that the evidence was insufficient to show that, as the judge instructed the jury, "an act or omission of Birnbaum was a substantially contributing factor to the death of Mr. Matsuyama." The "substantial contributing factor" test is useful in cases in which damage has multiple causes, including but not limited to cases with multiple tortfeasors in which it may be impossible to say for certain that any *individual* defendant's conduct was a but-for cause of the

---

[41] [The court explained that there are two categories of pain and suffering that a lost chance plaintiff might suffer. First, the delay in treatment may cause pain and suffering greater than would have been incurred in the absence of malpractice and prompt treatment. Second, there is the pain and suffering that any victim of gastric cancer would suffer in the course of death. The first category would not be subject to discount by the lost chance percentage, while the second category would. Here, the court found that the jury was only instructed on and awarded damages for the first category.]

harm, even though it can be shown that the defendants, in the aggregate, caused the harm. The substantial contributing factor test is less appropriate, however, as an instruction as to cause in a loss of chance case in which one defendant's malpractice alone is alleged to have caused the victim's diminished likelihood of a more favorable outcome. The proper test in a loss of chance case concerning the conduct of a single defendant is whether that conduct was the but-for cause of the loss of chance.

In the circumstances of this case, the judge's use of the "substantial contributing factor" test did not prejudice the defendant. The judge instructed the jury that the word "substantial" "doesn't mean that Mr. Matsuyama's chance of survival was fifty percent or greater, only that there was a fair chance of survival or cure had Dr. Birnbaum not been negligent and had he conformed to the applicable standard of care." The judge's formulation did not use the words "but-for cause," but his definition of "substantial" clearly focused the jury's attention on the idea that Birnbaum's negligence, if any, had to be a but-for cause of Matsuyama's losing a "fair chance of survival."

. . .

Judgment affirmed.

NOTES AND QUESTIONS

1.   What is the difference between asking whether the plaintiff (1) proved that because of D's negligence decedent lost a 37.5% chance to survive (worth $875,000), and (2) proved to a 37.5% probability that decedent died due to defendant's negligence?

2.   Suppose that if diagnosed promptly, patient's chance of survival is 99%. Because of a negligent delay in diagnosis, patient's chance of survival is reduced to 97%, and the patient dies. What is the percentage of lost opportunity of survival? What is the probability that the physician's negligence caused the patient's death?

In answering this question, consider 100 persons all of whom suffered the same delay in diagnosis. At the end of the day, how many of those 100 would have died? Of those who did die, what percentage would have died because of the negligent delay in diagnosis?

3.   The *Matsuyama* court limits its recognition of lost chance to the medical malpractice context. Are the court's reasons for doing so persuasive?

Should the lost chance approach have been available against Siegrist in *Farwell*, p. 135 supra, if there had been expert testimony that, if brought to a hospital immediately, the decedent would have had a 35% chance to survive? A 75% chance? Might the *Matsuyama* court's analysis extend to retaining a termite contractor to try to save a house from termite damage? See Hardy v. Southwestern Bell Telephone Co., 910 P.2d 1024 (Okla.1996)(refusing to extend lost chance beyond medical situations to case against telephone company alleging that failure of 911 emergency system led to death of heart-attack victim).

4.   If the jury in a case involving solely a credibility dispute concludes that it is 80% likely that the plaintiff is the one telling the truth, should it be told to award the plaintiff 80% of the agreed upon damages? See generally Levmore, Probabilistic Recoveries, Restitution, and Recurring Wrongs, 19 J. Legal Stud. 691 (1990).

5.   In footnote 33, the court states that it does not decide whether the ultimate harm, i.e., death in *Matsuyama*, must be suffered for a lost chance claim to be asserted. Does that undercut the court's claim that it is recognizing lost chance as a legally compensable harm? Most courts do not permit recovery for lost chance in this situation. See, e.g., Alberts v. Schultz, 975 P.2d 1279 (N.M.1999).

For a case permitting recovery for a lost chance before the outcome to be avoided had occurred, see Dickhoff ex rel. Dickhoff v. Green, 836 N.W.2d 321 (Minn.2013). The dissent took the majority to task for this decision:

> Imagine, for example, a patient who undergoes surgery for which the doctor negligently fails to disclose a 20% chance of death on the operating table. But the patient survives the surgery and does not die on the operating table. Although the patient surely would not have been indifferent to the increased 20% chance of death in choosing to undergo the surgery, having escaped harm the patient has not suffered a compensable injury.

Is the dissent correct that the patient has not suffered a compensable injury?

6.   If a court adopts the lost chance approach and awards proportional damages in less-than-even chance cases, should it also award proportional damages in a case in which the evidence establishes a 75% probability that the defendant's negligence caused the loss of the leg? See DeHanes v. Rothman, 727 A.2d 8 (N.J.1999), in which the jury found that if defendant physician in the emergency room had exercised due care and diagnosed decedent's heart attack, decedent would have had a 70% chance to survive. Although the case went off on other issues, the court noted in passing that the trial judge reduced the jury's verdict "to reflect the lost chance of seventy percent." Was that correct? The court in Doll v. Brown, 75 F.3d 1200 (7th Cir.1996), was much more explicit. In an employment discrimination case, the court said that if a plaintiff with a 25% chance of success can recover 25% of damages, then "he should be entitled to 75 percent of his damages if he had a 75 percent chance of survival—not 100 percent of his damages on the theory that by establishing a 75 percent chance he proved injury by a preponderance of the evidence." Despite a few cases like *Doll* and significant academic support for proportional liability, most courts have not adopted this reform, i.e., extending proportional recovery to cases where a greater than 50% likelihood of loss occurred. See, e.g., Estate of Dormaier v. Columbia Basin Anesthesia, P.L.L.C., 313 P.3d 431 (Wash.Ct.App.2013)(holding plaintiff's recovery in a similar case in which the probability of better outcome is greater than 50% is for the full amount of wrongful death damages).

The fairness concern about "one-way" proportional liability has been cited by some courts as a reason to decline adopting a lost chance theory: "If a plaintiff whose decedent had a 49% chance of survival, which was lost through negligent treatment, is permitted to recover 49% of the value of the decedent's life, then a plaintiff whose decedent had a 51% chance of survival which was lost through negligent treatment, perhaps ought to have recovery limited to 51% of the value of the life lost." Fennell v. Southern Maryland Hospital Center, Inc., 580 A.2d 206, 214 (Md.1990). The court also was concerned that the logic of lost chance would require recovery even if the plaintiff never suffered the adverse outcome, the confusion and misunderstanding that would be engendered by use of such statistics at trials, and the impact of such a change on the cost of medical services. What is the most persuasive of the Fennell reasons?

7. *Reasonable medical certainty.* Many courts require that experts state that they hold their opinions to a "reasonable degree of medical [or scientific] certainty," as the *Matsuyama* court apparently does with regard to the probability that the patient would have a successful outcome. In *Alberts*, cited in note 5 above, the court states that reasonable probability is equivalent to the preponderance-of-the-evidence standard. If that is so, then why require a witness to testify to reasonable certainty or probability? In Bara v. Clarksville Memorial Health Systems, Inc., 104 S.W.3d 1 (Tenn.Ct.App.2002), the court held that use of the reasonable-degree-of-certainty term in instructing the jury was error. Drawing on academic commentary, which criticizes the uncertainty of the term as well as the absence of any equivalent concept in the medical or scientific community, the court explained that all elements of a case, including causation established through expert testimony, must be proved by a preponderance of the evidence.

Introduction to Joint and Several Liability

The basic doctrine. So far we have been dealing with cases in which the focus was on the causal contribution of a single defendant. We turn now to cases in which more than one relevant cause may be involved in the harm that befell plaintiff. One example would be a case in which two cars collide and one of the cars goes up on the sidewalk and hits a pedestrian. The proof shows that if either driver had been careful the accident would have been averted. In other words, the negligence of each driver was essential to plaintiff's harm.

In this type of case the two drivers were traditionally held subject to "joint and several liability" (not a terribly accurate term of art). This meant that the plaintiff might sue them together or separately and recover the full extent of the damages against either one. If plaintiff's harm was $50,000, and both defendants were found negligent, the judgment traditionally provided that the plaintiff was to recover $50,000 against D1 and D2. Plaintiff could then collect the entire

$50,000 from whichever defendant plaintiff chose—usually the one from whom it was easier to collect the entire award. The plaintiff did not care whether one of the defendants was insolvent because any solvent defendant was liable for the entire award. By the mid-20th century when "contribution" claims were first recognized, a defendant that paid more than its "share" could seek contribution from the other defendant(s). At the time, shares were determined on a pro rata basis— equal shares for each defendant(s). Because the plaintiff could recover full damages in a suit against one of the drivers, joint and several liability also placed the burden of pursuing other potential tortfeasors on the defendant. This result was justified when contributory negligence barred a plaintiff from any recovery on the basis that, as between two (or more) culpable defendants and an innocent plaintiff, the defendants should bear the risk of another's insolvency.

By contrast to joint and several liability, "several liability" made each defendant liable for only its "share" of the plaintiff's harm. Insolvency, thus, is a risk borne by the plaintiff as is the burden of pursuing all responsible parties.

Since the latter part of the 20th century, there has been substantial reform to what once was a near-universal rule of joint and several liability. Today, neither joint and several liability nor several liability reflects the majority rule. Instead, more than half the states use a "hybrid" that contains elements of both of these doctrines. In Chapter VII, we elaborate on the impact of reform in this area.

B. MULTIPLE DEFENDANTS

Summers v. Tice
Supreme Court of California, 1948.
33 Cal.2d 80, 199 P.2d 1.

■ CARTER, JUSTICE [after stating the facts and upholding the negligence determinations].

[Plaintiff and defendants Tice and Simonson were hunting quail when both defendants fired in plaintiff's direction. One shot struck plaintiff's eye and another his lip. Both defendants were using the same gauge shotgun and the same size shot. The trial judge, sitting without a jury, found both defendants negligent and found that plaintiff was in no way at fault. Unable to decide which defendant's shot hit the plaintiff, the judge awarded judgment against both defendants, who appealed.]

The problem presented in this case is whether the judgment against both defendants may stand. It is argued by defendants that they are not joint tort feasors, and thus jointly and severally liable, as they were not acting in concert, and that there is not sufficient evidence to show which defendant was guilty of the negligence which caused the injuries—the shooting by Tice or that by Simonson. Tice argues that there is evidence to show that the shot which struck plaintiff came from Simonson's gun because of admissions allegedly made by him to third persons and no evidence that they came from his gun. Further in connection with the latter contention, the court failed to find on plaintiff's allegation in his complaint that he did not know which one was at fault—did not find which defendant was guilty of the negligence which caused the injuries to plaintiff.

Considering the last argument first, we believe it is clear that the court sufficiently found on the issue that defendants were jointly liable and that thus the negligence of both was the cause of the injury or to that legal effect. It found that both defendants were negligent and "That as a direct and proximate result of the shots fired by *defendants, and each of them,* a birdshot pellet was caused to and did lodge in plaintiff's right eye and that another birdshot pellet was caused to and did lodge in plaintiff's upper lip." In so doing the court evidently did not give credence to the admissions of Simonson to third persons that he fired the shots which it was justified in doing. It thus determined that the negligence of both defendants was the legal cause of the injury—or that both were responsible. Implicit in such finding is the assumption that the court was unable to ascertain whether the shots were from the gun of one defendant or the other or one shot from each of them. The one shot that entered plaintiff's eye was the major factor in assessing damages and that shot could not have come from the gun of both defendants. It was from one or the other only.

It has been held that where a group of persons are on a hunting party, or otherwise engaged in the use of firearms, and two of them are negligent in firing in the direction of a third person who is injured thereby, both of those so firing are liable for the injury suffered by the third person, although the negligence of only one of them could have caused the injury. [ ]; Oliver v. Miles, [110 So. 666 (Miss.1926)]; [ ]. The same rule has been applied in criminal cases [ ] and both drivers have been held liable for the negligence of one where they engaged in a racing contest causing an injury to a third person [ ]. These cases speak of the action of defendants as being in concert as the ground of decision, yet it would seem they are straining that concept and the more reasonable basis appears in *Oliver v. Miles,* supra. There two persons were hunting together. Both shot at some partridges and in so doing shot across the highway injuring plaintiff who was traveling on it. The court stated they were acting in concert and thus both were liable. The court then stated: "We think that . . . each is liable for the resulting injury to the boy, although no one can say definitely who actually shot him. *To hold otherwise would be to exonerate both from liability, although each was negligent, and the injury resulted from such negligence."* [Emphasis added.]

. . .

When we consider the relative position of the parties and the results that would flow if plaintiff was required to pin the injury on one of the defendants only, a requirement that the burden of proof on that subject be shifted to defendants becomes manifest. They are both wrongdoers—both negligent toward plaintiff. They brought about a situation where the negligence of one of them injured the plaintiff, hence it should rest with them each to absolve himself if he can. The injured party has been placed by defendants in the unfair position of pointing to which defendant caused the harm. If one can escape the other may also and plaintiff is remediless. Ordinarily defendants are in a far better position to offer evidence to determine which one caused the injury. This reasoning has recently found favor in this court. In a quite analogous situation this court held that a patient injured while unconscious on an operating table in a hospital could hold all or any of the persons who had any connection with the operation even though he could not select the particular acts by the particular person which led to his disability. *Ybarra v. Spangard*, [p. 101 supra]. There the court was considering whether the patient could avail himself of res ipsa loquitur, rather than where the burden of proof lay, yet the effect of the decision is that plaintiff has made out a case when he has produced evidence which gives rise to an inference of negligence which was the proximate cause of the injury. It is up to defendants to explain the cause of the injury. It was there said: "If the doctrine is to continue to serve a useful purpose, we should not forget that 'the particular force and justice of the rule, regarded as a presumption throwing upon the party charged the duty of producing evidence, consists in the circumstance that the chief evidence of the true cause, whether culpable or innocent, is practically accessible to him but inaccessible to the injured person.'" [ ] Similarly in the instant case plaintiff is not able to establish which of defendants caused his injury.

. . .

It is urged that plaintiff now has changed the theory of his case in claiming a concert of action; that he did not plead or prove such concert. From what has been said it is clear that there has been no change in theory. The joint liability, as well as the lack of knowledge as to which defendant was liable, was pleaded and the proof developed the case under either theory. We have seen that for the reasons of policy discussed herein, the case is based upon the legal proposition that, under the circumstances here presented, each defendant is liable for the whole damage whether they are deemed to be acting in concert or independently.   *holding*

The judgment is affirmed. — *disposition*

■ GIBSON, C.J., SHENK, J., EDMONDS, J., TRAYNOR, J., SCHAUER, J., and SPENCE, J., concurred.

NOTES AND QUESTIONS

1.   Under the common law before comparative fault, if the damages were $20,000, each defendant would be "jointly and severally liable" for the full amount, although plaintiff could not obtain more than one satisfaction of his $20,000 judgment. Under today's practice, the factfinder, even if unable to determine causation, would assess a comparative fault percentage for each defendant—then the state statute on joint and several (or several) liability would be applied to those findings. How might the faults differ here?

2.   Is it essential to the analysis that the two defendants were hunting as a team? What if they had been independent negligent hunters who never met one another until after the accident?

3.   How should the cause issue be analyzed if the judge found that although either pellet might have hit the plaintiff, only Tice's behavior had been negligent, so that the innocent Simonson could not be liable to plaintiff even if his pellet had done the harm? In Garcia v. Joseph Vince Co., 148 Cal.Rptr. 843 (App.1978), plaintiff fencer was hurt by a defective saber. Plaintiff could not identify which of two manufacturers was the source of the defective saber because it had been put back into a pile of sabers. His effort to invoke *Summers v. Tice* was rejected, and the case was dismissed.

4.   What result would the court reach if three defendants had fired negligently at the same time? What if only one of the three had been negligent? In what way is this latter hypothetical like *Ybarra*, p. 101 supra? In what way is it different?

5.   Suppose that one minute after Tice fired and hit Summers in the eye, blinding it, Simonson fired and hit Summers in his now-blind eye. Who would be liable for what? Suppose that, instead of Simonson firing, Summers had an incurable eye disease that would have blinded him a month after Tice shot him in the eye. For what would Tice be liable?

In the famous case of Dillon v. Twin State Gas & Electric Co., 163 A. 111 (N.H.1932), a boy lost his balance while sitting on a girder 19 feet above a bridge. In an effort to avoid falling, he grabbed hold of a negligently exposed wire and was electrocuted. The court concluded that if the jury found that the boy would have been killed by the fall without regard to the wire, any award against the defendant utility for the exposed wire should be reduced drastically. Is that sound? For extended discussion of these issues, see Dillof, Doomed Steamers and Merged Fires: The Problem of Preempted Innocent Threats in Torts, 30 Ga.St.U.L.Rev. 703 (2014).

Hymowitz v. Eli Lilly & Co.

Court of Appeals of New York, 1989.
73 N.Y.2d 487, 539 N.E.2d 1069, 541 N.Y.S.2d 941.

■ WACHTLER, CHIEF JUDGE.

Plaintiffs in these appeals allege that they were injured by the drug diethylstilbestrol (DES) ingested by their mothers during pregnancy. They seek relief against defendant DES manufacturers. While not class actions, these cases are representative of nearly 500 similar actions pending in the courts in this State; the rules articulated by the court here, therefore, must do justice and be administratively feasible in the context of this mass litigation. . . .

I.

The history of the development of DES and its marketing in this country has been repeatedly chronicled [ ]. Briefly, DES is a synthetic substance that mimics the effect of estrogen, the naturally formed female hormone. It was invented in 1937 by British researchers, but never patented.

In 1941, the Food and Drug Administration (FDA) approved the new drug applications (NDA) of 12 manufacturers to market DES for the treatment of various maladies, not directly involving pregnancy. In 1947, the FDA began approving the NDAs of manufacturers to market DES for the purpose of preventing human miscarriages; by 1951, the FDA had concluded that DES was generally safe for pregnancy use, and stopped requiring the filing of NDAs when new manufacturers sought to produce the drug for this purpose. In 1971, however, the FDA banned the use of DES as a miscarriage preventative, when studies established the harmful latent effects of DES upon the offspring of mothers who took the drug. Specifically, tests indicated that DES caused vaginal adenocarcinoma, a form of cancer, and adenosis, a precancerous vaginal or cervical growth.

Although strong evidence links prenatal DES exposure to later development of serious medical problems, plaintiffs seeking relief in court for their injuries faced two formidable and fundamental barriers to recovery in this State; not only is identification of the manufacturer of the DES ingested in a particular case generally impossible, but, due to the latent nature of DES injuries, many claims were barred by the Statute of Limitations before the injury was discovered.

The identification problem has many causes. All DES was of identical chemical composition. Druggists usually filled prescriptions from whatever was on hand. Approximately 300 manufacturers produced the drug, with companies entering and leaving the market continuously during the 24 years that DES was sold for pregnancy use. The long latency period of a DES injury compounds the identification problem; memories fade, records are lost or destroyed, and witnesses die. Thus the pregnant women who took DES generally never knew who produced the drug they took, and there was no reason to attempt to discover this fact until many years after ingestion, at which time the information is not available.

. . .

The second barrier to recovery, involving the Statute of Limitations, arose from the long-standing rule in this State that the limitations period accrued upon exposure in actions alleging personal injury caused by toxic substances. [Following a case in which the court refused to change that rule for DES cases, the legislature provided that the statute began to run upon the discovery of "the latent effects of exposure to any substance," and for one year revived causes of action for exposure to DES that had been barred.]

It is estimated that eventually 800 DES cases will be brought under the revival portion of this recent statute. . . .

The present appeals are before the court in the context of summary judgment motions. In all of the appeals defendants moved for summary judgment dismissing the complaints because plaintiffs could not identify the manufacturer of the drug that allegedly injured them. In three of the appeals defendants also moved on Statute of Limitations grounds, arguing that the revival of the actions was unconstitutional under the State and Federal Constitutions, and that the complaints, therefore, are time barred and should be dismissed. The trial court denied all of these motions. On the Statute of Limitations issue, the trial court also granted plaintiffs' cross motions, dismissing defendants' affirmative defenses that the actions were time barred. The Appellate Division affirmed in all respects and certified to this court the questions of whether the orders of the trial court were properly made. [ ] We answer these questions in the affirmative.

II.

In a products liability action, identification of the exact defendant whose product injured the plaintiff is, of course, generally required [ ]. In DES cases in which such identification is possible, actions may proceed under established principles of products liability [ ]. The record now before us, however, presents the question of whether a DES plaintiff may recover against a DES manufacturer when identification of the producer of the specific drug that caused the injury is impossible.

A.

As we noted [ ], the accepted tort doctrines of alternative liability and concerted action are available in some personal injury cases to permit recovery where the precise identification of a wrongdoer is impossible. However, we agree with the near unanimous views of the high State courts that have considered the matter that these doctrines in their unaltered common-law forms do not permit recovery in DES cases [ ].

The paradigm of alternative liability is found in the case of [*Summers v. Tice*]. In *Summers,* plaintiff and the two defendants were hunting, and defendants carried identical shotguns and ammunition. During the hunt, defendants shot simultaneously at the same bird, and plaintiff was struck by bird shot from one of the defendants' guns. The court held that where two defendants breach a duty to the plaintiff, but there is uncertainty regarding which one caused the injury, "the burden is upon each such actor to prove that he has not caused the harm" [ ]; cf., *Ravo v. Rogatnick*, ([p. 457 infra] [successive tortfeasors may be held jointly and severally liable for an injury to the plaintiff that is, practically, indivisible]). The central rationale for shifting the burden of proof in such a situation is that without this device both defendants will be silent, and plaintiff will not recover; with alternative liability, however, defendants will be forced to speak, and reveal the culpable party, or else be held jointly and severally liable themselves. Consequently, use of the alternative liability doctrine generally requires that the defendants have better access to information than does the plaintiff, and that all possible tortfeasors be before the court [ ]. It is also recognized that alternative liability rests on the notion that where there is a small number of possible wrongdoers, all of whom breached a duty to the plaintiff, the likelihood that any one of them injured the plaintiff is relatively high, so that forcing them to exonerate themselves, or be held liable, is not unfair [ ].

In DES cases, however, there is a great number of possible wrongdoers, who entered and left the market at different times, and some of whom no longer exist. Additionally, in DES cases many years elapse between the ingestion of the drug and injury. Consequently, DES defendants are not in any better position than are plaintiffs to identify the manufacturer of the DES ingested in any given case, nor is there any real prospect of having all the possible producers before the court. Finally, while it may be fair to employ alternative liability in cases involving only a small number of potential wrongdoers, that fairness disappears with the decreasing probability that any one of the defendants actually caused the injury. This is particularly true when applied to DES where the chance that a particular producer caused the injury is often very remote [ ]. Alternative liability, therefore, provides DES plaintiffs no relief.

Nor does the theory of concerted action, in its pure form, supply a basis for recovery. This doctrine, seen in drag racing cases, provides for joint and several liability on the part of all defendants having an understanding, express or tacit, to participate in "a common plan or design to commit a tortious act" [ ]. As . . . the present record reflects, drug companies were engaged in extensive parallel conduct in developing and marketing DES [ ]. There is nothing in the record, however, beyond this similar conduct to show any agreement, tacit or otherwise, to market DES for pregnancy use without taking proper steps to ensure the drug's safety. Parallel activity, without more, is insufficient to establish the agreement element necessary to maintain a concerted action claim [ ]. Thus this theory also fails in supporting an action by DES plaintiffs.

In short, extant common-law doctrines, unmodified, provide no relief for the DES plaintiff unable to identify the manufacturer of the drug that injured her. This is not a novel conclusion; in the last decade a number of courts in other jurisdictions also have concluded that present theories do not support a cause of action in DES cases. Some courts, upon reaching this conclusion, have declined to find any judicial remedy for the DES plaintiffs who cannot identify the particular manufacturer of the DES ingested by their mothers (see, Zafft v. Eli Lilly & Co., 676 S.W.2d 241 [Mo.1984] [en banc]; Mulcahy v. Eli Lilly & Co., 386 N.W.2d 67 [Iowa 1986] [stating that any change in the law to allow for recovery in nonidentification DES cases should come from the Legislature]). Other courts, however, have found that some modification of existing doctrine is appropriate to allow for relief for those injured by DES of unknown manufacture (e.g., [Sindell v. Abbott Laboratories, 607 P.2d 924 (Cal.1980) Collins v. Eli Lilly & Co., 342 N.W.2d 37 (Wis.1984); Martin v. Abbott Laboratories, 689 P.2d 368 (Wash.1984)]).

We conclude that the present circumstances call for recognition of a realistic avenue of relief for plaintiffs injured by DES. These appeals present many of the same considerations that have prompted this court in the past to modify the rules of personal injury liability, in order "to achieve the ends of justice in a more modern context" [ ], and we perceive that here judicial action is again required to overcome the " 'inordinately difficult problems of proof' " caused by contemporary products and marketing techniques [ ].

Indeed, it would be inconsistent with the reasonable expectations of a modern society to say to these plaintiffs that because of the insidious nature of an injury that long remains dormant, and because so many manufacturers, each behind a curtain, contributed to the devastation, the cost of injury should be borne by the innocent and not the wrongdoers. This is particularly so where the Legislature consciously created these expectations by reviving hundreds of DES cases. Consequently, the ever-evolving dictates of justice and fairness, which are the heart of our common-law system, require formation of a remedy for injuries caused by DES [ ].

We stress, however, that the DES situation is a singular case, with manufacturers acting in a parallel manner to produce an identical, generically marketed product, which causes injury many years later, and which has evoked a legislative response reviving previously barred actions. Given this unusual scenario, it is more appropriate that the loss be borne by those that produced the drug for use during pregnancy, rather than by those who were injured by the use, even where the precise manufacturer of the drug cannot be identified in a particular action. We turn then to the question of how to fairly and equitably apportion the loss occasioned by DES, in a case where the exact manufacturer of the drug that caused the injury is unknown.

B.

The past decade of DES litigation has produced a number of alternative approaches to resolve this question. Thus, in a sense, we are now in an enviable position; the efforts of other courts provided examples for contending with this difficult issue, and enough time has passed so that the actual administration and real effects of these solutions now can be observed. With these useful guides in hand, a path may be struck for our own conclusion.

[The court decided to adopt a version of the market share concept. In *Sindell*—the first case to adopt such an approach—the "central justification" was the "belief that limiting a defendant's liability to its market share will result, over the run of cases, in liability on the part of a defendant roughly equal to the injuries the defendant actually caused." After *Sindell*, the California court held, in Brown v. Superior Court, 751 P.2d 470 (Cal.1988), that a manufacturer's liability is several only, and, in cases in which all manufacturers in the market are not joined for any reason, liability will still be limited to market share, resulting in a less than 100% recovery for a plaintiff. The *Hymowitz* court also noted that determining the market shares in the years after *Sindell* "proved difficult and engendered years of litigation. After attempts at using smaller geographical units, it was eventually determined that the national market provided the most feasible and fair solution, and this national market information was compiled."]

[The court then traced the variations on *Sindell* developed in Wisconsin and Washington, involving such issues as how to determine market shares; how to handle absent defendants; when to allow named defendants to exculpate themselves; and whether to make liability joint and several or only several.]

Turning to the structure to be adopted in New York, we heed both the lessons learned through experience in other jurisdictions and the realities of the mass litigation of DES claims in this State. Balancing these considerations, we are led to the conclusion that a market share theory, based upon a national market, provides the best solution. As California discovered, the reliable determination of any market smaller than the national one likely is not practicable. Moreover, even if it were possible, of the hundreds of cases in the New York courts, without a doubt there are many in which the DES that allegedly caused injury was ingested in another State. Among the thorny issues this could present, perhaps the most daunting is the spectre that the particular case could require the establishment of a separate market share matrix. We feel that this is an unfair, and perhaps impossible burden to routinely place upon the litigants in individual cases.

[The court rejected approaches that required "individualized and open-ended assessment" in each case because it feared that the large number of cases pending in New York would unduly burden the courts.]

Consequently, for essentially practical reasons, we adopt a market share theory using a national market. We are aware that the adoption of a national market will likely result in a disproportion between the liability of individual manufacturers and the actual injuries each manufacturer caused in this State. Thus our market share theory cannot be founded upon the belief that, over the run of cases, liability will approximate causation in this State [ ]. Nor does the use of a national market provide a reasonable link between liability and the risk created by a defendant to a particular plaintiff [ ]. Instead, we choose to apportion liability so as to correspond to the overall culpability of each defendant, measured by the amount of risk of injury each defendant created to the public-at-large. Use of a national market is a fair method, we believe, of apportioning defendants' liabilities according to their total culpability in marketing DES for use during pregnancy. Under the circumstances, this is an equitable way to provide plaintiffs with the relief they deserve, while also rationally distributing the responsibility for plaintiffs' injuries among defendants.

To be sure, a defendant cannot be held liable if it did not participate in the marketing of DES for pregnancy use; if a DES producer satisfies its burden of proof of showing that it was not a member of the market of DES sold for pregnancy use, disallowing exculpation would be unfair and unjust. Nevertheless, because liability here is based on the overall risk produced, and not causation in a single case, there should be no exculpation of a defendant who, although a member of the market producing DES for pregnancy use, appears not to have caused a particular plaintiff's injury. It is merely a windfall for a producer to escape liability solely because it manufactured a more identifiable pill, or sold only to certain drugstores. These fortuities in no way diminish the culpability of a defendant for marketing the product, which is the basis of liability here.

Finally, we hold that the liability of DES producers is several only, and should not be inflated when all participants in the market are not before the court in a particular case. We understand that, as a practical matter, this will prevent some plaintiffs from recovering 100% of their damages. However, we eschewed exculpation to prevent the fortuitous avoidance of liability, and thus, equitably, we decline to unleash the same forces to increase a defendant's liability beyond its fair share of responsibility.[3]

---

[3] . . .

We are confronted here with an unprecedented identification problem, and have provided a solution that rationally apportions liability. We have heeded the practical lessons learned by other jurisdictions, resulting in our adoption of a national market theory with full knowledge that it concedes the lack of a logical link between liability and causation in a single case. The dissent ignores these lessons, and, endeavoring to articulate a theory it perceives to be closer

III.

The constitutionality of the revival statute remains to be considered [ ]. This section revives, for the period of one year, actions for damages caused by the latent effects of DES, tungsten-carbide, asbestos, chlordane, and polyvinylchloride. Defendants argue that the revival of barred DES claims was unconstitutional as a denial of both due process and equal protection, under the State and Federal Constitutions. . . .

[After extended discussion, the court rejected the constitutional challenges.]

Accordingly, in each case the order of the Appellate Division should be affirmed, with costs, and the certified question answered in the affirmative.

■ MOLLEN, JUDGE (concurring in *Hymowitz* and *Hanfling;* and dissenting in part in *Tigue* and *Dolan*.)

. . .

. . . I would adopt a market share theory of liability, based upon a national market, which would provide for the shifting of the burden of proof on the issue of causation to the defendants and would impose liability upon all of the defendants who produced and marketed DES for pregnancy purposes, except those who were able to prove that their product could not have caused the injury. Under this approach, DES plaintiffs, who are unable to identify the actual manufacturer of the pill ingested by their mother, would only be required to establish, (1) that the plaintiff's mother ingested DES during pregnancy; (2) that the plaintiff's injuries were caused by DES; and (3) that the defendant or defendants produced and marketed DES for pregnancy purposes. Thereafter, the burden of proof would shift to the defendants to exculpate themselves by establishing, by a preponderance of the evidence, that the plaintiff's mother could not have ingested their particular pill. Of those defendants who are unable to exculpate themselves from liability, their respective share of the plaintiff's damages would be measured by their share of the national market of DES produced and marketed for pregnancy purposes during the period in question.

---

to traditional law, sets out a construct in which liability is based upon chance, not upon the fair assessment of the acts of defendants. Under the dissent's theory, a manufacturer with a large market share may avoid liability in many cases just because it manufactured a memorably shaped pill. Conversely, a small manufacturer can be held jointly liable for the full amount of every DES injury in this State simply because the shape of its product was not remarkable, even though the odds, realistically, are exceedingly long that the small manufacturer caused the injury in any one particular case. Therefore, although the dissent's theory based upon a "shifting the burden of proof" and joint and several liability is facially reminiscent of prior law, in the case of DES it is nothing more than advocating that bare fortuity be the test for liability. When faced with the novel identification problem posed by DES cases, it is preferable to adopt a new theory that apportions fault rationally, rather than to contort extant doctrines beyond the point at which they provide a sound premise for determining liability.

I would further note that while, on the one hand, the majority would not permit defendants who produced DES for pregnancy purposes to exculpate themselves, the majority at the same time deprives the plaintiffs of the opportunity to recover fully for their injuries by limiting the defendants' liability for the plaintiff's damages to several liability. In my view, the liability for the plaintiff's damages of those defendants who are unable to exculpate themselves should be joint and several thereby ensuring that the plaintiffs will receive full recovery of their damages, as they are entitled to by any fair standard. . . .

. . . [T]his approach, unlike that taken by the majority, does not represent an unnecessary and radical departure from basic principles of tort law. By characterizing this approach as "nothing more than advocating that bare fortuity be the test for liability" [ ], the majority fails to perceive that this is no more and no less than a basic principle of tort law; i.e., a plaintiff may not recover for his or her injuries from a defendant who could not have caused those injuries. When the majority eliminates this fundamental causative factor as a basis for recovery, it effectively indulges in the act of judicial legislating. . . .

Judged by the aforesaid standard, I conclude that the trial courts' orders in [*Tigue & Margolies v. Squibb & Sons* and in *Dolan v. Lilly & Co.*], to the extent that they denied the summary judgment motions of the defendant The Upjohn Company (Upjohn) in both actions and the defendant Rexall Drug Company (Rexall) in the *Tigue* action, were improper. In *Tigue,* Mrs. Tigue, the plaintiff's mother, testified that the DES pill she ingested while she was pregnant with the plaintiff was a white, round tablet [ ]. Similarly, Myrna Margolies' mother testified that the DES pill she ingested was a dark red, hard, round pill [ ]. Mr. Margolies, the plaintiff's father, also recalled that the pills were a reddish color and Mrs. Margolies' obstetrician stated that the DES pill he prescribed to his patients was not an Upjohn product. Moreover, in the *Dolan* action, Mrs. Dolan, the plaintiff's mother, stated that the DES pill she took was a white, round, hard tablet [ ]. This fact was corroborated by Mr. Dolan's testimony [ ]. Finally, it was established that Upjohn's DES pill which was produced and marketed for pregnancy purposes, was in the form of a "perle" which is a pharmaceutical term for a dose form consisting of a soft elastic capsule containing a liquid center [ ]. Based on the evidence submitted in support of Upjohn's summary judgment motions in these two cases, I would conclude that the plaintiffs have failed to adduce sufficient proof in admissible form to raise a triable issue of fact as to whether their mothers ingested an Upjohn DES pill. Accordingly, Upjohn's motion for summary judgment in those actions should have been granted.

. . .

■ ALEXANDER, TITONE and HANCOCK, JJ., concur with WACHTLER, C.J.

■ MOLLEN, J., [concurring and dissenting].

■ SIMONS, KAYE and BELLACOSA, JJ., taking no part.

NOTES AND QUESTIONS

1. Why is *Hymowitz* a case about factual causation? In what way is it different from *Stubbs* and *Zuchowicz*?

The *Hymowitz* court states that "strong evidence links prenatal DES exposure" to the vaginal adenocarcinoma and adenosis suffered by plaintiffs. In fact, these diseases only occur in young women who were exposed in utero to DES. This circumstance is known as a "signature disease" because the existence of the disease is a "signature" of exposure to the agent.

2. In the DES cases, various state courts have had to consider a market-share analysis because they almost uniformly rejected the traditional theories plaintiffs put forth. In addition to rejecting *Summers v. Tice,* the court, as noted, also refused to adopt the "concert of action" theory. This theory has been used more broadly than in the drag race cases. In Orser v. Vierra, 60 Cal.Rptr. 708 (App.1967), for example, several men negligently fired in the plaintiff's direction. D1 and D2 alternately fired with the gun that was identified as the one causing the fatal injury. D3 was firing at the same time with a different gun. D3 was held jointly and severally liable with the others—although his bullet could not have caused the injury—because he knew the others were acting tortiously and encouraged them by doing the same thing.

The *Sindell* court, in the influential California DES case, rejected the concert of action analogy on the ground that in cases like *Orser*, there was an allegation that the defendant knew others were acting tortiously. In *Sindell,* however, there was no allegation that "each defendant knew the other defendants' conduct was tortious toward plaintiff, and that they assisted and encouraged one another to inadequately test DES and to provide inadequate warnings. Indeed, it seems dubious whether liability on the concert of action theory can be predicated upon substantial assistance and encouragement given by one alleged tortfeasor to another pursuant to a tacit understanding to fail to perform an act." All the cases cited by plaintiff had involved "conduct by a small number of individuals whose actions resulted in a tort against a single plaintiff, usually over a short span of time, and the defendant held liable was either a direct participant in the acts which caused damages, or encouraged and assisted the person who directly caused the injuries by participating in a joint activity."

A third theory rejected by the DES cases has been industry-wide liability or "enterprise liability." The plaintiff relied on Hall v. E.I. Du Pont De Nemours & Co., 345 F.Supp. 353 (E.D.N.Y.1972), in which the defendants were six blasting cap manufacturers "comprising virtually the entire blasting cap industry in the United States" and their trade association. The claim resulted from blasts allegedly due to inadequate warnings and other safety precautions. The *Sindell* court, for example, saw *Hall* as a case in which "there was evidence that defendants, acting independently, had adhered to an industry-wide standard with regard to the safety features of blasting caps, that they had in effect delegated some functions of safety investigation and design, such as labelling, to their trade association, and that there was industry-wide cooperation in the manufacture and design of blasting caps."

Hall itself had cautioned against application of the doctrine to large numbers of producers. The difference between six and 200 was too great. Moreover, there was no showing of delegation in the DES situation. There was one further distinction, according to the *Sindell* court:

> Equally important, the drug industry is closely regulated by the Food and Drug Administration, which actively controls the testing and manufacture of drugs and the methods by which they are marketed, including the contents of warning labels. To a considerable degree, therefore, the standards followed by drug manufacturers are suggested or compelled by the government. Adherence to those standards cannot, of course, absolve a manufacturer of liability to which it would otherwise be subject. [ ] But since the government plays such a pervasive role in formulating the criteria for the testing and marketing of drugs, it would be unfair to impose upon a manufacturer liability for injuries resulting from the use of a drug which it did not supply simply because it followed the standards of the industry.

Do the distinctions recognized by the *Sindell* court require the exploration of a new theory for DES cases? Note that, in all three of the theories rejected by *Sindell*, defendants would be jointly and severally liable for plaintiff's damages.

3.   The judges agree on using a national market share. What are the benefits of that approach? The drawbacks?

Conley v. Boyle Drug Co., 570 So.2d 275 (Fla.1990), decided that the market "should be as narrowly defined as the evidence in a given case allows. Thus, where it can be determined that the DES ingested by the mother was purchased from a particular pharmacy, that pharmacy should be considered the relevant market." This definition was consistent with allowing exculpation by defendants who did not market in the region in which the DES was purchased. Also, the narrower the market, "the greater the likelihood that liability will be imposed only on those drug companies who could have manufactured the DES which caused the plaintiff's injuries."

Conley demanded that plaintiff show due diligence in trying to find the specific source of the DES before she would be allowed to bring a market share action. Market share liability was a "theory of last resort" to be used only where need could be shown.

How does the *Conley* approach compare with the *Sindell* and *Hymowitz* approaches in terms of fairness? Administrative feasibility? All market-share approaches were rejected in Smith v. Eli Lilly & Co., 560 N.E.2d 324 (Ill.1990), as "too great a deviation from our existing tort principles." Of the courts that have addressed market share, they have split almost evenly, but less than 20 states have confronted the issue. See Restatement (Third) of Torts § 28, rptrs. note to cmt. p.

4.   The judges in *Hymowitz* disagree over whether each defendant should be permitted to try to exculpate itself. Who has the better of that argument? Suppose a defendant wanted to exculpate itself by showing that although it marketed DES for pregnancy, it did not do so during the time that plaintiff's mother took the drug?

5.   The judges disagree over whether to use several liability or joint and several liability. Recall that several liability means that the plaintiff cannot collect the share of insolvent or absent defendants. Who has the better of that argument?

6.   *Other possible applications.* In the wake of the DES cases, plaintiffs have tried to extend market share liability to other products, with little success.

Numerous asbestos plaintiffs have sought to invoke market share liability. Most have been unsuccessful. Thus, in Goldman v. Johns-Manville Sales Corp., 514 N.E.2d 691 (Ohio 1987), the court observed that the essential condition required for market share treatment was "fungibility"— all the products made pursuant to a single formula. "In contrast, asbestos is not a 'product,' but rather a generic name for a family of minerals." Asbestos-containing products "do not create similar risks of harm because there are several varieties of asbestos fibers, and they are used in various quantities, even in the same class of product." Why should fungibility be required?

The fungibility concern also played out in a childhood vaccine case. In Shackil v. Lederle Laboratories, 561 A.2d 511 (N.J.1989), the court, 4–2, refused to extend market share liability to manufacturers of diphtheria-typhoid-pertussis vaccine when plaintiff could not identify the producer of the particular dose. The court noted that the pertussis portion of the vaccine causes almost all the adverse reactions. There were then three major different types of the pertussis component, each with a different risk factor. Although one version was most likely responsible for the child's illness, at least one of the defendants also marketed one of the other vaccines at the same time. Should plaintiff have sought market share liability against only those who marketed the likely cause? A legislative approach to vaccine injuries is discussed in Chapter XII.

In In re Methyl Tertiary Butyl Ether (MTBE) Products Liability Litigation, 379 F.Supp.2d 348 (S.D.N.Y.2005), a federal court in New York conducted consolidated proceedings over many cases alleging groundwater contamination due to MTBE, a chemical gasoline additive. Relying on factors from the Third Restatement, the court found that the product was fungible, plaintiffs were unable to identify the manufacturers, and the clear causal relation between the product and the harm justified imposing market share liability in cases from states that had accepted market share as well as in several that had not decided the issue.

7.   For an argument that liability under both alternative liability and market share liability can be justified by "evidential grouping" of

defendants who contributed to the tortious risk, rather than inquiring into causation for each defendant, see Geistfeld, The Doctrinal Unity of Alternative Liability and Market-Share Liability, 155 U.Pa.L.Rev. 447 (2006). Geistfeld surveys other areas in which ordinary causal rules are relaxed, such as multiple sufficient causes, and finds they provide a principle for evidential grouping. Suppose that a plaintiff can prove only that each defendant acted tortiously and could have been a cause of plaintiff's harm, and at least one was a cause. Application of individualized but-for causation would leave plaintiff remediless—as it would in both *Summers* and DES cases. In such cases, Geistfeld argues evidential grouping of all such defendants is appropriate, and plaintiff need not identify which defendant actually caused the harm.

8.   *The statute of limitations and the statute of repose.* The *Hymowitz* case involved long lapses of time between the sale and the harm, which challenge the application of traditional rules on statutes of limitation. Statutes of limitation specify the amount of time a victim has in which to file suit. We address them in more detail at p. 505 infra. By contrast with statutes of limitations, which are keyed to the time of exposure or injury, statutes of repose are measured from the time of sale or manufacture of a product. We address them further in the Chapter on products liability, p. 646 infra.

C. THE SPECIAL CASE OF TOXIC HARMS

The causal relation issue has been central to a wide variety of extensively publicized concerns about toxics in the environment: among others, claims based on asbestos, Agent Orange, hazardous wastes, and atomic test fallout. These toxic harm controversies, along with silicone breast implants and drug cases such as DES, Bendectin, and Vioxx have posed a number of distinctive issues, not all about factual causation, for the tort system that are discussed in the following excerpt and the notes that follow it.

Environmental Liability and the Tort System
Robert L. Rabin.
24 Houston Law Review 27, 27–32 (1987).

. . .

. . . Essentially, environmental liability stands out in bold relief from the generality of everyday risks embraced by tort law because of three critical characteristics that are found, singly or in combination, in every case of harm from toxics or other pollutants. I will refer to these characteristics of environmental liability as problems of *identification, boundaries* and *source.*

(1) *Problems of Identification.* Through the centuries of common law development, the identification of a tortious injury has hardly ever been a problem. At earliest common law, it was the unwanted intrusion on the land of another or the physical violation of a right to bodily

integrity. Well into the twentieth century, one finds remarkably little change on this score. Auto accidents and overcharged coke bottles are the modern-day counterpart of trespassers and runaway buggies from the pre-industrial era. The focus is consistently on an accidental injury, the relatively sudden event in which the victim's bodily security or property is violated. If problems of causation exist, they are ordinarily of the "whodunit" variety, rather than issues of whether the victim actually suffered identifiable harm that can be isolated from the everyday risks of living.

But it is precisely this latter inquiry which characterizes the case of environmental harm. Toxics of all sorts—impure water, hazardous chemicals, defective synthetics—often breed disease rather than cause immediate injury. As a consequence, the tort system is severely tested. Since diseases do not occur instantaneously, there are serious time-lag issues. And because diseases are frequently a product of the background risks of living (or at least intertwined with those risks), technical information is essential to establish attribution. Thus, *identification*, ordinarily a routine issue of cause in fact at common law, is a costly enterprise that relies on types of evidence and probability judgments which can be regarded as ill-suited to traditional resolution through the adversary process.

(2) *Problems of Boundaries.* Let us assume that through epidemiological studies, laboratory tests or rough mortality data it can be established that a particular widespread incidence of disease was "caused" by the release of an identifiable toxic substance. At first blush, environmental liability may then appear to be similar to a classical mass tort episode—akin to a commercial airline disaster or the collapse of a hotel balcony. But appearances are deceiving; once again, the case of environmental harm frequently creates problems that place special stress on the tort system.

The crux of the matter, again, is the accident/disease distinction. The harm suffered in an airplane crash is extensive but it is also bounded. Most of the victims die, and, apart from derivative loss, there are virtually no post-generational consequences. Contrast the toxic tort scenario. In cases like Agent Orange and hazardous waste dump exposure, the claims are potentially unbounded. Victims of exposure not yet ill fear that it is only a matter of time before they show signs of pathology, *in utero* exposure is an overriding concern, and generations not yet conceived may suffer genetic damage.

Moreover, these are only the most peripheral claims. Even with respect to first-generation, identifiable victims, the *ex ante* assessment of limits on liability is often highly open-ended. Unlike an airplane or public facilities disaster, the aggregate exposure can be hard to define in advance. In addition, the extent of harm may be unpredictable because the need for post-exposure treatment is extensive (degeneration rather than instant death is, by and large, far more common in toxic tort episodes than mass accident cases) and the array of disorders is far more wide-ranging.

By *boundaries,* then, I have in mind an *ex ante* assessment of the magnitude of harm. Mass accident torts are rare at common law, and in fact, put the flexibility of the tort system to the test when they occur. But they pose nothing like the challenge of unconfined liability intrinsic to many environmental harms. In common law terms, valuation of damages is the crux of the matter. Asbestos and the emerging toxic tort cases claim victims in the thousands, not the low hundreds. And, the intrinsic vagaries of chemically induced diseases introduce bizarre pathologies that are costly to treat and raise intergenerational concerns which vex a torts process designed for more modest purposes. In sum, it is both the two-party structure of traditional tort litigation and the underlying premise of sudden accidental injury that are confounded by environmental harm.

(3) *Problems of Source.* A generation ago, tort lawyers viewed the frontiers of causal responsibility as defined by cases like *Summers v. Tice*, the classic accident situation in which the victim could not identify which of his two careless hunting companions fired the shotgun pellet which entered his eye. *Summers* seems almost an ancient artifact bearing witness to the practices of an earlier epoch when compared with the source-related issues presented by toxic tort and pollution cases. To venture for a moment into the world of conjecture (or, perhaps, nightmare), suppose at some future date uncertainty over the harmful effects of chlorofluorocarbon emissions is resolved through an extraordinarily sharp rise in the incidence of skin cancer. To continue in a speculative vein, assume that the multitude of victims can properly pursue a class action. Would the action be appropriately brought against the thousands of emitters of chlorofluorocarbons including the producers of aerosols, foams, solvents, freezers and insulation materials? Should the multinational chemical companies producing the constituent products be joined? What about the host governments that approve (or, at least, allow) the processes to be undertaken? The prospects stagger the imagination.

But one need not create a parade of future horribles to illustrate the problem. The vast array of asbestos producers and insurers, or the typical participants in the hazardous waste chain of distribution— generators, transporters and operators of sites—are present-day examples of the singular difficulties in dealing with problems of *source* in environmental liability cases.

Here, too, the long-standing premises of tort law are challenged by the rise of toxic and pollutant harms. Because tort law has traditionally been concerned with accidents, the search for a responsible source has never raised overwhelming difficulties. At most, the classic single-party focus of responsibility is extended slightly along a horizontal axis in cases like *Summers v. Tice* or a multi-car collision. Under other circumstances, the single-party focus may be extended slightly along a vertical (production/distribution) axis in cases where a defective product may be the responsibility of an assembler and manufacturers of component parts. But these modest variations on the two-party tort configuration in which some*one* is responsible for the harm clearly are of small consequence to the system.

By contrast, environmental torts evoke an entirely different perspective on liability, one which is virtually unknown at common law. Frequently, environmental harm is a consequence of the aggregate risk created by a considerable number of independently acting enterprises. It may be that the risk generated by any single source is, in fact, inconsequential. Or, it may be that the risk inherent in the product is substantial, but it soon merges into a common pool. Whatever the case, environmental harm is very often *collective* harm.

Acid rain, chlorofluorocarbons, Agent Orange, and asbestos fibers confound the private law perspective in a dual sense. Not only are they potentially the source of widespread harm, but they are frequently produced by a vast number of discrete enterprises, each making independent decisions about the extent to which they will degrade or endanger the commons. Traditional tests of causal responsibility—the but-for principle, substantial factor causation, *pro rata* joint and several liability—are operating in foreign territory when they are employed in such cases. They are premised on a wrongful act that in itself triggers accidental harm, an act that can be isolated and pinned down as consequential.

In view of these distinctive characteristics, it is small wonder that environmental liability has achieved special recognition in discourse about standards of liability and the efficacy of the torts process. Automobiles and power lawnmowers may wreak havoc, but their dangers are readily cognizable. We understand how they work and why they go awry. Toxic substances evoke the special apprehensions of unseen risks. They emanate from sources that are hard to identify. They attack us unaware, planting the seeds of future debilitating disease. They run a course that we cannot discern. Translated into legal terms, they pose unique challenges to a tort system premised on adversary treatment of easily identifiable two-party accidents.

NOTES AND QUESTIONS

1. In a following section, the article points out that not all cases of environmental harm exhibit the same distinctive characteristics. The article discusses three scenarios: (1) individualized harm such as Ferebee v. Chevron Chemical Co., 736 F.2d 1529 (D.C.Cir.1984), in which an agricultural worker claimed toxic poisoning from exposure to a herbicide; (2) multiple party harm in which injuries occurred to residents of a discrete and limited geographical area; and (3) mass tort claims such as the hundreds of thousands of cases arising from asbestos exposure.

2. *Mass tort claims: aggregation issues.* The last category, in particular, places singular strains on the tort system—partly because of causation-related issues, but also due to the procedural difficulties created by the enormous volume of cases. The complexities in aggregating mass tort claims are discussed in, among others, In re Rhone-Poulenc Rorer, Inc., 51 F.3d 1293 (7th Cir.1995)(rejecting HIV-infected hemophiliacs' class action against blood solids suppliers); R. Nagareda, Mass Torts in a World of Settlement (2007); and Coffee, Class Wars: The Dilemma of the Mass Tort Class Action, 95 Colum.L.Rev. 1343 (1995).

In Castano v. American Tobacco Co., 84 F.3d 734 (5th Cir.1996), the court overturned the certification of a nationwide class of nicotine-dependent tobacco plaintiffs. Relying heavily on *Rhone-Poulenc Rorer*, the court pointed out that variations in applicable state law, as well as serious doubts that the Rule 23(b)(3) class action requirements of superiority over individual treatment and predominance of common issues were satisfied, led to the conclusion that the tobacco litigation was not then suited for aggregate treatment.

After the de-certification of a nationwide class action in *Castano*, plaintiffs' attorneys filed a large number of statewide class actions against the tobacco industry with almost no greater success. See Rabin, Tobacco Control Strategies: Past Efficacy and Future Promise, 41 Loy.L.A.L.Rev. 1721, 1733–35 (2008).

In Amchem Products, Inc. v. Windsor, 521 U.S. 591 (1997), the Court affirmed, 6–2, the court of appeals, which had thrown out a major class action settlement of asbestos-related claims—again involving interpretation of the requirements of Rule 23(b)(3). The plaintiff class included both already injured and "exposure-only" victims; claimants presented a wide array of diseases. The majority quoted approvingly from the Third Circuit opinion:

> Class members were exposed to different asbestos-containing products, for different amounts of time, in different ways, and over different periods. Some class members suffer no physical injury or have only asymptomatic pleural changes, while others suffer from lung cancer, disabling asbestosis, or from mesothelioma. . . . Each has a different history of cigarette smoking, a factor that complicates the causation inquiry.

> The [exposure-only] plaintiffs especially share little in common, either with each other or with the presently injured class members. It is unclear whether they will contract asbestos-related disease and, if so, what disease each will suffer. They will also incur different medical expenses because their monitoring and treatment will depend on singular circumstances and individual medical histories.

Although the benefits of settlement were not to be ignored, the majority went on to point out that differences in applicable state law and doubts about adequate representativeness of the named parties compounded its concerns about the settlement—which it proceeded to vacate.

In Ortiz v. Fibreboard Corp., 527 U.S. 815 (1999), the Court rejected the lower courts' approval of a proposed global settlement of another asbestos class action. The majority held that the record before the trial judge did not justify certifying the class because it failed to "support the essential premises of mandatory limited fund actions." The record relied on below "failed to demonstrate that the fund was limited except by the agreement of the parties, and it showed exclusions from the class and allocations of assets at odds with the concept of limited fund treatment and the structural protections of Rule 23(a) explained in *Amchem*."

Mass tort class actions have generally received a more favorable reaction in state courts. After a deeply ideological battle, the Class Action Fairness Act of 2005, Pub.L.No. 109–2, 119 Stat. 4 (codified in various sections of 28 U.S.C.) was enacted. In addition to regulating various aspects of consumer class actions, the Act expands federal court subject matter jurisdiction for putative class actions that would permit defendants to remove to federal court many mass toxic substances cases initially brought in state court. See generally Herr & McCarthy, The Class Action Fairness Act of 2005—Congress Again Wades into Complex Litigation Management Issues, 228 F.R.D. 673 (2005).

For a succinct treatment of Rule 23 provisions for class actions in the context of mass tort claims, see J. Eggen, Toxic Torts (5th ed.2015). The topic is generally given more detailed consideration in advanced courses.

With the decline of class actions in mass torts involving personal injury, other devices have been employed or developed to permit aspects of a mass tort to be treated collectively for pretrial and settlement purposes. In the litigation over Vioxx, a drug for the pain of arthritis that was found to also cause heart attacks, pretrial proceedings for all federal cases were consolidated in a single court in New Orleans. A global settlement of almost $5 billion was eventually reached that raised several difficult ethical issues about subordinating individual plaintiff rights to the collective interest of all claimants, not to mention the interests of their lawyers.

The story behind Vioxx, the New Drug Application process, Merck's marketing and aspirations for the drug, a subsequent clinical study and the concerns it raised internal to Merck, Merck's spin on the heart effects found in that study, and the difficulties of the FDA in effectively regulating drugs in the post-approval period is compellingly told in McDarby v. Merck & Co., Inc., 949 A.2d 223 (N.J.Sup.Ct.App.Div.2008). For contrasting views on the tension between facilitating settlement of mass torts and respecting litigant autonomy raised in the Vioxx settlement and by the ALI Principles of the Law of Aggregate Litigation (2010), compare R. Nagareda, Mass Torts in a World of Settlement (2007) with Erichson & Zipursky, Consent Versus Closure, 96 Cornell L.Rev. 265 (2011).

3. *Future claimants.* For an especially useful survey of the entire range of issues raised by mass torts episodes, see Judicial Conference of the United States & Federal Judicial Center, Report of the Advisory Committee on Civil Rules and the Working Group on Mass Torts (1999). With regard to future claimants, the Report comments:

> Particularly troublesome problems arise from injuries that may not become manifest until many years after exposure to the causal event. Injuries from exposure to asbestos, for example, may not occur until decades have passed. The resulting substantive law issues include whether remedies should be awarded to "exposure only" victims for medical monitoring, fear of future injury, and risk of future injury. A related problem is that statutes of limitations may force plaintiffs to file claims before the fact or extent of injury can be known, substantially expanding the number of claims filed. These accelerated filings lead to the problem of finding methods to defer consideration of plaintiffs with no present needs in favor of those who have serious present injuries.
>
> The mirror image of these questions arises from the desire of defendants to achieve closure—to buy "global peace"—by resolving all present and future claims at once. Any procedure that would purport to bind future claimants would have to provide them with adequate representation and at least some form of notice. Representation problems arise partly from the difficulty of finding lawyers who are experienced, capable of vigorously litigating the claims, and free from disabling conflicts between present and future claimants. It also is difficult, if not impossible, to provide meaningful notice to people who may not be aware of their past exposure. It has been suggested that one means of addressing this problem might be to follow the approach of Rule 23(b)(3) class actions by providing future claimants an opportunity to opt out of a settlement or even a litigated judgment after they become aware of actual injury. But such opt-out provisions raise questions of their own, and could discourage settlement by making global peace difficult, if not impossible, for defendants to obtain.
>
> Another concern arises when there is a perceptible risk that a defendant lacks sufficient assets to compensate fully all present and future claimants. Inclusion of future claimants becomes a question not merely of achieving peace for the defendant but also of ensuring that future claimants have an opportunity for compensation reasonably equal to that of present claimants.

4. *Medical monitoring.* Should a long-time heavy smoker who has not suffered any smoking-related disease be able to assert an equitable claim that would provide medical monitoring to facilitate an early diagnosis of lung cancer or other smoking-related disease? In Caronia v. Philip Morris USA, Inc., 5 N.E.3d 11 (N.Y.2013), the court answered a certified question on that issue from the Second Circuit Court of Appeals. Splitting 4–2, the majority declined to recognize such a claim and explained that a predicate for such relief was some existing injury or disease caused by defendants. The "increased risk" faced by plaintiffs was not such a cognizable injury. Acknowledging that other courts are split on this question, the court listed several policy reasons for its decision: 1) the "floodgates" concern that could result in " 'tens of millions' of potential plaintiffs" seeking monitoring; 2) siphoning money away from physical injury victims to plaintiffs who may never suffer any smoking-related disease; and 3) the complexity of setting up a system to provide medical monitoring to plaintiffs and the inappropriateness of doing so by a common law court.

A spirited dissent argued that there should be a remedy for those suffering an enhanced risk of cancer caused by the tortious conduct of defendants. Quoting a California case that recognized medical monitoring, the court asserted that "monitoring claims promote the 'important public health interest in fostering access to medical testing for individuals whose exposure to toxic chemicals creates an enhanced risk of disease, particularly in light of the value of early diagnosis and treatment for many cancer patients.' " Providing medical monitoring could also reduce costs (including the liability to which defendants would be subject) by early diagnosis that permits more successful and economical treatment. Medical monitoring could also enhance deterrence because claims for disease present grave difficulties of proof of causation given other potential causes (recall *Stubbs*, p. 338 supra, and Rabin's "Problems of Identification"). Finally, the "floodgates" concern could be addressed by carefully setting the elements of a medical monitoring claim so as to constrain its limits.

In Donovan v. Philip Morris USA, Inc., 914 N.E.2d 891, 902 (Mass. 2009), the court recognized medical monitoring and set forth the elements of such a claim:

> (1) The defendant's negligence (2) caused (3) the plaintiff to become exposed to a hazardous substance that produced, at least, subcellular changes that substantially increased the risk of serious disease, illness, or injury (4) for which an effective medical test for reliable early detection exists, (5) and early detection, combined with prompt and effective treatment, will significantly decrease the risk of death or the severity of the disease, illness or injury, and (6) such diagnostic medical examinations are reasonably (and periodically) necessary, conformably with the standard of care, and (7) the present value of the reasonable cost of such tests and care, as of the date of the filing of the complaint.

Is the *Donovan* medical monitoring claim sufficiently constrained to avoid courts being inundated with these claims? In that regard, consider that millions of Americans have been occupationally exposed to asbestos. Might the number of claims depend on whether the relief was a system providing medical monitoring for plaintiffs or money damages to pay the cost of such monitoring in the future?

For another skeptical view of monitoring liability see *Metro-North*, p. 268 supra, in which the Court, after rejecting recovery for emotional distress, barred, 7–2, the recovery of lump-sum medical monitoring costs. The Court concluded that the cases allowing recovery "do not endorse a full-blown traditional tort law cause of action for lump-sum damages—of the sort that the Court of Appeals seems to have endorsed here." Rather, those courts were seen as suggesting court-supervised funds or other limitations on traditional tort damages. The Court noted the "uncertainty among professionals about just which tests are most usefully administered and when. [ ] And in part those difficulties can reflect the fact that scientists will not always see a medical need to provide systematic scientific answers to the relevant legal question, namely, whether an exposure calls for extra monitoring." After some uncertainty about the benefits of CT scans for early detection of lung cancer see Jane E. Brody, *What an Extra Eye on Cancer Can Do for You*, N.Y. Times, Aug. 16, 2005, at D7, both a United States task force on preventive care and the American Cancer Society recommended annual CT scanning, which cost $300–$400 for heavy smokers. See Deborah Kotz, *Heavy Smokers Urged to Have CT Scans for Lung Cancer*, Boston Globe, Dec. 31, 2013.

Currently courts applying the law from approximately 20 different states have decided the medical monitoring matter, splitting 2–1 in favor of such claims. See Schwartz, Recovery of Damages for Expense of Medical Monitoring to Detect or Prevent Future Disease or Condition, 17 A.L.R.5th 327.

5.   *Fear of future injury and risk of future injury.* As the excerpt from the Advisory Committee report, quoted in note 3 supra, indicates, these types of injury claims, like medical monitoring, tend to be characteristic of toxic harm cases. Nonetheless, they raise cross-cutting issues that apply more generally to the conceptual framework of accidental harm cases. We have considered fear of future injury claims, p. 268 supra, in the section on duty to compensate for emotional distress, and we addressed enhanced risk of future injury claims, p. 343 supra, in the section on causation in conjunction with probabilistic harm issues.

6.   There have been a number of useful case studies of the range of perplexing issues raised by mass tort episodes. In particular, see J. Sanders, Bendectin on Trial: A Study of Mass Tort Litigation (1998); M. Green, Bendectin and Birth Defects: The Challenges of Mass Toxic Substances Litigation (1996); M. Angell, Science on Trial: The Clash of Medical Evidence and the Law in the Breast Implant Case (1996); and P. Schuck, Agent Orange on Trial: Mass Toxic Disasters in the Courts (1986).

7.   Would causation issues be more fairly and efficiently decided under an administrative compensation scheme than through tort litigation? See Rabin, Some Thoughts on the Efficacy of a Mass Toxics Administrative Compensation Scheme, 52 Md.L.Rev. 951 (1993). No-fault and social insurance replacements for the tort system are discussed generally in Chapter XII.

CHAPTER VI

PROXIMATE CAUSE (SCOPE OF LIABILITY)

In the cases presented in this Chapter, either the plaintiff has made out the elements previously discussed—duty, breach of duty, and cause in fact—or else they are sufficiently in dispute that the defendant cannot establish the absence of any of them as a matter of law. Instead, the defendant will argue that even a negligent defendant who actually caused the harm in question should not be liable for the plaintiff's harm. The legal formulation of the claim is that the defendant's admitted or assumed negligence was not the proximate cause (or "legal cause") of the plaintiff's harm. The cases in which this claim is given serious consideration tend to have one feature in common—something quite unexpected has contributed either to the occurrence of the harm or to its severity.

Because "proximate cause" generally has little to do with proximity of time or geography and equally little to do with factual causation, the Third Restatement of Torts employs a new term, "scope of liability," in place of proximate cause. The Restatement explains: "[Scope of liability] terminology more accurately describes the concerns of this Chapter: Tort law does not impose liability on an actor for all harm factually caused by the actor's tortious conduct." Restatement (Third) of Torts: Liability for Physical and Emotional Harm ch. 6 Special Note (2010). Nevertheless, the Restatement also includes proximate cause terminology because of its widespread usage in court opinions, and we do so here, as well.

A. UNEXPECTED HARM

Benn v. Thomas

Supreme Court of Iowa, 1994.
512 N.W.2d 537.

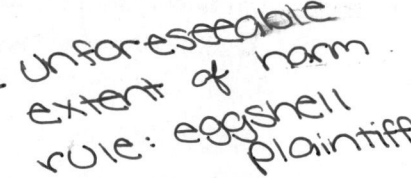

unforeseeable - extent of harm
rule: eggshell plaintiff

■ Considered by McGIVERIN, C.J., and HARRIS, LARSON, SNELL, and ANDREASEN, JJ.

■ McGIVERIN, CHIEF JUSTICE.

The main question here is whether the trial court erred in refusing to instruct the jury on the "eggshell plaintiff" rule in view of the fact that plaintiff's decedent, who had a history of coronary disease, died of a heart attack six days after suffering a bruised chest and fractured ankle in a motor vehicle accident caused by defendant's negligence. The court of appeals concluded that the trial court's refusal constituted reversible error. We agree with the court of appeals and reverse the judgment of the trial court and remand for a new trial.

[Benn's executor sued defendant for Loras Benn's injuries and his death in 1989 after defendant's vehicle rear-ended the van in which decedent was a passenger.]

At trial, the estate's medical expert, Dr. James E. Davia, testified that Loras had a history of coronary disease and insulin-dependent diabetes. Loras had a heart attack in 1985 and was at risk of having another. Dr. Davia testified that he viewed "the accident that [Loras] was in and the attendant problems that it cause[d] in the body as the straw that broke the camel's back" and the cause of Loras's death. Other medical evidence indicated the accident did not cause his death.

Based on Dr. Davia's testimony, the estate requested an instruction to the jury based on the "eggshell plaintiff" rule, which requires the defendant to take his plaintiff as he finds him, even if that means that the defendant must compensate the plaintiff for harm an ordinary person would not have suffered. [Plaintiff requested the following charge:]

> If Loras Benn had a prior heart condition making him more susceptible to injury than a person in normal health, then the Defendant is responsible for all injuries and damages which are experienced by Loras Benn, proximately caused by the Defendant's actions, even though the injuries claimed produced a greater injury than those which might have been experienced by a normal person under the same circumstances.

[ ]

[The trial judge denied that request and instead gave the following general charge:]

> The conduct of a party is a proximate cause of damage when it is a substantial factor in producing damage and when the damage would not have happened except for the conduct. "Substantial" means the party's conduct has such an effect in producing damage as to lead a reasonable person to regard it as a cause.

Special Verdict Number 4 asked the jury: "Was the negligence of Leland Thomas a proximate cause of Loras Benn's death?" The jury answered this question, "No." The jury returned a verdict for $17,000 for Loras's injuries but nothing for his death. In its special verdict, the jury determined the defendant's negligence in connection with the accident did not proximately cause Loras's death. The court of appeals reversed the trial court's judgment for $17,000 and remanded the case because the charge given to the jury failed to convey the applicable law.]

A tortfeasor whose act, superimposed upon a prior latent condition, results in an injury may be liable in damages for the full disability. [ ] This rule deems the injury, and not the dormant condition, the proximate cause of the plaintiff's harm. [ ] This precept is often referred to as the "eggshell plaintiff" rule, which has its roots in cases such as Dulieu v. White & Sons, [1901] 2 K.B. 669, 679, where the court observed:

> If a man is negligently run over or otherwise negligently injured in his body, it is no answer to the sufferer's claim for damages that he would have suffered less injury, or no injury at all, if he had not had an unusually thin skull or an unusually weak heart. [ ]
>
> . . .

Defendant contends that plaintiff's proposed instruction was inappropriate because it concerned damages, not proximate cause. Although the eggshell plaintiff rule has been incorporated into the Damages section of the Iowa Uniform Civil Jury Instructions, we believe it is equally a rule of proximate cause. See Christianson v. Chicago, St. Paul, Minneapolis & Omaha Ry. Co., 69 N.W. 640, 641 (Minn.1896)("Consequences which follow in unbroken sequence, without an intervening efficient cause, from the original negligent act, are natural and proximate; and for such consequences the original wrongdoer is responsible, even though he could not have foreseen the particular results which did follow.").

Defendant further claims that the instructions that the court gave sufficiently conveyed the applicable law. . . .

We agree that the jury might have found the defendant liable for Loras's death as well as his injuries under the instructions as given. But the proximate cause instruction failed to adequately convey the existing law that the jury should have applied to this case. The eggshell plaintiff rule rejects the limit of foreseeability that courts ordinarily require in the determination of proximate cause. [ ] Once the plaintiff establishes that the defendant caused some injury to the plaintiff, the rule imposes liability for the full extent of those injuries, not merely those that were foreseeable to the defendant. Restatement (Second) of Torts § 461 (1965)("The negligent actor is subject to liability for harm to another although a physical condition of the other . . . makes the injury greater than that which the actor as a reasonable man should have foreseen as a probable result of his conduct.").

The instruction given by the court was appropriate as to the question of whether defendant caused Loras's initial personal injuries, namely, the fractured ankle and the bruised chest. This instruction alone, however, failed to adequately convey to the jury the eggshell plaintiff rule, which the jury reasonably could have applied to the cause of Loras's death.

Defendant maintains "[t]he fact there was extensive heart disease and that Loras Benn was at risk any time is not sufficient" for an instruction on the eggshell plaintiff rule. Yet the plaintiff introduced substantial medical testimony that the stresses of the accident and subsequent treatment were responsible for his heart attack and death. Although the evidence was conflicting, we believe that it was sufficient for the jury to determine whether Loras's heart attack and death were the direct result of the injury fairly chargeable to defendant Thomas's negligence. [ ]

. . .

To deprive the plaintiff estate of the requested instruction under this record would fail to convey to the jury a central principle of tort liability.

. . .

The record in this case warranted an instruction on the eggshell plaintiff rule. We therefore affirm the decision of the court of appeals. We reverse the judgment of the district court and remand the cause to the district court for a new trial consistent with this opinion.

NOTES AND QUESTIONS

1.   Do questions of cause in fact exist in this case? Why didn't plaintiff's proving that decedent suffered a bruised chest and fractured ankle resolve any factual cause issues in this case?

2.   Why is the instruction the trial court gave erroneous?

3.   In Steinhauser v. Hertz Corp., 421 F.2d 1169 (2d Cir.1970), although the 14-year-old plaintiff sustained no bodily injury in a minor automobile accident, she began, within minutes, to behave in "an unusual way." In the following days "things went steadily worse." She was institutionalized for a period and diagnosed with a "chronic schizophrenic reaction." The court cited a variety of events in plaintiff's life that occurred shortly before the accident and might have given her "a predisposition to schizophrenia which, however, requires a 'precipitating factor' to produce an outbreak." The court held that the trial judge had committed prejudicial error by failing to charge that plaintiff was entitled to recover for the schizophrenia if the jury concluded that it had been "precipitated" by the accident. At the same time, the court observed that the existence of the prior tendencies might greatly affect damages (recall *Dillon v. Twin State*, p. 374 supra). Defendants were entitled to explore the possibility that plaintiff would have developed schizophrenia in any event. On this point, the court concluded that although this kind of prediction may be "taxing" for those "who have devoted their lives to psychiatry, it is one for which a jury is ideally suited." Does *Steinhauser* identify one factual cause issue in *Benn*?

4.   *Suicide.* Courts have historically resisted imposing liability in the case of suicide, often concluding that the decedent's acts are the proximate

cause of harm not the defendant's negligence. More recently, that resistance has diminished in some cases in which the defendant's negligence has severely injured a person who later commits suicide. In *Fuller v. Preis*, 322 N.E.2d 263 (N.Y.1974), the victim was a 43-year-old surgeon who sustained injuries in an automobile accident that left him subject to seizures and caused a physical deterioration. Meanwhile, his wife, who had been partially paralyzed by polio, suffered "nervous exhaustion." Seven months after the crash he learned that his mother had cancer. One of his suicide notes warned his family to destroy it because "it would alter the outcome of the 'case'—i.e., it's worth a million dollars to you all." The court held that the required "irresistible impulse" did not necessarily mean a "sudden impulse." The jury could find that the irresistible impulse that "caused decedent to take his life also impelled the acquisition of the gun and the writing of the suicide notes." But see *Maloney v. Badman*, 938 A.2d 883 (N.H.2007)(severely ill Crohn's disease patient committed suicide with pain killers and tranquilizers prescribed by defendant that violated the standard of care and resulted in his being reprimanded by state medical disciplinary committee; nevertheless, suicide is held to be a superseding cause of death).

5. *Emotional distress.* In discussing claims based on emotional distress, courts often say that to be actionable the harm must be such that it would cause distress in the ordinarily sensitive person or the reasonably constituted person. Recall *Gammon*, p. 276 supra. If that standard is met in a case, should it also limit the amount of plaintiff's damages or should plaintiff recover the harm that plaintiff actually sustained even if it is greater than what an "ordinarily sensitive person" would have suffered? The Third Restatement provides that when plaintiffs suffer greater damages than those that were foreseeable because of pre-existing "physical or mental condition[s]," the plaintiff may recover for all such harm. Restatement (Third) of Torts: Liability for Physical Harm § 31 (2010). What might be the rationale for this position?

6. *Secondary harm.* In Stoleson v. United States, 708 F.2d 1217 (7th Cir.1983), plaintiff worked in a munitions plant and was found to have suffered heart problems from negligently being exposed to nitroglycerine. Although the harm was temporary and should have stopped when plaintiff ceased working at the factory, she developed hypochondria after the episode and was unable to function normally. The court adverted to the possibility that the plaintiff's condition was brought about by medical advice given to her after the exposure to nitroglycerine had ended:

> If a pedestrian who has been run down by a car is taken to a hospital and because of the hospital's negligence incurs greater medical expenses or suffers more pain and suffering than he would have if the hospital had not been negligent, he can collect his incremental as well as his original damages from the person who ran him down, since they would have been avoided if that person had used due care.

Is the original wrongdoer liable if the hospital staff reasonably chooses a course of treatment that does not work—if it later appears that another reasonable choice would in fact have done the job? Why? In Miyamoto v. Lum, 84 P.3d 509 (Haw. 2004), the court held irrelevant whether subsequent medical treatment is rendered negligently or innocently.

Does the principle from the medical aggravation cases extend to transportation to the hospital for needed attention? In Pridham v. Cash & Carry Building Center, Inc., 359 A.2d 193 (N.H.1976), plaintiff, who had been seriously injured by defendant's negligence, died when the ambulance driver transporting him to a hospital suffered a heart attack and the ambulance swerved into a tree. The trial judge charged that the defendant was liable for further injuries resulting from "normal efforts of third persons in rendering aid . . . which the other's injury reasonably requires irrespective of whether such acts are done in a proper or in a negligent manner." The charge was upheld on appeal from a plaintiff's judgment. If medical services "are rendered negligently, the rule based on questions of policy makes the negligence of the original tortfeasor a proximate cause of the subsequent injuries suffered by the victim." The ambulance trip was a "necessary step in securing medical services required by the accident at Cash & Carry." Should it matter whether the ambulance was racing to the hospital or proceeding in the normal stream of traffic?

7.   In Wagner v. Mittendorf, 134 N.E. 539 (N.Y.1922), the defendant negligently broke plaintiff's leg. While plaintiff was recovering, through no fault of his own, his crutch slipped and the leg was rebroken. The court held the defendant liable for that aggravation. Why? What if the plaintiff must use crutches permanently and is killed ten years later in a fire because of his inability to run away?

In re an Arbitration Between Polemis and Another and Furness, Withy & Co., Ltd.

Court of Appeal, 1921.
3 K.B. 560, [1921] All E.R. 40.

[The owners of the ship Thrasyvoulos sought to recover damages from the defendants who chartered the ship. The contract of charter was read to hold the defendant charterers responsible for damage caused by fire due to their negligence. Stevedores, for whose conduct the defendants were responsible, were moving benzine from one hold to another by means of a sling. The stevedores had placed wooden boards across an opening above one hold to make a temporary platform to facilitate the transfer. "When the sling containing the cases of benzine was being hoisted up, owing to the negligence of the stevedores the rope by which the sling was hoisted or the sling itself came in contact with the boards, causing one of the boards to fall into the hold, and the fall was immediately followed by a rush of flames, the result being the total destruction of the ship."

The case was heard by arbitrators who found "that the fire arose from a spark igniting petrol vapour in the hold; that the spark was caused by the falling board coming into contact with some substance in the hold; . . . [and] that the causing of the spark could not reasonably have been anticipated from the falling of the board though some damage to the ship might reasonably have been anticipated." Damages were set at almost £200,000.

Subject to the court's opinion on the law, the arbitrators decided that the owners were entitled to recover the full loss from the charterers. The court was required to accept the arbitrators' findings. Although the case arose in the contract context, none of the three opinions mentions this point, and all rely on tort cases in their analyses.]

■ BANKES, L.J.

. . . According to the one view, the consequences which may reasonably be expected to result from a particular act are material only in reference to the question whether the act is or is not a negligent act; according to the other view, those consequences are the test whether the damages resulting from the act, assuming it to be negligent, are or are not too remote to be recoverable. Sir F. Pollock in his Law of Torts, 11th ed., pp. 39, 40, refers to this difference of view, and calls attention to the fact that the late Mr. Beven, in his book on Negligence, supports the view founded on Smith v. London and South Western Ry. Co. . . .

In the present case the arbitrators have found as a fact that the falling of the plank was due to the negligence of the defendants' servants. The fire appears to me to have been directly caused by the falling of the plank. Under these circumstances I consider that it is immaterial that the causing of the spark by the falling of the plank could not have been reasonably anticipated. The appellants' junior counsel sought to draw a distinction between the anticipation of the extent of damage resulting from a negligent act, and the anticipation of the type of damage resulting from such an act. He admitted that it could not lie in the mouth of a person whose negligent act had caused damage to say that he could not reasonably have foreseen the extent of the damage but he contended that the negligent person was entitled to rely upon the fact that he could not reasonably have anticipated the type of damage which resulted from his negligent act. I do not think that the distinction can be admitted. Given the breach of duty which constitutes the negligence, and given the damage as a direct result of that negligence, the anticipations of the person whose negligent act has produced the damage appear to me to be irrelevant. I consider that the damages claimed are not too remote.

. . .

For these reasons I think that the appeal fails, and must be dismissed with costs.

■ SCRUTTON, L.J.

. . .

The second defense is that the damage is too remote from the negligence, as it could not be reasonably foreseen as a consequence. . . . To determine whether an act is negligent, it is relevant to determine whether any reasonable person would foresee that the act would cause damage; if he would not, the act is not negligent. But if the act would or might probably cause damage, the fact that the damage it in fact causes is not the exact kind of damage one would expect is immaterial, so long as the damage is in fact directly traceable to the negligent act, and not due to the operation of independent causes having no connection with the negligent act, except that they could not avoid its results. Once the act is negligent, the fact that its exact operation was not foreseen is immaterial. . . . In the present case it was negligent in discharging cargo to knock down the planks of the temporary staging, for they might easily cause some damage either to workmen, or cargo, or the ship. The fact that they did directly produce an unexpected result, a spark in an atmosphere of petrol vapour which caused a fire, does not relieve the person who was negligent from the damage which his negligent act directly caused.

Appeal dismissed.

■ [The concurring opinion of WARRINGTON, L J., is omitted.]

NOTES AND QUESTIONS

1. In the cited case of Smith v. London and South Western Ry., the facts as stated on appeal (L.R. 6 C.P. 14) were as follows:

It was proved that the defendants' railway passed near the plaintiff's cottage, and that a small strip of grass extended for a few feet on each side of the line, and was bounded by a hedge which formed the boundary of the defendants' land; beyond the hedge was a stubble-field, bounded on one side by a road, beyond which was the plaintiff's cottage. About a fortnight before the fire the defendants' servants had trimmed the hedge and cut the grass and left the trimmings and cut grass along the strip of grass. On the morning of the fire the company's servants had raked the trimmings and cut-grass into small heaps. The summer had been exceedingly dry, and there had been many fires about in consequence. On the day in question, shortly after two trains had passed the spot, a fire was discovered upon the strip of grass land forming part of the defendants' property; the fire spread to the hedge and burnt through it, and caught the stubble-field, and a strong wind blowing at the time, the flames ran across the field for 200 yards, crossed the road, and set fire to and burnt the plaintiffs cottage.

How are *Polemis* and *Smith* similar? Are they similar enough to warrant the same approach? The plaintiff won in *Smith*.

2. Might the appellant's junior counsel have been seeking to avoid the result in the railroad fire case when he made his argument distinguishing "type" and "extent" of harm?

3. Might the "eggshell plaintiff" rule apply to the *Polemis* case?

4. How might the case have been analyzed if the claim was that it was negligent to have gasoline vapors in the hold?

Overseas Tankship (U.K.) Ltd. v. Mort's Dock & Engineering Co., Ltd. (The Wagon Mound)

Privy Council, 1961.
[1961] A.C. 388.

■ VISCOUNT SIMONDS.

[Plaintiffs respondents owned a wharf in Sydney Harbour, Australia, and were refitting the ship Corrimal. At a different wharf, about 600 feet away, the ship Wagon Mound, chartered by defendants, was taking on bunkering oil. A large quantity of bunkering oil spilled into the bay and some of it concentrated near plaintiffs' property. Defendants set sail, making no effort to disperse the oil. When plaintiffs' manager became aware of the condition he stopped all welding and burning until he could assess the danger. Based on discussions with the manager at the Wagon Mound berth and his own understanding about furnace oil in open waters, he felt he could safely order activities to be resumed with all precautions taken to prevent flammable material from falling off the wharf into the oil.

For two days work proceeded and there was no movement of the oil. Then, oil under or near the wharf was ignited and a fire spread, causing extensive damage to the wharf and plaintiffs' equipment. The trial judge found that floating on the oil underneath the wharf was a piece of debris on which lay some cotton waste or rag that had caught fire from molten metal falling from the wharf, and that this set the floating oil afire either directly or by first setting fire to a wooden pile coated with oil.

The trial judge awarded judgment to the plaintiffs and the Full Court of the Supreme Court of New South Wales dismissed the defendants' appeal.]

The trial judge also made the all-important finding, which must be set out in his own words: "The *raison d'être* of furnace oil is, of course, that it shall burn, but I find the defendant did not know and could not reasonably be expected to have known that it was capable of being set afire when spread on water." This finding was reached after a wealth of evidence, which included that of a distinguished scientist, Professor Hunter. It receives strong confirmation from the fact that at the trial the respondents strenuously maintained that the appellants had discharged petrol into the bay on no other ground than that, as the spillage was set alight, it could not be furnace oil. An attempt was made before their Lordships' Board to limit in some way the finding of fact, but it is clear that it was intended to cover precisely the event that happened.

One other finding must be mentioned. The judge held that apart from damage by fire the respondents had suffered some damage from the spillage of oil in that it had got upon their slipways and congealed upon them and interfered with their use of the slips. He said: "The evidence of this damage is slight and no claim for compensation is made in respect of it. Nevertheless it does establish some damage, which may be insignificant in comparison with the magnitude of the damage by fire, but which nevertheless is damage which, beyond question, was a direct result of the escape of the oil." It is upon this footing that their Lordships will consider the question whether the appellants are liable for the fire damage. . . .

. . .

There can be no doubt that the decision of the Court of Appeal in *Polemis* plainly asserts that, if the defendant is guilty of negligence he is responsible for all the consequences whether reasonably foreseeable or not. The generality of the proposition is perhaps qualified by the fact that each of the Lords Justices refers to the outbreak of fire as the direct result of the negligent act. There is thus introduced the conception that the negligent actor is not responsible for consequences which are not "direct," whatever that may mean. . . .

. . . If the line of relevant authority had stopped with *Polemis,* their Lordships might, whatever their own views as to its unreason, have felt some hesitation about overruling it. But it is far otherwise. . . .

. . .

Enough has been said to show that the authority of *Polemis* has been severely shaken though lip-service has from time to time been paid to it. In their Lordships' opinion it should no longer be regarded as good law. It is not probable that many cases will for that reason have a different result, though it is hoped that the law will be thereby simplified, and that in some cases, at least, palpable injustice will be avoided. For it does not seem consonant with current ideas of justice or morality that for an act of negligence, however slight or venial, which results in some trivial foreseeable damage the actor should be liable for all consequences however unforeseeable and however grave, so long as they can be said to be "direct." It is a principle of civil liability, subject only to qualifications which have no present relevance, that a man must be considered to be responsible for the probable consequences of his act. To demand more of him is too harsh a rule, to demand less is to ignore that civilized order requires the observance of a minimum standard of behaviour.

This concept applied to the slowly developing law of negligence has led to a great variety of expressions which can, as it appears to their Lordships, be harmonized with little difficulty with the single exception of the so-called rule in *Polemis*. For, if it is asked why a man should be responsible for the natural or necessary or probable consequences of his act (or any other similar description of them) the answer is that it is not because they are natural or necessary or probable, but because, since they have this quality, it is judged by the standard of the reasonable man that he ought to have foreseen them. Thus it is that over and over again it has happened that in different judgments in the same case, and sometimes in a single judgment, liability for a consequence has been imposed on the ground that it was reasonably foreseeable or, alternatively, on the ground that it was natural or necessary or probable. The two grounds have been treated as coterminous, and so they largely are. But, where they are not, the question arises to which the wrong answer was given in *Polemis*. For, if some limitation must be imposed upon the consequences for which the negligent actor is to be held responsible—and all are agreed that some limitation there must be—why should that test (reasonable foreseeability) be rejected which, since he is judged by what the reasonable man ought to foresee, corresponds with the common conscience of mankind, and a test (the "direct" consequence) be substituted which leads to nowhere but the never-ending and insoluble problems of causation. . . .

. . .

It is, no doubt, proper when considering tortious liability for negligence to analyze its elements and to say that the plaintiff must prove a duty owed to him by the defendant, a breach of that duty by the defendant, and consequent damage. But there can be no liability until the damage has been done. It is not the act but the consequences on which tortious liability is founded. Just as (as it has been said) there is no such thing as negligence in the air, so there is no such thing as liability in the air. Suppose an action brought by A for damage caused by the carelessness (a neutral word) of B, for example, a fire caused by the careless spillage of oil. It may, of course, become relevant to know what duty B owed to A, but the only liability that is in question is the liability for damage by fire. It is vain to isolate the liability from its context and to say that B is or is not liable, and then to ask for what damage he is liable. For his liability is in respect of that damage and no other. If, as admittedly it is, B's liability (culpability) depends on the reasonable foreseeability of the consequent damage, how is that to be determined except by the foreseeability of the damage which in fact happened—the damage in suit? And, if that damage is unforeseeable so as to displace liability at large, how can the liability be restored so as to make compensation payable?

But, it is said, a different position arises if B's careless act has been shown to be negligent and has caused some foreseeable damage to A.

Their Lordships have already observed that to hold B liable for consequences however unforeseeable of a careless act, if, but only if, he is at the same time liable for some other damage however trivial, appears to be neither logical nor just. This becomes more clear if it is supposed that similar unforeseeable damage is suffered by A and C but other foreseeable damage, for which B is liable, by A only. A system of law which would hold B liable to A but not to C for the similar damage suffered by each of them could not easily be defended. Fortunately, the attempt is not necessary. For the same fallacy is at the root of the proposition. It is irrelevant to the question whether B is liable for unforeseeable damage that he is liable for foreseeable damage, as irrelevant as would the fact that he had trespassed on Whiteacre be to the question whether he has trespassed on Blackacre. Again, suppose a claim by A for damage by fire by the careless act of B. Of what relevance is it to that claim that he had another claim arising out of the same careless act? It would surely not prejudice his claim if that other claim failed: it cannot assist it if it succeeds. Each of them rests on its own bottom, and will fail if it can be established that the damage could not reasonably be foreseen. . . .

Their Lordships conclude this part of the case with some general observations. They have been concerned primarily to displace the proposition that unforeseeability is irrelevant if damage is "direct." In doing so they have inevitably insisted that the essential factor in determining liability is whether the damage is of such a kind as the reasonable man should have foreseen. This accords with the general view thus stated by Lord Atkin in *Donoghue v. Stevenson*: "The liability for negligence, whether you style it such or treat it as in other systems as a species of 'culpa,' is no doubt based upon a general public sentiment of moral wrongdoing for which the offender must pay." It is a departure from this sovereign principle if liability is made to depend solely on the damage being the "direct" or "natural" consequence of the precedent act. Who knows or can be assumed to know all the processes of nature? But if it would be wrong that a man should be held liable for damage unpredictable by a reasonable man because it was "direct" or "natural," equally it would be wrong that he should escape liability, however "indirect" the damage, if he foresaw or could reasonably foresee the intervening events which led to its being done. . . . Thus foreseeability becomes the effective test. . . .

. . .

Their Lordships will humbly advise Her Majesty that this appeal should be allowed, and the respondents' action so far as it related to damage caused by the negligence of the appellants be dismissed with costs. . . . The respondents must pay the costs of the appellants of this appeal and in the courts below.

NOTES AND QUESTIONS

1.   The Judicial Committee of the Privy Council had jurisdiction over appeals from the Commonwealth courts, whereas the House of Lords had jurisdiction over appeals from British courts. In the House of Lords, each judge delivers an opinion, but the Privy Council at the time of this case delivered but one opinion—and no dissents. Since the Privy Council was advising Her Majesty on the disposition, a single opinion was thought more useful. It is rumored that the Privy Council split 3–2 in *Wagon Mound*. See The Foresight Saga 3 (Haldane Society 1962).

2.   The court observes that "all are agreed" that there must be some limitation upon the consequences for which the negligent actor is held responsible. Would setting such a limit be facilitated by ascertaining its purpose?

3.   After *Wagon Mound,* is there room for a distinction between the "type" and the "extent" of harm? Suppose the defendant is driving negligently through skid row and runs down a person who appears to be one of the derelicts on the street. In fact, the victim is a successful and highly paid athlete who was posing as a derelict to work among the area's residents. How might Viscount Simonds respond to the defendant's argument that he could reasonably expect to have done only minor harm— and not the great harm suffered by this prosperous athlete and his or her family?

4.   In Smith v. Leech Brain & Co., [1962] 2 Q.B. 405 (Eng.), through the defendant's negligence in providing inadequate shielding, a worker was burned on the lip by a piece of molten metal. The burn was treated but did not heal. It ulcerated, developed into cancer that spread, and the worker died of cancer three years later. The judge found that the worker had probably become pre-disposed to cancer by ten years of work in the gas industry earlier in his life. He held that *Wagon Mound* did not alter the principle that a defendant must take his victim as he finds him:

> The test is not whether these employers could reasonably have foreseen that a burn would cause cancer and he would die. The question is whether these employers could reasonably foresee the type of injury he suffered, namely, the burn. What, in the particular case, is the amount of damage which he suffers as a result of that burn, depends upon the characteristics and constitution of the victim.

Is this approach consistent with *Wagon Mound?*

In proving that decedent suffered a burned lip, plaintiff showed that defendant's negligence had proximately caused at least some compensable harm, thereby completing the prima facie case for liability. The defendant was liable for at least some damages, so the remaining causal issues addressed the amount of damages. In the damages phase of the case, plaintiff had to prove that defendant's negligence was both a cause in fact and proximate cause of the cancer. The cancer was directly caused by the predicate compensable harm (the burned lip) as required by the eggshell skull rule, the same result reached in *Benn*, p. 395 supra, in which the plaintiff recovered for a heart attack that was directly caused by the predicate compensable harms (a bruised chest and fractured ankle). In *Wagon Mound*, by contrast, the only foreseeable harm created by the defendant's negligence involved the mucking up of the dock. That predicate compensable harm, however, did not cause the ensuing fire, and so the eggshell skull rule did not apply. On this view, the rule of proximate cause in the liability phase of the case (the foreseeability test) differs from the rule of proximate cause in the damages phase of the case (the directness test or eggshell skull rule). For defense of this approach, see Geistfeld, Tort Law: The Essentials 263–68 (2008).

   5.   If there is utility to the idea of different types of harm, what do we mean by "different types of harm"? Consider Darby v. National Trust [2001] EWCA (Civ) 189 (Eng.), in which the owner of a historic house had an ornamental lake in front of it in which rats regularly urinated. The owner failed to warn guests not to swim in the lake, which was negligent because of the risk of contracting Weil's disease, which is fatal. The plaintiff swam and died. However, plaintiff died not from Weil's but simply drowned. The court held that proximate cause was absent. Didn't the decedent suffer precisely the same type of harm (death) that was foreseeable due to the defendant's negligence?

   The Third Restatement provides: "An actor's liability is limited to those harms that result from the risks that made the actor's conduct tortious." Restatement (Third) of Torts: Liability for Physical and Emotional Harm § 29 (2010). How would section 29 apply to deciding *Darby*? Does that provide assistance in understanding the idea of "different types of harm"?

   6.   Recall *De Haen,* p. 83 supra, in which Judge Cardozo thought it important to identify the purposes behind the statute's requirement of a barrier around an open hole at a construction site. Is the statutory purpose question analogous to the proximate cause question presented in these cases?

   7.   Viscount Simonds puts forth the example of A and C who suffer damage at the hands of B. He suggests that a system that allowed A to recover for the negligently inflicted unforeseeable harm but denied such recovery to C "could not easily be defended." Why not? Is the problem allowing A to recover or not allowing C to recover?

   8.   The owners of the Corrimal brought a separate action against the charterers of the Wagon Mound. The trial judge held against plaintiffs on the negligence claim. The Privy Council reversed. Overseas Tankship (U.K.), Ltd. v. Miller Steamship Co. (Wagon Mound No. 2), [1967] 1 A.C. 617 (P.C.). The Privy Council read the trial judge's findings to suggest that the defendants might have foreseen a very slight danger of fire. This contrasted with the finding in No.1 that the defendant "did not know and could not reasonably be expected to have known that [the oil] was capable of being set afire when spread on water." The Privy Council reconciled the two cases by noting that in No.1, if the plaintiffs had tried "to prove that it was foreseeable by the engineers of the Wagon Mound that this oil could be set alight, they might have had difficulty in parrying the reply that then this must also have been foreseeable by their manager. Then there would have been contributory negligence," which would have been a complete defense. Does this suggest something about the nature of the adversary process and the purposes of litigation?

9. In an omitted footnote in *Zuchowicz*, p. 347 supra, Judge Calabresi addressed the need to "link" defendant's conduct to the plaintiff's harm. This "causal link" requires both 1) a but-for connection between defendant's tortious conduct and plaintiff's harm, and 2) that defendant's conduct increased "the chances of a similar accident in the future" if defendant repeated the conduct:

> The leading case involving this requirement is Berry v. Sugar Notch Borough, 43 A. 240 (Pa.1899). In *Berry*, a tree fell on a trolley car whose excess speed had caused the tram to be at that specific place when the tree fell. The court held that the requirement of causation was not met. This result was correct since, although the accident would not have occurred *but for* the trolley's speeding, speeding does not increase the probability of trees falling on trolleys. Other similar cases (termed "darting out" cases) involve speeders who but for their velocity would not have been at the particular spot when children darted out from behind trees, etc., and were hit. In such cases—assuming that, had the speeders been at the same spot at the same time, they would have been unable to avoid the collision even if they were driving within the speed limit—no liability results. [ ]

> ... Causal link says that, even if defendant's wrong was a *but for* cause of the injury in a given case, no liability ensues unless defendant's wrong increases the chances of such harm occurring in general. *But for* says even if what the defendant did greatly increased the risk of certain injuries occurring, unless it was a *sine qua non* of the specific harm that actually came about, no liability will be assessed.

B. SUPERSEDING CAUSES

In this section, we consider the role of intervening forces or actors in the proximate cause inquiry. Sometimes an unforeseeable force, such as an unprecedented storm, raises an issue about defendant's negligent conduct: is such a natural occurrence one that the defendant should have anticipated and taken precautions against? However, sometimes the defendant has been negligent and the claim is that an intervening force or third-party conduct is unforeseeable or has produced harm different from that for which the defendant should be held liable. Consider Gibson v. Garcia, 216 P.2d 119 (Cal.App.1950). There, plaintiff alleged that defendant Los Angeles Transit had negligently allowed a wooden power pole on a main road to deteriorate to such an extent that when a negligent driver crashed into it, it fell over onto the plaintiff who was walking by at the time. The court rejected the defendant's argument that, although it might be liable if the pole had simply fallen by itself, it should not be liable when the fall was caused by a negligent driver. Do you agree with the court? If so, can you imagine any situation in which you would exculpate the defendant because of what caused the pole to come down?

Doe v. Manheimer
Supreme Court of Connecticut, 1989.
212 Conn. 748, 563 A.2d 699.

■ Before PETERS, C.J., and SHEA, GLASS, COVELLO and HULL, JJ.

■ GLASS, ASSOCIATE JUSTICE.

The difficult issue in this case is whether a landowner may be liable in tort for damages arising from the rape of a pedestrian committed on the landowner's property behind brush and trees that shielded the area from view from the nearby public sidewalk and street.

I

[The plaintiff, who was working as a meter reader, was raped by an unidentified assailant at approximately 8:00 a.m. on property owned by the defendant. As she approached a male on the sidewalk, he pulled a gun from a satchel that contained other items suggesting that he had planned a rape.] He forced her from the sidewalk through a paved vacant lot that abutted the street. The man then forced her onto adjacent property owned by the named defendant (hereinafter defendant) some fifty to seventy feet from the sidewalk. The defendant's property extended approximately six and three-quarter feet from the side of his building to the lot boundary parallel to the building. The area into which the plaintiff was forced was bounded by the defendant's building on one side and a retaining wall in the rear. On the other side, overgrown sumac bushes and tall grass shielded the area from view from the sidewalk and street.

[The abductor assaulted and raped the plaintiff; she suffered serious emotional and psychiatric problems thereafter, which required hospitalization. She attempted suicide several times.

The neighborhood was a high crime area, with prostitution, drug dealing, derelicts, homeless and their detritus common. About three months earlier, another rape had occurred in a neighborhood building. Fourteen months earlier, the defendant's 90-year-old mother, Clara Manheimer, "had been bound, gagged and robbed in the package store at the front of the building on the defendant's property."

Plaintiff's expert, an environmental psychologist, opined that "the physical configuration of the specific site increased the risk of violent crimes between strangers by creating a 'protective' zone that reduced or eliminated visibility and, hence, served as an inducement for crime."] He summarized the results of his study by testifying that "I've analyzed the local site, the sub area, the presence of adult entertainment, activities, sexually oriented businesses. I've looked at prior crimes. . . . The fact that it is an area of the city with a relatively high incidence of crime. And I . . . assumed as a result of those observations that there was a persistent and inappropriate use of that site based on the evidence that it was periodically and frequently used by drunks. . . . There was fighting. Police came. A history of complaints. All those things indicate a condition of environmental disorder that I would contend is potentially related to increasing the risk of crime."

. . .

The plaintiff brought an action against the defendant for personal injuries sustained in the assault. . . . In essence, she claimed that the defendant had failed to remove the overgrown vegetation although he knew or should have known that, because the neighborhood was a high crime area, third persons might use the overgrowth to conceal the perpetration of crimes against pedestrians. She asserted that, had the overgrowth not been present, the area in which the assault occurred would have been visible to passing motorists and pedestrians. Consequently, she alleged, the overgrowth caused and contributed to the assault and the duration of the assault.

. . .

[T]he defendant rested without presenting evidence and moved for a directed verdict. . . . Thereafter, the jury returned a general verdict in favor of the plaintiff, and awarded her $540,000 in damages. . . . Subsequently, however, the trial court set aside the verdict on the defendant's motion. In setting aside the verdict, the trial court first observed that "[w]ithout the shielding [of the overgrowth], the rape most probably would not have occurred [on the defendant's property]." The court implicitly found that the defendant owed the plaintiff a duty of reasonable care, stating that, "[i]n the neighborhood described in the present case, a trier of fact may . . . find the occurrence of violence reasonably foreseeable in such a sheltered location to be perpetrated by someone lying in ambush or by someone also using the public right of way who harbors an intent to drag into concealment and out of public view some other party also using the public right of way to inflict harm." It also found that the "breach of duty whether common law or statutory . . . was the position of the sumac bush."

Despite finding a legally cognizable duty and a breach of that duty, the trial court nevertheless ruled that "the shielded bushing did not cause the injury. The rape and assault caused the injury and damages." "That shielding (which was described as the building, a retaining wall and sumac trees and/or bushes) could have been provided in that same place and time by some other validly positioned or placed appurtenance." The court concluded, therefore, that as a matter of law, the jury could not find that the defendant's maintenance of overgrowth on his property was a "substantial factor" in producing the plaintiff's injuries and, hence, the plaintiff had failed to establish proximate cause.

II

. . . On appeal, the plaintiff claims that the trial court erred in setting aside the verdict on the ground that the plaintiff had not established proximate cause as a matter of law. She asserts that evidence pertaining to the condition of the defendant's property, in connection with evidence that the neighborhood was a high crime area and that the specific site was frequented by trespassing street people and derelicts, created a question of fact for the jury whether the harm the plaintiff had suffered was reasonably foreseeable to the defendant. She avers, therefore, that the trial court erred in concluding that the criminal act of the unknown assailant was the supervening cause of the plaintiff's injuries as a matter of law. Further, she argues that the trial court's conclusion that the condition of the defendant's property was not a "substantial factor" in causing the plaintiff's injuries was inconsistent with its prior finding that "the occurrence of violence [was] reasonably foreseeable in such a sheltered location" and that "[w]ithout the shielding, the rape most probably would not have occurred there." Consequently, she claims, the court erred in setting aside the jury's verdict in her favor on the ground that she had failed to prove proximate cause. We are not persuaded.

A

. . .

[T]he "issue of proximate cause is ordinarily a question of fact for the trier." [ ] "Conclusions of proximate cause are to be drawn by the jury and not by the court." [ ] " 'It becomes a conclusion of law only when the mind of a fair and reasonable man could reach only one conclusion; if there is room for a reasonable disagreement the question is one to be determined by the trier of fact.' . . ." [ ] Thus, the trial court's judgment setting aside the jury's verdict may stand only if there was no "room for a reasonable disagreement" on the question of proximate cause.

B

To prevail on a negligence claim, a plaintiff must establish that the defendant's conduct "legally caused" the injuries. [ ] As we observed in [ ], "[l]egal cause is a hybrid construct, the result of balancing philosophic, pragmatic and moral approaches to causation." The first component of "legal cause" is "causation in fact." " 'Causation in fact' is the purest legal application of . . . legal cause. The test for cause in fact is, simply, would the injury have occurred were it not for the actor's conduct." [ ]

The second component of "legal cause" is proximate cause, which we have defined as " '[a]n actual cause that is a substantial factor in the resulting harm. . . .' [ ]" The "proximate cause" requirement tempers the "expansive view of causation [in fact] . . . by the pragmatic . . . shaping [of] rules which are feasible to administer, and yield a workable degree of certainty. [ ] Remote or trivial [actual] causes are generally rejected because the determination of the responsibility for another's injury is much too important to be distracted by explorations for obscure consequences or inconsequential causes." [ ] "In determining proximate cause, the point beyond which the law declines to trace a series of events that exist along a chain signifying actual causation is a matter of fair judgment and a rough sense of justice. See generally *Palsgraf v. Long Island R.R. Co.,* [p. 421 infra] (Andrews, J., dissenting)." [ ]

This court has often stated that the "test" of proximate cause is whether the defendant's conduct is a "substantial factor" in producing the plaintiff's injury. [ ]; but see [ ]. That negligent conduct is a "cause in fact," however, obviously does not mean that it is also a "substantial factor" for the purposes of a proximate cause inquiry. The "substantial factor" test, in truth, reflects the inquiry fundamental to all proximate cause questions; that is, " 'whether the harm which occurred was of the same general nature as the foreseeable risk created by the defendant's negligence.' [ ]; see Palsgraf v. Long Island R.[R.] Co., [ ]." [ ] In applying this test, we look " 'from the injury to the negligent act complained of for the necessary causal connection. [ ]' " [ ]

The "scope of the risk" analysis of "proximate cause" similarly applies where, as here, the risk of harm created by the defendant's negligence allegedly extends to an intervening criminal act by a third party. [ ] "We have consistently adhered to the standard of 2 Restatement (Second), Torts § 442B (1965) that a negligent defendant, whose conduct creates or increases the risk of a particular harm and is a substantial factor in causing that harm, is not relieved from liability by the intervention of another person, *except* where the harm is intentionally caused by the third person *and* is not within the scope of the risk created by the defendant's conduct [ ]." (Emphasis added.) [ ] "The reason [for the general rule precluding liability where the intervening act is intentional or criminal] is that in such a case the third person has deliberately assumed control of the situation, and all responsibility for the consequences of his act is shifted to him." 2 Restatement (Second), Torts § 442B, comment c. "Such tortious or criminal acts may in themselves be foreseeable, [however,] and so within the scope of the created risk. . . ." Id.; see also 2 Restatement (Second), Torts §§ 448 and 449.

C

Applying these principles, we first note that the defendant has not argued that his conduct was not a "cause in fact" of the plaintiff's injuries. The trial court found that the sexual assault most probably would not have occurred where it actually occurred had the overgrown vegetation not been present. The court also found that the jury could have found from the evidence that the rapist "by design and plan premeditated that the sexual assault would occur in that exact location." Further, there was evidence from which the jury could reasonably have found that the assault would not have [continued as long as it did] absent the shielding provided by the overgrowth. Under the circumstances, we have no reason to question the trial court's finding that the injury would not have occurred, where it actually occurred, were it not for the shielding created by the overgrowth. [ ]

We disagree with the plaintiff, however, that there was room for reasonable disagreement over the question whether the condition on the defendant's property proximately caused her injuries. [ ] The plaintiff argues that there was sufficient evidence for the jury to find that the impaired visibility created by the overgrowth, in conjunction with the manner in which the defendant's property was used and the unseemly character of the neighborhood, increased the risk of violent crime between strangers. She claims, therefore, that under § 442B of the Restatement, the assailant's act was within the "scope of the risk" created by the condition of the defendant's property. We are persuaded, however, that the plaintiff's application of § 442B of the Restatement is unduly broad. Contrary to her assertion, the harm she suffered cannot reasonably be understood as within the scope of the risk created by the defendant's conduct. We reach this conclusion on the basis of the applicable standards established in our cases as well as by reference to factually analogous precedents.

First, we decline to accept the plaintiff's argument suggesting that it was within the "scope of the risk" that the condition of the defendant's land might catalyze a criminal assault. The plaintiff presented expert testimony that conditions of "environmental disorder," such as those present on the defendant's property and within the surrounding neighborhood, stood in a direct and positive relationship with an increased risk of violent crimes between strangers. She also presented evidence tending to indicate that the assailant had planned the crime around the site. Thus, the plaintiff's theory of liability turns in part on the argument that because the overgrowth was instrumental, in a psychological and sociological sense, in fostering the criminal act, the defendant should be held liable.

This argument envisages the rapist's conduct as a "dependent intervening force"; that is, a predictable response or "reaction to the stimulus of a situation for which the actor has made himself responsible by his negligent conduct." 2 Restatement (Second), Torts § 441, comment c. This position is untenable. First, it is clear that § 442B contemplates *reasonably foreseeable* intervening misconduct, rather than *all* conduct that actually proceeds from a situation created by the defendant. [ ] We are not persuaded that a landowner should reasonably foresee that a condition on his property such as overgrown vegetation might provide a substantial incentive or inducement for the commission of a violent criminal assault between strangers. This is true although once such an incident does occur, it necessarily "could" have occurred. Violent crimes are actuated by a host of social and psychological factors. Although, as a matter of fact, it may be true that one of those actuating factors is mere opportunity for concealment, common experience informs us that such a factor is at most incidental. A prudent person who owns land abutting a public way would not, in our opinion, infer from his ordinary experience the possibility that overgrown vegetation will prompt or catalyze a violent criminal act. This theory ascribes far too much speculative imagination to a "reasonable" or "prudent" person. A person of ordinary caution is not required to be accomplished at making such recondite associations.

Moreover, in the present case, there was no evidence tending to demonstrate that the defendant had had any past experience that might reasonably have led him to perceive and act on the atypical association between "natural shields" such as overgrown vegetation and violent criminal activity. Indeed, the evidence showed that the prior "criminal activity" occurring in the vacant lot abutting his property and the scene of the crime generally was nonviolent, involving vagrancy and the public consumption of alcohol. The plaintiff has not directed our attention to evidence that any of the individuals who frequented the vacant lot threatened or assaulted any passersby or local residents, except to the extent that their mere presence and appearance was "threatening." Moreover, evidence that the defendant's mother had been robbed in the liquor store on the defendant's premises, and that a rape had occurred in a nearby building more than two months prior to the assault on the plaintiff, does not require a different conclusion. Both incidents occurred indoors. The fact that criminals will rob liquor stores is an unfortunate, but not extraordinary, fact of contemporary life, and cannot reasonably be seen as exciting the imagination of a prudent person to suppose that a violent sexual crime will occur behind nearby overgrown vegetation in the area of a vacant lot. Further, even if it is assumed that the defendant knew or should have known of the rape in the nearby building, the plaintiff has not presented evidence demonstrating anything distinctive about that inherently atrocious incident that might be reasonably understood as eliciting the type of sensitivity for which she would now hold the defendant accountable. In addition, that experts in environmental psychology . . . are attuned to the association between conditions of "environmental disorder," such as overgrown vegetation in a poor neighborhood, and crime is surely a product of special training, knowledge, interest and, especially, perspective.

Further, the theory of "catalyst" liability suggested by the plaintiff is far too ambitious. We are persuaded that such a principle would eliminate the role of "proximate cause" in "shaping rules which are feasible to administer, and yield a workable degree of certainty." [ ] Indeed, under this principle, for example, parents of a violent adult child might well be held liable to third persons injured by that child's crime if the victim only establishes a positive relationship between the parents' poor parenting skills and the child's violence. We have little doubt that, in any particular case, such a victim could establish a "cause in fact" in such a case. This hypothetical illustrates the fundamental weakness of the plaintiff's position: it renders "proximate cause" coextensive with "cause in fact." "Proximate cause," however, deals with liability, not physics. [ ]

No different result ensues from the plaintiff's less dramatic argument that the condition on the defendant's property, in connection with the "socio-chemistry" of the area, created a foreseeable "opportunity" for the commission of a violent crime and, hence, the harm inflicted on the plaintiff was within the "scope of the risk." Our cases make it clear that, to be within the "scope of the risk," the harm actually suffered must be of the same "general type" as that which makes the defendant's conduct negligent in the first instance. [ ] It is unexceptional to impose upon a landowner liability resulting from injuries caused directly and without intervening criminal conduct by "dangerous conditions" on the land. Thus, where the plaintiff stumbles on accumulated debris on the defendant's land, and injures himself, the defendant may be liable. [ ] We are not prepared, however, to extend the scope of the foreseeable risk presented by "obnoxious overgrowth" or accumulated debris beyond injury produced by physical contact with such conditions. Thus, the harm suffered by the plaintiff in this case was not of the same general type that allegedly made the defendant negligent.

Even if liability could extend beyond injury caused by physical contact with "dangerous conditions" on a defendant's property, the relationship between the "opportunity" of shielding and the plaintiff's harm in this case was accidental. As the trial court found, there could have been any number of natural or nonnatural conditions on the defendant's property that would have shielded the assault. We do not understand the plaintiff to contend that every conceivable item that could have shielded the occurrence of a violent crime should be deemed a basis for negligence because of the potential for crime endemic in an urban neighborhood. . . .

Our conclusion is supported by many cases in which we have declined to hold that the defendant's conduct in contributing to the harm, principally caused "in fact" by another person or force, was a "proximate cause" of the harm. . . .

[The court discussed earlier Connecticut cases as well as those from other jurisdictions.]

. . .

There is no error.

In this opinion the other Justices concurred.

NOTES AND QUESTIONS

1.   On factual causation, the trial court found that the plaintiff would not have been sexually assaulted on defendant's property absent the defendant's negligence in failing to clean up the property. Would factual causation have existed if, absent the defendant's negligence in failing to clean up, the assailant would have taken the plaintiff to another location and assaulted her similarly? How does the evidence of the rapist's premeditation bear on this question?

2.   Is the scope of the risk standard different from the reasonable foreseeability standard the court also employs?

3.   In Hines v. Garrett, 108 S.E. 690 (Va.1921), a train improperly carried the 18-year-old plaintiff a mile past her stop. The conductor told her to walk back to the depot, even though he knew she would have to walk through a disreputable area known as Hoboes' Hollow. In her action against the railroad for damages for rape, the court held that the intervening criminal conduct did not insulate the railroad from liability. Can *Hines* be reconciled with *Doe*?

4.   In Addis v. Steele, 648 N.E.2d 773 (Mass.App.Ct.1995), guests at an inn were injured when forced to jump from a second floor window to escape a late-night fire. Their claim of negligent failure to provide lights or reasonable escape paths withstood defendant's claim that it was not liable because the fire was set by an arsonist. The defendant's obligation was to anticipate fire from whatever source. It had failed in that respect and the actual source of this fire was irrelevant. Would the analysis be the same if the fire was started by the first recorded lightning in the region? If it was started by an overloaded electrical circuit and failed circuit breaker? Is *Addis* consistent with *Doe*?

Can *Addis* be reconciled with *Doe* on the grounds that arson is a reasonably foreseeable intervening event? Can it be reconciled with *Doe* on the grounds that the risk that made defendant negligent was an emergency condition such as a fire, regardless of its source? In a case involving the September 11 terrorist attacks on the World Trade Center, the trial court held that the fires caused by the attacks were foreseeable to the defendants who owned or leased the buildings. In re September 11 Litigation, 280 F.Supp.2d 279, 299–300 (S.D.N.Y.2013)("The duty of landowners and lessors to adopt fire-safety precautions applies to fires set by criminals. . . . [Consequently], the WTC Defendants owed a duty to the occupants to create and implement adequate fire safety measures, even in the case of a fire caused by criminals such as those who hijacked [the] flights . . . on September 11, 2001.").

5.   If foreseeability is to play a role in these cases, we must first decide what it is that needs to be foreseeable. Professor Clarence Morris has addressed this question in considering the role of unusual details in these cases:

> For example, in *Hines v. Morrow*, [236 S.W. 183 (Tex.App.1921)], two men were sent out in a service truck to tow a stalled car out of a mud hole. One of them, the plaintiff, made a tow rope fast and

tried to step from between the vehicles as the truck started. His artificial leg slipped into the mud hole in the road, which would not have been there had defendant-railroad not disregarded its statutory duty to maintain this part of the highway. He was unable to pull out his peg-leg and was in danger of being run over by the stalled car. He grabbed the tailgate of the service truck to use its forward force to pull him loose. A loop in the tow rope lassoed his good leg, tightened, and broke his good leg. As long as these details are considered significant facts of the case, the accident is unforeseeable. No doubt some judges would itemize the facts and hold that the railroad's neglect was not the proximate cause of the injury. As a matter of fact, courts have on occasion ruled that much less freakish injuries were unforeseeable. But in the peg-leg case, the court quoted with approval the plaintiff's lawyer's "description" of the "facts," which was couched in these words, "The case, stated in the briefest form, is simply this: Appellee was on the highway, using it in a lawful manner, and slipped into this hole, created by appellant's negligence, and was injured in undertaking to extricate himself." The court also adopted the injured man's answer to the railroad's attempt to stress unusual details: "Appellant contends [that] it could not reasonably have been foreseen that slipping into this hole would have caused the appellee to have become entangled in a rope, and the moving truck, with such dire results. The answer is plain: The exact consequences do not have to be foreseen."

In this . . . class of cases, foreseeability can be determined only after the significant facts of the case have been described. If official description of the facts of the case as formulated by the court is detailed, the accident can be called unforeseeable; if it is general, the accident can be called foreseeable. Since there is no authoritative guide to the proper amount of specificity in describing the facts, the process of holding that a loss is—or is not—foreseeable is fluid and often embarrasses attempts at accurate prediction.

Professor Morris cautioned that an advocate who pushes too far hurts rather than helps the cause: "A plaintiff's lawyer who insists on a too-general description appears to be trying to suppress important facts; a defense counsel who insists on a too-specific description appears to be taking advantage of mere technicality." C. Morris & C.R. Morris, Morris on Torts, 164–66 (2d ed.1980).

6.   In the next Chapter, we will examine the development of comparative negligence. That reform has generated considerable attention to its effect on superseding cause law. In Barry v. Quality Steel Products, Inc., 820 A.2d 258 (Conn.2003), the court held that there is no independent significance to intervening negligent third-party conduct for proximate cause purposes. If the plaintiff's harm is within the scope of the risk created by the defendant's tortious conduct, no separate instruction on intervening events and superseding causes should be employed. The court relied on the adoption of comparative fault (and comparative contribution) and cited other jurisdictions that have also diminished the role of superseding causes. The Restatement (Third) of Torts: Liability for Physical and Emotional Harm § 34 (2010) similarly employs the same standard for proximate cause when there are superseding causes as when there are not. A comment in the Third Restatement explains that, if it were not for the long history of special treatment of superseding causes, there would be no need for a separate section addressing them in the Third Restatement. In that respect, the Third Restatement goes beyond *Barry* and provides that even intervening actors who commit intentional torts are not superseding causes if the harm that occurs is within the scope of the risk. Is that sensible? Consistent with *Doe v. Manheimer*?

In addition to third-party conduct, courts sometimes concluded that a plaintiff's culpable conduct constituted a superseding cause. During the time when contributory negligence barred recovery, should it have mattered whether a plaintiff's conduct was classified as contributory negligence or a superseding cause? Does it matter after the adoption of comparative fault? At odds with the developments described in the prior paragraph, in Exxon Co., U.S.A. v. Sofec, Inc., 517 U.S. 830 (1996), p. 449 infra, an admiralty case, the Supreme Court held that there was no inconsistency between the adoption of comparative fault and consideration of a plaintiff's conduct as constituting a superseding cause. Thus, the plaintiff could be barred from recovery based on its employee's quite careless conduct—a superseding cause—in navigating a boat that was set loose due to defendant's negligence.

———

The Kinsman cases. Several of the issues raised in the foregoing proximate cause cases came together in Petition of Kinsman Transit Co., 338 F.2d 708 (2d Cir.1964). The Buffalo River "with many turns and bends" was full of floating ice in winter. A thaw had begun and two ice jams were moving downstream under a strong current. Because its crew responded inadequately to the impending danger, the Shiras, owned by Kinsman, was torn loose from its moorings at the Concrete Elevator dock operated by Continental and began floating downstream. The Shiras crashed into a properly moored ship, the Tewksbury, tearing it loose, and both ships (one 525 feet long and the other 425 feet long) careened down the river (whose channel was 177 feet wide) toward a lift bridge operated by the city, situated three miles from the Continental dock. Because of the city's negligence, the bridge was not raised, and the two ships crashed into it, destroying it and some surrounding property. The wreckage of the ships and the bridge formed a dam that caused the ice and the water to back up causing property to sustain flooding damage as far back upstream as the Continental dock. This case involved claims for the property damage. In a complex group of rulings, the trial judge found liability against Continental, Kinsman, and the City of Buffalo.

The court of appeals, in an opinion by Judge Friendly, affirmed. As to Kinsman, the timing of the negligence of the crew was such that what followed was foreseeable. (What new question would have been raised if the flooding had damaged property upstream from the dock?) As to the city, the majority once again concluded that the conditions that day made it reasonably foreseeable that a dam might be created at the bridge if the span were not lifted in time and that upriver flooding might result. (How would you analyze a case against the city brought by flooded property owners upstream from the dock?)

The difficult case was Continental, which was negligent because of failure to inspect a "deadman" device at its dock over an extended period of time. The court thought that the negligence in failing to maintain equipment was not time-specific. This raised the question of the liability of a defendant who could have foreseen the ships crashing into property as they made their way down the river, but not the flooding that actually occurred. Although Judge Friendly stated his agreement with the result in *Wagon Mound* because the defendant there "had no reason to believe that the floating furnace oil would burn," his opinion also conveyed the spirit of *Polemis*:

> On that view [*Wagon Mound*] simply applies the principle which excludes liability where the injury sprang from a hazard different from that which was improperly risked, [ ]. Although some language in the judgment goes beyond this, we would find it difficult to understand why one who had failed to use the care required to protect others in the light of expectable forces should be exonerated when the very risks that rendered his conduct negligent produced other and more serious consequences to such persons than were fairly foreseeable when he fell short of what the law demanded. Foreseeability of danger is necessary to render conduct negligent; where as here the damage was caused by just those forces whose existence required the exercise of greater care than was taken—the current, the ice, and the physical mass of the Shiras—the incurring of consequences other and greater than foreseen does not make the conduct less culpable or provide a reasoned basis for insulation.[9]

> . . .

> We see no reason why an actor engaging in conduct which entails a large risk of small damage and a small risk of other and greater damage, of the same general sort, from the same

---

[9] The contrasting situation is illustrated by the familiar instances of the running down of a pedestrian by a safely driven but carelessly loaded car, or of the explosion of unlabeled rat poison, inflammable but not known to be, placed near a coffee burner. [ ] Exoneration of the defendant in such cases rests on the basis that a negligent actor is responsible only for harm the risk of which was increased by the *negligent aspect* of his conduct. [ ]

. . .

forces, and to the same class of persons, should be relieved of responsibility for the latter simply because the chance of its occurrence, if viewed alone, may not have been large enough to require the exercise of care.

Was the harm that occurred due to the crew's negligence of the "same general sort" as might have been reasonably expectable from that negligence? Are you persuaded that the *Kinsman* facts are different from the cases in the court's footnote 9?

Kinsman II. Another set of claims arose from the closure of the bridge. 388 F.2d 821 (2d Cir.1968). Here the court rejected claims based on the higher costs of unloading ships due to the inability of tugs to reach them, and the costs of obtaining substitute grain to fulfil contracts when grain could not be moved to elevators above the bridge. The "instant claims occurred only because the downed bridge made it impossible to move traffic along the river. Under all the circumstances of this case, we hold that the connection between the defendants' negligence and the claimants' damages is too tenuous and remote to permit recovery":

> In the final analysis, the circumlocution whether posed in terms of "foreseeability," "duty," "proximate cause," "remoteness," etc. seems unavoidable. As we have previously noted [in *Kinsman I*], we return to Judge Andrews' frequently quoted statement [in *Palsgraf v. Long Island Railroad Co.,* immediately following] "It is all a question of expediency . . . of fair judgment, always keeping in mind the fact that we endeavor to make a rule in each case that will be practical and in keeping with the general understanding of mankind."

C. UNEXPECTED VICTIM — unexpected plaintiff

Palsgraf v. Long Island Railroad Co.

Court of Appeals of New York, 1928.
248 N.Y. 339, 162 N.E. 99.

■ CARDOZO, CH. J.

[Appeal from a judgment entered on a plaintiff's verdict. The Appellate Division affirmed, 3–2.]

Plaintiff was standing on a platform of defendant's railroad after buying a ticket to go to Rockaway Beach. A train stopped at the station, bound for another place. Two men ran forward to catch it. One of the men reached the platform of the car without mishap, though the train was already moving. The other man, carrying a package, jumped aboard the car, but seemed unsteady as if about to fall. A guard on the car, who had held the door open, reached forward to help him in, and another guard on the platform pushed him from behind. In this act, the package was dislodged, and fell upon the rails. It was a package of small size, about fifteen inches long, and was covered by a newspaper. In fact it contained fireworks, but there was nothing in its appearance to give notice of its contents. The fireworks when they fell exploded. The shock of the explosion threw down some scales at the other end of the platform, many feet away. The scales struck the plaintiff, causing injuries for which she sues.

The conduct of the defendant's guard, if a wrong in its relation to the holder of the package, was not a wrong in its relation to the plaintiff, standing far away. Relatively to her it was not negligence at all. Nothing in the situation gave notice that the falling package had in it the potency of peril to persons thus removed. Negligence is not actionable unless it involves the invasion of a legally protected interest, the violation of a right. "Proof of negligence in the air, so to speak, will not do" (Pollock, Torts [11th ed.], p. 455; [ ]). "Negligence is the absence of care, according to the circumstances" [ ]. The plaintiff as she stood upon the platform of the station might claim to be protected against intentional invasion of her bodily security. Such invasion is not charged. She might claim to be protected against unintentional invasion by conduct involving in the thought of reasonable men an unreasonable hazard that such invasion would ensue. These, from the point of view of the law, were the bounds of her immunity, with perhaps some rare exceptions, survivals for the most part of ancient forms of liability, where conduct is held to be at the peril of the actor [ ]. If no hazard was apparent to the eye of ordinary vigilance, an act innocent and harmless, at least to outward seeming, with reference to her, did not take to itself the quality of a tort because it happened to be a wrong, though apparently not one involving the risk of bodily insecurity, with reference to some one else. "In every instance, before negligence can be predicated on a given act, back of the act must be sought and found a duty to the individual complaining, the observance of which would have averted or avoided the injury" [ ]. "The ideas of negligence and duty are strictly correlative" [ ]. The plaintiff sues in her own right for a wrong personal to her, and not as the vicarious beneficiary of a breach of duty to another.

A different conclusion will involve us, and swiftly too, in a maze of contradictions. A guard stumbles over a package which has been left upon a platform. It seems to be a bundle of newspapers. It turns out to be a can of dynamite. To the eye of ordinary vigilance, the bundle is abandoned waste, which may be kicked or trod on with impunity. Is a passenger at the other end of the platform protected by the law against the unsuspected hazard concealed beneath the waste? If not, is the result to be any different, so far as the distant passenger is concerned, when the guard stumbles over a valise which a truckman or a porter has left upon the walk? The passenger far away, if the victim of a wrong at all, has a cause of action, not derivative, but original and primary.

His claim to be protected against invasion of his bodily security is neither greater nor less because the act resulting in the invasion is a wrong to another far removed. In this case, the rights that are said to have been violated, the interests said to have been invaded, are not even of the same order. The man was not injured in his person nor even put in danger. The purpose of the act, as well as its effect, was to make his person safe. If there was a wrong to him at all, which may very well be doubted, it was a wrong to a property interest only, the safety of his package. Out of this wrong to property, which threatened injury to nothing else, there has passed, we are told, to the plaintiff by derivation or succession a right of action for the invasion of an interest of another order, the right to bodily security. The diversity of interests emphasizes the futility of the effort to build the plaintiff's right upon the basis of a wrong to some one else. The gain is one of emphasis, for a like result would follow if the interests were the same. Even then, the orbit of the danger as disclosed to the eye of reasonable vigilance would be the orbit of the duty. One who jostles one's neighbor in a crowd does not invade the rights of others standing at the outer fringe when the unintended contact casts a bomb upon the ground. The wrongdoer as to them is the man who carries the bomb, not the one who explodes it without suspicion of the danger. Life will have to be made over, and human nature transformed, before prevision so extravagant can be accepted as the norm of conduct, the customary standard to which behavior must conform.

The argument for the plaintiff is built upon the shifting meanings of such words as "wrong" and "wrongful," and shares their instability. What the plaintiff must show is "a wrong" to herself, i.e., a violation of her own right, and not merely a wrong to some one else, nor conduct "wrongful" because unsocial, but not "a wrong" to any one. We are told that one who drives at reckless speed through a crowded city street is guilty of a negligent act and, therefore, of a wrongful one irrespective of the consequences. Negligent the act is, and wrongful in the sense that it is unsocial, but wrongful and unsocial in relation to other travelers, only because the eye of vigilance perceives the risk of damage. If the same act were to be committed on a speedway or a race course, it would lose its wrongful quality. The risk reasonably to be perceived defines the duty to be obeyed, and risk imports relation; it is risk to another or to others within the range of apprehension [ ]. This does not mean, of course, that one who launches a destructive force is always relieved of liability if the force, though known to be destructive, pursues an unexpected path. "It was not necessary that the defendant should have had notice of the particular method in which an accident would occur, if the possibility of an accident was clear to the ordinarily prudent eye" [ ]. Some acts, such as shooting, are so imminently dangerous to any one who may come within reach of the missile, however unexpectedly, as to impose a duty of prevision not far from that of an insurer. Even today, and much oftener in earlier stages of the law, one acts sometimes at one's peril [ ]. Under this head, it may be, fall certain cases of what is known as transferred intent, an act willfully dangerous to A resulting by misadventure in injury to B (Talmage v. Smith, 101 Mich. 370, 374 [1894]). These cases aside, wrong is defined in terms of the natural or probable, at least when unintentional (Parrot v. Wells, Fargo & Co. [The Nitro-Glycerine Case], 15 Wall. [82 U.S.] 524 [1872]). The range of reasonable apprehension is at times a question for the court, and at times, if varying inferences are possible, a question for the jury. Here, by concession, there was nothing in the situation to suggest to the most cautious mind that the parcel wrapped in newspaper would spread wreckage through the station. If the guard had thrown it down knowingly and willfully, he would not have threatened the plaintiff's safety, so far as appearances could warn him. His conduct would not have involved, even then, an unreasonable probability of invasion of her bodily security. Liability can be no greater where the act is inadvertent.

Negligence, like risk, is thus a term of relation. Negligence in the abstract, apart from things related, is surely not a tort, if indeed it is understandable at all [ ]. Negligence is not a tort unless it results in the commission of a wrong, and the commission of a wrong imports the violation of a right, in this case, we are told, the right to be protected against interference with one's bodily security. But bodily security is protected, not against all forms of interference or aggression, but only against some. One who seeks redress at law does not make out a cause of action by showing without more that there has been damage to his person. If the harm was not willful, he must show that the act as to him had possibilities of danger so many and apparent as to entitle him to be protected against the doing of it though the harm was unintended. Affront to personality is still the keynote of the wrong. Confirmation of this view will be found in the history and development of the action on the case. Negligence as a basis of civil liability was unknown to mediaeval law (8 Holdsworth, History of English Law, p. 449; Street, Foundations of Legal Liability, vol. 1, pp. 189, 190). For damage to the person, the sole remedy was trespass and trespass did not lie in the absence of aggression, and that direct and personal [ ]. Liability for other damage, as where a servant without orders from the master does or omits something to the damage of another, is a plant of later growth [ ]. When it emerged out of the legal soil, it was thought of as a variant of trespass, an offshoot of the parent stock. This appears in the form of action, which was known as trespass on the case [ ]. The victim does not sue derivatively, or by right of subrogation, to vindicate an interest invaded in the person of another. Thus to view his cause of action is to ignore the fundamental difference between tort and crime ([ ]). He sues for breach of a duty owing to himself.

The law of causation, remote or proximate, is thus foreign to the case before us. The question of liability is always anterior to the question of the measure of the consequences that go with liability. If there is no tort to be redressed, there is no occasion to consider what damage might be recovered if there were a finding of a tort. We may assume, without deciding, that negligence, not at large or in the abstract, but in relation to the plaintiff, would entail liability for any and all consequences, however novel or extraordinary ([ ]; Smith v. London & S.W. Ry. Co., L.R. 6 C.P. 14; [ ]; cf. Matter of Polemis, L.R. 1921, 3 K.B. 560; [ ]). There is room for argument that a distinction is to be drawn according to the diversity of interests invaded by the act, as where conduct negligent in that it threatens an insignificant invasion of an interest in property results in an unforeseeable invasion of an interest of another order, as, e.g., one of bodily security. Perhaps other distinctions may be necessary. We do not go into the question now. The consequences to be followed must first be rooted in a wrong.

The judgment of the Appellate Division and that of the Trial Term should be reversed, and the complaint dismissed, with costs in all courts.

■ ANDREWS, J. (dissenting).

Assisting a passenger to board a train, the defendant's servant negligently knocked a package from his arms. It fell between the platform and the cars. Of its contents the servant knew and could know nothing. A violent explosion followed. The concussion broke some scales standing a considerable distance away. In falling they injured the plaintiff, an intending passenger.

Upon these facts may she recover the damages she has suffered in an action brought against the master? The result we shall reach depends upon our theory as to the nature of negligence. Is it a relative concept—the breach of some duty owing to a particular person or to particular persons? Or where there is an act which unreasonably threatens the safety of others, is the doer liable for all its proximate consequences, even where they result in injury to one who would generally be thought to be outside the radius of danger? This is not a mere dispute as to words. We might not believe that to the average mind the dropping of the bundle would seem to involve the probability of harm to the plaintiff standing many feet away whatever might be the case as to the owner or to one so near as to be likely to be struck by its fall. If, however, we adopt the second hypothesis we have to inquire only as to the relation between cause and effect. We deal in terms of proximate cause, not of negligence.

. . .

But we are told that "there is no negligence unless there is in the particular case a legal duty to take care, and this duty must be one which is owed to the plaintiff himself and not merely to others." [ ] This I think too narrow a conception. Where there is the unreasonable act, and some right that may be affected there is negligence whether damage does or does not result. That is immaterial. Should we drive down Broadway at a reckless speed, we are negligent whether we strike an approaching car or miss it by an inch. The act itself is wrongful. It is a wrong not only to those who happen to be within the radius of danger but to all who might have been there—a wrong to the public at large. Such is the language of the street. . . .

It may well be that there is no such thing as negligence in the abstract. "Proof of negligence in the air, so to speak, will not do." In an empty world negligence would not exist. It does involve a relationship between man and his fellows. But not merely a relationship between man and those whom he might reasonably expect his act would injure. Rather, a relationship between him and those whom he does in fact injure. If his act has a tendency to harm some one, it harms him a mile away as surely as it does those on the scene. We now permit children to recover for the negligent killing of the father. It was never prevented on the theory that no duty was owing to them. A husband may be compensated for the loss of his wife's services. To say that the wrongdoer was negligent as to the husband as well as to the wife is merely an attempt to fit facts to theory. An insurance company paying a fire loss recovers its payment of the negligent incendiary. We speak of subrogation—of suing in the right of the insured. Behind the cloud of words is the fact they hide, that the act, wrongful as to the insured, has also injured the company. Even if it be true that the fault of father, wife or insured will prevent recovery, it is because we consider the original negligence not the proximate cause of the injury. [ ]

In the well-known *Polemis* Case [ ], Scrutton, L.J., said that the dropping of a plank was negligent for it might injure "workman or cargo or ship." Because of either possibility the owner of the vessel was to be made good for his loss. The act being wrongful the doer was liable for its proximate results. Criticized and explained as this statement may have been, I think it states the law as it should be and as it is. [ ]

The proposition is this: Every one owes to the world at large the duty of refraining from those acts that may unreasonably threaten the safety of others. Such an act occurs. Not only is he wronged to whom harm might reasonably be expected to result, but he also who is in fact injured, even if he be outside what would generally be thought the danger zone. There needs be duty due the one complaining but this is not a duty to a particular individual because as to him harm might be expected. Harm to some one being the natural result of the act, not only that one alone, but all those in fact injured may complain. We have never, I think, held otherwise. . . .

If this be so, we do not have a plaintiff suing by "derivation or succession." Her action is original and primary. Her claim is for a breach of duty to herself—not that she is subrogated to any right of action of the owner of the parcel or of a passenger standing at the scene of the explosion.

The right to recover damages rests on additional considerations. The plaintiff's rights must be injured, and this injury must be caused by the negligence. We build a dam, but are negligent as to its foundations. Breaking, it injures property down stream. We are not liable if all this happened because of some reason other than the insecure foundation. But when injuries do result from our unlawful act we are liable for the consequences. It does not matter that they are unusual, unexpected, unforeseen and unforeseeable. But there is one limitation. The damages must be so connected with the negligence that the latter may be said to be the proximate cause of the former.

These two words have never been given an inclusive definition. What is a cause in a legal sense, still more what is a proximate cause, depend in each case upon many considerations, as does the existence of negligence itself. Any philosophical doctrine of causation does not help us. A boy throws a stone into a pond. The ripples spread. The water level rises. The history of that pond is altered to all eternity. It will be altered by other causes also. Yet it will be forever the resultant of all causes combined. Each one will have an influence. How great only omniscience can say. You may speak of a chain, or if you please, a net. An analogy is of little aid. Each cause brings about future events. Without each the future would not be the same. Each is proximate in the sense it is essential. But that is not what we mean by the word. Nor on the other hand do we mean sole cause. There is no such thing.

Should analogy be thought helpful, however, I prefer that of a stream. The spring, starting on its journey, is joined by tributary after tributary. The river, reaching the ocean, comes from a hundred sources. No man may say whence any drop of water is derived. Yet for a time distinction may be possible. Into the clear creek, brown swamp water flows from the left. Later, from the right comes water stained by its clay bed. The three may remain for a space, sharply divided. But at last, inevitably no trace of separation remains. They are so commingled that all distinction is lost.

As we have said, we cannot trace the effect of an act to the end, if end there is. Again, however, we may trace it part of the way. A murder at Sarajevo may be the necessary antecedent to an assassination in London twenty years hence. An overturned lantern may burn all Chicago. We may follow the fire from the shed to the last building. We rightly say the fire started by the lantern caused its destruction.

A cause, but not the proximate cause. What we do mean by the word "proximate" is, that because of convenience, of public policy, of a rough sense of justice, the law arbitrarily declines to trace a series of events beyond a certain point. This is not logic. It is practical politics. Take our rule as to fires. Sparks from my burning haystack set on fire my house and my neighbor's. I may recover from a negligent railroad. He may not. Yet the wrongful act has directly harmed the one as the other. We may regret that the line was drawn just where it was, but drawn somewhere it had to be. We said the act of the railroad was not the proximate cause of our neighbor's fire. Cause it surely was. The words we used were simply indicative of our notions of public policy. Other courts think differently. But somewhere they reach the point where they cannot say the stream comes from any one source.

Take the illustration given in an unpublished manuscript by a distinguished and helpful writer on the law of torts. A chauffeur negligently collides with another car which is filled with dynamite, although he could not know it. An explosion follows. A, walking on the sidewalk nearby, is killed. B, sitting in a window of a building opposite, is cut by flying glass. C, likewise sitting in a window a block away, is similarly injured. And a further illustration. A nursemaid, ten blocks away, startled by the noise, involuntarily drops a baby from her arms to the walk. We are told that C may not recover while A may. As to B it is a question for court or jury. We will all agree that the baby might not. Because, we are again told, the chauffeur had no reason to believe his conduct involved any risk of injuring either C or the baby. As to them he was not negligent.

But the chauffeur, being negligent in risking the collision, his belief that the scope of the harm he might do would be limited is immaterial. His act unreasonably jeopardized the safety of any one who might be affected by it. C's injury and that of the baby were directly traceable to the collision. Without that, the injury would not have happened. C had the right to sit in his office, secure from such dangers. The baby was entitled to use the sidewalk with reasonable safety.

The true theory is, it seems to me, that the injury to C, if in truth he is to be denied recovery, and the injury to the baby is that their several injuries were not the proximate result of the negligence. And here not what the chauffeur had reason to believe would be the result of his conduct, but what the prudent would foresee, may have a bearing. May have some bearing, for the problem of proximate cause is not to be solved by any one consideration.

It is all a question of expediency. There are no fixed rules to govern our judgment. There are simply matters of which we may take account. We have in a somewhat different connection spoken of "the stream of events." We have asked whether that stream was deflected—whether it was forced into new and unexpected channels. [ ] This is rather rhetoric than law. There is in truth little to guide us other than common sense.

There are some hints that may help us. The proximate cause, involved as it may be with many other causes, must be, at the least, something without which the event would not happen. The court must ask itself whether there was a natural and continuous sequence between cause and effect. Was the one a substantial factor in producing the other? Was there a direct connection between them, without too many intervening causes? Is the effect of cause on result not too attenuated? Is the cause likely, in the usual judgment of mankind, to produce the result? Or by the exercise of prudent foresight could the result be foreseen? Is the result too remote from the cause, and here we consider remoteness in time and space. (Bird v. St. Paul F. & M. Ins. Co., 224 N.Y. 47 [1918], where we passed upon the construction of a contract—but something was also said on this subject.) Clearly we must so consider, for the greater the distance either in time or space, the more surely do other causes intervene to affect the result. When a lantern is overturned the firing of a shed is a fairly direct consequence. Many things contribute to the spread of the conflagration—the force of the wind, the direction and width of streets, the character of intervening structures, other factors. We draw an uncertain and wavering line, but draw it we must as best we can.

Once again, it is all a question of fair judgment, always keeping in mind the fact that we endeavor to make a rule in each case that will be practical and in keeping with the general understanding of mankind.

Here another question must be answered. In the case supposed it is said, and said correctly, that the chauffeur is liable for the direct effect of the explosion although he had no reason to suppose it would follow a collision. "The fact that the injury occurred in a different manner than that which might have been expected does not prevent the chauffeur's negligence from being in law the cause of the injury." But the natural results of a negligent act—the results which a prudent man would or should foresee—do have a bearing upon the decision as to proximate cause. We have said so repeatedly. What should be foreseen? No human foresight would suggest that a collision itself might injure one a block away. On the contrary, given an explosion, such a possibility might be reasonably expected. I think the direct connection, the foresight of which the courts speak, assumes prevision of the explosion, for the immediate results of which, at least, the chauffeur is responsible.

It may be said this is unjust. Why? In fairness he should make good every injury flowing from his negligence. Not because of tenderness toward him we say he need not answer for all that follows his wrong. We look back to the catastrophe, the fire kindled by the spark, or the explosion. We trace the consequences—not indefinitely, but to a certain point. And to aid us in fixing that point we ask what might ordinarily be expected to follow the fire or the explosion.

This last suggestion is the factor which must determine the case before us. The act upon which defendant's liability rests is knocking an apparently harmless package onto the platform. The act was negligent. For its proximate consequences the defendant is liable. If its contents were broken, to the owner; if it fell upon and crushed a passenger's foot, then to him. If it exploded and injured one in the immediate vicinity, to him also as to A in the illustration. Mrs. Palsgraf was standing some distance away. How far cannot be told from the record—apparently twenty-five or thirty feet. Perhaps less. Except for the explosion, she would not have been injured. We are told by the appellant in his brief "it cannot be denied that the explosion was the direct cause of the plaintiff's injuries." So it was a substantial factor in producing the result—there was here a natural and continuous sequence—direct connection. The only intervening cause was that instead of blowing her to the ground the concussion smashed the weighing machine which in turn fell upon her. There was no remoteness in time, little in space. And surely, given such an explosion as here it needed no great foresight to predict that the natural result would be to injure one on the platform at no greater distance from its scene than was the plaintiff. Just how no one might be able to predict. Whether by flying fragments, by broken glass, by wreckage of machines or structures no one could say. But injury in some form was most probable.

Under these circumstances I cannot say as a matter of law that the plaintiff's injuries were not the proximate result of the negligence. That is all we have before us. The court refused to so charge. No request was made to submit the matter to the jury as a question of fact, even would that have been proper upon the record before us.

The judgment appealed from should be affirmed, with costs.

■ POUND, LEHMAN and KELLOGG, JJ., concur with CARDOZO, CH. J.; ANDREWS, J., dissents in opinion in which CRANE and O'BRIEN, JJ., concur.

NOTES AND QUESTIONS

1. Motion for reargument was denied, 164 N.E. 564 (N.Y.1928), with the following opinion:

> If we assume that the plaintiff was nearer the scene of the explosion than the prevailing opinion would suggest, she was not so near that injury from a falling package, not known to contain explosives, would be within the range of reasonable prevision.

How close would have been close enough for the majority? The three original dissenters concurred in the denial of reargument.

2. In what way do the facts of *Palsgraf* differ from those of *Polemis* and *Wagon Mound*? How might the facts of *Wagon Mound* be altered to resemble *Palsgraf*?

3. Are there differences between the approach taken by Judge Cardozo and that taken by Viscount Simonds in *Wagon Mound*? Compare the reasons for limiting liability for negligence offered by Viscount Simonds and Judge Andrews.

4. What is the role of proximate cause in the Cardozo analysis?

5. How are the functions of judge and jury with regard to foreseeability of the risk of harm to plaintiff allocated under the Cardozo view? Under the Andrews view? Which, in your view, is the preferable allocation?

Professor Cardi, who examined how states address plaintiff-foreseeability, found that a majority of states treat this issue as an aspect of duty rather than scope of liability, with the law in a substantial number of the other states too unclear to categorize. While duty is a matter of law for the court, Cardi also found that courts that treat plaintiff foreseeability as a matter of duty split just about in half as to whether that issue should be decided by the fact-finder or by the court. See Cardi, The Hidden Legacy of *Palsgraf*: Modern Duty Law in Microcosm, 91 B.U.L.Rev. 1873, 1890–1911 (2011).

6. *Palsgraf* is surely one of a handful of the most famous U.S. torts cases of all time, perhaps the single most famous. It has been widely cited even by contemporary courts, and scholars remain interested in its legacy. Yet, often *Palsgraf* is cited for propositions that are far afield from the narrow duty ruling it adopted, and Judge Andrews' dissent is regularly invoked. As Prosser put it, "It has become fashionable to cite *Palsgraf* in every kind of negligence case, and most . . . must be disregarded as insignificant and immaterial." Prosser, *Palsgraf* Revisited, 52 Mich.L.Rev. 1, 8 (1953). Nevertheless, *Palsgraf* is often credited for directing courts to the element of duty as the appropriate basis for invoking policy concerns to limit liability instead of employing the proximate cause inquiry to serve that purpose, as would be necessary based on Judge Andrews' insistence on a duty owed to the entire world. See Geistfeld, The Principle of Misalignment: Duty, Damages, and the Nature of Tort Liability, 121 Yale L.J. 142, 177 (2011).

7. How might Judge Cardozo's suggested distinction between the risk of an insignificant invasion of property and the occurrence of bodily injury work? He suggests other distinctions might be desirable. Assume plaintiff is standing four feet from the railroad agents. Instead of the package falling on P's foot it hits the ground and explodes, taking out one of P's eyes. Would it make sense to distinguish between a risk to the feet and a risk to the eyes? What is the appropriate level of generality at which to describe harms? Recall C. Morris & C.R. Morris, p. 417 supra.

8. What outcome in *Palsgraf* under the different "type" of harm argument made in *Polemis*, p. 400 supra? Under the harm-within-the-risk test in the Third Restatement, p. 408 supra? How would those rules resolve the hypothetical in the previous note?

9. Toward the end of his opinion, Judge Cardozo says that to permit the plaintiff to sue "derivatively" to "vindicate an interest invaded in the person of another" would be to "ignore the fundamental difference between tort and crime." What does he mean?

10. Do the *Palsgraf* facts suggest any other theory on which plaintiff might have been more successful in a suit against the railroad? How should the case have been analyzed if plaintiff had argued that the railroad's negligence was the failure to secure adequately the weighing scale?

11. *Rescue.* Judge Cardozo had previously decided a case in which plaintiff was hurt while trying to rescue his cousin who had fallen from defendant's train due to the negligence of the crew. Wagner v. International

Railway Co., 133 N.E. 437 (N.Y.1921). The trial judge had charged that the negligence toward the cousin would not lead to liability to the rescuer unless the jury found that the train conductor had invited the plaintiff to partake in the rescue and had accompanied him with a lantern. Rejecting that approach, Judge Cardozo wrote:

> Danger invites rescue. The cry of distress is the summons to relief. The law does not ignore these reactions of the mind in tracing conduct to its consequences. It recognizes them as normal. It places their effects within the range of the natural and probable. The wrong that imperils life is a wrong to the imperiled victim; it is a wrong also to his rescuer. . . . The risk of rescue, if only it be not wanton, is born of the occasion. The emergency begets the man. The wrongdoer may not have foreseen the coming of a deliverer. He is accountable as if he had.

Is this consistent with *Palsgraf*? What about a case in which the area is so desolate that the defendant could not reasonably anticipate anyone around to attempt rescuing someone defendant is negligently harming or threatening? Judge Cardozo then turned to another issue:

> The defendant says that we must stop, in following the chain of causes, when action ceases to be "instinctive." By this, is meant, it seems, that rescue is at the peril of the rescuer, unless spontaneous and immediate. If there has been time to deliberate, if impulse has given way to judgment, one cause, it is said, has spent its force, and another has intervened. In this case, the plaintiff walked more than four hundred feet in going to Herbert's aid. He had time to reflect and weigh; impulse had been followed by choice; and choice, in the defendant's view, intercepts and breaks the sequence. We find no warrant for thus shortening the chain of jural causes. We may assume, though we are not required to decide, that peril and rescue must be in substance one transaction; that the sight of the one must have aroused the impulse to the other; in short, that there must be unbroken continuity between the commission of the wrong and the effort to avert its consequences. If all this be assumed, the defendant is not aided. Continuity in such circumstances is not broken by the exercise of volition. . . . The law does not discriminate between the rescuer oblivious of peril and the one who counts the cost. It is enough that the act, whether impulsive or deliberate, is the child of the occasion.

Should it matter whether a rescuer is bitten by a snake, struck by lightning, or hurt in the crash of a helicopter that has joined the search? Injuries to professional rescuers are discussed at p. 487 infra.

In Moore v. Shah, 458 N.Y.S.2d 33 (App.Div.1982), plaintiff alleged that he was a rescuer entitled to recovery—he donated his kidney to his father who had been hurt by defendant's malpractice. Although it was foreseeable that malpractice might create the need for a kidney and that a child might feel the need to donate a kidney to a parent in need, the court denied recovery. The donor's actions were not spontaneous or instantaneous; rather, the son's action was "deliberate and reflective, not made under the pressures and exigencies of an emergency situation, and significantly, at a time after defendant's alleged negligent acts." Why should the time frame matter? For a discussion of other kidney donation cases, all of which reach the same outcome as *Moore*, see Dabdoub v. Ochsner Clinic, 760 So.2d 347 (La.2000).

12. *Fire.* The fire rule to which Judge Andrews referred is unique to New York and originated in Ryan v. New York Central Railroad Co., 35 N.Y. 210 (1866). Sparks from defendant's negligently maintained engine ignited one of its sheds and the fire spread to other buildings, including plaintiff's. The court denied recovery:

> I prefer to place my opinion upon the ground that, in the one case, to wit, the destruction of the building upon which the sparks were thrown by the negligent act of the party sought to be charged, the result was to have been anticipated the moment the fire was communicated to the building; that its destruction was the ordinary and natural result of its being fired. In the second, third or twenty-fourth case, as supposed, the destruction of the building was not a natural and expected result of the first firing. That a building upon which sparks and cinders fall should be destroyed or seriously injured must be expected, but that the fire should spread and other buildings be consumed, is not a necessary or [a] usual result. That it is possible, and that it is not unfrequent, cannot be denied. The result, however, depends, not upon any necessity of a further communication of the fire, but upon a concurrence of accidental circumstances, such as the degree of the heat, the state of the atmosphere, the condition and materials of the adjoining structures and the direction of the wind. These are accidental and varying circumstances. The party has no control over them, and is not responsible for their effects.

Later New York cases have extended the liability somewhat, but the fundamental limitation remains. Does Judge Andrews adequately distinguish this line of cases? Virtually all other states reject this limitation.

13. For further reading on proximate cause, see L. Green, Rationale of Proximate Cause (1927); H. Hart & A. Honore, Causation in the Law (1959); C. Morris & C. Robert Morris, Morris on Torts, Ch. VII (2d ed.1980); Calabresi, Concerning Cause and the Law of Torts: An Essay for Harry Kalven, Jr., 43 U.Chi.L.Rev. 69 (1975); Kelley, Proximate Cause in Negligence Law: History, Theory, and the Present Darkness, 69 Wash.U.L.Q. 49 (1991).

CHAPTER VII

DEFENSES

A. THE PLAINTIFF'S FAULT

The foregoing chapters have explored the prima facie case that the plaintiff must present in order to establish liability for negligence (except for damages, a subject discussed in Chapter XI). But the common law has recognized several defenses against the plaintiff's claim. By far, the most common is the defendant's contention that even if defendant was negligent toward the plaintiff, the plaintiff was careless about his or her own safety and was "contributorily" negligent. This defense appears as early as 1809 in England and seems to have been well established in this country by 1850—the time of *Brown v. Kendall*, p. 40 supra. We have already encountered the defense in a number of cases, such as *Carroll Towing*, which set forth the Hand formula for reasonable care, p. 47 supra.

1. CONTRIBUTORY NEGLIGENCE

When the defense of contributory negligence was established, plaintiff was completely barred from recovery, as we saw in *Baltimore & Ohio Railroad v. Goodman*, p. 62 supra. Thus, traditional negligence law operated on an all or nothing basis. This meant that although both plaintiff and defendant acted negligently, plaintiff bore all of the costs of the accident. As we shall soon see, this feature of the system produced a range of legal doctrines to ease the impact of the contributory negligence defense on certain plaintiffs.

The common law elements of the contributory negligence defense parallel those of the basic negligence claim—except in the sense that any duty owed is to one's self rather than to others. The trier uses an adapted risk calculus to determine the reasonableness of the plaintiff's conduct. For example, rescuers who were hurt going to the aid of others would often be barred by a straightforward application of the ordinary risk calculus because the risks attending the attempted rescue outweighed the expected gain both to the victim and the rescuer. Nevertheless, the courts usually allowed these cases to reach juries by declaring them to involve issues on which reasonable persons could differ.

The conduct must be a factual cause of the plaintiff's harm. This requirement is illustrated by Hightower v. Paulson Truck Lines, Inc., 559 P.2d 872 (Or.1977), in which plaintiff's recovery was not affected, despite his having followed defendant's vehicle too closely on the highway, because defendant "suddenly slowed" without warning. A jury could have found that even if the plaintiff had been following at a reasonably safe distance, he still could not have stopped in time. Might plaintiffs have a more tolerant standard of causation applied to their contributory conduct? Isn't conduct that only poses a risk to oneself less culpable than when it exposes others to a risk of harm? When contributory negligence constituted a complete bar to recovery, many courts were more lenient in evaluating plaintiffs' conduct both with regard to reasonableness and causation.

The plaintiff's negligence must also be a proximate cause of the plaintiff's harm. For example, assume P is warned not to stand on a high platform because it is shaky and may not hold P's weight. Without justification P disregards the advice, stands on the platform, and is hurt when an adjacent wall collapses as the result of defendant's negligence and knocks P from the platform to the ground below. Assuming P is hurt, her negligence may have causally contributed to the injury, but was it a proximate cause or was the unexpected consequence one that absolves plaintiff of her unreasonable conduct?

Recall the determination in *Brown v. Kendall* that the plaintiff had the burden of proving freedom from contributory negligence. Virtually all states have switched that burden to the defendant. Is one approach more clearly appropriate than the other?

Statutes. A statute may have the purpose of protecting some group against its own inability to protect itself, in which case the statute may be interpreted as barring a defense of contributory negligence. See, e.g., Chainani v. Board of Education, 663 N.E.2d 283 (N.Y.1995), discussing a statute requiring school bus operators to instruct students in crossing streets, to flash red lights, and to wait until students disembarking from the bus have crossed the street. The court had already decided that the statutory purpose was to protect the school children against their own negligence, and now held that that purpose would be thwarted if a child's contributory negligence were a defense.

Limitations on contributory negligence. Even if contributory negligence was found in a particular case, several rules emerged over the years that limited the impact of such a finding in barring a plaintiff's recovery.

a. *Recklessness.* Virtually all courts decided that contributory negligence was a defense only in cases of negligence. If the misconduct of the defendant was more serious—recklessness or willful misconduct—the appropriate defense would have been "contributory recklessness" or "contributory willful misconduct." Contributory negligence was totally irrelevant in such cases and the plaintiff recovered all of his or her damages. Why?

Consider Second Restatement section 500, which provides the following approach to the common law aspects of recklessness, usually considered to be synonymous with willful or wanton misconduct:

The actor's conduct is in reckless disregard of the safety of another if he does an act or intentionally fails to do an act which it is his duty to the other to do, knowing or having reason to know of facts which would lead a reasonable man to realize, not only that his conduct creates an unreasonable risk of physical harm to another, but also that such risk is substantially greater than that which is necessary to make his conduct negligent.

b. *Last clear chance.* Contributory negligence was also disregarded under circumstances that came to be called "last clear chance." In these cases the plaintiff behaved carelessly and got into a dangerous situation that led to injury. In response to the defense of contributory negligence, plaintiff claimed that the defendant had, but failed to utilize, the "last clear chance" to avoid the injury to the negligent plaintiff. The doctrine is first applied in Davies v. Mann, 10 M. & W. 546, 152 Eng.Rep. 588 (1842), in which defendant ran into a donkey that plaintiff had carelessly left tied in the roadway.

Two types of dangerous situations triggered the doctrine of last clear chance. In one, the plaintiff had gotten into a position of "helpless peril" through her own negligence and was no longer able to take protective steps. In that situation most courts invoked last clear chance against a defendant who knew or should have known of the plaintiff's plight while still able to avoid the harm by the exercise of due care. The other type of last clear chance case involved an inattentive plaintiff who was oblivious to the danger that she could have avoided had she been reasonably attentive. Here, most courts required that before the doctrine could be applied the defendant had to have actual knowledge of plaintiff's danger in time to avoid harm by the exercise of due care.

Generally, the doctrine was regarded as having a chronological aspect. Thus, a claim that the defendant could not stop in time because of brake failure would not have invoked last clear chance because most courts required that the defendant be able to do something in the period after the plaintiff's peril starts

When last clear chance was held applicable, the fact that the plaintiff was contributorily negligent became totally irrelevant, and the plaintiff recovered all appropriate damages with no offset. The doctrine remains important in states that still retain contributory negligence. See Washington Metropolitan Area Transit Authority v. Johnson, 726 A.2d 172 (D.C.1999)(en banc).

c. *Refusal to impute contributory negligence.* We have already observed that on occasion the law will impute the negligence of one person to another. The most significant example of imputed negligence is respondeat superior, the doctrine that has given rise to the imposition of vicarious liability on employers. Recall the discussion in Chapter I. On the plaintiff's side, we have also seen examples of cases in which the courts have reached a similar result by calling one action derivative from another, thus giving the person bringing the second action only the rights that the first person had.

With the exception of derivative actions, virtually all imputed contributory negligence has been eliminated over the years. Thus, most courts continue to impute the negligence of an injured person to family members asserting consortium claims. Similarly, in wrongful death actions, the decedent's negligence is imputed to the survivors' suit. Courts are split on whether a bystander's claim for negligent infliction of emotional distress should bear the fault of the physical injury victim.

These imputation rules do not necessarily reflect a single ethical or economic rationale. Respondeat superior, for example, served the important function of providing a class of defendants who were more likely than their servants to be able to respond to the damage awards that the courts were imposing and might be able to make the entire operation safer. On the other hand, calling an action "derivative" rather than "independent" in the consortium and wrongful death cases appears to spring more from a notion of regarding the cluster of plaintiffs as a group, and then finding it unfair for the defendant to owe a greater obligation to some "indirect" plaintiffs than to the original victim.

d. *The jury's role.* Surely the most modern technique for ameliorating the perceived harshness of the all or nothing contributory negligence rule (prior to the adoption of comparative negligence) was the increased frequency with which courts found that reasonable persons could differ over the characterization of the plaintiff's conduct— so that a jury question was presented. Observers asserted that most juries rejected the judge's instruction to return a defense verdict if they found any contributory negligence, even the most minimal contributory fault, so long as it proximately related to the harm. The belief was that the jury simply reduced the plaintiff's damages by some amount rather than returning a defense verdict. Consider the following passage from Alibrandi v. Helmsley, 314 N.Y.S.2d 95 (N.Y.Civ.Ct.1970), involving a trial to the court, in which the judge assumed that defendant was negligent and concluded that the plaintiff was contributorily negligent. He then continued:

> Plaintiff's injuries were not trivial. I am as confident as one can be about these matters that, had the case been tried to a jury, the jury would have determined the sum of plaintiff's damages in a substantial amount, deducted a portion equivalent to the degree of his negligence, and returned a verdict for the difference. In short, as every trial lawyer knows, the jury would likely have ignored its instructions on contributory negligence and applied a standard of comparative negligence.
>
> It would be comfortable for me simply to guess what the jury's verdict would have been and then file a one-sentence decision holding defendants liable in that amount. Comfortable

but false. My duty is to apply the law as I understand it, and I do not understand that, no matter what a jury might do, a judge may pretend to make a decision on the basis of contributory negligence while actually deciding on comparative negligence.

Did the judge reach the right decision? Did the plaintiff's attorney commit malpractice by not demanding a jury in the case? Does the judge's analysis reflect badly on the legal system? The jury system?

Recently, researchers gathered empirical evidence supporting the *Alibrandi* judge's assessment of jury behavior. See Best & Donohue, Jury Nullification in Modified Comparative Negligence Regimes, 79 U.Chi.L.Rev. 945 (2012)(finding juries in modified comparative fault states were 67% less likely to assign comparative fault in excess of 50%, in which case recovery would be barred, than in pure comparative fault states, where such a finding results only in a proportional reduction).

From the plaintiff's standpoint, jury nullification did not solve the basic problem with contributory negligence. Sometimes plaintiff's negligence was so clear that no self-respecting judge could permit the issue to go to the jury. In other words, the device of sending a close case to the jury worked only when the closeness was in the question of whether plaintiff had been negligent at all—not in cases in which plaintiff's negligence was clear, but relatively minor. Of course, plaintiffs also faced the prospect that some juries might actually follow the judge's instructions.

2. COMPARATIVE NEGLIGENCE

Until the late 1960s, only a handful of states had abandoned the all or nothing contributory negligence approach. These few states adopted a system called "comparative negligence," in which a negligent plaintiff's recovery depended on how serious plaintiff's negligence was compared to the defendant's. Three principal versions had developed. In one, called "pure" comparative negligence, the plaintiff who is 90% to blame for an accident can recover 10% of the damages from the defendant who was found to be 10% at fault. (A defendant who was also hurt in that same accident could recover 90% of her damages from the plaintiff.) The second and third versions are lumped together as a "modified" system. Under one variant, a plaintiff who is at fault can recover as under the pure system but only so long as that negligence is "not as great as" the defendant's. Under the other variant, plaintiff can recover as under the pure system but only so long as that negligence is "no greater than" the defendant's. When does this distinction matter?

In addition to the states, the federal statute regulating injuries to railroad workers, discussed at p. 853 infra, used a pure system. Still, comparative negligence remained largely a reform proposal at the beginning of the 1970s.

Today, only a handful of states and the District of Columbia adhere to the traditional contributory negligence rule. In Coleman v. Soccer Ass'n of Columbia, 69 A.3d 1149 (Md. 2013), reform proponents made a full-scale effort to convince the court to adopt comparative fault, which it had declined to do 30 years previously. Once again, the court, in a 4–2 decision, refused to do so, explaining that the host of subsidiary questions that arise when comparative fault is adopted are better addressed at one time by the legislature, which is also the appropriate body for expressions of the state's public policy. A spirited dissent by Judge Harrell began:

> Paleontologists and geologists inform us that Earth's Cretaceous period (including in what is present day Maryland) ended approximately 65 million years ago with an asteroid striking Earth (the Cretaceous-Paleogene Extinction Event), wiping-out, in a relatively short period of geologic time, most plant and animal species, including dinosaurs. As to the last premise, they are wrong. A dinosaur roams yet the landscape of Maryland (and Virginia, Alabama, North Carolina and the District of Columbia), feeding on the claims of persons injured by the negligence of another, but who contributed proximately in some way to the occasion of his or her injuries, however slight their culpability. The name of that dinosaur is the doctrine of contributory negligence. With the force of a modern asteroid strike, this Court should render, in the present case, this dinosaur extinct.

Of the states that have adopted comparative negligence, about a dozen use the "pure" version, and almost all the others are divided between those adhering to the "not as great as" and the "no greater than" variants. (A few use "slight" and "gross.") This flood was undoubtedly due in part to growing unhappiness with the harshness of contributory negligence. But it seems to have received a considerable boost from efforts to undermine proponents of no-fault auto insurance, who were arguing that too many auto accident victims were receiving no tort compensation because of the contributory negligence rule. We discuss the no-fault approach in Chapter XII.

Although most of the action in the 1970s and early 1980s occurred in state legislatures, some courts in important states, including those of California, Florida, and Illinois, adopted comparative negligence by judicial decision. See, e.g., Li v. Yellow Cab Co. of California, 532 P.2d 1226 (Cal.1975), discussing at length the propriety of judicial action in this area. Those courts willing to change the rule emphasized the fact that the original doctrine was judicially created and thus was amenable to judicial change. They also stressed the power of the common law to grow and develop in response to newly perceived needs. In contrast, those courts that refused to make the change emphasized that the doctrine had been such a central part of negligence law for over a century that legislative consideration should occur before it was changed. Who had the better of this argument? Which body is better suited to lay out the subsidiary rules (see the Uniform Comparative Fault Act, p. 442 infra) that require determination once comparative negligence is adopted?

Recall that in *Hammontree v. Jenner,* p. 3 supra, the court rejected the plaintiff's suggestion that the court abandon the negligence approach in favor of strict liability principles on the ground that such a change required legislative action. Is there a distinction between the two situations? Is it possible to generalize from these two cases about the circumstances in which judicial reform of basic tort doctrine—as opposed to legislative reform—is appropriate? See generally Zacharias, The Politics of Torts, 95 Yale L.J. 698 (1986)(arguing that when legislative action is desirable, courts should decide cases in a way that is most likely to spur legislative action).

In the states that proceeded by legislation, the statutes were usually quite short and simply announced which version of comparative negligence was being adopted—most frequently a modified, rather than pure, version. No attempt was made to anticipate the many questions that would arise after any such basic change in the system was enacted. By contrast, virtually all the states that proceeded by judicial decision adopted the "pure version"—in large part because the choice of either modified version involved what might have appeared to be an arbitrary selection.

Adoption of comparative fault also affects the apportionment of liability among multiple tortfeasors. Recall that in the introduction to joint and several liability in Chapter V, p. 370, the impact of the adoption of comparative fault on joint and several liability was briefly explained. Modification of joint and several liability, in turn, raises a number of issues about apportioning liability among defendants and settling parties for contribution purposes where joint and several liability still operates, or among defendants, settling parties, and non-parties where several liability governs. These issues are addressed at p. 452 infra, in the materials following our discussion of the effect of comparative fault on apportioning liability between plaintiff and defendant.

Implementation issues. The courts, although perhaps discussing some of the impending problems more than the legislatures, also did not anticipate many of the complications that have emerged. We will explore the central issues raised by a comparative negligence approach through consideration of a model statute, a state statute with different provisions from the model statute, and discussion of the judicial issues that have arisen in the area. The model statute is the Uniform Comparative Fault Act (the UCFA) promulgated by the National Conference of Commissioners on Uniform State Laws (NCCUSL) in

1977.* The state statute is from Iowa, which enacted a comparative negligence statute modeled on the UCFA but which contains several significant differences.

Read the UCFA and the Iowa statutory provisions following it to learn the rights of your client C in the following situations (disregard insurance). Be sure to note the differences in the outcomes under the UCFA and the Iowa statute:

a.   There has been an accident in which A has suffered damages of $100,000 and has brought suit against B, C, and D. A trial has established that the relative shares of fault are A–40%; B–30%; C–10%; and D–20%. Assume all are solvent.

b.   At trial it appears that D is insolvent. Now what result?

c.   Same as a., except that C has also been hurt and has sustained damages of $25,000. *can only recover $22,500*

d.   Change the percentages in a. to A–50%; B–30%; C–10%; and D–10%. What happens if A's share is determined to be 51% (with a 1% reduction for C)?

e.   Suppose after judgment in the hypothetical described in a., A says to B, "Pay me $60,000." Does B have to do that or can B tender $30,000 and satisfy her obligations under the judgment?

[Handwritten margin notes:
UCFA   I
10k   *10k*
12k to C   10k
A 10k
B 7.5k
D 5k
to A
C 10k still
10k or *9k when 51%*
O   once 51%   if 50% still 10k
★ individually and jointly/severally liable]

Uniform Comparative Fault Act

12 Uniform Laws Annotated 33 (1981 Supp.).

Section 1.   [Effect of contributory fault]

(a) In an action based on fault seeking to recover damages for injury or death to person or harm to property, any contributory fault chargeable to the claimant diminishes proportionately the amount awarded as compensatory damages for an injury attributable to the claimant's contributory fault, but does not bar recovery. This rule applies whether or not under prior law the claimant's contributory fault constituted a defense or was disregarded under applicable legal doctrines, such as last clear chance.

(b) "Fault" includes acts or omissions that are in any measure negligent or reckless toward the person or property of the actor or others, or that subject a person to strict tort liability. The term also includes breach of warranty, unreasonable assumption of risk not constituting an enforceable express consent, misuse of a product for which the defendant otherwise would be liable, and unreasonable

---

* In 2003, NCCUSL promulgated a new uniform act, the Uniform Apportionment of Tort Responsibility Act, 5 ULA 12 (Supp.2005). It was enacted after all but five United States jurisdictions had adopted comparative negligence and so is unlikely to have broad impact. It was enacted in order to account for the substantial modification of joint and several liability since the UCFA. Its main differences from the UCFA are discussed below in the notes following the UCFA.

failure to avoid an injury or to mitigate damages. Legal requirements of causal relation apply both to fault as the basis for liability and to contributory fault.

Section 2.   [Apportionment of damages]

(a) In all actions involving fault of more than one party to the action, including third-party defendants and persons who have been released under Section 6, the court, unless otherwise agreed by all parties, shall instruct the jury to answer special interrogatories or, if there is no jury, shall make findings, indicating:

(1) the amount of damages each claimant would be entitled to recover if contributory fault is disregarded; and

(2) the percentage of the total fault of all of the parties to each claim that is allocated to each claimant, defendant, third-party defendant, and person who has been released from liability under Section 6. For this purpose the court may determine that two or more persons are to be treated as a single party.

(b) In determining the percentages of fault, the trier of fact shall consider both the nature of the conduct of each party at fault and the extent of the causal relation between the conduct and the damages claimed.

(c) The court shall determine the award of damages to each claimant in accordance with the findings, subject to any reduction under Section 6, and enter judgment against each party liable on the basis of rules of joint-and-several liability. For purposes of contribution under Sections 4 and 5, the court also shall determine and state in the judgment each party's equitable share of the obligation to each claimant in accordance with the respective percentages of fault.

(d) Upon motion made not later than [one year] after judgment is entered, the court shall determine whether all or part of a party's equitable share of the obligation is uncollectible from that party, and shall reallocate any uncollectible amount among the other parties, including a claimant at fault, according to their respective percentages of fault. The party whose liability is reallocated is nonetheless subject to contribution and to any continuing liability to the claimant on the judgment.

Section 3.   [Setoff]

A claim and counterclaim shall not be set off against each other, except by agreement of both parties. On motion, however, the court, if it finds that the obligation of either party is likely to be uncollectible, may order that both parties make payment into court for distribution. The court shall distribute the funds received and declare obligations discharged as if the payment into court by either party had been a payment to the other party and any distribution of those funds back to the party making payment had been a payment to him by the other party.

Section 4.   [Right of contribution]

(a) A right of contribution exists between or among two or more persons who are jointly and severally liable upon the same indivisible claim for the same injury, death, or harm, whether or not judgment has been recovered against all or any of them. It may be enforced either in the original action or by a separate action brought for that purpose. The basis for contribution is each person's equitable share of the obligation, including the equitable share of a claimant at fault, as determined in accordance with the provisions of Section 2.

(b) Contribution is available to a person who enters into a settlement with a claimant only (1) if the liability of the person against whom contribution is sought has been extinguished and (2) to the extent that the amount paid in settlement was reasonable.

Section 5.   [Enforcement of contribution]

(a) If the proportionate fault of the parties to a claim for contribution has been established previously by the court, as provided by Section 2, a party paying more than his equitable share of the obligation, upon motion, may recover judgment for contribution.

(b) If the proportionate fault of the parties to the claim for contribution has not been established by the court, contribution may be enforced in a separate action, whether or not a judgment has been rendered against either the person seeking contribution or the person from whom contribution is being sought.

(c) If a judgment has been rendered, the action for contribution must be commenced within [one year] after the judgment becomes final. If no judgment has been rendered, the person bringing the action for contribution either must have (1) discharged by payment the common liability within the period of the statute of limitations applicable to the claimant's right of action against him and commenced the action for contribution within [one year] after payment, or (2) agreed while action was pending to discharge the common liability and, within [one year] after the agreement, have paid the liability and commenced an action for contribution.

Section 6.   [Effect of release]

A release, covenant not to sue, or similar agreement entered into by a claimant and a person liable discharges that person from all liability for contribution, but it does not discharge any other persons liable upon the same claim unless it so provides. However, the claim of the releasing person against other persons is reduced by the amount of the released person's equitable share of the obligation, determined in accordance with the provisions of Section 2.

Iowa Code Chapter 668

Liability in Tort-Comparative Fault.

. . .

668.3.   [Effect of contributory fault]

1.   a. Contributory fault shall not bar recovery in an action by a claimant to recover damages for fault resulting in death or in injury to person or property unless the claimant bears a greater percentage of fault than the combined percentage of fault attributed to the defendants, third-party defendants and persons who have been released [settling parties], but any damages allowed shall be diminished in proportion to the amount of fault attributable to the claimant.

. . .

5.   If the claim is tried to a jury, the court shall give instructions and permit evidence and argument with respect to the effects of the answers to be returned to the interrogatories submitted under this section [inquiring into the percentages of comparative fault that the jury assigns to the parties].

. . .

668.4.   Joint and several liability

In actions brought under this chapter, the rule of joint and several liability shall not apply to defendants who are found to bear less than fifty percent of the total fault assigned to all parties. However, a defendant found to bear fifty percent or more of fault shall only be jointly and severally liable for economic damages and not for any noneconomic damage awards.

NOTES AND QUESTIONS

1.   *Pure or modified version?* The introductory notes by the NCCUSL commissioners make a number of arguments against the modified version. First, a party more at fault than the other who has to bear his own losses and also a share of the other party's losses is worse off than at common law. Second, if a plaintiff whose fault is greater than the defendant's is barred from recovery under a modified statute but is permitted to pursue a traditional common law claim, plaintiff might, in some cases, such as last clear chance, recover full damages: "The anomaly therefore arises that he may be better off if his negligence is found to be greater than that of the defendant and he thus recovers full damages. . . ." Finally, if the plaintiff is not permitted to pursue a common law claim, he may be worse off under the modified comparative negligence statute than he would have been with contributory negligence (and its ameliorative doctrines). Are these persuasive attacks on the modified version? What are the problems of the "pure" version? Why have 30 of the 36 jurisdictions legislatively adopting comparative negligence chosen a modified version? Unlike the UCFA, the 2003 Uniform Apportionment of Tort Responsibility Act adopts a modified

comparative negligence scheme, recognizing that it is the predominant scheme selected by legislatures.

In Sutton v. Piasecki Trucking, Inc., 451 N.E.2d 481 (N.Y.1983), plaintiff driver disregarded a stop sign and was hit by an approaching truck. Plaintiff was allocated 99% of the fault—and received 1% of his damages. Are awards such as this sensible? Are they likely to be recurring problems?

2.   *What is to be compared?* The comments to section 2 of the UCFA state that in setting fault percentages, the trier of fact should consider:

> such matters as (1) whether the conduct was mere inadvertence or engaged in with an awareness of the danger involved, (2) the magnitude of the risk created by the conduct, including the number of persons endangered and the potential seriousness of the injury, (3) the significance of what the actor was seeking to attain by his conduct, (4) the actor's superior or inferior capacities, and (5) the particular circumstances, such as the existence of an emergency requiring a hasty decision.

Making this comparison sometimes can produce widely varying appraisals. In Wright v. City of Knoxville, 898 S.W.2d 177 (Tenn.1995), for example, plaintiff girlfriend was riding in a car driven by defendant boyfriend and heading north. At an extremely busy intersection, the green arrow came on and boyfriend began to make a left turn into a westbound lane when he heard a siren. Because he could not locate the siren, he continued making the turn—and he collided with a police car that was driving east in the westbound lane to avoid traffic backed up at the light. The officer, who was responding to a call of "an accident with injuries," was moving at 10–15 miles per hour. Plaintiff sued both her boyfriend and the officer driving the police car. The judge sitting as trier of fact allocated 75% of the fault to the officer and 25% to the boyfriend. The court of appeals found that the boyfriend had violated a number of Tennessee traffic regulations and allocated 100% of the fault to him. The Supreme Court held that the officer should be assigned 25% of the fault because she had driven on the wrong side of the road with full knowledge that drivers would be turning directly at her. Despite the result in the *Knoxville* case, courts generally are reluctant to reassess the fact finder's allocation of percentages unless they are totally indefensible.

3.   *Reckless conduct.** What types of conduct should be compared? Under contributory negligence, the plaintiff's negligence generally was overlooked when the defendant's conduct had been reckless. The UCFA's sweep in section 1(b) is quite broad, reaching matters of liability and of

---

*   Up to this point we have used the term "comparative *negligence.*" That terminology becomes inaccurate when applied to culpable conduct other than negligence, such as recklessness or intentional conduct. Reflecting that concern, many courts and the UCFA, set out above, have employed "comparative fault." However, even that more expansive label is inadequate when strict liability is also included for apportionment purposes. Thus, the Restatement Third: Apportionment of Liability and the 2003 Uniform Act rely on "comparative responsibility." We continue to use the term comparative negligence for the sake of uniformity, despite the limited scope it conveys.

damage measurement. Even though few courts have adopted this draft legislation, virtually all states with pure versions have concluded that reckless conduct should be compared with plaintiff's negligence. E.g., Sorensen v. Allred, 169 Cal.Rptr. 441 (App.1980)(comparing defendant's drunk and speeding driving (55%) with plaintiff's careless left turn in front of defendant (45%)).

4. *The interplay of intent and negligence.* Although the vast majority of states will compare the plaintiff's negligence with the defendant's recklessness, what should they do when the defendant has committed an intentional tort or crime and the plaintiff has been negligent? Consider, for example, a defendant who commits an assault and battery on a plaintiff at a bar after the plaintiff acts unreasonably to provoke the attack. Of the few states that have addressed the issue, most have refused to compare the negligence of a plaintiff with the intentional tort of a defendant because intentional conduct is different "in kind" from negligent or reckless conduct and therefore may not be compared. In cases of intentional torts, contributory negligence is not an affirmative defense, so what would justify reducing the plaintiff's recovery on this ground? The comments to section 1 of the UCFA state that although the Act does not include intentional torts, courts are not precluded from making comparisons in such cases if they find it appropriate. We consider the related question of what to do when there are two defendants, one of whom has been negligent and the other of whom was an intentional tortfeasor or criminal in note 1, p. 453 infra.

5. *Plaintiff no-duty rules.* In those jurisdictions that permit comparisons between a negligent plaintiff and an intentional tortfeasor, might there be a role for no-duty rules applicable to a plaintiff's conduct? Thus, in the same way that courts adopted no-duty rules to exempt defendants from liability as reflected in Chapter III, courts can rule that a plaintiff had no duty to protect herself (however awkward it is to speak of a plaintiff's duty to herself). Thus, in Christensen v. Royal School District No. 160, 124 P.3d 283 (Wash.2005)(en banc), a 13-year-old student sued the school and principal as a result of a sexual relationship the student had with a teacher. Defendants claimed that her voluntary participation constituted contributory negligence. The court held that her consent could not constitute contributory fault. It cited two policy reasons: the same concerns for protection of minors that mandate statutory rape as a crime, regardless of consent, and the "solemn duty" of a school district to protect its minor students.

6. *Should the judgments be set off against each other?* The denial of setoffs in the UCFA is designed to cover situations in which insurance exists on both sides so that injured parties will maximize their recoveries. The issue arose in Jess v. Herrmann, 604 P.2d 208 (Cal.1979), in which the court, 4–3, denied setoff: if both drivers were adequately insured, the "setoff produces results detrimental to the interests *of both parties* and accords the insurance companies of the parties a fortuitous windfall simply because each insured happens to have an independent claim against the person he has injured."

7. *Should jurors be told the consequences of their verdict?* States disagree over whether juries should know the implications of their decisions. In H.E. Butt Grocery Co. v. Bilotto, 985 S.W.2d 22 (Tex.1998), the question was whether to use special verdicts that tell the jury the legal consequences of any verdict that it might render. The majority, 5–4, approved telling the jury. Justice Gonzalez, concurring at length, asserted that "most jurisdictions that have addressed the issue in the last twenty-five years have moved away from the rule against informing the jury of the legal effect of its answers." He quoted from Seppi v. Betty, 579 P.2d 683 (Idaho 1978):

> It would be incredibly naive to believe that jurors, after having listened attentively to testimony of the parties and a parade of witnesses and after having heard the arguments of counsel, will answer questions . . . without giving any thought to the effect those answers will have on the parties and to whether their answers will effectuate a result in accord with their own lay sense of justice. With respect to most questions, the jury would have to be extremely dullwitted not to be able to guess which answers favor which parties. In those instances where the legal effect of their answers is not so obvious, the jurors will nonetheless speculate, often incorrectly, and thus subvert the whole judicial process.

Some states address the question in their statutes. See, e.g., Iowa Code § 668.3.5, p. 445 supra. The 2003 Uniform Act has a similar provision in section 3.

The question of how much to tell the jury arises in other contexts as well. See, e.g., Weiss v. Goldfarb, 713 A.2d 427 (N.J.1998)(jury not to be told that hospital's statutory maximum liability is $10,000 in a case in which outside doctors are also being sued—and noting that the statute bars telling jury about cap on punitive damages); Lacy v. CSX Transportation, Inc., 520 S.E.2d 418 (W.Va.1999)(jury not to be told about operation of joint and several liability). Contra Kaeo v. Davis, 719 P.2d 387 (Haw.1986)(jury to be informed of effect of holding D1 99% at fault and D2 1% at fault in joint and several liability state).

8. *Damage caps.* Many states, as an aspect of tort reform, have enacted limitations on the total amount of damages that a plaintiff may recover. Often these limits are imposed only on non-economic damages such as pain and suffering, but occasionally on the plaintiff's entire damages. These caps create a question of statutory interpretation when the jury's award of damages is above the cap, but the plaintiff's comparative negligence would reduce the recovery to below that statutory cap. In Hall v. Brookshire Bros., 848 So.2d 559 (La.2003), the court read the statute imposing the cap to address the maximum amount the plaintiff could *recover* and thus held that the plaintiff's comparative share should first be deducted from the verdict amount, then the cap applied.

9. *Other changes wrought by comparative negligence.* The introduction of comparative negligence has forced courts to reconsider

almost every aspect of the negligence system, indeed many aspects of strict liability and intentional torts as well. Some defenses, such as last clear chance, were eliminated. Some other changes include:

a. *Res ipsa loquitur.* Under comparative negligence, what if the evidence clearly shows contributory negligence on plaintiff's part? In Montgomery Elevator Co. v. Gordon, 619 P.2d 66 (Colo.1980)(en banc), the court concluded that res ipsa could be used if the plaintiff's evidence showed only that the accident is ordinarily of the type caused by negligence and that the defendant had control of the instrumentality that caused such negligence. Such circumstantial proof of defendant's negligence does not foreclose the possibility that the accident was also caused by the plaintiff's contributory negligence. Under those conditions, the jury must then compare any evidence of negligence of the plaintiff with the inferred negligence of the defendant and decide what percentage of negligence is attributable to each party.

b. *Proximate cause.* Recall *Barry v. Quality Steel Products, Inc.*, p. 418 supra, in which the court held that, because of the adoption of apportionment based on comparative fault, innocent and negligent superseding causes should have no independent significance. Thus, so long as the harm was within the scope of the risk, negligent intervening actors could not be superseding causes. But see Exxon Co., U.S.A. v. Sofec, Inc., 517 U.S. 830 (1996)(holding that for admiralty purposes adoption of comparative fault does not prevent plaintiff's conduct from constituting a superseding cause because such a rule is not internally inconsistent with comparative fault).

c. *Rescue.* Since the introduction of comparative negligence, defendants have argued that rescuers—who were not barred from recovery by their negligence earlier unless rash or reckless—no longer need special protection. Most courts have agreed. See also Restatement (Third) of Torts: Liability for Physical and Emotional Harm § 32 cmt. d (2010)(stating that "social value and altruistic motivation" of a rescuer can be taken into account both as to whether the rescuer was negligent and, if so, in assigning comparative responsibility to that rescuer). But see Ouellette v. Carde, 612 A.2d 687 (R.I.1992), in which the court held that comparative negligence "does not fully protect the rescue doctrine's underlying policy of promoting rescue." The law "places a premium on human life, and one who voluntarily attempts to save a life of another should not be barred from complete recovery." Since the defendant did not allege that the plaintiff had acted rashly or recklessly, the trial judge should not have charged at all on the issue of plaintiff's negligence.

d. *The unlawful acts doctrine.* This doctrine holds that a plaintiff cannot recover damages when, at the time of the injury, the plaintiff was engaged in an illegal act. Thus, in Greenwald v. Van Handel, 88 A.3d 467 (Conn.2014), plaintiff was charged criminally with possession of child pornography. He sued the social worker who counseled him when he was a minor alleging that the defendant negligently failed to treat plaintiff for his behavior of viewing pornography on the Internet. That failure, plaintiff claimed, led to the behavior that resulted in his arrest. After engaging in a thorough discussion of the rule, its breadth, and exceptions, the court concluded it barred plaintiff's claim notwithstanding the adoption of comparative fault, explaining:

> [C]omparative negligence "has no application to the [wrongful conduct] rule precluding a plaintiff from recovering for injuries sustained as a direct result of his own illegal conduct of a serious nature. . . . That rule is not based on the theory that a plaintiff, with an otherwise cognizable cause of action, cannot recover for an injury to which he has contributed. . . . It rests, instead, upon the public policy consideration that the courts should not lend assistance to one who seeks compensation under the law for injuries resulting from his own acts when they involve a substantial violation of the law. . . . It simply means that proof of such an injury would not demonstrate any cause of action cognizable at law."

Id. at 476–77 (quoting Barker v. Kallash, 468 N.E.2d 39 (N.Y.1984)).

By contrast, in Estate of Kelley v. Moguls, Inc., 632 A.2d 360 (Vt.1993), the court held that the estate of a person who had killed himself by driving while drunk may assert a common law negligence action against the licensed vendor who supplied the alcohol. The defendant argued that this would encourage drunk driving and allow a wrongdoer to profit from his own wrong. The court responded that under comparative negligence plaintiff would not be made whole, and that it was appropriate that both parties in this situation be deterred from their conduct. See also Dugger v. Arredondo, 408 S.W.3d 825 (Tex.2013)(concluding in a suit against the friend of decedent whose use of heroin caused his death for failing to call 911 that the state's adoption of comparative fault and a narrower rule that barred claims by convicted felons for injuries arising from that conduct superseded the state's common law unlawful acts doctrine barring the claim); Ashmore v. Cleanweld Products, Inc., 672 P.2d 1230 (Or.App.1983)(relying on section 889 of the Second Restatement, which states that "[o]ne is not barred from recovery for an interference with his legally protected interests merely because at the time of the interference he was committing a tort or a crime," to conclude that 15-year-old bomb maker could maintain his action against product sellers of ingredients used to make the bomb; public policy against illegal manufacture of explosives "is best effectuated . . . through penal laws").

Should the unlawful acts doctrine bar an illegal immigrant from bringing any tort suit?

e.   *The role of seat belt nonusage.* After seat belts were first installed in automobiles—the regulatory mandate to install them in all cars occurred in 1968—the question arose of what impact a plaintiff's failure to use the belt should have in a tort suit.* At the time, contributory negligence was a complete bar to recovery, and both legislatures and courts were not

---

*   Such a "defense," if recognized, constituted a form of avoidable consequences, i.e., a failure to mitigate damages that occurred as a result of the initial accident, a subject we address at p. 461 infra.

sympathetic to barring a claim for any enhanced injuries caused by plaintiff's failure to use a seat belt. Some legislatures, when making it a crime not to use a belt or helmet, added a provision that makes the violation inadmissible in any civil action. Others provided that the violation, if causally related to the harm, may reduce civil damages but by no more than a small percentage. See, e.g., Meyer v. City of Des Moines, 475 N.W.2d 181 (Iowa 1991)(discussing the Iowa statute that limits the reduction in the plaintiff's recovery to 5%).

Some states, including California and New York, allow the failure to use safety devices to fully reduce recoverable damages, although the defendant is likely to bear the burden of showing what part of plaintiff's harm was due to the failure to use the safety equipment. See the extended discussion in Law v. Superior Court, 755 P.2d 1135 (Ariz.1988). Others reject any reduction. See Swajian v. General Motors Corp., 559 A.2d 1041 (R.I.1989):

> We recognize the safety-belt defense for what it is worth—a manifestation of public policy. This court believes that any attempt at reducing highway fatalities through promoting the increased use of safety belts is best accomplished by legislative action. Recent studies indicate that the vast majority of Rhode Islanders refuse to buckle up. [ ] If we were to impose a duty to wear safety belts, in essence this court would be condemning most motor-vehicle occupants as negligent. Such a determination, if desirable, is properly left to the Legislature. . . . Moreover, should recent safety-belt-use studies prove reliable, it could be argued that manufacturers should design vehicles in a manner safe for those who foreseeably will not wear safety belts. The above discussion smacks of public-policy considerations more appropriately addressed by the Legislature. In any event, we are doubtful that a contrary holding would encourage increased use of safety belts.

The Texas Supreme Court, which had decided in 1974 against any seat belt defense, reconsidered that rule 40 years later in *Nabors Well Services, Ltd. v. Romero*, 456 S.W.3d 553, 555–56 (Tex.2015):

> For more than forty years evidence of a plaintiff's failure to use a seat belt has been inadmissible in car-accident cases. That rule, which this Court first announced in 1974, offered plaintiffs safe harbor from the harshness of an all or nothing scheme that barred recovery for even the slightest contributory negligence. Moreover, the Court reasoned that although a plaintiff's failure to use a seat belt may exacerbate his injuries, it cannot *cause* a car accident, and therefore should not affect a plaintiff's recovery.

> In 1985 the Legislature jumped in to statutorily prohibit evidence of use or nonuse of seat belts in all civil cases. It repealed that law in 2003, leaving our rule to again stand alone. But much has changed in the past four decades. The Legislature has overhauled Texas's system for apportioning fault in negligence

cases—a plaintiff's negligence can now be apportioned alongside a defendant's without entirely barring the plaintiff's recovery. And unlike in 1974, seat belts are now required by law and have become an unquestioned part of daily life for the vast majority of drivers and passengers.

These changes have rendered our prohibition on seat-belt evidence an anachronism. The rule may have been appropriate in its time, but today it is a vestige of a bygone legal system and an oddity in light of modern societal norms. Today we overrule it and hold that relevant evidence of use or nonuse of seat belts is admissible for the purpose of apportioning responsibility in civil lawsuits.

Apportionment of Liability Among Multiple Defendants

Comparative fault may be understood as a method for apportioning liability between plaintiffs and defendants. Once the all or nothing rule of contributory negligence was replaced with comparative assessments, the doctrine of contribution—the apportionment of loss among defendants—also incorporated comparative notions. Thus, the UCFA provides, in section 4(a), p. 444, supra, for a right of contribution among jointly and severally liable defendants and determines the "equitable share" of each defendant through the assignment of a percentage of fault in section 2(a)(2). This means that if D1 is held 75% at fault and D2 25% at fault for the harm suffered by the plaintiff, the victim could still get full damages from either defendant, but they would ultimately share the loss in a 75–25 ratio if both were solvent.

In addition to contribution, indemnity is another method for apportioning among defendants but operates on an all or nothing basis. The classic situation for indemnity is master-servant, in which the master, who is liable only as a matter of law under respondeat superior, could seek indemnification. Recall Chapter I, p. 25.

The second recent change in the traditional pattern of apportioning liability among multiple defendants has been much more significant—replacing or modifying joint and several liability. Joint and several liability came under fire after the adoption of comparative fault, which meant that even culpable plaintiffs could recover damages, and because of perceived unfairness to some "peripheral" defendants who nevertheless were solvent when the other "primary" defendants were far more culpable and insolvent. Do you see why several liability obviates (under most circumstances) the need for contribution but not indemnity?

When all defendants are solvent, whether joint and several liability or several liability is applicable does not matter. (Do you see why plaintiff's solvency vel non doesn't matter?) However, in reality, insolvency often shapes litigation strategy in tort law. (Recall, e.g.,

Tarasoff, p. 150 supra, *Vince v. Wilson*, p. 181 supra, and *Reynolds v. Hicks*, p. 175 supra.)

Since the early 1980s, some 40 states, including Iowa in section 668.4, p. 445 supra, have made major legislative changes in the operation of joint and several liability. It is hard to capture the array of changes but they fit very roughly into the following categories:

1.   About a dozen states have abolished the doctrine, leaving a solvent defendant responsible only for his or her percentage-of-fault share of the plaintiff's damages.

2.   About a dozen have abolished the doctrine in cases in which the defendant is less than a specified threshold percentage at fault. In most of these the threshold is 50%.

3.   A few states, including California, have retained joint and several liability for economic damages but have abolished it for non-economic damages.

4.   A handful of states have abolished the doctrine when the plaintiff is partially at fault, but have retained it when the plaintiff is not at fault.

5.   A handful retain joint and several liability, but reallocate the percentage share of any insolvent defendant to the other parties in the case in proportion to their respective shares of fault. See section 2(d) of the Uniform Comparative Fault Act, p. 442 supra.

6.   A handful have abolished the doctrine in many kinds of torts, but have retained it in a few areas—most commonly toxic and environmental torts. (New York, for example, retains the doctrine in several listed situations, including motor vehicle and motorcycle cases, recklessness cases, and a variety of environmental cases.)

Which if any of these changes would you favor?

NOTES AND QUESTIONS

1.   *Apportionment among intentional and negligent defendants.* Many courts have permitted apportionment among defendants when one or more committed an intentional tort while others acted negligently. Recall the reluctance of courts to permit such apportionment between a negligent plaintiff and an intentional tortfeasor, note 4, p. 447 supra. In Veazey v. Elmwood Plantation Associates, Ltd., 650 So.2d 712 (La.1994), the plaintiff was raped in her apartment and brought an action against the management company for failure to exercise due care for the safety of residents. After the trial judge refused to permit any allocation of fault to the unidentified nonparty rapist, the supreme court split three ways. The majority concluded that it might be appropriate to compare negligence and intentional fault in some cases but that this case was not one of them. Three reasons motivated the majority. First, the defendant's duty to provide a safe place to live encompassed the very risk that injured plaintiff, and the defendant should not be able to reduce its liability when its failure

brought about the very harm feared. Second, any comparison would be against public policy because it would reduce the safety incentives of the management company, especially here since any "rational juror" would apportion most of the fault to the rapist at the "innocent plaintiff's expense." Finally, the court concluded that intentional torts are "fundamentally different" from negligence and the two cannot be compared in many situations, including this one.

The concurring justice asserted that the trial judge reached the right result because the two types of torts could never be compared. The dissenters thought that the two types of harm could be, and should be, compared in this case. One dissenter asserted that this "result—holding the negligent tortfeasor(s) responsible for the entirety of the damages because of the mere happenstance that a co-tortfeasor committed an intentional, as opposed to a negligent wrongdoing—is anomalous." That justice concluded that the fault should be apportioned 90% to the rapist and 10% to the defendant. Under the state law of joint and several liability this would have made the defendant liable for half the plaintiff's damages. Which of the three views seems most sound? Does your view depend on the state's approach to joint and several liability? Two years after *Veazey*, the legislature adopted the concurring approach and barred use of plaintiff's fault to reduce recovery against an intentional tortfeasor. La. Civ. Code Ann. art. 2323. See also Kansas State Bank & Trust Co. v. Specialized Transportation Services, Inc., 819 P.2d 587 (Kan.1991)(refusing to apportion where defendant negligently hired a school bus driver who attacked a student).

2. *The impact of several liability.* Remember that with joint and several liability, apportionment among intentional and negligent tortfeasors will not affect the total liability of the negligent tortfeasors to the plaintiff. This is especially important given the frequency with which intentional tortfeasors are judgment proof. Several liability changes this situation dramatically. Do you see why? Sometimes courts refuse to permit comparisons between negligent and intentional tortfeasors to preserve substantial recovery against the negligent tortfeasor. Sometimes, courts that permit comparison are motivated by a countervailing concern—to cushion the negligent tortfeasor from bearing most or all of the plaintiff's damages. Thus, in Chianese v. Meier, 774 N.E.2d 722 (N.Y.2002), plaintiff tenant was attacked in the hallway of her apartment building. The court upheld apportioning responsibility to both the owner (for negligent security) and the attacker. Despite the anomaly in comparing intent and negligence, the court was concerned that to do otherwise would deny the benefit of several liability to a negligent defendant when another party committed an intentional tort. What impact does permitting apportionment have on incentives to exercise reasonable care to prevent intentional torts? See Graves v. North Eastern Services, Inc., 345 P.3d 619, 634 (Utah 2015)(holding similarly to *Chianese* while acknowledging that such a rule would "dampen incentives of a defendant who has a duty to undertake due care in preventing acts of intentional misconduct").

3. *Apportioning greater fault to negligent than to intentional tortfeasors.* In a state that allows or requires comparison, is a jury ever justified in allocating more fault to the negligent defendant than to the person who committed an intentional tort? How is the jury to compare the two? In Scott v. County of Los Angeles, 32 Cal.Rptr.2d 643 (App.1994), the trial court entered judgment in favor of an abused child on a jury verdict that apportioned fault 99% to the county and the social worker and 1% to the abusive parent. The appellate court rejected that allocation, referring to a case in which another court had overturned a jury's allocation of 95% of the fault to a landlord who had been negligent in not protecting tenants from assaults and 5% against the two rapists.

Nash v. Port Authority of New York & New Jersey, 856 N.Y.S.2d 583 (App.2008), rev'd on other grounds sub nom. In re World Trade Center Bombing Litigation, 957 N.E.2d 733, 751 (N.Y.2011), reflects a contrasting approach to *Scott*. This case arose out of the first World Trade Center ("WTC") terrorist attack in 1993 when terrorists exploded a bomb in the parking garage. The case tells a chilling tale of how the WTC was recognized as a target for a terrorist attack as early as the 1980s by the Port Authority. The jury assigned defendant Port Authority 68% of the comparative fault, more than it assigned to the terrorists. The court declined to upset that ruling, relying on the "jury's exercise of its unique capacity to arrive at a more nuanced understanding of the nature and quality of the culpable conduct and its role in causing the plaintiff's harm" to justify this result. "[A]s this case so vividly illustrates, the blameworthiness of negligence may actually be increased by the heinousness of the wrongdoing it directly and foreseeably facilitates."

Consider the approach of the Restatement Third: Apportionment of Liability, section 14, which provides that a defendant who is negligent because of a "failure to protect the [plaintiff] from the specific risk of an intentional tort is jointly and severally liable" for the intentional tortfeasor's share of fault. How would section 14 affect cases like *Scott* or *Nash*? How would it affect a case against a towing company that negligently failed to tow a disabled car during which time the car was stolen by a thief who ran a red light and killed a pedestrian?

4. *What if one defendant is insolvent?* Reconsider the question posed about apportionment of liability in light of the UCFA and the Iowa comparative fault act, p. 442, supra. Suppose that, whether required or not, after judgment B pays A $60,000. What should B do after making that payment? Suppose that instead of suing B, C, and D, A sued only B and you represent B. What might you do to protect your client from paying more than her share? Since most states, as reflected in the Iowa statute, do not follow the UCFA, their treatment will depend on the state's law on joint and several liability. In states that retain the doctrine of joint and several liability, but do not follow the UCFA, the loss due to one defendant's insolvency will be spread among the remaining defendants through a contribution claim by the defendant who has paid more than its share. With several liability, the plaintiff will bear that loss. In Iowa, as in the many states that have some form of a hybrid of joint and several and several liability, the insolvent defendant's share of the damage will be shared among the plaintiff and the solvent defendants.

5. *Assigning fault to non-parties.* Many, but not all, jurisdictions that employ some form of several liability, permit comparative responsibility to be assigned to a non-party. The logic is that if defendant's liability is limited to its "share," determining the appropriate share requires consideration of all tortfeasors who bear responsibility for the harm, not just those joined in the suit. See, e.g., Landis v. Hearthmark, LLC, 750 S.E.2d 280 (W.Va.2013)(concluding that although the parental immunity doctrine precluded defendants from seeking contribution from parents, defendants could join parents as third-party defendants for an allocation of fault); Town of Kearny v. Brandt, 67 A.3d 601, 617 (N.J.2013)(upholding apportionment to party that had been dismissed from the case based on statute of repose). Section B19 of the Apportionment Restatement permits assignment of fault to non-parties so long as the non-party is identified and the defendant seeking to do so provides adequate notice to the other parties. The defendant bears the burden of proof of the non-party's liability. By contrast, the 2003 Uniform Apportionment of Tort Responsibility Act does not permit apportioning fault to non-parties.

6. *Partial settlements.* It is quite common for cases against two or more defendants to involve settlements with some but not all defendants. Consider the following hypothetical: A sues B, alleging B negligently drove his automobile into A, and also sues C, who served alcohol to B before the accident. Assume that at trial the jury will find damages to be $100,000 and that plaintiff is 10% at fault and each of the defendants is 45% at fault. B proposes a settlement with A of $25,000, which is the policy limit of B's liability insurance. B has no other assets. Should A settle with B:

a.   Under the UCFA?

The UCFA, in section 6, provides that when a tortfeasor settles with the plaintiff, the settling tortfeasor is released from any contribution claim by non-settling defendants. Those non-settlors receive a credit against any judgment for plaintiff in the amount of the settling party's "equitable share of the obligation," i.e., the amount of damages discounted by the comparative share of fault assigned to the settling party. Under this provision, A would recover a total of $70,000 if she settles with B. Yet, if she refuses to settle with B and goes to trial, she would recover more, because with the UCFA's reallocation provision in section 5(c), C would pay $45,000 plus 45/55 (82%) of B's $20,000 partial insolvency. Do you see why a comparative share credit for non-settling parties discourages settlement when one or more defendants is insolvent or partially insolvent?

b.   Under the Iowa statute?

Remember that, if any defendant is less than 50% comparatively at fault, that defendant is only severally liable. No contribution claim would exist for C because C would only be liable for its $45,000 comparative share of the damages. Thus, A would recover the same amount whether she settled with B or not.

c.   Under California (and a number of other states) law, which reduces the non-settling defendant's liability by the amount of a good faith settlement (i.e., one that did not involve any collusion between A and B)? (This system is known as a "pro tanto" or dollar-for-dollar credit for the non-settling defendant.)

Under the California system, C would receive a credit of only $25,000 for B's settlement, thus preserving the advantage of joint and several liability for A even if she settles with B. Do you see why the California scheme incentivizes early first settlements by jointly and severally liable defendants? Is there unfairness to the non-settling party when an entirely solvent defendant enters into a settlement with plaintiff for less than the settling defendant's comparative share of fault?

Apportionment on the Basis of Factual Causation

The discussion above about apportioning liability among plaintiff and defendants addressed only comparative *fault* as a basis of apportionment. Another basis for apportionment involves factual causation. Sometimes apportioning on the basis of causation is easy and it is performed without difficulty. Imagine two drivers who, driving negligently, simultaneously hit a careful pedestrian in a crosswalk: one driver hits the pedestrian on her right side, breaking her right arm, while the other hits the victim on her left side, breaking her left leg. In such an instance is there any role for comparative fault for apportioning liability? Contrast a situation in which each defendant is a cause of the entirety of plaintiff's harm. Thus, suppose the two negligent drivers collided with each other, resulting in the wheel of one of their cars flying off and hitting the careful pedestrian in the head, causing a concussion. Is there any role for apportionment on the basis of causation in such a case?

Sometimes, the causal role of the parties with regard to plaintiff's harm is not as clear as in the hypotheticals above. In Ravo v. Rogatnick, 514 N.E.2d 1104 (N.Y.1987), plaintiff suffered severe brain damage at birth. The evidence supported the view that the obstetrician's improper surgical technique during delivery resulted in hypoxia contributing to plaintiff's brain damage, as did the pediatrician's misdiagnosis and improper treatment. But the role of each was unclear; one expert testified she could not determine how much the pediatrician's negligence enhanced the brain injury. The pediatrician's defense was that he was not responsible for any of the child's brain damage, and thus he provided no evidence that might have permitted the jury to apportion on the basis of causation. The Court of Appeals affirmed a jury verdict finding both defendants liable for the entire injury and approved an instruction that permitted the jury to find both defendants liable if they were unable to determine how much of plaintiff's injury was caused by each. That result reflected section 433B(2) of the Second Restatement of Torts:

> Where the tortious conduct of two or more actors has combined to bring about harm to the plaintiff, and one or more of the actors seeks to limit his liability on the ground that the harm is capable of apportionment among them, the burden of proof as to the apportionment is upon each such actor.

What kind of apportionment does section 433B(2) address? What other basis of apportionment might nevertheless occur?

In *Ravo*, the jury assigned 80% of the fault to the obstetrician and 20% to the pediatrician. Damages were assessed at $2.75 million and the pediatrician argued that he should be liable for only $550,000. Because New York employed joint and several liability at the time, the court disagreed: This "aspect of the jury's determination of culpability merely defines the amount of contribution defendants may claim from each other, and does not impinge upon plaintiff's right to collect the entire judgment from either defendant."

Suppose that the jury in *Ravo* found that the pediatrician's negligence only enhanced the degree of the plaintiff's brain injury by 20%. How would such a finding affect the liability of the pediatrician by comparison to what he was held liable for in the case? Suppose that, rather than joint and several liability, the applicable rule was several liability and, as in *Ravo*, the jury was unable to apportion on the basis of causation but assigned 80% and 20% fault to the two doctors?

Do you understand why the Third Restatement recommends apportionment occur first, based on causation, and only after that is completed employing comparative fault to apportion? See Restatement (Third) of Torts: Apportionment of Liability § 26. All of these apportionment issues are discussed at length in Robertson, The Common Sense of Cause in Fact, 75 Tex.L.Rev. 1765 (1997).

Fritts v. McKinne

Court of Civil Appeals of Oklahoma, 1996.
934 P.2d 371.

■ STUBBLEFIELD, JUDGE.

. . .

David Fritts was seriously injured in a one-vehicle accident, which occurred during the early morning hours of February 20, 1990. David Fritts and his friend, David Manus, had been drinking prior to the accident. There was some dispute about which one of the two men was driving the Fritts pickup truck at the time of the accident. In any event, the vehicle hit a tree at approximately seventy miles per hour and overturned.

David Fritts sustained serious injuries as a result of the accident. He was diagnosed with a Lefort II fracture—literally all of his major facial bones were broken. He was placed in intensive care due to concern over the impact injury to his chest but later moved into a regular room.

[On February 25, 1990, Fritts underwent surgery to repair his facial fractures. During that surgery, defendant was performing a tracheostomy to allow Fritts to breathe during surgery. Fritts began bleeding profusely and died three days later. Plaintiff claimed that defendant negligently failed to identify and isolate the proper artery. Defendant claimed that the artery was anomalous—that it was in the neck area "when normally it should have been in the chest." He also asserted a comparative negligence defense based on the contention that Fritts was injured while driving drunk or was drunk while riding in a vehicle with Manus, who also was drunk.

At trial, plaintiff, Fritts's widow and administrator of his estate, objected to any mention of the use of drugs or alcohol. Defendant argued that such evidence was relevant to comparative negligence because "[his] injury arose in the automobile accident that he caused, because he [either drove] drunk or elected to ride with somebody who was driving drunk." Defendant also argued that the evidence was "relevant to the issue of damages—he would present expert testimony that Fritts had a substantially diminished life expectancy due to his drug and alcohol use." The trial court denied the plaintiff's motion to exclude the evidence. Much of the trial was devoted to evidence about Fritts's drunkenness at the time of the accident as well as his past drug and alcohol abuse.]

. . . Over plaintiff's objection, the trial court instructed the jury on the issue of Fritts's comparative negligence. These instructions included an instruction on "General Duty of Drivers," which stated that "[i]t is the duty of the driver of a motor vehicle to use ordinary care to prevent injury to himself or to other persons."

The jury returned a verdict in favor of Dr. McKinne. . . .

Plaintiff raises two interrelated propositions of error on appeal. She claims that the trial court erred in admitting evidence regarding her deceased husband's history of substance abuse and in allowing the jury to consider comparative negligence—based on the events of the automobile accident—as a basis for reducing or denying recovery on the medical negligence claim. . . .

appeal claims

. . . [Defendant] defended against the allegations of negligence by contending that, due to Fritts's unusual anatomy and the resultant injury to his artery from the high speed impact, the rupture of the artery was inevitable. This was a proper and appropriate defense. However, we conclude that the interjection of the issue of Fritts's possible negligence in the automobile accident, a matter unrelated to the medical procedures, was a substantial error that removed the jury's consideration from the relevant issues and led to an erroneous excursion into irrelevant and highly prejudicial matters.

There are limited circumstances under which reasonableness of patient conduct can be an appropriate consideration in medical negligence cases. For example, evidence of a patient's failure to reveal medical history that would have been helpful to his physician raises the issue of contributory negligence, particularly where the evidence also shows that the patient may have been advised of the importance of this information. [ ] A patient's furnishing of false information about his condition, failure to follow a physician's advice and instructions, or delay or failure to seek further recommended medical attention also are appropriate considerations in determining contributory negligence. . . .

Under the guise of a claim of contributory negligence, a physician simply may not avoid liability for negligent treatment by asserting that the patient's injuries were originally caused by the patient's own negligence. "Those patients who may have negligently injured themselves are nevertheless entitled to subsequent nonnegligent medical treatment and to an undiminished recovery if such subsequent nonnegligent treatment is not afforded." [ ]

P's right. →

Thus, aside from limited situations, negligence of a party which necessitates medical treatment is simply irrelevant to the issue of possible subsequent medical negligence. Herein, Dr. McKinne testified that, at the time of the surgery, which was five days after the accident, "alcohol was not a problem." Yet, from the time of his opening statement, the principal focus of the doctor's counsel was on the behavior of the decedent before and leading up to the automobile accident. . . .

Thus, we conclude that the submission of the issue of comparative negligence—decedent's conduct unrelated to his medical treatment— was error. We also find a strong probability that the erroneously given instructions misled the jurors and caused them to reach a result different from what they would have reached but for the flawed instructions.

. . .

Fritts's history of substance abuse is relevant to the issue of damages where there is evidence of its effect on probable life expectancy, and Plaintiff seeks damages based on loss of future earnings. However, like evidence of Fritts's drinking on the night of the accident, it was not proper for the jury to consider such evidence in regard to the claim of negligence against Dr. McKinne. Where evidence is admissible on a certain point only, the trial court should at least advise the jury to consider it on that point alone in order to assure that the evidence will not be applied improperly. [ ] Here, where the evidence is extremely inflammatory, bifurcation of trial of the liability and damages issues would have avoided completely the possibility of prejudice from the evidence.

We find that evidence of Fritts's intoxication and history of substance abuse, along with repeated references to it by defense counsel, was sufficiently prejudicial to Plaintiff's case as to have prevented a full and fair trial of the issues. Furthermore, the admission of relevant but inflammatory evidence, admissible for only one issue, was reversible error in the absence of limiting instructions or bifurcated trial.

[The judgment was reversed and remanded for a new trial.]

■ GOODMAN, P.J., and BOUDREAU, J., concur.

NOTES AND QUESTIONS

1.   What are the arguments for and against comparing in this type of situation? Do they involve questions of safety incentives?

2.   Suppose that defendant, after being sued by plaintiff, filed a claim for contribution against Manus, decedent's companion, alleging that his negligence in driving the car was also a cause of death. Would Manus's negligence be treated the same way as the court rules decedent's negligence should be treated?

3.   Should a physician sued for negligently treating a bullet wound be permitted to show that it had been inflicted while plaintiff, a robber, was trying to escape from the police? Recall the unlawful acts doctrine, p. 449 supra.

4.   Should the reluctance to compare plaintiff's conduct reflected in *Fritts* be limited to medical malpractice cases? Consider Wolfgang v. Mid-America Motorsports, Inc., 111 F.3d 1515 (10th Cir.1997), in which plaintiff professional car racer had negligently crashed on defendant racetrack. He sued only for harm due to a subsequent fire that was not extinguished quickly because of the track's alleged negligence. The court, using Kansas law, held that since plaintiff was suing only for the excess harm caused by the late rescue, the defendant could not show how plaintiff had been hurt.

3. AVOIDABLE CONSEQUENCES

During the era of contributory negligence there existed side-by-side a related doctrine called "avoidable consequences," which addressed the measure of damages but not issues of liability. Even if the accident were entirely the defendant's fault, the plaintiff's recovery would be reduced to the extent he failed to exercise due care to mitigate the harm done.

The clearest form of an avoidable consequences issue involved the plaintiff's failure to obtain medical attention or to follow medical advice. Courts generally refused to award damages for complications that could have been avoided by the exercise of due care after the accident. This situation may raise particularly sensitive issues. In Hall v. Dumitru, 620 N.E.2d 668 (Ill.App.Ct.1993), the court held a person under no duty to undergo surgery to mitigate the damages caused by defendant's negligence. Refusing to distinguish between major and minor surgery, the court thought the crucial line was between treatments that involved a "recognized risk" and those that did not. The duty to mitigate applied in the latter case, but not in the former:

> [I]f the proposed treatment could result in an aggravation of the existing condition or the development of an additional condition of ill health, or if the prospect for improved health is slight, then there should be no duty to undergo the treatment. If the risk is clearly remote, the exception should not apply. But the risk need not be significant or even probable in order to trigger the exception.

Once the grounds for an exception are established, the plaintiff need not articulate reasons for rejecting the procedure. "It is not the place of the court or the jury to evaluate a patient's reasons for declining surgery or treatment, if the risks are recognized." In the actual case the proposed surgery was a tubal ligation that involved "general anesthetic which alone has attendant risks which can be potentially harmful and life threatening. The procedure itself involves the use of a sharp instrument in close proximity to vital organs necessitating the use of carbon dioxide to inflate the abdomen. It is apparent from the record that a tubal ligation surgery involves risks to a woman's life or member. [ ] Therefore, the plaintiff was under no duty to undergo the surgery to mitigate her damages. . . ."

The reluctance to mitigate by treatment raises special problems when the reasons are based on religious beliefs. In Munn v. Algee, 924 F.2d 568 (5th Cir.1991), the court held that the decedent's religious beliefs would not justify her failure to accept a blood transfusion. The case is criticized in Note, Reason, Religion, and Avoidable Consequences: When Faith and the Duty to Mitigate Collide, 67 N.Y.U.L.Rev. 1111 (1992), which develops a "reasonable believer" notion under which the jury would be "instructed to assess the reasonableness of a plaintiff's mitigation efforts according to the standard of a reasonable, sincere adherent of the plaintiff's religious tenets." The note suggests an analogy to "eggshell skull. . . . From a policy standpoint . . . a victim of another's tortious conduct—whose religion constrains her from taking what others might deem reasonable, ameliorative steps—ought not be forced to choose between being spiritually or financially whole." But see Simons, The Puzzling Doctrine of Contributory Negligence, 16 Cardozo L.Rev. 1693 (1995), suggesting that the result in *Munn* is better explained on the ground that although "decedent's decision to honor her religious beliefs is *not* unreasonable, defendant has no duty to subsidize her choice to sacrifice her life in the name of religion."

Compare Tanberg v. Ackerman Investment Co., 473 N.W.2d 193 (Iowa 1991), in which plaintiff sustained a back injury due to defendant's negligence. His physician advised him to lose weight to mitigate the back pain. A jury found that plaintiff failed to make a reasonable effort to lose weight, and that plaintiff was 70% at fault for his damage compared to 30% for the tortfeasor. The court held the finding was plausible and affirmed after concluding that under the state's modified comparative negligence rule plaintiff recovered nothing. How would the UCFA handle this situation?

Another aspect of the avoidable consequences issue involves the failure to use seat belts or safety belts in automobiles, discussed p. 450 supra, or helmets with motorcycles. Because the mitigation precaution arose before the initial injury, this issue might be described as one of "anticipatory avoidable consequences." Regardless of when the untaken precaution arose, analytically this form of mitigation is the same as the conventional avoidable consequences doctrine. Under comparative fault, the issue is complicated. The problem is posed by assuming some numbers:

Defendant was solely to blame for a two-vehicle motorcycle crash in which the plaintiff, the other motorcyclist, was not wearing a helmet. Defendant offers unrebutted expert testimony that use of the helmet would have kept the damages at $20,000 instead of $200,000. Defendant was solely at fault for the initial accident and plaintiff was 20% at fault for the enhanced injuries. Suppose the plaintiff was 50% at fault in causing the initial accident and 60% at fault for the enhanced injuries?

In Meyer v. City of Des Moines, 475 N.W.2d 181 (Iowa 1991), which involved the failure to wear a helmet, the court noted that under the state's comparative negligence statute a plaintiff who was more than 50% at fault would get nothing. If failure to wear a helmet were treated as fault for this purpose, the plaintiff might get no recovery whatsoever—and the doctrine of avoidable consequences would be operating as comparative negligence. This was one among several reasons for excluding evidence of the failure to use a helmet.

Another current aspect of the doctrine of avoidable consequences occurs in the realm of toxic torts. In Champagne v. Raybestos-Manhattan, Inc., 562 A.2d 1100 (Conn.1989), plaintiff's job brought him into contact with asbestos. After being tested in 1975, he was warned that his chest X-ray had shown change, and he was "strongly advised [to] discontinue cigarette smoking." The jury could have found that plaintiff had continued smoking until his death despite repeated warnings. He left work in 1979, developed lung cancer in late 1984 or early 1985, and died in 1985 at age 60. An expert testified that the most likely cause of the cancer was "asbestos exposure along with the incidence of smoking." His basis for such an opinion was that the incidence of cancer in smokers exposed to asbestos is "from ten to sixty times more than the incidence of cancer in nonsmokers exposed to asbestos." The judge's charge allowed the jury to allocate comparative responsibility. The jury found for plaintiff but reduced the award by 75%. This part of the case was affirmed on appeal. The court held that the jury could reasonably have concluded that the decedent knew or should have known that his conduct was unreasonable and, consequently, there was no basis for upsetting the jury's decision. Is *Champagne* about avoidable consequences or a straightforward application of comparative negligence?

B. ASSUMPTION OF RISK

1. EXPRESS AGREEMENTS

Parties sometimes agree in advance that the defendant need not exercise due care for the safety of the plaintiff. These disclaimers are generally contained in a written contract, usually called an exculpatory or a hold-harmless agreement. If the plaintiff is later hurt by what is claimed to be defendant's negligence, the contract is usually at the center of any ensuing litigation. Such litigation generally raises two types of questions: (1) will the courts enforce even the most clearly drafted exculpatory clause, given the type of activity involved, and (2) if so, is the contractual language disclaiming liability sufficiently clear. The following case illustrates the nature of the inquiries.

Hanks v. Powder Ridge Restaurant Corp.

Supreme Court of Connecticut, 2005.
885 A.2d 734.

■ SULLIVAN, C.J.

The record reveals the following factual and procedural history. The defendants operate a facility [for skiing, snowboarding and snowtubing] in Middlefield, known as Powder Ridge. On February 16, 2003, the plaintiff brought his three children and another child to Powder Ridge to snowtube. Neither the plaintiff nor the four children had ever snowtubed at Powder Ridge, but the snowtubing run was open to the public generally, regardless of prior snowtubing experience, with the restriction that only persons at least six years old or forty-four inches tall were eligible to participate. Further, in order to snowtube at Powder Ridge, patrons were required to sign a "Waiver, Defense, Indemnity and Hold Harmless Agreement, and Release of Liability" (agreement). The plaintiff read and signed the agreement on behalf of himself and the four children. While snowtubing, the plaintiff's right foot became caught between his snowtube and the man-made bank of the snowtubing run, resulting in serious injuries that required multiple surgeries to repair.

Thereafter, the plaintiff filed the present negligence action against the defendants. Specifically, the plaintiff alleges that the defendants negligently caused his injuries [in a variety of ways that mainly involved changes that would have made the course safer for riders than it was].

[T]he defendants moved for summary judgment, claiming that the agreement barred the plaintiff's negligence claim as a matter of law. The trial court agreed and rendered summary judgment in favor of the defendants. Specifically, the trial court determined, pursuant to our decision in *Hyson v. White Water Mountain Resorts of Connecticut, Inc.,* [829 A.2d 827 (Conn.2003)], that the plaintiff, by signing the agreement, unambiguously had released the defendants from liability for their allegedly negligent conduct. . . .

The plaintiff raises two claims on appeal. First, the plaintiff claims that the trial court improperly concluded that the agreement clearly and expressly releases the defendants from liability for negligence. Specifically, the plaintiff contends that a person of ordinary intelligence reasonably would not have believed that, by signing the agreement, he or she was releasing the defendants from liability for personal injuries caused by negligence and, therefore, pursuant to *Hyson* [ ], the agreement does not bar the plaintiff's negligence claim. Second, the plaintiff claims that the agreement is unenforceable because it violates public policy. Specifically, the plaintiff contends that a recreational operator cannot, consistent with public policy, release itself from liability for its own negligent conduct where, as in the present case, the operator offers its services to the public generally, for a fee, and requires patrons to sign a standardized exculpatory agreement as a condition of participation. We disagree with the plaintiff's first claim, but agree with his second claim.

Before reaching the substance of the plaintiff's claims on appeal, we review this court's decision in *Hyson*. The plaintiff in *Hyson* was injured while snowtubing at the same resort and sued [one of the same defendants as in this case.] Prior to snowtubing at Powder Ridge, the plaintiff had signed an exculpatory agreement entitled "RELEASE FROM LIABILITY." [ ] The issue presented in *Hyson* was whether the exculpatory agreement released the defendant from liability for its negligent conduct and, consequently, barred the plaintiff's negligence claims as a matter of law. [ ] We concluded that it did not. [ ]

In arriving at this conclusion, we noted that there exists "widespread support in other jurisdictions for a rule requiring that any agreement intended to exculpate a party for its own negligence state so expressly"; [ ]; and that this court previously had acknowledged "the well established principle . . . that '[t]he law does not favor contract provisions which relieve a person from his own negligence. . . .'" [ ] Accordingly, we determined that "the better rule is that a party cannot be released from liability for injuries resulting from its future negligence in the absence of language that expressly so provides." [ ] This rule "prevents individuals from inadvertently relinquishing valuable legal rights" and "does not impose . . . significant cost[s]" on entities seeking to exculpate themselves from liability for future negligence. [ ] Examining the exculpatory agreement at issue in *Hyson,* we observed that "the release signed by the plaintiff [did] not specifically refer to possible negligence by the defendant" but, instead, only referred to "inherent and other risks involved in [snowtubing]. . . ."[3] [ ] Thus, "[a] person of ordinary intelligence reasonably could believe that, by signing this release, he or she was releasing the defendant only from liability for damages caused by dangers inherent in the activity of snowtubing." [ ] Accordingly, we concluded that the exculpatory agreement did not expressly release the defendants from liability for future negligence and, therefore, did not bar the plaintiff's claims. . . .

. . .

I

We first address the plaintiff's claim that the agreement does not expressly release the defendants from liability for personal injuries incurred as a result of their own negligence as required by *Hyson.* . . . We disagree.

. . .

The agreement at issue in the present case provides in relevant part: "I understand that there are inherent risks involved in snowtubing, including the risk of serious physical injury or death and *I fully assume all risks associated with [s]nowtubing,* even if due to the NEGLIGENCE of [the defendants] . . . including but not limited to: variations in the snow conditions; steepness and terrain; the presence of ice, moguls, bare spots and objects beneath the snowtubing surface such as rocks, debris and tree stumps; collisions with objects both on and off the snowtubing chutes such as hay bales, trees, rocks, snowmaking equipment, barriers, lift cables and equipment, lift towers, lift attendants, employees, volunteers, other patrons and spectators or their property; equipment or lift condition or failure; lack of safety devices or

---

[3]   That exculpatory agreement provided:

"SNOWTUBING
"RELEASE FROM LIABILITY
"PLEASE READ CAREFULLY BEFORE SIGNING

"1. I accept use of a snowtube and accept full responsibility for the care of the snowtube while in my possession.

"2. I understand that there are inherent and other risks involved in SNOWTUBING, including the use of lifts and snowtube, and it is a dangerous activity/sport. These risks include, but are not limited to, variations in snow, steepness and terrain, ice and icy conditions, moguls, rocks, trees, and other forms of forest growth or debris (above or below the surface), bare spots, lift terminals, cables, utility lines, snowmaking equipment and component parts, and other forms [of] natural or manmade obstacles on and/or off chutes, as well as collisions with equipment, obstacles or other snowtubes. Snow chute conditions vary constantly because of weather changes and snowtubing use. Be aware that snowmaking and snow grooming may be in progress at any time. These are some of the risks of SNOWTUBING. All of the inherent risks of SNOWTUBING present the risk of serious and/or fatal injury.

"3. I agree to hold harmless and indemnify Powder Ridge, White Water Mountain Resorts of Connecticut, Inc. and/or any employee of the aforementioned for loss or damage, including any loss or injuries that result from damages related to the use of a snowtube or lift.

"I, the undersigned, have read and understand the above release of liability." (Internal quotation marks omitted.) [ ]

inadequate safety devices; lack of warnings or inadequate warnings; lack of instructions or inadequate instructions; use of any lift; and the like. . . . I . . . *agree I will defend, indemnify and hold harmless* [the defendants] . . . from any and all claims, suits or demands by anyone arising from my use of the Powder Ridge snowtubing facilities and equipment including claims of NEGLIGENCE on the part of [the defendants]. . . . I . . . hereby release, and agree that *I will not sue* [the defendants] . . . for money damages for personal injury or property damage sustained by me while using the snowtubing facilities and equipment even if due to the NEGLIGENCE of [the defendants]. . . ." (Emphasis in original.)

We conclude that the agreement expressly and unambiguously purports to release the defendants from prospective liability for negligence. The agreement explicitly provides that the snowtuber *"fully assume[s] all risks associated with [s]nowtubing,* even if due to the NEGLIGENCE" of the defendants. (Emphasis in original.) Moreover, the agreement refers to the negligence of the defendants three times and uses capital letters to emphasize the term "negligence." Accordingly, we conclude that an ordinary person of reasonable intelligence would understand that, by signing the agreement, he or she was releasing the defendants from liability for their future negligence.

. . .

II

We next address the issue we explicitly left unresolved in *Hyson* [ ], namely, whether the enforcement of a well drafted exculpatory agreement purporting to release a snowtube operator from prospective liability for personal injuries sustained as a result of the operator's negligent conduct violates public policy. We conclude that it does and, accordingly, reverse the judgment of the trial court.

Although it is well established "that parties are free to contract for whatever terms on which they may agree"; [ ]; it is equally well established "that contracts that violate public policy are unenforceable." [ ] "[T]he question [of] whether a contract is against public policy is [a] question of law dependent on the circumstances of the particular case, over which an appellate court has unlimited review." [ ]

As previously noted, "[t]he law does not favor contract provisions which relieve a person from his own negligence. . . ." [ ] This is because exculpatory provisions undermine the policy considerations governing our tort system. "[T]he fundamental policy purposes of the tort compensation system [are] compensation of innocent parties, shifting the loss to responsible parties or distributing it among appropriate entities, and deterrence of wrongful conduct. . . . It is sometimes said that compensation for losses is the primary function of tort law . . . [but it] is perhaps more accurate to describe the primary function as one of determining when compensation [is] required. . . . An equally compelling function of the tort system is the prophylactic factor of preventing future harm. . . . The courts are concerned not only with compensation of the victim, but with admonition of the wrongdoer." [ ] Thus, it is consistent with public policy "to posit the risk of negligence upon the actor" and, if this policy is to be abandoned, "it has generally been to allow or require that the risk shift to another party better or equally able to bear it, not to shift the risk to the weak bargainer." [ ]

. . . A frequently cited standard for determining whether exculpatory agreements violate public policy was set forth by the Supreme Court of California in *Tunkl v. Regents of the University of California,* [383 P.2d 441 (Cal.1963)]. In *Tunkl,* the court concluded that exculpatory agreements violate public policy if they affect the public interest adversely; [ ]; and identified six factors (*Tunkl* factors) relevant to this determination: "[1] [The agreement] concerns a business of a type generally thought suitable for public regulation. [2] The party seeking exculpation is engaged in performing a service of great importance to the public, which is often a matter of practical necessity for some members of the public. [3] The party holds himself out as willing to perform this service for any member of the public who seeks it, or at least for any member coming within certain established standards. [4] As a result of the essential nature of the service, in the economic setting of the transaction, the party invoking exculpation possesses a decisive advantage of bargaining strength against any member of the public who seeks his services. [5] In exercising a superior bargaining power the party confronts the public with a standardized adhesion contract of exculpation, and makes no provision whereby a purchaser may pay additional reasonable fees and obtain protection against negligence. [6] Finally, as a result of the transaction, the person or property of the purchaser is placed under the control of the seller, subject to the risk of carelessness by the seller or his agents." [ ] The court clarified that an exculpatory agreement may affect the public interest adversely even if some of the *Tunkl* factors are not satisfied. [ ]

Various states have adopted the *Tunkl* factors to determine whether exculpatory agreements affect the public interest adversely and, thus, violate public policy. [ ] The Virginia Supreme Court, however, has determined that all exculpatory agreements purporting to release tortfeasors from future liability for personal injuries are unenforceable because "[t]o hold that it was competent for one party to put the other parties to the contract at the mercy of its own misconduct . . . can never be lawfully done where an enlightened system of jurisprudence prevails. Public policy forbids it. . . ." [ ]

Having reviewed the various methods for determining whether exculpatory agreements violate public policy, we conclude, as the *Tunkl* court itself acknowledged, that "[n]o definition of the concept of public interest can be contained within the four corners of a formula." [ ] Accordingly, we agree with the Supreme Courts of Maryland and

Vermont that "[t]he ultimate determination of what constitutes the public interest must be made considering the totality of the circumstances of any given case against the backdrop of current societal expectations." [ ] Thus, our analysis is guided, but not limited, by the *Tunkl* factors, and is informed by any other factors that may be relevant given the factual circumstances of the case and current societal expectations.

We now turn to the merits of the plaintiff's claim. The defendants are in the business of providing snowtubing services to the public generally, regardless of prior snowtubing experience, with the minimal restriction that only persons at least six years old or forty-four inches tall are eligible to participate. Given the virtually unrestricted access of the public to Powder Ridge, a reasonable person would presume that the defendants were offering a recreational activity that the whole family could enjoy safely. Indeed, this presumption is borne out by the plaintiff's own testimony. Specifically, the plaintiff testified that he "trusted that [the defendants] would, within their good conscience, operate a safe ride."

The societal expectation that family oriented recreational activities will be reasonably safe is even more important where, as in the present matter, patrons are under the care and control of the recreational operator as a result of an economic transaction. The plaintiff, in exchange for a fee, was permitted access to the defendants' snowtubing runs and was provided with snowtubing gear. As a result of this transaction, the plaintiff was under the care and control of the defendants and, thus, was subject to the risk of the defendants' carelessness. Specifically, the defendants designed and maintained the snowtubing run and, therefore, controlled the steepness of the incline, the condition of the snow and the method of slowing down or stopping patrons. Further, the defendants provided the plaintiff with the requisite snowtubing supplies and, therefore, controlled the size and quality of the snowtube as well as the provision of any necessary protective gear. Accordingly, the plaintiff voluntarily relinquished control to the defendants with the reasonable expectation of an exciting, but reasonably safe, snowtubing experience.

Moreover, the plaintiff lacked the knowledge, experience and authority to discern whether, much less ensure that, the defendants' snowtubing runs were maintained in a reasonably safe condition. As the Vermont Supreme Court observed, in the context of the sport of skiing, it is consistent with public policy "to place responsibility for maintenance of the land on those who own or control it, with the ultimate goal of keeping accidents to the minimum level possible. [The] [d]efendants, not recreational skiers, have the expertise and opportunity to foresee and control hazards, and to guard against the negligence of their agents and employees. They alone can properly maintain and inspect their premises, and train their employees in risk management. They alone can insure against risks and effectively spread the costs of insurance among their thousands of customers. Skiers, on the other hand, are not in a position to discover and correct risks of harm, and they cannot insure against the ski area's negligence.

"If the defendants were permitted to obtain broad waivers of their liability, an important incentive for ski areas to manage risk would be removed, with the public bearing the cost of the resulting injuries. . . . It is illogical, in these circumstances, to undermine the public policy underlying business invitee law and allow skiers to bear risks they have no ability or right to control." *Dalury v. S-K-I, Ltd.,* [670 A.2d 795 (Vt.1995)]. The concerns expressed by the court in *Dalury* are equally applicable to the context of snowtubing, and we agree that it is illogical to permit snowtubers, and the public generally, to bear the costs of risks that they have no ability or right to control.

Further, the agreement at issue was a standardized adhesion contract offered to the plaintiff on a "take it or leave it" basis. The "most salient feature [of adhesion contracts] is that they are not subject to the normal bargaining processes of ordinary contracts." [ ] Not only was the plaintiff unable to negotiate the terms of the agreement, but the defendants also did not offer him the option of procuring protection against negligence at an additional reasonable cost. [ ] (factor relevant to enforcement of contractual limit on liability is "whether the party seeking exculpation was willing to provide greater protection against tortious conduct for a reasonable, additional fee"). Moreover, the defendants did not inform prospective snowtubers prior to their arrival at Powder Ridge that they would have to waive important common-law rights as a condition of participation. Thus, the plaintiff, who traveled to Powder Ridge in anticipation of snowtubing that day, was faced with the dilemma of either signing the defendants' proffered waiver of prospective liability or forgoing completely the opportunity to snowtube at Powder Ridge. Under the present factual circumstances, it would ignore reality to conclude that the plaintiff wielded the same bargaining power as the defendants.

The defendants contend, nevertheless, that they did not have superior bargaining power because, unlike an essential public service, "[s]nowtubing is a voluntary activity and the plaintiff could have just as easily decided not to participate." We acknowledge that snowtubing is a voluntary activity, but we do not agree that there can never be a disparity of bargaining power in the context of voluntary or elective activities.[11] [ ] Voluntary recreational activities, such as snowtubing, skiing, basketball, soccer, football, racquetball, karate, ice skating, swimming, volleyball or yoga, are pursued by the vast majority of the

---

[11] We need not decide whether an exculpatory agreement concerning a voluntary recreational activity violates public policy if the *only* factor militating against enforcement of the agreement is a disparity in bargaining power because, in the present matter, there are additional factors that combine to render the agreement contrary to public policy. . . .

population and constitute an important and healthy part of everyday life. Indeed, this court has previously recognized the public policy interest of promoting vigorous participation in such activities. [ ]. In the present case, the defendants held themselves out as a provider of a healthy, fun, family activity. After the plaintiff and his family arrived at Powder Ridge eager to participate in the activity, however, the defendants informed the plaintiff that, not only would they be immune from claims arising from the inherent risks of the activity, but they would not be responsible for injuries resulting from their own carelessness and negligence in the operation of the snowtubing facility. We recognize that the plaintiff had the option of walking away. We cannot say, however, that the defendants had no bargaining advantage under these circumstances.

For the foregoing reasons, we conclude that the agreement in the present matter affects the public interest adversely and, therefore, is unenforceable because it violates public policy. Accordingly, the trial court improperly rendered summary judgment in favor of the defendants.

. . . We acknowledge that most states uphold adhesion contracts releasing recreational operators from prospective liability for personal injuries caused by their own negligent conduct. Put simply, we disagree with these decisions for the reasons already explained in this opinion. . . .

The judgment is reversed and the case is remanded for further proceedings according to law.

■ In this opinion KATZ, VERTEFEUILLE and ZARELLA, JS., concurred.

■ NORCOTT, J., with whom BORDEN and PALMER, JS., join, dissenting.

. . .

I begin by noting that "[i]t is established well beyond the need for citation that parties are free to contract for whatever terms on which they may agree. This freedom includes the right to contract for the assumption of known or unknown hazards and risks that may arise as a consequence of the execution of the contract. Accordingly, in private disputes, a court must enforce the contract as drafted by the parties and may not relieve a contracting party from anticipated or actual difficulties undertaken pursuant to the contract. . . ." [ ] Nevertheless, contracts that violate public policy are unenforceable. [ ]

In determining whether prospective releases of liability violate public policy, the majority adopts the Vermont Supreme Court's totality of the circumstances approach. See *Dalury v. S-K-I, Ltd.,* [ ]. Although it also purports to consider the widely accepted test articulated by the California Supreme Court in *Tunkl v. Regents of the University of California,* [ ], the majority actually accords the test only nominal consideration. Because I consider the *Tunkl* factors to be dispositive, I address them at length.

. . .

Applying the six *Tunkl* factors to the sport of snowtubing, I note that the first, second, fourth and sixth factors support the defendants, . . . while the third and fifth factors support the plaintiff. Accordingly, I now turn to a detailed examination of each factor as it applies to this case.

The first of the *Tunkl* factors, that the business is of a type thought suitable for regulation, cuts squarely in favor of upholding the release. . . . Indeed, the plaintiff points to no statutes or regulations that affect snowtubing. . . .

The second *Tunkl* factor also works in the defendants' favor. Snowtubing is not an important public service. Courts employing the *Tunkl* factors have found this second element satisfied in the contexts of hospital admission and treatment, residential rental agreements, banking, child care services, telecommunications and public education, including interscholastic sports. [ ] The public nature of these industries is undeniable and each plays an important and *indispensable* role in everyday life. Snowtubing, by contrast, is purely a recreational activity.

The fourth *Tunkl* factor also counsels against the plaintiff's position that snowtubing affects the public interest because snowtubing is not an essential activity. The plaintiff's only incentive for snowtubing was recreation, not some other important personal interest such as, for example, health care, banking or insurance. The plaintiff would not have suffered any harm by opting not to snowtube at Powder Ridge, because snowtubing is not so significant a service that a person in his position would feel compelled to agree to any terms offered rather than forsake the opportunity to participate. Furthermore, ". . . snowtubing occurs regularly at locations all across the state, including parks, backyards and golf courses." [ ] Thus, the plaintiff had ample opportunity to snowtube in an environment of his choosing, which he could have selected based on whatever safety considerations he felt were relevant. In the absence of a compelling personal need and a limited choice of facilities, I cannot conclude that the defendants enjoyed a significant bargaining advantage over the plaintiff.

Finally, the sixth *Tunkl* factor weighs against a determination that the release implicates the public interest. The plaintiff did not place his person or property under the defendants' control. Unlike the patient who lies unconscious on the operating table or the child who is placed in the custody of a day care service, the Powder Ridge patron snowtubes on his own, without entrusting his person or property to the defendants' care. In fact, the attraction of snowtubing and other recreational activities often is the lack of control associated with participating.

In contrast, the third and fifth *Tunkl* factors support the plaintiff's position. [The minimal restriction on age and height does not negate that the facility was open to a vast swath of the public.]

. . . "[The] most salient feature [of adhesion contracts] is that they are not subject to the normal bargaining processes of ordinary contracts." [ ] Although the plaintiff made no attempt to bargain as to the terms of the release, it defies logic to presume that he could have done so successfully. As the majority correctly notes, the defendants presented patrons with a "take it or leave it" situation, conditioning access to the snowtubing run on signing the release agreement . . .

[The court then observed that both the *Tunkl* factors and the approach of the vast majority of states in cases involving recreational activities support upholding this release. Participants in recreational activities, which are voluntary, can decide to forgo the activity if they don't want to release the activity from liability.]

. . . The average person is capable of reading a release agreement and deciding not to snowtube because of the risks that he or she is asked to assume. By contrast, in those fields implicating the public interest, the patron is at a substantial bargaining disadvantage. Few people are in a position to quibble over contractual obligations when seeking, for example, insurance, medical treatment or child care. A general characteristic of fields entangled with the public interest is their indispensability; snowtubing hardly is indispensable. Under the majority's reasoning, nearly any release affects the public interest, no matter how unnecessary or inherently dangerous the underlying activity may be. That position remains the distinct minority view, followed only by the courts of Vermont and Virginia. [ ]

The great weight of these numerous and highly persuasive authorities compels my conclusion that the release at issue herein does not violate public policy as it pertains to the sport of snowtubing. Accordingly, I conclude that the trial court properly granted summary judgment in the defendants' favor and I would affirm that judgment. I, therefore, respectfully dissent.

NOTES AND QUESTIONS

1.   *Tunkl* involved a release required of all patients entering a hospital. Is the court suggesting that the same analysis should apply to snowtubing? Is the dissent persuasive on how the *Tunkl* factors play out here?

2.   Consider the court's suggestion about how a reasonable person might have understood the release in the cited *Hyson* case. Given that understanding, what liability would have been waived by the release?

3.   Every day, consumers enter into contracts of adhesion—students who enroll in law school, for example, cannot negotiate the terms of the agreement to provide an education in exchange for tuition. Does the *Hanks* case raise questions about the enforceability of those contracts? If your answer is no, why not?

4.   *Post-injury releases.* The *Hanks* court's discussion is limited to pre-injury releases. Those written after injury are essentially settlement agreements and raise typical contract issues. As with the contracts mentioned in note 3, no question about the enforceability of those agreements on public policy grounds exist. Why?

5.   The court relies on fundamental tort law policies of compensation and deterrence to conclude that public policy bars enforcement of defendant's waiver of liability. Are there other fundamental policies the court fails to take into account? See BJ's Wholesale Club, Inc. v. Rosen, 80 A.3d 345 (Md.2013)("[i]n the absence of legislation to the contrary, exculpatory clauses are generally valid, and the public policy of freedom of contract is best served by enforcing the provisions of the clause.").

6.   No matter what the situation, courts generally agree that gross negligence or recklessness may never be disclaimed by agreement, no matter what words are used. Sommer v. Federal Signal Corp., 593 N.E.2d 1365 (N.Y.1992)(alarm company's failure to relay alarm). Similarly, strict product liability claims cannot be contractually disclaimed. Restatement (Third) of Torts: Products Liability § 18. Why should this be so if the activity is not one that implicates the *Tunkl* factors?

7.   Recall that the plaintiff in *Hanks* signed a release not only of his claims but also his children's. Even when releases are determined to be valid, whether adults signing releases can bind members of their family arises with increasing frequency. Compare Galloway v. State, 790 N.W.2d 252 (Iowa 2010)(holding that parental waivers of liability to their children are per se invalid because of the limited authority of parents over their children's legal affairs, reflecting independent legal protection for children from parental decisions while at the same time distinguishing adult releases) with BJ's Wholesale Club, Inc. v. Rosen, note 5 supra, (upholding a waiver signed by a parent based on the parent's responsibility for the "child's support, care, nurture, welfare, and education") and Zivich v. Mentor Soccer Club, Inc., 696 N.E.2d 201 (Ohio 1998)(holding that a parent's signature on a release to permit a child's participation in a soccer league bound the child and also barred the parents' derivative action for harm to the child—at least in cases involving nonprofit groups). See generally King, Exculpatory Agreements for Volunteers in Youth Activities—the Alternative to "Nerf (R)" Tiddlywinks, 53 Ohio St.L.J. 683 (1992)(arguing that denying immunity will deter volunteers, as the "choice for many may be between youth activities without a right to sue and no organized youth activities at all.").

8.   Before we turn to cases in which defendants claim that plaintiff's conduct shows an implied assumption of the risk, we should note briefly an intermediate area—cases in which defendants claim that a contract exists by virtue of a sign posted on defendant's land combined with plaintiff's conduct. The typical case involves a bailment at a parking lot with a large sign announcing that all cars are left at owner's risk. If the car is stolen, courts reject the claim that the bailment contract included the disclaimer, unless the defendant proves that the limitation—whether on a sign or on a claim check—was drawn to the plaintiff's attention. See, e.g., Berrios v.

United Parcel Service, 627 A.2d 701 (N.J.Super.Ct.Law Div. 1992)(stating general rule that unilateral disclaimers are not effective unless brought to the attention of plaintiff and citing courts adopting rule).

9. *The controversy over contract.* Among theorists, a debate rages on whether physician negligence should remain as a tort matter or left to the market through contract, including waivers of liability as an element of the contract. Adherents of contract tend to believe in the desirability of free markets to allocate risks. Critics argue that markets are flawed or an inappropriate mechanism for allocating malpractice risks. Compare, e.g., R. Thaler & C. Sunstein, Nudge ch. 14 (2008)(asserting that barring waivers requires patients to, in effect, purchase mandatory insurance and many would opt for waivers of liability and concomitant lower costs if given the choice) and Epstein, Contractual Principle Versus Legislative Fixes: Coming to Closure on the Unending Travails of Medical Malpractice, 54 DePaul L.Rev. 503, 505 (2005)(arguing that the medical malpractice system, based on tort law is broken and that patients and providers could do better determining allocation of risk through contract); with Baker & Lytton, Allowing Patients to Waive the Right to Sue for Medical Malpractice: A Response to Thaler and Sunstein, 104 Nw.U.L.Rev. 233 (2010)(contending that Thaler and Sunstein misapply the teachings of behavioral economics to medical malpractice and ignore or understate the benefits of the malpractice system) and Arlen, Contracting Over Liability: Medical Malpractice and the Cost of Choice, 158 U.Pa.L.Rev. 957 (2010)(identifying a variety of factors that would prevent even informed patients from contracting for a liability system with providers that would be as beneficial as what tort provides).

Could a patient make an informed decision about whether waiving a malpractice claim in exchange for, say, a 3% reduction in health care costs was in her best interest?

2.   IMPLIED ASSUMPTION OF RISK

In this section, no express language or agreement states the intentions or understandings of the parties. The defendant instead argues that the plaintiff implicitly assumed the risk by deciding to engage in the risky activity. The area is quite controversial, in part because of disagreement over whether the doctrine plays any useful role in negligence litigation. Throughout the materials in this section, consider whether the doctrine serves a purpose distinct from other aspects of the negligence framework we have considered up to this point.

Murphy v. Steeplechase Amusement Co.

Court of Appeals of New York, 1929.
250 N.Y. 479, 166 N.E. 173.

[Appeal from a judgment of the Appellate Division of the Supreme Court, affirming a judgment in favor of plaintiff entered upon a verdict.]

■ CARDOZO, CH. J.

The defendant, Steeplechase Amusement Company, maintains an amusement park at Coney Island, New York. One of the supposed attractions is known as "The Flopper." It is a moving belt, running upward on an inclined plane, on which passengers sit or stand. Many of them are unable to keep their feet because of the movement of the belt, and are thrown backward or aside. The belt runs in a groove, with padded walls on either side to a height of four feet, and with padded flooring beyond the walls at the same angle as the belt. An electric motor, driven by current furnished by the Brooklyn Edison Company, supplies the needed power.

Plaintiff, a vigorous young man, visited the park with friends. One of them, a young woman, now his wife, stepped upon the moving belt. Plaintiff followed and stepped behind her. As he did so, he felt what he describes as a sudden jerk, and was thrown to the floor. His wife in front and also friends behind him were thrown at the same time. Something more was here, as every one understood, than the slowly-moving escalator that is common in shops and public places. A fall was foreseen as one of the risks of the adventure. There would have been no point to the whole thing, no adventure about it, if the risk had not been there. The very name above the gate, the Flopper, was warning to the timid. If the name was not enough, there was warning more distinct in the experience of others. We are told by the plaintiff's wife that the members of her party stood looking at the sport before joining in it themselves. Some aboard the belt were able, as she viewed them, to sit down with decorum or even to stand and keep their footing; others jumped or fell. The tumbling bodies and the screams and laughter supplied the merriment and fun. "I took a chance," she said when asked whether she thought that a fall might be expected.

Plaintiff took the chance with her, but, less lucky than his companions, suffered a fracture of a knee cap. He states in his complaint that the belt was dangerous to life and limb in that it stopped and started violently and suddenly and was not properly equipped to prevent injuries to persons who were using it without knowledge of its dangers, and in a bill of particulars he adds that it was operated at a fast and dangerous rate of speed and was not supplied with a proper railing, guard or other device to prevent a fall therefrom. No other negligence is charged.

We see no adequate basis for a finding that the belt was out of order. It was already in motion when the plaintiff put his foot on it. He cannot help himself to a verdict in such circumstances by the addition of the facile comment that it threw him with a jerk. One who steps upon a moving belt and finds his heels above his head is in no position to discriminate with nicety between the successive stages of the shock, between the jerk which is a cause and the jerk, accompanying the fall, as an instantaneous effect. There is evidence for the defendant that power was transmitted smoothly, and could not be transmitted otherwise. If the movement was spasmodic, it was an unexplained and, it seems, an inexplicable departure from the normal workings of the mechanism. An aberration so extraordinary, if it is to lay the basis for a verdict, should rest on something firmer than a mere descriptive epithet, a summary of the sensations of a tense and crowded moment [ ]. But the jerk, if it were established, would add little to the case. Whether the movement of the belt was uniform or irregular, the risk at greatest was a fall. This was the very hazard that was invited and foreseen [ ].

Volenti non fit injuria. One who takes part in such a sport accepts the dangers that inhere in it so far as they are obvious and necessary, just as a fencer accepts the risk of a thrust by his antagonist or a spectator at a ball game the chance of contact with the ball [ ]. The antics of the clown are not the paces of the cloistered cleric. The rough and boisterous joke, the horseplay of the crowd, evokes its own guffaws, but they are not the pleasures of tranquility. The plaintiff was not seeking a retreat for meditation. Visitors were tumbling about the belt to the merriment of onlookers when he made his choice to join them. He took the chance of a like fate, with whatever damage to his body might ensue from such a fall. The timorous may stay at home.

A different case would be here if the dangers inherent in the sport were obscure or unobserved ([ ]; Tantillo v. Goldstein Bros. Amusement Co., 248 N.Y. 286 [1928]), or so serious as to justify the belief that precautions of some kind must have been taken to avert them [ ]. Nothing happened to the plaintiff except what common experience tells us may happen at any time as the consequence of a sudden fall. Many a skater or a horseman can rehearse a tale of equal woe. A different case there would also be if the accidents had been so many as to show that the game in its inherent nature was too dangerous to be continued without change. The president of the amusement company says that there had never been such an accident before. A nurse employed at an emergency hospital maintained in connection with the park contradicts him to some extent. She says that on other occasions she had attended patrons of the park who had been injured at the Flopper, how many she could not say. None, however, had been badly injured or had suffered broken bones. Such testimony is not enough to show that the game was a trap for the unwary, too perilous to be endured. According to the defendant's estimate, two hundred and fifty thousand visitors were at the Flopper in a year. Some quota of accidents was to be looked for in so great a mass. One might as well say that a skating rink should be abandoned because skaters sometimes fall.

There is testimony by the plaintiff that he fell upon wood, and not upon a canvas padding. He is strongly contradicted by the photographs and by the witnesses for the defendant, and is without corroboration in the testimony of his companions who were witnesses in his behalf. If his observation was correct, there was a defect in the equipment, and one not obvious or known. The padding should have been kept in repair to break the force of any fall. The case did not go to the jury, however, upon any such theory of the defendant's liability, nor is the defect fairly suggested by the plaintiff's bill of particulars, which limits his complaint. The case went to the jury upon the theory that negligence was dependent upon a sharp and sudden jerk.

The judgment of the Appellate Division and that of the Trial Term should be reversed. . . .

■ POUND, CRANE, LEHMAN, KELLOGG and HUBBS, JJ., concur; O'BRIEN, J., dissents on the authority of [*Tantillo v. Goldstein Bros. Amusement Co.*].

NOTES AND QUESTIONS

1. Why does Judge Cardozo say that even if the belt had jerked unexpectedly this fact would not have helped plaintiff's case? What might he have said if such a jerk made everyone on the belt fall and suffer broken limbs?

2. In what way did the defendant act negligently in *Murphy?*

3. Judge Cardozo suggests that *Murphy* might have been different if the Flopper caused so many accidents that its "inherent nature" made it "too dangerous to be continued without change." If one of every three patrons suffered a broken bone and such information was posted conspicuously at the entrance to the Flopper, and each prospective customer had to watch for ten minutes before getting on, how would that case differ from *Murphy?* For a critical assessment of *Murphy* and its contribution to the law of assumption of risk, see Simons, *Murphy v. Steeplechase Amusement Co.*: While the Timorous Stay at Home, the Adventurous Ride the Flopper, in R. Rabin & S. Sugarman (eds.), Torts Stories 179 (2003).

4. *Baseball spectators.* In Davidoff v. Metropolitan Baseball Club, 463 N.E.2d 1219 (N.Y.1984), the 14-year-old plaintiff was sitting in the first row behind first base during a professional game at Shea Stadium when she was badly injured by a foul ball. The court, 5–2, affirmed defendant stadium owner's summary judgment:

> Claims involving injuries sustained by spectators from misdirected baseballs were traditionally decided—and dismissed—on the ground of assumption of risk. However, with the enactment of [comparative negligence] in 1975, the absolute defense was no longer applicable and it became necessary to define the duty of care owed by a proprietor of a baseball field to its spectators. This we did . . . in [ ]:
>
> > [W]here a proprietor of a ball park furnishes screening for the area of the field behind home plate where the danger of being struck by a ball is greatest and that screening is of sufficient extent to provide adequate protection for as many spectators

as may reasonably be expected to desire such seating in the course of an ordinary game, the proprietor fulfills the duty of care imposed by law and, therefore, cannot be liable in negligence.

Here, there has been no showing by plaintiff that (1) defendants failed to erect a screen behind home plate providing adequate protection in that area, and (2) there are not sufficient seats behind the screen to accommodate as many spectators as reasonably may be expected to desire such seating. No evidence that the screen was inadequate was presented, and it is undisputed that there were unoccupied seats behind the screen at Shea on the day plaintiff was injured.

The fact that others have been injured in this unscreened area did not matter. Plaintiff's claim that notice of danger should raise a jury question "would require a baseball field proprietor to operate as an insurer of spectators unless there was a protective screen shielding every seat."

As the Nevada Supreme Court explained decisions like *Davidoff*, " 'the limited duty rule . . . identifies the duty of baseball stadium proprietors with greater specificity than the usual . . . standard provides.' [That is, it imposes a duty only to screen a portion of the seats.] In this sense, the limited duty rule does not eliminate the stadium owner's duty to exercise reasonable care under the circumstances to protect patrons against injury; rather, it defines that duty in detail." Turner v. Mandalay Sports Entertainment, LLC, 180 P.3d 1172 (Nev.2008)(quoting Benejam v. Detroit Tigers, Inc., 635 N.W.2d 219 (Mich.Ct.App.2001)).

The *Davidoff* dissenters argued that requiring screening only behind home plate "does nothing more than to artificially limit the liability of ball park owners." Moreover, even if the majority's focus on unoccupied screened seats made sense in a sandlot where spectators may move around, it "is utterly out of place when the setting is a major sports stadium where . . . all seats are individually assigned or allocated to a specific area." A fan who is "unable to secure a seat behind home plate must go home or fully assume responsibility for any consequences of remaining at the ball park no matter how unreasonable the risk of injury."

For apparently the first time, a state supreme court rejected the baseball rule. See Rountree v. Boise Baseball, LLC, 296 P.3d 373 (Idaho 2013)(finding no compelling reason to adopt the baseball rule as there had been only one instance of spectator injury in seven years and the defendant presented no statistics to suggest that spectator injury was a significant problem). By contrast with the *Rountree* rationale, an investigation by a sportswriter found that an average of 1,750 fans were hit by baseballs each year. The sportswriter observed "[t]hat's more often than a batter is hit by a pitch, which happened 1,536 times last season." David Glovin, *Baseball Caught Looking as Fouls Injure 1,750 Fans a Year*, Bloomberg Business, Sept. 9, 2014, http://www.bloomberg.com/news/articles/2014-09-09/baseball-caught-looking-as-fouls-injure-1-750-fans-a-year.

Would the result or the analysis in *Davidoff* change if the plaintiff had been a foreign tourist who had heard about baseball but did not know about its dangers? Does it matter whether the spectator is hurt during the first two minutes after taking a seat or after one hour?

Legislation. After adverse judgments against both the Chicago Cubs and White Sox, the Illinois legislature adopted protective legislation. Essentially, owners and operators of stadiums are not liable to those hit by a ball or bat unless they were sitting behind a negligently defective screen or they were hurt as the result of willful or wanton conduct. 745 Ill.Comp.Stat. 38/10. Colorado adopted similar legislation just as it got its first major league team. The legislation, Colo.Rev.Stat. § 13–21–120, asserts that professional baseball is a "wholesome and healthy family activity which should be encouraged," that the "state will derive economic benefit from spectators" who attend the games, and that it is thus in the state's interest to "encourage attendance at professional baseball games." Limiting the civil liability of team owners and stadium owners "will help contain costs, keeping ticket prices more affordable." When the legislatures in Illinois and Colorado were considering this legislation, who would you expect to have been lobbying against it?

Davenport v. Cotton Hope Plantation Horizontal Property Regime

Supreme Court of South Carolina, 1998.
333 S.C. 71, 508 S.E.2d 565.

■ TOAL, JUSTICE.

This is a comparative negligence case arising out of an accident in which respondent, Alvin Davenport, was injured while descending a stairway near his apartment. We granted certiorari to review the [decision of the court of appeals]. . . .

[Plaintiff rented from its owner a condominium unit on the top floor of a three-floor building within defendant's premises. Three stairways offered access: one at each end and one in the middle of the building. Plaintiff's unit was five feet from the middle stairway. For two months before his fall, plaintiff had been reporting to management that the middle stairway's floodlights were not working, but he continued using that stairway. One night, as plaintiff descended the middle stairway to go to work, he tripped and was hurt in the resulting fall. He testified that what he thought was a step turned out to be a shadow caused by the broken floodlights. The trial court directed a verdict against plaintiff based on assumed risk and also held that even if comparative negligence applied, plaintiff was more negligent than defendant as a matter of law. The court of appeals reversed on both points.]

The threshold question we must answer is whether assumption of risk survives as a complete bar to recovery under South Carolina's [modified] comparative negligence system. . . .

. . .

[This court] ultimately extended the defense [of assumption of risk] to negligence cases outside the traditional master-servant context. See, e.g., Smith v. Edwards, [195 S.E. 236 (S.C.1938)]. In *Smith*, the plaintiff died as a result of burns she suffered while receiving a "permanent wave" at a beauty shop. The defendant argued that the plaintiff had diabetes which made her peculiarly susceptible to the injuries, and consequently, she assumed the risk of injury. The plaintiff argued that under these facts, assumption of risk was not available as an affirmative defense. This Court disagreed, stating, "[assumption of risk] applies to any case . . . where the facts proved show that the person against whom the doctrine of assumption of risk is pleaded knew of the danger, appreciated it, and acquiesced therein." [ ]

Currently in South Carolina, there are four requirements to establishing the defense of assumption of risk: (1) the plaintiff must have knowledge of the facts constituting a dangerous condition; (2) the plaintiff must know the condition is dangerous; (3) the plaintiff must appreciate the nature and extent of the danger; and (4) the plaintiff must voluntarily expose himself to the danger. . . .

As noted by the Court of Appeals, an overwhelming majority of jurisdictions that have adopted some form of comparative negligence have essentially abolished assumption of risk as an absolute bar to recovery. [ ] In analyzing the continuing viability of assumption of risk in a comparative negligence system, many courts distinguish between "express" assumption of risk and "implied" assumption of risk. [ ] Implied assumption of risk is further divided into the categories of "primary" and "secondary" implied assumption of risk. [ ] We will discuss each of these concepts below.

Express assumption of risk applies when the parties expressly agree in advance, either in writing or orally, that the plaintiff will relieve the defendant of his or her legal duty toward the plaintiff. See Restatement (Second) of Torts § 496B (1965); [ ]. Thus, being under no legal duty, the defendant cannot be charged with negligence. [ ] Even in those comparative fault jurisdictions that have abrogated assumption of risk, the rule remains that express assumption of risk continues as an absolute defense in an action for negligence. [citing 16 cases and treatises] The reason for this is that express assumption of risk sounds in contract, not tort, and is based upon an express manifestation of consent. [ ]

. . .

Express assumption of risk is contrasted with implied assumption of risk which arises when the plaintiff implicitly, rather than expressly, assumes known risks. As noted above, implied assumption of risk is characterized as either primary or secondary. Primary implied assumption of risk arises when the plaintiff impliedly assumes those risks that are inherent in a particular activity. [ ] (student injured in a collision during football drill); [ ] (injured while watching softball game). Primary implied assumption of risk is not a true affirmative defense, but instead goes to the initial determination of whether the defendant's legal duty encompasses the risk encountered by the plaintiff. E.g., Perez v. McConkey, 872 S.W.2d 897 (Tenn.1994); [ ]. In *Perez*, the Tennessee Supreme Court summarized the doctrine in the following way:

> In its primary sense, implied assumption of risk focuses not on the plaintiff's conduct in assuming the risk, but on the defendant's general duty of care. . . . Clearly, primary implied assumption of risk is but another way of stating the conclusion that a plaintiff has failed to establish a prima facie case [of negligence] by failing to establish that a duty exists.

[ ] In this sense, primary implied assumption of risk is simply a part of the initial negligence analysis. [ ]

Secondary implied assumption of risk, on the other hand, arises when the plaintiff knowingly encounters a risk created by the defendant's negligence. [ ] It is a true defense because it is asserted only after the plaintiff establishes a prima facie case of negligence against the defendant. Secondary implied assumption of risk may involve either reasonable or unreasonable conduct on the part of the plaintiff. [The court quoted a lower court case that had discussed "secondary unreasonable implied assumption of the risk" in the context of a person who "dashed into a fire in order to save his hat." Such a risk could be found to be "out of all proportion to the advantage which he is seeking to gain."]⁴ Since express and primary implied assumption of risk are compatible with comparative negligence, we will refer to secondary implied assumption of risk simply as "assumption of risk."

As alluded to in [ ], assumption of risk and contributory negligence have historically been recognized as separate defenses in South Carolina. [ ] However, other courts have found assumption of risk functionally indistinguishable from contributory negligence and consequently abolished assumption of risk as a complete defense. [ ]

To date, the only comparative fault jurisdictions that have retained assumption of risk as an absolute defense are Georgia, Mississippi, Nebraska, Rhode Island, and South Dakota. [ ] Only the Rhode Island Supreme Court has provided a detailed discussion of why it believes the common law form of assumption of risk should survive under comparative negligence. [ ] In Kennedy v. Providence Hockey Club, Inc., [376 A.2d 329 (R.I.1977)], the Rhode Island Supreme Court distinguished between assumption of risk and contributory negligence, emphasizing the former was measured by a subjective standard while

---

⁴ Reasonable implied assumption of risk exists when the plaintiff is aware of a risk negligently created by the defendant but, nonetheless, voluntarily proceeds to encounter the risk; when weighed against the risk of injury, the plaintiff's action is reasonable. [ ]

the latter was based on an objective, reasonable person standard. The court further noted that it had in the past limited the application of assumption of risk to those situations where the plaintiff had actual knowledge of the hazard. The court then rejected the premise that assumption of risk and contributory negligence overlap:

> [C]ontributory negligence and assumption of the risk do not overlap; the key difference is, of course, the exercise of one's free will in encountering the risk. Negligence analysis, couched in reasonable hypotheses, has no place in the assumption of the risk framework. When one acts knowingly, it is immaterial whether he acts reasonably. [ ]

Rhode Island's conclusions are in sharp contrast with the West Virginia Supreme Court's opinion in King v. Kayak Manufacturing Corp., [387 S.E.2d 511 (W.Va.1989)]. Like Rhode Island, the West Virginia Supreme Court in *King* recognized that assumption of risk was conceptually distinct from contributory negligence. The court specifically noted that West Virginia's doctrine of assumption of risk required actual knowledge of the dangerous condition, which conformed with the general rule elsewhere in the country. [ ] In fact, the court cited Rhode Island's decision in *Kennedy* as evidence of this general rule. [ ] Nevertheless, the West Virginia court concluded that the absolute defense of assumption of risk was incompatible with its comparative fault system. The court therefore adopted a comparative assumption of risk rule, stating, "a plaintiff is not barred from recovery by the doctrine of assumption of risk unless his degree of fault arising therefrom equals or exceeds the combined fault or negligence of the other parties to the accident." [ ] The court explained that the absolute defense of assumption of risk was as repugnant to its fault system as the common law rule of contributory negligence. [ ]

A comparison between the approaches in West Virginia and Rhode Island is informative. Both jurisdictions recognize that assumption of risk is conceptually distinct from contributory negligence. However, Rhode Island focuses on the objective/subjective distinction between the two defenses and, therefore, retains assumption of risk as a complete bar to recovery. On the other hand, West Virginia emphasizes that the main purpose of its comparative negligence system is to apportion fault. Thus, West Virginia rejects assumption of risk as a total bar to recovery and only allows a jury to consider the plaintiff's negligence in assuming the risk. If the plaintiff's total negligence exceeds or equals that of the defendant, only then is the plaintiff completely barred from recovery.

Like Rhode Island and West Virginia, South Carolina has historically maintained a distinction between assumption of risk and contributory negligence, even when the two doctrines appear to overlap. [ ] Thus, the pertinent question is whether a plaintiff should be completely barred from recovery when he voluntarily assumes a known risk, regardless of whether his assumption of that risk was reasonable or unreasonable. Upon considering the purpose of our comparative fault system, we conclude that West Virginia's approach is the most persuasive model.

In [a 1984 South Carolina appellate case], Judge Sanders provided the following justification for adopting a comparative negligence system: "It is contrary to the basic premise of our fault system to allow a defendant, who is at fault in causing an accident, to escape bearing any of its cost, while requiring a plaintiff, who is no more than equally at fault or even less at fault, to bear all of its costs." [ ] By contrast, the main reason for having the defense of assumption of risk is not to determine fault, but to prevent a person who knowingly and voluntarily incurs a risk of harm from holding another person liable. [ ] Cotton Hope argues that the justification behind assumption of risk is not in conflict with South Carolina's comparative fault system. We disagree.

As stated by Judge Sanders, it is contrary to the premise of our comparative fault system to require a plaintiff, who is fifty-percent or less at fault, to bear all of the costs of the injury. In accord with this logic, the defendant's fault in causing an accident is not diminished solely because the plaintiff knowingly assumes a risk. If assumption of risk is retained in its current common law form, a plaintiff would be completely barred from recovery even if his conduct is reasonable or only slightly unreasonable. In our comparative fault system, it would be incongruous to absolve the defendant of all liability based only on whether the plaintiff assumed the risk of injury. Comparative negligence by definition seeks to assess and compare the negligence of both the plaintiff and defendant. This goal would clearly be thwarted by adhering to the common law defense of assumption of risk.

. . .

[The court concluded that] (1) although the absolute defense of assumption of risk has historically been treated as a separate defense from contributory negligence, it is incompatible with our comparative fault system; (2) a plaintiff's conduct in assuming a risk can be compared with the defendant's negligence; (3) a plaintiff's conduct in assuming the risk can be made a part our comparative fault system; (4) by abolishing assumption of risk as an absolute bar to recovery, South Carolina will not be adopting a policy that would encourage people to take unnecessary risks; and (5) even if Davenport assumed the risk of injury, he will not be barred from recovery unless his negligence exceeds the defendant's negligence.

We therefore hold that a plaintiff is not barred from recovery by the doctrine of assumption of risk unless the degree of fault arising therefrom is greater than the negligence of the defendant. . . . Express and primary implied assumption of risk remain unaffected by our decision.

. . .

Cotton Hope finally argues that we should affirm the trial court's ruling that, as a matter of law, Davenport was more than fifty-percent negligent. The trial court based its ruling on the fact that Davenport knew of the danger weeks before his accident, and he had a safe, alternate route. However, there was also evidence suggesting Cotton Hope was negligent in failing to properly maintain the lighting in the exterior stairway. In the light most favorable to Davenport, it could be reasonably concluded that Davenport's negligence in proceeding down the stairway did not exceed Cotton Hope's negligence. Thus, it is properly submitted for jury determination.

[The case was remanded for a new trial.]   *— remanded for new trial*

■ FINNEY, C.J., MOORE, WALLER and BURNETT, JJ., concur.

NOTES AND QUESTIONS

1. What were the trial judge's errors? What should happen on remand?

2. Why does "express" assumption of the risk remain compatible with comparative negligence?

3. Why does "primary" implied assumption of the risk remain compatible with comparative negligence?

4. With "secondary" implied assumption of the risk, does it matter why a person runs into a house that has been set afire by defendant's negligence? Whether to save a child or save his hat?

Recall *Moore v. Shah*, p. 432 supra, involving the donation of the kidney. Might *Moore* be analyzed as assumed risk?

5. New Jersey was the first state clearly to reject the existence of the term assumption of risk—and did so well before comparative negligence became popular. The history is set forth in McGrath v. American Cyanamid Co., 196 A.2d 238 (N.J.1963):

> In Meistrich v. Casino Arena Attractions, Inc., [ ], we pointed out that assumption of the risk was theretofore used in two incongruous senses: in one sense it meant the defendant was not negligent, while in its other sense it meant the plaintiff was contributorily negligent. We said that in truth there are but two issues—negligence and contributory negligence—both to be resolved by the standard of the reasonably prudent man, and that it was erroneous to suggest to the jury that assumption of the risk was still another issue.
>
> . . .
>
> In *Meistrich* we said the terminology of assumption of the risk should not be used when it is projected in its secondary sense, i.e., that of contributory negligence [ ]. We thought, however, that "[p]erhaps a well-guarded charge of assumption of risk in its primary sense will aid comprehension" [ ]. . . . Experience, however, indicates the term "assumption of risk" is so apt to

create mist that it is better banished from the scene. We hope we have heard the last of it. Henceforth let us stay with "negligence" and "contributory negligence."

Does the emergence of comparative negligence affect the analysis?

6. *Recreational sports participants.* In the 1990s, participants in amateur sports began suing each other for injuries incurred during the competition. Courts adopted different approaches to these suits, some modifying the negligence standard to reflect the rough and tumble of sports competition, while others employed the reasonable care standard, adapted to the circumstances. Frequently invoked in these opinions, but without agreement as to its appropriate role or nomenclature, is "assumption of risk" by participants.

The first major case was Knight v. Jewett, 834 P.2d 696 (Cal.1992). Plaintiff alleged that during halftime of a Super Bowl telecast, she and her friends decided to play an informal game of touch football on an adjoining dirt lot, using a "peewee" football. Each side included both men and women. No rules were explicitly discussed before the game. Plaintiff alleged that defendant, one of her opponents, played aggressively and that on the play before she was hurt she told him to "be careful" or she would stop playing. On the next play, he knocked plaintiff over from behind while defending on a pass play—and stepped on her hand, injuring it. The trial judge granted defendant summary judgment.

On appeal, the court affirmed. A four-judge majority modified the duty owed by participants, requiring that they only refrain from "intentionally injur[ing] another player or engag[ing] in conduct that is so reckless as to be totally outside the range of the ordinary activity involved in the sport." If a participant breaches that duty, affirmative defenses based on the plaintiff's conduct may be available depending on the facts. However, the *Knight* defendant's behavior was at most careless, and summary judgment was properly granted. See also Crawn v. Campo, 643 A.2d 600 (N.J.1994)(adopting a lenient duty standard and including, in support, the policy of avoiding a flood of unseemly litigation).

Some courts do not accept the *Knight* modification of the reasonable care duty. For a review of the development and history of the recreational sports rule and a critical analysis of it, see Feld v. Borkowski, 790 N.W.2d 72, 89–93 (Iowa 2010)(Appel, J., concurring and dissenting). Justice Appel made several arguments in favor of retaining a reasonable care standard: 1) the negligence standard is sufficiently flexible to take into account the circumstances of recreational sports competition and hence, most recreational sports injuries would not be the result of negligence; 2) the lack of evidence that a negligence standard was chilling competition in sports competition; 3) quoting a sports law text, "the evidence is accumulating that, on every level of competition, participants need to be restrained and not emboldened"; 4) rejecting the claim that the contact sports exception was necessary to prevent an "avalanche of litigation," citing the fact that over a 50 year period in Connecticut before it adopted the recreational sports exception in 1997 there were only two reported sports cases; and 5) that any impingement on robust competition was worth the cost of deterring unreasonable conduct and the consequent costs of injuries.

Is the disagreement between courts on the appropriate standard of care a reprise of the issue in *Bethel*, p. 53 supra, in which the court replaced the "utmost care" standard for a common carrier with reasonable care under the circumstances?

7. *The professional rescuer rule.* In a number of jurisdictions, firefighters and police officers face greater obstacles to recovery for negligently inflicted injuries they suffer in the course of employment. Thus, a firefighter injured in fighting a fire that was negligently started by a homeowner would be barred from recovery by this doctrine. Sometimes dubbed the "firefighter rule," courts rely on several different grounds for justification: 1) assumption of risk; 2) higher compensation in the form of a risk premium for professional rescuers; 3) professional rescuers on private land are licensees and only owed a duty not to avoid wanton or willful injury; 4) professional rescuers who are provided workers' compensation paid for by tax dollars should not be able to sue their "employers" in tort.

Significant variations exist among the states that do recognize this doctrine. Compare Levandoski v. Cone, 841 A.2d 208 (Conn.2004)(relying on rescuers' status as licensees to limit professional rescuer doctrine to those hurt on defendant's private property by conditions on the land) with Roberts v. Vaughn, 587 N.W.2d 249 (Mich.1998)(firefighter rule "bars firefighters' or police officers' recovery for injuries sustained as a result of the negligence that gave rise to their emergency duties") and Zanghi v. Niagara Frontier Transportation Commission, 649 N.E.2d 1167 (N.Y.1995)(barring firefighters and police officers from recovery when they are injured by hazards whose risks are intrinsic to the position for which they were hired).

8. For a broad review of the entire subject of assumed risk, see Sugarman, Assumption of Risk, 31 Val.U.L.Rev. 833 (1997).

C. PREEMPTION

Earlier, on p. 86 supra, we discussed the issue of whether courts should recognize a regulatory compliance defense as a matter of common law deference for cases in which a defendant's conduct has satisfied applicable regulatory standards. Here, we consider a related scenario with a constitutional foundation; in particular, whether federal law regulating an activity overrides or preempts state tort claims. The constitutional basis for federal law displacing state law is the Supremacy Clause, U.S.Const.art. VI, § 1, which makes federal law "the supreme law of the land," notwithstanding any contrary state law. As we will see, this preemption claim is often based on federal legislative/regulatory standards addressing the subject matter of a tort suit.

Riegel v. Medtronic, Inc.

Supreme Court of the United States, 2008.
552 U.S. 312, 128 S.Ct. 999, 169 L.Ed.2d 892.

■ JUSTICE SCALIA delivered the opinion of the Court.

We consider whether the pre-emption clause enacted in the Medical Device Amendments of 1976, 21 U.S.C. § 360k, bars common-law claims challenging the safety and effectiveness of a medical device given premarket approval by the Food and Drug Administration (FDA).

I

A

The Federal Food, Drug, and Cosmetic Act (FDCA), [ ], has long required FDA approval for the introduction of new drugs into the market. Until the statutory enactment at issue here, however, the introduction of new medical devices was left largely for the States to supervise as they saw fit. See *Medtronic, Inc. v. Lohr,* 518 U.S. 470, 475–476, 116 S.Ct. 2240, 135 L.Ed.2d 700 (1996).

The regulatory landscape changed in the 1960's and 1970's, as complex devices proliferated and some failed. Most notably, the Dalkon Shield intrauterine device, introduced in 1970, was linked to serious infections and several deaths, not to mention a large number of pregnancies. Thousands of tort claims followed. [ ] In the view of many, the Dalkon Shield failure and its aftermath demonstrated the inability of the common-law tort system to manage the risks associated with dangerous devices. [ ] Several States adopted regulatory measures, including California, which in 1970 enacted a law requiring premarket approval of medical devices. [ ]; [ ] (identifying 13 state statutes governing medical devices as of 1976).

Congress stepped in with passage of the Medical Device Amendments of 1976 (MDA), 21 U.S.C. § 360c *et seq.,* which swept back some state obligations and imposed a regime of detailed federal oversight. The MDA includes an express pre-emption provision that states:

> "Except as provided in subsection (b) of this section, no State or political subdivision of a State may establish or continue in effect with respect to a device intended for human use any requirement—
>
> > "(1) which is different from, or in addition to, any requirement applicable under this chapter to the device, and
> >
> > "(2) which relates to the safety or effectiveness of the device or to any other matter included in a requirement applicable to the device under this chapter." § 360k(a).

The exception contained in subsection (b) permits the FDA to exempt some state and local requirements from pre-emption.

The new regulatory regime established various levels of oversight for medical devices, depending on the risks they present. Class I, which includes such devices as elastic bandages and examination gloves, is subject to the lowest level of oversight: "general controls," such as labeling requirements. [ ] Class II, which includes such devices as powered wheelchairs and surgical drapes, *ibid.*, is subject in addition to "special controls" such as performance standards and postmarket surveillance measures, [ ].

The devices receiving the most federal oversight are those in Class III, which include replacement heart valves, implanted cerebella stimulators, and pacemaker pulse generators, [ ]. In general, a device is assigned to Class III if it cannot be established that a less stringent classification would provide reasonable assurance of safety and effectiveness, and the device is "purported or represented to be for a use in supporting or sustaining human life or for a use which is of substantial importance in preventing impairment of human health," or "presents a potential unreasonable risk of illness or injury." [ ]

Although the MDA established a rigorous regime of premarket approval for new Class III devices, it grandfathered many that were already on the market. Devices sold before the MDA's effective date may remain on the market until the FDA promulgates, after notice and comment, a regulation requiring premarket approval. [ ] A related provision seeks to limit the competitive advantage grandfathered devices receive. A new device need not undergo premarket approval if the FDA finds it is "substantially equivalent" to another device exempt from premarket approval. [ ] The agency's review of devices for substantial equivalence is known as the § 510(k) process, named after the section of the MDA describing the review. Most new Class III devices enter the market through § 510(k). In 2005, for example, the FDA authorized the marketing of 3,148 devices under § 510(k) and granted premarket approval to just 32 devices. [ ]

Premarket approval is a "rigorous" process. [ ] A manufacturer must submit what is typically a multivolume application. [ ] It includes, among other things, full reports of all studies and investigations of the device's safety and effectiveness that have been published or should reasonably be known to the applicant; a "full statement" of the device's "components, ingredients, and properties and of the principle or principles of operation"; . . . and a specimen of the proposed labeling. [ ] Before deciding whether to approve the application, the agency may refer it to a panel of outside experts, [ ], and may request additional data from the manufacturer, [ ].

The FDA spends an average of 1,200 hours reviewing each application, *Lohr,* [ ], and grants premarket approval only if it finds there is a "reasonable assurance" of the device's "safety and effectiveness," [ ]. The agency must "weig[h] any probable benefit to health from the use of the device against any probable risk of injury or illness from such use." [ ] It may thus approve devices that present great risks if they nonetheless offer great benefits in light of available alternatives. It approved, for example, under its Humanitarian Device Exemption procedures, a ventricular assist device for children with failing hearts, even though the survival rate of children using the device was less than 50 percent. [ ]

The premarket approval process includes review of the device's proposed labeling. The FDA evaluates safety and effectiveness under the conditions of use set forth on the label, [ ], and must determine that the proposed labeling is neither false nor misleading, [ ].

After completing its review, the FDA may grant or deny premarket approval. [ ] It may also condition approval on adherence to performance standards, 21 CFR § 861.1(b)(3), restrictions upon sale or distribution, or compliance with other requirements, § 814.82. The agency is also free to impose device-specific restrictions by regulation. [ ]

If the FDA is unable to approve a new device in its proposed form, it may send an "approvable letter" indicating that the device could be approved if the applicant submitted specified information or agreed to certain conditions or restrictions. [ ] Alternatively, the agency may send a "not approvable" letter, listing the grounds that justify denial and, where practical, measures that the applicant could undertake to make the device approvable. [ ]

Once a device has received premarket approval, the MDA forbids the manufacturer to make, without FDA permission, changes in design specifications, manufacturing processes, labeling, or any other attribute, that would affect safety or effectiveness. [ ] If the applicant wishes to make such a change, it must submit, and the FDA must approve, an application for supplemental premarket approval, to be evaluated under largely the same criteria as an initial application. [ ]

After premarket approval, the devices are subject to reporting requirements. [ ] These include the obligation to inform the FDA of new clinical investigations or scientific studies concerning the device which the applicant knows of or reasonably should know of, [ ], and to report incidents in which the device may have caused or contributed to death or serious injury, or malfunctioned in a manner that would likely cause or contribute to death or serious injury if it recurred, [ ]. The FDA has the power to withdraw premarket approval based on newly reported data or existing information and must withdraw approval if it determines that a device is unsafe or ineffective under the conditions in its labeling. [ ] (recall authority).

B

. . . The device at issue is an Evergreen Balloon Catheter marketed by defendant-respondent Medtronic, Inc. It is a Class III device that received premarket approval from the FDA in 1994; changes to its label received supplemental approvals in 1995 and 1996.

Charles Riegel underwent coronary angioplasty in 1996, shortly after suffering a myocardial infarction. [ ] His right coronary artery was diffusely diseased and heavily calcified. Riegel's doctor inserted the Evergreen Balloon Catheter into his patient's coronary artery in an attempt to dilate the artery, although the device's labeling stated that use was contraindicated for patients with diffuse or calcified stenoses. The label also warned that the catheter should not be inflated beyond its rated burst pressure of eight atmospheres. Riegel's doctor inflated the catheter five times, to a pressure of 10 atmospheres; on its fifth inflation, the catheter ruptured. [ ] Riegel developed a heart block, was placed on life support, and underwent emergency coronary bypass surgery.

Riegel and his wife Donna brought this lawsuit in April 1999, in the United States District Court for the Northern District of New York. Their complaint alleged that Medtronic's catheter was designed, labeled, and manufactured in a manner that violated New York common law, and that these defects caused Riegel to suffer severe and permanent injuries. The complaint raised a number of common-law claims. The District Court held that the MDA pre-empted Riegel's claims of strict liability; breach of implied warranty; and negligence in the design, testing, inspection, distribution, labeling, marketing, and sale of the catheter. [ ] It also held that the MDA pre-empted a negligent manufacturing claim insofar as it was not premised on the theory that Medtronic violated federal law. . . .

The United States Court of Appeals for the Second Circuit affirmed these dismissals. [ ] The court concluded that Medtronic was "clearly subject to the federal, device-specific requirement of adhering to the standards contained in its individual, federally approved" premarket approval application. [ ] The Riegels' claims were pre-empted because they "would, if successful, impose state requirements that differed from, or added to" the device-specific federal requirements. [ ] We granted certiorari. [ ]

II

Since the MDA expressly pre-empts only state requirements "different from, or in addition to, any requirement applicable . . . to the device" under federal law, § 360k(a)(1), we must determine whether the Federal Government has established requirements applicable to Medtronic's catheter. If so, we must then determine whether the Riegels' common-law claims are based upon New York requirements with respect to the device that are "different from, or in addition to" the federal ones, and that relate to safety and effectiveness. [ ].

We turn to the first question. In *Lohr,* a majority of this Court interpreted the MDA's pre-emption provision in a manner "substantially informed" by the FDA regulation set forth at [ ]. That regulation says that state requirements are pre-empted "only when the Food and Drug Administration has established specific counterpart regulations or there are other specific requirements applicable to a particular device. . . ." [ ] Informed by the regulation, we concluded that federal manufacturing and labeling requirements applicable across the board to almost all medical devices did not pre-empt the common-law claims of negligence and strict liability at issue in *Lohr*. The federal requirements, we said, were not requirements specific to the device in question—they reflected "entirely generic concerns about device regulation generally." [ ] While we disclaimed a conclusion that general federal requirements could never pre-empt, or general state duties never be pre-empted, we held that no pre-emption occurred in the case at hand based on a careful comparison between the state and federal duties at issue. [ ]

Even though substantial-equivalence review under § 510(k) is device specific, *Lohr* also rejected the manufacturer's contention that § 510(k) approval imposed device-specific "requirements." We regarded the fact that products entering the market through § 510(k) may be marketed only so long as they remain substantial equivalents of the relevant pre-1976 devices as a qualification for an exemption rather than a requirement. [ ]

Premarket approval, in contrast, imposes "requirements" under the MDA as we interpreted it in *Lohr*. Unlike general labeling duties, premarket approval is specific to individual devices. And it is in no sense an exemption from federal safety review—it *is* federal safety review. Thus, the attributes that *Lohr* found lacking in § 510(k) review are present here. While § 510(k) is " 'focused on *equivalence,* not safety,' " [ ], premarket approval is focused on safety, not equivalence. While devices that enter the market through § 510(k) have "never been formally reviewed under the MDA for safety or efficacy," *ibid.,* the FDA may grant premarket approval only after it determines that a device offers a reasonable assurance of safety and effectiveness, [ ]. And while the FDA does not " 'require' " that a device allowed to enter the market as a substantial equivalent "take any particular form for any particular reason," [ ], the FDA requires a device that has received premarket approval to be made with almost no deviations from the specifications in its approval application, for the reason that the FDA has determined that the approved form provides a reasonable assurance of safety and effectiveness.

III

We turn, then, to the second question: whether the Riegels' common-law claims rely upon "any requirement" of New York law applicable to the catheter that is "different from, or in addition to" federal requirements and that "relates to the safety or effectiveness of the device or to any other matter included in a requirement applicable to the device." § 360k(a). Safety and effectiveness are the very subjects of the Riegels' common-law claims, so the critical issue is whether New York's tort duties constitute "requirements" under the MDA.

A

In *Lohr,* five Justices concluded that common-law causes of action for negligence and strict liability do impose "requirement[s]" and would be pre-empted by federal requirements specific to a medical device. [ ] We adhere to that view. In interpreting two other statutes we have likewise held that a provision pre-empting state "requirements" pre-empted common-law duties. *Bates v. Dow Agrosciences LLC,* 544 U.S. 431, 125 S.Ct. 1788, 161 L.Ed.2d 687 (2005), found common-law actions to be pre-empted by a provision of the Federal Insecticide, Fungicide, and Rodenticide Act that said certain States " 'shall not impose or continue in effect *any requirements* for labeling or packaging in addition to or different from those required under this subchapter.' " *Id.,* [ ]. *Cipollone v. Liggett Group, Inc.,* 505 U.S. 504, 112 S.Ct. 2608, 120 L.Ed.2d 407 (1992), held common-law actions pre-empted by a provision of the Public Health Cigarette Smoking Act of 1969, 15 U.S.C. § 1334(b), which said that "[n]o requirement or prohibition based on smoking and health shall be imposed under State law with respect to the advertising or promotion of any cigarettes" whose packages were labeled in accordance with federal law. [ ]

Congress is entitled to know what meaning this Court will assign to terms regularly used in its enactments. Absent other indication, reference to a State's "requirements" includes its common-law duties. As the plurality opinion said in *Cipollone,* common-law liability is "premised on the existence of a legal duty," and a tort judgment therefore establishes that the defendant has violated a state-law obligation. [ ] And while the common-law remedy is limited to damages, a liability award " 'can be, indeed is designed to be, a potent method of governing conduct and controlling policy.' " [ ]

In the present case, there is nothing to contradict this normal meaning. To the contrary, in the context of this legislation excluding common-law duties from the scope of pre-emption would make little sense. State tort law that requires a manufacturer's catheters to be safer, but hence less effective, than the model the FDA has approved disrupts the federal scheme no less than state regulatory law to the same effect. Indeed, one would think that tort law, applied by juries under a negligence or strict-liability standard, is less deserving of preservation. A state statute, or a regulation adopted by a state agency, could at least be expected to apply cost-benefit analysis similar to that applied by the experts at the FDA: How many more lives will be saved by a device which, along with its greater effectiveness, brings a greater risk of harm? A jury, on the other hand, sees only the cost of a more dangerous design, and is not concerned with its benefits; the patients who reaped those benefits are not represented in court. As Justice Breyer explained in *Lohr,* it is implausible that the MDA was meant to "grant greater power (to set state standards 'different from, or in addition to' federal standards) to a single state jury than to state officials acting through state administrative or legislative lawmaking processes." [ ] That perverse distinction is not required or even suggested by the broad language Congress chose in the MDA, and we will not turn somersaults to create it.

. . .

For the foregoing reasons, the judgment of the Court of Appeals is *Affirmed.*

■ JUSTICE STEVENS, concurring in part and concurring in the judgment.

. . .

■ JUSTICE GINSBURG, dissenting.

The Medical Device Amendments of 1976 (MDA or Act), 90 Stat. 539, as construed by the Court, cut deeply into a domain historically occupied by state law. The MDA's preemption clause, 21 U.S.C. § 360k(a), the Court holds, spares medical device manufacturers from personal injury claims alleging flaws in a design or label once the application for the design or label has gained premarket approval from the Food and Drug Administration (FDA); a state damages remedy, the Court instructs, persists only for claims "premised on a violation of FDA regulations." *Ante,* at 1011.[1] I dissent from today's constriction of state authority. Congress, in my view, did not intend § 360k(a) to effect a radical curtailment of state common-law suits seeking compensation for injuries caused by defectively designed or labeled medical devices.

. . .

I

The "purpose of Congress is the ultimate touchstone of pre-emption analysis." *Cipollone* [ ]. Courts have "long presumed that Congress does not cavalierly pre-empt state-law causes of action." *Medtronic, Inc. v. Lohr,* [ ]. Preemption analysis starts with the assumption that "the historic police powers of the States [a]re not to be superseded . . . unless that was the clear and manifest purpose of Congress." [ ] "This assumption provides assurance that 'the federal-state balance' will not

---

[1]   The Court's holding does not reach an important issue outside the bounds of this case: the preemptive effect of § 360k(a) where evidence of a medical device's defect comes to light only after the device receives premarket approval.

be disturbed unintentionally by Congress or unnecessarily by the courts." [ ]

The presumption against preemption is heightened "where federal law is said to bar state action in fields of traditional state regulation." [ ] Given the traditional "primacy of state regulation of matters of health and safety," *Lohr,* [ ], courts assume "that state and local regulation related to [those] matters . . . can normally coexist with federal regulations," [ ].

Federal laws containing a preemption clause do not automatically escape the presumption against preemption. See *Bates v. Dow Agrosciences LLC,* 544 U.S. 431, 449, 125 S.Ct. 1788, 161 L.Ed.2d 687 (2005); [ ]. A preemption clause tells us that Congress intended to supersede or modify state law to some extent. In the absence of legislative precision, however, courts may face the task of determining the substance and scope of Congress' displacement of state law. Where the text of a preemption clause is open to more than one plausible reading, courts ordinarily "accept the reading that disfavors pre-emption." *Bates,* [ ].

II

. . .

"Absent other indication," the Court states, "reference to a State's 'requirements' includes its common-law duties." [ ] Regarding the MDA, however, "other indication" is not "[a]bsent." Contextual examination of the Act convinces me that § 360k(a)'s inclusion of the term "requirement" should not prompt a sweeping preemption of mine-run claims for relief under state tort law.

A

Congress enacted the MDA "to provide for the safety and effectiveness of medical devices intended for human use." [ ] A series of high-profile medical device failures that caused extensive injuries and loss of life propelled adoption of the MDA. Conspicuous among these failures was the Dalkon Shield intrauterine device, used by approximately 2.2 million women in the United States between 1970 and 1974. [ ] Aggressively promoted as a safe and effective form of birth control, the Dalkon Shield had been linked to 16 deaths and 25 miscarriages by the middle of 1975. [ ] By early 1976, "more than 500 lawsuits seeking compensatory and punitive damages totaling more than $400 million" had been filed. [ ] Given the publicity attending the Dalkon Shield litigation and Congress' awareness of the suits at the time the MDA was under consideration, I find informative the absence of any sign of a legislative design to preempt state common-law tort actions.

. . .

. . . The Court's construction of § 360k(a) has the "perverse effect" of granting broad immunity "to an entire industry that, in the judgment of Congress, needed more stringent regulation," *Lohr,* [ ], not exemption from liability in tort litigation.

. . .

B

Congress enacted the MDA after decades of regulating drugs and food and color additives under the Federal Food, Drug, and Cosmetic Act (FDCA), 52 Stat. 1040, as amended, 21 U.S.C. § 301 *et seq.* The FDCA contains no preemption clause, and thus the Court's interpretation of § 360k(a) has no bearing on tort suits involving drugs and additives. But § 360k(a)'s confinement to medical devices hardly renders irrelevant to the proper construction of the MDA's preemption provision the long history of federal and state controls over drugs and additives in the interest of public health and welfare. Congress' experience regulating drugs and additives informed, and in part provided the model for, its regulation of medical devices. I therefore turn to an examination of that experience.

[Justice Ginsburg related the history of the Food, Drug and Cosmetic Act from 1938 when the first premarketing approval process was mandated. Other amendments to the Act from that time until the MDA in 1976 mandated premarketing approval, but none contained an express preemption clause. That was true, even though when they were enacted, there was a background of tort suits about the newly regulated products, including medical devices at the time of the MDA. The reason for the express preemption clause in the MDA was that states had already been regulating medical devices, and it was this state regulation that was the target of § 360k(a) and (b), which were "to empower the FDA to exercise control over state premarket approval systems installed at a time when there was no preclearance at the federal level."]

In sum, state premarket regulation of medical devices, not any design to suppress tort suits, accounts for Congress' inclusion of a preemption clause in the MDA; no such clause figures in earlier federal laws regulating drugs and additives, for States had not installed comparable control regimes in those areas.

C

Congress' experience regulating drugs also casts doubt on Medtronic's policy arguments for reading § 360k(a) to preempt state tort claims. Section 360k(a) must preempt state common-law suits, Medtronic contends, because Congress would not have wanted state juries to second-guess the FDA's finding that a medical device is safe and effective when used as directed. [ ] The Court is similarly minded. [ ]

But the process for approving new drugs is at least as rigorous as the premarket approval process for medical devices. Courts that have considered the question have overwhelmingly held that FDA approval of a new drug application does not preempt state tort suits. Decades of drug regulation thus indicate, contrary to Medtronic's argument, that Congress did not regard FDA regulation and state tort claims as mutually exclusive.

III

Refusing to read § 360k(a) as an automatic bar to state common-law tort claims would hardly render the FDA's premarket approval of Medtronic's medical device application irrelevant to the instant suit. First, a "pre-emption provision, by itself, does not foreclose (through negative implication) any possibility of implied conflict preemption." [ ] Accordingly, a medical device manufacturer may have a dispositive defense if it can identify an actual conflict between the plaintiff's theory of the case and the FDA's premarket approval of the device in question. As currently postured, this case presents no occasion to take up this issue for Medtronic relies exclusively on § 360k(a) and does not argue conflict preemption.

Second, a medical device manufacturer may be entitled to interpose a regulatory compliance defense based on the FDA's approval of the premarket application. Most States do not treat regulatory compliance as dispositive, but regard it as one factor to be taken into account by the jury. [ ] In those States, a manufacturer could present the FDA's approval of its medical device as evidence that it used due care in the design and labeling of the product.

The Court's broad reading of § 360k(a) saves the manufacturer from any need to urge these defenses. Instead, regardless of the strength of a plaintiff's case, suits will be barred *ab initio*. The constriction of state authority ordered today was not mandated by Congress and is at odds with the MDA's central purpose: to protect consumer safety.

. . .

For the reasons stated, I would hold that § 360k(a) does not preempt Riegel's suit. I would therefore reverse the judgment of the Court of Appeals in relevant part.

NOTES AND QUESTIONS

1.   When Congress includes an express preemption clause, as it did in the Medical Device Amendments, courts must determine whether preemption is limited to state "positive" enactments, i.e., statutes and administrative regulations, or also includes common law tort claims.

Virtually every time the Supreme Court has been confronted with the question, it has read "requirement" in preemption statutes to include common law tort liability. In the cited *Cipollone* case, the Court for the first time faced this question under the 1969 amendments to the 1965 cigarette labeling act. It responded first by noting that the broad language of the statute in question "suggests no distinction between positive enactments and common law." Moreover, it was clear that "regulation can be as effectively exerted through an award of damages as through some form of preventive relief. The obligation to pay compensation can be, indeed is designed to be, a potent method of governing conduct and controlling policy." What is the opposing argument? Does Justice Ginsburg's dissent provide a persuasive claim that that is not what Congress meant in section 360k(a) of the Medical Device Amendments?

In Bates v. Dow Agrosciences LLC, 544 U.S. 431 (2005), the Court once again found that "requirement," this time contained in the Federal Insecticide, Fungicide, and Rodenticide Act (FIFRA), encompassed common law decisions. FIFRA preempts "any requirements for labeling or packaging in addition to or different from those" provided by the statute. The Court, however, added a novel twist in concluding that plaintiff's design defect claim was not preempted: even if a finding of design defect might induce the defendant manufacturer to change its label, that outcome was not a "requirement" of common law preempted by the statute. Only if the legal requirement, such as a warning claim, determines the labeling to be inadequate would it constitute a state law "requirement" preempted by the statute. Is this distinction between the consequences of design defect and warning defect claims convincing?

2.   In the cited *Lohr*, the Court decided that the section 510k "substantially equivalent" approval of devices did not constitute "a specific counterpart [regulation] or . . . other specific [requirement] applicable to a particular device," which was required for preemption under the Medical Device Amendments. What is the specific regulation or requirement applicable to the Medtronic catheter that results in the preemption in *Reigel*?

3.   As the explanation of *Bates* in note 1 reveals, a second critical question that arises when express preemption includes tort claims is the scope of preemption, i.e., which tort claims are preempted by the statutory language and which are not. After parsing the statutory language, the *Bates* Court concluded that failure to warn, fraud, deceptive trade practice, and express warranty claims were not preempted so long as they were not inconsistent with provisions in FIFRA barring false or misleading statements on product labeling. Similarly, in the cited *Cipollone* case, involving a claim for lung cancer against a tobacco company, the Court concluded that claims alleging failure to warn in advertising and promotional efforts were preempted under the federal cigarette warning legislation, but that claims based on express warranty, fraud, and misrepresentation were not preempted.

4.   The Court explains that plaintiff's doctor over-inflated the balloon catheter five times while treating plaintiff and that the catheter burst in his coronary artery on the fifth attempt. In addition, the device's labeling warned against use in patients, like plaintiff, with stenosis. Of what relevance are these facts?

5. The majority states: "State tort law that requires a manufacturer's catheters to be safer, but hence less effective, than the model the FDA has approved disrupts the federal scheme no less than state regulatory law to the same effect." Would state tort law that requires a safer design that is no less effective equally disrupt the federal scheme?

6. In footnote 1 of Justice Ginsburg's dissent, she identifies a significant limit to the majority's opinion. Does the majority's rationale offer any clues as to how it might decide such a case?

7. Even if there is no express preemption language in a statute, it may still impliedly preempt a state tort claim. A variety of grounds for this implied preemption exist, including a conflict between federal and state law, state law that frustrates the purpose of regulatory legislation, and Congress's enacting legislation that fully occupies a particular field, such as labor law. For example, in Buckman Co. v. Plaintiffs' Legal Committee, 531 U.S. 341 (2001), the Court addressed the question of preemption for state-law claims asserting that a medical device manufacturer committed fraud in the process of obtaining approval from the FDA to market its device. Finding that the FDA required sole control over policing and enforcing compliance with its pre-marketing regulations, the Court found such claims impliedly preempted based on their conflict with the FDA statutory and regulatory scheme. We address implied preemption in greater detail following these notes.

8. The preemption battleground covers many areas that had previously been litigated as common law tort cases, as suggested in the following cases: Bruesewitz v. Wyeth LLC, 562 U.S. 223 (2011)(concluding that the National Vaccine Act expressly preempts all state tort claims alleging that a vaccine is defectively designed); American Electric Power Co. v. Connecticut, 564 U.S. 410 (2011)(holding that federal environmental law displaces any federal common-law right to seek abatement of carbon dioxide emissions contributing to climate change but leaving open the availability of state nuisance claims); Garcia v. Vanguard Car Rental USA, Inc., 540 F.3d 1242 (11th Cir.2008)(federal statute displaces state law that imposes vicarious liability on car rental companies—like all car owners—for the negligence of those driving the car with permission, namely renters); Greene v. B.F. Goodrich Avionics Systems, Inc., 409 F.3d 784 (6th Cir.2005)(FAA regulation of aviation preempts a products liability claim against the manufacturer of gyroscope used in a helicopter); Farina v. Nokia Inc., 625 F.3d 97 (3d Cir.2010)(although tort claims against cell phone manufacturers are not expressly preempted by Federal Communications Act, such suits would impede congressional purpose in enacting the Act and hence are impliedly preempted); Pinney v. Nokia, Inc., 402 F.3d 430 (4th Cir.2005)(state tort claims against cell phone manufacturers are not preempted by the Federal Communications Act); Hodges v. Delta Airlines, Inc., 44 F.3d 334 (5th Cir.1995)(en banc)(negligence claim by passenger hit by falling case of rum against airline for allowing case to be stored in overhead bin was not preempted by Airline Deregulation Act); Greenlaw v. Garrett, 59 F.3d 994 (9th Cir.1995)(federal employee's state tort claims against former employer for sex discrimination were preempted by federal Civil Service Reform Act); BIC Pen Corp. v. Carter, 251 S.W.3d 500 (Tex.2008)(Consumer Product Safety Commission standard for child safety of butane lighters preempts state tort claims asserting a design defect). New areas of potential preemption seem to arise regularly.

————

Implied Preemption

One year after *Riegel*, the Court decided perhaps its most important preemption case: whether products liability suits against drug manufacturers are preempted by the extensive regulatory structure established in the Food, Drug, and Cosmetic Act (FDCA) for new prescription drugs. As the dissent in Wyeth v. Levine, 555 U.S. 555 (2009), explained, regulation of prescription drugs is at least as rigorous as for Class III medical devices under the Medical Device Amendments. But there was one important difference between *Riegel* and *Levine*. Congress placed no express preemption clause for prescription drugs in the FDCA. Thus, defendant's argument was that state tort law is impliedly preempted. More specifically, subjecting drug manufacturers to the regulatory dictates of the FDA and the judgment of state court juries could pose the dilemma for manufacturers of modifying the drug or its labeling to conform to a jury determination that was inconsistent with the terms by which the drug was approved by the FDA. Specifically, the language contained in a drug's labeling, which includes warnings, is an important aspect of the FDA's premarketing approval of a drug—after such approval, the drug must be sold with the approved labeling.

The plaintiff in *Wyeth v. Levine* received an anti-nausea drug, Phenergan, for severe migraine headaches. Phenergan must be injected, either intra-muscularly or intravenously. One intravenous method available is to insert an IV line and drip the drug into a vein ("IV drip"). Alternatively, the drug can be directly injected into a vein, using a needle, for quicker administration ("IV push"). But the drug must not be put or leaked into an artery—if it is, the drug is corrosive and can cause gangrene. After an earlier intramuscular injection did not provide relief, a physician's assistant administered an additional dose of Phenergan employing the IV push method. The physician's assistant either injected the drug erroneously into an artery or nicked an artery, permitting leakage of the drug into the artery. This likely occurred because the drug was injected into a blood vessel in the crook on the inside of the plaintiff's arm at the elbow—a location that the drug's labeling warned was inappropriate because both veins and arteries are in close proximity. Plaintiff developed gangrene, and much of her arm had to be amputated.

After settling a malpractice suit against her physicians, plaintiff sued Wyeth, the manufacturer of Phenergan. Plaintiff alleged that the warnings on the drug's label were inadequate, rendering the drug defective. Specifically, plaintiff wanted stronger warnings against using the IV push method. While the labeling had extensive information about the dangers of getting Phenergan into arterial blood, none specifically mentioned IV push as presenting a higher risk of such mishaps. Although the FDA and Wyeth had desultory communications about the drug's warnings over the years, in 1996 the FDA requested that Wyeth retain labeling proposed by Wyeth and in place since 1981.

At trial, the jury found for plaintiff and awarded her $7.4 million. The Vermont Supreme Court affirmed, rejecting Wyeth's federal implied preemption defense on the ground that FDA regulation sets a floor not a ceiling for safety.

Wyeth's implied preemption defense had two components. First, as mentioned above, making any change in Phenergan's labeling would put it in conflict with the FDA's requirement that the drug be sold only with its approved labeling. Second, permitting state court juries to decide whether prescription drugs were defective would frustrate Congress's purpose of delegating to the FDA, with its expertise, the determination of appropriate labeling for drugs, rather than having lay juries make these determinations.

A majority of the Court rejected Wyeth's implied preemption claims. Critical to the Court's reasoning was a regulation of the FDA that permits drug manufacturers to change the labeling of drugs without prior approval by the FDA, the CBE (changes being effected) regulation. It requires notification to the FDA and preserves the FDA's prerogative to reject the change if the FDA determines that it does not reflect supporting scientific evidence. In this case, there was no indication that the FDA would be opposed to or reverse a change in Phenergan's labeling that strengthened the warnings about IV push administration, a burden the Court placed on Wyeth, stating "absent clear evidence that the FDA would not have approved a change to Phenergan's label, we will not conclude that it was impossible for Wyeth to comply with both federal and state requirements."

Wyeth's second basis for preemption, frustration of congressional purpose, was also rejected. There was a long history of state tort litigation over prescription drugs and Congress had amended the FDCA a number of times, including an express preemption provision in 1976 in the Medical Device Amendments, and yet it had never added any express preemption language addressing prescription drugs.

Justice Breyer, concurring, made two short, yet important points:

State tort law will sometimes help the Food and Drug Administration (FDA) "uncover unknown drug hazards and [encourage] drug manufacturers to disclose safety risks." But it is also possible that state tort law will sometimes interfere with the FDA's desire to create a drug label containing a specific set of cautions and instructions. . . . The FDA may seek to determine whether and when state tort law acts as a help or a hindrance to achieving the safe drug-related medical care that Congress sought. [ ] It may seek to embody those determinations in lawful specific regulations describing, for example, when labeling requirements serve as a ceiling as well as a floor. And it is possible that such determinations would have preemptive effect. [ ] I agree with the Court, however, that such a regulation is not at issue in this case.

Justice Thomas also concurred, but with a novel and provocative position. In his view, the Court's use of implied preemption on the ground that state law obstructed congressional purpose was improper. Preemption divorced from statutory language was not, in his view, consistent with the Supremacy Clause in the Constitution, the foundational authority for having federal law displace state law.

Three dissenters offered a different perspective on the preemption issue from the majority. Based on statements made by plaintiff's attorney to the jury, the dissent viewed the case as about whether IV push should be retained as a method for administering Phenergan, and they found evidence that the FDA had assessed that issue and decided that the benefits of IV push outweighed its risks. The labeling had extensive warnings about the risks of the drug getting into an artery. Although the labeling did not explicitly address the higher risks of the IV push method, there were many cautionary statements that referred to the risks of intra-arterial injections, some of which could only have been about the IV push method. Thus, the label stated: "When administering any irritant drug intravenously, it is usually preferable to inject it through the tubing of an intravenous infusion set that is known to be functioning satisfactorily." The dissent concluded, "juries are ill-equipped to perform the FDA's cost-benefit-balancing function," which is why Congress delegated these decisions to the FDA and why Vermont cannot have a jury make a contrary determination.

NOTES AND QUESTIONS

1.   The majority, in explaining the history of this case, remarked that the trial judge, in an opinion on post-trial motions, stated that evidence in the case revealed at least 20 amputations similar to the plaintiff's since the 1960s. Is that evidence relevant to the implied preemption issue in the case?

2.   In the aftermath of *Levine*, the reaction of most courts to its scope is reflected in Mason v. SmithKline Beecham Corp., 596 F.3d 387 (7th Cir.2010). Plaintiff's decedent took defendant's antidepressant and committed suicide two days later. Plaintiff sued alleging inadequate warnings of the risk of suicide. (The issue of a causal connection between this class of antidepressants and suicide has long been controversial.) The lower court dismissed on preemption grounds. The court reversed, but not

until after it had canvassed the post-approval process in some detail, including three citizen petitions to change the labeling that were denied by the FDA, meetings between the FDA and defendant, and a call by the FDA for more research on the causal connection. *Levine* imposed the burden on defendant to establish by "clear evidence" that the FDA would have disapproved a proposed change in the drug's labeling, and the evidence marshaled by the defendant here did not meet this "stringent standard."

By contrast with *Mason* is In re Fosamax (Alendronate Sodium) Products Liability Litigation, 951 F.Supp.2d 695, 703 (D.N.J.2013). The plaintiff-patient alleged that she suffered a fracture of her femur due to her taking Fosamax, a drug used to treat osteoporosis in post-menopausal women. Eight months before she suffered her fracture, the manufacturer sought to change its labeling to add a warning about such fractures but the FDA rejected the request. The court concluded that the "FDA's rejection constitutes clear evidence that the FDA would not have approved a label change to the Precautions section of the label prior to [the plaintiff's] injury," and granted defendant's motion for judgment as a matter of law based on implied preemption.

3. In Pliva, Inc. v. Mensing, 131 S.Ct. 2567 (2011), the Court held (5–4) that the FDA's regulations governing the labeling of generic drugs impliedly preempt tort claims alleging that a generic-drug manufacturer has a duty to provide a warning that differs from the one contained on the branded drug. Plaintiffs alleged that the defendants, generic-drug manufacturers, should have provided stronger warnings on their labels related to the risk of a disorder caused by prolonged use of the drug. The defendants argued that they could not alter the warning in this manner because federal statutory provisions and FDA regulations required them to use the same label as the one used by the branded-drug manufacturer. The Court agreed with the defendants, concluding that it would be impossible for defendants to comply with both state and federal law. The Court recognized that under *Wyeth v. Levine*, plaintiffs' claims would not have been preempted if they were suing the brand-name manufacturer for the identical warning defect. The Court then observed that from the plaintiffs' perspective, it makes "little sense" that they are barred from recovering against a generic-drug manufacturer but not from the brand-name manufacturer. The Court concluded, however, that it was obligated to follow the express statutory and regulatory language governing the labeling requirements applicable to the two different types of drug manufacturers. Might there be "some sense" to permitting claims against brand-name manufacturers but barring such claims against generic manufacturers?

A proposed regulation by the FDA would give generic drug manufacturers the same ability to change the labeling as branded drug manufacturers and change the result in *Mensing*. The proposal has generated considerable resistance by the generic drug industry, which claims that opening them up to expensive suits would increase the costs of generic drugs. See Sabrina Tavernise, *Makers of Generic Drugs Challenge F.D.A. Plan for Updated Warnings*, N.Y. Times, March 27, 2015, at A13.

4. For a range of views on The Supreme Court's preemption jurisprudence affecting state tort claims from *Cipollone* to *Wyeth*, see Geistfeld, Tort Law in the Age of Statutes, 99 Iowa L.Rev. 957 (2014); Rabin, Conflicting Conceptions of Tort Preemption: Territorial Claims in the Domain of Accidental Harm, 74 Brook. L.Rev. 987 (2009); Sharkey, Products Liability Preemption: An Institutional Approach, 76 Geo.Wash.L.Rev. 449 (2008); Schuck, FDA Preemption of State Tort Law in Drug Regulation: Finding the Sweet Spot, 13 Roger Williams U.L.Rev. 73 (2008); Kessler & Vladeck, A Critical Examination of the FDA's Efforts to Preempt Failure-to-Warn Claims, 96 Geo.L.J. 461 (2008).

ERISA Preemption

The issue of when and whether health maintenance organizations and insurers can be sued for physical harm or death resulting from decisions wrongly denying medical treatment to their insureds has been percolating in the federal courts for years. In Aetna Health Inc. v. Davila, 542 U.S. 200 (2004), the Court resolved the issue. In *Davila*, plaintiffs, covered under employee benefit plans governed by ERISA, sued under state law after plan administrators refused to cover them for treatment decisions recommended by their physicians. The Supreme Court unanimously held that ERISA preempted the state law action. The majority distinguished and limited Pegram v. Herdrich, 530 U.S. 211 (2000), which held that, in making decisions involving both eligibility and treatment, an HMO is not acting within the scope of certain provisions of ERISA that would have preempted the claim because in that case the physicians were both treating physicians and administrators of the plan. That fact made the decision in *Pegram* a "mixed eligibility and treatment" decision. By contrast, in *Davila*, the decision was made only by administrators and only on the basis of whether the plan covered the proposed medical treatment. Justice Ginsburg, joined by Justice Breyer, concurred.

Justice Ginsburg noted the suggestion by the United States in its amicus brief that plaintiffs such as those in *Davila* might obtain adequate relief in claims under ERISA, a proposition that the federal courts had not previously believed to be the case. The concurrence also echoed a chorus of federal court opinions that had been unusually outspoken about the need for congressional action to overturn the pernicious effect of ERISA, which preempts state claims for damages when benefits are wrongfully denied but refuses to provide adequate relief in the private claims available under ERISA. See, e.g., Cicio v. Does, 321 F.3d 83, 106 (2d Cir.2003)(Calabresi, J., concurring and dissenting)("gaping wound" created by Supreme Court's decisions on broad scope of preemption combined with limited remedies available under ERISA require the Court to "start over from the beginning, or for Congress to wipe the slate clean"), vacated, 542 U.S. 933 (2004);

DiFelice v. Aetna U.S. Healthcare, 346 F.3d 442, 453 (3d Cir.2003)(Becker, J., concurring)(expressing concern that the distinction between eligibility decisions and mixed decisions is a "Serbonian bog" that entails "extraordinary subtleties and complexities of this area of the law that cry out for clarification by the Congress, or, failing that, by the Supreme Court"). For a variety of perspectives on the impact that the *Davila* decision has had on state tort claims, see Symposium, The Grand Irony of ERISA?: Intersectionality of ERISA Preemption and Remedial Issues, 26 Hofstra Labor & Employment L.J. 341 (2009).

D. STATUTES OF LIMITATION

Statutes of limitation play a significant role in tort lawsuits. They prescribe a time within which suit must be filed and impose a hefty penalty for failing to comply: those plaintiffs who do not file in time lose their claim. Statutes of limitation are, predominantly, true affirmative defenses. Defendant must plead and prove a violation (although often proof that the statute has run is straightforward).

Although a variety of rationales have been articulated to support statutes of limitation, the most persuasive are that they 1) serve to encourage more accurate resolution of litigation by avoiding faded memories and stale evidence; and 2) provide repose to those who might be sued by limiting the period in which they are subject to suit. Often less explicit is a vague sense that those who sleep on their rights and fail to file suit promptly are less deserving. Although statutes of limitation are harsh in barring claims, they are administratively efficient because they provide bright-line rules that are easily resolved.

Statutes of limitation operate by setting a prescribed period within which suit must be filed. That limit varies from state to state and across different types of claims. Tort suits generally have a statute of limitation of two or three years, although specific types of tort suits such as products liability or wrongful death may have a different period specified. The statute of limitations "clock" starts upon "accrual" of the claim, which ordinarily occurs when the victim is injured. The clock proceeds to run after accrual, and suit must be filed before the specified period runs out. Specified conditions or events may "toll" the running of the statutory clock: in many jurisdictions the statute is tolled during the minority of a child victim; or the statute may be tolled when a defendant fraudulently conceals facts that would reveal the existence of a claim, e.g., a doctor who lies to a patient about the cause of an adverse outcome.

With most traumatic injury claims, the time when the claim accrues concurs with the time when the victim can file suit. Thus, physical injury is necessary before such a victim can file suit—having suffered cognizable harm, both the final element of a tort claim is in place and the statute begins to run. But that is not universally so, as our prior encounter with *Hymowitz v. Eli Lilly & Co.*, p. 374 supra, revealed. Until the New York legislature adopted a discovery rule in place of the former rule that a claim accrued for statute of limitation purposes upon exposure, claims were barred by the statute before a victim could file suit—without some "injury," as defined by statute, no claim existed. This difficulty was particularly problematic in toxic injury cases, such as *Hymowitz*, in which exposures often preceded the development of disease by decades, far longer than the statute of limitations.

While the legislature addressed the matter in New York, more common is judicial modification of when accrual occurs in latent disease cases and some other litigation, such as medical malpractice. Typical is Griffin v. Unocal Corp., 990 So.2d 291 (Ala.2008). Plaintiff's decedent was exposed while at work to various chemicals manufactured by defendants. Ten years after retiring he developed leukemia, and five months later he died of the disease. A wrongful death suit against the chemical manufacturers was dismissed because suit was filed more than two years after decedent's last exposure, the time when the claim accrued. The Alabama Supreme Court reversed and adopted a discovery rule for accrual. The statute of limitations does not begin to run for toxic-exposure disease claims until the injury manifests itself by observable signs or symptoms, or is medically identifiable, even if the injured person is not personally aware of the injury or knows of its cause or origin. Most courts have adopted a discovery rule, although there is considerable variation in precisely what the victim must discover before accrual of the claim. See Grisham v. Philip Morris U.S.A., Inc., 151 P.3d 1151 (Cal.2007)(statute of limitations accrues for smokers in suit against tobacco companies when they are diagnosed with an illness).

What effect do discovery rules have on the purposes of statutes of limitations set forth at the outset of this discussion?

The statute of limitations works in conjunction with the single judgment rule discussed p. 16 supra to bar all claims that arise from the set of facts that comprise the plaintiff's claim. This requires plaintiff to recover for all harm, including future harm, in a single action. Consider the application of these rules to the asbestos context in which there are at least three different diseases, with varying latency periods and severity, that can be caused by the same asbestos exposure. Do you see the dilemma faced by asbestos victims when they first suffer symptoms of an asbestotic disease, particularly one of less severity?

Addressing a matter that several prior courts had confronted in the asbestos context, the California Supreme Court decided that the existence of one disease does not begin the running of the statute of limitations for other "separate" diseases that may be caused by exposure to the same substance. Pooshs v. Philip Morris USA, Inc., 250

P.3d 181 (Cal.2011). When the plaintiff smoker sued for lung cancer, the court held that the earlier discovery of COPD, for which the plaintiff had not sued, did not affect the statute of limitation for lung cancer. The court noted: "We limit our holding to latent disease cases, without deciding whether the same rule should apply in other contexts."

CHAPTER VIII

STRICT LIABILITY

In the first part of this Chapter, we consider the doctrinal developments that have led to the modern rules of strict liability for certain types of activities. In tracing this evolution of the common law, we will see the courts venturing beyond isolated cases—such as escaping fires, rampaging wild animals and straying cattle—to fashion a more comprehensive standard of liability without fault. In the late nineteenth century, for instance, continued reference to "the blasting cases" indicates the judicial affinity for narrow categorization. But as demonstrated by the following cases, the courts developed these narrowly defined rules of strict liability into a more general doctrine of strict liability for ultrahazardous, or abnormally dangerous, activity.

In the second part of the Chapter, we examine a variety of scholarly efforts to establish the theoretical underpinnings of strict liability. A plaintiff who can recover under negligence liability will typically choose to do so. Strict liability does not displace the default rule of negligence liability; it instead provides recovery for a plaintiff who is unable to prove negligence. What might explain or justify such a supplemental rule of liability? The literature addressing this issue consists of efforts both to identify the strands of strict liability in the case law and to advocate a broader reliance on strict liability for normative reasons. An examination of these theories reprises the apparent tension between strict liability and negligence and provides a bridge to the doctrine of strict products liability in the next chapter.

A. DOCTRINAL DEVELOPMENT

Fletcher v. Rylands
Exchequer Chamber, 1866.
L.R. 1. Ex. 265.

[Plaintiff Fletcher was a tenant mining coal under agreement with the landowner. Defendant Rylands was operating a cotton mill on nearby land.]

■ The judgment of the Court (WILLES, BLACKBURN, KEATING, MELLOR, MONTAGUE SMITH, and LUSH, JJ.), was delivered by BLACKBURN, J.

This was a special case stated by an arbitrator, under an order of nisi prius, in which the question for the court is stated to be whether the plaintiff is entitled to recover any, and, if any, what damages from the defendants, by reason of the matters therein before stated.

In the Court of Exchequer, the Chief Baron and Martin, B., were of opinion that the plaintiff was not entitled to recover at all, Bramwell,

B., being of a different opinion. The judgment in the Exchequer was consequently given for the defendants, in conformity with the opinion of the majority of the court. The only question argued before us was whether this judgment was right, nothing being said about the measure of damages in case the plaintiff should be held entitled to recover. We have come to the conclusion that the opinion of Bramwell, B., was right, and that the answer to the question should be that the plaintiff was entitled to recover damages from the defendants, by reason of the matters stated in the case, and consequently, that the judgment below should be reversed, but we cannot at present say to what damages the plaintiff is entitled.

It appears from the statement in the case, that the plaintiff was damaged by his property being flooded by water, which, without any fault on his part, broke out of a reservoir constructed on the defendants' land by the defendants' orders, and maintained by the defendants.

It appears from the statement in the case that the coal under the defendants' land had, at some remote period, been worked out; but this was unknown at the time when the defendants gave directions to erect the reservoir, and the water in the reservoir would not have escaped from the defendants' land, and no mischief would have been done to the plaintiff, but for this latent defect in the defendants' subsoil. And it further appears, that the defendants selected competent engineers and contractors to make their reservoir, and themselves personally continued in total ignorance of what we have called the latent defect in the subsoil; but that these persons employed by them in the course of the work became aware of the existence of the ancient shafts filled up with soil, though they did not know or suspect that they were shafts communicating with old workings.

It is found that the defendants, personally, were free from all blame, but that in fact proper care and skill was not used by the persons employed by them, to provide for the sufficiency of the reservoir with reference to these shafts. The consequence was, that the reservoir when filled with water burst into the shafts, the water flowed down through them into the old workings, and thence into the plaintiff's mine, and there did the mischief.

The plaintiff, though free from all blame on his part, must bear the loss, unless he can establish that it was the consequence of some default for which the defendants are responsible. The question of law therefore arises, what is the obligation which the law casts on a person who, like the defendants, lawfully brings on his land something which, though harmless whilst it remains there, will naturally do mischief if it escape out of his land. It is agreed on all hands that he must take care to keep in that which he has brought on the land and keeps there, in order that it may not escape and damage his neighbors, but the question arises whether the duty which the law casts upon him, under such circumstances, is an absolute duty to keep it in at his peril, or is, as the majority of the Court of Exchequer have thought, merely a duty to take all reasonable and prudent precautions, in order to keep it in, but no more. If the first be the law, the person who has brought on his land and kept there something dangerous, and failed to keep it in, is responsible for all the natural consequences of its escape. If the second be the limit of his duty, he would not be answerable except on proof of negligence, and consequently would not be answerable for escape arising from any latent defect which ordinary prudence and skill could not detect.

Supposing the second to be the correct view of the law, a further question arises subsidiary to the first, viz., whether the defendants are not so far identified with the contractors whom they employed, as to be responsible for the consequences of their want of care and skill in making the reservoir in fact insufficient with reference to the old shafts, of the existence of which they were aware, though they had not ascertained where the shafts went to.

We think that the true rule of law is, that the person who for his own purposes brings on his lands and collects and keeps there anything likely to do mischief if it escapes, must keep it in at his peril, and, if he does not do so, is prima facie answerable for all the damage which is the natural consequence of its escape. He can excuse himself by showing that the escape was owing to the plaintiff's default; or perhaps that the escape was the consequence of vis major, or the act of God; but as nothing of this sort exists here, it is unnecessary to inquire what excuse would be sufficient. The general rule, as above stated, seems on principle just. The person whose grass or corn is eaten down by the escaping cattle of his neighbor, or whose mine is flooded by the water from his neighbour's reservoir, or whose cellar is invaded by the filth of his neighbour's privy, or whose habitation is made unhealthy by the fumes and noisome vapours of his neighbour's alkali works, is damnified without any fault of his own; and it seems but reasonable and just that the neighbour, who has brought something on his own property which was not naturally there, harmless to others so long as it is confined to his own property, but which he knows to be mischievous if it gets on his neighbour's, should be obliged to make good the damage which ensues if he does not succeed in confining it to his own property. But for his act in bringing it there no mischief could have accrued, and it seems but just that he should at his peril keep it there so that no mischief may accrue, or answer for the natural and anticipated consequences. And upon authority, this we think is established to be the law whether the things so brought be beasts, or water, or filth, or stenches.

The case that has most commonly occurred, and which is most frequently to be found in the books, is as to the obligation of the owner of cattle which he has brought on his land, to prevent their escaping and doing mischief. The law as to them seems to be perfectly settled from early times; the owner must keep them in at his peril, or he will be answerable for the natural consequences of their escape; that is with regard to tame beasts, for the grass they eat and trample upon, though not for any injury to the person of others, for our ancestors have settled that it is not the general nature of horses to kick, or bulls to gore; but if the owner knows that the beast has a vicious propensity to attack man, he will be answerable for that too.

. . .

. . . But it was further said by Martin, B., that when damage is done to personal property, or even to the person, by collision, either upon land or at sea, there must be negligence in the party doing the damage to render him legally responsible; and this is no doubt true, and as was pointed out by Mr. Mellish during his argument before us, this is not confined to cases of collision, for there are many cases in which proof of negligence is essential, as for instance, where an unruly horse gets on the footpath of a public street and kills a passenger [ ]; or where a person in a dock is struck by the falling of a bale of cotton which the defendant's servants are lowering [ ]; and many other similar cases may be found. But we think these cases distinguishable from the present. Traffic on the highways, whether by land or sea, cannot be conducted without exposing those whose persons or property are near it to some inevitable risk; and that being so those who go on the highway, or have their property adjacent to it, may well be held to do so subject to their taking upon themselves the risk of injury from that inevitable danger; and persons who by the license of the owner pass near to warehouses where goods are being raised or lowered, certainly do so subject to the inevitable risk of accident. In neither case, therefore, can they recover without proof of want of care or skill occasioning the accident; and it is believed that all the cases in which inevitable accident has been held an excuse for what prima facie was a trespass, can be explained on the same principle, viz., that the circumstances were such as to show that the plaintiff had taken that risk upon himself. But there is no ground for saying that the plaintiff here took upon himself any risk arising from the uses to which the defendants should choose to apply their land. He neither knew what these might be, nor could he in any way control the defendants, or hinder their building what reservoirs they liked, and storing up in them what water they pleased, so long as the defendants succeeded in preventing the water which they there brought from interfering with the plaintiff's property.

The view which we take of the first point renders it unnecessary to consider whether the defendants would or would not be responsible for the want of care and skill in the persons employed by them, under the circumstances stated in the case.

. . .

Judgment for the plaintiff.

NOTES AND QUESTIONS

1. *The contractor's negligence.* Fletcher did not sue the contractor directly, perhaps because earlier cases had concluded that in such situations the contractor owed a duty only to the employer and not third parties. The leading case was Winterbottom v. Wright, 152 Eng.Rep. 402 (1842), discussed at p. 560 infra. The contractor may also have been bankrupt at the time of suit. Although Rylands had employed the contractor, there had as yet been no decision holding the employer of an independent contractor liable for the contractor's negligence. That did not come until Bower v. Peate, 1 Q.B.D. 321 (1876). Recall the discussion of vicarious liability in Chapter I. For these reasons, the negligence of the contractor was not relevant to the disposition of the case.

2. *Posture of the case.* In the Court of Exchequer, the defendant prevailed, 2–1. The majority found that the traditional actions for interference with real property—trespass and nuisance—were inapplicable. Within the writ system, trespass required direct and immediate invasion of the plaintiff's land, while in this case the invasion was indirect—the water flowed down and through intervening shafts and land. Nuisance, which is an unreasonable interference with the plaintiff's use and enjoyment of land, failed because a reservoir was lawful and nuisances at the time involved activities that created ongoing harm, such as noxious fumes, rather than a single occurrence. Nuisance is discussed in Chapter X and trespass in Chapter XIII.

The arbitrator below identified the legal questions to be resolved by the Court of Exchequer. While the case was before the arbitrator, a large dam in Yorkshire, built as a reservoir, failed, resulting in severe flooding and the death of over 200 people. Liability for bursting reservoirs took on significance that helps to explain why the arbitrator focused on the legal question of whether defendant was subject to strict liability. In rejecting this basis for liability, Martin, B., emphasized the fault requirement in collision cases and concluded that to "hold the defendant liable without negligence would be to constitute him an insurer, which, in my opinion, would be contrary to legal analogy and principle." Bramwell, B., dissented, arguing that plaintiff had a "right to be free from what has been called 'foreign' water, that is, water artificially brought or sent to him directly, or indirectly by its being sent to where it would flow to him." If one has a right to be free from injury, regardless of negligence, would the resultant rule of strict liability be limited to injuries caused by "foreign" water?

3. *A limiting principle?* In adopting a rule of strict liability, does Justice Blackburn persuasively identify its limitations? At one point he emphasizes that "but for" the defendants' act no mischief would have resulted. Is he saying that cause in fact suffices for finding liability for any act that harms another's land? Does the particular use of the land matter? If the reservoir had been made exclusively from material on the defendants' land and had been filled only with rainwater that fell on the land, would Justice Blackburn have imposed strict liability? How successful are his efforts to distinguish the highway injury cases, in which he admits that

negligence must be shown? What analysis if the flooding had caused part of a public highway to collapse, injuring a traveler or destroying a wagon?

4.   *Trespassing animals.* Are the trespassing animal cases relevant to this case? Under the Restatement (Third) of Torts: Liability for Physical and Emotional Harm § 21 (2010), the owner or possessor of animals, except for cats and dogs, is subject to strict liability for the physical harms caused by their intrusions onto another's land. See also id. § 22 (strict liability for wild animals); § 23 (strict liability for abnormally dangerous animals).

5.   The *Ryland* defendants appealed to the House of Lords.

Rylands v. Fletcher

House of Lords, 1868.
L.R. 3 H.L. 330.

■ THE LORD CHANCELLOR (LORD CAIRNS) [after stating the facts].

My Lords, the principles on which this case must be determined appear to me to be extremely simple. The Defendants treating them as the owners or occupiers of the close on which the reservoir was constructed, might lawfully have used that close for any purpose for which it might in the ordinary course of the enjoyment of land be used; and if, in what I may term the natural user of that land, there had been any accumulation of water, either on the surface or underground, and if, by the operation of the laws of nature, that accumulation of water had passed off into the close occupied by the Plaintiff, the Plaintiff could not have complained that that result had taken place. If he had desired to guard himself against it, it would have lain upon him to have done so, by leaving, or by interposing, some barrier between his close and the close of the Defendants in order to have prevented that operation of the laws of nature.

. . .

On the other hand if the Defendants, not stopping at the natural use of their close, had desired to use it for any purpose which I may term a non-natural use, for the purpose of introducing into the close that which in its natural condition was not in or upon it, for the purpose of introducing water either above or below ground in quantities and in a manner not the result of any work or operation on or under the land,— and if in consequence of their doing so, or in consequence of any imperfection in the mode of their doing so, the water came to escape and to pass off into the close of the Plaintiff, then it appears to me that that which the Defendants were doing they were doing at their own peril; and, if in the course of their doing it, the evil arose to which I have referred, the evil, namely, of the escape of the water and its passing away to the close of the Plaintiff and injuring the Plaintiff, then for the consequence of that, in my opinion, the Defendants would be liable. . . .

My Lords, these simple principles, if they are well founded, as it appears to me they are, really dispose of this case.

The same result is arrived at on the principles, referred to by Mr. Justice Blackburn. [Lord Cairns here quotes in full the paragraph starting "We think that the true rule of law is. . . ."—Eds.]

My Lords, in that opinion, I must say I entirely concur. Therefore, I have to move your Lordships that the judgment of the Court of Exchequer Chamber be affirmed, and that the present appeal be dismissed with costs.

LORD CRANWORTH:—My Lords, I concur with my noble and learned friend in thinking that the rule of law was correctly stated by Mr. Justice Blackburn in delivering the opinion of the Exchequer Chamber. If a person brings, or accumulates, on his land anything which, if it should escape, may cause damage to his neighbour, he does so at his peril. If it does escape, and cause damage, he is responsible, however careful he may have been, and whatever precautions he may have taken to prevent the damage.

. . .

Judgment of the Court of Exchequer Chamber affirmed.

NOTES AND QUESTIONS

1.   Where does Justice Blackburn's rationale stand after the decision of the House of Lords? Is there a difference between Justice Blackburn's "not naturally there" and Lord Cairns' "non-natural use"? Does Lord Cranworth agree with Lord Cairns?

2.   At the outset, most American courts were less than enthusiastic about recognizing a broad principle of strict liability, on the basis of *Rylands,* that would apply to cases involving neighboring landowners. Consider the leading case of Losee v. Buchanan, 51 N.Y. 476 (1873), in which defendant's steam boiler—used in connection with a paper manufacturing business—exploded and was catapulted onto plaintiff's land and through several of his buildings. Rejecting *Rylands* after concluding that the line of cases recognizing strict liability for harm caused by straying animals does not apply to inanimate objects, the court extolled the virtues of the fault principle in an industrializing society:

> By becoming a member of civilized society, I am compelled to give up many of my natural rights, but I receive more than a compensation from the surrender by every other man of the same rights and the security, advantage and protection which the laws give me. So, too, the general rules that I may have the exclusive and undisturbed use and possession of my real estate, and that I must so use my real estate as not to injure my neighbor, are much modified by the exigencies of the social state. We must have factories, machinery, dams, canals and railroads. They are demanded by the manifold wants of mankind, and lay at the basis

of all our civilization. If I have any of these upon my lands, and they are not a nuisance and are not so managed as to become such, I am not responsible for any damage they accidentally and unavoidably do my neighbor. He receives his compensation for such damage by the general good, in which he shares, and the right which he has to place the same things upon his lands. I may not place or keep a nuisance upon my land to the damage of my neighbor, and I have my compensation for the surrender of this right to use my own as I will by the similar restriction imposed upon my neighbor for my benefit. I hold my property subject to the risk that it may be unavoidably or accidentally injured by those who live near me; and as I move about upon the public highways and in all places where other persons may lawfully be, I take the risk of being accidentally injured in my person by them without fault on their part. Most of the rights of property, as well as of person, in the social state, are not absolute but relative, and they must be so arranged and modified, not unnecessarily infringing upon natural rights, as upon the whole to promote the general welfare.

Id. at 489.

Consider also Brown v. Collins, 53 N.H. 442 (1873), another leading contemporaneous American decision, similarly rejecting the strict liability rule of *Rylands* because it would "impose a penalty upon efforts, made in a reasonable, skillful, and careful manner, to rise above a condition of barbarism" and would serve as "an obstacle in the way of progress and improvement." But compare the favorable reception in Massachusetts, dating back to 1868, which is traced to the present in Clark-Aiken Co. v. Cromwell-Wright Co., Inc., 323 N.E.2d 876 (Mass.1975).

This dynamic changed following the catastrophic bursts of mining dams in California in the early 1880s and a dam holding back a recreational lake that flooded Jamestown, Pennsylvania in 1889. Since then, "a strong majority of states has approved *Rylands*." Shugerman, A Watershed Moment: Reversals of Tort Theory in the Nineteenth Century, 2 J.Tort L., issue 2, at 14–20 (2008). In adopting this rule of strict liability, courts employed various "moral arguments in favor of strict liability," including "an argument from fairness (those who profit from an activity should pay those they hurt); a social contract argument of reciprocity; and a rights argument in favor of the natural user over the unnatural innovator." Id. at 5.

3. *The non-natural use of land.* Do reservoirs necessarily involve a non-natural use of the land subject to the *Rylands* rule? In Turner v. Big Lake Oil Co., 96 S.W.2d 221, 225 (Tex.1936), the court observed that "this basis of the English rule is to be found in the meteorological conditions which obtain there. England is a pluvial country, where constant streams and abundant rains make the storage of water unnecessary for ordinary or general purposes." The court then reasoned that

In Texas we have conditions very different from those which obtain in England. A large portion of Texas is an arid or semi-arid region. West of the 98th meridian of longitude, where the rainfall is approximately 30 inches, the rainfall decreases until finally, in the extreme western part of the State, it is only about 10 inches. This land of decreasing rainfall is the great ranch or livestock region of the State, water for which is stored in thousands of ponds, tanks, and lakes on the surface of the ground. The country is almost without streams; and without the storage of water from rainfall in basins constructed for the purpose, or to hold waters pumped from the earth, the great livestock industry of West Texas must perish. No such condition obtains in England. With us the storage of water is a natural or necessary and common use of the land, necessarily within the contemplation of the State and its grantees when grants were made, and obviously the rule announced in *Rylands v. Fletcher*, predicated upon different conditions, can have no application here.

Id. at 226.

How does the "non-natural use" requirement apply to polluting activities? In Cities Service Co. v. State, 312 So.2d 799 (Fla.App.1975), Cities Service operated a phosphate rock mine in which it collected phosphate slimes in settling ponds. When a dam broke, one billion gallons of slime escaped into a creek and then into a river "killing countless numbers of fish and inflicting other damage." The State of Florida sought compensatory damages along with other relief, and the court decided to adopt the doctrine of *Rylands v. Fletcher*:

> In early days it was important to encourage persons to use their land by whatever means were available for the purpose of commercial and industrial development. In a frontier society there was little likelihood that a dangerous use of land could cause damage to one's neighbor. Today our life has become more complex. Many areas are overcrowded, and even the nonnegligent use of one's land can cause extensive damages to a neighbor's property. Though there are still many hazardous activities which are socially desirable, it now seems reasonable that they pay their own way.

Id. at 801. In State Dept. of Environmental Protection v. Ventron Corp., 468 A.2d 150, 157 (N.J.1983), the defendant's manufacturing processes had raised the mercury content of a nearby tidal estuary to the highest found in fresh water sediments anywhere in the world. The court adopted *Rylands* after concluding that "it is time to recognize expressly that the law of liability has evolved so that a landowner is strictly liable to others for harm caused by toxic wastes that are stored on his property and flow onto the property of others." How are the courts in these cases interpreting the "non-natural" use requirement of *Rylands?*

4. *Rylands v. Fletcher* has not led England to employ a full-throated rule of strict liability for anything escaping from one's land that causes harm to neighboring property, as might have been understood from Lord Cairns' opinion. Instead, subsequent cases employed a restrictive interpretation of non-natural use that eliminates common activities, such as supplying water or gas, regardless of the danger involved. A commonly accepted definition of non-natural use is contained in Lord Moulton's opinion in Rickards v. Lothian, [1913] A.C. 263: "It must be some special use bringing with it increased danger to others and must not merely be the ordinary use of the land or such a use as is proper for the general benefit of the community." Would this definition change the outcome in any of the cases discussed in note 3? More recently, the House of Lords intimated that the *Rylands* rule might be regarded as a special kind of private nuisance law, in which the interference with another's land is not continuous. Cambridge Water Co. v. Eastern Counties Leather Plc, [1994] 2 A.C. 264. Nuisance is covered in Chapter X.

5. For comprehensive treatment of the origins and impact of *Rylands*, see Abraham, *Rylands v. Fletcher*: Tort Law's Conscience, in R. Rabin & S. Sugarman (eds.), Torts Stories 207 (2003), concluding that "the story of *Rylands* lies in the idea of strict liability, and the power of that idea to influence our way of thinking about tort law, far out of proportion to the contemporary influence of this idea on the particulars of legal doctrine." *Rylands* has inspired a vast literature, including Bohlen, The Rule in *Rylands v. Fletcher*, 59 U.Pa.L.Rev. 298, 373, 423 (1911); Gregory, Trespass to Negligence to Absolute Liability, 37 Va.L.Rev. 359 (1951); Molloy, *Fletcher v. Rylands*—A Reexamination of Juristic Origins, 9 U.Chi.L.Rev. 266 (1941); Simpson, Legal Liability for Bursting Reservoirs: The Historical Context of *Rylands v. Fletcher*, 13 J. Legal Stud. 209 (1984); Shugerman, The Floodgates of Strict Liability: Bursting Reservoirs and the Adoption of *Rylands v. Fletcher* in the Gilded Age, 110 Yale L.J. 333 (2000). Particularly interesting in this earlier work are the views of Bohlen, arguing that "in England, the dominant class was the landed gentry, whose opinion the judges, who either sprang from this class or hoped to establish themselves and their families within—naturally reflected" (p. 318), and Molloy, reporting social and biographical data on the judges in *Rylands* that contradicts the "landed gentry" thesis.

6. Despite the early mixed reception given *Rylands,* American courts had previously applied strict liability to harms caused by certain entrepreneurial activities. The following case provides the context.

Sullivan v. Dunham
Court of Appeals of New York, 1900.
161 N.Y. 290, 55 N.E. 923.

[Defendant landowner employed two men to dynamite a 60-foot tree on the land. The blast hurled a fragment of wood 412 feet onto a highway where it struck plaintiff's decedent and killed her. The two blasters were also sued. The trial judge charged that negligence need not be proven to establish liability. Defendants appealed from a judgment entered on a plaintiff's verdict and affirmed by the appellate division.]

■ VANN, J. (after stating the facts).

The main question presented by this appeal is whether one who, for a lawful purpose and without negligence or want of skill, explodes a blast upon his own land and thereby causes a piece of wood to fall upon a person lawfully traveling in a public highway, is liable for the injury thus inflicted.

The statute authorizes the personal representative of a decedent to "maintain an action to recover damages for a wrongful act, neglect, or default, by which the decedent's death was caused, against a natural person who, or a corporation which, would have been liable to an action in favor of the decedent, by reason thereof, if death had not ensued." (Code Civ.Pro. § 1902.) It covers any action of trespass upon the person, which the deceased could have maintained if she had survived the accident. Stated in another form, therefore, the question before us is whether the defendants are liable as trespassers.

This is not a new question, for it has been considered, directly or indirectly, so many times by this court that a reference to the earlier authorities is unnecessary. In the leading case upon the subject, the defendant, in order to dig a canal authorized by its charter, necessarily blasted out rocks from its own land with gunpowder, and thus threw fragments against the plaintiff's house, which stood upon the adjoining premises. Although there was no proof of negligence, or want of skill, the defendant was held liable for the injury sustained. All the judges concurred in the opinion of Gardiner, J., who said:

> The defendants had the right to dig the canal. The plaintiff the right to the undisturbed possession of his property. If these rights conflict, the former must yield to the latter, as the more important of the two, since, upon grounds of public policy, it is better that one man should surrender a particular use of his land, than that another should be deprived of the beneficial use of his property altogether, which might be the consequence if the privilege of the former should be wholly unrestricted. The case before us illustrates this principle. For if the defendants in excavating their canal, in itself a lawful use of their land, could, in the manner mentioned by the witnesses, demolish the stoop of the plaintiff with impunity, they might, for the same purpose, on the exercise of reasonable care, demolish his house, and thus deprive him of all use of his property. The use of land by the proprietor is not therefore an absolute right, but qualified and limited by the higher right of others to the lawful possession of their property. To this possession the law prohibits all direct injury, without regard to its extent or the motives of the aggressor. . . . He may excavate a canal, but he cannot cast the dirt or stones upon the land of

his neighbor, either by human agency or the force of gunpowder. If he cannot construct the work without the adoption of such means, he must abandon that mode of using his property, or be held responsible for all damages resulting therefrom. He will not be permitted to accomplish a legal object in an unlawful manner. [Hay v. Cohoes Co., 2 N.Y. 159 (1849)].

This case was followed immediately by Tremain v. Cohoes Co. (2 N.Y. 163), a similar action against the same defendant, which offered to show upon the trial "that the work was done in the best and most careful manner." It was held that the evidence was properly excluded because the manner in which the defendant performed its work was of no consequence, as what it did to the plaintiff's injury was the sole question.

These were cases of trespass upon lands, while the case before us involves trespass upon the person of a human being, when she was where she had the same right to protection from injury as if she had been walking upon her own land. As the safety of the person is more sacred than the safety of property, the cases cited should govern our decision unless they are no longer the law.

The *Hay* case was reviewed by the Commission of Appeals in Losee v. Buchanan (51 N.Y. 476, 479) [1873], where it was held that one who, without negligence and with due care and skill, operates a steam boiler upon his own premises, is not liable to his neighbor for the damages caused by the explosion thereof. That was not a case of intentional but of accidental explosion. A tremendous force escaped, so to speak, from the owner, but was not voluntarily set free. The court, commenting upon the *Hay* case, said: "It was held that the defendant was liable for the injury, although no negligence or want of skill in executing the work was alleged or proved. This decision was well supported by the clearest principles. The acts of the defendant in casting the rocks upon plaintiff's premises were direct and immediate. The damage was the necessary consequence of just what the defendant was doing, and it was just as much liable as if it had caused the rocks to be taken by hand, or any other means, and thrown directly upon plaintiff's land."

The *Hay* case was expressly approved and made the basis of judgment in St. Peter v. Denison (58 N.Y. 416) [1874], where a blast, set off by a contractor with the state in the enlargement of the Erie canal, threw a piece of frozen earth against the plaintiff when he was at work upon the adjoining premises for the owner thereof. . . .

This case is analogous to the one before us, because the person injured did not own the land upon which he stood when struck, but he had a right to stand there the same as the plaintiff's intestate had a right to walk in the highway. We see no distinction in principle between the two cases.

. . .

When the injury is not direct, but consequential, such as is caused by concussion, which, by shaking the earth, injures property, there is no liability in the absence of negligence.

. . .

We think that the *Hay* case has always been recognized by this court as a sound and valuable authority. After standing for fifty years as the law of the state upon the subject it should not be disturbed, and we have no inclination to disturb it. It rests upon the principle, founded in public policy, that the safety of property generally is superior in right to a particular use of a single piece of property by its owner. It renders the enjoyment of all property more secure by preventing such a use of one piece by one man as may injure all his neighbors. It makes human life safer by tending to prevent a landowner from casting, either with or without negligence, a part of his land upon the person of one who is where he has a right to be. It so applies the maxim of *sic utere tuo* as to protect person and property from direct physical violence, which, although accidental, has the same effect as if it were intentional. It lessens the hardship by placing absolute liability upon the one who causes the injury. The accident in question was a misfortune to the defendants, but it was a greater misfortune to the young woman who was killed. The safety of travelers upon the public highway is more important to the state than the improvement of one piece of property, by a special method, is to its owner. . . .

. . .

The judgment is right and should be affirmed, with costs.

All concur, except GRAY, J., not voting.

NOTES AND QUESTIONS

1.   How might the *Sullivan* facts have been analyzed by Justice Blackburn? By Lord Cairns?

2.   Judge Vann states that courts will apply the maxim of *sic utere* so as "to protect person and property from direct physical violence, which, although accidental, has the same effect as if it were intentional." In *Losee*, the court refused to apply this maxim after observing that it "has many exceptions and limitations, made necessary by the exigencies of business and society." 51 N.Y. at 480. Is the exception recognized by *Losee* consistent with *Sullivan*?

3.   The different treatment accorded harms caused by debris and by concussion might be an artifact of the writ system. Direct harm from debris was recoverable in a trespass action, for which intent and fault were irrelevant; concussion damage was indirect, or consequential, and could be recovered only in an action on the case, for which a fault component developed. In the leading case of Booth v. Rome, W. & O.T.R.R. Co., 35 N.E. 592 (N.Y.1893), the court held the 1849 *Hay* case inapplicable to harm

suffered by concussion because there the defendant's act had caused direct harm to the plaintiff's property and was thus a trespass. In *Booth,* the court emphasized that the defendant was engaged in a "lawful act" on its own land. "The immediate act was confined to its own land, but the blasts, by setting the air in motion, or in some other unexplained way, caused an injury to plaintiff's house. . . . The blasting was necessary, was carefully done, and the injury was consequential. There was no technical trespass." The court added that "to exclude the defendant from blasting to adapt its lot to the contemplated uses, at the instance of the plaintiff, would not be a compromise between conflicting rights, but an extinguishment of the right of the one for the benefit of the other." Again, "public policy is sustained by the building up of towns and cities and the improvement of property. Any unnecessary restraint on freedom of action of a property owner hinders this."

The distinction between debris and concussion has virtually disappeared. It survived in New York until Spano v. Perini Corp., 250 N.E.2d 31, 34–35 (N.Y.1969), in which, referring to the second set of reasons in *Booth,* the court said:

> This rationale cannot withstand analysis. The plaintiff in *Booth* was not seeking, as the court implied, to "exclude the defendant from blasting" and thus prevent desirable improvements to the latter's property. Rather, he was merely seeking compensation for the damage which was inflicted upon his own property as a result of that blasting. The question, in other words, was not *whether* it was lawful or proper to engage in blasting but *who* should bear the cost of any resulting damage— the person who engaged in the dangerous activity or the innocent neighbor injured thereby. Viewed in such a light, it clearly appears that *Booth* was wrongly decided and should be forthrightly overruled.

4. Does this rationale for strict liability apply to unintended explosions of stored dynamite? In Heeg v. Licht, 80 N.Y. 579 (1880), plaintiff's buildings were damaged when defendant's powder magazine exploded for no apparent reason. The case was argued as one of nuisance, a theory of liability discussed in detail in Chapter X. The court observed that the occurrence of the explosion "tends to establish that the magazine was dangerous and liable to cause damage to the property of persons residing in the vicinity." The court divided the cases of liability for a legitimate business into two groups. Some uses of land produce inconvenience and injury to others, such as "slaughter houses, fat and offal boiling establishments, hog-styles, or tallow manufactories, in or near a city." Another group of uses involves dangerous acts done on one's premises that might harm those passing by or residing nearby. Here the court cited Hay v. Cohoes Co., and concluded that "a single individual should surrender the use of his land for especial purposes injurious to his neighbor. . . ." A person "has no more right to keep a magazine of powder upon his premises, which is dangerous to the detriment of his neighbor, than he is authorized to engage in any other business which may occasion serious consequence."

Strict liability was expressly adopted in the leading case of Exner v. Sherman Power Const. Co., 54 F.2d 510, 514 (2d Cir.1931).

> When, as here, the defendant, though without fault, has engaged in the perilous activity of storing large quantities of a dangerous explosive for use in his business, we think there is no justification for relieving it of liability, and that the owner of the business, rather than a third party who has no relation to the explosion, other than that of injury, should bear the loss.

The court also noted that the rule from *Rylands v. Fletcher* "has not been followed in America to the full extent of all its implications, . . . yet in the so-called 'blasting' cases an absolute liability, without regard to fault, has uniformly been imposed by the American courts wherever there has been an actual invasion of property by rocks or debris." Id. at 513.

5. Based on the cases involving dynamite blasts and burst reservoirs, is there a more comprehensive standard for determining whether strict liability applies? According to sections 519 and 520 in the first Restatement of Torts, these cases involve an "ultrahazardous activity," defined as involving a risk that "cannot be eliminated by the exercise of the utmost care" and "is not a matter of common usage." In section 519, the Second Restatement reframed the standard by providing that one who "carries on an abnormally dangerous activity is subject to liability for harm . . . resulting from the activity, although he has exercised the utmost care to prevent the harm." In determining whether an activity is "abnormally dangerous," section 520 listed six factors for consideration:

(a) existence of a high degree of risk of some harm to the person, land or chattels of others;

(b) likelihood that the harm that results from it will be great;

(c) inability to eliminate the risk by the exercise of reasonable care;

(d) extent to which the activity is not a matter of common usage;

(e) inappropriateness of the activity to the place where it is carried on; and

(f) extent to which its value to the community is outweighed by its dangerous attributes.

In Dyer v. Maine Drilling & Blasting, Inc., 984 A.2d 210, 216 (Me.2009), the court observed that "almost every other state" has "adopt[ed] strict liability in blasting and other abnormally dangerous activity cases," and so the court decided that it, too, would "adopt strict liability under the Restatement's six factor test." This test is central to the case that follows.

Indiana Harbor Belt Railroad Co. v.
American Cyanamid Co.

United States Court of Appeals, Seventh Circuit, 1990.
916 F.2d 1174.

■ Before POSNER, MANION and KANNE, CIRCUIT JUDGES.

■ POSNER, CIRCUIT JUDGE.

American Cyanamid Company, the defendant in this diversity tort suit governed by Illinois law, is a major manufacturer of chemicals, including acrylonitrile, a chemical used in large quantities in making acrylic fibers, plastics, dyes, pharmaceutical chemicals, and other intermediate and final goods. On January 2, 1979, at its manufacturing plant in Louisiana, Cyanamid loaded 20,000 gallons of liquid acrylonitrile into a railroad tank car that it had leased from the North American Car Corporation. The next day, a train of the Missouri Pacific Railroad picked up the car at Cyanamid's siding. The car's ultimate destination was a Cyanamid plant in New Jersey served by Conrail rather than by Missouri Pacific. The Missouri Pacific train carried the car north to the Blue Island railroad yard of Indiana Harbor Belt Railroad, the plaintiff in this case, a small switching line that has a contract with Conrail to switch cars from other lines to Conrail, in this case for travel east. The Blue Island yard is in the Village of Riverdale, which is just south of Chicago and part of the Chicago metropolitan area.

The car arrived in the Blue Island yard on the morning of January 9, 1979. Several hours after it arrived, employees of the switching line noticed fluid gushing from the bottom outlet of the car. The lid on the outlet was broken. After two hours, the line's supervisor of equipment was able to stop the leak by closing a shutoff valve controlled from the top of the car. No one was sure at the time just how much of the contents of the car had leaked, but it was feared that all 20,000 gallons had, and since acrylonitrile is flammable at a temperature of 30 degrees Fahrenheit or above, highly toxic, and possibly carcinogenic [ ], the local authorities ordered the homes near the yard evacuated. The evacuation lasted only a few hours, until the car was moved to a remote part of the yard and it was discovered that only about a quarter of the acrylonitrile had leaked. Concerned nevertheless that there had been some contamination of soil and water, the Illinois Department of Environmental Protection ordered the switching line to take decontamination measures that cost the line $981,022.75, which it sought to recover by this suit.

[After some procedural tangles, the district judge granted plaintiff summary judgment on its strict liability claim and dismissed plaintiff's negligence claim. Defendant appealed and plaintiff cross-appealed.]

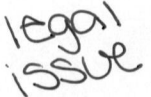

The question whether the shipper of a hazardous chemical by rail should be strictly liable for the consequences of a spill or other accident to the shipment en route is a novel one in Illinois [despite earlier confusion that might have suggested otherwise].

The parties agree that the question whether placing acrylonitrile in a rail shipment that will pass through a metropolitan area subjects the shipper to strict liability is, as recommended in Restatement (Second) of Torts § 520, comment *l* (1977), a question of law, so that we owe no particular deference to the conclusion of the district court. They also agree ... that the Supreme Court of Illinois would treat as authoritative the provisions of the Restatement governing abnormally dangerous activities. The key provision is section 520, which sets forth six factors to be considered in deciding whether an activity is abnormally dangerous and the actor therefore strictly liable.

The roots of section 520 are in nineteenth-century cases. The most famous one is Rylands v. Fletcher, 1 Ex. 265, aff'd, L.R. 3 H.L. 300 (1868), but a more illuminating one in the present context is Guille v. Swan, 19 Johns. (N.Y.) 381 (1822). A man took off in a hot-air balloon and landed, without intending to, in a vegetable garden in New York City. A crowd that had been anxiously watching his involuntary descent trampled the vegetables in their endeavor to rescue him when he landed. The owner of the garden sued the balloonist for the resulting damage, and won. Yet the balloonist had not been careless. In the then state of ballooning it was impossible to make a pinpoint landing.

Guille is a paradigmatic case for strict liability. (a) The risk (probability) of harm was great, and (b) the harm that would ensue if the risk materialized could be, although luckily was not, great (the balloonist could have crashed into the crowd rather than into the vegetables). The confluence of these two factors established the urgency of seeking to prevent such accidents. (c) Yet such accidents could not be prevented by the exercise of due care; the technology of care in ballooning was insufficiently developed. (d) The activity was not a matter of common usage, so there was no presumption that it was a highly valuable activity despite its unavoidable riskiness. (e) The activity was inappropriate to the place in which it took place—densely populated New York City. The risk of serious harm to others (other than the balloonist himself, that is) could have been reduced by shifting the activity to the sparsely inhabited areas that surrounded the city in those days. (f) Reinforcing (d), the value to the community of the activity of recreational ballooning did not appear to be great enough to offset its unavoidable risks.

These are, of course, the six factors in section 520. They are related to each other in that each is a different facet of a common quest for a proper legal regime to govern accidents that negligence liability cannot adequately control. The interrelations might be more perspicuous if the six factors were reordered. One might for example start with (c), inability to eliminate the risk of accident by the exercise of due care. [ ] The baseline common law regime of tort liability is negligence. When it is a workable regime, because the hazards of an activity can be avoided by being careful (which is to say, nonnegligent), there is no need to switch to strict liability. Sometimes, however, a particular type of accident cannot be prevented by taking care but can be avoided, or its consequences minimized, by shifting the activity in which the accident occurs to another locale, where the risk or harm of an accident will be less (e), or by reducing the scale of the activity in order to minimize the number of accidents caused by it (f). [ ] By making the actor strictly liable—by denying him in other words an excuse based on his inability to avoid accidents by being more careful—we give him an incentive, missing in a negligence regime, to experiment with methods of preventing accidents that involve not greater exertions of care, assumed to be futile, but instead relocating, changing, or reducing (perhaps to the vanishing point) the activity giving rise to the accident. [ ] The greater the risk of an accident (a) and the costs of an accident if one occurs (b), the more we want the actor to consider the possibility of making accident-reducing activity changes; the stronger, therefore, is the case for strict liability. Finally, if an activity is extremely common (d), like driving an automobile, it is unlikely either that its hazards are perceived as great or that there is no technology of care available to minimize them; so the case for strict liability is weakened.

The largest class of cases in which strict liability has been imposed under the standard codified in the Second Restatement of Torts involves the use of dynamite and other explosives for demolition in residential or urban areas. [ ] Explosives are dangerous even when handled carefully, and we therefore want blasters to choose the location of the activity with care and also to explore the feasibility of using safer substitutes (such as a wrecking ball), as well as to be careful in the blasting itself. Blasting is not a commonplace activity like driving a car, or so superior to substitute methods of demolition that the imposition of liability is unlikely to have any effect except to raise the activity's costs.

Against this background we turn to the particulars of acrylonitrile. Acrylonitrile is one of a large number of chemicals that are hazardous in the sense of being flammable, toxic, or both; acrylonitrile is both, as are many others. A table in the record, [ ], contains a list of the 125 hazardous materials that are shipped in highest volume on the nation's railroads. Acrylonitrile is the fifty-third most hazardous on the list. . . . The plaintiff's lawyer acknowledged at argument that the logic of the district court's opinion dictated strict liability for all 52 materials that rank higher than acrylonitrile on the list, and quite possibly for the 72 that rank lower as well, since all are hazardous if spilled in quantity while being shipped by rail. Every shipper of any of these materials would therefore be strictly liable for the consequences of a spill or other accident that occurred while the material was being shipped through a metropolitan area. The plaintiff's lawyer further acknowledged the irrelevance, on her view of the case, of the fact that Cyanamid had leased and filled the car that spilled the acrylonitrile; all she thought important is that Cyanamid introduced the product into the stream of commerce that happened to pass through the Chicago metropolitan area. Her concession may have been incautious. One might want to distinguish between the shipper who merely places his goods on his loading dock to be picked up by the carrier and the shipper who, as in this case, participates actively in the transportation. But the concession is illustrative of the potential scope of the district court's decision.

No cases recognize so sweeping a liability. Several reject it, though none has facts much like those of the present case. . . .

[The court discussed Siegler v. Kuhlman, 502 P.2d 1181 (Wash.1972), in which the trailer of defendant's gasoline truck broke away and rolled down onto a highway on which plaintiff motorist was traveling. Plaintiff's car went into a pool of gasoline spilled from the trailer and the resulting explosion "obliterated the plaintiff's decedent and her car"—and evidence of what happened. Although the *Siegler* court used strict liability, Judge Posner suggested that res ipsa loquitur would have sufficed. He also noted that the suit was against the transporter of the gasoline rather than its manufacturer.]

So we can get little help from precedent, and might as well apply section 520 to the acrylonitrile problem from the ground up. To begin with, we have been given no reason, whether the reason in *Siegler* or any other, for believing that a negligence regime is not perfectly adequate to remedy and deter, at reasonable cost, the accidental spillage of acrylonitrile from rail cars. [ ] Acrylonitrile could explode and destroy evidence, but of course did not here, making imposition of strict liability on the theory of the *Siegler* decision premature. More important, although acrylonitrile is flammable even at relatively low temperatures, and toxic, it is not so corrosive or otherwise destructive that it will eat through or otherwise damage or weaken a tank car's valves although they are maintained with due (which essentially means, with average) care. No one suggests, therefore, that the leak in this case was caused by the inherent properties of acrylonitrile. It was caused by carelessness—whether that of the North American Car Corporation in failing to maintain or inspect the car properly, or that of Cyanamid in failing to maintain or inspect it, or that of the Missouri Pacific when it had custody of the car, or that of the switching line itself in failing to notice the ruptured lid, or some combination of these possible failures of care. Accidents that are due to a lack of care can be prevented by taking care; and when a lack of care can (unlike *Siegler*) be shown in court, such accidents are adequately deterred by the threat of liability for negligence.

. . . For all that appears from the record of the case or any other sources of information that we have found, if a tank car is carefully maintained the danger of a spill of acrylonitrile is negligible. If this is right, there is no compelling reason to move to a regime of strict liability, especially one that might embrace all other hazardous materials shipped by rail as well. . . . If the vast majority of chemical spills by railroads are preventable by due care, the imposition of strict liability should cause only a slight, not as [amici] argue a substantial, rise in liability insurance rates, because the incremental liability should be slight. The amici have momentarily lost sight of the fact that the feasibility of avoiding accidents simply by being careful is an argument against strict liability.

. . .

The district judge and the plaintiff's lawyer make much of the fact that the spill occurred in a densely inhabited metropolitan area. Only 4,000 gallons spilled; what if all 20,000 had done so? Isn't the risk that this might happen even if everybody were careful sufficient to warrant giving the shipper an incentive to explore alternative routes? Strict liability would supply that incentive. But this argument overlooks the fact that, like other transportation networks, the railroad network is a hub-and-spoke system. And the hubs are in metropolitan areas. Chicago is one of the nation's largest railroad hubs. In 1983, the latest year for which we have figures, Chicago's railroad yards handled the third highest volume of hazardous-material shipments in the nation. East St. Louis, which is also in Illinois, handled the second highest volume. [ ] With most hazardous chemicals (by volume of shipments) being at least as hazardous as acrylonitrile, it is unlikely—and certainly not demonstrated by the plaintiff—that they can be rerouted around all the metropolitan areas in the country, except at prohibitive cost. Even if it were feasible to reroute them one would hardly expect shippers, as distinct from carriers, to be the firms best situated to do the rerouting. Granted, the usual view is that common carriers are not subject to strict liability for the carriage of materials that make the transportation of them abnormally dangerous, because a common carrier cannot refuse service to a shipper of a lawful commodity. Restatement, supra, § 521. Two courts, however, have rejected the common carrier exception. National Steel Service Center, Inc. v. Gibbons, 319 N.W.2d 269 (Iowa 1982); Chavez v. Southern Pacific Transportation Co., 413 F.Supp. 1203, 1213–14 (E.D.Cal.1976). If it were rejected in Illinois, this would weaken still further the case for imposing strict liability on shippers whose goods pass through the densely inhabited portions of the state.

The difference between shipper and carrier points to a deep flaw in the plaintiff's case. Unlike *Guille* and unlike *Siegler*, and unlike the storage cases, beginning with *Rylands* itself, here it is not the actors— that is, the transporters of acrylonitrile and other chemicals—but the manufacturers, who are sought to be held strictly liable. [ ] A shipper can in the bill of lading designate the route of his shipment if he likes, 49 U.S.C. § 11710(a)(1), but is it realistic to suppose that shippers will become students of railroading in order to lay out the safest route by which to ship their goods? Anyway, rerouting is no panacea. Often it will increase the length of the journey, or compel the use of poorer track, or both. When this happens, the probability of an accident is increased, even if the consequences of an accident if one occurs are reduced; so the expected accident cost, being the product of the probability of an accident and the harm if the accident occurs, may rise. [ ] It is easy to see how the accident in this case might have been prevented at reasonable cost by greater care on the part of those who handled the tank car of acrylonitrile. It is difficult to see how it might have been prevented at reasonable cost by a change in the activity of transporting the chemical. This is therefore not an apt case for strict liability.

[Although an argument might have been made that Cyanamid should be treated as a "shipper-transporter" subject to rules more onerous than those imposed on "shippers," the court found it had not been made in this case and was waived.] Which is not to say that had it not been waived it would have changed the outcome of the case. The very fact that Cyanamid participated actively in the transportation of the acrylonitrile imposed upon it a duty of due care and by doing so brought into play a threat of negligence liability that, for all we know, may provide an adequate regime of accident control in the transportation of this particular chemical.

In emphasizing the flammability and toxicity of acrylonitrile rather than the hazards of transporting it, as in failing to distinguish between the active and the passive shipper, the plaintiff overlooks the fact that ultrahazardousness or abnormal dangerousness is, in the contemplation of the law at least, a property not of substances, but of activities: not of acrylonitrile, but of the transportation of acrylonitrile by rail through populated areas. . . . Whatever the situation under products liability law (section 402A of the Restatement), the manufacturer of a product is not considered to be engaged in an abnormally dangerous activity merely because the product becomes dangerous when it is handled or used in some way after it leaves his premises, even if the danger is foreseeable. [ ] The plaintiff does not suggest that Cyanamid should switch to making some less hazardous chemical that would substitute for acrylonitrile in the textiles and other goods in which acrylonitrile is used. Were this a feasible method of accident avoidance, there would be an argument for making manufacturers strictly liable for accidents that occur during the shipment of their products (how strong an argument we need not decide). Apparently it is not a feasible method.

. . . Brutal though it may seem to say it, the inappropriate use to which land is being put in the Blue Island yard and neighborhood may be, not the transportation of hazardous chemicals, but residential living. The analogy is to building your home between the runways at O'Hare.

The briefs hew closely to the Restatement, whose approach to the issue of strict liability is mainly allocative rather than distributive. By this we mean that the emphasis is on picking a liability regime (negligence or strict liability) that will control the particular class of accidents in question most effectively, rather than on finding the deepest pocket and placing liability there. . . .

The case for strict liability has not been made. Not in this suit in any event. . . .

[Although the improper grant of summary judgment normally requires a remand for trial of that part of the case, this case was different because no new facts were suggested that would warrant strict liability. Defendant conceded that if the strict liability claim fell, the negligence claim had to be remanded for trial.]

The judgment is reversed (with no award of costs in this court) and the case remanded for further proceedings, consistent with this opinion, on the plaintiff's claim for negligence.

NOTES AND QUESTIONS

1. Why is the Restatement section framed in terms of activities rather than "acts," as in negligence? Consider in this regard the differences among the activities of manufacturing, transportation, and storage of dangerous chemicals. Does each activity have the same characteristics that are relevant for purposes of strict liability?

2. For reasons explained by David Rosenberg, Judge Posner's interpretation of the Restatement Second rule is based on

> what is commonly referred to as the activity-level justification for strict liability. Essentially, this justification responds to problems that courts encounter when applying the negligence rule beyond the conventional, relatively straightforward questions of care, such as whether Cyanamid reasonably maintained and operated the tank car. Undertaking to assess the reasonableness of activity-level-type decisions, such as Cyanamid's choices of when, where, and how much acrylonitrile to produce and ship by rail, risks overwhelming judicial resources. Indeed, courts often shy away from tackling this set of especially complex and elusive issues, thereby allowing actors to engage in excessive levels of risky activity free from the check of tort liability. Strict liability can remedy this problem. "By making the actor strictly liable," Judge Posner explained, "we give him an incentive, missing in a negligence regime, to experiment with methods of preventing accidents that involve not greater exertions of care, assumed to be futile, but instead relocating, changing, or reducing (perhaps to the vanishing point) the activity giving rise to the accident."

Rosenberg, The Judicial Posner on Negligence Versus Strict Liability: *Indiana Harbor Belt Railroad Co. v. American Cyanamid Co.*, 120 Harv.L.Rev. 1210, 1212 (2007).

The activity-level rationale for strict liability is based on the premise that courts may not be able to evaluate adequately all components of risky behavior, leaving these "activities" immune from negligence liability and better suited for strict liability. Did Judge Posner's analysis adequately recognize this difficulty? According to Rosenberg,

> [t]esting the efficacy of strict liability by determining whether the defendant had reasonable options for reducing its activity level— in *Indiana Harbor Belt,* for example, rerouting chemical-laden tank cars—involves precisely the negligence-style cost-benefit analysis of activity level that generally proves too expensive and complex for courts to perform effectively and that justifies turning to strict liability in the first place.

Id. at 1215.

3. Aside from its impact on the magnitude of risk, why should the location of an activity be relevant to strict liability? In Yukon Equipment, Inc. v. Fireman's Fund Insurance Co., 585 P.2d 1206 (Alaska 1978), which involved the explosion of a building used to store explosives, the court rejected location as a reason for limiting strict liability:

> The reasons for imposing absolute liability on those who have created a grave risk of harm to others by storing or using explosives are largely independent of considerations of locational appropriateness. We see no reason for making a distinction between the right of a homesteader to recover when his property has been damaged by a blast set off in a remote corner of the state, and the right to compensation of an urban resident whose home is destroyed by an explosion originating in a settled area. In each case, the loss is properly to be regarded as a cost of the business of storing or using explosives. Every incentive remains to conduct such activities in locations which are as safe as possible, because there the damages resulting from an accident will be kept to a minimum.

How might Judge Posner respond?

4. The first Restatement used the term "ultrahazardous" rather than "abnormally dangerous" activity and framed the liability as a rule instead of a standard based on a list of factors. According to that version, strict liability was to be imposed if the activity

(a) necessarily involves a risk of serious harm to the person, land or chattels of others which cannot be eliminated by the exercise of the utmost care, and

(b) is not a matter of common usage.

How does this version differ from the one used by the court? Would its use have altered the result of the principal case?

The Third Restatement section 20 reverts to the first Restatement's two-element test, although it retains the "abnormally dangerous" language from the Second Restatement. (The first element is modified to require "a foreseeable and highly significant risk of physical harm even when reasonable care is exercised by all actors.") The Third Restatement observes that two omitted factors that were contained in the Second

Restatement, locational appropriateness and value to the community, may have some bearing on the two requirements retained for strict liability. The location of the activity may affect the magnitude of the risk posed, and socially valuable, albeit risky, activities may be in more common usage, as with commercial airplane travel.

5. In Torchia v. Fisher, 468 A.2d 1061 (N.J.1983), the court held the owner of a stolen airplane liable for ground damage to plaintiffs under a statute construed to create "absolute liability." The court concluded that "as between an unsuspecting homeowner or person on the ground and the plane's owner, the Legislature could rationally decide to place the loss on the owner, for whom the plane served some purpose."

Contrary to a view taken in the first Restatement, most courts now refuse to hold owners or pilots of falling aircraft strictly liable for harm to land, persons or chattels on the ground. See, e.g., Crosby v. Cox Aircraft Co. of Washington, 746 P.2d 1198 (Wash.1987). The framers of the Second Restatement, however, after much debate, adopted a special provision making the owner and operator of any aircraft liable for harm caused to land, persons or chattels on the ground by the aircraft itself or any object falling therefrom "even if he has exercised the utmost care to prevent it." A comment to the section observed that despite great strides, the safety records did not indicate "that the ordinary rules of negligence should be applied." The comment also stressed that those on the ground have "no place to hide from falling aircraft and are helpless to select any locality for their residence or business in which they will not be exposed to the risk, however minimized it may be." Section 520A, cmt. c.

The Third Restatement reviews the Second Restatement debate, characterizes *Crosby* as undoubtedly correct in concluding that aviation does not fit the formal Restatement criteria for an abnormally dangerous activity, and concludes:

> In light of all of this, the issue of strict liability for aviation ground damage can be regarded as difficult. Even so, the doctrinal argument against strict liability that almost all airline crashes are due to negligence confirms that the strict-liability issue is no longer one that has major practical significance (and similarly explains why there are so few modern cases considering the issue). In these circumstances, the issue is left open in this Restatement.

Restatement (Third) of Torts: Liability for Physical and Emotional Harm § 20 cmt. k, rptrs. note (2010). Is the rule regarding ground damage caused by airplanes relevant to the issue of whether strict liability should apply to the rail transport of dangerous chemicals?

6. In 1973, an explosion occurred in the Southern Pacific railroad yards near Roseville, California. Eighteen boxcars laden with bombs, all belonging to the United States, exploded, causing widespread damage and injury, and triggering several lawsuits. In Chavez v. Southern Pacific Transportation Co., 413 F.Supp. 1203 (E.D.Cal.1976), cited in *Harbor Belt*, the railroad argued that where a carrier is required to accept dangerous cargo, it is "unjust" to impose strict liability. The judge concluded that California courts would not create such an exception even though Second Restatement section 521 did reject strict liability in such a situation:

> If California predicated liability solely upon the "fairness" rationale appearing in [Green v. General Petroleum Corp., 270 P. 952 (Cal.1928)], it might well find that strict liability was inappropriate. Under the *Green* rationale strict liability is imposed because the ultrahazardous factor intentionally exposes others to a serious danger—an anti-social act is being redressed. Where the carrier has no choice but to accept dangerous cargo and engage in an ultrahazardous activity, it is the public which is requiring the carrier to engage in the anti-social activity. The carrier is innocent.
>
>   But, there is no logical reason for creating a "public duty" exception when the rationale for subjecting the carrier to absolute liability is the carrier's ability to distribute the loss to the public. Whether the carrier is free to reject or bound to take the explosive cargo, the plaintiffs are equally defenseless. Bound or not, Southern Pacific is in a position to pass along the loss to the public. Bound or not, the social and economic benefits which are ordinarily derived from strict liability are achieved. . . . A more efficient allocation of resources results. Thus, the reasonable inference to be drawn from the adoption of the risk distribution rationale in Smith v. Lockheed Propulsion Co., [56 Cal.Rptr. 128 (App.1967)] is that California would . . . find carriers engaging in ultrahazardous activity are subject to strict liability.

Chavez is discussed at p. 536 infra, in the excerpt from Rabin, The Ideology of Enterprise Liability. For an extensive discussion of the carrier issue, see National Steel Service Center, Inc. v. Gibbons, 319 N.W.2d 269 (Iowa 1982), also rejecting the Second Restatement's position.

    7. *Defenses.* There have been relatively few cases involving defenses in this branch of strict liability. Why might this be? Second Restatement section 523 states that plaintiff's assumption of the risk of harm from the activity "bars his recovery for the harm." Section 524 states that contributory negligence is not a defense to strict liability except when the plaintiff's conduct involves "knowingly and unreasonably subjecting himself to the risk of harm from the activity. . . ." An illustration to section 524 states that if a driver is so intent on passing the truck ahead that the driver fails to see "Danger, Dynamite" plainly marked on the truck, and collides with the truck causing an explosion, the driver is not barred by contributory negligence. The driver who has read the sign, however, is barred from recovery.

    The Restatement sections were prepared before the emergence of comparative negligence. Should a state that has adopted comparative fault for negligence cases extend it to this type of strict liability case? An increasing number of cases support comparative negligence as an appropriate partial defense in strict liability. See, e.g., Maddy v. Vulcan

Materials Co., 737 F.Supp. 1528 (D.Kan.1990)(abnormally dangerous activities); Johnson v. Swain, 787 S.W.2d 36 (Tex.1989)(parties stipulated that comparative negligence is the relevant defense in a wild-animal case). The Restatement (Third) of Torts: Apportionment of Liability section 7 provides: "Plaintiff's . . . negligence that is a legal cause of an indivisible injury to the plaintiff reduces the plaintiff's recovery in proportion to the share of responsibility the fact finder assigns to the plaintiff (or other person for whose negligence the plaintiff is responsible)."

B. THEORETICAL PERSPECTIVES

Strict liability can be seriously regarded as a comprehensive alternative to the fault principle only if it is grounded in a broader-based foundation than the cases involving abnormally dangerous activities. The various formulations of enterprise liability adopted by the courts, initially in the abnormally dangerous activity cases, but more extensively in defective products litigation, supply one set of basic elements for such a theory. These elements, along with other insights drawn from economics and moral theory, served as the basis for a substantial body of tort scholarship in recent years aimed at illuminating the principles of strict liability.

This section offers selections from that literature, beginning with a historical perspective arguing that the evolving strict liability case law that has been considered in the preceding section can be seen as reflecting a fundamental shift in focus from a corrective justice to a collective justice perspective—a shift in which enterprise liability emerges as a dominant theme in explaining modern strict liability.

The Ideology of Enterprise Liability
Robert L. Rabin.
55 Maryland Law Review 1190, 1194–99 (1996).

In the nineteenth century, strict liability for accidental harm is generally identified with two sources—*Rylands v. Fletcher* and the blasting cases. Neither reflects a different perspective on the ideological source of rights and duties in tort, as I see it, from the principles of fault liability that were developing contemporaneously. The point is nicely illustrated by the opinion of Justice Blackburn in *Rylands*, as he attempted to reconcile his position that fault was irrelevant in that case with cases involving "traffic on the highways," in which he observed that a showing of fault was a necessary condition to liability. "Traffic on the highways" became a metaphor for situations in which individuals are injured while pursuing their daily lives in public rather than enjoying the privacy of their own domicile. To the nineteenth century judicial mind, still dominated by interpersonal notions of neighborliness rooted in property rights, one's domicile remained sacrosanct:

The person whose grass or corn is eaten down by the escaping cattle of his neighbour, or whose mine is flooded by the water from his neighbour's reservoir, or whose cellar is invaded by the filth of his neighbour's privy, or whose habitation is made unhealthy by the fumes and noisome vapours of his neighbour's alkali works, is damnified without any fault of his own; and it seems but reasonable and just that the neighbour, who has brought something on his own property which was not naturally there, harmless to others so long as it is confined to his own property, but which he knows to be mischievous if it gets on his neighbour's, should be obliged to make good the damage which ensues if he does not succeed in confining it to his own property.

Blackburn's emphasis on "doing right" by one's neighbor is just as focused on moralistic judgment about appropriate private behavior as is the code of personal conduct at the foundation of the fault principle.

The blasting cases reveal similar origins in trespassory notions of protecting private rights in land. As later cases, such as *Sullivan v. Dunham*, shifted the focus to protection of those injured in public by blasting activities, these decisions also blurred the meaning of "trespass," drawing on still other venerable precedents of liability for "direct" acts. But the critical point, in reading turn-of-the-century blasting cases like *Sullivan*, is that there is not the slightest evidence of attention to risk-bearing, creating incentives to safer conduct, or other utilitarian concerns. Instead, in these opinions, norms of interpersonal conduct remain deeply ingrained: "As the safety of the person is more sacred than the safety of property, the cases cited [recognizing that the use of land by the proprietor is not an absolute right, but limited by the higher right of others to lawfully possess their property] should govern our decision. . . ."[30]

Rights qualified and rights absolute, *sic utere tuo*[31] as a guiding principle, trespass as a buffer against invasive conduct—these are the touchstones of strict liability as traditionally conceived. It is a discourse

---

[30] [ ] But cf. Losee v. Buchanan, 51 N.Y. 476, 479 (1873)(rejecting strict liability in a case involving explosion of a steam boiler on grounds that a growing industrialized society required a more limited foundation for responsibility than strict liability—namely, fault). Cases like *Losee* planted the seed for a collective-based notion of fault, but the ripening of utilitarian considerations in fault cases did not really become evident until the mid-twentieth century. Consider in particular the influence of what came to be known as the Learned Hand test for negligence, United States v. Carroll Towing Co., 159 F.2d 169, 173 (2d Cir.1947)(establishing a calculus in which due care of a barge owner was to be assessed as "a function of three variables: (1) the probability that she will break away; (2) the gravity of the resulting injury if she does, (3) the burden of adequate precautions")—although it is far from clear that Judge Hand had presentday economic efficiency considerations in mind when he spelled out his formula.

[31] The complete phrase is "*Sic utere tuo ut alienum non laedas*," or "use your own so as not to injure another's property." Cochran's Law Lexicon 271 (5th ed. 1973).

grounded in ethical norms of interpersonal conduct.[32] It is akin to Oliver Wendell Holmes's contemporaneous account in The Common Law, forging a foreseeability-based rationale for fault liability in a pre-modern society free of industrial injuries, product mishaps, and impulses to view accidental harm as a collective concern.

Flash forward to 1973. A federal district court in California, in *Chavez v. Southern Pacific Transportation Co.*, entertained a number of lawsuits arising out of an explosion of eighteen boxcars filled with bombs in a railroad yard in Roseville, California.[35] The carrier argued a "public duty" defense—that it was required to accept the cargo by the federal government and consequently should not be strictly liable. The court responded in terms revealing the paradigm shift that has occurred:

> If California predicated liability solely upon the "fairness" rationale appearing in . . . [Green v. General Petroleum Corp., 270 P. 952 (Cal.1928)], it might well find that strict liability was inappropriate. Under the *Green* rationale strict liability is imposed because the ultrahazardous actor intentionally exposes others to a serious danger—an anti-social act is being redressed. Where the carrier has no choice but to accept dangerous cargo and engage in an ultrahazardous activity, it is the public which is requiring the carrier to engage in the anti-social activity. The carrier is innocent.
>
> But, there is no logical reason for creating a "public duty" exception when the rationale for subjecting the carrier to absolute liability is the carrier's ability to distribute the loss to the public. Whether the carrier is free to reject or bound to take the explosive cargo, the plaintiffs are equally defenseless. Bound or not, Southern Pacific is in a position to pass along the loss to the public. Bound or not, the social and economic benefits which are ordinarily derived from imposing strict liability are achieved.

The federal district court in *Chavez* relied on *Smith v. Lockheed Propulsion Co.*, a 1967 case involving reverberation damage from rocket testing, that had in turn relied on *Luthringer v. Moore*, a 1948 case involving personal injuries from fumigation in an adjoining building. To complete the strict liability lineage, *Luthringer* relied on *Green*, cited in

---

[32]   The ethical basis for these norms of interpersonal conduct has in fact taken a variety of forms. Compare, e.g., George P. Fletcher, Fairness and Utility in Tort Theory, 85 Harv. L. Rev. 537, 546–51 (1972) [hereinafter Fletcher, Fairness and Utility] as amplified in George P. Fletcher, Corrective Justice for Moderns, 106 Harv. L. Rev. 1658, 1677–78 (1993) [hereinafter Fletcher, Corrective Justice] (reviewing Jules Coleman, Risks and Wrongs (1992))(emphasizing nonreciprocity of risk posed by intersecting activities) with Richard A. Epstein, A Theory of Strict Liability, 2 J. Legal Stud. 151, 200–04 (1973) and Richard A. Epstein, Defenses and Subsequent Pleas in a System of Strict Liability, 3 J. Legal Stud. 165, 168–69 (1974)(articulating a causation-based theory).

[35]   Chavez v. Southern Pac. Transp. Co., 413 F. Supp. 1203, 1205 (E.D.Cal.1976).

the passage above. In 1928, as the quote suggests, the *Green* court was still operating in a world of interpersonal ethical dictates. Significantly, the *Green* court relied on a California Civil Code provision that read "[o]ne must so use his own rights as not to infringe upon the rights of another." Two decades later, the *Luthringer* court's opinion was wholly opaque, revealing not the slightest clue as to why—beyond the hazardous nature of the fumigant and the uncommon character of fumigation (satisfying the then-existing Restatement standards)— liability was to be strict. Twenty-eight years later, however, *Chavez* clarified the reasoning and firmly anchored strict liability in collective justice/enterprise liability ideology.

Thus we find, well into the twentieth century, that there is no necessary connection between strict liability and an ideology of enterprise liability. That the recent enterprise liability literature suggests otherwise, is explained by the near single-minded preoccupation with the dynamic development of products liability law beginning in the 1960s. That development, of course, explicitly turned on the "revolution" of enthroning strict liability as a replacement for liability based on fault. But, as developments in the more prosaic domain of traditional strict liability reveal, the relational nexus rather is between enterprise liability and a radically different way of thinking about the social function of the tort system—in particular, viewing tort as a redistributive and regulatory mechanism—that has evolved independently of doctrinal change.

In a similar vein, consider that most ancient and ubiquitous form of strict liability—vicarious liability. In earlier times, before vicarious liability came to be taken for granted, scholars debated the origins of this imperfection in the design of responsibility based on fault. Baty, a staunch opponent of the concept, identified nine separate justifications for vicarious liability, which he then proceeded to annihilate with relish. Without reciting his litany, it is interesting to note the singular commitment to corrective justice embodied in the various pre-modern explanations for the concept. To name just a few: a control theory, emphasizing responsibility for close personal supervision over the work of an employee; a retribution theory, an explanation offered by Holmes in The Common Law, based on vicarious liability as a form of payment in place of forfeiting entitlement to the services of a wrongdoing servant; an identification theory, a somewhat mystical (and conclusory) conception of the master and servant as a single entity for legal purposes; an evidentiary theory, serving as a kind of offshoot of res ipsa loquitur that emphasizes the master's superior ability to identify the wrongful actor responsible for a victim's injury; a profit-based theory, turning on the fairness of linking the burdens of a vagrant employee's labors with the correlative benefits derived from his services; and others.

By contrast, in the more modern writers such as Atiyah and Harper and James, one finds clear reference to the ideology of enterprise liability as the contemporaneous underpinning for vicarious liability. Summarizing the early writing of Guido Calabresi, Atiyah's treatise on vicarious liability, published at the dawn of the modern products liability era, offers both risk-spreading and safety incentives rationales for holding employers responsible for the tortious acts of their employees. In like fashion, Calabresi's mentor, Fleming James, offered an explicitly distributional justification a decade earlier. Old wine, it seems, had been poured into new bottles.

NOTES AND QUESTIONS

1. The introduction to this article discusses contributions to the enterprise liability literature, including Priest, The Invention of Enterprise Liability: A Critical History of the Intellectual Foundations of Modern Tort Law, 14 J. Legal Stud. 461 (1985). In discussing Priest's views, Rabin describes enterprise liability as characterized by "the twin notions that an enterprise should bear the risks of accidents it produces because (1) an enterprise has superior risk-bearing capacity compared to victims who would otherwise bear the costs of accidents, and (2) an enterprise is generally better placed to respond to the safety incentives created by liability rules than is the party suffering harm." In what sense does this rationale better fit strict liability than liability based on negligence? To what extent is it consistent with the doctrine of abnormally dangerous activities in Restatement Second §§ 519–20, p. 523 supra? See generally, Shugerman, A Watershed Moment: Reversals of Tort Theory in the Nineteenth Century, 2 Journal of Tort Law, Issue 1, Article 2 (2008), discussing the complementarity of moral and economic approaches in the evolving nineteenth century judicial approach to strict liability.

2. Compare Keating, The Theory of Enterprise Liability and Common Law Strict Liability, 54 Vand.L.Rev. 1285 (2001), taking issue with the Restatement Second approach, carried over into the Restatement Third, for being "limited to a set of special cases"—strict liability, that is, limited to abnormally dangerous activities:

> The distinctive modern form of strict liability—enterprise liability—is a particular articulation of what it means to make agency the basis of responsibility. Two propositions form the core of enterprise liability. First, activities should bear their characteristic accident costs. Fault liability pins the costs of the nonnegligent accidents that are the long-run price of an activity's presence in the world on the random victims of the activity. Enterprise liability pins those accident costs on the activity—the enterprise—which imposed the nonnegligent risks responsible for the injuries at issue. Second, enterprise liability holds that an enterprise's accident costs should be distributed among the members of the enterprise. The costs of an injury should be shared by those who profit from the activity responsible for the

injury; they should not be concentrated on the injured party, or be dispersed across unrelated activities. These two propositions are often linked to a particular conception of fairness. Fairness requires a just distribution of burdens and benefits. It therefore gives rise to a presumption that the costs of the accidental physical injuries characteristic of an activity should be borne by those who benefit from the activity, whether or not they are culpably responsible for precipitating the injuries at issue. These propositions are also frequently linked to economic ideas of allocative efficiency and loss-spreading.

3. The safety incentives rationale was developed into a full-blown theory of general, or optimal, deterrence in Guido Calabresi, The Costs of Accidents (1970), which explored the risk-spreading rationale as well. More recent contributions to the enterprise liability literature include Croley & Hanson, Rescuing the Revolution: The Revived Case for Enterprise Liability, 91 Mich.L.Rev. 683 (1993); V. Nolan & E. Ursin, Understanding Enterprise Liability: Rethinking Tort Reform for the Twenty-First Century (1995); Keating, The Idea of Fairness in the Law of Enterprise Liability, 95 Mich.L.Rev. 1266 (1997); and Geistfeld, Should Enterprise Liability Replace the Rule of Strict Liability for Abnormally Dangerous Activities?, 45 UCLA L.Rev. 611 (1998).

4. In reading the selection that follows, consider whether the risk-spreading/safety incentives characterization provides a persuasive underpinning for enterprise liability. What, if anything, does it leave out as a satisfying explanation for strict liability more generally? We return to these questions in the notes and questions following this excerpt and in the case law development of strict liability for defective products in Chapter IX; in particular, consider Justice Traynor's influential concurring opinion in *Escola v. Coca Cola Bottling Co. of Fresno*, p. 564 infra.

A Goals-Oriented Approach to Strict Tort Liability for Abnormally Dangerous Activities

Joseph H. King, Jr.
48 Baylor Law Review 341, 349–61 (1996).

B.   Goals of Strict Tort Liability

Most authorities would agree that multiple goals have animated and influenced the evolution of strict liability. There is, however, less agreement on what those goals should be and the relative weight they should accord. The absence of a single normative predicate or a meta-prioritization for strict liability has resulted in an uncertain and unstable legal system with courts and commentators oscillating between various goals, when goals are mentioned at all. The uncertainty has been compounded by the failure of both the Restatement and the courts to meaningfully incorporate these goals into the criteria for strict liability. The challenge is to identify the best combination of goals to guide decisions on the question of strict liability for dangerous activities.

1.   Loss-Spreading

A central goal of strict liability is to spread losses caused by accidental injuries among a broad class of persons. This loss-spreading or distributive justice goal helps to assure that the effects of otherwise devastating losses are ameliorated by diffusing them among a broad array of appropriate entities and individuals. Fleming James articulated this loss-spreading goal in terms of the marginal utility of money, which he explained with his "bottom dollar" thesis. A person's bottom dollar is that person's most valuable dollar, and each added dollar has decreasing value to that person. In other words, "(a)s one loses wealth, each additional dollar imposes a greater sacrifice." The underlying premise for loss-spreading is that accident costs should be "collectively, not individually, borne," because a loss causes less social and economic disruption if it is shared by many people.

Under the loss-spreading goal, the decision whether to impose strict liability hinges partially on whether the actor engaging in the injurious activity.is an appropriate party to incur and then redistribute, or "spread," a loss. This loss-spreading function would thus depend on the extent to which the actor was able to anticipate and evaluate the underlying risk, take appropriate steps to accumulate resources to insure against the loss, and then systematically recapture those outlays by passing them on to suitable consumers. This loss-spreading goal should not, however, be considered in isolation. The fact that other avenues for compensating injuries exist—such as workers' compensation, Social Security disability benefits, and first-party insurance—must also be taken into account. Various institutions too often operate insularly and even at cross purposes. The relative inefficiency of strict tort liability should be compared with other systems. Less than half of each insurance premium dollar reaches accident victims. This is an important factor to keep in mind when considering non-tort loss-spreading alternatives.

As strict liability matured as a discrete liability-producing concept, its primary focus shifted from the deterrent goals central under fault-based liability to the direction of loss-spreading. Although some commentators continue to minimize the centrality of loss-spreading under strict liability, loss-spreading is increasingly regarded as one of the dominant rationales for strict liability. Professor Gregory, an influential commentator on strict liability during the formative years between the two Restatements, noted that perhaps the strongest argument for strict "enterprise" liability stemmed from the fact that industry was the most practical institution to administer a loss-bearing system.

If loss-spreading were the only goal of a tort compensation system, and if a broader distribution of a loss were better, then there would be no stopping point short of government liability for all accidents. This is one reason why other goals should be incorporated into the matrix for determining strict liability. Vindication of other goals not only serves the interests of these other goals, but also provides a manageable "stopping point" that is otherwise absent when loss-spreading is the only goal.

2.   Loss Avoidance (or Risk Reduction)

A second goal of strict liability is loss avoidance or reduction. This goal, sometimes referred to as the "primary" reduction of accident costs, aims at imposing liability in a way that reduces the number and severity of accidents.[67] This goal requires appraisal of the actor's ability to systematically evaluate the risks of his activities and make sound cost-benefit decisions about the manner of operations as well as the level and location of the activity, safeguards, and alternatives. Calabresi describes this general deterrence function as seeking to impose accident costs on those engaging in the injurious activities who could "reduce accident costs most cheaply."[68]

Even commentators who view the loss avoidance goal as central to strict liability would probably agree that it must nevertheless be applied in conjunction with other considerations. Thus, the need and effectiveness of general deterrence should be assessed in the context of other potential means for reducing accidents, such as collective ("specific") deterrence through direct governmental regulation of the activity. Moreover, other goals must inevitably be taken into account when one cannot make, in Calabresi's classic oxymoron, "intelligent intuitive choices" of the best or cheapest cost avoiders (or best cost benefit analysts).

There are several reasons why the loss avoidance goal, albeit entitled to consideration, should be accorded less weight than loss-spreading considerations. First, a contradiction lurks in the goal. On one hand, strict liability may be imposed on a defendant even if that defendant is innocent.[71] Yet, the very existence of loss avoidance goals by definition assumes that some aspect of the defendant's activity could

---

[67] Calabresi, [The Costs of Accidents (1970)] at 26. Calabresi and Hirschoff have also articulated the goal more broadly in terms of seeking "minimization of the sum of accident costs and of accident avoidance costs." Guido Calabresi & Jon T. Hirschoff, Toward a Test for Strict Liability in Torts, 81 Yale L.J. 1055, 1084 (1972).

[68] Calabresi, [The Costs of Accidents (1970)] at 135. Under this formulation, the judge or jury need not evaluate (or second guess) the defendant's conduct in terms of the relative costs of the accident and its avoidance. Instead, the judge or jury would decide which of the parties was the best cost-benefit analyst—the one "in the best position to make the cost-benefit analysis . . . and to act on the decision once it is made." Calabresi & Hirschoff, supra note 67, at 1060.

. . .

[71] Some commentators have argued that strict liability is not really a morally neutral concept at all. They argue that the community sense of morality would find abnormally dangerous activities "blameworthy" if there were not some provision for compensation for the injuries caused by such activities. See generally Robert E. Keeton, Conditional Fault in the Law of Torts, 72 Harv. L. Rev. 401, 427 (1959) . . .

have been changed for the better. Perhaps this apparent contradiction could be finessed by asserting that, under strict liability, the threat of liability operates not as a deterrent, but rather as an incentive to promote safer conduct. This semantic sleight of hand leaves one still wondering. Perhaps strict liability promotes loss reduction and prevention through incentives and disincentives that affect defendants' activities, a sphere that negligence law may not address comprehensively. Nonetheless, how much the threat of strict liability adds to loss reduction beyond the reduction already produced by negligence liability is questionable.

Secondly, serious questions exist about the efficacy of general deterrence. These concerns are relevant in applying strict liability. Deterrence, or loss avoidance incentives, requires an often unattainable knowledge of relevant risks by responsible decisionmakers. Moreover, the message of deterrence is often quite attenuated under the tort system. The extent of the injury will often not coincide with the appropriate level of deterrence in any particular case. Similar injuries are not compensated similarly. There is an absence of predictable outcomes of litigation and standards of behavior are not effectively communicated to appropriate decisionmakers. Furthermore, various theories of disordered behavior suggest that there are inherent psychological limitations on the efficacy of deterrence or rational response to incentives. Thus, according to some theories of disordered behavior, dangerous conduct may be the product of organic brain impairment, genetic factors, biochemical factors, or the product of internalized, often unconscious, determinants. Even behavioral theorists who contend that "people behave as they do because they have learned that behavior" would confront factors in the torts system that may confound deterrence. These factors stem from the fact that the torts system lacks the celerity and consistency of outcome so important to reinforce behavior, and relies on punishment rather than more potentially influential positive rewards.

Third, the threat of liability can frequently over-deter, producing negative results. One example is the do-it-yourselfer who chooses a more dangerous alternative to an activity which has been forced out of availability. This idea is sometimes more broadly conceived as the "theory of the second best" under which high prices or unavailability of products or services causes consumers to turn to substitutes that are less safe.[81] Thus, the goal of reducing the incidence or severity of accidental losses, if pursued solely to alter the conduct of the defendant, may be subverted by strict liability. On the other hand, if the availability of alternatives to the activity in question is considered, in

---

[81] Mark Geistfeld, Implementing Enterprise Liability: A Comment on Henderson and Twerski, 67 N.Y.U. L. Rev. 1157, 1170–71 (1992). "(T)he theory of the second best shows that if individuals make choices from a set of activities, regulations designed to achieve efficient behavior with respect to one activity may lead to greater overall inefficiency if enough people switch from regulated to unregulated activities." Id. at 1170.

the context of the goal of loss allocation, as a means of educating consumers about the true costs so that they might intelligently opt for less costly alternatives, the goal of loss avoidance may be better served. The limitations of the loss avoidance goal underscore the importance of considering an array of goals in applying strict liability.

Notwithstanding reservations about the goal of loss avoidance, it may still make sense to consider this objective when deciding whether to impose strict liability. Strict liability was developed in part because of the difficulties encountered by plaintiffs attempting to prove negligence. If it is true that much of the negligence that occurs cannot be proven, then strict liability may afford significant deterrence against this kind of occult negligence, and thus offer more effective deterrence than traditional negligence law.

Strict liability for dangerous activities may also fill a gap created by the failure of negligence theory, at least in some situations, to adequately address and evaluate the level of a defendant's activity, rather than merely the quality of that activity, in the application of the due care standard. According to Steven Shavell, in order to evaluate the reasonableness of a defendant's activity level, "(c)ourts would, by definition, have to decide on the appropriate level of activity, and their competence to do this is problematic." To the extent that negligence law does not or cannot realistically be expected to evaluate activity levels when assessing due care, then strict liability may operate to fill that void. Thus, even if courts and juries are not appropriate institutions to evaluate the reasonableness of enterprise activity levels, those engaging in such activities may be sufficiently experienced and positioned to systematically consider their own activity level when faced with potential strict liability. Strict liability may therefore create incentives not simply with respect to the manner of the activity's conduct, but also for relocating, changing, or reducing the activity. Accordingly, a relevant consideration in strict liability is the degree to which the actor responsible for an injury is capable of systematically evaluating the risks and benefits of conducting the underlying enterprise at present levels.

3.   Loss Allocation (or Internalization)

A third goal of strict liability is loss allocation. The objective is for a loss to be initially borne (or "internalized") by the enterprise whose activities engendered it and whose activities are sufficiently connected to the loss to make it appropriate to reflect the loss in the cost of the enterprise's services. Such added charges will constitute a signal to interested service consumers, owners or shareholders, managers, and employees of the enterprise, of the true costs of the activities of that enterprise. This will promote better informed choices by these interested parties, thereby encouraging investment in safety and discouraging or moderating consumption and investment in relatively more hazardous products and services (or at least making such consumption and investment more discriminating). Thus, internalization of costs through loss allocation will induce price-mediated adjustments in production and activity levels, with reduction of the incidence of accidents. In turn, society will ideally move closer to an optimal allocation of its limited resources. Liability thus prevents enterprise costs from being externalized and avoids forcing society to unwittingly subsidize the dangerous enterprise.

Loss allocation is inextricably intertwined with other goals. It is essentially the emanation of loss-spreading, delineating the route along which spreading must take place. Loss allocation also serves to inform enterprises and consumers of the true costs of an activity so that they may appropriately adjust their activity levels, selection of services and products, and manner of operation in ways that reduce the net cost of accidents.

Notwithstanding the positive effects of the loss allocation goal, if taken too far, loss allocation can have a serious downside. Forcing enterprises to internalize too many costs can inhibit economic development and technological innovation. Also, forcing too many costs on an enterprise may foster efforts to avoid liability by substituting unregulable modes of behavior. These attempts to avoid loss allocation might include sales of goods and services in "black markets" and other "clandestine production and distribution" methods. In addition, as a greater proportion of the costs of accidents are shifted to enterprises, a concomitantly smaller percentage of their resources will be available to entrepreneurs and managers to develop and nurture the enterprise. In this era of fierce international competition and declining profit margins, continued dissipation of the resources available to decisionmakers to manage and develop their enterprises will have a profound rippling effect. Domestic enterprises will be less able to compete against international competitors who are far less burdened by potential liability. It also affects the vitality of the free enterprise system, which depends on managers having a critical mass of resources necessary to animate their entrepreneurial discretion.

4.   Administrative Efficiency

A fourth goal of strict liability is to achieve an acceptable level of administrative costs. Sometimes this goal is expressed in terms of reducing the "tertiary" costs of accidents, meaning the systemic transaction costs involved in imposing liability. This tertiary goal "tells us to question constantly whether an attempt to reduce accident costs, either by reducing accidents themselves or by reducing their secondary effects, costs more than it saves."

Strict liability would produce administrative savings with simplified liability determinations by removing the need for proving fault, an expensive exercise often requiring expert testimony. It would also improve the overall administrative integrity of the system by promoting recovery in cases where the evidence was destroyed or unavailable, which sometimes occurs in accidents arising out of abnormally dangerous activities. For strict liability to realize its potential for administrative efficiency, however, the rules for identifying liability-producing activities must be simplified and conformed to the goals of strict liability. Professor Henderson identifies several process norms that must be satisfied in order for liability rules to provide a coherent guide to judges and juries: the rules must be comprehensible, encompass verifiable facts, and lend themselves to common law adjudication.

Even if strict liability cases are more efficiently resolved than their negligence cousins, adoption of strict liability may in some respects increase overall transaction costs. Broadening the reach of strict liability will increase the number of tort claims. That in turn may magnify the overall inefficiencies of the tort system. The challenge is to formulate a standard for strict liability that vindicates its goals while keeping administrative costs at an acceptable level. . . .

5.   Fairness

Another goal frequently invoked for strict liability is fairness. One dimension of this goal is embodied in George Fletcher's paradigm of reciprocity.[101] This paradigm represents, according to Fletcher, one of two ways of looking at tort liability, the other being the paradigm of reasonableness, which animates fault-based liability. The paradigm of reciprocity focuses on the relative magnitude and quality of the risks created by the activities of the defendant and those of the victim. According to this paradigm, "a victim has a right to recover for injuries caused by a risk greater in degree and different in order from those created by the victim and imposed on the defendant—in short, for injuries resulting from non-reciprocal risks." This fairness rationale is more commonly stated simply as a belief that between two innocent persons, the initiator who benefits from the ultimately injurious activity should be liable.

Strict liability is, however, subject to some serious reservations in terms of fairness. Fletcher's reciprocity paradigm has been criticized as "temporally bound" with a misplaced focus. Instead of tying liability to the goal of cheapest cost avoidance, Fletcher's paradigm is said to advance a "philosophical theory of desert . . . (with) new risks . . . less deserving" than existing ones. There is no clear understanding or consensus on what is meant by "fairness." One might also question the fairness of a rule requiring consumers to pay higher prices so that accident victims can be compensated at levels reflecting their pre-accident physical and economic prospects. Is it really "fair" to charge everyone more for abnormally dangerous services so that economically-advantaged members of society can maintain their economic level in the

---

[101] See Fletcher, [Fairness and Utility in Tort Theory, 85 Harv.L.Rev. 537 (1972)], at 540–42. Fletcher apparently views fairness as also encompassing other concerns and thus too broad to be coterminous with his paradigm of reciprocity. Id. at 541.

event the activity harms one of them? And is it fair to compensate victims of abnormally dangerous activities but not victims of accidents arising from more benign or generic sources?

Fairness, whatever that term connotes, probably does not figure centrally among the goals of strict liability, at least as a conceptually distinct rationale. Indeed, fairness may actually embrace other goals. For example, perhaps Fletcher's paradigm of reciprocity is better characterized not in terms of fairness, but as normatively advancing a whole range of strict liability goals. Thus, an imbalance in risk creation between actor and victim may suggest an absence of notice to the victim or lack of a reasonable opportunity or ability to prepare for or endure a loss, a fact relevant to the goals of loss-spreading, loss avoidance, and loss allocation.

6.   Protection of Individual Autonomy

Protection of individual autonomy is also occasionally mentioned by some writers as a goal of strict liability. . . .

NOTES AND QUESTIONS

1.   *Economic theories.* Are the goals that King identifies as loss avoidance and loss allocation distinct? As the author indicates, these goals serve as the foundation for the general deterrence theory, spelled out by Guido Calabresi in The Costs of Accidents (1970), and further explained in the cited Calabresi & Hirschoff. Another seminal contribution to the economic vantage point was Coase, The Problem of Social Cost, 3 J. Law & Econ. 1 (1960), discussed at p. 696 infra, in the context of nuisance law. Coase addressed issues of causation from the perspective of both intersecting activities resulting in harm to one of the parties and loss allocation under conditions of perfect information about risk. He set the stage for later analysis of appropriate liability rules in situations where costless bargaining and access to information were impaired. The Costs of Accidents is examined thirty-five years later, from a variety of perspectives, in Symposium, Calabresi's *The Costs of Accidents:* A Generation of Impact on Law and Scholarship, 64 Md.L.Rev. 1–754 (2005).

See also L. Kaplow & S. Shavell, Fairness Versus Welfare (2002). The third chapter of the book provides a systematic analysis of tort law from the perspective of welfare economics, including a critique of competing "fairness" perspectives.

2.   At one point, King observes that loss allocation is "inextricably intertwined with other goals." Can you think of situations in which the loss allocation goal and the loss-spreading goal would lead to different liability rules? At another point, he asserts that loss avoidance "should be accorded less weight than loss-spreading." Are his arguments for this proposition convincing?

3.   Gary Schwartz systematically reviewed the empirical evidence bearing on the economists' claims for the deterrent effect of tort law and their many critics' claims that tort law does not effectively deter. Schwartz,

Reality in the Economic Analysis of Tort Law: Does Tort Law Really Deter?, 42 UCLA L.Rev. 377 (1994). He concluded that neither polar position was correct: "tort law, while not as effective as economic models suggest, may still be somewhat successful in achieving its stated deterrence goals." See also D. Dewees, D. Duff & M. Trebilcock, Exploring the Domain of Accident Law: Taking the Facts Seriously (1996)(examining systematically the extant empirical literature on deterrence through tort rules).

4. The excerpt from Richard Posner, Economic Analysis of Law, which follows, will expand on the economic perspective in the context of a comparison between strict liability and negligence. But first consider some non-economic perspectives.

5. *Moral theories.* Several writers have objected to the focus on economics because other values have been diluted or disregarded. Among the critics of the economic approach to tort liability is Professor George Fletcher, as indicated in the King excerpt. In Fairness and Utility in Tort Theory, 85 Harv.L.Rev. 537 (1972), he objected that "the thrust of the academic literature is to convert the tort system into something other than a mechanism for determining the just distribution of accident losses. . . . Discussed less and less are precisely those questions that make tort law a unique repository of intuitions of corrective justice: What is the relevance of risk-creating conduct to the just distribution of wealth? What is the rationale for an individual's 'right' to recover for his losses? What are the criteria for justly singling out some people and making them, and not their neighbors, bear the costs of accidents?"

Fletcher developed an approach—briefly described by King—that built on a variety of cases, including the *Rylands* case, the ultrahazardous group, and *Vincent v. Lake Erie Transportation Co.*, reprinted at p. 969 infra:

> The general principle expressed in all of these situations governed by diverse doctrinal standards is that a victim has a right to recover for injuries caused by a risk greater in degree and different in order from those created by the victim and imposed on the defendant—in short, for injuries resulting from nonreciprocal risks. . . . For example, a pilot or an airplane owner subjects those beneath the path of flight to nonreciprocal risks of harm. Conversely, cases of nonliability [*i.e.*, in which there is no such "right" to recover] are those of reciprocal risks, namely those in which the victim and the defendant subject each other to roughly the same degree of risk. For example, two airplanes flying in the same vicinity subject each other to reciprocal risks of a mid-air collision. Of course, there are significant problems in determining when risks are nonreciprocal. . . .

Professor Fletcher then sketched a paradigm of reasonableness opposing the paradigm of reciprocity. The reasonableness paradigm "represents a rejection of non-instrumentalist values and a commitment to the community's welfare as the criterion for determining both who is entitled to receive and who ought to pay compensation. Questions that are distinct under the paradigm of reciprocity—namely, is the risk nonreciprocal and was it unexcused—are collapsed in this paradigm into a single test: was the risk unreasonable?"

Although the paradigm of reciprocity bears resemblance to strict liability and that of reasonableness to negligence, Fletcher asserted that the reciprocity cases cut across these lines and that many cases now handled under negligence lend themselves to analysis under both paradigms—in particular, because liability is warranted between reciprocal risk-creators when one party negligently harms the other. Much of the article was devoted to analyzing groups of cases to suggest how they fit into one or the other of the paradigms.

At one point Fletcher flatly rejected assignments of liability based on access to insurance or the ability to invoke the market mechanism to distribute losses: "This is an argument of distributive rather than corrective justice, for it turns on the defendant's wealth and status, rather than his conduct. Using the tort system to redistribute negative wealth (accident losses) violates the premise of corrective justice, namely that liability should turn on what the defendant has done, rather than on who he is. [ ] What is at stake is keeping the institution of taxation distinct from the institution of tort litigation."

Calabresi responded to Fletcher in Calabresi & Hirschoff, Toward a Test for Strict Liability in Torts, cited in the King excerpt. Posner responded in Strict Liability: A Comment, 2 J. Legal Stud. 205 (1973).

6. Fletcher, Corrective Justice for Moderns, 106 Harv.L.Rev. 1658 (1993), revisits the nonreciprocal risk thesis, now arguing that tort law should be understood as a "middle position" between criminal law and contract law:

> [C]ases of strict liability reflect criminal law. The influence begins early in the law of torts under the writ of trespass and carries forward in the various situations in which we perceive the defendant's action as aggression that dominates the interests of a plaintiff insulated by her rights. In contrast, the influence of private law thinking breaks through in the collaborative principle underlying the law of negligence. By entering into certain spheres of risk-taking, plaintiff and defendant both come under duties to act with a view to the costs and benefits of their actions. They become a unit, acting under an implicit obligation to optimize the consequences of their actions.

He elaborates on the distinction between dominance and collaboration with three airplane operators' liability examples. In the first two, where harm occurs to passengers or owners of other planes, the parties have entered into a collaborative enterprise and thus fall under a negligence system. In the third, involving homeowners in the path of flight, the situation is one of dominance and strict liability applies. Does the dominance-collaboration perspective appear consistent with Fletcher's earlier nonreciprocity-reciprocity perspective?

7.   King's last-mentioned goal, which he characterizes as protection of individual autonomy, was perhaps most prominently expounded (albeit not referred to in King's discussion) by Richard Epstein. The economic approach (and Fletcher's right-based reciprocity analysis) were rejected by Epstein in favor of a strict liability approach that relied heavily on notions of causation, which he developed in a series of articles: Epstein, A Theory of Strict Liability, 2 J. Legal Stud. 151 (1973); Defenses and Subsequent Pleas in a System of Strict Liability, 3 J. Legal Stud. 165 (1974); and Nuisance Law: Corrective Justice and Its Utilitarian Constraints, 8 J. Legal Stud. 49 (1979).

As summarized by John Borgo in Causal Paradigms in Tort Law, 8 J. Legal Stud. 419 (1979), Epstein's theory was predicated on a strongly articulated baseline of property and individual autonomy rights (recall the excerpt from Epstein, p. 131 supra):

> founded exclusively upon the concept of corrective justice: that is, upon the notion that when one man harms another the victim has a moral right to demand, and the injurer a moral duty to pay to him, compensation for the harm. The right and duty are only prima facie, for the concept of corrective justice has embedded within itself a number of excuses and justifications for harming another. Should any of these obtain in a particular case, the injurer may invoke them to defeat his victim's claim. But in their absence, the mere fact that he had harmed the victim obligates the injurer to pay compensation. This obligation arises from the causal relation between the injurer's conduct and the victim's harm. When A injures B, he puts him in a worse position than before the injury. This fact justifies B's demand that A make him whole, even though he would not be obligated to honor a similar demand made by someone whose harm he has not caused. Thus the notion of a man causing another's harm provides the basis for ascribing moral responsibility in everyday life. Therefore, . . . it ought to provide the basis for imposing tort liability.

The theories developed by Epstein and Fletcher are criticized in Schwartz, The Vitality of Negligence and the Ethics of Strict Liability, 15 Ga.L.Rev. 963, 977–1005 (1981). See also Posner, The Concept of Corrective Justice in Recent Theories of Tort Law, 10 J. Legal Stud. 187 (1981).

For a thoroughgoing assessment of the evolving approach of Epstein to strict liability over a forty-year period, see the symposium issue offering a variety of critical perspectives on his views, The Torts Scholarship of Richard Epstein, 3 J. Tort Law, Issue 1 (2010). In a response paper, Epstein largely reiterates his earlier version as applicable to cases involving strangers, but would allow for "some of negligence" complemented by contract, arbitration and a strong version of assumed risk in consensual relationship cases. Epstein, Toward a General Theory of Tort Law: Strict Liability in Context, 3 J. Tort Law, Issue 1, Article 6 (2010).

8.   In Pricelessness and Life: An Essay for Guido Calabresi, 64 Md.L.Rev. 159 (2005), Professor Gregory Keating draws on safety and feasibility norms established in a number of federal statutory schemes in proposing rejection of conceptualizing accident law in market terms. Keating argues that accident law

> encompasses norms that prescribe especially stringent precaution—more than efficient precaution—against "significant" risks of accidental death. These norms require that the risks of some activities be reduced either to the greatest extent "feasible," or to the point where the activity can be called "safe." These norms embrace nonmarket criteria for trading life against other goods and embody a moral value different from the value of efficiency embraced by the market. . . .
>
> Feasible and safe precaution are animated by the competing value of interpersonal fairness. They flow from the proposition that the burdens and benefits of risky activities must be justifiable to those who are burdened by the activities. Feasible and safe precaution take safety to be an especially important good—a pre-condition of a decent life.

9. For wide-ranging collections of essays by law-and-philosophy scholars interested in the tort system, see J. Oberdiek (ed.), Philosophical Foundations of Tort Law (2014); G. Postema (ed.), Philosophy and the Law of Torts (2001), and D. Owen (ed.), Philosophical Foundations of Tort Law (1995). For extensive readings on economic, moral, historical, and other approaches to the analysis of tort law, see the collections of essays in R. Rabin (ed.), Perspectives on Tort Law (4th ed.1995); S. Levmore & C. Sharkey (ed.), Foundations of Tort Law (2d ed.2009).

Economic Analysis of Law

Richard A. Posner.
226–31 (8th ed.2010).

Strict tort liability means that someone who causes an accident is liable for the victim's damages even if the injurer could not have avoided inflicting the injury by the exercise of due care (PL might be $150 and B $300). As a first approximation, strict liability has the same effects on safety as negligence liability, provided that there is a defense of contributory negligence, as there usually is though often under a different name. (Why is the defense actually *more* important for strict liability than for negligence?) If B is smaller than PL, the strictly liable defendant will take precautions to avoid the accident, just as the defendant in a negligence system will, in order to reduce his net costs. Less obviously, if B is larger than PL, the strictly liable defendant will not take precautions, just as under negligence. True, he will have to pay the victim's damages. But those damages, discounted by the probability of the accident, are less than the cost of avoidance; in other words, the expected cost of liability (= PL) is less than the cost of avoidance, so avoidance doesn't pay.

But there are significant economic differences between negligence and strict liability. One way to avoid an auto accident is to drive more carefully, but another is to drive less. Rarely will a court in a negligence case try to determine the optimal level of the activity that gave rise to the accident. When a driver is in an accident, the court will not inquire whether the benefit of the particular trip (maybe it was to the grocery store to get some gourmet food for his pet iguana) was equal to or greater than the costs, including the expected accident cost to other users of the road; or whether driving was really cheaper than walking or taking the train when all social costs are reckoned in. Such a judgment is too difficult for a court to make in an ordinary tort case. Only if the benefits of the activity are obviously very slight, as where a man runs into a burning building to retrieve an old hat and does so as carefully as he can in the circumstances but is seriously burned nonetheless, will the court find that engaging in the activity was itself negligence, even though once the decision to engage in the activity was made, the actor (plaintiff or defendant) conducted himself with all possible skill and circumspection. . . .

The courts' inability to determine optimal activity levels except in simple cases is potentially a serious shortcoming of a negligence system. In contrast, potential injurers subject to a rule of strict liability will automatically take into account possible changes in activity level, as well as possible changes in expenditures on care, in deciding whether to prevent accidents. . . .

. . .

The problem with using this analysis to support a universal rule of strict liability is that changes in activity level by victims are also a method of accident avoidance, and one that is encouraged by negligence liability but discouraged by strict liability. . . .

Only when a class of activities can be identified in which activity-level changes by potential injurers are the most efficient method of accident prevention is there a compelling argument for imposing strict liability. Conversely, in a class of activities in which activity-level changes by potential victims are the most efficient method of accident prevention, there is a strong argument for a rule of no liability, as when the doctrine of assumption of risk is applied to participation in dangerous sports.

Through the concept of ultrahazardous activities, tort law imposes strict liability on activities that involve a high degree of danger that cannot feasibly be prevented by the actor's being careful or potential victims' altering their behavior. An example is strict liability for injuries by wild animals. If my neighbor has a pet tiger, there is little I can do (at reasonable cost) to protect myself. And there is only so much the owner can do, in the way of being careful, to keep the tiger under control. The most promising precaution may consist simply of his not having a tiger—an activity-level change. But suppose we're speaking not of a neighbor's tiger but of the zoo's. Is it likely that the best way of controlling accidents to visitors at zoos is not to have dangerous animals in zoos—just gentle ones? The social cost of this particular activity change would be prohibitive, because dangerous animals are major zoo attractions. So courts have made an exception to the rule of strict liability for injuries caused by wild animals in zoos, circuses, and other animal parks and shows. Not that strict liability would actually induce zoos not to keep dangerous animals. (Why not?) But then what point would imposing strict liability have?

Another area of strict liability for ultrahazardous activities is blasting with explosives. No matter how careful the construction company is, there will be accidents; and since construction goes on everywhere, it is unlikely that the best way to minimize these accidents is for potential victims to alter their activities. The best way may be for the companies to switch to alternative methods of demolition that are less dangerous; and strict liability gives them a financial incentive to consider such alternatives.

There is a tendency to apply the "ultrahazardous" label to any new activities (often called nonnatural), such as reservoirs in England or ballooning in early nineteenth-century America. New activities tend to be dangerous because there is little experience with coping with whatever dangers they present. For the same reason, the dangers may not be avoidable simply by taking care—yet the fact that the activities are new implies that there are good substitutes for them. Hence the best method of accident control may be to cut back on the scale of the activity—to slow its spread while more is learned about how to conduct it safely.

The distinction between care and activity is not the only dimension along which negligence and strict liability differ. Another is the relative cost of administering the two legal standards. The trial of a strict liability case is simpler than that of a negligence case because there is one less issue, negligence; and the fewer the issues, the easier it should be to settle the case without a trial. On both counts we can expect litigation costs to be lower under strict liability than under negligence— for the same number of claims. But, as in the case when comparative negligence is substituted for contributory negligence, the number may not be the same. In principle, under strict liability, every accident to which there is more than one party gives rise to a claim, not just every accident in which the defendant may have been negligent. If the accident rate in some activity will fall dramatically if strict liability is imposed, because accident costs exceed the costs of avoiding them through changes in the level of the activity, there may well be fewer claims under strict liability; and since the average cost of processing claims should be lower under strict liability, the substitution of strict liability for negligence will be an unequivocal economic gain. But if most of the accidents that occur in some activity are unavoidable in an economic sense either by taking greater care or by reducing the amount of the activity (because the costs of greater care, or less activity, exceed any savings in reduced accident costs), the main effect of switching from negligence to strict liability will be to increase the number of damages claims.

Another difference is that strict liability operates to insure victims of unavoidable accidents. It is a gain only if the cost of insurance through the tort system is less than the cost to potential victims of buying accident insurance policies in the insurance market; almost certainly it is greater. All sides of the no-fault debate agree that the tort system is a very costly method of providing insurance; the debate is over whether it provides another good, the deterrence of non-cost-justified accidents. A related point is that . . . the size of, and economic rents earned in, an industry subject to strict liability will be smaller than if the industry were subject to negligence.

Courts make mistakes; which regime—strict liability or negligence—is more robust against them? On the one hand, an erroneous finding that an injurer is not negligent cannot have misallocative consequences under strict liability, because the injurer's negligence is not an issue. On the other hand, the consequences of a mistaken ascription of causation, or an overestimation of damages, are worse under strict liability. Under negligence, a person is sanctioned only for inefficient conduct; under strict liability, he may be sanctioned for efficient conduct, and if the actual costs of that conduct are exaggerated, the conduct may be deterred. Suppose the cost of some precaution is 10, the expected accident cost under an error-free regime of strict liability is 9 (and this is the number used to determine whether failure to take the precaution is negligence), but the expected accident cost (really the expected legal-judgment cost) given errors as to causation or damages favoring plaintiffs is 11. Then the conduct will be deterred under strict liability (because $10 < 11$) but not under negligence (because $10 > 9$), unless mistakes as to causation or damages infect the determination of the standard of care.

Because of the many important differences between negligence and strict liability, we would not expect the tort system to opt all for one or all for the other. Nor would we expect the balance between the two regimes to be the same at all times. . . .

It would be a mistake, despite their differences, to dichotomize negligence and strict liability. Negligence has a strict liability component. . . . Being careful means having attitudes, acquiring skills and knowledge, etc., that reduce the probability of a careless slip but do not eliminate it; to eliminate it would require an excessive investment in care. The law, though, does not recognize "optimal negligence" (meaning what?), and it has been argued that as a result it creates a bias in favor of preventing accidents by making capital expenditures rather than by making expenditures on careful operation of existing equipment and facilities (can you see why?).[6] Does strict liability avoid this problem?

How, finally, to explain the greater role of strict liability in contract law than in tort law? The difference may reflect the greater availability of market insurance in tort cases (and hence the lesser value of providing insurance through the legal system) and the fact that contract cases are less likely than tort cases to involve an interactive mishap that either party could have prevented though possibly at very different costs. Ordinarily one of the parties to a contract is performer and the other payor. The former has complete control over performance, the latter complete control over payment. The presumption is therefore that a breach, whether in payment or performance, is preventable at lower cost by the promisor than by the promisee, or if not preventable then insurable by the former at lower cost. In contrast, most tort situations are collisions of one sort or another and there is no basis for a general presumption, such as would warrant a general rule of strict liability, that the injurer was in a better position than the victim to have prevented the collision.

NOTES AND QUESTIONS

1. Can you think of other major differences between strict liability and negligence in addition to those mentioned by Posner?

2. What empirical evidence would be useful in resolving the comparative advantages of each that he discusses? See Geistfeld, Should Enterprise Liability Replace the Rule of Strict Liability for Abnormally Dangerous Activities?, 45 UCLA L.Rev. 611, 639–45 (1998)(identifying the relevant empirical issues and using the available data to engage in a heuristic assessment finding that strict liability would be efficient only if it reduced risk by at least 20 percent relative to the level that obtains under negligence liability).

3. Posner elaborates on the activity-level rationale for strict liability made by Steven Shavell in Strict Liability Versus Negligence, 9 J.Legal Stud. 1 (1980). Posner also relied on this rationale for strict liability in *Indiana Harbor Belt*, p. 524 supra, and cited to this article. Shavell's conclusion that only strict liability can control activity-level decisions is confusing in an important respect that requires clarification. In Shavell's analysis, an "activity" is any component of risky behavior that is not regulated by negligence liability. In principle, negligence is capable of addressing all forms of risky behavior. In practice, however, negligence is rarely employed and therefore largely ineffective for regulating certain types of risky behavior due to the complexity of the care decisions and the concomitant problems of proof. Consider the decision of the defendant in *Rylands v. Fletcher*, p. 514 supra, to locate the reservoir in an area riddled with abandoned mine shafts. Was that decision unreasonable? To prove as

---

[6]   Mark F. Grady, Why Are People Negligent? Technology, Nondurable Precautions, and the Medical Malpractice Explosion, 82 Nw. U. L. Rev. 293 (1988).

much, plaintiff would have to show that defendant's manufacturing concern, which required the reservoir, could be reasonably located elsewhere. Could a plaintiff realistically prove that the cost of relocating an entire manufacturing operation would be reasonable in light of the ensuing safety benefits? If not, then the defendant's decision of where to locate the reservoir would be effectively immune from negligence liability, making it an "activity-level" decision for purposes of Shavell's analysis.

4.   Posner's defense of strict liability draws heavily on examples of "abnormally dangerous activities." Does his development of the differences between strict liability and negligence suggest that he would favor a more general limitation of strict liability to those situations? Would King's set of goals supporting strict liability suggest a limitation to abnormally dangerous activities?

5.   Would Posner subscribe to the enterprise liability rationale for strict liability discussed in the Rabin excerpt and the notes following? Which of the goals discussed by King would Posner regard as appropriate?

CHAPTER IX

LIABILITY FOR DEFECTIVE PRODUCTS

A. INTRODUCTION

No area of personal injury law has changed as dramatically in the past century as the law governing liability for defective products. Nineteenth century products liability law languished in the shadow of the privity doctrine, which required a contractual relationship between the parties as the basis for a duty of due care. As the following landmark case reveals, the privity requirement was eventually undermined by a cluster of categorical exceptions created in response to the growing influence of the negligence principle. But as we shall see, the judicial impulse to refashion the liability rules in this area was not exhausted by consolidation of the negligence principle. Instead, the courts later began to construct a system with elements of strict liability—a process that continues to lend a dynamic, and controversial, character to products liability law. The materials in this section, then, provide an excellent opportunity for exploring the fundamental compensation and deterrence issues underlying these different forms of tort liability. At the same time, products liability is of particular interest because of the interplay between contract and tort law in shaping the approach to the subject.

MacPherson v. Buick Motor Co.
Court of Appeals of New York, 1916.
217 N.Y. 382, 111 N.E. 1050.

Appeal, by permission, from a judgment of the Appellate Division . . . affirming a judgment in favor of plaintiff entered upon a verdict.

■ CARDOZO, J.

The defendant is a manufacturer of automobiles. It sold an automobile to a retail dealer. The retail dealer resold to the plaintiff. While the plaintiff was in the car, it suddenly collapsed. He was thrown out and injured. One of the wheels was made of defective wood, and its spokes crumbled into fragments. The wheel was not made by the defendant; it was bought from another manufacturer. There is evidence, however, that its defects could have been discovered by reasonable inspection, and that inspection was omitted. There is no claim that the defendant knew of the defect and willfully concealed it. The case, in other words, is not brought within the rule of Kuelling v. Roderick Lean Mfg. Co., [75 N.E. 1098 (N.Y.1905)]. The charge is one, not of fraud, but of negligence. The question to be determined is whether the defendant owed a duty of care and vigilance to any one but the immediate purchaser.

The foundations of this branch of the law, at least in this state, were laid in Thomas v. Winchester (6 N.Y. 397 [1852]). A poison was falsely labeled. The sale was made to a druggist, who in turn sold to a customer. The customer recovered damages from the seller who affixed the label. "The defendant's negligence," it was said, "put human life in imminent danger." A poison falsely labeled is likely to injure any one who gets it. Because the danger is to be foreseen, there is a duty to avoid the injury. Cases were cited by way of illustration in which manufacturers were not subject to any duty irrespective of contract. The distinction was said to be that their conduct, though negligent, was not likely to result in injury to any one except the purchaser. We are not required to say whether the chance of injury was always as remote as the distinction assumes. Some of the illustrations might be rejected today. The principle of the distinction is for present purposes the important thing.

Thomas v. Winchester became quickly a landmark of the law. In the application of its principle there may at times have been uncertainty or even error. There has never in this state been doubt or disavowal of the principle itself. The chief cases are well known, yet to recall some of them will be helpful. Loop v. Litchfield (42 N.Y. 351 [1870]) is the earliest. It was the case of a defect in a small balance wheel used on a circular saw. The manufacturer pointed out the defect to the buyer, who wished a cheap article and was ready to assume the risk. The risk can hardly have been an imminent one for the wheel lasted five years before it broke. In the meanwhile the buyer had made a lease of the machinery. It was held that the manufacturer was not answerable to the lessee. *Loop v. Litchfield* was followed in Losee v. Clute (51 N.Y. 494 [1873]), the case of the explosion of a steam boiler. That decision has been criticized [ ]; but it must be confined to its special facts. It was put upon the ground that the risk of injury was too remote. The buyer in that case had not only accepted the boiler, but had tested it. The manufacturer knew that his own test was not the final one. The finality of the test has a bearing on the measure of diligence owing to persons other than the purchaser [ ].

These early cases suggest a narrow construction of the rule. Later cases, however, evince a more liberal spirit. First in importance is Devlin v. Smith (89 N.Y. 470 [1882]). The defendant, a contractor, built a scaffold for a painter. The painter's servants were injured. The contractor was held liable. He knew that the scaffold, if improperly constructed, was a most dangerous trap. He knew that it was to be used by the workmen. He was building it for that very purpose. Building it for their use, he owed them a duty, irrespective of his contract with their master, to build it with care.

From *Devlin v. Smith* we pass over intermediate cases and turn to the latest case in this court in which *Thomas v. Winchester* was followed. That case is Statler v. George A. Ray Mfg. Co., [88 N.E. 1063 (N.Y.1909)]. The defendant manufactured a large coffee urn. It was installed in a restaurant. When heated, the urn exploded and injured the plaintiff. We held that the manufacturer was liable. We said that the urn "was of such a character inherently that, when applied to the purposes for which it was designed, it was liable to become a source of great danger to many people if not carefully and properly constructed."

It may be that *Devlin v. Smith* and *Statler v. George A. Ray Mfg. Co.* have extended the rule of *Thomas v. Winchester*. If so, this court is committed to the extension. The defendant argues that things imminently dangerous to life are poisons, explosives, deadly weapons— things whose normal function it is to injure or destroy. But whatever the rule in *Thomas v. Winchester* may once have been, it has no longer that restricted meaning. A scaffold [*Devlin v. Smith*], is not inherently a destructive instrument. It becomes destructive only if imperfectly constructed. A large coffee urn [*Statler*] may have within itself, if negligently made, the potency of danger, yet no one thinks of it as an implement whose normal function is destruction. What is true of the coffee urn is equally true of bottles of aerated water (Torgesen v. Schultz, [84 N.E. 956 (N.Y.1908)]).

. . .

We hold, then, that the principle of *Thomas v. Winchester* is not limited to poisons, explosives, and things of like nature, to things which in their normal operation are implements of destruction. If the nature of a thing is such that it is reasonably certain to place life and limb in peril when negligently made, it is then a thing of danger. Its nature gives warning of the consequences to be expected. If to the element of danger there is added knowledge that the thing will be used by persons other than the purchaser, and used without new tests, then, irrespective of contract, the manufacturer of this thing of danger is under a duty to make it carefully. That is as far as we are required to go for the decision of this case. There must be knowledge of a danger, not merely possible, but probable. It is possible to use almost anything in a way that will make it dangerous if defective. That is not enough to charge the manufacturer with a duty independent of his contract. Whether a given thing is dangerous may be sometimes a question for the court and sometimes a question for the jury. There must also be knowledge that in the usual course of events the danger will be shared by others than the buyer. Such knowledge may often be inferred from the nature of the transaction. But it is possible that even knowledge of the danger and of the use will not always be enough. The proximity or remoteness of the relation is a factor to be considered. We are dealing now with the liability of the manufacturer of the finished product, who puts it on the market to be used without inspection by his customers. If he is negligent, where danger is to be foreseen, a liability will follow. We are not required at this time to say that it is legitimate to go back of the manufacturer of the finished product and hold the manufacturers of the component parts. To make their negligence a cause of imminent danger, an independent cause must often intervene; the manufacturer of the finished product must also fail in his duty of inspection. It may be that in those circumstances the negligence of the earlier members of the series is too remote to constitute, as to the ultimate user, an actionable wrong [ ]. We leave that question open. We shall have to deal with it when it arises. The difficulty which it suggests is not present in this case. There is here no break in the chain of cause and effect. In such circumstances, the presence of a known danger, attendant upon a known use, makes vigilance a duty. We have put aside the notion that the duty to safeguard life and limb, when the consequences of negligence may be foreseen, grows out of contract and nothing else. We have put the source of the obligation where it ought to be. We have put its source in the law.

From this survey of the decisions, there thus emerges a definition of the duty of a manufacturer which enables us to measure this defendant's liability. Beyond all question, the nature of an automobile gives warning of probable danger if its construction is defective. This automobile was designed to go fifty miles an hour. Unless its wheels were sound and strong, injury was almost certain. It was as much a thing of danger as a defective engine for a railroad. The defendant knew the danger. It knew also that the car would be used by persons other than the buyer. This was apparent from its size; there were seats for three persons. It was apparent also from the fact that the buyer was a dealer in cars, who bought to resell. The maker of this car supplied it for the use of purchasers from the dealer just as plainly as the contractor in *Devlin v. Smith* supplied the scaffold for use by the servants of the owner. The dealer was indeed the one person of whom it might be said with some approach to certainty that by him the car would not be used. Yet the defendant would have us say that he was the one person whom it was under a legal duty to protect. The law does not lead us to so inconsequent a conclusion. Precedents drawn from the days of travel by stage coach do not fit the conditions of travel today. The principle that the danger must be imminent does not change, but the things subject to the principle do change. They are whatever the needs of life in a developing civilization require them to be.

. . .

In England the limits of the rule are still unsettled. Winterbottom v. Wright (10 M. & W. 109) [1842] is often cited. The defendant undertook to provide a mail coach to carry the mail bags. The coach broke down from latent defects in its construction. The defendant, however, was not the manufacturer. The court held that he was not liable for injuries to a passenger. . . .

There is nothing anomalous in a rule which imposes upon A, who has contracted with B, a duty to C and D and others according as he knows or does not know that the subject-matter of the contract is intended for their use. We may find an analogy in the law which measures the liability of landlords. If A leases to B a tumble-down house he is not liable, in the absence of fraud, to B's guests who enter it and are injured. This is because B is then under the duty to repair it, the lessor has the right to suppose that he will fulfill that duty, and, if he omits to do so, his guests must look to him [ ]. But if A leases a building to be used by the lessee at once as a place of public entertainment, the rule is different. There injury to persons other than the lessee is to be foreseen, and foresight of the consequences involves the creation of a duty [ ].

. . .

We think the defendant was not absolved from a duty of inspection because it bought the wheels from a reputable manufacturer. It was not merely a dealer in automobiles. It was a manufacturer of automobiles. It was responsible for the finished product. It was not at liberty to put the finished product on the market without subjecting the component parts to ordinary and simple tests [ ]. Under the charge of the trial judge nothing more was required of it. The obligation to inspect must vary with the nature of the thing to be inspected. The more probable the danger, the greater the need of caution. There is little analogy between this case and Carlson v. Phenix Bridge Co., [30 N.E. 750 (N.Y.1892)], where the defendant bought a tool for a servant's use. The making of tools was not the business in which the master was engaged. Reliance on the skill of the manufacturer was proper and almost inevitable. But that is not the defendant's situation. Both by its relation to the work and by the nature of its business, it is charged with a stricter duty.

Other rulings complained of have been considered, but no error has been found in them.

The judgment should be affirmed with costs.

■ HISCOCK, CHASE and CUDDEBACK, JJ., concur with CARDOZO, J., and HOGAN, J., concurs in result; WILLARD BARTLETT, CH. J., reads dissenting opinion; POUND, J., not voting.

[The dissenting opinion stressed that the earlier cases could all be explained by the "inherently dangerous" analysis and that the court should not go beyond that formulation.]

NOTES AND QUESTIONS

1. *The privity requirement.* Earlier analyses had understood the English case of *Winterbottom v. Wright* to stand for the proposition that manufacturers, suppliers, and repairers of chattels could be liable for their negligence only to those with whom they had contracted. In that case, Lord Abinger had stated:

> There is no privity of contract between these parties; and if the plaintiff can sue, every passenger, or even any person passing along the road, who was injured by the upsetting of the coach, might bring a similar action. Unless we confine the operation of such contracts as this to the parties who entered into them, the most absurd and outrageous consequences, to which I can see no limit, would ensue.

How might Judge Cardozo respond to that assertion?

2.   *Winterbottom* was decided shortly before the writ system was abolished in the mid-nineteenth century. Eliminating the writ system did not render the prior case law irrelevant, and courts continued to require privity in a negligence action unless the case fell into one of the previously recognized exceptions involving products that were "inherently dangerous" or otherwise placed human life in "imminent danger." This inquiry forced the courts to confront a difficult issue: How to determine whether a product was "imminently or inherently dangerous" and not subject to the privity requirement, as distinguished from defective products like the coach in *Winterbottom* that were not exempted from this requirement. Based on Judge Cardozo's survey of the case law, do you think that the courts had adequately answered this question? Did he think that this was the proper question for resolving the issue of duty for a product manufacturer? According to his analysis, what is the attribute of the product that creates a tort duty?

3.   Assess the meaning and significance of Judge Cardozo's statement that "We have put the source of the obligation where it ought to be. We have put its source in the law."

4.   *Extending the duty.* What arguments might justify imposing a duty on Buick but not on the wheel manufacturer? In Smith v. Peerless Glass Co., 181 N.E. 576 (N.Y.1932), a soda bottle exploded and hurt plaintiff. The court treated the bottle maker as the manufacturer of a component part and brought it within the *MacPherson* principle.

The doctrine of *MacPherson* came to be accepted generally throughout the United States. It covered injuries to bystanders including pedestrians hurt by a careening car or tire, property damage, cases where damage was not "reasonably certain," and the duty of repairers as well as manufacturers. Other developments included treating a retailer who sold a product under its own brand name as though it were the manufacturer, and thus holding it liable for negligent manufacture. Also, manufacturers who incorporated component parts in the final product were held liable for the negligence of the subcontractors. Eventually, courts began holding architects and builders liable for negligence in construction that hurt patrons or tenants. As per *MacPherson*, the courts in these cases based the duty on the foreseeable risk of physical harm posed by a defect in the product.

5.   *Development of negligence liability.* After *MacPherson*, the plaintiff in a tort suit had to show that the defect was attributable to negligence by the defendant seller. To establish negligence, plaintiffs frequently invoked the evidentiary doctrine of res ipsa loquitur, discussed on p. 93 supra. In effect, the plaintiff argued that the mere existence of the defect establishes negligence on someone's part. The plaintiff then had to show that the defendant, rather than someone else, was responsible for the defect. This argument was extraordinarily successful. "[O]nce the cause of the injury is proved to lie with the defendant, once it is brought home to his plant, the jury finds for the plaintiff." Prosser, The Assault Upon the Citadel (Strict Liability to the Consumer), 69 Yale L.J. 1099, 1115 (1960). Is this a proper application of res ipsa loquitur?

   6. *Warranty development.* As courts were extending *MacPherson*, they also developed an alternative approach based on the implied warranty of merchantability or quality. According to this doctrine, the nature of a sales transaction implies certain duties or responsibilities on the seller's part and a corresponding set of rights held by the buyer. Because the duties and rights spring from the sales transaction, the implied warranty appears to be a rule of contract law. Such a contractual understanding of the doctrine was held by courts and lawyers in the mid-nineteenth century, and a contractual conceptualization of the implied warranty fit well with the privity requirement adopted by *Winterbottom*. The implied warranty, however, was originally a tort doctrine. Consider Ryan v. Progressive Grocery Stores, Inc., 175 N.E. 105 (N.Y.1931), in which plaintiff was seriously injured when he swallowed a pin embedded in a slice of the bread that his wife had purchased from defendant. This sales transaction implied certain things about the bread, including a valid title and the product's ability to perform safely its intended function. These implied representations created reasonable expectations concerning material facts—the plaintiffs reasonably expected to own a loaf of edible bread. The seller would frustrate these reasonable expectations either by not conveying valid title to the bread (defect of title) or by conveying bread that was not fit for human consumption (defect of quality), regardless of whether the seller exercised reasonable care. If either type of defect caused injury to the consumer, the seller had completed a tort—the consumer was foreseeably injured by reasonably relying on the seller's misrepresentation of a material fact. Hence, "[t]he warranty of title stood anciently upon the same footing as the warranty of quality." The footing was in tort. Ames, The History of Assumpsit, 2 Harv.L.Rev. 1, 10 (1888).

   The tort rationale for the implied warranty remained obscure until courts in the early twentieth century invoked the doctrine to apply strict tort liability to the sale of contaminated food, an issue of pressing national concern. The courts looked to the ancient English rule that strictly obligated sellers to supply "wholesome" food. This doctrine had existed for centuries before *Winterbottom* was decided, but the doctrine had only been applied to cases involving buyers and sellers and appeared to fit comfortably with the *Winterbottom* privity requirement. However, the nature of the food cases made it easier to conceptualize the implied warranty as a matter of tort law, leading courts to impose strict liability upon the seller of contaminated food. See, e.g., Jacob E. Decker & Sons, Inc. v. Capps, 164 S.W.2d 828, 829 (Tex.1942)("A majority of the American courts that have followed this holding have not based such warranty upon an implied term in the contract between buyer and seller, . . . but have imposed it as a matter of public policy in order to discourage the sale of unwholesome food.").

In efforts to permit warranty recoveries, courts resorted to many devices to avoid the lack-of-privity barrier. One author catalogued 29 theories used to achieve the result, mostly in food cases. Gillam, Products Liability in a Nutshell, 37 Or.L.Rev. 119, 153–55 (1957). As a tort doctrine, is the implied warranty inherently limited by the privity requirement? Does it only apply to contaminated food?

7.   Would the tort version of the implied warranty improve upon the negligence-based approach following *MacPherson* that relied almost exclusively on the evidentiary doctrine of res ipsa loquitur? Consider this question in the context of the next case.

Escola v. Coca Cola Bottling Co. of Fresno

Supreme Court of California, 1944.
24 Cal.2d 453, 150 P.2d 436.

■ GIBSON, CHIEF JUSTICE.

[Plaintiff, a waitress, was injured when a soda bottle broke in her hand as she moved it from the case to the refrigerator. She testified that she had handled it carefully. The defendant bottler used pressure to bottle carbonated beverages. An engineer from the bottle manufacturer (which was not sued) testified at the trial about how bottles are tested and called these tests "pretty near" infallible. The majority affirmed a plaintiff's judgment and held that plaintiff had properly benefited from res ipsa loquitur in her negligence action. The following three paragraphs give the flavor of the majority opinion.]

It thus appears that there is available to the industry a commonly used method of testing bottles for defects not apparent to the eye, which is almost infallible. Since Coca Cola bottles are subjected to these tests by the manufacturer, it is not likely that they contain defects when delivered to the bottler which are not discoverable by visual inspection. Both new and used bottles are filled and distributed by defendant. The used bottles are not again subjected to the tests referred to above, and it may be inferred that defects not discoverable by visual inspection do not develop in bottles after they are manufactured. Obviously, if such defects do occur in used bottles there is a duty upon the bottler to make appropriate tests before they are refilled, and if such tests are not commercially practicable the bottles should not be re-used. This would seem to be particularly true where a charged liquid is placed in the bottle. It follows that a defect which would make the bottle unsound could be discovered by reasonable and practicable tests.

Although it is not clear in this case whether the explosion was caused by an excessive charge or a defect in the glass, there is a sufficient showing that neither cause would ordinarily have been present if due care had been used. Further, defendant had exclusive control over both the charging and inspection of the bottles. Accordingly, all the requirements necessary to entitle plaintiff to rely on the doctrine of res ipsa loquitur to supply an inference of negligence are present.

It is true that defendant presented evidence tending to show that it exercised considerable precaution by carefully regulating and checking the pressure in the bottles and by making visual inspections for defects in the glass at several stages during the bottling process. It is well settled, however, that when a defendant produces evidence to rebut the inference of negligence which arises upon application of the doctrine of res ipsa loquitur, it is ordinarily a question of fact for the jury to determine whether the inference has been dispelled.

[One justice concurred separately.]

■ TRAYNOR, J.

I concur in the judgment, but I believe the manufacturer's negligence should no longer be singled out as the basis of a plaintiff's right to recover in cases like the present one. In my opinion it should now be recognized that a manufacturer incurs an absolute liability when an article that he has placed on the market, knowing that it is to be used without inspection, proves to have a defect that causes injury to human beings. [*MacPherson v. Buick Motor Co.*] established the principle, recognized by this court, that irrespective of privity of contract, the manufacturer is responsible for an injury caused by such an article to any person who comes in lawful contact with it. [ ] In these cases the source of the manufacturer's liability was his negligence in the manufacturing process or in the inspection of component parts supplied by others. Even if there is no negligence, however, public policy demands that responsibility be fixed wherever it will most effectively reduce the hazards to life and health inherent in defective products that reach the market. It is evident that the manufacturer can anticipate some hazards and guard against the recurrence of others, as the public cannot. Those who suffer injury from defective products are unprepared to meet its consequences. The cost of an injury and the loss of time or health may be an overwhelming misfortune to the person injured, and a needless one, for the risk of injury can be insured by the manufacturer and distributed among the public as a cost of doing business. It is to the public interest to discourage the marketing of products having defects that are a menace to the public. If such products nevertheless find their way into the market it is to the public interest to place the responsibility for whatever injury they may cause upon the manufacturer, who, even if he is not negligent in the manufacture of the product, is responsible for its reaching the market. However intermittently such injuries may occur and however haphazardly they may strike, the risk of their occurrence is a constant risk and a general one. Against such a risk there should be general and constant protection and the manufacturer is best situated to afford such protection.

The injury from a defective product does not become a matter of indifference because the defect arises from causes other than the negligence of the manufacturer, such as negligence of a submanufacturer of a component part whose defects could not be revealed by inspection [ ] or unknown causes that even by the device of res ipsa loquitur cannot be classified as negligence of the manufacturer. The inference of negligence may be dispelled by an affirmative showing of proper care. If the evidence against the fact inferred is "clear, positive, uncontradicted, and of such a nature that it cannot rationally be disbelieved, the court must instruct the jury that the nonexistence of the fact has been established as a matter of law." (Blank v. Coffin, [126 P.2d 868 (Cal.1942)].) An injured person, however, is not ordinarily in a position to refute such evidence or identify the cause of the defect, for he can hardly be familiar with the manufacturing process as the manufacturer himself is. In leaving it to the jury to decide whether the inference has been dispelled, regardless of the evidence against it, the negligence rule approaches the rule of strict liability. It is needlessly circuitous to make negligence the basis of recovery and impose what is in reality liability without negligence. If public policy demands that a manufacturer of goods be responsible for their quality regardless of negligence there is no reason not to fix that responsibility openly.

. . .

The retailer, even though not equipped to test a product, is under an absolute liability to his customer, for the implied warranties of fitness for proposed use and merchantable quality include a warranty of safety of the product. [ ] This warranty is not necessarily a contractual one [ ], for public policy requires that the buyer be insured at the seller's expense against injury. [ ] The courts recognize, however, that the retailer cannot bear the burden of this warranty, and allow him to recoup any losses by means of the warranty of safety attending the wholesaler's or manufacturer's sale to him. [ ] Such a procedure, however, is needlessly circuitous and engenders wasteful litigation. Much would be gained if the injured person could base his action directly on the manufacturer's warranty.

The liability of the manufacturer to an immediate buyer injured by a defective product follows without proof of negligence from the implied warranty of safety attending the sale. Ordinarily, however, the immediate buyer is a dealer who does not intend to use the product himself, and if the warranty of safety is to serve the purpose of protecting health and safety it must give rights to others than the dealer. In the words of Judge Cardozo in the *MacPherson* case: "The dealer was indeed the one person of whom it might be said with some approach to certainty that by him the car would not be used. Yet, the defendant would have us say that he was the one person whom it was under a legal duty to protect. The law does not lead us to so inconsequent a solution." While the defendant's negligence in the *MacPherson* case made it unnecessary for the court to base liability on warranty, Judge Cardozo's reasoning recognized the injured person as the real party in interest and effectively disposed of the theory that the liability of the manufacturer incurred by his warranty should apply only to the immediate purchaser. It thus paves the way for a standard of liability that would make the manufacturer guarantee the safety of his product even when there is no negligence.

This court and many others have extended protection according to such a standard to consumers of food products, taking the view that the right of a consumer injured by unwholesome food does not depend "upon the intricacies of the law of sales" and that the warranty of the manufacturer to the consumer in absence of privity of contract rests on public policy. [ ] Dangers to life and health inhere in other consumers' goods that are defective and there is no reason to differentiate them from the dangers of defective food products. [ ]

In the food products cases the courts have resorted to various fictions to rationalize the extension of the manufacturer's warranty to the consumer: that a warranty runs with the chattel; that the cause of action of the dealer is assigned to the consumer; that the consumer is a third party beneficiary of the manufacturer's contract with the dealer. They have also held the manufacturer liable on a mere fiction of negligence: "Practically he must know it [the product] is fit, or bear the consequences if it proves destructive." [ ] Such fictions are not necessary to fix the manufacturer's liability under a warranty if the warranty is severed from the contract of sale between the dealer and the consumer and based on the law of torts [ ] as a strict liability. [ ] Warranties are not necessarily rights arising under a contract. An action on a warranty "was, in its origin, a pure action of tort," and only late in the historical development of warranties was an action in assumpsit allowed. (Ames, The History of Assumpsit, 2 Harv.L.Rev. 1, 8; 4 Williston on Contracts (1936) § 970.) . . .

As handicrafts have been replaced by mass production with its great markets and transportation facilities, the close relationship between the producer and consumer of a product has been altered. Manufacturing processes, frequently valuable secrets, are ordinarily either inaccessible to or beyond the ken of the general public. The consumer no longer has means or skill enough to investigate for himself the soundness of a product, even when it is not contained in a sealed package, and his erstwhile vigilance has been lulled by the steady efforts of manufacturers to build up confidence by advertising and marketing devices such as trade marks. [ ] Consumers no longer approach products warily but accept them on faith, relying on the reputation of the manufacturer or the trade mark. [ ] Manufacturers have sought to justify that faith by increasingly high standards of inspection and a readiness to make good on defective products by way of replacements and refunds. [ ] The manufacturer's obligation to the consumer must keep pace with the changing relationship between them; it cannot be escaped because the marketing of a product has become so complicated as to require one or more intermediaries. Certainly there is greater reason to impose liability on the manufacturer than on the retailer who is but a conduit of a product that he is not himself able to test.

The manufacturer's liability should, of course, be defined in terms of the safety of the product in normal and proper use, and should not extend to injuries that cannot be traced to the product as it reached the market.

NOTES AND QUESTIONS

1.   What were the majority's justifications for employing res ipsa loquitur to affirm the jury verdict? Are they persuasive? Consider the possibility that a recycled bottle contained a hairline fracture that caused the bottle to explode. Is the majority correct that if there were no "commercially practicable" test for identifying such defects, then "the bottles should not be re-used"? Does the exercise of reasonable care require the wholesale elimination of risk? What were Justice Traynor's objections to the use of res ipsa loquitur? In his view, if the doctrine were applied properly, what would be the outcome in cases like *Escola*?

2.   Consider separately each sentence in the first paragraph of Justice Traynor's opinion. What justifications for strict liability are presented? Are other justifications presented elsewhere in the opinion?

3.   How does *MacPherson* support Justice Traynor's theory of liability? After *MacPherson*, the tort duty was no longer based on the intrinsic properties of the product (was it inherently dangerous?), but instead depended on whether a defect created a foreseeable risk of physical harm. Does this holding have implications for the rule that limited the implied warranty to food cases? Compare Llewellyn, On Warranty of Quality, and Society: II, 37 Colum.L.Rev. 341, 404–05 (1937)("This is not a question of food. This is a question of consumer. Of helpless consumer. . . . [A] gathering of some hundred cases, from 1850 to [1937] . . . demonstrate that food and drink, in part, were only typical of a general trend.").

4.   Warranty doctrine as a basis for strict tort liability was not fully separated from the food cases until the 1960 decision in Henningsen v. Bloomfield Motors, Inc., 161 A.2d 69 (N.J.1960). A defect in the steering mechanism of a recently acquired Plymouth caused the car to spin out of control, seriously injuring plaintiff driver. Echoing Justice Traynor's language in *Escola*, the court held that

> under modern marketing conditions, when a manufacturer puts a new automobile in the stream of trade and promotes its purchase by the public, an implied warranty that it is reasonably suitable

for use as such accompanies it into the hands of the ultimate purchaser. Absence of agency between the manufacturer and the dealer who makes the ultimate sale is immaterial.

For related reasons, the court struck down express disclaimers limiting liability that were "imposed upon the automobile consumer" in "a standardized form designed for mass use" as contrary to public policy.

For the moment, it appeared that the move beyond negligence to strict liability might be grounded in warranty, rather than the tort theory urged by Traynor. The common law tort version of the implied warranty had been codified in the Uniform Sales Act and then in the Uniform Commercial Code (UCC), which eliminates some ordinary contractual defenses involving privity.* The UCC might have become the primary source of liability for defective products. See the classic contemporaneous article, Prosser, The Assault on the Citadel, 69 Yale L.J. 1099 (1960). But Traynor was to have the final word on this issue.

5. *Subsequent California developments.* Beginning in the early 1960s, a series of California decisions foreshadowed similar developments in other jurisdictions that have now become accepted by the overwhelming majority of states.

a. *Majority acceptance of* Escola. Greenman v. Yuba Power Products, Inc., 377 P.2d 897 (Cal.1963). Following his concurrence in *Escola*, Justice Traynor continued to argue for strict liability in a series of other cases. In *Greenman*, he finally persuaded the entire court in a ruling that affirmed plaintiff's judgment against defendant manufacturer. While using a lathe in the manner intended by defendant manufacturer, plaintiff was hurt when a piece of wood flew up and struck him in the forehead. Experts had testified that the lathe was of defective design and manufacture because the set screws were inadequate to hold the wood. As in *Escola*, none of the parties had made an argument concerning strict liability. Three new justices had been appointed to the court since *Escola*, but the three remaining members accepted Justice Traynor's position despite their earlier refusal to do so. Writing for a unanimous court, Traynor stated: "We need not recanvass the reasons for imposing strict liability on the manufacturer. They have been fully articulated. . . ."

b. *Retailers.* Vandermark v. Ford Motor Co., 391 P.2d 168 (Cal.1964). Plaintiff bought a new Ford from defendant retailer. The brakes soon locked, pulling the car to the right and into a pole, hurting plaintiff and his sister, who also sued the retailer. Expert testimony suggested that the defect was not caused by the retailer but by a wrong-sized part or

---

* The UCC relaxes the privity requirement only with respect to "horizontal privity"— that is, extensions beyond the immediate purchaser to other product users. The UCC drafters offered three versions of § 2–318 from which the states were to pick one. Under all three versions of § 2–318, whatever warranties the seller does extend with the product are extended to certain classes of people who may reasonably be expected to "use, consume or be affected by the goods." Version A extends the warranties to "any natural person who is in the family or household of his buyer or who is a guest in his home . . . who is injured in person. . . ." Version B extends to "any natural person . . . who is injured in person. . . ." Version C extends to "any person . . . who is injured. . . ." Most state legislatures adopted Version A, but in some of these states the courts considered themselves free to expand such protection.

improper assembly or adjustment during the manufacturing process. In the landmark opinion that first applied strict products liability to non-manufacturing retailers and distributors, Justice Traynor justified strict liability in terms of its ability to promote product safety:

> In some cases the retailer may be the only member of [the overall producing and marketing] enterprise reasonably available to the injured plaintiff. In other cases the retailer himself may play a substantial part in insuring that the product is safe or may be in a position to exert pressure on the manufacturer to that end; the retailer's strict liability thus serves as an added incentive to safety. Strict liability on the manufacturer and retailer alike affords maximum protection to the injured plaintiff and works no injustice to the defendants, for they can adjust the costs of such protection between them in the course of their continuing business relationship.

Id. at 171–72. The court then held that contractual disclaimers of this tort duty are unenforceable: "Regardless of the obligations [defendant] assumed by contract, it is subject to strict liability in tort because it is in the business of selling automobiles, one of which proved to be defective and caused injury to human beings." Id. at 172.

       c.   *Bystanders.* Elmore v. American Motors Corp., 451 P.2d 84 (Cal.1969). Plaintiff Elmore purchased a new Rambler manufactured by one defendant and sold by the other. It veered across the road and into the oncoming car of Waters. Occupants of both cars were either hurt or killed and suits were brought against both defendants. In one of the first opinions to address the issue of whether the tort duty is limited to consumers or instead extends to bystanders, the *Elmore* court observed that bystanders such as Waters were entitled to the same strict liability protections as those in the Elmore car:

> If anything, bystanders should be entitled to greater protection than the consumer or user where injury to bystanders from the defect is reasonably foreseeable. Consumers and users, at least, have the opportunity to inspect for defects and to limit their purchases to articles manufactured by reputable manufacturers and sold by reputable retailers, whereas the bystander ordinarily has no such opportunities. . . .
>
> An automobile with a defectively connected drive shaft constitutes a substantial hazard on the highway not only to the driver and passenger of the car but also to pedestrians and other drivers. The public policy which protects the driver and passenger of the car should also protect the bystander, and where a driver or passenger of another car is injured due to defects in the manufacture of an automobile and without any fault of their own, they may recover from the manufacturer of the defective automobile.

Id. at 89. Finally, for the reasons suggested in *Vandermark*, the court concluded that the retailer was liable to bystanders as well as customers.

6. *Extension to other types of defendants.* Courts have had to determine whether strict liability extends to persons other than commercial sellers of new goods.

a. *Used-goods sellers.* Most courts have declined to impose strict liability on sellers of used goods—even for claims that the product contained the defect when it was first marketed. In Tillman v. Vance Equipment Co., 596 P.2d 1299 (Or.1979), the court noted that of its three reasons for strict liability—spreading the risk, satisfying reasonable buyer expectations, and risk reduction—only the first applied to dealers in used products. The second did not apply because these sellers generally make no particular representations about the quality of their goods. The third did not apply because these dealers have no direct relationship to the manufacturers or distributors of the goods. Providing an adequate remedy for the victim "cannot provide the sole justification for imposing liability without fault on a particular class of defendants." What does this rule imply about the loss-spreading rationale for strict liability? See Brody v. Overlook Hospital, 317 A.2d 392, 398 (N.J.App.1974)(recognizing that the "loss spreading" rationale provides "only the part of a makeweight argument" in favor of strict liability).

Even if a used goods seller is not subject to strict liability, it can be liable for negligence. In Wilke v. Woodhouse Ford, Inc., 774 N.W.2d 370 (Neb.2009), the court held that "a commercial dealer of used vehicles has a duty to conduct a reasonable inspection of the vehicle prior to sale in order to determine whether there are any patent defects which would make the vehicle unsafe for ordinary operation." The *Wilke* principle is applicable across many other products liability contexts—even if a seller or other product distributor is not subject to strict liability, it may be liable for negligence.

b. *Successors.* A question that overlaps the law of torts and corporations involves the liability of successor corporations for defective products marketed by businesses before they were bought by the successor. The Restatement (Third) of Torts: Products Liability section 12 adopts the traditional approach to successor liability, imposing liability on the successor if the acquisition "(a) is accompanied by an agreement for the successor to assume such liability; or (b) results from a fraudulent conveyance to escape liability for the debts or liabilities of the predecessor; or (c) constitutes a consolidation or merger with the predecessor; or (d) results in the successor becoming a continuation of the predecessor." Several courts, beginning with the California Supreme Court in Ray v. Alad Corp., 560 P.2d 3 (Cal.1977), adopted more expansive theories of liability for successors who acquired all of the assets of a predecessor for cash. More typical of recent decisions, however, is the Court of Appeals in Semenetz v. Sherling & Walden, Inc., 851 N.E.2d 1170 (N.Y.2006), which declined to adopt a product line exception—the same expansive theory adopted in *Ray*—to the traditional successor liability rules. The court was concerned that if successors were liable for the predecessor's torts, the market for small businesses would dry up, and those businesses would be forced to sell their assets piecemeal and then dissolve, thereby reducing the number of small businesses. See generally Cupp, Redesigning Successor Liability, 1999 U.Ill.L.Rev. 845 (arguing in favor of common law expansion of successor liability); Green, Successor Liability: The Superiority of Statutory Reform to Protect Products Liability Claimants, 72 Cornell L.Rev. 17 (1986)(contending that the common law is not well situated to solve the problem of manufacturers that sell their assets, distribute the proceeds, and become unavailable to respond to injured consumers and that a preferable solution lies in legislative action); Matheson, Successor Liability, 96 Minn.L.Rev. 371, 373–74 (2011)(characterizing the current law on successor liability as the "worst of all possible worlds" and proposing a federal statutory solution that would limit successor liability to "a transfer of substantially all assets" between the predecessor and successor companies).

c.	*Other nonsellers*. Strict liability has been extended beyond pure commercial "sellers" to include a wide variety of suppliers and those who aid suppliers, including commercial lessors. Price v. Shell Oil Co., 466 P.2d 722 (Cal.1970). Some courts have extended the doctrine to franchisors who impose quality control upon their franchisees. See Kosters v. Seven-Up Co., 595 F.2d 347 (6th Cir.1979)(imposing strict liability on the franchisor for the franchisee's defective design of a carton for carrying soda bottles where the franchisor had consented to the use of that type of carton). Strict liability has been imposed on commercial sellers who give products away or provide free samples as part of a promotion. See McKisson v. Sales Affiliates, Inc., 416 S.W.2d 787 (Tex.1967)(strict liability for breach of warranty, despite absence of sale). On the other hand, courts have been reluctant to apply the doctrine to companies that finance purchases by others. See, e.g., Nath v. National Equipment Leasing Corp., 439 A.2d 633 (Pa.1981)(refusing to apply strict liability in a suit by a worker whose hand was injured in the machine his employer had financed through defendant).

d.	*Irregular sellers*. Strict liability has been limited to sellers who were in the business of selling the product involved. In Sprung v. MTR Ravensburg Inc., 788 N.E.2d 620 (N.Y.2003), plaintiff sued the custom fabricator of a retractable floor installed in a large turbine assembly plant where plaintiff was employed. When trying to open the doors of the retractable floor from a pit below it, two panels of the floor came out of their enclosure and fell on plaintiff, injuring him. Although this was the defendant's only sale of such a retractable floor, the court held that the defendant was subject to strict liability as it was in the business of designing and constructing custom sheet-metal products.

7.	*Existence of defect at time of sale or commercial distribution*. In Welge v. Planters Lifesavers Co., 17 F.3d 209, 212 (7th Cir.1994), plaintiff was hurt when a glass jar of peanuts shattered as he tried to re-fasten its plastic lid. The fragments of the jar were preserved and the experts agreed that it "must have contained a defect but they could not find the fracture that had precipitated the shattering of the jar and they could not figure out when the defect . . . had come into being." The case revolved around efforts to identify when the defect developed in the jar: Was it before or after the retail sale? Defendants—K-Mart, the retailer; Planters who filled the jar;

and the jar manufacturer—argued that actions of the plaintiff or others after the sale had created the weakness, and so the product was not defective when sold by any of the defendants. Plaintiff's evidence suggested that nothing untoward had occurred to the jar after purchase by Karen Godfrey, the person with whom plaintiff boarded. The court concluded that summary judgment against plaintiff was inappropriate:

> The question is when the defect was introduced. It could have been at any time from the manufacture of the glass jar . . . to moments before the accident. But testimony by Welge and Karen Godfrey, if believed—and at this stage in the proceedings we are required to believe it—excludes all reasonable possibility that the defect was introduced into the jar after Godfrey plucked it from a shelf in the K-Mart store. From the shelf she put it in her shopping cart. The checker at the check-out counter scanned the bar code without banging the jar. She then placed the jar in a plastic bag. Godfrey carried the bag to her car and put it on the floor. She drove directly home, without incident. After the bar-code portion of the label was removed, the jar sat on top of the refrigerator except for the two times Welge removed it to take peanuts out of it. Throughout this process it was not, so far as anyone knows, jostled, dropped, bumped, or otherwise subjected to stress beyond what is to be expected in the ordinary use of the product. Chicago is not Los Angeles; there were no earthquakes. *Jaws reference* Chicago is not Amityville either; no supernatural interventions are alleged. So the defect must have been introduced earlier, when the jar was in the hands of the defendants.

As to when the defect might have developed before sale and the implications for liability of the three defendants, the court held that it did not matter:

> The strict liability element in modern products liability law comes precisely from the fact that a seller subject to that law is liable for defects in his product even if those defects were introduced, without the slightest fault of his own for failing to discover them, at some anterior stage of production. [ ] So the fact that K-Mart sold a defective jar of peanuts to Karen Godfrey would be conclusive of K-Mart's liability. . . . In exactly the same way, Planter's liability would be unaffected by the fact, if it is a fact, that the defect was due to [the jar manufacturer] rather than to itself. To repeat an earlier and fundamental point, a seller who is subject to strict products liability is responsible for the consequences of selling a defective product even if the defect was introduced without any fault on his part by his supplier or by his supplier's supplier.

Against which defendant is the plaintiff's case strongest? Would res ipsa loquitur have applied against each of the three defendants?

8.   *Causation.* In cases of strict products liability, plaintiffs must establish both factual cause and proximate cause, just as they must do in

negligence cases. See Restatement (Third) of Torts: Products Liability § 15 ("Whether a product defect caused harm to persons or property is determined by the prevailing rules and principles governing causation in tort."). For example, proximate cause was at issue in Stahlecker v. Ford Motor Co., 667 N.W.2d 244 (Neb.2003). Plaintiffs alleged that a defective tire failed and rendered the car inoperable while female decedent was driving alone in a remote area. Plaintiffs claimed that because of the tire failure a stranger was able to assault and murder decedent. The court held that even if the tire were defective, the stranger's acts negated proximate cause.

9. *Emotional distress and pure economic loss.* Recall Chapter IV and the rules on bystander recovery for emotional distress, as well as the rules governing pure economic loss. Should these limitations of the negligence duty also limit the strict liability duty? In cases of pure emotional distress, courts have largely applied these limitations to claims of strict products liability. For example, "[m]ost jurisdictions permit an emotional distress claim in strict products liability for bystanders under similar guidelines" to the *Dillon* standard adopted by "roughly half the states" in cases of negligence liability, which is discussed on p. 276 supra. D. Owen & M. Davis, 3 Owen & Davis on Products Liability § 25:9 (4th ed.2014). By contrast, in cases of pure economic loss, courts have limited the duty for reasons specific to products liability as discussed in further detail at p. 672 infra.

10. Early in the development of strict liability for defective products, Professor Kalven sounded a note of caution:

> The idea of enterprise liability has been in the wind for years, originally in an effort to explain the doctrines of agency. On this view what is important is that the defendant is an enterprise, that is, systematically engaged in generating the risks, and has access to the mechanism of the market. The first characteristic is thought to make him a good target for the deterrence of the tort sanction—liability is imposed in the quest for safety and accident prevention; the second characteristic is thought to make him a superior risk bearer able to pass on the loss into channels of wide distribution. There is undoubted power in these policy notions and this is not the place to debate them seriously. We would merely note that the premises now have considerable reach, and if we are serious about enterprise liability, a good part of contemporary tort law will need to be revised accordingly, and very little of its once spacious domain is likely to be left to the negligence principle.

Kalven, Tort Law—Tort Watch, 34 J.Am. Trial L. Ass'n 1, 57 (1972).

If the rationale stems from injuries caused by profit-making businesses, why limit strict liability to only those injuries caused by defective products? The enterprise liability rationale would seem to lead inexorably to a general rule of strict liability for all product-caused injuries, but courts have not gone that far.

Reviewing the major breakthroughs of American products liability law, one is struck by the courts' systematic elimination of conceptual barriers to plaintiffs' recovery. . . . Their next logical step would be to eliminate the plaintiff's need to show any type of defect at all. Such a move would be tantamount to imposing true strict liability for generic product hazards, something that many courts claim rhetorically to have done, but which none, in fact, yet has accomplished.

Henderson & Twerski, Closing the American Products Liability Frontier: The Rejection of Liability Without Defect, 66 N.Y.U.L.Rev. 1263, 1329 (1991). The requirement of defect limits the scope of strict products liability for reasons that are not made apparent by the enterprise rationale for strict liability. In reading the following set of materials from the Second and Third Restatements, consider how each one treats the issue of defect.

The Restatements

Early in the development of the modern approach, the American Law Institute promulgated section 402A of the Restatement (Second) of Torts, a most influential section that provided an early black letter formulation of the new approach. The section, published in 1965, provided:

> (1) One who sells any product in a defective condition unreasonably dangerous to the user or consumer or to his property is subject to liability for physical harm thereby caused to the ultimate user or consumer, or to his property, if
>
>> (a) the seller is engaged in the business of selling such a product, and
>>
>> (b) it is expected to and does reach the user or consumer without substantial change in the condition in which it is sold.
>
> (2) The rule stated in Subsection (1) applies although
>
>> (a) the seller has exercised all possible care in the preparation and sale of his product, and
>>
>> (b) the user or consumer has not bought the product from or entered into any contractual relation with the seller.

The mixed contract-tort heritage of strict products liability, suggested in *Escola*, is reflected in the Restatement's definition of a defect. Plaintiff must demonstrate that the product causing the injuries was in a "defective condition unreasonably dangerous" to person or property at the time it left defendant's possession. The Restatement's comments define the requisite defective state in terms of a consumer's expectations—the traditional contract approach. See cmt i. The Restatement then acknowledges that "[t]here is nothing in this Section which would prevent any court from treating the [tort] rule stated as a matter of 'warranty' to the user or consumer," although such a "'warranty' is a very different kind of warranty from those usually found in the sale of goods, and . . . is not subject to the various contract rules which have grown up to surround such sales." Id. at cmt. m.

Although section 402A was widely adopted after 1965, it was promulgated as the area was first developing. In the succeeding years, other approaches began to emerge in cases that either rejected the Second Restatement's approach or elaborated upon issues it had not addressed. The dozen or so pages devoted to the problem of defective products in the Second Restatement subsequently led to a body of case law requiring over 300 pages of exposition in the Restatement (Third) of Torts: Products Liability, which was adopted by the American Law Institute in 1998 after several years of debate. The Products Liability Restatement apparently took a quite different approach.

Section 1 provides that "One engaged in the business of selling or otherwise distributing products who sells or distributes a defective product is subject to liability for harm to persons or property caused by the defect."

Section 2 provides that for purposes of determining whether a product is defective, there are three types of defects. A product:

> (a) contains a manufacturing defect when the product departs from its intended design even though all possible care was exercised in the preparation and marketing of the product;

or (b) is defective in design when the foreseeable risks of harm posed by the product could have been reduced or avoided by the adoption of a reasonable alternative design by the seller or other distributor, or a predecessor in the commercial chain of distribution, and the omission of the alternative design renders the product not reasonably safe;

or (c) is defective because of inadequate instructions or warnings when the foreseeable risks of harm posed by the product could have been reduced or avoided by the provision of reasonable instructions or warnings by the seller or other distributor, or a predecessor in the commercial chain of distribution, and the omission of the instructions or warnings renders the product not reasonably safe.

Section 3 provides a provision complementary to its section 2 for establishing the existence of a defect:

> It may be inferred that the harm sustained by the plaintiff was caused by a product defect existing at the time of sale or distribution, without proof of a specific defect, when the incident that harmed the plaintiff:
>
> > (a) was of a kind that ordinarily occurs as a result of product defect; and

(b) was not, in the particular case, solely the result of causes other than product defect existing at the time of sale or distribution.

Sometimes referred to as the "malfunction" theory of defect, section 3 primarily encompasses manufacturing defects whose existence cannot be directly proved, but also includes design defects that cause a product to fail in ways that it clearly should not. Thus, if a homeowner climbs a brand-new ladder and then falls to the ground after each rung breaks in half, section 3 would permit a finding of defect without concern for whether a manufacturing or design defect was responsible and without requiring the plaintiff to point to either a specific manufacturing or design defect.

What appear to be the essential differences between the approaches in the two Restatements? What type of defect was involved in the early cases of contaminated food, shattering wheels, and exploding soda bottles? Is this type of defect treated differently in the two Restatements? Might section 3 of the Products Liability Restatement capture the cases that the "defective condition unreasonably dangerous" language in section 402A was meant to address? If so, and if the Third Restatement's standards for design and warning defects are essentially congruent with negligence, is there any difference between the law of products liability in the Second Restatement and in the Third Restatement? Many critics of the Third Restatement have claimed that it guts the strict liability established in the Second Restatement. For an argument otherwise, see Green, The Unappreciated Congruity of the Second and Third Torts Restatements on Design Defects, 74 Brook.L.Rev. 807 (2009).

Keep both approaches in mind as we consider recent developments in liability for defective products. Be sure to note in each situation which Restatement—if either—is being analyzed by the court.

B. MANUFACTURING DEFECTS

The most common and straightforward cases of defective products involve the aberrational mass-produced item that has come off the assembly line different from (and more dangerous than) the intended product. These defects can take various forms. Materials or component parts of the product can be flawed or contaminated; the product can be improperly assembled or constructed; or the product can be improperly packaged. These defects can also occur after the product has been constructed or manufactured. Delivery of the product by a seller can create the defect, as when soda bottles are mishandled during delivery and incur hairline fractures that unduly weaken the bottle, causing it to explode when lifted by the consumer. The defect is generally apparent in the flawed unit by the time of trial, and courts have concluded that strict liability should follow.

According to the Products Liability Restatement section 2 cmt. a, "imposing strict liability on manufacturers for harm caused by manufacturing defects encourages greater investment in product safety than does a regime of fault-based liability under which, as a practical matter, sellers may escape their appropriate share of responsibility." Is this rationale different from the activity-level rationale for the rule of strict liability for abnormally dangerous activities, discussed in note 3, p. 554 supra?

To prove that the product departed from its blueprint or design specifications, usually the plaintiff need only compare the allegedly defective product to the design. That comparison may require expert testimony. In some cases, the plaintiff is unable to identify the specific defect. The product can be destroyed in the accident or the particular product may have been lost or sold, making it impossible to determine whether it had a manufacturing defect. Lacking direct evidence of defect, the plaintiff can still try to prove that the product was defective by relying on circumstantial proof, as per the malfunction theory of defect.

In McCorvey v. Baxter Healthcare Corp., 298 F.3d 1253 (11th Cir.2002), a catheter, in its usual condition for use, spontaneously erupted and fragmented inside the patient's bladder. The district court dismissed the case because plaintiff did not produce any evidence of the existence of a defect in the catheter. The court of appeals reversed, holding that the plaintiff was entitled to the benefit of an inference of a defect when the product "malfunctions during normal operation." Plaintiff did not have the burden to eliminate other potential causes, so long as the product "malfunctions during normal operation."

The malfunction theory does not reduce the plaintiff's evidentiary burden. "[T]he law reports brim with decisions that recite the propriety of the doctrine as a general proposition but hold it inapplicable to the facts. The opinions in such cases frequently note that . . . the law will not allow plaintiffs or juries to rely on guess, conjecture, or speculation." Owen, Manufacturing Defects, 53 S.C.L.Rev. 851, 878 (2002). For example, in Price v. General Motors Corp., 931 F.2d 162 (1st Cir.1991), plaintiffs alleged that their car suddenly swerved from the highway into a utility pole. The car had been "inadvertently destroyed" before major investigation could be conducted. The court upheld summary judgment for defendant:

> Even if the Price vehicle leaked power steering fluid, the leak could as well have been due to inadequate maintenance, improper repairs to any of several hoses and seals, or defective non-GMC replacement parts, as it could to an original . . . manufacturing defect. The Prices purchased their 1981 Citation second-hand in 1983, after it had been driven more than 63,000 miles; they drove it approximately 15,000 additional miles. Appellants offered no evidence relating to the

maintenance and repair history of the vehicle prior to their purchase. . . . Finally, appellants' own expert conceded that he had no way of knowing whether any of the mechanical parts in the power steering mechanism were original.

Id. at 165–66. Would the outcome be different if the car were new? For thorough discussion of the malfunction doctrine and its evidentiary requirements, see Metropolitan Property & Casualty Insurance Co. v. Deere & Co., 25 A.3d 571 (Conn.2011). Recall that the malfunction theory of defect is recognized in section 3 of the Products Liability Restatement, p. 576 supra.

C. DESIGN DEFECTS

A commonly shared design is the defining characteristic of a product line. Consequently, an allegation of defective design implicates the entire product line, substantially expanding the manufacturer's liability exposure as compared to product-specific defects attributable to manufacturing flaws or mishandling. One design feature can be the subject of numerous lawsuits, potentially subjecting a manufacturer to aggregate liabilities of an amount that could cause bankruptcy.

Not only does the potential scope of liability exceed that involved with product-specific defects, but the liability rules governing defective product design are also more complex and ambiguous than those governing construction or manufacturing defects. As one court observed, "the determination of when a product is actionable because of the nature of its design" is one of " 'the most agitated controversial question[s]' . . . in products liability law." Pritchett v. Cottrell, Inc., 512 F.3d 1057, 1063 (8th Cir.2008).

In a highly influential line of cases, the California Supreme Court developed the rule of strict products liability for defective design. In the first case, Cronin v. J.B.E. Olson Corp., 501 P.2d 1153 (Cal.1972), a bakery truck driver was injured when, in a crash, the metal bread trays came forward and struck him in the back. Defendant appealed from a judgment for plaintiff on the ground that the trial judge's charge on strict liability omitted the requirement that any defect in the product must be found to be "unreasonably dangerous" as required by section 402A. The court disagreed. It thought the phrase "burdened the injured plaintiff with proof of an element which rings of negligence. . . . A bifurcated standard is of necessity more difficult to prove than a unitary one. But merely proclaiming that the phrase 'defective condition unreasonably dangerous' requires only a single finding would not purge that phrase of its negligence complexion":

> We recognize that the words "unreasonably dangerous" may also serve the beneficial purpose of preventing the seller from being treated as the insurer of its products. However, we think that such protective end is attained by the necessity of

proving that there was a defect in the manufacture or design of the product and that such defect was a proximate cause of the injuries.

Although the court assumed that *Greenman* (note 5.a, p. 569 supra) had involved a manufacturing defect, it saw "no difficulty in applying the *Greenman* formulation to the full range of products liability situations, including those involving 'design defects.'" Indeed, the *Greenman* opinion described the defect as one of design. According to the *Cronin* court: "A defect may emerge from the mind of the designer as well as from the hand of the workman." Although it may be "easier to see the 'defect' in a single imperfectly fashioned product than in an entire line badly conceived, a distinction between manufacture and design defects is not tenable." The court accordingly rejected the Restatement's "unreasonably dangerous" standard for both types of defects.

A large number of states followed *Cronin* in dropping the "unreasonably dangerous" phrase from the definition of defect. Does the Products Liability Restatement section 2, p. 576 supra, appear to reinstate this requirement in its definition of a design defect?

Consider how a case like *Cronin* would be resolved under the malfunction theory of defect set forth in section 3 of the Products Liability Restatement, p. 576 supra. In Smoot v. Mazda Motors of America, Inc., 469 F.3d 675, 681 (7th Cir.2006), the court considered whether plaintiff could make out a prima facie case of defect under the malfunction theory and observed that "[i]t would make no difference, so far as application of the doctrine was concerned, if a car accelerated when the brake was depressed because the brake had been manufactured negligently or designed improperly." Is this reasoning any different from that employed by *Cronin*? Note that at the time when *Cronin* was decided, products liability cases routinely involved malfunctioning products like contaminated food and exploding soda bottles. If the product does not malfunction, how should courts determine whether the design is defective?

The Barker Case

In Barker v. Lull Engineering Co., 573 P.2d 443 (Cal.1978), plaintiff was hurt when the high-lift loader he was operating overturned on a slope. Among other alleged design defects was that the loader was not equipped with outriggers that would have provided additional stability as a load was being lifted, increasing the center of gravity of the loader. The regular operator of the loader—concerned about the danger involved in the proposed lift on sloping ground—called in sick on that day, leaving it to plaintiff, an inexperienced substitute, to operate the loader. The court reversed a defense judgment because the trial judge, ruling before *Cronin* had been decided, used the "unreasonably dangerous" language in the charge to the jury. The court also found error in the trial judge's limitation of liability to situations in which the product was used in the "intended" manner. Such a limitation would prevent liability in cases of automobile crashes or in situations in which products are widely used for purposes for which they are not "intended," such as standing on chairs or using a screwdriver to pry open the lid of a paint can. The appropriate limiting phrase would require the product to be used in the "intended or a reasonably foreseeable manner." Id. at 452.

The court then discussed how plaintiffs might show that a product was defectively designed. "First, our cases establish that a product may be found defective in design if the plaintiff demonstrates that the product failed to perform as safely as an ordinary consumer would expect when used in an intended or reasonably foreseeable manner." Id. at 454.

But this would not be the exclusive means for determining whether a design defect exists because in many situations consumers "have no idea how safe the product could be made." Id. This led to a second, alternative, formulation: that design defect could be shown "if through hindsight the jury determines that the product's design embodies 'excessive preventable danger,' or, in other words, if the jury finds that the risk of danger inherent in the challenged design outweighs the benefits of such design." The jury was to consider

> among other relevant factors, the gravity of the danger posed by the challenged design, the likelihood that such danger would occur, the mechanical feasibility of a safer alternative design, the financial cost of an improved design, and the adverse consequences to the product and to the consumer that would result from an alternative design.

Id. at 455.

On this second prong, the defendant had the burden of producing evidence and persuading the trier of fact that the product should not be judged defective. Plaintiff and amicus argued that this second prong was equivalent to demanding a showing of negligence. The court disagreed. In many cases it is true that a showing of defect "may also demonstrate that the manufacturer was negligent in choosing such a design. As we have indicated, however, in a strict liability case, as contrasted with a negligent design action, the jury's focus is properly directed to the condition of the product itself, and not to the reasonableness of the manufacturer's conduct." Id. at 457.

Barker plays a central role in the case that follows.

Soule v. General Motors Corporation

Supreme Court of California, 1994.
8 Cal.4th 548, 882 P.2d 298, 34 Cal.Rptr.2d 607.

■ BAXTER, JUSTICE.

Plaintiff's ankles were badly injured when her General Motors (GM) car collided with another vehicle. She sued GM, asserting that defects in her automobile allowed its left front wheel to break free, collapse rearward, and smash the floorboard into her feet. GM denied any defect and claimed that the force of the collision itself was the sole cause of the injuries. Expert witnesses debated the issues at length. Plaintiff prevailed at trial, and the Court of Appeal affirmed the judgment.

We granted review to resolve three questions. First, may a product's design be found defective on grounds that the product's performance fell below the safety expectation of the ordinary consumer (see [*Barker*]), if the question of how safely the product should have performed cannot be answered by the common experience of its users? . . .

We reach the following conclusions: The trial court erred by giving an "ordinary consumer expectations" instruction in this complex case. Moreover, the court should have granted GM's request for a special instruction explaining its correct theory of legal cause. However, neither error warrants reversal unless it caused actual prejudice, and both errors were harmless on this record. We will therefore affirm the Court of Appeal's judgment.

[During a slight drizzle one afternoon, plaintiff was driving her Camaro on the street "apparently" not wearing her seat belt. An approaching Datsun suddenly skidded into plaintiff's path. The Datsun's left rear quarter struck plaintiff's car in the area of the left front wheel at a combined closing speed estimated variously at from 30 to 70 miles per hour. "The collision bent the Camaro's frame adjacent to the wheel and tore loose the bracket that attached the wheel assembly (specifically, the lower control arm) to the frame. As a result, the wheel collapsed rearward and inward. The wheel hit the underside of the 'toe pan'—the slanted floorboard area beneath the pedals—causing the toe pan to crumple, or 'deform,' upward into the passenger compartment." In addition to various minor injuries, plaintiff sustained two fractured ankles, including a compound compression fracture of her left ankle, which caused permanent injury.

The "failed bracket" was retrieved but the rest of the Camaro was acquired by a salvage dealer, repaired and resold. In the ensuing suit, plaintiff "asserted a theory of strict tort liability for a defective product. She claimed the severe trauma to her ankles was not a natural consequence of the accident, but occurred when the collapse of the Camaro's wheel caused the toe pan to crush violently upward against her feet. Plaintiff attributed the wheel collapse to a manufacturing defect, the substandard quality of the weld attaching the lower control arm bracket to the frame. She also claimed that the placement of the bracket, and the configuration of the frame, were defective designs because they did not limit the wheel's rearward travel in the event the bracket should fail."

The "available physical and circumstantial evidence left room for debate about the exact angle and force of the impact and the extent to which the toe pan had actually deformed. The issues of defect and causation were addressed through numerous experts produced by both sides in such areas as biomechanics, metallurgy, orthopedics, design engineering, and crash-test simulation."

Plaintiff presented evidence of improper welding techniques and of a design on Ford Mustangs of comparable years that were said to "provide protection against unlimited rearward travel of the wheel should a bracket assembly give way." GM denied the claims of poor welding and design defect, and argued that the Ford design was "not distinctly safer for all collision stresses to which the vehicle might be subjected." One witness asserted that at least one recent Ford product had adopted the Camaro's design. GM also argued that the force of the collision was the sole cause of the ankle injuries—that plaintiff's unrestrained body went forward and downward at the moment of impact, causing the ankle injury "before significant deformation of the toe pan occurred."

The trial court gave a conventional "ordinary consumer expectations" charge that required plaintiff to show "(1) the manufacturer's product failed to perform as safely as an ordinary consumer would expect, (2) the defect existed when the product left the manufacturer's possession, (3) the defect was a 'legal cause' of plaintiff's 'enhanced injury,' and (4) the product was used in a reasonably foreseeable manner." As noted earlier, the judge denied GM's requested instruction on causation.

The jury made special findings that the Camaro contained a "defect (of unspecified nature) which was a 'legal cause' of plaintiff's 'enhanced injury.'" The jury found that plaintiff was at fault for not wearing a seat belt but that it was not a legal cause of her enhanced injuries. The jury awarded $1.65 million. The court of appeal affirmed.]

DISCUSSION

. . .

In *Barker*, we offered two alternative ways to prove a design defect, each appropriate to its own circumstances. The purposes, behaviors, and dangers of certain products are commonly understood by those who ordinarily use them. By the same token, the ordinary users or consumers of a product may have reasonable, widely accepted minimum expectations about the circumstances under which it should perform safely. Consumers govern their own conduct by these expectations, and products on the market should conform to them.

In some cases, therefore, "ordinary knowledge . . . as to . . . [the product's] characteristics" [section 402A], may permit an inference that the product did not perform as safely as it should. If the facts permit such a conclusion, and if the failure resulted from the product's design, a finding of defect is warranted without any further proof. The manufacturer may not defend a claim that a product's design failed to perform as safely as its ordinary consumers would expect by presenting expert evidence of the design's relative risks and benefits.[3]

However, as we noted in *Barker*, a complex product, even when it is being used as intended, may often cause injury in a way that does not engage its ordinary consumers' reasonable minimum assumptions about safe performance. For example, the ordinary consumer of an automobile simply has "no idea" how it should perform in all foreseeable situations, or how safe it should be made against all foreseeable hazards. [*Barker*]

An injured person is not foreclosed from proving a defect in the product's design simply because he cannot show that the reasonable minimum safety expectations of its ordinary consumers were violated. Under *Barker*'s alternative test, a product is still defective if its design embodies "excessive preventable danger" [ ], that is, unless "the benefits of the . . . design outweigh the risk of danger inherent in such design" [ ]. But this determination involves technical issues of feasibility, cost, practicality, risk, and benefit [ ], which are "impossible" to avoid [ ]. In such cases, the jury must consider the manufacturer's evidence of competing design considerations [ ] and the issue of design defect cannot fairly be resolved by standardless reference to the "expectations" of an "ordinary consumer."

As we have seen, the consumer expectations test is reserved for cases in which the everyday experience of the product's users permits a conclusion that the product's design violated minimum safety assumptions, and is thus defective regardless of expert opinion about the merits of the design.

It follows that where the minimum safety of a product is within the common knowledge of lay jurors, expert witnesses may not be used to demonstrate what an ordinary consumer would or should expect. Use of expert testimony for that purpose would invade the jury's function [ ], and would invite circumvention of the rule that the risks and benefits of a challenged design must be carefully balanced whenever the issue of

---

[3]   For example, the ordinary consumers of modern automobiles may and do expect that such vehicles will be designed so as not to explode while idling at stoplights, experience sudden steering or brake failure as they leave the dealership, or roll over and catch fire in two-mile-per-hour collisions. If the plaintiff in a product liability action proved that a vehicle's design produced such a result, the jury could find forthwith that the car failed to perform as safely as its ordinary consumers would expect, and was therefore defective.

design defect goes beyond the common experience of the product's users.[4]

By the same token, the jury may not be left free to find a violation of ordinary consumer expectations whenever it chooses. Unless the facts actually permit an inference that the product's performance did not meet the minimum safety expectations of its ordinary users, the jury must engage in the balancing of risks and benefits required by the second prong of *Barker*.

Accordingly, as *Barker* indicated, instructions are misleading and incorrect if they allow a jury to avoid this risk-benefit analysis in a case where it is required. [ ] Instructions based on the ordinary consumer expectations prong of *Barker* are not appropriate where, as a matter of law, the evidence would not support a jury verdict on that theory. Whenever that is so, the jury must be instructed solely on the alternative risk-benefit theory of design defect announced in *Barker*.[5]

GM suggests that the consumer expectations test is improper whenever "crashworthiness," a complex product, or technical questions of causation are at issue. Because the variety of potential product injuries is infinite, the line cannot be drawn as clearly as GM proposes. But the fundamental distinction is not impossible to define. The crucial question in each individual case is whether the circumstances of the product's failure permit an inference that the product's design performed below the legitimate, commonly accepted minimum safety assumptions of its ordinary consumers.

GM's argument

GM argues at length that the consumer expectations test is an "unworkable, amorphic, fleeting standard" which should be entirely abolished as a basis for design defect. In GM's view, the test is deficient and unfair in several respects. First, it defies definition. Second, it focuses not on the objective condition of products, but on the subjective, unstable, and often unreasonable opinions of consumers. Third, it ignores the reality that ordinary consumers know little about how safe

---

[4] Plaintiff insists that manufacturers should be forced to design their products to meet the "objective" safety demands of a "hypothetical" reasonable consumer who is fully informed about what he or she should expect. Hence, plaintiff reasons, the jury may receive expert advice on "reasonable" safety expectations for the product. However, this function is better served by the risk-benefit prong of *Barker*. There, juries receive expert advice, apply clear guidelines, and decide accordingly whether the product's design is an acceptable compromise of competing considerations. On the other hand, appropriate use of the consumer expectations test is not necessarily foreclosed simply because the product at issue is only in specialized use, so that the general public may not be familiar with its safety characteristics. If the safe performance of the product fell below the reasonable, widely shared minimum expectations of those who do use it, perhaps the injured consumer should not be forced to rely solely on a technical comparison of risks and benefits. By the same token, if the expectations of the product's limited group of ordinary consumers are beyond the lay experience common to all jurors, expert testimony on the limited subject of what the product's actual consumers do expect may be proper. [ ]

[5] Plaintiff urges that any limitation on use of the consumer expectations test contravenes *Greenman's* purpose to aid hapless consumers. But we have consistently held that manufacturers are not insurers of their products; they are liable in tort only when "defects" in their products cause injury. . . .

the complex products they use can or should be made. Fourth, it invites the jury to isolate the particular consumer, component, accident, and injury before it instead of considering whether the whole product fairly accommodates the competing expectations of all consumers in all situations [ ]. Fifth, it eliminates the careful balancing of risks and benefits which is essential to any design issue.

In its amicus curiae brief, the Product Liability Advisory Council, Inc. (Council) makes similar arguments. The Council proposes that all design defect claims be resolved under a single risk-benefit analysis geared to "reasonable safety."

We fully understand the dangers of improper use of the consumer expectations test. However, we cannot accept GM's insinuation that ordinary consumers lack any legitimate expectations about the minimum safety of the products they use. In particular circumstances, a product's design may perform so unsafely that the defect is apparent to the common reason, experience, and understanding of its ordinary consumers. In such cases, a lay jury is competent to make that determination.

Nor are we persuaded by the Council's proposal. In essence, it would reinvest product liability claims with the requirement of "unreasonable danger" that we rejected in *Cronin* and *Barker*.

When use of the consumer expectations test is limited as *Barker* intended, the principal concerns raised by GM and the Council are met. Within these limits, the test remains a workable means of determining the existence of design defect. We therefore find no compelling reason to overrule the consumer expectations prong of *Barker* at this late date, and we decline to do so.[7]

Applying our conclusions to the facts of this case, however, we agree that the instant jury should not have been instructed on ordinary consumer expectations. Plaintiff's theory of design defect was one of technical and mechanical detail. It sought to examine the precise behavior of several obscure components of her car under the complex circumstances of a particular accident. The collision's exact speed, angle, and point of impact were disputed. It seems settled, however, that plaintiff's Camaro received a substantial oblique blow near the left front wheel, and that the adjacent frame members and bracket assembly absorbed considerable inertial force.

An ordinary consumer of automobiles cannot reasonably expect that a car's frame, suspension, or interior will be designed to remain intact in any and all accidents. Nor would ordinary experience and

---

[7]   GM observes that some other states have rejected the consumer expectations test. (E.g., Prentis v. Yale Mfg. Co. [365 N.W.2d 176, 185–186 (Mich.1984)] [adopting pure negligence theory for product injury]; [ ]). But a substantial number of jurisdictions expressly recognize, consistent with *Barker*, that a product's design is defective if it either violates the minimum safety expectations of an ordinary consumer or contains dangers which outweigh its benefits. [ ]

understanding inform such a consumer how safely an automobile's design should perform under the esoteric circumstances of the collision at issue here. Indeed, both parties assumed that quite complicated design considerations were at issue, and that expert testimony was necessary to illuminate these matters. Therefore, injection of ordinary consumer expectations into the design defect equation was improper.

We are equally persuaded, however, that the error was harmless, because it is not reasonably probable defendant would have obtained a more favorable result in its absence. . . .

[The court stressed that "the consumer expectations theory was never emphasized at any point." The case was "tried on the assumption that the alleged design defect was a matter of technical debate. Virtually all the evidence and argument on design defect focused on expert evaluation of the strengths, shortcomings, risks, and benefits of the challenged design, as compared with a competitor's approach." Neither "plaintiff's attorney nor any expert witness on her behalf told the jury that the Camaro's design violated the safety expectations of the ordinary consumer."]

Under these circumstances, we find it highly unlikely that a reasonable jury took that path. We see no reasonable probability that the jury disregarded the voluminous evidence on the risks and benefits of the Camaro's design, and instead rested its verdict on its independent assessment of what an ordinary consumer would expect. Accordingly, we conclude, the error in presenting that theory to the jury provides no basis for disturbing the trial judgment.[8]

. . .

Instructional error in a civil case is prejudicial "where it seems probable" that the error "prejudicially affected the verdict." [ ]

. . .

The trial court erred when it instructed on the consumer expectations test for design defect. . . . However, [the] error caused [no] actual prejudice. Accordingly, the judgment of the Court of Appeal, upholding the trial court judgment in favor of plaintiff, is affirmed.

---

[8] In a separate argument . . . both GM and the Council urge us to reconsider *Barker's* holding . . . that under the risk-benefit test, the manufacturer has the burden of proving that the utility of the challenged design outweighs its dangers. [ ] We explained in *Barker* that placement of the risk-benefit burden on the manufacturer is appropriate because the considerations which influenced the design of its product are "peculiarly within . . . [its] knowledge." . . . GM argues that *Barker* unfairly requires the manufacturer to "prove a negative"—i.e., the absence of a safer alternative design. The Council suggests our "peculiar knowledge" rationale is unrealistic under liberal modern discovery rules. We are not persuaded. *Barker* allows the evaluation of competing designs, but it does not require proof that the challenged design is the safest possible alternative. The manufacturer need only show that given the inherent complexities of design, the benefits of its chosen design outweigh the dangers. Moreover, modern discovery practice neither redresses the inherent technical imbalance between manufacturer and consumer nor dictates that the injured consumer should bear the primary burden of evaluating a design developed and chosen by the manufacturer. GM and the Council fail to convince us that *Barker* was incorrectly decided in this respect.

■ KENNARD, GEORGE, WERDEGAR and BOREN (assigned) JJ., concur.

■ MOSK, ACTING CHIEF JUSTICE, concurring [in the majority opinion on consumer expectations and writing separately on another issue].

■ ARABIAN, JUSTICE, concurring [on the court's resolution of the applicability of the consumer expectations test] and dissenting [on another issue].

NOTES AND QUESTIONS

1. Plaintiff asserted claims alternatively based on a manufacturing defect and a design defect; she needed to prevail on only one to succeed in her suit. How would plaintiff's proof for each of these two claims be different?

2. *The consumer expectations test.* In Pruitt v. General Motors Corp., 86 Cal.Rptr.2d 4, 5 (App.1999), the plaintiff was hurt when an air bag deployed in a "low impact collision." After a judgment for defendant, the appellate court upheld the trial court's refusal to charge on the consumer expectations test because the "deployment of an air bag is, quite fortunately, not part of the 'everyday experience' of the consuming public. Minimum safety standards for air bags are not within the common knowledge of lay jurors. Jurors are in need of expert testimony to evaluate the risks and benefits of the challenged design." To the examples in *Soule*'s footnote 3, the *Pruitt* court added "air bags inflating for no apparent reason while one is cruising down the road at 65 miles per hour." How different is that from what actually happened? In Romine v. Johnson Controls, Inc., 169 Cal.Rptr.3d 208 (App.2014), plaintiff's car was hit from behind by a vehicle traveling around 40 mph. The seat collapsed, badly injuring her. The court held that "[r]ear-end collisions are common and within the average consumer's ordinary experience. Consumers have expectations about whether a vehicle's driver's seat will collapse rearward in a rear-end collision, regardless of the speed of the collision." Id. at 219–20.

Compare Morton v. Owens-Corning Fiberglas Corp., 40 Cal.Rptr.2d 22 (App.1995), in which a former insulation installer sued asbestos suppliers after contracting mesothelioma—a cancer of the lining that surrounds the lungs. Plaintiff succeeded before the jury on a consumer expectations approach. On appeal, defendant argued that such a test was inapplicable in an asbestos case because of its complexity. The court held the consumer expectations test applicable, stating that the question was whether "the circumstances of the product's failure permit an inference that the product's design performed below the legitimate, commonly accepted minimum safety assumptions of its ordinary consumers." Id. at 24. What does the court mean by this statement? The asbestos performed its intended function of retarding fires in the insulation materials, and so there was no malfunction of the type discussed in *Pruitt*. In what respect, then, did the asbestos violate "commonly accepted minimum safety assumptions"? Is it because the hazards posed by asbestos so clearly violate the second prong of the *Barker* test that expert testimony about the matter is not required?

3. *From consumer expectations to the risk-utility test.* The *Soule* court suggests that some car accidents are properly subject to the consumer expectations test. What do they have in common? How would these cases be resolved under the malfunction theory of defect set forth in section 3 of the Products Liability Restatement, p. 576 supra? When the court states that the consumer expectations test is proper for cases in which "the circumstances of the product's failure permit an inference that the product's design performed below the legitimate, commonly accepted minimum safety assumptions of its ordinary consumers," does it mean that the consumer expectations test is congruent with section 3? Under this interpretation, the consumer at minimum expects that the product will not malfunction. Does this interpretation help to explain when the consumer expectations test is appropriately invoked in California after *Soule*?

If a product does not malfunction, what does the ordinary consumer reasonably expect about its safety performance? Consider footnote 4 in *Soule*, where the court discusses the "reasonable safety expectations" of a well-informed hypothetical consumer and concludes that she is "better served by the risk-benefit prong of *Barker*." An ordinary consumer who is well informed about the relevant issues would expect the product design to pass this prong of *Barker*, and so the concept of reasonable consumer expectations provides a rationale for the risk-utility test in cases that do not involve malfunctioning products. See M. Geistfeld, Principles of Product Liability 44–48 (2d ed.2011).

4. *Reasonable alternative design ("RAD").* "The reasonableness of choosing from among various alternative product designs and adopting the safest one if it is feasible is considered the 'heart' of design defect cases." Banks v. ICI Americas, Inc., 450 S.E.2d 671 (Ga.1994). "The essential inquiry, therefore, is whether the design chosen was a reasonable one from among the feasible choices of which the manufacturer was aware or should have been aware."

The approach in *Banks* has been formalized in the Products Liability Restatement section 2 cmt. f, which requires the plaintiff to "prove that a reasonable alternative design would have reduced the foreseeable risks of harm. . . ." Sometimes "the feasibility of a reasonable alternative design is obvious and understandable to lay persons and therefore expert testimony is unnecessary to support a finding that the product should have been designed differently and more safely." Other products already on the market may serve "a similar function at lower risk and at comparable cost." (One exception to the necessity for a RAD involves the malfunction theory of defect; the other exception is for the irreducibly unsafe product discussed in note 8 infra.)

The comment is explicit about some other criteria that play a role in the reasonableness balancing but recognizes that they will vary from case to case: a "broad range of factors may be considered in determining whether an alternative design is reasonable and whether its omission renders a product not reasonably safe." These factors include "among others" the "magnitude and probability of the foreseeable risks of harm, the instructions and warnings accompanying the product, and the nature and strength of consumer expectations regarding the product, including expectations arising from product portrayal and marketing." In addition, the relative advantages and disadvantages of the product and its proposed alternative must be considered. These include the impact on production costs and on "product longevity, maintenance, repair and esthetics; and the range of consumer choice among products":

> Moreover, the factors interact with one another. For example, evidence of the magnitude and probability of foreseeable harm may be offset by evidence that the proposed alternative design would reduce the efficiency and utility of the product. On the other hand, evidence that a proposed alternative design would increase production costs may be offset by evidence that product portrayal and marketing created substantial expectations of performance or safety, thus increasing the probability of foreseeable harm. . . . On the other hand, it is not a factor under Subsection (b) that the imposition of liability would have negative effect on corporate earnings or would reduce employment in a given industry.

How might the plaintiff in a case like *Soule* go about proving a RAD? Few states have joined California in shifting the burden of proof to defendants on the issue of "excessive preventable danger." Indeed, in Ray v. BIC Corp., 925 S.W.2d 527, 533 (Tenn.1996), the court characterized the position as "aberrant."

5. The combined effect of the RAD requirement in the Products Liability Restatement and expert gatekeeping spawned by *Daubert*, p. 357 supra is illustrated in Unrein v. Timesavers, Inc., 394 F.3d 1008 (8th Cir.2005). Plaintiff was injured by an industrial sander when she reached into it to dislodge two boards that were stuck together. Her hand got caught in the nip point, and the machine drew her arm in up to her elbow. Her expert provided an alternative design; he testified that the nip point should have been guarded and suggested a number of ways to accomplish this, including safety trip cords that were in "widespread use," according to the expert. The court affirmed the trial court's exclusion of the expert's testimony on *Daubert* grounds, stating "he did not prepare drawings showing how it would be integrated into the . . . sander or present photographs showing its use with similar machines." Id. at 1012.

6. Can plaintiff prove a RAD by invoking one product category to show that another category, by comparison, is unreasonably dangerous? In Dreisonstok v. Volkswagenwerk, A.G., 489 F.2d 1066 (4th Cir.1974), plaintiff passengers were hurt when the microbus in which they were riding left the road and ran into a tree. One distinctive feature of the microbus was that its passenger compartment was at the very front of the vehicle. Plaintiffs' negligence claim alleged that the design was defective because it provided less protection than that available in a "standard American made vehicle, which is a configuration with the passengers in the middle and the motor in the front." The court, reversing a plaintiffs' judgment, rejected the claim, observing: "If a person purchases a convertible . . . he cannot expect and the Court may not impose on the manufacturer the duty to provide him with the exact kind of protection in a rollover accident as in the 'standard American passenger car.'" The court continued:

> Price is, also, a factor to be considered, for, if a change in design would appreciably add to cost, add little to safety, and take an article out of the price range of the market to which it was intended to appeal, it may be "unreasonable" as well as "impractical" for the Courts to require the manufacturer to adopt such change. Of course, if an article can be made safer and the hazard of harm may be mitigated "by an alternate design or device at no substantial increase in price," then the manufacturer has a duty to adopt such a design but a Cadillac may be expected to include more in the way of both conveniences and "crashworthiness" than the economy car. Moreover, in a "crashworthy" case, it is necessary to consider the circumstances of the accident itself. As *Dyson* puts it, "it could not reasonably be argued that a car manufacturer should be held liable because its vehicle collapsed when involved in a head-on collision with a large truck, at high speed." In summary, every case such as this involves a delicate balancing of many factors in order to determine whether the manufacturer has used ordinary care in designing a car, which, giving consideration to the market purposes and utility of the vehicle, did not involve unreasonable risk of injury to occupants within the range of its "intended use."

> Applying the foregoing principles to the facts of this particular case, it is clear that there was no violation by the defendant of its duty of ordinary care in the design of its vehicle. The defendant's vehicle, described as "a van type multipurpose vehicle," was of a special type and particular design. This design was uniquely developed in order to provide the owner with the maximum amount of either cargo or passenger space in a vehicle inexpensively priced and of such dimensions as to make possible easy maneuverability. To achieve this, it advanced the driver's seat forward, bringing such seat in close proximity to the front of the vehicle, thereby adding to the cargo or passenger space. This, of course, reduced considerably the space between the exact front of the vehicle and the driver's compartment. All of this was readily discernible to any one using the vehicle; in fact, it was, as we have said, the unique feature of the vehicle. The usefulness of the design is vouchsafed by the popularity of the type. It was of special utility as a van for the transportation of light cargo, as a family camper, as a station wagon and for use by passenger groups too large for the average passenger car. It was a design duplicated in the construction of the large trucking tractors, where there was the same purpose of extending the cargo space without unduly lengthening the tractor-trailer coupling. There was no evidence in the record that there was any practical way of

improving the "crashability" of the vehicle that would have been consistent with the peculiar purposes of its design.

Id. at 1072–74.

The court concluded that the microbus was to be compared only with comparable vehicles. Here, the defense had presented unrefuted testimony that the safety of the microbus "was equal to or superior to that of other vehicles of like type." Id. at 1075.

7. *Distinguishing one product category from another.* In Evans v. Lorillard Tobacco Co., 990 N.E.2d 997 (Mass.2013), plaintiff's mother died from lung cancer caused by smoking Newport brand cigarettes. Plaintiff sued defendant manufacturer, alleging, in part, that the cigarettes were defectively designed and accompanied by an inadequate warning. To prove defective design, plaintiff presented evidence that a low tar, low nicotine cigarette was a reasonable alternative design to defendant's Newport brand. In affirming the jury verdict of compensatory damages (reduced by remittitur to $35 million), the court rejected defendant's argument that the alternative design was "not truly a cigarette, and that the jury essentially found that all cigarettes were defective, thereby imposing categorical product liability on all cigarettes." Id. at 1016. The court agreed that the jury may not impose categorical liability, but it rejected the proposition "that every cigarette, to be a cigarette, must contain levels of tar that cause a high risk of cancer and levels of nicotine that are addictive." The court recognized that the design proffered by plaintiff was not a reasonable alternative for the ordinary consumer who was already "addicted to nicotine, whose freedom of choice was physiologically impaired by the effects of nicotine." It nevertheless concluded that plaintiff's proposed design was a reasonable alternative for "the subclass of cigarette consumers who are not yet addicted." To do otherwise as argued by defendant would "place addictive chemicals outside the reach of product liability and give them special protection akin to immunity based solely on the strength of their addictive qualities." Id. at 1019.

The court's decision to rely on addiction to distinguish between classes of consumers is novel. In prior cases, courts had summarily rejected plaintiffs' arguments that cigarettes with lower levels of tar and nicotine are a reasonable alternative design to ordinary cigarettes. E.g., Adamo v. Brown & Williamson Tobacco Corp., 900 N.E.2d 966 (N.Y.2008)(ruling that "[t]he only 'utility' of a cigarette is to gratify smokers' desires for a certain experience, and plaintiffs did not prove, or try to prove, that light cigarettes perform this function as well as regular cigarettes"). The court in *Evans* observed that *Adamo* "did not address the issue of addiction and, therefore, did not discuss whether the gratification of 'smokers' desires for a certain experience' was the gratification of a craving arising from nicotine addiction, or whether the utility of a cigarette to a nonaddicted consumer is the same as to one who is addicted."

8. *The irreducibly unsafe product.* Despite cases like *Dreisonstok*, courts have not ruled out the possibility that the dangers that inhere in a category of products could render any product within the category unreasonably dangerous or defective, regardless of its particular design features. Consequently, the Products Liability Restatement recognizes a narrow exception to the RAD requirement in cases of the irreducibly unsafe product. O'Brien v. Muskin Corp., 463 A.2d 298 (N.J.1983), illustrated this issue. Plaintiff was hurt when he dove into an above-ground swimming pool that was properly filled with 3½ feet of water. The trial judge submitted a warning claim to the jury, which decided for defendant. The judge's refusal to submit a design defect claim was reversed on appeal. The court recognized that if there was no reasonable alternative, "recourse to a unique design is more defensible." Nonetheless:

> The evaluation of the utility of a product also involves the relative need for that product; some products are essentials, while others are luxuries. A product that fills a critical need and can be designed only one way should be viewed differently from a luxury item. Still other products, including some for which no alternative exists, are so dangerous and of such little use that under the risk-utility analysis, a manufacturer would bear the cost of liability of harm to others. That cost might dissuade a manufacturer from placing the product on the market, even if the product has been made as safely as possible. Indeed, plaintiff contends that above-ground pools with vinyl liners are such products and that manufacturers who market those pools should bear the cost of injuries they cause to foreseeable users.

> . . . The trial judge should have permitted the jury to consider whether, because of the dimensions of the pool and slipperiness of the bottom, the risks of injury so outweighed the utility of the product as to constitute a defect. . . . Viewing the evidence in the light most favorable to plaintiff, even if there are no alternative methods of making bottoms for above-ground pools, the jury might have found that the risk posed by the pool outweighed its utility.

Id. at 306.

The majority then turned to emphasize a main difference between them and the dissenter:

> [The dissenter] would find that no matter how dangerous a product may be, if it bears an adequate warning, it is free from design defects if there is no known alternative. Under that hypothesis, manufacturers, merely by placing warnings on their products, could insulate themselves from liability regardless of the number of people those products maim or kill. By contrast, the majority concludes that the judicial, not the commercial, system is the appropriate forum for determining whether a product is defective, with the resultant imposition of strict liability upon those in the commercial chain.

Id. at 306–07.

What does "defective" mean in this context? What analysis if, after several years of warnings that all reasonable people recognize as more than adequate in substance, size and placement, ten people per year in New

Jersey still dive into these pools and are paralyzed? Recall the *Dreisonstok* case, note 6 supra, in which the court refused to compare the microbus design with that of dissimilar—safer—vehicles. What if 1,000 people accidentally cut themselves badly on sharp knives in New Jersey each year?

Other states have rejected *O'Brien*. In Baughn v. Honda Motor Co., 727 P.2d 655 (Wash.1986), for example, the court held that a manufacturer of "mini-trail bikes" could not be held liable for injuries suffered when the bikes were used on public roads in disregard of explicit warnings against such usage. Plaintiff relied on *O'Brien* for the proposition that the case should go to the jury to weigh the risk and utility of the bikes. The court insisted that the product was not defective as a matter of law when its warnings (which were found adequate) were followed. Should it matter if 10% of the users of these bikes are killed in highway accidents?

The New Jersey legislature sought to restrict *O'Brien* by providing that there is no liability when there is no "practical and technically feasible alternative design that would have prevented the harm without substantially impairing the reasonably anticipated or intended function of the product." An exception was created where the court found by "clear and convincing evidence" that "(1) the product is egregiously unsafe or ultra-hazardous; (2) the ordinary user or consumer of the product cannot reasonably be expected to have knowledge of the product's risks, or the product poses a risk of serious injury to persons other than the user or consumer; and (3) the product has little or no usefulness." N.J.S.A. 2A:58C–3.

The Products Liability Restatement states that liability may flow even if a product has no RAD if its value is deemed to be minimal. It recognized that some courts had imposed categorical liability for generic products with a "manifestly unreasonable design." Section 2, comments d and e, accepted this approach as to prank exploding cigars but rejected it for "[c]ommon and widely distributed products such as alcoholic beverages, firearms, and above-ground swimming pools. . . ." What about all-terrain vehicles? Lawn darts with sharp pointed ends? Compare Parish v. Jumpking, Inc., 719 N.W.2d 540, 544 (Iowa 2006)(adopting the approach of the Products Liability Restatement and concluding that a trampoline is a type of "common and widely distributed product" not subject to categorical liability).

Camacho v. Honda Motor Co., Ltd.
Supreme Court of Colorado, 1987.
741 P.2d 1240.

■ KIRSHBAUM, JUSTICE.

[In March 1978, plaintiff bought a new Honda Hawk motorcycle. In an intersection accident with a car, plaintiff suffered severe leg injuries. Plaintiff and his wife sued the various parties in the chain of distribution, claiming that the absence of crash bars to protect the legs made the product defective under a strict liability analysis. Negligence and breach of warranty claims were not before the court. Two mechanical engineers testified at depositions that "the state of the art in mechanical engineering and motorcycle design was such that effective leg protection devices were available in March 1978 and that several manufacturers other than Honda had made such devices available as optional equipment; that, although room for further improvement of crash bars existed in March 1978, crash bars then available from manufacturers other than Honda provided some protection in low-speed collisions and, in particular, would have reduced or completely avoided the serious leg injuries" that plaintiff suffered. The trial court granted Honda summary judgment. The court of appeals affirmed on the ground that the danger "would have been fully anticipated by or within the contemplation of the ordinary user or consumer."]

. . .

In Roberts v. May, [583 P.2d 305 (Colo.App.1978)], the Court of Appeals recognized the applicability of the "crashworthiness" doctrine in Colorado. Under this doctrine, a motor vehicle manufacturer may be liable in negligence or strict liability for injuries sustained in a motor vehicle accident where a manufacturing or design defect, though not the cause of the accident, caused or enhanced the injuries. [ ] The doctrine was first recognized in the landmark case of Larsen v. General Motors Corp., 391 F.2d 495 (8th Cir.1968), in which the court noted that a manufacturer's duty encompassed designing and building a product reasonably fit and safe for its intended use, that automobiles are intended for use on the roadways and that injury-producing collisions are a frequent, foreseeable and statistically expectable result of such normal use. Incumbent upon the automobile manufacturer was a duty of reasonable care in the design and manufacture of its product, including a duty to use reasonable care to minimize the injurious effects of a foreseeable collision by employing common-sense safety features. [ ] The crashworthiness doctrine has been adopted by the vast majority of courts in other jurisdictions which have considered the issue. [ ] We agree with the reasoning of those decisions, as did the Court of Appeals in its consideration of this case, and adopt the crashworthiness doctrine for this jurisdiction.

The crashworthiness doctrine has been applied to accidents involving motorcycles. [ ] Honda argues, however, that motorcycles are inherently dangerous motor vehicles that cannot be made perfectly crashworthy and, therefore, that motorcycle manufacturers should be free of liability for injuries not actually caused by a defect in the design or manufacture of the motorcycle. We find no principled basis to conclude that liability for failure to provide reasonable, cost-acceptable safety features to reduce the severity of injuries suffered in inevitable accidents should be imposed upon automobile manufacturers but not upon motorcycle manufacturers. The use of motorcycles for transportation over roadways is just as foreseeable as the use of automobiles for such purpose. The crashworthiness doctrine does not require a manufacturer to provide absolute safety, but merely to provide some measure of reasonable, cost-effective safety in the foreseeable use of the product. [ ] Honda acknowledges that motorcycle accidents are just as foreseeable as automobile accidents and that motorcycle riders face a much greater risk of injury in the event of an accident than do occupants of automobiles. In view of the important goal of encouraging maximum development of reasonable, cost-efficient safety features in the manufacture of all products, the argument that motorcycle manufacturers should be exempt from liability under the crashworthiness doctrine because serious injury to users of that product is foreseeable must be rejected. [ ]

III.

In determining the extent of liability of a product manufacturer for a defective product, this court has adopted the doctrine of strict products liability as set forth in [section 402A].

Honda asserts that as a matter of law a motorcycle designed without leg protection devices cannot be deemed "in a defective condition unreasonably dangerous to the user" because the risk of motorcycle accidents is foreseeable to every ordinary consumer and because it is obvious that motorcycles do not generally offer leg protection devices as a standard item. In support of this argument Honda relies on comment *i* to section 402A, which states in pertinent part:

> i. Unreasonably dangerous. The rule stated in this Section applies only where the defective condition of the product makes it unreasonably dangerous to the user or consumer. . . . The article sold must be dangerous to an extent beyond that which would be contemplated by the ordinary consumer who purchases it, with the ordinary knowledge common to the community as to its characteristics.

The trial court and the Court of Appeals in essence applied this consumer contemplation test in dismissing the Camachos' claims.

In *Cronin v. J.B.E. Olson Corp.*, [ ], the California Supreme Court declined to require an injured person to establish that a product is unreasonably dangerous as a requisite to recovery for injuries in a strict liability design defect context. In Union Supply Co. v. Pust, [583 P.2d 276 (Colo.1978)], this court rejected the *Cronin* rationale, recognizing that requiring a party who seeks recovery on the basis of an alleged defective product to establish that the product is unreasonably dangerous appropriately places reasonable limits on the potential liability of manufacturers. However, we also held in *Pust* that the fact that the dangers of a product are open and obvious does not constitute a defense to a claim alleging that the product is unreasonably dangerous. We noted that adoption of such a principle would unfairly elevate the assumption of risk defense to a question of law.[6] The obvious and foreseeable consumer contemplation test employed by the trial court and approved by the Court of Appeals is substantially similar to the open and obvious standard specifically rejected in *Pust*. It is not the appropriate standard in Colorado for measuring whether a particular product is in a defective condition unreasonably dangerous to the consumer or user.

A consumer is justified in expecting that a product placed in the stream of commerce is reasonably safe for its intended use, and when a product is not reasonably safe a products liability action may be maintained. [ ] Of course, whether a given product is reasonably safe and, therefore, not unreasonably dangerous, necessarily depends upon many circumstances. Any test, therefore, to determine whether a particular product is or is not actionable must consider several factors. While reference to "reasonable" or "unreasonable" standards introduces certain negligence concepts into an area designed to be free from these concepts [ ], that difficulty is much less troublesome than are the problems inherent in attempting to avoid dealing with the competing interests involved in allocating the risk of loss in products liability actions. . . .

These considerations strongly suggest that the consumer contemplation concept embodied in comment *i*, while illustrative of a particular problem, does not provide a satisfactory test for determining whether particular products are in a defective condition unreasonably dangerous to the user or consumer. In the final analysis, the principle of products liability contemplated by section 402A is premised upon the concept of enterprise liability for casting defective products into the stream of commerce. [ ] The primary focus must remain upon the nature of the product under all relevant circumstances rather than upon the conduct of either the consumer or the manufacturer. [ ] Total reliance upon the hypothetical ordinary consumer's contemplation of an obvious danger diverts the appropriate focus and may thereby result in a finding that a product is not defective even though the product may easily have been designed to be much safer at little added expense and no impairment of utility. [ ] Uncritical rejection of design defect claims in all cases wherein the danger may be open and obvious thus

---

[6]   Where the obviousness of the danger inherent in the ordinary use of a product is not dispositive of whether the product is unreasonably dangerous, the plaintiff's appreciation of the danger may nonetheless rise to the level of assumption of the risk. Assumption of the risk is an affirmative defense to strict liability, requiring a showing of more than ordinary contributory negligence in that the plaintiff must have voluntarily and unreasonably proceeded to encounter a known danger the specific hazards of which the plaintiff had actual subjective knowledge. [ ] The question of whether a plaintiff had actual knowledge of the specific hazards comprising the danger is ordinarily a fact question which should be left for the jury and not precluded by the conclusion that the danger should have been obvious. . . .

contravenes sound public policy by encouraging design strategies which perpetuate the manufacture of dangerous products. [ ]

In Ortho Pharmaceutical Corp. v. Heath, 722 P.2d 410 (Colo.1986), we recently recognized that exclusive reliance upon consumer expectations is a particularly inappropriate means of determining whether a product is unreasonably dangerous under section 402A where both the unreasonableness of the danger in the design defect and the efficacy of alternative designs in achieving a reasonable degree of safety must be defined primarily by technical, scientific information.[8] Moreover, manufacturers of such complex products as motor vehicles invariably have greater access than do ordinary consumers to the information necessary to reach informed decisions concerning the efficacy of potential safety measures. [ ] The principles that have evolved in the law of products liability have in part been developed to encourage manufacturers to use information gleaned from testing, inspection and data analysis to help avoid the "massive problem of product accidents." [ ]

. . . In *Ortho* we noted that the following factors are of value in balancing the attendant risks and benefits of a product to determine whether a product design is unreasonably dangerous:

(1) The usefulness and desirability of the product—its utility to the user and to the public as a whole.

(2) The safety aspects of the product—the likelihood that it will cause injury and the probable seriousness of the injury.

(3) The availability of a substitute product which would meet the same need and not be as unsafe.

(4) The manufacturer's ability to eliminate the unsafe character of the product without impairing its usefulness or making it too expensive to maintain its utility.

(5) The user's ability to avoid danger by the exercise of care in the use of the product.

(6) The user's anticipated awareness of the dangers inherent in the product and their avoidability because of general public knowledge of the obvious condition of the

---

[8] Honda asserts that the application of the consumer expectation test is particularly appropriate in the context of motorcycle design defect claims because the motorcycle purchaser who is injured in an accident has bargained for the condition about which he complains and because the element of conscious consumer choice is invariably present in contradistinction to those claims involving accidents occurring in the workplace. We cannot agree that the purchaser of a motorcycle bargains for the risk of serious leg injury; rather, the purchaser bargains for a motorized vehicle the purpose of which is to provide an economical, open-air, maneuverable form of transportation on the roadways. Cf. Wade, On the Nature of Strict Liability for Products, 44 Miss.L.J. 825, 839–40 (1973)(noting that a plaintiff who has cut his finger on a sharp knife should not be able to maintain a cause of action against the manufacturer of the knife on the theory that the knife was unsafe because it was sharp, because the very purpose of a knife is to cut); Page, Generic Product Risks: The Case Against Comment k and For Strict Tort Liability, 58 N.Y.U.L.Rev. 853, 857 (1983). . . .

product, or of the existence of suitable warnings or instructions.

(7) The feasibility, on the part of the manufacturer, of spreading the loss by setting the price of the product or carrying liability insurance.

[*Ortho*] (relying on [Wade's article, cited in footnote 8]). The factors enumerated in *Ortho* are applicable to the determination of what constitutes a product that is in a defective unreasonably dangerous condition. By examining and weighing the various interests represented by these factors, a trial court is much more likely to be fair to the interests of both manufacturers and consumers in determining the status of particular products.

The question of the status of the motorcycle purchased by Camacho involves in part the interpretation of mechanical engineering data derived from research and testing—interpretation which necessarily includes the application of scientific and technical principles. In addition, the question posed under the crashworthiness doctrine is not whether the vehicle was obviously unsafe but rather whether the degree of inherent dangerousness could or should have been significantly reduced. The record contains some evidence to support the conclusion that Honda could have provided crash bars at an acceptable cost without impairing the motorcycle's utility or substantially altering its nature and Honda's failure to do so rendered the vehicle unreasonably dangerous under the applicable danger-utility test. It is far from certain, however, that the ultimate answer to this question can be determined on the basis of the limited facts thus far presented to the trial court.

. . .

The Camachos proffered evidence that the Honda Hawk motorcycle could have been equipped with crash bars which would mitigate injuries in low-speed, angled-impact collisions such as the one in which Camacho was involved. The Camachos' expert witnesses' interpretation of research and testing data indicated that the maneuverability of the motorcycle could be retained by making the crash bars no wider than the handlebars, that the stability of the motorcycle could be retained by mounting the crash bars relatively close to the center of gravity and that the addition of crash bars would not impair the utility of the motorcycle as a fuel efficient, open-air vehicle nor impair the safety of the motorcycle in accidents which varied in kind from the accident involving Camacho. These conclusions are all strenuously disputed by Honda. However, precisely because the factual conclusions reached by expert witnesses are in dispute, summary judgment as to whether the design strategies of Honda were reasonable is improper.

The judgment is reversed, and the case is remanded to the Court of Appeals with directions to remand the case to the trial court for further proceedings consistent with the views expressed in this opinion.

[Three justices concurred in Justice Kirshbaum's opinion.]

■ VOLLACK, JUSTICE, dissenting

Because I believe that the court of appeals correctly affirmed the trial court's order, I respectfully dissent.

The issue before the court is what test should apply in determining whether a product has a design defect causing it to be in a defective condition that is unreasonably dangerous. After arriving at the appropriate test, we must decide whether the court of appeals correctly affirmed the trial court's summary judgment order. . . .

. . .

II.

We have not before decided what test should apply in determining whether a product is "unreasonably dangerous" in a design defect case. I believe the appropriate test is defined in [comment *i* to § 402A]: "The article sold must be dangerous to an extent beyond that which would be contemplated by the ordinary consumer who purchases it, with the ordinary knowledge common to the community as to its characteristics" [hereinafter the consumer contemplation test].

Some jurisdictions have adopted this test; others have adopted it in part or rejected it. [ ]

. . .

Other jurisdictions have adopted a variation of the consumer expectation test. Dart v. Wiebe Mfg., Inc., [709 P.2d 876 (Ariz.1985)] (where consumer expectation test is sufficient to resolve a case, that test is to be used; where that test "fails to provide a complete answer," application of risk/benefit factors is appropriate [ ]); Nichols v. Union Underwear Co., 602 S.W.2d 429 (Ky.1980)(consumer expectation or knowledge is just one factor to be considered by a jury in determining whether a product is unreasonably dangerous. [ ]); Knitz v. Minster Machine Co., [432 N.E.2d 814 (Ohio 1982)](product is of defective design "if (1) it is more dangerous than an ordinary consumer would expect when used in an intended or reasonably foreseeable manner, or (2) if the benefits of the challenged design do not outweigh the risk inherent in such design." [ ]).

Other states have rejected the consumer expectation test. Prentis v. Yale Mfg. Co., [365 N.W.2d 176 (Mich.1984)]("[W]e adopt, forthrightly, a pure negligence, risk utility test in products liability actions against manufacturers of products, where liability is predicated upon defective design." [ ]); Turner v. General Motors Corp., 584 S.W.2d 844 (Tex.1979)(risk-utility test will be applied "when the considerations of utility and risk are present in the state of the evidence." [ ]).

III.

. . .

The cases discussed demonstrate that states have taken a variety of approaches to resolve this question. Because of the nature of the product here, I believe the appropriate test is the consumer contemplation or consumer expectation test. The facts presented in this case differ from cases which involve the defective condition of products such as automobile brakes, prescription drugs, and gas tanks. With those types of products, the ordinary consumer is not capable of assessing the danger of the product. On the other hand, an ordinary consumer is necessarily aware that motorcycles can be dangerous. The plaintiff had the choice to purchase other motorcycles by other manufacturers which carried additional safety features, and instead elected to purchase this particular motorcycle and ride it without leg protection devices. The conclusion follows that the trial court's ruling and the court of appeals' decision were correct.

. . .

I also believe the majority incorrectly relies on [*Ortho*]. I believe the risk benefit test cited by the majority and applied in *Ortho* is an appropriate test for products such as drugs, because their danger "is defined primarily by technical, scientific information," and because some drugs are unavoidably unsafe in some respect. [ ] A consumer of drugs cannot realistically be expected to foresee dangers in prescribed drugs which even scientists find to be complex and unpredictable. On the other hand, the purchaser of a motorcycle knows that the purchase and use of "an economical, open-air, maneuverable form of transportation," [ ], presents the risk of accidents and resulting injuries due to the open-air nature of the motorcycle.

Because I believe that the correct test under facts such as these is the consumer contemplation test, I would affirm the court of appeals' decision. Accordingly, I respectfully dissent.

I am authorized to state that JUSTICE ERICKSON and JUSTICE ROVIRA join in this dissent.

NOTES AND QUESTIONS

1. *The crashworthiness doctrine.* Explain the crashworthiness doctrine in terms of the underlying tort duty. Why does the manufacturer's tort duty extend to safety precautions that would protect the occupants of motor vehicles from injuries they might suffer in a crash?

In cases that involve a breach of this duty, courts must resolve a difficult causal question. The manufacturer is liable only for the injuries that were caused by the defect, such as a malfunctioning airbag, but not for the injuries that were or would have been caused by the underlying crash. How, then, can the plaintiff prove the extent to which the defect enhanced her injuries? The Products Liability Restatement section 16 cmt. d, reflecting most courts' resolution of this matter, provides that once the plaintiff proves that enhanced injuries occurred, the burden of proof on their magnitude is placed on the defendant. The result is that if the defendant is unable to prove the amount of enhanced injuries, it will be liable for the entirety of the plaintiff's harm, subject to comparative responsibility apportionment discussed at p. 638, infra. To trigger this rule, the plaintiff must prove that the defect caused at least some compensable harm.

2. *Consumer expectations and patent dangers.* Under the consumer expectations test, can the victim ever win a claim based on defective design when hurt by a danger that was "open and obvious"? Consider the expectations of the consumer in a case like *Camacho*. Given the obvious absence of leg guards, the consumer cannot expect the motorcycle to perform as if it had the guards. The product, therefore, cannot malfunction in this sense and is not subject to liability under the formulation of the consumer expectations test that limits strict liability to product malfunctions. For a product that does not malfunction, can the consumer still have a reasonable expectation that it should perform even better as required by the risk-utility test? Recall the discussion in note 3, p. 589 supra, which describes why the ordinary consumer can reasonably expect that the product design passes the risk-utility test. As *Camacho* put it: "A consumer is justified in expecting that a product placed in the stream of commerce is reasonably safe for its intended use, and when a product is not reasonably safe a products liability action may be maintained." Consumer expectations can justify liability for patent dangers under the risk-utility test, even though these dangers do not constitute product malfunctions that violate the consumer expectations test. For a discussion of events that led a state to overturn its "open and obvious" rule in a motorcycle leg guard case, see Satcher v. Honda Motor Co., 52 F.3d 1311 (5th Cir.1995)(Mississippi law).

In Hernandez v. Tokai Corp., 2 S.W.3d 251 (Tex.1999), a child was burned after a sibling gained access to a disposable lighter and started a fire. Defendant argued that the weight of authority in other jurisdictions is to reject disposable lighter design defect claims as a matter of law. The court responded that this was true in jurisdictions employing a consumer expectations test (do you see why?) but not in courts employing a risk-utility analysis.

3. *Applying the risk-utility test.* The *Camacho* court stated that "the record contains some evidence to support the conclusion that Honda could have provided crash bars at an acceptable cost without impairing the motorcycle's utility or substantially altering its nature." If the motorcycle cost $10,000, how much could the crash bars cost and still be an "acceptable cost"? Is the cost of the motorcycle a relevant criterion for a risk-utility analysis of crash bars? Might we instead want to know how much the crash bars cost and how much risk they could avoid? Can you frame this inquiry in terms of the Hand formula for negligence, discussed at p. 47 supra? What is the significance of the fact that other manufacturers offered the crash bars? Is it relevant that they offered them as optional equipment?

4. *Balancing risk and utility.* Under the risk-utility test how do the *Barker* factors, p. 580 supra, differ from the seven-factor test used in *Camacho*? Does either test tell jurors how to balance these factors? If defendant argued that the crash bars simply cost too much, how would the jury have responded? The conventional wisdom among defense lawyers is that "[i]f you do argue this, you're almost certain to lose on liability, and you can expose yourself to punitive damages as well." Schwartz, The Myth of the Ford Pinto case, 43 Rutgers L.Rev. 1013, 1067 (1991). Would the jury be more sympathetic to cost arguments if the risk-utility test were framed in terms of consumer expectations? Compare Potter v. Chicago Pneumatic Tool Co., 694 A.2d 1319 (Conn.1997)(rejecting the risk-utility test in the Products Liability Restatement on the ground that it is not rooted in the protection of consumer expectations and then using the risk-utility test to define consumer expectations of complex product designs).

5. *Voluntary product standards.* To what extent are standards promulgated by voluntary associations such as Underwriters Laboratories relevant for a design defect case? In Robinson v. G.G.C., Inc., 808 P.2d 522 (Nev.1991), plaintiff was an employee of a supermarket. While working on defendant's box crushing machine, his hand was caught in the mechanism that crushed cardboard boxes. The machine included a removable safety screen that prevented foreign objects from intruding into the crushing mechanism, but the screen could be removed and the machine operated without it as occurred when plaintiff was injured. The American National Standards Institute ("ANSI"), a voluntary association of predominantly industry members that facilitates the adoption of "voluntary consensus standards," had a standard for such machines requiring an interlock that prevented operation when the point of operation guard was removed. The court held that this standard was admissible even though it was not promulgated until several years after defendant's machine had been designed and sold.

Notwithstanding their role in *Robinson*, a cautionary tale about voluntary standards is contained in Alan Schwarz, *As Injuries Rise, Scant Oversight of Helmet Safety*, N.Y. Times, Oct. 20, 2010, at A1. The article discusses the toll of head injuries that occur to children playing tackle football in Pop Warner, high school, and other community leagues. It goes on to address the role of standards for football helmets, promulgated by an association made up of trade members and physicians, that have not been updated since 1973 and which do not address protection against concussions but are limited to the risks of severe forces capable of causing skull fractures. The standards were, however, frequently influential in suits against manufacturers whose helmets meet the standards.

6. *Food products.* Some courts use a foreign/natural test to determine when food is defective. See, e.g., Mexicali Rose v. Superior Court, 822 P.2d 1292 (Cal.1992), in which plaintiff was injured when he swallowed a chicken bone while eating a chicken enchilada at defendant's restaurant. The court unanimously agreed that plaintiff should be able to sue in negligence, but rejected, 4–3, defective products and breach of warranty theories on the facts of the case. The majority would have permitted all three theories if the harm had been caused by a "foreign" object, such as a piece of glass or wire.

The Products Liability Restatement takes a different approach to food defects. Despite rejecting the consumer expectations test for design defects, the Restatement revives that test for food cases, and draws largely on cases involving customers who choke on chicken bones in chicken salad or fish bones in chowder. Though plaintiffs in these cases might have claimed a manufacturing defect, it was difficult to tell if this was an aberration from a norm or an intrinsic (albeit unwanted) part of a designed dish. Section 7 provides that "a harm-causing ingredient of the food product constitutes a defect if a reasonable consumer would not expect the food product to contain that ingredient."

The Iowa Supreme Court explained the basis for its decision to employ a consumer expectations test:

> The "foreign-natural" test . . . does not recommend itself to us as being logical or desirable. It is true one can expect a T-bone in T-bone steak, chicken bones in roast chicken, pork bone in a pork chop, pork bone in spare ribs, a rib bone in short ribs of beef, and fish bones in a whole baked or fried fish, but the expectation is based not on the naturalness of the particular bone to the meat, fowl, or fish, but on the type of dish served containing the meat, fowl, or fish. There is a distinction between what a consumer expects to find in a fish stick and in a baked or fried fish, or in a chicken sandwich made from sliced white meat and in roast chicken. The test should be what is reasonably expected by the consumer in the food as served, not what might be natural to the ingredients of that food prior to preparation.

Kolarik v. Cory International Corp., 721 N.W.2d 159 (Iowa 2006).

Does this rule have broader implications? Much like a food recipe ordinarily does not fully specify every characteristic or component of the ingredients (like the size of chicken bones), any product design is likely to be incomplete in important respects. A tire manufacturer can describe the components and proper assembly of the tire, but not specify how long the tire is intended to function. What if the tire fails after 2,000 miles? As one court found, "[c]ommon experience indicates that no owner of a tire expects it to fail with less than 2,000 miles on its treads." McCann v. Atlas Supply Co., 325 F.Supp. 701, 704 (W.D.Pa.1971). In effect, consumer expectations supply the default definition for product defects, enabling them to fill the gap of incomplete product designs in food and other cases—a foundational role that unifies consumer expectations with the more particularized definitions of defective design, such as the risk-utility test, applicable to other cases.

7. What is the source of consumer expectations? Can they depend on how the seller markets the product, even if the marketing claims are insufficient to create an express warranty? In Denny v. Ford Motor Co., 662 N.E.2d 730 (N.Y.1995), a jury could have found that an off-road vehicle that had certain advantages off the normal highway had been advertised and sold as appropriate for normal driving. The features that made it useful for off-road driving—high center of gravity, narrow track width, and short wheel base—made it dangerous when drivers took evasive action on paved roads. The court developed a dual-purpose doctrine under which a product that might pass the risk-utility test for one purpose could be defective under a consumer expectations test if marketed as suitable for another purpose that might not be appropriate. The court grounded the consumer expectations test in the implied warranty of merchantability.

See also Castro v. QVC Network, Inc., 139 F.3d 114 (2d Cir.1998), in which the defendant advertised a pan on television as fit for cooking 25-pound turkeys. In fact, the pan was fit for many other purposes but was allegedly inadequate for this one because its handles were too small. Plaintiff was burned when the pan tipped over due to the small handles. The court, using New York law and following *Denny*, held that a "jury could have found that the roasting pan's overall utility for cooking low-volume foods outweighed the risk of injury when cooking heavier foods, but that the product was nonetheless unsafe for the purpose for which it was marketed and sold—roasting a twenty-five pound turkey—and, as such, was defective under the consumer expectations test." What gave rise to this expectation—the kind of knowledge that comes with everyday experience or the defendant's marketing of the product?

For an argument and evidence that manufacturers exploit consumers' cognitive limitations to influence their perceptions of product risk, with special reference to the tobacco industry, see Hanson & Kysar, Taking Behavioralism Seriously: The Problem of Market Manipulation, 74 N.Y.U.L.Rev. 630 (1999); Hanson & Kysar, Taking Behavioralism Seriously: Some Evidence of Market Manipulation, 112 Harv.L.Rev. 1420 (1999).

8. *Bystander expectations?* Recall that the consumer expectations test is a product of the contract/warranty heritage of strict products liability that protects both purchasers and users (the "consumer") from defective products. Can the test accommodate the expectations of a bystander who is injured by someone else's use of the product? See, e.g., Ewen v. McLean Trucking Co., 706 P.2d 929 (Or.1985)(consumer expectations test does not include expectations of pedestrian injured by truck but is limited to the expectations ordinary consumers would have at the time of purchase). Should it make any difference if the victim (or user) is a child? In Horst v. Deere & Co., 769 N.W.2d 536 (Wis.2009), a father driving a riding lawnmower backed up over his two-year-old son, severing both feet. Wisconsin continues to employ the consumer expectations test for defect. The plaintiff argued for a "bystander expectations" test, but the court held otherwise. Switching to a bystander standard would produce a vague, amorphous test that would leave the jury with virtually unlimited discretion in deciding whether a defect exists. Moreover, the uncertainty about the standard for a defect would dilute the deterrence incentives for product manufacturers. Would it?

In these cases, the bystander can still pursue a claim for negligent design against the manufacturer. Would that be any different from a claim under the risk-utility test?

9. Based on a survey of the case law, one court concluded that

> Some form of a risk-utility test is employed by an overwhelming majority of the jurisdictions in this country. Some of these jurisdictions exclusively employ a risk-utility test, while others do so with a hybrid of the risk-utility and the consumer expectations test, or an explicit either-or option. States that exclusively employ the consumer expectations test are a decided minority.

Branham v. Ford Motor Co., 701 S.E.2d 5, 14–15 (S.C.2010). Although the consumer expectations test is exclusively used by only a "decided minority" of jurisdictions, the test, in one form or another, continues to be recognized by a substantial majority of jurisdictions. See id. at 14 n.12 (citing 17 different states as exclusively relying on the risk-utility test). For another review of the case law and conclusion that a plaintiff can prove defective design under either the consumer expectations test or the risk-utility test, depending on the evidence, see Tincher v. Omega Flex, Inc., 104 A.3d 328 (Pa.2014).

Are these differences more apparent than real? In jurisdictions that employ both tests, "courts . . . have been very sensitive to the limitations of the consumer expectations test and have confined its application to cases that instantiate res ipsa-like product failures i.e., where a product fails to perform its manifestly intended function." Twerski & Henderson, Manufacturer's Liability for Defective Product Designs: The Triumph of Risk-Utility, 74 Brook.L.Rev. 1061, 1101 (2009). Recall that the malfunction theory of defect is recognized in section 3 of the Products Liability Restatement, p. 576 supra. "To the extent that a court recognizes that if a product does not fall within section 3 the plaintiff must establish that the product fails to meet risk-utility norms, the law of that jurisdiction is perfectly congruent with the Products Liability Restatement." Twerski & Henderson, supra, at 1101.

10. Did "strict liability" play a role in the decision in *Camacho?* In *Soule?* Would either be decided differently under a negligence analysis? Recall that section 2(b) of the Products Liability Restatement, p. 576 supra, does not use either conceptual label.

Can strict liability have a distinctive role in the causal inquiry? In *Evans v. Lorillard Tobacco Co.*, discussed at note 7, p. 592 supra, plaintiff proved defective design by showing that a low tar, low nicotine cigarette was a reasonable alternative design to defendant's Newport brand. Defendant argued that the design defect could not have caused the plaintiff's mother's injury because she had "tried and rejected a brand of cigarettes with lower tar and nicotine." The court concluded otherwise, reasoning that a plaintiff "may establish causation by proving that the defect caused her injury; the plaintiff need not prove that she would have used a reasonable alternative design had one been available." The plaintiff had accordingly established causation because "the evidence was essentially undisputed that the tar and nicotine in Newport brand cigarettes caused [the] lung cancer." How does this ruling satisfy the traditional rule of but-for causation, which asks whether the injury would have occurred if the defendant had not acted tortiously? As defendant had proven, if it had supplied low tar, low nicotine cigarettes, the plaintiff's mother would still have smoked the Newport brand, so how did the defective design cause the injury? See M. Geistfeld, Principles of Products Liability 211–14 (2d ed.2011)(distinguishing the causal rule in negligence cases from the causal rule under strict liability, which "simply asks whether the tortious risk for which the defendant is strictly responsible caused the plaintiff's injury").

11. Regardless of the test employed in a particular case, the jury evaluates the design on a case-by-case basis. Dawson v. Chrysler Corp., 630 F.2d 950 (3d Cir.1980), voiced two significant critiques of this approach. First, because each individual jury decides design defects de novo, the verdict in one case is not binding on the next case, and so product manufacturers are denied the guidance of uniform standards. The second problem is that common law adjudication may miss the forest for the trees. The court discussed these concerns in the course of upholding a judgment for $2 million for a driver who was crushed after his car skidded sideways into a pole and wrapped around it. Evidence showed that using a firmer side frame would have added 200–250 pounds to the weight of the car and $300 to its cost:

> The result of such arrangement is that while the jury found Chrysler liable for not producing a rigid enough vehicular frame, a factfinder in another case might well hold the manufacturer liable for producing a frame that is too rigid. Yet, as pointed out at trial, in certain types of accidents—head-on collisions—it is desirable to have a car designed to collapse upon impact because the deformation would absorb much of the shock of the collision, and divert the force of deceleration away from the vehicle's passengers. In effect, this permits individual juries applying varying laws in different jurisdictions to set nationwide automobile safety standards and to impose on automobile manufacturers conflicting requirements. It would be difficult for members of the industry to alter their design and production behavior in response to jury verdicts in such cases, because their response might well be at variance with what some other jury decides is a defective design. Under these circumstances, the law imposes on the industry the responsibility of insuring vast numbers of persons involved in automobile accidents.

> Equally serious is the impact on other national social and economic goals of the existing case-by-case system of establishing automobile safety requirements. As we have become more dependent on foreign sources of energy, and as the price of that energy has increased, the attention of the federal government has been drawn to a search to find alternative supplies and the means

of conserving energy. More recently, the domestic automobile industry has been struggling to compete with foreign manufacturers which have stressed smaller, more fuel-efficient cars. Yet, during this same period, Congress has permitted a system of regulation by ad hoc adjudications under which a jury can hold an automobile manufacturer culpable for not producing a car that is considerably heavier, and likely to have less fuel efficiency.

Id. at 962–63

The court concluded that letting individual juries impose liability for defective designs was not "fair or efficient." Because Congress had permitted the common law to continue, and "because Congress is the body best suited to evaluate and, if appropriate, to change that system, we decline today to do anything in this regard except to bring the problem to the attention of the legislative branch."

D. SAFETY INSTRUCTIONS AND WARNINGS

After having considered the design of the product, we turn to the search for defects based on the words—instructions and warnings—that accompany (or are omitted from) the product, whether on the package, on the product or in an insert that comes with the product. These words may reduce risk by instructing users in how to obtain the benefits from the product's intended use and in the care required for safe use. Words may also alert potential buyers and users to irreducible dangers in the product, dangers that cannot be reasonably reduced by the manufacturer nor avoided by consumers no matter how careful they may be. Warnings of side effects of pharmaceuticals are common examples of the latter. Keep in mind these differing roles of warnings as you proceed through this section.

A threshold issue: Common knowledge and the duty to warn. If the ordinary consumer already knows about the risk in question, the manufacturer has no duty to warn. In Brown Forman Corp. v. Brune, 893 S.W.2d 640 (Tex.App.1994), the court held that no notice was required on a bottle of tequila to warn against the dangers of drinking a large quantity in a short period of time. The underage plaintiff, already intoxicated from other drinking, died after drinking unmixed tequila from a glass, and then the bottle, "heavily and rapidly." The dangers were apparent even to an 18-year-old person. Nor would a warning have averted what happened. Is this a harder case than one based on the lack of warning that a knife is sharp?

Nor is there a duty to warn about the dangers of riding unrestrained in the cargo bed of a pickup truck. In Maneely v. General Motors Corp., 108 F.3d 1176, 1180 (9th Cir.1997), the court, using California law, noted the pervasiveness of "buckle-up" campaigns and the "manifest danger" of "being ejected from the vehicle during a crash or being slammed against an unforgiving hard surface of the vehicle itself." From all of this "we conclude that the dangers of riding unrestrained in a moving motor vehicle have become common knowledge and are firmly engraved upon the public consciousness." (As to design defect, the consumer expectations test would yield the same result. The truck passed a risk-utility analysis because the design's benefits outweighed its dangers as a matter of law: To redesign a pickup truck to provide protective seats "and occupant packaging" would "transform the cargo-hauling pickup truck into just another passenger-carrying vehicle and would eliminate its utility in carrying cargo." Id. at 1181.)

In Emery v. Federated Foods, Inc., 863 P.2d 426 (Mont.1993), 2½-year-old Chad choked on marshmallows. The court held, 5–2, that a jury should decide whether it was common knowledge that young children were at risk in eating marshmallows because marshmallows expand "when they are soaked with the liquid secretions that are present in the breathing tubes of the lungs." Further, an "aspirated marshmallow fragment might not be reachable with a finger and could be difficult to dislodge with a Heimlich maneuver." Id. at 432.

We turn now to cases in which defendant does not contest the need for a warning. The issue, rather, is whether the warning adequately conveyed the requisite information.

Hood v. Ryobi America Corp.
United States Court of Appeals, Fourth Circuit, 1999.
181 F.3d 608.

■ Before WILKINSON, CHIEF JUDGE, and WIDENER and KING, CIRCUIT JUDGES.

■ WILKINSON, CHIEF JUDGE.

. . .

Hood purchased a Ryobi TS-254 miter saw in Westminster, Maryland on February 25, 1995, for the purpose of performing home repairs. The saw was fully assembled at the time of purchase. It had a ten-inch diameter blade mounted on a rotating spindle controlled by a finger trigger on a handle near the top of the blade. To operate the saw, the consumer would use that handle to lower the blade through the material being cut.

Two blade guards shielded nearly the entire saw blade. A large metal guard, fixed to the frame of the saw, surrounded the upper half of the blade. A transparent plastic lower guard covered the rest of the blade and retracted into the upper guard as the saw came into contact with the work piece.

A number of warnings in the operator's manual and affixed to the saw itself stated that the user should operate the saw only with the blade guards in place. For example, the owner's manual declared that the user should "KEEP GUARDS IN PLACE" and warned: "ALWAYS USE THE SAW BLADE GUARD. Never operate the machine with the guard removed"; "NEVER operate this saw without all guards in place and in good operating condition"; and "WARNING: TO PREVENT POSSIBLE SERIOUS PERSONAL INJURY, NEVER PERFORM ANY CUTTING OPERATION WITH THE UPPER OR LOWER BLADE GUARD REMOVED." The saw itself carried several decals stating "DANGER: DO NOT REMOVE ANY GUARD. USE OF SAW WITHOUT THIS GUARD WILL RESULT IN SERIOUS INJURY"; "OPERATE ONLY WITH GUARDS IN PLACE"; and "WARNING . . . DO NOT operate saw without the upper and lower guards in place."

The day after his purchase, Hood began working with the saw in his driveway. While attempting to cut a piece of wood approximately four inches in height Hood found that the blade guards prevented the saw blade from passing completely through the piece. Disregarding the manufacturer's warnings, Hood decided to remove the blade guards from the saw. Hood first detached the saw blade from its spindle. He then unscrewed the four screws that held the blade guard assembly to the frame of the saw. Finally, he replaced the blade onto the bare spindle and completed his cut.

Rather than replacing the blade guards, Hood continued to work with the saw blade exposed. He worked in this fashion for about twenty minutes longer when, in the middle of another cut, the spinning saw blade flew off the saw and back toward Hood. The blade partially amputated his left thumb and lacerated his right leg.

Hood admits that he read the owner's manual and most of the warning labels on the saw before he began his work. He claims, however, that he believed the blade guards were intended solely to prevent a user's clothing or fingers from coming into contact with the saw blade. He contends that he was unaware that removing the blade guards would permit the spinning blade to detach from the saw. But Ryobi, he claims, was aware of that possibility. In fact, another customer had sued Ryobi after suffering a similar accident in the mid-1980s.

[In Hood's diversity case he] raised claims of failure to warn and defective design under several theories of liability. On cross-motions for summary judgment the district court entered judgment for the defendants on all claims, finding that in the face of adequate warnings Hood had altered the saw and caused his own injury. [ ] Hood appeals.

II.

A manufacturer may be liable for placing a product on the market that bears inadequate instructions and warnings or that is defective in design. Moran v. Fabergé, Inc., [332 A.2d 11 (Md.1975)]; [ ]. Hood asserts that Ryobi failed adequately to warn of the dangers of using the saw without the blade guards in place. Hood also contends that the design of the saw was defective. We disagree on both counts.[1]

A.

Hood first complains that the warnings he received were insufficiently specific. Hood admits that Ryobi provided several clear and conspicuous warnings not to operate the saw without the blade guards. He contends, however, that the warnings affixed to the product and displayed in the operator's manual were inadequate to alert him to the dangers of doing so. In addition to Ryobi's directive "never" to operate a guardless saw, Hood would require the company to inform of the actual consequences of such conduct. Specifically, Hood contends that an adequate warning would have explained that removing the guards would lead to blade detachment.

We disagree. Maryland does not require an encyclopedic warning. ← *Maryland's law* Instead, "a warning need only be one that is reasonable under the circumstances." Levin v. Walter Kidde & Co., [248 A.2d 151 (Md.1968)]. A clear and specific warning will normally be sufficient—"the manufacturer need not warn of every mishap or source of injury that the mind can imagine flowing from the product." [ ]; see *Levin*, [ ] (declining to require warning of the danger that a cracked syphon bottle might explode and holding "never use cracked bottle" to be adequate as a matter of law). In deciding whether a warning is adequate, Maryland law asks whether the benefits of a more detailed warning outweigh the costs of requiring the change. [*Moran*].

Hood assumes that the cost of a more detailed warning label is minimal in this case, and he claims that such a warning would have prevented his injury. But the price of more detailed warnings is greater than their additional printing fees alone. Some commentators have observed that the proliferation of label detail threatens to undermine the effectiveness of warnings altogether. See James A. Henderson, Jr. & Aaron D. Twerski, Doctrinal Collapse in Products Liability: The Empty Shell of Failure to Warn, 65 N.Y.U. L.Rev. 265, 296–97 (1990). As manufacturers append line after line onto product labels in the quest for the best possible warning, it is easy to lose sight of the label's communicative value as a whole. Well-meaning attempts to warn of every possible accident lead over time to voluminous yet impenetrable labels—too prolix to read and too technical to understand.

By contrast, Ryobi's warnings are clear and unequivocal. Three labels on the saw itself and at least four warnings in the owner's manual direct the user not to operate the saw with the blade guards removed. Two declare that "serious injury" could result from doing so. This is not a case where the manufacturer has failed to include any

---

[1] Hood raises these claims under three theories of recovery: strict liability, negligence, and breach of warranty. The principles of Maryland law governing these three theories, at least as relevant to this case, are virtually identical.

warnings at all with its product. [ ] Ryobi provided warnings sufficient to apprise the ordinary consumer that it is unsafe to operate a guardless saw—warnings which, if followed, would have prevented the injury in this case.

It is apparent, moreover, that the vast majority of consumers do not detach this critical safety feature before using this type of saw. Indeed, although Ryobi claims to have sold thousands of these saws, Hood has identified only one fifteen-year-old incident similar to his. Hood has thus not shown that these clear, unmistakable, and prominent warnings are insufficient to accomplish their purpose. Nor can he prove that increased label clutter would bring any net societal benefit. We hold that the warnings Ryobi provided are adequate as a matter of law.

[The court then rejected plaintiff's claim based on design defect, discussed in the notes that follow.]

Warned never to operate his miter saw without the blade guards in place, Hood nonetheless chose to detach those guards and run the saw in a disassembled condition. We hold that Ryobi is not liable for Hood's resulting injuries under any of the theories of recovery raised here. The judgment of the district court is therefore affirmed.

NOTES AND QUESTIONS

1. *The standard for adequacy.* According to the court, an adequate warning must be "reasonable under the circumstances." Is that any different from the standard for negligence? Several cases have developed criteria for determining the adequacy of a warning, with a leading formulation supplied by Pittman v. Upjohn Co., 890 S.W.2d 425, 429 (Tenn.1994):

> A reasonable warning not only conveys a fair indication of the dangers involved, but also warns with the degree of intensity required by the nature of the risk. [ ] Among the criteria for determining the adequacy of a warning are: 1. the warning must adequately indicate the scope of the danger; 2. the warning must reasonably communicate the extent or seriousness of the harm that could result from misuse of the [product]; 3. the physical aspects of the warning must be adequate to alert a reasonably prudent person to the danger; 4. a simple directive warning may be inadequate when it fails to indicate the consequences that might result from failure to follow it and, . . . 5. the means to convey the warning must be adequate. [ ]

Why are these factors appropriate? How does the warning in *Hood* fare under them?

2. *Content of the communication.* If the manufacturer merely warned "use product safely to avoid injury," then doing so would clearly be inadequate. An adequate warning conveys whatever detailed information the consumer must know in order to use the product safely. Why does the

court reject plaintiff's argument that Ryobi should have told him about the precise danger of removing the guard? If a user thinks that a warning is addressed to getting fingers or clothing caught in the machine, and thinks correctly that such a peril can be avoided, and Ryobi knows another (not widely known) reason for keeping the guard on, why shouldn't it have to tell the user about that peril as well?

Courts in other cases have found warnings to be defective for not adequately disclosing more detailed information. In Ragans v. Miriam Collins-Palm Beach Laboratories Co., 681 So.2d 1173 (Fla.App.1996), plaintiff hairstylist was using a permanent wave kit that she had used 30–50 times before. It contained wave lotion in a clear bottle and neutralizer in a white plastic bottle. The activator came in a tube that said "ADD TO CLEAR BOTTLE ONLY." The instructions also stated that adding the activator "to other than wave lotion can cause serious injury." Plaintiff inadvertently poured a few drops of activator into the neutralizer bottle. "The resulting mixture reacted explosively and shot out of the neutralizer bottle with enough force to hit the ceiling" and cause severe chemical burns and permanent facial injuries. The court concluded that a jury question was presented because the words failed to warn of the dangerous consequences of not following the five-word direction above. Neither did a leaflet inside the box which, in step number 5, again simply warned of "serious injury."

3. *Information costs.* What limits the amount of detail that must be provided by an adequate warning? *Hood* suggests that safety information, in addition to its benefits, also involves the cost of acquiring and retaining the information—often called "information costs." In *Moran v. Fabergé, Inc.*, a 1975 case cited in *Hood*, the court stated that the "cost of giving an adequate warning is usually so minimal, amounting only to the expense of adding some more printing to a label, that this balancing process will almost always weigh in favor of an obligation to warn of latent dangers, if the manufacturer is otherwise required to do so." Can *Hood* be reconciled with *Moran*?

To see why cases like *Moran* contain no discussion of information costs, one must recognize that courts first formulated the warning doctrine before the Internet had become widely available. In light of the ensuing proliferation of easily accessible information, is it realistic to assume that supplying more and more detailed information is always better for the consumer?

In one of the first cases to address this issue, Cotton v. Buckeye Gas Products Co., 840 F.2d 935 (D.C.Cir.1988), plaintiff was hurt when propane tanks on the job site exploded. He argued that the labels were inadequate. In the course of rejecting the claims, the court observed:

> The primary cost [of added warning] is, in fact, the increase in time and effort required for the user to grasp the message. The inclusion of each extra item dilutes the punch of every other item. Given short attention spans, items crowd each other out; they get lost in fine print. . . .

> [Plaintiff] discounts altogether the warnings in the pamphlet, without even considering what the canister warning would have looked like if Buckeye had supplemented it not only with the special items he is personally interested in—in hindsight—but also with all other equally valuable items (i.e., "equally" in terms of the scope and probability of the danger likely to be averted and the incremental impact of the information on user conduct). If every foreseeable possibility must be covered, "[T]he list of foolish practices warned against would be so long, it would fill a volume." [ ]

Id. at 938.

Is this analysis relevant to Mr. Hood's claim? Despite the concerns expressed by the *Cotton* court, warnings have proliferated to such an extent that consumers may be more inclined to omit reading them. Might a manufacturer be subject to liability for providing too elaborate a set of warnings, such that they diluted the essential message about the most serious risks based on the communicative requirement of an adequate warning?

4. *Method of the communication.* In addition to the content of a warning, courts consider the method by which the manufacturer communicates that content to the user. In Johnson v. Johnson Chemical Co., 588 N.Y.S.2d 607 (App.1992), plaintiff was hurt when an anti-roach fogger exploded while plaintiff was using it in the kitchen—with the pilot light on the stove still lit, despite a warning to shut off pilot lights among other possible sources of flame. Defendant argued that the adequacy of the warning was irrelevant because plaintiff had not read it. The court responded:

> This argument loses its persuasive force . . . once it is understood that the intensity of the language used in the text of a warning is only one of the factors to be considered in deciding whether such warning is adequate. A second factor to be considered is the prominence with which such language is displayed. [ ] For example, the warning "harmful if swallowed" is less intense than the warning, "swallowing will result in death"; however, the former, less intense warning, when displayed prominently in block letters on the front label of a product, may be ultimately more effective than the latter, more intense warning, when [the latter is] displayed unobtrusively in small letters in the middle of a 10-page package insert [ ]. A consumer such as [plaintiff] who, by her own admission, tends to ignore one sort of label, might pay heed to a different, more prominent or more dramatic label.

Is the required method of disclosure limited to written English? In Farias v. Mr. Heater, Inc., 684 F.3d 1231 (11th Cir.2012), the Spanish-speaking plaintiff's home was damaged by a fire caused by a propane gas heater that she had been improperly using indoors. Plaintiff brought suit against the manufacturer and distributors of the heater, alleging that the warning was defective for not providing instructions in Spanish. In affirming summary judgment for defendants, the court concluded that the English language and pictorial warnings on the box that contained the heater accurately, clearly, and unambiguously warned against indoor use of the product. Thus, defendants were under no obligation under Florida law to provide Spanish-language warnings, absent evidence that the heater was specifically marketed in any way to Spanish-speaking customers in Florida through use of Hispanic media. Compare Campos v. Firestone Tire & Rubber Co., 485 A.2d 305, 310 (N.J.1984)("In view of the unskilled or semi-skilled nature of the work and the existence of many in the work force who do not read English, warnings in the form of symbols might have been appropriate. . . ."). Does this concern for the method of communication reflect the importance of reducing the consumer's information costs?

5. *Causation and the "heeding presumption."* A number of states have adopted a presumption that the ordinary consumer will read and heed an adequate warning. This "heeding presumption" places the burden on the defendant to show that the user would not have followed an adequate warning if one had been given. See, e.g., Coffman v. Keene Corp., 628 A.2d 710, 717 (N.J.1993), in which the defendant argued that the presumption could not be justified empirically because "it is nearly impossible to go through a day without consciously ignoring warnings designed to protect health and safety." The court did not dispute this assertion, but concluded that the presumption is justified because it would operate as a "powerful incentive" to manufacturers by subjecting them to liability for an inadequate warning without the jury needing to speculate on whether an adequate warning would have prevented plaintiff's injury. Compare General Motors Corp. v. Saenz, 873 S.W.2d 353 (Tex.1993), in which the court rejected a heeding presumption where plaintiffs claimed that they had not been adequately warned about the dangers of overloading a truck. Although warnings to that effect were placed in the owner's manual and in the door jamb, plaintiffs argued that the wording was inadequate. The court found no reason to conclude that if the wording had been better the accident would not have happened.

6. *Interplay of design and warning.* When, if ever, can the supplier choose to give a safety instruction instead of redesigning the product to make it safer? Assume that in *Camacho*, p. 594 supra, Honda, after rejecting the advice of its marketing department, had placed in large print on every motorcycle that lacked leg guards the following conspicuous statement: "WARNING. THIS PRODUCT CONTAINS NO LEG GUARDS. ANY ACCIDENT IS LIKELY TO CAUSE THE OCCUPANT SERIOUS LEG INJURIES." Might this have affected the design-defect issue in *Camacho*? As this question suggests, warnings effectively make product risks open and obvious to the consumer. As *Camacho* illustrates, even for dangers that are patent to the ordinary consumer, the manufacturer can still be liable for defective design. Consequently, a warning about a particular product risk does not necessarily absolve the manufacturer from the duty to eliminate that risk with a reasonable redesign of the product.

In the design part of the case, the *Hood* court declared that Maryland imposed "no duty to predict that a consumer will violate clear, easily understandable safety warnings such as those Ryobi included with this product." Does this mean that the manufacturer can reasonably expect that consumers will always understand and comply with product warnings? If so, then what risk would remain for purposes of product design?

In Hansen v. Sunnyside Products, Inc., 65 Cal.Rptr.2d 266 (App.1997), plaintiff was injured when defendant's household cleanser, which contained hydrofluoric acid, came through a tiny hole in a glove she was wearing to protect against contact with the cleanser. In an effort to show that the design was not defective, the defendant sought to present evidence about the warnings on the package in an effort to show that the warnings had prevented harm in the past. The court agreed that this evidence was admissible because it might help the jury to decide the design question:

> We do not think that the risk to the consumer of the design of many household products can be rationally evaluated without considering the product's warnings. Thus, for example, what is the risk of the design of a power saw, or other power tools or equipment, without considering the product's directions and warnings? We dare say that the risk would be astronomically, and irrationally high.

Id. at 278.

A warning affects how consumers use the product and therefore the amount of risk that is the subject of the manufacturer's design decision, leading the court to conclude that "whereas an adequate warning will avoid liability on a failure to warn theory, it is but one factor to be weighed in the balance in a design defect case." Can these issues be framed in terms of the risk-utility test for defective design? See M. Geistfeld, Principles of Products Liability 164–69 (2d ed.2011)(arguing that the risk to be eliminated by redesign is defined by the magnitude of the foreseeable risk stemming from consumers' imperfect compliance with the warning and that the utility of redesign includes elimination of the burden that consumers would incur to follow the warning).

7. *Products dangerous for another exposed class.* Sometimes a product that is appropriate for one class of consumers is dangerous for another group that is exposed to the product. In Hernandez v. Tokai Corp., 2 S.W.3d 251, 259 (Tex.1999), a child was badly burned due to her five-year-old sister's playing with a disposable cigarette lighter. The court noted that a "product intended for adults need not be designed to be safe for children solely because it is possible for the product to come into a child's hands. . . . The risk that adults, for whose use the products were intended, will allow children access to them, resulting in harm, must be balanced against the products' utility to their intended users." If the product design is deemed appropriate for adults, might a warning still be needed about the risks posed to children? Compare Bean v. BIC Corp., 597 So.2d 1350 (Ala.1992)(jury question whether warnings on package and lighter were adequate), with Kirk v. Hanes Corp., 16 F.3d 705 (6th Cir.1994)(Michigan law imposes no duty to warn because danger of lighter is obvious to adult buyers). In 1993, the Consumer Product Safety Commission issued one of its few regulations, applicable to lighters, requiring that they be designed so they defeated efforts of 85% of children who attempted to use them in a test specified by the CPSC. 16 C.F.R. 1210.1 et seq.

8. *The addressee.* An important question in judging the need for, and adequacy of, warnings is to whom they are addressed. The normal rule is that they must reach the person who is likely to use the product. Thus, under the sophisticated user doctrine, a manufacturer has no duty to warn when the class of foreseeable users already has specialized knowledge of the danger. In Carrel v. National Cord & Braid Corp., 852 N.E.2d 100 (Mass.2006), a camper at a Boy Scout camp grabbed a bungee cord attached to a "zip line." A knot by which the bungee cord was attached to the zip line came undone and the resulting recoil hit the plaintiff-camper in the eye. Plaintiff claimed that the warning did not adequately disclose the risk that some types of knots could easily become undone due to certain latent properties of the bungee cord. On appeal of a defense verdict, the court held that the Boy Scouts, who operated the camp, and its consultant-specialist, who purchased the cord at issue, were sufficiently knowledgeable to justify an instruction on the sophisticated user rule. The Boy Scouts ran this "adventure" program across the country, it conducted training courses, it had national safety standards, and it employed specialists to inspect and ensure compliance with the standards.

The following case involves another important context in which the addressee of the warning is at issue.

State v. Karl

Supreme Court of Appeals of West Virginia, 2007.
220 W.Va. 463, 647 S.E.2d 899.

■ DAVIS, CHIEF JUSTICE.

[A] drug manufacturer asks this Court to adopt the learned intermediary doctrine as an exception to the general duty of manufacturers to warn consumers of the dangerous propensities of their products. After thorough consideration of the learned intermediary doctrine in light of the current state of the prescription drug industry and physician/patient relationships, we decline to adopt this doctrine. [ ]

I.

FACTUAL AND PROCEDURAL HISTORY

[Because of the procedural posture of the case], the facts have not been conclusively determined below. Nevertheless, it appears to be undisputed that on May 19, 1999, Mrs. Nancy J. Gellner was prescribed the drug Propulsid by her primary care physician, Daniel J. Wilson, M.D., a respondent to this proceeding (hereinafter referred to as "Dr. Wilson").... Propulsid was manufactured and distributed by [petitioner] Janssen.... Mrs. Gellner died suddenly on the third day after she began taking Propulsid.

On May 17, 2001, Mrs. Gellner's estate (hereinafter referred to as "the Estate"), a respondent herein, filed a products liability/medical malpractice action against Janssen and Dr. Wilson. . . . On August 26, 2004, Janssen filed a motion for summary judgment asserting that, under the learned intermediary doctrine, it had fulfilled its duty to warn by providing warnings regarding Propulsid to Dr. Wilson. . . . [T]he circuit court denied Janssen's motion by order entered on June 13, 2006. [Janssen sought discretionary appellate review, which was granted.]

. . .

III.

DISCUSSION

The issue raised in this original jurisdiction action is one of first impression. . . .

"The learned intermediary doctrine provides an exception to the general rule imposing a duty on manufacturers to warn consumers about the risks of their products." [ ]

The learned intermediary doctrine stands for the proposition that

a drug "manufacturer is excused from warning each patient who receives the product when the manufacturer properly warns the prescribing physician of the product's dangers." [ ] Hence, a drug manufacturer's duty to warn consumers about the dangers of its prescription drugs extends only to the prescribing physician or healthcare provider, who acts as a "learned intermediary" between the manufacturer and the ultimate consumer and assumes responsibility for advising individual patients of the risks associated with the drug.

[ ]

Some authorities have suggested that the number of jurisdictions having adopted the doctrine is an overwhelming majority, but those authorities have either included lower court decisions, or have included jurisdictions where federal circuit courts applying state law have concluded that the doctrine would be adopted. [The court then cited cases from other jurisdictions revealing disagreement regarding how large a majority of state courts had explicitly adopted the learned intermediary doctrine.]

Our own research has yielded a markedly different result. Considering decisions of only the highest state courts, we find that a mere twenty-one states have expressly adopted the learned intermediary doctrine. In one additional state, North Carolina, the doctrine has been adopted by statute. [ ] Thus, the total number of jurisdictions recognizing the learned intermediary doctrine, either by decision of the highest court or by statute, is only twenty-two, [and six other high courts have intimations that they look favorably on the doctrine].

On the other hand, the highest courts of the remaining twenty-two states ... have not adopted the learned intermediary doctrine. Likewise, the District of Columbia Court of Appeals and the Supreme Court of Puerto Rico have not adopted the learned intermediary doctrine. Thus, while the doctrine is widely applied among lower courts, the number of high courts who have followed suit and expressly adopted the doctrine, while admittedly in the majority, do not make up the *overwhelming majority* that has often been suggested by courts and commentators.

Among the primary justifications that have been advanced for the learned intermediary doctrine are (1) the difficulty manufacturers would encounter in attempting to provide warnings to the ultimate users of prescription drugs; (2) patients' reliance on their treating physicians' judgment in selecting appropriate prescription drugs; (3) the fact that it is physicians who exercise their professional judgment in selecting appropriate drugs; (4) the belief that physicians are in the best position to provide appropriate warnings to their patients; and (5) the concern that direct warnings to ultimate users would interfere with doctor/patient relationships. For example, the Supreme Court of Washington has explained that

> The reasons for this rule should be obvious. Where a product is available only on prescription or through the services of a physician, the physician acts as a "learned intermediary" between the manufacturer or seller and the patient. It is his duty to inform himself of the qualities and characteristics of those products which he prescribes for or administers to or uses on his patients, and to exercise an independent judgment, taking into account his knowledge of the patient as well as the product. The patient is expected to and, it can be presumed, does place primary reliance upon that judgment. The physician decides what facts should be told to the patient. Thus, if the product is properly labeled and carries the necessary instructions and warnings to fully apprise the physician of the proper procedures for use and the dangers involved, the manufacturer may reasonably assume that the physician will exercise the informed judgment thereby gained in conjunction with his own independent learning, in the best interest of the patient. It has also been suggested that the rule is made necessary by the fact that it is ordinarily difficult for the manufacturer to communicate directly with the consumer.

Terhune v. A.H. Robins Co., 90 Wash.2d 9, 14, 577 P.2d 975, 978 (1978) (footnote omitted).

We find these justifications for the learned intermediary doctrine to be largely outdated and unpersuasive. At the outset, we note that the learned intermediary doctrine is not a modern doctrine. Rather, its origins may be traced as far back as 1925. [The court recounted the development of the learned intermediary rule.]

We note the lengthy history of the learned intermediary doctrine because the very age of the doctrine requires us to pause and engage in a thorough examination, even though the doctrine has been widely accepted. Significant changes in the drug industry have post-dated the adoption of the learned intermediary doctrine in the majority of states in which it is followed. We refer specifically to the initiation and intense proliferation of direct-to-consumer advertising, along with its impact on the physician/patient relationship, and the development of the Internet as a common method of dispensing and obtaining prescription drug information.

When the learned intermediary doctrine was developed, direct-to-consumer advertising of prescription drugs was utterly unknown. "Historically, prescription drug advertising in the United States was directed primarily to prescribers, who were once the sole decision-makers when choosing prescription medications." [ ] ("Originally, pharmaceutical manufacturers advertised to physicians directly via medical journals or pharmaceutical representatives. The general public was less aware of what name brand drugs were on the market."). As one court has aptly observed,

> Our medical-legal jurisprudence is based on images of health care that no longer exist. At an earlier time, medical advice was received in the doctor's office from a physician who most likely made house calls if needed. The patient usually paid a small sum of money to the doctor. Neighborhood pharmacists compounded prescribed medicines. Without being pejorative, it is safe to say that the prevailing attitude of law and medicine was that the "doctor knows best." [ ]
>
> . . .
>
> For good or ill, that has all changed. Medical services are in large measure provided by managed care organizations. Medicines are purchased in the pharmacy department of supermarkets and often paid for by third-party providers. Drug manufacturers now directly advertise products to consumers on the radio, television, the Internet, billboards on public transportation, and in magazines.

Perez v. Wyeth Labs. Inc., 161 N.J. 1, 4, 734 A.2d 1245, 1246–47 (1999).

. . .[14]

Since the 1997 proliferation of drug advertising, only four high courts have adopted the learned intermediary doctrine. *See Vitanza v.*

---

[14] [The court provided a table containing the amount of direct-to-consumer advertising from 1989 to 2001 that revealed spending increased from $12 million to $2.38 billion.]

Upjohn Co., 257 Conn. 365, 778 A.2d 829 (2001); *McCombs v. Synthes,* 277 Ga. 252, 587 S.E.2d 594 (2003); *Larkin v. Pfizer, Inc.,* 153 S.W.3d 758 (Ky.2004); *Freeman v. Hoffman-La Roche, Inc.,* 260 Neb. 552, 618 N.W.2d 827 (2000). In deciding to adopt the learned intermediary doctrine, none of those courts gave thorough consideration to the changes that have occurred in the prescription drug industry with respect to direct-to-consumer advertising. We, however, find such changes to be a significant factor in deciding this issue, especially the impact direct-to-consumer advertising has had on the physician/patient relationship. [ ]

. . .

In rejecting the application of the learned intermediary doctrine to drugs that had been the subject of direct-to-consumer advertising, the Supreme Court of New Jersey opined, and we agree, that such advertising obviates each of the premises upon which the doctrine rests:

> These premises: (1) reluctance to undermine the doctor patient-relationship; (2) absence in the era of "doctor knows best" of need for the patient's informed consent; (3) inability of drug manufacturer to communicate with patients; and (4) complexity of the subject; are all (with the possible exception of the last) absent in the direct-to-consumer advertising of prescription drugs.

> First, with rare and wonderful exceptions, the " 'Norman Rockwell' image of the family doctor no longer exists." [ ] Informed consent requires a patient-based decision rather than the paternalistic approach of the 1970s. [ ]

> Second, because managed care has reduced the time allotted per patient, physicians have considerably less time to inform patients of the risks and benefits of a drug. Sheryl Gay Stolberg, *Faulty Warning Labels Add to Risk in Prescription Drugs,* N.Y. Times, June 4, 1999, at A27. "In a 1997 survey of 1,000 patients, the F.D.A. found that only one-third had received information from their doctors about the dangerous side effects of drugs they were taking." [ ]

> Third, having spent $1.3 billion on advertising in 1998, . . . drug manufacturers can hardly be said to "lack effective means to communicate directly with patients," [ ], when their advertising campaigns can pay off in close to billions in dividends.

> . . .

> When all of its premises are absent, as when direct warnings to consumers are mandatory, the learned intermediary doctrine, "itself an exception to the manufacturer's traditional duty to warn consumers directly of the risk associated with any product, simply drops out of the

calculus, leaving the duty of the manufacturer to be determined in accordance with general principles of tort law." *Edwards v. Basel Pharms.*, 116 F.3d 1341, 1343 (10th Cir.1997) (discussing question of adequacy of nicotine patch warning under Texas law certified in *Edwards v. Basel Pharms.*, 933 P.2d 298 (Okla.1997)). . . .

Perez v. Wyeth Labs. Inc., 161 N.J. 1, 18–19, 734 A.2d 1245, 1255–56. [ ]

Many jurisdictions have addressed the shortcomings of the learned intermediary doctrine by developing various exceptions.

> [C]ourts have recognized exceptions [to the learned intermediary doctrine] regarding: (1) vaccine inoculations; *Davis v. Wyeth Laboratories, Inc.*, [399 F.2d 121, 131 (9th Cir.1968)]; (2) oral contraceptives; *MacDonald v. Ortho Pharmaceutical Corp.*, 394 Mass. 131, 135–36, 475 N.E.2d 65, *cert. denied*, 474 U.S. 920, 106 S.Ct. 250, 88 L.Ed.2d 258 (1985); (3) contraceptive devices; *Hill v. Searle Laboratories*, [884 F.2d 1064, 1070–71 (8th Cir.1989)]; (4) drugs advertised directly to consumers; *Perez v. Wyeth Laboratories, Inc.*, [161 N.J. 1, 21, 734 A.2d 1245, 1257 (1999)]; (5) overpromoted drugs; *Proctor v. Davis*, 291 Ill.App.3d 265, 279–84, 225 Ill.Dec. 126, [136–40,] 682 N.E.2d 1203, [1212–16,] *cert. denied*, 175 Ill.2d 553, 228 Ill.Dec. 725, 689 N.E.2d 1146 (1997); and (6) drugs withdrawn from the market; *Nichols v. McNeilab, Inc.*, 850 F.Supp. 562, 565 ([E.D.] Mich.1993).

Vitanza v. Upjohn Co., 257 Conn. at 393, 778 A.2d at 846–47. [ ]

Even the version of the learned intermediary doctrine contained in the Restatement (Third) of Torts incorporates the foregoing exceptions by including a general exception to cover those circumstances where the manufacturer knows or should know that a physician will not be in a position to provide an adequate warning:

> (d) A prescription drug or medical device is not reasonably safe due to inadequate instructions or warnings if reasonable instructions or warnings regarding foreseeable risks of harm are not provided to:
>
> > (1) prescribing and other health-care providers who are in a position to reduce the risks of harm in accordance with the instructions or warnings; or
> >
> > (2) the patient when the manufacturer knows or has reason to know that health-care providers will not be in a position to reduce the risks of harm in accordance with the instructions or warnings.

Restatement (Third) of Torts: Products Liability 6(d), at 145 (1998). In Comment *e* to 6, the American Law Institute discusses some circumstances under which direct warnings to patients may be warranted under subsection 6(d)(2). Ultimately, though, the Institute commented that it "leaves to developing case law whether exceptions to the learned intermediary rule in these or other situations should be recognized." Restatement (Third) of Torts: Products Liability 6 cmt. e, at 149. . . .

Given the plethora of exceptions to the learned intermediary doctrine, we ascertain no benefit in adopting a doctrine that would require the simultaneous adoption of numerous exceptions in order to be justly utilized. This is particularly so when our existing law of comparative contribution among joint tortfeasors is adequate to address issues of liability among physicians and drug companies in those cases where patients sue for injuries related to the use of prescription drugs.

Furthermore, we believe that if drug manufacturers are able to adequately provide warnings to consumers under the numerous exceptions to the learned intermediary doctrine, then they should experience no substantial impediment to providing adequate warnings to consumers in general. "There is no question that pharmaceutical manufacturers believe they have very effective methods to communicate directly with consumers." *Larkin v. Pfizer, Inc.,* 153 S.W.3d at 771 (Wintersheimer, J., dissenting).

Finally, because it is the prescription drug manufacturers who benefit financially from the sales of prescription drugs and possess the knowledge regarding potential harms, and the ultimate consumers who bear the significant health risks of using those drugs, it is not unreasonable that prescription drug manufacturers should provide appropriate warnings to the ultimate users of their products.

> Public policy dictates that the manufacturer should warn the ultimate user of the harmful effects of its pharmaceuticals since it involves a person's health. The knowledge of pharmaceutical side effects goes well beyond the scope of the average individual. The benefit in warning the consumer directly [far outweighs] the costs. It is not as though the manufacturer must incur costs to discover the risks as they are already known. It is only a matter of adding the consumer to the list of who to warn. . . .

> . . . Since the early 1980's, direct-to-consumer advertising has boomed into a very profitable venture for pharmaceutical manufacturers. Yet, consumers' exposure to harm has increased as a result. They are surrounded by various prescription advertisements in all forms of print and broadcast media. Advertisements directed to consumers, however, often supply partial or incomplete information. Additionally, self-diagnosis by the consumer has resulted from these advertisements, as well as patient-demand for the brand-name drugs. *It is in the best interest of the general public that manufacturers have a duty to warn the ultimate user of side*

effects and risks. Courts are increasingly motivated to protect the consumer, and require manufacturers to warn more than just the physician.

. . .

Pharmaceutical manufacturers spend millions to make millions more. They are pushing their products onto the general public like never before. Consequently, consumers need more protection. As a response to the changing times, courts have diminished the manufacturer's shield of the learned intermediary doctrine. They have imposed a duty to warn the consumer in addition to the physician. In doing so, the goal of product liability to protect the ultimate user from harm, is more attainable. In the end, the burden should be on the one producing health care, not the one consuming it.

[ ] West Virginia physicians naturally have duties and responsibilities regarding their role in providing prescription medicines to consumers. It would be unreasonable not to require the manufacturers of those medicines to accept similar responsibilities.

Based upon the foregoing, we now hold that, under West Virginia products liability law, manufacturers of prescription drugs are subject to the same duty to warn consumers about the risks of their products as other manufacturers. We decline to adopt the learned intermediary exception to this general rule.

. . .

Writ denied.

■ Albright, Justice, dissenting:

. . .

Rather than trying to enervate the near-majority of jurisdictions that have already adopted the doctrine, the majority should have earnestly analyzed whether any of the rationales which underlie the doctrine remain valid today. What the majority overlooks by emphasizing the direct marketing of drugs to consumers is that the doctrine may still serve a useful purpose for prescription drugs that are not heavily marketed and in those circumstances where a physician's expertise is relied upon to make the all-important selection of which particular drug(s) to prescribe; to interpret contraindicative information; and to interpret the myriad of warning-related information distributed by a pharmaceutical manufacturer.

. . .

Consistent with comment e to the *Restatement (Third) of Torts,* I would follow the American Institute of Law's [*sic*] proposal that prescription drugs which are marketed via the mass media should be treated as a distinct category. Because government regulations already require that these heavily-marketed drugs must include appropriate risk-related information as part of the advertising materials, there is an established procedure for requiring that the manufacturers of such drugs disclose pertinent warning-related information concurrent with the marketing of these pharmaceuticals. Where the need for the doctrine's adoption is most clear is where the drugs at issue were not the subject of a massive advertising campaign and/or where the physician did in fact assume the role of a "learned intermediary" in advising and recommending that the plaintiff/patient use a particular drug. And, in the case of a defective drug, the manufacturer should always be required to advise both the pharmacies and all the direct purchasers of the drug at issue as to the nature of the product concerns.

Because I believe that the issue of adequate pharmaceutical warnings is one that will largely depend on the unique circumstances of the case, I think it was unwise to completely cast aside the learned intermediary doctrine. Furthermore, by attaching undue importance to the effects of direct marketing, the majority downplays the continuing and vital role that a physician plays in the decision as to which prescription drugs are appropriate for a given patient based upon that particular individual's specific medical needs. In those circumstances where the physician has received extensive warning material regarding the effects of a specific drug and makes an individualized decision to prescribe that medication based on such information, there is a valid and continuing rationale for permitting the learned intermediary doctrine to operate. Where on the other hand, a physician advises against the use of a specific drug and the consumer insists on a particular medication based on his or her exposure to a massive advertising campaign for a specific drug, the need for the doctrine's application is arguably reduced. But to presume, as the majority appears to, that the mere presence of pharmaceutical advertising in our society relegates the role of the physician to a mere dispensary of prescriptions is simply not true. In those cases where the medications are prescribed in a traditional fashion with the physician carefully weighing the advantages and disadvantages of a given drug for a patient presenting with specific concerns, to deny on an across-the-board basis the application of the learned intermediary doctrine—a doctrine that has been applied throughout this country for years—seems both precipitous and unwarranted. Accordingly, I dissent.

■ MAYNARD, JUSTICE, concurring:

Suppose Patient John Doe visits his small-town West Virginia doctor. Further suppose he is prescribed a drug by his doctor that causes him serious injury. Suppose that the drug is one that is heavily advertised. Patient Doe then sues his West Virginia doctor and the drug manufacturer for the injury caused by the drug. If this Court were to adopt the learned intermediary doctrine, the West Virginia doctor would remain in the lawsuit, but the drug manufacturer would not remain in the suit and would not be liable for damages if the drug manufacturer could show that it warned the doctor of the risks of injury associated with the drug. Thus, a small-town West Virginia doctor would become solely responsible for the injury to Patient Doe while an out-of-state multi-million dollar drug manufacturer is off the hook. This would be the result if the dissenting Justices had their way in this case. This result simply would be unfair.

One need only look at the massive amounts of direct-to-consumer advertising done by drug manufacturers in this country to understand this truth. Americans cannot watch an hour of television or skim through a magazine without being bombarded by commercials and advertisements extolling the benefits of Viagra, Vioxx, Prilosec, Claritin, Paxil, Zocor, Celebrex, Flonase, Allegra, Pravachol, Zyrtec, Singulair, Lipitor, Nasonex, Lamisil, and others. The fact is that drug manufacturers spend about four billion dollars annually on direct-to-consumer pharmaceutical advertising. Thanks to these expensive advertising campaigns, we consumers are well educated about the salutary effects of these drugs. There is no reason why we should not be just as educated about their potential risks. In sum, because of direct-to-consumer advertising, drug manufacturers have a ready forum in which to warn health care consumers about the risks of their products. For this reason, they should not be exempt from the general duty to warn that this State places on manufacturers. It is a simple matter of fairness.

. . .

■ STARCHER, J., concurring.

. . .

NOTES AND QUESTIONS

1.   Notwithstanding the majority's tallying of courts that have accepted and not accepted the learned intermediary doctrine, *Karl* is the first decision by a state high court to reject it. Numerous exceptions, as detailed by the court, had developed and a significant number of states still have not definitively addressed and resolved the question. Compare Centocor, Inc. v. Hamilton, 372 S.W.3d 140 (Tex.2012)(expressly adopting for the first time the learned intermediary rule in the prescription drug context and discussing, without adopting, the direct-to-consumer advertising exception).

2.   The policy ground explained by the cited *Terhune* court reflects that physicians are gatekeepers for prescription drugs and therefore need to know the relevant therapeutic benefits and risks of those drugs. Is that rationale relevant for determining whether it would be detrimental to provide that information *as well* to patients? How about the other reasons for the learned intermediary rule set forth by the court?

3.   As the court states, one of the exceptions to the learned intermediary rule involves oral contraceptives, in part because the choice of

contraception is a matter significantly of consumer choice. Might the cases under this exception have extended more broadly to "well patients"—those who see a physician because they wish to enhance their quality of life, rather than because they "need" medical treatment? Should the "well patient" category include patients who seek prescription drugs for such matters as baldness and erectile dysfunction as well as contraception?

4. In learned intermediary cases, there may be further variations on the warning doctrine. In the first, the physician is given adequate instructions and fails to convey that information to the patient. For example, in Pustejovsky v. Pliva, Inc., 623 F.3d 271 (5th Cir.2010), the physician had not read the drug's labeling (which included all necessary warnings), leading the court to affirm dismissal of the warning claim because the plaintiff had no evidence to demonstrate that an adequate warning would have reached her doctor. What claims might the patient have against the physician? In the second, the physician was given inadequate information. The patient in these cases can directly sue the manufacturer for not adequately warning the physician. Suppose the physician testifies that even with an adequate warning, she still would have prescribed the medicine in question. See Boehm v. Eli Lilly & Co., 747 F.3d 501 (8th Cir.2014)(concluding that the drug manufacturer was not liable because of the lack of factual causation). Does the plaintiff in such a case have a claim against the physician? Is there room here for a heeding presumption?

5. *Pharmaceutical design defect claims.* For the most part, the risks of pharmaceuticals are addressed through warnings. In part, this is because, drugs that may be beneficial for one class of patients can be dangerous for another. For example, thalidomide, a horrific teratogen that caused severe birth defects in the 1960s, is now used to treat the symptoms of leprosy. If these side effects are warned against adequately, could the product nevertheless be defectively designed because its side effects for pregnant women exceeded its therapeutic benefits for lepers? Or that another drug has a better benefit-risk ratio than the challenged drug? Or that the challenged drug should have been designed differently? Note that a finding of defective design would effectively eliminate this drug option from the market due to the threat of punitive damages in future cases, depriving one class of consumers (lepers) from therapeutic benefits due to the risk faced by another class (pregnant women).

This issue is addressed by the Second Restatement in an inscrutable comment, comment k, which exempts "unavoidably dangerous products" from strict liability because they have benefits that necessarily come with dangers that cannot be eliminated. Comment k caused considerable confusion for the courts, which the Products Liability Restatement sought to resolve by providing in section 6 (c) that:

> A prescription drug or medical device is not reasonably safe due to defective design if the foreseeable risks of harm posed by the drug or medical device are sufficiently great in relation to its foreseeable therapeutic benefits that reasonable health-care-providers, knowing of such foreseeable risks and therapeutic

benefits, would not prescribe the drug or medical device for any class of patients.

Under this approach, thalidomide cannot be defectively designed because of its therapeutic benefits for one class (lepers), despite the risk posed to another class (pregnant women). To what extent does the role of the prescribing physician, discussed in the preceding notes, ensure that thalidomide will be prescribed only for the relevant class of consumers and not those unduly at risk?

In Freeman v. Hoffman-La Roche, Inc., 618 N.W.2d 827 (Neb.2000), the plaintiff alleged that she had suffered serious side effects from Accutane, which had been prescribed for her chronic acne. The court rejected section 6(c) for several reasons. Among them, the court objected to the result that liability for any drug was defeated for all plaintiffs if the drug was suitable for "any class of patients." For further critical commentary of section 6(c), see Conk, Is There a Design Defect in the Restatement (Third) of Torts: Products Liability?, 109 Yale L.J. 1087 (2000). For a defense of section 6(c), see Henderson & Twerski, Drug Designs are Different, 111 Yale L.J. 151 (2001). For an assessment of why drug designs might be different from other product designs and the associated implications for an appropriate design rule for drugs, see Green, Prescription Drugs, Alternative Designs, and the Restatement (Third): Preliminary Reflections, 30 Seton Hall L.Rev. 207 (1999).

6. *Allergic reactions.* Courts have treated allergic reactions as a separate class of harm, often holding that a manufacturer has no duty to change a product's design to guard against allergic reactions when the product's benefit to the public outweighs the harm it may cause to the idiosyncratic few. Liability for failure to warn may be imposed, however, when the number of allergic sufferers is substantial, although some courts do not even require a substantial number before imposing a duty to warn. Comment k to section 2 of the Products Liability Restatement states: "Essentially, this reflects the same risk-utility balancing undertaken in warnings cases generally." Are there reasons why allergic reactions should be treated differently from other types of harms caused by products that are beneficial for one class of consumers but detrimental for another?

––––––––

The following case discusses the question of liability where the claim is that there was a failure to warn even though the information about the risk that came to pass was unknown (and not reasonably knowable) at the time the product was distributed. The court bases its decision on the implied warranty of merchantability, which under Massachusetts law is "congruent in nearly all respects with the principles expressed in the Restatement (Second) of Torts § 402A" rule of strict products liability. Back v. Wickes Corp., 378 N.E.2d 964, 969 (Mass.1978).

Vassallo v. Baxter Healthcare Corporation

Supreme Judicial Court of Massachusetts, 1998.
428 Mass. 1, 696 N.E.2d 909.

■ Before WILKINS, C.J., and ABRAMS, LYNCH, GREANEY and MARSHALL, JJ.

■ GREANEY, JUSTICE.

[Plaintiff claimed that silicone gel breast implants, manufactured by a company since bought by defendant, had been negligently designed, accompanied by negligent product warnings, and that they breached the implied warranty of merchantability, with the consequence that she was injured. Her husband claimed loss of consortium. A jury returned verdicts on the negligence and warranty counts in favor of the plaintiffs. On direct appeal, the court upheld the judgment entered on the negligence verdict.]

Because the plaintiffs' recoveries can be upheld on the jury's findings of negligence, we need not address the defendants' claims of error concerning the breach of warranty count. We take this opportunity, however, to consider the defendants' argument that we should change our products liability law concerning the implied warranty of merchantability from what is stated in Hayes v. Ariens Co., 462 N.E.2d 273 (Mass.1984), and that the law should be reformulated to adopt a "state of the art" standard that conditions a manufacturer's liability on actual or constructive knowledge of the risks.

Our current law, regarding the duty to warn under the implied warranty of merchantability, presumes that a manufacturer was fully informed of all risks associated with the product at issue, regardless of the state of the art at the time of the sale, and amounts to strict liability for failure to warn of these risks. [ ] This rule has been justified by the public policy that a defective product, "unreasonably dangerous due to lack of adequate warning[s], [is] not fit for the ordinary purposes for which [it is] used regardless of the absence of fault on [a defendant's] part." [ ]

At trial, the defendants requested a jury instruction that a manufacturer need only warn of risks "known or reasonably knowable in light of the generally accepted scientific knowledge available at the time of the manufacture and distribution of the device." The judge declined this request, and instead gave an instruction using language taken almost verbatim from that in [*Hayes*]. While the judge's instruction was a correct statement of our law, we recognize that we are among a distinct minority of States that applies a hindsight analysis to the duty to warn.

The majority of States, either by case law or by statute, follow the principle expressed in Restatement (Second) of Torts § 402A comment *j* (1965), which states that "the seller is required to give warning against [a danger], if he has knowledge, or by the application of reasonable, developed human skill and foresight should have knowledge, of the . . . danger." [ ]; [Products Liability Restatement, Reporters' Note to § 2 comment *m*, at 104 (1998)] ("An overwhelming majority of jurisdictions supports the proposition that a manufacturer has a duty to warn only of risks that were known or should have been known to a reasonable person."). At least three jurisdictions that previously applied strict liability to the duty to warn in a products liability claim have reversed themselves, either by statute or by decision, and now require knowledge, or reasonable knowability as a component of such a claim. [Colorado]; Feldman v. Lederle Labs., [479 A.2d 374 (N.J.1984)]; La.Rev.Stat. Ann. § 9:2800.59(B)(West 1997). The change in the law of New Jersey is particularly relevant, because we relied in part on New Jersey law in formulating the strict liability standard expressed in the *Hayes* decision. See [*Hayes*] citing Beshada v. Johns-Manville Products Corp., [447 A.2d 539 (N.J.1982)].

The thin judicial support for a hindsight approach to the duty to warn is easily explained. The goal of the law is to induce conduct that is capable of being performed. This goal is not advanced by imposing liability for failure to warn of risks that were not capable of being known. [ ]

The [Products Liability Restatement § 2(c)] reaffirms the principle expressed in Restatement (Second) of Torts, at § 402A comment *j*, by stating that a product "is defective because of inadequate instructions or warnings when the foreseeable risks of harm posed by the product could have been reduced or avoided by the provision of reasonable instructions or warnings . . . and the omission of the instructions or warnings renders the product not reasonably safe." The rationale behind the principle is explained by stating that "[u]nforeseeable risks arising from foreseeable product use . . . by definition cannot specifically be warned against." [ ] However, comment *m* also clarifies the manufacturer's duty "to perform reasonable testing prior to marketing a product and to discover risks and risk-avoidance measures that such testing would reveal. A seller is charged with knowledge of what reasonable testing would reveal." [ ]

We have stated that liability under the implied warranty of merchantability in Massachusetts is "congruent in nearly all respects with the principles expressed in Restatement (Second) of Torts § 402A." [ ] The main difference has been our application of a hindsight approach to the duty to warn of (and to provide adequate instructions regarding) risks associated with a product. We recognize that this approach has received substantial criticism in the literature. . . .

In recognition of the clear judicial trend regarding the duty to warn in products liability cases, and the principles stated in Restatement (Third) of Torts: Products Liability, supra at § 2(c) and comment *m*, we hereby revise our law to state that a defendant will not be held liable under an implied warranty of merchantability for failure to warn or provide instructions about risks that were not reasonably foreseeable at the time of sale or could not have been discovered by way of reasonable testing prior to marketing the product. A manufacturer will be held to the standard of knowledge of an expert in the appropriate field, and will remain subject to a continuing duty to warn (at least purchasers) of risks discovered following the sale of the product at issue. In accordance with the usual rule governing retroactivity in this type of action, the standard just expressed will apply to all claims on which a final judgment has not been entered, or as to which an appeal is pending or the appeal period has not expired, and to all claims on which an action is commenced after the release of this opinion. [ ]

[The court noted that the jury's sustainable verdict on negligence in failing to warn of known risks precluded the defendant from taking advantage of the change in the law. The judgment was affirmed.]

NOTES AND QUESTIONS

1.   What are the arguments for and against a hindsight approach? In the cited *Beshada* case, workers injured by handling asbestos products before 1960 sued the manufacturers of asbestos. Defendants argued that the medical profession did not recognize these particular health hazards from asbestos until the 1960s.* Plaintiffs responded that, even if true, this fact was no defense to a strict liability claim. The New Jersey court agreed: "Strict liability focuses on the product, not the fault of the manufacturer." The court found that this rule was consistent with the three main reasons underlying its adoption of strict liability—risk spreading, accident avoidance, and reducing administrative costs by avoiding "complicated, costly, confusing and time-consuming" trials about the distant past. On the second point, the court stated that the " 'state of the art' at a given time is partly determined by how much industry invests in safety research. By imposing on manufacturers the costs of failure to discover hazards, we create an incentive for them to invest more actively in safety research." In addition, "fairness" suggested that "manufacturers not be excused from liability because their prior inadequate investment in safety rendered the hazards of their product unknowable." Why doesn't the premarketing "reasonable testing," duty, referred to by the *Vassallo* court, adequately address the safety research incentive asserted in *Beshada*? Recall in this regard the rationale for strict liability based on the difficulty of proving negligence, discussed at p. 530, supra.

In the cited *Feldman* case, the New Jersey court reversed course. Plaintiff's teeth were discolored by a drug that was prescribed for respiratory infections. No warning was given about this side effect until

---

*   The idea that the asbestos industry did not know of the danger involved in *Beshada* was suspect from the beginning. See generally P. Brodeur, Outrageous Misconduct: The Asbestos Industry on Trial (1985); see also Bragg v. Owens-Corning Fiberglas Corp., 734 A.2d 643, 651 n.16 (D.C.App.1999)(noting that Pliny the Elder "reported a lung disease in slaves weaving asbestos").

late in the course of the plaintiff's use of the product. Defendant claimed that the danger had only then become apparent and could not have been warned about earlier. The court concluded that as to design and warning questions, "generally conduct should be measured by knowledge at the time the manufacturer distributed the product." The courts should ask when the manufacturer had "actual or constructive knowledge of the danger." For purposes of this determination, the manufacturer is "held to the standard of an expert in the field." This approach implies the "notion that at least in some fields, such as those impacting on public health, a manufacturer may be expected to be informed and affirmatively to seek out information concerning the public's use of its own product." The court "restrict[ed] *Beshada* to the circumstances giving rise to its holding," without further elaboration about what those circumstances were.

The *Feldman* court did, however, shift the burden of proof to the defendant on the question of whether and when the relevant technical information became available:

> The defendant is in a superior position to know the technological material or data in the particular field or specialty. The defendant is the expert, often performing self-testing. It is the defendant that injected the product in the stream of commerce for its economic gain. As a matter of policy the burden of proving the status of knowledge in the field at the time of distribution is properly placed on the defendant.

479 A.2d at 388.

Does the shift in the burden of proof and the emphasis on the defendant as "an expert in the field" undermine any practical difference between *Beshada* and *Feldman*? See generally Rabin, Indeterminate Risk and Tort Reform: Comment on Calabresi and Klevorick, 14 J.Legal Stud. 633 (1985). How could a defendant show that a risk was not known at some point in the past?

In James v. Bessemer Processing Co., 714 A.2d 898 (N.J.1998), workers who reconditioned container drums sued chemical and petroleum manufacturers for failing to warn that the drums contained toxic products. The court, after noting that plaintiffs could proceed under either strict liability or negligence, undertook to identify the differences:

> In cases proceeding under a theory of strict liability, knowledge of the harmful effects of a product will be imputed to a manufacturer on a showing that "knowledge of the defect existed within the relevant industry." [ ] Once proof of such knowledge in the industry has been established, triggering the duty to warn, the plaintiff must show that an adequate warning was not provided. When proceeding under a theory of negligence, the plaintiff must demonstrate that the specific defendant knew or should have known of the potential hazards of the product.

Id. at 908. Is this an intelligible distinction given that the manufacturer in these cases is held to an expert standard of care?

After either theory is established, the "heeding presumption" comes into play so that a plaintiff need "introduce evidence that the defendant's failure to warn . . . led to plaintiff's exposure only if it becomes necessary to defeat a defendant's attempt to rebut the heeding presumption with its own proofs." Can the heeding presumption function as a causal rule of strict liability? Consider a drug that is defective for not adequately warning users about the risk of a serious side effect. Suppose that even if the ordinary consumer had been adequately warned of this risk, she would still ingest the drug because of its therapeutic benefits. Under these conditions, how can the warning defect be the cause of injury for a plaintiff who suffers from the side effect? See note 10, p. 606 supra (explaining how a causal rule of strict liability simply asks whether the tortious risk for which defendant is strictly responsible caused plaintiff's injury).

2. Compare Green v. Smith & Nephew AHP, Inc., 629 N.W.2d 727 (Wis.2001). Plaintiff hospital worker had an allergic reaction to latex gloves. The court held that the state followed the consumer expectations test "exclusively," rejecting the Products Liability Restatement. Accordingly, whether the manufacturer knew or "could have known" about the risk of its product was irrelevant because the consumer did not expect the product to cause such an allergic reaction. The court rejected a requirement that the risk be foreseeable because that smacked of negligence. Following the *Beshada* rationale, but without citing it, the court stated: "Where a manufacturer places a defective and unreasonably dangerous product into the stream of commerce, the manufacturer and not the injured consumer, should bear the costs of the risks posed by the product." Id. at 752. The court also rejected the Restatement's requirement that plaintiff show a reasonable alternative design. One justice dissented on the merits.

Under this formulation of the consumer expectations test, does it matter whether strict liability will promote the safety objective? How would the *Vassallo* court respond? Recall the earlier discussion about the loss-spreading rationale for strict liability, which is not an independently sufficient reason for liability. See note 6.a, p. 571 supra. If spreading injury costs were sufficient, would there be any reason to limit liability to defective products?

3. *State of the art.* According to the Products Liability Restatement section 2 rptrs. note to cmt. d, "the term 'state of the art' has been variously defined by a multitude of courts. For some, it refers to industry custom or industry practice; for others, it means the safest existing technology that has been adopted for use; for others it means cutting edge technology," all of which would be relevant to the RAD requirement discussed at note 4, p. 589 supra. The *Vassallo* court uses the term in yet another way—to refer to the state of knowledge concerning product risks.

How do these various meanings of "state of the art" apply in the following two cases: (a) in the months before a product with an unknown risk is marketed in the United States, a small company in Finland had discovered that very risk and, without public announcement, had begun preparing a new product that avoided the risk; (b) a few weeks before defendant's product was marketed, the risk had first been reported in a Finnish scientific journal?

4. *Post-sale warning obligations.* Even if defendants are not liable for the unknown risks that cause injuries after their product is marketed, do they have an obligation to warn once the first hint of trouble appears? If not, when does the obligation arise? The *Vassallo* court suggested that manufacturers have a continuing duty to warn after sale. Recall the affirmative duty imposed on those who non-negligently create a risk of harm, p. 133 supra.

In Lovick v. Wil-Rich, 588 N.W.2d 688 (Iowa 1999), an experienced farmer was injured in 1993 when a design defect caused a linkage to break and the wing of a farm cultivator to fall unexpectedly. Defendant began marketing this type of cultivator in 1971. Plaintiff's model was made in 1981, and he bought it in "the late 80s." In 1983, defendant received the first report of a falling wing. Since that time it had received eight more. In 1988, it began attaching warnings to new cultivators. In 1994, it began trying to notify owners of existing cultivators of the danger and providing a back-up safety kit. Plaintiff introduced evidence that John Deere, defendant's competitor, had begun a safety program in 1983 for its similarly designed cultivator after learning of instances of wing malfunction. Deere's efforts included trying to locate owners of previously sold cultivators and equipping them with a safety latch and upgraded warning. The court stated that defendant, although it learned of Deere's 1983 actions in 1987, did not start its campaign until 1994 "essentially due to the practical difficulties of identifying and locating the owners and users of previously sold cultivators." The trial judge submitted to the jury "a general reasonableness standard of care instruction." The jury returned a verdict for compensatory and punitive damages.

On appeal, the court rejected defendant's first argument that it owed no duty as to dangers discovered after the sale. The court noted that most states to address the issue had recognized such a duty, although other courts had rejected a post-sale duty. See Patton v. Hutchinson Wil-Rich Mfg. Co., 861 P.2d 1299 (Kan.1993), noting contrary cases in an opinion in which it upheld a post-sale duty to warn in a case involving the same model cultivator as in *Lovick*.

The *Lovick* court then turned to the nature of that duty. Although the rationale for a duty to warn after the sale was "nearly identical" to those supporting a duty to warn at the time of sale, "the parameters of those duties must be separately identified." The court noted that section 10 of the Products Liability Restatement states that a reasonable seller would warn if:

> (1) "the seller knows or reasonably should know that the product poses a substantial risk of harm to persons or property"; (2) those who would benefit from the warning can be identified and are likely unaware of the risk; (3) "a warning can be effectively be communicated to and acted upon" by recipients; and (4) the "risk

of harm is sufficiently great to justify the burden of providing a warning."

The court agreed that negligence is the proper standard in this area. Nonetheless, the general reasonableness charge that the trial court had given to the jury was inadequate to convey the different considerations that apply to post-sale warnings. In future cases, trial judges should charge on all four factors to help the jury focus on the unique features of this obligation.

Should the duty to warn include the duty to pay for the safety kits that Deere and Wil-Rich were providing? The *Patton* court, supra, although imposing a duty to warn, refused to impose a duty to retrofit or to recall the product. Administrative agencies are "better able to weigh the benefits and costs involved in locating, recalling, and retrofitting products." 861 P.2d at 1316. This approach is widely followed by other courts and adopted by the Products Liability Restatement.

5. *Subsequent remedial measures.* When a defendant manufacturer takes steps, after an accident, to make the product safer, rule 407 of the Federal Rules of Evidence prohibits the plaintiff from using those subsequent remedial measures to prove that the product was defective or the manufacturer negligent. Without this prohibition, those who might make a situation safer may fail to do so, concerned that those actions will be used against them later in court. In Diehl v. Blaw-Knox, 360 F.3d 426 (3d Cir.2004), plaintiff worked for a contractor widening roads. Plaintiff sued when equipment made by defendant manufacturer ran over him. After the accident, the contractor redesigned the machine to make it safer. The court held that it was prejudicial error for the trial judge to have excluded this evidence. The policy behind that rule was not implicated here, because a person not subject to liability had made the change.

6. *Misrepresentation.* So far the discussion in this section has revolved around cases in which either there was no warning at all or the warning was claimed to be inadequate. What about words that affirmatively mislead? Section 9 of the Products Liability Restatement addresses this issue by providing that a seller or distributor who "makes a fraudulent, negligent, or innocent misrepresentation of fact concerning the product is subject to liability for harm to persons or property caused by the misrepresentation." The comments make clear that this section intended no change in existing law.

The earlier formulation is found in section 402B of the Second Restatement, which provides that a seller is liable for physical harm to one who justifiably relies on a material misrepresentation, even if the maker is not negligent in misrepresenting and even if the person hurt did not buy the product from the seller. What justifies this rule of strict liability? For an extended consideration of section 402B and its relation to warranty theories, see American Safety Equipment Corp. v. Winkler, 640 P.2d 216 (Colo.1982) and Hauter v. Zogarts, 534 P.2d 377 (Cal.1975).

E. DEFENSES

Early in the development of strict products liability, courts recognized that the consumer's "misuse" of a product could absolve the manufacturer from liability. Unfortunately, the term proved to be confusing because it was employed to perform several functions without courts fully articulating those multiple meanings. Indeed, some of those misuses were not truly affirmative defenses, but instead addressed whether plaintiff had established a prima facie case of products liability.

For example, the issue of product misuse can be relevant to whether a defect existed in the first place. Imagine, to invoke an egregious example, a consumer who uses a screwdriver as a toothpick. In a suit against the manufacturer alleging a design defect, the manufacturer might claim misuse by the plaintiff. But, it is plain, isn't it, that the screwdriver is not defective in the first place. The harder question is why? Is the screwdriver not defective because the manufacturer did not intend for it to be used as a toothpick? Prior to the development of the crashworthiness doctrine discussed in *Camacho*, p. 594 supra, car manufacturers asserted such a "misuse defense" when an injured driver claimed that the car was defective because it was not designed to be crashworthy. According to the manufacturers, the car was not intended to be involved in crashes, and so such "misuse" was outside of their tort duty. Based on the crashworthiness doctrine, courts have extended the design obligation beyond intended uses to foreseeable ones, which includes car crashes. Based on the concept of foreseeability, the manufacturer is obligated to design or warn against foreseeable misuses of the product, the type of conduct at issue in *Ryobi*, p. 609 supra.

The extent of uses that a manufacturer must anticipate can be affected by the marketing scheme employed. In Lugo v. LJN Toys, Ltd., 552 N.E.2d 162 (N.Y.1990), a playmate threw a detachable part of a doll made by defendant into the eye of plaintiff. The claim was that the doll was a replica of a well-known television cartoon character, Voltron, who overcame enemies by hurling his shield at them. The detachable part of the doll that was thrown was variously described as a "shield," "blade," or "star." The court held that summary judgment was properly denied. Product suppliers had to anticipate uses that were "unintended but reasonably foreseeable." Here, plaintiff "has submitted expert evidence that, based upon customs and standards in the toy safety community, the part was defective because detachable from the doll and that throwing it was foreseeable because of the extensive television exposure in which Voltron did so."

A second, and not entirely unrelated, reliance on the misuse doctrine is with regard to proximate cause. In Price v. Blaine Kern Artista, Inc., 893 P.2d 367 (Nev.1995), plaintiff entertainer had bought an oversized caricature head mask of the first President George Bush made by defendant. While plaintiff was performing in Las Vegas, he either tripped or was pushed from behind and was hurt by the shifting weight of the mask when he fell. His negligence action claimed a defective design in that the mask did not have a safety harness to support the head and neck in case of a fall. Defendant argued that it was not a foreseeable use of the mask if plaintiff had been deliberately pushed by a drunk or by a political foe of President Bush. The court disagreed, holding that a fact question was presented whether defendant should have foreseen the possibility of some sort of violent reaction by intoxicated or politically volatile persons, "ignited by the sight of an oversized caricature of prominent political figures." Id. at 370. See also Briscoe v. Amazing Products, Inc., 23 S.W.3d 228 (Ky.App.2000), in which a high school student, knowing the danger of the product, threw drain cleaner at her rival. The court held that the defendants in the product chain were not required to anticipate that use of the product.

Finally, the term "misuse" is often invoked by courts to describe unreasonable but foreseeable consumer behavior—a true affirmative defense. When section 402A was promulgated in the 1960s, contributory negligence barred the plaintiff's recovery in negligence actions. This rule posed a problem in product cases. If plaintiffs could never recover for foreseeable product misuse, then this bar to recovery would effectively eliminate the manufacturer's obligation to consider the risk of foreseeable product misuse when designing the product. Consequently, section 402A cmt. n, which is discussed in the next case, sharply limits the role of contributory negligence in product cases. Today, comparative fault or responsibility is applied in the products liability context in the overwhelming majority of states. Product misuse no longer necessarily bars recovery, but issues now emerge about what, exactly, should be compared. The following material addresses common situations in which courts must make such a comparison and further discusses the treatment of defenses to products liability in the Second Restatement and in the subsequent Products Liability Restatement.

Because product cases have raised issues in the prima facie case unlike those we have previously considered, it should not be surprising that differences might appear in the area of defenses, as well. As you read this section, consider whether the crucial lines are (1) those that divide product-derived harms from others, (2) those that separate strict liability from negligence, or (3) those that distinguish among personal injury, property damage, and economic harm. State statutes may explicitly cover products liability—as in the case below—or courts may extend either common law or statutory principles of comparative fault to products cases.

1. CONTRIBUTORY NEGLIGENCE, COMPARATIVE RESPONSIBILITY, AND ASSUMPTION OF RISK

General Motors Corporation v. Sanchez

Supreme Court of Texas, 1999.
997 S.W.2d 584.

■ JUSTICE GONZALES delivered the opinion for a unanimous Court.

The principal question in this case is when does the doctrine of comparative responsibility apply in a products liability case. . . .

I

Because there were no witnesses, relatively little is known first hand about the circumstances of the accident that is the basis of this litigation. Lee Sanchez, Jr. left his home to feed a pen of heifers in March 1993. The ranch foreman found his lifeless body the next morning and immediately called Sanchez's father. Apparently, Sanchez's 1990 Chevy pickup had rolled backward with the driver's side door open pinning Sanchez to the open corral gate in the angle between the open door and the cab of the truck. Sanchez suffered a broken right arm and damaged right knee where the gate crushed him against the door pillar, the vertical metal column to which the door is hinged. He bled to death from a deep laceration in his right upper arm.

The family, his estate, and his wife sued General Motors Corporation and the dealership that sold the pickup for negligence, products liability, and gross negligence based on a defect in the truck's transmission and transmission-control linkage. The plaintiffs presented circumstantial evidence to support the following theory of how the accident happened. Sanchez drove his truck into the corral and stopped to close the gate. He mis-shifted into what he thought was Park, but what was actually an intermediate, "perched" position between Park and Reverse where the transmission was in "hydraulic neutral." Expert witnesses explained that hydraulic neutral exists at the intermediate positions between the denominated gears, Park, Reverse, Neutral, Drive, and Low, where no gear is actually engaged. Under this scenario, as Sanchez walked toward the gate, the gear shift slipped from the perched position of hydraulic neutral into Reverse and the truck started to roll backwards. It caught Sanchez at or near the gate and slammed him up against it, trapping his right arm and knee. He was pinned between the gate and the door pillar by the pressure the truck exerted while idling in Reverse. Struggling to free himself, Sanchez severed an artery in his right arm and bled to death after 45 to 75 minutes.

[At trial, G.M. presented alternative theories.]

The jury rejected G.M.'s theories and found that G.M. was negligent, the transmission was defectively designed, and G.M.'s warning was [inadequate]. The jury also found that Sanchez was fifty percent responsible for the accident, but the trial court disregarded this finding. The trial court rendered judgment for actual and punitive damages of $8.5 million for the plaintiffs. [The court of appeals, en banc, affirmed.]

. . .

III

The jury found that Sanchez was fifty percent responsible for his accident. G.M. argues that this finding should be applied to reduce its liability for damages whether in negligence or strict liability. However, the plaintiffs argue that Sanchez's actions amounted to no more than a failure to discover or guard against a product defect and, because of our decision in Keen v. Ashot Ashkelon, Ltd., [748 S.W.2d 91 (1988) (failure to discover or guard against a defect is no defense to a strict liability claim)], such negligence does not constitute a defense to strict liability. To review the plaintiffs' claim, we must first consider the effect of the 1987 revisions to Chapter 33 of the Civil Practice and Remedies Code upon our decision in *Keen*.

[Before 1987, negligence cases were submitted under the statutory comparative negligence system. *Keen* was decided at the time this statute was in effect, but it did not apply to *Keen* because the statute only governed negligence actions and *Keen* included a strict liability claim. Hence, *Keen* was decided under common law principles— including "the rule in comment *n* to § 402A of the Restatement (Second) of Torts, that negligent failure to discover or guard against a product defect is not a defense."]

In 1987, the Legislature changed Chapter 33 from comparative negligence to comparative responsibility. Under comparative responsibility, a court reduces a claimant's damages recovery by the "percentage of responsibility" attributed to him by the trier of fact. The new statute expressly included suits based on strict tort liability. It defined "Percentage of responsibility" as the percentage that a party "cause[d] or contribute[d] to cause in any way, whether by *negligent act or omission*, . . . [or] by *other conduct or activity violative of the applicable legal standard*" the harm for which damages are sought. Thus, as the emphasized language indicates, the new statute applies to a claimant's conduct that violated the duty to use ordinary care or some other applicable legal standard.

G.M. contends that the 1987 revisions of Chapter 33 effectively overrule *Keen*. It is not quite that simple. Implicit in this Court's holding in *Keen* was that a consumer has no duty to discover or guard against a product defect. The 1987 changes to Chapter 33, which apportion responsibility based on a breach of a legal duty or other applicable legal standard, do not impose a new duty on plaintiffs. The statute merely says that if a claimant breaches an existing duty, then comparative responsibility shall apply. Accordingly, if a plaintiff's failure to discover or guard against a product defect breaches no duty, the statute does not apply.

Thus, *Keen*'s viability after the 1987 revisions depends on whether a plaintiff in a strict liability case has a duty to take steps to discover and guard against product defects. [A later court] refused to recognize such a failure as a defense, relying in part on comment *n* to section 402A of the Restatement (Second):

> Contributory negligence of the plaintiff is not a defense when such negligence consists merely in a failure to discover the defect in the product, or to guard against the possibility of its existence. On the other hand the form of contributory negligence which consists in voluntarily and unreasonably proceeding to encounter a known danger, and commonly passes under the name of assumption of risk, is a defense under this Section as in other cases of strict liability. If the user or consumer discovers the defect and is aware of the danger, and nevertheless proceeds unreasonably to make use of the product and is injured by it, he is barred from recovery.

We note that comment "*n*" was not carried forward in the Restatement (Third). The position of Restatement (Third), section 17(a), is that a plaintiff's conduct should be considered to reduce a damages recovery if it fails to conform to applicable standards of care, similar to the Texas 1987 statutory scheme. However, comment *d* to Restatement (Third) states:

> [W]hen the defendant claims that the plaintiff failed to discover a defect, there must be evidence that the plaintiff's conduct in failing to discover a defect did, in fact, fail to meet a standard of reasonable care. In general, a plaintiff has no reason to expect that a new product contains a defect and would have little reason to be on guard to discover it.

We believe that a duty to discover defects, and to take precautions in constant anticipation that a product might have a defect, would defeat the purposes of strict liability. Thus, we hold that a consumer has no duty to discover or guard against a product defect, but a consumer's conduct other than the mere failure to discover or guard against a product defect is subject to comparative responsibility. Public policy favors reasonable conduct by consumers regardless of whether a product is defective. A consumer is not relieved of the responsibility to act reasonably nor may a consumer fail to take reasonable precautions regardless of a known or unknown product defect. We therefore disapprove of *Keen* to the extent it suggests that the failure to discover or guard against a product defect is a broad category that includes all conduct except the assumption of a known risk. Because we conclude that a consumer has no duty to discover or guard against a product defect, we next determine whether the decedent's conduct in this case was merely the failure to discover or guard against a product defect or some other negligence unrelated to a product defect.

The truck's owner's manual describes safety measures designed to ensure that the truck would not move when parked: (1) set the parking brake; (2) place the truck completely in Park; (3) turn off the engine; (4) remove the key from the ignition; and (5) check that Park is fully engaged by pulling down on the gear shift. Sanchez's father testified that his son probably read the entire owner's manual. The plaintiff's own experts agreed at trial that Sanchez failed to perform any of the safety measures described in the owner's manual and that performing any one of them would have prevented the accident. This evidence is sufficient to support the jury's negligence finding.

Regardless of any danger of a mis-shift, a driver has a duty to take reasonable precautions to secure his vehicle before getting out of it. The danger that it could roll, or move if the engine is running, exists independently of the possibility of a mis-shift. For instance, the driver could inadvertently leave a vehicle in gear or a mechanical problem unrelated to a product defect could prevent Park from fully engaging. A moving vehicle without a driver is a hazard to public safety. The state licenses drivers who have demonstrated the minimum knowledge and skill necessary to safely operate a motor vehicle. Many, perhaps most, consumer products may be operated without a license, including lawn and garden equipment, household appliances, and powered hand tools. It follows then that, because of this licensing requirement, as well as other special duties imposed on drivers, more is expected of an operator of a motor vehicle than of users of most other consumer products. Thus, although we do not expect the average driver to have the engineering background to discover defects in their car's transmission, we do expect the reasonably prudent driver to take safety precautions to prevent a runaway car. Sanchez had a responsibility to operate his truck in a safe manner. The fact that the precautions demanded of a driver generally would have prevented this accident does not make Sanchez's negligence a mere failure to discover or guard against a mis-shift.

We recognize that there may be some tension between how we apply the law to the facts of this case and the *Keen* majority's characterization of the plaintiff's conduct in that case. As discussed previously, the *Keen* analysis was flawed from the outset because it recognized only two categories of plaintiff conduct: mere failure to discover or guard against a defect and assumption of the risk. All conduct that was not assumption of the risk was categorized as failure to discover or guard against a defect and thus no defense. Today, we hold that a plaintiff's conduct other than the mere failure to discover or guard against a product defect is subject to comparative responsibility.

Sanchez's actions amounted to conduct other than a mere failure to discover or guard against a product defect. We hold as a matter of law that such conduct must be scrutinized under the duty to use ordinary care or other applicable duty. We conclude that there was legally sufficient evidence to support the jury's verdict that Sanchez breached the duty to use ordinary care and was fifty percent responsible for the accident.

[The court reversed the punitive damage award and remanded for entry of the award for actual damages reduced by 50 percent.]

NOTES AND QUESTIONS

1.   The court concludes that "a consumer has no duty to discover or guard against a product defect" because such a duty "would defeat the purposes of strict liability." How is the court conceptualizing the "purposes of strict liability"? Is the court's no-duty holding different from the Products Liability Restatement's position that ordinarily consumers have no reason to expect a new product is defective?

Is this issue related to section 402A comment n, quoted in *Sanchez*? Under comment n, the consumer's failure to discover a defect is not a defense, unlike assumption of risk. At most, the failure to discover a defect involves constructive knowledge—the consumer should have known of the defect—unlike the actual knowledge required by assumption of risk. By eliminating an affirmative defense based on the consumer's constructive knowledge of defect, does comment n effectively foreclose any limitation of liability based on the premise that the consumer should have known of the defect?

2.   Which of the decedent's actions provided the basis for the court to conclude that a jury could find that his conduct involved more than a failure to discover a product defect? How do the two Restatements differ on this type of defense?

3.   Does *Sanchez* mean that any time a consumer fails to follow a manufacturer's instructions or warnings, comparative responsibility may be assigned to the consumer?

4.   *The comparative exercise.* How does the jury determine the respective percentages of responsibility? Courts have struggled with this issue. In Daly v. General Motors Corp., 575 P.2d 1162, 1172 (Cal.1978), an early influential products case involving crashworthiness, the court, 4–3, applied comparative fault (which it thought might better be termed "equitable apportionment of loss"). The dissent lamented that:

> The majority's assumption that a jury is capable of making a fair apportionment between a plaintiff's negligent conduct and a defendant's defective product is no more logical or convincing than if a jury were to be instructed that it should add a quart of milk (representing plaintiff's negligence) and a metal bar three feet in length (representing defendant's strict liability for a defective product), and that the two added together equal 100 percent—the total fault for plaintiff's injuries; that plaintiff's quart of milk is then to be assigned its percentage of the 100 percent total and defendant's metal bar is to be assigned the remaining percentage

of the total. Either the jury or the trial judge will then subtract from the total amount of plaintiff's damages an amount equal to the percentage of total fault allocated to plaintiff.

Id. at 1178.

Consider the comparative approach adopted in the 1987 Texas legislation quoted in *Sanchez*. How can "cause"—at least factual cause—be compared? What might the legislature have meant in its use of "cause or contribute"? The Apportionment Restatement rejects causation as a basis for assigning comparative percentages, as well as fault and negligence, adopting instead the "general and neutral term," responsibility. " 'Assigning shares of responsibility' may be a less confusing phrase because it suggests that the factfinder, after considering the relevant factors, assigns shares of responsibility rather than compares incommensurate quantities. Nevertheless, the term 'comparative responsibility' is used pervasively by courts and legislatures to describe percentage-allocation systems." Restatement (Third) of Torts: Apportionment of Liability § 8 cmt. a.

In Zuern v. Ford Motor Company, 937 P.2d 676 (Ariz.App.1996), plaintiffs sued Ford, claiming their car's uncrashworthy condition caused serious injury to their five-year-old son. The driver of another car admitted full responsibility for rear-ending plaintiffs' car, and was, in fact, sent to prison for drunk driving. At trial, Ford adduced evidence of the driver's intoxication and conviction, and, based on that evidence, "Ford's counsel told the jury in closing argument that it should assess 'by far the largest degree of fault' to [the other driver] and urged the jury, as 'the conscience of the community,' to 'figure out what we are going to do with drunk drivers in this community.' " The jury allocated fault 70% to the driver and 30% to Ford. In explaining why it upheld the trial court's admission of this evidence, the court of appeals observed that a state statute "requires the trier to assess 'degrees of fault,' not just degrees of causation. Although causation (or physical contribution to the injury) is a necessary condition precedent to consideration of a person's fault . . . once causation is found the trier of fact must determine and apportion 'the relative degrees of fault' of all parties and non-parties." How would pure causal apportionment work in this case? Would the alternative approach adopted by the court work when the defendant is subject to strict liability? If the term "fault" is replaced by "responsibility," is the approach any different from the one adopted by the Apportionment Restatement?

5. *Enhanced injuries.* In many cases, plaintiffs do not allege that the product defect caused the entirety of their injury, but simply that it enhanced what would otherwise have been a less serious harm. For example, in Binakonsky v. Ford Motor Co., 133 F.3d 281 (4th Cir.1998), plaintiffs' decedent, driving drunk, had hit an oak tree head on, and his Ford van caught on fire. Plaintiffs, alleging that this fire—and not the crash—had killed him, claimed that a design defect had caused the fire. The majority explained that the defense of contributory negligence did not apply to strict products liability claims under Maryland law. It then explained why assumption of risk should not bar plaintiff's present suit:

Assumption of risk, sometimes called a form of contributory negligence, is a defense to claims based on strict liability. The defense is available against a plaintiff who unreasonably uses a product despite a known risk of danger. . . . Drunk driving is an unreasonable use of a car, and it is common knowledge that a driver who strikes a tree will cause damage. For this reason, a drunk driver, such as Binakonsky, assumes the risk of injury from the initial impact.

It is not generally known however, that plastic lines and connectors and the lack of an anti-siphoning device will cause a vehicle to burst into a devastating post-collision fire. Moreover, Ford gave no warning about the likelihood of such fire. For these reasons the plaintiffs are entitled to the reasonable inference that Binakonsky did not assume the risk of a lethal fire.

Id. at 289. Should the decedent's negligence in causing the accident reduce the recovery from Ford for the enhanced injuries?

The difficulty of this issue is revealed by Jahn v. Hyundai Motor Co., 773 N.W.2d 550 (Iowa 2009), in which plaintiff was injured when another car went through a stop sign and collided with plaintiff's car. The air bag then failed due to a defect, enhancing the plaintiff's injuries. Departing from its ruling in an earlier case, the court concluded that plaintiff's fault should be considered in the final allocation of liability for the enhanced injury. Suppose the jury apportions responsibility as 50–50 between plaintiff and the crashworthiness defendant and finds the initial injuries were $100,000 and enhanced injuries $250,000. What will be the amount of the judgment against the defendant? What should the allocation be if the jury cannot apportion the initial injury from the enhanced injury, in which case defendant is liable for the entire injury, as discussed in note 1, p. 601 supra?

Rejecting the "majority rule," D'Amario v. Ford Motor Co., 806 So.2d 424 (Fla.2001), held that the "principles of comparative fault concerning apportionment of fault as to the cause of the underlying crash will not ordinarily apply in crashworthiness or enhanced injury cases." The court distinguished the injuries caused initially by the crash, for which any fault of the driver or others would be compared, from the enhanced harm resulting from the uncrashworthiness of the vehicle. The court exempted these latter injuries from apportionment by analogizing a plaintiff's negligence in a crashworthiness case to pre-presentment negligence by a patient in a medical malpractice case, p. 458 supra. Is that persuasive? In 2011, the Florida legislature overturned the rule in *D'Amario* in an amendment to its comparative fault statute. Fla. Stat. Ann. § 768.81(3)(b).

6. *Apportionment among defendants.* Suppose the plaintiff has prevailed against the retailer and the manufacturer in the case of a metal sliver in a can of tuna fish. How should liability be apportioned between these defendants? See Godoy v. Abamaster of Miami, Inc., 754 N.Y.S.2d 301 (App.Div.2003)(concluding as a matter of law that downstream distributors that had "moved the product through the stream of commerce without knowledge of the defect" were entitled to full indemnification from upstream suppliers). The Apportionment Restatement in section 13 cmt. d, states that when one defendant is vicariously liable for another defendant's negligence, the two should be submitted together to the jury for a single apportionment of responsibility. Do you see why? What if the defective product is a car with a loose wheel that should have been found by the retailer during its final check before delivering the car—and the plaintiff has recovered a judgment against both the manufacturer and the retailer?

2. OTHER AFFIRMATIVE DEFENSES

Disclaimers and contractual waivers. The Products Liability Restatement addresses the validity of disclaimers in section 18: "disclaimers and limitations of remedies by product sellers or other distributors, waivers by product purchasers, and other similar contractual exculpations, oral or written, do not bar or reduce otherwise valid products liability claims against sellers or other distributors of new products for harm to persons." This section adopts and extends comment m to section 402A of the Second Restatement, which stated that "The consumer's cause of action [in tort] . . . is not affected by any disclaimer or other agreement. . . ." The Products Liability Restatement section 18 cmt. a justifies this rule on the ground that "[i]t is presumed that the ordinary product user or consumer lacks sufficient information and bargaining power to execute a fair contractual limitation of rights to recover."

Courts, however, have adopted distinct approaches regarding the enforceability of disclaimers. By far the most prevalent one is consistent with the Products Liability Restatement, although some courts distinguish between disclaimers of negligence liability, recall *Hanks*, p. 464 supra, and strict liability. Thus, in Westlye v. Look Sports, Inc., 22 Cal.Rptr.2d 781 (App.1993), the court held that express assumption of the risk would bar plaintiff's negligence action but not her strict liability claim for the failure of her ski boot bindings to release when she fell. The court reasoned that "one purpose of strict liability in tort is to prevent a manufacturer from defining the scope of his responsibility for harm caused by his products." Allowing a defense of disclaimer in the products area would contravene this fundamental end of strict liability.

By contrast, in Mohney v. USA Hockey, Inc., 77 F.Supp.2d 859 (N.D. Ohio 1999), rev'd on other grounds, 5 F.App'x 450 (6th Cir.2001), the court held that a disclaimer barred a strict liability claim against a hockey equipment manufacturer: "[S]ince strict liability requires a lesser showing of culpability than does negligence, it stands to reason that if a plaintiff can waive a negligence claim, he can also waive a strict liability claim." See generally Ausness, "Waive" Goodbye to Tort Liability: A Proposal to Remove Paternalism from Product Sales Transactions, 37 San Diego L.Rev. 293 (2000), arguing for allowing waivers of liability by consumers in product sales cases involving personal injuries. Assuming that the ordinary consumer does not have the information required to execute a fair limitation of liability, on what basis could a court determine whether the individual plaintiff was sufficiently informed?

Statutes of repose. Statutes of repose are similar to statutes of limitation in that after the passage of a specified period of time, a claim is barred unless previously filed. Statutes of repose are different in that the time begins to run when the product is first sold (or sometimes when manufactured), rather than when the claim accrued, as with statutes of limitation. The application of statutes of repose is illustrated in Tanges v. Heidelberg North America, Inc., 710 N.E.2d 250 (N.Y.1999). Plaintiff was hurt by defendant's printing press, which had been first sold by defendant ten years and three months before plaintiff was injured while using it. Due to choice of law principles, Connecticut law applied, and a Connecticut statute provided that any claim involving a product had to be brought within three years after the injury and not "later than ten years from the date that the party last parted with possession or control of the product." Id. at 251. The *Tanges* court explained:

> Statutes of repose are theoretically and functionally distinct from typical time limitations. The former are an increasingly common feature of comprehensive products liability codifications. States use the enhanced repose concept as a tool to alleviate the increasing cost burden borne by manufacturers and sellers seeking to obtain products liability insurance. [ ] Unlike the usual limitation provision, which does not begin to run until a cause of action accrues [ ], a statute of repose begins to run when the specific event or events takes place, regardless of whether a potential claim has accrued or, indeed, whether any injury has occurred.

Id. at 253. Based on the statute, the court concluded that plaintiff's claim was extinguished before it had been filed.

Perhaps the most prominent statute of repose is one enacted on the federal level that takes effect 18 years after the manufacturer of a general aviation aircraft delivers the aircraft "to its first purchaser or lessee." General Aviation Revitalization Act of 1994 (GARA), Pub.L.No. 103–298, 108 Stat. 1552, 49 U.S.C. § 40101 note.

Preemption. As we saw in Chapter VII, an increasing number of federal statutes and regulations are reducing the scope of state tort liability. The principal case on the preemption defense, *Riegel,* p. 488 supra, involved a defective product claim, although there was no legal significance to the underlying tort claim being a products liability action. Most recent Supreme Court decisions on preemption of tort claims have occurred in the products liability context. See Chapter VII, Section C.

F. Work-Related Injuries

Almost all of the main cases in this Chapter have involved claims brought by ordinary consumers—either the purchaser or someone who had permission to use the product. Recall *MacPherson* (car), *Soule* (car), *Camacho* (motorcycle), *Hood* (home saw), *Karl* (prescription drug), and *Vassallo* (breast implant). Outside of the employment context, this conception of the consumer has evident logic. Unlike a mere product user, the purchaser pays for any product safety precautions, such as an airbag, via the associated increase in product price and related costs. In making the purchase decision, the buyer presumably gives equal consideration to the welfare of other users, such as family members or friends. One who buys an automobile expects it to be safe for all occupants, not merely the driver. The interests of the parties coincide, making it defensible to conceptualize the consumer as including both the buyer and any reasonably foreseeable user of the product. Does this rationale apply to work-related injuries? In purchasing or otherwise modifying the product, does the employer adequately consider the interests of the employees who will use the product and face the threat of injury? In this section we consider these special problems, including the impact of workers' compensation, a subject we cover in detail in Chapter XII.

Although workers' tort suits against their employers for accidental injuries are barred because of the "exclusive remedy" provision of workers' compensation statutes, workers injured on the job may sue third parties for having violated any tort obligations owed to them—as though the compensation system did not exist. (In a few states, suits are barred against any third party contributing to the compensation system.) Moreover, the worker may accept compensation benefits and pursue the tort action simultaneously without waiving one or the other, although, as we shall see, the worker ordinarily must return the duplicative compensation benefits after recovering in tort. This has undoubtedly occurred in many cases that we have considered, especially in the defective product area.

Jones v. Ryobi, Ltd.

United States Court of Appeals, Eighth Circuit, 1994.
37 F.3d 423.

■ Before Fagg, Circuit Judge, Heaney, Senior Circuit Judge, and Loken, Circuit Judge.

■ Fagg, Circuit Judge.

Jennifer Jones was employed at Business Cards Tomorrow (BCT) as the operator of a small printing press known as an offset duplicator. Jones seriously injured her left hand when she caught it in the moving parts of the press. Alleging negligence and strict product liability for defective design, Jones brought this diversity lawsuit against Ryobi,

Ltd. (the manufacturer) and A.B. Dick Corporation (the distributor). At trial, Jones dropped her negligence claims but she later moved to amend her complaint to reassert her negligence claim against the distributor. The district court denied Jones's motion to amend. At the close of Jones's case, the manufacturer and the distributor moved for judgment as a matter of law (JAML). The district court granted the manufacturer's and the distributor's motions for JAML. Jones appeals and we affirm.

The press involved in Jones's injury operates by passing blank paper through several moving parts, imprinting an image on the paper, and dispensing the printed paper through upper and lower "eject wheels." To avoid streaking the freshly printed image, on each job the operator must adjust the eject wheels to ensure the wheels do not touch the freshly printed area. The press was manufactured and sold to BCT equipped with both a plastic guard that prevented the operator from reaching into the moving parts to adjust the eject wheels, and an electric interlock switch that automatically shut off the press if the guard was opened. Sometime after the press was manufactured and delivered to BCT, the guard was removed and the interlock switch was disabled to allow the press to run without the guard. Because this modification increased production by saving the few seconds required to stop and to restart the press when the operator adjusted the eject wheels, the modification was a common practice in the printing industry.

Jones learned to operate the press by watching other BCT employees. Jones testified she knew the guard was missing and knew it was dangerous to have her hands near the unguarded moving parts, but her supervisor pressured her to save time by adjusting the eject wheels while the press was running. Jones feared she would be fired if she took the time to stop the press. While Jones was adjusting the eject wheels on the running press, a noise startled her. Jones jumped and her left hand was caught in the press's moving parts and crushed.

In granting the manufacturer's and the distributor's motions for JAML, the district court relied on the open and obvious nature of the asserted danger. See Restatement (Second) of Torts § 402A cmt. *i* (1965)(consumer expectation test). The district court did not reach the manufacturer's and the distributor's other grounds for JAML. We review the district court's grant of JAML de novo; thus, we may affirm on another ground. [ ] Because we conclude the district court's grant of JAML was proper on an alternate ground, we need not consider the ground relied on by the district court.

To recover on a theory of strict liability for defective design under Missouri law, Jones must prove she was injured as a direct result of a defect that existed when the press was sold. [ ] Jones had the burden to show the press had not been modified to create a defect that could have proximately caused her injury. [ ] Jones failed to meet this burden because her evidence showed the press had been substantially modified by removing the safety guard and disabling the interlock switch, and showed the modification caused her injury. When a third party's modification makes a safe product unsafe, the seller is relieved of liability even if the modification is foreseeable. [ ] Jones did not show who modified the press, but her evidence clearly showed that a third party, not the manufacturer or the distributor, was responsible for the modification.

Although the manufacturer provided tools for general maintenance of the press that could also be used to remove the guard, we do not believe this made the manufacturer responsible for the guard's removal. Jones produced no evidence that any representative of the manufacturer or the distributor removed the guard or instructed BCT to remove the guard from the press involved in Jones's injury. Indeed, the distributor's service representative testified he told BCT's owner several times the guard should be replaced, but BCT's owner shrugged off the suggestion. Because BCT knew the guard was missing and the interlock switch was disabled, but did not follow the distributor's advice to repair the disabled safety features, the distributor's service work on the press did not extend the distributor's liability to defects that were not present when the press was sold. [ ]

Jones argues the modification rule does not apply because the press was not safe even before the modification. We disagree. The press was safe before the modification because the press would not run without the safety guard covering the moving parts. The fact BCT encouraged Jones to operate the press without the safety features to increase production does not show the press was sold "in a defective condition [and thus] was unreasonably dangerous when put to a reasonably anticipated use." [ ] Although several witnesses testified the press operated more efficiently without the safety guard and interlock switch, other witnesses testified similar presses operated satisfactorily with the designed safety features intact. The press could be operated safely without removing the guard because the eject wheels did not have to be adjusted while the press was running. Jones's expert witness opined the press was unsafe as designed, but the expert based his view on the printing industry's tendency to disable the press's safety features to achieve greater production. Thus, the expert's testimony does not show the press was unreasonably dangerous when used in the same condition as when it was sold. [ ]

Because Jones's evidence showed a third party's modification, not a defect existing when the press was sold, was the sole cause of her injury, her strict product liability claim for defective design fails as a matter of law. [ ] The district court thus properly granted the manufacturer's and the distributor's JAML motions.

. . .

Accordingly, we affirm.

■ HEANEY, SENIOR CIRCUIT JUDGE, dissenting.

Viewing the evidence in the light most favorable to Jones, as we must, I cannot subscribe to the majority's opinion that the offset duplicator was safe as originally manufactured.

The rule to which Missouri adheres, as correctly stated by the majority, is that a manufacturer is not liable where a modification is foreseeable, but the modification renders a safe product unsafe. . . .

. . . The critical question, thus, is whether the duplicator as manufactured was unreasonably dangerous.

The testimony of Dr. Creighton, Jones's expert witness, is alone sufficient to support the inference that the offset duplicator was not safe as originally designed. . . . He testified that the duplicator's guard, in addition to not being fail-safe, was made of material "that will break . . . readily," did not allow for proper ventilation of the internal components of the machine, and invited removal. He further testified that the design of the eject wheels, which essentially requires operators to make manual adjustments while the offset duplicator is running, was "absolutely not safe," indeed "the worst of situations from a human factors standpoint." The duplicator could have been equipped, he noted, with external adjustment handles to enable operators to make adjustments to the eject wheels without placing their hands in close proximity to the moving parts of the machine.

Further, although not direct proof that the duplicator was defectively designed, the fact that an overwhelming majority of machines had their guards removed after their delivery is evidence that the duplicator was incapable of operating efficiently according to industry standards. According to [a representative of the former distributor of the product] nearly ninety-eight percent of all machines he came into contact with had their safety covers removed. [ ] Indeed, [he] testified that he told duplicator operators in effect to remove the guard in order to alleviate problems with ink emulsification that occurred as a result of humidity which frequently became trapped inside the plastic shield. [ ]

The majority does not address (nor need it, given the focus of its opinion) the open-and-obvious defense on which the district court relied in granting the defendants' motion for judgment as a matter of law. I touch on it briefly [to show that it will not support affirmance.]

We have held that the obviousness of a defect or danger is material to the issue of whether a product is unreasonably dangerous. [ ] It does not, however, alone constitute a defense to a submissible case of strict liability under section 402A. [The question under Missouri law] is not simply whether the danger was open and obvious, but whether the product was unreasonably dangerous taking into account the obviousness of the danger.

There is no question in my mind that there was sufficient evidence from which a jury, taking into account the obviousness of the conceded danger, could conclude that the offset duplicator was unreasonably dangerous. . . .

In my judgment there was sufficient evidence to support the inference that the offset duplicator was unreasonably dangerous and thus was defectively designed. This case should have met its fate in the hands of the jury members, not the district court's and not now ours.

NOTES AND QUESTIONS

1. With regard to the trial court's basis for dismissing the case—an open and obvious danger—recall *Camacho*, p. 594 supra. Could a jury find that the duplicator was dangerous beyond the expectations of an ordinary user or purchaser? Considering the testimony of the plaintiff's expert, was the dangerous condition of the duplicator open and obvious? How persuasive is the dissent on this issue?

2. What is the significance of the fact that defendant distributor knew that BCT had removed the guard and tried "several times" to persuade management to put it back? Even if the manufacturer did not know about BCT's practices, should it be enough that the manufacturer knew of the "common practice" in the industry to remove the guards? Suppose the distributor's representatives tried to sell the machine by encouraging buyers to remove the guard? Should it matter whether the defendant manufacturer was aware of the distributor's approach?

3. Is it relevant why the industry removed the guards? Does it matter whether it was to (a) save ten seconds three times a day, (b) increase production by 20%, or (c) improve the quality of the end product? What does it mean to say that a guard "invites removal"?

4. If a manufacturer has no duty to design a product that takes into account foreseeable substantial modifications, what is the nature of a duty to market a reasonably safe product? What about the rule that the manufacturer's tort duty includes foreseeable product misuses, discussed at p. 636 supra? How might the plaintiff show that the press was "not safe" when it left the hands of the manufacturer and the distributor?

5. *Statutory change.* Although the majority of courts may favor the approach of the dissent to substantial modification in *Ryobi*, the situation is less clear when statutory developments are considered. As we have noted in connection with joint and several liability, p. 452 supra, and will describe more generally in Chapter XII, legislative changes to common law tort decisions have become more common recently. About a quarter of the states have adopted statutes aimed at protecting suppliers of goods that have been altered after the supplier distributed them. Some of these protect suppliers only when the alteration was not foreseeable. But several others apply to any substantial alteration.

6.   To what extent can the problem of alteration be resolved by product warnings? Consider this question in the context of the following case.

Liriano v. Hobart Corp.

Court of Appeals of New York, 1998.
92 N.Y.2d 232, 700 N.E.2d 303, 677 N.Y.S.2d 764.

■ CIPARICK, JUDGE.

In Robinson v. Reed-Prentice Div. of Package Mach. Co., [403 N.E.2d 440 (N.Y.1980)], we held that a manufacturer is not responsible for injuries resulting from substantial alterations or modifications of a product by a third party that render the product defective or otherwise unsafe. The present case certifies the issue of whether a plaintiff, whose design claim is barred by the substantial modification defense stated in *Robinson*, may nevertheless maintain a claim for failure to warn of the consequences of such modification. Finding the issue to be an open one, the United States Court of Appeals for the Second Circuit certified the following question to our Court:

> Can manufacturer liability exist under a failure to warn theory in cases in which the substantial modification defense would preclude liability under a design defect theory, and if so, is such manufacturer liability barred as a matter of law on the facts of this case, viewed in the light most favorable to the plaintiff?

We answer the first part of the certified question in the affirmative and decline to answer the second part. . . .

[In 1993, Liriano, a 17-year-old recent immigrant, was employed in the meat department of a "Super" grocery store. He lost his right hand and lower forearm when his hand was caught in a meat grinder manufactured and sold by defendant in 1961. The safety guard had been removed from the grinder while it was in Super's possession and there was no warning on the grinder about the danger of using it without a guard. In 1962, after Hobart became aware that a significant number of purchasers of its meat grinders had removed the safety guards, it began issuing warnings on its meat grinders concerning removal of the safety guard.

Liriano sued Hobart under theories of negligence and strict products liability for, among other things, defective product design and failure to warn. Hobart impleaded Super. At trial the jury apportioned liability 5% to Hobart and 95% to Super. It then allocated 33 1/3% of the total responsibility to plaintiff. The trial judge entered a judgment that was conformed to reflect the jury's allocations.]

A manufacturer who places a defective product on the market that causes injury may be liable for the ensuing injuries [ ]. A product may be defective when it contains a manufacturing flaw, is defectively designed or is not accompanied by adequate warnings for the use of the product [ ]. A manufacturer has a duty to warn against latent dangers resulting from foreseeable uses of its product of which it knew or should have known [ ]. A manufacturer also has a duty to warn of the danger of unintended uses of a product provided these uses are reasonably foreseeable [ ].

A manufacturer is not liable for injuries caused by substantial alterations to the product by a third party that render the product defective or unsafe [*Robinson*]. Where, however, a product is purposefully manufactured to permit its use without a safety feature, a plaintiff may recover for injuries suffered as a result of removing the safety feature [Lopez v. Precision Papers, 492 N.E.2d 1214 (N.Y.1986)].

[Hobart argued that *Robinson* should apply to failure-to-warn claims as well as design claims.] Several intermediate appellate courts have interpreted *Robinson* to mean that, where a substantial alteration of a product occurs, an injured party is also precluded from asserting a claim for failure to warn [ ]. Relying on *Robinson* and these lower court decisions, Hobart urges that the plaintiff's failure-to-warn claim should be barred as a matter of law. *Robinson*, however, did not resolve the issue of whether preclusion of a claim for defective design because of substantial alteration by a third party should also bar a claim for failure to warn.

This Court's rationale in *Robinson* stemmed from the recognition that a manufacturer is responsible for a "purposeful design choice" that presents an unreasonable danger to the user [*Robinson.*] This responsibility derives from the manufacturer's superior position to anticipate reasonable uses of its product and its obligation to design a product that is not harmful when used in that manner. However, this duty is not open-ended, and it is measured as of the time the product leaves the manufacturer's premises. Thus, a manufacturer is not required to insure that subsequent owners and users will not adapt the product to their own unique uses. That kind of obligation is much too broad and would effectively impose liability on manufacturers for all product-related injuries [ ].

While this Court stated that principles of foreseeability are inapplicable where there has been a substantial modification of the product, that discussion was limited to the manufacturer's responsibility for defective design where there had been a substantial alteration of a product by a third party [ ]. Thus, this Court stated that a manufacturer's duty "does not extend to *designing* a product that is impossible to abuse or one whose safety features may not be circumvented" and the manufacturer need not trace its "product through every link in the chain of distribution to insure that users will not adapt the product to suit their own unique purposes" [ ] [emphasis added].

Hobart and amici argue that the rationale of *Robinson* is equally applicable to failure-to-warn claims where a substantial modification of the product occurs and that application of the failure-to-warn doctrine in these circumstances would undermine *Robinson*'s policy justification and destroy its purpose. This Court is not persuaded that the existence of a substantial modification defense precludes, in all cases, a failure-to-warn claim.

The factors militating against imposing a duty to design against foreseeable post-sale product modifications are either not present or less cogent with respect to a duty to warn against making such modifications. The existence of a design defect involves a risk/utility analysis that requires an assessment of whether "if the design defect were known at the time of the manufacture, a reasonable person would conclude that the utility of the product did not outweigh the risk inherent in marketing a product designed in that manner" [ ]. Such an analysis would be unreasonably complicated, and may very well be impossible to measure, if a manufacturer has to factor into the design equation all foreseeable post-sale modifications. Imposition of a duty that is incapable of assessment would effectively result in the imposition of absolute liability on manufacturers for all product-related injuries [see *Robinson*]. This Court has drawn a policy line against that eventuality.

These concerns are not as strongly implicated in the context of a duty to warn. Unlike design decisions that involve the consideration of many interdependent factors, the inquiry in a duty to warn case is much more limited, focusing principally on the foreseeability of the risk and the adequacy and effectiveness of any warning. The burden of placing a warning on a product is less costly than designing a perfectly safe, tamper resistant product. Thus, although it is virtually impossible to design a product to forestall all future risk-enhancing modifications that could occur after the sale, it is neither infeasible nor onerous, in some cases, to warn of the dangers of foreseeable modifications that pose the risk of injury.

Furthermore, this Court has held that a manufacturer may be liable for failing to warn against the dangers of foreseeable misuse of its product [ ]. No material distinction between foreseeable misuse and foreseeable alteration of a product is evident in this context. Thus, the rationale of [*Lugo*] should apply to both situations.[2]

This Court has also recognized that, in certain circumstances, a manufacturer may have a duty to warn of dangers associated with the use of its product even after it has been sold. Such a duty will generally

---

[2] True, issues of foreseeability, obviousness, proximate cause or the adequacy of warnings can be troublesome in failure-to-warn cases, as has been noted by various commentators [ ]. Those difficulties do not, however, negate the duty to warn against foreseeable product misuse which is well established in this Court's precedents as well as contemporary products liability jurisprudence.

arise where a defect or danger is revealed by user operation and brought to the attention of the manufacturer; the existence and scope of such a duty are generally fact-specific (see, Cover v. Cohen, [473 N.Y.S.2d 378 (N.Y.1984)]; [ ].)[3]

The justification for the post-sale duty to warn arises from a manufacturer's unique (and superior) position to follow the use and adaptation of its product by consumers (see, [*Cover*]). Compared to purchasers and users of a product, a manufacturer is best placed to learn about post-sale defects or dangers discovered in use. A manufacturer's superior position to garner information and its corresponding duty to warn is no less with respect to the ability to learn of modifications made to or misuse of a product. Indeed, as in this case, Hobart was the only party likely to learn about the removal of the safety guards and, as it ultimately did, pass along warnings to customers.

This Court therefore concludes that manufacturer liability can exist under a failure-to-warn theory in cases in which the substantial modification defense as articulated in *Robinson* might otherwise preclude a design defect claim.

We should emphasize, however, that a safety device built into the integrated final product is often the most effective way to communicate that operation of the product without the device is hazardous. Thus, where the injured party was fully aware of the hazard through general knowledge, observation or common sense, or participated in the removal of the safety device whose purpose is obvious, lack of a warning about that danger may well obviate the failure to warn as a legal cause of an injury resulting from that danger [ ]. Thus, in appropriate cases, courts could as a matter of law decide that a manufacturer's warning would have been superfluous given an injured party's actual knowledge of the specific hazard that caused the injury [ ]. Nevertheless, in cases where reasonable minds might disagree as to the extent of plaintiff's knowledge of the hazard, the question is one for the jury [ ].

Similarly, a limited class of hazards need not be warned of as a matter of law because they are patently dangerous or pose open and obvious risks, [ ]. Where a danger is readily apparent as a matter of common sense, "there should be no liability for failing to warn someone of a risk or hazard which he [or she] appreciated to the same extent as a warning would have provided" [ ]. Put differently, when a warning would have added nothing to the user's appreciation of the danger, no duty to warn exists as no benefit would be gained by requiring a warning. On the other hand, the open and obvious defense generally

---

[3]   As we noted in *Cover*, the post-sale duty of a manufacturer to warn involves the weighing of a number of factors: including the degree of danger the problem involves, the number of reported incidents, the burden of providing the warning, as well as the burden and/or ability to track a product post-sale. [ ]

should not apply when there are aspects of the hazard which are concealed or not reasonably apparent to the user.

This is particularly important because requiring a manufacturer to warn against obvious dangers could greatly increase the number of warnings accompanying certain products. If a manufacturer must warn against even obvious dangers, "[t]he list of foolish practices warned against would be so long, it would fill a volume" [ ]. Requiring too many warnings trivializes and undermines the entire purpose of the rule, drowning out cautions against latent dangers of which a user might not otherwise be aware. Such a requirement would neutralize the effectiveness of warnings as an inexpensive way to allow consumers to adjust their behavior based on knowledge of a product's inherent dangers.

While important to warning law, the open and obvious danger exception is difficult to administer [ ]. The fact-specific nature of the inquiry into whether a particular risk is obvious renders bright-line pronouncements difficult, and in close cases it is easy to disagree about whether a particular risk is obvious. It is hard to set a standard for obviousness that is neither under nor overinclusive. Because of the factual nature of the inquiry, whether a danger is open and obvious is most often a jury question [ ]. Where only one conclusion can be drawn from the established facts, however, the issue of whether the risk was open and obvious may be decided by the court as a matter of law.

[The court declined to answer the second question because failure-to-warn "liability is intensely fact-specific, including but not limited to such issues as feasibility and difficulty of issuing warnings in the circumstances [ ]; obviousness of the risk from actual use of the product; knowledge of the particular product user; and proximate cause." The factual record was being developed in the federal court. Thus, "any remaining question posed is appropriately addressed by the Second Circuit in light of the substantive law question we have now resolved."]

Accordingly, the certified question should be answered as follows: manufacturer liability for failure to warn may exist in cases where the substantial modification defense would preclude liability on a design defect theory.

■ KAYE, C.J., and TITONE, BELLACOSA, SMITH, LEVINE and WESLEY, JJ., concur.

NOTES AND QUESTIONS

1.   If, as the court states about its *Robinson* decision, the "principles of foreseeability are inapplicable where there has been a substantial modification of the product," why is a product that "is purposefully manufactured to permit its use without a safety feature" different?

In the cited *Lopez* case, plaintiff forklift operator was injured when an object fell onto his unprotected head. The overhead guard had been removed in the workplace. In the suit against the manufacturer, the court distinguished *Robinson*, stating in full:

> The record presents triable issues of fact concerning whether the forklift, as marketed with an attached but removable overhead safety guard, was "not reasonably safe" [ ] for the uses intended or reasonably anticipated by the manufacturer [ ].
>
> . . . [*Robinson*] does not compel a different result. In contrast with the detaching of the removable safety guard in this case, *Robinson* involved "[m]aterial alterations [i.e. cutting a 6-inch by 14-inch access hole in the safety gate of a plastic molding machine] which work[ed] a substantial change in the condition in which the product was sold by destroying the functional utility of a key safety feature" [ ]. There is evidence in this record that the forklift was purposefully manufactured to permit its use without the safety guard.

492 N.E.2d at 1215.

2. Why does *Robinson* bar a design defect claim in *Liriano*? Is the court's treatment of the distinction between design and warning in this context persuasive? When the reasons for *Robinson* are considered in warning cases, why are they "not present or less cogent"?

3. Other courts have responded differently to the alteration problem than have Missouri and New York. Consider Anderson v. Nissei ASB Machine Co., 3 P.3d 1088 (Ariz.App.1999), involving a machine for making plastic bottles. The machine came with safety doors that left a six-inch space through which hands could fit. It also came with "purge guards" that were attached to the safety doors with three small screws (not rivets) and that reduced the open space from six inches to three inches. Opening or jarring the safety doors automatically shut down the machine. Once shut down, the machine took as long as two hours to restart. Workers faced the problem of how to remove "drool"—molten waste material that quickly hardens into rock-like lumps—from the machine. If it were not removed at least every 15 minutes, the drool would damage the machine and render it inoperable. Defendant's manual did not mention drool or how to remove it. The workers developed their own system: inserting a stick with a long hook into the three-inch gap left by the purge guard and dragging out the drool. If the stick hit or jarred the doors, the machine would shut down. As frequently happened with this machine model, someone in the factory (other than plaintiff) removed the purge guards so that it would be easier to get the drool out without jarring the machine. An expert testified that increasing the open space from three to six inches made removal much easier. As plaintiff reached into the six-inch gap of the operating machine his hand and forearm were crushed.

The court, 2–1, upheld a jury finding that the machine was defective as marketed. The court focused on the ease of removal of the purge guards and the defendant's failure to warn or address the issue of drool. Because the modification was essential to keep the machine running and purge-guard removal was common in the industry, a jury could find that the removal was foreseeable, and the product defective. The court distinguished the New York position in *Robinson* on the ground that the modification here was not simply to increase the employer's productivity but to make the machine function adequately for the purpose for which it was sold. Also, in *Robinson* there was no defect in the design of the safety gate. The court disagreed with *Jones v. Ryobi*, because Missouri law denied recovery even in cases of foreseeable dangerous modification. See also Spurgeon v. Julius Blum, Inc., 816 F.Supp. 1317 (C.D.Ill.1993)(suggesting that the requisite foreseeability may be established by showing that a machine guard is easily removed, difficult to replace, must be removed frequently for cleaning, or that the guard inhibits the task that the machine is to perform).

4. On remand in *Liriano*, on the warning question, the Second Circuit found a jury question. 170 F.3d 264 (2d Cir.1999). Judge Calabresi noted that—taking the facts most favorably to the plaintiff—Liriano, who was 17 years old at the time of the accident, had "recently immigrated" to the United States, had been employed at Super for one week, had not been instructed in the operation of the grinder, and had used it only two or three times previously. In addition, the danger was not visible to the operator. Defendant argued that the danger of grinders was so widely understood that no warning was necessary.

But the court observed that a warning may do more "than exhort its audience to be careful." Beyond showing danger, a warning can also explain ways to avoid harm. The court used the distinction between two signs: "Danger—Steep Grade" and "Steep Grade Ahead—Follow Suggested Detour to Avoid Dangerous Areas." Thus, even if the danger of the grinder was obvious, informing users of the availability of guards and their benefits was additional information that a factfinder might determine was not obvious. On causation, the court invoked a "heeding presumption."

Concurring, Judge Newman observed that a warning might have spurred the plaintiff to ask others for help. He also noted that it was easier for a driver to avoid a steep grade than for a worker to refuse to work on a dangerous product. Reasonable minds might differ on "avoiding use of a machine from which a safety guard had been removed and requesting a machine with the guard in place."

5. *The bulk supplier.* As we saw earlier with regard to learned intermediaries, p. 617 supra, and sophisticated users, p. 617 supra, the addressee of a warning can influence the duty to warn. For work-related injuries, the issue frequently involves one company that supplies a product in bulk to a large enterprise where it will be used by many workers. In these cases, does the supplier have a duty to warn the employer, the employees, or both? Under the bulk supplier defense, the duty is owed only to the employer and not the employees. In Humble Sand & Gravel, Inc. v. Gomez, 146 S.W.3d 170 (Tex.2004), the court adopted the bulk supplier defense. Relying on the Second and Third Restatements, the court developed a list of factors to be employed in determining whether the defense applied: 1) the likelihood of serious injury from a supplier's failure to warn the employees or other product users; 2) the burden on a supplier of giving a warning directly to the employees or other product users; 3) the feasibility and effectiveness of such a warning; 4) the reliability of employers in conveying the warning to their own employees; 5) the existence and efficacy of other protections; and 6) the social utility of requiring, or not requiring, suppliers to warn end users of the product. Id. at 192–94. The court held that the burden of proof was on the supplier, in light of the factors identified, to establish that the warning demanded by plaintiff would not have been effective in preventing harm to individual users.

For a case in which the manufacturer of a dangerous liquid bulk product was held at a minimum to owe a duty to stop supplying downstream repackagers who omitted necessary warnings, see Hunnings v. Texaco, Inc., 29 F.3d 1480 (11th Cir.1994). Plaintiff's claim could also encompass a requirement that defendant instruct "downstream distributors to notify retailers to discontinue the practice of packaging mineral spirits in milk containers, [ ], or curtailing business with customers who were known to distribute the product to errant retailers." Id. at 1487.

6. *Defenses in the employment setting.* As one might imagine, the defenses to products liability claims for work-related injuries can involve unique issues. These issues return us to the question of how employers incorporate employees' personal safety into their own calculus of costs, an issue discussed at the outset of this section. The interaction of tort liability with workers' compensation systems, discussed in the following section, may also affect judicial attitudes in this area.

a.   *The employer as buyer.* To what extent should a product supplier be able to transfer responsibility for employees' personal injuries through its negotiations with an employer? Consider cases in which employers or their agents have negotiated waivers and expressly assumed the risks entailed by a product. These sellers may assert that the employer's explicit assumption of risk should apply to an injured employee as well. Courts disagree on whether to recognize this defense. Compare Ferragamo v. Mass. Bay Transp. Auth., 481 N.E.2d 477 (Mass.1985)(concluding that plaintiff employee who was injured by a defect in defendant's product was not bound by disclaimer in contract between defendant and plaintiff's employer as buyer of the product), with Buettner v. R.W. Martin & Sons, Inc., 47 F.3d 116 (4th Cir.1995)(holding that a disclaimer that a used product was sold "as is" could be enforced against the employee as well as her employer, and that a statutory provision rendering limitations of remedies in personal injury cases prima facie unconscionable applied only to consumer goods).

A related issue is whether product suppliers should be obliged to evaluate the risks to employees created by the absence of safety features that employer purchasers have bargained away. Should an employer's purchasing decisions limit the tort rights of its employees? Even if the employer has made an informed choice, has the employee done the same?

In Scarangella v. Thomas Built Buses, Inc., 717 N.E.2d 679 (N.Y.1999), plaintiff employee of a school bus company (Huntington) was hurt when one of the company's buses, built by defendant, backed into her in the bus yard. The new bus had been bought without an optional back-up alarm. Clifford, the chief operating officer of Huntington, testified that he made what the court called "a considered decision" not to purchase the "screaming alarms" because he intended to park the buses at yards in the middle of residential neighborhoods and had been experiencing problems with neighbors concerned with noise pollution. With a "tremendous amount" of backing up in the yard and in the absence of alarms, Clifford ordered drivers to be careful and to use their ordinary horns. Clifford also considered the risk to be minimal because "the only significant incidence of operating buses in reverse was in positioning buses in and backing them out of the yard." Because of a blind spot that was created when buses were moving in reverse, the drivers "were instructed as part of their training not to operate the buses in reverse except in the yard." The trial judge's directed verdict for defendant was affirmed on appeal. After reviewing its prior cases on when a product without an optional safety device is defective, the court concluded:

> The product is not defective where the evidence and reasonable inferences therefrom show that: (1) the buyer is thoroughly knowledgeable regarding the product and its use and is actually aware that the safety feature is available; (2) there exist normal circumstances of use in which the product is not unreasonably dangerous without the optional equipment; and (3) the buyer is in a position, given the range of uses of the product, to balance the benefits and the risks of not having the safety device in the specifically contemplated circumstances of the buyer's use of the product. In such a case, the buyer, not the manufacturer, is in the superior position to make the risk-utility assessment, and a well-considered decision by the buyer to dispense with the optional safety equipment will excuse the manufacturer from liability.

Id. at 683.

The court found that all three factors had been established as a matter of law and that no jury questions remained. It did observe that had the accident occurred outside of the yard or had the plaintiff submitted evidence of "some incidence of buses backing up outside the yard, at least a triable issue might have been created as to whether there was an actual separate and distinct normal use of the buses without back-up alarms which was reasonably safe." When the court says that the buyer was in a "superior position" relative to the manufacturer, does it adequately account for the risk faced by the user/employee?

Should the court have reached the same result if suit had been brought by a student run over by a bus that was backing up in a school yard? Would the student have recourse that the plaintiff in *Scarangella* would not have?

b. *The employee's behavior.* Some Ohio cases have considered assumption of risk in the workplace context. In Cremeans v. Willmar Henderson Manufacturing Co., 566 N.E.2d 1203 (Ohio 1991), plaintiff's job was to load fertilizer at Sohio's plant. The loader had been designed by defendant Willmar to be sold with a protective cage for the driver, known as a ROPS. Because the loader could not fit into the fertilizer room to scoop the fertilizer if it had the cage, Sohio ordered it without the protective covering. In the bill of sale, the defendant insisted that Sohio assume any liability arising from the removal of the cage. "Cremeans continued to operate the [uncaged] loader in the fertilizer bins even though he was aware of the potential for an avalanche. Cremeans continued to operate the loader because it was his job." If the loader had had its ROPS, plaintiff "would not have sustained his injury." (How might the *Scarangella* court have analyzed this case?)

A divided court refused to apply assumption of risk against Cremeans. The plurality thought:

> The record in this case demonstrates that Cremeans encountered the risks associated with the use of the Willmar loader because he was required to do so in the normal performance of his job duties and responsibilities and that Cremeans was injured during the execution of such duties and responsibilities. Therefore, his assumption of the risk was neither voluntary nor unreasonable and, hence, . . . Cremeans is not barred from recovery on his products liability claim based upon strict liability in tort. This is so regardless of the fact that it was Cremeans's employer, and not Willmar, who required Cremeans to perform the particular job duty which resulted in the injury. Given the facts of this case, to wit, that Willmar knew that the loader it was selling to Sohio was not equipped with a necessary safety device and, in fact, demanded indemnity from Sohio before agreeing to make the sale, the issue is even clearer.
>
> . . . Thus, Cremeans was put at risk either solely as a result of the product defect, or by the combination of the defect and the conduct of Cremeans's employer, Sohio. In either event, the economic pressures associated with the reality of today's workplace inevitably came to bear on Cremeans's decision to encounter the risk.

Id. at 1208.

For the dissenters, "[t]he unbelievably bad result of the majority opinion here is that the manufacturer becomes an insurer of his product whenever an employer coerces his workers into exposing themselves to unconscionable risk of injury." Why is that result "unbelievably bad"? Does the indemnity contract alter that characterization?

Is the plurality's concern with the "economic pressures" placed upon the employee analogous to courts' worries in the consumer situation about consumers' bargaining powers?

After *Cremeans*, Ohio adopted legislation providing in part that when plaintiff establishes a strict liability defect, a showing that the victim "expressly or impliedly assumed a risk" is a "complete bar" to recovery of damages. Ohio Rev. Code Ann. § 2307.711(B)(2). Would that alter the result in *Cremeans*?

Meshing Compensation and Tort

In our study of products liability cases involving work-related injuries, we have not yet considered a very important aspect—the interplay between tort law and workers' compensation. The following excerpt discusses that relationship. In recent years, along with the increasing number of suits brought by injured workers against third parties, these third parties have sought to recoup all or part of their tort payments from the employer or, alternatively, to have some portion of responsibility for plaintiff's harm apportioned to the employer. The question in these cases is whether the exclusivity provision in the typical workers' compensation statute bars actions for contribution or indemnity by defendants who would have been jointly liable with the employer under traditional tort rules, yet who have been held solely liable for the full extent of the injury. To what extent is the latter action simply an indirect suit by the employee that should be barred by the statute? The modification of joint and several liability and the prevalence of several liability or hybrid systems creates another layer of issues about and complexity to this matter. The following discussion of alternative approaches to this problem was prepared before the substantial modification of joint and several liability.

Enterprise Responsibility for Personal Injury Vol. II

Approaches to Legal and Institutional Change

Report to the American Law Institute (1991).
187–92.

III. The Policy Options

A.   The Dominance of WC Policy

At this time the great majority of states still deny the third-party manufacturer any contribution at all from the negligent employer toward the full tort damages awarded to the injured employee.

The policy rationale for this position is that the employer, which has been promised full immunity from fault-based tort liability in return for financing no-fault WC benefits for its employees, should not face any erosion in that legal protection through the device of the employee's suing a third party and the third party's forcing the employer to foot a share of the resulting tort award. But the practical consequence is that even in cases in which the employer was negligent, the employer will emerge scot-free from any financial contribution to compensate the injuries if tort liability happens to be fixed on a third party and if part of the proceeds are then used to satisfy the employer's lien for its WC payments.

As we noted, from the point of view of compensation policy this result is neutral because the injured worker ends up with full tort damages and no more. From the point of view of administration this position is the most economical because it avoids any need to resolve an often contentious dispute over whether and to what extent the employer was at fault in the accident, as compared with the responsibility of worker and manufacturer. But the price of such administrative saving is a potentially serious gap and distortion in effective prevention. In these kinds of cases the employer faces no legal-financial impact from its misuse of "defective" products; instead, all such incentives are trained on the manufacturer to build costly safeguards into its products in order to avoid the hazards created by a minority of employers who are prepared to disregard the safety and health of their employees.

B.   The Dominance of Tort Policy

In response to that concern, courts in a few jurisdictions have moved to a legal position which effectively ignores the WC exclusivity principle in this context and simply applies a new tort law approach, apportioning burdens among all negligent actors. In effect, these courts are prepared to bear the additional administrative price of establishing and comparing the employer's responsibility for the injury in order to secure the basic tort function of creating a financial incentive for all parties to avoid the legal risk by taking reasonable steps to prevent the injury from occurring in the first place.

The problem in that approach is its focusing on the apparently sensible tort disposition of the immediate case while overlooking the broader policy trade-off within the WC system as a whole. Under tort law the manufacturer will be liable in full for any injuries (in the workplace or otherwise) caused by its products which are defective. . . . By contrast, under WC the employer has immunity from direct tort suit for full damages even where it has been at fault because the same employer is obligated to pay for guaranteed but limited WC benefits to all employees who are hurt on the job, even when the employer was not at fault—indeed, even in cases where the injury was due to the fault of the employee himself or of a judgment-proof outside party. But now, simply because a particular injured employee may happen to have a valid tort claim against a third party, the employer will be required to shoulder an additional financial burden for injuries in its workplace over and above what the community has decided was appropriate under its WC policy.

C.   Substantive Blend of Tort and WC Policy

Recognition of that problem has led a few states to a solution that appeared to mesh more successfully the principles and policies of the WC and tort regimes. The employer would be required to contribute a share of the injured worker's damage award against the third-party manufacturer, but only up to the amount of the employer's financial exposure to pay WC benefits for the injury. In effect, the limited employer contribution to tort damages would offset what otherwise would be the employer's WC lien against the tort award. The simplest legal mechanism for accomplishing that result is to allow the third party to assert the amount of the employer's WC payment as a setoff against the employee's tort claim and to reduce correspondingly the employer's lien against the employee's tort award.

The positive virtue of this substantive policy blend is that the employer continues to bear its expected WC share of the cost of workplace injuries. As a result, the happenstance of third-party tort litigation will not relieve the employer of the normal financial incentive it faces under WC to adopt feasible precautions to avoid injuries to its employees. However, the negative flip side of this new policy is that an additional and expensive contest over the employer's fault in managing its workplace is introduced into what otherwise would be a more straightforward dispute between the employee and the manufacturer about the safety of a particular product. Moreover, complex and often contentious calculations are necessary in order to work out the appropriate reductions and setoffs whenever there is a compromise settlement (rather than an itemized adjudication) of such a tort claim, often involving only partial tort damages where full WC benefits have already been paid.

D.   Administrative Accommodation of WC and Tort

To avoid some of these difficulties we endorse a different tack toward the same objective, an approach contained in the proposed Uniform Product Liability Act.

State WC legislation should be altered by eliminating any subrogation right of the employer against the injured worker's tort award. At the same time, product liability law should be altered by reducing the size of tort damages by the amount of WC benefits payable by the employer to the employee.

Note that there are substantial differences between this resolution of the problem and that embodied in Model C above. Under this proposal the manufacturer's tort liability would be reduced only by the WC benefit actually payable by the employer, rather than by some appropriate measure of the culpable employer's share of the larger tort award. At the same time, all employers, not only culpable employers, would lose their subrogation right against the worker's tort award. The aim is to exclude not simply the contentious issue of the employer's comparative fault, but also the very presence of the employer from the tort contest between injured worker and third-party manufacturer. . . . In contrast with the current offset-lien rule in the vast majority of jurisdictions, we would shift a somewhat greater share of the current burden of compensating workers to the considerably cheaper-to-administer WC insurance regime, away from the increasingly expensive tort litigation/liability insurance system. In the long run such a move would enure to the benefit of employers as well, because the manufacturers' rising expenses for product liability insurance and legal fees are eventually incorporated in the prices firms charge customers for their products; and in the case of workplace products, the customers are those very employers.

————

To evaluate the reform proposed by the Enterprise Responsibility Report, consider the final allocations of liability in the many jurisdictions that have replaced joint and several liability with several liability. When a defendant is subject only to several liability, apportionment of comparative fault is required for all potentially liable tortfeasors, including immune parties and other non-parties who have not been joined. Otherwise, the "share" of the severally liable defendant cannot be determined. In these circumstances, the comparative responsibility of a severally liable product manufacturer can be reduced by the employer's responsibility for the injury under workers' compensation. As the Apportionment of Liability Restatement explains:

> The workers' compensation and tort systems are separate systems. The former entails a statutorily imposed arrangement between employees and employers that the employer will pay benefits for any occupational injury, regardless of the employer's liability under tort law. Employees benefit from this system because they are assured some compensation in the event of an occupational injury. Employers benefit because workers' compensation benefits are considerably less than tort damages, and workers compensation is the exclusive remedy against the employer for occupational injuries. The tort system, with several liability and submission of all legally responsible persons to the factfinder for a determination of comparative responsibility, imposes liability on the independent tortfeasor only for its comparative-responsibility share of the plaintiff-employee's damages. Thus, the plaintiff-employee's workers' compensation benefits can be conceptualized as a settlement of tort liability between the plaintiff-employee and the employer, analogous to a preaccident resolution of liability under [rules governing contractual arrangement of liability]. Consistent with the rules regarding partial settlements in [this Restatement], plaintiff would be entitled to both the workers' compensation payment and the recovery of the independent tortfeasor's comparative share of liability. No subrogation claim would be permitted, to continue the analogy, because a settling tortfeasor is not entitled to contribution and because both the employer and the

independent tortfeasor have each paid their legally imposed share of the plaintiff-employee's injury. This result is consistent with the principles set forth in this Restatement. It also has the fortuitous effect of facilitating settlement of the plaintiff-employee's suit against the independent tortfeasor by obviating the need for negotiating with the employer for an adjustment of its subrogation claim based on uncertainties about establishing liability or other parameters that might affect the employer's recovery of its subrogation claim. Some state statutes or policies expressed in state regulatory rules or judicial decisions may produce a different result from that provided in this Comment.

Restatement (Third) of Torts: Apportionment Liab. § B19 cmt. l.

Is this result any different from the approach endorsed by The Enterprise Responsibility Report? To the extent that comparative responsibility makes the employer partially liable for an employee's injuries caused by a defective product, would employers have an adequate financial incentive for considering employee interests when purchasing products? Workers' compensation is considered in Chapter XII.

G. PRODUCT/SERVICE HYBRID TRANSACTIONS

Royer v. Catholic Medical Center

Supreme Court of New Hampshire, 1999.
741 A.2d 74.

■ BROCK, C.J.

[Plaintiff underwent a total knee replacement at defendant CMC, during which a prosthetic knee provided by defendant was surgically implanted. When he complained of pain in the knee, his doctors discovered that the prosthesis was defective. He underwent a second operation during which the defective prosthesis was removed and a second one implanted. Plaintiff alleged that CMC "was strictly liable to [Royer] because it had sold a prosthesis with a design defect that was in an unreasonably dangerous condition." The defendant moved to dismiss, arguing, inter alia, that it was not a "seller of goods" for purposes of strict products liability. The trial court granted CMC's motion to dismiss the complaint.]

In New Hampshire, "[o]ne who sells any product in a defective condition unreasonably dangerous to the user or consumer or to his property is subject to [strict] liability for physical harm thereby caused" if, inter alia, "the seller is engaged in the business of selling such a product." [section 402A] If the defendant merely provides a service, however, there is no liability absent proof of a violation of a legal duty. [ ] In this case, we are asked to determine whether a health care provider that supplies a defective prosthesis in the course of delivering health care services is a "seller" of prosthetic devices, or is merely providing a professional service.

In deciding this issue of first impression, we are guided by the principles that have supported the development of a cause of action for strict liability in New Hampshire. "Strict liability for damages has traditionally met with disfavor in this jurisdiction." Bruzga v. PMR Architects, [693 A.2d 401, 404–05 (N.H.1997)]. As a general rule,

> strict liability is available only where the Legislature has provided for it or in those situations where the common law of this state has imposed such liability and the Legislature has not seen fit to change it. [ ]
>
> . . .
>
> The reasons for the development of strict liability in tort were the lack of privity between the manufacturer and the buyer, the difficulty of proving negligence against a distant manufacturer using mass production techniques, and the better ability of the mass manufacturer to spread the economic risks among consumers.

[Bruzga]. Particularly crucial to our adoption of strict liability in the context of defective products was the practical impossibility of proving legal fault in many products liability cases. [ ]

Although we have adopted a cause of action for strict products liability, we have recognized limits to the doctrine. [ ] In Bruzga, we rejected an argument that strict liability should extend to architects and building contractors who allegedly designed and "manufactured" a defective building. [ ] After determining that the reasons supporting strict liability did not apply to architects and contractors, we concluded that architects and contractors provide a professional service. [ ] Although we acknowledged that a building contractor "supplies" a structure to the purchaser, we declined to extend strict products liability to contractors because they are "engaged primarily in the rendition of a service." [ ]

A majority of the jurisdictions that have addressed whether a health care provider who supplies a defective prosthesis is subject to strict liability have declined to extend strict liability, similarly reasoning that the health care provider primarily renders a service, and that the provision of a prosthetic device is merely incidental to that service. [The court cited supporting and disagreeing cases.] The defendant urges us to adopt this rationale.

The plaintiffs argue, however, that the distinction between selling products and providing services is a legal fiction. The defendant, according to the plaintiffs, acted both as a seller of the prosthetic knee and as a provider of professional services in the transaction. Because the defendant charged separately for the prosthesis and earned a profit on the "sale," the plaintiffs argue that the defendant should be treated no differently than any other distributor of a defective product. The defendant, according to the plaintiffs, primarily supplied a prosthesis, while the surgeon provided the professional "services."

Although a defendant may both provide a service and sell a product within the same transaction for purposes of strict liability, [ ] the dispositive issue in this case is not whether the defendant "sold" or transferred a prosthetic knee, but whether the defendant was an entity "engaged in the business of selling" prosthetic knees so as to warrant the imposition of liability without proof of legal fault. "[T]he language of 402A, . . . as with other nonstatutory declarations, is a common law pronouncement by the court, which always retains the right and the duty to test the reason behind a common law rule in determining the applicability of such a rule to the facts before it." [ ] We find the reasoning of both *Bruzga* and the majority of courts that have declined to extend strict liability to health care providers who supply defective prostheses to be persuasive.

. . .

. . . "[T]he essence of the transaction between the retail seller and the consumer relates to the article sold. The seller is in the business of supplying the product to the consumer. It is that, and that alone, for which he is paid." [ ] A patient, by contrast, does not enter a hospital to "purchase" a prosthesis, "but to obtain a course of treatment in the hope of being cured of what ails him." [ ] Indeed, "to ignore the ancillary nature of the association of product with activity is to posit surgery, or . . . any medical service requiring the use of a physical object, as a marketing device for the incorporated object." [ ]

We decline to ignore the reality of the relationship between Ira Royer and CMC, and to treat any services provided by CMC as ancillary to a primary purpose of selling a prosthetic knee. Rather, the record indicates that in addition to the prosthesis, Royer was billed for a hospital room, operating room services, physical therapy, a recovery room, pathology laboratory work, an EKG or ECG, X-rays, and anesthesia. Thus, it is evident that Ira Royer entered CMC not to purchase a prosthesis, but to obtain health care services that included the implantation of the knee, with the overall objective of restoring his health. [ ] Necessary to the restoration of his health, in the judgment of his physicians, was the implantation of the prosthesis. We do not find this scenario, as [plaintiff urges], analogous to one in which a plaintiff purchases a defective tire from a retail tire distributor and has the distributor install the tire. [ ]

Moreover, the policy rationale underlying strict liability, as in *Bruzga*, does not support extension of the doctrine under the facts of this case. With respect to the inherent difficulty of proving negligence in many products liability cases, this rationale fails in the context of non-manufacturer cases alleging a design defect. Because "ordinarily there is no possibility that a distributor other than the manufacturer created a design defect[,] . . . strict liability would impose liability when there is no possibility of negligence." [ ] The plaintiffs do not allege in this case that the defendant altered the prosthesis in any way. Further, holding health care providers strictly liable for defects in prosthetic devices necessary to the provision of health care would likely result in higher health care costs borne ultimately by all patients, [ ], and "place an unrealistic burden on the physicians and hospitals of this state to test or guarantee the tens of thousands of products used in hospitals by doctors," [ ]. Additionally, "research and innovation in medical equipment and treatment would be inhibited." [ ] We find that the "peculiar characteristics of medical services[,] . . . [which] include the tendency to be experimental, . . . a dependence on factors beyond the control of the professional[,] and a lack of certainty or assurance of the desired result," [ ], outweigh any reasons that might support the imposition of strict liability in this context.

"In short, medical services are distinguished by factors which make them significantly different in kind from the retail marketing enterprise at which 402A is directed." [ ] We conclude that where, as here, a health care provider in the course of rendering health care services supplies a prosthetic device to be implanted into a patient, the health care provider is not "engaged in the business of selling" prostheses for purposes of strict products liability. Accordingly, the trial court did not err in granting the defendant's motion to dismiss.

. . .

Affirmed.

All concurred.

NOTES AND QUESTIONS

1.   Why would the plaintiff bring suit against the hospital as opposed to the device manufacturer? Apparently, the suit was brought against CMC because the prosthesis manufacturer had filed for bankruptcy. The case for strict liability for non-negligent retailers and others in the chain of distribution, discussed in note 5.b, p. 569 supra, has never been as strong as the case for holding manufacturers liable. Manufacturers are, after all, responsible for almost all defects. Acknowledging wasteful administrative costs when a retailer is sued instead of or in addition to the manufacturer, the Products Liability Restatement identifies both manufacturer bankruptcy and a lack of jurisdiction over the manufacturer in the plaintiff's home state as grounds for imposing what might otherwise be redundant strict liability on retailers and others in the chain of distribution. In the end, however, the Restatement retains full strict liability for non-manufacturing sellers. Restatement (Third) of Torts: Products Liability § 1 cmt. e (1998). Several states have enacted limitations on the strict liability of retailers. See, e.g., Wash. Rev.Code § 7.72.040(2)(a) (permitting suit based on strict liability against non-manufacturing sellers

if jurisdiction cannot be obtained in the state against a solvent manufacturer). Might the concern with imposing strict liability on non-manufacturing sellers have influenced the court in *Royer*? Is that concern particularly acute for medical devices and prescription drugs?

2. Should it matter that the prosthetic knee was provided by the hospital in connection with services? Is the court's "research and innovation" argument persuasive? Is it also applicable to strict liability of the manufacturer? Are there justifications for strict liability that might have produced a different result in this case?

3. Is the court's claim that this case is not analogous to a suit against a retail distributor who sold and installed a defective tire persuasive? Can *Vandermark v. Ford Motor Co.*, p. 569 supra, or *Ryan v. Progressive Grocery Stores*, p. 563 supra, be reconciled with the court's reluctance to impose strict liability "when there is no possibility of negligence" (on the part of a non-manufacturer in the distribution chain)?

4. Should an action based on strict liability lie against a physician or surgeon who made a reasonable decision that turned out in hindsight to have been wrong and harmful? How might liability for harm arising from services be cabined by the equivalent of the "defect" requirement employed in the product context? What if it were shown that the three best surgeons in the world would have made the right choice? See the extensive discussion about extending strict liability to services in Hoven v. Kelble, 256 N.W.2d 379 (Wis.1977), which refused to extend strict liability to diagnoses and decisions made by medical providers.

5. In Murphy v. E.R. Squibb & Sons, Inc., 710 P.2d 247 (Cal.1985), the court, 4–3, rejected a strict liability action against a pharmacist who filled prescriptions for DES. The court had already concluded that doctors who prescribed the drug were not strictly liable: "[T]he doctor prescribed the medication only as an aid to effect a cure and was not in the business of selling the drug." Here, plaintiff asserted that the pharmacist simply reads a prescription, fills the container with the proper dosage, types the label, attaches it to the container, and exchanges the container for payment. The plaintiff argued that a pharmacist was the functional equivalent of "an experienced clerk at a hardware store." The defense stressed the professional aspects of pharmacists.

The plurality expressed concern that if strict liability were imposed, some pharmacists would refuse to stock drugs that carried even remote risks. Furthermore, a pharmacist who has a choice might stock only the more expensive products of an established manufacturer in order to be able to secure indemnity. Some pharmacies at the time were owned by large chains, but most were not. (Should that matter?) One concurring justice, although recognizing that most customers used pharmacists as retailers, rejected strict liability because drugs are dispensed "only at the direction of a prescriber who is himself exempt from such liability." The dissenters found the focus on professional status "elitist." For them, the sale aspect dominated the transaction and all the policies of strict liability would be furthered by imposing it on pharmacists.

Compare Cottam v. CVS Pharmacy, 764 N.E.2d 814 (Mass.2002), in which plaintiff claimed that the pharmacy had inadequately warned of the drug's dangers. The court adhered to the rule that there is no duty to warn of dangers in a prescription that was properly filled. But here the pharmacy had undertaken to offer some warnings and thus became obligated to provide all appropriate warnings.

6. Soon after the movement toward strict liability began, one court hesitated. In Wights v. Staff Jennings, Inc., 405 P.2d 624 (Or.1965), the wife of the purchaser sued the manufacturer for injuries suffered when a pleasure boat exploded. Although reversing a judgment for the defendant, Justice O'Connell declined to follow the approach taken by Justice Traynor in *Escola* and *Greenman*:

> Substantially the same reasons for imposing strict liability upon sellers of defective chattels have been advanced in several other cases and in various texts and articles. Summarized, the thesis is that a loss resulting from the use of defendant's defective goods "is a casualty produced by the hazards of defendant's enterprise, so that the risk of loss is properly a risk of that enterprise," a view commonly described as the theory of enterprise liability. The theory is a corollary of the broader thesis urged by some writers, particularly Harper and James on Torts, that compensation of the victim rather than fault of the defendant should be the objective in the adjudication of accident cases.[11]
>
> . . .
>
> The rationale of risk spreading and compensating the victim has no special relevancy to cases involving injuries resulting from the use of defective goods. The reasoning would seem to apply not only in cases involving personal injuries arising from the sale of defective goods, but equally to any case where an injury results from the risk creating conduct of the seller in any stage of the production and distribution of goods. Thus a manufacturer would be strictly liable even in the absence of fault for an injury to a person struck by one of the manufacturer's trucks being used in transporting his goods to market. It seems to us that the enterprise liability rationale employed in the *Escola* case proves too much and that if adopted would compel us to apply the principle of strict liability in all future cases where the loss could be distributed.

Id. at 628. How substantial is this concern? Can it be answered? The *Wights* court also had reservations about retaining common law damages if enterprise liability were to be adopted. Are the safety considerations of

---

[11] "It is the principal job of tort law today to deal with these [human] losses. They fall initially on people who as a class can ill afford them, and this fact brings great hardship upon the victims themselves and causes unfortunate repercussions to society as a whole. The best and most efficient way to deal with accident loss, therefore, is to assure accident victims of substantial compensation, and to distribute the losses involved over society as a whole or some very large segment of it. Such a basis for administering losses is what we have called social insurance." 2 Harper and James, Law of Torts, § 13.2, pp. 762–63 (1956).

Escola applicable to driving a truck? Soon after *Wights*, Oregon adopted the emerging law of strict products liability.

H. The Intersection of Tort and Contract

So far we have been focusing on the role of tort law when victims have been physically harmed by allegedly defective products. By contrast, the course in contracts involves cases in which plaintiffs with disappointed economic expectations seek damages under common law contract or UCC theories. Although these are the two major categories of cases, two smaller but important categories remain: claims in tort by plaintiffs seeking to recover for pure economic loss, and claims in contract and under the UCC for personal injury. As we turn first to the role of tort law in product-related economic harm cases, recall the discussion of such cases in the negligence context in Chapter IV.

East River Steamship Corp. v. Transamerica Delaval Inc.

Supreme Court of the United States, 1986.
476 U.S. 858, 106 S.Ct. 2295, 90 L.Ed.2d 865.

■ JUSTICE BLACKMUN delivered the opinion of the Court.

[Defendant Delaval made turbines, each costing $1.4 million, for four supertankers, each costing $125 million. East River and three other plaintiffs were the separate charterers of each ship for 20–22 years from the owner. Each charterer assumed responsibility for the cost of any repairs. When the first ship made its maiden voyage, the high-pressure turbine malfunctioned, but the ship was able to get to port. Inspection revealed that an essential ring had virtually disintegrated and had caused additional damage to other parts of the turbine. Eventually, the ship was permanently and satisfactorily repaired. As a result of this experience, the second and third ships were inspected. The same condition was discovered and satisfactory repairs were made. These problems are involved in the first three counts of the complaint. (The fourth count, involving another design claim, is not relevant here.)

The problem with the fourth ship was that a valve between the high-pressure and low-pressure turbines was installed backwards. Because of that error, steam entered the low-pressure turbine and damaged it. This condition was repaired. This episode is the subject of the fifth count—which alleged negligence.

The charterers' complaints invoked the admiralty jurisdiction and set forth tort claims for the cost of repairing the ships and for income lost while the ships were out of service. The district court granted Delaval summary judgment and the court of appeals affirmed. The Supreme Court granted certiorari to resolve a conflict among the courts of appeals sitting in admiralty.]

In this admiralty case, we must decide whether a cause of action in tort is stated when a defective product purchased in a commercial transaction malfunctions, injuring only the product itself and causing purely economic loss. The case requires us to consider preliminarily whether admiralty law, which already recognizes a general theory of liability for negligence, also incorporates principles of products liability, including strict liability. Then, charting a course between products liability and contract law, we must determine whether injury to a product itself is the kind of harm that should be protected by products liability or left entirely to the law of contracts.

[The Court concluded that the claims fell within the admiralty jurisdiction since the wrongs alleged occurred on or near the high seas or navigable waters. This meant that admiralty substantive law applied. Absent a statute, the general maritime law, as developed by the judiciary from state and federal sources, applied. The Supreme Court joined the courts of appeals in recognizing concepts of products liability based on both negligence and strict liability. But this acceptance of products liability into maritime law "is only the threshold determination to the main issue in this case."]

IV.

Products liability grew out of a public policy judgment that people need more protection from dangerous products than is afforded by the law of warranty. See Seely v. White Motor Co., [403 P.2d 145, 149 (Cal.1965)]. It is clear, however, that if this development were allowed to progress too far, contract law would drown in a sea of tort. See G. Gilmore, The Death of Contract 87–94 (1974). We must determine whether a commercial product injuring itself is the kind of harm against which public policy requires manufacturers to protect, independent of any contractual obligation.

A

The paradigmatic products-liability action is one where a product "reasonably certain to place life and limb in peril," distributed without reinspection, causes bodily injury. See, e.g., [*MacPherson*]. The manufacturer is liable whether or not it is negligent because "public policy demands that responsibility be fixed wherever it will most effectively reduce the hazards to life and health inherent in defective products that reach the market." [*Escola*] (concurring opinion).

For similar reasons of safety, the manufacturer's duty of care was broadened to include protection against property damage. [ ] Such damage is considered so akin to personal injury that the two are treated alike. See [*Seely*].

In the traditional "property damage" cases, the defective product damages other property. In this case, there was no damage to "other" property. Rather, the first, second, and third counts allege that each supertanker's defectively designed turbine components damaged only the turbine itself. Since each turbine was supplied by Delaval as an integrated package, each is properly regarded as a single unit. "Since all but the very simplest of machines have component parts, [a contrary] holding would require a finding of 'property damage' in virtually every case where a product damages itself. Such a holding would eliminate the distinction between warranty and strict products liability." [ ] The fifth count also alleges injury to the product itself. Before the high-pressure and low-pressure turbines could become an operational propulsion system, they were connected to piping and valves under the supervision of Delaval personnel. [ ] Delaval's supervisory obligations were part of its manufacturing agreement. The fifth count thus can best be read to allege that Delaval's negligent manufacture of the propulsion system—by allowing the installation in reverse of the astern guardian valve—damaged the propulsion system. [ ] Obviously, damage to a product itself has certain attributes of a products-liability claim. But the injury suffered—the failure of the product to function properly—is the essence of a warranty action, through which a contracting party can seek to recoup the benefit of its bargain.

B

The intriguing question whether injury to a product itself may be brought in tort has spawned a variety of answers. At one end of the spectrum, the case that created the majority land-based approach, *Seely* (defective truck), held that preserving a proper role for the law of warranty precludes imposing tort liability if a defective product causes purely monetary harm. [ ]

At the other end of the spectrum is the minority land-based approach, whose progenitor, Santor v. A and M Karagheusian, Inc., [207 A.2d 305, 312–313 (N.J.1965)] (marred carpeting), held that a manufacturer's duty to make nondefective products encompassed injury to the product itself, whether or not the defect created an unreasonable risk of harm. The courts adopting this approach, including the majority of the Courts of Appeals sitting in admiralty that have considered the issue, [ ] find that the safety and insurance rationales behind strict liability apply equally where the losses are purely economic. These courts reject the *Seely* approach because they find it arbitrary that economic losses are recoverable if a plaintiff suffers bodily injury or property damage, but not if a product injures itself. They also find no inherent difference between economic loss and personal injury or property damage, because all are proximately caused by the defendant's conduct. Further, they believe recovery for economic loss would not lead to unlimited liability because they think a manufacturer can predict and insure against product failure. [ ]

Between the two poles fall a number of cases that would permit a products-liability action under certain circumstances when a product injures only itself. These cases attempt to differentiate between "the disappointed users . . . and the endangered ones," Russell v. Ford Motor Co., [575 P.2d 1383, 1387 (Or.1978)], and permit only the latter to sue in tort. The determination has been said to turn on the nature of the defect, the type of risk, and the manner in which the injury arose. [ ] The Alaska Supreme Court allows a tort action if the defective product creates a situation potentially dangerous to persons or other property, and loss occurs as a proximate result of that danger and under dangerous circumstances. [ ]

We find the intermediate and minority land-based positions unsatisfactory. The intermediate positions, which essentially turn on the degree of risk, are too indeterminate to enable manufacturers easily to structure their business behavior. Nor do we find persuasive a distinction that rests on the manner in which the product is injured. We realize that the damage may be qualitative, occurring through gradual deterioration or internal breakage. Or it may be calamitous. [ ] But either way, since by definition no person or other property is damaged, the resulting loss is purely economic. Even when the harm to the product itself occurs through an abrupt, accident-like event, the resulting loss due to repair costs, decreased value, and lost profits is essentially the failure of the purchaser to receive the benefit of its bargain—traditionally the core concern of contract law. See E. Farnsworth, Contracts § 12.8, pp. 839–840 (1982).

We also decline to adopt the minority land-based view espoused by [*Santor* and other cases]. Such cases raise legitimate questions about the theories behind restricting products liability, but we believe that the countervailing arguments are more powerful. The minority view fails to account for the need to keep products liability and contract law in separate spheres and to maintain a realistic limitation on damages.

C

Exercising traditional discretion in admiralty, [ ], we adopt an approach similar to *Seely* and hold that a manufacturer in a commercial relationship has no duty under either a negligence or strict products-liability theory to prevent a product from injuring itself.

"The distinction that the law has drawn between tort recovery for physical injuries and warranty recovery for economic loss is not arbitrary and does not rest on the 'luck' of one plaintiff in having an accident causing physical injury. The distinction rests, rather, on an understanding of the nature of the responsibility a manufacturer must undertake in distributing his products." [*Seely*] When a product injures only itself the reasons for imposing a tort duty are weak and those for leaving the party to its contractual remedies are strong.

The tort concern with safety is reduced when an injury is only to the product itself. When a person is injured, the "cost of an injury and the loss of time or health may be an overwhelming misfortune," and one the person is not prepared to meet. [*Escola*] (concurring opinion). In contrast, when a product injures itself, the commercial user stands to lose the value of the product, risks the displeasure of its customers who find that the product does not meet their needs, or, as in this case, experiences increased costs in performing a service. Losses like these can be insured. [ ] Society need not presume that a customer needs special protection. The increased cost to the public that would result from holding a manufacturer liable in tort for injury to the product itself is not justified. Cf. [*United States v. Carroll Towing Co.*]

Damage to a product itself is most naturally understood as a warranty claim. Such damage means simply that the product has not met the customer's expectations, or, in other words, that the customer has received "insufficient product value." [ ] The maintenance of product value and quality is precisely the purpose of express and implied warranties. See UCC § 2–313 (express warranty), § 2–314 (implied warranty of merchantability), and § 2–315 (warranty of fitness for a particular purpose). Therefore, a claim of a nonworking product can be brought as a breach-of-warranty action. Or, if the customer prefers, it can reject the product or revoke its acceptance and sue for breach of contract. See UCC §§ 2–601, 2–608, 2–612.

Contract law, and the law of warranty in particular, is well suited to commercial controversies of the sort involved in this case because the parties may set the terms of their own agreements. The manufacturer can restrict its liability, within limits, by disclaiming warranties or limiting remedies. See UCC §§ 2–316, 2–719. In exchange, the purchaser pays less for the product. Since a commercial situation generally does not involve large disparities in bargaining power, [ ] we see no reason to intrude into the parties' allocation of the risk.

While giving recognition to the manufacturer's bargain, warranty law sufficiently protects the purchaser by allowing it to obtain the benefit of its bargain. [ ] The expectation damages available in warranty for purely economic loss give a plaintiff the full benefit of its bargain by compensating for forgone business opportunities. [ ] Recovery on a warranty theory would give the charterers their repair costs and lost profits, and would place them in the position they would have been in had the turbines functioned properly.[9] [ ] Thus, both the nature of the injury and the resulting damages indicate it is more natural to think of injury to a product itself in terms of warranty.

A warranty action also has a built-in limitation on liability, whereas a tort action could subject the manufacturer to damages of an indefinite amount. The limitation in a contract action comes from the agreement of the parties and the requirement that consequential damages, such as lost profits, be a foreseeable result of the breach. See

---

[9]   In contrast, tort damages generally compensate the plaintiff for loss and return him to the position he occupied before the injury. [ ] Tort damages are analogous to reliance damages, which are awarded in contract when there is particular difficulty in measuring the expectation interest. [ ]

Hadley v. Baxendale, 9 Ex. 341, 156 Eng.Rep. 145 (1854). In a warranty action where the loss is purely economic, the limitation derives from the requirements of foreseeability and of privity, which is still generally enforced for such claims in a commercial setting. [ ]

In products-liability law, where there is a duty to the public generally, foreseeability is an inadequate brake. Cf. Petitions of Kinsman Transit Co., 388 F.2d 821 (C.A.2 1968). [ ] Permitting recovery for all foreseeable claims for purely economic loss could make a manufacturer liable for vast sums. It would be difficult for a manufacturer to take into account the expectations of persons downstream who may encounter its product. In this case, for example, if the charterers—already one step removed from the transaction—were permitted to recover their economic losses, then the companies that subchartered the ships might claim their economic losses from the delays, and the charterers' customers also might claim their economic losses, and so on. "The law does not spread its protection so far." Robins Dry Dock & Repair Co. v. Flint, 275 U.S. 303, 309 (1927).

And to the extent that courts try to limit purely economic damages in tort, they do so by relying on a far murkier line, one that negates the charterers' contention that permitting such recovery under a products-liability theory enables admiralty courts to avoid difficult linedrawing. Cf. [*Ultramares Corp. v. Touche*]; [ ].

D

For the first three counts, the defective turbine components allegedly injured only the turbines themselves. Therefore, a strict products-liability theory of recovery is unavailable to the charterers. Any warranty claims would be subject to Delaval's limitation, both in time and scope, of its warranty liability. . . .

. . .

Similarly, in the fifth count, alleging the reverse installation of the astern guardian valve, the only harm was to the propulsion system itself rather than to persons or other property. Even assuming that Delaval's supervision was negligent, as we must on this summary judgment motion, Delaval owed no duty under a products-liability theory based on negligence to avoid causing purely economic loss. [ ] Thus, whether stated in negligence or strict liability, no products-liability claim lies in admiralty when the only injury claimed is economic loss.

. . . [W]e affirm the entry of judgment for Delaval.

NOTES AND QUESTIONS

1.   What is the impact of choosing between tort and contract in this type of case? Although it is not binding on state courts, *East River* has been widely accepted.

2. As the *East River* opinion intimates, the line between economic harm and harm to other property is indistinct when a defective component part causes damage to the larger product in which it is incorporated. Would *East River* have been a different case if the turbine caused a vibration that, over time, destroyed the ship? Would it matter whether Delaval was also the shipmaker? The Products Liability Restatement addresses this matter in section 21 comment e:

> [W]hen a component part of a machine or a system destroys the rest of the machine or system, the characterization process becomes more difficult. When the product or system is deemed to be an integrated whole, courts treat such damage as harm to the product itself. When so characterized, the damage is excluded from the coverage of this Restatement. A contrary holding would require a finding of property damage in virtually every case in which a product harms itself and would prevent contractual rules from serving their legitimate function in governing commercial transactions.

Consider, in this regard, Jimenez v. Superior Court, 58 P.3d 450 (Cal.2002). Plaintiff homeowners sued the manufacturers of windows installed in mass produced homes when the windows failed and caused damage to other parts of the plaintiffs' home. The court, 6–1, distinguished *Seely* and held that the window was a product distinct from the home, which therefore constituted other property. Thus, plaintiffs could maintain their strict liability claim against the window manufacturer. The dissent criticized the majority's conclusory reasoning, observing that, given the ubiquity of complex products, the problem of components that damage the product should be governed by *Seely*'s approach of preserving the role of contract.

A number of "other property" cases have a distinctly agricultural flavor. In Grams v. Milk Products, Inc., 699 N.W.2d 167, 170 (Wis.2005), plaintiffs, who raised calves, purchased a "milk replacer," which was designed to provide nutrition to calves early in their lives. Defendant's product resulted in plaintiffs' calves failing to thrive, appearing gaunt and hungry, and in a tripled mortality rate. The court held, with a single dissent, that plaintiffs were limited to contract because their claims "are the result of disappointed expectations of a bargained-for product's performance." If the milk replacer caused one of the plaintiffs to contract cancer, would suit against the seller be a result of "disappointed expectations" about the product's performance? The dissent thought that the harm suffered by the calves involved other property and therefore plaintiffs should be permitted to pursue their tort claims.

3. In *Seely*, a dissenting judge said that he found it "hard to understand how one might . . . award a traveling salesman lost earnings if a defect in his car causes his leg to break in an accident but deny that salesman his lost earnings if the defect instead disables only his car before any accident occurs." How might Justice Blackmun respond?

4. Does the economic loss rule of *East River* entail a trade-off between effectuating private arrangements and providing greater incentives for safety? Compare Washington Water Power Co. v. Graybar Electric Co., 774 P.2d 1199, 1209 (Wash.1989)(rejecting *East River's* analysis on the ground that the "increased certainty [of identifying the line between tort and contract] comes at too high a price"), with Bocre Leasing Corp. v. General Motors Corp., 645 N.E.2d 1195, 1198 (N.Y.1995)(adopting *East River* and rejecting a tort claim for pure economic loss, despite the fact that the alleged defect created a serious risk of personal injury, in part because "any product put into the stream of commerce has the theoretical potential to injure persons and property, [and so] the incentive to provide safe products is always present").

5. What are the strengths and weaknesses of the *Santor* approach? Of the "intermediate" approach? Of the Court's approach?

New Jersey largely abandoned its *Santor* approach in Alloway v. General Marine Industries, L.P., 695 A.2d 264 (N.J.1997), a case involving an economic loss claim based on a boat that, because of a defective seam in its bottom, sank while docked. After lengthy discussion, the court rejected the applicability of a tort regime to the plaintiff's purchase of a luxury boat, holding that "[b]y providing for express and implied warranties, the U.C.C. amply protects all buyers—commercial purchasers and consumers alike—from economic loss arising out of the purchase of a defective product." The court did, however, reserve judgment on the applicability of warranty to (1) a case in which the product posed a risk of personal injury or property damage, as well as to (2) a case in which "the parties are of unequal bargaining power, the product is a necessity, no alternative source for the product is readily available, and the purchaser cannot reasonably insure against consequential damages." Two justices concurred on the latter score, arguing that "a gross inequality of bargaining power will supplant the exclusivity of the U.C.C. remedy."

Is tort liability more justifiable when the buyer is an individual? Consider Jones, Product Defects Causing Commercial Loss: The Ascendancy of Contract over Tort, 44 U. Miami L.Rev. 731, 797 (1990), concluding that when individual consumers are the buyers, "because of limitations on consumer knowledge and because of disparities in consumer wealth, it cannot be said that contractual reallocations of risk are economically efficient and socially acceptable in the general run of manufacturer-consumer transactions." Professor Jones then maintains that when the buyer is a commercial enterprise, contracting is economically efficient and any social concerns are minimal. In such cases, the role of tort law is "redundant and perverse. It is used by litigants and courts to undermine allocations of risks agreed to by the parties and to substitute judicial solutions for contractual arrangements that are almost certainly superior in terms of both fairness and efficiency."

6. How similar are the problems in cases like *East River* and those raised in the *532 Madison Ave.* case, p. 319 supra? Consider, on this question, Paramount Aviation Corp. v. Agusta, 288 F.3d 67 (3d Cir.2002). Plaintiff management company agreed to manage a helicopter (supply pilots, perform maintenance, etc.) owned by a third party. The helicopter crashed allegedly due to a defect or negligent maintenance by the helicopter manufacturer. The management company sued the manufacturer for economic loss (lost profits on its management contract and on other such contracts because similar helicopters were grounded until the cause of crash was determined). Based on New Jersey law in this diversity case, the district court held that the only remedy for plaintiff was that provided in the UCC. On appeal, the court reversed, holding that the UCC only bars claims for economic loss when the plaintiff is in the chain of distribution of the product, which it was not on these facts. Thus, subject to limitations on recovery of economic loss for negligence and for strict liability under the governing New Jersey law (to be addressed on remand), plaintiff could proceed on these claims.

7. *The asbestos exception and beyond?* In Aas v. Superior Court, 12 P.3d 1125 (Cal.2000), legislatively overruled, Cal. Code § 942, homeowners brought tort claims for construction defects against the developer, contractor and subcontractors who had built their homes. The court held, 5–2, that since no damage had yet occurred—the only claims being for cost of repairs and diminished value—no tort action would lie pursuant to the economic loss rule. Courts, however, have adopted a very different approach in cases involving the owners of buildings in which asbestos has been found. The owners have sued manufacturers for the cost of abatement—removing the asbestos, effectively a cost of "repair." Such cases would appear to be squarely within the economic loss rule barring tort claims, but courts have concluded otherwise. As the Products Liability Restatement section 21 cmt. e explains:

> One category of claims stands apart. In the case of asbestos contamination in buildings, most courts have taken the position that the contamination constitutes harm to the building as other property. The serious health threat caused by asbestos contamination has led the courts to this conclusion. Thus, actions seeking recovery for the costs of asbestos removal have been held to be within the purview of products liability law rather than commercial law.

Would a better explanation of these cases be that the costs of abatement constitute something similar to pre-injury mitigation of personal injury damages, p. 463 supra, that, in fairness, should be borne by defendant?

Lloyd v. General Motors Corp., 916 A.2d 257 (Md.2007), reveals a far larger role for the "asbestos exception" than one might have initially thought. Plaintiffs sued for the cost of repairing a defect in their automobiles that could result in the seatback collapsing in a rear-end collision, thereby propelling the occupant backward with risks of spine compression injuries, including paraplegia. The court held that plaintiffs could maintain their tort actions, as an exception to the economic loss rule, relying in part on the asbestos exception. Referring to an earlier case, in which the court permitted a tort suit to proceed against the general contractor and others of a building that had inadequate fire protection, the court wrote:

[A] plaintiff should not "have to wait for a personal tragedy to occur in order to recover damages to remedy or repair defects[.] In the final analysis, the cost to the developer for a resulting tragedy could be far greater than the cost of remedying the condition." [ ] If, therefore, the conduct complained of creates a risk of death or personal injury, this Court continued, "the action will lie for recovery of the reasonable cost of correcting the dangerous condition in a tort action seeking purely economic loss." [ ] The Court [in *Whiting-Turner*, 517 A.2d at 345] explained:

> "it is the serious nature of the risk that persuades us to recognize the cause of action in the absence of actual injury. Accordingly, conditions that present a risk to general health, wealth, or comfort but fall short of presenting a clear danger of death or personal injury will not suffice. A claim that defective design or construction has produced a drafty condition that may lead to a cold or pneumonia would not be sufficient."

Id. at 267. The *Lloyd* court concluded that the allegations in the complaint met the "serious-nature" standard.

8. *Introduction to personal injury litigation based on non-tort theories.* The remaining category involves suits for personal injury that are brought based on legal theories other than tort law. These suits are typically brought under a warranty provision of the UCC and may be asserted alone or in addition to tort claims.

a. *Implied warranties.* The implied warranty sections of the UCC, §§ 2–314 and 2–315, generally involve aberrationally defective products— either manufacturing defects or defects of the sort dealt with in section 3 of the Products Liability Restatement, see p. 576 supra. Recall the *Ryan* case, p. 563 supra, involving a pin in a loaf of bread. Why might a plaintiff prefer to proceed on a warranty theory rather than tort law—especially where the contract theories may offer privity problems and less attractive damage awards because of limits on punitive damages or on nonpecuniary awards? One answer is the statute of limitations. The UCC's statute of limitations contained in section 2–725 is four years from the delivery of the goods. The tort limitation usually is shorter but generally runs only from the time of the plaintiff's injury or perhaps discovery of that injury. It is not difficult to imagine situations in which plaintiffs might find one avenue barred while the other is still open.

b. *Express warranty.* This is potentially a very important basis for liability under the UCC—with a tort analog. If a manufacturer makes an express warranty about the quality or attributes of the product, anyone hurt if such a representation or warranty turns out to be false may recover damages—even without fault on the maker's part. In some states this may be true even though the victim did not know about the warranty and did not rely on it in using the product. See U.C.C. §§ 2–313, 2–316; see also Note, Express Warranties Under the Uniform Commercial Code: Is There a Reliance Requirement?, 66 N.Y.U.L.Rev. 468 (1991). Note that the product need not be defective; it may be perfectly adequate. The claim is based on the failure of the product to live up to what the supplier claimed for it. Recall the discussion earlier of the *Denny* and *Castro* cases, pp. 604–605 supra.

9. *Introduction to warranty defenses.* We have seen that courts tend to use a comparative approach to defenses in tort cases. What happens when the case is brought under the UCC? The UCC nowhere contemplates shared responsibility; it speaks in terms of proximate cause, suggesting that once a buyer discovers a defect or should reasonably have discovered it, there can no longer be reasonable reliance on the warranty, and thus no recovery. See U.C.C. § 2–314 cmt. 13; § 2–316 cmt. 8; § 2–715 cmt. 5.

A few courts have adopted this approach. See Erdman v. Johnson Bros. Radio & Television Co., 271 A.2d 744 (Md.1970)(no warranty liability for fire where plaintiffs continued using a television set after seeing sparks coming from it).

Other courts have developed a comparative fault approach to warranty cases analogous to what the state would do in a tort action. See West v. Caterpillar Tractor Co., 547 F.2d 885 (5th Cir.1977)(developing a partial defense to avoid the anomaly of permitting negligent defendants sued in tort to reduce their liability under comparative negligence, but not permitting innocent defendants sued in warranty a similar reduction where the plaintiff carelessly failed to observe the danger).

10. *The interplay between tort and contract: a reprise.* In Rardin v. T & D Machine Handling, Inc., 890 F.2d 24, 25 (7th Cir.1989), Rardin bought a press from Whiteacre that was "Sold As Is, Where Is." The press had to be moved and for that task Whiteacre hired defendant. The contract between Rardin and Whiteacre provided that Whiteacre was liable for damage to the press incurred by fault or negligence of Whiteacre's "employees, agents, contractors or representatives." During the move the press was damaged due to the negligence of defendant. Rardin incurred costs to repair the press and lost profits during the time it took to put the press in working order. Rardin settled with Whiteacre for the damage to the press. Rardin's negligence action under Illinois law against defendant for lost profits was rejected in an opinion by Judge Posner.

The court analogized the problem to one in which A takes a watch to B retail store for repair and B sends it out to C for the actual repair. Through negligence C damages the watch and it does not always tell time accurately. As a result, A misses an important meeting with his creditors and is thrown into bankruptcy, losing everything. The court assumed that "but for C's negligence A would have made the meeting and averted the bankruptcy, just as but for T & D's negligence the press would have arrived in working condition. The issue is not causation; it is duty."

The court stated that the "basic reason why no court (we believe) would impose liability on C in a suit by A is that C could not estimate the consequences of his carelessness, ignorant as he was of the circumstances of A, who is B's customer." Although in "a perfect world of rational actors and complete information," there would be no negligence, "it is not realistic to assume that *every* responsible citizen can and will avoid *ever* being negligent. In fact, all that taking care does is make it less likely that one will commit a careless act. In deciding how much effort to expend on being careful—and therefore how far to reduce the probability of a careless accident—the potential injurer must have at least a rough idea of the extent of liability. C in our example could not form such an idea. He does not know the circumstances of the myriad owners of watches sent him to repair. He cannot know what costs he will impose if through momentary inattention he negligently damages one of the watches in his charge." Id. at 26.

The court thought that two further points "argue against liability." The first was that A could have protected himself by a contract with B. "The fact that B would in all likelihood refuse to give such a guaranty for a consideration acceptable to A is evidence that liability for all the consequences of every negligent act is not in fact optimal." Second, A could have taken steps by "reducing his dependence on his watch." He could have left a margin of error for getting to the meeting in time or "consulted another timepiece."

The court asserted that the "spirit of *Hadley v. Baxendale* . . . broods over this case. . . ." The contract measure of damages in that case did not extend to lost profits from down time. The plaintiff mill owners could have protected themselves from this loss by having a spare shaft available. Although it is "generally true that consequential damages are recoverable in tort law although not in contract law, [a cited case] shows that the classification of a case as a tort case or a contract case is not decisive on this question."

Judge Posner noted that the "economic loss" doctrine followed by Illinois, other states, and *East River* "rests on the insight . . . that contractual-type limitations on liability may make sense in many tort cases that are not contract cases only because there is no privity of contract between the parties." He also noted that the doctrine "is not the only tort doctrine that limits for-want-of-a-nail-the-kingdom-was-lost liability. It is closely related to the doctrine . . . that bars recovery for economic loss even if the loss does not arise from a commercial relationship between the parties—even if for example a negligent accident in the Holland Tunnel backs up traffic for hours, imposing cumulatively enormous and readily monetizable costs of delay"—referring to an example offered by the court in *Kinsman II*, p. 421 supra.

This rejection of liability was "in tension with other doctrines of tort law that appear to expose the tortfeasor to unlimited liability. One is the principle that allows recovery of full tort damages in a personal-injury suit for injury resulting from a defective or unreasonably dangerous product—a form of legal action that arises in a contractual setting and indeed originated in suits for breach of warranty." A second example was the "thin-skull" plaintiff rule. Judge Posner saw three explanations for this tension:

The first difference is that the potential variance in liability is larger when the victim of a tort is a business, because businesses vary in their financial magnitude more than individuals do; more precisely, physical capital is more variable than human capital. The second is that many business losses are offset elsewhere in the system; Rardin's competitors undoubtedly picked up much or all of the business he lost as a result of the delay in putting the press into operation, so that his loss overstates the social loss caused by T & D's negligence. [ ] Third, tort law is a field largely shaped by the special considerations involved in personal-injury cases, as contract law is not. Tort doctrines are, therefore, prima facie more suitable for the governance of such cases than contract doctrines are.

Judge Posner noted that tort liability might still extend to "purely economic loss" in some cases. Among these he noted "suits against an attorney or accountant for professional malpractice or negligent misrepresentation that causes business losses to the plaintiff. [ ] These cases are distinguishable, however, as ones in which the role of the defendant is, precisely, to guarantee the performance of the other party to the plaintiff's contract, usually a seller. The guaranty would be worth little without a remedy, necessarily in tort (or in an expansive interpretation of the doctrine of third-party beneficiaries) against the guarantor."

Finally, Judge Posner found support in *H.R. Moch Co. v. Rensselaer Water Co.*, p. 173 supra. "The city was acting as the agent of its residents in negotiating with the water company, and the water company was entitled to assume that, if it was to be the fire insurer for the city's property, the city would compensate it accordingly." Similarly, in this case, because Whiteacre was acting as Rardin's agent in dealing with the defendant handler, the defendant was "entitled to assume that, if it was to be an insurer of Rardin's business losses, Whiteacre on behalf of Rardin would compensate it accordingly."

The extended analysis "underscores the desirability—perhaps urgency—of harmonizing the entire complex and confusing pattern of liability and nonliability for tortious conduct in contractual settings." But that was a task for the Supreme Court of Illinois.

CHAPTER X

NUISANCE

Nuisance protects interests in the use and enjoyment of land. Nuisance actions have a long history of affording landowners protection against offensive uses of real property.

The subject is given separate consideration here for two main reasons. Most important, courts have long regarded nuisance as a functionally distinct category of tort. "[N]uisance, as a general term, describes the consequences of conduct, the inconvenience to others, rather than the type of conduct involved. It is a field of tort liability rather than a single type of tortious conduct." Copart Indus. v. Consolidated Edison Co. of New York, 362 N.E.2d 968, 971 (N.Y.1977). As a consequence, nuisance actions cut across the boundaries of the intentional and unintentional tort categories and involve instances of both fault and strict liability. In addition, the modern cases, in particular, provide the common law foundation for much of contemporary environmental law, including statutes and regulations seeking the reduction of hazardous waste and pollution. Nuisance also informs zoning laws governing land use. For all of these reasons, the judicially fashioned liability rules in this area deserve special attention.

Our brief treatment of basic doctrine will place considerable emphasis on the Second Restatement approach, which brought some semblance of order to a confused body of case law. Frequently, courts cite to Prosser's comment that "[t]here is no more impenetrable jungle in the entire law than that which surrounds the word 'nuisance.'" Some of this confusion can be avoided by distinguishing at the outset between private and public nuisance. Despite the overlapping terminology, the interests protected by each action and the corresponding elements in establishing a prima facie case are quite different, and we treat them separately in this Chapter.

A. PRIVATE NUISANCE

Section 822 of the Second Restatement of Torts states the general rule that one is subject to liability for conduct that is a legal cause of an invasion of another's interest in the private use and enjoyment of land if the invasion is either: (a) intentional and unreasonable, or (b) unintentional and arising out of negligent or reckless conduct or abnormally dangerous conditions or activities. The latter category, unintentional nuisances, is governed primarily by the rules relating to the underlying negligence, recklessness, or abnormally dangerous activity on which the nuisance is based, with the added requirement that the injury be related to an invasion of interests in the use and enjoyment of land.

By far the more significant category of nuisances is that which the Second Restatement defines as intentional. Section 825 extends that category to situations in which there is knowledge that the conduct is invading, or is substantially certain to invade, another's interest in the use and enjoyment of land. Virtually all conduct of a continuing nature, then, such as the typical instances of industrial pollution, would be intentional after an initial invasion.

An intentional invasion satisfies the "unreasonableness" requirement, according to section 826, if "(a) the gravity of the harm outweighs the utility of the actor's conduct, or (b) the harm caused by the conduct is serious and the financial burden of compensating for this and similar harm to others would not make the continuation of the conduct not feasible." "Gravity of harm" and the "utility of the conduct" are in turn elaborated as follows:

§ 827   Gravity of Harm—Factors Involved

In defining the gravity of the harm from an intentional invasion of another's interest in the use and enjoyment of land, the following factors are important:

(a) The extent of the harm involved;

(b) the character of the harm involved;

(c) the social value that the law attaches to the type of use or enjoyment invaded;

(d) the suitability of the particular use or enjoyment invaded to the character of the locality; and

(e) the burden on the person harmed of avoiding the harm.

§ 828   Utility of the Conduct—Factors Involved

In determining the utility of conduct that causes an intentional invasion of another's interest in the use and enjoyment of land, the following factors are important:

(a) The social value that the law attaches to the primary purpose of the conduct;

(b) the suitability of the conduct to the character of the locality; and

(c) the impracticability of preventing or avoiding the invasion.

These lists of factors are not intended to be exhaustive, and the relative weight to be given each factor is dependent on the circumstances of the particular case. Obviously, this formulation gives the courts considerable discretion in determining the final outcome of a balancing test.

The first Restatement of Torts included only the test for unreasonableness contained in Restatement (Second) section 826(a)—

whether the gravity of the harm outweighs the utility of the conduct. If this were the sole standard, it could be questioned whether there would be much difference between the tests for intentional and unintentional nuisance—even though "unreasonableness" is to be determined, in the case of intentional nuisances, with reference to the gravity of the harm actually suffered, and in the case of unintended harm, with reference to the likelihood of injury multiplied by the prospective extent of the harm. As comment k to section 822 explains, the negligent, reckless, and abnormally dangerous standards of unintentional nuisances incorporate in some form a balancing of harm against the utility of the conduct, as in the concept of unreasonable risk. And this balancing is made explicit for intentional invasions in section 826.

But section 826(a) is not the sole test in the Second Restatement. An intentional invasion may now be unreasonable under section 826(b) even though the utility of the conduct outweighs the gravity of the harm, if the harm is serious and the defendant could afford to compensate the plaintiff and others similarly harmed while continuing to be engaged in its activity. Similarly, section 829A declares that the gravity of an invasion outweighs its utility (and hence is unreasonable under section 826) whenever the harm caused is both substantial and greater than the plaintiff "should be required to bear without compensation." Thus, an invasion, particularly one causing harm "physical in character," may be so grievous that it outweighs as a matter of law any utility arising from the activity.

At this point it should be evident that the rules governing intentional nuisance involve both negligence and strict liability: liability for an intentional invasions that is unreasonable under section 826(a) is a form of negligence, whereas the intentional invasions governed by section 826(b) are reasonable but nevertheless subject to a compensatory obligation, a form of strict liability. Apart from the standards of liability, however, what remedies are available to an aggrieved party? Compensatory damages or an injunction that requires the defendant to stop engaging in the nuisance-creating activity? In the nuisance context, the question of remedial alternatives often is critical, since continuance of the nuisance will impair the plaintiff's use and enjoyment of land but there may be a very substantial difference between the harm suffered by the plaintiff and the cost to defendant of ceasing its activity. Should injunctive relief be generally available? The following case deals with this important issue, and also provides the opportunity to go beyond this general introduction and explore in greater detail some fundamental questions about the threshold rules of liability.

Boomer v. Atlantic Cement Co.

Court of Appeals of New York, 1970.
26 N.Y.2d 219, 257 N.E.2d 870, 309 N.Y.S.2d 312.

■ BERGAN, J.

Defendant operates a large cement plant near Albany. These are actions for injunction and damages by neighboring land owners alleging injury to property from dirt, smoke and vibration emanating from the plant. A nuisance has been found after trial, temporary damages have been allowed; but an injunction has been denied.

The public concern with air pollution arising from many sources in industry and in transportation is currently accorded ever wider recognition accompanied by a growing sense of responsibility in State and Federal Governments to control it. Cement plants are obvious sources of air pollution in the neighborhoods where they operate.

But there is now before the court private litigation in which individual property owners have sought specific relief from a single plant operation. The threshold question raised by the division of view on this appeal is whether the court should resolve the litigation between the parties now before it as equitably as seems possible; or whether, seeking promotion of the general public welfare, it should channel private litigation into broad public objectives.

A court performs its essential function when it decides the rights of parties before it. Its decision of private controversies may sometimes greatly affect public issues. Large questions of law are often resolved by the manner in which private litigation is decided. But this is normally an incident to the court's main function to settle controversy. It is a rare exercise of judicial power to use a decision in private litigation as a purposeful mechanism to achieve direct public objectives greatly beyond the rights and interests before the court.

Effective control of air pollution is a problem presently far from solution even with the full public and financial powers of government. In large measure adequate technical procedures are yet to be developed and some that appear possible may be economically impracticable.

It seems apparent that the amelioration of air pollution will depend on technical research in great depth; on a carefully balanced consideration of the economic impact of close regulation; and of the actual effect on public health. It is likely to require massive public expenditure and to demand more than any local community can accomplish and to depend on regional and interstate controls.

A court should not try to do this on its own as a by-product of private litigation and it seems manifest that the judicial establishment is neither equipped in the limited nature of any judgment it can pronounce nor prepared to lay down and implement an effective policy for the elimination of air pollution. This is an area beyond the circumference of one private lawsuit. It is a direct responsibility for government and should not thus be undertaken as an incident to solving a dispute between property owners and a single cement plant—one of many—in the Hudson River valley.

The cement making operations of defendant have been found by the court at Special Term to have damaged the nearby properties of plaintiffs in these two actions. That court, as it has been noted, accordingly found defendant maintained a nuisance and this has been affirmed at the Appellate Division. The total damage to plaintiffs' properties is, however, relatively small in comparison with the value of defendant's operation and with the consequences of the injunction which plaintiffs seek.

The ground for the denial of injunction, notwithstanding the finding both that there is a nuisance and that plaintiffs have been damaged substantially, is the large disparity in economic consequences of the nuisance and of the injunction. This theory cannot, however, be sustained without overruling a doctrine which has been consistently reaffirmed in several leading cases in this court and which has never been disavowed here, namely that where a nuisance has been found and where there has been any substantial damage shown by the party complaining an injunction will be granted.

The rule in New York has been that such a nuisance will be enjoined although marked disparity be shown in economic consequence between the effect of the injunction and the effect of the nuisance.

The problem of disparity in economic consequence was sharply in focus in Whalen v. Union Bag & Paper Co., [101 N.E. 805 (N.Y.1913)]. A pulp mill entailing an investment of more than a million dollars polluted a stream in which plaintiff, who owned a farm, was "a lower riparian owner." The economic loss to plaintiff from this pollution was small. This court, reversing the Appellate Division, reinstated the injunction granted by the Special Term against the argument of the mill owner that in view of "the slight advantage to plaintiff and the great loss that will be inflicted on defendant" an injunction should not be granted [ ]. "Such a balancing of injuries cannot be justified by the circumstances of this case," Judge Werner noted [ ]. He continued: "Although the damage to the plaintiff may be slight as compared with the defendant's expense of abating the condition, that is not a good reason for refusing an injunction" [ ].

Thus the unconditional injunction granted at Special Term was reinstated. The rule laid down in that case, then, is that whenever the damage resulting from a nuisance is found not "unsubstantial," viz., $100 a year, injunction would follow. This states a rule that had been followed in this court with marked consistency [ ].

. . .

Although the court at Special Term and the Appellate Division held that injunction should be denied, it was found that plaintiffs had been damaged in various specific amounts up to the time of the trial and damages to the respective plaintiffs were awarded for those amounts. The effect of this was, injunction having been denied, plaintiffs could maintain successive actions at law for damages thereafter as further damage was incurred.

The court at Special Term also found the amount of permanent damage attributable to each plaintiff, for the guidance of the parties in the event both sides stipulated to the payment and acceptance of such permanent damage as a settlement of all the controversies among the parties. The total of permanent damages to all plaintiffs thus found was $185,000. This basis of adjustment has not resulted in any stipulation by the parties.

This result at Special Term and at the Appellate Division is a departure from a rule that has become settled; but to follow the rule literally in these cases would be to close down the plant at once. This court is fully agreed to avoid that immediately drastic remedy: the difference in view is how best to avoid it.*

One alternative is to grant the injunction but postpone its effect to a specified future date to give opportunity for technical advances to permit defendant to eliminate the nuisance; another is to grant the injunction conditioned on the payment of permanent damages to plaintiffs which would compensate them for the total economic loss to their property present and future caused by defendant's operations. For reasons which will be developed the court chooses the latter alternative.

If the injunction were to be granted unless within a short period— e.g., 18 months—the nuisance be abated by improved methods, there would be no assurance that any significant technical improvement would occur.

The parties could settle this private litigation at any time if defendant paid enough money and the imminent threat of closing the plant would build up the pressure on defendant. If there were no improved techniques found, there would inevitably be applications to the court at Special Term for extensions of time to perform on showing of good faith efforts to find such techniques.

Moreover, techniques to eliminate dust and other annoying byproducts of cement making are unlikely to be developed by any research the defendant can undertake within any short period, but will depend on the total resources of the cement industry nationwide and throughout the world. The problem is universal wherever cement is made.

---

* Respondent's investment in the plant is in excess of $45,000,000. There are over 300 people employed there.

For obvious reasons the rate of the research is beyond control of defendant. If at the end of 18 months the whole industry has not found a technical solution a court would be hard put to close down this one cement plant if due regard be given to equitable principles.

On the other hand, to grant the injunction unless defendant pays plaintiffs such permanent damages as may be fixed by the court seems to do justice between the contending parties. All of the attributions of economic loss to the properties on which plaintiffs' complaints are based will have been redressed.

The nuisance complained of by these plaintiffs may have other public or private consequences, but these particular parties are the only ones who have sought remedies and the judgment proposed will fully redress them. The limitation of relief granted is a limitation only within the four corners of these actions and does not foreclose public health or other public agencies from seeking proper relief in a proper court.

It seems reasonable to think that the risk of being required to pay permanent damages to injured property owners by cement plant owners would itself be a reasonably effective spur to research for improved techniques to minimize nuisance.

The power of the court to condition on equitable grounds the continuance of an injunction on the payment of permanent damages seems undoubted. [ ]

The damage base here suggested is consistent with the general rule in those nuisance cases where damages are allowed. "Where a nuisance is of such a permanent and unabatable character that a single recovery can be had, including the whole damage past and future resulting therefrom, there can be but one recovery" (66 C.J.S., Nuisances, § 140, p. 947). It has been said that permanent damages are allowed where the loss recoverable would obviously be small as compared with the cost of removal of the nuisance [ ].

. . .

Thus it seems fair to both sides to grant permanent damages to plaintiffs which will terminate this private litigation. The theory of damage is the "servitude on land" of plaintiffs imposed by defendant's nuisance. (See United States v. Causby, 328 U.S. 256, 261, 262, 267 [1946], where the term "servitude" addressed to the land was used by Justice Douglas relating to the effect of airplane noise on property near an airport.)

The judgment, by allowance of permanent damages imposing a servitude on land, which is the basis of the actions, would preclude future recovery by plaintiffs or their grantees.

This should be placed beyond debate by a provision of the judgment that the payment by defendant and the acceptance by plaintiffs of permanent damages found by the court shall be in compensation for a servitude on the land.

Although the Trial Term has found permanent damages as a possible basis of settlement of the litigation, on remission the court should be entirely free to re-examine this subject. It may again find the permanent damage already found; or make new findings.

The orders should be reversed, without costs, and the cases remitted to Supreme Court, Albany County to grant an injunction which shall be vacated upon payment by defendant of such amounts of permanent damage to the respective plaintiffs as shall for this purpose be determined by the court.

■ JASEN, J. (dissenting).

I agree with the majority that a reversal is required here, but I do not subscribe to the newly enunciated doctrine of assessment of permanent damages, in lieu of an injunction, where substantial property rights have been impaired by the creation of a nuisance.

It has long been the rule in this State, as the majority acknowledges, that a nuisance which results in substantial continuing damage to neighbors must be enjoined. [ ]

To now change the rule to permit the cement company to continue polluting the air indefinitely upon the payment of permanent damages is, in my opinion, compounding the magnitude of a very serious problem in our State and Nation today.

In recognition of this problem, the Legislature of this State has enacted the Air Pollution Control Act (Public Health Law, §§ 1264–1299m) declaring that it is the State policy to require the use of all available and reasonable methods to prevent and control air pollution (Public Health Law, § 1265).

The harmful nature and widespread occurrence of air pollution have been extensively documented. Congressional hearings have revealed that air pollution causes substantial property damage, as well as being a contributing factor to a rising incidence of lung cancer, emphysema, bronchitis and asthma.

The specific problem faced here is known as particulate contamination because of the fine dust particles emanating from defendant's cement plant. The particular type of nuisance is not new, having appeared in many cases for at least the past 60 years. [ ] It is interesting to note that cement production has recently been identified as a significant source of particulate contamination in the Hudson Valley. This type of pollution, wherein very small particles escape and stay in the atmosphere, has been denominated as the type of air pollution which produces the greatest hazard to human health. We have thus a nuisance which not only is damaging to the plaintiffs, but also is decidedly harmful to the general public.

I see grave dangers in overruling our long-established rule of granting an injunction where a nuisance results in substantial continuing damage. In permitting the injunction to become inoperative upon the payment of permanent damages, the majority is, in effect, licensing a continuing wrong. It is the same as saying to the cement company, you may continue to do harm to your neighbors so long as you pay a fee for it. Furthermore, once such permanent damages are assessed and paid, the incentive to alleviate the wrong would be eliminated, thereby continuing air pollution of an area without abatement.

It is true that some courts have sanctioned the remedy here proposed by the majority in a number of cases, but none of the authorities relied upon by the majority are analogous to the situation before us. In those cases the courts, in denying an injunction and awarding money damages, granted their decision on a showing that the use to which the property was intended to be put was primarily for the public benefit. Here, on the other hand, it is clearly established that the cement company is creating a continuing air pollution nuisance primarily for its own private interest with no public benefit.

This kind of inverse condemnation [ ] may not be invoked by a private person or corporation for private gain or advantage. Inverse condemnation should only be permitted when the public is primarily served in the taking or impairment of property. [ ] The promotion of the interests of the polluting cement company has, in my opinion, no public use or benefit.

Nor is it constitutionally permissible to impose servitude on land, without consent of the owner, by payment of permanent damages where the continuing impairment of the land is for a private use. [ ] This is made clear by the State Constitution (art. I, § 7, subd. [a]) which provides that "[p]rivate property shall not be taken for *public use* without just compensation" (emphasis added). It is, of course, significant that the section makes no mention of taking for a *private* use.

In sum, then, by constitutional mandate as well as by judicial pronouncement, the permanent impairment of private property for private purposes is not authorized in the absence of clearly demonstrated public benefit and use.

I would enjoin the defendant cement company from continuing the discharge of dust particles upon its neighbors' properties unless, within 18 months, the cement company abated this nuisance.

   . . .

■ CHIEF JUDGE FULD and JUDGES BURKE and SCILEPPI concur with JUDGE BERGAN; JUDGE JASEN dissents in part and votes to reverse in a separate opinion; JUDGES BREITEL and GIBSON taking no part.

NOTES AND QUESTIONS

1. *Intentional nuisance.* In *Boomer*, the defendant argued at the trial level that it was not committing a nuisance. The trial judge found that the defendant "took every available and possible precaution to protect the plaintiffs from dust." Nonetheless, the court found a nuisance because the "discharge of large quantities of dust upon each of the properties and excessive vibration from blasting deprived each party of the reasonable use of his property and thereby prevented his enjoyment of life and liberty therein." 287 N.Y.S.2d 112 (Albany Cty.1967). The defendant in *Boomer* knew to a substantial certainty that those nearby would be subjected to dust and vibration, and continued the operation after having actual knowledge of the harm. Notice that by this analysis, the defendant is deemed to have intended the nuisance under the prevailing definition of intent in tort law. See p. 899 infra. Thus the overwhelming majority of alleged industrial nuisances are "intentional." In what sense is the harm intended here?

2. *The unreasonableness requirement.* Because the vast majority of industrial nuisances are "intentional," liability in these cases typically turns on the question whether the invasion of plaintiff's property was "unreasonable." This problem was explored at length in Jost v. Dairyland Power Cooperative, 172 N.W.2d 647 (Wis.1969), in which sulfur dioxide gas was discharged into the atmosphere by defendant's power plant, damaging nearby crops. The farmers sued and the defendant sought to prove that it had used due care in the construction and operation of its plant and that the "social and economic utility of the Alma plant outweighed the gravity of damage to the plaintiffs." The trial judge's rejection of such proof as to liability was affirmed. The court found crop damage of several hundred dollars and then, turning to liability, concluded:

> [T]he court properly excluded all evidence that tended to show the utility of the Dairyland Cooperative's enterprise. Whether its economic or social importance dwarfed the claim of a small farmer is of no consequence in this lawsuit. It will not be said that, because a great and socially useful enterprise will be liable in damages, an injury small by comparison should go unredressed. We know of no acceptable rule of jurisprudence that permits those who are engaged in important and desirable enterprises to injure with impunity those who are engaged in enterprises of lesser economic significance. Even the government or other entities, including public utilities, endowed with the power of eminent domain—the power to take private property in order to devote it to a purpose beneficial to the public good—are obliged to pay a fair market value for what is taken or damaged. To contend that a public utility, in the pursuit of its praiseworthy and legitimate enterprise, can, in effect, deprive others of the full use of their property without compensation, poses a theory unknown to the law of Wisconsin, and in our opinion would constitute the taking of property without due process of law.

Is the court's reasoning consistent with the approach taken in the initial Restatement p. 686 supra? In the Second Restatement? In *Boomer*? Recall that under the Second Restatement, an intentional nuisance is "unreasonable" if the defendant's conduct was unreasonable *or* if the harm suffered by plaintiff was unreasonable, defined as a serious harm that the defendant would be able to compensate without having to cease the (reasonable) activity. For a comprehensive discussion of the case law and law review literature on *Boomer* and private nuisance in the succeeding two decades (including a tally of the cases adopting some version of the Second Restatement approach to balancing the utilities), see Lewin, *Boomer* and the American Law of Nuisance: Past, Present, and Future, 54 Alb.L.Rev. 189 (1990). For a case providing the flavor of nuisance controversies—and resolutions—prior to the adoption of strict liability analysis, see Waschak v. Moffat, 109 A.2d 310 (Pa.1954). On the analog to governmental takings, see Halper, Untangling the Nuisance Knot, 26 B.C.Envtl.Aff.L.Rev. 89 (1998).

3. *Examples of unreasonable interferences.* A considerable body of nuisance law deals with land use disputes that lack the broader environmental aspects of the *Boomer* case. Typically, these cases deal with the loss of commercial value of adjoining property. In Fontainebleau Hotel Corp. v. Forty-Five Twenty-Five, Inc., 114 So.2d 357 (Fla.App.1959), a Miami Beach hotel sought an injunction to prevent a neighboring hotel from building a 14-floor addition that would block a considerable amount of sunlight from plaintiff's property. Another involves a loss of economic value of residential property, such as the numerous efforts to enjoin a funeral parlor from locating in a neighborhood. See, e.g., Travis v. Moore, 377 So.2d 609 (Miss.1979). At times, the claims combine allegations of loss of market value with pain and suffering. See Weinhold v. Wolff, 555 N.W.2d 454 (Iowa 1996), involving a successful claim for damages from noxious odors emanating from a neighboring hog feeding and confinement facility. Hard feelings and spiteful behavior are not uncommon in these cases. Consider Tarlton v. Kaufman, 199 P.3d 263 (Mont.2008), in which defendants, who had complained unsuccessfully about their neighbors' yard lights, built a 26-foot-high fence that they covered with dark material. Plaintiffs brought a nuisance action, claiming it was a "spite fence" that had no function, was unsightly, and reduced their property value, which the court held stated a claim. Contrast Wernke v. Halas, 600 N.E.2d 117 (Ind.App.1992), in which the court held that nailing a toilet seat to a tree and placing offensive graffiti on a fence facing the plaintiffs' property might constitute "unsightliness or lack of aesthetic virtue" but did not rise to the level of a nuisance.

For a case merging the environmental and commercial aspects of nuisance law, see Prah v. Maretti, 321 N.W.2d 182 (Wis.1982), in which the court upheld the claim of the owner of a solar-heated residence against a neighbor's proposed construction that would have interfered with the plaintiff's solar access. See also Vogel v. Grant-Lafayette Electric Cooperative, 548 N.W.2d 829 (Wis.1996)(allowing a nuisance claim for stray voltage from defendant's electric power grid that caused plaintiffs' cattle to exhibit "violent or erratic behavior" and to produce less milk). Detailed consideration of these dimensions of nuisance law is beyond the scope of a Torts course; the residential and commercial aspects of nuisance law—and zoning law, as well—are taken up in courses in Land Use and Property.

4. *Basis of liability.* Did the defendant in *Boomer* act negligently, or is the liability strict in the sense that despite the defendant's exercise of reasonable care, it was still obligated to compensate plaintiffs for their harm? See Copart Indus. v. Consolidated Edison Co. of New York, 362 N.E.2d 968, 973 (N.Y.1977)("it is obvious that [*Boomer* did not involve] a nuisance in which the substance of the wrong was negligence").

As discussed on p. 549 supra, strict liability is sometimes justified in terms of causal responsibility. Contrast the following two views on assigning causal responsibility. Professor Fletcher, in the 1972 article discussed at p. 547 supra, argues that a victim of harm

> has a right to recover for injuries caused by a risk greater in degree and different in order from those created by the victim and imposed on the defendant—in short, for injuries resulting from non-reciprocal risks.

In Coase, The Problem of Social Cost, 3 J.L. & Econ. 1 (1960), referred to earlier at p. 546 supra, the author challenges widely accepted notions of causal direction:

> The question is commonly thought of as one in which A inflicts harm on B and what has to be decided is: how should we restrain A? But this is wrong. We are dealing with a problem of a reciprocal nature. To avoid the harm to B would inflict harm on A. The real question that has to be decided is: should A be allowed to harm B or should B be allowed to harm A? . . . [An] example is afforded by the problem of straying cattle which destroy crops on neighboring land. If it is inevitable that some cattle will stray, an increase in the supply of meat can only be obtained at the expense of a decrease in the supply of crops. The nature of the choice is clear: meat or crops.

Is one of these formulations more helpful than the other in thinking about nuisance cases? In thinking about accidental harm cases more generally?

5. *The substantial harm requirement.* The "live and let live rule" exempts prima facie nuisances from liability on the ground that the conflicting uses are widespread and involve low-level harms. The rule was famously justified by Baron Bramwell:

> There must be, then, some principle on which such cases must be excepted. It seems to me that that principle may be deduced from the character of these cases, and is this, viz., that those acts necessary for the common and ordinary use and occupation of land and houses may be done, if conveniently done, without subjecting those who do them to an action. . . . There is an obvious necessity for such a principle as I have mentioned. It is as much

for the advantage of one owner as of another; for the very nuisance the one complains of, as the result of the ordinary use of his neighbour's land, he himself will create in the ordinary use of his own, and the reciprocal nuisances are of a comparatively trifling character. The convenience of such a rule may be indicated by calling it a rule of give and take, live and let live. . . .

Bamford v. Turnley, (1862) 122 Eng.Rep. 27, 32–33.

Consider this rule in relation to the different approaches to causal responsibility discussed in note 4. Does it support either one? Both?

6. *Other limits on the type of harm.* Recall that the trial court in *Rylands*, p. 513 supra, decided that there was no nuisance because the act was not a continuing harm. Although most nuisances have been accompanied by continuing harm, this is no longer considered an essential element.

Liability, however, is limited by the type of harm. In Adams v. Star Enterprise, 51 F.3d 417 (4th Cir.1995), property owners brought suit against defendant oil distribution facility for a major discharge of oil that created a plume extending underground to near their property—although not yet actually contaminating their property. They sought damages for emotional distress and diminished property value on, among other theories, private nuisance. Applying Virginia law, the court held that there could be no recovery on a nuisance theory absent some evidence of physically perceptible harm. Here the plume was "incapable of detection" from plaintiffs' properties.

What are some of the problems associated with allowing such claims to go forward on the grounds of depreciation of property values without "physically perceptible harm"? In Adkins v. Thomas Solvent Co., 487 N.W.2d 715 (Mich.1992), which held that property owners living near a contaminated site could not recover for the diminution of their property values in the absence of evidence demonstrating that contaminants had migrated to their property, the majority reasoned that:

> If any property owner in the vicinity of the numerous hazardous-waste sites that have been identified can advance a claim seeking damages when unfounded public fears of exposure cause property depreciation, the ultimate effect might be a reordering of the polluter's resources for the benefit of the persons who have suffered no cognizable harm at the expense of those claimants who have been subjected to a substantial and unreasonable interference in the use and enjoyment of property.

The dissent, however, would have allowed a nuisance action on a showing "that the defendants actually contaminated soil and ground water in the neighborhood of plaintiffs' homes with toxic chemicals and industrial wastes, that the market perception of the value of plaintiffs' homes was actually adversely affected by the contamination of the neighborhood, and thus that plaintiffs' loss was causally related to defendants' conduct." Who has the better argument? In contrast, a few courts have been willing to allow a nuisance action without evidence of physical harm. See, e.g., Omega

Chemical Co. v. United Seeds, 560 N.W.2d 820 (Neb.1997)(finding a nuisance where accumulated snow on defendant's roof merely threatened harm to the plaintiff). What about situations involving continuing noxious odors, high noise levels, or strong vibrations? Do these meet the threshold requirement of physically perceptible harm? Should they?

7. *Extrasensitive plaintiffs.* What if the plaintiff is particularly sensitive or vulnerable to a particular use of land? Where the exposure leads to an individual claim of personal injury, nuisance law typically holds that the harm suffered should be determined by reference to a "normal" person in the community. Why might this be? For an early case articulating the general approach, see Rogers v. Elliott, 15 N.E. 768 (Mass.1888)(denying relief to plaintiff who suffered harm from ringing of church bells because of his highly nervous condition). Is this approach contrary to the eggshell plaintiff rule considered at p. 395 supra? Compare the treatment of the super-sensitive plaintiff in emotional distress cases, p. 281 supra.

8. *Coming to the nuisance.* In *Boomer,* the defendant came to the area more recently than the plaintiffs. Is this relevant? Sometimes the defendant establishes its facility in an isolated area only to find the nearby town expanding and others moving closer to it. The question raised is whether a plaintiff who has knowingly encountered the nuisance is barred from suing. Restatement (Second) of Torts section 840D says that this is "not in itself sufficient to bar his action, but it is a factor to be considered in determining whether the nuisance is actionable." How might this be a relevant factor? Might there be an underlying concern about first-comers exercising extraterritorial controls over large areas of land? Might the price plaintiff paid for the land be relevant? The issue is discussed in Wittman, First Come, First Served: An Economic Analysis of "Coming to the Nuisance," 9 J. Legal Stud. 557 (1980).

9. *Nuisance and zoning laws.* The law of private nuisance has occasionally been characterized as a form of judicial zoning. Although the court of appeals in *Boomer* does not mention it, the appellate division opinion notes that the area was zoned. 294 N.Y.S.2d 452 (App.Div.1968). Apparently before the defendant began operations in 1962, the town zoned the defendant's property to permit quarrying and business, so that defendant's activity was lawful. Should the zoning be relevant to whether the defendant is liable for any nuisance? Is it proper for a court to find a common law nuisance when the defendant has obeyed legislative zoning requirements? For an extensive discussion of the subject, see Ellickson, Alternatives to Zoning: Covenants, Nuisance Rules, and Fines as Land Use Controls, 40 U.Chi.L.Rev. 681 (1973).

Boomer was held inapplicable in Little Joseph Realty, Inc. v. Town of Babylon, 363 N.E.2d 1163 (N.Y.1977), in which plaintiff sued to enjoin the continuing operation of an asphalt plant that emitted "great quantities of dust and soot" onto defendant's adjoining property. The lower court determined that the plant, which violated the town's zoning ordinance, was a nuisance, and ordered it enjoined unless certain remedial devices were installed—and they were. On appeal, reversed. New York's long-standing rule that structures built on adjoining or nearby property in violation of zoning ordinances were enjoinable at the demand of a specially damaged neighbor was not changed by *Boomer.*

The court remarked that *Boomer* involved a private dispute between two parties in which it was proper to adjust "competing uses with a view towards maximizing the social value of each." But zoning "is far more comprehensive. Its design is, on a planned basis, to serve as a 'vital tool for maintaining a civilized form of existence' for the benefit and welfare of an entire community. . . . It follows that, when a continuing use flies in the face of a valid zoning restriction, it must, subject to the existence of any appropriate equitable defenses, be enjoined unconditionally." This does not mean that "risk-utility considerations have not entered into the adoption of a zoning law's restriction on use. It is rather that presumptively they have already been weighed and disposed of by the Legislature which enacted them."

   10. *Intersection with environmental regulatory schemes.* One legislative remedy available in New York against air pollution at the time of *Boomer* was Public Health Law §§ 1264–98, establishing an administrative body to determine standards for pollution and to promulgate regulations accordingly. The Commissioner of Health was to investigate and determine violations. His conclusions were subject to administrative and judicial review. Failure to take corrective action subjected the offender to penalties not to exceed $1,000 plus $200 for each day of continued violation. The Commissioner could also seek an injunction. The act expressly stated that it was supplementary to any other existing remedies, but at the same time provided that the rules and regulations promulgated under the statute were "not intended to create in any way new or enlarged rights or to enlarge existing rights." Any determination by the Commissioner that pollution existed or that a regulation had been violated "shall not create by reason thereof any presumption of law or finding of fact which shall inure to or be for the benefit of any person other than the state." New York had also entered interstate compacts to combat water and air pollution. (N.Y. Public Health Law §§ 1299–1299s.) Does the existence of these procedures affect your views of the majority decision?

   Since 1970, the federal government has assumed a major presence in the field of regulatory control of environmental pollution. A wide variety of statutory schemes have been enacted in an effort to develop a more comprehensive approach to many of the environmental harms associated with air and water pollution, hazardous wastes, and toxic substances (among others). For the most part, these enactments have not been interpreted as preempting private nuisance actions under state common law, but there are exceptions. In International Paper Co. v. Ouellette, 479 U.S. 481 (1987), for example, the Supreme Court held that the Clean Water Act preempts state nuisance law when applied to an out-of-state source.

   At the state level, most states have enacted pollution control statutes that either specifically preserve nuisance actions or have been interpreted by the courts to preserve such actions. As in the federal system, however, there are exceptions. In San Diego Gas & Electric Co. v. Superior Court,

920 P.2d 669 (Cal.1996), in which a group of homeowners alleged that electric and magnetic fields (EMF) emitted from the utility's electric power lines had caused them emotional distress, made their homes uninhabitable, and destroyed the market value of their homes, the court rejected their private nuisance action, holding that an award of damages would impermissibly interfere with the Public Utility Commission's policy on power line electric and magnetic fields. Recall the discussion of the preemption defense at p. 487 supra. Is there reason to think it would play out differently in the nuisance context? For an overview of the preemption issue and an argument that nuisance law should be retained as a supplemental remedy rather than being preempted by pollution control statutes, see Heimert, Keeping Pigs Out of Parlors: Using Nuisance Law to Affect the Location of Pollution, 27 Envtl.L. 403 (1997).

11. *Remedial considerations.* Turning now to questions of remedy for private nuisance, what relief did the trial judge award in *Boomer*? How did the court of appeals alter the remedy granted by the lower courts?

In the *Union Bag* case, cited in *Boomer,* the plaintiff's harm was assessed at $100 per year. Plaintiff enforced his injunction, and the mill, which represented an investment of $1,000,000, was permanently closed. Why was the pre-*Boomer* New York rule on injunctive relief on its face so favorable to plaintiffs? Did it embody a distinctive view about property rights in land?

In the *Jost* case the court also awarded damages:

> [Plaintiffs'] avenue for compensation is for permanent and continuing nuisance as may be reflected in a diminution of market value. Of course, permitting a recovery now for a permanent loss of market value presupposes that the degree of nuisance will not increase. If such be the case, an award of damages for loss of market value is final. If, however, the level of nuisance and air pollution should be increased above the level that may now be determined by a jury, with a consequent additional injury the plaintiffs would have the right to seek additional permanent damage to compensate them for the additional diminished market value.

What should happen in *Boomer* and *Jost* if, after paying permanent damages, the defendant reduces the harm being inflicted—either by closing down the operation or by installing newly developed control devices? But what is the defendant's incentive in *Boomer* to install any new devices at all? What if the plaintiff in *Jost* switches to crops that are less profitable but impervious to sulfur dioxide gas?

12. *Bargaining in the shadow of the law.* In the article discussed in note 4, Coase goes on to argue that in the absence of transaction costs (i.e., costs associated with striking a bargain) the rule of liability does not matter from an economic efficiency standpoint. In a *Boomer* situation, if the polluter is liable he will invest more in pollution control measures only when doing so is cheaper than paying damages or going out of business. If the polluter is not liable, the victim will "bribe" him to invest in pollution control equipment where doing so costs less than the damage the victim would otherwise suffer. Whatever the liability rule, the choice between pollution control measures and victim harm will result in precisely the same amount of resources being invested in elimination of the harm— although, of course, the distributional consequences will differ. Since there are almost invariably transaction costs—consider the costs of getting the parties together in *Boomer*—the rights and remedies recognized by nuisance law do generally make a considerable difference.

13. *Conceptualizing entitlements.* In an influential article, Property Rules, Liability Rules, and Inalienability: One View of the Cathedral, 85 Harv.L.Rev. 1089 (1972), Calabresi and Melamed discuss a framework of rules that the law uses to protect "entitlements"—decisions regarding which of two or more conflicting parties will prevail. These rules yield the traditional results of no liability, damages, or injunctive relief.

An entitlement is protected by a "property" rule when a person who wishes to obtain the entitlement must purchase it at a price determined by the holder. Thus, the New York rule regarding injunctions for nuisances, before *Boomer,* provided an entitlement in cases of "not unsubstantial" damage to the neighbors of a polluter that was protected by a property rule: A polluter who wished to continue operations had to buy the right to do so. Alternatively, an entitlement protected by a property rule could be given to the polluter. This would be the case if the courts adopted a rule of no liability for pollution damage.

Two other alternatives are possible. The entitlement held by the neighbors or by the polluters might be protected only by a "liability" rule, which is the case when one of the parties in conflict can purchase the entitlement at an objectively determined price. This rule corresponds to the imposition of damages by a court. *Boomer* is an example of an entitlement in the plaintiffs protected by a liability rule (the third alternative)— defendant polluter can continue operations as long as damages are paid in satisfaction of the entitlement.

The fourth alternative, giving the polluter an entitlement protected by a liability rule, is rarely recognized as a possibility. The leading nuisance case employing this approach, Spur Industries, Inc. v. Del E. Webb Development Co., 494 P.2d 700 (Ariz.1972), involved a conflict between defendant's pre-existing cattle feedlot operation and plaintiff's residential subdivision, which expanded toward the feedlot until the flies and odors drifting onto the development made sale of more units impossible and provoked numerous complaints from existing residents. The court found that the feedlot was an enjoinable nuisance, but held that because of the "coming to the nuisance" aspect of the case, plaintiff developer would be required to indemnify defendant Spur for the cost of "moving or shutting down." The court reasoned:

> It does not seem harsh to require a developer, who has taken advantage of the lesser land values in a rural area as well as the availability of large tracts of land on which to build and develop a

new town or city in the area, to indemnify those who are forced to leave as a result.

The court emphasized, however, that:

> this relief to Spur is limited to a case wherein a developer has, with foreseeability, brought into a previously agricultural or industrial area the population which makes necessary the granting of an injunction against a lawful business and for which the business has no adequate relief.

Is the remedy accorded in *Spur* likely to be useful or applicable in many cases? Consider that here the homeowners' individual interests were represented by the development company. If an action were brought by an individual or by a class, how would compensation to the feedlot be apportioned among all the homeowners affected? What about homeowners who failed to join in the action?

What factors should be considered in deciding who gets an entitlement? In deciding whether the entitlement should be protected by a property rule or a liability rule? See generally E. Rabin, Nuisance Law: Rethinking Fundamental Assumptions, 63 Va.L.Rev. 1299 (1977); Lewin, Compensated Injunctions and the Evolution of Nuisance Law, 71 Iowa L.Rev. 775 (1986).

B. PUBLIC NUISANCE

Public nuisance has a long history, dating back to offenses to the Crown in medieval times. More recently, public nuisance has been employed in attempts to attack public health hazards, as the next case illustrates. Unlike private nuisance, public nuisance does not protect interests in the use and enjoyment of private land. As you work through these materials, consider whether other differences between public and private nuisance make common usage of "nuisance" unfortunate, with its implication that these two torts share at least a common core.

State of Rhode Island v. Lead Industries Association, Inc.

Supreme Court of Rhode Island, 2008.
951 A.2d 428.

■ CHIEF JUSTICE WILLIAMS, for the Court.

OPINION

In this landmark lawsuit, filed in 1999, the then Attorney General, on behalf of the State of Rhode Island (the state), filed suit against various former lead pigment manufacturers. . . .

. . .

I
Facts and Travel

It is undisputed that lead poisoning constitutes a public health crisis that has plagued and continues to plague this country, particularly its children. The General Assembly has declared that although "[c]hildhood lead poisoning is completely preventable," [ ], it is "the most severe environmental health problem in Rhode Island." [ ] Indeed, Providence has received the unfavorable nickname "the lead paint capital" because of its disproportionately large number of children with elevated blood-lead levels. [ ]

A
Dangers of Lead Poisoning

Lead is a toxic chemical that contributes to the "most common environmental disease of young children." . . . Contact with low levels of lead may lead to "permanent learning disabilities, reduced concentration and attentiveness and behavior problems, problems which may persist and adversely affect the child's chances for success in school and life." . . . Children exposed to elevated levels of lead can suffer from comas, convulsions, and even death. [ ]

Lead was widely used in residential paints in the United States until the mid-1970s. . . . In the United States, children most often are lead-poisoned by ingesting lead paint chips from deteriorating walls or inhaling lead-contaminated surface dust. [ ]

. . .

C
Legislative Responses

[The court explained several efforts, both at the federal and state levels, to attend to the risk of lead poisoning. . . . In Rhode Island, the legislature enacted the Lead Poisoning Prevention Act (LPPA), "to reduce exposure to environmental lead and prevent childhood lead poisoning, the most severe environmental health problem in Rhode Island." A decade later, the legislature supplemented the LPPA with the Lead Hazard Mitigation Act (LHMA), which required landlords to attend to lead paint that existed in their rental units. "[S]ince 1994, there has been a dramatic decrease in the incidence of lead poisoning among Rhode Island children. . . . [T]he progress has proven to be a "public health success story."]

. . .

D
Attorney General's Lawsuit

. . .

The state alleged that the manufacturers or their predecessors-in-interest had manufactured, promoted, distributed, and sold lead pigment for use in residential paint, despite that they knew or should have known, since the early 1900s, that lead is hazardous to human health. . . . The state further alleged that defendants' actions caused it to incur substantial damages. As such, the state asserted, defendants were liable for public nuisance. . . . The state also requested equitable relief to protect children in Rhode Island. The state sought compensatory and punitive damages, in addition to an order requiring defendants to (1) abate lead pigment in all Rhode Island buildings accessible to children and (2) fund educational and lead-poisoning prevention programs.

. . .

The jury . . . found that the "cumulative presence of lead pigment in paints and coatings on buildings throughout the State of Rhode Island" constituted a public nuisance. The jury further found that defendants . . . were liable for causing or substantially contributing to the creation of the public nuisance. Lastly, the jury concluded that those . . . defendants "should be ordered to abate the public nuisance." . . .

. . .

II
Analysis

. . .

1
History of Public Nuisance

. . .

Today, public nuisance and private nuisance are separate and distinct causes of action, but both torts are inextricably linked by their joint origin as a common writ, dating to twelfth-century English common law. [ ] In its earliest form, nuisance was a criminal writ used to prosecute individuals or require abatement of activities considered to "be '*nocumentum iniuriousum propter communem et publicam utiliatem*'—a nuisance by reason of the common and public welfare." [ ] Public nuisance, or common nuisance as it originally was called, was "an infringement of the rights of the Crown." 4 Restatement (Second) *Torts* § 821B, cmt. *a* at 87 (1979). Although the earliest cases involved encroachments on the royal domain, public nuisance law evolved to include "the invasion of the rights of the public." [ ]

By the fourteenth century, courts began to apply public nuisance principles to protect rights common to the public, including "roadway safety, air and water pollution, disorderly conduct, and public health * * *." [ ] Nuisance became a "flexible judicial remedy" that allowed courts to address conflicts between land use and social welfare at a time when government regulations had not yet made their debut. [ ]

It was not until the sixteenth century that the crime of public nuisance largely was transformed into the tort that is familiar in our courts today. [ ] However, additional parameters were necessary to limit the reach of the new tort. A private party seeking to bring a public nuisance claim was required to demonstrate that he or she had "suffered a 'particular' or 'special' injury that was not common to the public." [ ]; *see also* 4 Restatement (Second) *Torts* § 821B, cmt. *a* at 87–88 [ ].

Ultimately, "[a]t common law public nuisance came to cover a large, miscellaneous and diversified group of minor offenses * * *." [ ] Notably, all these offenses involved an "interference with the interests of the community at large—interests that were recognized as rights of the general public entitled to protection." [ ]

Public nuisance as it existed in English common law made its way to Colonial America without change. [ ] In time, public nuisance became better known as a tort, and its criminal counterpart began to fade away in American jurisprudence. As state legislatures started enacting statutes prohibiting particular conduct and setting forth criminal penalties there was little need for the broad, vague, and anachronistic crime of nuisance. [ ]

The criminal origins of public nuisance in Rhode Island still can be found in statutes designating certain criminal activities and the places in which they are conducted as "common nuisances." *See, e.g.,* [ ] (defining the unlicensed manufacture or distribution of intoxicating liquor as a common nuisance); [ ] (defining slaughterhouses, rendering plants, garbage plants, and brick kilns as common nuisances if located within 300 feet of any public park or public hospital); [ ] (defining the burning of decaying and waste substances as a nuisance); [ ] (defining certain facilities used in the distribution of illegal drugs as common nuisances); [ ] (defining unauthorized boxing matches as common nuisances).

2

Public Nuisance in Rhode Island

. . .

This Court has defined public nuisance as "an unreasonable interference with a right common to the general public." [ ] "[I]t is behavior that unreasonably interferes with the health, safety, peace, comfort or convenience of the general community." . . .

Although this Court previously has not had the opportunity to address all the elements of public nuisance, to the extent that we have addressed this common law cause of action, our definition largely is consistent with that of many other jurisdictions, the Restatement (Second) of Torts, and several scholarly commentators.

The Restatement (Second) defines public nuisance, in relevant part, as follows:

> "(1) A public nuisance is an unreasonable interference with a right common to the general public.

> "(2) Circumstances that may sustain a holding that an interference with a public right is unreasonable include the following:

> "(a) Whether the conduct involves a significant interference with the public health, the public safety, the public peace, the public comfort or the public convenience * * *." 4 Restatement (Second) Torts § 821B at 87.

> . . .

This Court recognizes three principal elements that are essential to establish public nuisance: (1) an unreasonable interference; (2) with a right common to the general public; (3) by a person or people with control over the instrumentality alleged to have created the nuisance when the damage occurred. After establishing the presence of the three elements of public nuisance, one must then determine whether the defendant caused the public nuisance. We will address each element in turn.

. . .

3

Whether the Presence of Lead Paint Constitutes a Public Nuisance

. . .

. . . [W]e cannot ascertain allegations in the complaint that support each of these elements. The state's complaint alleges simply that "[d]efendants created an environmental hazard that continues and will continue to unreasonably interfere with the health, safety, peace, comfort or convenience of the residents of the [s]tate, thereby constituting a public nuisance." Absent from the state's complaint is any allegation that defendants have interfered with a public right as that term long has been understood in the law of public nuisance. Equally problematic is the absence of any allegation that defendants had control over the lead pigment at the time it caused harm to children.

. . .

A necessary element of public nuisance is an interference with a public right—those indivisible resources shared by the public at large, such as air, water, or public rights of way. The interference must deprive all members of the community of a right to some resource to which they otherwise are entitled. *See* 4 Restatement (Second) *Torts* § 821B, cmt. *g* at 92. The Restatement (Second) provides much guidance in ascertaining the fine distinction between a public right and an aggregation of private rights. "Conduct does not become a public nuisance merely because it interferes with the use and enjoyment of land by a large number of persons." [ ] [In another part of its opinion, the court quoted more extensively from the Restatement's explanation of what constitutes a public right:

> " 'A public right is *one common to all members of the general public.* It is collective in nature and not like the individual right that everyone has not to be assaulted or defamed or defrauded or negligently injured. Thus the pollution of a stream that merely deprives fifty or a hundred lower riparian owners of the use of the water for purposes connected with their land does not for that reason alone become a public nuisance. If, however, the pollution prevents the use of a public bathing beach or kills the fish in a navigable stream and so deprives all members of the community of the right to fish, it becomes a public nuisance.' 4 Restatement (Second) *Torts* § 821B, cmt. *g* at 92 (emphasis added)."]

Although the state asserts that the public's right to be free from the hazards of unabated lead had been infringed, this contention falls far short of alleging an interference with a public right as that term traditionally has been understood in the law of public nuisance. The state's allegation that defendants have interfered with the "health, safety, peace, comfort or convenience of the residents of the [s]tate" standing alone does not constitute an allegation of interference with a public right. [ ] The term public right is reserved more appropriately for those indivisible resources shared by the public at large, such as air, water, or public rights of way. [ ] Expanding the definition of public right based on the allegations in the complaint would be antithetical to the common law and would lead to a widespread expansion of public nuisance law that never was intended, as we discuss *infra.* . . .

The right of an individual child not to be poisoned by lead paint is strikingly similar to other examples of nonpublic rights cited by courts, the Restatement (Second), and several leading commentators. *See Beretta U.S.A. Corp.,* 290 Ill.Dec. 525, 821 N.E.2d at 1114 (concluding that there is no public right to be "free from unreasonable jeopardy to health, welfare, and safety, and from unreasonable threats of danger to person and property, caused by the presence of illegal weapons in the city of Chicago"); 4 Restatement (Second) *Torts* § 821B, cmt. *g* at 92 (the individual right that everyone has not to be assaulted or defamed or defrauded or negligently injured is not a public right); Gifford, [Public Nuisance as a Mass Products Liability Tort, 71 U.Cin.L.Rev. 741, 815 (2003)] (there is no common law public right to a certain standard of living, to a certain standard of medical care, or to a certain standard of housing).

In the words of one commentator:

"Despite the tragic nature of the child's illness, the exposure to lead-based paint usually occurs within the most private and intimate of surroundings, his or her own home. Injuries occurring in this context do not resemble the rights traditionally understood as public rights for public nuisance purposes—obstruction of highways and waterways, or pollution of air or navigable streams." Gifford, 71 U.Cin.L.Rev. at 818.

The enormous leap that the state urges us to take is wholly inconsistent with the widely recognized principle that the evolution of the common law should occur gradually, predictably, and incrementally. Were we to hold otherwise, we would change the meaning of public right to encompass all behavior that causes a widespread interference with the private rights of numerous individuals.

The Illinois Supreme Court recently hypothesized on the effect of a broader recognition of public right. In *Beretta,* the Illinois Supreme Court considered whether there was a public right to be "free from unreasonable jeopardy to health, welfare, and safety, and from unreasonable threats of danger to person and property, caused by the presence of illegal weapons in the city of Chicago." *Beretta U.S.A. Corp.,* 290 Ill.Dec. 525, 821 N.E.2d at 1114. In concluding that there was not, the court acknowledged the far-reaching effects of a decision otherwise. *Id.* 290 Ill.Dec. 525, 821 N.E.2d at 1116. The court speculated that

"[i]f there is public right to be free from the threat that others may use a lawful product to break the law, that right would include the right to drive upon the highways, free from the risk of injury posed by drunk drivers. This public right to safe passage on the highways would provide the basis for public nuisance claims against brewers and distillers, distributing companies, and proprietors of bars, taverns, liquor stores, and restaurants with liquor licenses, all of whom could be said to contribute to an interference with the public right." *Id.*

In taking the analogy a step further, the court considered the effect of other product misuse, stating:

"Similarly, cell phones, DVD players, and other lawful products may be misused by drivers, creating a risk of harm to others. In an increasing number of jurisdictions, state legislatures have acted to ban the use of these otherwise legal products while driving. A public right to be free from the threat that other drivers may defy these laws would permit nuisance liability to be imposed on an endless list of manufacturers, distributors, and retailers of manufactured products that are intended to be, or are likely to be, used by drivers, distracting them and causing injury to others." *Id.*

Like the *Beretta* court, we see no reason to depart from the long-standing principle that a public right is a right of the public to shared resources such as air, water, or public rights of way.

Even had the state adequately alleged an interference with a right common to the general public, which we conclude it did not, the state's complaint also fails to allege any facts that would support a conclusion that defendants were in control of the lead pigment at the time it harmed Rhode Island's children.

[In another part of the court's opinion, it had explained the requirement that defendant control the nuisance:]

As an additional prerequisite to the imposition of liability for public nuisance, a defendant must have *control* over the instrumentality causing the alleged nuisance *at the time the damage occurs*. Put simply, "[o]ne who controls a nuisance is liable for damages caused by that nuisance." *Friends of the Sakonnet v. Dutra,* 749 F.Supp. 381, 395 (D.R.I.1990) (*Dutra II*)(applying Rhode Island law); *see also Citizens for Preservation of Waterman Lake,* 420 A.2d at 59 (declining to impose liability for public nuisance when plaintiff "failed to produce any evidence directly bearing on the amount of noise created by trucks *under [defendant's] control*") (emphasis added).

. . .

Indeed, control at the time the damage occurs is critical in public nuisance cases, especially because the principal remedy for the harm caused by the nuisance is abatement. [ ] ("Injunctions or abatements have been the traditional remedies where the state brings suit for a public nuisance * * *."); *see also National Gypsum Co.,* 637 F.Supp. at 656 ("The defendants, after the time of manufacture and sale, no longer had the power to abate the nuisance. Therefore, a basic element of the tort of nuisance is absent, and the plaintiff cannot succeed on this theory of relief."); [ ]."]

The state filed suit against defendants in their capacity "either as the manufacturer of * * * lead pigment * * * or as the successors in interest to such manufacturers" for "the cumulative presence of lead pigment in paints and coatings in or on buildings throughout the [s]tate of Rhode Island." For the alleged public nuisance to be actionable, the state would have had to assert that defendants not only manufactured the lead pigment but also controlled that pigment at the time it caused injury to children in Rhode Island—and there is no allegation of such control.

The New Jersey Supreme Court applied these same elements to the lead paint litigation in that jurisdiction and likewise held that public nuisance was an improper cause of action. The court emphasized that were it "to permit these complaints to proceed, [it] would stretch the concept of public nuisance far beyond recognition and would create a new and entirely unbounded tort antithetical to the meaning and inherent theoretical limitations of the tort of public nuisance." *In re Lead Paint Litigation,* [924 A.2d 484, 494 (N.J.2007)]. We agree.

We conclude, therefore, that there was no set of facts alleged in the state's complaint that, even if proven, could have demonstrated that defendants' conduct, however unreasonable, interfered with a public right or that defendants had control over the product causing the alleged nuisance at the time children were injured. Accordingly, we need not decide whether defendants' conduct was unreasonable or whether defendants caused an injury to children in Rhode Island.

. . .

Finally, our decision that defendants' conduct does not constitute a public nuisance as that term has for centuries been understood in Anglo-American law does not leave Rhode Islanders without a remedy. For example, an injunction requiring abatement may be sought against landlords who allow lead paint on their property to decay. [ ] In addition, the LPPA provides for penalties and fines against those property owners who violate its rules or procedures. [ ] The LHMA further authorizes a private cause of action to be brought on behalf of households with at-risk occupants to seek injunctive relief to compel property owners to comply with the act. [ ]

Apart from these actions, the proper means of commencing a lawsuit against a manufacturer of lead pigments for the sale of an unsafe product is a products liability action. The law of public nuisance never before has been applied to products, however harmful. Courts in other states consistently have rejected product-based public nuisance suits against lead pigment manufacturers, expressing a concern that allowing such a lawsuit would circumvent the basic requirements of products liability law. [ ]

Public nuisance focuses on the abatement of annoying or bothersome activities. Products liability law, on the other hand, has its own well-defined structure, which is designed specifically to hold manufacturers liable for harmful products that the manufacturers have caused to enter the stream of commerce.

Undoubtedly, public nuisance and products liability are two distinct causes of action, each with rational boundaries that are not intended to overlap.

A product-based public nuisance cause of action bears a close resemblance to a products liability action, yet it is not limited by the strict requirements that surround a products liability action. Courts presented with product-based public nuisance claims have expressed their concern over the ease with which a plaintiff could bring what properly would be characterized as a products liability suit under the guise of product-based public nuisance. The New Jersey Supreme Court, in rejecting the public nuisance claims against lead pigment manufacturers wrote that "[w]e cannot help but agree with the observation that, were we to find a cause of action here, 'nuisance law would become a monster that would devour in one gulp the entire law of tort.' " *In re Lead Paint Litigation,* 924 A.2d at 505 [ ].

. . .

It is essential that these two causes of action remain just that—two separate and distinct causes of action. Addressing this distinction and the danger of a product-based public nuisance suit against gun manufacturers, wholesalers, and retailers, a New York appellate court explained that

> "giving a green light to a common-law public nuisance cause of action today will * * * likely open the courthouse doors to a flood of limitless, similar theories of public nuisance, not only against these defendants, but also against a wide and varied array of other commercial and manufacturing enterprises and activities." *People v. Sturm, Ruger & Co., Inc.,* 309 A.D.2d 91, 761 N.Y.S.2d 192, 196 (N.Y.App.Div.2003).

The Rhode Island General Assembly has recognized that lead paint has created a public health hazard and, pursuant to its power to legislate, has adopted several statutory schemes to address this problem. Collectively, the LPPA and the LHMA reflect the General Assembly's chosen means of responding to the state's childhood lead poisoning problem. The legislative body made clear policy decisions about how to reduce lead hazards in Rhode Island homes, buildings, and other dwellings and who should be responsible. Importantly, the General Assembly has recognized that landlords, who are in control of the lead pigment at the time it becomes hazardous, are responsible for maintaining their premises and ensuring that the premises are lead-safe. Quite tellingly, the General Assembly's chosen means of remedying childhood lead poisoning in Rhode Island did not include an authorization of an action for public nuisance against the manufacturers of lead pigments, despite the fact that this action seeking to impose liability on various lead pigment manufacturers was well under way at the time the LHMA was enacted. Indeed, even the trial justice recognized the absence of legislation governing defendants' actions. He found the LPPA inapplicable because it does not "address in any fashion the actions of these defendants" and because "[t]he statutes and regulations do not authorize the existence of the claimed public nuisance." By focusing on the party in control of the instrumentality at the time the harm occurs, the General Assembly's enactments are wholly consistent with the law of public nuisance in this state and all other jurisdictions.

Conclusion

For the foregoing reasons, we conclude that the trial justice erred in denying defendants' motion to dismiss.

NOTES AND QUESTIONS

1. *Posture of the case.* Before trial, the court granted two motions relating to the state's claim for compensatory damages that resulted in the dismissal of all claims for compensatory damages. Thus, the only relief to which the state was entitled after the jury verdict was an order requiring defendants to abate the nuisance. In an omitted portion of the supreme court's opinion, the court declined to address the state's appeal of the damages dismissal on the ground that it was unnecessary in light of the resolution of the court's determination that no nuisance claim existed.

2. *Control.* The court requires that the defendant be in control of the instrumentality that causes the nuisance. Is control one of the Second Restatement's elements quoted by the court? Why is control at the time of trial required if the defendant had control when the nuisance was first created? Would this have been a different case if the state's claim for compensatory damages had survived?

Suppose that a shoddily constructed building poses an imminent danger of collapsing, and, as a result, the city demolishes it. The city sues the contractor to recover the costs of the demolition on a public nuisance theory, and the contractor defends on the ground that it had no control of the building (and therefore the nuisance) at the time of its demolition because title had passed to the owner. Has the city sued the wrong party? Asserted the wrong tort theory? Or should the city win the suit against the contractor?

3. *Relation to products liability.* Consider a products liability claim, rather than a public nuisance claim, by the state. In what way would the issues be different? Would the state prevail? Suppose that instead of a products suit by the state, a group of landlords who were required to abate the lead paint in their rental properties sued for the costs of abatement asserting private nuisance and products liability actions. What result? What result in a products liability suit by a child in Rhode Island who suffers lead poisoning from exposure to peeling paint?

4. *Private claims for public nuisance.* Private parties may bring a public nuisance claim, but, as the *Lead Industry Association* court explained, they must establish that the defendant is responsible for a nuisance that has caused them to suffer a "special injury" different in kind from that suffered by other members of the public. The Second Restatement, in comment j to section 821C, has this to say about the reason for the special-injury requirement: "The reasons for this rule in the damage action are that it is to prevent the bringing of a multiplicity of actions by many members of the public and the bringing of actions for trivial injury." When individuals suffer personal injury or property damage, courts recognize special injury and permit public nuisance suits. Thus, in Anderson v. W.R. Grace & Co., 628 F.Supp. 1219 (D.Mass.1986), the case made famous in Jonathan Harr's 1996 book, *A Civil Action*, the court permitted plaintiffs suffering from a variety of diseases to maintain a public nuisance claim for damages.

5. *Intersection with statutes.* What role do the two state statutes addressing lead poisoning play in the court's decision? One equivalent to implied preemption? Some other role? Is the court persuasive in its explanation of why the statute has a role to play in whether a public nuisance claim exists? As discussed in note 10, p. 699 supra, most statutes do not impliedly preempt tort claims for private nuisance. Does the nature of public nuisance make implied preemption more likely?

6. *Gun distribution.* Beginning in the late 1990s, a substantial number of municipalities sued the handgun industry alleging that the distribution and sales practices of the industry—and the consequent use of handguns for criminal purposes—constituted a public nuisance. In a limited number of cases, the courts were receptive. See, e.g., City of Gary v. Smith & Wesson Corp., 801 N.E.2d 1222 (Ind.2003), in which the court held that the municipality's complaint, alleging that defendant manufacturers had knowledge that some retail sellers engaged in practices that included blatant violations of gun regulations, stated a cause of action for public nuisance. The *Lead Industries* opinion cites two that concluded otherwise. For a discussion of the cases, see Kinter, Bad Apples and Smoking Barrels: Private Actions for Public Nuisance Against the Gun Industry, 90 Iowa L.Rev. 1163 (2005). In any case, in late 2005, Congress put an end to these suits in the Protection of Lawful Commerce in Arms Act, 15 U.S.C. § 7901 et seq.

7. *Global warming.* In Connecticut v. American Elec. Power Co., 131 S.Ct. 813 (2010), several public entities sued eight electrical utilities, including the five largest carbon emitters in the United States, that operated fossil-fuel generating plants. Plaintiffs sought abatement of the defendants' contributions to global warming. In a ruling with potentially wide-ranging implications for tort litigation involving climate change, the Court concluded (8–0) that federal environmental law displaces any federal common-law right to abate carbon dioxide emissions. The Court also left for consideration on remand the issue of whether federal law preempts related tort claims based on state nuisance law. Relying in part on *American Electric Power*, the court in U.S. v. EME Homer City Generation L.P., 823 F.Supp.2d 274 (W.D.Penn.2011) concluded that a state-law claim for public nuisance (not involving climate change) is preempted by the Clean Air Act (CAA). But cf. Little v. Louisville Gas & Elec. Co., 33 F.Supp.3d 791 (W.D.Ky.2014)(discussing nuisance cases without differentiating between private and public nuisances and concluding that "since the Supreme Court's ruling in [*American Electric Power*] that the CAA displaces federal common-law claims, courts have increasingly interpreted the CAA's savings clause to permit individuals to bring state common-law tort claims against polluting entities"). For a discussion of the preemption question, see Gallisdorfer, Note, Clean Air Act Preemption of State Common Law: Greenhouse Gas Nuisance Claims After *AEP v. Connecticut*, 99 Va.L.Rev.131 (2013). For analysis of the role that tort liability could play in the regulation of large-scale catastrophic risks, see Farber, Tort Law in the Era of Climate Change, Katrina, and 9/11: Exploring Liability for Extraordinary Risks, 43 Val.U.L.Rev. 1075 (2009).

CHAPTER XI

DAMAGES AND INSURANCE

Our emphasis so far has been on the doctrinal development of negligence and strict liability, with principal attention to legal liability in various fact patterns. By and large, tort defendants are less concerned with the concept of liability than with the consequences of that liability—the imposition of damages. Corporations and businesses often treat tort liability as a cost of doing business, and so they are primarily concerned only about the total annual cost of tort liability. One potential exception is that adverse publicity about a case, particularly one involving product quality, may cause significant harm to a company's good will. Similarly, a defendant charged with professional malpractice may worry about liability because a small adverse judgment or even the filing of suit may tarnish, for example, a physician's reputation in some communities and produce considerable emotional harm.

We begin this chapter with an introduction to the basic items of recoverable damages and highlight the central problems of damage measurement. We then examine how tort law interacts with the institution of insurance. The role of insurance in the course so far has been obscured by the collateral source rule, a common law doctrine that permits full recovery even when the plaintiff has insurance coverage for claimed tort damages, such as medical expenses. The role of insurance is further obscured by an evidence rule that excludes proof concerning the defendant's insurance coverage for tort liabilities. These rules prevent insurance from factoring into the jury's determination of damages, and yet both forms of coverage substantially influence the practice of tort law in a manner that might not otherwise be apparent from a study of the doctrinal bases for liability.

A. DAMAGES

1. COMPENSATORY DAMAGES

The fundamental goal of damage awards in the unintentional tort area is to return the plaintiff as closely as possible to his or her condition before the accident. This is achieved by measuring certain items of harm in past and future terms. The total amount of these past and future damages is usually awarded in a single lump-sum award pursuant to the common law single judgment rule, which provides that plaintiff sue only once for the harm she has suffered. Plaintiff generally has no further legal recourse after she recovers a judgment, even if she sustains unanticipated harm that is related to the defendant's tortious conduct. Thus, in Fetter v. Beale (1697) 91 Eng.Rep. 1122 (K.B.), plaintiff sued defendant and recovered £11 for bruises suffered from defendant's battery. Thereafter, "part of his skull by reason of the said battery came out of his head," and he brought a second suit to recover damages for that injury. The court entered judgment for defendant, blaming plaintiff for suing too quickly in the first action. What if the statute of limitations was about to run on plaintiff's claim? What should the law do if the plaintiff makes an unexpected recovery shortly after winning an award that anticipated a continuing disability?

Instead of accepting projections and predictions, the law might have required plaintiff to sue at regular intervals for harm incurred since the last suit. Such a procedure has obvious advantages and disadvantages, including better accuracy in determining the amount of the damages and the time and expense of repeated litigation over damages. See generally Henderson, Designing a Responsible Periodic-Payment System for Tort Awards: Arizona Enacts a Prototype, 32 Ariz.L.Rev. 21, 25–26 (1990)(describing the attributes and benefits of a system that would pay an injured plaintiff periodically). The principal cases in this chapter all involve the single judgment and single payment approach.

Seffert v. Los Angeles Transit Lines

Supreme Court of California, 1961.
56 Cal.2d 498, 364 P.2d 337, 15 Cal.Rptr. 161.

■ PETERS, J.

Defendants appeal from a judgment for plaintiff for $187,903.75[*] entered on a jury verdict. Their motion for a new trial for errors of law and excessiveness of damages was denied.

At the trial plaintiff contended that she was properly entering defendants' bus when the doors closed suddenly catching her right hand and left foot. The bus started, dragged her some distance, and then threw her to the pavement. Defendants contended that the injury resulted from plaintiff's own negligence, that she was late for work and either ran into the side of the bus after the doors had closed or ran after the bus and attempted to enter after the doors had nearly closed.

The evidence supports plaintiff's version of the facts. Several eyewitnesses testified that plaintiff started to board the bus while it was standing with the doors wide open. Defendants do not challenge the sufficiency of the evidence. They do contend, however, that prejudicial errors were committed during the trial and that the verdict is excessive.

[Here Justice Peters rejected the defendants' contention that the trial judge had made certain erroneous legal rulings during the trial. He continued:]

---

[*]   [In 2015 dollars this amount is approximately $1.5 million.—Eds.]

One of the major contentions of defendants is that the damages are excessive, as a matter of law. There is no merit to this contention.

The evidence most favorable to the plaintiff shows that prior to the accident plaintiff was in good health, and had suffered no prior serious injuries. She was single, and had been self-supporting for 20 of her 42 years. The accident happened on October 11, 1957. The trial took place in July and August of 1959.

As already pointed out, the injury occurred when plaintiff was caught in the doors of defendants' bus when it started up before she had gained full entry. As a result she was dragged for some distance. The record is uncontradicted that her injuries were serious, painful, disabling and permanent.

The major injuries were to plaintiff's left foot. The main arteries and nerves leading to that foot, and the posterior tibial vessels and nerve of that foot, were completely severed at the ankle. The main blood vessel which supplies blood to that foot had to be tied off, with the result that there is a permanent stoppage of the main blood source. The heel and shin bones were fractured. There were deep lacerations and an avulsion[3] which involved the skin and soft tissue of the entire foot.

These injuries were extremely painful. They have resulted in a permanently raised left heel, which is two inches above the floor level, caused by the contraction of the ankle joint capsule. Plaintiff is crippled and will suffer pain for life.[4] Although this pain could, perhaps, be alleviated by an operative fusion of the ankle, the doctors considered and rejected this procedure because the area has been deprived of its normal blood supply. The foot is not only permanently deformed but has a persistent open ulcer on the heel, there being a continuous drainage from the entire area. Medical care of this foot and ankle is to be reasonably expected for the remainder of plaintiff's life.

Since the accident, and because of it, plaintiff has undergone nine operations and has spent eight months in various hospitals and rehabilitation centers. These operations involved painful skin grafting and other painful procedures. One involved the surgical removal of gangrenous skin leaving painful raw and open flesh exposed from the heel to the toe. Another involved a left lumbar sympathectomy in which plaintiff's abdomen was entered to sever the nerves affecting the remaining blood vessels of the left leg in order to force those blood vessels to remain open at all times to the maximum extent. Still another operation involved a cross leg flap graft of skin and tissue from plaintiff's thigh which required that her left foot be brought up to her right thigh and held at this painful angle, motionless, and in a cast for a month until the flap of skin and fat, partially removed from her thigh,

---

[3]   Defined in Webster's New International Dictionary (2d ed.) as a "tearing asunder; forcible separation."

[4]   Her life expectancy was 34.9 years from the time of trial.

but still nourished there by a skin connection, could be grafted to the bottom of her foot, and until the host site could develop enough blood vessels to support it. Several future operations of this nature may be necessary. One result of this operation was to leave a defective area of the thigh where the normal fat is missing and the muscles exposed, and the local nerves are missing. This condition is permanent and disfiguring.

Another operation called a debridement, was required. This involved removal of many small muscles of the foot, much of the fat beneath the skin, cleaning the end of the severed nerve, and tying off the severed vein and artery.

The ulcer on the heel is probably permanent, and there is the constant and real danger that osteomyelitis may develop if the infection extends into the bone. If this happens the heel bone would have to be removed surgically and perhaps the entire foot amputated.

Although plaintiff has gone back to work, she testified that she has difficulty standing, walking or even sitting, and must lie down frequently; that the leg is still very painful; that she can, even on her best days, walk not over three blocks and that very slowly; that her back hurts from walking; that she is tired and weak; that her sleep is disturbed; that she has frequent spasms in which the leg shakes uncontrollably; that she feels depressed and unhappy, and suffers humiliation and embarrassment.

Plaintiff claims that there is evidence that her total pecuniary loss, past and future, amounts to $53,903.75. This was the figure used by plaintiff's counsel in his argument to the jury, in which he also claimed $134,000 for pain and suffering, past and future. Since the verdict was exactly the total of these two estimates, it is reasonable to assume that the jury accepted the amount proposed by counsel for each item.

The summary of plaintiff as to pecuniary loss, past and future, is as follows:

Doctor and Hospital Bills	$10,330.50	
Drugs and other medical expenses stipulated to in the amount of	2,273.25	
Loss of earnings from time of accident to time of trial	5,500.00	$18,103.75
Future Medical Expenses:		
$2,000 per year for next 10 years	20,000.00	
$200 per year for the 24 years thereafter	4,800.00	
Drugs for 34 years	1,000.00	25,800.00
		43,903.75
Possible future loss of earnings		10,000.00
Total Pecuniary Loss		$53,903.75

There is substantial evidence to support these estimates. The amounts for past doctor and hospital bills, for the cost of drugs, and for a past loss of earnings, were either stipulated to, evidence was offered on, or is a simple matter of calculation. These items totaled $18,103.75. While the amount of $25,800 estimated as the cost of future medical expense, for loss of future earnings and for the future cost of drugs, may seem high, there was substantial evidence that future medical expense is certain to be high. There is also substantial evidence that plaintiff's future earning capacity may be substantially impaired by reason of the injury. The amounts estimated for those various items are not out of line, and find support in the evidence.

This leaves the amount of $134,000 presumably allowed for the nonpecuniary items of damage, including pain and suffering, past and future. It is this allowance that defendants seriously attack as being excessive as a matter of law.

It must be remembered that the jury fixed these damages, and that the trial judge denied a motion for new trial, one ground of which was excessiveness of the award. These determinations are entitled to great weight. The amount of damages is a fact question, first committed to the discretion of the jury and next to the discretion of the trial judge on a motion for new trial. They see and hear the witnesses and frequently, as in this case, see the injury and the impairment that has resulted therefrom. As a result, all presumptions are in favor of the decision of the trial court. [ ] The power of the appellate court differs materially from that of the trial court in passing on this question. An appellate court can interfere on the ground that the judgment is excessive only on the ground that the verdict is so large that, at first blush, it shocks the conscience and suggests passion, prejudice or corruption on the part of the jury. The proper rule was stated in Holmes v. Southern Cal. Edison Co., [177 P.2d 32 (Cal.App.1947)], as follows: "The powers and duties of a trial judge in ruling on a motion for new trial and of an appellate court on an appeal from a judgment are very different when the question of an excessive award of damages arises. The trial judge sits as a thirteenth juror with the power to weigh the evidence and judge the credibility of the witnesses. If he believes the damages awarded by the jury to be excessive and the question is presented it becomes his duty to reduce them. [ ] When the question is raised his denial of a motion of new trial is an indication that he approves the amount of the award. An appellate court has no such powers. It cannot weigh the evidence and pass on the credibility of the witnesses as a juror does. To hold an award excessive it must be so large as to indicate passion or prejudice on the part of the jurors." . . .

There are no fixed or absolute standards by which an appellate court can measure in monetary terms the extent of the damages suffered by a plaintiff as a result of the wrongful act of the defendant. . . . The amount to be awarded is "a matter on which there legitimately may be a wide difference of opinion" [ ]. . . .

While the appellate court should consider the amounts awarded in prior cases for similar injuries, obviously, each case must be decided on its own facts and circumstances. Such examination demonstrates that such awards vary greatly. (See exhaustive annotations in [ ].) Injuries are seldom identical and the amount of pain and suffering involved in similar physical injuries varies widely. These factors must be considered. [ ] Basically, the question that should be decided by the appellate courts is whether or not the verdict is so out of line with reason that it shocks the conscience and necessarily implies that the verdict must have been the result of passion and prejudice.

In the instant case, the nonpecuniary items of damage include allowances for pain and suffering, past and future, humiliation as a result of being disfigured and being permanently crippled, and constant anxiety and fear that the leg will have to be amputated. While the amount of the award is high, and may be more than we would have awarded were we the trier of the facts, considering the nature of the injury, the great pain and suffering, past and future, and the other items of damage, we cannot say, as a matter of law, that it is so high that it shocks the conscience and gives rise to the presumption that it was the result of passion or prejudice on the part of the jurors.

Defendants next complain that it was prejudicial error for plaintiff's counsel to argue to the jury that damages for pain and suffering could be fixed by means of a mathematical formula predicated upon a per diem allowance for this item of damages. The propriety of such an argument seems never to have been passed upon in this state. In other jurisdictions there is a sharp divergence of opinion on the subject. [ ] It is not necessary to pass on the propriety of such argument in the instant case because, when plaintiff's counsel made the argument in question, defendants' counsel did not object, assign it as misconduct or ask that the jury be admonished to disregard it. Moreover, in his argument to the jury, the defendants' counsel also adopted a mathematical formula type of argument. This being so, even if such argument were error (a point we do not pass upon), the point must be deemed to have been waived, and cannot be raised properly, on appeal. [ ]

The judgment appealed from is affirmed.

■ GIBSON, C.J., WHITE, J., and DOOLING, J., concurred.

■ TRAYNOR, J. I dissent.

Although I agree that there was no prejudicial error on the issue of liability, it is my opinion that the award of $134,000 for pain and suffering is so excessive as to indicate that it was prompted by passion, prejudice, whim, or caprice.

Before the accident plaintiff was employed as a file clerk at a salary of $375 a month. At the time of the trial she had returned to her job at the same salary and her foot had healed sufficiently for her to walk. At the time of the accident she was 42 years old with a life expectancy of 34.9 years.

During closing argument plaintiff's counsel summarized the evidence relevant to past and possible future damages and proposed a specific amount for each item. His total of $187,903.75 was the exact amount awarded by the jury.

His proposed amounts were as follows:

. . .

Total Pecuniary Loss		$ 53,903.75
Pain and Suffering:		
From time of accident to time of trial (660 days) @ $100 a day . . .	$66,000.00	
For the remainder of her life (34 years) @ $2,000 a year	68,000.00	134,000.00
Total proposed by counsel		$187,903.75

The jury and the trial court have broad discretion in determining the damages in a personal injury case. [ ] A reviewing court, however, has responsibilities not only to the litigants in an action but to future litigants and must reverse or remit when a jury awards either inadequate or excessive damages. [ ]

The crucial question in this case, therefore, is whether the award of $134,000 for pain and suffering is so excessive it must have resulted from passion, prejudice, whim or caprice. "To say that a verdict has been influenced by passion or prejudice is but another way of saying that the verdict exceeds any amount justified by the evidence." (Zibbell v. Southern Pacific Co., [116 P. 513 (Cal.1911)]; [ ].)

There has been forceful criticism of the rationale for awarding damages for pain and suffering in negligence cases. [ ] Such damages originated under primitive law as a means of punishing wrongdoers and assuaging the feelings of those who had been wronged. [ ] They become increasingly anomalous as emphasis shifts in a mechanized society from ad hoc punishment to orderly distribution of losses through insurance and the price of goods or of transportation. Ultimately such losses are borne by a public free of fault as part of the price for the benefits of mechanization. [ ]

Nonetheless, this state has long recognized pain and suffering as elements of damages in negligence cases [ ]; any change in this regard must await reexamination of the problem by the Legislature. Meanwhile, awards for pain and suffering serve to ease plaintiffs' discomfort and to pay for attorney fees for which plaintiffs are not otherwise compensated.

It would hardly be possible ever to compensate a person fully for pain and suffering. "No rational being would change places with the injured man for an amount of gold that would fill the room of the court, yet no lawyer would contend that such is the legal measure of damages." ([*Zibbell*]; see 2 Harper and James, The Law of Torts 1322.) "Translating pain and anguish into dollars can, at best, be only an arbitrary allowance, and not a process of measurement and consequently the judge can, in his instructions give the jury no standard to go by; he can only tell them to allow such amount as in their discretion they may consider reasonable. . . . The chief reliance for reaching reasonable results in attempting to value suffering in terms of money must be the restraint and common sense of the jury. . . ." (McCormick, Damages, § 88, pp. 318–319.) Such restraint and common sense were lacking here.

A review of reported cases involving serious injuries and large pecuniary losses reveals that ordinarily the part of the verdict attributable to pain and suffering does not exceed the part attributable to pecuniary losses. [ ] The award in this case of $134,000 for pain and suffering exceeds not only the pecuniary losses but any such award heretofore sustained in this state even in cases involving injuries more serious by far than those suffered by plaintiff. [ ] In *McNulty v. Southern Pacific Co.* [ ], the court reviewed a large number of cases involving injuries to legs and feet, in each of which the total judgment, including both pecuniary loss and pain and suffering did not exceed $100,000. Although excessive damages is "an issue which is primarily factual and is not therefore a matter which can be decided upon the basis of awards made in other cases" [ ], awards for similar injuries may be considered as one factor to be weighed in determining whether the damages awarded are excessive. [ ].

The excessive award in this case was undoubtedly the result of the improper argument of plaintiff's counsel to the jury. Though no evidence was introduced, though none could possibly be introduced on the monetary value of plaintiff's suffering, counsel urged the jury to award $100 a day for pain and suffering from the time of the accident to the time of trial and $2,000 a year for pain and suffering for the remainder of plaintiff's life.

The propriety of counsel's proposing a specific sum for each day or month of suffering has recently been considered by courts of several jurisdictions. [ ] The reasons for and against permitting "per diem argument for pain and suffering" are reviewed in [ ] [1959 Florida decision holding such argument is permissible] and *Botta v. Brunner*, [1958 New Jersey decision holding such argument to be an "unwarranted intrusion into the domain of the jury"].

The reason usually advanced for not allowing such argument is that since there is no way of translating pain and suffering into monetary terms, counsel's proposal of a particular sum for each day of suffering represents an opinion and a conclusion on matters not disclosed by the evidence, and tends to mislead the jury and result in excessive awards. The reason usually advanced for allowing "per diem argument for pain and suffering" is that it affords the jury as good an arbitrary measure as any for that which cannot be measured.

Counsel may argue all legitimate inferences from the evidence, but he may not employ arguments that tend primarily to mislead the jury. [ ] A specified sum for pain and suffering for any particular period is bound to be conjectural. Positing such a sum for a small period of time and then multiplying that sum by the number of days, minutes or seconds in plaintiff's life expectancy multiplies the hazards of conjecture. Counsel could arrive at any amount he wished by adjusting either the period of time to be taken as a measure or the amount surmised for the pain for that period.

. . .

The misleading effect of the per diem argument was not cured by the use of a similar argument by defense counsel. Truth is not served by a clash of sophistic arguments. (See Michael and Adler, The Trial of an Issue of Fact, 34 Colum.L.Rev. 1224, 1483–1484.) Had defendant objected to the improper argument of plaintiff's counsel this error would be a sufficient ground for reversal whether or not the award was excessive as a matter of law. Defendant's failure to object, however, did not preclude its appeal on the ground that the award was excessive as a matter of law or preclude this court's reversing on that ground and ruling on the impropriety of counsel's argument to guide the court on the retrial. [ ]

I would reverse the judgment and remand the cause for a new trial on the issue of damages.

■ SCHAUER, J., and MCCOMB, J., concurred.

NOTES AND QUESTIONS

1. *Standard of proof.* Did the evidence show that the plaintiff, more likely than not, would suffer the amount of damages for future injuries awarded by the jury? How would such a standard affect the plaintiff's ability to recover damages for future injuries, such as lost wages? Recognizing that such proof is often unavailable and the concomitant unfairness that would exist if defendants could avoid liability on these grounds, courts employ a standard of proof in the damages phase of the case that differs from the standard applicable to the prima facie case. The plaintiff is required to establish the amount of damages with "as much certainty as the nature of the tort and the circumstances permit." Restatement (Second) of Torts § 912 (1979).

2. *Past pecuniary losses.* The most easily proven category of recoverable damages is past pecuniary losses—in *Seffert* those incurred for doctors, hospitals, drugs, and lost earnings. Most of the medical expenses are established by bills, and these are ordinarily accepted. See p. 774 infra. Lost earnings may be a bit more complicated to establish, especially for self-employed persons, but can usually be reconstructed without much difficulty.

One recurrent problem in awarding lost earnings is the question of taxation. Although some percentage of the gross wages lost would have been taxed if the plaintiff had in fact earned them, Congress has decided that compensatory damage awards for physical injury (but not pure emotional harm) are not taxable. What, if anything, should the judge charge the jury on this question? Some courts say nothing and let the jury think whatever it might on the subject. Others charge the jury that the award of lost earnings is not taxable and that the jury should not worry about being sure that plaintiff gets enough to pay the taxes. See Lanzano v. City of New York, 519 N.E.2d 331 (N.Y.1988). In an effort to remove the ambiguity about when and how the jury should be told about the tax implications, one court has decided that "the measurement of after-tax income is the 'more accurate and therefore proper, measure of damages'" and that the plaintiff has the burden of proving that sum. Caldwell v. Haynes, 643 A.2d 564 (N.J.1994).

3. *Future pecuniary losses.* As *Seffert* shows, physical harm may cause losses into the future. To take the easiest case, the evidence shows that the plaintiff will need a specific drug for the next five years. There are of course no bills yet. But the jury must calculate the cost now. How much will the drug cost over the next five years? What is the expected rate of inflation for the prescription drug market? If the plaintiff requires physical therapy or psychological counseling in the future, how long will the course of treatment be needed? If any of these expenses appear likely to be life-long, life expectancy tables will be used.* Should the trier then consider health factors unrelated to the accident, such as smoking, and reduce plaintiff's life expectancy and damages accordingly?

Even more complicated than determining future medical expenses is the task of calculating the plaintiff's future earnings. For example, assume that at the time of her injury, a plaintiff had been earning $50,000 a year but now will not be able to work again. (Of course, in some litigation the permanence of plaintiff's disability will be hotly contested, but assume our plaintiff is completely disabled.) In order to decide how large her award should be, the court must first determine how many years she would have worked had she not been injured. The plaintiff might have died in an unrelated accident shortly after trial, in which case she hardly would have worked at all, or she could live into her nineties and have a long, productive career. Perhaps she smokes and so would have a shorter life expectancy than others her age who do not smoke. This question is further complicated

---

* Life expectancy is determined based on standardized tables that provide the average remaining years of life for all persons of a given age. They are broken down by gender and other characteristics that reflect different life expectancies. Life expectancy is determined as of the time of trial, because future damages are awarded from that time.

by the increasing unpredictability of retirement ages. Given these uncertainties, attorneys may begin with the average work career of an employee in plaintiff's field and present evidence on whether there is reason to believe the plaintiff's career would have varied from the norm.

Should the average work career (or other matters) be determined based on tables that combine both genders or on gender-specific statistics? Which would be more accurate? Fairer? These questions are addressed in Chamallas, Questioning the Use of Race-Specific and Gender-Specific Economic Data in Tort Litigation: A Constitutional Argument, 63 Fordham L.Rev. 73 (1994), which argues that employing race- and sex-based data to determine lost earnings capacity in a judicial proceeding continues existing discrimination, is bad social policy, and violates the Equal Protection Clause of the Fourteenth Amendment. See also Wriggins, Damages in Tort Litigation: Thoughts on Race and Remedies, 1865–2007, 27 Rev.Litig. 37 (2007). In McMillan v. City of New York, 253 F.R.D. 247 (E.D.N.Y.2008), Judge Weinstein accepted the Chamallas argument and held that race-specific actuarial tables could not be used in a case brought by an African-American victim of a ferry crash. The tables showed shorter life expectancies for African-Americans than for those of other races. Judge Weinstein applied this ruling in a recent case involving a child injured by lead-paint poisoning. "Posed is the question, can statistics based on the ethnicity (in this case, 'Hispanic') of a child be relied upon to find a reduced likelihood of his obtaining higher education, resulting in reduced damages in a tort case? The answer is no." G.M.M. v. Kimpson, 2015 WL 4572470 (E.D.N.Y.2015).

Lost earnings for a badly injured or deceased child who has no prior work experience are particularly hard to determine. Consider Greyhound Lines, Inc. v. Sutton, 765 So.2d 1269 (Miss.2000), holding in a wrongful death action that future income for a child with no earnings record should be calculated based on a "rebuttable presumption that the deceased child's income would have been the equivalent of the national average as set forth by the United States Department of Labor," although either side could rebut by presenting relevant evidence that might include such things as "precocity, mental and physical health, intellectual development, and relevant family circumstances."

A related set of issues involves adults who are either unemployed or underemployed. In these cases, the harm is understood as the lost earning capacity, and so a plaintiff may recover for what she would have been able to earn with the earning capacity that defendant has harmed. Thus, in Martinez v. Shapland, 833 P.2d 837 (Colo.App.1992), the plaintiff was unemployed at the time of trial. Nevertheless, the court held that she was entitled to an instruction on lost earnings capacity based on her prior employment as a nurse's aide. How should damages be calculated for a plaintiff under a legal disability preventing work, such as incarceration or undocumented alien status? Compare Silva v. Wilcox, 223 P.3d 127 (Colo.App.2009)(deciding that immigration status is relevant and admissible, thereby leaving to the jury the decision whether to award anything for lost wages, to discount the amount of lost wages, or to award all lost wages), with Hoffman Plastic Compounds, Inc. v. NLRB, 535 U.S. 137 (2002)(holding that backpay could not be awarded by the National Labor Relations Board to an undocumented alien who was fired in violation of federal law because such an award would be in contravention of policy expressed in the Immigration Reform and Control Act of 1986, which makes it unlawful for employers knowingly to hire undocumented workers or for employees to use fraudulent documents to establish employment eligibility).

Even if the plaintiff had been fully employed, the award for lost earnings cannot be set by multiplying her current wage by the number of years she had left to work. A worker's wages rarely remain stable over the course of a lifetime. What about promotions and merit raises? Even without these personal achievements, the plaintiff's wages could be expected to rise. In the decades after World War II, increases in productivity resulted in an overall rise in wages for workers as a class. Apart from these "real" increases in workers' wages, many workers have contractual cost of living adjustments that automatically increase their wages in relation to the consumer price index so that general inflation also raises wages. And what about fringe benefits such as medical coverage, pensions, and retirement plans?

What if the plaintiff claims to have lost an opportunity for great financial success? In Snow v. Villacci, 754 A.2d 360, 362 (Me.2000), plaintiff was enrolled in a 25-month program to become a "financial consultant" at a major brokerage house. In the 20th month, his success "was possible but not assured." At that time he was injured by defendant and lost 14 weeks of work. Although the firm gave him extra time, plaintiff alleged that he was unable to complete the program. The claimed consequence was that although the firm retained him in another capacity, he was unable to complete the program and would not be allowed another chance to do so. The court held that if plaintiff could show that he had been deprived of a special opportunity to which he had already been given access, and would have succeeded but for the injury, he might be able to recover for this loss. The court noted that, because the case had been decided on summary judgment, it had no occasion to consider how far into the future any recovery might reach. See also Cook v. Cook, 607 S.E.2d 459, 467 (W.Va.2004)(Davis, J. concurring)(explaining the difference between lost future income and loss of an earnings opportunity).

After the plaintiff has presented evidence about the amount of damages, the defendant is likely to pose countervailing considerations. Shouldn't the plaintiff, who no longer has to commute, or buy business clothes or uniforms, and thus no longer incurs the cost of these expenses, have them deducted from her award for future earnings? Moreover, as mentioned above, the plaintiff's lump-sum award is tax-free, so her lost future earnings arguably should be based only on after-tax earnings. Often a court will offset some of these variables, declaring, for instance, that lost fringe benefits will be roughly equal to the decrease in work-related expenses.

4. *Discounting to present value.* Assume that after considering all of these factors, the trier of fact determines that the plaintiff would have worked for the next five years and that her after-tax salary in those years would be $50,000, $52,000, $55,000, $58,000, and $60,000 for a total of $275,000. Our calculations are not yet done. To award the plaintiff a lump sum of $275,000 would be to overcompensate her, because by investing the total amount at the outset, she could earn interest on the lump sum that, combined with the initial amount of principal, would exceed her lost future earnings. To adjust for this earning potential, the court must reduce the plaintiff's award to its present value. In other words, the trier of fact must determine the amount of money the plaintiff should be awarded today so that, if invested prudently, it will earn interest sufficient to support a pay-out over five years equal to what her income-stream would have been. Although the original lump-sum award is tax-free, the interest earned on it is not, so the original award will have to be high enough to earn interest that will cover the taxes and still provide an equivalent payout.

Thus, in order to determine the proper award, the factfinder must decide upon a discount rate, which is in effect the estimated return on a prudent investment for the next five years. Each party will present evidence as to why its estimate of this uncertain figure is the better one. Adding to the complexity is the inflation rate. Although the plaintiff may earn additional money through interest, that money may be worth less because of inflation. Plaintiff will argue that her award should not be discounted because the inflation rate and the return on investment cancel each other out. Do they?

Courts are divided on how to handle this issue. Some accept the "total offset" rationale. See Kaczkowski v. Bolubasz, 421 A.2d 1027, 1038–39 (Pa.1980)("[A]s a matter of law . . . future inflation shall be presumed equal to future interest rates with these factors offsetting"). Other courts adopt the theory that the market interest rate reflects three factors: risk, protection from inflation, and the "real interest rate." The risk element should not be considered in the tort award, because the plaintiff should make only "safe" investments to ensure compensation. That leaves the real interest rate and the inflationary rate. In determining the discount rate for a tort award, these courts believe that the real interest rate is the proper rate to use for discounting, allowing inflation to be offset by the "inflationary interest rate." Otherwise, a total offset would overcompensate the plaintiff. Under this approach, if the annual real interest rate were 2%, a damages award of $1,000 for an injury ten years from now would be about $820 today. For comprehensive discussions of these issues, see Jones & Laughlin Steel Corp. v. Pfeifer, 462 U.S. 523 (1983) and Brody, Inflation, Productivity, and the Total Offset Method of Calculating Damages for Lost Future Earnings, 49 U.Chi.L.Rev. 1003 (1982).

5. *Pain and suffering.* We turn now to the nonpecuniary losses that formed the core of the *Seffert* case. What is the theoretical justification for awarding damages in this type of case for pain and suffering?

Among the articles cited by Justice Traynor, Jaffe's offered the sharpest attack on pain and suffering awards. Jaffe, Damages for Personal

Injury: The Impact of Insurance, 18 Law & Contemp.Probs. 219 (1953). Jaffe recognized that when the defendant's conduct is "reprehensible, damages are an apt instrument of punishment" because criminal law is a clumsy way to handle "unsocial activity. . . . To pay money to one's victim is a salutary humiliation." But justification was harder when the defendant's behavior was negligent rather than willful. The usual justification here is that, although there is no way to measure the loss in question, plaintiff has in fact lost "something" and the wrongdoer should not escape liability because of the difficulty of valuation.

But Jaffe challenged this rationale, arguing that "[p]ain is a harm, an 'injury,' but neither past pain nor its compensation has any consistent economic significance. The past experience is not a loss except in so far as it produced present deterioration. . . . Insurance aside, it is doubtful justice seriously to embarrass a defendant, though negligent, by real economic loss in order to do honor to plaintiff's experience of pain." Id. at 224–25. See also King, Pain and Suffering, Noneconomic Damages, and the Goals of Tort Law, 57 SMU L.Rev. 163 (2004).

Are there other arguments supporting recovery for pain and suffering that are not mentioned here? Consider the plaintiff in *Seffert*, who prior to the injury had substantially different choices available to her as compared to her condition following the accident. "Self-altering injuries constrain one's ability to maintain [or pursue] a set of commitments. These constraints are harms." Williams, Self-Altering Injury: The Hidden Harms of Hedonic Adaptation, 96 Cornell L.Rev. 535 (2011); see also Ogus, Damages for Lost Amenities: For a Foot, a Feeling or a Function?, 35 Mod.L.Rev. 1 (1972).

Compare Kwasny v. United States, 823 F.2d 194 (7th Cir.1987), in which the court affirmed an award under the Federal Tort Claims Act. In passing, Judge Posner observed:

> We disagree with those students of tort law who believe that pain and suffering are not real costs and should not be allowable items of damages in a tort suit. No one likes pain and suffering and most people would pay a good deal of money to be free of them. If they were not recoverable in damages, the cost from negligence would be less to the tortfeasors and there would be more negligence, more accidents, more pain and suffering, and hence higher social costs.

Do you agree? Is the deterrence argument more powerful than the compensation argument for pain and suffering awards? Can damages for pain and suffering be justified on deterrence grounds even if people would not insure, in advance, against the prospect of such losses? For discussion of these issues, see Croley & Hanson, The Nonpecuniary Costs of Accidents: Pain-and-Suffering Damages in Tort Law, 108 Harv.L.Rev. 1785 (1995); Schwartz, Proposals for Products Liability Reform: A Theoretical Synthesis, 97 Yale L.J. 353, 362–67 (1988). For an assessment of pain and suffering in the broader context of intangible loss recovery in tort, see

Rabin, Pain and Suffering and Beyond: Some Thoughts on Recovery for Intangible Loss, 55 DePaul L.Rev. 359 (2005).

6. *Judicial review.* Recall that the *Seffert* court employed a limited "shocks the conscience" standard to determine if the damage award was so excessive as to permit an appellate court to interfere. Can a verdict be so "excessive" as to call for reduction even if it does not shock the judicial conscience? In the mid-1980s New York enacted a statute that directed the appellate division to "determine that an award is excessive or inadequate if it deviates materially from what would be reasonable compensation." N.Y. CPLR § 5501(c). Whatever the standard, it functions differently for trial judges and appellate judges for reasons discussed by *Seffert.* Do you think that one is more likely to affirm the verdict than the other?

7. *Remittitur and additur.* When a court is persuaded that a verdict is excessive, two options exist. One is to grant a new trial in which damages (and perhaps liability as well) will be retried before another jury. Another device is to grant a remittitur, by which the court conditionally grants a new trial, unless the plaintiff consents to a reduction of the damage award to an amount that the court believes is not excessive. Consider a plaintiff's decisionmaking calculus when a court orders a remittitur.

The complement of a remittitur is an additur, employed when the court believes that the damages awarded are inadequate as a matter of law. Again, a new trial is ordered unless the defendant agrees to an adjustment upward in the amount of damages awarded. Additurs are less frequently invoked in state courts and never used in federal court because the Supreme Court decided that they violate the Seventh Amendment right to a jury trial. See Dimick v. Schiedt, 293 U.S. 474 (1935).

8. *Per diems and other monetary guides.* Courts are divided over the wisdom of giving the jury some monetary guidelines when it considers pain and suffering. Most states permit arguments using monetary guidelines. A few permit the argument but without numbers. E.g., Friedman v. C & S Car Service, 527 A.2d 871 (N.J.1987). On the other hand, in Carchidi v. Rodenhiser, 551 A.2d 1249, 1252 (Conn.1989), the court, noting that it had already barred plaintiffs from naming the amount sought in the complaint and did not permit *per diem* arguments, barred the plaintiff's attorney in closing arguments from giving the jury any number that would be an appropriate award for pain and suffering because of the "risk of improper influence upon a jury." *Carchidi* was overturned by a statute providing that in any damage action counsel for any party "shall be entitled to specifically articulate to the trier of fact during closing arguments, in lump sums or by mathematical formulae, the amount of past and future economic and noneconomic damages claimed to be recoverable." Conn.Gen.Stat. § 52–216b(a). The jury is to be told that the numbers are arguments but not evidence. § 52–216b(b).

9. *Discounting awards for intangible losses.* However the sum for intangible awards is arrived at, there is the further question of discounting. The great majority of courts do not discount these awards because of the "incongruity of discounting to present value damages that are, by their very nature, so speculative and imprecise." The use of time-unit arguments may lend an "aura of rationality" to this type of award but does not convert the award into one for economic loss. To allow discounting here "would add to the time, expense, and complexity of civil trials without any corresponding enhancement of the reliability, accuracy, or fairness of damages awards." Friedman v. C & S Car Service, 527 A.2d 871, 875 (N.J.1987); see also Levine v. Wyeth, 944 A.2d 179 (Vt.2006), aff'd on other grounds, 555 U.S. 555 (2009). But see Gretchen v. United States, 618 F.2d 177 (2d Cir.1980)(discounting the award).

10. *Variability of pain and suffering awards.* Empirical studies have found that the severity of injury is a good predictor of the size of a pain and suffering award. Injury severity, however, explains only part of these awards. "Vertical equity"—the degree to which more severe types of injury receive more compensation, on average, than less severe ones—"is rather good. The main problem is the absence of 'horizontal equity'—the extent of variation within a single category." Bovbjerg, Sloan & Blumstein, Valuing Life and Limb in Tort: Scheduling "Pain and Suffering," 83 Nw.U.L.Rev. 908, 924 (1989). "Similarly injured plaintiffs who experience similar pain and endure similar suffering are often awarded vastly differing amounts of damages." Leebron, Final Moments: Damages for Pain and Suffering Prior to Death, 64 N.Y.U.L.Rev. 256, 310 (1989).

11. *The precedential value of prior awards.* In Blumstein, Bovbjerg & Sloan, Beyond Tort Reform: Developing Better Tools for Assessing Damages for Personal Injury, 8 Yale J.Reg. 171 (1991), the authors observe that liability decisions rely on precedent to narrow the range of choice, while with damages we give jurors no guidance from prior results. In their view, prior awards should be collected and analyzed. Information "on the spectrum of prior damage awards should be provided to juries, judges, or both, as an aid to decisionmaking." The jury should be told that if it wants to make an award in the top (or bottom) quartile of past results it must justify that result by pointing to facts in its case that tilt it to the high (or low) side of the range. "An unexplained outlier should constitute a prima facie case for either remittitur or additur by the trial judge or an appellate holding of inadequacy or excessiveness of the judgment." For a similar approach, using the analogy of prison sentencing guidelines, see Levin, Pain and Suffering Guidelines: A Cure for Damages Measurement "Anomie," 22 U.Mich.J.L. Reform 303 (1989). Do these efforts resemble Justice Traynor's view in *Seffert*? See also Avraham, Putting a Price on Pain-and-Suffering Damages: A Critique of the Current Approaches and a Preliminary Proposal for Change, 100 Nw.U.L.Rev. 87 (2006)(recommending that pain and suffering awards be based on a non-binding multiplier of medical expenses incurred by the victim); and Sanders, Why Do Proposals Designed to Control Variability in General Damages (Generally) Fall on Deaf Ears? (And Why This is too Bad), 55 DePaul L.Rev. 489 (2006).

In Jutzi-Johnson v. United States, 263 F.3d 753 (7th Cir.2001), the family of a prisoner who committed suicide in jail sued under the Federal Tort Claims Act. In discussing the damages phase of the case, Judge Posner argued in dictum that the trier of fact (here the judge because of the nature of the suit) should consider comparable awards in other Federal Tort Claim Act cases at the first instance rather than hold these until post-trial motions or the appellate stage. He did not address what might be "comparable" or what methodology might be employed to determine comparability. Continuing the theme sounded in *Jutzi-Johnson,* Judge Posner in Arpin v. United States, 521 F.3d 769 (7th Cir.2008), required the trial judge, as finder of fact, in a Federal Tort Claims Act case to explain the basis for a $7 million award to a widow and adult children for loss of consortium. Although Illinois law does not favor consideration of comparable awards, this was a procedural matter and therefore governed by federal law. The court also suggested that the consideration of similar cases might begin by determining the ratio of compensatory to consortium damages in other cases and then deciding whether an adjustment from that overall ratio is appropriate based on the facts of the instant case. If this approach is sound, should it be limited to judges as triers of fact or extended to juries as well?

12. *Size of damage awards.* Given the severity of plaintiff's injury, the combined damage award in *Seffert* was so small as to be almost quaint by today's standards. Compare Meals v. Ford Motor Co., 417 S.W.3d 414 (Tenn. 2013)(upholding jury verdict of $43.8 million, including $39.5 million in non-economic damages, for spinal fracture suffered by a six-year old caused by a defect in defendant's automobile). A study of jury awards in medical malpractice cases (in which damage awards are generally higher than in other categories of torts) for metropolitan New York City, California, and Florida in the mid-1990s found that the largest five percent of jury awards to the most seriously injured were above $40 million in New York City, above $13 million in Florida, and approximately $40 million in California. Notably, the authors also found that those awards were reduced significantly after verdict by remittitur, statutory damage caps in California, comparative fault, and settlement. Vidmar et al., Jury Awards for Medical Malpractice and Post-Verdict Adjustments of Those Awards, 48 DePaul L.Rev. 265 (1998).

13. *Statutory change—caps on awards.* In an effort to reduce the size of damage awards, some states set maximum amounts that may be awarded for "pain and suffering." The movement began in the mid-1970s when California enacted Civil Code § 3333.2, which limited pain and suffering awards in cases brought against health care providers to $250,000. (The amount has not changed, although it would require $1,109,000 to be equivalent in 2015 dollars.) Other states have enacted damage caps—some of which are also limited to malpractice cases, but many of which are applicable across all tort actions. These statutory changes are addressed in greater detail in the discussion of incremental tort reform, at p. 824 infra.

McDougald v. Garber

Court of Appeals of New York, 1989.
73 N.Y.2d 246, 536 N.E.2d 372, 538 N.Y.S.2d 937.

■ WACHTLER, CHIEF JUDGE.

[Defendants' malpractice left plaintiff in a "permanently comatose condition." In her suit for damages the parties agreed that, if liability were established, she would be entitled to the usual pecuniary damage items—past and future loss of earning capacity, and medical expenses, including custodial care. The parties also agreed that plaintiff could not recover damages for conscious pain and suffering unless she were found to have been aware of experiencing them, but they disagreed over whether she had the requisite level of awareness. "At trial, defendants sought to show that Mrs. McDougald's injuries were so severe that she was incapable of either experiencing pain or appreciating her condition. Plaintiffs, on the other hand, introduced proof that Mrs. McDougald responded to certain stimuli to a sufficient extent to indicate that she was aware of her circumstances."

The judge charged that to "experience suffering" there must be "some level of awareness. . . . If, however, you conclude that there is some level of perception or that she is capable of an emotional response at some level, then damages for pain and suffering should be awarded." In addition, the judge charged:

> Damages for the loss of the pleasures and pursuits of life, however, require no awareness of the loss on the part of the injured person. Quite obviously, Emma McDougald is unable to engage in any of the activities which constitute a normal life, the activities she engaged in prior to her injury. . . . Loss of the enjoyment of life may, of course, accompany the physical sensation and emotional responses that we refer to as pain and suffering, and in most cases it does. It is possible, however, for an injured person to lose the enjoyment of life without experiencing any conscious pain and suffering. Damages for this item of injury relate not to what Emma McDougald is aware of, but rather to what she has lost. What her life was prior to her injury and what it has been since September 7, 1978 and what it will be for as long as she lives.

Defendants objected that this item was not a separate recoverable item and, in any event, required awareness of loss.

In addition to pecuniary awards, the jury awarded $1 million for conscious pain and suffering and $3.5 million for loss of enjoyment of life. The judge reduced these amounts to a single award of $2 million. The appellate division affirmed the award as modified. The only issues now before the court on appeal involve "nonpecuniary damages," which the court defined as those damages "awarded to compensate an injured person for the physical and emotional consequences of the injury, such as pain and suffering and the loss of the ability to engage in certain activities."]

   . . .

We begin with the familiar proposition that an award of damages to a person injured by the negligence of another is to compensate the victim, not to punish the wrongdoer [ ]. The goal is to restore the injured party, to the extent possible, to the position that would have been occupied had the wrong not occurred [ ]. To be sure, placing the burden of compensation on the negligent party also serves as a deterrent, but purely punitive damages—that is, those which have no compensatory purpose—are prohibited unless the harmful conduct is intentional, malicious, outrageous, or otherwise aggravated beyond mere negligence [ ].

Damages for nonpecuniary losses are, of course, among those that can be awarded as compensation to the victim. This aspect of damages, however, stands on less certain ground than does an award for pecuniary damages. An economic loss can be compensated in kind by an economic gain; but recovery for noneconomic losses such as pain and suffering and loss of enjoyment of life rests on "the legal fiction that money damages can compensate for a victim's injury" [ ]. We accept this fiction, knowing that although money will neither ease the pain nor restore the victim's abilities, this device is as close as the law can come in its effort to right the wrong. We have no hope of evaluating what has been lost, but a monetary award may provide a measure of solace for the condition created [ ].

Our willingness to indulge this fiction comes to an end, however, when it ceases to serve the compensatory goals of tort recovery. When that limit is met, further indulgence can only result in assessing damages that are punitive. The question posed by this case, then, is whether an award of damages for loss of enjoyment of life to a person whose injuries preclude any awareness of the loss serves a compensatory purpose. We conclude that it does not.

Simply put, an award of money damages in such circumstances has no meaning or utility to the injured person. An award for the loss of enjoyment of life "cannot provide [such a victim] with any consolation or ease any burden resting on him. . . . He cannot spend it upon necessities or pleasures. He cannot experience the pleasure of giving it away" [ ].

We recognize that, as the trial court noted, requiring some cognitive awareness as a prerequisite to recovery for loss of enjoyment of life will result in some cases "in the paradoxical situation that the greater the degree of brain injury inflicted by a negligent defendant, the smaller the award the plaintiff can recover in general damages" [ ]. The force of this argument, however—the temptation to achieve a balance between injury and damages—has nothing to do with meaningful compensation for the victim. Instead, the temptation is rooted in a desire to punish the defendant in proportion to the harm inflicted. However relevant such retributive symmetry may be in the criminal law, it has no place in the law of civil damages, at least in the absence of culpability beyond mere negligence.

Accordingly, we conclude that cognitive awareness is a prerequisite to recovery for loss of enjoyment of life. We do not go so far, however, as to require the fact finder to sort out varying degrees of cognition and determine at what level a particular deprivation can be fully appreciated. With respect to pain and suffering, the trial court charged simply that there must be "some level of awareness" in order for plaintiff to recover. We think that this is an appropriate standard for all aspects of nonpecuniary loss. No doubt the standard ignores analytically relevant levels of cognition, but we resist the desire for analytical purity in favor of simplicity. A more complex instruction might give the appearance of greater precision but, given the limits of our understanding of the human mind, it would in reality lead only to greater speculation.

We turn next to the question whether loss of enjoyment of life should be considered a category of damages separate from pain and suffering.

IV.

There is no dispute here that the fact finder may, in assessing nonpecuniary damages, consider the effect of the injuries on the plaintiff's capacity to lead a normal life. Traditionally, in this State and elsewhere, this aspect of suffering has not been treated as a separate category of damages; instead, the plaintiff's inability to enjoy life to its fullest has been considered one type of suffering to be factored into a general award for nonpecuniary damages, commonly known as pain and suffering.

Recently, however, there has been an attempt to segregate the suffering associated with physical pain from the mental anguish that stems from the inability to engage in certain activities, and to have juries provide a separate award for each. [ ]

Some courts have resisted the effort, primarily on the ground that duplicative and therefore excessive awards would result [ ]. Other courts have allowed separate awards, noting that the types of suffering involved are analytically distinguishable [ ]. Still other courts have questioned the propriety of the practice but held that, in the particular case, separate awards did not constitute reversible error [ ].

In this State, the only appellate decisions to address the question are the decision . . . now under review and the decision of the Second Department in *Nussbaum v. Gibstein* [which the court reverses at the same time it decides *McDougald*]. Those courts were persuaded that the distinctions between the two types of mental anguish justified separate awards and that the potential for duplicative awards could be mitigated by carefully drafted jury instructions. In addition, the courts opined that separate awards would facilitate appellate review concerning the excessiveness of the total damage award.

We do not dispute that distinctions can be found or created between the concepts of pain and suffering and loss of enjoyment of life. If the term "suffering" is limited to the emotional response to the sensation of pain, then the emotional response caused by the limitation of life's activities may be considered qualitatively different [ ]. But suffering need not be so limited—it can easily encompass the frustration and anguish caused by the inability to participate in activities that once brought pleasure. Traditionally, by treating loss of enjoyment of life as a permissible factor in assessing pain and suffering, courts have given the term this broad meaning.

If we are to depart from this traditional approach and approve a separate award for loss of enjoyment of life, it must be on the basis that such an approach will yield a more accurate evaluation of the compensation due to the plaintiff. We have no doubt that, in general, the total award for nonpecuniary damages would increase if we adopted the rule. That separate awards are advocated by plaintiffs and resisted by defendants is sufficient evidence that larger awards are at stake here. But a larger award does not by itself indicate that the goal of compensation has been better served.

The advocates of separate awards contend that because pain and suffering and loss of enjoyment of life can be distinguished, they must be treated separately if the plaintiff is to be compensated fully for each distinct injury suffered. We disagree. Such an analytical approach may have its place when the subject is pecuniary damages, which can be calculated with some precision. But the estimation of nonpecuniary damages is not amenable to such analytical precision and may, in fact, suffer from its application. Translating human suffering into dollars and cents involves no mathematical formula; it rests, as we have said, on a legal fiction. The figure that emerges is unavoidably distorted by the translation. Application of this murky process to the component parts of nonpecuniary injuries (however analytically distinguishable they may be) cannot make it more accurate. If anything, the distortion will be amplified by repetition.

Thus, we are not persuaded that any salutary purpose would be served by having the jury make separate awards for pain and suffering and loss of enjoyment of life. We are confident, furthermore, that the trial advocate's art is a sufficient guarantee that none of the plaintiff's losses will be ignored by the jury.

. . .

[A new trial was ordered as to nonpecuniary damages.]

■ TITONE, JUDGE (dissenting).

The majority's holding represents a compromise position that neither comports with the fundamental principles of tort compensation nor furnishes a satisfactory, logically consistent framework for compensating nonpecuniary loss. Because I conclude that loss of enjoyment of life is an objective damage item, conceptually distinct from conscious pain and suffering, I can find no fault with the trial court's instruction authorizing separate awards and permitting an award for "loss of enjoyment of life" even in the absence of any awareness of that loss on the part of the injured plaintiff. Accordingly, I dissent.

It is elementary that the purpose of awarding tort damages is to compensate the wronged party for the actual loss he or she has sustained [ ]. Personal injury damages are awarded "to restore the injured person to the state of health he had prior to his injuries because that is the only way the law knows how to recompense one for personal injuries suffered" [ ]. Thus, this court has held that "[t]he person responsible for the injury must respond for all damages resulting directly from and as a natural consequence of the wrongful act" [ ].

The capacity to enjoy life—by watching one's children grow, participating in recreational activities, and drinking in the many other pleasures that life has to offer—is unquestionably an attribute of an ordinary healthy individual. The loss of that capacity as a result of another's negligent act is at least as serious an impairment as the permanent destruction of a physical function, which has always been treated as a compensable item under traditional tort principles [ ]. Indeed, I can imagine no physical loss that is more central to the quality of a tort victim's continuing life than the destruction of the capacity to enjoy that life to the fullest.

Unquestionably, recovery of a damage item such as "pain and suffering" requires a showing of some degree of cognitive capacity. Such a requirement exists for the simple reason that pain and suffering are wholly subjective concepts and cannot exist separate and apart from the human consciousness that experiences them. In contrast, the destruction of an individual's capacity to enjoy life as a result of a crippling injury is an objective fact that does not differ in principle from the permanent loss of an eye or limb. As in the case of a lost limb, an essential characteristic of a healthy human life has been wrongfully taken, and, consequently, the injured party is entitled to a monetary award as a substitute, if, as the majority asserts, the goal of tort compensation is "to restore the injured party, to the extent possible, to the position that would have been occupied had the wrong not occurred" [ ].

Significantly, this equation does not suggest a need to establish the injured's awareness of the loss. The victim's ability to comprehend the degree to which his or her life has been impaired is irrelevant, since, unlike "conscious pain and suffering," the impairment exists independent of the victim's ability to apprehend it. Indeed, the majority reaches the conclusion that a degree of awareness must be shown only after injecting a new element into the equation. Under the majority's formulation, the victim must be aware of the loss because, in addition to being compensatory, the award must have "meaning or utility to the injured person." [ ] This additional requirement, however, has no real foundation in law or logic. "Meaning" and "utility" are subjective value judgments that have no place in the law of tort recovery, where the primary goal is to find ways of quantifying, to the extent possible, the worth of various forms of human tragedy.

Moreover, the compensatory nature of a monetary award for loss of enjoyment of life is not altered or rendered punitive by the fact that the unaware injured plaintiff cannot experience the pleasure of having it. The fundamental distinction between punitive and compensatory damages is that the former exceed the amount necessary to replace what the plaintiff lost [ ]. As the Court of Appeals for the Second Circuit has observed, "[t]he fact that the compensation [for loss of enjoyment of life] may inure as a practical matter to third parties in a given case does not transform the nature of the damages" (Rufino v. United States, 2nd Cir., 829 F.2d 354, 362).

. . .

In the final analysis, the rule that the majority has chosen is an arbitrary one, in that it denies or allows recovery on the basis of a criterion that is not truly related to its stated goal. In my view, it is fundamentally unsound, as well as grossly unfair, to deny recovery to those who are completely without cognitive capacity while permitting it for those with a mere spark of awareness, regardless of the latter's ability to appreciate either the loss sustained or the benefits of the monetary award offered in compensation. In both instances, the injured plaintiff is in essentially the same position, and an award that is punitive as to one is equally punitive as to the other. Of course, since I do not subscribe to the majority's conclusion that an award to an unaware plaintiff is punitive, I would have no difficulty permitting recovery to both classes of plaintiffs.

Having concluded that the injured plaintiff's awareness should not be a necessary precondition to recovery for loss of enjoyment of life, I also have no difficulty going on to conclude that loss of enjoyment of life is a distinct damage item which is recoverable separate and apart from the award for conscious pain and suffering. . . .

In fact, while "pain and suffering compensates the victim for the physical and mental discomfort caused by the injury; . . . loss of enjoyment of life compensates the victim for the limitations on the person's life created by the injury," a distinctly objective loss [ ]. In other words, while the victim's "emotional response" and "frustration and anguish" are elements of the award for pain and suffering, the "limitation of life's activities" and the "inability to participate in activities" that the majority identifies are recoverable under the "loss of enjoyment of life" rubric. Thus, there is no real overlap, and no real basis for concern about potentially duplicative awards where, as here, there is a properly instructed jury.

Finally, given the clear distinction between the two categories of nonpecuniary damages, I cannot help but assume that permitting separate awards for conscious pain and suffering and loss of enjoyment of life would contribute to accuracy and precision in thought in the jury's deliberations on the issue of damages. Indeed, the view that itemized awards enhance accuracy by facilitating appellate review has already been expressed by the Legislature in enacting [special verdict procedures]. In light of the concrete benefit to be gained by compelling the jury to differentiate between the specific objective and subjective elements of the plaintiff's nonpecuniary loss, I find unpersuasive the majority's reliance on vague concerns about potential distortion owing to the inherently difficult task of computing the value of intangible loss. My belief in the jury system, and in the collective wisdom of the deliberating jury, leads me to conclude that we may safely leave that task in the jurors' hands.

. . . Accordingly, I would affirm the order below affirming the judgment.

■ SIMONS, KAYE, HANCOCK and BELLACOSA, JJ., concur with WACHTLER, C.J. TITONE, J., dissents and votes to affirm in a separate opinion in which ALEXANDER, J., concurs.

NOTES AND QUESTIONS

1. *Loss of life's pleasures.* At one point the majority talks of efforts to "segregate the suffering associated with physical pain from the mental anguish that stems from the inability to engage in certain activities." This makes clear that New York seeks to compensate both the pain and the loss of pleasure under the same rubric.

Other states, however, segregate these items, calling the loss of pleasure "loss of enjoyment of life" or "hedonic damages." In Fantozzi v. Sandusky Cement Products Co., 597 N.E.2d 474 (Ohio 1992), the court approved a separate charge to the jury addressing "the plaintiff's inability, presently and prospectively, to perform the usual activities of life, such as the basic mechanical bodily movements that accommodate walking, climbing stairs, feeding oneself, driving a car, etc.":

> The claim of damages for deprivation or impairment of life's usual activities has, in other jurisdictions, been applied to a wide variety of pleasurable activities shown to have been curtailed by the injuries received by the plaintiff. Such damages include loss of ability to play golf, dance, bowl, play musical instruments, engage in specific outdoor sports, along with other activities. These types of experiences are all positive sensations of pleasure, the loss of which could provide a basis for an award of damages to the

plaintiff in varying degrees depending upon his involvement, as shown by the evidence. Such proof differs from the elements of mental suffering occasioned by the plaintiff's injury such as nervousness, grief, shock, anxiety, and so forth. Although the loss of the ability to engage in a usual pleasant activity of life is an emotional experience, it is a loss of a positive experience rather than the infliction of a negative experience.

Id. at 485–86.

The court thought that the use of more and narrower categories "would help the jury understand exactly what claimed damages it is addressing. This adds more clarity and objectivity to this part of the jury determination." To avoid double recoveries, the court mandated an elaborate two-paragraph instruction detailing how the jury should avoid double counting. Do you think this separation will create more rational jury discussions of intangible loss? Is it relevant that plaintiffs generally press for recognition of new damage categories while defendants argue against them?

What role does physical impairment play in determining damages, including those for loss of enjoyment of life? In Golden Eagle Archery, Inc. v. Jackson, 116 S.W.3d 757 (Tex.2003), the court addressed the implications of physical impairment and whether it represented a distinct or overlapping head of damage. The court concluded that physical impairment encompasses (and therefore overlaps with) lost earnings capacity, pain and suffering, and loss of enjoyment of life, and instructed lower courts to take steps to avoid jury instructions on damages that might compensate for the same harm twice. Can a plaintiff suffer loss of enjoyment of life without physical impairment?

How should courts handle the case of a woman with a scar across her face that deters her from playing golf—something she did weekly for 20 years before the accident? Suppose she cannot play as well as she did before because her arm hurts every time she swings? Suppose she continues to play but obtains diminished satisfaction because her coordination has suffered?

2. *Compensation and cognition.* How does the compensatory role of tort law fit into the discussion in *McDougald*? Is it a "paradoxical situation" that the worse a person is hurt the less likely that person may be able to recover anything for pain and suffering? Might this also be true in wrongful death cases? Under the dissent's approach, what is recoverable if the victim died instantly?

An omitted part of the dissent raised another issue. Damages for pain and suffering are available only during the period of cognitive awareness. But damages for loss of enjoyment of life are to compensate for losses "over a natural life span." With respect to the latter, the dissent asked, under the majority's approach if plaintiff is "entitled to recover an award representing his entire lifetime's loss notwithstanding that he was conscious of the loss for only a few moments before lapsing into cognitive oblivion?" Might the majority limit recovery to the period of awareness? Under this approach, how would these damages be determined?

3.   *Compensation and adaptation.* Behavioral research has shown that those who suffer losses have a significant ability to adapt to the circumstances—often with less consequence to their happiness than the uninjured might expect. Legal scholarship addressing the implications of this research for hedonic damages includes Bagenstos & Schlanger, Hedonic Damages, Hedonic Adaptation, and Disability, 60 Vand.L.Rev. 745 (2007), and Sunstein, Illusory Losses, 37 J. Legal Stud. S157 (2008). Professors Bagenstos and Schlanger recommend that hedonic damages not be awarded, while Professor Sunstein advocates damage guidelines for hedonic loss be provided to juries. To evaluate these proposals, consider someone who is rendered a quadriplegic by the defendant's negligence. Even if the victim adapts and ends up being largely as happy as she had been before the accident, has she nevertheless experienced any loss of life's pleasures that ought to be compensated?

4.   *Recipient of the compensation.* The dissent addresses the issue of who is likely to get to spend the pain and suffering award in this type of case. Should that matter?

5.   *Framing the compensation problem.* How one thinks about the compensatory problem can be a matter of perspective. In one study using experimental data, the authors compared the implications of thinking about compensating specific injuries from an *ex post* perspective of "making whole" and an *ex ante* perspective of how much money healthy persons would want to sell their good health for the same injuries. Those viewing the matter from the *ex ante* perspective tended to award about twice as much as those viewing the injury from the "making whole" perspective. McCaffery, Kahneman & Spitzer, Framing the Jury: Cognitive Perspectives on Pain and Suffering Awards, 81 Va.L.Rev. 1341 (1995). Which perspective makes more sense for purposes of tort law?

Note that the results from this study do not directly translate into the negligence context, because the study involved compensation for the certainty of injury and not an accidental harm. Courts all reject the "golden rule" argument that the jury should determine damages by considering how much someone would accept in exchange for suffering the plaintiff's injury with certainty. Is it possible to frame the compensation problem in terms of risk?

6.   *The function of deterrence.* To what extent should the deterrent function of tort law affect the outcome in *McDougald*? The court expresses the concern that compensatory damages not be employed to punish the defendant. Can punishment be distinguished from deterrence?

Relatedly, can the function of compensation be distinguished from the function of deterrence in these cases? Individuals are willing to pay money to avoid suffering injuries of the type involved in *McDougald*, and that amount can be used to calculate the damages award with an approach routinely used by federal regulatory agencies. To conduct cost-benefit analyses of proposed health-and-safety regulations as required by executive order, a federal agency must calculate the expected safety benefits of reduced morbidity and mortality. To estimate the monetary benefit of a saved life, the agency compares the underlying risk of harm to the individual's willingness to pay to eliminate that risk. Suppose the agency finds that individuals are willing to pay up to $79 to reduce a 1-in-100,000 chance of dying. These individuals equate the $79 payment with the expected cost of injury that they would otherwise face (the probability of injury P multiplied by the severity of injury L). Consequently,

$$\$79 = P \cdot L$$
$$\$79 = (1/100,000) \cdot L$$
$$\$7,900,000 = L.$$

This measure, known as the "value of a statistical life or VSL" is addressed by a substantial body of academic literature. "Current agency practice provides a VSL ranging from roughly $5 million to $9 million per statistical life." Office of Information & Regulatory Affairs, Regulatory Impact Analysis: A Primer (2011), https://www.whitehouse.gov/omb/inforeg_regpol_agency_review.

For argument that a VSL measure based on the risk created by defendant appropriately links the compensatory and deterrence functions of tort law, see Geistfeld, Placing a Price on Pain and Suffering: A Method for Helping Juries Determine Tort Damages for Nonmonetary Injuries, 83 Cal.L.Rev. 775 (1995). See also Miller, Willingness to Pay Comes of Age: Will the System Survive?, 83 Nw.U.L.Rev. 876 (1989); Viscusi, Pain and Suffering in Product Liability Cases: Systematic Compensation or Capricious Awards?, 8 Int'l Rev.L. & Econ. 203 (1988); Wilt v. Buracker, 443 S.E.2d 196 (W.Va.1993)(discussing at length the nature of expert economic testimony that values life by drawing on studies about willingness to pay to avoid injury, and rejecting such testimony in favor of treating hedonic damages as part of general damages); Montalvo v. Lapez, 884 P.2d 345 (Haw.1994)(same).

This approach, however, does not fully solve the potential conflict between compensation and deterrence. Individuals impute a substantial cost to premature death, and yet as *McDougald* illustrates, the requirement of consciousness can bar tort recovery for the loss of life's pleasures. The shortfall is most pronounced in cases of wrongful death. Does this limitation of compensatory damages mean that a dutyholder must take *less* care for fatal risks than nonfatal risks that involve substantially higher damage awards? Consider the standard of reasonable care, $B < PL$, as formulated by Judge Hand in *Carroll Towing*, p. 47 supra. Should the threatened loss L be defined by the compensatory damages measure, in which case the low compensatory damages for wrongful death would imply a lower level of reasonable care B? For discussion of the associated issues, see Geistfeld, The Principle of Misalignment: Duty, Damages, and the Nature of Tort Liability, 121 Yale L.J. 142 (2011) (arguing that the standard of reasonable care relies on a legal valuation of the threatened loss that should substantially exceed the compensatory damages measure); Note, Hedonic Damages for Wrongful Death: Are

Tortfeasors Getting Away with Murder?, 78 Geo.L.J. 1687, 1687 (1990)(arguing "that to deter negligent behavior adequately, tortfeasors should be held liable for what may be the most substantial cost they impose on accident victims—'hedonic damages,' or the loss of the value of life that results from premature death"). As illustrated by these issues, premature death poses particularly hard problems for the tort system.

Damages in the Event of Death

Although no claim could be prosecuted at common law once a person died, statutes were enacted to reverse that rule. In the event of death, two potential claims are provided, a survival action and, when the tortious conduct is responsible for the victim's death, a wrongful death action. Each of these claims is explored below.

Survival actions. Survival statutes provide for recovery of damages that the deceased could have obtained before death. The right to sue is held by the deceased person's estate. The measurement of past lost income and medical expense—that is, loss suffered between the time of injury and the time of death—is similar to non-death cases. The survival action also typically allows recovery for pain and suffering sustained by the decedent. In a case in which the victim is very badly burned as a result of the defendant's negligence, remains conscious in excruciating pain for a day or two, and then dies, why should the estate in a survivor action be able to receive compensation for that pain?

In Sander v. Geib, Elston, Frost P.A., 506 N.W.2d 107 (S.D.1993), defendant's negligence in reading a Pap smear test led to a failure to detect cervical cancer until it was too late to save decedent, a 34-year-old wife and mother of three children. She underwent some radiation therapy but was found unsuitable for any radical procedures because the cancer was too far advanced. The court does not recount evidence of physical pain in its opinion. In a suit for her death, the jury made an award that was assumed to include $1 million for her pain and suffering. In rejecting a claim of excessiveness, the court responded:

> [Decedent] greatly suffered many faces of pain during the year following the realization that she would die from the very disease which the pap smear was designed to detect. The enormity of [decedent's] knowledge of her impending, unalterable doom, her confusion, fear, misery, depression, helplessness, physical pain and mental terror, her sure knowledge that she would never live to witness the adulthood of her children or old age with her husband, all were proper considerations for the jury and surely had a powerful influence upon it.

Is each of these considerations proper? The defendant's strategy was to focus on denying liability. As a result it "did not argue damages in closing arguments to the jury." Was this a mistake?

Are courts in cases like *Sander* compensating for something other than pain and suffering? Can awards such as those in these cases nevertheless be justified?

In a jurisdiction that permits an injured plaintiff to recover for loss of enjoyment of life, should it also be recoverable in a survival action? In Durham v. Marberry, 156 S.W.3d 242 (Ark.2004), plaintiffs' decedent was killed instantly in a collision with a mobile home transport. Based on an amendment to the Arkansas survival actions that authorized recovery "for the decedent's loss of life as an independent element of damages," plaintiffs sought recovery for those damages. The trial court granted summary judgment to defendants on the claim for loss-of-life damages on the ground that some period of survival is required before they are recoverable.

> On appeal, the [defendants] concede that loss-of-life damages are a new element of damages, but they now argue that damages for loss of life are the equivalent of, and synonymous with, damages for the loss of enjoyment of life, and these types of damages are incurred pre-death and require a period of conscious life between injury and death.

> There is some confusion amongst both case law and legal scholarship as to the definition of "loss of enjoyment of life" damages. Some cases and scholars have used the term "loss of enjoyment of life" to describe damages that compensate a pre-death loss of the ability to enjoy life's activities while still living. Still others have used this term to mean the loss of the enjoyment of being alive that is incurred at the point of death forward. So the term "loss of enjoyment of life" is confusing and, at times, has been used in a way that is equivalent to "loss of life."

> [The court then discussed two cases that had distinguished between the conscious appreciation that one's life expectancy has been shortened, a harm that might be conceptualized as an element of pain and suffering, and loss of life, which, whether appreciated or not, denies the decedent the rewards and pleasures of the years of lost life.]

> Clearly, then, loss-of-life damages and damages for loss of enjoyment of life are not the same, though some courts and scholars have used the term "loss of enjoyment of life" to mean both. . . .

> . . .

> Loss-of-life damages seek to compensate a decedent for the loss of the value that the decedent would have placed on his or her own life. "Survival" actions have traditionally included those damages suffered by the decedent between injury and death. Nonetheless, Ark. Code Ann. section 16–62–101 makes

no distinction between "personal injury" or "death" when it speaks of the term "injury." In other words, when a person is killed instantaneously, as was Miss Durham, her injury *is* her death, which is compensated by loss-of-life damages.

In sum, because the legislature chose to amend the survival statute to add loss-of-life damages as a separate and independent element in addition to all other elements of damage already allowed by law, the appellants are correct that loss-of-life damages are a new element of damages. Moreover, . . . since loss-of-life damages can only begin accruing at the point when life is lost, at death, there is no reason to believe the legislature intended to require the decedent to live for a period of time between injury and death. Therefore, we hold that it is not necessary for a decedent to live for a period of time between injury and death in order to recover loss-of-life damages. . . .

In addition to Arkansas, a handful of other states permit recovery of loss of enjoyment of life damages (sometimes referred to as "hedonic" damages) as a distinct item; three of them, in addition to Arkansas, permit recovery of loss-of-life damages. See E. Posner & Sunstein, Dollars and Death, 72 U.Chi.L.Rev. 537 (2005); Dorn v. Burlington N. Santa Fe R.R. Co., 397 F.3d 1183 (9th Cir.2005)(affirming jury instruction on hedonic damages, despite the absence of any Montana Supreme Court case adopting it).

Wrongful death actions. Wrongful death and survival actions are often brought together. In wrongful death actions, the liability is based on defendant's violation of the decedent's tort right, but the right to recover is held by the statutorily specified beneficiaries (not the decedent's estate) for their injuries that are compensable under the statute.

The major item of damages traditionally has been the economic loss to the beneficiaries, because in many states only "pecuniary" loss is recoverable. Pecuniary loss is measured in one of two ways, depending on the statutory language. The "loss to dependent's measure" bases recovery on the financial support lost by the decedent's dependents. The "loss to the estate" measure does not directly account for the lost support to dependents, but instead compensates for the extent to which the decedent's estate was diminished by the premature death, an amount that presumably would have been ultimately passed onto the dependents but for the wrongful death. Under either measure, the damages are not wholly determined by the decedent's lost wages as such. From that lost income figure the amount the decedent would have spent personally for food, clothing, and other personal consumption has to be deducted. Until recently, many states imposed small caps on wrongful death awards. These have been eliminated or made more generous. See, e.g., Neiman v. American National Property & Casualty

Co., 613 N.W.2d 160 (Wis.2000), noting that in 1995 the state had a cap on wrongful death awards of $150,000. This was raised in 1998 to $500,000 for a deceased minor and to $350,000 for a deceased adult. What justifies any limit in such cases?

New York has been the state most closely identified with a strict interpretation of the requirement that the damages be "pecuniary." The statutory language states in relevant part that the damages awardable in death cases are such sum as the trier "deems to be fair and just compensation for the pecuniary injuries resulting from the decedent's death to the persons for whose benefit the action is brought." The paradoxical impact that such a requirement can produce is illustrated in a case with expert economic testimony about the value of the life of an 84-year-old woman. The defense expert had testified that the woman's savings level would remain constant, and that during her expected seven years of life, she would consume more of her income than could have been generated through interest. He concluded that the "distributees are actually financially better off as a result of [the decedent's] death." Accepting that testimony, the judge, as trier of fact, awarded funeral expenses as the only recoverable item for her wrongful death. "Crass though it may seem (and if crass it is, it is because of the current state of the law), the Court finds that the only pecuniary loss suffered" was an $8,000 funeral bill. He noted that other states had expanded recovery to include loss of society and urged a change in New York law. See the extended report of Hubbard v. State, in N.Y.L.J., June 29, 2000, at 1.

Why is the estate entitled to recover even the $8,000 funeral costs, since they would have been incurred in any case? As suggested by this question, wrongful death damages in some cases can be zero.

A majority of states now permit recovery of nonpecuniary damages for the loss of relationship by designated survivors in wrongful death cases. Fewer permit recovery for the grief of family members. See Perry & Adar, Wrongful Abortion: A Wrong in Search of a Remedy, 5 Yale J. Health Pol'y, L. & Ethics 507, 533 nn. 119–20 & 123–24 (2005)(listing state statutes and courts interpreting general wrongful death statutes). For discussion of one statute permitting nonpecuniary recoveries, see In re Air Crash Near Nantucket Island, Massachusetts, on October 31, 1999, 462 F. Supp.2d 360 (E.D.N.Y.2006)(Death on the High Seas Act, amended in 2000 to permit recovery for "loss of care, comfort, and companionship").

Wrongful death of a child. The issue involved when children are killed revolves even more clearly around the split between states that limit recovery to pecuniary harm and those that do not.

For an effort to avoid a "pecuniary damages" statutory limitation, see Green v. Bittner, 424 A.2d 210 (N.J.1980), involving the wrongful death of a high school senior. The trial judge told the jury to consider the services the child had performed around the house and those that she might have undertaken to provide her parents as she grew older. From this, the jury was to subtract the value of food, clothing, and education that the family would have spent on her until her majority. The jury returned a verdict of no damages. The trial judge upheld the verdict, observing that the "jury in this particular case followed literally the language of the statute." On appeal, the court reversed:

> We hold that [in addition to the usual items] the jury should be allowed, under appropriate circumstances, to award damages for the parents' loss of their child's companionship as they grow older, when it may be most needed and valuable, as well as the advice and guidance that often accompanies it. As noted later, these other losses will be confined to their pecuniary value, excluding emotional loss. Given this expansion of permissible recovery, a verdict finding no damages for the death of a child should ordinarily be set aside by the trial court and a new trial ordered. To sustain such a verdict "would result in a return to the outmoded doctrine that a child is a liability—not an asset." [ ]

In discussing the nature of the recoverable loss of "guidance, advice and counsel," the court stressed:

> The loss of guidance, advice and counsel is similarly to be confined to its pecuniary element. It is not the loss simply of the exchange of views, no matter how perceptive, when child and parent are together; it is certainly not the loss of the pleasure which accompanies such an exchange. Rather it is the loss of that kind of guidance, advice and counsel which all of us need from time to time in particular situations, for specific purposes, perhaps as an aid in making a business decision, or a decision affecting our lives generally, or even advice and guidance needed to relieve us from unremitting depression. It must be the kind of advice, guidance or counsel that could be purchased from a business adviser, a therapist, or a trained counselor, for instance. That some of us obtain the same benefit without charge from spouses, friends or children does not strip it of pecuniary value.

Consider the damages the plaintiffs might have recovered for loss of consortium if, instead of being killed, their daughter survived, but in a vegetative state. Is there an anomaly in the difference in the damages available if she survives or is killed?

For a wide-ranging historical discussion of how tort law has measured damages in these cases, see V. Zelizer, Pricing the Priceless Child: The Changing Social Value of Children (1994).

2. PUNITIVE DAMAGES

Until now we have been exploring the nature of compensatory damages. We turn now to the question of whether damages that do not seek to compensate should also be available in certain kinds of cases. Almost all states have concluded that sometimes damages may be awarded to punish the defendant or to make an example of that defendant so that others will avoid such serious misconduct. At the extreme, outrageous intentional conduct would warrant this type of treatment. We consider this when we cover intentional torts in Chapter XIII. Most states have expanded the availability of punitive damages to other types of serious misconduct. The jury has total discretion, in a case that meets the requisite standard for punitive damages, about whether or not to award them, although the amount of the award is subject to limitation under both state law and the U.S. Constitution.

a. THE COMMON LAW

Mathias v. Accor Economy Lodging, Inc.

United States Court of Appeals, Seventh Circuit, 2003.
347 F.3d 672.

■ Before POSNER, KANNE, and EVANS, CIRCUIT JUDGES.

■ POSNER, J.

The plaintiffs brought this diversity suit governed by Illinois law against affiliated entities (which the parties treat as a single entity, as shall we) that own and operate the "Motel 6" chain of hotels and motels. One of these hotels (now a "Red Roof Inn," though still owned by the defendant) is in downtown Chicago. The plaintiffs, a brother and sister, were guests there and were bitten by bedbugs, which are making a comeback in the U.S. as a consequence of more conservative use of pesticides. [ ] The plaintiffs claim that in allowing guests to be attacked by bedbugs in a motel that charges upwards of $100 a day for a room and would not like to be mistaken for a flophouse, the defendant was guilty of "willful and wanton conduct" and thus under Illinois law is liable for punitive as well as compensatory damages. [ ] The jury agreed and awarded each plaintiff $186,000 in punitive damages though only $5,000 in compensatory damages. The defendant appeals, complaining primarily about the punitive-damages award. . . .

The defendant argues that at worst it is guilty of simple negligence, and if this is right the plaintiffs were not entitled by Illinois law to any award of punitive damages. It also complains that the award was excessive—indeed that any award in excess of $20,000 to each plaintiff would deprive the defendant of its property without due process of law. The first complaint has no possible merit, as the evidence of gross negligence, indeed of recklessness in the strong sense of an unjustifiable failure to avoid a *known* risk, [ ], was amply shown. In 1998, EcoLab, the extermination service that the motel used, discovered bedbugs in several rooms in the motel and recommended that it be hired to spray every room, for which it would charge the motel only $500; the motel refused. The next year, bedbugs were again discovered in a room but EcoLab was asked to spray just that room. The motel tried to negotiate "a building sweep [by EcoLab] free of charge," but, not surprisingly, the negotiation failed. By the spring of 2000, the motel's manager "started noticing that there were refunds being given by my desk clerks and reports coming back from the guests that there were ticks in the rooms and bugs in the rooms that were biting." She looked in some of the rooms and discovered bedbugs. . . .

Further incidents of guests being bitten by insects and demanding and receiving refunds led the manager to recommend to her superior in the company that the motel be closed while every room was sprayed, but this was refused. This superior, a district manager, was a management-level employee of the defendant, and his knowledge of the risk and failure to take effective steps either to eliminate it or to warn the motel's guests are imputed to his employer for purposes of determining whether the employer should be liable for punitive damages. [] The employer's liability for compensatory damages is of course automatic on the basis of the principle of respondeat superior, since the district manager was acting within the scope of his employment.

The infestation continued and began to reach farcical proportions. . . . By July, the motel's management was acknowledging to EcoLab that there was a "major problem with bed bugs" and that all that was being done about it was "chasing them from room to room." . . . Desk clerks were instructed to call the "bedbugs" "ticks," apparently on the theory that customers would be less alarmed. . . .

It was in November that the plaintiffs checked into the motel. They were given Room 504, even though the motel had classified the room as "DO NOT RENT UNTIL TREATED," and it had not been treated. Indeed, that night 190 of the hotel's 191 rooms were occupied, even though a number of them had been placed on the same don't-rent status as Room 504. . . .

Although bedbug bites are not as serious as the bites of some other insects, they are painful and unsightly. Motel 6 could not have rented any rooms at the prices it charged had it informed guests that the risk of being bitten by bedbugs was appreciable. Its failure either to warn guests or to take effective measures to eliminate the bedbugs amounted to fraud and probably to battery as well []. . . . There was, in short, sufficient evidence of "willful and wanton conduct" within the meaning that the Illinois courts assign to the term to permit an award of punitive damages in this case.

But in what amount? [The court then explains why this question implicates the federal constitutional requirements of due process as prescribed by the U.S. Supreme Court, an issue addressed by the next principal case, p. 757 infra.]

We must consider why punitive damages are awarded and why the Court has decided that due process requires that such awards be limited. The second question is easier to answer than the first. The term "punitive damages" implies punishment, and a standard principle of penal theory is that "the punishment should fit the crime" in the sense of being proportional to the wrongfulness of the defendant's action, though the principle is modified when the probability of detection is very low (a familiar example is the heavy fines for littering) or the crime is potentially lucrative (as in the case of trafficking in illegal drugs). Hence, with these qualifications, which in fact will figure in our analysis of this case, punitive damages should be proportional to the wrongfulness of the defendant's actions.

Another penal precept is that a defendant should have reasonable notice of the sanction for unlawful acts, so that he can make a rational determination of how to act; and so there have to be reasonably clear standards for determining the amount of punitive damages for particular wrongs.

And a third precept, the core of the Aristotelian notion of corrective justice, and more broadly of the principle of the rule of law, is that sanctions should be based on the wrong done rather than on the status of the defendant; a person is punished for what he does, not for who he is, even if the who is a huge corporation.

What follows from these principles, however, is that punitive damages should be admeasured by standards or rules rather than in a completely ad hoc manner, and this does not tell us what the maximum ratio of punitive to compensatory damages should be in a particular case. To determine that, we have to consider why punitive damages are awarded in the first place. [ ]

England's common law courts first confirmed their authority to award punitive damages in the eighteenth century, [ ], at a time when the institutional structure of criminal law enforcement was primitive and it made sense to leave certain minor crimes to be dealt with by the civil law. And still today one function of punitive-damages awards is to relieve the pressures on an overloaded system of criminal justice by providing a civil alternative to criminal prosecution of minor crimes. An example is deliberately spitting in a person's face, a criminal assault but because minor readily deterrable by the levying of what amounts to a civil fine through a suit for damages for the tort of battery. Compensatory damages would not do the trick in such a case, and this for three reasons: because they are difficult to determine in the case of acts that inflict largely dignitary harms; because in the spitting case they would be too slight to give the victim an incentive to sue, and he might decide instead to respond with violence—and an age-old purpose of the law of torts is to provide a substitute for violent retaliation against wrongful injury—and because to limit the plaintiff to compensatory damages would enable the defendant to commit the offensive act with impunity provided that he was willing to pay, and again there would be a danger that his act would incite a breach of the peace by his victim.

When punitive damages are sought for billion-dollar oil spills and other huge economic injuries, the considerations that we have just canvassed fade. . . . Our case is closer to the spitting case. The defendant's behavior was outrageous but the compensable harm done was slight and at the same time difficult to quantify because a large element of it was emotional. And the defendant may well have profited from its misconduct because by concealing the infestation it was able to keep renting rooms. Refunds were frequent but may have cost less than the cost of closing the hotel for a thorough fumigation. The hotel's attempt to pass off the bedbugs as ticks, which some guests might ignorantly have thought less unhealthful, may have postponed the instituting of litigation to rectify the hotel's misconduct. The award of punitive damages in this case thus serves the additional purpose of limiting the defendant's ability to profit from its fraud by escaping detection and (private) prosecution. If a tortfeasor is "caught" only half the time he commits torts, then when he is caught he should be punished twice as heavily in order to make up for the times he gets away.

. . . It is here that the defendant's aggregate net worth of $1.6 billion becomes relevant. A defendant's wealth is not a sufficient basis for awarding punitive damages. [ ] That would be discriminatory and would violate the rule of law, as we explained earlier, by making punishment depend on status rather than conduct. Where wealth in the sense of resources enters is in enabling the defendant to mount an extremely aggressive defense against suits such as this and by doing so to make litigating against it very costly, which in turn may make it difficult for the plaintiffs to find a lawyer willing to handle their case, involving as it does only modest stakes, for the usual 33–40 percent contingent fee.

. . .

All things considered, we cannot say that the award of punitive damages was excessive, albeit the precise number chosen by the jury was arbitrary. It is probably not a coincidence that $5,000 + $186,000 = $191,000/191 = $1,000: i.e., $1,000 per room in the hotel. But as there are no punitive-damages guidelines, corresponding to the federal and state sentencing guidelines, it is inevitable that the specific amount of punitive damages awarded whether by a judge or by a jury will be arbitrary. (Which is perhaps why the plaintiffs' lawyer did not suggest a number to the jury.) The judicial function is to police a range, not a point. [ ]

But it would have been helpful had the parties presented evidence concerning the regulatory or criminal penalties to which the defendant exposed itself by deliberately exposing its customers to a substantial risk of being bitten by bedbugs. That is an inquiry recommended by the Supreme Court. [ ] But we do not think its omission invalidates the award. We can take judicial notice that deliberate exposure of hotel guests to the health risks created by insect infestations exposes the hotel's owner to sanctions under Illinois and Chicago law that in the aggregate are comparable in severity to the punitive damage award in this case.

. . .

AFFIRMED.

NOTES AND QUESTIONS

1. *Punitive damages as punishment.* The widely recognized rationales for punitive damages involve retribution and deterrence. To what extent is the court's rationale for the amount of the award based on the concern for punishment? Punitive damages are sometimes called "extracompensatory damages," a label that deemphasizes the retributive rationale for these awards.

2. *The Pinto case.* The retributive rationale for punitive damages is illustrated by a highly publicized case involving a defective automobile. In 1972, a Ford Pinto was struck in the rear by another car, resulting in the gas tank rupturing and a horrific fire. The driver of the Pinto was killed, and a teenage passenger was badly burned. A lawsuit resulted, and in 1978 the jury awarded the passenger $2.5 million in compensatory damages and $125 million ($458 million in 2015 dollars) in punitive damages, which the trial court subsequently reduced to $3.5 million. Grimshaw v. Ford Motor Co., 174 Cal.Rptr. 348 (App.1981). An internal company memorandum surfaced that many understood as revealing that Ford had compared the costs of deaths and burn injuries for which it would be liable against the costs of a safer fuel system. Because the cost of liability was less than the cost of redesigning the Pinto fuel system, Ford apparently decided to do nothing about the safety problem. According to the appellate court, "[t]here was evidence that Ford could have corrected the hazardous design defects at minimal cost but decided to defer correction of the shortcomings by engaging in a cost-benefit analysis balancing human lives and limbs against corporate profits." Id. at 384. Moreover, Ford's valuation of a life— $200,000—in that memorandum was regarded as both unconscionable in placing a value on life and deplorably low. That balancing of costs and lives justified, in the court's view, not only compensatory liability but the harsh punitive damage award as well. The *Grimshaw* case became a cause célèbre in the media, has been (and continues to be) used as a case study of corporate (ir)responsibility, and Ford and the Pinto were widely and harshly criticized by commentators. The Pinto was repeatedly characterized at the time as a "firetrap." Ford was, a few years after

Grimshaw, criminally prosecuted in Indiana over another death that occurred in a Pinto, although the case resulted in Ford's acquittal.

Many question, however, whether Ford deserved to be punished on these facts. The substantial misunderstanding by the public of the Ford Pinto and the *Grimshaw* case is insightfully unpacked in Schwartz, The Myth of the Ford Pinto Case, 43 Rutgers L.Rev. 1013 (1991). The cost-benefit memorandum was never permitted to be introduced in the *Grimshaw* case and was not about the design of the Pinto; it was prepared in response to a proposed safety rule applicable to all later-manufactured cars by the National Highway Traffic Safety Administration (NHTSA). Moreover, Ford's use of the $200,000 figure to value a life was consistent with usage by NHTSA in its regulatory efforts. The Pinto was, overall, no more dangerous than other cars of its subcompact class. While it did have a higher rate of fatalities due to rear-end fire crashes, it made up for that deficiency in other aspects—its overall death rate in accidents was "respectabl[e]" by comparison with competitor cars.

The most significant problem with the case, according to Professor Schwartz, involves the paradox of tort law embracing cost-benefit analysis in its negligence standard, even when personal injury and death are at stake, while the public (and the *Grimshaw* court) finds this type of analysis to be abominable:

> [T]he process of balancing the magnitude of the risk against the cost of risk prevention has been embedded in negligence law since the nineteenth century, and was rendered official by the *First Restatement of Torts* and Learned Hand's opinion in *United States v. Carroll Towing Co.* Indeed, many scholars have interpreted the products liability risk-benefit standard precisely as a very modern manifestation of very traditional negligence reasoning.
>
>   . . .
>
> [For that reason, the] punitive damage award in the Ford Pinto case is . . . difficult to justify. To a large extent it rested on the premise that Ford had behaved reprehensibly when it balanced safety against cost in designing the Pinto. However, the process by which manufacturers render such trade-off design decisions seems not only to be anticipated but endorsed by the prevailing risk-benefit standard for design liability. Accordingly, the Pinto jury's decision that punitive damages were appropriate—a decision that was affirmed by the trial judge and the court of appeal—raises serious questions about the operational viability of the risk-benefit standard itself.

Id. at 1037–38 & 1067. In the course of the article, Schwartz recounts discussions with trial lawyers that led him to conclude that while defense lawyers can justify a design decision by arguing that an alternative design would impair the usefulness of the product (or make it less safe in other respects), "one argument that you should almost never make is that the manufacturer deliberately included a dangerous feature in the product's design because of the high monetary cost that the manufacturer would have incurred in choosing another design. If you do argue this, you're almost certain to lose on liability, and you can expose yourself to punitive damages as well." Id. at 1038.

What problems does this practice pose for the deterrence objective of tort law? Compare Viscusi, Pricing Lives for Corporate Risk Decisions, 68 Vand.L.Rev. 1117 (2015)(arguing that the widely publicized 2014 ignition-switch recall by General Motors reflected an "inattention to systematic thinking about product safety [that] can be traced to the hostile treatment of corporate risk analyses by the courts").

The Pinto case reveals the difficulties posed by the retributive rationale for punitive damages. As illustrated by the intentional torts, a defendant who consciously disregarded the plaintiff's tort right is properly subject to punitive damages. The Pinto case shows why this standard is much harder to apply in cases of accidental harms.

3. *Behavior that merits punitive damages.* What is the appropriate culpability standard for triggering a punitive award? All agree that ordinary negligence does not suffice. All also agree that the defendant's ability and willingness to pay compensatory damages does not bar an award of punitive damages (otherwise one could sexually assault another in exchange for paying the "price" of compensatory damages). Outside of these matters, the behavior that merits punitive damages is more difficult to define.

For example, under California Civil Code section 3294, "where the defendant has been guilty of oppression, fraud, or malice, express or implied, the plaintiff, in addition to actual damages, may recover damages for the sake of example and by way of punishing the defendant." To clarify the ambiguity inherent in these terms (which were at issue in the Pinto case), section 3294 was subsequently amended to define these three terms:

(1) "Malice" means conduct which is intended by the defendant to cause injury to the plaintiff or despicable conduct which is carried on by the defendant with a willful and conscious disregard of the rights or safety of others.

(2) "Oppression" means despicable conduct that subjects a person to cruel and unjust hardship in conscious disregard of that person's rights.

(3) "Fraud" means an intentional misrepresentation, deceit, or concealment of a material fact known to the defendant with the intention on the part of the defendant of thereby depriving a person of property or legal rights or otherwise causing injury.

In addition, section 3294 requires that the oppression, fraud or malice be "proven by clear and convincing evidence."

Would these definitions change the analysis of the Pinto case? Compare Owens-Illinois, Inc. v Zenobia, 601 A.2d 633 (Md. 1992)(adopting majority rule that punitive damages for defective products cannot be based on implied malice but instead requires actual malice based on proof showing "(1) actual knowledge of the defect on the part of the defendant, and (2) the defendant's conscious or deliberate disregard of the foreseeable harm flowing from the defect"); Hillrichs v. Avco Corp., 514 N.W.2d 94 (Iowa 1994)("[A]n award of punitive damages is inappropriate when room exists for reasonable disagreement over the relative risks and utilities of the conduct and device at issue.").

Should punitive damages be awarded based solely on proof that defendant knowingly violated the law? Note that such a standard would apply to most drivers on the freeway who are choosing to exceed the legal speed limit. Compare Ross v. Louise Wise Serv., Inc., 868 N.E.2d 189 (N.Y. 2007)("punitive damages may be sought when the wrongdoing was deliberate and has the character of outrage frequently associated with crime").

4. *Liability for punitive damages when the tortfeasor dies.* The overwhelming majority of states deny recovery of punitive damages from the estate of a deceased tortfeasor. For confirmation of the majority rule, see Crabtree v. Estate of Crabtree, 837 N.E.2d 135 (Ind.2005). To what extent is this view based on the retributive rationale for punitive damages? In Haralson v. Fisher Surveying, Inc., 31 P.3d 114 (Ariz.2001), the court, 3–2, adopted the minority rule that permits the estate of a dead tortfeasor to be held liable for punitive damages. A concurring opinion stressed the importance of deterring drunk driving and concluded that whether the driver lives or dies should not change the result.

5. *Punitive damages and deterrence.* For reasons emphasized in *Mathias*, punitive damages can also serve a deterrent purpose. Isn't that, however, one purpose of compensatory damages? Consider the paradox that in one area in which compensatory damages are thought inadequate to provide appropriate deterrence—wrongful death—punitive damages are often not permitted. Nevertheless, the deterrence rationale for punitive damages is that they should be employed when there will be under-enforcement of tort claims, either because the tortfeasor won't be discovered 100% of the time or because the harm to each injured person is small, and the costs of pursuing a claim prevent defendant from being forced to pay for all of the harm caused. For example, if the defendant expects to incur liability in only 1/3 of all meritorious cases, then total damages must be three times the amount of compensatory damages in order to give defendant an adequate financial incentive for avoiding the wrongdoing. See Polinsky & Shavell, Punitive Damages: An Economic Analysis, 111 Harv.L.Rev. 869 (1998)(arguing that punitive damages can be justified from a deterrence perspective when defendant has a significant chance of otherwise escaping liability); see also Craswell, Deterrence and Damages: The Multiplier Principle and Its Alternatives, 97 Mich.L.Rev. 2185 (1999). According to the *Mathias* court, what is the multiplier that might explain the jury verdict? Are there other instances of under-enforcement that you can think of that would be appropriate for punitive damages?

6. *Employer liability for punitive damages.* When plaintiffs seek to impose punitive damages on employers based on vicarious liability, states have adopted varying positions. In some states, punitive damages flow with

vicarious liability. Other states follow the Second Restatement section 909, which provides:

> Punitive damages can properly be awarded against a master or other principal because of an act by an agent if, but only if,
>
> (a) the principal or a managerial agent authorized the doing and the manner of the act, or
>
> (b) the agent was unfit and the principal or a managerial agent was reckless in employing or retaining him, or
>
> (c) the agent was employed in a managerial capacity and was acting in the scope of employment, or
>
> (d) the principal or a managerial agent of the principal ratified or approved the act.

The Restatement justifies this limited approach as "result[ing] from the reasons for awarding punitive damages, which make it improper ordinarily to award punitive damages against one who himself is personally innocent and therefore liable only vicariously." The Restatement (Third) of Agency section 7.03 cmt. e (2006) endorses the Second Restatement approach, while observing that the difference between that rule and the slight majority that permit punitive damages based on vicarious liability may not be all that great, especially in the case of organizations. Consider this reasoning as applied to *Mathias*.

7.   *The passage of time.* In Fischer v. Johns-Manville Corp., 512 A.2d 466 (N.J.1986), plaintiff recovered punitive damages in an asbestos case based on knowledge of the dangers of asbestos and suppression of that information by the two defendants some 40 years previously. Should the long passage of time between act and damage award influence the availability of punitive damages as a matter of retribution? How about deterrence? Are the considerations different for compensatory damages?

8.   *Governmental liability.* What do the purposes of punitive damages suggest about holding the government liable for such damages? The Federal Tort Claims Act provides that the "United States . . . shall not be liable . . . for punitive damages." 28 U.S.C. § 2674.

9.   *Comparative responsibility.* The general view is that in a comparative fault state, the plaintiff's compensatory award should be reduced to reflect any fault, but punitive awards should not be reduced. See Clark v. Cantrell, 529 S.E.2d 528 (S.C.2000). Why might that be?

10.   *The practice of punitive damages.* A considerable body of empirical inquiry into the frequency and magnitude of punitive damages and the types of cases in which they are awarded has been conducted in recent years. The results of those studies are quite consistent:

- Punitive damages are awarded in four to six percent of trials in which plaintiffs are successful (plaintiffs are successful overall in 40–60% of trials, so the rate of punitive damages is half of the above for all cases tried).

- Punitive damages are awarded more frequently and at a higher rate in commercial litigation than in tort cases. One study found 254 punitive damages awards in tort cases tried in 2005, comprising less than 2% of all tort trials, and 446 such awards in commercial cases, comprising 7.6% of such trials.

- The only category of personal injury torts in which punitive damages are awarded at a higher rate than the rate in commercial litigation is intentional torts.

- The median award of punitive damages is modest, around $70,000 in current dollars.

- The mean award of punitive damages is quite a bit higher (because of high-end awards), in excess of $500,000.

- The typical amount of punitive damages awarded by juries and judges equals the amount of compensatory damages.

See Langton & Cohen, Bureau of Justice Statistics, Special Report: Civil Bench and Jury Trials in State Courts, 2005 (2008), available at http://bjs. ojp.usdoj.gov/content/pub/pdf/cbjtsc05.pdf; Eisenberg et al., Juries, Judges, and Punitive Damages: Empirical Analyses Using the Civil Justice Survey of State Courts 1992, 1996, and 2001 Data, 3 J. Empirical Leg. Stud. 263 (2006); Eisenberg et al., The Predictability of Punitive Damages, 26 J. Legal Stud. 623 (1997); Eisenberg et al., Judges, Juries, and Punitive Damages, 87 Cornell L.Rev. 743 (2002). For discussion of the problematic manner in which juries often compute these awards, see Sunstein, Kahneman & Schkade, Assessing Punitive Damages (with Notes on Cognition and Valuation in Law), 107 Yale L.J. 2071 (1998); Schkade, Sunstein & Kahneman, Deliberating About Dollars: The Severity Shift, 100 Colum.L.Rev. 1139 (2000).

11. *Statutory change.* A majority of the states have placed statutory limitations on punitive damage awards, including a more demanding burden of proof and maximum dollar amounts above which punitive damages may not be recovered. These statutory changes are addressed in greater detail in the discussion of incremental tort reform, at p. 824 infra.

b. CONSTITUTIONAL LIMITATIONS

In seven opinions dating back to 1989 and including the following principal case, the Supreme Court has addressed the extent to which the U.S. Constitution places limits on punitive damages awards. The following case involves automobile insurance. As the next section explains, automobile liability insurance provides that the insurer will cover certain tort liabilities incurred by the insured. It also provides that the insurer will hire and pay for a lawyer to defend the insured in a lawsuit involving any claim that is potentially covered by the policy. When the insurer is providing the defense in a case that exposes the plaintiff/policyholder to uncovered liabilities, courts have imposed a duty on the insurer with regard to settlement that requires the insurer to take into account adequately the policyholder's uninsured interests. An insurer that breaches this duty is liable for the entire judgment, even if it exceeds the limits of the policy. The breach of this duty can also subject the insurer to punitive damages. The following case arose in this context.

State Farm Mutual Automobile Insurance Co. v. Campbell

Supreme Court of the United States, 2003.
538 U.S. 408, 123 S.Ct. 1513, 155 L.Ed.2d 585.

■ JUSTICE KENNEDY delivered the opinion of the Court.

We address once again the measure of punishment, by means of punitive damages, a State may impose upon a defendant in a civil case. The question is whether, in the circumstances we shall recount, an award of $145 million in punitive damages, where full compensatory damages are $1 million, is excessive and in violation of the Due Process Clause of the Fourteenth Amendment to the Constitution of the United States.

I

In 1981, Curtis Campbell (Campbell) was driving with his wife, Inez Preece Campbell, in Cache County, Utah. He decided to pass six vans traveling ahead of them on a two-lane highway. Todd Ospital was driving a small car approaching from the opposite direction. To avoid a head-on collision with Campbell, who by then was driving on the wrong side of the highway and toward oncoming traffic, Ospital swerved onto the shoulder, lost control of his automobile, and collided with a vehicle driven by Robert G. Slusher. Ospital was killed, and Slusher was rendered permanently disabled. The Campbells escaped unscathed.

In the ensuing wrongful death and tort action, Campbell insisted he was not at fault. Early investigations did support differing conclusions as to who caused the accident, but "a consensus was reached early on by the investigators and witnesses that Mr. Campbell's unsafe pass had indeed caused the crash." [ ] Campbell's insurance company, petitioner State Farm Mutual Automobile Insurance Company (State Farm), nonetheless decided to contest liability and declined offers by Slusher and Ospital's estate (Ospital) to settle the claims for the policy limit of $50,000 ($25,000 per claimant). State Farm also ignored the advice of one of its own investigators and took the case to trial, assuring the Campbells that "their assets were safe, that they had no liability for the accident, that [State Farm] would represent their interests, and that they did not need to procure separate counsel." [ ] To the contrary, a jury determined that Campbell was 100 percent at fault, and a judgment was returned for $185,849, far more than the amount offered in settlement.

At first State Farm refused to cover the $135,849 in excess liability. Its counsel made this clear to the Campbells: " 'You may want to put for sale signs on your property to get things moving.' " [ ] Nor was State Farm willing to post a supersedeas bond to allow Campbell to appeal the judgment against him. Campbell obtained his own counsel to appeal the verdict. During the pendency of the appeal, in late 1984, Slusher, Ospital, and the Campbells reached an agreement whereby Slusher and Ospital agreed not to seek satisfaction of their claims against the Campbells. In exchange the Campbells agreed to pursue a bad faith action against State Farm and to be represented by Slusher's and Ospital's attorneys. The Campbells also agreed that Slusher and Ospital would have a right to play a part in all major decisions concerning the bad faith action. No settlement could be concluded without Slusher's and Ospital's approval, and Slusher and Ospital would receive 90 percent of any verdict against State Farm.

In 1989, the Utah Supreme Court denied Campbell's appeal in the wrongful death and tort actions. [ ] State Farm then paid the entire judgment, including the amounts in excess of the policy limits. The Campbells nonetheless filed a complaint against State Farm alleging bad faith, fraud, and intentional infliction of emotional distress. The trial court initially granted State Farm's motion for summary judgment because State Farm had paid the excess verdict, but that ruling was reversed on appeal. 840 P.2d 130 (Utah App.1992). On remand State Farm moved *in limine* to exclude evidence of alleged conduct that occurred in unrelated cases outside of Utah, but the trial court denied the motion. At State Farm's request the trial court bifurcated the trial into two phases conducted before different juries. In the first phase the jury determined that State Farm's decision not to settle was unreasonable because there was a substantial likelihood of an excess verdict.

Before the second phase of the action against State Farm we decided BMW of North America, Inc. v. Gore, 517 U.S. 559 (1996), and refused to sustain a $2 million punitive damages award which accompanied a verdict of only $4,000 in compensatory damages. Based on that decision, State Farm again moved for the exclusion of evidence of dissimilar out-of-state conduct. [ ] The trial court denied State Farm's motion. [ ]

The second phase addressed State Farm's liability for fraud and intentional infliction of emotional distress, as well as compensatory and punitive damages. The Utah Supreme Court aptly characterized this phase of the trial:

> State Farm argued during phase II that its decision to take the case to trial was an "honest mistake" that did not warrant punitive damages. In contrast, the Campbells introduced evidence that State Farm's decision to take the case to trial was a result of a national scheme to meet corporate fiscal goals

by capping payouts on claims company wide. This scheme was referred to as State Farm's "Performance, Planning and Review," or PP & R, policy. To prove the existence of this scheme, the trial court allowed the Campbells to introduce extensive expert testimony regarding fraudulent practices by State Farm in its nation-wide operations. Although State Farm moved prior to phase II of the trial for the exclusion of such evidence and continued to object to it at trial, the trial court ruled that such evidence was admissible to determine whether State Farm's conduct in the Campbell case was indeed intentional and sufficiently egregious to warrant punitive damages. [ ]

Evidence pertaining to the PP & R policy concerned State Farm's business practices for over 20 years in numerous States. Most of these practices bore no relation to third-party automobile insurance claims, the type of claim underlying the Campbells' complaint against the company. The jury awarded the Campbells $2.6 million in compensatory damages and $145 million in punitive damages, which the trial court reduced to $1 million and $25 million respectively. Both parties appealed.

The Utah Supreme Court sought to apply the three guideposts we identified in [*Gore*], and it reinstated the $145 million punitive damages award. Relying in large part on the extensive evidence concerning the PP & R policy, the court concluded State Farm's conduct was reprehensible. The court also relied upon State Farm's "massive wealth" and on testimony indicating that "State Farm's actions, because of their clandestine nature, will be punished at most in one out of every 50,000 cases as a matter of statistical probability," [ ], and concluded that the ratio between punitive and compensatory damages was not unwarranted. Finally, the court noted that the punitive damages award was not excessive when compared to various civil and criminal penalties State Farm could have faced, including $10,000 for each act of fraud, the suspension of its license to conduct business in Utah, the disgorgement of profits, and imprisonment. [ ] We granted certiorari. [ ]

II

We recognized in *Cooper Industries, Inc. v. Leatherman Tool Group, Inc.,* 532 U.S. 424 (2001), that in our judicial system compensatory and punitive damages, although usually awarded at the same time by the same decisionmaker, serve different purposes. [ ] Compensatory damages "are intended to redress the concrete loss that the plaintiff has suffered by reason of the defendant's wrongful conduct." [ ] By contrast, punitive damages serve a broader function; they are aimed at deterrence and retribution. [ ]

While States possess discretion over the imposition of punitive damages, it is well established that there are procedural and substantive constitutional limitations on these awards. [ ] The Due

Process Clause of the Fourteenth Amendment prohibits the imposition of grossly excessive or arbitrary punishments on a tortfeasor. [*Cooper Industries, supra*] The reason is that "[e]lementary notions of fairness enshrined in our constitutional jurisprudence dictate that a person receive fair notice not only of the conduct that will subject him to punishment, but also of the severity of the penalty that a State may impose." [ ] To the extent an award is grossly excessive, it furthers no legitimate purpose and constitutes an arbitrary deprivation of property. [ ]

Although these awards serve the same purposes as criminal penalties, defendants subjected to punitive damages in civil cases have not been accorded the protections applicable in a criminal proceeding. This increases our concerns over the imprecise manner in which punitive damages systems are administered. We have admonished that "[p]unitive damages pose an acute danger of arbitrary deprivation of property. Jury instructions typically leave the jury with wide discretion in choosing amounts, and the presentation of evidence of a defendant's net worth creates the potential that juries will use their verdicts to express biases against big businesses, particularly those without strong local presences." [ ] Our concerns are heightened when the decisionmaker is presented, as we shall discuss, with evidence that has little bearing as to the amount of punitive damages that should be awarded. Vague instructions, or those that merely inform the jury to avoid "passion or prejudice," [ ], do little to aid the decisionmaker in its task of assigning appropriate weight to evidence that is relevant and evidence that is tangential or only inflammatory.

In light of these concerns, in *Gore, supra,* we instructed courts reviewing punitive damages to consider three guideposts: (1) the degree of reprehensibility of the defendant's misconduct; (2) the disparity between the actual or potential harm suffered by the plaintiff and the punitive damages award; and (3) the difference between the punitive damages awarded by the jury and the civil penalties authorized or imposed in comparable cases. [ ] We reiterated the importance of these three guideposts in *Cooper Industries* and mandated appellate courts to conduct *de novo* review of a trial court's application of them to the jury's award. [ ] Exacting appellate review ensures that an award of punitive damages is based upon an " 'application of law, rather than a decisionmaker's caprice.' " [ ]

III

Under the principles outlined in *BMW of North America, Inc. v. Gore,* this case is neither close nor difficult. It was error to reinstate the jury's $145 million punitive damages award. We address each guidepost of *Gore* in some detail.

A

"[T]he most important indicium of the reasonableness of a punitive damages award is the degree of reprehensibility of the defendant's conduct." [*Gore*] We have instructed courts to determine the reprehensibility of a defendant by considering whether: the harm caused was physical as opposed to economic; the tortious conduct evinced an indifference to or a reckless disregard of the health or safety of others; the target of the conduct had financial vulnerability; the conduct involved repeated actions or was an isolated incident; and the harm was the result of intentional malice, trickery, or deceit, or mere accident. [ ] The existence of any one of these factors weighing in favor of a plaintiff may not be sufficient to sustain a punitive damages award; and the absence of all of them renders any award suspect. It should be presumed a plaintiff has been made whole for his injuries by compensatory damages, so punitive damages should only be awarded if the defendant's culpability, after having paid compensatory damages, is so reprehensible as to warrant the imposition of further sanctions to achieve punishment or deterrence. [ ]

Applying these factors in the instant case, we must acknowledge that State Farm's handling of the claims against the Campbells merits no praise. The trial court found that State Farm's employees altered the company's records to make Campbell appear less culpable. State Farm disregarded the overwhelming likelihood of liability and the near-certain probability that, by taking the case to trial, a judgment in excess of the policy limits would be awarded. State Farm amplified the harm by at first assuring the Campbells their assets would be safe from any verdict and by later telling them, postjudgment, to put a for-sale sign on their house. While we do not suggest there was error in awarding punitive damages based upon State Farm's conduct toward the Campbells, a more modest punishment for this reprehensible conduct could have satisfied the State's legitimate objectives, and the Utah courts should have gone no further.

This case, instead, was used as a platform to expose, and punish, the perceived deficiencies of State Farm's operations throughout the country. The Utah Supreme Court's opinion makes explicit that State Farm was being condemned for its nationwide policies rather than for the conduct directed toward the Campbells. . . .

The Campbells contend that State Farm has only itself to blame for the reliance upon dissimilar and out-of-state conduct evidence. The record does not support this contention. From their opening statements onward the Campbells framed this case as a chance to rebuke State Farm for its nationwide activities. . . .

A State cannot punish a defendant for conduct that may have been lawful where it occurred. [ ] Nor, as a general rule, does a State have a legitimate concern in imposing punitive damages to punish a defendant for unlawful acts committed outside of the State's jurisdiction. Any proper adjudication of conduct that occurred outside Utah to other persons would require their inclusion, and, to those parties, the Utah courts, in the usual case, would need to apply the laws of their relevant jurisdiction. [ ]

Here, the Campbells do not dispute that much of the out-of-state conduct was lawful where it occurred. They argue, however, that such evidence was not the primary basis for the punitive damages award and was relevant to the extent it demonstrated, in a general sense, State Farm's motive against its insured. [ ] This argument misses the mark. Lawful out-of-state conduct may be probative when it demonstrates the deliberateness and culpability of the defendant's action in the State where it is tortious, but that conduct must have a nexus to the specific harm suffered by the plaintiff. A jury must be instructed, furthermore, that it may not use evidence of out-of-state conduct to punish a defendant for action that was lawful in the jurisdiction where it occurred. [ ] A basic principle of federalism is that each State may make its own reasoned judgment about what conduct is permitted or proscribed within its borders, and each State alone can determine what measure of punishment, if any, to impose on a defendant who acts within its jurisdiction. [ ]

For a more fundamental reason, however, the Utah courts erred in relying upon this and other evidence: The courts awarded punitive damages to punish and deter conduct that bore no relation to the Campbells' harm. A defendant's dissimilar acts, independent from the acts upon which liability was premised, may not serve as the basis for punitive damages. A defendant should be punished for the conduct that harmed the plaintiff, not for being an unsavory individual or business. Due process does not permit courts, in the calculation of punitive damages, to adjudicate the merits of other parties' hypothetical claims against a defendant under the guise of the reprehensibility analysis, but we have no doubt the Utah Supreme Court did that here. [ ] Punishment on these bases creates the possibility of multiple punitive damages awards for the same conduct; for in the usual case nonparties are not bound by the judgment some other plaintiff obtains. [ ]

The same reasons lead us to conclude the Utah Supreme Court's decision cannot be justified on the grounds that State Farm was a recidivist. Although "[o]ur holdings that a recidivist may be punished more severely than a first offender recognize that repeated misconduct is more reprehensible than an individual instance of malfeasance," [ ], in the context of civil actions courts must ensure the conduct in question replicates the prior transgressions. [ ]

The Campbells have identified scant evidence of repeated misconduct of the sort that injured them. Nor does our review of the Utah courts' decisions convince us that State Farm was only punished for its actions toward the Campbells. Although evidence of other acts need not be identical to have relevance in the calculation of punitive damages, the Utah court erred here because evidence pertaining to claims that had nothing to do with a third-party lawsuit was introduced at length. Other evidence concerning reprehensibility was even more tangential. For example, the Utah Supreme Court criticized State Farm's investigation into the personal life of one of its employees and, in a broader approach, the manner in which State Farm's policies corrupted its employees. . . .

B

Turning to the second *Gore* guidepost, we have been reluctant to identify concrete constitutional limits on the ratio between harm, or potential harm, to the plaintiff and the punitive damages award. [ ] We decline again to impose a bright-line ratio which a punitive damages award cannot exceed. Our jurisprudence and the principles it has now established demonstrate, however, that, in practice, few awards exceeding a single-digit ratio between punitive and compensatory damages, to a significant degree, will satisfy due process. . . . While these ratios [in earlier cases] are not binding, they are instructive. They demonstrate what should be obvious: Single-digit multipliers are more likely to comport with due process, while still achieving the State's goals of deterrence and retribution, than awards with ratios in range of 500 to 1, [ ], or, in this case, of 145 to 1.

Nonetheless, because there are no rigid benchmarks that a punitive damages award may not surpass, ratios greater than those we have previously upheld may comport with due process where "a particularly egregious act has resulted in only a small amount of economic damages." [ ] The converse is also true, however. When compensatory damages are substantial, then a lesser ratio, perhaps only equal to compensatory damages, can reach the outermost limit of the due process guarantee. The precise award in any case, of course, must be based upon the facts and circumstances of the defendant's conduct and the harm to the plaintiff.

In sum, courts must ensure that the measure of punishment is both reasonable and proportionate to the amount of harm to the plaintiff and to the general damages recovered. In the context of this case, we have no doubt that there is a presumption against an award that has a 145–to–1 ratio. The compensatory award in this case was substantial; the Campbells were awarded $1 million for a year and a half of emotional distress. This was complete compensation. The harm arose from a transaction in the economic realm, not from some physical assault or trauma; there were no physical injuries; and State Farm paid the excess verdict before the complaint was filed, so the Campbells suffered only minor economic injuries for the 18-month period in which State Farm refused to resolve the claim against them. The compensatory damages for the injury suffered here, moreover, likely were based on a component which was duplicated in the punitive award. Much of the distress was caused by the outrage and humiliation the Campbells suffered at the actions of their insurer; and it is a major role of punitive damages to condemn such conduct. Compensatory damages, however, already contain this punitive element. See Restatement (Second) of Torts § 908, Comment *c,* p. 466 (1977)("In many cases in which compensatory damages include an amount for emotional distress, such as humiliation or indignation aroused by the defendant's act, there is no clear line of demarcation between punishment and compensation and a verdict for a specified amount frequently includes elements of both").

. . .

The remaining premises for the Utah Supreme Court's decision bear no relation to the award's reasonableness or proportionality to the harm. They are, rather, arguments that seek to defend a departure from well-established constraints on punitive damages. While States enjoy considerable discretion in deducing when punitive damages are warranted, each award must comport with the principles set forth in *Gore.* Here the argument that State Farm will be punished in only the rare case, coupled with reference to its assets (which, of course, are what other insured parties in Utah and other States must rely upon for payment of claims) had little to do with the actual harm sustained by the Campbells. The wealth of a defendant cannot justify an otherwise unconstitutional punitive damages award. [ ] The principles set forth in *Gore* must be implemented with care, to ensure both reasonableness and proportionality.

C

The third guidepost in *Gore* is the disparity between the punitive damages award and the "civil penalties authorized or imposed in comparable cases." [ ] We note that, in the past, we have also looked to criminal penalties that could be imposed. [ ] The existence of a criminal penalty does have bearing on the seriousness with which a State views the wrongful action. When used to determine the dollar amount of the award, however, the criminal penalty has less utility. Great care must be taken to avoid use of the civil process to assess criminal penalties that can be imposed only after the heightened protections of a criminal trial have been observed, including, of course, its higher standards of proof. Punitive damages are not a substitute for the criminal process, and the remote possibility of a criminal sanction does not automatically sustain a punitive damages award.

Here, we need not dwell long on this guidepost. The most relevant civil sanction under Utah state law for the wrong done to the Campbells appears to be a $10,000 fine for an act of fraud, [ ], an amount dwarfed by the $145 million punitive damages award. The Supreme Court of Utah speculated about the loss of State Farm's business license, the disgorgement of profits, and possible imprisonment, but here again its references were to the broad fraudulent scheme drawn from evidence of out-of-state and dissimilar conduct. This analysis was insufficient to justify the award.

IV

An application of the *Gore* guideposts to the facts of this case, especially in light of the substantial compensatory damages awarded (a portion of which contained a punitive element), likely would justify a punitive damages award at or near the amount of compensatory damages. The punitive award of $145 million, therefore, was neither reasonable nor proportionate to the wrong committed, and it was an irrational and arbitrary deprivation of the property of the defendant. The proper calculation of punitive damages under the principles we have discussed should be resolved, in the first instance, by the Utah courts.

The judgment of the Utah Supreme Court is reversed, and the case is remanded for proceedings not inconsistent with this opinion.

■ JUSTICE SCALIA, dissenting.

I adhere to the view expressed in my dissenting opinion in [*Gore*], that the Due Process Clause provides no substantive protections against "excessive" or " 'unreasonable' " awards of punitive damages. I am also of the view that the punitive damages jurisprudence which has sprung forth from *BMW v. Gore* is insusceptible of principled application; accordingly, I do not feel justified in giving the case *stare decisis* effect. [ ] I would affirm the judgment of the Utah Supreme Court. [For largely these same reasons, Justice Thomas separately dissented.]

■ JUSTICE GINSBURG, dissenting.

Not long ago, this Court was hesitant to impose a federal check on state-court judgments awarding punitive damages. In [a 1989 case], the Court held that neither the Excessive Fines Clause of the Eighth Amendment nor federal common law circumscribed awards of punitive damages in civil cases between private parties. [ ] Two years later, in [ ], the Court observed that "unlimited jury [or judicial] discretion . . . in the fixing of punitive damages may invite extreme results that jar one's constitutional sensibilities," [ ]; the Due Process Clause, the Court suggested, would attend to those sensibilities and guard against unreasonable awards, [ ]. Nevertheless, the Court upheld a punitive damages award in [in one of these cases] "more than 4 times the amount of compensatory damages, . . . more than 200 times [the plaintiff's] out-of-pocket expenses," and "much in excess of the fine that could be imposed." . . .

It was not until 1996, in [*Gore*], that the Court, for the first time, invalidated a state-court punitive damages assessment as unreasonably large. [ ] If our activity in this domain is now "well-established," see [Court's opinion part III B], it takes place on ground not long held.

In *Gore,* I stated why I resisted the Court's foray into punitive damages "territory traditionally within the States' domain." [ ] I adhere to those views. . . .

I

The large size of the award upheld by the Utah Supreme Court in this case indicates why damage-capping legislation may be altogether fitting and proper. Neither the amount of the award nor the trial record, however, justifies this Court's substitution of its judgment for that of Utah's competent decisionmakers. In this regard, I count it significant that, on the key criterion "reprehensibility," there is a good deal more to the story than the Court's abbreviated account tells.

[Justice Ginsburg recounted other evidence at length.]

State Farm's "policies and practices," the trial evidence thus bore out, were "responsible for the injuries suffered by the Campbells," and the means used to implement those policies could be found "callous, clandestine, fraudulent, and dishonest." [ ]; [ ] (finding "ample evidence" that State Farm's reprehensible corporate policies were responsible for injuring "many other Utah consumers during the past two decades"). The Utah Supreme Court, relying on the trial court's record-based recitations, understandably characterized State Farm's behavior as "egregious and malicious." [ ]

. . .

When the Court first ventured to override state-court punitive damages awards, it did so moderately. The Court recalled that "[i]n our federal system, States necessarily have considerable flexibility in determining the level of punitive damages that they will allow in different classes of cases and in any particular case." [*Gore*] Today's decision exhibits no such respect and restraint. No longer content to accord state-court judgments "a strong presumption of validity," [ ], the Court announces that "few awards exceeding a single-digit ratio between punitive and compensatory damages, to a significant degree, will satisfy due process." [ ] Moreover, the Court adds, when compensatory damages are substantial, doubling those damages "can reach the outermost limit of the due process guarantee." [ ] In a legislative scheme or a state high court's design to cap punitive damages, the handiwork in setting single-digit and 1-to-1 benchmarks could hardly be questioned; in a judicial decree imposed on the States by this Court under the banner of substantive due process, the numerical controls today's decision installs seem to me boldly out of order.

. . .

NOTES AND QUESTIONS

1. *History of the case.* On remand from the Supreme Court's decision, the Utah Supreme Court unanimously found the "blameworthiness of State Farm's behavior toward the Campbells to be several degrees more offensive than the Supreme Court's less than condemnatory phrase that State Farm's behavior 'merits no praise.'" The court reviewed the evidence and the standards that it had used. It concluded that the conduct was "so egregious" as to warrant a punitive award that was $9 million—nine times the compensatory award. Campbell v. State Farm Mutual Automobile Insurance Co., 98 P.3d 409 (Utah 2004). For an illuminating case study of the 20-year *Campbell* litigation from initial traffic accident through Supreme Court decision, see J. Stempel, Litigation Road: The Story of *Campbell v. State Farm* (2008).

2. *Reprehensibility.* Although the *Campbell* Court emphasized that reprehensibility is the most important factor in the constitutional inquiry, it did not specify how that factor relates to the others. Does greater reprehensibility justify punitive awards at the upper end of the single-digit ratio, or awards above that amount? In Boeken v. Philip Morris Inc., 127 Cal.App.4th 1640 (App.2005), the court found that all five reprehensibility factors mentioned in *Campbell* established that defendant tobacco manufacturer's fraudulent misconduct was "highly reprehensible," justifying a punitive damages award nine times greater than compensatory damages. In a subsequent case involving "the same defendant, same causes of action, same counsel, and much of the same conduct as this case," the court upheld a punitive award 33 times greater than compensatory damages. Bullock v. Philip Morris, Inc., 42 Cal.Rptr.3d 140 (App.2006). Unlike *Boeken*, the court in *Bullock* was able to rely on a decision recently issued by the California Supreme Court stating that a punitive damages award that exceeds the single-digit ratio is not necessarily unconstitutional but instead requires special justification. Simon v. San Paolo Holding Co., 113 P.3d 63 (Cal.2005). What would constitute such special justification?

3. *Defendant's wealth.* The *Campbell* Court stated that a defendant's wealth "cannot justify an otherwise unconstitutional punitive damages award." Can it justify a higher award of punitive damages than if the defendant were of less substantial means? Might the answer to this question depend on whether the defendant's misconduct involved obtaining a financial advantage, such as in *Campbell*, or involved malicious personal behavior such as assault and battery?

The role of wealth has been important at the state level. Some state courts or statutes appear to require the plaintiff to prove defendant's wealth as part of the case for punitive damages. See, e.g., Herman v. Sunshine Chemical Specialties, Inc., 627 A.2d 1081 (N.J.1993); Adams v. Murakami, 813 P.2d 1348 (Cal.1991). But see Hall v. Wal-Mart, 959 P.2d 109 (Utah 1998), in which the defendant challenged a punitive award of $25,000 for lack of proof of wealth. The court, 3–2, held that this was not necessary in every case. It relied heavily on Kemezy v. Peters, 79 F.3d 33 (7th Cir.1996), in which Judge Posner observed:

> The reprehensibility of a person's conduct is not mitigated by his not being a rich person, and plaintiffs are never required to apologize for seeking damages that if awarded will precipitate the defendant into bankruptcy. A plea of poverty is a classic appeal to the mercy of the judge or jury, and why the plaintiff should be required to make the pleas on behalf of his opponent eludes us. . . . The defendant who cannot pay a large award of punitive

damages can point this out to the jury so that they will not waste their time and that of the bankruptcy courts by awarding an amount that exceeds his ability to pay.

The *Hall* court did note, however, that a plaintiff might be well advised to present evidence on this question when requesting a very large punitive award because an award that might otherwise be presumptively excessive under prevailing standards "can be justified by the defendant's relative wealth." The dissenters objected that the majority had read "relative wealth" out of the state's list of seven factors to be used whenever punitive damages were considered.

Although it has sometimes been suggested that punitive awards may not exceed some percentage of the defendant's assets, courts appear to focus more on the conduct in question. See Rufo v. Simpson, 103 Cal.Rptr.2d 492 (App.2001)(affirming two punitive damage awards of $12.5 million against O.J. Simpson, who the jury found committed two murders).

4. *Harms to non-parties.* According to *Campbell*, evidence of misconduct unrelated to and different from that directed to the plaintiffs may not be considered to determine the reprehensibility of the defendant's conduct. Suppose that State Farm adopted a policy that its claims agents should engage in fraudulent conduct in order to defend any claims for which State Farm was the insurer. Would such a policy be admissible to demonstrate State Farm's reprehensibility?

After *Campbell*, in Philip Morris USA v. Williams, 549 U.S. 346 (2007), the Supreme Court confronted the question of the role of harm to other persons in determining the proper amount of punitive damages. On top of an $820,000 compensatory damage award to a cigarette smoker, the jury awarded $79.5 million in punitive damages, which were reduced to $32 million by the trial judge. The Oregon Supreme Court rejected the defendant's argument that the trial court erred by failing to give an instruction that defendant could not be punished for the harm it had done to others. Plaintiff's counsel made just such an argument to the jury. The U.S. Supreme Court ruled that the Due Process Clause barred consideration of harm to others in awarding punitive damages. Adjudicating the existence and number of others harmed, the seriousness of harm suffered, and the culpability of defendant's conduct toward others would be nearly impossible. Without requiring such proof and affording defendant the opportunity to respond denies defendant fundamental procedural protection. Drawing a fine distinction, the Court held that a jury may consider the harm inflicted on others in assessing the reprehensibility of the defendant's conduct and in deciding on the proper ratio between compensatory and punitive damages. At the same time, a jury may not punish a defendant for harm to others. Dissenting, Justice Stevens tartly commented, "This nuance eludes me." Id. at 360.

5. *Deterrence.* In one of the pre-*Campbell* cases, TXO Production Corp. v. Alliance Resources Corp., 509 U.S. 443 (1993), the Court upheld a West Virginia punitive award of $10 million, 526 times larger than the compensatory award of $19,000. The Court rejected a constitutional challenge based on the disparity. The Court quoted approvingly a passage from an earlier West Virginia case:

> For instance, a man wildly fires a gun into a crowd. By sheer chance, no one is injured and the only damage is to a $10 pair of glasses. A jury reasonably could find only $10 in compensatory damages, but thousands of dollars in punitive damages in order to discourage future bad acts.

Can *TXO* be reconciled with *Campbell* and *Williams*? To what extent does the concern for deterrence justify a departure from the single-digit ratio? In *Mathias*, p. 747 supra, the two punitive damage awards were each 37.2 times the amount of compensatory damages. In concluding that the awards satisfied the constitutional requirements of due process, the court observed that *Campbell* "did not lay down a . . . single-digit ratio rule—it said merely that "there is a presumption against an award that has a 145-to-1 ratio." 347 F.3d at 676.

Consider *Williams* in relation to the deterrence rationale for punitive damages, which would justify treble damages in the event that defendant expected to be sued in only 1/3 of all meritorious cases. See note 5, p. 754 supra. To what extent is this rationale based on the unconstitutional argument that defendant should be punished for harms to non-parties (the 2/3 meritorious cases that are not litigated)? Compare Geistfeld, Punitive Damages, Retribution, and Due Process, 81 S.Cal.L.Rev. 263 (2008)(arguing that punitive awards that only vindicate the plaintiff's individual tort right as required by *Williams* also sufficiently promote general deterrence in mass markets).

6. *The impact of* Campbell *and* Williams. A recent empirical study found that *Campbell* has generally reduced the size of blockbuster punitive awards—those exceeding $100 million—and has reduced the likelihood that a punitive award will exceed the single-digit ratio. See Viscusi & McMichael, Shifting the Fat Tail of Blockbuster Punitive Damage Awards, 11 J. Empirical Stud. 350 (2014). The potential impact of *Williams* on large punitive damage awards is illustrated by Bullock v. Philip Morris USA, Inc., 71 Cal.Rptr.3d 775, 802–07 (App.2008), in which the court overturned a $28 billion punitive damage award that had been reduced to $28 million on a remittitur by the trial court on the basis of a jury instruction inconsistent with the due process limitations established in *Williams*.

7. *The binding ratio in maritime cases.* Citing the sources and data referred to in note 10, p. 755 supra, the Supreme Court concluded in Exxon Shipping Co. v. Baker, 554 U.S. 471 (2008), that much of the criticism of these awards is unjustified and that overall they have been awarded with "restraint." Nevertheless, the Court expressed concern about their unpredictability and the variance in amounts, reflecting large outlier awards. Ruling for the first time on punitive damages as a matter of federal common law—because the case was governed by maritime law—the Court concluded that the best solution for narrowing the variance is to limit the ratio of punitive to compensatory awards. Based on the studies it cited finding a median ratio below 1–1, the Court adopted a maximum limit of a

1–1 ratio for maritime law. The Court's decision brought the long-running litigation over the Exxon Valdez oil spill in Alaska in 1989 to a conclusion. For an insightful and highly critical analysis of the case, see Sharkey, The Exxon Valdez Litigation Marathon: A Window on Punitive Damages, 7 U.St. Thomas L.J. 25 (2010).

Professors Eisenberg, Heise, and Wells, on whose work the Court relied for its variance and unpredictability assessments, subsequently disaggregated their data based on the size of the punitive damage award. They found the largest ratios in the cases with the smallest punitive damage awards, with mean ratios of 100–1 in cases with awards under $1,000, declining to 1.5–1 for awards in excess of $10,000. Eisenberg et al., Variability in Punitive Damages: An Empirical Assessment of the U.S. Supreme Court's Decision in *Exxon Shipping v. Baker* (2009). Cornell Law School Research Paper No. 09–011, available at http://ssrn.com/abstract= 1392438. What are the implications of these findings for the reasoning in *Baker*?

Binding only in maritime cases, *Baker* has not had much influence beyond that area. See Line v. Ventura, 38 So.3d 1 (Ala.2009), in which defendant challenged a punitive damage award of $550,000 in light of compensatory damages amounting to $200,000. The court responded to defendant's effort to invoke *Baker*, "We reject [this] argument in light of the *Baker* Court's explicit limitation of its holding to federal maritime common law." See also Myers v. Central Fla. Investments, Inc., 592 F.3d 1201 (11th Cir.2010)(challenge to punitive damages awarded in a ratio of about 5–1 in which court stated that *Baker* had no effect on Florida punitive damages law).

8. *Repetitive awards.* In W.R. Grace & Co. v. Waters, 638 So.2d 502 (Fla.1994), a mass tort action involving asbestos products, the court refused to bar multiple awards of punitive damages. The court noted that other courts have "unanimously" rejected the idea that such damages be awarded only once—perhaps to the first successful plaintiff:

> We acknowledge the potential for abuse when a defendant may be subjected to repeated punitive damage awards arising out of the same conduct. Yet, like the many other courts which have addressed the problem, we are unable to devise a fair and effective solution. Were we to adopt the position advocated by Grace, our holding would not be binding on other state courts or federal courts. This would place Floridians injured by asbestos on an unequal footing with the citizens of other states with regard to the right to recover damages from companies who engage in extreme misconduct. Any realistic solution to the problems caused by the asbestos litigation in the United States must be applicable to all fifty states. It is our belief that such a uniform solution can only be effected by federal legislation.

Although the lower court had suggested that Grace could use the fact of prior awards as mitigation before this jury, "advising the jury of previous punitive damage awards would actually hurt its cause" as it tries to argue that it should not be punished at all. The *Grace* court sought to meet this concern by ordering lower courts to bifurcate the proceeding. The first step would permit evidence on: (1) liability, (2) the amount of compensatory damages and (3) liability for punitive damages. If the jury determines that punitive damages are appropriate, the second step would permit evidence on the amount of such damages, including any prior awards. This would permit defendant to "build a record for a due process argument based on the cumulative effect of prior awards." More than a dozen states use this type of bifurcation. See also Owens-Corning Fiberglas Corp. v. Ballard, 749 So.2d 483 (Fla.1999)(upholding a punitive award of $31 million in an asbestos case).

For an extended consideration of the problem of exposure to repeated punitive awards, see Dunn v. HOVIC, 1 F.3d 1371 (3d Cir.1993)(en banc), holding, 8–5, that repeated awards are not per se unconstitutional, although repeated awards may be relevant in assessing constitutional attacks on the awards—either on the ground that the total sum is too high or on the ground that the particular defendant cannot afford to pay them. The dissenting opinion of Judge Weis emphasized that even within a single state, early punitive awards risked leaving later victims without recovery for even their compensatory damages.

Is the concern about repetitive awards of punitive damages mitigated by the Court's statements in *Campbell* that conduct outside the state ordinarily is not proper for consideration in deciding punitive damages? Is it a satisfactory resolution?

9.   *The view from abroad.* Adam Liptak, *Foreign Courts Wary of U.S. Punitive Damages*, N.Y. Times, March 26, 2008, at A1 reports on the negative attitude of the rest of the world about punitive damages in the United States. The article discusses the Italian Supreme Court's refusal to permit enforcement of a United States judgment because the idea of using damages in a civil case to punish is so antithetical to Italian notions of justice. Similarly, Helmut Koziol reports on the refusal of the German Supreme Court to enforce a United States judgment for $400,000 in punitive damages. Koziol, Punitive Damages—A European Perspective, 68 La.L.Rev. 741, 742 (2008).

10.   For commentary on the Court's entry into regulating punitive damages on constitutional grounds, see Colby, Clearing the Smoke from *Philip Morris v. Williams*: The Past, Present, and Future of Punitive Damages, 118 Yale L.J. 392 (2008)(arguing that the constitutional question differs depending on whether the damages punish private wrongs or public wrongs); Geistfeld, Constitutional Tort Reform, 38 Loy.L.A.L.Rev. 1093 (2005)(considering the extent to which use of the Due Process Clause to regulate punitive damages may extend to other areas of tort law); Hines, Due Process Limitations on Punitive Damages: Why *State Farm* Won't Be the Last Word, 37 Akron L.Rev. 779 (2004)(identifying the significance of reprehensibility, defendant's wealth, and repetitive award of punitive damages for the same conduct as requiring future attention by the Court).

B. TORT LAW AND INSURANCE

Inevitably a course on tort law emphasizes accidental injuries caused by others. In the real world, however, we often accidentally hurt ourselves or suffer injury at the hands of natural forces that are not subject to tort law. As society has grown more affluent, individuals have increasingly sought to insure themselves and their families against the financial burden of these misfortunes. The institution of life insurance, which is several hundred years old, was developed to permit a person to protect others against the financial consequences of the insured's premature death. In the twentieth century, individuals for the first time could procure insurance against the expenses of hospitalization, unusual medical expenses, and disruption of labor income as the result of an accident or illness. These lines of insurance are called "first-party" insurance because the underlying loss is suffered directly by the insured (the first party). Liability insurance, taken out to protect the insured against the economic impact of having to pay damages to another person, is called "third-party" insurance because the underlying loss is suffered by a third person (the tort plaintiff), the cost of which is then shifted via the imposition of legal liability to the insured (as tort defendant). Liability insurance did not appear until the end of the nineteenth century. See generally K. Abraham, The Liability Century 14–38 (2008).

Although first-party and third-party insurance cover different situations and serve different goals, they may co-exist in the same insurance policy. For example, homeowner's insurance provides first-party coverage protecting the policyholder from damage to the insured property caused by fire and other specified perils. A homeowner with a mortgage may be required to purchase such insurance to secure the value of the loan. The policy, however, also has a third-party aspect—coverage that protects the insured against legal liability incurred in non-vehicular contexts, regardless of whether the conduct occurred on the insured premises.

The conventional automobile insurance policy also contains both types of insurance.

First-party coverage:

> Medical Payments coverage provides protection against specified amounts of hospital and medical costs for each person injured in the policyholder's vehicle (usually a relatively small amount, e.g., $5,000).

> Collision insurance covers the cost of repairs to a policyholder's car after an accident, regardless of whether the policyholder was at fault.

> Comprehensive coverage protects the policyholder's car against the perils of fire, theft, flood, vandalism, or malicious mischief.

Personal Injury Protection—available only in no-fault states discussed infra p. 854.

Third-party coverage:

Bodily Injury Liability provides coverage when the policyholder (or other lawful operator) is found to be at fault and legally liable for the personal injury of a third party. The amount of coverage usually varies in multiples of thousands of dollars of coverage per person and per occurrence. For example, bodily injury coverage of $100,000/$300,000 would provide protection up to $100,000 for each person, and up to $300,000 for all persons, injured in an accident in which the policyholder (or other lawful operator) is at fault. BI coverage also obligates the insurer to defend the policyholder against third-party bodily injury claims.

Property Damage Liability coverage compensates third parties for loss of or damage to their property (whether a picket fence or a car) inflicted by the policyholder's vehicle under circumstances in which the policyholder (or other lawful operator) is found to be at fault. Here, too, the insurer is obligated to defend the policyholder against third-party claims.

Some coverage provisions are hybrids that are comprised of both first- and third-party coverage:

Uninsured Motorists coverage provides specified amounts of protection to the policyholder and occupants of his or her car against personal injury and property damage losses incurred in an accident in which the other driver is uninsured and is determined to be at fault. (Underinsured motorist coverage operates in a similar fashion.)

First-party insurance is offered with a variety of coverage limitations (or policy limits) and deductible amounts. Deductibles are not generally available under third-party insurance.

Regardless of whether a policy contains both forms of coverage, first-party insurance fundamentally differs from third-party insurance, requiring us to consider how each type interacts with tort law.

1. TORT LAW AND FIRST-PARTY INSURANCE

Beyond the voluntarily acquired first-party insurance already discussed, universal governmental programs protect individuals against certain risks. These include coverage of medical costs for those over age 65 through Medicare, benefit programs for disabled persons of whatever age (SSDI)—some stressing long term disabilities and others temporary conditions—and attempts to cushion the financial shocks of unemployment and retirement. Still other government programs help those injured in occupational accidents. We discuss workers' compensation in Chapter XII.

All studies indicate that non-tort first-party sources of aid are already significant and becoming more so as first-party insurance becomes more widespread. According to the U.S. Census Bureau, over 90% of all Americans were covered by some form of health insurance in 2015. The impact of these private and governmental programs on the damages to be awarded in a tort action depends on the collateral source rule and the doctrine of subrogation addressed in the next two sections.

a.   THE COLLATERAL SOURCE RULE

Kenney v. Liston
Supreme Court of Appeals of West Virginia, 2014.
760 S.E.2d 434.

■ KETCHUM, J.

[Defendant drove while intoxicated and badly injured plaintiff. Defendant admitted liability, and so the trial involved only the determination of damages.] As a result of the collision, the plaintiff incurred medical bills in excess of $70,000.00. West Virginia law permits a plaintiff to recover the necessary and reasonable medical expenses for an injury from a tortfeasor. Proof that a medical bill was incurred is *prima facie* evidence the expense was necessary and reasonable. [ ] The plaintiff therefore sought to recover the entire billed amount as his necessary and reasonable medical expenses.

Prior to trial, the defendant filed a motion *in limine* and asserted that only a portion of each medical bill had been paid, either by the plaintiff (as co-pays or deductibles) or by the plaintiff's health insurance carrier (Blue Cross/Blue Shield). By an agreement between the plaintiff's medical providers and his health insurance carrier, the medical bills were discounted, reduced, or adjusted downward. Because of the agreement with the health insurance carrier, the remaining, unpaid portions of the medical bills were "written off" by the plaintiff's medical providers.

The defendant asserted that the plaintiff's damages "should be limited to the amounts actually paid by Plaintiff . . . and amounts paid on Plaintiff's behalf by any collateral source," such as the plaintiff's health insurance carrier. . . . The defendant contends that since the full bills were neither paid nor actually incurred by the plaintiff or the plaintiff's health insurance carrier, the plaintiff should not be allowed to introduce evidence of those written-off amounts at trial.

The circuit court denied the defendant's motion *in limine* because the discounts or write-offs were a collateral source to the plaintiff. The circuit court reasoned that under the collateral source rule, the plaintiff was entitled to recover damages for the value of any reasonable and necessary medical services he received, "whether such services are rendered gratuitously or paid for by another." [] . . . Because of the collateral source rule, and because the evidence would tend to be misleading and prejudicial, the circuit court prevented the defendant from offering any evidence that the bills for the plaintiff's medical services were either reduced by the provider or paid by the health insurer at a discounted rate.

. . . The jury awarded the plaintiff compensatory damages totaling $325,272.92. The verdict included $74,061.00 for the plaintiff's past medical expenses, an amount almost equal to the total amount of the plaintiff's medical bills.

. . .

The defendant now appeals and asks that we vacate the circuit court's judgment order in its entirety and grant the parties a new trial. . . .

The question presented concerns how to calculate the "reasonable value" of the plaintiff's medical services in light of the collateral source rule. The defendant argues that the collateral source rule does not apply to the difference in value between the amount billed and the amount paid. The plaintiff responds that the collateral source rule protects the entire amount initially billed, so long as it was necessary and reasonable, because any discounts or written-off amounts were as a result of a collateral source: the plaintiff's health insurance. In addition, the plaintiff argues that W.Va.Code § 57–5–4j provides that the medical bills that he incurred are *prima facie* evidence that the amounts billed were necessary and reasonable.

The collateral source rule is a long-standing principle in West Virginia law and has been "a staple of American tort law since before the Civil War."[9] "The collateral source rule excludes payments from other sources to plaintiffs from being used to reduce damage awards imposed upon culpable defendants." [] The collateral source rule protects payments made to or benefits conferred upon an injured party from sources other than the tortfeasor by denying the tortfeasor any corresponding offset or credit against the injured party's damages. Even though these collateral sources mitigate the injured party's loss, they do not reduce the tortfeasor's liability. [] . . .

The law is clear that, "A tort victim who has incurred medical expenses, suffered lost wages, or experienced other compensable loss,

---

[9]   Michael I. Krauss & Jeremy Kidd, Collateral Source and Tort's Soul, 48 U. Louisville L.Rev. 1,4 (2009). The collateral source rule first appeared in America in The Propeller Monticello v. Mollison, 58 U.S. 152 (1854). The term "collateral source" derives from language used in 1870, in Harding v. Town of Townshend, 43 Vt. 536, 538 (1870) ("The policy of insurance is collateral to the remedy against the defendant, and was procured solely by the plaintiff and at his expense, and to the procurement of which the defendant was in no way contributory.").

may sue the tortfeasor for the entire amount of the victim's injuries even if those losses have been neutralized by first-party insurance, by the victim's relatives, by the victim's employer, or through the kindness of strangers." [ ] A tortfeasor cannot take advantage of a contract or relationship "between an injured party and a third person, no matter whether the source of the funds received is an insurance company, an employer, a family member, or other source." [ ] . . .

The collateral source rule is both a rule of evidence and a rule of damages.

"As a rule of evidence, [the collateral source rule] precludes the defendant in a personal injury or wrongful death case from introducing evidence that some of the plaintiff's damages have been paid by a collateral source." [ ] Because the likelihood of misuse by the jury clearly outweighs the probative value of evidence of collateral benefits, the "induction of collateral sources into the jury's consciousness for whatever purpose is to be avoided." [ ] The theory is "that the jury may well reduce the damages based on the amounts that the plaintiff has been shown to have received from collateral sources." [ ] For example, "[c]alling attention to the fact that a plaintiff had [hospitalization or medical] insurance can be prejudicial error because the jury may conclude that plaintiff sustained no damages for which he was entitled to recover if his medical bills were paid by insurance." [ ]

As a rule of damages, the collateral source rule "precludes the defendant from offsetting the judgment against any receipt of collateral sources by the plaintiff." [ ] The "rationale for this rule is that the party at fault should not be able to minimize his damages by offsetting payments received by the injured party through his own independent arrangements." [ ] "[T]he wrongdoer should not benefit from the expenditures made by the injured party or take advantage of contracts or other relations that may exist between the injured party and third persons." [ ]

. . .

Examples of collateral sources that are inadmissible to reduce a defendant's liability, in both our jurisprudence and that of other states, are legion. Benefits to a plaintiff protected by the collateral source rule come from sources as diverse as life insurance [ ], health insurance [ ], accident insurance [ ], workers' compensation [ ], sick pay [ ], vacation pay [ ], gratuitous nursing care by a relative [ ], charity [ ], remarriage [ ], disability insurance [ ], veteran's and military hospitals [ ], tax savings [ ], private or government pension programs such as Social Security [ ], or other government programs like Medicare and Medicaid [ ]. The cases from this jurisdiction and others are clear: "Only benefits received from the original tortfeasor, the tortfeasor's agent, or a joint tortfeasor reduce a tort defendant's liability." [ ]

We turn now to the specific question at hand: does the collateral source rule protect the amounts discounted from the plaintiff's medical bill or written off by the medical provider? We hold that it does, because the amount of the medical expense that was discounted or written off can be considered both a benefit of the plaintiff's bargain with his health insurance carrier, and a gratuitous benefit arising from the plaintiff's bargain with the medical provider. "A creditor's forgiveness of debt—that is what a write-down in the present context amounts to—is often considered equivalent to payment in other contexts, e.g., income tax, credit bids at foreclosure, etc. In other words, a creditor's partial forgiveness of a tort victim's medical bills via a write-down is properly considered a third-party 'payment,' evidence of which is barred by the collateral source rule." [ ] . . .

A majority of jurisdictions that have considered this question hold that a plaintiff can present to the jury the amount that a health care provider initially billed for the services necessarily rendered, and not merely amounts that were later paid. [ ] The tortfeasor cannot offer evidence that part of the bill was discounted or written off. Further, the plaintiff is not limited to recovering only expenditures made or obligations actually incurred. The plaintiff may recover the full amount of his or her reasonable and necessary medical expenses, even if those expenses were later discounted and a portion written off by the health care provider. Regardless of how, or even whether, the plaintiff's obligation to the medical provider was later discharged, the plaintiff became liable for the bills when the services were received; the plaintiff is therefore entitled to recover the value of the services. "The damage is sustained when the plaintiff incurs the liability, and the method by which that liability is later discharged has no effect on the measure of damages." [ ]

. . .

The public policies behind the collateral source rule are wide ranging. For one, "it is better for injured plaintiffs to receive the benefit of collateral sources in addition to actual damages than for defendants to be able to limit their liability for damages merely by the fortuitous presence of these sources." [ ] The Supreme Court of Virginia has said:

> The collateral source rule is designed to strike a balance between two competing principles of tort law: (1) a plaintiff is entitled to compensation sufficient to make him whole, but no more; and (2) a defendant is liable for all damages that proximately result from his wrong. A plaintiff who receives a double recovery for a single tort enjoys a windfall; a defendant who escapes, in whole or in part, liability for his wrong enjoys a windfall. *Because the law must sanction one windfall and deny the other, it favors the victim of the wrong rather than the wrongdoer.* [ ]

The collateral source rule is a central part of the tort system's goal of "requiring tortfeasors to make right their wrongful acts." [ ] The primary unifying principle of tort law is one of corrective justice, that is, the law establishes a legal duty for a tortfeasor to repair any damage or losses carelessly inflicted upon a victim. As the drafters of the *Restatement (Second) of Torts* recognized, "it is the tortfeasor's responsibility to compensate for *all* harm that he causes," [ ] not merely the net loss to the injured party.

We are persuaded that a defendant owes to an injured plaintiff a duty to make right for his or her wrongful acts, and so must pay the plaintiff compensation for all losses proximately caused by any negligence or wrongdoing. It is the defendant's responsibility to repair the damage he or she has done to the plaintiff, and the plaintiff's receipt of benefits from collateral sources, whether from affection, philanthropy, contract, social services, or others cannot relieve the defendant of this obligation. "The collateral source rule requires the injured party to be made whole exclusively by the tortfeasor and not by a combination of compensation from the tortfeasor and collateral sources."

In light of the above, we hold that the rule that collateral source benefits are not subtracted from a plaintiff's recovery applies to proceeds or benefits from sources such as insurance policies, whether maintained by the plaintiff or a third party; employment benefits; services or benefits rendered gratuitously (whether free, discounted, or later written off); and social legislation benefits. The law does not differentiate between the nature of these collateral source benefits, so long as they did not come from the defendant or a person acting for the defendant.

. . .

In this case, the defendant does not deny that the plaintiff would have been liable for the total amount billed by his medical providers absent his health insurance coverage. Whether the plaintiff took benefits from his health insurer in the form of medical expense payments or in the form of discounts and write-offs because of agreements between his health insurer and his health care providers is irrelevant. Those amounts written off are as much of a benefit for which the plaintiff paid consideration as are the actual cash payments made by his health insurer to the health care providers. This is the very purpose of the collateral source rule: to prevent a defendant from reaping the benefits of a plaintiff's preparation and protection.

Accordingly, we find no error in the circuit court's decision to apply the collateral source rule and prohibit the defendant from introducing evidence of the plaintiff's discounted medical bills.

. . .

Affirmed.

■ BENJAMIN, J., concurs. . . .

■ LOUGHERY, J., dissenting.

. . .

The majority concludes that the "write-off" or discount is a benefit the plaintiff received from her insurer because she paid the premium and her insurer extinguished her liability for the full price of her medical care through a combination of cash payments and the negotiated "write off" or discount. However, the majority ignores the fact that the plaintiff was never liable for the inflated bill because at the time the charges were incurred, the medical provider and the insurer had already agreed on a different price for the services rendered. . . . Furthermore, the "write off" or discount does not primarily benefit the plaintiff and to the extent that it does, it was not intended as compensation for the plaintiff's injuries. . . .

Given the current complexities of health care pricing structures, it is simply absurd to conclude that the amount billed for a certain procedure reflects the "reasonable value" of that medical service. Like retailers who raise the price of their goods by twenty-five percent before having a ten percent off sale, medical providers utilize the same sort of tactic to ensure a profit. In fact, "[b]ecause so many patients, insured, uninsured, and recipients under government health care programs, pay discounted rates, hospital bills have been called 'insincere,' in the sense that they would yield truly enormous profits if those prices were actually paid." [ ]

One authority reports that hospitals historically billed insured and uninsured patients similarly. [ ] With the advent of managed care, some insurers began demanding deep discounts, and hospitals shifted costs to less influential patients. [ ] This authority reports that insurers generally pay about forty cents per dollar of billed charges and that hospitals accept such amounts in full satisfaction of the billed charges. [ ]

. . .

The collateral source rule should not be extended to permit plaintiffs to receive compensation for medical expenses that were never paid by anyone. The rule was intended to prevent tortfeasors from unfairly receiving a discount on the damages they are required to pay merely because a plaintiff was wise or fortunate enough to have procured insurance coverage. Limiting the amounts which can be recovered as damages for medical expenses to those amounts actually paid, as opposed to fictitious amounts generated by medical providers to ensure they can still make a profit after giving a substantial discount, does not thwart the rationale behind the collateral source rule. If tortfeasors are automatically required to compensate plaintiffs for their medical expenses at the highest possible price, regardless of the actual amounts paid, those costs will inevitably be passed on to the public through higher insurance premiums. "Tort law . . . is not designed to be a Las Vegas game of chance; it serves no useful purpose to turn the tort system into a lottery where everyone pays high insurance premiums so that enormous windfalls can be allocated randomly." [ ] Accordingly, I respectfully dissent from the majority's decision in this case.

NOTES AND QUESTIONS

1. *Rationales for the rule.* As illustrated by *Kenney*, the evolving dynamics of health care delivery has forced courts to reconsider the collateral source rule. Is there a single underlying explanation for the collateral source rule? Should the rule apply equally to a gift from a brother, a loan from that brother repayable if and when the tort suit succeeds, a reduced hospital bill, and a payment from a health insurer?

In addition to the rationales discussed in *Kenney*, courts have justified the collateral source rule in compensatory terms:

> The collateral source rule also recognizes the inadequacies of damage awards for personal injuries. That is because "[l]egal 'compensation' for personal injuries does not actually compensate. Not many people would sell an arm for the average or even the maximum amount that juries award for loss of an arm. Moreover the injured person seldom gets the compensation he 'recovers,' for a substantial attorney's fee usually comes out of it. The Rule helps to remedy these problems inherent in compensating the tort victim." [ ] Since collateral sources only cover economic damages like medical costs and lost earnings, there is no possibility of a double recovery for intangibles like pain and suffering "which can be translated into monetary loss only with great difficulty." [ ] Rather than overcompensating a plaintiff, the collateral source rule "partially provides a somewhat closer approximation to full compensation for his injuries." [ ]

Arambula v. Wells, 85 Cal.Rptr.2d 584 (Ct.App.1999).

2. In contrast to the approach taken by *Kenney*, many courts do not apply the collateral source rule in these cases, enabling the defendant to introduce evidence about write-offs of the billed amount in order to limit plaintiff's recovery for medical expenses to the amount actually paid by the health insurer. For example, in Howell v. Hamilton Meats & Provisions, Inc., 257 P.3d 1130, 1137 (Cal.2011), the court distinguished reasonable expenses from actual expenses: "a plaintiff may recover as economic damages *no more* than the reasonable value of the medical services received and is not entitled to recover the reasonable value if his or her actual loss was less." These courts recognize that the collateral source rule can prevent the defendant from reducing damages on the basis of a gratuitous benefit that a third party has conferred on the plaintiff, but hold that the write-offs do not fall into this category. E.g., id. at 337 ("Medical providers that agree to accept discounted payments by managed care organizations or other health insurers as full payment for a patient's care do so not as a gift to the patient or insurer, but for commercial reasons and as a result of

negotiations. [H]ospitals and medical groups obtain commercial benefits from their agreements with health insurance organizations; the agreements guarantee the providers prompt payment of the agreed rates and often have financial incentives for plan members to choose the providers' services.").

All agree that the collateral source rule prevents the defendant tortfeasor from asserting a claim to the benefits conferred on the plaintiff by collateral sources like first-party insurance. Courts instead disagree on whether benefits created by the insurance contract can always be legitimately claimed by the plaintiff (as per *Kenney*) or instead sometimes inure only to a third party (the medical providers that agree to accept discounts or write-offs), in which case the collateral source rule is not triggered. Thus, in Acuar v. Letourneau, 531 S.E.2d 316 (Va.2000), the court concluded that defendant could not deduct from its liability "any part of the benefits [plaintiff] received from his contractual arrangement with his health insurance carrier, whether those benefits took the form of medical expense payments or amounts written off because of agreements between his health insurance carrier and his health care providers. Those amounts written off are as much of a benefit for which [plaintiff] paid consideration as are the actual cash payments made by his health insurance carrier to the health care providers."

3. *Public benefits.* Should the *Kenney* result be different when the plaintiff receives insurance benefits from a public program like Medicare or Medicaid that is funded by tax revenues? In Wills v. Foster, 892 N.E.2d 1018 (Ill.2008)(identifying different approaches and citing cases), the court held that Medicaid/Medicare discounts should not be treated differently from private insurance. Other courts, recognizing that the benefit-of-the-bargain theory has different implications for these two forms of insurance, have reached a contrary result. In Stayton v. Delaware Health Corp., 117 A.3d 521 (Del.2015), the court concluded that the collateral source rule applies to provider write-offs for private insurance but not for Medicare payments. Plaintiff was severely burned as a consequence of defendant's negligence and was billed a total of $3,683,797.11 by the hospital and other health care providers. The same bill showed that Medicare had paid the providers $262,550.17 in full satisfaction of the charges. The court first recognized that "[t]he fact that the written off portion of [plaintiff's] medical bills is thirteen times the amount paid gives us pause. It reflects the purchasing power of Medicare, given the size of its beneficiary population. It also reflects the way in which the realities of today's healthcare economy diverge from the traditional underpinnings of the collateral source rule." The court then concluded that the collateral source rule does not apply to the Medicare payments, enabling the defendant to introduce evidence limiting the tort damages to the amount the insurer actually paid for the services.

> [W]e follow the view that provider write-offs are not payments made to or benefits conferred on the injured party. The $3,421,246.94 that [plaintiff's] healthcare providers wrote off was paid by no one. Any benefit that [plaintiff's] healthcare providers

conferred in writing off over ninety percent of their collective charges was conferred on federal taxpayers, as a consequence of Medicare's purchasing power. Thus, the collateral source rule does not apply to the amounts written off by Stayton's healthcare providers.

Should other government programs be treated differently? In Washington v. Barnes Hospital, 897 S.W.2d 611 (Mo.1995), as a result of defendant's malpractice, plaintiffs' brain-damaged child would need special education for life. Plaintiffs proved what such a private education would cost. The court held that the defendant was improperly prevented from arguing that public education was available for that need. Although most courts had sided with the plaintiffs' position, this court disagreed:

> Here plaintiffs need not purchase the public school benefits, nor work for them as an employment benefit, nor contract for them. Hence the "benefit of the bargain" rationale does not apply. Nor are these benefits provided as a gift by a friend or family member to assist plaintiffs specifically, such that it would be inequitable to transfer the value of the benefit from plaintiffs to defendants. Nor is this a benefit that is dependent upon plaintiffs' indigence or other special status. Instead, public school programming is available to all by law. While to some extent public schools are funded by plaintiffs' tax dollars, they are also funded by defendants' tax dollars and no windfall results to either. We reject the concept that the collateral source rule should be utilized solely to punish the defendant. Damages in our tort system are compensatory not punitive.

On remand, plaintiffs "may respond to this evidence with arguments" concerning "the inadequacy [of public school], the risk of its continued availability, etc."

Is this case analogous to one in which plaintiff insists on being treated at the most expensive hospital by the most expensive physicians? Should a plaintiff who goes to an "economy" hospital be entitled to recover the difference between that hospital's charges and the luxury hospital's? A medium-priced hospital's? How would these issues be resolved by the majority in *Kenney*? The dissent?

4. *Measuring the loss.* The measure of damages for pecuniary loss requiring replacement is the reasonable value of the replacement goods or services. Ordinarily, the amount charged and paid is presumed to represent the reasonable value. A defendant may, however, challenge the reasonableness of those amounts, thereby requiring the plaintiff to prove their reasonableness. See, e.g., Kent v. Baptist Memorial Hospital-North Mississippi, Inc., 853 So.2d 873 (Miss.App.2003). Because the amount charged and paid is not necessarily equal to the reasonable value, even if a court decides that the collateral source rule does not apply to write-offs of health care bills, it must still determine whether the paid amount represents a reasonable value for those services. See *Stayton*, 117 A.3d at 531–34 (surveying the different approaches that courts have adopted for resolving this issue and concluding that the actual amount paid should be used as a reasonable value for the services).

5. *Statutory change.* The collateral source rule has been the subject of statutory modification in varying degrees in about half of the states. The nature of these changes is considered at p. 824 infra. In New York, for example, money already received from most collateral insurance sources is to be deducted from the plaintiff's judgment, except that plaintiff is to receive credit for having paid premiums for up to two years. The effect of this statutory modification can be profound as illustrated by a case involving the September 11 terrorist attacks on the World Trade Center. The owner of the properties sued a number of aviation defendants, claiming that their negligence proximately caused destruction of the buildings. The trial court rejected this claim on the ground that even if the defendants were liable for the billions of dollars of property damage incurred by the plaintiff, the amount of property insurance received by plaintiff reduced the permitted tort recovery to zero. In re Sept. 11 Litigation, 957 F.Supp.2d 501 (S.D.N.Y.2013).

6. *A windfall?* Insofar as the collateral source rule permits a plaintiff to receive double recovery for a loss—once from the defendant, and again from an insurer—the legislature's rationale for modifying the rule is easy to understand. The extent to which a plaintiff actually receives such a windfall, however, depends on the doctrine of "subrogation," the subject of the next section.

b.   SUBROGATION

Frost v. Porter Leasing Corp.

Supreme Judicial Court of Massachusetts, 1982.
386 Mass. 425, 436 N.E.2d 387.

■ Before HENNESSEY, C.J., and WILKINS, LIACOS, ABRAMS and O'CONNOR, JJ.

■ HENNESSEY, CHIEF JUSTICE.

[Frost was injured in a motor vehicle accident. He and his wife sued the other driver for medical expenses incurred, pain and suffering, impaired earning capacity, and future expenses. His wife's claim was for loss of consortium. While this case was pending, Frost received medical expense benefits of $22,700 under a union health insurance plan paid for by his employer. The insurer, Union Labor, intervened in the Frosts' tort action, claiming a right of subrogation (i.e., a right to reimbursement) from plaintiff, its insured, for any of the medical expense damages recovered in this action. The insurer made no claim directly against the other driver. The Frosts then settled their tort claim for a lump sum of $250,000. In this phase of the case, the trial judge concluded that the insurer had a right of subrogation in the proceeds of the settlement to the extent it had paid Frost, less a share of the costs the Frosts had incurred in obtaining the settlement.]

A Superior Court judge has reported the question "[w]hether a group insurer which provides medical and hospital expenses benefits to an insured has a right of subrogation in a recovery by the insured against a tortfeasor for personal injuries even though the group insurance policy contains no express provision entitling the insurer to subrogation rights." We conclude that the insurer has no right, in the absence of a subrogation clause, to share in the insured's recovery against the tortfeasor.

. . .

Subrogation is an equitable adjustment of rights that operates when a creditor or victim of loss is entitled to recover from two sources, one of which bears a primary legal responsibility. If the secondary source (the subrogee) pays the obligation, it succeeds to the rights of the party it has paid (the creditor or loss victim, called the subrogor) against the third, primarily responsible party. [ ] The doctrine of subrogation applies, within limits to be discussed shortly, to payments under policies of insurance. Upon payment, the insurer is entitled to share the benefit of any rights of recovery the insured may have against a tortfeasor for the same loss covered by the insurance. [ ] If the insured recovers from the tortfeasor, the insurer's right becomes a right to the proceeds in the hands of the insured.[6] [ ]

An insurer's right of subrogation may be reserved in an agreement between the insurer and the insured, [ ] or may arise by implication, as a matter of [common] law [ ].[7] Here, Union Labor admits that Frost's insurance policy contained no provision for subrogation. Union Labor's claim is one of implied subrogation, and we express no opinion on the ability of parties to fix their rights by contract. [ ]

The reason for implied subrogation under contracts of insurance is to prevent an unwarranted windfall to the insured. [ ] If the insured recovers from both the insurer and the tortfeasor, his compensation may exceed his actual loss. Duplicative recovery is "a result which the law has never looked upon with favor." [ ] It is contrary to the indemnity purposes that underlie many insurance contracts, and produces a form of unjust enrichment. [ ] Further, duplicative recoveries by particular accident victims cause an inefficient distribution of the overall resources available for accident compensation. Subrogation returns any excess to the insurer, who can then recycle it in the form of lower insurance costs. See Fleming, The Collateral Source Rule and Loss Allocation in Tort Law, 54 Cal.L.Rev. 1478, 1481–1484 (1966).

Nevertheless, rights of subrogation do not arise automatically upon payment of benefits under any contract of insurance. The availability of

---

[6]   If the tortfeasor has settled with the insured, with knowledge of the insurer's claim, some courts have permitted the insurer to proceed against the tortfeasor. [ ]

[7]   In addition, statutes may provide for subrogation. [ ]

subrogation has generally depended on the type of coverage involved. Courts have readily implied rights of subrogation under policies covering property damage. [ ] The insurer's obligation under a policy of property insurance is viewed only as a duty to indemnify the insured for actual loss, and not as an absolute liability to pay a certain sum of money upon the happening of an event. [ ] Moreover, the insured's loss is generally liquidated, and tort recovery is comparable, if not identical, to insurance coverage. [ ] Therefore, the insured's actual loss, and the amount of any excess compensation from the combination of insurance proceeds and tort recovery, can be determined with certainty.

On the other hand, courts have not recognized implied rights of subrogation in the area of "personal insurance," a category that has included medical expense benefits as well as life insurance and other forms of accident insurance. [ ] Personal insurance is said to be less a contract of indemnity than a form of investment, imposing on the insurer an absolute duty to pay if the named condition occurs. [ ] Further the insured's receipt of both tort damages and insurance benefits may not produce a measurably duplicative recovery. The insured is likely to have suffered intangible losses that are insusceptible to precise measurement, and the two sources of his recovery may cover different ranges of loss and be differently affected by considerations such as fault. [ ]

Commentators have objected to the courts' classification of medical expense policies with other forms of personal insurance, and have argued that subrogation rights should be implied upon payment of benefits for medical and hospital expenses. They point out that medical coverage, like property insurance, is designed to indemnify the insured for quantifiable economic losses, and bears little similarity to an investment. [ ]

Although we recognize the indemnity character of medical and hospital expense benefits, we do not feel that the principles that support subrogation under policies of property insurance would be served by extending implied rights of subrogation into the field of insurance for personal injuries. Subrogation rights, as we have said, are implied to prevent unwarranted compensation and to facilitate sound distribution of compensation resources. If medical expenses are isolated from the other consequences of an accident, excess compensation of an insured accident victim may appear definite and quantifiable. However, when subrogation is based on broad principles of equity and efficiency, rather than on the contract of the parties, isolation of medical expenses is artificial, and the accident victim's position should be viewed as a whole. [ ] Subrogation played no part in the bargain between insurer and insured,[8] and in this circumstance, the courts should not intervene

---

[8]   Union Labor points out that the premiums for Frost's policy were paid by Frost's employer rather than by Frost himself. The fact that the benefits do not flow to the party who has paid premiums, however, should not detract from the force of legitimate expectations, both

to adjust the rights of the parties unless all the adverse consequences of the accident have been offset. [ ]

When the insured's losses are viewed in their entirety, duplicative compensation is both uncertain and unlikely. [ ] The insured may be faced with property damage, pain and suffering, and diminished earning capacity, in addition to medical bills. The costs of litigation, or the decision to settle, may reduce his overall recovery. Yet the insurer's implied right of subrogation must be limited to excessive recovery if it is to conform to the purposes that justify it. Further, when the insured has not agreed to subrogation, doubt should be resolved in his favor. [ ]

Perhaps a formula could be devised by which subrogation could be confined to recapture of duplicative compensation. The insurer might, for example, be permitted to recover if it could demonstrate that the insured's net recovery (insurance proceeds and tort recovery, less costs of collection) exceeded fair compensation for the insured's losses. [ ] However, the costs of implementing the formula could well undercut its justifications, particularly when, as here, the insured had reached a lump-sum settlement with the tortfeasor. [ ] If the inquiry covered the insured's overall loss from the accident—as in fairness it should—determination of the extent of excess recovery could be equally as complex as the personal injury trial the original parties sought to avoid by settlement. [ ] Thus, litigation over subrogation would impose additional burdens on the insured, and cut into his overall compensation for injury. Moreover, this added step in the adjustment of rights would detract from any generalized benefits that subrogation might bring to the sound use and distribution of resources available to compensate loss. Much of the "windfall" produced by overlapping coverage would be absorbed by the costs of dividing it, rather than recycled to reduce the costs of insurance. [ ]

For these reasons, we conclude that, in the absence of a subrogation agreement between the insurer and the insured, an insurer that has paid medical or hospital expense benefits has no right to share in the proceeds of the insured's recovery against a tortfeasor. Accordingly, we answer the reported question in the negative.

So ordered.

■ WILKINS, JUSTICE (concurring).

I agree with the conclusion of the court that, in the absence of a provision for subrogation in the applicable insurance policy, an insurer providing health insurance is not entitled to subrogation as to amounts paid or payable by a tortfeasor to the insured. I do not reach this result because of the asserted problems of administration of such a system of subrogation to which the court makes reference. The problems are manageable, and most are not substantial. I reach my conclusion on the

of the beneficiary and of the one who has paid. This is particularly true when, as here, the policy is an employment benefit, bargained for by the insured's union.

ground that, in fairness to an insured, a policy should disclose the possibility of subrogation claims. A person or group purchasing coverage for medical costs should know the limitations of such coverage, and, as a realistic matter, a lay person cannot be expected to have knowledge of a common law right of subrogation.

I reject the implications of the opinion that subrogation presents substantial problems with respect to insurance payments made for medical expenses incurred as the result of injuries caused by a third party wrongdoer. The amount of the insured's loss, the insurer's payment, and the tort recovery are known with certainty. The subrogated insurer should acknowledge a proportionate reduction in its claim to reflect the services and expenses of the claimant's attorney in collecting on the tort claim. If the claim is settled, as most are, the subrogated insurer should accept a proportionate and reasonable reduction in its subrogation claim to reflect the discount that the claimant accepted in order to obtain a settlement. Assuming prompt assertion of the subrogation claim, the amount to be paid to the insurer on its subrogation claim can be readily determined in most cases as part of the settlement process.

Subrogation is a reasonable method of assisting in holding down the costs of health insurance. It prevents an undeserved windfall to the insured. It is appropriate to consider the matter of medical expenses apart from other aspects of the injured person's claim. Whatever uncertainty may exist with respect to other elements of damages, the amount paid under the medical insurance policy can be ascertained and dealt with independently. I see no justification for denying subrogation, as the court seems to suggest, because, in settling a case, the claimant may not have been made whole on all elements of his damages. The claimant can be and is made whole on his medical costs, to the extent of his coverage. A health insurer should not be obliged to forbear asserting subrogation rights in order to assist in making the claimant whole on some other aspect of his damages, such as lost wages and pain and suffering, for which the insured has not purchased coverage from the health insurer.

NOTES AND QUESTIONS

1.   How does the majority distinguish between "property" insurance and "personal" insurance? What consequences flow from that distinction? Would the same result follow if plaintiff had obtained a judgment instead of having settled?

2.   Under the concurrence's view, when would subrogation be allowed? How would legal expenses be allocated?

3.   *Express subrogation.* Notwithstanding the situation in *Frost*, virtually all first-party health and automobile insurance policies now contain subrogation clauses permitting the insurer to recover payments

made to the insured from a third-party tortfeasor. Why do insurers insert into the policy an express right of subrogation?

4. *The problem of settlement.* The concurrence in *Frost* suggests that when subrogation is allowed, the amount should be reduced if the underlying tort claim is settled rather than litigated. Why? Why, in that instance, would the insurer "accept a proportionate and reasonable reduction in its subrogation claim," as suggested by the concurrence?

In that connection, consider Smith v. Marzolf, 375 N.E.2d 995 (Ill.App.1978), in which plaintiff was injured by defendant's negligence. Plaintiff was entitled to up to $50,000 of first-party benefits from Aetna for his medical bills and lost income. Plaintiff sued defendant, and plaintiff's wife also sued for loss of consortium. The parties agreed to settle the case by allocating $10,000 to plaintiff's claim and $65,000 to his wife's. Aetna objected that it had already paid plaintiff almost $17,000 and future payments up to the $50,000 limit were likely. Plaintiff and defendant then rewrote their settlement to give plaintiff $17,000 and his wife $58,000. Aetna still objected. The trial judge called the settlement "absolutely ridiculous" and a fraud on Aetna's subrogation rights. The refusal to permit the settlement was upheld on appeal because plaintiff had breached his duties to Aetna. Is it clear why Aetna should be involved in these settlement talks?

5. *Allocation of settlement proceeds.* If there had been a right of subrogation, how much of the $250,000 settlement in *Frost* should be allocated to medical expenses paid by Union Labor?

In Assoc. Hosp. Serv. of Phil. v. Pustilnik, 396 A.2d 1332 (Pa.1979), the court held that when a tort plaintiff as "subrogor settles, he waives his right to a judicial determination of his losses, and conclusively establishes the settlement amount as full compensation for his damages." To understand the implications of this approach, consider a tort claim seeking compensatory damages of $250,000 for medical expenses and $1 million for pain and suffering. Suppose the plaintiff settles for $250,000. Because the settlement constitutes full compensation of *all* damages, the health insurer can recover every dollar it paid for the plaintiff policyholder's medical expenses (all of which were fully compensated by the tort settlement) up to the $250,000 settlement amount. Thus, if the insurer paid $250,000 for plaintiff's medical expenses, then the insurer would be entitled to the entire $250,000 settlement, less its pro rata share of legal fees. How might this approach affect the plaintiff's incentive to settle the case? Why would a plaintiff settle a case for anything less than the amount that would provide full compensation?

Most courts reject this approach, requiring instead that the plaintiff must be "made whole" before the insurer can assert any subrogation right. Any remaining sums, above the "make whole" amount, provide the funds from which the insurer can seek subrogation. As one court explained,

> neither subrogation nor reimbursement should detract from the primary goal of compensatory damages: to compensate a party for the full extent of his or her losses. Moreover, the equitable

interests [with regard to subrogation], apply equally to reimbursement. . . . [T]here is no risk of the insured receiving a "double recovery" for the same loss if he or she has not been made whole. Similarly, reimbursement to the insurer from the insured would not hold the wrongdoer or tortfeasor accountable for the loss. Finally, in considering the equities between the parties, we note that any potential loss incurred by the insure[r] is a loss that it was paid to assume by the very nature of an insurance contract.

York v. Sevier Cty. Ambulance Auth., 8 S.W.3d 616 (Tenn.1999).

Under this approach, how should the court determine the amount that would make the plaintiff "whole"? Does the amount of compensatory damages alleged in the complaint provide a defensible number? If so, how might such a rule affect pleading practices?

6.   *Insurer v. Insurer.* Suppose plaintiff's house is badly burned by defendant's negligence, plaintiff's insurer pays plaintiff the $90,000 agreed value of the damage, and plaintiff has no other uncovered losses. What are the implications of the collateral source rule and subrogation if plaintiff's insurer proceeds against defendant?

In DiLullo v. Joseph, 792 A.2d 819 (Conn.2002), a tenant's negligence caused harm to landlord's property. After the landlord's insurer paid for the loss, it sought subrogation from the tenant. Suppose the tenant had been insured (he was not): The landlord's insurer would be suing the tenant's insurer to determine which insurance company would bear the loss. This possibility is not fanciful. In Wasko v. Manella, 849 A.2d 777 (Conn.2004), a guest negligently set fire to the host's house and caused substantial fire damage. After paying the host, the host's fire insurer sought subrogation against the guest. The unanimous court allowed the claim, reasoning in part that houseguests ordinarily are covered against such claims by their own liability insurance (a coverage included in their homeowners policy). What can be said for—and against—having the host's insurer seek subrogation from the guest's insurer?

7.   *Toting up the costs.* On the costs of subrogation, consider the following excerpt from Conard, The Economic Treatment of Automobile Injuries, 63 Mich.L.Rev. 279, 311 (1964):

Consider the case of a one thousand dollar hospital bill incurred by a Blue Cross policyholder. When his bill is paid by Blue Cross, the cost to all Blue Cross policyholders combined is about 1,080 dollars. Assume further that Blue Cross obtains reimbursement by virtue of subrogation from Drivers' Liability Company, which has insured the tortfeasor. Blue Cross will presumably pay at least twenty-five per cent in collection expenses and will net about 750 dollars out of the one thousand dollars paid by Drivers' Liability. But the policyholders of Drivers' Liability will have incurred corresponding premium costs of sixteen hundred dollars, since liability insurers work at an expense rate equivalent to about sixty per cent of payouts. The net effect of the subrogation is to make liability insurance policyholders pay sixteen hundred dollars in order to save 750 dollars for health insurance policyholders. Probably a large majority of the health insurance policyholders are also liability insurance policyholders, who have their costs doubled by subrogation without any increase of their benefits. The principal beneficiaries of the shift are insurance companies and lawyers.

Professor Conard derived the cost figures used in his passage from other studies that he summarized at pp. 290–91 of his article:

The Michigan study also estimated total expenses of the damage system, adding to lawyers' fees the litigation expenses of claimants themselves, the costs of selling and administering insurance, and the costs of keeping courts open for injury cases. This summation indicated that the operating costs of the damage system are about 120 percent of the net benefits that go to the injury victims themselves; the net amounts that the victims get are less than the total retained by insurance companies, law offices, and courts. Presumably, the cost ratio would be even higher in such states as New York and Illinois, where it appears that the legal expenses are substantially higher than in Michigan.

In contrast, private loss insurance systems (embracing principally life insurance and health insurance) showed average costs of about twenty-two percent of net benefits. In some Blue Cross systems the operating costs drop to less than five per cent of the net benefits, and in Social Security programs they drop to about two percent.

Although the percentages have changed some since Conard wrote, the overall pattern persists. See O'Connell & Barker, Compensation for Injury and Illness: An Update of the Conard-Morgan Tabulations, 47 Ohio St.L.J. 913 (1986); see also Priest, The Current Insurance Crisis and Modern Tort Law, 96 Yale L.J. 1521, 1560 (1987):

The administrative costs of insurance delivered through tort law are vastly greater than the administrative costs of any first-party insurance regime. Blue Cross-Blue Shield first-party health insurance administration costs are 10% of benefits; SSI disability insurance administrative costs are 8% of benefits; Workers' Compensation disability insurance administration costs are (a much-criticized) 21% of benefits. In contrast, tort law administrative costs are estimated to be 53% of net plaintiff benefits.

The last figure is drawn from J. Kakalik & N. Pace, Costs and Compensation Paid in Tort Litigation (1986) and is broken down further there at p. 70:

The legal fees and expenses paid by plaintiffs as a percent of total compensation were essentially the same for auto tort (31 percent) and other tort cases (30 percent). However, defendants' costs of litigation differ significantly. For auto tort cases, which are often straightforward, defense legal fees and expenses were an estimated 16 percent of total compensation. For other (nonauto) tort cases, which are often more complex, defense legal fees and expenses were much higher—28 percent of total compensation paid.

The plaintiffs' net compensation as a percentage of the total expenditures was 52 percent for auto torts and 43 percent for all other torts. This difference primarily reflects the higher defendants' litigation costs for nonauto torts.

Why might cost differences exist between first-party and third-party insurance? We return shortly to some possible implications of these cost differences.

8. *Subrogation and the collateral source rule.* Is the justification for the collateral source rule dependent on the right of reimbursement or subrogation of insurers? In an omitted portion of *Kenney*, p. 774 supra, the court observed that "[s]ometimes, as in fire insurance or collision automobile insurance, the insurance company is subrogated to the rights of the third party. This additional reason for keeping the tortfeasor's liability alive is not necessary, however, as the [collateral source] rule applies to insurance not involving subrogation, such as life or health policies."

Under the formulation of the collateral source rule adopted by *Kenney*, if the health insurer in that case were then to assert its subrogation rights against the tort plaintiff/policyholder, what is the final distribution of the tort judgment among plaintiff, defendant, and health insurer?

c.   FIRST-PARTY INSURANCE AND THE EXTENT OF TORT LIABILITY

Due to the collateral source rule, the extent of a defendant's tort liability is not affected by the plaintiff's first-party insurance coverage. Should the extent of liability be more dependent on first-party insurance? Do any tort doctrines effectively recognize as much? These issues are explored in this section.

The Collateral Source Rule and Loss Allocation in Tort Law

John Fleming.
54 Cal.L.Rev. 1478, 1546–49 (1966).

Two most perplexing features haunt the present state of American law. One arises directly from the last-mentioned fact that such reimbursement [via subrogation] to the other [collateral] fund cannot in general be technically accomplished without the aid of the collateral source rule, that is, precluding the tortfeasor from arguing that his liability has been reduced by the collateral subvention. Thus, whereas the collateral source rule is often enough invoked by courts wholly indifferent as to whether this will result in double recovery, there are others which at least condone it on the ground that, in the individual case, double recovery will be avoided by subrogation or some other like technique for passing the excess on to the collateral source. Finally, one also occasionally encounters a court purposefully insisting on the collateral source rule precisely in order to accomplish such a shifting of the loss.

Turning from double recovery to a consideration of other alternatives, we note that these differ from the former in posing a decision as to which of two sources of compensation to treat as the primary and which as the secondary. In contrast to cumulation of benefits, they force a confrontation with a basic policy orientation whether accident losses generally, or any particular accident loss, should be absorbed by the tortfeasor or by a collateral source, whether in accordance with the regime of tort law or the regime of private or social insurance. It calls for a fixing of priorities pursuant to relevant contemporary social and economic values as to loss allocation. In particular, the following criteria can be isolated as most important in their bearing on this assignment: (1) the reprehensiveness of the defendant's conduct, (2) the desirability of attributing the cost to the loss-causing enterprise for reasons of accident-prevention, proper cost allocation, etc., and (3) the function and, more important still, the economic base of the particular collateral compensation regime.

Not surprisingly, the predominant response has been to regard the tortfeasor as the primary source of compensation. Imbued with the philosophic values of a culture that has traditionally regarded tort law as the only and proper system for allocating accident losses, it is still widely considered as almost axiomatic that if an injurer's conduct justifies his being compelled to relieve the injured from the loss he has inflicted, it is also sufficient reason for his relieving anybody else who might otherwise have undertaken the job of reparation. This approach, dominated by lingering notions of promoting an individualistic morality against "wrongdoers," is reinforced by the impression that it would also reduce the cost to the community in general, and the plaintiff in particular, in maintaining the collateral fund. It is strongest in cases of private insurance, where to reduce the tortfeasor's liability would look like diverting the fruit of the plaintiff's own thrift into the pockets of one who least "deserves" it; but it has also found ardent advocates among social security organizations ever watchful to save the public purse.

These primarily moralistic postulates are gradually yielding in their appeal to an economic value system which places in the forefront the high collection costs of reshifting the loss from a collateral source to the tortfeasor, the attendant wastefulness of multiple insurance and, most important of all perhaps, an awareness that in these days, when tort liability qualifies as a significant source of compensation only in cases of defendants who can pass on the loss through liability insurance or pricing of their goods or services, the question is not so much whether a wrongdoer deserves to be relieved as which of several competing "risk communities" should bear the loss. Loss-bearing has become collectivized, whether it falls on the defendant or some other regime, like insurance or social security, to fill the role as conduit for distribution. While this focus does not provide ready-made solutions, still less generally valid answers, it stimulates a probe all along the line whether in any particular case there is sufficient justification for going to the trouble and expense of shifting the loss to the tortfeasor from some other regime that has already footed the bill and could as well or even better absorb it. Social security, for example, because of its broad base of contributors, has a strong claim for displacing *pro tanto* any "risk pool" represented by tort defendants. On the other hand, very special hazards presented by certain enterprises (for example, nuclear power stations) may make it advisable, for reasons of proper economic cost allocation as well as in the interest of maximizing accident prevention, to assign the ultimate loss to that enterprise rather than spread it on a broader base where these advantages would be lost. If deterrence in the old crude sense has any continuing appeal as a justification for tort liability, it will be confined to situations where it can realistically perform an admonitory function, namely, only against defendants guilty of serious misconduct. Somewhat paradoxically, tort law would shrink, at least in this respect, to its original starting-point as an adjunct of the criminal law in sanctioning immoral conduct. In several European countries, especially Scandinavia and Britain, vast encroachments on the erstwhile primacy of tort liability have already taken place along these lines. In the United States, this process of emancipation from the paralyzing legacy of largely obsolete folklore is still in its infancy, but is bound to gain increasing momentum as social security and other collateral regimes are assuming a greater role in the business of meeting accident costs.

In the upshot, there is thus emerging a second tier of principles of loss allocation; the first being concerned with the traditional problem of whether the person injured should be compensated at all, and the second with whether the tortfeasor rather than some other available fund should bear the ultimate burden of compensation. As a result, in many instances tort liability will become only an *excess* or a *guarantee* liability, its function being merely to allot responsibility for compensation to a person (labelled "tortfeasor") *to the extent that the cost of compensation has not been met by another source.*

In many ways this development represents a much more dramatic innovation than the sensational trend of recent years towards strict liability in the consumer protection area. It is more important by far because it adds an entirely new element to the grammar of loss allocation. Tort liability has ceased to be the sole point of reference in any inquiry, legislative or judicial, as to how particular accident losses should be absorbed.

NOTES AND QUESTIONS

1.   What are the arguments in favor of Fleming's suggestion? Is the point limited to "social security"? What about cases in which the plaintiff has private medical and hospital coverage and private income-protection insurance?

2.   Fleming suggests that cases involving "very special hazards" might well be treated differently. Why might this be? Why should this reasoning apply only to "very special hazards"?

3.   What are the strongest general arguments against "displacing" tort law?

4.   What view of Fleming's approach might be taken by those who emphasize the deterrent value of tort law?

5.   Consider whether the legal resolutions of the following fact patterns support Fleming's argument.

Fire cases. Throughout the course, although we are primarily concerned with personal injuries, we occasionally consider cases involving property damage. For the most part, we have not drawn distinctions between the two types of cases. But might the role of first-party loss insurance in some situations explain the outcomes of certain property damage cases?

The 1866 *Ryan* case, p. 433 supra, creating the unique New York fire rule on proximate cause, may be an early example. The following passage indicates that the availability of insurance weighed heavily with the court:

> To sustain such a claim as the present, and to follow the same to its legitimate consequences, would subject to a liability against which no prudence could guard, and to meet which no private fortune would be adequate. Nearly all fires are caused by negligence, in its extended sense. In a country where wood, coal, gas and oils are universally used, where men are crowded into cities and villages, where servants are employed, and where children find their home in all houses, it is impossible that the most vigilant prudence should guard against the occurrence of accidental or negligent fires. A man may insure his own house or his own furniture, but he cannot insure his neighbor's building or furniture, for the reason that he has no interest in them. To hold that the owner must not only meet his own loss by fire, but that he must guarantee the security of his neighbors on both sides, and to an unlimited extent, would be to create a liability which would be the destruction of all civilized society. No community could long exist, under the operation of such a principle. In a commercial country, each man, to some extent, runs the hazard of his neighbor's conduct, and each, by insurance against such hazards, is enabled to obtain a reasonable security against loss. To neglect such precaution, and to call upon his neighbor, on whose premises a fire originated, to indemnify him instead, would be to award a punishment quite beyond the offense committed. It is to be

considered, also, that if the negligent party is liable to the owner of a remote building thus consumed, he would also be liable to the insurance companies who should pay losses to such remote owners. The principle of subrogation would entitle the companies to the benefit of every claim held by the party to whom a loss should be paid.

A defendant at that time could not obtain insurance against liability. Does that justify the court's analysis? Recall the *Losee* case, p. 515 supra, decided in 1873, involving similar considerations about extended liability.

Even before *Ryan,* legislatures had addressed the relation between fire insurance and liability, as in Mass. Laws 1840, Ch. 85:

> When any injury is done to a building or other property, of any person or corporation, by fire communicated by a locomotive engine of any railroad corporation, the said railroad corporation shall be held responsible, in damages, to the person or corporation so injured; and any railroad corporation shall have an insurable interest in the property for which it may be so held responsible in damages, along its route, and may procure insurance thereon in its own behalf.

What was the philosophy underlying the statute? Must negligence be shown? In 1895 the statute was amended by Ch. 293, to provide that if held liable the railroad "shall be entitled to the benefit of any insurance effected upon such property by the owner thereof, less the cost of premium and expense of recovery." Why the change? How would the 1895 act work if the property is fully insured by the owner?

Water company cases. Although New York's fire rule may have been unique, the *Moch* case, p. 173 supra, which relied to some extent on *Ryan,* is followed in the majority of states, although its influence has waned in recent years. Might the prevalence of fire insurance covering improved property explain the result? By the time of *Moch,* water companies could obtain liability insurance—and they could probably raise their rates without fear of competition or of losing customers. If they sustained losses due to tort liability for fires they could probably make those up by raising rates without bringing sanctions from government rate regulators. But, what is the likely relationship between property owners and water users in a large city? Who are the likely winners if there is liability? If there is no liability? The rationale that liability would be catastrophic in a case such as *Moch* is difficult to support, because in those states permitting recovery against negligent water companies in fire cases, there is no showing that the rule adversely affected the economy. Should actual or available insurance play any part in judicial analysis? Recall the famous concurrence by Justice Traynor in *Escola v. Coca Cola Bottling Co.,* p. 564 supra, in which he relied on the availability of liability insurance to justify strict liability.

In Weinberg v. Dinger, 524 A.2d 366 (N.J.1987), the court overruled earlier decisions that had refused to impose liability on water companies that negligently failed to supply water to fight fires. The water companies contended that "since property owners are invariably insured against loss from fire damage, a rule imposing liability on water companies would simply create a windfall for property-insurance carriers whose subrogated rights would permit them to recoup from water companies sums paid out pursuant to property insurance policies." The court observed that it was aware that increased water costs were "ultimately borne by the consumer [and that liability insurance] constitutes a less efficient method of insuring against fire loss than is afforded by property insurance." (Recall our earlier discussion of the cost differential between the two.) Nonetheless, the court overruled the earlier cases and imposed a duty of due care on water companies. Next, however, it concluded that the action should not lie for insured property losses:

> [W]e abrogate the water company's immunity for losses caused by the negligent failure to maintain adequate water pressure for fire fighting only to the extent of claims that are uninsured or underinsured [so as to avoid the carrier's subrogation claims against the water company]. This determination is made without prejudice to the right of a subrogation claimant, either in this or other litigation, to offer proof tending to demonstrate that any increase in water rates resulting from liability for subrogation claims would be substantially offset by reductions in fire-insurance premiums. If insurance rates were set on the basis of risk and experience, one would expect a high correlation between the increase in water company liability rates and the decrease in fire-insurance rates occasioned by the abrogation of water company immunity in cases like this. If that correlation were to be proven in subsequent litigation, we would be prepared to reconsider our denial of the carrier's right to subrogation against a water company.

Id. at 378–79.

One justice dissented from the decision to retain immunity in subrogation cases. Another dissenter opposed any retreat from the pre-existing immunity of water companies.

Is it likely that the demanded showing can be made? If the showing is made, why might that influence the majority to eliminate what remains of New Jersey's immunity for water companies? Is it relevant that the state's water companies are subject to the jurisdiction of the state's public utility commission?

The majority observed in passing that the argument for immunity did not address cases in which personal injury occurred during the fire. The case before the court involved only property damage—and there is apparently no reported case against a water company involving personal injury or death from fire. What is there about claims against water companies that might effectively limit them to property damage claims?

Do the foregoing cases support Professor Fleming's argument that widespread first-party insurance should limit the extent of tort liability? Would such limitation be more defensible for some types of harms, such as property damage, than for others, such as bodily injury? If so, what does that distinction say about the underlying rationale for tort liability?

2. TORT LAW AND LIABILITY INSURANCE

We now consider the development and impact of liability (or third-party) insurance. Virtually every private defendant sued in the cases we have read in this course was probably covered by insurance protecting, at least to some extent, against the financial consequences of an adverse liability judgment. Indeed, these cases were probably defended by attorneys hired by the liability insurer. To be sure, some very large companies self-insure and defend cases themselves with in-house counsel or retain outside counsel. Large government defendants—states and the federal government—often self-insure as well, relying on the taxing power to fund liability losses. But smaller governments, such as towns and cities, often use private liability insurers to protect against crushing losses, as do small businesses and individuals.

Although judicial opinions in tort cases rarely mention either first-party or liability insurance, the importance of insurance for tort law is undeniable. Recently, courts have been somewhat more explicit in referring to the prevalence of liability insurance, but not to whether the particular defendant was insured.

Judge Friendly was particularly explicit about the role of liability insurance in affecting attitudes toward the boundaries of tort liability. In *Kinsman I,* discussed at p. 419 supra, Judge Friendly observed that "[w]here the [liability] line will be drawn will vary from age to age; as society has come to rely increasingly on insurance and other methods of loss-sharing, the point may lie further off than a century ago." Also, in *Steinhauser,* p. 398 supra, after noting the broad acceptance of the "thin-skull" doctrine, he stated "[t]he seeming severity of this doctrine is mitigated by the prevalence of liability insurance which spreads the risks."

Judge Friendly's observations are fully reflected in the analysis employed by many courts, as in *Randi W.*, p. 141 supra, that expressly consider the availability of liability insurance for determining whether a new tort duty should be adopted. All else being equal, liability insurance reduces the cost of risky behavior for the insured, thereby reducing the burden of the proposed tort duty and making it easier to justify. Judge Friendly's observations undoubtedly also go far to explain such judicial developments as the family-purpose doctrine, p. 24 supra, and the changes in intrafamily liability, p. 216 supra. Recall also the fire, water, and other property cases discussed in the notes after the Fleming excerpt, p. 791 supra.

a.   HISTORICAL BACKGROUND

We emphasize in this section the development of the institution of liability insurance, considering most extensively the development of automobile insurance because it has the longest history of involvement with accident law. (Liability insurance also made possible the development of workers' compensation—a subject we consider in Chapter XII.)

Automobile insurance. The development of the automobile created an immediate awareness of the dangers of the product along with a concern about financial responsibility for accidents. Although courts continued to rely on substantive law that was developed during the days of the horse and buggy, the new problem was solvency of those who now had the power to do much more harm than previously. At first the courts tried to expand the group of responsible defendants by creating doctrines such as the "family purpose" doctrine (owner of a car held vicariously liable to strangers for torts of anyone using the car to carry out a family purpose) and "joint enterprise" (each member of a group venture vicariously liable for the torts of their driver). These doctrines have survived. See Nelson v. Johnson, 599 N.W.2d 246 (N.D.1999), observing that the family purpose doctrine "is founded on the theory that the driver of a family car, in pursuit of recreation or pleasure, is engaged in the owner's business and is viewed as either the agent or servant of the owner. [ ] The respondeat superior theoretical basis for the doctrine is a fiction created in furtherance of the public policy of giving an injured party a cause of action against a financially responsible defendant. [ ] Under the family purpose doctrine, the owner of the vehicle is not liable for his own negligence, but is vicariously liable for the tortious acts of the driver."

These steps helped but did not assure financial responsibility because car owners did not always have the resources to respond in damages and also because of the gap left when the owner permitted a non-family member to drive the car. Under the traditional law of bailments the owner was not responsible for the negligence of the bailee unless there had been a negligent entrustment in the first instance. Recall *Vince,* p. 181 supra. Many states met this latter concern by adopting legislation making the owner liable for the negligence of *any* person operating the car with the express or implied permission of the owner—even if the owner used due care in selecting the permittee. In Oliveira v. Lombardi, 794 A.2d 453 (R.I.2002), the court interpreted the state's vicarious-liability-for-owners statute to apply to commercial parties who lease their cars on a long-term basis to others. Some states extended vicarious liability to car rental companies. Congress overturned those statutes in a 2005 transportation bill, the Graves Amendment, that bars vicarious liability for car rental companies. 49 U.S.C.A. § 30106. What is the federal interest in state laws regarding the vicarious liability of car rental companies?

The market for liability insurance began to emerge along with the automobile at the start of the twentieth century. Why might a person who bought a car decide to carry liability insurance? Which owners would be most likely to buy such insurance? At the outset, automobile insurance was known as "indemnity" insurance—the company agreed that if the insured was required to pay a victim for an accident, and actually did pay, the insurer would reimburse (indemnify) the insured for that amount. If the amount of the judgment exceeded the personal assets of the insured, then to the extent of the insured's insolvency, the victim was left without full recovery. In these cases, the insurer had to reimburse the insured only for whatever amount the victim had been able to wring from the insured. Apparently, insurers sometimes colluded with insureds to transfer the insured's assets to others so as to avoid all payments to victims. Soon, the policies were converted to "liability" policies, under which the insurer became obligated to pay the victim for the tort damages up to the policy limits once the insured's liability was established.

Automobile policies had to take into account judicial impositions of liability that deviated from the paradigm case in which the owner and the driver were the same person. Two contract provisions emerged. One covered liability for the negligence of anyone driving the car, as explained above. The other, known as the "drive-other-car" clause, provided that the insured was protected when driving any car with the permission of its owner. These provisions were necessary because, from the outset, automobile liability insurance was written for particular vehicles rather than for individual drivers.

During this early period of liability insurance, a driver's decision of whether to acquire coverage was completely voluntary. But as early as the 1920s, states became concerned about the insolvency of many negligent motorists. States began a series of legislative efforts to encourage motorists to carry liability insurance. Financial responsibility laws were enacted, requiring that after a judgment of liability in a first accident, a motorist could continue to drive only after giving proof of adequate insurance or assets to be able to pay relatively small future judgments. Some states required this showing immediately after involvement in an accident rather than waiting until a first judgment of liability.

Both forms of legislation were problematic, however, because there was no requirement that this level of solvency exist *before* the first negligently caused accident. The statutes came into play only after the initial accident—for which the motorist might be unable to respond. A few states sought to fill this gap by denying driving privileges after a first accident unless the owner could show ability to pay for *that* accident if later found liable for it. The hope was that fear of this outcome would encourage the acquisition of insurance before any accident. Other states tried to ameliorate the insolvency problem by creating "unsatisfied judgment funds" to which victims would have recourse up to limited maximum amounts, if they could not collect judgments from those liable for the injuries.

In 1927, Massachusetts required that motorists demonstrate a minimum amount of non-cancellable liability coverage before being permitted to register their cars. No state followed that route until New York and North Carolina in the mid-1950s. (As this movement might have been gaining momentum, the "no-fault" movement was getting started and drew attention away from compulsory insurance, as we shall see in Chapter XII.) Among the problems of compulsory insurance, in addition to such gaps as hit-and-run accidents and out-of-state drivers, was what to do with a driver who was unable to obtain the required insurance from any private carrier. The answer has been to place such a person in an "assigned risk" pool—a group made up of the insurers in the state who write liability insurance—which must accept the coverage unless the applicant's driving record is badly flawed.

To counter the increasing regulation of the insurance field caused by increased concern for uncompensated victims, insurers began offering, as part of their liability coverage, a clause that provided financial protection against being injured by negligent uninsured motorists. In effect, the insurer stood in the shoes of the uninsured motorist in a tort claim by the insured. In addition, liability insurers added "med pay" provisions offering modest medical benefits to all persons injured in an accident without regard to fault.

By this point, the original justification for automobile liability insurance—protecting persons of means against having their funds diminished by their negligent harming of others—had given way to a highly regulated form of virtually compulsory insurance to assure that victims of negligent motorists would be compensated to some extent. (That extent, however, might be low. New York requires that motorists carry a minimum amount of liability insurance of $25,000 for bodily injury to one person, $50,000 for bodily injury to all persons, $10,000 for property damage in any one accident, and mandatory "no-fault" coverage of $50,000.) Using the same framework as uninsured motorist coverage, insureds may now acquire "underinsured motorist" coverage. This coverage provides insureds additional protection in cases in which the person who negligently hurts them has lower, even if legally adequate, liability limits in his or her policy than those in the insured's policy. These policies are considered at length in Doyle v. Metropolitan Property & Casualty Insurance Co., 743 A.2d 156 (Conn.1999), Prudential Property & Casualty Co. v. Szeli, 635 N.E.2d 282 (N.Y.1994), and Butzberger v. Foster, 89 P.3d 689 (Wash.2004).

Despite the blandishments and compulsion, nationwide 12.6% of American motorists were uninsured during the period 2010–12. That figure varies significantly from the state with the highest rate, Oklahoma with 26% uninsured, to Massachusetts, the lowest-rate state, with only 4%. Insurance Research Council, Uninsured Motorists 2014 Edition (Dec.2014). What factors might affect variations in the incidence?

We have been tracing common law and legislative efforts to enhance the likelihood that negligent motorists will be able to respond in damages to their victims. Why was there no comparable concern during that period for victims of auto accidents in which fault could not be established? Or for those injured by the negligence of non-motorists?

Non-auto liability insurance. The development of automobile liability insurance has been the subject of more legislation than has the development of liability insurance for medical malpractice, defective products, or liability for defective premises. Unless they self-insure, larger enterprises usually rely upon a standard form of commercial general liability (CGL) coverage to protect against liability to a third party for bodily injury or property damage. For specific risks, such as pollution or product liability, the insured may have to purchase coverage separately (a "special purpose" coverage). Smaller companies often buy combined liability and first-party property coverage called "commercial multi-peril" coverage. Physicians buy professional liability coverage—either from private insurers or, more recently, from "mutual" insurance companies formed by physicians' associations to compete with the commercial carriers.

The volume of non-auto liability insurance has grown dramatically. In 1958, medical malpractice premiums were $895 million. As of 1999, they were about $6 billion and after peaking at $10.1 billion in 2006, declined to $8.5 billion in 2013. Other premiums, for policies covering such things as products liability and other forms of commercial liability excluding auto and medical, totaled $784 million in 1958. By 1999, these totaled $27.1 billion. From 2004 through 2013, these premiums were fairly stable running in the range of $40–$46 billion. Best's Aggregates & Averages (2014).

Although there have been alleged "crises" in the pricing of these policies, they have remained in the private sector with no legislative efforts to coerce the acquisition of coverage. Why, for example, not require some minimum liability coverage as a condition of practicing medicine? From time to time, in response to instability in the premiums and curtailed availability of these liability policies, legislatures have changed substantive tort rules to make liability harder to establish or to impose limits on recoverable damages, which, in turn, has made the relevant insurance either cheaper or more readily available. Might some of the instability in liability markets be due to the voluntary nature of this insurance with the safer manufacturers (or physicians) opting out and choosing to self-insure, leaving the more dangerous and the untested newer entrants in the liability insurance markets? This thesis, based on the economic principle of "adverse selection," is developed in Priest, The Current Insurance Crisis in Modern Tort Law,

96 Yale L.J. 1521 (1987). For explanation of the insurance underwriting "cycle" and why it produces periodic "crises" in the market for medical malpractice insurance, see T. Baker, The Medical Malpractice Myth (2005). For general discussion of the perceived insurance crisis of the mid-1980s, see Abraham, Making Sense of the Liability Insurance Crisis, 48 Ohio St.L.J. 399 (1987).

b.   THE PROBLEM OF MORAL HAZARD

When insurance markets first developed, some critics saw these policies as creating temptations: life insurance was a form of gambling, fire insurance was an invitation to arson. Among several safeguards developed to allay such concerns, courts and legislatures have adopted an "insurable interest" requirement, which limits what may be insured by whom. A person may insure his or her own life, those closely related to that person may do so, and creditors may protect their loans by taking out life insurance on the debtor. The interest that the insured has in the subject covered by these insurance policies avoids the "moral hazard" that would exist if, for example, one were permitted to insure a stranger's house against fire or a neighbor's life. Perhaps the dangers are best suggested by Liberty National Life Insurance Co. v. Weldon, 100 So.2d 696 (Ala.1957), in which the defendant issued a life insurance policy on a young child to her aunt who, under state law, did not have the requisite insurable interest in the child. The aunt killed the child in an attempt to recover the insurance proceeds. (The court upheld an award to the child's parents in their wrongful death action against the insurance company for its negligence in issuing the illegal policy to the aunt.) "Moral hazard" is now a term of art; it refers to the possibility that those who are insured for a risk will take less care to avoid the harm than they would have if they bore the full cost of that harm. Lacking sufficient "skin in the game," an insured does not have the requisite financial incentives for exercising costly precautions that would reduce the chance of loss. Thus, many health insurance policies have deductibles and co-payments that make the insured responsible for a portion of the medical expenses, thereby reducing the likelihood that the insured will ignore cost and overuse medical services.

Similarly, some courts initially thought that liability insurance would create moral hazard by making the insured careless about the safety of others. This concern is borne out occasionally in reported cases. In Herschensohn v. Weisman, 119 A. 705 (N.H.1923), plaintiff passenger told defendant that he was driving carelessly and was assured, "Don't worry. I carry insurance for that." See also Breeden v. Frankfort Marine, Accident & Plate Glass Insur. Co., 119 S.W. 576, 581 (Mo.1909)("In our judgment, when a carrier knows that a third person is required to furnish the means from his own pocket with which to pay for the injuries done by his negligence to the passenger, then that consideration has a direct and potent influence in encouraging negligence on the part of the carrier."). Despite such cases and the possibility of a diminished sense of responsibility, courts have concluded that "liability insurance is ... favored, because it facilitates the compensation of successful plaintiffs." Abraham, Liability Insurance and Accident Prevention: The Evolution of an Idea, 64 Md.L.Rev. 573 (2005).

The moral hazard problem, however, is more pronounced in other contexts. As is true for other contracts, courts will not enforce an express provision of an insurance contract if doing so would be contrary to public policy. For some types of tort claims, coverage of the liabilities would be contrary to public policy for reasons related to moral hazard. In Taylor v. Superior Court, 598 P.2d 854 (Cal.1979), the court observed that section 533 of the California Insurance Code provides that an insurer is not liable for a "willful act of the insured," which state courts have equated with an intent to harm. The section "reflects a fundamental public policy of denying coverage for willful wrongs. [ ] The parties to an insurance policy therefore cannot contract for such coverage." See also J.C. Penney Casualty Insurance Co. v. M.K., 804 P.2d 689 (Cal.1991)(even if the policy provides coverage to defendant for a claim of sexual molestation, the state's public policy bars insurance coverage for such a claim).

Courts have struggled over the question of whether coverage for punitive damages violates public policy. (Recall from our earlier discussion in this chapter that these damages are ordinarily justified on grounds of deterrence and retribution.) For cases in which the insurance policy does not exclude coverage for a claim of punitive damages (which it often does), New York has decided that its "public policy precludes insurance indemnification for punitive damages awards, whether the punitive damages are based on intentional actions or actions which, while not intentional, amount to 'gross negligence, recklessness, or wantonness' [ ] or 'conscious disregard of the rights of others or for conduct so reckless as to amount to such disregard' [ ]." Home Insurance Co. v. American Home Products Corp., 550 N.E.2d 930 (N.Y.1990). Several other states concur in a line of cases extending back to the early 1960s, when courts first confronted the issue in deciding whether the third-party provisions of automobile insurance indemnify the policyholder for punitive damages incurred as a result of drunk driving.

This position is most easily justified under the early formulations of punitive damages that limited the liability to outrageous behavior. But because the rules regarding punitive damages have evolved, some now argue that states have been permitting punitive damages too readily—for such conduct as gross negligence and in vicarious liability situations—and have not been reviewing jury awards sufficiently carefully. Recall the discussion earlier in this Chapter, p. 753 supra. If a defendant might now be held liable for punitive damages for conduct that is not "all that different" from negligence, is noninsurability still justifiable?

A different argument for the insurability of punitive damages relies on the incentives that a third-party liability insurer has with respect to these forms of tort liability. Moral hazard inefficiently increases the cost of insurance due to the increased number of insurance payouts, incentivizing the insurer to cut these costs and lower premiums to match those of competitors in the marketplace. For this reason, liability insurance excludes coverage for intentional harms or otherwise limits coverage to accidents, each of which would bar coverage for a considerable number of punitive damages claims involving outrageous behavior, such as assault and battery.

In addition to policy exclusions, liability insurers employ a variety of different mechanisms to combat moral hazard, such as underwriting, experience rating, coverage design, loss control, ex-post auditing, and external control measures. See generally Baker & Siegelman, The Law and Economics of Liability Insurance: A Theoretical and Empirical Review, in D. Schwarcz & P. Siegelman (eds.), Research Handbook on the Economics of Insurance Law (2015). Experience rating, for example, sets premiums on the basis of the insured's previous liability experience. Under this approach, an insured subject to prior awards of punitive damages would have to pay higher premiums for procuring liability coverage in the future, creating a financial incentive to avoid incurring punitive damages in the first instance. In First Nat'l Bank v. Fid. & Deposit Co., 389 A.2d 359 (Md.1978), the court concluded that punitive damages are insurable in part because "those who are demonstrated by experience to be poor risks encounter substantial difficulty in obtaining insurance, a fact such persons know."

In light of the incentives that insurers have for ameliorating the problem of moral hazard, should courts invoke public policy as the reason for not enforcing insurance contracts that cover punitive damages? See Baker, Reconsidering Insurance for Punitive Damages, 1998 Wis.L.Rev. 101 (arguing that "there is no need for courts to act on deterrence grounds to prohibit insurance for punitive damages" because the "twin problems of moral hazard and adverse selection provide insurers with adequate incentive to address the deterrence objection"); see also Sharkey, Revisiting the Noninsurable Costs of Accidents, 64 Md.L.Rev. 409, 427 (2005)(identifying 25 states that permit insurance coverage for punitive damages either by statute or court decision and nine states that hold such coverage contravenes public policy).

The argument for the insurability of punitive damages depends on the extent to which insurers can combat moral hazard through express exclusions of coverage in the policy. To evaluate this issue, note that an express provision in the insurance policy that excludes coverage for intentional harms (or otherwise limits coverage to "accidents") does not necessarily negate coverage for all intentional torts. Part of the reason involves the definition of intent employed by tort law. In some cases, the intent requirement can be satisfied without culpable behavior on the defendant's part, transforming these intentional torts (like "innocent" trespasses) into forms of strict liability. See note 1, p. 945 infra. In cases like this, a court can conclude that the defendant/policyholder did not have the intent (or culpable purpose) to cause harm, thereby permitting coverage for these intentional torts under the policy. These cases show why the meaning of "intent" in tort law can differ from the meaning employed by insurance law, although another factor confounds this analysis. By denying coverage on grounds that the defendant/policyholder intended the loss, a court knows that the ruling may effectively deny full recovery to the tort plaintiff. Many believe this factor often influences the judicial interpretation of insurance contracts, thereby undermining the way in which policy exclusions can address particular problems of insurability, such as moral hazard.

The associated issues are illustrated by two lines of cases involving persons who are mentally impaired. These cases are summarized in Cooperative Fire Insurance Ass'n v. Combs, 648 A.2d 857 (Vt.1994), which involved a shooting death and an insurance policy that excluded coverage of liability resulting from "an intentional act of an insured." The parties stipulated that the shooter-insured was "insane." One line of cases holds that "an insane person cannot act intentionally as a matter of law" for insurance purposes, and the second holds that "so long as there is evidence that the insured understood the physical nature and consequences of his action, he is capable of intent even though he may not be capable of distinguishing between right and wrong or of controlling his conduct." Even under this second view, "there will be coverage if the insured is so mentally ill that he does not, in fact, know what he is doing, as when, for instance, he points a pistol thinking he is peeling a banana." The court adopted the first view. What are the consequences of adopting the first view for the victims, the insured, and the insurer? The second view?

The reasons for the various positions are explored in Hanover Insurance Co. v. Talhouni, 604 N.E.2d 689 (Mass.1992)(upholding coverage for insured who assaulted stranger while on a "bad trip" from LSD and who "was completely out of touch with reality, was hallucinating and delusional, and did not know that he was assaulting another human being"); Municipal Mutual Insurance Co. v. Mangus, 443 S.E.2d 455 (W.Va.1994)(denying coverage where insured shot neighbor: "he knew he was picking up a gun and not a banana; that when he went outside with that gun, he knew he was pointing the gun at a man and knew that man was Rickey Fields"); Auto-Owners Insurance Co. v. Churchman, 489 N.W.2d 431 (Mich.1992)(holding that even though "an insane or mentally ill insured may be unable to form the criminal intent necessary to be charged with murder, such an individual can still intend or expect the results of the injuries he causes" and insurance coverage is excluded). What do these cases suggest about the ability of insurers to combat moral hazard?

c. THE IMPACT OF LIABILITY INSURANCE ON TORT LITIGATION

The jury is not to be told whether the defendant is insured. Why? When the defendant has insurance, the plaintiff's attorney would like to ask prospective jurors if they have any ties with insurance companies. Should such questions be permitted?

In Roman v. Mitchell, 413 A.2d 322 (N.J.1980), the court split 4–3 over the trial judge's action in excluding voir dire questions asking whether any prospective jurors held stock in, or were employed by, a casualty insurance company. The majority thought that the questions "tend to emphasize unduly the fact of insurance coverage. Absent some indication that a basis for asking them exists, they should ordinarily be rejected by the trial court." The majority feared that asking such questions, even in good faith, "can prejudice a defendant's right to a fair trial." One dissenter argued that modern jurors know about the existence of liability insurance and will not use the information to render excessive verdicts. Aren't all of these issues, at bottom, empirical questions? The dissent also noted that insurance companies frequently advertised in national magazines to remind the public of the widespread incidence of liability insurance and to urge that jurors use restraint in awards. See also Taylor v. Republic Automotive Parts, Inc., 950 S.W.2d 318 (Mo.App.1997).

In Rodgers v. Pascagoula Public School District, 611 So.2d 942 (Miss.1992), defendant school district admitted liability for a bus crash, and the jury awarded nothing for pain and suffering or other non-economic damages. The court ordered additur. Three concurring justices observed:

> I am compelled to question how a jury composed of taxpayers can be expected to render a fair award of damages when operating under the assumption that they, the taxpayers, would ultimately foot the bill. . . . How can we continue [the policy of excluding mention of insurance] because of the presumed prejudice to an insurer when that same insurer can capitalize upon the gross prejudice that a jury of taxpayers will have toward assessing damages for the plaintiff? . . . [In this type of case] I believe that evidence of liability coverage should be admitted to ensure a fair and adequate award, untainted by any misconceptions that it could lighten the pocketbooks of taxpaying jurors.

What is this "misconception"? How would the concurrence eliminate it?

Although the defendant's liability insurance is not ordinarily discussed in the courtroom, it can still exert substantial influence on the tort suit. As discussed earlier in the context of automobile insurance, liability insurance often provides the sole funding for a defendant to satisfy the plaintiff's tort judgment. To the extent that the judgment exceeds the limits of the defendant's liability insurance, the plaintiff must collect from the defendant's personal assets. Doing so is not ordinarily a problem when the defendant is a large, solvent corporation. Matters are different with respect to small businesses or individuals. "Most Americans are judgment-proof not because we are poor, but because state and federal laws entitle us to be judgment-proof." Gilles, The Judgment-Proof Society, 63 Wash. & Lee L.Rev. 603, 607 (2006). For example, bankruptcy law protects substantial personal assets (like a residential home) from collection by creditors, including the tort plaintiff. Thus, "[i]n the absence of liability insurance, plaintiffs are effectively barred from bringing suit unless the tortfeasor is an asset-rich corporation or an affluent individual who neglects to take elementary precautions to protect his or her assets from tort liability." Id. at 606; see also Zeiler et al., Physicians' Insurance Limits and Malpractice Payments: Evidence from Texas Closed Claims, 1990–2003, 36 J.Legal Stud. S9 (2007)(reporting results of empirical study finding that for physicians in Texas over the studied period, "policy limits often act as effective caps on recovery [for medical malpractice], and that personal contributions by physicians to close claims were rare"). For these reasons, tort litigation routinely centers on the limits of the defendant's insurance policy rather than the full amount of tort damages sought by plaintiff.

To be sure, the plaintiff can sometimes collect from the personal assets of the defendant. Based on a series of interviews conducted with personal injury lawyers in Connecticut and Florida, Professor Baker found that plaintiffs often impute special value to these payments.

> "Blood money" is a term many of my respondents used for . . . money paid directly to plaintiffs by defendants out of their own pockets. As their term reflects, blood money hurts defendants in a way that money paid on behalf of a defendant by a liability insurance company cannot. For that reason, blood money is an entirely different currency than what lawyers refer to as "insurance money."

Baker, Blood Money, New Money, and the Moral Economy of Tort Law in Action, 35 Law & Soc'y Rev. 275, 276 (2001). Due to this difference in the "moral currency" of different sources of compensation, there is a "strong norm against paying blood money in a negligence case, [and so] the plaintiff's legal claim to blood money motivates all the repeat players in the litigation process to arrive at a settlement within the liability insurance limits." Consequently, "[r]eal money from real people accounts for a very small fraction of tort settlement dollars." Id. at 277.

In order to gain access to a defendant's liability insurance, plaintiffs often attempt to shape their complaints to avoid contractual or legislative exclusions of coverage. See, e.g., American Employer's Insurance Co. v. Smith, 163 Cal.Rptr. 649 (App.1980), in which an arsonist was sued for negligence. Joined with that action was a suit by the defendant's insurer contesting coverage for the claim. The insurer argued that the claim against the arsonist, its insured, should be dismissed since the insured clearly was guilty of intentional wrongdoing. The court rejected this argument, concluding that "it is not a defense to negligence to contend that the conduct was willful or the harm intended." But the court left open the question of whether the plaintiff could satisfy any judgment through the defendant's insurance. Under this approach, resolution of the tort claim does not answer the insurance question, which can be separately litigated in a coverage action between the tort defendant/policyholder and liability insurer. Any findings in the underlying tort suit (the arsonist was negligent) would not be binding in the subsequent coverage suit (enabling the insurer to prove that the arson was intentional). Due to the considerable costs created by the collateral litigation, courts have adopted other approaches. In Landry v. Leonard, 720 A.2d 907 (Me.1998), plaintiff cab driver sued a robber for negligence. The court held that the insurer did not have to defend the suit because the policy excluded coverage of bodily injury "which is expected or intended by the 'insured.'" The court also held that the negligence action failed. Given the "intentional act of robbing Landry with the use of a dangerous weapon, a finding of negligence for that act is excluded." See also Boyles v. Kerr, 855 S.W.2d 593 (Tex.1993)(alleging that defendant, who secretly taped his sexual relations with plaintiff and then showed the tapes to others, had behaved negligently). See Pryor, The Stories We Tell: Intentional Harm and the Quest for Insurance Funding, 75 Tex.L.Rev. 1721 (1997). For discussion of how liability insurance affects other aspects of the day-to-day world of tort litigation, see Baker, Liability Insurance as Tort Regulation: Six Ways that Liability Insurance Shapes Tort Law in Action, 12 Conn.Ins.L.J. 1 (2006).

Skilled plaintiff's lawyers know that the amount that can be obtained from the defendant's liability insurer can sometimes exceed the policy limits of the insurance. Recall *Campbell*, p. 757 supra, the case in which the insureds recovered punitive damages from their insurer for failure to settle a tort claim against them. To satisfy the underlying judgment owed to the tort plaintiffs, the insureds (as tort defendants) agreed to give the tort plaintiffs 90% of any verdict against the insurer. That verdict involved a substantial punitive award, giving the tort plaintiffs an ultimate recovery far in excess of the tort defendants' policy limits. The availability of such a claim against an insurer for its settlement practices—so called "bad faith" refusal-to-settle claims—is addressed in the following case.

Pavia v. State Farm Mutual
Automobile Insurance Co.

Court of Appeals of New York, 1993.
82 N.Y.2d 445, 626 N.E.2d 24, 605 N.Y.S.2d 208.

■ TITONE, JUDGE.

[One evening in April 1985, Carmine Rosato, a 16-year-old, picked up the 19-year-old plaintiff and another youth in a car belonging to Rosato's mother. The car was insured by defendant with a $100,000 liability limit. Rosato, whose learner's permit did not authorize driving at night, turned a corner apparently at an excessive speed and encountered a double-parked car. In his efforts to avoid that car he collided with a car driven by Amerosa. Plaintiff was seriously hurt.]

. . .

In October 1985, Pavia commenced a personal injury action against the Rosatos and Mr. Amerosa. The record reveals that as early as March 1986 a line unit representative at State Farm responsible for a preliminary investigation of plaintiff's claim, concluded that the Rosatos were 100% liable for the accident. By August 1986, a State Farm claims representative responsible for handling the case on a daily basis was in receipt of medical reports attesting to the severity of plaintiff's injuries. A physical examination of plaintiff conducted by State Farm's physicians on April 27, 1987 confirmed those findings. New developments in the case against the Rosatos surfaced on June 9, 1987—the date that Carmine Rosato was deposed. Through Rosato's testimony, State Farm was led to believe that the double-parked car may have been backing up, suggesting that Rosato's quick maneuvering may have been justified under an "emergency defense"; that witnesses not previously identified could support this version of the incident; that Pavia failed to wear a seat belt; and that drugs were being used in the car that night, possibly supporting an assumption of the risk defense. By letter dated June 10, 1987, counsel retained for the Rosatos by State Farm acknowledged that the liability forecast was "extremely unfavorable," but recommended that a further inquiry be conducted in light of these new leads.

On June 26, 1987, admittedly without having read Rosato's deposition, plaintiff's counsel wrote to State Farm demanding the full $100,000 policy limit in settlement of the personal injury action and requiring acceptance of the offer within thirty days. The offer expired without response from State Farm. By this time, however, State Farm had embarked on a thorough investigation of the potential defenses illuminated by Rosato's deposition. In fact, State Farm had hired an investigator to locate the supposed witnesses who would corroborate Rosato's version of how the events leading to the accident unfolded. By November 1987, State Farm's efforts to locate those witnesses were abandoned because the search had proved fruitless. On December 1,

1987, State Farm's Claims Committee, whose members had the authority to offer payments in excess of $50,000, convened for the first time to discuss the reports generated by the claim representative assigned to the case. On December 16, 1987, the Committee authorized its counsel to offer plaintiff the full policy limits. This offer was conveyed to plaintiff's attorney by counsel retained by State Farm on the Rosatos' behalf on January 7, 1988 during a "settle or select" conference, but was rejected as "too late."

The trial of the underlying personal injury action commenced in March 1988. The jury returned a plaintiff's verdict in the amount of $6,322,000, attributing 85% of the fault to Carmine Rosato and 15% to co-defendant Amerosa. Supreme Court reduced the verdict upon State Farm's motion to $5,000,000 and the Appellate Division modified that judgment by further reducing the verdict to $3,880,000 upon plaintiff's stipulation.

The Rosatos subsequently assigned all causes of action they might have against State Farm to plaintiff by executing an assignment agreement, which included a covenant by plaintiff that he would not execute the excess portion of the judgment against the Rosatos. The Rosatos and plaintiff then commenced this action, alleging essentially that State Farm acted in bad faith by "failing to accept [plaintiff's] policy limits settlement offer within a reasonable time despite the clear liability and obvious damages exceeding the policy limits."

At the ensuing trial on the bad faith action, the jury was presented solely with the following question: "Did the defendant, State Farm, act in gross disregard of the interests of Carmine Rosato and Joanne Rosato, their insured, in that there was a deliberate or reckless decision to disregard the interest of their insured?" The jury answered affirmatively, and Supreme Court entered an "excess" judgment against State Farm in the amount of $4,688,030—the amount of the jury verdict in the underlying personal injury action as modified by the Appellate Division, less $110,000 already paid by State Farm and Amerosa's insurer, plus interest and costs.

The Appellate Division affirmed, holding that the trial court properly charged the jury that, in order to find bad faith, State Farm must have acted in "gross disregard" of the Rosatos' interests, and properly rejected the standard urged by State Farm—that bad faith required "an extraordinary showing of disingenuous or dishonest failure" to carry out the insurance contract [ ]. The court also rejected State Farm's contention that the evidence adduced at trial was insufficient as a matter of law to present a jury question on the "bad faith" issue, noting that State Farm "possessed the information necessary to accurately assess both the magnitude of Frank Pavia's injuries and the Rosatos' potential exposure well before the June 26, 1987 settlement offer was received" [ ]. Despite our conclusion that the courts below properly applied the "gross disregard" standard, as a matter of law the finding of bad faith is not supported by this record.

II.

The notion that an insurer may be held liable for the breach of its duty of "good faith" in defending and settling claims over which it exercises exclusive control on behalf of its insured is an enduring principle, well-settled in this State's jurisprudence [ ]. The duty of "good faith" settlement is an implied obligation derived from the insurance contract [ ]. Naturally, whenever an insurer is presented with a settlement offer within policy limits a conflict arises between, on the one hand, the insurer's interest in minimizing its payments and on the other hand, the insured's interest in avoiding liability beyond the policy limits [ ]. By refusing to settle within the policy limits, an insurer risks being charged with bad faith on the premise that it has "advanced its own interest by compromising those of its insured". . . . [ ].

At the root of the "bad faith" doctrine is the fact that insurers typically exercise complete control over the settlement and defense of claims against their insureds, and, thus, under established agency principles may fairly be required to act in the insured's best interests [ ]. On the other hand, a countervailing policy consideration exists in the courts' understandable reluctance to expose insurance carriers to liability far beyond the bargained-for policy limits for conduct amounting to a mere mistake in judgment. Thus, established precedent clearly bars a "bad faith" prosecution for conduct amounting to ordinary negligence [ ]. Indeed, in [ ], this Court held that even where an insurer had withdrawn from its insured's defense on the erroneous belief that the policy of insurance had lapsed, the error in judgment could not form the predicate for a bad faith action [ ].

Beyond that principle, the courts have had some difficulty selecting a standard for actionable "bad faith" because of the need to balance the insured's rightful expectations of "good faith" against the insurer's equally legitimate contract expectations. Consequently, a divergence of authority has arisen concerning whether a bad faith finding may be predicated on a showing of the insurer's recklessness or "gross disregard" for the insured's interests [ ], or whether a heightened showing of intentionally harmful, dishonest or disingenuous motive is required [ ].

Faced squarely with the question for the first time, we reject defendant's proposed requirement of a "sinister motive" on the part of the insurer [ ], and hold instead that, in order to establish a prima facie case of bad faith, the plaintiff must establish that the insurer's conduct constituted a "gross disregard" of the insured's interests—that is, a deliberate or reckless failure to place on equal footing the interests of its insured with its own interests when considering a settlement offer [ ]. In other words, a bad faith plaintiff must establish that the defendant insurer engaged in a pattern of behavior evincing a conscious or knowing indifference to the probability that an insured would be held personally accountable for a large judgment if a settlement offer within the policy limits were not accepted.

The gross disregard standard, which was utilized by the trial court here, strikes a fair balance between two extremes by requiring more than ordinary negligence and less than a showing of dishonest motives. The former would remove the latitude that insurers must be accorded in investigating and resisting unfounded claims, while the latter would be all but impossible to satisfy and would effectively insulate insurance carriers from conduct that, while not motivated by malice, has the potential to severely prejudice the rights of its insured. The intermediate standard accomplishes the two-fold goal of protecting both the insured's and the insurer's financial interests.

III.

Having established the proper legal standard, we necessarily shift to the sufficiency of plaintiff's proof in this case. Naturally, proof that a demand for settlement was made is a prerequisite to a bad faith action for failure to settle [ ]. However, evidence that a settlement offer was made and not accepted is not dispositive of the insurer's bad faith. It is settled that an insurer "cannot be compelled to concede liability and settle a questionable claim" [ ] simply "because an opportunity to do so is presented" [ ]. Rather, the plaintiff in a bad faith action must show that "the insured lost an actual opportunity to settle the claim" [ ] at a time when all serious doubts about the insured's liability were removed.

Bad faith is established only "where the liability is clear and the potential recovery far exceeds the insurance coverage" [ ]. However, it does not follow that whenever an injury is severe and the policy limits are significantly lower than a potential recovery the insurer is obliged to accept a settlement offer. The bad faith equation must include consideration of all of the facts and circumstances relating to whether the insurer's investigatory efforts prevented it from making an informed evaluation of the risks of refusing settlement. In making this determination, courts must assess the plaintiff's likelihood of success on the liability issue in the underlying action, the potential magnitude of damages and the financial burden each party may be exposed to as a result of a refusal to settle. Additional considerations include the insurer's failure to properly investigate the claim and any potential defenses thereto, the information available to the insurer at the time the demand for settlement is made, and any other evidence which tends to establish or negate the insurer's bad faith in refusing to settle. The insured's fault in delaying or ceasing settlement negotiations by misrepresenting the facts also factors into the analysis [ ].

Application of the aforementioned principles here leads us to the conclusion that plaintiffs have failed to establish a prima facie case of bad faith. Plaintiffs' allegations of bad faith stem principally from defendant State Farm's failure to abide by a settlement deadline unilaterally established by plaintiff Pavia's counsel and its delay in ultimately offering the policy limits in settlement.

However, defendant's failure to respond to the letter and overall delay under the circumstances of this case cannot serve as a basis for recovery. Permitting an injured plaintiff's chosen timetable for settlement to govern the bad faith inquiry would promote the customary manufacturing of bad faith claims, especially in cases where an insured of meager means is covered by a policy of insurance which could finance only a fraction of the damages in a serious personal injury case. Indeed, insurers would be bombarded with settlement offers imposing arbitrary deadlines and would be encouraged to prematurely settle their insureds' claims at the earliest possible opportunity in contravention of their contractual right and obligation of thorough investigation.

Here, plaintiff's time-limited settlement offer came at a relatively early point in the litigation. Moreover, at the time the 30-day settlement demand was made, there remained several significant questions about the insured's liability, which defendant was entitled to investigate and explore. That defendant could have acted more expeditiously does not convert inattention into a gross disregard for the insured's rights, particularly where, as here, there is no contention that the insurer failed to carry out an investigation, to evaluate the feasibility of settlement [ ], or to offer the policy limits before trial after the weakness of the insured's litigation position was clearly and fully assessed.

The facts that State Farm's preliminary liability forecasts were unfavorable and that the investigation ultimately proved those forecasts accurate certainly do not establish that the insurer was unjustified in engaging in further investigation and failing to effectuate an early settlement. On the contrary, State Farm's failure to conduct the continuing inquiry could have constituted a breach of its obligation to investigate and defend its insured. Moreover, State Farm should not be penalized for the delay in processing the claim and offering the full policy limits in settlement which resulted from its pursuit of an investigation prompted by its insured's representations which ultimately did not materialize [ ].

By any view of the evidence, State Farm's failure to promptly respond to the time-restricted demand did not amount to more than ordinary negligence—an insufficient predicate for a bad faith action. Evident as it may be with hindsight that State Farm should have responded to the settlement offer by at least requesting an extension, its failure to do so was not evidence of willful neglect of the insured's rights, but instead amounted to mistaken judgment or administrative delay in confirming what it had suspected it would do all along—settle for the policy limits. Thus, this record lacks any pattern or indicia of reckless or conscious disregard for the insured's rights upon which we could uphold a bad faith judgment.

. . . [The Appellate Division's order was reversed and the complaint dismissed.]

■ KAYE, C.J., and SIMONS, HANCOCK, BELLACOSA, SMITH and LEVINE, JJ., concur.

NOTES AND QUESTIONS

1. *The duty to defend and the duty to indemnify.* For cases in which the insurer might be obliged to indemnify the policyholder/defendant for the liability in a tort suit, why does the policy give the insurer a right to defend the suit? The policy also imposes a duty on the insurer to defend these suits. Why might that be?

Although liability insurance ordinarily includes both duties, the insurer's duty to indemnify covered liabilities is different from the duty to defend against those liabilities. Twin City Fire Ins. Co. v. Ben Arnold-Sunbelt Beverage Co. of S.C., 433 F.3d 365 (4th Cir.2005), explains how these two obligations are handled when it is unclear whether the policy would cover the legal liabilities incurred by the policyholder/defendant:

> When a party with insurance coverage is sued, the insured notifies the insurance company of the suit. The insurance company, in turn, typically chooses, retains, and pays private counsel to represent the insured as to all claims. If the suit involves some claims that are covered under the insurance policy and some claims that are not covered, the insurance company typically will send a reservation of rights letter to the insured stating what claims the insurance company believes are covered and what claims it believes are not covered.

Because the insurer can have a duty to defend a case in which it will not necessarily have a duty to indemnify, the insurer can have a conflict of interest. Why not defend the case in a manner that leaves the insured exposed only to those forms of liability that are not covered by the policy? A reservation of rights letter informs the policyholder of this potential conflict but does not otherwise resolve it, so the court then had to "examine whether, under South Carolina law, such a reservation of rights letter automatically triggers a conflict of interest entitling the insured to reject counsel tendered by the insurance company and instead to choose and retain its own counsel and to have the insurance company pay for that counsel."

The court considered whether to adopt a per se rule permitting the insured to hire private counsel in all of these cases, or to instead require the trial judge to determine if a conflict exists. After canvassing the different approaches taken by other courts, the court adopted the rule requiring judicial examination and concluded that in the case at hand, the reservation of rights by the insurer did not create a conflict permitting the insured to hire private counsel.

Would an insured be entitled to independent counsel whenever a claim for punitive damages is asserted and the jurisdiction bars insurance coverage for such damage? Who should pay for this defense? Even if the insurer pays for the defense, is that cost ultimately borne by policyholders as a group via an increase in premiums? As between a lay insured and sophisticated insurer, who is in the better position of procuring effective counsel at the lowest cost? See Galanter, Why the "Haves" Come Out Ahead: Speculations on the Limits of Legal Change, 9 Law & Soc'y Rev. 95 (1974)(identifying various methods by which repeat players in litigation— the "haves"—can derive advantages and benefits for their position).

2. *The defense attorney's conflict of interest.* To what extent does the attorney-client relationship mitigate any conflicts of interest between the insurer and insured? The answer critically depends on which party is the client of the attorney hired by the insurer to defend the case against the insured. This issue is addressed by the Restatement (Third) of the Law Governing Lawyers section 134 cmt. f (2000):

> It is clear in an insurance situation that a lawyer designated to defend the insured has a client-lawyer relationship with the insured. The insurer is not, simply by the fact that it designates the lawyer, a client of the lawyer. Whether a client-lawyer relationship also exists between the lawyer and the insurer is determined under [other provisions]. . . .
>
>   . . .
>
> Material divergence of interest might exist between a liability insurer and an insured, for example, when a claim substantially in excess of policy limits is asserted against an insured. If the lawyer knows or should be aware of such an excess claim, the lawyer may not follow directions of the insurer if doing so would put the insured at significantly increased risk of liability in excess of the policy coverage. Such occasions for conflict may exist at the outset of the representation or may be created by events that occur thereafter. The lawyer must address a conflict whenever presented. To the extent that such a conflict is subject to client consent (see § 122(2)(c)), the lawyer may proceed after obtaining client consent under the limitations and conditions stated in § 122.
>
> When there is a question whether a claim against the insured is within the coverage of the policy, a lawyer designated to defend the insured may not reveal adverse confidential client information of the insured to the insurer concerning that question (see § 60) without explicit informed consent of the insured [ ]. . . .
>
> With respect to events or information that create a conflict of interest between insured and insurer, the lawyer must proceed in the best interests of the insured, consistent with the lawyer's duty not to assist client fraud [ ] and, if applicable, consistent with the lawyer's duties to the insurer as co-client [ ]. If the designated lawyer finds it impossible so to proceed, the lawyer must

withdraw from representation of both clients as provided in
§ 32; [ ]. . . .

States take different approaches to this question. Compare, e.g., In re
Rules of Professional Conduct, 2 P.3d 806 (Mont.2000) (defense counsel
represents only the insured) with, e.g., Cincinnati Insurance Co. v. Wills,
717 N.E.2d 151 (Ind.1999)(in-house counsel for insurer could represent
both insured and insurer, at least until a conflict between them arose).
Considerable scholarly disagreement also exists about who defense counsel
is representing. Compare Silver & Syverud, The Professional
Responsibilities of Insurance Defense Lawyers, 45 Duke L.J. 255
(1995)(dual co-equal clients) with Pepper, Applying the Fundamentals of
Lawyers' Ethics to Insurance Defense Practice, 4 Conn.Ins.L.J. 27 (1997–
98)(concluding that there is an irresolvable tension between the lawyer's
ethical obligation to defend the insured and the obligations and rights
provided in the insurance agreement, such that neither a "single client" nor
"dual client" model is satisfactory) and Baker, Liability Insurance Conflicts
and Defense Lawyers: From Triangles to Tetrahedrons, 4 Conn.Ins.L.J. 101
(1997–98)(insured is primary client whose interests take precedence over
insurer).

Even if the court concludes that the attorney's only client is the
insured and not the insurer paying for the defense, does the attorney still
realistically face any conflicts? Consider in this regard the volume of
business that an insurer can send to a defense attorney. For extensive and
critical view of insurers' practices in these areas, see Smith, The
Miscegenetic Union of Liability Insurance and Tort Process in the Personal
Injury Claims System, 54 Cornell L.Rev. 645 (1969).

3. *The insurer's duty of good faith to the policyholder.* Although the
defense attorney owes the tort defendant an ethical duty of loyalty, and
although the insurer must notify the policyholder/defendant about any
potential conflicts of interest in a reservation-of-rights letter, the conflict is
not wholly eliminated. To what extent does *Pavia* resolve the residual
conflict by imposing a tort duty of good faith on the insurer? Is the court
persuasive in arguing that a standard of "ordinary negligence" is
inappropriate for this duty?

In many jurisdictions, the insurer breaches the duty to settle by
rejecting a "reasonable" settlement offer—one that would be acceptable to
the insurer if it were fully liable for the claims in question. How might
settlements be affected by a system that made insurers strictly liable for
any failure to accept a settlement offer within the policy limits if the case
then goes to trial and results in a jury verdict subjecting the
defendant/policyholder to liability in excess of the policy limits? Suppose
such a rule were coupled with a limitation on damages to the amount that
the plaintiff could have obtained from the insured for any excess award?

Should an insurer be liable for not offering the insured the chance to
pay something now in order to avoid a possibly greater liability later? In
Parich v. State Farm Mutual Automobile Insurance Co., 919 F.2d 906 (5th
Cir.1990), the insurer refused a $37,000 settlement offer on a $25,000

policy limit without first asking the insured whether he would contribute the extra $12,000. The case went to trial, resulting in a judgment against the insured for some $400,000. The insurer was held liable for the entire judgment. What if the insurer in that case had asked the insured to provide the extra $12,000, and the insured had refused?

For discussion of how settlement negotiations can create a variety of conflicts between insurers and insureds, and possible ways to resolve them, see Syverud, The Duty to Settle, 76 Va.L.Rev 1113 (1990). For an empirical study of the impact of bad faith claims on the amounts paid in settlements, see Browne, Pryor & Puelz, The Effect of Bad-Faith Laws on First-Party Insurance Claims Decisions, 33 J.Legal Stud. 355 (2004)(finding a correlation between the availability of bad faith claims and the amounts paid in settlements). See generally Symposium on the Law of Bad Faith in Contract and Insurance, 72 Tex.L.Rev. 1203 (1994).

4. *Punitive damages redux.* The New York Court of Appeals refused to extend bad faith claims for underlying judgments involving punitive damages. In Soto v. State Farm Insurance Co., 635 N.E.2d 1222 (N.Y.1994), defendant's insureds were found liable for $420,000 in compensatory damages and $450,000 in punitive damages in connection with a fatal automobile accident. The insurer defended the case on the ground that the driver did not have the insured-owner's permission to drive the car. The jury found that the driver (the insured's live-in boyfriend) had permission—and was drunk at the time of the accident. After the judgment, defendant paid plaintiffs the full amount of the compensatory award (not just the $100,000 policy limits). The insureds (now the driver had been established as an insured as well) assigned to the tort plaintiffs the insureds' claim that their insurer acted in bad faith when it refused a pretrial offer from plaintiffs to settle for the policy limits of $50,000 for each of two deaths. In this suit, plaintiff-assignees sought payment of the punitive award as well.

The court rejected the claim, even though "for purposes of measuring the amounts recoverable in a bad-faith action against an insurer, [a punitive award] is no different in principle from an award of excess personal injury damages; both are unindemnified liabilities to which the insured would not have been exposed if the insurer had acted in good faith to reach a fair pretrial settlement." Nonetheless, the state's goal of "preserving the condemnatory and retributive character of punitive damage awards . . . cannot be reconciled with a conclusion that would allow the insured wrongdoer to divert the economic punishment to an insurer because of the insurer's unrelated, independent wrongful act in improperly refusing a settlement within policy limits":

> Our system of civil justice may be organized so as to allow a wrongdoer to escape the punitive consequences of his own malfeasance in order that the injured plaintiff may enjoy the advantage of a swift and certain pretrial settlement. However, the benefit that a morally culpable wrongdoer obtains as a result of this system, i.e., being released from exposure to liability for punitive damages, is no more than a necessary incident of the

process. It is certainly not a right whose loss need be made subject to compensation when a favorable pretrial settlement offer has been wasted by a reckless or faithless insurer.

Id. at 1225.

California accepted *Soto* in PPG Industries, Inc. v. Transamerica Insurance Co., 975 P.2d 652 (Cal.1999). By a 4–3 vote, the court held that an insured's liability for punitive damages was not a recoverable item of damage in a suit for the insurer's negligent failure to settle. The insured was the proximate cause of its liability for punitive damages, and it was against public policy to allow indemnity for that liability. Moreover, passing along this liability would make all the other policyholders pay for these damages. The dissent feared that the result would encourage insurers to breach their duty to settle "when the claim of its insured's victim is deemed to expose the insured to a relatively small sum in compensatory damages and a relatively large sum in punitive damages." The dissent thought that the insurer should be liable for all the damages proximately caused by its negligent failure to settle.

5.   *The bad faith setup.* Because a breach of the duty to settle can subject the insurer to liability in excess of the policy limits, the tort plaintiff has a strong incentive to induce such a breach. What tactics might enable the plaintiff to accomplish this objective? Did the tort plaintiff in *Pavia* engage in such behavior? Consider Schmidt, The Bad Faith Setup, 29 Tort & Ins.L.J. 705, 705 (1994):

> Creative plaintiffs' attorneys often seek to expand the insurer's policy limits by staging facts that would give rise to bad faith liability. Sometimes these attorneys play "dirty pool" in their attempts to set insurers up for bad faith claims, using such techniques as making policy limits offers with unreasonable time limits, making offers before there has been adequate time for investigation or discovery, and backing out of settlement agreements under pretexts they blame on the insurer.

Does this objective give the tort defendant/policyholder an incentive to collude with the tort plaintiff? How are these issues addressed by *Pavia*? Note that a defendant/policyholder who colludes with the plaintiff in a "bad faith setup" runs the risk of voiding coverage under the policy, either by breaching a "duty to cooperate" clause in the policy or by breaching the independent duty of good faith owed by the policyholder to the insurer. Consequently, "[i]nequitable conduct on the part of the insured may be the basis of an estoppel defense by the insurer or of a 'comparative bad faith' defense based on application of comparative fault principles." Id. at 717.

6.   *The insurer's duty of good faith to the tort plaintiff.* In contrast to cases such as *Pavia* in which the tort defendant/insured sues his or her own insurer for bad faith in the settlement process, some tort plaintiffs have sued the liability insurer of the defendant, claiming that the liability insurer owes a good faith duty to the tort plaintiff in settling the matter. The viability of such a cause of action is controversial. See Moradi-Shalal v. Fireman's Fund Insurance Cos., 758 P.2d 58 (Cal.1988), overruling Royal

Globe Insurance Co. v. Superior Court, 592 P.2d 329 (Cal.1979), which had relied on the insurer's statutory obligation to act in good faith as the basis for recognizing a new tort duty running to the tort plaintiff to settle the claim in good faith. For what harms might a plaintiff recover damages in such a suit?

A study of the impact of *Royal Globe* on claims and recoveries by automobile accident victims found "sharp increases" in the proportion of accident victims who made claims for personal injuries and the average payment received while *Royal Globe* was in effect. Those effects were reversed, however, after *Royal Globe* was overruled. See A. Hawken, S. Carroll & A. Abrahamse, The Effects of Third-Party, Bad Faith Doctrine on Automobile Insurance Costs and Compensation (2001).

7. *The role of liability insurers with respect to settlements covered by the policy.* The addition of insurers to the claims mix is treated in detail in H.L. Ross, Settled Out of Court: The Social Process of Insurance Claims Adjustments (1980 ed.). Consider the following excerpts from pp. 237–40:

> In order to process successfully vast numbers of cases, organizations tend to take on the characteristics of "bureaucracy" in the sociological sense of the term: operation on the basis of rules, government by a clear hierarchy, the maintenance of files, etc. Such an organizational form produces competence and efficiency in applying general rules to particular cases, but it is not well suited to making complex and individualized decisions. One form of response of bureaucracies to such demands involves a type of breakdown. There will be long delays, hewing to complicated and minute procedures, and a confusion of means with ends. A common and perhaps more constructive response is to simplify the task. This was the tack taken by the claims men I studied. Phone calls and letters replaced personal visits; only a few witnesses, rather than all possible, would be interviewed; and the law of negligence was made to lean heavily on the much simpler traffic law.

> Traffic laws are simple rules, deliberately so because their purpose is to provide a universal and comprehensible set of guidelines for safe and efficient transportation. Negligence law is complex, its purpose being to decide after the fact whether a driver was unreasonably careless. However, all levels of the insurance company claims department will accept the former rules as generally adequate for the latter purpose. The underlying reason for this is the difficulty if not impossibility of investigating and defending a more complex decision concerning negligence in the context of a mass operation. In the routine case, the stakes are not high enough to warrant the effort, and the effort is not made. The information that a given insured violated a specific traffic law and was subsequently involved in an accident will suffice to allocate fault. No attempt is made to analyze why this took place or how. The legal concepts of negligence and fault in action

contain no more substance than the simple and mechanical procedures noted here provide.

The law of damages is also simplified in action. Although the measurement of special damages appears rather straightforward even in formal doctrine, some further simplification occurs in action when, for instance, life table calculations are used to compute future earnings. More important, the measurement of pain, suffering, and inconvenience is thoroughly routinized in the ordinary claim. The adjuster generally pays little attention to the claimant's privately experienced discomforts and agonies; I do not recall ever having read recitals of these matters in the statements, which are the key documents in the settlement process and in which all matters considered relevant to the disposition of a claim are recorded. The calculation of general damages is for the most part a matter of multiplying the medical bills by a tacitly but generally accepted arbitrary constant. This practice is justified by claims men on the theory that pain and suffering are very likely to be a function of the amount of medical treatment experienced. There is of course a grain of truth in this theory, but it also contains several sources of error. Types of injury vary considerably in the degree of pain and suffering, the necessity for treatment, and the fees charged for treatment; and the correlations between these elements are low. I believe that the more important reason for the use of the formula is again that all levels of the claims department find it acceptable in justifying payment over and beyond special damages. The formula provides a conventional measurement for phenomena that are so difficult to evaluate as to be almost unmeasurable. It provides a rule by which a rule-oriented organization can proceed, though the rule is never formalized. This simplification also meets the comparable needs of plaintiffs' attorneys and is acceptable to them as well. Because of the mutual acceptability of the formula, attorneys will try to capitalize on it by adding to the use and cost of medical treatment, a procedure known as "building" the file, and adjusters will argue concerning the reasonableness of many items that purport to be medical expenses and thus part of the base to which the formula is applied.

Is this passage reassuring? Disillusioning?

CHAPTER XII

A SURVEY OF ALTERNATIVES

In recent years, tort reform activity has been largely concentrated on efforts to adopt incremental changes in the existing system. We begin with a brief discussion of the principal types of initiatives in this category. There is logic to our consideration of these strategies immediately after the chapter on damages and insurance. As will become evident, the dominant incremental reform measures in recent years have been addressed to the remedial, or damages/insurance, side of the tort system, rather than aimed at altering substantive tort doctrine.

After examining incremental tort reform measures in greater detail, we will consider a wide variety of alternatives to the tort system. Some, such as workers' compensation and auto no-fault plans, are designed to replace all or a substantial part of tort law in major areas of injury activity. Others, such as vaccine and birth defect compensation schemes, focus on narrower areas of accidental harm. At the other extreme from these focused plans, we examine comprehensive no-fault and social insurance proposals that would replace much or all of tort law in accident-related injury and disease cases. The common theme in these diverse plans is that they are intended to serve as tort replacement measures. Their premise is that a better system than tort law can be designed to address the problem of accidental harm.

What are the dimensions of that problem? National Safety Council data indicate that in 2013 in a total U.S. population of about 316 million, there were some 130,800 accidental deaths—the three major categories being 35,500 motor vehicle deaths, 65,800 deaths in the home, and 2,240 workplace deaths not involving motor vehicles. An estimated 39.6 million medically consulted injuries occurred, principally in the home (19.9 million), on the job (4.8 million), or in motor vehicles (4.3 million). In 2012, unintentional injuries were the fifth largest cause of death overall, and were the biggest killer of those aged up to 44 (except those under one).

The National Safety Council report also estimates the pecuniary costs associated with accidental death and injury. The total of $820.6 billion for all accidents includes $388.4 billion in wage and productivity loss, $219.8 billion in medical expenses, and $133.3 billion in administrative costs (insurance, police and legal costs). The motor vehicle looms large in these figures, with total cost of automobile accidents pegged at $288.1 billion, including $90.8 billion in wage and productivity losses. By comparison, worker injuries were estimated at $206.1 billion and home injuries at $226.1 billion. See National Safety Council, Injury Facts (2015 ed.).

How do these accident figures translate into tort claims? A National Center for State Courts survey of 31 states representing 62% of the U.S. population estimated that about 416,000 tort claims were filed in 2006. Between 1996 and 2008, the number of tort suits filed declined by approximately one-third. See Bureau of Justice Statistics, Conference of State Court Administrators & National Center for State Courts, Examining the Work of State Courts, 2006 & 2009: A National Perspective from the Court Statistics Project (2007 & 2010). A sample of the overall claims (relying on 2002 data) found that 53% were auto cases, 40% involved "other torts" (legal and other professional malpractice, premises liability, intentional torts, and defamation), 4% involved products liability, and 3% were in the medical malpractice area. See National Center for State Courts, Examining the Work of State Courts (2007).

About 2% of tort cases go to trial. Galanter, The Vanishing Trial: An Examination of Trials and Related Matters in Federal and State Courts, 1 J.Empirical Legal Stud. 459, 465 (2004). Of claims reaching trial, plaintiffs prevailed in 64% of automobile cases, 55% of asbestos cases, but only 23% of medical malpractice cases. Civil Justice Survey of State Courts, 2005 (Bureau of Justice Statistics Bulletin (April 2009)). The number of cases reaching trial in federal court has declined 79% from its 1985 peak and represents only 2% of claims filed. Factors in that decline are greater mass settlement of tort claims and the increased use of alternative dispute resolution. Just 3.5% of federal tort cases were resolved through arbitration in 1992 whereas one-seventh of federal cases are now referred to ADR proceedings. Galanter, supra. The most common type of tort trial involved one individual suing another (42% of all tort cases—and a large majority of auto cases—fall in this category). Individuals sue businesses in 28% of the cases, and about 11% involve suits by individuals against government agencies or hospitals. Civil Justice Survey of State Courts, 2005.

To put tort cases in context, a 1995 Department of Justice study found that tort claims constituted about 10% of all civil filings—the largest category of civil filings being domestic relations cases (41%). Among tort cases, 2013 data from the Court Statistics Project at the National Center for State Courts, based on newly filed, reopened and reactivated filings in four states ((Alabama, Kansas, New Hampshire, and Pennsylvania), indicated 54% auto, 5% products liability, 4% medical malpractice, and just over 1% premises liability, with the remainder in scattered categories other than accidental harm. From another perspective, recall the data from a 1991 Rand study, p. 1 supra, indicating that tort liability payments comprise only 11% of total compensation for loss from all sources in accidental harm cases. For comprehensive discussion of the interrelationship between tort and other sources of payment in accidental harm cases, see Abraham & Liebman, Private Insurance, Social Insurance, and Tort Reform:

Toward a New Vision of Compensation for Illness and Injury, 93 Colum.L.Rev. 75 (1993).

Although a study estimated that injury victims in 1985 obtained about 46% of the premiums paid by defendants in tort suits, that percentage varied from 52% of total expenditures received by plaintiffs in auto cases to an average of 43% in other accident cases. The study estimated that the legal fees and expenses of injury victims constitute about 30–31% of the total compensation paid to plaintiffs, and that defendants' legal fees and expenses average about 16% of the total compensation paid to plaintiffs in auto cases and 28% in non-auto cases. The study also estimated that defendants' legal expenses had been growing annually at a rate of 6% in auto cases and 15% in non-auto cases during the prior five years. Trend data were not available for plaintiffs' legal fees and expenses. See J. Kakalik & N. Pace, Costs and Compensation Paid in Tort Litigation (1986). Unfortunately, no more recent comprehensive study of claims and costs in tort litigation has been published.

A system that pays one dollar in benefits for one dollar of premiums is not likely to be the goal. This point is made in Brandau, Compensating Highway Accident Victims—Who Pays the Insurance Cost?, 37 Ins. Counsel J. 598 (1970). Adverting to figures on the relative efficiency of various reparation systems, the author suggested (p. 605) that:

> [T]he concept of efficiency often used in describing systems seems to imply that an absolutely efficient system would pay out $1.00 in benefits for every dollar it collected in payments. This is not the case. Such a system would ultimately prove to be very inefficient. Some expense is necessary to determine whether persons applying for benefits are qualified. Any system needs a control to determine eligibility for payments or else the system will be fraught with fraud. Of course, to the extent that there are extensive eligibility requirements, the expense of administering a program goes up. The justification of this expense is not a matter of efficiency, but rather a matter of judgment whether the eligibility requirements are worth the expense of administering the program.

Can the due care issue in negligence cases be regarded as an "eligibility requirement," in Brandau's terms? What about the causation issues in toxic tort cases? Assess the fault system and the tort system generally in Brandau's terms. Keep these considerations in mind as we consider other techniques for meeting the financial consequences of accidents.

A. INCREMENTAL TORT REFORM

Within the last 40 years, we can trace three periods of legislative activity related to aspects of tort reform. The first, in the mid-1970s, was centered on medical malpractice. Physicians complained of high malpractice insurance premiums: some left high-risk specialties; others "went bare"—dropped their liability coverage; some went on strike and marched to demand relief. Virtually all state legislatures responded—although with little uniformity. Among the common changes in malpractice cases were: placing caps on the amount that could be awarded for pain and suffering; regulating fees of plaintiffs' attorneys; shortening statutes of limitation; requiring periodic payments as to future awards; and altering or eliminating the collateral source rule.

One prominent example was California, which enacted the Medical Injury Compensation Reform Act (MICRA) in 1975. The Act limited recovery for pain and suffering in medical malpractice cases to a maximum of $250,000. Cal.Civ. Code § 3333.2. Also, in any case in which the award of future damages exceeded $50,000, the judge was required, at the request of either party, to direct that the money be paid periodically. If the victim died before the judgment was satisfied, the defendant might be relieved of paying for future medical expenses. The payments for future lost earnings would not be affected by death. Cal. Code Civ.Pro. § 667.7. Maximum percentages for contingent fees were set. Cal.Bus. & Prof. Code § 6146. Lastly, the Act provided that if all or part of the victim's medical bills had been paid by the victim's own insurance or some other source unrelated to the defendant, the jury should be told this—but not told what to do with the information. Subrogation was eliminated. Cal.Civ. Code § 3333.1.

The second wave of activity occurred in the mid-1980s, as the result of increasingly large damage awards, soaring insurance premiums, and, for a growing number of enterprises, the complete unavailability of liability insurance. The extent of this crisis was questioned by critics of the insurance industry (who blamed the industry's problems on the lowering of interest rates, which reduced the investment income of insurers, from their highs of the early 1980s). Whatever the truth, between 1985 and 1988, 48 state legislatures responded with some variety of tort reform legislation. These enactments addressed the concerns of tort defendants generally, unlike the physician-specific statutes of the mid-1970s.

The principal changes were in the damages and insurance areas. A large number of states enacted limitations in one form or another on recovery for non-economic loss (pain and suffering and/or punitive damages), on joint and several liability, and on the collateral source rule. In all, during this second wave, 30 states changed their joint and several liability rules and 23 placed some type of ceiling on pain and suffering awards. Another 25 placed limits on punitive damage awards—either eliminating them, placing caps on them, requiring that they not exceed some fixed ratio to compensatory awards, or requiring that some percentage of the punitive award be paid to the state. Other areas of change involved limitations on plaintiff lawyers' attorneys' fees, adoption of special legislation covering dram shop and social host liability for drunken driving, and requirements of periodic payments in large-award cases. These developments are discussed in Sanders & Joyce, "Off to the Races": The 1980s Tort Crisis and the Law Reform Process, 27 Hous.L.Rev. 207 (1990).

Generalization is difficult because each state took its own distinctive approach to tort reform. Even when states began with the same agenda, legislative compromise often produced quite disparate results. The Washington legislature, for example, limited the amount recoverable for all non-monetary losses in personal injury cases by a formula keyed to the state's average wage and the victim's life expectancy. On the other hand, some states enacted flat caps on non-economic damages, such as Maryland's $350,000.

New York adopted a comprehensive tort reform package that, among other things, altered the collateral source rule and provided for periodic payments. It also provided that most defendants who were held less than 50% at fault were liable to the plaintiff only for that percentage of the award for pain and suffering. California, by voter initiative, abolished all joint and several liability for non-economic damages, p. 453 supra.

In the same period when these across-the-board limitations were being enacted, several states adopted measures to protect defendants in products liability cases. The most common provision was adoption of a statute of repose—a statute that protected sellers whose products caused harm more than a certain number of years after they put the product into the stream of commerce. Some states adopted similar legislation for architects and builders. A typical length of time was 10 or 12 years. This made it possible for the statute of repose to have run before the victim was hurt. See, e.g., Arsenault v. Pa-Ted Spring Co., 523 A.2d 1283 (Conn.1987)(claim involving 14-year-old product barred by 10-year statute of repose). A few states adopted "useful life" statutes in which the trier of fact must determine the average expected useful life of a generic product to determine if the injury in the case came from the normal aging of the product in question or from a "defect." See Note, The Evolution of Useful Life Statutes in the Products Liability Reform Effort, 1989 Duke L.J. 1689. Note also that some states legislated to make the "open and obvious" nature of a danger relevant in products cases.

All of these reform efforts were undertaken by state legislatures. The products area, however, raises unique problems in terms of the utility of seeking reform at the state level, as opposed to the federal level. It may well be that state courts developed and expanded tort liability doctrines in this area in part because they had little control over the development of the common law and did not want their citizens to face barriers that citizens in other states did not face. The state "home-cooking" focus was never made clearer than in Blankenship v. General Motors Corp., 406 S.E.2d 781 (W.Va.1991). In response to questions certified by a federal district court, the court announced that it would adopt the doctrine of crashworthiness in an appropriate case. Although the court stated its doubts about much of existing products law, it also observed that:

> West Virginia is a small rural state with .66 percent of the population of the United States. Although some members of this Court have reservations about the wisdom of many aspects of tort law, as a court we are utterly powerless to make the *overall* tort system for cases arising in interstate commerce more rational: Nothing that we do will have any impact whatsoever on the set of economic trade-offs that occur in the *national* economy. And, ironically, trying unilaterally to make the American tort system more rational through being uniquely responsible in West Virginia will only punish our residents severely without, in any regard, improving the system for anyone else.

> . . .

> . . . In light of the fact that all of our sister states have adopted a cause of action for lack of crashworthiness, General Motors is *already* collecting a product liability premium every time it sells a car anywhere in the world, including West Virginia. [ ] West Virginians, then, are already paying the product liability insurance premium when they buy a General Motors car, so this Court would be both foolish and irresponsible if we held that while West Virginians must pay the premiums, West Virginians can't collect the insurance after they're injured.

The court announced further that if the federal courts were in doubt in any future crashworthiness case in which there was a real split of authority among the states, West Virginia would adopt the rule most favorable to plaintiffs.

How do you react to this position? Should a legislator in West Virginia react any differently if pressed to adopt legislation that would cut back on product liability rules that now favor plaintiffs? The author of *Blankenship* had published a book three years earlier advocating the Supreme Court take on reforming products liability. R. Neely, The Products Liability Mess: How Business Can Be Rescued From State Court Politics (1988). For a skeptical view that favoritism of state residents played a significant role in the development of strict products liability, see Schwartz, Considering the Proper Federal Role in American Tort Law, 38 Ariz.L.Rev. 917 (1996).

After a brief hiatus, a third wave of tort reform activity arose in the early 1990s—once again featuring packages of reform targeted at some combinations of caps on non-economic loss and punitive damages, limitations on collateral source recovery, elimination of joint and several liability, and in some instances, restrictions on the contingency fee. See B. Franklin, Learning Curve: Lawyers Must Confront Impact of Changes on Litigation Strategies, 81 A.B.A.J. 62 (Aug.1995).

In the subsequent two decades, tort reform proponents expanded their agenda to include class action reform (adopted by 11 states), jury service reform (adopted by 14), decreasing the bond posting requirements for the filing of an appeal (adopted by 41), and attorney "sunshine" rules (adopted by 22) that require legislative approval of large contingency fee contracts to retain attorneys for litigation on behalf of the state. Currently, 40 states have modified joint and several liability rules, 23 have instituted caps on non-economic damages (another 6 enacted limitations that were struck down), and 32 have reformed punitive damages. See ATRA, Tort Reform Record (June 2015).

Texas provides a relatively recent example of enactment of wholesale adoption of incremental reform. In 2003, the state adopted H.B. 4, Act of June 2, 2003 (codified at Tex.Civ.Prac. & Rem. Code Ann. 42.004). The Act imposed a non-economic damages cap of $250,000 in medical malpractice cases for care providers and a separate $250,000 cap for hospital facilities. The Act also modified joint and several liability rules, introduced a 15-year statute of repose for products liability cases, reformed attorney's fees, reduced the bond posting requirements for appeals of judgments, and provided for interlocutory appeals of orders of class certification. Texas's legislation is unusual in that it was accompanied by an amendment to the state constitution to ensure that the legislature had not exceeded its authority.

In 2005, reform was also enacted at the federal level. The Class Action Fairness Act, 28 U.S.C. §§ 1332(d), 1453, and 1711–15, expands removal from state courts in diversity cases by granting federal courts original jurisdiction over certain class actions in which the amount in controversy exceeds $5 million and in which liberalized diversity requirements are met. The Act was enacted because of a perception that state courts were too liberal in certifying class actions, which impose strong incentives on defendants to settle in order to avoid a huge adverse judgment. The Act also discourages the practice of including coupons as part of a settlement by requiring judges to calculate attorney's fees based on the value of the coupons redeemed rather than issued. Congress also shielded gun manufacturers from suits seeking to hold them liable for unlawful acts committed with their products by enacting the Protection of Lawful Commerce in Arms Act, Pub. L. No. 109–92, 119 Stat. 2095 (codified at 15 U.S.C. § 7901 et seq.). The grant of immunity was in response to a growing number of suits against the manufacturers, by both individuals and municipalities. See, e.g., Ileto v. Glock Inc., 349 F.3d 1191 (9th Cir.2003)(finding that individual plaintiffs had stated a claim for public nuisance because gun manufacturers had intentionally supplied the black market in weapons by over-saturating the legal market).

————

Have the incremental tort reform measures been effective in addressing "the tort law crisis"? The effect of MICRA on trial outcomes was examined in the RAND Corporation Report, Capping Non-Economic Awards in Medical Malpractice Trials: California Jury Verdicts Under MICRA (2004). Researchers reviewed 257 plaintiff verdicts in California malpractice trials from 1995 to 1999 to determine how the caps affected plaintiff recoveries and attorneys' fees. (RAND did not attempt to study the impact of caps on the number of claims filed or on the settlement process.) The study concluded that total payout by defendants was reduced some 30% by the cap on non-economic damages. In cases where the cap was triggered, awards were reduced by 37%. The report also analyzed what the payouts would have been had the liability limit been tied to the Consumer Price Index instead of remaining fixed at $250,000. Although that would have resulted in roughly a tripling of the cap—to over $700,000 for each year studied—overall savings to defendants would have been reduced only by 21%. The cap would have been triggered in 19% of cases instead of 45%.

Because MICRA also imposed a sliding scale for attorney's fees— with lawyers working on contingency to collect a maximum of 40% of the first $50,000 recovered, one-third of the next $50,000, 25% of the next $500,000, and 15% of any amount beyond that—for large judgments, attorneys are paid considerably less than the standard rate of one-third. A reduction in the fee percentage combined with smaller overall judgments led to a 60% reduction in attorney's fees—$56 million was charged instead of $140 million. For a strong endorsement of the MICRA approach by a former president of the American Medical Association, see Palmisano, Health Care in Crisis: The Need for Medical Liability Reform, 5 Yale J. Health Pol'y L. & Ethics 371 (2005)("California's MICRA provides a prime example of the type of reforms that are necessary if we are to fix the medical liability crisis that currently pervades the United States health care system."). For a critical perspective on the impact of MICRA-type reforms, see Paik, Black, & Hyman, The Receding Tide of Medical Malpractice Litigation Part 2: Effect of Damage Caps, 10 J. Empirical Stud. 639 (2013), finding "strong evidence that damage caps reduce both claim rates and payout per claim, with a large combined impact on payout per physician." In another study, Paik, Black, Hyman, & Silver, Will Tort Reform Bend the Health Care Cost Curve: Evidence from Texas, 9 J. Empirical Legal

Stud. 173 (2012), the authors conclude that there is no evidence that MICRA-type tort reform measures in Texas helped bend the health care cost curve. See also Boehm, Debunking Medical Malpractice Myths: Unraveling the False Premises Behind "Tort Reform," 5 Yale J. Health Pol'y L. & Ethics 357 (2005).

The perception that common law tort doctrine became less expansive, beginning in the 1980s, is explored, with an attempt at explanation, in Schwartz, The Beginning and Possible End of the Rise of Modern American Tort Law, 26 Ga.L.Rev. 601 (1992). See also Henderson & Eisenberg, The Quiet Revolution in Products Liability Law: An Empirical Study of Legal Change, 37 UCLA L.Rev. 479 (1990)(locating the onset of stabilization in the products area in the mid-1980s). Evidence of the impact of either tort reform or the retrenchment in tort doctrine or both is found in the decline of tort cases filed in recent years set out at p. 822 supra.

The constitutionality of many of these reform efforts, particularly the enactment of caps on damages, has often been challenged—in some cases successfully—on a variety of state constitutional grounds. Recent successful challenges include Estate of Michelle Evette McCall v. U.S., 134 So.3d 894 (Fla.2014)(concluding that state's statutory cap on wrongful death non-economic damages recoverable in medical malpractice actions violates the right to equal protection under state constitution); Lewellen v. Franklin, 441 S.W.3d 136 (Mo.2014)(holding that state statute that imposed a cap on punitive damages of $500,000 or five times net amount of judgment awarded to plaintiff violates state constitutional right to a trial by jury); Montgomery v. Potter, 341 P.3d 660 (Okla.2014)(concluding that state statute barring uninsured motorists from recovering certain non-economic damages is an unconstitutional special law); Schroeder v. Weighall, 316 P.3d 482 (Wash.2014)(concluding that a state statute eliminating medical malpractice actions from general tolling of cause of action brought by minor until minor reached age of majority violated state constitution's prohibition against special privileges and immunities because there is no reasonable basis for the statutory distinction); Douglas v. Cox Retirement Props., 302 P.3d 789 (Okla.2013)(concluding that state legislation entitled Comprehensive Lawsuit Reform Act of 2009 violated single-subject requirement of state constitution and was void in its entirety); Wall v. Marouk, 302 P.3d 775 (Okla.2013)(concluding that state statute requiring patient to attach expert affidavit of merit in support of claim for medical malpractice was impermissible special law that violated patient's state constitutional right of access to courts). At the same time, courts continue to find that other tort-reform statutes do not violate a plaintiff's state constitutional rights. See e.g., Zauflik v. Pennsbury School Dist., 104 A.3d 1096 (Pa.2014)(finding that statutory damages cap applicable to claims against governmental entities did not violate equal protection, open courts provision of state constitution, or constitutional right to jury trial).

Statutes that award some portion of punitive damages to the state, which at least 12 states have passed, are another target of constitutional challenges. Victorious plaintiffs have asserted that this forfeiture of a fraction of their tort judgment amounts to an unconstitutional taking of their property. In Kirk v. Denver Publishing Co., 818 P.2d 262 (Colo.1991), the Colorado Supreme Court struck down a statute requiring recipients of punitive damages to contribute one-third to the state's general fund. Most state statutes, however, have withstood such challenges. See, e.g., Gordon v. State, 608 So.2d 800 (Fla.1992); see generally Sharkey, Punitive Damages as Societal Damages, 113 Yale L.J. 347 (2003).

B. OCCUPATIONAL INJURIES—WORKERS' COMPENSATION

Occupational injuries emerged as a serious problem in this country after the Civil War. The rapid pace of industrialization brought a steadily increasing number of accidental injuries and deaths. Along with other accidental injury claims, workers' claims were handled in the tort system until the early years of the twentieth century. Within a decade, however, beginning in 1910, a majority of states enacted workers' compensation laws, replacing the tort remedy with a no-fault compensation scheme. The following excerpt describes these developments and discusses the basic features of the system.

Workers' Compensation: Strengthening the Social Compact
Orin Kramer & Richard Briffault.
13–27, 73–75 (1991).

A. Basic Terms: No-Fault and Exclusive Remedy

At the heart of workers' compensation is a basic quid pro quo: employers must provide employees who suffer work-related injuries or disease with medical and income benefits regardless of whether the employee or the employer was at fault for the injury; employees, in turn, must treat workers' compensation benefits as their exclusive remedy against the employer and give up any common law tort claims against their employers. This no-fault principle embodies two fundamental concerns.

First, it is argued that fault should not be relevant because, as a matter of social justice, business should bear the financial burden of work-related accidents, much like any other cost of production. As Theodore Roosevelt put it, "Exactly as the working man is entitled to his wages, so should he be entitled to indemnity for the injuries sustained in the natural course of his labor." Moreover, making business bear the costs of industrial accidents maximizes employer interest in occupational safety and health and thus reduces the frequency and severity of injury.

Second, no-fault provides greater efficiency. By eliminating fault and making workers' compensation the employee's exclusive remedy, compensation can be provided on a swift, certain and self-executing basis, at minimal administrative cost and without the expense, delays, uncertainties, and adversarial confrontation of attorney involvement and common law litigation. The recent upsurge in attorney involvement due to external pressures and changes in the system now jeopardizes the goal of a low administrative cost, litigation-free, self-executing mechanism.

B. Origins: Meeting the Challenge of the Industrial Revolution and Overcoming the Restrictions of the Common Law

The Industrial Revolution was accompanied by an enormous upsurge in work-related accidents. The rapid expansion and development of manufacturing, mining, steel mills, and railroads, the deployment of dangerous heavy machinery and high-speed industrial processes, and the employment of large numbers of new, relatively unskilled workers all resulted in unprecedented levels of workplace injuries.

1. The "Unholy Trinity" of Employer Common Law Defenses

Under common law, the employer had a duty to provide a reasonably safe place in which to work and reasonably safe tools, appliances, and working materials. Therefore, in theory the employee who sustained a work-related injury, or his survivors, could bring a tort action for damages against the employer if the injury reflected a breach of the employer's duty of reasonable care. In practice, however, 19th century employers were largely immunized from liability for industrial accidents by three other common law doctrines.

First, under the "fellow servant" rule, an employee could not recover damages from the employer if another employee had contributed to the injury. Since in the large factories, mines and mills of an industrial economy the employer almost inevitably acts through other employees, the fellow servant rule was a nearly insuperable barrier to recovery.

Second, under the principle of "contributory negligence," the injured employee could not recover damages if he had in any way negligently contributed to his own injury.

Third, under the doctrine of "assumption of risk," employees were held to have assumed the risk of injury from the customary and observable dangers attendant upon their jobs.

Reformers, concerned about the plight of injured workers and their families, sought to overcome the harsh effects of this "unholy trinity" of employer common law defenses, and around the turn of the century courts and legislatures in several states modified or abandoned one or more of these three rules. However, this liberalization of the common law was of limited benefit to most injured workers since it still left in place the need to prove fault, and that often proved to be as high a hurdle to vault as the "unholy trinity" of defenses.

2.   The Burden of Fault

Under the fault system, an employee, or his survivors, needed to hire a lawyer, persuade fellow workers to testify against their employer, and attempt to survive without wages or money for medical bills until the litigation was resolved. Moreover, for many accidents it was difficult to prove that the employer had violated an established standard of care. As a result, although in some cases employees won generous awards, including damages for pain and suffering, in most cases they received little or nothing. One early 20th century study of workers killed on the job found that in 37% of the cases the families of the victims received no compensation, and that in another 42% of the cases the families received less than $500, or well under the average annual salary of $791.

Fault-based litigation, even without the "unholy trinity," was a costly and uncertain gamble for most workers. Employers, too, were troubled by rising levels of litigation and the prospect of serious damages in the few but increasing number of cases in which workers prevailed.

3.   The Adoption of Workers' Compensation

Workers' compensation was pioneered in Germany in the late 19th century. The first American workers' compensation measure was a federal statute adopted in 1908 that provided a limited program for federal workers and served as a forerunner of the current Federal Employees Compensation Act. In 1910, New York enacted the first state workers' compensation program, but the New York Court of Appeals found that the imposition of liability without fault was unconstitutional and invalidated the statute. The first effective state workers' compensation law was passed in Wisconsin in 1911. To avoid the constitutional issue, the state made workers' compensation elective. As an incentive to employer participation, the legislature provided for the waiver of the "unholy trinity" defenses for employers not participating in the program.

The Wisconsin model of "elective" workers' compensation was sustained in the courts and spread rapidly to other states. By the end of 1911, 10 states had adopted workers' compensation, and by 1917 it was on the books in 37 states. Since the enactment of legislation by

Mississippi in 1949, there has been a workers' compensation program in every state.

By eliminating the requirement of proof of fault, workers' compensation laws enormously simplified the process of providing medical and disability compensation for injured workers. Employees no longer need plead and prove through costly litigation a standard of reasonable care for the operations of the workplace or of industrial equipment, or establish by a preponderance of the evidence that their employers had violated such a standard. The elimination of fault also removes the element of opprobrium from the employer as the duty to compensate is not based on misconduct but treated as a cost of production. Finally, the no-fault system was intended to eliminate the adversarial atmosphere that surrounds litigation and thus improve the quality of employer-employee relations.

C. Evolution: The Expansion of Coverage, the Redefinition of Compensable Injury, and the Enhancement of Benefits

Although most states have had workers' compensation programs for more than 70 years, the system has undergone considerable change, particularly in recent decades. State legislatures have repeatedly amended their laws, modifying programs, and experimenting with new provisions. State courts have also played an important role in interpreting and often liberalizing the effects of state laws.

1. The Pace and Direction of Change

The general direction of state legislatures and courts has been expansion: the inclusion of more workers and workplaces, the liberalization of the definition of compensable injury, the addition of new benefits, and the enhancement of existing benefits. The pace of change accelerated markedly following the publication of the Report of the National Commission on State Workmen's Compensation Laws in 1972 and the increased attention in the 1970s and early 1980s to the problems of occupational disease. Nor has the rate of change slackened significantly since the 1970s. Between 1982 and 1987, there were approximately 900 amendments to state workers' compensation laws, and an additional 155 changes were made in 1988 alone.

Many of these changes have advanced the societal goal of fair and adequate compensation for injured workers. But these changes have also added markedly to the costs of workers' compensation systems. In most states, the current workers' compensation system is, by design, more generous and thus considerably more costly than workers' compensation was in 1911 or 1972.

The expansion of workers' compensation coverage and the enhancement of benefits must be taken into account in assessing the costs of the system and the proper levels of premium for workers' compensation insurance. Indeed, a significant component of the current problems besetting workers' compensation is the failure of the regulatory system in some jurisdictions to respond to the real costs of an expanded compensation system.

2.   Expansion of Coverage of Workers and Employers

Initially, workers' compensation was limited to large firms, firms engaged in "hazardous" or "ultra-hazardous" activities, and to limited categories of workers. Moreover, long after the constitutionality of no-fault had been revisited and sustained by most state courts, many states continued to make workers' compensation elective. In 1950, 77% of American workers were covered by workers' compensation laws. As late as 1968, 24 states had significant size-of-firm restrictions, and 23 states still permitted elective coverage.

Among the "essential recommendations" of the National Commission on State Workmen's Compensation Laws was universal workers' compensation coverage. The Commission called for the elimination of "elective" coverage, of the exemption of small employers, of the exemption of any class of employees, and for the extension of coverage to traditionally non-covered workers such as agricultural workers, household workers and government employees.

Although there has not been total state compliance with the National Commission's recommendations, and many states continue to exempt certain categories of workers and employees, the percentage of the work force covered by workers' compensation has grown to 87%. Only three states continue to make the program elective for covered workers. In only four states are fewer than 75% of employees under workers' compensation. In 23 states, more than 90% of all employees are covered by workers' compensation, and in four states and the District of Columbia coverage is universal.

3.   Expansion of the Definition of Compensable Injury

a.   The Concept of Work-Relatedness

Workers' compensation did not and does not make the employer absolutely responsible for employee health care and disabilities. (For a description of the structure of workers' compensation benefits, see Appendix.) The employer's duty extends only to work-related injuries: injuries which, according to the language of virtually every state law, "arise out of and in the course of employment." In other words, although workers' compensation eliminates the requirement of employer fault, it continues to require proof of *work-related cause*.

i.   The Model of the Traumatic Accident

When workers' compensation was first adopted, it did not seem that proof of work-related causation would entail anything like the complexities and ambiguities implicit in fault-based compensation. The prevalent cause of work-related injury was the traumatic accident: a sudden, unexpected event which resulted in immediate injury. Since the place and physical cause of most injuries are readily apparent, it was assumed that employers and administrators could easily distinguish between work-related and non-work-related accidents, without resort to protracted dispute resolution processes, litigation or attorneys. And for the overwhelming majority of claims, that remains the case.

ii. Traditional Gray Areas

There were, of course, always gray areas in determining the work-relatedness of even simple traumatic accidents. Injuries occurring on the employer's premises but outside the production process, such as during coffee breaks or lunch time; injuries involving employee violation of work rules or willful misconduct; and injuries occurring during commutation or off-premises have been a regular source of dispute. But these are a tiny fraction of compensation claims, and in most states these issues have been resolved by court decision or statutory amendment.

iii. Soft Tissue Injuries and Aggravation of Existing Conditions

More numerically significant and more conceptually difficult than the traditional gray areas are soft tissue injuries that result from repeated activity, such as straining, bending, twisting or lifting, over a period of time. In these instances, it is more difficult to determine when the injury has occurred and whether the injury is the result of on-the-job or off-the-job activity. By one count, in 1988 approximately 48% of workplace injuries were the result of repetitive motion.

In aggravation of existing conditions cases, the injury may have occurred on the job, but its severity in terms of medical bills and time lost from work may be a result of a prior injury, unusual personal susceptibility or environmental factors unrelated to work. In this case the employer may seek to limit its liability to the work-related component of the injury. Today in many states the employer is responsible for the full extent of work-related injury, consistent with the well-established doctrine that the employer "takes the employee as he finds him."

Although soft tissue injuries and aggravation of existing conditions claims have added significant new costs to workers' compensation coverage, the real challenge to the work-relatedness requirement and to the system's ability to resolve the causation question without resort to extensive administrative or litigated proceedings has been occupational disease.

b. The Challenge of Occupational Disease

i. Initial Limitations on Coverage

Some occupational diseases do not fit within the national model of traumatic accidents. The onset of illness may not occur at the workplace or during the course of employment. Often illness will not result until years after exposure to the causative agent. The manifestations of occupational disease may not be distinctive and may be difficult to distinguish from those of non-occupational ailments or the aging process. The causation of disease may be complex and may involve the interaction of work, heredity, environment, personal lifestyle and other factors.

Most early workers' compensation laws did not provide compensation for disease or only provided coverage for specified, or "scheduled" diseases, like "black lung," silicosis or byssinosis ("brown lung"). These diseases were uniquely occupation-related in the sense that while many workers in an occupation eventually contracted the illness, few people not employed in that occupation ever suffered from the disease.

Moreover, recovery for occupational disease in some states was limited by procedural requirements. Statutes of limitations that ran from the time of last exposure to the disease-causing agent effectively blocked recovery in cases of long latency illnesses. Minimum exposure rules and recency of exposure requirements which had no scientific basis also restricted the availability of coverage, as did statutory provisions affecting the responsibilities of particular employers where the worker was exposed to the disease-causing hazard during a succession of jobs in an industry.

ii.   The Expansion of Coverage

In recent decades, the situation has changed dramatically. In the wake of liberalizing court decisions and the recommendation of the National Commission on State Workmen's Compensation Laws, all 50 states now provide workers' compensation for any work-caused illness. Moreover, many states have relaxed their procedural restrictions, for example, by starting statute of limitations requirements from the onset of the first manifestation of illness rather than from the last exposure to the causative agent. This makes it far easier for workers suffering from diseases with long latency periods to bring claims.

The workers' compensation system is now caught in a vise. On the one hand, expanding scientific and medical knowledge has suggested associations between certain workplace materials, conditions and processes and an increased risk of contracting many ordinary diseases, such as cancer, heart disease, lung diseases, dermatitis, hypertension, and degenerative diseases such as arthritis. Given the complex causation of these diseases, whether the risk actually results in illness may often turn on non-work-related factors.

On the other hand, state workers' compensation laws, although they have abandoned the "scheduled disease" approach, still continue to require that, to be compensable, a disease must result from factors "peculiar to the trade or occupation" and not be an "ordinary disease of life."

The result has been increased litigation over causation and the existence and scope of coverage in the area of occupational disease. In these cases, both claimants and employers or insurers make complex medical and legal arguments. These cases are marked by the claims of conflicting experts, the so-called "dueling doctors," with considerable litigation costs and uncertainty of outcome for all parties.

The overall trend has been to relax the claimant's burden of proof and permit recovery even where work-related factors are a contributing but not the sole cause of disease. In some cases, liability has been found even where work-related contributing causation was only "reasonably probable" in light of current medical knowledge. This means that the employer will have to pay the full costs of an illness which is at best only partially work-related.

It is critical to recognize that occupational diseases today represent only a modest cost in the workers' compensation system. In most states, only about 2% of claims involve work-related illness, and the majority of those claims involve conditions that can be handled easily by the system. However, these claims have a disproportionate impact on total workers' compensation costs. The special issues with respect to the proof of causation drive up administrative costs, while the average indemnity benefit for occupational disease is five times greater than for traumatic injuries.

Moreover, today's claims may be only the leading edge of future occupational disease filings. Scientific knowledge continues to expand our understanding of the relationship between work conditions and health and to provide new bases for claims for compensation. Most significantly, several observers have noted that "a new type of claim is on the horizon," one that portends steeply increased administrative and compensation burdens for the workers' compensation system in future years: mental stress.

iii. The Special Case of Mental Stress

Over the last decade, the number of mental stress claims has exploded, rising from virtually zero to more than 10% of all occupational disease claims. In California, the number of mental stress claims rose 511% from 1980 to 1987. Mental stress now accounts for approximately 25% of all occupational disease claims in California making it the leading source of occupational disease claims in the nation's largest state.

The earliest workers' compensation claims for mental injury grew out of cases based on some physical event, either a traumatic physical accident which resulted in subsequent psychiatric harm, or acute mental stress which led to a physical injury such as a heart attack. These "physical-mental" and "mental-physical" cases have been largely supplanted in notoriety by the so-called "mental-mental" cases in which a highly subjective mental or emotional injury results from a mental or emotional cause, without any physical accident or impairment.

Mental stress claims incorporate all the causation difficulties of some occupational disease claims, but taken to an extreme degree. Most mental stress claims have no single precipitating cause. A study of mental stress claims in California found that 90% are the result of cumulative events.

Few mental stress claims stem from conditions peculiar or unique to particular workplaces or occupations. Rather, a California study found that most such claims are due to non-specific "job pressures" or "harassment," features "pandemic to workplaces." Many mental stress claims involve the aggravation of pre-existing conditions and the interaction of workplace and non-workplace factors.

Mental stress claims are highly subjective, difficult to diagnose, assess, quantify or disprove. Medical knowledge with respect to the cause and treatment of mental stress is imprecise. Standards for determining when a mental or emotional problem rises to the level of illness are uncertain. And there is no uniform or agreed upon definition of what constitutes a compensable psychiatric injury.

The lack of determinate standards and the absence of physical symptoms make the resolution of mental stress claims particularly contentious. Employers and insurers are often skeptical of mental stress claims: a California Workers Compensation Institute study found that "antagonism and suspicion characterize claims management in mental stress cases." The subjectivity of the asserted injury makes mental stress claims especially litigable. In California 99% of mental stress cases are litigated.

Although nationwide there are still relatively few mental stress claims, this may only be the tip of the iceberg. The potential for claims growth is enormous. Virtually every employee is subject to some level of stress. The National Institute of Mental Health estimates that one person in five suffers from some psychiatric disorder. All told, 75% of corporate medical directors consider stress to be fairly pervasive.

A series of forces has contributed and will continue to contribute to the growth of workplace stress. The pace of work is accelerating and job security declining in a more competitive economic environment. Many employees have unfulfilled expectations about work and the quality of life. There has been an expansion of service sector jobs such as secretarial and office-manager, which some have suggested to be particularly stressful.

Social mores have changed so that acknowledgement of mental and emotional illness has become more acceptable, and the acceptance of psychiatric treatment has lost much of its former stigma. The broad and unlimited medical coverage under most state workers' compensation statutes, compared to the more limited coverage of psychiatric treatment under many private health plans, makes workers' compensation a particularly attractive target for mental stress claims.

Moreover, the rapid growth of mental stress claims has occurred despite the fact that in only eight states have appellate courts adopted an expansive definition of compensable mental stress claims. That broader definition provides coverage for stress that constitutes only a gradual increase over ordinary workplace stress and is not unusual in nature or degree. Courts in 21 other states permit compensation only if the mental stress is attributable to a sudden or frightening event, or if stress levels are in excess of ordinary employment conditions. Seven state appellate courts have ruled that "mental-mental" claims are not compensable, while courts in 14 states and the District of Columbia have yet to establish a legal standard for "mental-mental" claims. If more state courts adopt the expansive approach, the number of mental stress claims could soar.

On the other hand, several states have taken steps recently to adopt more objective standards and require that compensable stress derive from unusual workplace conditions. As of this year, Colorado will limit coverage to stress resulting from traumatic or extraordinary events. California's recent reforms require that mental stress claims be based on actual events and exclude compensability for injuries resulting from personnel actions of the employer. Oregon has required "clear and convincing evidence" to establish mental stress claims. But whether these measures are sufficient to check the potential magnitude of mental stress exposure remains to be seen.

4. The Expansion of Benefits

Workers' compensation provides medical benefits, indemnity benefits that compensate for lost wages during the period of recuperation and for permanent disability, and death benefits to the families of occupational injury victims. In the last two decades the levels of indemnity benefits have been very significantly enhanced. Moreover, a new benefit, mandatory vocational rehabilitation, is now provided in most states. Together, the enhancement in benefit levels and the addition of a new benefit have increased costs and contributed to the strains besetting the system.

a. The Enhancement of Benefit Levels

Indemnity benefits replace some specified percentage of lost wages, subject to a statutory ceiling on amount. Initially, benefits were relatively low, since the purpose of workers' compensation in its early years was, in part, not to make up for lost wages but to "prevent hardship." In 1920, only 20 states replaced as much as 60% of lost wages. By the 1960s, about two-thirds of the states had adopted the goal of replacing two-thirds of the injured worker's lost gross wages, but low statutory ceilings held down the amounts actually paid. In 46 states the benefit levels lagged so far below wage levels that a disabled worker earning the state average weekly wage could not receive a benefit that would produce the legislated wage replacement rate. Inevitably, there was a widespread sense that benefit levels were inadequate and that fair treatment of injured employees required a substantial increase in benefits.

i.   The Modernization of Benefit Levels

The 1972 Report of the National Commission on State Workmen's Compensation Laws precipitated a major modernization of benefit levels. The Report called on the states to adopt the goal of replacing two-thirds of pre-injury gross pay (or 80% of net wages) and to raise the statutory maximum to no lower than the state average weekly wage. Workers' compensation benefits are exempt from federal income taxation. Two-thirds of gross, or 80% of net, is designed to replace lost wages while maintaining a proper incentive to return to work. All states responded at least in part to the Report's recommendations. Currently, 48 states and the District of Columbia provide for replacement of two-thirds or more of gross wages, or 80% of net wages. In 31 states the statutory maximum for *temporary* disability is at or above the state average weekly wage, while in 29 states the statute maximum for *permanent* disability is at or above the state average weekly wage.

ii.   Continuing Increases

Approximately 40 states fix the statutory maximum in terms of the state average weekly wage itself, rather than as a specified dollar amount, so that benefit levels track inflation-driven wage increases. As a result of automatic adjustments and statutory amendments, benefit levels rose in 43 states and the District of Columbia in 1988 and in 42 states in 1989.

iii.   Benefit Levels and Benefit Utilization

Increasing benefit levels has two effects on workers' compensation claim costs. First, benefit increases directly raise costs when injured workers file for compensation. Second, benefit increases create incentives for greater utilization: More claims will be filed, and workers may stay out of work longer, thus extending the duration of the benefits period. Studies have found that a 20% increase in indemnity benefits is associated with a 7% increase in indemnity benefit filings and a 24% increase in the duration of indemnity claims. The impact on benefits utilization is particularly significant for less serious claims. In short, a 10% increase in benefit levels is associated with a 5% increase in utilization on top of the benefit increase, so that a 10% increase in benefits will raise aggregate payments by 15%. Most of that increased utilization is due to increased claim frequency, but some is attributable to increases in the duration of disability.

The enhancement of benefit levels in recent years has had a significant impact on the percentage of payroll devoted to workers' compensation and to mounting concerns among employers regarding the system's cost. For many years, workers' compensation amounted to an average of well under 1% of payroll, and there was little annual growth. In 1946 benefits were 0.54% of payroll, in 1960 they were 0.59% of payroll, and as late as 1972 they were still only 0.68%. But over the next decade and a half the percentage of payroll devoted to workers' compensation benefits doubled, to 1.39% in 1986. Today total average compensation costs are closer to 2% of payroll. And there is no sign that benefit growth is abating.

. . .

b.   Vocational Rehabilitation: Growth of a New Benefit

Another area of change in the workers' compensation social contract has been vocational rehabilitation. Most state workers' compensation programs now make some provision for the costs of vocational rehabilitation services for eligible employees, although there is an enormous variance in the quality, extent and utilization of rehabilitation programs. Several states, including California and Florida, make vocational rehabilitation mandatory. In these states, rehabilitation has become a substantial and rising component of claim costs.

Vocational rehabilitation consists of the provision of services which attempt to maximize the ability of an injured worker to compete in the labor market. Rehabilitation is of great potential benefit to both employees and employers. It can serve to complete the employee's economic and psychological recovery from a disabling accident and improve employee morale, while mitigating the disability expenses attributable to injury and reducing the costs of hiring and training new workers to replace skilled but injured employees.

But vocational services can be quite expensive. Indeed, both utilization and claim costs have soared in the states with mandatory vocational rehabilitation, far outpacing increases in indemnity claims and costs generally. In California, the number of cases involving vocational rehabilitation rose from 5,236 in 1978 to 32,579 in 1987, a 440% increase. And vocational rehabilitation claims have risen at an even faster pace than utilization, with total claim costs escalating 775% in the same period. By contrast, over the same period personal disability claims rose only 33%, and personal disability claim costs 180%. When California first adopted mandatory rehabilitation in 1975, it was estimated that vocational rehabilitation would account for 2.7% of claim costs. Today vocational rehabilitation accounts for 13% of every benefit dollar. In Florida, 18% of all lost-time cases involve rehabilitation.

. . .

APPENDIX: WORKERS' COMPENSATION BENEFITS PROVIDED

Medical Benefits

In all U.S. jurisdictions, except for the Virgin Islands, there are no limits on medical coverage for conditions resulting from occupational disease or job-related injury. Medical coverage includes costs for physicians, hospitals, nursing service, physical therapy, dentists, chiropractors, and prosthetic devices.

Permanent Total Disability

Permanent total disability benefits are provided for those claimants whose job-related injury or occupational disease has rendered them permanently unable to engage in substantially remunerative employment. As in temporary total disability cases, claimants usually receive a wage-substitute benefit of 66 2/3% of their full or average weekly wage up to a statutory maximum rate. Permanent total disability claimants, however, are paid for a lifetime in most states and have higher total dollar amounts than temporary total disability claimants. Permanent total disability benefits continue until the claimant returns to substantially remunerative employment, dies, or exhausts the maximum dollar or time amount set by statute. For some statutorily defined severe injuries, such as total blindness, claimants are entitled to continued benefits in some states even if they successfully attain employment after being declared permanently and totally disabled.

Temporary Total Disability

Temporary inability to return to former employment constitutes a condition of temporary total disability, the most commonly awarded disability compensation. Claimants usually receive a wage-substitute benefit of 66 2/3% of the worker's pre-injury wage up to a statutory maximum rate. Temporary total disability payment often requires a waiting period of a few days to a few weeks before payment begins.

Waiting Period

Statutes provide that a waiting period must elapse during which income benefits are not available. The waiting period affects compensation only, since medical and hospital care are provided immediately. For most states the period is either three or seven days, while the remainder fall somewhere in between. If a worker's disability continues, most states provide for payment retroactive to the date of the injury. The retroactive period varies by state from five days to six weeks, with the norm being two to three weeks.

Temporary and Permanent Partial Disability

Partial disability compensation is payable to claimants who have suffered a negative effect on their earnings, earning capacity, or employability due to a job-related injury but are still able to engage in some remunerative employment. Some states calculate payment for earning capacity loss in the same manner as they calculate actual earnings losses, disregarding considerations of future earning capacity.

Vocational Rehabilitation

Vocational rehabilitation is designed to return injured workers to the labor market as rapidly as possible. All but two states (Indiana and South Carolina) have incorporated rehabilitation into their workers' compensation systems. The rehabilitation benefit usually provides an allowance for maintenance—board, lodging and travel, or as much as weekly compensation equivalent to temporary total disability—and payment for physical and vocational rehabilitation. Time limits of six-months to two years accompany the benefits. In some states continued payment of compensation is contingent upon a claimant attempting rehabilitation, while in others claimants are referred for rehabilitation review to determine whether they would be helped by rehabilitation. Compensation is payable until the claimant can return to remunerative employment or until it is determined that the injured worker failed to cooperate with vocational rehabilitation.

Medical Impairment—Permanent Partial Disability

Permanent partial disability awards are provided to give an injured worker an incentive to return to work, or simply to provide a cash award. Non-scheduled awards, or those not fixed by a statute, can be based strictly on medical impairment or the medical impairment's effect upon that individual's earning capacity.

Scheduled awards compensate injured workers through statutorily designated awards for injury. Schedules typically include payments for loss of arm, hand, leg, foot, eye, hearing in one or both ears, toes, and digits of the hand. Massachusetts only schedules benefits for the first six categories, and Georgia, Minnesota, and Nevada have no schedules at all.

Survivor Benefits

Weekly compensation benefits and burial allowances are paid to surviving dependents of workers killed in the course of employment or through occupational disease. Benefits are usually equivalent to 66 2/3% of the deceased worker's average weekly wage. About one-third of the states provide a limit on the total death award, and most states end death benefits to a surviving spouse upon remarriage. Surviving children lose benefits when they reach majority, or, if they are full-time students, at age 21, 23, or 25.

NOTES AND QUESTIONS

1. As the excerpt indicates, the first compulsory coverage plan adopted in the United States, enacted by New York early in the twentieth century, succumbed to constitutional attack in Ives v. South Buffalo Railway Co., 94 N.E. 431 (N.Y.1911). After reviewing the possible reasons

for the legislature's enactment of the law, the court concluded that the scheme violated the Due Process Clauses of both the state and federal Constitutions. The following excerpt from the opinion reflects its tone:

> If the argument in support of this statute is sound we do not see why it cannot logically be carried much further. Poverty and misfortune from every cause are detrimental to the state. It would probably conduce to the welfare of all concerned if there could be a more equal distribution of wealth. Many persons have much more property than they can use to advantage and many more find it impossible to get the means for a comfortable existence. If the legislature can say to an employer, "you must compensate your employee for an injury not caused by you or by your fault," why can it not go further and say to the man of wealth, "you have more property than you need and your neighbor is so poor that he can barely subsist; in the interest of natural justice you must divide with your neighbor so that he and his dependents shall not become a charge upon the State?" The argument that the risk to an employee should be borne by the employer because it is inherent in the employment, may be economically sound, but it is at war with the legal principle that no employer can be compelled to assume a risk which is inseparable from the work of the employee, and which may exist in spite of a degree of care by the employer far greater than may be exacted by the most drastic law. If it is competent to impose upon an employer, who has omitted no legal duty and has committed no wrong, a liability based solely upon a legislative fiat that his business is inherently dangerous, it is equally competent to visit upon him a special tax for the support of hospitals and other charitable institutions, upon the theory that they are devoted largely to the alleviation of ills primarily due to his business. In its final and simple analysis that is taking the property of A and giving it to B, and that cannot be done under our Constitutions.

New York promptly amended its state constitution to authorize the legislature to adopt a compensation system, and the Supreme Court held that a compulsory compensation system, at least as applied to "hazardous employment," did not violate the federal Constitution. New York Central Railroad Co. v. White, 243 U.S. 188 (1917). The most common reaction to the threat of judicial invalidation was to avoid the compulsory compensation approach and to allow employers to choose whether to participate in the system, but, as noted in the excerpt, to stack the tort rules against employers who opted out of workers' compensation.

2. Insurance arrangements under workers' compensation are summarized in Enterprise Responsibility for Personal Injury, Vol. I, The Institutional Framework, Report to the American Law Institute (1991) at p. 121:

> Rather than simply establish substantive rights and liabilities regarding workplace injuries, workers' compensation laws always require as well that funds be available to satisfy fully all potential

claims that might be brought. Larger firms that can demonstrate the capacity to do so are permitted to self-insure (only about 1 percent of firms do so, but their companies comprise nearly 20 percent of payroll coverage). All other employers must purchase WC insurance through private carriers (about 60 percent of coverage) or state funds (about 20 percent).

3. The trend towards expansion of coverage and enhancement of benefits that the Kramer & Briffault excerpt details was reversed for most of the 1990s. Spieler & Burton, Compensation for Disabled Workers: Workers' Compensation, in T. Thomason, J. Burton, & D. Hyatt (eds.), New Approaches to Disability in the Workplace 205 (1998). Both the benefits and the costs of workers' compensation underwent an unprecedented decline from their respective peaks in 1992 and 1993. Spieler and Burton enumerate five causes for these reductions. First, the level of cash benefits provided was statutorily diminished—partially through cutting back on the maximum time-periods for temporary total disability payments, but most importantly through reforms in permanent partial disability payments. Second, rules governing compensability altered significantly; so-called mental-mental claims were restricted, claims based on the aggravation of a pre-existing condition were limited, and threshold requirements for permanent total disability eligibility were raised. Furthermore, statutory changes tightened the standards of proof and evidentiary requirements for compensation. Third, reliance on traditional health care cost containment methods helped to reduce the costs of compensation. Fourth, principles of disability management—supported by the Americans with Disabilities Act—encouraged employers to provide workers with jobs to which they could return after they had been injured. Finally, employees began to resort to remedies outside workers' compensation—and within the common law tort system. How do these changes compare with those we have seen proposed in other areas? Spieler and Burton argue that workers' compensation must be conceived of according to the two—conflicting—principles of adequacy and affordability, and that, in the 1990s, adequacy was disregarded in favor of affordability.

During the late 1990s and early 2000s, the downward trend in benefits and costs reached its nadir and swung back. The 2000s saw steady expansion of workers compensation benefits until the recession of 2008, when growth in benefits stalled and employer costs declined substantially. Data from 2011 and 2012 indicate that growth may be picking up again. In 2012, 128 million workers, or 90% of the total workforce, were covered by workers' compensation, with the employees of small farms and household workers earning less than a threshold amount representing the largest uncovered classes. While this is an increase of 1.6% over 2011, it is still 4.7% fewer workers than were covered in 2008. In 2012, the level of disbursements totaled $61.8 billion; this represented an increase in benefits of 1.3% from 2011 (and 5.7% from 2010). Of the amount disbursed, 50% was supplied for medical care, and the rest took the form of cash compensation to disabled workers or their survivors. The premiums paid to insurers or self-insurance funds totaled over $83.2 billion, an increase of

6.9% from 2011 (and up 14.3% from 2010). See I. Sengupta, M. Baldwin, & V. Reno, Workers' Compensation: Benefits, Coverage, and Costs, 2012 (National Academy of Social Insurance 2014).

    4.   The amount levied against each employer varies with the risks involved in the particular industry—and, when there is sufficient experience, among firms within an industry—and is measured in terms of a percentage of the employer's payroll. In hazardous industries the rate may be 25%, but if clerical or office positions make up the bulk of an industry's payroll, the basic rates may be well below one percent of payroll. The overall national average in recent years has been about 1.5 percent. These basic rates may be altered for large employers on the basis of safety inspections or past safety experience. For a study of the injury prevention effects of workers' compensation, see M. Moore & W.K. Viscusi, Compensation Mechanisms for Job Risks: Wages, Workers' Compensation, and Product Liability (1990), concluding that the system has a substantial impact on job safety—reducing workplace fatalities alone by about 25% from the expected level without the system in effect. How would you expect the safety incentives of workers' compensation to fare as compared with the tort system?

    5.   The problems of "arising out of" and "in the course of" the employment cause occasional difficulty, as this sample of cases suggests.

    a.   In Capizzi v. Southern District Reporters, Inc., 459 N.E.2d 847 (N.Y.1984), plaintiff was on a business trip when she slipped and fell in the bathtub of her motel room. The court held that her injuries were compensable because she "was required to work and stay at a place distant from home, placed in a new environment thereby creating a greater risk of injury, and was engaged in a reasonable activity . . . attendant to, although not directly related to her employment duties. . . ."

    b.   In Guillory v. Interstate Gas Station, 653 So.2d 1152 (La.1995), the claimant was shot by her estranged husband while she was at work. The court held that the harm did not arise out of the employment and thus was not covered.

    c.   In Pierre v. Seaside Farms, Inc., 689 S.E.2d 615 (S.C.2010), the claimant, a migrant farm worker, slipped and fell on the sidewalk outside his employer-provided residence. The South Carolina Workers' Compensation Commission denied his claim for benefits, citing the fact that the claimant was not working at the time of the accident nor was he required by contract to live at the farm. The South Carolina Supreme Court reversed, finding that the injury was compensable because it was within the scope of the claimant's employment. Three factors contributed to its determination. First, the nature of the work (i.e., low-wage farm work) effectively required the claimant to live on the farm. Second, the claimant was making reasonable use of the employer-provided premises at the time of the accident. Finally, the claimant's injury was "causally related to his employment in that it was due to conditions under which he lived, i.e., a wet sidewalk outside his building."

6. *Going and coming.* Suppose an employee is injured on the way to or from work. When is the injury arising out of and in the course of the employment? Compare the following illustrative cases.

a.   In Price v. W.C.A.B., 693 P.2d 254 (Cal.1984), a worker's injuries were held within the scope of the statute when he arrived early at his place of employment and was hit by a car while waiting for the premises to be unlocked. The going and coming rule which would have barred compensation did not apply because the worker had finished his local commute at the time of the injury. And even though he was pouring oil into his car when he was injured, this personal act was within the course of employment under the "dual purpose rule." Under that rule, where an employee is mixing his own business with his employer's, " 'no nice inquiry will be made as to which business he was actually engaged in at the time of injury, unless it clearly appears that neither directly nor indirectly could he be serving his employer.' [ ]." Here, the employee was "serving the interests of his employer by waiting near the premises to begin work early."

b.   In Santa Rosa Junior College v. W.C.A.B., 708 P.2d 673 (Cal.1985), a teacher was taking work home from campus when he was killed in a car accident. If he had been required by his employer to work at home, his home would have been considered a second jobsite and injuries sustained in traveling from one jobsite to the other would have been within the scope of the statute. Here, the decision to work at home was voluntary and the teacher's death was not compensable. What if the employer expected more work of the employee than could be performed during the working day?

7.   Closely related to the "scope" question is a series of statutory defenses excluding workers who are injured while engaging in "willful misconduct" or in specified misconduct, such as when an employee is injured in the course of committing a crime. These defenses are usually limited to deliberate exposure to danger and are construed narrowly to exclude instinctive behavior and bad judgment. Some violations of work rules are analyzed under this exclusion. Even if violation of such a rule falls short of being willful misconduct, it may bring disqualification under another statutory defense—unreasonable failure to observe safety rules or to use safety devices. This defense exists in almost half of the states. In some, violation will bar all compensation recovery; in others it will reduce compensation by 10, 15, or 50%. A. Larson, 1A Law of Workmen's Compensation ch. 34–39.

Over half the states provide a statutory defense if the worker was intoxicated at the time of the injury. In most of these, intoxication can serve as a complete bar to compensation, but in a few it will serve only to reduce the award. The major difference among the statutes is the extent of causal connection required between the intoxication and the injury: this ranges from no requirement of causal connection to a requirement of demonstrating that intoxication was the "sole cause" of the injury. Larson, § 36.03[3]. Is it consistent with the theory of the compensation acts to reduce the worker's benefits for misbehavior?

8. Several states increase the employee's compensation when injury results from the employer's violation of safety rules. In RTE Corp. v. Department of Industry, Labor & Human Relations, 276 N.W.2d 290 (Wis.1979), the court affirmed a 15% increase in the compensation award because the worker's death had resulted from the employer's violation of a safety regulation whose purpose was to prevent the kind of injury the worker sustained. Is it consistent with workers' compensation theory to increase an award if the employer has violated a safety order?

California Labor Code section 4553 requires that the compensation award be increased by one-half (together with costs and expenses not to exceed $250) if the worker's injury resulted from "serious and willful misconduct" of the employer. Such misconduct has been defined as "more than negligence, however gross. The type of conduct necessary to invoke the penalty . . . is that of a 'quasi criminal nature, the intentional doing of something either with the knowledge that it is likely to result in serious injury, or with a wanton and reckless disregard of its possible consequences. . . .' " American Smelting & Refining Co. v. W.C.A.B., 144 Cal.Rptr. 898 (App.1978).

9. *Permanent partial disability.* The following statute from New York demonstrates the scheduling approach to permanent partial disability.

New York Workers' Compensation Law
Section 15.

. . .

3. Permanent partial disability. In case of disability partial in character but permanent in quality the compensation shall be sixty-six and two-thirds per centum of the average weekly wages and shall be paid to the employee for the period named in this subdivision, as follows:

Member lost	Number of weeks' compensation
a. Arm	312
b. Leg	288
c. Hand	244
d. Foot	205
e. Eye	160
f. Thumb	75
g. First finger	46
h. Great toe	38
i. Second finger	30
j. Third finger	25
k. Toe other than great toe	16
l. Fourth finger	15

m.   Loss of hearing. Compensation for the complete loss of the hearing of one ear, for sixty weeks, for the loss of hearing of both ears, for one hundred and fifty weeks.

. . .

r.   Total loss of use. Compensation for permanent total loss of use of a member shall be the same as for loss of the member.

s.   Partial loss or partial loss of use. Compensation for permanent partial loss or loss of use of a member may be for proportionate loss or loss of use of the member. . . .

t.   Disfigurement.

1.   The board may award proper and equitable compensation for serious facial or head disfigurement, not to exceed twenty thousand dollars, including a disfigurement continuous in length which is partially in the facial area and also extends into the neck region as described in paragraph two hereof.

2.   The board, if in its opinion the earning capacity of an employee has been or may in the future be impaired, may award compensation for any serious disfigurement in the region above the sterno clavicular articulations anterior to and including the region of the sterno cleido mastoid muscles on either side, but no award under subdivisions one and two shall, in the aggregate, exceed twenty thousand dollars.

3.   Notwithstanding any other provision hereof, two or more serious disfigurements, not continuous in length, resulting from the same injury, if partially in the facial area and partially in the neck region as described in paragraph two hereof, shall be deemed to be a facial disfigurement.

u.   Total or partial loss or loss of use of more than one member or parts of members. In any case in which there shall be a loss or loss of use of more than one member or parts of more than one member set forth in paragraphs a through t, inclusive, of this subdivision, but not amounting to permanent total disability, the board shall award compensation for the loss or loss of use of each such member or part thereof, which awards shall be fully payable in one lump sum upon the request of the injured employee.

v.   Additional compensation for impairment of wage earning capacity in certain permanent partial disabilities. Notwithstanding any other provision of this subdivision, additional compensation shall be payable for impairment of wage earning capacity for any period after the termination of an award under paragraph a, b, c, or d, of this subdivision for the loss or loss of use of fifty per centum or more of a member, provided such impairment of earning capacity shall be due solely thereto. . . .

w.   Other cases. In all other cases of permanent partial disability, the compensation shall be sixty-six and two-thirds percent of the difference between the injured employee's average weekly wages and his or her wage-earning capacity thereafter in the same employment or otherwise. Compensation under this paragraph shall be payable during the continuance of such permanent partial disability, but subject to reconsideration of the degree of such impairment by the board on its own motion or upon application of any party in interest. . . .

———

What are the strengths and weaknesses of this approach? Does it seem appropriate that both a construction worker and a law professor would receive the same benefits for loss of an arm—assuming both are above the average weekly wage ceiling—under the statute? Does it seem proper that the law professor would receive these benefits even if she suffered no loss of earning capacity? What justification might be offered for the scheduling of permanent partial disability benefits?

10. *Lump sums.* In death cases, most states provide lump sum payments to close out accounts when widows or widowers remarry. This raises the general question of lump sum payments in lieu of the periodic payments in some injury situations, too. In many states the lump sum has become common since it is at least superficially attractive to everyone concerned: the claimant, who gets one very large award; the attorney, who thus finds it easier to collect a fee; the employer, who can dispose of the matter once and for all and probably at a lower cost; and the court or administering agency, which avoids further litigation and supervision of the claim. Lump summing, however, does not meet one of the primary goals of the compensation system, provision of a regular benefit payment to take the place of lost wages. The objection is that the worker will find the lump sum soon spent, leaving him or her with no further recourse and in no better position than if there had been no compensation scheme at all. Are the lump sum problems of compensation systems different from those of the common law?

11. *Opting out.* Up to this point we have been dealing with cases in which the injured worker has sought coverage under a workers' compensation scheme. Sometimes, however, an injured worker may wish to avoid the rule that if an injury is compensable within the system, there may be no other remedy against the employer or co-workers. Although compensation plans originally provided the injured worker's only practical hope of recovery, the modern worker is much more likely to succeed in a tort action against the employer—if allowed to pursue it. In such a case, coverage may be a detriment to the worker.

a.   In some cases the worker claims to be outside the scope of employment at the time of injury, while the employer argues for coverage. For example, in Mason v. Lake Dolores Group, LLC, 11 Cal.Rptr.3d 914 (App.2004), plaintiff worked at defendant water amusement park. One day when the park was closed he reported for work but had not clocked in. He asked a co-employee to turn on the water, and he rode his favorite water slide. The water supply was in fact insufficient, and he crashed into the restraining wall at the bottom and was rendered paraplegic. The trial court granted judgment n.o.v. on the ground that workers' compensation was the exclusive remedy. The court of appeal reversed. The jury had found that plaintiff's injury did not arise out of and in the course of the employment.

Even though the statute calls upon courts to "liberally construe" the provision to extend coverage, here there was substantial evidence to support the jury's finding. He was not "testing" the water or doing anything that was conceivably beneficial to defendant. Defendant "had expressly prohibited" all of its employees from using the slides when the park was closed and the slides had been turned off.

Nor were the injuries a "reasonable expectancy of his employment." The statute bars compensation for injuries that "arise out of voluntary participation in any off-duty recreational, social, or athletic activity not constituting part of the employee's work-related duties, except where these activities are a reasonable expectancy of, or are expressly or impliedly required by, the employment. . . ."

The court also stated that "[t]he mere fact that an employee is performing a personal act when injured does not per se "bring him without the purview of the compensation law." [ ] But the act, "however characterized, must be work-related, or reasonably contemplated by the employment. Mason's was not."

The jury had placed 52% of the fault on defendant, 38% on plaintiff, and 10% on others. The fault issues were not involved in the appeal and plaintiff's judgment for $4.4 million was reinstated.

Should the statutory command that coverage be "liberally construed" be affected by whether the worker seeks to be included or excluded from coverage? Should it be affected by whether the worker has a valid tort claim?

b.   Another way to escape the exclusive remedy bar in many states is to prove that the employer committed an intentional tort. See the extended discussion in Magliulo v. Superior Court, 121 Cal.Rptr. 621 (App.1975), allowing a tort action to a waitress whose employer allegedly hit her in anger and threw her down.

Liability in tort for reckless conduct falling short of intentional wrongdoing on the part of the employer has been denied, in the absence of less limiting statutory language. See e.g. Bardere v. Zafir, 477 N.Y.S.2d 131 (App.Div.), aff'd on other grounds, 472 N.E.2d 37 (N.Y.1984), in which the court held that an employer's conduct in removing safety features from a machine to increase its speed, with knowledge that a worker might come in contact with the dangerous machine, was insufficient to establish an intentional tort and overcome the exclusive remedy of workers' compensation.

In Cole v. Fair Oaks Fire Protection District, 729 P.2d 743 (Cal.1987), the court declined to allow an employee to sue an employer in tort based on a claim of intentional infliction of emotional distress. As a result of a sustained campaign of harassment and humiliation, including an unjustified demotion by his employer in retaliation for his union activities, the plaintiff suffered a severe stroke that rendered him unable to move, care for himself, or communicate other than by blinking his eyes. The court rejected the worker's claim that the intent element of the tort could be satisfied by a showing that the defendant proceeded with *reckless* disregard to the possibility of causing emotional injury to the plaintiff. The court did not stop there. It went on to hold that even a showing of *purposeful* infliction of emotional distress would not allow the claimant to avoid the exclusivity provisions of workers' compensation. This, according to the majority opinion, could have the effect of transforming virtually every negative personnel decision into a tort claim.

Can the claimant in *Cole* also argue that the injury arose from activities outside the scope of his employment? The court rejected this argument, noting: "[T]he allegations in the instant case as to the *conduct* of the employer and the assistant chief reflect matters which can be expected to occur with substantial frequency in the working environment . . . Disciplinary hearings and demotions and friction in negotiations as to grievances are also an inherent part of the employment setting as are decisions to seek disability retirement and demands to appear at meetings which interfere with personal arrangements." The California Supreme Court seemed most concerned that a contrary holding would open the floodgates to tort claims arising out of common employer-employee exchanges. Do you share this concern? Is there a principled way to side with *Cole* while limiting tort liability in common cases of employee demotion, discipline, or firing?

A trio of cases decided in recent years reveal the full spectrum of approaches to when an injured employee can bypass workers' compensation and proceed in tort based on the culpability of the employer's actions. At the most restrictive end of that spectrum is Franklin Corp. v. Tedford, 18 So.3d 215 (Miss.2009). The employer permitted employees to be exposed to excessive glue vapors by failing to install ventilation equipment or to provide personal protective equipment. The Mississippi Supreme Court required that there be "an actual intent to injure" (effectively, purpose) in order for the employee to make a tort claim outside workers' compensation. Helf v. Chevron U.S.A., Inc., 203 P.3d 962 (Utah 2009), hews a more middle ground, requiring that the employer or supervisor have a purpose to harm *or* expect that harm will occur. The court makes an effort to distinguish the "substantially certain" standard, which it claims only involves a probability of injury in contrast with an expectation or knowledge that injury is "virtually certain" to occur. The court finds its test satisfied on the facts of the case. While the employer was not trying to harm the plaintiff, it put her in a situation—cleaning toxic sludge with a different and cheaper method—that the employer knew released toxic and noxious gases. Reflecting the most lenient position is Hannifan v. American National Bank of Cheyenne, 185 P.3d 679 (Wyo.2008). The court requires that the defendant's conduct be "wanton and willful" for the plaintiff to avoid the exclusive remedy bar to tort. High walls in a coal mine created a risk of rocks coming loose and cascading down onto those working in the mine, which is what happened to plaintiff. The court explains that in the context of the workplace wanton and willful means that "the co-employee had knowledge of the dangerous condition and demonstrated a disregard of the risks through intentional acts." These circumstances and the supervisors' knowledge of them were sufficient for the jury to find wanton or willful conduct.

12. Sometimes, even though an injury falls within the scope of the statute, the particular harm suffered by the worker is not covered. "Non-disabling" injuries are often not compensable. The most obvious example is the refusal of compensation systems to pay anything for conventional pain and suffering. Other examples include injury to sexual organs; loss of taste, smell or sensation; and psychic damage.

The fact that a compensation scheme excludes these types of injury does not mean that tort law is available. Thus, in Fetterhoff v. Western Block Co., 373 N.Y.S.2d 920 (App.Div.1975), a worker who alleged that his work-related injury had left him permanently unable to have sexual intercourse was barred from suing in tort even though his loss of sexual function was not compensable under workers' compensation. In Moss v. Southern Excavation, Inc., 611 S.W.2d 178 (Ark.1981), a worker who lost the non-compensable senses of taste and smell in an accident that was covered by workers' compensation was barred from suing in tort for these losses.

13. The exclusiveness of the workers' compensation remedy applies not only to covered workers but also to plaintiffs who claim harm derivatively through the injured employee. Compensation schemes do not provide benefits to spouses or children of workers who are injured, or to the non-dependent relatives of workers who are killed. Generally, these family members are not permitted to bring tort actions against the employer for loss of consortium or wrongful death.

14. See Chapter IX, p. 647 supra, for general consideration of the problems of meshing workers' compensation and tort in the context of third-party products liability cases.

15. *The "sharing economy"*—One recent flashpoint for workers' compensation litigation relates to the employment status—and thus the eligibility for workers' compensation—of those working for car services like Uber and Lyft. For a recent article on the status of this litigation, see D. MacMillan, Uber Appeals Class-Action Ruling for Lawsuit, Wall St.J., Sept. 15, 2015. These questions are sure to continue to arise as companies look to profit from the new "sharing economy," built on the work of independent contractors outside the traditional business environment. See G. Bensinger, *Startups Scramble to Define "Employee,"* Wall St. J., July 30, 2015.

16. For a regulatory perspective that critically considers the role of the Occupational Safety and Health Administration (OSHA) in managing the risks from workplace hazards, see I. Urbina, *As OSHA Emphasizes Safety, Long-Term Health Risks Fester*, N.Y. Times, March 31, 2013, at A1.

Railroad Workers

While the states were grappling with problems of workers' injuries, Congress confronted the special situation of persons employed in interstate commerce as that term was understood at the turn of the twentieth century. In 1908 Congress passed the Federal Employers' Liability Act (FELA), 45 U.S.C. §§ 51–60. The Act provided that interstate railroads were liable to negligently injured employees and that any attempt by the employer to contract out of liability would be void. The original version of the Act barred assumption of risk in some situations; a 1939 amendment was held to have "obliterated" the doctrine. Tiller v. Atlantic Coast Line R. Co., 318 U.S. 54 (1943). Comparative negligence applies in all actions against the employer, unless the employer has violated a safety statute—in which case the worker's fault is not considered.

Several Supreme Court decisions in the 1940s and 1950s made the injured railroad worker's path much easier than that of a plaintiff in a common law negligence action. In addition to the elimination of the three major defenses, the task of establishing causation was eased.

In a more recent case, Norfolk S. Ry. Co. v. Sorrell, 549 U.S. 158 (2007), the Court continued its interpretive tradition, holding that under FELA the same standard of factual causation, which is a relaxed one, that is applicable to a defendant's negligence is applicable to a plaintiff's contributory negligence, as well.

Most recently, in CSX Transport, Inc. v. McBride, 131 S.Ct. 2630 (2011), the Supreme Court considered whether the plaintiff must submit to the jury evidence of proximate cause to recover under FELA. The Court held that no proximate cause instruction was appropriate and that the plaintiff need only show that defendant's negligence "played any part in bringing about the [plaintiff's] injury."

Railroad workers have steadfastly opposed a compensation system to replace FELA.

C. MOTOR VEHICLE INJURIES

Not long after the automobile became part of daily life, the first doubts were raised about the adequacy of legal treatment of automobile accidents. We have already considered the legal theory underlying the fault system and the impact on it of the institution of insurance. Before considering current no-fault alternatives, we review briefly the history of proposed changes—both because they frame the basic issues and because they helped shape the legislation that followed.

1. THE PAST

The earliest thinking about extensions of the no-fault concept began shortly after the passage of the workers' compensation statutes. Writers saw that incongruities would occur: if a trolley car collided with an automobile, the employees on the trolley car would be eligible for compensation, but the trolley passengers and car occupants would have to prove fault. Professor Jeremiah Smith in his article, Sequel to Workmen's Compensation Acts, 27 Harv.L.Rev. 235, 363 (1914), concluded that the fault system and the compensation system could not live together in harmony: "In the end, one or the other of the two conflicting theories is likely to prevail. There is no probability, during the present generation, of a repeal of the Workmen's Compensation Acts." Smith then speculated on the creation of a state insurance law that would protect all, not only workers, against accident and disease. "It may include damage wholly due to a natural cause, such as a stroke of lightning. Whether legislation of the above description *ought* to be enacted is a question upon which no opinion is here intimated. Our immediate point is that the Workmen's Compensation legislation will inevitably give rise to a plausible agitation for such further legislation."* Fifteen years after Professor Smith wrote, some lawyers and social scientists undertook an empirical analysis of automobile injuries in 8,849 cases across the United States. Their findings were remarkably similar to those of recent studies: "payments do not increase in proportion to the losses sustained; temporary disability cases with small losses are considerably overpaid, those with larger losses are slightly overpaid, while permanent disability cases of earners—the class with the largest losses and greatest need—receive just about enough to meet the losses incurred up to the time of our investigations and get nothing to apply against the continued medical expense or wage loss resulting from their impaired earning ability." They were concerned about delay and uncompensated victims at a time when first-party insurance for injuries was unusual, and tort law was the one available resource; workers' compensation was available only when a person was hurt on the job. The study is presented in Report by the Committee to Study Compensation for Automobile Accidents to the Columbia University Council for Research into the Social Sciences (1932).

The study suggested a workers' compensation model after considering its relevance to the automobile situation (pp.134–36):

> In many respects there is a close analogy between the industrial situation where workmen's compensation has been developed and the motor vehicle situation where the application of a like principle is now being discussed. Accidents are inevitable, whether in industry or in the operation of motor vehicles. It has been accepted as sound policy that the major part of the cost of accidents to employees should be borne by the industry, and it is proposed that the major part of the cost of those caused by the operation of motor vehicles should be cast upon the persons for whose benefit the motor vehicles are being operated. The conditions calling for the application of the compensation plan are similar: The failure of the common law system to measure up to a fair estimate of social necessity.

Compensation was to be paid from compulsory insurance carried by every vehicle owner for the benefit of those harmed by the vehicle. The

---

* Indeed, within two years plans began to appear. See Ballantine, A Compensation Plan for Railway Accident Claims, 29 Harv.L.Rev. 705 (1916), proposing a plan to cover injuries to passengers on railroads and street railways.

amount of compensation was to be scheduled much as with workers' compensation payments. The group recognized that the amounts of compensation would present different problems because of the greater diversity of potential automobile victims as compared to workers.

The major breakthrough occurred in 1965, with the publication of Basic Protection for the Traffic Victim, by Professors Robert E. Keeton and Jeffrey O'Connell. Not only did the authors attack the operation of the common law fault system in auto cases, they also proposed a new approach and presented a 37-page draft statute practically ready for introduction into state legislatures. Suddenly, no-fault legislation became a political possibility.

Briefly, they utilized a first-party structure building on the medical payments provision that would cover medical expenses and 85% of wage loss up to a total of $10,000, although lost wage payments would be limited to $750 per month. A deductible of $100 or 10% of the work loss, whichever was larger, was imposed to keep small claims from burdening the system and to reduce moral hazard. Those who wanted greater no-fault protection would be able to buy it. In any tort action against another driver, the judgment would exclude the first $10,000 of economic loss and the first $5,000 of pain and suffering. In suits against other defendants, such as railroads or car manufacturers, no deductions or exclusions would be made but the no-fault insurer would be reimbursed to prevent double recovery. For a short summary of the plan, see Keeton & O'Connell, Basic Protection Automobile Insurance, 1967 U.Ill.L.F. 400.

The impetus for change in Massachusetts was the great public outcry about high insurance rates. Its liability premiums were the highest in the country. Also, the state was the home of Professor Robert Keeton, who had co-authored the Keeton-O'Connell plan. In 1970, Massachusetts adopted a plan that was traceable to that work.

The statute required compulsory no-fault coverage for all medical expenses and 75% of lost earnings incurred within two years up to a combined sum of $2,000. The act made no general provision for collateral sources but did require a worker to use up (subject to later reimbursement) any wage continuation protection before recovering for lost wages. Another provision correlated workers' compensation benefits with the no-fault benefits.

Tort actions for damages were permitted with an exclusion for the first $2,000 of the award. Pain and suffering was recoverable in a tort action if one of the following existed: medical and hospital expenses over $500, death, loss of body member, permanent disfigurement, loss of sight or hearing, or a "fracture." Compulsory liability insurance was continued at low limits to cover the tort action. Insureds could choose a deductible of up to $2,000 for their own losses. An assigned claims plan protected pedestrians and others who were hurt in the state by cars that didn't carry the no-fault coverage. The statute also regulated policy cancellations and renewals and provided explicitly for merit driving discounts and surcharges for moving violations and involvement in accidents.

2.   THE NEW YORK EXPERIENCE

a.   BACKGROUND

As soon as Massachusetts acted, the scene shifted to New York. In 1970, the state's Insurance Department had prepared a study of the operation of the tort system in auto cases. Automobile Insurance . . . for Whose Benefit?, A Report to Governor Nelson A. Rockefeller by the Insurance Department of the State of New York (1970). The study concluded that the system had failed. Among its points (pp. 17–44):

1.   One in four persons suffering bodily injury in auto accidents obtained "nothing whatever" from the fault system. Significant here is that New York did not adopt comparative negligence until 1973.

2.   Determinations "are made either by an overburdened judiciary on stale facts or else by insurance adjusters in a bargaining process. Part lottery and part bazaar, the fault insurance system is unreliable and unpredictable."

3.   Data showed, as in earlier studies, that benefits were malapportioned, with small claims being overcompensated to get rid of them with payments for pain and suffering far in excess of the economic loss sustained. Large claims, however, were being badly underpaid. "The seriously injured receive a sort of negative 'pain and suffering.' "

4.   Benefits were not coordinated with other support systems. Thus, 91% of workers in New York in 1970 were covered by health insurance and most were also covered by income continuation plans. The collateral source rule operated to provide double recoveries when these persons were hurt. Workers with good fringe benefits received no reduction in their auto premiums. Instead, they got "a chance at redundant payment" if injured in the future.

5.   Physical rehabilitation was delayed under the fault system because of the cost involved and the question of whether the victim would be able to pay for rehabilitation if no tort recovery were obtained.

6.   The system was inefficient because 56 cents of each premium dollar went to operating expenses of the system. Of the 44 cents that reached victims, 8 cents covered economic losses already covered by another source, 21.5 cents covered pain and suffering, and only 14.5 cents was for net economic loss not otherwise covered.

7.   Finally the litigation system bred overreaching and dishonesty. Insurers deal "with thousands of claimants who are adversaries the company never expects to see again, and is doing so in situations that afford no clear line between rigorous bargaining and downright dishonesty. . . . Too often, especially where injuries are

serious, the insurer can simply wait out the injured victim to obtain a more favorable settlement." The highly abstract standard of "fault" and the indeterminate measure of damages "offer rich rewards to the claimant who will lie, the attorney who will inflame, the adjuster who will chisel and the insurance company which will stall or intimidate."

The study also discussed several problems of insurance administration. How many of the enumerated concerns are likely to be unique to auto accidents?

Consider the following discussion of how to evaluate an existing reparation system, taken from A. Conard et al., Automobile Accident Costs and Payments 106–07 (1964):

> No valid evaluation of reparation systems can be made which measures them by a single dimension. Some are better than others for procuring medical treatment, some for maintaining subsistence, some for compensating total loss, some for deterring negligence, some for raising the price of hazardous activities, some for spreading broadly the pain of loss, some for economy of operation. If any of the major elements in the scheme is knocked out, some important function will remain unperformed.

> This does not mean that nothing in the picture can be changed. In fact, a great many elements in the picture are quite recent. Workmen's compensation entered about fifty years ago; social security was added about twenty-five years ago for survivors' benefits and within the last ten years for disability benefits; hospital and medical insurance is largely a growth of the last fifteen years. It seems probable that further changes will be made in reparation systems, which might include the shifting of functions from one system to another, and altering the linkage between benefits and burdens. When such changes are made, they should be made with a clear perception of the plurality of functions to be performed, and of the plurality of systems now performing them.

For an extended discussion of the issues underlying the adoption of any no-fault proposal, see Blum & Kalven, Ceilings, Costs, and Compulsion in Auto Compensation Legislation, 1973 Utah L.Rev. 341.

b.   THE NEW YORK STATUTE

The New York statute provides one of the most generous sets of no-fault benefits and one of the most significant limitations on tort actions of any of the 20-odd state statutes adopting some version of auto no-fault. The statute was adopted in 1973, and amended frequently to meet problems that appeared during its first years of operation. The statute that follows is the current version. The cross-references to articles six and eight of the Vehicle and Traffic Law are to provisions for compulsory insurance and other devices relating to financial security arrangements.

In reading the statute, keep in mind some general questions. Among those, who would get compensated under the statute if they were not compensated before? How does the amount of recovery compare with that currently available under tort? If the act is likely to be more expensive than the current system, where will the money come from? If there are savings, who will benefit? What about collateral sources and subrogation? Does the act internalize the costs of auto accidents so that the motoring activity pays for them? Is internalization important? What are the alternatives to internalizing the costs? Is the act conducive to fraudulent claims? More so than the existing system? What, if anything, remains of the tort action? Should safety be left to other parts of the legal system? What conception of justice does the statute reflect? How does that conception line up with your own? Is the act likely to have any effect on driving safety?

When reading a statute, lawyers and judges are usually looking for answers to specific questions. In reading this statute, assume a client who is asking about her rights under New York's current legislation. V is a 25-year-old commercial artist. Although she owns a car that is properly insured under the statute, she was hurt while walking home from a neighborhood movie house one evening. She was run over by a car owned and operated by D, who was probably negligent, and who possessed the proper insurance under the statute. V sustained a broken left arm (she is left-handed) and also sustained a four-inch-long permanent scar on her left forearm. The fracture healed perfectly. She had medical bills of $4,000, of which $2,500 was covered and paid by the group medical policy that she received as a fringe benefit at her office. She was out of work, without pay, for a month and a half. Her salary was $3000 per month.

(a) What are V's rights?

(b) What if V owned no car?

(c) What if V had driven to and from the movie and collided with D's car?

(d) Some tests on D's new car have suggested that the crash might have been due to a defective steering column. Does it matter if the crash was due to the defect rather than D's negligence?

New York Insurance Law
Article 51.

§ 5101. Title

This article shall be known and may be cited as the "Comprehensive Motor Vehicle Insurance Reparations Act."

§ 5102. Definitions

In this chapter:

(a) "Basic economic loss" means, up to fifty thousand dollars per person of the following combined items, subject to the limitations of section five thousand one hundred eight of this article:

(1) All necessary expenses incurred for: (i) medical, hospital, . . . surgical, nursing, dental, ambulance, x-ray, prescription drug and prosthetic services; (ii) psychiatric, physical therapy (provided that treatment is rendered pursuant to a referral) and occupational therapy and rehabilitation; (iii) any non-medical remedial care and treatment rendered in accordance with a religious method of healing recognized by the laws of this state; and (iv) any other professional health services; all without limitation as to time, provided that within one year after the date of the accident causing the injury it is ascertainable that further expenses may be incurred as a result of the injury. For the purpose of determining basic economic loss, the expenses incurred under this paragraph shall be in accordance with the limitations of section five thousand one hundred eight of this article.

(2) Loss of earnings from work which the person would have performed had he not been injured, and reasonable and necessary expenses incurred by such person in obtaining services in lieu of those that he would have performed for income, up to two thousand dollars per month for not more than three years from the date of the accident causing the injury. An employee who is entitled to receive monetary payments, pursuant to statute or contract with the employer, or who receives voluntary monetary benefits paid for by the employer, by reason of the employee's inability to work because of personal injury arising out of the use or operation of a motor vehicle, is not entitled to receive first party benefits for "loss of earnings from work" to the extent that such monetary payments or benefits from the employer do not result in the employee suffering a reduction in income or a reduction in the employee's level of future benefits arising from a subsequent illness or injury.

(3) All other reasonable and necessary expenses incurred, up to twenty-five dollars per day for not more than one year from the date of the accident causing the injury.

(4) "Basic economic loss" shall not include any loss incurred on account of death; subject, however, to the provisions of paragraph four of subsection (a) of section five thousand one hundred three of this article.

(5) "Basic economic loss" shall also include an additional option to purchase, for an additional premium, an additional twenty-five thousand dollars of coverage, [which may be keyed to economic loss or medical bills as the buyer wishes and which comes into play after the first $50,000 is exhausted.] This optional coverage shall be made

available and notice with explanation of such coverage [shall be provided by an insurer at the first policy renewal after the effective date of the statute].

(b) "First party benefits" means payments to reimburse a person for basic economic loss on account of personal injury arising out of the use or operation of a motor vehicle, less:

(1) Twenty percent of lost earnings computed pursuant to paragraph two of subsection (a) of this section.

(2) Amounts recovered or recoverable on account of such injury under state or federal laws providing social security disability benefits, or workers' compensation benefits, or disability benefits under article nine of the workers' compensation law, or medicare benefits, other than lifetime reserve days and provided further that the medicare benefits utilized herein do not result in a reduction of such person's medicare benefits for a subsequent illness or injury.

(3) Amounts deductible under the applicable insurance policy.

(c) "Non-economic loss" means pain and suffering and similar non-monetary detriment.

(d) "Serious injury" means a personal injury which results in death; dismemberment; significant disfigurement; a fracture; loss of a fetus; permanent loss of use of a body organ, member, function or system; permanent consequential limitation of use of a body organ or member; significant limitation of use of a body function or system; or a medically determined injury or impairment of a non-permanent nature which prevents the injured person from performing substantially all of the material acts which constitute such person's usual and customary daily activities for not less than ninety days during the one hundred eighty days immediately following the occurrence of the injury or impairment.

(e) "Owner" [is defined broadly].

(f) "Motor vehicle" [is very broadly defined and includes fire and police vehicles, but excludes motorcycles].

(g) "Insurer" means the insurance company or self-insurer, as the case may be, which provides the financial security required by article six or eight of the vehicle and traffic law.

(h) "Member of his household" means a spouse, child or relative of the named insured who regularly resides in his household.

(i) "Uninsured motor vehicle" means a motor vehicle, the owner of which is (i) a financially irresponsible motorist . . . or (ii) unknown and whose identity is unascertainable.

(j) "Covered person" means any pedestrian injured through the use or operation of, or any owner, operator or occupant of, a motor vehicle which has in effect the financial security required by . . . the vehicle and traffic law . . . or any other person entitled to first party benefits.

(k) "Bus" means both a bus and a school bus as defined in sections one hundred four and one hundred forty-two of the vehicle and traffic law.

(l) "Compensation provider" means the state insurance fund, or the person, association, corporation or insurance carrier or statutory fund liable under state or federal laws for the payment of workers' compensation benefits or disability benefits under article nine of the workers' compensation law.

(m) "Motorcycle" [is defined by reference to other statutes].

§ 5103. Entitlement to first party benefits; additional financial security required

(a) Every owner's policy of liability insurance issued on a motor vehicle in satisfaction of the requirements of article six or eight of the vehicle and traffic law shall also provide for . . . the payment of first party benefits to:

(1) Persons, other than occupants of another motor vehicle or a motorcycle, for loss arising out of the use or operation in this state of such motor vehicle. In the case of occupants of a bus other than operators, owners, and employees of the owner or operator of the bus, the coverage for first party benefits shall be afforded under the policy or policies, if any, providing first party benefits to the injured person and members of his household for loss arising out of the use or operation of any motor vehicle of such household. In the event there is no such policy, first party benefits shall be provided by the insurer of such bus.

(2) The named insured and members of his household, other than occupants of a motorcycle, for loss arising out of the use or operation of (i) an uninsured motor vehicle or motorcycle, within the United States, its territories or possessions, or Canada; and (ii) an insured motor vehicle or motorcycle outside of this state and within the United States, its territories or possessions, or Canada.

(3) Any New York resident who is neither the owner of a motor vehicle with respect to which coverage for first party benefits is required by this article nor, as a member of a household, is entitled to first party benefits under paragraph two of this subsection, for loss arising out of the use or operation of the insured or self-insured motor vehicle outside of this state and within the United States, its territories or possessions, or Canada.

(4) The estate of any covered person, other than an occupant of another motor vehicle or a motorcycle, a death benefit in the amount of two thousand dollars for the death of such person arising out of the use or operation of such motor vehicle which is in addition to any first party benefits for basic economic loss.

(b) An insurer may exclude from coverage required by subsection (a) hereof a person who:

(1) Intentionally causes his own injury.

(2) Is injured as a result of operating a motor vehicle while in an intoxicated condition or while his ability to operate such vehicle is impaired by the use of a drug within the meaning of section eleven hundred ninety-two of the vehicle and traffic safety law; provided, however, that an insurer shall not exclude such person from coverage with respect to necessary emergency health services rendered in a general hospital ... including ambulance services attendant thereto and related to medical screening. Notwithstanding any other law, where the covered person is found to have violated section eleven hundred ninety-two of the vehicle and traffic law, the insurer has a cause of action for the amount of first party benefits paid or payable on behalf of such covered person against such covered person.

(3) Is injured while he is: (i) committing an act which would constitute a felony, or seeking to avoid lawful apprehension or arrest by a law enforcement officer, or (ii) operating a motor vehicle in a race or speed test, or (iii) operating or occupying a motor vehicle known to him to be stolen, or (iv) operating or occupying any motor vehicle owned by such injured person with respect to which the coverage required by subsection (a) hereof is not in effect, or (v) a pedestrian, through being struck by any motor vehicle owned by such injured pedestrian with respect to which the coverage required by subsection (a) hereof is not in effect, or (vi) repairing, servicing or otherwise maintaining a motor vehicle if such conduct is within the course of a business of repairing, servicing or otherwise maintaining a motor vehicle and the injury occurs on the business premises.

(c) Insurance offered by any company to satisfy the requirements of subsection (a) hereof shall be offered (1) without a deductible and (2) with a family deductible of up to two hundred dollars (which deductible shall apply only to the loss of the named insured and members of his household). The superintendent may approve a higher deductible in the case of insurance policies providing additional benefits or pursuant to a plan designed and implemented to coordinate first party benefits with other benefits. . . .

. . .

(f) Every owner's policy of liability insurance issued on a motorcycle or an all terrain vehicle in satisfaction of the requirements of article six or eight of the vehicle and traffic law shall also provide for ... the payment of first party benefits to persons, other than the occupants of such motorcycle or all terrain vehicle, another motorcycle or all terrain vehicle, or any motor vehicle, for loss arising out of the use or operation of the motorcycle or all terrain vehicle within this state. Every insurer and self-insurer may exclude from the coverage required by this subsection a person who intentionally causes his own injury or is injured while committing an act which would constitute a felony or while seeking to avoid lawful apprehension or arrest by a law enforcement officer.

(g) [A general health insurer may, with the consent of the superintendent of insurance] upon a showing that the company or corporation is qualified to provide for all of the items of basic economic loss specified in paragraph one of subsection (a) of section five thousand one hundred two of this article, provide coverage for such items of basic economic loss to the extent that an insurer would be required to provide under this article. Where a policyholder elects to be covered under such an arrangement the insurer providing coverage for the automobile shall be furnished with the names of all persons covered by the company or corporation under the arrangement and such persons shall not be entitled to benefits for any of the items of basic economic loss specified in such paragraph. The premium for the automobile insurance policy shall be appropriately reduced to reflect the elimination of coverage for such items of basic economic loss. Coverage by the automobile insurer of such eliminated items shall be effected or restored upon request by the insured and payment of the premium for such coverage. All companies and corporations providing coverage for items of basic economic loss pursuant to the authorization of this subsection shall have only those rights and obligations which are applicable to an insurer subject to this article.

. . .

§ 5104. Causes of action for personal injury

(a) Notwithstanding any other law, in any action by or on behalf of a covered person against another covered person for personal injuries arising out of negligence in the use or operation of a motor vehicle in this state, there shall be no right of recovery for non-economic loss, except in the case of a serious injury, or for basic economic loss. The owner, operator or occupant of a motorcycle which has in effect the financial security required by article six or eight of the vehicle and traffic law . . . shall not be subject to an action by or on behalf of a covered person for recovery for non-economic loss, except in the case of a serious injury, or for basic economic loss.

(b) In any action by or on behalf of a covered person, against a non-covered person, where damages for personal injuries arising out of the use or operation of a motor vehicle or a motorcycle may be recovered, an insurer which paid or is liable for first party benefits on account of such injuries has a lien against any recovery to the extent of benefits paid or payable by it to the covered person. No such action may be compromised by the covered person except with the written consent of the insurer, or with the approval of the court, or where the amount of such settlement exceeds fifty thousand dollars. The failure of such person to commence such action within two years after accrual gives the insurer a cause of action for the amount of first party benefits paid or payable against any person who may be liable to the covered person for his personal injuries. The insurer's cause of action shall be in addition to the cause of action of the covered person except that in any action subsequently commenced by the covered person for such injuries, the amount of his basic economic loss shall not be recoverable.

(c) Where there is no right of recovery for basic economic loss, such loss may nevertheless be pleaded and proved to the extent that it is relevant to the proof of non-economic loss.

§ 5105. Settlement between insurers

(a) Any insurer liable for the payment of first party benefits to or on behalf of a covered person and any compensation provider paying benefits in lieu of first party benefits which another insurer would otherwise be obligated to pay pursuant to subsection (a) of section five thousand one hundred three of this article . . . has the right to recover the amount paid from the insurer of any other covered person to the extent that such other covered person would have been liable, but for the provisions of this article, to pay damages in an action at law. In any case, the right to recover exists only if at least one of the motor vehicles involved is a motor vehicle weighing more than six thousand five hundred pounds unloaded or is a motor vehicle used principally for the transportation of persons or property for hire. However, in the case of occupants of a bus other than operators, owners, and employees of the owner or operator of the bus, an insurer which, pursuant to paragraph one of subsection (a) of section five thousand one hundred three of this article, provides coverage for first party benefits for such occupants under a policy providing first party benefits to the injured person and members of his household for loss arising out of the use or operation of any vehicle of such household, shall have no right to recover the amount of such benefits from the insurer of such bus.

(b) The sole remedy of any insurer or compensation provider to recover on a claim arising pursuant to subsection (a) hereof, shall be the submission of the controversy to mandatory arbitration pursuant to procedures promulgated or approved by the superintendent. Such procedures shall also be utilized to resolve all disputes arising between insurers concerning their responsibility for the payment of first party benefits.

(c) The liability of an insurer imposed by this section shall not affect or diminish its obligations under any policy of bodily injury liability insurance.

§ 5106. Fair claims settlement

(a) Payments of first party benefits and additional first party benefits shall be made as the loss is incurred. Such benefits are overdue if not paid within thirty days after the claimant supplies proof of the fact and amount of loss sustained. If proof is not supplied as to the entire claim, the amount which is supported by proof is overdue if not paid within thirty days after such proof is supplied. All overdue payments shall bear interest at the rate of two percent per month. If a valid claim or portion was overdue, the claimant shall also be entitled to recover his attorney's reasonable fee, for services necessarily performed in connection with securing payment of the overdue claim, subject to limitations promulgated by the superintendent in regulations.

(b) Every insurer shall provide a claimant with the option of submitting any dispute involving the insurer's liability to pay first party benefits, or additional first party benefits, the amount thereof or any other matter which may arise pursuant to subsection (a) of this section to arbitration pursuant to simplified procedures to be promulgated or approved by the superintendent. . . .

(c) An award by an arbitrator shall be binding except where vacated or modified by a master arbitrator in accordance with simplified procedures to be promulgated or approved by the superintendent. The grounds for vacating or modifying an arbitrator's award by a master arbitrator shall not be limited to those grounds for review set forth in article seventy-five of the civil practice law and rules. The award of a master arbitrator shall be binding except for the grounds for review set forth in article seventy-five of the civil practice law and rules, and provided further that where the amount of such master arbitrator's award is five thousand dollars or greater, exclusive of interest and attorney's fees, the insurer or the claimant may institute a court action to adjudicate the dispute de novo.

§ 5107. Coverage for non-resident motorists

(a) Every insurer authorized to transact or transacting business in this state, or controlling or controlled by or under common control by or with such an insurer, which sells a policy providing motor vehicle liability insurance coverage or any similar coverage in any state or Canadian province, shall include in each such policy coverage to satisfy the financial security requirements of article six or eight of the vehicle and traffic law and to provide for the payment of first party benefits pursuant to subsection (a) of section five thousand one hundred three of this article when a motor vehicle covered by such policy is used or operated in this state.

(b) Every policy described in subsection (a) hereof shall be construed as having the coverage required by subsection (a) of section five thousand one hundred three of this article.

§ 5108. Limit on charges by providers of health services

[Charges for health services specified in § 5102(a)(1) are not to exceed charges for those procedures set forth in schedules prepared for workers' compensation injuries. No provider of health services "may demand or request any payment in addition to" the authorized charges.

Insurers are to report "any patterns of overcharging" within 30 days after they learn of them.]

§ 5109. Unauthorized providers of health services

[Establishes procedures for investigating and suspending authorization for payment to health care providers found to be incompetent or engaged in fraudulent practices.]

NOTES AND QUESTIONS

1. *Is it constitutional?* A unanimous court rejected constitutional challenges to the statute in Montgomery v. Daniels, 340 N.E.2d 444 (N.Y.1975). The court observed that all line drawing raises questions of why the line was not drawn somewhere else; the test to be used was whether there is a reasonable connection between the perceived problem and the remedy adopted. Reviewing criticisms of the fault law of automobile accidents, the court found the statute responsive. As for equal protection, the court found all the classifications to have a "reasonable basis."

Finally, the court held that abrogation of any tort claim entailed the abolition of any correlative right to a jury trial; the statute did not replace the jury with another fact finder but instead changed the substantive right. This point had been a problem in 1911 when the court held the then-new workers' compensation law unconstitutional in *Ives v. South Buffalo Ry. Co.*, note 1, p. 843 supra. But the *Montgomery* court observed that "Jurisprudence has marched many strides in the intervening years. Reliance on *Ives* is misplaced."

No-fault legislation has survived constitutional attack in most jurisdictions. See, e.g., Dimond v. District of Columbia, 792 F.2d 179 (D.C.Cir.1986).

2. *Death cases.* The original statute provided that basic economic loss did not cover losses due to death. In 1977, section 5103(a)(4) was added to allow for $2,000 in death benefits in addition to basic economic loss. The drafters were concerned about a possible constitutional problem caused by Article I, Section 16 of the New York Constitution: "The right of action now existing to recover damages for injuries resulting in death, shall never be abrogated; and the amount recoverable shall not be subject to any statutory limitation." The drafters of the statute left death claims out of the statute but allowed recovery for economic loss that occurred before death and added a flat sum for death benefits to cover funeral expenses. The wrongful death action is left intact with the first party insurer subrogated to any tort recovery. Note that section 5102(d) includes death within "serious injury."

3. *First-party benefits—Who is eligible?* Before considering the wisdom of the legislation, we must understand how it works. Consider whether the statute provides coverage in the following situations. (In each assume that the person was hurt in a motor vehicle accident, unless that point is in doubt.)

    a. An inattentive driver crashes into a tree.

  b. An intoxicated driver crashes into a tree.

  c. .A passenger is hurt when the driver of his car, who is intoxicated, drives off the road. May the passenger recover first-party benefits?

4. *What constitutes "use or operation"?* Section 5102(b) defines "first party benefit" in terms of "injury arising out of the use or operation of a motor vehicle." "Use or operation," under insurance department regulations "includes the loading or unloading of such vehicle but does not include conduct within the course of a business of repairing, servicing, or otherwise maintaining motor vehicles, unless the conduct occurs off the business premises." Boundaries always cause litigation. Consider, for example, Walton v. Lumbermens Mutual Casualty Co., 666 N.E.2d 1046 (N.Y.1996). A truck driver was hurt while unloading his truck at a supermarket when the supermarket's lift collapsed. Although the driver may have been "using" the truck at the time of the injury, his injury did not arise "out of the use or operation" of the vehicle. The use must be the "proximate cause of the injury" before the statute applies. The court approved an earlier case denying benefits to a victim hurt when the gas stove she was using in her "mini-motor home" exploded.

5. *First-party benefits—What is recoverable?* Once the question of eligibility is resolved, the next question becomes the amount of benefits that an eligible victim may recover.

  a. What is the relationship between "first party benefits" and "basic economic loss"?

  b. Are any medical or other out-of-pocket expenses excluded from the victim's recovery?

  c. What is the maximum wage loss that a covered person may be paid after losing $4,000 in one month? The gross figure of $4,000 should be reduced by 20%. Since that amount exceeds $2,000, it should be reduced to the $2,000 maximum. (The $2,000 maximum in section 5102(a)(2) was raised from $1,000 in 1991.) See Kurcsics v. Merchants Mutual Insurance Co., 403 N.E.2d 159 (N.Y.1980), which overturned an insurance department regulation that had limited the benefits to 80% of the statutory maximum.

  d. What role do deductibles play in the scheme? Recall sections 5103(c) and (g).

6. *First-party benefits—Special case of motorcycles.* The legislature originally excluded motorcyclists from having to provide coverage for themselves or their riders because of the high cost of such coverage. In 1977, the legislature added "or a motorcycle" to section 5103(a)(1) and added "other than occupants of a motorcycle" to section 5103(a)(2). At the same time the legislature added section 5103(f) providing that motorcycle liability policies must provide for payment of first-party benefits to persons "other than occupants of such motorcycle, or any motor vehicle" for loss arising from the use of the motorcycle.

In Carbone v. Visco, 497 N.Y.S.2d 524 (App.Div.1985), the court ruled that an injured motorcyclist is not entitled to first-party benefits under the statute. Although a motorcyclist is required to maintain liability insurance under the financial security provisions of the Insurance Law, first-party benefits under the policy are provided only to pedestrians.

7. *First-party benefits—Whose insurer pays?* This problem is often phrased as whether the insurance "follows the car or follows the family." Consider which insurer pays if C, who owns a car and has a proper insurance policy:

   a. Drives off the road into a tree.

   b. Is a passenger in a friend's car when it goes into a tree.

   c. Is walking across the street and is run down by Y's car. Does it matter whether Y has insurance?

   d. Is hurt when C's car collides with Y's car. Is section 5105 relevant?

   e. The original version did not mention separate treatment for buses. What is the purpose of the provision in section 5103(a)(1)?

Does it matter whether the insurance follows the car or the family?

8. *What is the role of arbitration?* As the statute and cases indicate, much of the work is handled by arbitrators. Resort to the courts is to be minimized—although when the decision of the master arbitrator (whose role is outlined in section 5106(c) and detailed in regulations) awards at least $5,000, the disgruntled litigant may obtain a trial *de novo.*

Judicial review of the master arbitrator's decision is generally limited to determining whether the decision was arbitrary and capricious and whether it had a rational or plausible basis.

9. *Serious injury—Is a tort action available?*

Before a claim for pain and suffering can be pursued, the trial court must determine whether the plaintiff has established a prima facie case of serious injury. Licari v. Elliott, 441 N.E.2d 1088 (N.Y.1982). Determining what constitutes a "serious injury" under the statute has not been easy.

In three cases decided together, the court considered whether herniated discs are "serious injury" for purposes of the New York statute. In Pommells v. Perez, 830 N.E.2d 278 (N.Y.2005), the unanimous court reviewed the history and philosophy of the no-fault statute, its perception of the growing incidence of claims of fraud in the administration of the statute and congestion in the courts, and the difficulty of deciding which soft-tissue injuries should be treated as "serious injury." The court upheld dismissals in two of the cases. In one, the ground was that there had been a long "gap in treatment" during which plaintiff had sustained other adverse medical events that raised serious doubt about causation. In the second, the court focused on evidence that the problems with the discs had been degenerative before the accident, casting doubt on the causation element. In the third case, the court reinstated the action on the ground that the "gap in treatment" here had been plausibly explained: "a plaintiff need not incur the additional expense of consultation, treatment or therapy, merely to establish the seriousness or causal relation of his injury. Unlike [the first case], plaintiff's cessation of treatment was explained sufficiently to raise an issue of fact and survive summary judgment."

10. *What happens to the uncovered victim?* Several lower court cases have struggled with the question of when, if ever, persons who do not qualify as "covered persons" may bring tort actions. Most commonly, these are uninsured drivers, or members of the family of an uninsured driver, who are hurt in a multi-vehicle collision. In each case, the victim has claimed the right to sue in tort under pre-1973 rules on the ground that the statute should not be read to change the common law more than it specifies—and it is silent on the tort rights of uncovered persons.

Several views are possible, including: tort law remains fully applicable; tort law is totally barred; and uncovered persons may sue in tort only if they sustain "serious injury." The Court of Appeals has yet to provide an authoritative interpretation, despite conflicting lower court opinions.

What about passengers who are also injured? See Millan v. Yan Yee Lau, 420 N.Y.S.2d 529 (App.Term 1979), concluding that the uninsured driver should "at the very least" be limited by the threshold requirement of serious injury in section 5102(d) but the "innocent" passengers in the uninsured vehicle should retain their common law tort action.

In Carbone v. Visco, note 6 supra, the court held that the injured motorcyclist, who was not covered by first-party benefits, "is entitled to pursue his common law remedies in an action against defendants as owner and operator of a motor vehicle involved in the accident. Under these circumstances, he is not required to comply with the 'serious injury' provision of Insurance Law § 5104."

11. *Meshing auto no-fault, workers' compensation, and tort law.* The massive effort to draft no-fault legislation for the motor vehicle was so absorbing and complex that no one seemed to consider the problem of meshing the various systems as they are removed from the operation of tort law. Although section 5102(b)(2) provided that first-party benefits do not include amounts recovered or recoverable under workers' compensation, the statute ignored the work-related motor vehicle accident. The courts were quickly engulfed by this problem.

After some uncertainty, the legislature amended the Workers' Compensation Law to provide that the compensation carrier shall have no lien on the proceeds of any recovery as to benefits it paid "which were in lieu of first-party benefits which another insurer would have otherwise been obligated to pay" under the no-fault law. "The sole remedy" of the compensation carrier is the settlement process contained in section 5105, but only if at least one vehicle involved weighs more than 6,500 pounds unloaded or is a motor vehicle used principally for the transportation of persons or property for hire; except that as to occupants of a bus or school bus (other than operator or employee) a compensation carrier has no right to proceed under section 5105. For an extended discussion of the interplay of these regimes, see Johnson v. Buffalo & Erie County Private Industry Council, 636 N.E.2d 1394 (N.Y.1994), and Kesick v. Ulster County Self Insurance Plan, 665 N.Y.S.2d 454 (App.Div.1997).

12. *Meshing no-fault benefits and uninsured motorist coverage.* When the covered person is the victim of a hit-and-run driver or an identified but uninsured motorist, the covered person's insurance policy is likely to provide for no-fault benefits and for tort damages, if fault can be established, under the uninsured motorist coverage. What happens when, after the insurer has paid no-fault benefits, the victim seeks recovery under the uninsured motorist coverage? Given that the goal of supplemental uninsured motorist coverage is "to give insureds the same level of protection that would have been available to others under the policy if the insureds were the tortfeasors who caused personal injuries," courts—at the request of insurers—have declined to allow victims to double recover. Raffelini v. State Farm Mutual Auto Insurance Co., 878 N.E.2d 583 (N.Y.2007). But the courts have held that to the extent the victim has suffered "serious injury," the tort recovery is for pain and suffering so there is no double recovery. Adams v. Government Employees Insurance Co., 383 N.Y.S.2d 319 (App.Div.1976), and Sinicropi v. State Farm Insurance Co., 391 N.Y.S.2d 444 (App.Div.1977).

13. *First-party pain and suffering?* Traditionally, we have thought about pain and suffering as an adjunct to a negligence action. One of the stumbling blocks to the development of automobile no-fault plans has been the future of pain and suffering. In a thoroughgoing no-fault plan that abolished all tort recovery, would there be any place for pain and suffering?

To the extent that mixed no-fault plans have allowed tort actions for pain and suffering, how much of this is explained by the felt need to preserve the opportunity for injured victims to recover this item of damages? Has that need been perceived in terms of the desirability of the plaintiff obtaining the funds—or because of the sense that, in this civilized form of vengeance, the money must come from the defendant? Some have stressed the role of vengeance in personal injury law—particularly in something as personal as automobile driving. See Ehrenzweig, A Psychoanalysis of Negligence, 47 Nw.U.L.Rev. 855 (1953), and Linden, Faulty No Fault: A Critique of the Ontario Law Reform Commission Report on Motor Vehicle Accident Compensation, 13 Osgoode Hall L.J. 449 (1975). But see Hasson, Blood-Feuds, Writs and Rifles—A Reply to Professor Linden, 14 Osgoode Hall L.J. 445 (1976). Could one also justify retaining pain and suffering for deterrence purposes? Or is the deterrence rationale of lesser importance in the auto injury context?

Despite all these considerations, it is not clear how much of the desire to retain access to the tort action for all, or at least serious, injuries has been based on the assumption that such a step is essential to preserve recovery for pain and suffering. For an extensive discussion of first-party insurance coverage for pain and suffering and of the market for such insurance, see Croley & Hanson, The Nonpecuniary Costs of Accidents: Pain-and-Suffering Damages in Tort Law, 108 Harv.L.Rev. 1785 (1995).

14. *Critical questions about the statute.*

Having worked through much of the detail of the operation of the New York no-fault scheme, consider the following broader questions:

    a.   Why make the first-party benefits compulsory? Why not eliminate the tort action in the smaller cases (or all cases) and allow individuals to decide for themselves whether to obtain insurance?

    b.   Once the decision is made to compel substantial first-party protection, why compel the purchase of liability insurance?

    c.   Is $50,000 an appropriate limit on first-party benefits? Why might a state make the figure $5,000? $500,000? In addition to complaints about the tort system mentioned in the Report, p. 856 supra, some have objected to this aspect of the tort system because it is regressive. See Hasson, Blood-Feuds, Writs and Rifles—A Reply to Professor Linden, supra, suggesting that no-fault systems are less regressive than negligence law: "Under the negligence system both a rich man and a poor man pay the same premium but there is no limit as to how much the rich person can recover under the negligence system." By way of contrast, he noted that as to lost income in no-fault systems, "a rich man would have to pay more than a person with a modest income to obtain adequate protection against future loss of income."

    d.   Should first-party benefits be primary as against private collateral sources such as health and accident insurance? Why not make the statutory benefits primary as against state workers' compensation payments? Is the deductible arrangement sound?

    e.   Is the statute likely to increase accidents?

    f.   If some limitation on tort law is desired, is the statute's approach to that limitation sound?

    g.   Might the goal of eliminating small cases have been achieved by excluding the first $10,000 of pain and suffering from the plaintiff's award?

15. For an extended argument rejecting the analogy between the work accident and the auto accident, see W. Blum & H. Kalven, Jr., Public Law Perspectives on a Private Law Problem—Auto Compensation Plans 25–27 (1965). Their basic point was that the existence of the contractual relationship made the work accident a special case. Why might that be?

16. *No-fault in the states.* As noted earlier, the Massachusetts version of no-fault provided minimal no-fault benefits but did bar some tort actions. As the states began to adopt no-fault statutes in the 1970s, they tended to follow one of two paths. (No state adopted a "pure" no-fault plan that totally abolished tort—as had been proposed in 1968 by some insurers.) About half of the states that did act, adopted what are called "add-on" statutes because they do not change tort law in any way. Instead, they provide for low first-party benefits to help meet medical expenses and lost wages. If the plaintiff does pursue an available tort action, the first-party insurer is entitled to have its payments reimbursed from the tort award.

The other half of the states that acted, adopted what are called "mixed" plans. These plans provide some first-party benefits—in amounts varying from small to large—and also bar some plaintiffs from access to the traditional tort system. The generosity of the first-party benefits is usually commensurate with the difficulty of the tort barrier. Massachusetts, as we have seen, adopted a mixed plan with small benefits and a relatively minor barrier to tort actions. Consider how the Massachusetts plan would be changed if the no-fault benefits were raised from $2,000 to $20,000, and the tort exclusion were raised to $20,000. New York's approach is found only in Michigan, which provides even more generous no-fault benefits than New York and comparable restrictions on the tort action. (If a pedestrian who does not own a car is hit by an uninsured motorist, every no-fault state has some mechanism for providing no-fault benefits to the pedestrian.)

17. *No-fault and property damage.* Our concern has been primarily with the personal injury aspect of no-fault. If that can be handled to the satisfaction of the public, it is unlikely that leaving property damage in the tort system will cause an insoluble problem. Many motor vehicles on the road today are being bought on time payments. Financing companies insist that the vehicle be insured against damage and have comprehensive coverage to protect the lender's interest in the car in case the buyer defaults on the payments. Thus, when property damage occurs it is almost entirely covered by first-party insurance and does not present serious dislocations. The amount of possible damage is readily ascertained and is unlikely to be great. It will be correlated with ability to bear the loss: the most expensive cars are usually owned by those who can most easily bear the loss—with or without insurance. But these people are also most likely to have their own insurance even if it is not required.

As matters now stand, property damage is generally excluded from coverage in no-fault states and tort law remains in effect. These cases are much easier to settle out of court than are personal injury actions—particularly since smaller sums are involved and most of the disputes are between insurance companies.

18. The RAND Institute for Civil Justice conducted a careful examination of the history of automobile no-fault statutes. See J. Anderson, P. Heaton, & S. Carroll, The U.S. Experience with No-Fault Automobile Experience: A Retrospective (2010). The study examines how no-fault legislation has performed over the years. Not well, it turns out, as no-fault failed to stem increasing insurance premiums, indeed contributing to greater increases in automobile insurance premiums than in non no-fault states. The primary reason is higher medical care costs in no-fault states, in terms of both greater utilization and higher prices paid for equivalent services. The authors were unable to determine the extent to which this finding was an artifact of medical care costs being shifted from health insurance to automobile no-fault insurance or truly reflected greater utilization and higher costs.

19. See generally Schwartz, Auto No-Fault and First-Party Insurance: Advantages and Problems, 73 S.Cal.L.Rev. 611 (2000), reviewing auto no-fault at length and concluding that hybrid plans that retain tort are so seriously compromised that proponents of auto no-fault plans should press for a pure version.

For a comprehensive discussion of the failure of no-fault, see N. Engstrom, An Alternative Explanation for No-Fault's Demise, 61 DePaul L.Rev. 303 (2012). Engstrom reviews the history and success (or failure) of auto no-fault at length, concluding that no-fault's demise should be attributed not just to its failure to succeed on the merits in terms of cost and accident prevention, but also to the closing of the "policy window" that encouraged no-fault's adoption and to a more fundamental tension—which Engstrom terms adversarial equilibrium—causing no-fault and tort to converge. According to Engstrom, this convergence produced benefits to the tort system, making it more attractive, and negatives to no-fault schemes, making them less attractive.

D. FOCUSED NO-FAULT SCHEMES

Workers' compensation established a pattern for addressing perceived deficiencies in the common law tort system. Although it has not overridden the legislative impulse to adopt incremental changes such as those discussed at the beginning of this chapter, the workers' compensation approach—blocking out a category of accidental harm for no-fault treatment—has been an often-used strategy for effecting focused tort reform. In this section, we examine the principal areas other than workplace and motor vehicle injuries in which either the federal government or a state has decided to replace or to supplement the tort system with a no-fault scheme. At the same time, we will look at some of the major no-fault proposals that have been suggested but not yet adopted.

In analyzing the focused no-fault schemes discussed below, consider the rationale for developing alternatives to the tort system, the efficacy of the schemes presented, the nature of the trade-offs involved, and the wisdom of piecemeal revisions in the tort area. Are the programs that have been instituted special responses to egregious tort system performance? Could or should similar schemes be adopted more generally? What are the limits of this approach to reform? On these questions, see generally Rabin, Some Reflections on the Process of Tort Reform, 25 San Diego L.Rev. 13 (1988).

The following excerpt describes some of the major no-fault legislation and proposals adopted since 1970.

The Renaissance of Accident Law Plans Revisited

Robert L. Rabin.
64 Maryland Law Review 699, 703–13 (2005).

. . .

[N]onfault legislative reform of traditional tort took on a new character after the mid-1970s. It became narrower in focus and more the product of classic interest group politics (which had been notably absent in the case of much of the consumer/environmental legislation enacted in the immediately preceding years, as well as the auto no-fault movement).

A. Legislative Nonfault Systems: Post-1970

1. *Black Lung Disease Compensation.* . . . The Black Lung Benefits Act provides benefit payments and medical treatment for coal miners totally disabled from black lung disease (pneumoconiosis).[25] A series of events led to the creation of the program. The 1960s witnessed a decline in coal production and coal prices throughout the nation.[26] Unemployment rates among coal mine workers rose significantly. Traditionally in the industry, a welfare and retirement benefits fund had been maintained by the large coal miners' union, United Mine Workers of America (UMWA), and funded through a price-per-coal-tonnage tax paid by mine owners. The fall in revenues and rise in unemployment rendered the fund an inadequate source of benefits. At the same time, a grassroots movement began among miners that pushed black lung disease to the forefront of union issues. The workers' compensation programs of most states did not provide benefits for occupational disease, and despite pressure by these grassroots groups, UMWA failed to get an occupational benefits provision added to the mine workers' contract during labor negotiations. Finally, in 1968, a mine explosion occurred at a large mine site in Farmington, West Virginia, killing 78 miners and bringing national attention to the issue of coal mine safety.

By the end of the 1960s, Congress faced political pressure from a variety of sources to take action on mine safety generally, and more specifically on the provision of black lung benefits. The UMWA, which was itself under strong attack by smaller miners' unions, lobbied for a federal black lung benefits program. At the same time, mine owners fought against any federal action that would put more economic pressure on the already declining coal industry. Additionally, state legal and health professional groups opposed any move to shift workers' compensation away from state control. In the end, the union interest prevailed on the federalism issue, and the Coal Mine Health and Safety

---

[25] 30 U.S.C. §§ 901–945 (2000). This compensation scheme began with the passage of the Federal Coal Mine Health and Safety Act of 1969, Pub. L. No. 91–173, 83 Stat. 742.

[26] Peter S. Barth, The Tragedy of Black Lung: Federal Compensation for Occupational Disease 4 (1987).

Act of 1969 in essence plugged the occupational-disease hole in the state workers' compensation programs, at least for coal miners afflicted with black lung disease.[37]

To receive benefits, a miner (or the miner's dependent survivors) must prove that he suffers from black lung disease, that he is totally disabled from the disease, and that he contracted the disease from coal mining-related employment. Under most circumstances, it is the last employer of the claimant who is responsible for benefits.[39] Compensation under the scheme is scheduled at a percentage of the pay rate for federal employees (GS-2, step 1); for FY 2003, benefits came to $535 per month with graduated increases for dependents. Medical benefits are recoverable in full. Surviving spouses receive benefits on the same monthly schedules as do the miners themselves, though there is a provision that allows beneficiaries to request lump-sum payment.

. . . The design features just sketched out are strikingly similar to the workers' compensation model: scheduled income replacement benefits for a specified, permanently disabling condition; medical expenses recoverable in full; no recovery for intangible loss; periodic payments; and funding by employer contribution.[44] In a perhaps fitting turn, then, the compensation gap created by the coverage limitations of existing state workers' compensation programs—limitations precluding

---

[37] [Barth] at 27–30. The contours of the federal black lung program have changed over time, influenced by lobbying efforts on behalf of the coal miners, and then responsive to concerns about steeply rising costs. See id. at 38–50. Title IV of the 1969 Act created a benefits program for underground coal miners who were totally disabled from black lung disease and for the dependents of coal miners who had died from the disease. Federal Coal Mine Health and Safety Act of 1969, tit. IV, 83 Stat. at 792–93. The 1972 amendments expanded the definition of "total disability" to include those miners unable to obtain gainful employment because of black lung disease. Black Lung Benefits Act of 1972, Pub. L. No. 92–303, § 4(a), 86 Stat. 150, 153–54. These amendments extended benefits to surface miners and to survivors of miners with black lung disease even if the miner had died of another cause. §§ 3(a), 4(b)(2), 86 Stat. at 153–54. The amendments also provided that a negative chest x-ray could not be the sole basis for a denial of benefits and it created a rebuttable presumption of the presence of black lung where the claimant could prove 15 years of underground coal mine employment and total disability due to respiratory or pulmonary impairment. § 4(c), (f), 86 Stat. at 154.

The criteria for benefits were expanded even more by the 1977 amendments. Black Lung Benefits Reform Act of 1977, Pub. L. No. 95–239, 92 Stat. 95 (1978). The definition of "miner" was rewritten to include individuals who work in or around coal mine or coal preparation facilities and who were exposed to coal dust. Id. § 2(b), 92 Stat. at 95. The most recent amendments, the Black Lung Benefits Amendments of 1981, have made eligibility for benefits more difficult. Pub. L. No. 97–119, tit. II, 95 Stat. 1643 (1981). The 1981 amendments overturned some of the provisions passed in 1972, including the rebuttable presumption of eligibility for 15-year coal mine employees. Id. § 202(b)(1), 95 Stat. at 1643. The 1981 law also reinstated the requirement that survivor claimants prove that their spouse's death was caused by black lung disease. § 203(a)(4), 95 Stat. at 1644.

[39] . . . The principal limitation is that the miner must have been employed by the operator for a cumulative period of not less than a year. [ ]

In addition to direct benefit payments, coal mine operators are required to pay an excise tax to support the Black Lung Disability Trust Fund. [ ]. The Fund is used to pay administrative costs and claimant benefits in cases where the liable operator has defaulted on payments or cannot be identified. [ ].

[44] See generally Orin Kramer & Richard Briffault, Workers Compensation: Strengthening the Social Compact (1991).

recovery for occupational disease—came to be filled by federal legislation referenced to the workers' compensation model.

2. *Childhood Vaccine-Related Injury Compensation.* The National Childhood Vaccine Injury Act of 1986[45] was created in response to an upsurge in tort claims. In the early 1980s, several reports were issued estimating the number of children seriously or fatally injured by adverse reactions to vaccines.[47] The number of lawsuits filed against vaccine manufacturers and health care providers increased during this time and a handful of large verdicts were entered.[48] These events led a number of companies to leave the industry.[49] In response to a perceived crisis of vaccine shortages, Congress created a no-fault alternative to tort liability. The goal of the program was to provide compensation for victims of vaccine-related injuries while giving protections to private vaccine manufacturers so they could continue making products deemed essential to the public welfare without a looming threat of massive tort awards.[51]

The Act established a compensation fund that is financed through an excise tax on each dose of vaccine distributed. Under the Act, a person claiming a vaccine-related injury must file a petition for compensation in the United States Court of Federal Claims. A special master evaluates the claim to determine whether it meets the criteria for benefits from the compensation fund. To qualify for compensation the claimant must show: (1) that she has suffered an injury listed on the Vaccine Injury Table; (2) that the vaccine significantly aggravated a pre-existing condition; or (3) that the vaccine caused an injury not listed on the Table.[55] For eligible claimants, the statute covers all actual medical expenses, rehabilitation costs, and lost earning power, based on the average earnings of workers in the nonfarm sector of the economy. Compensation for pain and suffering may also be awarded up to a limit of $250,000. Eligible claimants have the option of rejecting the

---

[45] Pub. L. No. 99–660, tit. III, 100 Stat. 3755 (codified as amended at 42 U.S.C. §§ 300aa–1 to 300aa–34 (2000)).

[47] E.g., Office of Technology Assessment, U.S. Cong., Compensation for Vaccine-Related Injuries: A Technical Memorandum (1980); Am. Med. Ass'n Bd. of Trustees, Report of the Ad Hoc Commission on Vaccine Injury Compensation, 49 Conn. Med. 172 (1985).

[48] See, e.g., Toner v. Lederle Labs., 828 F.2d 510, 511 (9th Cir.1987) (affirming a jury award of $1,131,200 in a negligence claim against a vaccine manufacturer); Johnson v. Am. Cyanamid Co., 718 P.2d 1318, 1320, 1327 (Kan. 1986) (reversing a $10,000,000 jury verdict against a vaccine manufacturer).

[49] Daniel A. Cantor, Striking a Balance Between Product Availability and Product Safety: Lessons from the Vaccine Act, 44 Am. U. L. Rev. 1853, 1858 (1995) (noting that six manufacturers ceased production of vaccines in the mid-1980s out of fear of financial exposure to tort liability).

[51] [ ] For a more detailed treatment of the politics of the enactment of the Act, see Thomas F. Burke, Lawyers, Lawsuits, and Legal Rights: The Battle over Litigation in American Society 142–70 (2002).

[55] [ ] The Injury Table lists certain vaccines with corresponding adverse events and time intervals between the administration of the vaccine and the occurrence of the event. [ ] Where a claimant is asserting an injury not listed on the Vaccine Injury Table, she bears the burden of proving that the vaccine did in fact cause the injury. [ ] For injuries listed on the Table, causation is presumed and need not be proved by the claimant. [ ]

compensation offer and pursuing a tort claim, but it is a seriously constrained tort option.[58] Likewise, those claimants deemed ineligible for compensation are free to seek tort relief.

The Childhood Vaccine Act, and the next-to-be discussed birth-related compensation schemes, introduced a new plot element into the narrative of nonfault compensation: legislative responsiveness to the perception of a public health crisis. On that score, a similar view can be taken of the ill-fated Swine Flu Vaccine Act.[60] How was certainty of financial exposure—the sine qua non of continuing market presence by the key suppliers—to be achieved? In the Childhood Vaccine Act, as earlier, the quest for certainty culminated in an insurance scheme that for all practical purposes banished tort from the playing field and replaced it with responsibility primarily limited to economic loss, tight ceilings on high-end recovery, and funding by flat contributions.

In context, the vaccine plan can be viewed as narrowly focused. Just as neurological birth defect litigation, next discussed, was a relatively small island in the sea of medical malpractice litigation, so too were childhood vaccine cases but a minor contributor to the volume of drug defect litigation. Nonetheless, in what came to be perceived as a crisis atmosphere, the individual rights perspective of tort yielded to a collective, insurance-based model of compensation.

3. *Birth-Related Neurological Injury Compensation.* Beginning in the 1970s, the nation experienced a rise in medical malpractice lawsuits.[61] The upsurge of tort litigation triggered increases in medical malpractice insurance premiums and decreases in insurance availability for practicing physicians. Malpractice claims for birth-related injuries are brought at a relatively high rate, and they often

---

[58] [ ] The Act puts three main constraints on claimants who choose to pursue the tort option. First, in accordance with the Restatement (Second) of Torts, it permits manufacturers to use the provision of an adequate warning as a defense against liability. [ ]; Restatement (Second) of Torts § 402A cmt. k (1965). Second, the Act adopts the "learned intermediary" doctrine, which requires an adequate warning only to the person who administers the vaccine. [ ] Finally, the Act allows a manufacturer's compliance with Federal Food, Drug and Cosmetic Act regulations to shield it against punitive damages. [ ]

[60] National Swine Flu Immunization Program of 1976, Pub. L. No. 94–380, 90 Stat. 1113 (originally codified at 42 U.S.C. § 247b(j)–(*l*) (repealed 1978)). It should be noted that this was a governmental liability replacement scheme, rather than a privately funded no-fault plan. In February of 1976, military servicemen in New Jersey were diagnosed with a strain of flu virus related to swine flu. In re Swine Flu Immunization Prods. Liab. Litig., 533 F. Supp. 567, 571–72 (D. Colo. 1980). Congress enacted the Swine Flu Act with the goal of preventing an epidemic within the U.S. similar to that of 1918–19, which took more than 500,000 American lives. Id. The Act sought to have the entire adult population of the U.S. inoculated by November of 1976. Id. at 571. During the same time period, the country was experiencing a collapse of the commercial liability insurance market for vaccine manufacturers. Id. at 572. Thus, as part of the Act, Congress implemented a vicarious liability provision that replaced tort liability of the manufacturers. The provision created a cause of action against the government for any claims of negligence or wrongful death, but made all damage awards final and left claimants with no alternate cause of action in tort. National Swine Flu Immunization Program, [ ]; see also Swine Flu, 533 F. Supp. at 571.

[61] See Paul C. Weiler, Medical Malpractice on Trial 26–27 (1991).

result in large monetary awards.[63] The high risk of financial exposure led malpractice insurance companies in many states to raise premiums and severely limit their coverage for obstetricians.[64] In two states, Florida and Virginia, legislatures responded to this move by the insurance companies, by enacting no-fault birth-related neurological injury compensation plans.[65] In both states, a compensation fund was created through contributions from participating physicians and hospitals.[66]

The programs provide full compensation for the child's necessary and reasonable medical expenses, including hospital, rehabilitative, residential, special equipment, and custodial care, as well as the costs of filing a claim, including attorney's fees.[67] Under the Virginia plan, families are compensated for the child's lost earnings—assessed from ages eighteen to sixty-five and calculated at fifty percent of the average weekly wage of nonfarm, private sector workers. There is no comparable provision for recovery of unrealized earnings in Florida. In Florida, families may receive a lump-sum pain and suffering award capped at $100,000; Virginia has no provision for recovery of intangible loss.

A 1997 study of the Florida and Virginia schemes found that families have continued to file malpractice lawsuits, even for injuries that could be eligible for no-fault compensation.[70] Although both schemes aspired to make no-fault an exclusive remedy against participating physicians apart from exceptional situations, the Florida statute has been judicially interpreted to leave the tort option open under many circumstances. Indeed, in Florida, roughly half of the claimants studied filed their initial claim in the tort system. The study also found that twenty-seven percent of the families who filed a no-fault claim but were deemed ineligible for compensation then chose to pursue a tort remedy. By contrast, in Virginia, where the option restriction is considerably more stringent, the study found that approximately only fourteen percent of the families initially filed a tort claim. Currently,

---

[63] See Frank A. Sloan et al., The Road from Medical Injury to Claims Resolution: How No-Fault and Tort Differ, 60 Law & Contemp. Probs. 35, 37 (1997); see also Frank Sloan et al., Suing for Medical Malpractice 191–93 (1993).

[64] See, e.g., David J. Nye et al., The Causes of the Medical Malpractice Crisis: An Analysis of Claims Data and Insurance Company Finances, 76 Geo. L.J. 1495, 1495–98 (1988) (discussing the malpractice insurance "crisis" that obstetricians faced in the mid-1980s); Peter H. White, Note, Innovative No-Fault Tort Reform for an Endangered Specialty, 74 Va. L. Rev. 1487, 1488 (1988) (noting that in 1986, Virginia's two largest malpractice insurance carriers refused to write any new policies for obstetricians, and a third carrier adopted a national policy under which it would terminate coverage for all obstetric practices with less than ten doctors).

[65] Florida Birth-Related Neurological Injury Compensation Plan, Fla. Stat. Ann. §§ 766.301–.316 (West 1997 & Supp. 2004); Virginia Birth-Related Neurological Injury Compensation Act, Va. Code Ann. §§ 38.2–5000 to 5021 (Michie 2002).

[66] These contributions are annual flat fees with no provision for experience rating. [ ]; [ ]

[67] [ ]; [ ] Both states reduce state payments by the amount paid by private insurance policies or other government programs. [ ]; [ ]

[70] Sloan et al., supra note 63, at 46.

Florida and Virginia remain the only two states that have such no-fault systems in place. . . .

Like the black lung and vaccine programs, these schemes are designed to remove the key discretionary elements of intangible loss, future wage replacement, and unlimited ceilings on recovery that characterize tort. The birth defect compensation plans also abandon—even more than black lung—any effort to tie financing obligations to risk-creating conduct, relying instead on flat-levy funding. The tradeoffs on the dimensions of risk prevention, spreading, and administrative cost considerations . . . are quite explicitly encoded in the statutory framework.

4. *September 11th Victim Compensation.* Perhaps the most dramatic nonfault scheme enacted since . . . 1970 was a consequence of the greatest trauma to American society in the same period, the events of September 11, 2001. Within two weeks of the terrorist acts, Congress established the September 11th Victim Compensation Fund (the Fund), adopting a no-fault compensation scheme for the personal injury victims and survivors of those who perished.[76] The Fund is unprecedented in a variety of ways that I have spelled out in detail elsewhere.[77] For present purposes, I would simply contrast it to a model that can be gleaned, in rough outline, from the legislative compensation schemes discussed above—noting, at the outset, the most obvious difference: that the Fund was an ex post response to a discrete event rather than an ex ante model for a category of continuing injury victims.[78]

In sharp contrast to the traditional model, the Fund rejects the tradeoff central to the conception of workers' compensation: that in return for benefits available without reference to fault, those eligible under the scheme are limited to recovery of economic loss—with the wage loss component of any such recovery further subject to scheduled limitations based on type of harm and ceilings reflecting notions of horizontal equity. As I have indicated, other no-fault compensation schemes enacted since [1970] adopt the workers' compensation premise—although, in some instances, allowing for relatively modest, fixed-sum pain and suffering. Instead, the Fund was designed to allow recovery of economic loss, defined to include not just medical expenses and loss of present earnings, but "loss of business or employment opportunities"—presumably future lost income—"to the extent recovery for such loss is allowed under applicable State law." Along with this strikingly open-ended, individualized approach to future economic loss,

---

[76] Air Transportation Safety and System Stabilization Act, Pub. L. No. 107–42, tit. IV, § 405(b)(2), 115 Stat. 230, 237 (2001) (reprinted at 49 U.S.C. § 40101 note (Supp. I 2001)).

[77] See Robert L. Rabin, The Quest for Fairness in Compensating Victims of September 11, 49 Clev. St. L. Rev. 573, 574–81 (2001) [hereinafter Quest for Fairness].

[78] . . .

A second critical difference is that the Fund is government financed, rather than enterprise or activity financed, as in the earlier-discussed no-fault schemes. . . .

the Fund provided for non-economic loss recovery, not in the fixed-sum, limited terms found in some no-fault schemes (assuming any non-economic loss is recognized), but with allowance of "losses for physical and emotional pain, suffering, inconvenience, physical impairment, mental anguish, disfigurement, loss of enjoyment of life, loss of society and companionship, loss of consortium (other than loss of domestic service), hedonic damages, injury to reputation, and all other nonpecuniary losses of any kind or nature."[81]

This sweeping provision for non-economic loss—exceeding even the bounds of traditional tort recovery for pain and suffering—was subsequently redefined in fixed-sum terms in the regulations adopted by the Special Master appointed to administer the Fund.[82] The Special Master also established a schedule of "presumed economic loss" that gave sharper definition to recovery for lost income, as well as establishing a presumptive ceiling on recovery—albeit an extraordinarily high one—the ninety-eighth percentile of individual income in the United States in 2000.

The question remains whether the Fund, with its distinctly tortcentric perspective on recovery, as contrasted against the workers' compensation model grounded in social welfare notions of horizontal equity, represents the direction for the future. In my view, there is good reason to think that the Fund model will have a very limited shelf life, and that any future resort to no-fault replacement of tort is likely to reflect the principles first established nearly a century ago in the workers' compensation model.[84] On this score, the Special Master's regulations are particularly revealing. As indicated above, the statutory language adopting an individualized, case-by-case approach to lost income and non-economic loss in claims of survivors—tantamount to the most liberal version of wrongful death recovery schemes in tort—was simply overridden by the Special Master in an effort to reshape the structure of benefits under the Fund in more traditional, categorical terms, through reliance on presumptions, scheduling and capping of damage awards.[85]

Moreover, the hybrid tort/compensation model adopted by Congress for September 11 redress can well be regarded as sui generis. In its rush to judgment, Congress was particularly concerned about the solvency of the airlines—and, in fact, capped the aggregate liability in

---

[81] [ ] In contrast to these tort-type provisions, the Act does have a strong preclusive provision regarding collateral sources. [ ] On the scheme's embrace of certain tort principles and rejection of others, see Rabin, Quest for Fairness, supra note 77, at 576–81.

[82] [ ] The regulations presume non-economic losses of $250,000 for decedents, plus $100,000 for the spouse and each dependent of the deceased. [ ]

[84] See generally Robert L. Rabin, The September 11th Victim Compensation Fund: A Circumscribed Response or an Auspicious Model?, 53 DePaul L. Rev. 769 (2003).

[85] The Special Master's regulations were upheld against a challenge that he had exceeded the authority conferred upon him by the enabling statute. Schneider v. Feinberg, 345 F.3d 135 (2d Cir.2003).

tort for those who chose to opt out of the Fund at the insurance limits of the airlines and other potential defendants. Because there was a general sense that these aggregate claims—including property damage tort claims outside the Fund—might far exceed insurance limits, the tort option could well have been viewed as creating a limited fund for victims that would fall far short of traditional tort recovery. Hence the impulse to build tort-type compensation into the Fund option. In addition, in the immediate aftermath of the tragedy, there clearly was a sense that the victims were stand-ins for all Americans—that they should be viewed as heroes, martyrs, or both—and afforded whatever special recognition could be attached to the extinguishment of their lives.

Note, too, that this special sense of generosity was very quickly exhausted. Efforts to extend Fund-type recoveries retroactively to the surviving families of earlier acts of terrorism that might well have been regarded as similar in character—the Oklahoma City bombing and the earlier bombing at the World Trade Center—were to no avail. A related no-fault fund for smallpox vaccination victims, established with little fanfare after September 11, was designed along traditional lines.[89] And more generally, the state crime victim compensation statutes, which might be regarded as broadly analogous in purpose to any future provision for victims of terrorist-related activity, are far more modestly designed to meet the immediate out-of-pocket needs of eligible claimants.

NOTES AND QUESTIONS

1.   The official report on the work of the September 11th Victim Compensation Fund provides a wealth of data on the performance of the program. See K. Feinberg, et al., Department of Justice, Final Report of the Special Master for the Victim Compensation Fund of 2001 (2004). The Fund distributed just under $6 billion in claims by survivors for 2,880 deceased victims. It distributed slightly more than $1 billion to 2,680 injury victims, bringing the total distributions to over $7 billion. The average award to surviving families was $2.1 million, with a range between $250,000 and $7.1 million. Awards to those suffering personal injury ranged between $500 and $8.6 million. Ninety-seven percent of eligible

---

[89]   Smallpox Emergency Personnel Protection Act of 2003, Pub. L. No. 108–20, 117 Stat. 638 (codified at 42 U.S.C.A. § 239 (Supp. 2004)). The Act provides no-fault benefits to health care workers and other emergency personnel who suffer injury or death after receiving the vaccine. [ ] Claimants are eligible for lost-income reimbursement at a rate of 66–2/3% of their income at the time of the injury (75% when there are dependents). [ ] Lost-income payments are capped at $50,000 annually, and the lifetime lost-income benefit is not to exceed the death-benefit received by police officers and firefighters under the Public Safety Officers' Benefits (PSOB) Program, currently $275,658. [ ]; [ ]. The lifetime-benefit cap does not apply to claimants who suffer "permanent and total disability." § 265(c)(3)(B), [ ] The scheme provides a death benefit for survivors of the decedent in the amount of the PSOB death benefit, less any benefits paid for lost income. § 266(a), 117 Stat. at 643–44. Reasonable medical expenses are also covered. [ ] All benefits are secondary to other public-benefit programs. [ ] There is no provision for non-economic loss.

claimants opted to participate in the Fund, and administrative costs associated with overall program management were 1.2% of total awards. The RAND Institute for Civil Justice also published a report surveying more generally compensation to September 11th victims from private insurance and charitable sources, as well as governmental programs. See L. Dixon & R. Stern, Compensation for Losses from the 9/11 Attacks (2004).

2. Are you persuaded by the author's assertion that the Victim Compensation Fund's "tortcentric" no-fault model is "likely to have a very limited shelf life"? In the event of another massive loss of life from a terrorist attack is it likely that Congress would reject the VCF model? Should it do so? In 2010, Congress enacted the James Zadroga 9/11 Health and Compensation Act of 2010, Pub. L. No. 111–347, 124 Stat. 3623 (2011), providing no-fault compensation to first responders and bystanders whose long-latency toxic exposures had not qualified for redress under the original September 11 Fund.

3. More generally, is there a convincing argument for creating a no-fault scheme for designated categories of victims, such as victims of terrorism (or victims of vaccine-related injuries, or injuries in the workplace), rather than leaving tort as the exclusive avenue of compensation—as it would be for other injury victims? See Rabin, The September 11th Victim Compensation Fund: A Circumscribed Response or an Auspicious Model?, 53 DePaul L.Rev. 769 (2003). For a critical assessment of the Fund, arguing that its implementation undermined the process values of tort, see Hadfield, Framing the Choice between Cash and the Courthouse: Experiences with the 9/11 Victim Compensation Fund, 42 Law & Soc.Rev. 645 (2008).

4. As indicated by the discussion of occupational disease claims under workers' compensation, p. 835 supra, no-fault schemes providing compensation for toxic exposures can raise difficult eligibility issues. See generally Rabin, Some Thoughts on the Efficacy of a Mass Toxics Administrative Compensation Scheme, 52 Md.L.Rev. 951 (1993). Is the problem of creating well-defined boundaries as to what constitutes a "compensable event"—i.e., regarding scope of coverage under a scheme— likely to be surmountable? Experience suggests that even the narrowly focused Vaccine Act, discussed in the preceding article, has been problematic on this score. In 1995, the Department of Health and Human Services promulgated new regulations reducing the number of potentially eligible recipients through narrower definitions of compensable events in the vaccine injury table, despite a 5–4 vote against the revisions by the Advisory Commission on Childhood Vaccines and the protests of parents' groups. Through July 1, 2015, a total of 14,000 petitions had been adjudicated, with over $3.18 billion awarded for damages and attorney's fees. Out of all the claims filed, however, only 4150 were actually compensated, meaning that more than 70% of all claims filed by petitioners had been dismissed. (These figures do not include the autism claims discussed just below.) For current performance data, see Health Resources and Services Administration, U.S. Dep't of HHS, National Vaccine Injury

Compensation Program Statistics Report, available at http://www.hrsa. gov/vaccinecompensation/statisticsreport.pdf.

Illustrating the complicated eligibility issue explained in this note is a trio of high profile Childhood Vaccine Act cases. For several years, claims that childhood vaccines, especially those containing mercury in the preservative thimerosal, cause autism have been accumulating. Three test cases addressed the issue of whether in children with a genetic predisposition, a combination of thimerosal-containing vaccines and the MMR vaccine could cause autism. In three separate cases, three special masters (who serve as the equivalent of trial judges) wrote lengthy comprehensive opinions explaining why the plaintiff's evidence was insufficient to establish causation. Snyder ex rel. Snyder v. Secretary of Dept. of HHS, 2009 WL 332044 (Fed. Cl.), rev. denied, 88 Fed.Cl. 706 (Fed. Cl. 2009); Cedillo v. Secretary of Dept. of HHS, 2009 WL 331968 (Fed. Cl.), rev. denied, 89 Fed.Cl. 158 (Fed. Cl. 2009); Hazlehurst v. Secretary of Dept. of HHS, 2009 WL 332306 (Fed. Cl. 2009), aff'd, 604 F.3d 1343 (Fed. Cir.2010). Three additional cases decided in 2010 put an additional nail in the coffin of claims that thimerosal is responsible for autism. These cases, unlike the earlier trio of cases, addressed the more general question of whether thimerosal employed in any vaccine caused autism. Once again, three special masters, writing separately, found that plaintiffs' evidence was insufficient to meet the causal standard in the Vaccine Act. Mead ex rel. Mead v. Secretary of Dept. of HHS, 2010 WL 892248 (Fed. Cl. 2010); Dwyer ex rel. Dwyer v. Secretary of Dept. of HHS, 2010 WL 892250 (Fed. Cl. 2010); King ex rel. King v. Secretary of Dept. of HHS, 2010 WL 892296 (Fed. Cl. 2010).

An extensive analysis of largely untapped material concerning the Vaccine Court's performance over the past three decades concludes that this specialized tribunal has largely failed to expedite adjudications and rationalize compensation decisions. See N. Engstrom, A Dose of Reality for Specialized Courts: Lessons from the VICP, 163 U.Pa.L.Rev. 1631 (2015)(also discussing implications of these findings for proposals to move medical malpractice claims from the tort system into specialized "health courts").

Federal no-fault programs like the Vaccine Injury Compensation Program (VICP) raise issues of preemption. In 2011, the Supreme Court decided in Bruesewitz v. Wyeth LLC, 562 U.S. 223 (2011), that the National Childhood Vaccine Injury Act (NCVIA) preempted design defect vaccine-related tort claims under state law. The NCVIA specifically preempts manufacturing and warning defect claims only when the vaccine was properly prepared and accompanied by proper directions and warnings (i.e., if a plaintiff can show negligent preparation or warning, she can still sue in tort). But the same provision says nothing about design defects. The Court relied on absence of language regarding design defects in this provision, along with the structure of the Act, to determine that design defect claims were impliedly preempted.

5. *Liability of nuclear power operators.* Congress imposed a tort/no-fault hybrid on the operators of nuclear power plants with the Price-

Anderson Act, Pub.L. No. 85–256, 71 Stat. 576 (1957)(codified at 42 U.S.C. § 2210). The Act was an early response to perceived deficiencies of the common law tort model in dealing with potential mass tort liability. Its express intent was to encourage investment in nuclear energy research and operations by a private sector daunted by the prospect of multimillion-dollar claims and a constrained insurance market.

The Act imposes a set of statutory constraints on possible catastrophic tort liability in the event of a nuclear accident, with damages paid out of a common fund. The system is financed through a combination of private insurance and mandatory contributions, which in effect set the limit on total liability for any nuclear incident. In accordance with amendments to the Act, each nuclear licensee is required to purchase roughly $375 million of private liability insurance. In addition, each licensee must contribute $96 million to a common compensation fund in the event of a nuclear accident at any plant. The liability limit of the fund, with over 100 plants in operation, is approximately $12.6 billion at present.

The Price-Anderson funding scheme closely resembles a no-fault model to the extent that it relies substantially on a pooling mechanism to compensate aggrieved parties, thus de-emphasizing the importance of individual responsibility. This pooling mechanism, in conjunction with the lack of an experience or risk-rating provision in the statute, blunts the incentives for optimal safety investment by individual firms. But at the same time the non-tort sanctions on suboptimal safety that would result from a serious nuclear accident, including the destruction of the facility itself, are very powerful (and a stringent regulatory scheme addresses the safety aspects of operating and maintaining a nuclear power plant).

Price-Anderson maintains some of the distinctive flavor of tort law with respect to establishing liability. All claims are consolidated in federal court. In the event of an "extraordinary nuclear occurrence," the Act creates strict liability for licensees and abrogates the defense of contributory negligence. The claims process retains a two-party character, with each individual claimant bearing the burden of establishing causation and particularizing proof of economic and non-economic harm. In light of the time and expense required to establish those elements, the Price-Anderson approach, in practice, might prove to be almost as inefficient as the standard common law tort approach.

6.   The Public Readiness and Emergency Preparedness Act, P.L. 109–148 was enacted as part of the appropriation bill for the Department of Defense for 2006. It includes immunity from lawsuits under state and federal law for manufacturers and distributors of pandemic and epidemic products (including vaccines), in the event that the Health and Human Services Department (HHS) secretary declares a public health emergency as a result of a disease or other health condition. The only exception to this immunity is for "willful misconduct."

The legislation also provides a process for establishing an emergency compensation fund to compensate individuals whose injuries or death are directly caused by the administration or use of a product covered by an emergency declaration. But it does not provide any specific funding for this eventuality. For an assessment of this legislation's ability to accomplish its goals while providing compensation to victims, see L. Mayer, Note, Immunity for Immunizations: Tort Liability, Biodefense, and Bioshield II, 59 Stan.L.Rev. 1753 (2007).

7. The Oil Pollution Act, P.L. 101–380, was enacted in 1990 to mitigate civil liability from oil spills off the coast of the United States, among other purposes. The Act limits liability from oil spills in tank vessels to $10 million; in offshore facilities (except deepwater ports) to $75 million; and in onshore facilities and deepwater ports to $350 million. These limits do not apply to any costs of removal, for which the responsible party is fully liable. Further, these limits do not apply where the incident was caused by "gross negligence or willful misconduct of, or the violation of an applicable Federal safety, construction, or operating regulation by the responsible party." The liability limitations of the act are codified in 33 U.S.C.A. § 2704.

The Oil Pollution Act was the subject of much debate following the oil spill at the Deepwater Horizon well in the Gulf of Mexico in April 2010. In 2014, the District Court for the Eastern District of Louisiana, where the claims related to the spill were centralized through multi-district litigation, held that OPA liability limits would not apply because the responsible party violated a federal safety regulation and this violation was the proximate cause of the accident. See In re Oil Spill by Oil Rig Deepwater Horizon in Gulf of Mexico on April 20, 2010, 21 F.Supp.3d 657 (E.D.La.2014).

For consideration of the various claims and damages arising from the Deepwater Horizon spill, see R. Force, M. Davies, & J. Force, Deepwater Horizon: Removal Costs, Civil Damages, Crimes, Civil Penalties, and State Remedies in Oil Spill Cases, 85 Tul.L.Rev. 889 (2011).

In another twist on ad hoc compensation schemes, British Petroleum (BP), at the urging of the U.S. Justice Department, hired Kenneth Feinberg to administer a $20 billion compensation fund to handle claims from the spill. The fund had mixed success. See Campbell Robertson & John Schwartz, *How a Gulf Settlement that BP Once Hailed Became Its Target*, N.Y. Times, April 26, 2014.

8. *Note on liability of international air carriers.* The Warsaw Convention, Convention for the Unification of Certain Rules Relating to International Transportation by Air, Oct. 12, 1929, 49 Stat. 3000, T.S. No. 876 (1934), note following 49 U.S.C. § 1502, is a multilateral treaty that regulates the liability of international air carriers. The Convention was drafted in 1929 and the United States became a signatory in 1934. Its terms apply to the international carriage of persons, luggage, or goods, by aircraft. The Supreme Court has noted that the Convention's principal purpose was to provide uniform liability limitations and foster the growth of commercial aviation. Trans World Airlines, Inc. v. Franklin Mint Corp., 466 U.S. 243, 256 (1984).

The Convention establishes a system of strict liability for personal injuries and cargo losses that occur on international flights and limits the damages that passengers may recover. As originally drafted, the Convention limited recovery for loss of life or injury to $8,300. The maximum recovery amount was subsequently increased to $75,000. In 1999, the Convention was replaced by the Montreal Convention, ratified by the U.S. Senate in 2003, which sets a maximum recovery determined in accordance with a blend of several currencies equivalent to about $155,000 in U.S. dollars, as of 2010. For a general description of the replacement convention, see Moore, The New Montreal Convention, Major Changes in International Air Law: An End to the Warsaw Convention, 9 Tul. J.Int'l & Comp.Law 223 (2001). The Warsaw Convention's limitations on damages were not applicable in cases of willful misconduct by an international air carrier or its employees. Importantly, the Montreal Convention limits on damages do not apply unless the airline proves that it was not negligent. Because of this limitation, the awards for the victims of a negligent plane crash can substantially differ, depending on which country's law applies to their claims. "The national approaches vary widely. Some countries do not allow compensation for wrongful-death cases. Courts in the United States, on the other hand, are generally highly favorable to families." Mouawad & Clark, Germanwings Crash Settlements are Likely to Vary by Passenger Nationality, N.Y.Times, March 29, 2015, at A9. According to one expert, "settlements in air disasters average $4.5 million for an American case, $1.6 million for a British case, $1.4 million for a Spanish case, and $1.3 million for a German case." Id.

Punitive damages are unavailable, even in the case of willful misconduct under both the Warsaw and Montreal Conventions. In re Korean Air Lines Disaster, 932 F.2d 1475 (D.C.Cir.), cert. denied, 502 U.S. 994 (1991); In re Air Disaster at Lockerbie, Scotland, 928 F.2d 1267 (2d Cir.), cert. denied, 502 U.S. 920 (1991). Is there anything distinctive about international travel that would justify strict liability? A damages cap?

An "accident" must take place to trigger liability under the Warsaw Convention.* The Supreme Court initially took a restrictive view of that requirement. In Air France v. Saks, 470 U.S. 392 (1985), a passenger suffered permanent deafness allegedly caused by negligent maintenance and operation of the aircraft's pressurization system. Emphasizing the need for an unusual or unexpected event external to the passenger, as opposed to an irregularity in the passenger's internal reaction to the normal operation of the aircraft, the Court held that her injury was not the result of an accident. The Supreme Court revisited the accident requirement in Olympic Airways v. Husain, 540 U.S. 644 (2004). There, the court held that a flight attendant's refusal three times to move an asthma sufferer away from the plane's smoking section was "unexpected and unusual" conduct and constituted an accident. The Court upheld the aircraft's liability for the heart attack the passenger suffered mid-flight. But in Caman v. Continental Airlines, Inc., 455 F.3d 1087 (9th Cir.2006), the court

---

* The Supreme Court has held that liability of carriers to passengers on international flights is limited to the remedies under the Warsaw Convention. No alternative remedies under, for example, state law are available even if the injury does not result from an accident or a non-compensable personal injury is suffered. El Al Israel Airlines v. Tseng, 525 U.S. 155 (1999).

suggested a further refinement, holding that an airline passenger's suffering deep vein thrombosis on a flight did not constitute an "accident" for purposes of the Act. Plaintiff claimed the airline was negligent for failing to warn of the danger. The court reasoned that the airline's failure to warn was an omission rather than an act of commission and therefore not an "event," as required by *Air France* for an accident to exist. The Montreal Convention states the expectation that it will be interpreted consistently with the Warsaw Convention with regard to the accident requirement and the "bodily injury" provision addressed in the next paragraph.

In Eastern Airlines, Inc. v. Floyd, 499 U.S. 530 (1991), the Supreme Court determined that the Convention does not permit recovery for mental or psychic injuries unaccompanied by physical injury or physical manifestation of injury. For a review of case law under the Warsaw Convention addressing the issue of recovery of psychological damages that are accompanied by some physical harm, see Chester, The Aftermath of the Airplane Accident: Recovery of Damages for Psychological Injuries Accompanied by Physical Injuries under the Warsaw Convention, 84 Marq.L.Rev. 227 (2000).

9. *Health care and no-fault.* In 1973, Professors Havighurst and Tancredi presented a model for applying no-fault insurance to medical malpractice claims. "Medical Adversity Insurance"—A No-Fault Approach to Medical Malpractice and Quality Assurance, 51 Milbank Memorial Fund Q. 125, reprinted in 1974 Ins.L.J. 69. That model was expanded two years later in Havighurst, "Medical Adversity Insurance"—Has Its Time Come?, 1975 Duke L.J. 1233. Medical Adversity Insurance (MAI) was designed to reduce the overall administrative cost of malpractice litigation by removing certain injuries from the fault system.

MAI policies would specify "adverse outcomes," or "compensable events," for which a patient could recover without proof of fault. The lists would be created by medical experts who, on the basis of their experience, would identify adverse results that were probably avoidable: "An event would be added to the list if medical opinion indicated that the event was usually or frequently—though by no means invariably—avoidable under good-quality medical care and that the frequency of the event could be expected to diminish if providers' attention were directed more strongly to the quality of the outcomes being achieved."

In order to recover under the MAI system a patient would have to show that he or she had suffered a designated compensable event (DCE). Negligence would be irrelevant and, because the listed adverse outcomes would be highly specific, cause would not be a problem. The two most complex malpractice issues would thus be avoided. Case-by-case inquiries would ask only whether an adverse outcome had occurred, and what damages had resulted. The damages allowed under the system would depend on the policies issued, but Professor Havighurst suggested these would include at least all medical expenses, and wage losses subject to weekly limits.

The MAI scheme was not designed to replace the present fault system, but to remove a large number of cases from it. Not all victims of malpractice would suffer compensable events on MAI lists. If an unlisted event occurred, the patient would have to resort to the fault system.

Is the causation problem in medical cases manageable? Does a medical no-fault proposal based on the compensable event approach overcome the causation difficulties? Does it raise other problems?

For a comprehensive analysis of the pros and cons of medical no-fault, see P. Weiler, Medical Malpractice on Trial 132–58 (1991). Professor Weiler reviewed the case for no-fault from a variety of perspectives—compensation, administration, and prevention—and concluded that such a system, if it offered broad coverage of serious harms, has great appeal when compared to the present tort approach. Nonetheless, the problems of coverage/causation are sufficiently troublesome to have led him to propose as "an intermediate step" an elective no-fault system (for further discussion of this concept, see note 10 infra).

Assuming, however, that the present system were to be retained, Weiler offered another proposal, organizational liability. As he stated it:

> The technique I favor is to make the hospital or other health care organization primarily liable for all *accidental* (negligent, not intentional) injuries inflicted on patients due to malpractice committed by anyone affiliated with the institution, whether or not the actor is technically an employee of the hospital. In other words, for purposes of personal injury policy, the relationship of hospital and affiliated physicians should be deemed to be the functional equivalent of the relationship of an HMO to its staff physicians. In the HMO context, individual obstetricians or surgeons are not expected personally to pay the large malpractice premium required for their medical specialties, which are much riskier than those of the pediatrician or internist. Likewise, we do not expect that the pilots or mechanics working for an airline company should personally pay the substantial premiums that would be required for insurance against instances of careless behavior in these jobs, slipups that are far riskier than those which might be committed by a flight attendant or passenger agent working for the same airline. Instead, under this proposal each doctor in every specialty is treated as a member of a single firm engaged in the enterprise of health care, with the organization responsible for collecting revenues from the patients who receive the benefits of its services and for purchasing the insurance required to protect against the risk of serious injuries that occur. The analogy, again, is to pilots or mechanics, who are assumed as a matter of course to be parts of the larger enterprise of air travel, with the firm assuming immediate responsibility for injuries caused by the mistakes of its workers, and paying for those costs through revenues collected from all passengers on its flights.

Is the analogy to airline workers apt? From a deterrence perspective, would you expect organizational liability to be more or less effective than the existing tort system? Does it raise fairness concerns between large and small hospitals? High and low risk practitioners? For hospitals held liable for independent contractor physicians over which the hospital has limited control? For a summary version of Weiler's work in the area, which grew out of the Harvard Medical Practice Study, Patients, Doctors and Lawyers: Medical Injury, Malpractice Litigation and Patient Compensation in New York (1990), see Weiler, The Case for No-Fault Medical Liability, 52 Md.L.Rev. 908 (1993).

Later studies by the Harvard Medical Practice group included a comparison of the Swedish approach to compensation of medical injuries— an elective no-fault system—with empirical data on the costs of medical malpractice in Utah and Colorado, two states that were contemplating implementation of a medical no-fault system; see Studdert, et al., Can the United States Afford a "No-Fault" System of Compensation for Medical Injury?, 60 Law & Contemp.Probs. 1 (1997); see also Studdert, Brennan & Thomas, Beyond Dead Reckoning: Measures of Medical Injury Burden, Malpractice Litigation, and Alternative Compensation Models from Utah and Colorado, 33 Ind.L.Rev. 1643 (2000)(replicating the earlier Harvard study (which had been based on New York data) in Utah and Colorado, and concluding, once again, that "the link between no-fault and error reduction is quite compelling," and that "eliminating the specter of litigation would also remove the principal barrier to the free flow of information about medical errors"). For further analysis of the data from these studies, see Mello & Brennan, Deterrence of Medical Errors: Theory and Evidence for Malpractice Reform, 80 Tex.L.Rev. 1595 (2002). For discussion of health courts and no-fault liability, see Barringer, Studdert, Kachalia & Mello, Administrative Compensation of Medical Injuries: A Hardy Perennial Blooms Again, 33 J.Health Politics, Pol'y & L. 725 (2008). A critical view of the prospects for medical malpractice reform through specialized courts and no-fault, through the lens of the Vaccine Injury Compensation Program, is offered in N. Engstrom, A Dose of Reality for Specialized Courts: Lessons from the VICP, 163 U.Pa.L.Rev. 1631 (2015).

10. *Neo no-fault and early offers.* Professor Jeffrey O'Connell was a leading advocate of a wide range of privately negotiated no-fault alternatives to the tort system for many years, in some instances backed by legislatively imposed conditions. See J. O'Connell & C. Kelly, The Blame Game: Injuries, Insurance and Injustice (1986), in which he and a co-author advocate adoption of a universal "neo no-fault" scheme in which tort defendants would have the option within 180 days of offering a claimant periodic payment of the claimant's net economic losses. The claimant would be required to accept such an offer once tendered. For an illustration of one of his tailored schemes, see O'Connell, A Neo No-Fault Contract in Lieu of Tort: Pre-accident Guarantees of Post-accident Settlement Offers, 73 Cal.L.Rev. 898 (1985)(describing the widely adopted Scholastic Lifetime Medical and Disability Policy, which provides for no-fault settlement offers for economic loss in cases of catastrophic injury to high school athletes).

O'Connell discusses his approach to the products liability area in O'Connell, Balanced Proposals for Product Liability Reform, 48 Ohio St.L.J. 317 (1987); see also J. O'Connell & C. Robinette, A Recipe for Balanced Tort Reform: Early Offers with Swift Settlements (2008).

The proposal is spelled out in the context of medical malpractice claims in Robinette, The Synergy of Early Offers and Medical Explanations/Apologies, 103 Nw.U.L.Rev. 2007 (2009):

> The early offers proposal functions quite simply. Under it, a medical malpractice defendant has the option to offer an injured claimant within a defined statutory period (for example, within 180 days of a claim) a settlement of periodic payments. In total, these payments would cover the claimant's net wage loss and medical expenses (including rehabilitation), plus a reasonable attorney's fee—presumptively 10% of the recovery, an amount that reflects the reduced legal load created by the shortened process. Pain and suffering is not included. The early offer option is totally voluntary—defendants are never forced to make an early offer, and, if no offer is made, traditional common-law principles apply to both liability and damages. If, however, the defendant does make an early offer, that offer triggers strong incentives for the claimant: a claimant who declines an early offer will be subject to a higher burden of proof (either "clear and convincing" or even "beyond a reasonable doubt"), and the defendant will be held to a higher standard of misconduct ("gross negligence"), at trial.

What are the pros and cons of such an approach? For discussion of Professor O'Connell's singular role in initiating no-fault proposals, see Rabin, Jeffrey O'Connell and the Compensation Principle in Accident Law: Institutional and Intellectual Perspectives, 6 J. Tort Law 3 (2013).

E. COMPREHENSIVE NO-FAULT AND BEYOND

As we have seen, the academic and political efforts in this country have been addressed primarily to piecemeal revision of tort law. Conceding that limited reform efforts may be politically expedient, however, it does not necessarily follow that considerations of policy, logic, or fairness favor piecemeal revision over system-wide change. At the outset of the no-fault movement, Jeremiah Smith argued this point in his landmark article, Sequel to Workmen's Compensation, 27 Harv.L.Rev. 235 (1913):

> If the fundamental general principle of the modern common law of torts (that fault is requisite to liability) is intrinsically right or expedient, is there sufficient reason why the legislature should make the workmen's case an exception to this general principle? On the other hand, if this statutory rule as to workmen is intrinsically just or expedient, is there sufficient reason for refusing to make this statutory rule the

test of the right of recovery on the part of persons other than workmen when they suffer hurt without the fault of either party?

In this section, we focus on comprehensive systems of compensation. We begin by examining the New Zealand experience. An interesting combination of factors led that country to assume a pioneering role in replacing its tort system with a comprehensive no-fault scheme covering all types of accidental injuries.

The New Zealand experience. In 1967, a Royal Commission headed by Justice Woodhouse, appointed to consider workers' compensation, concluded that employment injuries could not be separated from other injuries. It proposed abolishing the common law of accidental injuries and replacing it with a unified scheme based on five basic propositions: that all citizens must be protected against income loss and permanent disability; compensation should be related to the nature of the injury and not its cause; the scheme must stress physical and vocational recovery along with compensation; benefits should be paid for the duration of the incapacity; and the plan must be expeditious.

It should be stressed that the proposal of the Royal Commission was not a response to any public outcry against the existing tort system. No group, whether victims, physicians, manufacturers, motorists, or insurers had complained about the insurance premiums they were paying, the way their tort claims were being resolved in the courts, or any similar grievance. Rather, the Royal Commission perceived the common law to be a "lottery" in which some claimants received awards while others had to subsist on social welfare payments. There was also too little conscious attention to safety. The Royal Commission concluded that a new approach was needed. "If the scheme can be said to have a single purpose it is 24-hour insurance for every member of the work force, and for the housewives who sustain them." The emphasis was to be on accident prevention and rehabilitation, with compensation a third consideration.

The final version of the Accident Compensation Act became effective in 1974. Although the Act was amended several times, it remained essentially the same until the passage of the Accident Rehabilitation and Compensation Act 1992, which substantially altered the original program. It may help in considering the discussion that follows to realize that New Zealand has a population of about three million persons and is about the size of Oregon or Colorado. For a comparison of demographic and accident data, see Franklin, Personal Injury Accidents in New Zealand and the United States: Some Striking Similarities, 27 Stan.L.Rev. 653 (1975).

The original Act abolished virtually all common law tort actions. In their place, the program provided for compensation to individuals who experienced a "personal injury by accident." This phrase was interpreted to include occupational disease and illness but to exclude ordinary sickness. Courts also found it difficult to distinguish between "medical, surgical, dental or first aid misadventure," which was covered by the statute, and "damage to the body or mind caused exclusively by disease, infection, or the aging process," which was excluded by the statute.

Compensation was and still is provided to accident victims out of one of three compensation schemes. Workers are protected against accidental injury under the earners' scheme, receiving 80% of lost earnings for the duration of a disability as well as all reasonable medical and rehabilitation expenses. Similar protection is afforded them under the scheme during off-hours. Those injured in motor vehicle accidents—other than earners who are protected under the earners' scheme—receive compensation for medical costs and lost earning capacity out of a fund supported by flat levies on motor vehicle owners. Non-workers, such as the elderly, homemakers, children and students, who are injured in accidents not involving motor vehicles, are compensated for medical costs out of the general treasury. In addition to payments for lost earnings and medical costs, the Act also used to provide for two different types of lump sum payments. The first provided for payments of up to $17,000 NZ* (as of 1991) for loss of bodily part or function and the second provided for a payment of up to $10,000 NZ for pain and suffering, disfigurement and the loss of capacity for enjoying life if the loss was sufficiently serious in nature and duration.

The 1992 revisions significantly changed some of the Act's most important provisions. First, the 1992 revisions limited the types of injuries covered under the Act by restricting the definition of accident and by changing the phrase "personal injury by accident" to "personal injury by an accident" such that a specific, identifiable accident must be a cause of the injury in order for it to be compensable. Therefore, coverage no longer exists when an injury cannot be attributed to any identifiable external event. Second, the amendments to the Act excluded coverage for mental distress not associated with physical injury to the person seeking compensation. Third, the revisions sharply changed the compensation system for "medical misadventure." Although the original Act provided for compensation for medical misadventures without defining the operative phrase, the revised Act included a comprehensive definition of the phrase which required the injured party to prove something approaching negligence before he or she could receive compensation. Finally, the 1992 revisions eliminated the lump sum payments and replaced them with a much more modest "independence allowance" of up to $40 NZ per week.

In addition to these changes in the coverage and benefit provisions of the Act, the 1992 revisions significantly changed the Act's funding mechanisms. While employers continued to pay for employee injuries

---

* $11,390 in U.S. currency as of 2015.

sustained on the job, employee injuries that occurred off the job were compensated through insurance paid for by employees themselves. Flat levies on automobile owners continued to make up a large portion of the fund used to compensate motor vehicle injuries, but the 1992 revisions also provided for a $0.02/liter gasoline tax aimed at promoting a greater "user-pays" element within the Act. Finally, the 1992 revisions created a new account called the Medical Misadventure Account, funded through premiums paid by health professionals, for the purpose of compensating victims of medical misadventures. This change marked the first time since the passage of the Act that a risk-creating class was directly held accountable to persons injured by the class. All of these changes arguably marked a distinct philosophical departure from the purposes of the original Act.

What are your reactions to the New Zealand approach? Do obvious practical, philosophical, or other problems occur to you? For a highly critical response to the 1992 amendments, arguing that the plan lost much of the social insurance philosophy that once informed it, see Palmer, The Design of Compensation Systems: Tort Principles Rule, O.K.?, 29 Val.L.Rev. 1115 (1995). For a detailed description and critique of the 1992 revisions, see Miller, An Analysis and Critique of the 1992 Changes to New Zealand's Accident Compensation Scheme, 52 Md.L.Rev. 1070 (1993).

With the passage of the Accident Insurance Act 1998, New Zealand experimented with partial privatization of the system in the area of workers' compensation. It reversed that course only two years later with the Accident Insurance (Transitional Provisions) Act 2000. It retreated further back toward the principles espoused by the original Woodhouse Commission with the enactment of the Injury Prevention, Rehabilitation and Compensation Act 2001. The act gives independent weight to restoring the victim's health, independence, and labor force participation, and so it allows for greater expenditure on rehabilitation than a scheme that focuses solely on monetary outcomes. As amended in 2005, the Act also reincorporates the option of lump-sum payouts and removes the requirement that the injured party prove something like negligence in order to receive compensation for a medical misadventure. For a discussion of some of these permutations, see Duncan, Advancing in Employment: The Way Forward for Vocational Rehabilitation, 35 Vict.U. Wellington L.Rev. 801 (2004); Todd, Privatization of Accident Compensation: Policy and Politics in New Zealand, 39 Washburn L.J. 404 (2000).

The most extended discussion of the entire philosophy of the New Zealand development and its passage through the political process, is to be found in G. Palmer, Compensation for Incapacity: A Study of Law and Social Change in New Zealand and Australia (1979). As the title suggests, Australia seriously considered the New Zealand development, but lost interest after a change of national government. For a discussion of New Zealand's system with a particular focus on medical treatment injuries and emotional harm claims, see Schuck, Tort Reform, Kiwi-Style, 27 Yale L. & Pol'y Rev. 187 (2008).

Over the years, there was much discussion about adding sickness coverage to the existing act. An early chairman of the ACC suggested that the different treatment was an "anomaly" caused by the influence of the common law. Removing the anomaly would be "a matter of political philosophy and of economics. Political philosophy will determine the extent to which a country will devote a portion of its resources to the care of the disabled. Economics will dictate how far that philosophy can reasonably be applied." Might there be reasons for compensating disability from accident differently from disability due to sickness? The subject is discussed in P. Cane, Atiyah's Accidents, Compensation and the Law (8th ed.2013), Chapter 1.

Social insurance proposals. For a detailed proposal that would go beyond New Zealand and compensate for all disability, whether accident-related or not, see S. Sugarman, Doing Away with Personal Injury Law (1989). As the title suggests, Sugarman would eliminate personal injury law virtually across-the-board, with the sole exception of a limited punitive damage action for intentional torts. His book surveyed the literature on the workings of tort law and concluded that the system was a substantial failure from both the perspectives of compensation and deterrence.

Sugarman's comprehensive strategy would extend employment-based income replacement and health benefits to covered beneficiaries, whatever the source of their disability, in cases involving short-term needs (six months or less). In cases involving longer-term income replacement, as well as most cases of disability experienced by the various categories of non-employed persons, coverage would be provided by an expanded Social Security system. The tort system would be abandoned, along with pain and suffering damages, although in serious cases awards for pain and suffering on the original New Zealand model might be permitted. Accident prevention strategies would be left to the regulatory system. Anticipating the argument that his comprehensive plan was politically infeasible, Sugarman also outlined a first-step proposal that would concentrate on replacing the tort system in short-term injury cases and on limiting its applicability in longer-term cases through elimination of the collateral source rule and restrictions on pain and suffering recovery.

Does this outline of Sugarman's proposal suggest that the New Zealand approach may be, in fact, too modest in its coverage? See also P. Atiyah, The Damages Lottery (1997). Social insurance schemes currently in operation, including the Social Security Disability program, are discussed in Abraham & Liebman, Private Insurance, Social Insurance, and Tort Reform: Toward a New Vision of Compensation for Illness and Injury, 93 Colum.L.Rev. 75 (1993).

For an earlier effort to combine the benefits of social insurance for accidents and the advantages of internalized costs, see Franklin, *Replacing the Negligence Lottery: Compensation and Selective Reimbursement*, 53 Va.L.Rev. 774 (1967). This essay views the fault system as a lottery. Persons similarly injured may recover, if anything, very different amounts depending on the defendant's behavior and the origin of the injury. Persons committing the same wrongful act may be subject to very different liabilities depending upon the extent of the injury caused, if any, and to whom. Briefly, the goal was to separate the functions of compensation and deterrence, by having the former achieved through a social insurance fund and the latter through uninsurable fines and enterprise reimbursements of the fund for injury-creating activity. A somewhat similar proposal is offered in Pierce, *Encouraging Safety: The Limits of Tort Law and Government Regulation*, 33 Vand.L.Rev. 1281 (1980).

Professors Blum and Kalven argue that in large part "corrective justice is concerned not with deterring the wrongdoer, but with satisfying the victim's feeling of indignation. If the victim recovers only from the fund, he will not gain the satisfaction of seeing his wrong righted. Nor will it be much different if, after paying the victim, the fund later recovers from the tortfeasor." Blum & Kalven, *The Empty Cabinet of Dr. Calabresi—Auto Accidents and General Deterrence*, 34 U.Chi.L.Rev. 239, 268–69 (1967). Do you think victims care about the source of their benefits? For those that do, does the current system, with its reliance on liability insurance, satisfy that desire? The authors also urge that the law "not break sharply with the moral traditions of the society" and that the burden of satisfying indignation not be left solely to criminal law. What are these "moral traditions"?

The social insurance aspects of the Franklin, Pierce, Sugarman, and New Zealand proposals may all be traced to the influential Beveridge Report of 1942 on Social Insurance and Allied Services in Great Britain. Cmd. 6404. Speaking of workers' compensation, Beveridge said (pp. 38–39):

> The pioneer system of social security in Britain was based on a wrong principle and has been dominated by a wrong outlook. It allows claims to be settled by bargaining between unequal parties, permits payment of socially wasteful lump sums instead of pensions in cases of serious incapacity, places the cost of medical care on the workman or charity or poor relief, and over part of the field, large in the numbers covered, though not in the proportion of the total compensation paid, it relies on expensive private insurance. There should be no hesitation in making provision for the results of industrial accident and disease in the future, not by a continuance of the present system of individual employer's liability, but as one branch of a unified Plan for Social Security. If the matter were

now being considered in a clear field, it might well be argued that the general principle of a flat rate of compensation for interruption of earnings adopted for all other forms of interruption, should be applied also without reserve or qualification to the results of industrial accident and disease, leaving those who felt the need for greater security, by voluntary insurance, to provide an addition to the flat subsistence guaranteed by the State. If a workman loses his leg in an accident, his needs are the same whether the accident occurred in a factory or in the street; if he is killed, the needs of his widow and other dependents are the same, however the death occurred. Acceptance of this argument and adoption of a flat rate of compensation for disability, however caused, would avoid the anomaly of treating equal needs differently and the administrative and legal difficulties of defining just what injuries were to be treated as arising out of and in the course of employment. Interpretation of these words has been a fruitful cause of disputes in the past; whatever words are chosen, difficulties and anomalies are bound to arise. A complete solution is to be found only in a completely unified scheme for disability without demarcation by the cause of disability.

Although Beveridge did not ultimately recommend a totally unified scheme, subsequent writers have adopted his theoretical exposition. Reconsider the central premises of the U.S. tort system for addressing responsibility for accidental harm in light of Beveridge's theoretical exposition.

CHAPTER XIII

Intentional Harm

The first torts, although not denominated as such within the medieval writ system, involved intentional harms, starkly illustrated by physical attacks and the theft of property. Prior to the emergence of centralized legal systems, individuals needed to protect themselves from the threats posed by others. These self-help remedies ultimately evolved into ritualized systems of revenge, such as blood feuds between clans or families seeking to exact "an eye for an eye." Consequently, when the common law first emerged in medieval England, the government needed to suppress violent behavior and the ensuing cycle of revenge and retaliation, resulting in a body of rules that protected one from being intentionally harmed by another.

The long history of intentional torts has produced specific types of torts, such as assault, battery, and false imprisonment, each with their own special rules. These rules reflect early procedure and the writ system but still have implications for questions of pleading and proof today, as we shall see. Beginning with false imprisonment and carrying through to intentional infliction of emotional harm and government liability, we will also see how courts have responded to distinctly contemporary injury claims by expanding the boundaries of intentional tort doctrine.

In our study of the personal injuries that a defendant allegedly caused "intentionally," we focus on what the defendant sought to achieve, or knew would occur, rather than on whether the defendant intended the act that ultimately caused harm. Thus the definition of "intent" in the Restatement (Third) Torts: Liability for Physical and Emotional Harm section 1 requires that "(a) the person acts with the purpose of producing [the] consequence" or (b) "the person acts knowing that the consequence is substantially certain to result."

Note that this definition is the final point on a continuum in the Restatement that begins with strict liability followed by negligence, recklessness, and the intentional torts. Strict liability for abnormally dangerous activities involves reasonably careful behavior that nevertheless creates abnormal risk (section 20). Negligence is defined as "failing to exercise reasonable care under all the circumstances" (section 3). A person acts recklessly (section 2) if:

(a) the person knows of the risk of harm created by the conduct or knows facts that make the risk obvious to another in the person's situation, and

(b) the precaution that would eliminate or reduce the risk involves burdens that are so slight relative to the magnitude of the risk as to render the person's failure to adopt the precaution a demonstration of the person's indifference to the risk.

In defining intent, we no longer speak of risk—the characteristic attribute of an accidental harm—but rather of "purpose" to bring about consequences, or knowledge that such consequences are "substantially certain" to occur. Based on these definitions, the defendant's blameworthiness or culpability apparently changes on the continuum of strict liability, negligence, recklessness, and the intentional torts. Strict liability does not impugn the behavior in any respect, while the conduct governed by negligence, recklessness, and the intentional torts typically involves increasing levels of culpability. One who physically attacks another is obviously more blameworthy than one who accidentally harms another.

In studying the intentional torts, consider whether the defendant is always a "bad" actor whose conduct merits condemnation. Are the intentional torts limited to culpable behavior, or are there instances in which the defendant incurs liability without any personal fault or blameworthiness—a form of strict liability? Consider further the implications that your conclusion might have for the torts governing accidental harms. Insofar as the intentional torts subject both culpable and nonculpable behavior to liability, what would you expect with respect to the tort rules governing accidental harms?

A plaintiff who can frame a case as an intentional tort may reap benefits beyond pleading and proof: contributory negligence and even contributory recklessness are not defenses to intentional misconduct, and punitive damages are more readily available.* Also, although liability for negligently inflicted harm may be discharged in bankruptcy, this does not apply to "willful and malicious injury." 11 U.S.C. § 523(a)(6).** But as discussed in Chapter XI, p. 804 supra, most

---

* In Clark v. Cantrell, 529 S.E.2d 528 (S.C.2000), the court applied comparative fault in a case involving a reckless defendant—and reduced the compensatory but not the punitive award. Would that be appropriate for intentional torts? Traditionally, courts have not recognized contributory negligence as a defense to intentional wrongdoing. Some courts are rethinking that rule in an era of comparative responsibility. Compare, e.g., Bonpua v. Fagan, 602 A.2d 287 (N.J.App.1992) (comparing negligence of plaintiff in provoking fight with defendant's intentional battery), with, e.g., Cartwright v. Equitable Life Assurance Society, 914 P.2d 976 (Mont.1996) (refusing to compare plaintiff's negligence with defendant's fraud).

** The role of bankruptcy in tort law was clarified in Kawaauhau v. Geiger, 523 U.S. 57 (1998), in which malpractice plaintiffs sought to deny a discharge in bankruptcy to a physician who had been more than negligent in his conduct, which led to amputation of plaintiff's leg below the knee. Defendant was uninsured and, after the adverse judgment, sought protection under the bankruptcy laws. The Supreme Court unanimously held that the statute allowed discharge here since the underlying conduct was at most reckless. Given the narrow words used by Congress, the defendant must intend the consequences as well as the act that led to the harm: "The word 'willful' in (a)(6) modifies the word 'injury,' indicating that nondischargeability takes a deliberate or intentional injury, not merely a deliberate act that leads to injury."

The Court also noted that section 523(a)(9), added in 1984, bars discharge for liability incurred for "death or personal injury caused by the debtor's operation of a motor vehicle [since extended to boats and airplanes] if such operation was unlawful because the debtor was

liability insurance policies exclude coverage for intentional torts, which often results in the defendant having insufficient assets to pay for the plaintiff's tort judgment. Consider how these factors might affect a plaintiff's strategic decision concerning the best way to frame the tort claim.

A. BASIC DOCTRINE

1. INTENT

Garratt v. Dailey

Supreme Court of Washington, 1955.
46 Wash.2d 197, 279 P.2d 1091.

■ HILL, JUSTICE.

The liability of an infant for an alleged battery is presented to this court for the first time. Brian Dailey (age five years, nine months) was visiting with Naomi Garratt, an adult and a sister of the plaintiff, Ruth Garratt, likewise an adult, in the backyard of the plaintiff's home, on July 16, 1951. It is plaintiff's contention that she came out into the backyard to talk with Naomi and that, as she started to sit down in a wood and canvas lawn chair, Brian deliberately pulled it out from under her. The only one of the three persons present so testifying was Naomi Garratt. (Ruth Garratt, the plaintiff, did not testify as to how or why she fell.) The trial court, [sitting as factfinder], unwilling to accept this testimony, adopted instead Brian Dailey's version of what happened, and made the following findings:

> "III . . . that while Naomi Garratt and Brian Dailey were in the back yard the plaintiff, Ruth Garratt, came out of her house into the back yard. Some time subsequent thereto defendant, Brian Dailey, picked up a lightly built wood and canvas lawn chair which was then and there located in the back yard of the above described premises, moved it sideways a few feet and seated himself therein, at which time he discovered the plaintiff, Ruth Garratt, about to sit down at the place where the lawn chair had formerly been, at which time he hurriedly got up from the chair and attempted to move it toward Ruth Garratt to aid her in sitting down in the chair; that due to the defendant's small size and lack of dexterity he was unable to get the lawn chair under the plaintiff in time to prevent her from falling to the ground. That plaintiff fell to the ground and sustained a fracture of her hip, and other injuries and damages as hereinafter set forth.

---

intoxicated from using alcohol, a drug, or another substance." This addition would not have been needed if section 523(a)(6) covered cases of recklessness.

"IV. That the preponderance of the evidence in this case establishes that when the defendant, Brian Dailey, moved the chair in question *he did not have any wilful or unlawful purpose* in doing so; that *he did not have any intent to injure the plaintiff, or any intent to bring about any unauthorized or offensive contact with her person* or any objects appurtenant thereto; that the circumstances which immediately preceded the fall of the plaintiff established that the defendant, *Brian Dailey, did not have purpose, intent or design to perform a prank or to effect an assault and battery upon the person of the plaintiff.*" (Italics ours, for a purpose hereinafter indicated.)

It is conceded that Ruth Garratt's fall resulted in a fractured hip and other painful and serious injuries. To obviate the necessity of a retrial in the event this court determines that she was entitled to a judgment against Brian Dailey, the amount of her damage was found to be eleven thousand dollars. Plaintiff appeals from a judgment dismissing the action and asks for the entry of a judgment in that amount or a new trial.

The authorities generally, but with certain notable exceptions [ ], state that, when a minor has committed a tort with force, he is liable to be proceeded against as any other person would be. [ ]

In our analysis of the applicable law, we start with the basic premise that Brian, whether five or fifty-five, must have committed some wrongful act before he could be liable for appellant's injuries.

. . .

It is urged that Brian's action in moving the chair constituted a battery. A definition (not all-inclusive but sufficient for our purpose) of a battery is the intentional infliction of a harmful bodily contact upon another. . . .

We have in this case no question of consent or privilege. We therefore proceed to an immediate consideration of intent and its place in the law of battery. . . .

. . .

We have here the conceded volitional act of Brian, i.e., the moving of a chair. Had the plaintiff proved to the satisfaction of the trial court that Brian moved the chair while she was in the act of sitting down, Brian's action would patently have been for the purpose or with the intent of causing the plaintiff's bodily contact with the ground, and she would be entitled to a judgment against him for the resulting damages. Vosburg v. Putney, [50 N.W. 403 (Wis.1891)].

The plaintiff based her case on that theory, and the trial court held that she failed in her proof and accepted Brian's version of the facts rather than that given by the eyewitness who testified for the plaintiff. After the trial court determined that the plaintiff had not established her theory of a battery (i.e., that Brian had pulled the chair out from under the plaintiff while she was in the act of sitting down), it then became concerned with whether a battery was established under the facts as it found them to be.

. . .

A battery would be established if, in addition to plaintiff's fall, it was proved that, when Brian moved the chair, he knew with substantial certainty that the plaintiff would attempt to sit down where the chair had been. If Brian had any of the intents which the trial court found, in the italicized portions of the findings of fact quoted above, that he did not have, he would of course have had the knowledge to which we have referred. The mere absence of any intent to injure the plaintiff or to play a prank on her or to embarrass her, or to commit an assault and battery on her would not absolve him from liability if in fact he had such knowledge. [ ] Without such knowledge, there would be nothing wrongful about Brian's act in moving the chair, and, there being no wrongful act, there would be no liability.

While a finding that Brian had no such knowledge can be inferred from the findings made, we believe that before the plaintiff's action in such a case should be dismissed there should be no question but that the trial court had passed upon that issue; hence, the case should be remanded for clarification of the findings to specifically cover the question of Brian's knowledge, because intent could be inferred therefrom. If the court finds that he had such knowledge, the necessary intent will be established and the plaintiff will be entitled to recover, even though there was no purpose to injure or embarrass the plaintiff. [ ] If Brian did not have such knowledge, there was no wrongful act by him, and the basic premise of liability on the theory of a battery was not established.

It will be noted that the law of battery as we have discussed it is the law applicable to adults, and no significance has been attached to the fact that Brian was a child less than six years of age when the alleged battery occurred. The only circumstance where Brian's age is of any consequence is in determining what he knew, and there his experience, capacity, and understanding are of course material.

. . .

Remanded for clarification.

■ SCHWELLENBACH, DONWORTH, and WEAVER, JJ., concur.

NOTES AND QUESTIONS

1.   According to the court, what must Brian have "intended" in order to be held liable for a battery? Suppose he wasn't thinking about plaintiff one way or the other—he simply grabbed the nearest chair, despite the fact that she was about to sit in it, because he was eager to sit down. Would he have had the requisite intent?

Aside from Brian's testimony, how could the plaintiff prove that he had either the desire to cause harm or knowledge that his conduct was substantially certain to injure the plaintiff? On remand, the trial court found that Brian did have the necessary intent, and entered judgment for the plaintiff for $11,000. The judgment was affirmed on appeal. 304 P.2d 681 (Wash.1956). Brian's legal liabilities in the case were indemnified by his parents' homeowner's insurance, which may explain why the plaintiff sued a young child. This type of insurance is discussed at p. 772 supra.

2.   Suppose Brian did not believe to a "substantial certainty" that plaintiff was about to sit down. Might he still be liable on a negligence theory for the failure to exercise reasonable care? Can you construct versions of the facts that clarify the distinctions between intentional, reckless, and negligent misconduct? Might Brian's age make it more difficult to establish negligence than intentional wrongdoing here? See Price v. Kitsap Transit, 886 P.2d 556 (Wash.1994)(holding that children below the age of 6 are conclusively presumed to be unable to comprehend risk sufficiently to be held negligent).

3.   Suppose Brian did know to a "substantial certainty" that plaintiff was about to sit in the chair. Does it make sense to have a separate tort category of "intentional torts" for such cases? What about a car manufacturer that knows to a substantial certainty that numerous purchasers of its automobiles each year will suffer bodily injury? The Third Restatement, in comment e to section 1, suggests that the "substantial certainty" test be limited "to situations in which the defendant has knowledge to a substantial certainty that the conduct will bring about harm to a particular victim or to someone within a small class of potential victims within a localized area."

The relevant difference, according to Simons, Statistical Knowledge Deconstructed, 92 B.U.L.Rev. 1 (2012), is between "individualized knowledge"—the awareness that a particular act is substantially certain to harm someone—and "statistical knowledge"—the awareness that one's multiple acts over time will, to a high statistical likelihood, ultimately harm one or more persons from a large class of potential victims. While individualized knowledge is sufficient to satisfy the substantial certainty test for intent, statistical knowledge is not.

4.   In the cited case of *Vosburg v. Putney*, the court held that one schoolboy who lightly kicked another in the leg was liable for a battery despite the lack of any subjective intention to do harm. Moreover, the defendant was held liable for extraordinary harm that resulted because of the exacerbation of a pre-existing injury, the court tersely stating that "the wrongdoer is liable for all injuries resulting directly from the wrongful act, whether they could or could not have been foreseen by him." This statement apparently refers to the eggshell plaintiff rule, discussed at p. 395 supra, which requires a defendant who is otherwise liable to pay for injuries of this type. Is it appropriate to apply a rule for determining damages to cases in which the defendant denies liability altogether?

Vosburg has remained a great favorite of torts afficionados over the years. See its centennial celebration, including a sociolegal history of the case, Zile, *Vosburg v. Putney*: A Centennial Story, 1992 Wis.L.Rev. 877, and commentary by James A. Henderson (at p. 853), Robert L. Rabin (at p. 863), and J. Willard Hurst (at p. 875).

5.   *Cause-in-fact.* The basic rule is that plaintiff must prove that defendant's intentional tortious conduct was an actual cause of the harm. Consider the following passage from Malone, Ruminations on Cause-In-Fact, 9 Stan.L.Rev. 60, 72–73 (1956):

> Some rules of law are tremendously exacting and rest upon time-honored moral considerations. They are safeguards for well-established interests of others, and their mantle of protection embraces a large variety of risks. He who violates such a rule will be held responsible for any harm that can be causally associated in any plausible way with his wrongdoing. The court, for instance, will seldom hesitate to allow the jury a free range of speculation on the cause issue at the expense of an intentional wrongdoer who is charged with having physically injured another person.

Malone also suggests that in fire cases "Sound judgment may dictate, for instance, that an arsonist be held responsible for a fire contribution that has a much smaller damaging potential than could be recognized in the case of a householder whose lamp was tipped over by the wind." Can these views be justified? Consider in this regard the extent to which these different torts ordinarily embody differing degrees of culpability, as discussed at the outset of this Chapter.

6.   *Proximate cause.* In a negligence action, the scope of a defendant's liability is limited to those harms that were proximately caused by the negligent conduct. How should this requirement regarding the scope of liability apply to intentional torts? In Baker v. Shymkiv, 451 N.E.2d 811 (Ohio 1983), the plaintiff and decedent, her husband, came home to find a trench being built across their driveway by defendant. An angry confrontation occurred. At this point, plaintiff left to call the police. When she returned three minutes later, she found her husband lying face down in a mud puddle while the defendants were driving away. He was pronounced dead of a heart attack shortly thereafter. The trial judge charged that although the defendants were trespassers, they would not be liable for the death unless that harm could have been foreseen or reasonably anticipated by the wrongdoer. The Court of Appeals reversed a defense judgment, and the Ohio Supreme Court unanimously affirmed. Quoting from an earlier case, the court reasoned that when confronted with an innocent victim and an intentional wrongdoer, it is not surprising that the interest of the victim in attaining full compensation "is placed above the interest of the wrongdoer in protecting himself against potentially speculative damage awards."

Should intentional wrongdoers be held liable for more extended consequences than negligent parties? Consider Restatement (Third) Torts: Liability for Physical and Emotional Harm § 33(b): "An actor who intentionally or recklessly causes physical harm is subject to liability for a broader range of harms than the harms for which the actor would be liable if only acting negligently." Is that a helpful standard? How might it be operationalized in a jury instruction? See generally Note, The Tie That Binds: Liability of Intentional Tort-Feasors for Extended Consequences, 14 Stan.L.Rev. 362 (1962).

7. *Punitive damages.* In intentional tort cases, the defendant is often, but not always, responsible for both compensatory damages and punitive damages as well. As discussed in Chapter XI, p. 747 supra, the standard for punitive damages is triggered by reckless conduct. Consequently, intentional tort situations have been considered the paradigm case for award of such damages. Should a distinction be drawn between cases involving intent to injure and cases like *Vosburg* in which defendant intended no serious harm?

8. *Intent and insanity.* In Williams v. Kearbey, 775 P.2d 670 (Kan.App.1989), defendant, a minor, shot and injured two people at his junior high school. The wounded individuals brought successful battery actions. The jury found that the defendant was insane at the time of the shootings. Defendant argued that because of this fact, he should not be held civilly liable for his torts. The court followed the majority rule that a defendant's insanity does not establish a defense to liability. That rule reflected a policy decision "to impose liability on an insane person rather than leaving the loss on the innocent victim."

Does this rule follow from the definition of intent? To the extent that the defendant's insanity involved deluded motivations for the attack, is it relevant to the question whether he had the desire or purpose to shoot plaintiffs? What does this rule imply about the claim that the intentional torts are necessarily limited to blameworthy or culpable behavior?

9. *Victim compensation statutes.* The vast majority of valid intentional tort cases founder on the insolvency of the perpetrator, whose conduct is often subject to criminal liability as well. Statutes may provide some aid to victims of crimes from the state or local treasury, an idea that originated in Great Britain. California, in 1965, was the first state to enact a comprehensive victim compensation statute. Since then, at least 35 states have enacted some form of victim compensation program. These programs differ from one another significantly, both in scope and in the amount of reparations. For a detailed survey of the various state compensation programs, see D. Parent, B. Auerbach, & K. Carlson, Compensating Crime Victims: A Summary of Policies and Practices (National Institute of Justice 1992). The philosophical justifications for victim compensation programs are criticized in Henderson, The Wrongs of Victim's Rights, 37 Stan.L.Rev. 937 (1985).

––––––––––

In *Garratt,* the court offered two foundational observations before launching into its discussion of intent. First, the opinion defined the tort of battery, establishing the prima facie case as "the intentional infliction of a harmful bodily contact upon another." Next, the court observed that the most common defenses to battery were not involved: "We have in this case no question of consent or privilege." The following cases discuss the related torts of assault and battery in greater detail.

2.   ASSAULT AND BATTERY

Picard v. Barry Pontiac-Buick, Inc.

Supreme Court of Rhode Island, 1995.
654 A.2d 690.

■ LEDERBERG, JUSTICE.

[During an annual inspection, defendant dealer informed plaintiff Picard that the brakes on her mother's automobile would have to be replaced. Plaintiff took the vehicle to another inspection station, a repair shop, where it passed inspection. Plaintiff became upset about the dealer's work and contacted a local television news "troubleshooter" reporter. The dealer called the repair shop and requested that the car's inspection sticker be "pulled," because it had bad brakes. This culminated in the plaintiff returning to the repair shop with the automobile, along with representatives of the dealer, for the brakes to be reinspected. Picard took along a camera and photographed an employee of the dealer, who was also a defendant, as he was inspecting the brakes. There was a dispute as to what happened next. Plaintiff testified that defendant lunged at her and spun her around; defendant denied touching her and testified that he "pointed at plaintiff and said, 'who gave you permission to take my picture?' then walked around the car to plaintiff, placed his index finger on the camera and again asked, 'who gave you permission to take my picture?'" The defendant denied grabbing plaintiff or threatening her in any way. In further testimony, which was less than entirely consistent, plaintiff and her doctor claimed permanent damage to her back as a consequence of the altercation.

At trial to the court, plaintiff prevailed and was awarded $60,366 in compensatory damages and an additional $6,350 in punitive damages. Defendant appealed, arguing "1) that plaintiff failed to prove an assault and battery; 2) that plaintiff failed to prove that defendant's actions in fact caused the alleged harm to her; and 3) that the damage awards were grossly excessive and inappropriate as a matter of law." The supreme court vacated the award and remanded for a new trial on damages.]

. . .

The defendant contended that plaintiff failed to prove the occurrence of an assault because plaintiff was not placed in reasonable fear of imminent bodily harm. Further, defendant argued that plaintiff failed to prove a battery because the evidence failed to establish that defendant intended to inflict an unconsented touching of plaintiff. We disagree with both contentions.

Assault and battery are separate acts, usually arising from the same transaction, each having independent significance. [ ] "An assault is a physical act of a threatening nature or an offer of corporal injury which puts an individual in reasonable fear of imminent bodily harm." [ ] It is a plaintiff's apprehension of injury which renders a defendant's act compensable. [ ]; see also W. Page Keeton et al., Prosser and Keeton on the Law of Torts § 10, at 43 (5th ed. 1984)("[t]he damages recoverable for [assault] are those for the plaintiff's mental disturbance, including fright, humiliation and the like, as well as any physical illness which may result from them"). This apprehension must be the type of fear normally aroused in the mind of a reasonable person. [ ]

The plaintiff testified that she was frightened by defendant's actions. A review of the attendant circumstances attests that such a reaction was reasonable. The defendant admitted approaching plaintiff, and the photograph taken that day clearly showed defendant pointing his finger at plaintiff as defendant approached her. Because plaintiff's apprehension of imminent bodily harm was reasonable at that point, plaintiff has established a prima facie case of assault.

We have defined battery as an act that was intended to cause, and in fact did cause, "an offensive contact with or unconsented touching of or trauma upon the body of another, thereby generally resulting in the consummation of the assault. . . . An intent to injure plaintiff, however, is unnecessary in a situation in which a defendant willfully sets in motion a force that in its ordinary course causes the injury." [ ]

In the instant case, defendant contended that a battery did not occur because defendant did not intend to touch or injure plaintiff. Rather, defendant argued, the evidence showed that he intended to touch plaintiff's camera, not plaintiff's person, and therefore the contact was insufficient to prove battery. With this contention we must disagree. Even if this court were to accept defendant's characterization of the incident, a battery had nonetheless occurred. The defendant failed to prove that his actions were accidental or involuntary. Therefore, defendant's offensive contact with an object attached to or identified with plaintiff's body was sufficient to constitute a battery As noted in the comments to the Restatement (Second) Torts § 18, comment c at 31 (1965): "Unpermitted and intentional contacts with anything so connected with the body as to be customarily regarded as part of the other's person and therefore as partaking of its inviolability is actionable as an offensive contact with his person. There are some things such as clothing or a cane or, indeed, anything directly grasped by the hand which are so intimately connected with one's body as to be universally regarded as part of the person." The defendant's contact with the camera clutched in plaintiff's hand was thus sufficient to constitute a battery. We conclude, therefore, that plaintiff has proven the elements of assault and battery.

. . .

[The court next determined that the medical evidence in support of the claim for compensatory damages was inadequate and that the amount of damages awarded was excessive. In addition, the punitive damage award could not stand because "there was no proof of malice or bad faith."]

In conclusion, we deny in part and sustain in part the defendant's appeal. We affirm the judgment of the Superior Court in respect to the defendant's commission of assault and battery, but we vacate the awards of compensatory and punitive damages. We remand the case to the Superior Court for a new trial on the damages sustained by the plaintiff.

NOTES AND QUESTIONS

1.   For an interesting early case illustrating an assault claim, see I. de S. v. W. de S., Y.B. Lib. Ass. folio 99, pl. 60 (1348), in which defendant, enraged at being told by plaintiff that the tavern was closed for the night, swung his hatchet at her, but missed, as she stuck her head out of the window of the establishment. The court rejected the argument that no harm had been done, concluding that an actionable assault had occurred.

As illustrated by this case, a defendant can commit an assault without committing a battery. What might justify liability in these cases? Consider how the individual being assaulted is likely to respond to the threat.

2.   *Conditional threats.* Suppose defendant in *Picard* had gestured menacingly and threatened to harm plaintiff if she took a picture of him— but before she had actually done so. Would his actions have constituted an assault? In Tuberville v. Savage, 86 Eng.Rep. 684 (1669), the court held that the statement, "if it were not assize time, I would run this sword through you," did not amount to an assault because of its conditional nature. Threats conditioned on the occurrence of future events, even if unjustifiable, are not assaults.

Due to this requirement, the threat must be of an *imminent* battery. If the harmful contact were not imminent, would the threatened party ordinarily have time to seek protection from the police? Why might this be a better resolution of the problem?

3.   Note that the *Picard* court echoed *Garratt* in holding that an intent to injure is not required to establish a battery. What precisely was the intent required to establish not just an assault but a battery as well in *Picard*?

4.   Once tortious conduct amounting to an assault and battery was established in *Picard*, did the court act consistently when it reversed the punitive damage award because of the failure to establish "malice and bad faith"?

Wishnatsky v. Huey

Court of Appeals of North Dakota, 1998.
584 N.W.2d 859.

■ PER CURIAM.

Martin Wishnatsky appealed a summary judgment dismissing his battery action against David W. Huey, and an order denying his motion for an altered judgment. We conclude, as a matter of law, that no battery occurred, and we affirm the judgment and the order.

On January 10, 1996, Huey, an assistant attorney general, was engaged in a conversation with attorney Peter B. Crary in Crary's office. Without knocking or announcing his entry, Wishnatsky, who performs paralegal work for Crary, attempted to enter the office. Huey pushed the door closed, thereby pushing Wishnatsky back into the hall. Wishnatsky reentered the office and Huey left.

Wishnatsky brought an action against Huey, seeking damages for battery. Huey moved for summary judgment of dismissal. The trial court granted Huey's motion and a judgment of dismissal was entered. Wishnatsky moved to alter the judgment. The trial court denied Wishnatsky's motion.

Wishnatsky appealed, contending the evidence he submitted in response to Huey's motion for summary judgment satisfies the elements of a battery claim and the trial court erred in granting Huey's motion. Wishnatsky also contends Huey is not entitled to prosecutorial or statutory immunity.

. . .

"In its original conception [battery] meant the infliction of physical injury." [ ] By the Eighteenth Century, the requirement of an actual physical injury had been eliminated:

At Nisi Prius, upon evidence in trespass for assault and battery, Holt, C.J. declared,

> 1. That the least touching of another in anger is a battery. 2. If two or more meet in a narrow passage, and without any violence or design of harm, the one touches the other gently, it is no battery. 3. If any of them use violence against the other, to force his way in a rude inordinate manner, it is a battery; or any struggle about the passage, to that degree as may do hurt, is a battery. [ ]

Cole v. Turner, Pasch. 3 Ann., 6 Mod. 149, 90 Eng.Rep. 958 (1704). Blackstone explained:

> The least touching of another's person willfully, or in anger, is a battery; for the law cannot draw the line between different degrees of violence, and therefore totally prohibits the first and lowest stage of it: every man's person being sacred, and no

other having a right to meddle with it, in any the slightest manner.

3 William Blackstone, Commentaries *120. On the other hand, "in a crowded world, a certain amount of personal contact is inevitable, and must be accepted." [Prosser & Keeton].

The American Law Institute has balanced the interest in unwanted contacts and the inevitable contacts in a crowded world in Restatement (Second) of Torts §§ 18, 19 (1965):

18.   Battery: Offensive Contact

(1) An actor is subject to liability to another for battery if

(a) he acts intending to cause a harmful or offensive contact with the person of the other or a third person, or an imminent apprehension of such a contact, and

(b) an offensive contact with the person of the other directly or indirectly results.

(2) An act which is not done with the intention stated in Subsection (1,a) does not make the actor liable to the other for a mere offensive contact with the other's person although the act involves an unreasonable risk of inflicting it and, therefore, would be negligent or reckless if the risk threatened bodily harm.

. . .

19.   What Constitutes Offensive Contact

A bodily contact is offensive if it offends a reasonable sense of personal dignity.

Comment *c* to section 18 notes that the contact need not be "directly caused by some act of the actor" and also notes that "the essence of the plaintiff's grievance consists in the offense to the dignity involved in the unpermitted and intentional invasion of the inviolability of his person and not in any physical harm done to his body." Comment *a* to section 19 explains what kind of conduct offends a reasonable sense of personal dignity:

In order that a contact be offensive to a reasonable sense of personal dignity, it must be one which would offend the ordinary person and as such one not unduly sensitive as to his personal dignity. It must, therefore, be a contact which is unwarranted by the social usages prevalent at the time and place at which it is inflicted.

Huey moved for summary judgment of dismissal, because, among other things, "as a matter of law, a battery did not occur on January 10, 1996." Huey supported the motion with his affidavit stating in part:

8.   That Attorney Crary and I had settled into a serious discussion about the case and had established a good rapport

when the door to his office suddenly swung open without a knock. An unidentified individual carrying some papers then strode in unannounced. I had not been told that anyone would be entering Attorney Crary's office during the private meeting. . . . I subsequently learned that the individual's name is Martin Wishnatsky.

Wishnatsky responded to Huey's motion for summary judgment with an affidavit of Crary and with his own affidavit stating in part:

1.   I am a born-again Christian and cultivate holiness in my life. [A]s a result I am very sensitive to evil spirits and am greatly disturbed by the demonic. However, in Christ there is victory.

2.   On January 9, 1996, Mr. David Huey of the North Dakota Attorney General's office, visited the ministry where I was working at 16 Broadway in Fargo, North Dakota with an ex parte court order.

3.   The following morning I entered the office of Peter Crary, an attorney for whom I do paralegal work, to give him certain papers that had been requested. Mr. Crary was speaking with Mr. David Huey at the time. As I began to enter the office Mr. Huey threw his body weight against the door and forced me out into the hall. I had not said a word to him. At the same time, he snarled: "You get out of here." This was very shocking and frightening to me. In all the time I have been working as an aide to Mr. Crary, I have never been physically assaulted or spoken to in a harsh and brutal manner. My blood pressure began to rise, my heart beat accelerated and I felt waves of fear in the pit of my stomach. My hands began to shake and my body to tremble. Composing myself, I reentered the office, whereupon Mr. Huey began a half-demented tirade against me and stormed out into the hall. I looked at Mr. Crary in wonder.

We certainly agree with the Supreme Court's determination that when Wishnatsky attempted to enter the room in which Huey was conversing with Crary, "Huey apparently reacted in a rude and abrupt manner in attempting to exclude Wishnatsky from that conversation." Wishnatsky v. Huey, [560 N.W.2d 878 (N.D.1997)]. As a matter of law, however, Huey's "rude and abrupt" conduct did not rise to the level of battery.

The evidence presented to the trial court demonstrates Wishnatsky is "unduly sensitive as to his personal dignity." Restatement (Second) of Torts § 19 cmt. *a* (1965). Without knocking or otherwise announcing his intentions, Wishnatsky opened the door to the office in which Huey and Crary were having a private conversation and attempted to enter. Huey closed the door opened by Wishnatsky, thereby stopping Wishnatsky's forward progress and pushing him back into the hall. The bodily contact was momentary, indirect, and incidental. Viewing the evidence in the light most favorable to Wishnatsky, and giving him the benefit of all favorable inferences which can reasonably be drawn from the evidence, we conclude Huey's conduct in response to Wishnatsky's intrusion into his private conversation with Crary, while "rude and abrupt," would not "be offensive to a reasonable sense of personal dignity." In short, an "ordinary person . . . not unduly sensitive as to his personal dignity" intruding upon a private conversation in Wishnatsky's manner would not have been offended by Huey's response to the intrusion. We conclude that Huey's conduct did not constitute an offensive-contact-battery, as a matter of law, and the trial court did not err in granting Huey's motion for summary judgment dismissing Wishnatsky's action.

. . .

Affirmed.

■ HOBERG, C.J., WILLIAM F. HODNY, SURROGATE JUDGE, and DEBBIE G. KLEVEN, DISTRICT JUDGE, concur.

NOTES AND QUESTIONS

1.   In the leading case of Alcorn v. Mitchell, 63 Ill. 553 (1872), a disappointed litigant spat upon his adversary in the courthouse. The court allowed nominal compensatory and fairly substantial punitive damages in the subsequent action for the trespassory act. What are the justifications for extending battery actions beyond actual physical harm? Consider the historical origins of this tort, which took root in a culture that had embraced the retaliatory norm of "getting even." Is an underlying concern for physical violence present in *Huey*? If not, what is the interest that is protected by the tort of offensive battery? Compare Kumar v. Gate Gourmet, Inc., 325 P.3d 193 (Wash.2014)(holding that plaintiff employees sufficiently alleged a claim for offensive battery against defendant employer for "deceiving them into eating food in violation of their religious beliefs, knowing that this would cause an offensive contact").

2.   Under section 19 of the Second Restatement, "A bodily contact is offensive if it offends a reasonable sense of personal dignity." Consider that section's application in Vitale v. Henchey, 24 S.W.3d 651 (Ky.2000). The patient's son, who held a medical power of attorney, consented by telephone to an operation on his 95-year-old mother to be performed by two identified surgeons. Subsequently, at the request of these two surgeons, a third surgeon performed the operation. From earlier conversations with one of the two authorized surgeons, the son had reason to think that the third surgeon was "too aggressive, not compassionate"—and he testified that he would not have consented to surgery by the third surgeon. Plaintiff did not prove that the treatment provided by the unauthorized surgeon violated the accepted standard of care. The court, 5–2, held that such a showing was not required and upheld the battery claim against all three surgeons, even though no physical harm from the substitution could be shown. As to damages, the court stated that nominal damages were available in this

situation. On what basis is the element of intent established against the two surgeons who did not perform the operation?

3. *Reconsidering intent.* Suppose that D comes up behind a person he is quite certain is his friend and applies their traditional greeting of a slap on the back. If the other person turns out to be a stranger, has D committed an intentional tort? Remarkably, despite centuries of intentional tort jurisprudence, courts have not resolved the question of whether battery requires an intent *only* to make contact or, in addition, to make contact that is harmful or offensive. See Simons, A Restatement (Third) of Intentional Torts?, 48 Ariz.L.Rev. 1061, 1066–70 (2006). Compare City of Watauga v. Gordon, 434 S.W.3d 586 (Tex.2014)("Although a specific intent to inflict injury is without question an intentional tort, and many batteries are of this type, a specific intent to injure is not an essential element of battery."), with Carlsen v. Koivumaki, 227 Cal.App.4th 879 (2014)(holding that to establish a battery, plaintiff must prove that "the defendant touched the plaintiff, or caused the plaintiff to be touched, with the intent to harm or offend the plaintiff").

Because a battery involves either a harmful or offensive contact, a defendant can be liable for a battery without specifically intending to cause physical harm or offense. As *Huey* illustrates, the offensiveness of a contact is determined objectively, and so a defendant can be liable for an offensive battery by intending to cause a physical contact that the law deems to be offensive, even if the defendant did not have the specific intent to cause offense. Does this possibility explain *Vosburg v. Putney*, note 4 p. 904 supra, in which the defendant student committed a battery by slightly kicking the plaintiff while class was in session? Note in this regard that "[l]iability in battery . . . extends to harmful bodily contacts even though only offensive contacts were intended." *Gordon*, 434 S.W.3d at 586.

In cases like this, the defendant can incur liability because of the single intent to cause a bodily contact without having a secondary intent to cause physical harm or offense to the plaintiff. The law instead deems the contact to be offensive, regardless of the defendant's specific intent about the matter. The requirement of a single intent, however, poses difficulty in other cases involving physical harms. Consider a manufacturer that distributes a reasonably safe drug that could cause adverse side effects that were not reasonably foreseeable at the time of sale. The manufacturer intends for consumers to come into physical contact with the drug, thereby satisfying the single-intent requirement. If a consumer who ingests the drug were then injured by the unforeseen side effect, the contact in question would also be harmful. Under the single-intent formulation, the drug manufacturer would be liable for battery, even though the conduct in question would not be subject to negligence liability. To avoid this outcome, liability for battery must instead require the dual intent to cause (1) a physical contact, and (2) harm or offense as a result of that contact. The requirement of a dual intent, however, would seem to bar recovery in the cases of offensive battery discussed in the prior paragraph.

This problem is discussed extensively in the Restatement (Third) of Torts: Intentional Torts to Persons section 102 cmt. b (Tent. Draft No.1

2015), which "endorses the single-intent rule" because it "affords greater protection to the plaintiff's interest in bodily integrity, and can be understood as imposing a modest degree of strict liability, insofar as the actor is liable although he might have genuinely and even reasonably believed that the contact he caused would not cause harm or offense." The Restatement Third recognizes that a particular class of cases

> may raise the greatest doubts about the single-intent approach. In these cases, where the intentional contact is insufficient to satisfy the objective-offense requirement, but no category of consent (actual, apparent, or implied-in-law) precludes liability, the single-intent approach will impose liability if the contact causes bodily harm. Does such a minor and inoffensive contact properly warrant intentional tort liability? In many of these cases . . . the risk of physical injury is extremely low; thus, a negligence claim would be unlikely to succeed. On the other hand, insofar as the single-intent rule is meant to afford very strong protection to a person's right of bodily autonomy, liability even in this class of cases may be justifiable.

Id. cmt. f. Would this rule justifiably impose battery liability on a drug manufacturer that non-negligently distributed a drug with unforeseeable side effects? As discussed in Chapter IX, p. 629 supra, unforeseeable risks of this type are not subject to strict products liability in the vast majority of jurisdictions.

3. FALSE IMPRISONMENT

Like assault and battery, false imprisonment was initially formulated to address the problem of violence and public disorder in medieval England. An egregious example of false imprisonment involves the modern crime of kidnapping. And like the other intentional torts, false imprisonment has evolved over time.

Lopez v. Winchell's Donut House

Illinois Appellate Court, 1984.
126 Ill.App.3d 46, 466 N.E.2d 1309.

■ LORENZ, JUSTICE.

Plaintiff appeals from an order of the circuit court granting defendant corporation's motion for summary judgment. Plaintiff contends that the trial court erred in entering summary judgment against her because a genuine issue of material fact existed concerning her charge that she was falsely detained and imprisoned. For the reasons which follow, we affirm the trial court's decision.

Count I of plaintiff's unverified two-count complaint alleged that plaintiff was employed as a clerk in defendant's donut shop in Woodridge, Illinois, for approximately three years; that on or about April 8, 1981, defendant, through its agents and employees, Ralph Bell and James Cesario, accused her of selling donuts without registering sales and thereby pocketing defendant's monies; and that she was falsely detained and imprisoned against her will in a room located on defendant's premises, with force, and without probable and reasonable cause, by defendant's employees. Count I of her complaint also alleged that as a result of defendant's employees' wilful and wanton false imprisonment, she was exposed to public disgrace; greatly injured in her good name and reputation; suffered, and still suffers, great mental anguish, humiliation and shock; wrongfully terminated from her employment; required to seek medical attention; all of which prevented her from attending to her usual affairs.

[Defendant's answer consisted of an affirmative defense that it had reasonable grounds to believe that plaintiff had engaged in retail theft and that its inquiry as to whether she had failed to ring up certain retail sales was conducted "in a reasonable manner and for a reasonable length of time." Defendant then moved for summary judgment.]

The motion included portions of plaintiff's deposition which disclosed the following. James Cesario telephoned plaintiff at her home at 4:30 p.m. on April 9, 1981, and asked her to come down to the donut shop; he did not explain his reasons for wanting her to do so. As a result of this call, plaintiff walked to the store from her home, arriving ten minutes later. Upon her arrival at the store, Cesario asked her to accompany him into the baking room, which was located at the rear of the store; Ralph Bell was also present in the room. After Cesario asked plaintiff to sit down, she indicated that they (Cesario and Bell) closed the door and locked it by putting a "little latch on." She stated that the two men told her that they had proof that spotters going from store to store had purchased two dozen donuts from her, but that her register had not shown the sale. After refusing her request to view the "proof," plaintiff stated that she was "too upset" to respond to their questioning regarding the length of time that her alleged "shorting" of the cash drawer had been going on.

She further stated that defendant's employees never told her that she had to answer their questions or face the loss of her job; never directly threatened to fire her; and made no threats of any kind to her during the interrogation. She further testified that she at no time during the interrogation feared for her safety; that she at no time refused to answer any question put to her; that there was never a point in the interrogation that she said, "I want to leave" and was prevented from doing so; and that she got up, left the room and went home when she first decided to do so.

Plaintiff's written response to defendant's motion for summary judgment did not contradict the statements that she had made in her discovery deposition. In her affidavit filed in support of her response to defendant's motion for summary judgment, plaintiff averred that (1) she left the baking room after she began to shake, and when she felt that she was becoming ill; and (2) she was terminated from her employment by defendant.

The trial court entered summary judgment for defendant. Plaintiff appeals from that order. . . .

. . .

Plaintiff asserts that the trial court erred in granting defendant's motion for summary judgment as there exists a genuine issue of material fact. She posits that she felt compelled to remain in the baking room so that she could protect her reputation by protesting her innocence to the two men, and that she left the room once she began to shake and feel ill. Additionally, she attributes her "serious emotional upset" to her feelings of intimidation that she contends were caused by: James Cesario's sitting directly next to her during questioning, yellow pad and pencil in hand; Ralph Bell's repeated statement that his briefcase contained proof of her guilt; and his raised voice.

The common law tort of false imprisonment is defined as an unlawful restraint of an individual's personal liberty or freedom of locomotion. [ ] Imprisonment has been defined as "any unlawful exercise or show of force by which a person is compelled to remain where he does not wish to remain or to go where he does not wish to go." [ ] In order for a false imprisonment to be present, there must be actual or legal intent to restrain. [ ]

Unlawful restraint may be effected by words alone, by acts alone or both [ ]; actual force is unnecessary to an action in false imprisonment. [ ] The Restatement of Torts specifies ways in which an action may bring about the confinement required as an element of false imprisonment, including (1) actual or apparent physical barriers; (2) overpowering physical force, or by submission to physical force; (3) threats of physical force; (4) other duress; and (5) asserted legal authority. Restatement (Second) of Torts §§ 38–41 (1965).

It is essential, however, that the confinement be against the plaintiff's will and if a person voluntarily consents to the confinement, there can be no false imprisonment. [ ] "Moral pressure, as where the plaintiff remains with the defendant to clear himself of suspicion of theft, . . . , is not enough; nor, as in the case of assault, are threats for the future. . . . Any remedy for such wrongs must lie with the more modern tort of the intentional infliction of mental distress." [ ]

Plaintiff principally relies on the court's decision in *Marcus v. Liebman* (1978) [ ], for support of her position that summary judgment should not have been granted in the instant case. In *Marcus v. Liebman*, the court extensively examined the concept that threats of a future action are not enough to constitute confinement. [ ] There, the defendant psychiatrist threatened to have plaintiff committed to the Elgin State Hospital, and the *Marcus* court found that this was a present threat, constituting false imprisonment, as opposed to a threat of future action. The court in *Marcus* concluded that the lower court had incorrectly directed a verdict for the defendant, and reversed and remanded the case for trial on the question of imprisonment. The court noted that plaintiff was already voluntarily committed to the psychiatric wing of a private hospital when the defendant made the threat to commit her to a state mental hospital and reasoned, "[A]t the time the alleged threat was made plaintiff was already confined. It was certainly reasonable for the plaintiff to believe that before her release [from the private hospital], commitment procedures could have been concluded." [ ]

Our analysis of the *Marcus* decision, as well as the other cases cited by plaintiff, does not support plaintiff's position. All of these cases are easily distinguishable from the present case, as in each, either physical restraint or present threats of such were present.

In the case at bar, we are confronted with plaintiff's testimony, given under oath, that she voluntarily accompanied James Cesario to the baking room; that she stayed in the room in order to protect her reputation; that she was never threatened with the loss of her job; that she was never in fear of her safety; and that at no time was she prevented from exiting the baking room. Her affidavit, in which she averred that she left the baking room after she began to shake and when she felt that she was becoming ill, does not place into issue material facts which she had previously removed from contention. [ ] In her discovery deposition, given under oath, she stated that she "got up and left" when Ralph Bell asked her how long the cash register "shorting" had been going on.

In the tort of false imprisonment, it is not enough for the plaintiff to have felt "compelled" to remain in the baking room in order to protect her reputation (see Prosser, Torts, § 11); for the evidence must establish a restraint against the plaintiff's will, as where she yields to force, to the threat of force or the assertion of authority. (See Restatement (Second) of Torts §§ 38–41 (1965).) In the present case, our search of the record reveals no evidence that plaintiff yielded to constraint of a threat, express or implied, or to physical force of any kind. Also, absent evidence that plaintiff accompanied Cesario against her will, we cannot say that she was imprisoned or unlawfully detained by defendant's employees. Finally, we find no merit to plaintiff's argument that defendant's affirmative defense constituted an admission of an unlawful restraint.

For the reasons stated above, we conclude that the trial court properly granted defendant's motion for summary judgment, as there exists no question of material fact in the present case.

AFFIRMED.

■ MEJDA, P.J., and SULLIVAN, J., concur.

NOTES AND QUESTIONS

1. In *Lopez,* what appear to be the elements in the prima facie case of false imprisonment? What was the crux of the defendant's affirmative defense?

2. *Complete confinement.* Would summary judgment have been warranted if Bell and Cesario had told plaintiff that they weren't through questioning her when she decided to leave? What if they said that she was free to leave but if she did so she was fired? What role does the locking of the door play?

"To make the actor liable for false imprisonment, the other's confinement within the boundaries fixed by the actor must be complete." Restatement (Second) of Torts § 36(1). The confinement is complete if the plaintiff, to escape, is "required to run any risk of harm to his person or to his chattels or of subjecting himself to any substantial liability to a third person. . . ." Id. cmt. a. In Shen v. Leo A. Daly Co., 222 F.3d 472 (8th Cir.2000), the Taiwanese government refused to permit plaintiff to leave the country until defendant, his former employer, satisfied certain obligations. The court held that confinement within a country did not amount to false imprisonment. The court observed that although "it is difficult to define exactly how close the level of restraint must be, in this case the country of Taiwan is clearly too great an area within which to be falsely imprisoned."

3. The circumstances under which defendants have sought to restrain the freedom of movement of others defy generalization. On the overambitious efforts of two "high-powered" car repossessors, see National Bond & Investment Co. v. Whithorn, 123 S.W.2d 263 (Ky.1938). For a bizarre case involving the leader of a religious sect who did not allow the plaintiff to leave a yacht where she had been domiciled against her will except for occasional accompanied trips on shore, see Whittaker v. Sandford, 85 A. 399 (Me.1912). The court reduced the jury award of $1,100 to $500:

> The plaintiff, if imprisoned, was by no means in close confinement. She was afforded all the liberties of the yacht. She was taken on shore by her husband to do shopping and transact business at a bank. She visited neighboring islands with her husband and children, on one of which they enjoyed a family picnic. The case lacks the elements of humiliation and disgrace that frequently attend false imprisonment. She was respectfully treated as a guest in every way, except that she was restrained from quitting the yacht for good and all.

Id. at 403. Is the size of the damages award in this case related to the plaintiff's gender? What if the plaintiff had been a husband? Would his ability to go shopping and enjoy a family picnic lead the jury or judge to evaluate the "elements of humiliation and disgrace" in the same way? Should they?

4. *False arrest.* A special case of false imprisonment applies to arrests made by a police officer or other person who was not legally entitled to do so. Whether the plaintiff can establish liability critically depends on whether the defendant had "probable cause" for making the arrest. The rules governing when a law enforcement officer or other person acts lawfully in making an arrest, in the context of a survey of the historical development of the false imprisonment tort, are discussed in D. Dobbs et al., Handbook on Torts §§ 7.17–.18, at 153–57 (2d ed.2016).

5. *Malicious prosecution.* False arrest does not apply to cases in which the defendant was legally entitled to make the arrest because the warrant and legal forms were proper, but no basis existed for the arrest in the first place because the prosecution was initiated without probable cause and for improper purposes. This claim, called an action for malicious prosecution, permits the arrested individual, after exoneration, to bring an action for expenses and humiliation caused by the malicious prosecution. One of the crucial and much-litigated elements is the showing of a favorable termination for the malicious prosecution plaintiff in the earlier proceeding. See Smith-Hunter v. Harvey, 734 N.E.2d 750 (N.Y.2000)(state no longer requires plaintiff to show innocence; any favorable termination "not inconsistent with innocence" will suffice). For an example of the interplay between false arrest and malicious prosecution in the shoplifting context, see Soares v. Ann & Hope of Rhode Island, Inc., 637 A.2d 339 (R.I.1994), upholding a claim that a store initiated criminal proceedings without probable cause.

A more restricted form of this action lies in many states against persons who wrongfully file civil actions. The history of these actions is traced in Note, Groundless Litigation and the Malicious Prosecution Debate: A Historical Analysis, 88 Yale L.J. 1218 (1979). In Zamos v. Stroud, 87 P.3d 802 (Cal.2004), the unanimous court held that an attorney may be held liable for malicious prosecution for continuing to prosecute a lawsuit once it has been discovered to lack probable cause. Lack of probable cause in this situation is defined as a case that any reasonable attorney would agree is totally and completely without merit. Perhaps not surprisingly, parties who are disgruntled with the tort system are often plaintiffs in malicious prosecution cases. The medical community's experiences with such actions are discussed in Yardley, Malicious Prosecution: A Physician's Need for Reassessment, 60 Chi.-Kent L.Rev. 317 (1984).

Special Problems of Shoplifting

The arrest of a suspected shoplifter presents special legal problems because a private citizen is usually the arrester. The problem is significant economically. Retailers in 2014 lost an estimated $44 billion, roughly 1.4% of annual retail sales, to "shoplifting, employee and vendor theft, and administrative error collectively known as inventory shrink." National Retail Federation, Retailers Estimate Shoplifting, Incidents of Fraud at $44 billion in 2014 (June 23, 2015), at https://nrf.com/media/press-releases/retailers-estimate-shoplifting-incidents-of-fraud-cost-44-billion-2014. These losses are hard to itemize and are uninsurable.

In most states, the misdemeanor of petty larceny covers theft of merchandise worth less than $50 or $100. Thus, the shopkeeper's suspicion is usually that someone has committed a misdemeanor. There is no time to get an officer or a warrant. At common law, even a peace officer had no privilege to arrest for a misdemeanor committed in the officer's presence—unless the officer had a warrant—if the misdemeanor involved no breach of the peace.

Even states that have liberalized the common law misdemeanor arrest rules for police officers may require that the offense have occurred in the officer's presence—an unlikely event in shoplifting cases, unless the officer is not in uniform. For a "citizen's arrest," most states require that the misdemeanor have been committed in the citizen's presence and that the person arrested be guilty. In these states, even if a suspected theft occurs in the presence of a store employee, the shopkeeper still arrests at his or her peril: the arrested person must be proven guilty. Even in more lenient states, the shopkeeper must establish that a misdemeanor had indeed occurred. Thus, if a suspect refuses to open packages or explain suspicious conduct, these rules present the shopkeeper with the choice of making a possibly unlawful citizen's arrest or letting the suspect go. A similar dilemma is presented if the shopkeeper seeks only to retrieve goods without making an arrest: if, in fact, the suspect has obtained the goods legally, the shopkeeper's reasonable belief that they were stolen will not protect against liability for battery if force is used to retrieve the goods.

Nor can the shopkeeper solve the problem by seeking the assistance of a police officer. The shopkeeper who detains the suspect against his or her will until a police officer arrives has in effect made an arrest. If, instead, the shopkeeper chases a suspect down the street shouting, "Stop that man; he is a thief!," and a police officer arrests him, the shopkeeper will be deemed to have instigated the arrest and will be subject to the standards of a citizen's arrest, even though the police officer may be protected as having made the arrest on reasonable grounds.

In 1960, New York enacted General Business Law section 218:

> In any action for false arrest, false imprisonment, unlawful detention, defamation of character, assault, trespass, or invasion of civil rights, brought by any person by reason of having been detained on or in the immediate vicinity of the premises of a retail mercantile establishment for the purpose of investigation or questioning . . . as to the ownership of any merchandise, . . . it shall be a defense to such action that the person was detained in a reasonable manner and for not more than a reasonable time to permit such investigation or questioning by a peace officer . . . or by the owner of the retail

mercantile establishment . . . , his authorized employee or agent, and that such officer, owner, employee or agent had reasonable grounds to believe that the person so detained . . . was committing or attempting to commit larceny on such premises of such merchandise. . . . As used in this section, "reasonable grounds" shall include, but not be limited to, knowledge that a person has concealed possession of unpurchased merchandise of a retail mercantile establishment . . . and a "reasonable time" shall mean the time necessary to permit the person detained to make a statement or to refuse to make a statement, and the time necessary to examine employees and records of the mercantile establishment relative to the ownership of the merchandise. . . .

Similar statutes exist in most states. See, e.g., Calif. Penal Code § 490.5(f). How does the New York statute compare with the common law approach in employee theft cases taken by the *Lopez* court? Are there better alternatives?

In 1991, New York adopted legislation allowing merchants to impose civil penalties of five times the value of the stolen property or a minimum of $75 but not exceeding $500 on shoplifters who make restitution of the value of the stolen goods; in return for agreeing to an informal settlement, the shoplifter gets no criminal record. McKinney's General Obligations Law § 11–105. Increased private efforts to combat shoplifting, and the role of the 1991 New York statute in those efforts, are detailed in Andrea Elliott, *Stores Fight Shoplifting with Private Security*, N.Y. Times, June 17, 2003, at A1. The article features the "private jail" at Macy's, replete with chain-link holding cells, halogen lights, body searches, and handcuffs. A substantial number of cases are resolved without referral to law enforcement officials.

Suits for false imprisonment are apparently an infrequent occurrence. Bourque v. Stop & Shop Companies, Inc., 814 A.2d 320 (R.I.2003), provides a possible explanation: stores that detain suspected shoplifters obtain waivers of claims from those detained. The *Borque* court, however, held the waiver was ineffective because the plaintiff was coerced into signing it. If these waivers are almost always obtained through coercion, is there any point to obtaining them anyway?

4. INTENTIONAL INFLICTION OF EMOTIONAL DISTRESS

In contrast to the other intentional torts, the tort of intentional infliction of emotional distress (IIED) is relatively new. Traditionally, courts were reluctant to recognize such an action for at least two reasons: the difficulties in assuring that actual harm had occurred—an issue that also applied to negligently inflicted emotional distress, p. 262 supra—and the belief that a certain amount of verbal abuse is a part of everyday life. This reluctance was still discernible in a 1948 case in which the defendant loudly and repeatedly on a crowded street called the pregnant plaintiff a "god-damned son of a bitch" and "a dirty crook." Plaintiff alleged general physical harm resulting from the shock. A split court refused relief on the ground that there is "no right to recover for bad manners" in the absence of an assault or defamation because of the "speculative" and "sentimental" nature of the injury and the difficulty of measuring damages. Bartow v. Smith, 78 N.E.2d 735 (Ohio 1948), overruled by Yeager v. Local Union 20, 453 N.E.2d 666 (Ohio 1983).

During this period, other courts were granting relief not only for intentional infliction of emotional distress involving some physical injury, but also when it caused emotional distress alone—at least where the actor's behavior was particularly offensive. In State Rubbish Collectors Ass'n v. Siliznoff, 240 P.2d 282 (Cal.1952), the plaintiff sued for nonpayment of notes and the defendant's cross-complaint asked that the notes be cancelled because of duress. He also sought damages because plaintiff's members had coerced him to sign the notes to pay for a garbage collection contract he had signed with a customer—even though defendant did not belong to plaintiff association. He testified that the encounter was so distressing that he became ill and vomited several times. A jury award of both compensatory and punitive damages was upheld unanimously. For the court, Justice Traynor first concluded that "a cause of action is established when it is shown that one, in the absence of any privilege, intentionally subjects another to the mental suffering incident to serious threats to his physical well-being, whether or not the threats are made under such circumstances as to constitute a technical assault." When mental suffering is a major element of the damages, it is anomalous to deny recovery on the ground that no physical injury followed:

> There are persuasive arguments and analogies that support the recognition of a right to be free from serious, intentional, and unprivileged invasions of mental and emotional tranquility. If a cause of action is otherwise established, it is settled that damages may be given for mental suffering naturally ensuing from the acts complained of [ ], and in the case of many torts, such as assault, battery, false imprisonment, and defamation, mental suffering will frequently constitute the principal element of damages. [ ] In cases where mental suffering constitutes a major element of damages it is anomalous to deny recovery because the defendant's intentional misconduct fell short of producing some physical injury.

> It may be contended that to allow recovery in the absence of physical injury will open the door to unfounded claims and a flood of litigation, and that the requirement that there be physical injury is necessary to insure that serious mental suffering actually occurred. The jury is ordinarily in a better position, however, to determine whether outrageous conduct

results in mental distress than whether that distress in turn results in physical injury. From their own experience jurors are aware of the extent and character of the disagreeable emotions that may result from the defendant's conduct, but a difficult medical question is presented when it must be determined if emotional distress resulted in physical injury. . . .

To what extent does this rationale apply to threatening situations that do not quite measure up to assaults? Compare Restatement (Third) of Torts: Liability for Physical and Emotional Harm § 46 cmt. a ("The outrage tort originated as a catchall to permit recovery in the narrow instance when an actor's conduct exceeded all permissible bounds of a civilized society but an existing tort claim was unavailable.").

Womack v. Eldridge

Supreme Court of Virginia, 1974.
215 Va. 338, 210 S.E.2d 145.

■ Before I'ANSON, C.J., and CARRICO, HARRISON, COCHRAN, HARMAN, POFF and COMPTON, JJ.

■ I'ANSON, CHIEF JUSTICE.

Plaintiff, Danny Lee Womack, instituted this action against the defendant, Rosalie Eldridge, to recover compensatory and punitive damages for mental shock and distress allegedly caused by the defendant's willful, wanton, malicious, fraudulent and deceitful acts and conduct toward him. The question of punitive damages was stricken by the trial court and the jury returned a verdict for the plaintiff in the amount of $45,000. The trial court set aside the verdict . . . on the ground that there could be no recovery for emotional distress in the absence of "physical damage or other bodily harm." We granted plaintiff a writ of error. . . .

Plaintiff assigned numerous errors, but the controlling question is whether one who by extreme and outrageous conduct intentionally or recklessly causes severe emotional distress to another is subject to liability for such emotional distress absent any bodily injury.

The evidence shows that defendant had been engaged in the business of investigating cases for attorneys for many years. She was employed by Richard E. Seifert and his attorney to obtain a photograph of the plaintiff to be used as evidence in the trial of Seifert, who was charged with sexually molesting two young boys. On May 27, 1970, about 8 a.m., defendant went to plaintiff's home and upon gaining admittance told him that she was a Mrs. Jackson from the newspaper and that she was writing an article on Skateland. Defendant asked plaintiff, who was a coach at Skateland, if she could take a picture of him for publication with the article, and he readily consented.

Shortly thereafter defendant delivered the photograph to Seifert's counsel while he was representing Seifert at his preliminary hearing. Seifert's counsel showed plaintiff's photograph to the two young boys and asked if he was the one who molested them. When they replied that he was not, counsel withdrew the photograph and put it in his briefcase. However, the Commonwealth's Attorney then asked to see the photograph and requested additional information about the person shown in it. Defendant was then called to the stand and she supplied the plaintiff's name and address. Plaintiff's photograph in no way resembled Seifert, and the only excuse given by defendant for taking plaintiff's picture was that he was at Skateland when Seifert was arrested. However, the offenses alleged against Seifert did not occur at Skateland.

The Commonwealth's Attorney then directed a detective to go to plaintiff's home and bring him to court. The detective told plaintiff that his photograph had been presented in court; that the Commonwealth's Attorney wanted him to appear at the proceedings; and that he could either appear voluntarily then or he would be summoned. Plaintiff agreed to go voluntarily. When called as a witness, plaintiff testified as to the circumstances under which defendant had obtained his photograph. He also said that he had not molested any children and that he knew nothing about the charges against Seifert.

A police officer questioned plaintiff several times thereafter. Plaintiff was also summoned to appear as a witness before the grand jury but he was not called. However, he was summoned to appear several times at Seifert's trial in the circuit court because of continuances of the cases.

Plaintiff testified that he suffered great shock, distress and nervousness because of defendant's fraud and deceit and her wanton, willful and malicious conduct in obtaining his photograph and turning it over to Seifert's attorney to be used in court. He suffered great anxiety as to what people would think of him and feared that he would be accused of molesting the boys. He had been unable to sleep while the matter was being investigated. While testifying in the instant case he became emotional and incoherent. Plaintiff's wife also testified that her husband experienced great shock and mental depression from the involvement.

. . .

The precise issue presented on this appeal has not been decided by this court.

Courts from other jurisdictions are not in accord on whether there can be a recovery for emotional distress unaccompanied by physical injury. However, most of the courts which have been presented with the question in recent years have held that there may be a recovery against one who by his extreme and outrageous conduct intentionally or recklessly causes another severe emotional distress. . . .

The Restatement (Second) of Torts, section 46 at 71, provides: "(1) One who by extreme and outrageous conduct intentionally or recklessly causes severe emotional distress to another is subject to liability for such emotional distress, and if bodily harm to the other results from it, for such bodily harm." In comment (i) to the Restatement it is expressly stated that this rule also covers a situation where the actor knows that distress is certain, or substantially certain, to result from his conduct.

. . .

A great majority of cases allowing recovery for such a cause of action do so when the act was intentional and the wrongdoer desired the emotional distress or knew or should have known that it would likely result. [ ]

We adopt the view that a cause of action will lie for emotional distress, unaccompanied by physical injury, provided four elements are shown: One, the wrongdoer's conduct was intentional or reckless. This element is satisfied where the wrongdoer had the specific purpose of inflicting emotional distress or where he intended his specific conduct and knew or should have known that emotional distress would likely result. Two, the conduct was outrageous and intolerable in that it offends against the generally accepted standards of decency and morality. This requirement is aimed at limiting frivolous suits and avoiding litigation in situations where only bad manners and mere hurt feelings are involved. Three, there was a causal connection between the wrongdoer's conduct and the emotional distress. Four, the emotional distress was severe.

"It is for the court to determine, in the first instance, whether the defendant's conduct may reasonably be regarded as so extreme and outrageous as to permit recovery, or whether it is necessarily so. Where reasonable men may differ, it is for the jury, subject to the control of the court, to determine whether, in the particular case, the conduct has been sufficiently extreme and outrageous to result in liability." Restatement (Second) of Torts, *supra,* at 77.

In the case at bar, reasonable men may disagree as to whether defendant's conduct was extreme and outrageous and whether plaintiff's emotional distress was severe. Thus, the questions presented were for a jury to determine. A jury could conclude from the evidence presented that defendant willfully, recklessly, intentionally and deceitfully obtained plaintiff's photograph for the purpose of permitting her employers to use it as a defense in a criminal case without considering the effect it would have on the plaintiff. There is nothing in the evidence that even suggests that plaintiff may have been involved in the child molesting cases. The record shows that the only possible excuse for involving the plaintiff was that Seifert was arrested at the place where plaintiff was employed. A reasonable person would or should have recognized the likelihood of the serious mental distress that would be caused in involving an innocent person in child molesting cases. If the two boys had hesitated in answering that the man in the photograph was not the one who had molested them, it is evident that the finger of suspicion would have been pointed at the plaintiff.

Defendant contended in her brief, and in oral argument before us . . . that the action of the Commonwealth's Attorney in causing plaintiff's name to be revealed was an intervening cause which absolved her of any liability.

We will not consider those contentions because defendant did not assign cross-error. [ ]

For the reasons stated, the judgment of the court below is reversed, the jury verdict reinstated, and final judgment hereby entered for the plaintiff.

NOTES AND QUESTIONS

1.   Suppose the evidence indicated that defendant had been hired without knowledge of the use to which the photograph would be put. Would the Restatement standard of liability, as interpreted by the court, be satisfied? Suppose, instead, defendant knew that it was to be used for purposes of identification in a criminal case—but nothing more. Would the standard be satisfied? Suppose she knew that the photo was to be used to incriminate plaintiff in a case in which he had no involvement—but she took the picture on the street. Would plaintiff have had a colorable claim?

2.   What result if plaintiff had claimed intentional infliction of emotional distress against Seifert's attorney?

3.   In Russo v. White, 400 S.E.2d 160 (Va.1991), the court affirmed dismissal of the plaintiff's claim in a case in which she alleged that the defendant had made 340 "hang-up" phone calls to her in a two-month period after she refused to go out with him more than once. The court emphasized that plaintiff had not suffered any physical injury as a result of the stress and that defendant had not spoken during the calls. Asserting that the IIED tort, although recognized since *Womack,* is "not favored" in Virginia, the court quoted from Givelber, The Right to Minimum Social Decency and the Limits of Evenhandedness: Intentional Infliction of Emotional Distress by Outrageous Conduct, 82 Colum.L.Rev. 42, 42–43 (1982), in arguing:

> [IIED] "differs from traditional intentional torts in an important respect: it provides no clear definition of the prohibited conduct."
> . . . Assault, battery, and false imprisonment "describe specific forms of behavior," but the term "outrageous" "does not objectively describe an act or series of acts; rather, it represents an evaluation of behavior. The concept thus fails to provide clear guidance either to those whose conduct it purports to regulate, or to those who must evaluate that conduct."

Does this argument persuasively distinguish the IIED tort from other intentional torts, particularly offensive battery? How does IIED compare with negligence in specifying prohibited behavior? Does the argument significantly undermine the legitimacy of the IIED tort or instead justify greater judicial oversight? See Restatement (Third) of Torts: Liability for Physical and Emotional Harm § 46 cmt. g (recognizing that "courts play a more substantial screening role on the question of extreme and outrageous conduct than they usually do, as a balance to the open-ended nature of this claim and the wide range of behavior to which it might plausibly apply").

4.   *The "extreme and outrageous" standard.* In an effort to make the standard of liability more concrete, Restatement Second section 46, cmt. d. states "the case is one in which the recitation of the facts to an average member of the community would arouse his resentment against the actor, and lead him to exclaim, 'Outrageous!' " The Restatement Third section 46 cmt. d retains this standard because it "has been widely adopted, has been employed satisfactorily, and has become familiar." While recognizing that "[s]pecific rules for when conduct is extreme and outrageous cannot be stated, nor can categories of conduct be identified for formulation into universal rules," the Restatement Third concludes that the case law provides sufficient guidance:

> Whether an actor's conduct is extreme and outrageous depends on the facts of each case, including the relationship of the parties, whether the actor abused a position of authority over the other person, whether the other person was especially vulnerable and the actor knew of the vulnerability, the motivation of the actor, and whether the conduct was repeated or prolonged.

Id.

For these reasons, the extreme and outrageous behavior that is subject to liability "describes a very small slice of human behavior." Id. cmt. a. In particular, "[o]rdinary insults and indignities are not enough for liability to be imposed, even if the actor desires to cause emotional harm." Id. cmt. d.

5.   *The extrasensitive plaintiff.* As discussed in the prior note, courts will consider whether the defendant knew that plaintiff was "especially vulnerable." Should courts give any further recognition to the unusually sensitive plaintiff who is severely injured by a stimulus that would not cause the requisite harm in a reasonable person? Consider a stimulus that would ordinarily cause such harm for a reasonable person and subjects defendant to liability. Should defendant then be liable for the extraordinary harm suffered by an unusually sensitive plaintiff? Recall the eggshell rule that awards such damages for physical harms, discussed at p. 395 supra.

6.   *Credit practices.* One type of situation that recurs frequently is the bill-collector case. The extent to which a creditor may utilize self-help in attempting to collect a debt is problematic. Surely a creditor may write a letter warning the alleged debtor that unless the amount claimed to be due is paid within a certain number of days, a suit will be filed. Surely a creditor may not beat the alleged debtor to a pulp in efforts to collect money. Where should the line be drawn? Is it clear that some self-help

should be encouraged so that every creditor who wants to collect money need not initiate a lawsuit? On the assumption that physical violence is never permissible, we may confine our speculation to the words used and the ways in which they are communicated. Consider the following acts allegedly committed by a collection agency seeking repayment of a loan in Sherman v. Field Clinic, 392 N.E.2d 154, 156 (Ill.App.1979):

> telephoning plaintiffs' residence 10–20 times per day 3 days per week and 5–6 times per day 2 other days per week; sending numerous letters to plaintiffs' residence; making numerous telephone calls to Mr. Sherman at his place of business, though only Mrs. Sherman was responsible for any debts due the Clinic; threatening to "embarrass" Mr. Sherman by contacting his employers and co-workers; threatening to garnish half of Mr. Sherman's wages; frequently using profane and obscene language in calls to Mr. Sherman; calling and speaking to Mrs. Sherman's 15 year old daughter, plaintiff Deborah Billy, in connection with the debt, though only Mrs. Sherman was responsible for any debts due the Clinic; frequently making threats to the daughter that Mr. and Mrs. Sherman would be sent to jail for not paying the bill; and frequently using abusive language in calls to Mrs. Sherman.

To evaluate the propriety of each of the alleged acts if done alone, consider the following questions: (1) What is the basic purpose of the defendant's conduct? Does it "intend" to cause emotional harm? Physical harm? Should the courts focus on the harm that actually ensues, what the defendant intended to cause, or on what a reasonable defendant should have foreseen from its conduct? (2) Should the identity of the defendant matter? This case involves a collection agency attempting to collect a debt owed to a medical clinic. Often a suit involves a retail merchant who has sold items on credit and is attempting to collect the debt itself or, as in *Sherman*, with the help of a credit collection agency. Should each of these parties have the same self-help privilege? (3) If the alleged debtor denies owing the claimed amount, should that situation be treated differently from one in which the debtor admits the debt but claims financial difficulties and wants to delay repayment? (4) Should it matter if the creditor has had serious difficulties in locating the debtor?

7. *Racial harassment in the workplace.* Courts have upheld IIED claims in cases of racial insults and harassment, including such cases in the workplace.* See, e.g., Turley v. ISG Lackawana, Inc., 774 F.3d 140 (2d Cir.2014)(finding that plaintiff employee proved that his supervisor engaged in "extreme and outrageous" conduct by repeatedly failing over a three-year period to respond to ongoing instances of racially motivated harassment of plaintiff, blocking others from investigating the harassment, and encouraging others to participate in the harassment). Some courts have denied relief for harassment in the workplace on the ground that the employer's words and actions, while offensive, did not constitute "extreme and outrageous" conduct. See, e.g., Patterson v. McLean Credit Union, 805

---

*   In some jurisdictions, the workers' compensation bar to tort claims extends to common law actions for IIED.

F.2d 1143 (4th Cir.1986)(concluding that plaintiff's allegations that her supervisor gave her too much work, required her to sweep and dust, and commented that blacks are slower than whites, did not rise to level of "extreme and outrageous" conduct), aff'd in part, vacated in part and remanded on different grounds, 491 U.S. 164 (1989). The tort system's response to verbal harassment in the workplace is discussed and criticized in Austin, Employer Abuse, Worker Resistance, and the Tort of Intentional Infliction of Emotional Distress, 41 Stan.L.Rev. 1 (1988). See also Delgado, Words That Wound: A Tort Action for Racial Insults, Epithets, and Name-Calling, 17 Harv.C.R.-C.L.L.Rev. 133 (1982); Love, Discriminatory Speech and the Tort of Intentional Infliction of Emotional Distress, 47 Wash. & Lee L.Rev. 123 (1990).

Cases of workplace discrimination also implicate various federal statutes that make an employer liable for specified discriminatory acts. The purpose of these statutes is to eliminate these forms of discrimination in the workplace and provide employees with compensation for the harms they suffer as a result of their employers engaging in the prohibited discriminatory practices. For example, the Civil Rights Reform Act of 1991, Pub.L. 102—166, 105 Stat. 1071, makes claims for racial harassment on the job actionable under 42 U.S.C. § 1981, an antidiscrimination statute passed during the Reconstruction era, which gives all persons equal rights "to make and enforce contracts." Employees who have been victimized by racial discrimination can also bring an action under Title VII of the Civil Rights Act of 1964, 42 U.S.C. § 2000e et seq.; however, Title VII's framework for resolution imposes several procedural obstacles not present in a section 1981 action.

Scholars have long recognized the connection between these statutes and tort law. See, e.g., Oppenheimer, Negligent Discrimination, 141 U.Pa.L.Rev. 899 (1993)(articulating a negligence-based theory of employer liability under Title VII). Since the late 1980s, courts and scholars have expressly labeled federal employment discrimination statutes as "federal torts," and courts have increasingly applied tort concepts to these statutes. In 2011, the U.S. Supreme Court declared: "[W]e start from the premise that when Congress creates a federal tort it adopts the background of general tort law." Staub v. Proctor Hosp., 131 S.Ct. 1186, 1192 (2011). Although these statutes importantly differ from tort law, if they implicate terms or concepts that are part of tort law, the Court interprets these statutory provisions in light of their common law meaning, unless the statutory language dictates otherwise. For extended discussion of the relation between these statutes and tort law, see generally Symposium, Torts and Civil Rights Law: Migration and Conflict, 75 Ohio St.L.J. 1021 (2014).

8. *Sexual harassment in the workplace.* The law dealing with statutory claims for sexual harassment in the workplace has been dynamic. Courts have long held that employers violate Title VII if employment benefits are conditioned on sexual favors—so-called "quid pro quo" cases. In 1986, the Supreme Court broadened the Title VII standard to permit claims if discriminatory conduct created an "abusive working environment."

Meritor Savings Bank v. Vinson, 477 U.S. 57 (1986). The interplay between Title VII and the IIED tort in the sexual harassment area is nicely illustrated by Kanzler v. Renner, 937 P.2d 1337 (Wyo.1997), in which plaintiff, a police dispatcher, was harassed and stalked by a fellow police officer over an extended period of time. The Title VII claim failed because defendant was not her employer or supervisor as required by the statute, and the co-defendant police department took appropriate measures when apprised of the situation. But this did not preclude a common law claim by plaintiff against defendant Renner. In denying his motion for summary judgment, the court provided a list of factors to assist in determining the merit of a workplace claim of "outrageous conduct" subject to tort liability: 1) abuse of power, 2) repeated incidents/pattern of harassment, 3) unwelcome touching/offensive non-negligible physical contact, and 4) retaliation for refusing or reporting sexually motivated advances.

The subject of sexual harassment has received extensive scholarly treatment. See, e.g., C. MacKinnon, Sexual Harassment of Working Women (1979); Ehrenreich, Pluralist Myths and Powerless Men: The Ideology of Reasonableness in Sexual Harassment Law, 99 Yale L.J. 1177 (1990); Estrich, Sex at Work, 43 Stan.L.Rev. 813 (1991).

Constitutional Defense

The fine line between outrageous conduct and free expression has given rise to serious First Amendment concerns, which are addressed in the next case. In reading the case it is important to know that in New York Times Co. v. Sullivan, 376 U.S. 254 (1964), the Court held that in libel cases, public officials (later expanded to include public figures) who sue for false statements that harm their reputations must prove that the defendant made the statement knowing that it was false, or recklessly uttered it without caring whether it was true or false. Proof of either prong constitutes "actual malice." The case is reprinted in the next Chapter at p. 1062 infra.

Hustler Magazine v. Falwell

Supreme Court of the United States, 1988.
485 U.S. 46, 108 S.Ct. 876, 99 L.Ed.2d 41.

■ CHIEF JUSTICE REHNQUIST delivered the opinion of the Court.

Petitioner Hustler Magazine, Inc., is a magazine of nationwide circulation. Respondent Jerry Falwell, a nationally known minister who has been active as a commentator on politics and public affairs, sued petitioner and its publisher, petitioner Larry Flynt. . . .

The inside front cover of the November 1983 issue of Hustler Magazine featured a "parody" of an advertisement for Campari Liqueur that contained the name and picture of respondent and was entitled "Jerry Falwell talks about his first time." This parody was modeled after actual Campari ads that included interviews with various celebrities about their "first times." Although it was apparent by the end of each interview that this meant the first time they sampled Campari, the ads clearly played on the sexual double entendre of the general subject of "first times." Copying the form and layout of these Campari ads, Hustler's editors chose respondent as the featured celebrity and drafted an alleged "interview" with him in which he states that his "first time" was during a drunken incestuous rendezvous with his mother in an outhouse. The Hustler parody portrays respondent and his mother as drunk and immoral, and suggests that respondent is a hypocrite who preaches only when he is drunk. In small print at the bottom of the page, the ad contains the disclaimer, "ad parody—not to be taken seriously." The magazine's table of contents also lists the ad as "Fiction; Ad and Personality Parody."

Soon after the November issue of Hustler became available to the public, respondent brought this diversity action in the United States District Court for the Western District of Virginia against Hustler Magazine, Inc., Larry C. Flynt, and Flynt Distributing Co. Respondent stated in his complaint that publication of the ad parody in Hustler entitled him to recover damages for libel, invasion of privacy, and intentional infliction of emotional distress. The case proceeded to trial. At the close of the evidence, the District Court granted a directed verdict for petitioners on the invasion of privacy claim. The jury then found against respondent on the libel claim, specifically finding that the ad parody could not "reasonably be understood as describing actual facts about [respondent] or actual events in which [he] participated." [ ] The jury ruled for respondent on the intentional infliction of emotional distress claim, however, and stated that he should be awarded $100,000 in compensatory damages, as well as $50,000 each in punitive damages from petitioners [Hustler Magazine and Flynt]. Petitioners' motion for judgment notwithstanding the verdict was denied.

On appeal, the [Fourth Circuit] affirmed the judgment against petitioners. . . .[3] . . .

This case presents us with a novel question involving First Amendment limitations upon a State's authority to protect its citizens from the intentional infliction of emotional distress. We must decide whether a public figure may recover damages for emotional harm caused by the publication of an ad parody offensive to him, and doubtless gross and repugnant in the eyes of most. Respondent would have us find that a State's interest in protecting public figures from emotional distress is sufficient to deny First Amendment protection to speech that is patently offensive and is intended to inflict emotional injury, even when that speech could not reasonably have been

---

[3] Under Virginia law, in an action for intentional infliction of emotional distress a plaintiff must show that the defendant's conduct (1) is intentional or reckless; (2) offends generally accepted standards of decency or morality; (3) is causally connected with the plaintiff's emotional distress; and (4) caused emotional distress that was severe. [ ]

interpreted as stating actual facts about the public figure involved. This we decline to do.

At the heart of the First Amendment is the recognition of the fundamental importance of the free flow of ideas and opinions on matters of public interest and concern. "[T]he freedom to speak one's mind is not only an aspect of individual liberty—and thus a good unto itself—but also is essential to the common quest for truth and the vitality of society as a whole." [ ] We have therefore been particularly vigilant to ensure that individual expressions of ideas remain free from governmentally imposed sanctions. The First Amendment recognizes no such thing as a "false" idea. [ ] As Justice Holmes wrote, "[W]hen men have realized that time has upset many fighting faiths, they may come to believe even more than they believe the very foundations of their own conduct that the ultimate good desired is better reached by free trade in ideas—that the best test of truth is the power of the thought to get itself accepted in the competition of the market. . . ." [ ]

The sort of robust political debate encouraged by the First Amendment is bound to produce speech that is critical of those who hold public office or those public figures who are "intimately involved in the resolution of important public questions or, by reason of their fame, shape events in areas of concern to society at large." [ ] Justice Frankfurter put it succinctly in Baumgartner v. United States, 322 U.S. 665, 673–674 (1944), when he said that "[o]ne of the prerogatives of American citizenship is the right to criticize public men and measures." Such criticism, inevitably, will not always be reasoned or moderate; public figures as well as public officials will be subject to "vehement, caustic, and sometimes unpleasantly sharp attacks," [*New York Times*]. "[T]he candidate who vaunts his spotless record and sterling integrity cannot convincingly cry 'Foul!' when an opponent or an industrious reporter attempts to demonstrate the contrary." [ ]

Of course, this does not mean that any speech about a public figure is immune from sanction in the form of damages. Since [*New York Times*] we have consistently ruled that a public figure may hold a speaker liable for the damage to reputation caused by publication of a defamatory falsehood, but only if the statement was made "with knowledge that it was false or with reckless disregard of whether it was false or not." [ ] False statements of fact are particularly valueless; they interfere with the truth-seeking function of the marketplace of ideas, and they cause damage to an individual's reputation that cannot easily be repaired by counter speech, however persuasive or effective. [ ] But even though falsehoods have little value in and of themselves, they are "nevertheless inevitable in free debate," [ ], and a rule that would impose strict liability on a publisher for false factual assertions would have an undoubted "chilling" effect on speech relating to public figures that does have constitutional value. "Freedoms of expression require 'breathing space.' " [ ] This breathing space is provided by a constitutional rule that allows public figures to recover for libel or defamation only when they can prove both that the statement was false and that the statement was made with the requisite level of culpability.

Respondent argues, however, that a different standard should apply in this case because here the State seeks to prevent not reputational damage, but the severe emotional distress suffered by the person who is the subject of an offensive publication. [ ] In respondent's view, and in the view of the Court of Appeals, so long as the utterance was intended to inflict emotional distress, was outrageous, and did in fact inflict serious emotional distress, it is of no constitutional import whether the statement was a fact or an opinion, or whether it was true or false. It is the intent to cause injury that is the gravamen of the tort, and the State's interest in preventing emotional harm simply outweighs whatever interest a speaker may have in speech of this type.

Generally speaking the law does not regard the intent to inflict emotional distress as one which should receive much solicitude, and it is quite understandable that most if not all jurisdictions have chosen to make it civilly culpable where the conduct in question is sufficiently "outrageous." But in the world of debate about public affairs, many things done with motives that are less than admirable are protected by the First Amendment. In [Garrison v. Louisiana, 379 U.S. 64 (1964)], we held that even when a speaker or writer is motivated by hatred or ill-will his expression was protected by the First Amendment:

> Debate on public issues will not be uninhibited if the speaker must run the risk that it will be proved in court that he spoke out of hatred; even if he did speak out of hatred, utterances honestly believed contribute to the free interchange of ideas and the ascertainment of truth. [ ]

Thus while such a bad motive may be deemed controlling for purposes of tort liability in other areas of the law, we think the First Amendment prohibits such a result in the area of public debate about public figures.

Were we to hold otherwise, there can be little doubt that political cartoonists and satirists would be subjected to damages awards without any showing that their work falsely defamed its subject. Webster's defines a caricature as "the deliberately distorted picturing or imitating of a person, literary style, etc. by exaggerating features or mannerisms for satirical effect." [ ] The appeal of the political cartoon or caricature is often based on exploration of unfortunate physical traits or politically embarrassing events—an exploration often calculated to injure the feelings of the subject of the portrayal. The art of the cartoonist is often not reasoned or evenhanded, but slashing and one-sided. . . .

. . .

Despite their sometimes caustic nature, from the early cartoon portraying George Washington as an ass down to the present day, graphic depictions and satirical cartoons have played a prominent role in public and political debate. [Thomas] Nast's castigation of the Tweed Ring, Walt McDougall's characterization of presidential candidate James G. Blaine's banquet with the millionaires at Delmonico's as "The Royal Feast of Belshazzar," and numerous other efforts have undoubtedly had an effect on the course and outcome of contemporaneous debate. Lincoln's tall, gangling posture, Teddy Roosevelt's glasses and teeth, and Franklin D. Roosevelt's jutting jaw and cigarette holder have been memorialized by political cartoons with an effect that could not have been obtained by the photographer or the portrait artist. From the viewpoint of history it is clear that our political discourse would have been considerably poorer without them.

Respondent contends, however, that the caricature in question here was so "outrageous" as to distinguish it from more traditional political cartoons. There is no doubt that the caricature of respondent and his mother published in Hustler is at best a distant cousin of the political cartoons described above, and a rather poor relation at that. If it were possible by laying down a principled standard to separate the one from the other, public discourse would probably suffer little or no harm. But we doubt that there is any such standard, and we are quite sure that the pejorative description "outrageous" does not supply one. "Outrageousness" in the area of political and social discourse has an inherent subjectiveness about it which would allow a jury to impose liability on the basis of the jurors' tastes or views, or perhaps on the basis of their dislike of a particular expression. An "outrageousness" standard thus runs afoul of our longstanding refusal to allow damages to be awarded because the speech in question may have an adverse emotional impact on the audience. . . .

. . .

Admittedly, these oft-repeated First Amendment principles, like other principles, are subject to limitations. We recognized in [FCC v. Pacifica Foundation, 438 U.S. 726 (1978)] that speech that is " 'vulgar,' 'offensive,' and 'shocking' " is "not entitled to absolute constitutional protection under all circumstances." [ ] In Chaplinsky v. New Hampshire, 315 U.S. 568 (1942), we held that a state could lawfully punish an individual for the use of insulting " 'fighting' words—those which by their very utterance inflict injury or tend to incite an immediate breach of the peace." [ ] These limitations are but recognition of the observation in [Dun & Bradstreet, Inc. v. Greenmoss Builders, 472 U.S. 749 (1985)] that this Court has "long recognized that not all speech is of equal First Amendment importance." But the sort of expression involved in this case does not seem to us to be governed by any exception to the general First Amendment principles stated above.

We conclude that public figures and public officials may not recover for the tort of intentional infliction of emotional distress by reason of publications such as the one here at issue without showing in addition that the publication contains a false statement of fact which was made with "actual malice," i.e., with knowledge that the statement was false or with reckless disregard as to whether or not it was true. This is not merely a "blind application" of the *New York Times* standard, [ ], it reflects our considered judgment that such a standard is necessary to give adequate "breathing space" to the freedoms protected by the First Amendment.

Here it is clear that respondent Falwell is a "public figure" for purposes of First Amendment law.[5] The jury found against respondent on his libel claim when it decided that the Hustler ad parody could not "reasonably be understood as describing actual facts about [respondent] or actual events in which [he] participated." [ ] The Court of Appeals interpreted the jury's finding to be that the ad parody "was not reasonably believable," [ ], and in accordance with our custom we accept this finding. Respondent is thus relegated to his claim for damages awarded by the jury for the intentional infliction of emotional distress by "outrageous" conduct. But for reasons heretofore stated this claim cannot, consistently with the First Amendment, form a basis for the award of damages when the conduct in question is the publication of a caricature such as the ad parody involved here. The judgment of the Court of Appeals is accordingly

Reversed.

■ JUSTICE KENNEDY took no part in the consideration or decision of this case.

■ JUSTICE WHITE, concurring in the judgment.

As I see it, the decision in [*New York Times*] has little to do with this case, for here the jury found that the ad contained no assertion of fact. But I agree with the Court that the judgment below, which penalized the publication of the parody, cannot be squared with the First Amendment.

NOTES AND QUESTIONS

1. Why wasn't the *New York Times* standard violated here? Wasn't the ad depiction a false statement of fact made with "actual malice"? If it wasn't a false statement of fact, as Justice White suggests in his concurring opinion, why does *New York Times* have any relevance to the case?

2. Is the interest in providing breathing room for political satire sufficient to override the plaintiff's interests in avoiding the humiliation and embarrassment to which he was subjected?

---

[5] Neither party disputes this conclusion. Respondent is the host of a nationally syndicated television show and was the founder and president of a political organization formerly known as the Moral Majority. He is also the founder of Liberty University in Lynchburg, Virginia, and is the author of several books and publications. [ ]

3. The Court mentions a number of situations where expression is sometimes subject to limitation—obscenity; "fighting words"; vulgar, offensive, shocking material. Is the depiction here distinguishable?

4. Would you expect the *Falwell* Court's holding to be limited to public figures? What if Hustler parodied, in similar fashion, an anonymous bank clerk? The distinction between public and private figures has received extensive treatment in defamation law. We return to it in the next Chapter.

5. Should the law protect some minimal level of "civility" in public discourse? See generally R. Smolla, Jerry Falwell v. Larry Flynt: The First Amendment on Trial (1988); LeBel, Emotional Distress, the First Amendment, and "This Kind of Speech": A Heretical Perspective on *Hustler Magazine v. Falwell*, 60 Colo.L.Rev. 315 (1989); and Post, The Constitutional Concept of Public Discourse: Outrageous Opinion, Democratic Deliberation, and *Hustler Magazine v. Falwell*, 103 Harv.L.Rev. 601 (1990).

6. In Snyder v. Phelps, 562 U.S. 443 (2011), the father of a soldier killed in Iraq brought suit claiming defamation, invasion of privacy, and IIED against Westboro Baptist Church and several of its members. The case arose out of a well-publicized protest by the fundamentalist church, which frequently expressed, in outrageous terms, its disapproval of leniency toward gays and other aspects of modern society. Defendants picketed the solder's funeral, carrying signs with "Fag Troops," "Thank God for Dead Solders," "Priests Rape Boys," and other similar epithets. At trial, the jury awarded plaintiff $2.9 million in compensatory damages and a total of $8 million in punitive damages based on, among others, the IIED claim. Distinguishing between private and public speech, the latter of which is entitled to the highest First Amendment protection, the Supreme Court concluded that the defendants' speech concerned public matters. Although the speech took place at an individual's funeral, it consisted of a condemnation of several aspects of modern society. Thus, the Court held, 8–1, that state tort law could not impose liability on defendants for speech protected by the First Amendment, notwithstanding the outrageousness finding by the jury.

5. INTENTIONAL INTERFERENCE WITH FAMILY RELATIONSHIPS

For centuries, courts recognized two actions for intentional interference with the marital relation. The action for "criminal conversation" is based on adultery—"sexual intercourse of an outsider with husband or wife." Historically, the action was available only to husbands because of the early property rights approach to the relationship between husband and wife. In recent times, some states have extended the action to wives as well. But as some have expanded the action, a majority of the states have abolished the action entirely, either legislatively or judicially. In Neal v. Neal, 873 P.2d 871 (Idaho 1994), the court, after rejecting the historical justification for the tort, explained its decision to abolish it:

Revenge, which may be a motive for bringing the cause of action, has no place in determining the legal rights between two parties. Further, this type of suit may expose the defendant to the extortionate schemes of the plaintiff, since it could ruin the defendant's reputation. Deterrence is not achieved; the nature of the activities underlying criminal conversation, that is sexual activity, are not such that the risk of damages would likely be a deterrent. Finally, since the injuries suffered are intangible, damage awards are not governed by any true standards, making it more likely that they could result from passion or prejudice.

The second tort, for "alienation of affections," applies to behavior that enables outsiders, through any means, to drive a wedge between family members. See, e.g., Kirk v. Koch, 607 So.2d 1220 (Miss.1992)(jury could have found that defendant "directly and intentionally interfered" with plaintiff's marriage despite lack of showing of sexual relations or affectionate conduct between defendant and plaintiff's spouse). Again, most states have abolished this action, through judicial decision or by the enactment of "heart balm" statutes that prohibit suits based on alienation grounds. In many states, these statutes also preclude actions based upon breach of promise to marry and upon seduction.

In Veeder v. Kennedy, 589 N.W.2d 610 (S.D.1999), the court noted that 34 states had abandoned the alienation action by statute, but that only five had done so by judicial decision. In this case, the court again reviewed arguments against the action but retained it, affirming a judgment for compensatory and punitive damages totaling $265,000. The case involved a relationship between defendant bank manager and a married employee. The majority rejected arguments made by earlier judges that the "underlying rationale for alienation suits, that is, the preservation of the marriage, is ludicrous. And it is folly to hope any longer that a married person who has become inclined to philander can be preserved within an affectionate marriage by the threat of an alienation suit." The majority in *Veeder* declined to abolish the action, partly because it found legislative support for the action and thought that any abolition should come from the legislature, but also because it found value in the action, quoting a member of the court in a 1981 case:

> Finally, because we happen to be living in a period of loose morals and frequent extramarital involvements is no reason for a court to put its stamp of approval on this conduct; and I feel certain that a case will arise in the future where some party has so flagrantly broken up a stable marriage that we would rue the day that an alienation suit was not available to the injured party.

See also Bland v. Hill, 735 So.2d 414 (Miss.1999), in which a state that had already abolished criminal conversation retained the alienation action. The dissenters observed:

> Over the years, courts have increasingly been required to delve into matters which are not ideally suits for judicial intervention. . . . As it applies to two spouses, the judicial system cannot be called upon to make one spouse love another. When the marriage breaks down, it is usually the fault of both spouses.

> Hence, this Court is called upon under an archaic cause of action to put a price tag on the heart (love) by analyzing the love between two spouses . . . together with a third party and that party's role in allegedly breaking up the marriage that for all practical purposes was already heading for a divorce court.

The dissenters also noted that as early as 1935, states were abolishing this action "in response to a wide public sentiment . . . that such actions had been so abused, made the means of exploitation and blackmail, that the existence of such causes of action had become of greater injury than of benefit to society."

In McDermott v. Reynolds, 530 S.E.2d 902 (Va.2000), plaintiff attempted to avoid a statutory bar to claims for alienation of affections by arguing that defendant had "flaunted outwardly" his adulterous relationship with plaintiff's wife, constituting grounds for an intentional infliction of emotional distress claim recognized in the state [see *Womack*, p. 924 supra]. The court rejected what it took to be a back-door effort to evade the statutory bar, concluding that when the legislature enacted the provision "it manifested an intent to abolish common law actions seeking damages for a particular type of conduct, regardless of the name that a plaintiff assigns to it."

Compare Doe v. Zwelling, 620 S.E.2d 750 (Va.2005), a case in which plaintiff successfully maneuvered around the abolition of claims for alienation of affections. Defendant therapist counseled plaintiff's wife and then separately saw plaintiff in an effort to resolve marital difficulties. Plaintiff confided intimate details of the couple's relationship to defendant, insisting that they be kept confidential. Defendant used those details to malign plaintiff with his spouse and then entered into a relationship with her. After plaintiff's marriage fell apart, he sued alleging professional malpractice by the therapist. Distinguishing *McDermott* as a case in which the only harm arose from the effect of defendant's conduct on the plaintiff's marriage, the court reversed the trial court's dismissal of plaintiff's complaint. Plaintiff could proceed on claims of professional malpractice for harms caused to interests other than the marriage. The court identified failing to keep intimate confidences and providing inappropriate therapy to a patient—recommending psychotropic drugs and Eastern meditation—as harms independent of the marriage relationship.

At the same time when actions for criminal conversation and alienation are finding less favor, other actions are finding new support. In Stone v. Wall, 734 So.2d 1038 (Fla.1999), the court recognized an action for intentional interference with the parent-child relationship. The plaintiff father who had custody of his child sued members of the family of his deceased ex-wife for having failed to return the child from a visit and then concealing the child. The court began by noting that an ancient action gave the "father an action for the abduction of his heir." Though the action was extended to the kidnapping of any child, it was not given to mothers because they had no property right in their children. In the modern day, the court thought any parent or person with custodial rights should have such an action against those who interfere with such rights. The court noted that most states recognize the claim. The court observed that states widely recognized claims for "intentional interference with business relationships . . . because 'economic relations are entitled to freedom from unreasonable interference.' [ ] We find that the parental custody relationship should be entitled to no less legally recognized protection from unreasonable interference." See also Khalifa v. Shannon, 945 A.2d 1244 (Md.2008).

6. TRESPASS TO LAND

At early common law, every unauthorized entry by a person or object onto another's land that resulted from a voluntary act was subject to liability as a trespass. Obviously, a person who was carried against his will onto the land of another would not have satisfied the requirement of voluntary conduct and therefore could not be held to have committed a trespass.

As indicated by the New York blasting cases, p. 518 supra, many courts required actual physical entry by a tangible object, since the interest that plaintiff sought to protect was the exclusive possession of his land. As plaintiffs came to allege trespassory invasions resulting from objects—such as exploding boilers and flying debris—rather than people, many courts began to distinguish between "direct" and "indirect," or trespassory and non-trespassory harms. This distinction, which was borrowed from the common law writ system in which it was not limited to invasions of land, created great confusion. Again, the New York cases, considered earlier, offer examples. Modern trespass doctrine has largely obliterated the historical distinction between direct and indirect trespassory invasions of land.

With this background in mind, consider the following case.

Martin v. Reynolds Metals Co.

Supreme Court of Oregon, 1959.
221 Or. 86, 342 P.2d 790.

■ Before MCALLISTER, C.J., and LUSK, WARNER, PERRY, SLOAN, O'CONNELL and MILLARD, JJ.

■ O'CONNELL, J.

[Plaintiffs sued for trespass, claiming damage to their farmland from the operation of defendant's nearby aluminum reduction plant. The trial judge awarded plaintiffs $71,500 for damages to their land, which could no longer be used to raise livestock because the cattle were poisoned by ingesting the fluoride compounds that became airborne from the plant and settled on the plaintiffs' land. (The daily emanation of fluorides from the plant averaged 800 pounds.) The judge also awarded $20,000 for the deterioration of the land through growth of brush and weeds resulting from the lack of grazing. The judge rejected punitive damages. The damages covered the period from August 1951 through the end of 1955. If the action were properly brought in trespass, with its six-year statute of limitations, the award was permissible. But if the action were one of nuisance, then damages were recoverable for only 1954 and 1955, because of the two-year statute of limitations.]

The gist of the defendant's argument is as follows: a trespass arises only when there has been a "breaking and entering upon real property," constituting a direct, as distinguished from a consequential, invasion of the possessor's interest in land; and the settling upon the land of fluoride compounds consisting of gases, fumes and particulates is not sufficient to satisfy these requirements.

Before appraising the argument we shall first describe more particularly the physical and chemical nature of the substance which was deposited upon plaintiffs' land. In reducing alumina (the oxide of aluminum) to aluminum the alumina is subjected to an electrolytic process which causes the emanation of fluoridic compounds consisting principally of hydrogen fluoride, calcium fluoride, iron fluoride and silicon tetrafluoride. The individual particulates which form these chemical compounds are not visible to the naked eye. A part of them were captured by a fume collection system which was installed in November, 1950; the remainder became airborne and a part of the uncaptured particles eventually were deposited upon plaintiffs' land.

. . .

Trespass and private nuisance are separate fields of tort liability relating to actionable interference with the possession of land. They may be distinguished by comparing the interest invaded; an actionable invasion of a possessor's interest in the exclusive possession of land is a trespass; an actionable invasion of a possessor's interest in the use and enjoyment of his land is a nuisance. [ ]

The same conduct on the part of a defendant may and often does result in the actionable invasion of both of these interests, in which case the choice between the two remedies is, in most cases, a matter of little consequence. Where the action is brought on the theory of nuisance alone the court ordinarily is not called upon to determine whether the conduct would also result in a trespassory invasion. In such cases the courts' treatment of the invasion solely in terms of the law of nuisance does not mean that the same conduct could not also be regarded as a trespass. Some of the cases relied upon by the defendant are of this type; cases in which the court holds that the interference with the plaintiff's possession through soot, dirt, smoke, cinders, ashes and similar substances constitute a nuisance, but where the court does not discuss the applicability of the law of trespass to the same set of facts. [ ]

However, there are cases which have held that the defendant's interference with plaintiff's possession resulting from the settling upon his land of effluents emanating from defendant's operations is exclusively nontrespassory. [ ] Although in such cases the separate particles which collectively cause the invasion are minute, the deposit of each of the particles constitutes a physical intrusion and, but for the size of the particle, would clearly give rise to an action of trespass. The defendant asks us to take account of the difference in size of the physical agency through which the intrusion occurs and relegate entirely to the field of nuisance law certain invasions which do not meet the dimensional test, whatever that is. In pressing this argument upon us the defendant must admit that there are cases which have held that a trespass results from the movement or deposit of rather small objects over or upon the surface of the possessor's land.

[The court cites examples such as molten lead, soot, and gunshot pellets.]

And liability on the theory of trespass has been recognized where the harm was produced by the vibration of the soil or by the concussion of the air which, of course, is nothing more than the movement of molecules one against the other. . . . The view recognizing a trespassory invasion where there is no "thing" which can be seen with the naked eye undoubtedly runs counter to the definition of trespass expressed in some quarters. [ ] It is quite possible that in an earlier day when science had not yet peered into the molecular and atomic world of small particles, the courts could not fit an invasion through unseen physical instrumentalities into the requirement that a trespass can result only from a *direct* invasion. But in this atomic age even the uneducated know the great and awful force contained in the atom and what it can do to a man's property if it is released. In fact, the now famous equation $E = mc^2$ has taught us that mass and energy are equivalents and that our concept of "things" must be reframed. If these observations on science in relation to the law of trespass should appear theoretical and unreal in the abstract, they become very practical and real to the possessor of land when the unseen force cracks the foundation of his house. The force is just as real if it is chemical in nature and must be awakened by the intervention of another agency before it does harm.

If, then, we must look to the character of the instrumentality which is used in making an intrusion upon another's land we prefer to emphasize the object's energy or force rather than its size. Viewed in this way we may define trespass as any intrusion which invades the possessor's protected interest in exclusive possession, whether that intrusion is by visible or invisible pieces of matter or by energy which can be measured only by the mathematical language of the physicist.

We are of the opinion, therefore, that the intrusion of the fluoride particulates in the present case constituted a trespass.

. . .

. . . The modern law of trespass can be understood only as it is seen against its historical background. Originally all types of trespass, including trespass to land, were punishable under the criminal law because the trespasser's conduct was regarded as a breach of the peace. When the criminal and civil aspect of trespass were separated, the civil action for trespass was colored by its past, and the idea that the peace of the community was put in danger by the trespasser's conduct influenced the courts' ideas of the character of the tort. Therefore, relief was granted to the plaintiff where he was not actually damaged, partly at least as a means of discouraging disruptive influences in the community. Winfield on Torts (4th ed.) p. 305 expresses the idea as follows:

> The law, on the face of it, looks harsh, but trespass was so likely in earlier times to lead to a breach of the peace that even unwitting and trivial deviations on to another person's land were reckoned unlawful. At the present day there is, of course, much greater respect for the law in general and appreciation of the security which it affords, and the theoretical severity of the rules as to land trespass is hardly ever exploited in practice.

. . . If then, we find that an act on the part of the defendant in interfering with the plaintiff's possession, does, or is likely to result in arousing conflict between them, that act will characterize the tort as a trespass, assuming of course that the other elements of the tort are made out. . . .

Probably the most important factor which describes the nature of the interest protected under the law of trespass is nothing more than a feeling which a possessor has with respect to land which he holds. It is a sense of ownership; a feeling that what one owns or possesses should not be interfered with, and that it is entitled to protection through law. This being the nature of the plaintiff's interest, it is understandable why actual damage is not an essential ingredient in the law of trespass.

As pointed out in 1 Harper & James, Torts, § 1.8, p. 26, the rule permitting recovery in spite of the absence of actual damages "is probably justified as a vindicatory right to protect the possessor's proprietary or dignitary interest in his land."

We think that a possessor's interest in land as defined by the considerations recited above may, under the appropriate circumstances, be violated by a ray of light, by an atomic particle, or by a particulate of fluoride and, contrariwise, if such interest circumscribed by these considerations is not violated or endangered, the defendant's conduct, even though it may result in a physical intrusion, will not render him liable in an action of trespass. [ ]

We hold that the defendant's conduct in causing chemical substances to be deposited upon the plaintiffs' land fulfilled all of the requirements under the law of trespass.

The defendant contends that trespass will not lie in this case because the injury was indirect and consequential and that the requirement that the injury must be direct and immediate to constitute a trespass was not met. We have held that the deposit of the particulates upon the plaintiff's land was an intrusion within the definition of trespass. That intrusion was direct. The damages which flowed from it are consequential, but it is well established that such consequential damage may be proven in an action of trespass. [ ] The distinction between direct and indirect invasions where there has been a physical intrusion upon the plaintiff's land has been abandoned by some courts. [ ] Since the invasion in the instant case was direct it is not necessary for us to decide whether the distinction is recognized in this state.

. . .

It is also urged that the trial court erred in failing to enter a special finding requested by the defendant. The requested finding in effect stated that it was impossible in the operation of an aluminum reduction plant to capture all fluorides which are created in the manufacturing process; that the fume collection system was in operation during the period in question; and that it was the most efficient of the systems known in aluminum reduction plants in the United States.

It is argued that since the trial court elected to enter special rather than general findings it was required by ORS 17.430 to enter findings on all material issues which, it is claimed, would include the issue defined in the requested findings. The complaint alleged that the defendant "carelessly, wantonly and willfully continuously caused to be emitted," from its plant the poisonous compounds. This allegation was denied in the defendant's answer. The issue thus raised, as to the character of defendant's conduct in making the intrusion upon plaintiffs' land, would be material only with respect to the claim for punitive damages which, as we have already indicated, was rejected by the trial court. Since we hold that the intrusion in this case constituted a trespass it is immaterial whether the defendant's conduct was careless, wanton and willful or entirely free from fault. Therefore, the refusal to enter the requested finding is not error.

The judgment of the lower court is affirmed.

[The concurring opinion of MCALLISTER, C.J., is omitted.]

NOTES AND QUESTIONS

1. *Culpability and intent.* To establish a trespass, the plaintiff must show that defendant intentionally entered onto the land, or committed the equivalent of an entry, without the owner's permission. Does the requisite intent necessarily mean that defendant knew of the trespass? For example, what if defendant held the honest but mistaken belief that she was on her own property? See Baugh v. CBS, Inc., 828 F.Supp. 745, 756 (N.D.Cal.1993)("Trespass is a strict liability tort in the sense that the defendant's motivation or good faith belief is irrelevant.").

Although liability for trespass does not depend on culpable behavior or the specific intent to injure the landowner's interest in exclusive possession, the strictness of this tort is mitigated to some extent through a series of privileges that shield from liability activity that would otherwise constitute a trespass. These privileges may arise out of the consent of the possessor (Restatement (Second) sections 167–175), or may be afforded as a matter of law because of the purposes for which the actor enters the premises (sections 176–211). The scope of these privileges, however, is in general quite narrow and limited to specific types of situations. Thus, despite the increased flexibility these privileges afford to defendants, no overarching principle of reasonableness has developed in the area of intentional, as compared to unintentional, trespasses.

2. *Nominal damages.* Because the gist of the action for trespass to land is considered to be the intrusion or "breaking of the close," nominal damages (typically $1) can be recovered even if no demonstrable harm could be shown.

Why would an owner sue for trespass when only nominal damages are available? When ownership of property is in doubt, trespass suits have been used to resolve controversies over ownership—the purpose of the suit—rather than recovering damages. See Pfeiffer v. Grossman, 15 Ill. 53 (1853)(owner may bring trespass action against neighbor over disputed boundary and recover nominal damages if successful). Consider also the other remedies that become available once the plaintiff has established an entitlement to compensatory damages. An award of nominal damages, for example, gives plaintiff the option to seek injunctive relief that would prohibit the defendant from trespassing in the future. See, e.g., Lambert v. Holmberg, 712 N.W.2d 268, 275 (Neb.2006)(discussing cases "involving continuous and repeated trespasses" in which injunctive relief was awarded "without requiring the landowner to show anything other than nominal damages"). An award of nominal damages might also enable the plaintiff to obtain a substantial punitive damages award that is intended to punish and deter trespasses of this type. See, e.g., Jacque v. Steenberg Homes, Inc., 563 N.W.2d 154 (Wis.1997)(upholding $100,000 punitive award for case in which plaintiffs received nominal compensatory damages of $1 for defendant's trespass following plaintiffs' refusal to permit defendant to cross their land).

In contrast to intentional trespasses, the Restatement (Second) of Torts section 165 states that unintended intrusions—those resulting from reckless or negligent conduct or from abnormally dangerous activities—are subject to liability only if the intrusion causes actual harm.

3.   *Intangible invasions and claims for nuisance.* A tangible entry onto the land would clearly harm the plaintiff's interest in exclusive possession, explaining why the common law first adopted this requirement. An intangible entry would not ordinarily cause dispossession of the land, but only affect the plaintiff's ability to use or enjoy the land—the interest protected by the tort of nuisance. Because *Martin* involved an intangible invasion, the issue was not whether plaintiff had a viable cause of action but whether a claim for trespass could be maintained in addition to a claim for private nuisance.

Why does it matter whether trespass is also available? As *Martin* reveals, sometimes there is a difference in the statute of limitations and a continuing condition can result in greater damages being available under the tort with the longer limitations period. In addition, some jurisdictions have so-called right-to-farm laws that limit nuisance but not trespass claims against farmers. See John Larkin, Inc. v. Marceau, 959 A.2d 551 (Vt.2008)(developer sued neighboring orchard owner in trespass for spraying pesticides; state statute adopted a presumption that agricultural activities did not constitute a nuisance). Yet a third difference is that an intentional invasion of land is subject to nuisance liability only if it is "unreasonable," which requires the plaintiff to prove either that "(a) the gravity of the harm outweighs the utility of the actor's conduct, or (b) the harm caused by the conduct is serious and the financial burden of compensating for this and similar harm to others would not make the continuation of the conduct not feasible." Restatement (Second) of Torts § 826. This requirement, which is extensively covered in Chapter X, is considerably more demanding than the requirements for trespass described in the preceding notes.

Under the court's expansive view of the trespass action, what types of cases would be exclusively nuisance actions? If the plant in *Martin* had emitted a noxious stench, would the court have regarded the harm as actionable in trespass? In nuisance? What about a continuing abrasive level of noise? In a case decided two years after *Martin*, the Oregon Supreme Court held that a trespass is not established by "the use on three occasions of vile and obscene language and gestures directed at plaintiff by the defendant while plaintiff was in her house or on the property." Wilson v. Parent, 365 P.2d 72, 73 (Or.1961). Why wouldn't this allegation satisfy the requirements for trespass as described in *Martin*?

Martin is adopted and the question of overlap between trespass and nuisance discussed at length in Borland v. Sanders Lead Co., Inc., 369 So.2d 523 (Ala.1979)(action in trespass for lead pollution emitted from defendant's smelter). But see Babb v. Lee County Landfill SC, 747 S.E.2d 468 (S.C.2013)(adhering to the traditional "dimensional test," requiring a physical, tangible object for trespass and rejecting plaintiffs' trespass claims based on defendant landfill's emission of noxious odors); Johnson v. Paynesville Farmers Union Coop. Oil Co., 817 N.W.2d 693 (Minn.2012)(rejecting trespass claim and only permitting a nuisance claim in case involving the drift of pesticide spray from the defendant's commercial farm onto plaintiff's neighboring organic farm, based on the concern that trespass claims involving intangible objects would blur the line between trespass and nuisance).

4. *Intangible invasions and the requirement of actual harm.* In order to maintain the difference between trespass and nuisance claims in cases involving intangible invasions, some courts have required proof of actual harm. E.g., Tally Bissell Neighbors, Inc. v. Eyrie Shotgun Ranch, 228 P. 3d 1134, 1141 (Mont.2010). Without such a requirement, an apartment dweller who is annoyed by the classical music played by her neighbor could establish trespass on land. Trespass presumes nominal damages, enabling the plaintiff to receive injunctive relief that would prohibit the neighbor from future emissions of these sounds into plaintiff's apartment. Such an outcome is barred by the requirement that the plaintiff must suffer some actual physical harm in order to recover in trespass for an intangible invasion, thereby protecting the role of nuisance law in resolving claims involving conflicting uses of land. See also John Larkin, Inc. v. Marceau, 959 A.2d 551 (Vt.2008)(recognizing trespass claims for intrusion of intangible particulates but requiring actual damage to the property); Bradley v. American Smelting & Refining Co., 709 P.2d 782 (Wash.1985)(adopting *Martin* in a case involving deposit of airborne particles from a copper smelter, but requiring "actual and substantial damage" as a safeguard against mass trivial claims by neighboring landowners).

5. Traditionally, a special corner of the world of trespass to land has been occupied by claims of incursions by non-domesticated animals. The Restatement (Third) of Torts: Liability for Physical and Emotional Harm section 21 addresses these claims, providing strict liability for intrusions by livestock and other non-domesticated animals.

7. CONVERSION AND TRESPASS TO CHATTELS

Conversion and trespass to chattels are both concerned with protection of ownership rights in personal property. By contrast, the trespass and nuisance torts we considered in the last section and Chapter X protect rights relating to real property (land or fixtures permanently attached to it). Lying at the intersection of tort and property law, these four torts often receive little attention in both courses.

In recent years, both conversion and trespass to chattels have been brought to bear on interferences with new technology, such as computer systems, with varying success. Among the issues these cases raise is whether conversion and trespass to chattels apply to intangible personal property as well as the degree of interference required to satisfy each of these torts. While addressing the history and traditional role of these torts, this section focuses on their modern application.

Thyroff v. Nationwide Mutual Insurance Co.

Court of Appeals of New York, 2007.
8 N.Y.3d 283, 864 N.E.2d 1272.

■ GRAFFEO, J.

The United States Court of Appeals for the Second Circuit has certified a question to us that asks whether the common-law cause of action of conversion applies to certain electronic computer records and data. Based on the facts of this case, we hold that plaintiff may maintain a conversion claim.

I

Plaintiff Louis Thyroff was an insurance agent for defendant Nationwide Mutual Insurance Company. In 1988, the parties had entered into an Agent's Agreement that specified the terms of their business relationship. As part of the arrangement, Nationwide agreed to lease Thyroff computer hardware and software, referred to as the agency office-automation (AOA) system, to facilitate the collection and transfer of customer information to Nationwide. In addition to the entry of business data, Thyroff also used the AOA system for personal e-mails, correspondence and other data storage that pertained to his customers. On a daily basis, Nationwide would automatically upload all of the information from Thyroff's AOA system, including Thyroff's personal data, to its centralized computers.

The Agent's Agreement was terminable at will and, in September 2000, Thyroff received a letter from Nationwide informing him that his contract as an exclusive agent had been cancelled. The next day, Nationwide repossessed its AOA system and denied Thyroff further access to the computers and all electronic records and data. Consequently, Thyroff was unable to retrieve his customer information and other personal information that was stored on the computers.

Thyroff initiated an action against Nationwide in the United States District Court for the Western District of New York, asserting several causes of action, including a claim for the conversion of his business and personal information stored on the computer hard drives. In response to Nationwide's motion to dismiss, District Court held that the complaint failed to state a cause of action for conversion. . . .

In his appeal to the United States Court of Appeals for the Second Circuit, Thyroff sought reinstatement of his conversion cause of action, along with other relief. Nationwide countered that a conversion claim cannot be based on the misappropriation of electronic records and data because New York does not recognize a cause of action for the conversion of intangible property. The Second Circuit determined that the issue was unresolved in New York and therefore certified the following question of law to this Court: is a claim for the conversion of electronic data cognizable under New York law?[2]

II

"The hand of history lies heavy upon the tort of conversion" (Prosser, *The Nature of Conversion,* 42 Cornell LQ 168, 169 [1957]). [The court explained the evolution of the "ancient doctrine," dating back to the Norman conquest, which concerned protection of ownership rights in personal property. Claims denominated as trover, detinue, and trespass de bonis asportatis developed. Like trespass to real property, these torts were subsumed in the common law writ system and eventually expanded, similarly to the way in which trespass on the case emerged from trespass vi et armis. (Although an interesting saga, we need not delve further into these historical forms of action to understand modern use of conversion and trespass to chattels.)]

[handwritten margin note: common law action to recover value of personal property wrongfully disposed of by another person]

Trover gave way slowly to the tort of conversion, which was created to address "some interferences with chattels for which the action of trover would not lie," such as a claim dealing with a right of future possession (Restatement [Second] of Torts § 222A, Comment *b*). The technical differences between trover and conversion eventually disappeared. The Restatement (Second) of Torts now defines conversion as an intentional act of "dominion or control over a chattel which so seriously interferes with the right of another to control it that the actor may justly be required to pay the other the full value of the chattel" (*id.* § 222A [1]).

III

As history reveals, the common law has evolved to broaden the remedies available for the misappropriation of personal property. As [historical methods for resolving disputes] became incompatible with emerging societal values, the law changed. Similarly, the courts became willing to consider new species of personal property eligible for conversion actions.

Conversion and its common-law antecedents were directed against interferences with or misappropriation of "goods" that were tangible, personal property. This was consistent with the original notions

---

[2]   The Second Circuit also extended an opportunity for us to determine who is the proper owner of the electronic information at issue. Because Thyroff's conversion claim was dismissed pursuant to Federal Rules of Civil Procedure rule 12(b)(6) and a reviewing court must construe all facts and inferences in Thyroff's favor, we presume that he is the owner of the data for the purpose of resolving the certified question.

associated with the appeals of robbery and larceny, trespass and trover because tangible property could be lost or stolen [ ]. By contrast, real property and all manner of intangible rights could not be "lost or found" in the eyes of the law and were not therefore subject to an action for trover or conversion [ ].

Under this traditional construct, conversion was viewed as "the 'unauthorized assumption and exercise of the right of ownership over goods belonging to another to the exclusion of the owner's rights' " [ ]. Thus, the general rule was that "an action for conversion will not normally lie, when it involves intangible property" because there is no physical item that can be misappropriated [ ].

Despite this long-standing reluctance to expand conversion beyond the realm of tangible property, some courts determined that there was "no good reason for keeping up a distinction that arose wholly from that original peculiarity of the action" of trover (that an item had to be capable of being lost and found) and substituted a theory of conversion that covered "things represented by valuable papers, such as certificates of stock, promissory notes, and other papers of value" [ ]. This, in turn, led to the recognition that an intangible property right can be united with a tangible object for conversion purposes (*see Agar v. Orda,* 264 N.Y. 248, 251, 190 N.E. 479 [1934]; [ ]).

In *Agar,* which involved the conversion of intangible shares of stock, this Court applied the so-called "merger" doctrine because:

> "for practical purposes [the shares] are merged in stock certificates which are instrumentalities of trade and commerce. . . . Such certificates 'are treated by business men as property for all practical purposes.' . . . Indeed, this court has held that the shares of stock are so completely merged in the certificate that conversion of the certificate may be treated as a conversion of the shares of stock represented by the certificate" [ ].

More recently, we concluded that a plaintiff could maintain a cause of action for conversion where the defendant infringed on the plaintiff's intangible property right to a musical performance by misappropriating a master recording—a tangible item of property capable of being physically taken [ ].

IV

We have not previously had occasion to consider whether the common law should permit conversion for intangible property interests that do not strictly satisfy the merger test. Although some courts have adhered to the traditional rules of conversion (*see e.g. Allied Inv. Corp. v. Jasen,* 354 Md. 547, 562, 731 A.2d 957, 965 [1999] [interests in partnership and corporation]; *Northeast Coating Tech., Inc. v. Vacuum Metallurgical Co., Ltd.,* 684 A.2d 1322, 1324 [Me.1996] [interest in information contained in prospectus]; *Montecalvo v. Mandarelli,* 682

A.2d 918, 929 [R.I.1996] [partnership interest]), others have taken a more flexible view of conversion and held that the cause of action can embrace intangible property (*see e.g. Kremen v. Cohen,* 337 F.3d 1024, 1033–1034 [9th Cir.2003] [Internet domain name; applying California law]; *Shmueli v. Corcoran Group,* 9 Misc.3d 589, 594, 802 N.Y.S.2d 871 [Sup.Ct., N.Y. County 2005] [computerized client/investor list]; *see generally Town & Country Props., Inc. v. Riggins,* 249 Va. 387, 396–397, 457 S.E.2d 356, 363–364 [1995] [person's name]).[8]

A variety of arguments have been made in support of expanding the scope of conversion. Some courts have decided that a theft of intangible property is a violation of the criminal law and should be civilly remediable (*see National Sur. Corp. v. Applied Sys., Inc.,* 418 So.2d at 850); that virtual documents can be made tangible "by the mere expedient of a printing key function" (*Shmueli v. Corcoran Group,* 9 Misc.3d at 592, 802 N.Y.S.2d 871); that a writing is a document whether it is read on the computer or printed on paper (*see Kremen v. Cohen,* 325 F.3d 1035, 1048 [9th Cir.2003, Kozinski, J., dissenting from certification]); and that the expense of creating intangible, computerized information should be counterbalanced by the protection of an effective civil action (*see National Sur. Corp. v. Applied Sys., Inc.,* 418 So.2d at 850).

On the other hand, the primary argument for retaining the traditional boundaries of the tort is that it "seem[s] preferable to fashion other remedies, such as unfair competition, to protect people from having intangible values used and appropriated in unfair ways" [ ]. Nonetheless, advocates of this view readily concede that "[t]here is perhaps no very valid and essential reason why there might not be conversion of" intangible property [ ] and that there is "very little practical importance whether the tort is called conversion, or a similar tort with another name" because "[i]n either case the recovery is for the full value of the intangible right so appropriated" [ ]. The lack of a compelling reason to prohibit conversion for redress of a misappropriation of intangible property underscores the need for reevaluating the appropriate application of conversion.

V

"[I]t is the strength of the common law to respond, albeit cautiously and intelligently, to the demands of commonsense justice in an evolving society" ([ ]; *see Hymowitz v. Eli Lilly & Co.,* 73 N.Y.2d 487, 507, 541

---

[8] At least one court has approved of the use of conversion by referencing the merger doctrine (*see e.g. Astroworks, Inc. v. Astroexhibit, Inc.,* 257 F.Supp.2d 609, 618 [S.D.N.Y.2003] [conversion of idea that was represented by an Internet Web site]). Conversion claims have also been approved without consideration of the historical limits of the cause of action (*see e.g. Cole v. Control Data Corp.,* 947 F.2d 313, 318 [8th Cir.1991] [computer software program]; *Quincy Cablesystems, Inc. v. Sully's Bar, Inc.,* 650 F.Supp. 838, 848 [D.Mass.1986] [satellite cable signals]; *Charter Hosp. of Mobile, Inc. v. Weinberg,* 558 So.2d 909, 912 [Ala.1990] [addiction treatment program]; *National Sur. Corp. v. Applied Sys., Inc.,* 418 So.2d 847, 850 [Ala.1982] [computer program]; *Mundy v. Decker, 1999 WL 14479,* *4, 1999 Neb App LEXIS 3, *10–12 [Ct.App.1999] [WordPerfect documents]).

N.Y.S.2d 941, 539 N.E.2d 1069 [1989], *cert. denied* 493 U.S. 944, 110 S.Ct. 350, 107 L.Ed.2d 338 [1989]). That time has arrived. The reasons for creating the merger doctrine and departing from the strict common-law limitation of conversion inform our analysis. The expansion of conversion to encompass a different class of property, such as shares of stock, was motivated by "society's growing dependence on intangibles" [ ]. It cannot be seriously disputed that society's reliance on computers and electronic data is substantial, if not essential. Computers and digital information are ubiquitous and pervade all aspects of business, financial and personal communication activities. Indeed, this opinion was drafted in electronic form, stored in a computer's memory and disseminated to the Judges of this Court via e-mail. We cannot conceive of any reason in law or logic why this process of virtual creation should be treated any differently from production by pen on paper or quill on parchment. A document stored on a computer hard drive has the same value as a paper document kept in a file cabinet.

The merger rule reflected the concept that intangible property interests could be converted only by exercising dominion over the paper document that represented that interest [ ]. Now, however, it is customary that stock ownership exclusively exists in electronic format. Because shares of stock can be transferred by mere computer entries, a thief can use a computer to access a person's financial accounts and transfer the shares to an account controlled by the thief. Similarly, electronic documents and records stored on a computer can also be converted by simply pressing the delete button (*cf. Kremen v. Cohen,* 337 F.3d at 1034 ["It would be a curious jurisprudence that turned on the existence of a paper document rather than an electronic one. Torching a company's file room would then be conversion while hacking into its mainframe and deleting its data would not" (emphasis omitted)]).

Furthermore, it generally is not the physical nature of a document that determines its worth, it is the information memorialized in the document that has intrinsic value. A manuscript of a novel has the same value whether it is saved in a computer's memory or printed on paper. So too, the information that Thyroff allegedly stored on his leased computers in the form of electronic records of customer contacts and related data has value to him regardless of whether the format in which the information was stored was tangible or intangible. In the absence of a significant difference in the value of the information, the protections of the law should apply equally to both forms—physical and virtual.

In light of these considerations, we believe that the tort of conversion must keep pace with the contemporary realities of widespread computer use. We therefore answer the certified question in the affirmative and hold that the type of data that Nationwide allegedly took possession of—electronic records that were stored on a computer and were indistinguishable from printed documents—is subject to a claim of conversion in New York. Because this is the only type of intangible property at issue in this case, we do not consider whether any of the myriad other forms of virtual information should be protected by the tort.

Accordingly, the certified question should be answered in the affirmative.

■ CHIEF JUDGE KAYE and JUDGES CIPARICK, READ, SMITH, PIGOTT and JONES concur.

NOTES AND QUESTIONS

1. Restatement (Second) of Torts section 242 addresses conversion of intangible property. Subsection 1 provides for liability when the intangible right is merged in a tangible document. Subsection 2 provides:

> (2) One who effectively prevents the exercise of intangible rights of the kind customarily merged in a document is subject to a liability similar to that for conversion, even though the document is not itself converted.

Would Thyroff have been able to maintain his conversion claim under subsection 2?

2. *The difference between conversion and trespass to chattels.* Critical to Thyroff's conversion claim was that Nationwide had exercised dominion over Thyroff's files to his exclusion. Why is such dispossession required?

Historically, the difference between conversion and trespass to chattels developed because the former entitled the victim to recover the full value of the goods taken—the idea of a forced sale, adopted by section 222A of the Restatement. By contrast, the remedy for trespass to chattels is the actual damage caused by the interference or harm to the property.

There are a variety of degrees of interference with an owner's use of property. The Restatement states the standard for sufficient dominion for conversion, as opposed to trespass to chattels, as whether it is severe enough that it is reasonable to require the defendant to pay the full value of the property to the plaintiff. Restatement (Second) of Torts § 222A(1). Lesser interferences may be subject to a trespass to chattels claim.

3. Suppose that a law clerk for Judge Graffeo who vehemently disagreed with the outcome in *Thyroff* absconded with the file containing the draft opinion just before it was issued. Conversion? If so, what measure of damages? Who would be entitled to recover? Suppose that the court backed up all data files every night and there was a one-day earlier version of the opinion available to the court?

4. *Interference with computer systems.* In Intel Corp. v. Hamidi, 71 P.3d 296 (Cal.2003), a disaffected former employee sent mass e-mails to employees at his former employer on six occasions. The e-mails, which were sent through the employer's e-mail system, were harshly critical of the employer's employment practices. The employer brought suit alleging

trespass to chattels and asserting that the e-mails had disrupted its employees, causing diminished productivity. The court reversed summary judgment for the employer, relying on the fact that the e-mails caused no harm to the employer's computer system or disruption of the system's operation. The reduced productivity, reasoned the court, was not a consequence of the sending of the e-mails but of their content. In the course of its opinion, the court distinguished spammers whose mass e-mails interfere with the operation of Internet service providers' computer systems or the use of the e-mail system by subscribers. The court cited approvingly CompuServe, Inc. v. Cyber Promotions, Inc., 962 F.Supp. 1015 (S.D. Ohio 1997), the first case to find a spammer liable for trespass to chattels. In Register.com, Inc. v. Verio, Inc., 356 F.3d 393 (2d Cir.2004), the court affirmed a preliminary injunction barring defendant from using "search robots" to search plaintiff's website. Plaintiff registered new Internet domain names and defendant's search robots trolled plaintiff's website daily. The lower court's finding that these searches could interfere with and potentially shut down plaintiff's computer system justified a finding of trespass to chattels. See also Sotelo v. DirectRevenue, LLC, 384 F.Supp.2d 1219 (N.D.Ill.2005)(downloading spyware that "bombards" users with pop-up advertisements, obscuring the web page being viewed, constitutes sufficient harm to constitute trespass to chattels).

5. D, who fails to see a stop sign, crashes into P's car, damaging it so severely that it is totaled. Is D liable for conversion? Recall that conversion is an intentional tort; even though the intent element does not require an intent to do harm, it does, like trespass, require an intent to intrude or interfere with the property. D, in this situation, may be liable for negligence, but is not liable for conversion or, if the damages were less severe, for trespass to chattels. The larger point here is that even if conversion and trespass to chattels do not afford a remedy when there is interference with personal property, other torts may be available.

6. Is a mugger who takes a pedestrian's wallet, removes the credit cards and cash, and discards the wallet in a mailbox liable for conversion? For trespass to chattels? Would it make a difference if the mugger, instead of putting the wallet in a mailbox, burned it so that it could not provide evidence against the mugger? See Montgomery v. Devoid, 915 A.2d 270 (Vt.2006)(historically only identifiable currency and other fungible goods subject to conversion but extending conversion to all dispossessions of currency); see also D. Dobbs et al., Handbook on Torts § 44.2, at 1153 (2d ed.2016)("when the defendant commits an affirmative act and physically takes control of particular paper monies he is guilty of conversion, even if the particular bills or coins cannot be identified"). If the victim can identify the currency stolen after the thief uses it to buy goods, can the victim recover that currency from someone who innocently accepted the currency from the thief? Remember that the intent required for conversion does not require an intent to do harm, only an intent to assert a right to the property inconsistent with the owner's. Thus, the beneficiaries of Robin Hood's wealth redistribution are equally subject to liability for conversion as he would be. In cases of "innocent" conversion the tort functions as a form of strict liability.

7. Does a physician who uses cells from a patient's tissue that are removed in the course of medical treatment commit conversion? In Moore v. The Regents of the University of California, 793 P.2d 479 (Cal.1990), a physician and his University employer saved and developed cells harvested from a patient, Moore, with a rare form of leukemia after a splenectomy and follow-up treatment. The defendants were able to create a lucrative cell line that they patented, all the while concealing what they were doing from Moore. After Moore found out about this development, he sued asserting a number of theories, among them conversion. The trial court dismissed his complaint. The California Supreme Court, in a case that generated four separate opinions, held that conversion was not available—the patient's claim for conversion of his cells was novel, and the policy of avoiding interference with scientific research counseled against extending the conversion tort. The court noted the widespread distribution of cell lines among researchers and expressed concern, given the breadth of the conversion tort, about the impact of potential liability on innocent researchers who obtained cell lines from others. The court did find that both as a matter of informed consent and the fiduciary duty owed by physicians to patients, that the plaintiff stated a cause of action for the failure to inform him of his physician's research and economic interests in using excised human biological material. To what measure of damages would Moore be entitled if successful at trial?

8. DEFENSES AND PRIVILEGES

We have seen that defenses play important roles in negligence and strict liability. So, too, with intentional torts.

a. CONSENT

The plaintiff's consent to an intentional invasion of a legally protected interest ordinarily bars recovery. "It is a fundamental principle of the common law that *volenti non fit injuria*—to one who is willing, no wrong is done. The attitude of the courts has not, in general, been one of paternalism." R. Keeton et al., Prosser and Keeton on the Law of Torts § 18, at 112 (5th ed.1984).

Consent demarcates an important limit of tort liability, distinguishing tortious behavior from socially acceptable behavior. "For example, consent turns trespass into a dinner party; a battery into a handshake; a theft into a gift; an invasion of privacy into an intimate moment; a commercial appropriation of name and likeness into a biography." Hurd, The Moral Magic of Consent, 2 Legal Theory 121, 122 (1996).

Earlier, in the section on assumed risk as a defense to claims of negligence, we encountered the concept of "consent" as a recurring theme in the cases. The plaintiff can expressly assume a risk under a contract, as in cases such as *Hanks*, p. 464 supra, or can impliedly assume a risk by choosing to engage in the activity, as in cases such as *Murphy*, p. 475 supra. In these cases, the courts must decide issues that are somewhat analogous to the claim, now to be considered in the context of intentional harms, that plaintiff consented to the defendant's invasive or offensive contact. Think about whether the defense claimed in the following case and notes rests on a rationale similar to that offered in the accidental harm situations previously considered (and in medical malpractice informed consent cases as well, p. 117 supra).

<h1 style="text-align:center">Hart v. Geysel</h1>

Supreme Court of Washington, 1930.
159 Wash. 632, 294 P. 570.

■ MAIN, J.

This action was brought by the administrator of the estate of Hamilton I. Cartwright, deceased, who died as the result of a blow received in a prize fight. [The complaint alleged that plaintiff's decedent and defendant engaged in a prize fight and that plaintiff died as a result of the encounter. A statute made the fight illegal. The complaint contained no allegations that the mutual combat was undertaken in anger, that there was malicious intent to seriously injure, or that there was excessive force. The trial court granted defendant's demurrer to the complaint.]

[T]he adjudicated cases, as well as the text-writers, are in conflict. One line supports what is known as the majority rule, and the other, the minority. The majority rule has been stated as follows:

> Where the parties engage in mutual combat in anger, each is civilly liable to the other for any physical injury inflicted by him during the fight. The fact that the parties voluntarily engaged in the combat is no defense to an action by either of them to recover damages for personal injuries inflicted upon him by the other.

This rule is supported by the cases of [ ].

The minority rule has been stated as follows:

> Where parties engage in a mutual combat in anger, the act of each is unlawful and relief will be denied them in a civil action; at least, in the absence of a showing of excessive force or malicious intent to do serious injury upon the part of the defendant.

The cases of [ ] support this rule.

. . .

The facts in the case now before us do not bring it within the authorities supporting the majority rule, because here there are no facts which show anger, malicious intent to injure, or excessive force. It may be stated that the facts of this case do not contain one element of the minority rule, that of anger. It is unnecessary, as we view it, in the present case to adopt either rule. It is sufficient to say that in our opinion one who engages in prize fighting, even though prohibited by positive law, and sustains an injury, should not have a right to recover any damages that he may sustain as the result of the combat, which he expressly consented to and engaged in as a matter of business or sport. To enforce the criminal statute against prize fighting, it is not necessary to reward the one that got the worst of the encounter at the expense of his more fortunate opponent. This view is supported by the rule tentatively adopted [in section 75 of a draft of the first Restatement of Torts. The court quoted from a comment to that section:]

> Notwithstanding the numerical weight of authority against the view that an assent to a breach of the peace is a legally effective consent to such invasions of interest of personality as are involved therein the minority view is preferred for the following reasons:
>
> The majority view is obviously an exception to the general principle that one who has sufficiently expressed his willingness to suffer a particular invasion has no right to complaint if another acts upon his consent so given. The very nature of rights of personality, which are in freedom to dispose of one's interests of personality as one pleases, fundamentally requires this to be so. There is a further principle, applicable not only in tort law but throughout the whole field of law, and perhaps more conspicuously in other subjects, to the effect that no man shall profit by his own wrongdoing.
>
> The majority view is an exception to both of these two fundamental principles. Clearly if a plaintiff has consented to being struck by another in the course of a brawl, his right to the control of his person and to determine by whom and how it shall be touched has not been invaded. And it is equally clear that if he has so expressed his consent to the blow that, were he not party to a breach of the peace, his assent would be an operative consent and so bar his liability, he is profiting by the illegality of his conduct if because he is party to the breach of the peace he gains a right of action which but for his criminal joinder therein he would not have had.
>
> . . .

The judgment will be affirmed.

■ MITCHELL, C.J., and PARKER, TOLMAN, BEALS, MILLARD and BEELER, JJ., concur.

[Two dissenters favored the majority rule.]

NOTES AND QUESTIONS

1. Do the "two fundamental principles" that the Restatement draft identifies to support the minority view—and which lead the *Geysel* court to recognize a consent defense—seem equally persuasive? If prize-fighting had been legal in the state would either or both principles still have equivalent persuasive force?

2. In *Vosburg v. Putney*, note 4, p. 904 supra, the court remarked that the case might have been different if the schoolboy kick had occurred in the playground instead of the classroom. Does the possibility that "consent" might have barred recovery in such a situation suggest still another rationale for the defense? Can a person jostled by others during rush hour on a subway bring battery actions against the offenders? Are these considerations relevant to *Wishnatsky*, p. 910 supra?

3. *Apparent or implied consent.* "If words or conduct are reasonably understood by another to be intended as consent, they constitute apparent consent and are as effective as consent in fact." Restatement (Second) of Torts § 892. In O'Brien v. Cunard S.S. Co., 28 N.E. 266 (Mass.1891), plaintiff, a ship passenger, brought a battery action against defendant based on an alleged unconsented vaccination by the ship's surgeon, acting in anticipation of a quarantine order as the ship neared Boston. In determining whether plaintiff consented, the court observed:

> She was one of a large number of women who were vaccinated on that occasion, without, so far as appears, a word of objection from any of them. They all indicated by their conduct that they desired to avail themselves of the provisions made for their benefit. There was nothing in the conduct of the plaintiff to indicate to the surgeon that she did not wish to obtain a card which would save her from detention at quarantine, and to be vaccinated, if necessary, for that purpose. Viewing his conduct in the light of the surrounding circumstances, it was lawful; and there was no evidence tending to show that it was not.

Is the court suggesting that consent, as a protection of the plaintiff's interest in freedom from invasive conduct, is an objective inquiry, rather than a determination of the individual plaintiff's own subjective expectations? Aside from drawing reasonable inferences from the plaintiff's conduct, what can a defendant rely on for determining whether consent has been given? Compare *Matthies*, p. 117 supra, on informed consent in the context of medical malpractice.

4. *Scope of consent.* What if a woman consents to sexual intercourse based on false statements by the male? In Barbara A. v. John G., 193 Cal.Rptr. 422 (App.1983), John, who represented Barbara in a family law matter, had sex with her after telling her that he "couldn't possibly get anyone pregnant." Barbara understood that statement to mean John was sterile, which he was not, and she suffered an ectopic pregnancy. John sued Barbara for unpaid attorney fees, and she counterclaimed, alleging, among other claims, battery. The court held that two grounds vitiated John's consent defense: 1) impregnating plaintiff went beyond the scope of her

consent; and 2) consent obtained through fraud is invalid. Recall that the Virginia legislature, in the statutes quoted in *McDermott*, along with most other states, also abolished the tort of seduction, which consists of persuading a woman through fraud or false promises of marriage to engage in sexual intercourse. The interest protected by the seduction tort, however, was the chaste character of the woman.

The scope of consent can also be relevant in cases of implied consent. In a professional football game, plaintiff safety was near defendant fullback on pass coverage. When the pass was intercepted on the opposite side of the field, plaintiff tried to block defendant, and fell to the ground. "Acting out of anger and frustration, but without specific intent to injure, [defendant] stepped forward and struck a blow with his right forearm to the back of the kneeling plaintiff's head with sufficient force to cause both players to fall forward to the ground." The statute of limitations barred suit for an intentional tort, but plaintiff asserted claims of recklessness and negligence. The judge held, after trial, that plaintiff, who had 13 years of experience in professional football, "must have recognized and accepted the risk that he would be injured by such an act" as defendant committed, and the case was decided on assumption of risk. On appeal, the court reversed and remanded for an assessment of plaintiff's rights in view of the official players' code and customs of the sport: "The general customs of football do not approve the intentional punching or striking of others." Hackbart v. Cincinnati Bengals, Inc., 601 F.2d 516 (10th Cir.1979). See Nielsen, Controlling Sports Violence: Too Late for the Carrots—Bring on the Big Stick, 74 Iowa L.Rev. 681 (1989). Recall the rule that sports participants assume the inherent risks of the sport, discussed at p. 486 supra.

b.   SELF-DEFENSE

Courvoisier v. Raymond

Supreme Court of Colorado, 1896.
23 Colo. 113, 47 P. 284.

[Some rowdy men entered defendant's building after midnight without permission. With his gun drawn, he ejected them. Then they and other men gathered in the street outside as defendant stood at the steps in front of his building. Defendant claimed that when plaintiff emerged from out of the crowd, defendant thought he was a member of the crowd, and shot him. Plaintiff obtained a judgment against defendant. Further facts are stated in the opinion.]

■ HAYT, C. J.

. . . The parties expelled from the building, upon reaching the rear of the store, were joined by two or three others. In order to frighten these parties away, the defendant fired a shot in the air; but, instead of retreating, they passed around to the street in front, throwing stones and brickbats at the defendant, whereupon he fired a second, and perhaps a third, shot. The first shot fired attracted the attention of plaintiff, Raymond, and two deputy sheriffs, who were at the tramway depot across the street. These officers started towards Mr. Courvoisier, who still continued to shoot; but two of them stopped, when they reached the men in the street, for the purpose of arresting them, Mr. Raymond alone proceeding towards the defendant, calling out to him that he was an officer, and to stop shooting. Although the night was dark, the street was well lighted by electricity, and, when the officer approached him, defendant shaded his eyes, and, taking deliberate aim, fired, causing the injury complained of. The plaintiff's theory of the case is that he was a duly-authorized police officer, and in the discharge of his duties at the time; that the defendant was committing a breach of the peace; and that the defendant, knowing him to be a police officer, recklessly fired the shot in question. The defendant claims that the plaintiff was approaching him at the time in a threatening attitude, and that the surrounding circumstances were such as to cause a reasonable man to believe that his life was in danger, and that it was necessary to shoot in self-defense, and that defendant did so believe at the time of firing the shot.

. . .

The next error assigned relates to the instructions given by the court to the jury, and to those requested by the defendant and refused by the court. The second instruction given by the court was clearly erroneous. The instruction is as follows: "The court instructs you that if you believe, from the evidence, that, at the time the defendant shot the plaintiff, the plaintiff was not assaulting the defendant, then your verdict should be for the plaintiff." The vice of this instruction is that it excluded from the jury a full consideration of the justification claimed by the defendant. The evidence for the plaintiff tends to show that the shooting, if not malicious, was wanton and reckless; but the evidence for the defendant tends to show that the circumstances surrounding him at the time of the shooting were such as to lead a reasonable man to believe that his life was in danger, or that he was in danger of receiving great bodily harm at the hands of the plaintiff, and the defendant testified that he did so believe. He swears that his house was invaded, shortly after midnight, by two men, whom he supposed to be burglars; that, when ejected, they were joined on the outside by three or four others; that the crowd so formed assaulted him with stones and other missiles, when, to frighten them away, he shot into the air; that, instead of going away, some one approached him from the direction of the crowd; that he supposed this person to be one of the rioters, and did not ascertain that it was the plaintiff until after the shooting. He says that he had had no previous acquaintance with plaintiff; that he did not know that he was a police officer, or that there were any police officers in the town of South Denver; that he heard nothing said at the time, by the plaintiff or any one else, that caused him to think the plaintiff was an officer; that his eyesight was greatly impaired, so that he was obliged to use glasses; and that he was without glasses at the time of the shooting, and for this reason could not see distinctly. He then adds: "I saw a man come away from the bunch of men, and come up towards me, and as I looked around I saw this man put his hand to his hip pocket. I didn't think I had time to jump aside, and therefore turned around and fired at him. I had no doubts but it was somebody that had come to rob me, because, some weeks before, Mr. Wilson's store was robbed. It is next door to mine."

By this evidence two phases of the transaction are presented for consideration: First. Was the plaintiff assaulting the defendant at the time plaintiff was shot? Second. If not, was there sufficient evidence of justification for the consideration of the jury? The first question was properly submitted, but the second was excluded by the instruction under review. The defendant's justification did not rest entirely upon the proof of assault by the plaintiff. A riot was in progress, and the defendant swears that he was attacked with missiles, hit with stones, brickbats, etc.; that he shot plaintiff, supposing him to be one of the rioters. We must assume these facts as established in reviewing the instruction, as we cannot say what the jury might have found had this evidence been submitted to them under a proper charge. By the second instruction, the conduct of those who started the fracas was eliminated from the consideration of the jury. If the jury believed, from the evidence, that the defendant would have been justified in shooting one of the rioters, had such person advanced towards him, as did the plaintiff, then it became important to determine whether the defendant mistook plaintiff for one of the rioters; and, if such a mistake was in fact made, was it excusable, in the light of all the circumstances leading up to and surrounding the commission of the act? If these issues had been resolved by the jury in favor of the defendant, he would have been entitled to a judgment. Morris v. Platt, 32 Conn. 75 [1864]; [ ]. The opinion in the first of the cases above cited contains an exhaustive review of the authorities, and is very instructive. The action was for damages resulting from a pistol-shot wound. The defendant justified under the plea of self-defense. The proof for the plaintiff tended to show that he was a mere bystander at a riot, when he received a shot aimed at another; and the court held that, if the defendant was justified in firing the shot at his antagonist, he was not liable to the plaintiff, for the reason that the act of shooting was lawful under the circumstances. Where a defendant, in a civil action like the one before us, attempts to justify on a plea of necessary self-defense, he must satisfy the jury, not only that he acted honestly in using force, but that his fears were reasonable under the circumstances, and also as to the reasonableness of the means made use of. In this case, perhaps, the verdict would not have been different, had the jury been properly instructed; but it might have been, and therefore the judgment must be reversed. Reversed.

NOTES AND QUESTIONS

1. *Nature of the defense.* Is the defendant's argument here that he did not "intend" to shoot plaintiff? If that is not his claim, why should the jury be allowed to find no liability? Can the case be reconciled with the *Garratt* court's holding (see p. 901 supra) that defendant Brian could be taken to have the requisite intent even if he did not "mean" to harm plaintiff? What is the interplay between the prima facie claim of battery and the counter of self-defense in these cases?

These issues turn on the important distinction between excuses and justifications. In cases of excuse, the defendant does not deny that the conduct was wrongful but instead argues that the liability should be excused. Unlike criminal law, tort law does not recognize excuses such as insanity, creating a significant strain of strict fault liability within the intentional torts. An excuse only means that the defendant was not personally blameworthy or truly at "fault," which is not a requirement for tort liability, unlike criminal liability. The affirmative defenses in tort law instead justify or privilege certain forms of conduct, enabling the defendant to avoid liability by proving that he engaged in such conduct and therefore did not act wrongful in the first instance. Without wrongful behavior—or violation of another's tort right—there is no basis for subjecting the defendant to liability.

2. *The requirement of reasonable force.* The privilege of self-defense only entitles one to use reasonable force when she reasonably believes that another is about to commit an actionable battery on her (or to defend others who reasonably appear to be threatened by such an imminent attack). To be reasonable, the force "must not be disproportionate in extent to the harm from which the actor is seeking to protect. . . ." Restatement (Second) of Torts § 63 cmt. j. If the actor exercises excessive force, then she commits an assault or battery by doing so, but only to the extent that the force is unreasonable.

Consider the following hypothetical from Morris on Torts 35 (2d ed.1980):

> Suppose Bellicose advances on Quiet, saying, "Quiet, put up your fists; I'm going to knock the living daylights out of you." Quiet meets this threat with a quick blow on the point of Bellicose's chin, and Bellicose goes down. Bellicose then stands and staggers, obviously *hors de combat.* Nevertheless, the aroused Quiet delivers a second blow that breaks Bellicose's nose.

To what extent, if any, has either party employed unreasonable force? The authors explore whether by combining consent and self-defense, it may be possible for Quiet to escape liability. Is *Hart v. Geysel* relevant?

3. *Innocent victims.* In the cited *Morris v. Platt,* the innocent bystander was hit by an errant shot fired in legitimate self-defense. Does that case raise the same issue as in *Courvoisier*? Does the issue of whether a defendant employs reasonable force in self-defense depend on the number of innocent victims who might be harmed as a result?

In Crabtree v. Dawson, 83 S.W. 557 (Ky.1904), defendant had just ejected a man from a party. The man then threatened to come back and attack defendant. Shortly thereafter, in a poorly lighted area, the plaintiff came running toward the doorway and the defendant, believing that this was the same man returning and that self-defense was called for, struck plaintiff. What if defendant's belief was reasonable though mistaken? What if he honestly but unreasonably believed self-defense was necessary? Could defendant's conduct be subjected to conventional negligence analysis centering on the question of reasonable care?

c.   PROTECTION OF PROPERTY

Katko v. Briney

Supreme Court of Iowa, 1971.
183 N.W.2d 657.

■ MOORE, CHIEF JUSTICE.

[In 1957, defendant wife had inherited farmland on which her grandparents and parents had lived. No one occupied the house after the death of her parents. Defendant husband attempted to care for the land, but kept no machinery on it. Between 1957 and 1967 "there occurred a series of trespassing and housebreaking events with loss of some household items, the breaking of windows and 'messing up of the property in general.'" In July 1967, the events that gave rise to this case occurred. A jury returned a verdict for plaintiff and against defendants husband and wife for $20,000 actual and $10,000 punitive damages. The trial judge rejected motions for judgment notwithstanding the verdict and for a new trial. Further facts appear in the opinion.]

The primary issue presented here is whether an owner may protect personal property in an unoccupied boarded-up farm house against trespassers and thieves by a spring gun capable of inflicting death or serious injury.

We are not here concerned with a man's right to protect his home and members of his family. Defendants' home was several miles from the scene of the incident to which we refer infra.

Plaintiff's action is for damages resulting from serious injury caused by a shot from a 20-gauge spring shotgun set by defendants in a bedroom of an old farm house which had been uninhabited for several years. Plaintiff and his companion, Marvin McDonough, had broken and entered the house to find and steal old bottles and dated fruit jars which they considered antiques.

. . .

Defendants through the years boarded up the windows and doors in an attempt to stop the intrusions. They had posted "no trespass" signs on the land several years before 1967. The nearest one was 35 feet from the house. On June 11, 1967 defendants set "a shotgun trap" in the north bedroom. After Mr. Briney cleaned and oiled his 20-gauge shotgun, the power of which he was well aware, defendants took it to the old house where they secured it to an iron bed with the barrel pointed at the bedroom door. It was rigged with wire from the doorknob to the gun's trigger so it would fire when the door was opened. Briney first pointed the gun so an intruder would be hit in the stomach but at Mrs. Briney's suggestion it was lowered to hit the legs. He admitted he did so "because I was mad and tired of being tormented" but "he did not intend to injure anyone". He gave no explanation of why he used a loaded shell and set it to hit a person already in the house. Tin was nailed over the bedroom window. The spring gun could not be seen from the outside. No warning of its presence was posted.

Plaintiff lived with his wife and worked regularly as a gasoline station attendant in Eddyville, seven miles from the old house. He had observed it for several years while hunting in the area and considered it as being abandoned. He knew it had long been uninhabited. In 1967 the area around the house was covered with high weeds. Prior to July 16, 1967 plaintiff and McDonough had been to the premises and found several old bottles and fruit jars which they took and added to their collection of antiques. On the latter date about 9:30 p.m. they made a second trip to the Briney property. They entered the old house by removing a board from a porch window which was without glass. While McDonough was looking around the kitchen area plaintiff went to another part of the house. As he started to open the north bedroom door the shotgun went off striking him in the right leg above the ankle bone. Much of his leg, including part of the tibia, was blown away. Only by McDonough's assistance was plaintiff able to get out of the house and after crawling some distance was put in his vehicle and rushed to a doctor and then to a hospital. He remained in the hospital 40 days.

[After some doubt, plaintiff's leg was saved but was permanently deformed and shortened. He wore a cast for one year and a brace for another year. His medical bills totaled about $3,600.]

III. Plaintiff testified he knew he had no right to break and enter the house with intent to steal bottles and fruit jars therefrom. He further testified he had entered a plea of guilty to larceny in the nighttime of property of less than $20 value from a private building. He stated he had been fined $50 and costs and paroled during good behavior from a 60-day jail sentence. Other than minor traffic charges this was plaintiff's first brush with the law. On this civil case appeal it is not our prerogative to review the disposition made of the criminal charge against him.

IV. The main thrust of defendants' defense in the trial court and on this appeal is that "the law permits use of a spring gun in a dwelling or warehouse for the purpose of preventing the unlawful entry of a burglar or thief." They repeated this contention in their exceptions to the trial court's instructions 2, 5 and 6. They took no exception to the trial court's statement of the issues or to other instructions.

In the statement of issues the trial court stated plaintiff and his companion committed a felony when they broke and entered defendants' house. In instruction 2 the court referred to the early case history of the use of spring guns and stated under the law their use was prohibited except to prevent the commission of felonies of violence and where human life is in danger. The instruction included a statement that breaking and entering is not a felony of violence.

[Instruction 5 told the jury "that one may use reasonable force in the protection of his property, but such right is subject to the qualification that one may not use such means of force as will take human life or inflict great bodily injury. Such is the rule even though the injured party is a trespasser and is in violation of the law himself." Instruction 6 stated in part that "An owner of premises is prohibited from willfully or intentionally injuring a trespasser by means of force that either takes life or inflicts great bodily injury; and therefore a person owning a premise is prohibited from setting out 'spring guns' and like dangerous devices which will likely take life or inflict great bodily injury, for the purpose of harming trespassers. . . . The only time when such conduct of setting a 'spring gun' or a like dangerous device is justified would be when the trespasser was committing a felony of violence or a felony punishable by death, or where the trespasser was endangering human life by his act."]

The overwhelming weight of authority, both textbook and case law, supports the trial court's statement of the applicable principles of law.

Prosser on Torts, Third Edition, pages 116–118 [1964], states:

> * * * the law has always placed a higher value upon human safety than upon mere rights in property, it is the accepted rule that there is no privilege to use any force calculated to cause death or serious bodily injury to repel the threat to land or chattels, unless there is also such a threat to the defendant's personal safety as to justify a self-defense. * * * Spring guns and other man-killing devices are not justifiable against a mere trespasser, or even a petty thief. They are privileged only against those upon whom the landowner, if he were present in person would be free to inflict injury of the same kind.

[The court observed that Second Restatement section 85 and another treatise agreed with Prosser.]

In Hooker v. Miller, 37 Iowa 613 [1873], we held defendant vineyard owner liable for damages resulting from a spring gun shot although plaintiff was a trespasser and there to steal grapes. At pages 614–15, this statement is made: "This court has held that a mere trespass against property other than a dwelling is not a sufficient justification to authorize the use of a deadly weapon by the owner in its defense; and that if death results in such a case it will be murder, though the killing be actually necessary to prevent the trespass." [ ] At page 617 this court said: "(T)respassers and other inconsiderable violators of the law are not to be visited by barbarous punishments or prevented by inhuman inflictions of bodily injuries."

[The court cited several cases from other states to the same effect.]

The legal principles stated by the trial court in instructions 2, 5 and 6 are well established and supported by the authorities cited and quoted supra. There is no merit in defendants' objections and exceptions thereto. Defendants' various motions based on the same reasons stated in exceptions to instructions were properly overruled.

V.   Plaintiff's claim and the jury's allowance of punitive damages, under the trial court's instructions relating thereto, were not at any time or in any manner challenged by defendants in the trial court as not allowable. We therefore are not presented with the problem of whether the $10,000 award should be allowed to stand.

We express no opinion as to whether punitive damages are allowable in this type of case. If defendants' attorneys wanted that issue decided it was their duty to raise it in the trial court.

. . .

Under our law punitive damages are not allowed as a matter of right. [ ] When malice is shown or when a defendant acted with wanton and reckless disregard of the rights of others, punitive damages may be allowed as punishment to the defendant and as a deterrent to others. Although not meant to compensate a plaintiff, the result is to increase his recovery. He is the fortuitous beneficiary of such an award simply because there is no one else to receive it.

. . .

Study and careful consideration of defendants' contentions on appeal reveal no reversible error.

Affirmed.

■ All Justices concur except LARSON, J., who dissents.

■ LARSON, JUSTICE (dissenting).

. . .

It is my feeling that the majority oversimplifies the impact of this case on the law, not only in this but other jurisdictions, and that it has not thought through all the ramifications of this holding.

. . .

[T]his appeal presents two vital questions which are as novel as they are difficult. They are, (1) is the owner of a building in which are kept household furniture, appliances, and valuables, but not occupied by a person or persons, liable in damages to an intruder who in the nighttime broke into and entered the building with the intent to steal and was shot and seriously injured by a spring gun allegedly set by the owner to frighten intruders from his property, and (2) if he is liable for compensatory damages, is this a proper case for the allowance of exemplary or punitive damages?

. . .

Although I am aware of the often-repeated statement that personal rights are more important than property rights, where the owner has stored his valuables representing his life's accumulations, his livelihood business, his tools and implements, and his treasured antiques as appears in the case at bar, and where the evidence is sufficient to sustain a finding that the installation was intended only as a warning to ward off thieves and criminals, I can see no compelling reason why the use of such a device alone would create liability as a matter of law.

[The dissent thought the jury instructions erroneous because they failed to recognize a defense to the intentional tort claims "if the defendant did not intend to cause serious harm or fatal injury." He also objected to allowing punitive damages to a plaintiff engaged in criminal activity.]

Being convinced that there was reversible error in the court's instructions, that the issue of intent in placing the spring gun was not clearly presented to the jury, and that the issue as to punitive damages should not have been presented to the jury, I would reverse and remand the matter for a new trial.

The majority seem to ignore the evident issue of punitive policy involved herein and uphold the punitive damage award on a mere technical rule of civil procedure.

NOTES AND QUESTIONS

1.   Should the result have been different if defendant and his wife were occupying the house that evening? What if they occasionally occupied it, but were not there that night? What if plaintiff can establish that he was unarmed and interested solely in stealing more fruit jars?

2.   Should the result be different if the defendant erected signs, "These premises protected by spring gun"? For sharply divergent comments on this problem, see Palmer, The Iowa Spring Gun Case: A Study in American Gothic, 56 Iowa L.Rev. 1219 (1971); Posner, Wounding or Killing to Protect a Property Interest, 14 J.L.&Econ. 201 (1971); Comment, Use of Mechanical Devices in the Defense of Property, 24 S.Cal.L.Rev. 133 (1972).

3.   Posner argued that neither blanket permission nor blanket prohibition of the use of deadly force to protect property is likely to be the optimal rule. He proposed a "reasonableness test" to determine whether the use of deadly force is justified to protect property interests. The following considerations would be relevant:

(1) the value of the property at stake measured against the costs of human life and limb;

(2) the existence of an adequate legal remedy as an alternative to the use of force;

(3) the location of the property in terms of the difficulty of protecting it by other means;

(4) the kind of warning given;

(5) the deadliness of the device used;

(6) the character of the conflicting activities;

(7) the cost of avoiding interference by other means.

Posner maintained that "the dominant purpose of rules of liability is to channel people's conduct, and in such a way that the value of interfering activities is maximized." Is this an area in which the legal rule is likely to have an impact in shaping behavior? Is Posner's formulation likely to allow more, or less, use of force to protect property than the widely adopted rule absolutely prohibiting the use of deadly force except to prevent felonies of violence, felonies punishable by death, and acts that threaten imminent human injury? Is the role of the jury under Posner's test a factor that influences your assessment of it? If so, which way does it cut? For a wide-ranging economic analysis of intentional torts, see Landes & Posner, An Economic Theory of Intentional Torts, 1 Int'l Rev.L.&Econ. 127 (1981).

4. *Recapture of chattels.* Property in the form of chattels is movable, creating the opportunity of recapture by the owner. The owner can recapture the chattel by exercising reasonable force only if "he acts promptly after his dispossession or after his timely discovery of it." Restatement (Second) of Torts § 103. If one's bike is stolen, for example, he cannot use force to recapture the bike after seeing it on the street a couple of months later. After the passage of time, the current possessor of the bike may sincerely believe that he owns it. Perhaps the possessor purchased it from someone else, not knowing that it was stolen. The owner's effort to recapture the bike at this point is likely to cause the other to defend possession of the bike, with the consequent possibilities of escalating violence. At this point, the bike owner must seek help from the police or otherwise file a tort claim, illustrating once again how tort rules are sometimes formulated to prevent problematic self-help remedies not otherwise required by the exigencies of the moment.

d.   Private Necessity

Suppose a private party uses, or in an extreme case, destroys the property of another in order to preserve his or her person or property of greater value. Is there a privilege to do so?

In the leading case of Ploof v. Putnam, 71 A. 188 (Vt.1908), plaintiff moored his sloop at a dock on defendant's private island in order to avoid the hazards of a storm. Defendant's servant cut loose the sloop, which, as a result, was battered by the storm. The sloop and its contents were destroyed; plaintiff and his family were injured. In plaintiff's suit for damages, defendant argued that he was simply protecting his private property from use by plaintiff. The court awarded damages to plaintiff, recognizing a privilege, born of necessity, to use defendant's property. Because plaintiff had a right to use the property, defendant's servant violated that right and was subject to liability.

Assuming a privilege exists, there is the further question whether the party exercising the privilege should nonetheless be liable for damages if in fact the "taking" of another's property results in damage. To be more precise, is necessity an "incomplete" privilege that gives the defendant the right to use another's property but only on the condition that defendant pays for any consequent damage? In *Ploof,* that issue would have been whether defendant had a claim for any damage done to the dock. The issue is raised by the famous case that follows.

Vincent v. Lake Erie Transportation Co.

Supreme Court of Minnesota, 1910.
109 Minn. 456, 124 N.W. 221.

■ O'BRIEN, J.

The steamship Reynolds, owned by the defendant, was for the purpose of discharging her cargo on November 27, 1905, moored to plaintiffs' dock in Duluth. While the unloading of the boat was taking place a storm from the northeast developed, which at about ten o'clock p.m., when the unloading was completed, had so grown in violence that the wind was then moving at fifty miles per hour and continued to increase during the night. There is some evidence that one, and perhaps two, boats were able to enter the harbor that night, but it is plain that navigation was practically suspended from the hour mentioned until the morning of the twenty ninth, when the storm abated, and during that time no master would have been justified in attempting to navigate his vessel, if he could avoid doing so. After the discharge of the cargo the Reynolds signaled for a tug to tow her from the dock, but none could be obtained because of the severity of the storm. If the lines holding the ship to the dock had been cast off, she would doubtless have drifted away; but, instead, the lines were kept fast, and as soon as one parted or chafed it was replaced, sometimes with a larger one. The vessel lay upon the outside of the dock, her bow to the east, the wind and waves striking her starboard quarter with such force that she was constantly being lifted and thrown against the dock, resulting in its damage, as found by the jury, to the amount of $500.

We are satisfied that the character of the storm was such that it would have been highly imprudent for the master of the Reynolds to have attempted to leave the dock or to have permitted his vessel to drift away from it. . . . Nothing more was demanded of them than ordinary prudence and care, and the record in this case fully sustains the contention of the appellant that, in holding the vessel fast to the dock, those in charge of her exercised good judgment and prudent seamanship.

It is claimed by the respondent that it was negligence to moor the boat at an exposed part of the wharf, and to continue in that position after it became apparent that the storm was to be more than usually severe. We do not agree with this position. The part of the wharf where the vessel was moored appears to have been commonly used for that purpose. It was situated within the harbor at Duluth, and must, we think, be considered a proper and safe place, and would undoubtedly have been such during what would be considered a very severe storm. The storm which made it unsafe was one which surpassed in violence any which might have reasonably been anticipated.

The appellant contends by ample assignments of error that, because its conduct during the storm was rendered necessary by prudence and good seamanship under conditions over which it had no control, it cannot be held liable for any injury resulting to the property of others, and claims that the jury should have been so instructed. An analysis of the charge given by the trial court is not necessary, as in our opinion the only question for the jury was the amount of damages which the plaintiffs were entitled to recover, and no complaint is made upon that score.

The situation was one in which the ordinary rules regulating property rights were suspended by forces beyond human control, and if, without the direct intervention of some act by the one sought to be held liable, the property of another was injured, such injury must be attributed to the act of God, and not to the wrongful act of the person sought to be charged. If during the storm the Reynolds had entered the harbor, and while there had become disabled and been thrown against the plaintiffs' dock, the plaintiffs could not have recovered. Again, if while attempting to hold fast to the dock the lines had parted, without any negligence, and the vessel carried against some other boat or dock in the harbor, there would be no liability upon her owner. But here those in charge of the vessel deliberately and by their direct efforts held her in such a position that the damage to the dock resulted, and, having thus preserved the ship at the expense of the dock, it seems to us that her owners are responsible to the dock owners to the extent of the injury inflicted.

. . .

Theologians hold that a starving man may, without moral guilt, take what is necessary to sustain life; but it could hardly be said that the obligation would not be upon such person to pay the value of the property so taken when he became able to do so. And so public necessity, in times of war or peace, may require the taking of private property for public purposes; but under our system of jurisprudence compensation must be made.

Let us imagine in this case that for the better mooring of the vessel those in charge of her had appropriated a valuable cable lying upon the dock. No matter how justifiable such appropriation might have been, it would not be claimed that, because of the overwhelming necessity of the situation, the owner of the cable could not recover its value.

This is not a case where life or property was menaced by any object or thing belonging to the plaintiffs, the destruction of which became necessary to prevent the threatened disaster. Nor is it a case where, because of the act of God, or unavoidable accident, the infliction of the injury was beyond the control of the defendant, but is one where the defendant prudently and advisedly availed itself of the plaintiffs' property for the purpose of preserving its own more valuable property, and the plaintiffs are entitled to compensation for the injury done.

Order affirmed.

■ LEWIS, J. (dissenting).

I dissent. It was assumed on the trial before the lower court that appellant's liability depended on whether the master of the ship might, in the exercise of reasonable care, have sought a place of safety before the storm made it impossible to leave the dock. The majority opinion assumes that the evidence is conclusive that appellant moored its boat at respondents' dock pursuant to contract, and that the vessel was lawfully in position at the time the additional cables were fastened to the dock, and the reasoning of the opinion is that, because appellant made use of the stronger cables to hold the boat in position, it became liable under the rule that it had voluntarily made use of the property of another for the purpose of saving its own.

In my judgment, if the boat was lawfully in position at the time the storm broke, and the master could not, in the exercise of due care have left that position without subjecting his vessel to the hazards of the storm, then the damage to the dock, caused by the pounding of the boat, was the result of an inevitable accident. If the master was in the exercise of due care, he was not at fault. The reasoning of the opinion admits that if the ropes, or cables, first attached to the dock had not parted, or if, in the first instance, the master had used the stronger cables, there would be no liability. If the master could not, in the exercise of reasonable care, have anticipated the severity of the storm and sought a place of safety before it became impossible, why should he be required to anticipate the severity of the storm, and, in the first instance, use the stronger cables?

I am of the opinion that one who constructs a dock to the navigable line of waters, and enters into contractual relations with the owner of a vessel to moor the same, takes the risk of damage to his dock by a boat caught there by a storm, which event could not have been avoided in the exercise of due care, and further, that the legal status of the parties in such a case is not changed by renewal of cables to keep the boat from being cast adrift at the mercy of the tempest.

■ JAGGARD, J.

I concur with LEWIS, J.

NOTES AND QUESTIONS

1.   Is it important to the majority that defendant continued to replace the fraying lines? Why does the dissent regard this behavior as inconsequential? Is one position more consistent with the act of God defense than the other?

2.   Is *Vincent* an intentional tort case? Would the definition of intent utilized in *Garratt* and the Restatement apply here? Why does the majority think that the defendant should be held liable? Does the rationale bear any similarity to the basis for strict liability?

3.   Suppose there had been only a one percent chance that securing the vessel would result in damage to the dock. Would the case then be one of unintended harm? If so, would defendant still have been liable— assuming the likelihood of harm to the dock was far less than the expected harm to the (unsecured) boat? Can the liability rules governing these two situations be reconciled? See Seavey, Negligence—Subjective or Objective?, 41 Harv.L.Rev. 1 (1927).

4.   Is the pre-existing contractual relationship between the parties in *Vincent* of any relevance to the assignment of liability? On this score, do you agree with the assumed risk argument at the end of the dissenting opinion? Why does the majority make no reference to the contract? In a case like *Ploof,* where the parties had no contractual relationship, should the result be different?

5.   Consider the following analysis from Morris on Torts 41–42 (2d ed.1980):

> A justification for liability may possibly be brought to light by comparing the *Vincent* case to Cordas v. Peerless Transportation Co., [27 N.Y.S.2d 198 (N.Y.City Ct.1941)]. In the *Cordas* case, a pursued armed bandit jumped into a taxi-cab and ordered the driver to get going. The driver started the cab, shifted into neutral, suddenly slammed on his brakes to throw the bandit off-balance, and leaped out. The cab veered onto the sidewalk and injured a pedestrian. The court held the driver was not liable to the pedestrian in spite of the great likelihood that the driver's intentional act, done in a congested downtown locale, would cause injury and was done to save his own hide.

> The cab case differs from the dock case in several ways. The cab driver's conduct was fraught with only a possibility of injury; the ship captain's conduct was sure to injure the dock. The cab driver had much less time for deliberation than did the mariner. Another distinction may, however, have great significance. If the wharfinger could not hold the mariner responsible, he might have

been tempted to cut the ship loose and risk liability for whatever harm might befall the ship or crew. That risk might not materialize; if the ship happened to weather the storm without damage, the dock owner would then incur no liability. He was sure that his dock would be harmed if the ship remained fast. But if he were assured of compensation for damage to the dock, he would have no incentive to cast the ship loose. In the cab case, however, the pedestrian could do nothing to impede the cab driver from executing his plan of escape. No promise of compensation is needed to affect the pedestrian's behavior; he need not be given assurance of compensation to encourage cooperation.

Do these considerations seem critical? In Fletcher, Corrective Justice for Moderns, 106 Harv.L.Rev. 1658, 1670–71 (1993), the author argues that the key to the case is "the inroad made by the emergency situation on the plaintiff's property rights. The plaintiff is forced, under the circumstances, to keep his dock open to someone who finds himself there when the storm comes up. Because his rights are compromised in the interests of another person, tort law makes up for what he loses under the law of property."

In B. Fried, The Progressive Assault on Laissez Faire: Robert Hale and the First Law and Economics Movement 85 (1998), Professor Fried discussed Robert Hale's view of *Vincent*:

> As Hale noted . . . this decision not only deprived plaintiff of the absolute right to exclude the defendant but also deprived plaintiff of the right to exact whatever defendant would have paid for the right not to be excluded. "The abrogation of the absolute power to exclude in view of the emergency abrogates likewise the power to take advantage of the shipowner's special needs, just as the power to appropriate property by eminent domain denies the owner the opportunity to take advantage of the taker's special needs."

Are these perspectives helpful approaches to *Vincent*? See also E. Weinrib, The Idea of Private Law 196–203 (1995)(employing a restitutionary perspective to explain *Vincent*).

For an enlightening explanation of the trial, appeal, and the majority and dissenting opinions in *Vincent*, see Sugarman, *Vincent v. Lake Erie Transportation Co.*: Liability for Harm Caused by Necessity, in R. Rabin & S. Sugarman (eds.), Torts Stories 259 (2003).

6. Consider the following example from the Restatement (Second) of Torts section 73:

> A, while driving B, a child of three, in a sleigh, is pursued by a pack of wolves which are rapidly closing upon him. To gain time A throws B to the wolves. The time consumed by the wolves in devouring B enables A to reach shelter a few seconds before the pack can reach him. A is subject to liability under a wrongful death statute for the death of B.

Do you agree that A should be held liable? What are the damages in the wolf case if there is liability? Is the situation distinguishable from *Vincent* and *Cordas*? Should the wolf example be decided differently if A's action were taken to save the lives of seven others as well as his own?

7.   *Public necessity.* Sometimes private property is destroyed for the protection of the general public. In Harrison v. Wisdom, 7 Heisk. (55 Tenn.) 99 (1872), the defendants were residents of a town being approached by the Federal army. The defendants destroyed plaintiff's liquor supply to keep it from the troops. The court concluded that in cases of necessity involving protection of the public, "a private mischief is to be endured rather than a public inconvenience." Also, "Necessity, says Lord Coke, makes that lawful which would be otherwise unlawful: 8 Coke, 69." Should it matter whether the troops ever reached the town?

The same approach was adopted in Surocco v. Geary, 3 Cal. 69 (1853), in which the defendant, who was alcalde of San Francisco ordered the destruction of plaintiff's house to prevent the spread of a major fire. The suit was not for the damage to the house, which would clearly have been destroyed anyway, but rather for chattels that the plaintiff could have removed before the house caught fire, but were lost when the house was blown up. The court denied recovery, saying that in such situations "individual rights of property give way to the higher laws of impending necessity." Are these cases consistent with *Vincent*? As far as compensation is concerned, are there reasons to distinguish between private and public necessity? For an overview of this subject, see Christie, The Defense of Necessity Considered from the Legal and Moral Points of View, 48 Duke L.J. 975 (1999).

The court in *Geary* denied that this was a "taking" of private property in the constitutional sense, a view that was sustained in United States v. Caltex (Philippines), Inc., 344 U.S. 149 (1952), in which the armed forces destroyed valuable property belonging to the plaintiff to keep it from falling into enemy hands. The Court, 7–2, held that there was no compensable taking. The majority noted that "The terse language of the Fifth Amendment is no comprehensive promise that the United States will make whole all who suffer from every ravage and burden of war. This Court has long recognized that in wartime many losses must be attributed solely to the fortunes of war, and not to the sovereign." Justices Black and Douglas dissented on the ground that the property was taken as clearly as are food and animals requisitioned for military use: "Whenever the Government determines that one person's property . . . is essential to the war effort and appropriates it for the common good, the public purse, rather than the individual, should bear the loss."

In Muskopf v. Corning Hospital District, 359 P.2d 457 (Cal.1961), Justice Traynor noted that abolishing governmental immunity "does not mean that the state is liable for all harms that result from its activities. . . . Thus the harm resulting from free competition among individuals is not actionable, nor is the harm resulting from the diversion of business by the state's relocation of a highway." Why must the state pay for property it takes to build a new highway but not for business losses caused to merchants along the old route? Should the state be able to claim reimbursement from those whose property values increase because of the new highway? What about paying dairy farmers when the state legalizes the sale of oleomargarine? In the same vein, should the government compensate those who are hurt by decreased government spending or emphasis in their fields? Those who lose their jobs may receive unemployment benefits but how about those harmed derivatively, like the restaurants and gas stations near a defense plant that is closed down?

There is a vast literature on compensable takings, a subject explored in courses on Property and Constitutional Law.

B. ADJUDICATING FOREIGN CONDUCT IN UNITED STATES COURTS

American courts increasingly have encountered requests to adjudicate cases stemming from conduct taking place in foreign countries. Where personal jurisdiction is established, foreign plaintiffs have found in the Alien Tort Claims Act (ATCA), 28 U.S.C. § 1350, a limited vehicle to have cases of civil liability for intentional torts and crimes adjudicated in federal court. The development of the ATCA action is recounted in Wiwa v. Royal Dutch Petroleum Co., 226 F.3d 88 (2d Cir.2000). That case involved civil suits brought against international Shell Oil defendants for the executions of several Nigerians, including prominent author Ken Saro Wiwa, arising out of disputes over the development of oil resources in the homeland of the Ogoni people. Plaintiffs alleged that, although the government of Nigeria tortured and executed the claimants and their decedents, these abuses were "instigated, orchestrated, planned, and facilitated by Shell Nigeria under the direction of the defendants," who were said to have "provided money, weapons, and logistical support to the Nigerian military . . . participated in the fabrication of murder charges . . . , and bribed witnesses to give testimony." The defendants argued that the case should be pursued in England because of forum non conveniens.* The plaintiffs asserted that in addition to the ATCA, the 1991 passage of the Torture Victim Prevention Act, 28 U.S.C. § 1350, argued for keeping their cases in the United States. In addressing those issues, the court extensively reviewed the scope of these statutes:

> The Alien Tort Claims Act was adopted in 1789 as part of the original Judiciary Act. In its original form, it made no assertion about legal rights; it simply asserted that "[t]he district courts shall have original jurisdiction of any civil action by an alien for a tort only, committed in violation of the law of nations or a treaty of the United States." 28 U.S.C. § 1350. For almost two centuries, the statute lay relatively dormant, supporting jurisdiction in only a handful of cases. See, e.g., Filartiga v. Pena-Irala, 630 F.2d 876, 887 & n. 21 (2d

---

* Forum non conveniens permits a court that has jurisdiction of the parties and of a case to dismiss it because an alternative court provides a significantly more convenient forum for adjudicating the case.

Cir.1980) (identifying only two previous cases that had relied upon the ATCA for jurisdiction). As the result of increasing international concern with human rights issues, however, litigants have recently begun to seek redress more frequently under the ATCA. See, e.g., Abebe-Jira v. Negewo, 72 F.3d 844 (11th Cir.1996) (alleging torture of Ethiopian prisoners); Kadic v. Karadzic, 70 F.3d 232 (2d Cir.1995) (alleging torture, rape, and other abuses orchestrated by Serbian military leader); In re Estate of Ferdinand Marcos, 25 F.3d 1467 (9th Cir.1994) (alleging torture and other abuses by former President of Philippines); Tel-Oren v. Libyan Arab Republic, 726 F.2d 774 (D.C.Cir.1984) (alleging claims against Libya based on armed attack upon civilian bus in Israel); *Filartiga*, (alleging torture by Paraguayan officials); Xuncax v. Gramajo, 886 F.Supp. 162 (D.Mass.1995) (alleging abuses by Guatemalan military forces).

These suits produced several important decisions interpreting the meaning and scope of the 1789 Act. For example, in [*Filartiga v. Pena-Irala*], this court held that deliberate torture perpetrated under the color of official authority violates universally accepted norms of international human rights law, and that such a violation of international law constitutes a violation of the domestic law of the United States, giving rise to a claim under the ATCA whenever the perpetrator is properly served within the borders of the United States. More recently, we held in [*Kadic v. Karadzic*], that the ATCA reaches the conduct of private parties provided that their conduct is undertaken under the color of state authority or violates a norm of international law that is recognized as extending to the conduct of private parties.

In passing the Torture Victim Prevention Act [TVPA], Congress expressly ratified our holding in *Filartiga* that the United States courts have jurisdiction over suits by aliens alleging torture under color of law of a foreign nation, and carried it significantly further. While the 1789 Act expressed itself in terms of a grant of jurisdiction to the district courts, the 1991 Act (a) makes clear that it creates liability under U.S. law where under "color of law, of any foreign nation" an individual is subject to torture or "extra judicial killing," and (b) extends its remedy not only to aliens but to any "individual," thus covering citizens of the United States as well. [ ] The TVPA thus recognizes explicitly what was perhaps implicit in the Act of 1789—that the law of nations is incorporated into the law of the United States and that a violation of the international law of human rights is (at least with regard to torture) ipso facto a violation of U.S. domestic law. [ ]

Whatever may have been the case prior to passage of the TVPA, we believe plaintiffs make a strong argument in contending that the present law, in addition to merely permitting U.S. District Courts to entertain suits alleging violation of the law of nations, expresses a policy favoring receptivity by our courts to such suits.

. . .

One of the difficulties that confront victims of torture under color of a nation's law is the enormous difficulty of bringing suits to vindicate such abuses. Most likely, the victims cannot sue in the place where the torture occurred. Indeed, in many instances, the victim would be endangered merely by returning to that place. It is not easy to bring such suits in the courts of another nation. Courts are often inhospitable. Such suits are generally time consuming, burdensome, and difficult to administer. In addition, because they assert outrageous conduct on the part of another nation, such suits may embarrass the government of the nation in whose courts they are brought. Finally, because characteristically neither the plaintiffs nor the defendants are ostensibly either protected or governed by the domestic law of the forum nation, courts often regard such suits as "not our business."

The new formulations of the Torture Victim Protection Act convey the message that torture committed under color of law of a foreign nation in violation of international law is "our business," as such conduct not only violates the standards of international law but also as a consequence violates our domestic law.

The court reversed the lower court's granting of defendants' motion to dismiss on the grounds of forum non conveniens after finding that defendants failed to show the relevant factors tilted strongly in favor of adjudication in the foreign forum.

In Sosa v. Alvarez-Machain, 542 U.S. 692 (2004), the Supreme Court addressed a question decided in the *Filartiga* case, cited in *Wiwa*, but unnecessary to the outcome in *Wiwa*: whether the ATCA merely extends the subject matter jurisdiction of federal courts or whether it also creates a substantive cause of action for violations of international law. A Mexican national was abducted and transported by Mexican officials to the United States by Mexican officials, where he was lawfully arrested by DEA agents. After his trial in the United States for murder ended in his acquittal, the plaintiff sued his Mexican abductors (among others). No claim was available under applicable state law (and no claim was made under the TVPA because the plaintiff had not been tortured). The Supreme Court, 6–3, held that although the ATCA was passed with the understanding that it would permit federal courts to recognize claims based on then-widely accepted common law violations of international law, such as piracy and interference with safe passage, the ATCA was primarily jurisdictional. Federal courts should not recognize claims for violations of any international law norm with less definite content and acceptance than those recognized when the Act was enacted. Based on that limited scope of the ATCA, the Court ruled that plaintiff had no claim under the ATCA because "a single illegal detention of less than a day, followed by the transfer of custody to lawful authorities and a prompt arraignment, violates no norm of customary international law."

The federal circuit courts have split on the issue of whether the ATCA, which is now conventionally called the Alien Tort Statute (ATS), recognizes corporate liability. In Kiobel v. Royal Dutch Petroleum Co., 621 F.3d 111 (2d Cir.2010), the court recognized that *Sosa* requires courts to apply norms of international law, which must be "specific, universal and obligatory." Because "corporate liability is not a discernible—much less a universally recognized—norm of customary international law," the *Kiobel* court concluded that corporations cannot be held liable under the ATS. This ruling conflicted with the holdings in a number of other circuits that recognized claims of corporate liability under the ATS. E.g., Flomo v. Firestone Natural Rubber Co., 643 F.3d 1013 (7th Cir.2011) (Posner, J.)("If a corporation complicit in Nazi war crimes could be punished criminally for violating customary international law, as we believe it could be, then a fortiori if the board of directors of a corporation directs the corporation's managers to commit war crimes, engage in piracy, abuse ambassadors or use slave labor, the corporation can be civilly liable"). The Supreme Court affirmed *Kiobel* without resolving the issue of corporate liability, concluding instead that the presumption against the extraterritorial application of U.S. law required dismissal of the ATS claims because "all the relevant conduct took place outside of the United States." Kiobel v. Royal Dutch Petroleum Co., 133 S.Ct. 1659, 1669 (2013). The Court then provided some guidance about the type of conduct governed by the ATS:

> Even where the claims touch and concern the territory of the United States, they must do so with sufficient force to displace the presumption against extraterritorial application. . . . Corporations are often present in many countries, and it would reach too far to say that mere corporate presence suffices. If Congress were to determine otherwise, a statute more specific than the ATS would be required.

Id. Although *Kiobel* addressed the extraterritorial application of the ATS, it left open the question whether the statute recognizes corporate liability.

In contrast, the TPVA allows civil lawsuits against "an individual" who engages in torture or killings, leading to the question of whether that term could apply not only to natural persons but also to other juridical entities. In Mohamad v. Palestinian Authority, 132 S.Ct. 1702 (2012), relying on a dictionary definition of "individual," the Court ruled that corporations are not individuals for purposes of the statute.

The Anti-Terrorism Act (ATA), 28 U.S.C. § 2331 et seq., complements the TPVA and allows Americans injured by an "act of international terrorism" to sue foreign entities in U.S. courts. It has served as a basis for liability in several prominent terrorist attacks, including against Libya for its role in the 1988 downing of Pan-Am Flight 103 over Lockerbie, Scotland. See Rein v. Socialist People's Libyan Arab Jamahiriya, 995 F.Supp. 325 (E.D.N.Y.1998).

Among other questions, Boim v. Holy Land Foundation for Relief and Development, 549 F.3d 685 (7th Cir.2008), cert. denied, 558 U.S. 981 (2009), raised the issue of whether the ATA extends to those who engage in aiding and abetting. Hamas terrorists murdered a U.S. (and Israeli) citizen in Israel. His parents sued three organizations and an individual who contributed to Hamas. In an en banc opinion by Judge Posner, on appeal from a plaintiff's verdict, the majority decided there is no implied secondary liability (e.g., aiding or abetting) under the ATA, but that the statute does proscribe donations to terrorist organizations (what one might think of otherwise as aiding and abetting). On a related issue, the court held that the scienter required is knowledge (or deliberate indifference to the fact) that the organization engages in terrorist acts. And on a contested causation issue, the court invoked a version of the multiple sufficient causes paradigm (see supra p. 346) in holding that as long as the donation by a defendant would have been necessary even if some other contributions are ignored, defendant can be found to be a cause in fact. The majority also held that donations to the humanitarian causes of Hamas are equally a cause because they permit the organization to shift money from charity to terrorism. One of the dissenters, Judge Rovner, criticized the latter causation aspect as well as the conclusion that secondary liability does not exist in the statute and the failure to require intent to assist in terrorist activities.

Subsequent developments in the case law have not "disturbed the reasoning that Judge Posner applied to this question in *Boim.* . . . The principle is that when a tortfeasor acts with the knowledge that its conduct will, in concert with that of others, result in harm that would not otherwise occur, it is appropriate to hold each tortfeasor accountable." Linde v Arab Bank, PLC, 97 F.Supp.3d 287 (E.D.N.Y 2015)(upholding jury verdict finding that defendant bank violated the

ATA through its "deliberate indifference" in financing a series of terrorist activities by Hamas that injured plaintiffs).

Compare Presbyterian Church of Sudan v. Talisman Energy, Inc., 582 F.3d 244 (2d Cir.2009). Canadian oil companies were engaged in developmental activities in Sudan in the midst of the civil war. The government engaged in a practice of clearing a corridor of all natives in areas where the oil companies wanted to explore. This forced relocation was the basis for an ATS claim against the defendant companies for aiding and abetting. The court decided that international law must be the source of the standard for aiding and abetting and that it requires assistance rendered with a *purpose* to facilitate the violations. The court considered and rejected a series of alleged acts by the defendant that assisted the Sudanese government in its human rights abuses.

A major practical hurdle to suits under both the ATS and the ATA is the difficulty of finding assets of foreign defendants upon which a judgment can be executed. See Note, Sue and Be Recognized: Collecting § 1350 Judgments Abroad, 107 Yale L.J. 2177 (1998).

Suits naming foreign countries as defendants are limited by the Foreign Sovereign Immunities Act of 1976 (FSIA), 28 U.S.C. §§ 1602–11, which provides immunity from suit, subject to a number of exceptions. In Peterson v. Islamic Republic of Iran, 264 F.Supp.2d 46 (D.D.C.2003), plaintiffs were able to pursue claims under the FSIA's state-sponsored terrorism exception to immunity. There, the Iranian regime was held liable for its support of the terrorist organization Hezbollah in connection with the 1983 bombing of a Marines' barracks in Beirut that resulted in 241 deaths. However, limitations to the state-sponsored terrorism exception barred most claims against Saudi Arabian princes and officials for allegedly financing al Qaeda in In re Terrorist Attacks on September 11, 2001, 538 F.3d 71 (2d Cir.2008). Even where immunity has been abrogated, courts may interpret an international agreement as preventing suit in U.S. courts. See Roeder v. Islamic Republic of Iran, 333 F.3d 228 (D.C.Cir.2003).

C. GOVERNMENT LIABILITY

In Chapter III, we considered the circumstances in which various governmental entities might retain a common law or statutory immunity from tort liability. In this section, we consider claims against government officials that usually involve deliberate interference with claimed legal and civil rights of citizens. Our earlier focus was liability for negligence. Now we address cases that raise the issue of abuse of power by government officials. Nevertheless, the civil rights claims addressed below often overlap with common law tort claims that might also be made by plaintiffs in these cases. Recall *Town of Castle Rock, Colorado v. Gonzales* and *DeShaney v. Winnebago County Department of Social Services*, pp. 258–259 supra.

1.   THE FEDERAL CIVIL RIGHTS ACTION

a.   ELEMENTS OF THE STATUTORY CLAIM

In the years following the end of the Civil War, widespread violence and lawlessness raged in the South. Murders, whippings and other atrocities were perpetrated by members of the Ku Klux Klan and other vigilante groups against blacks and Union sympathizers. Although virtually all of these acts of terrorism were violations of state and local law, law enforcement officials did little to intervene and, in some cases, they tacitly condoned the illegal acts and even conspired with the outlaws. In response to this situation, Congress, under its power to enforce the recently ratified Fourteenth Amendment, passed the Ku Klux Klan Act of 1871. Section 1 of the Act, now codified as 42 U.S.C. § 1983, provides:

> Every person who, under color of any statute, ordinance, regulation, custom, or usage, of any State or Territory, subjects, or causes to be subjected, any citizen of the United States or other person within the jurisdiction thereof to the deprivation of any rights, privileges, or immunities secured by the Constitution and laws, shall be liable to the party injured in an action at law, suit in equity, or other proper proceeding for redress.

The section lay dormant until Monroe v. Pape, 365 U.S. 167 (1961), in which plaintiffs alleged that "13 Chicago police officers broke into [their] home in the early morning, routed them from bed, made them stand naked in the living room, and ransacked every room, emptying drawers and ripping mattress covers." Further, Mr. Monroe was taken to the police station and held for ten hours without being arraigned or allowed to call his family or attorney. He was released without charges being filed. Plaintiffs alleged that the officers had no search or arrest warrants. They sued the officers and the City of Chicago under section 1983, claiming that defendants acted "under color of the statutes, ordinances, regulations, customs and usages" of the city and state.

On appeal, the Court upheld the complaint. Although the original purposes of the statute were to "override certain kinds of state laws" and to "provide a remedy where state law was inadequate," the "purposes were much broader. The *third* aim was to provide a federal remedy where the state remedy, though adequate in theory, was not available in practice." The federal remedy was held "supplementary to the state remedy, and the latter need not be first sought and refused before the federal one is invoked." Thus, the fact that Illinois law outlawed unreasonable searches and seizures did not bar the suit.

The Court then concluded that the officers had acted "under color of" state law, relying on an earlier case in which a plurality had concluded that "misuse of power, possessed by virtue of state law and made possible only because the wrongdoer is clothed with the authority of state law, is action taken 'under color of' state law."

To state a claim under section 1983, a plaintiff must show that a "person" acting under color of state law, custom, or usage deprived him or her of a federally protected constitutional right. Each of the elements of the prima facie case discussed in *Monroe* has led to extensive litigation, but the principles established by *Monroe* have been generally followed. For an overview of the historical development of section 1983 doctrine, see Eisenberg, Section 1983: Doctrinal Foundations and An Empirical Study, 67 Cornell L.Rev. 482 (1982). See also Weinberg, The *Monroe* Mystery Solved: Beyond the "Unhappy History" Theory of Civil Rights Litigation, 1991 B.Y.U.L.Rev. 737 (explaining the development of section 1983 litigation in terms of the Bill of Rights jurisprudence of the Warren Court).

"Every person." In Monell v. New York City Department of Social Services, 436 U.S. 658 (1978), the Court held that "every person" was broad enough to include municipal corporations as potential defendants.* The Court went on to say that "a local government may not be sued under § 1983 for an injury inflicted solely by its employees or agents. Instead, it is when execution of a government's policy or custom, whether made by its lawmakers or by those whose edicts or acts may fairly be said to represent official policy, inflicts the injury that the government as an entity is responsible under § 1983." Thus, it is often said that vicarious liability is inapplicable in section 1983 actions; rather a policy or custom of the governmental employer that was a cause of the harm must be shown.

Will this limitation insulate governmental entities from liability very often?** In Pembaur v. City of Cincinnati, 475 U.S. 469 (1986), the Court held that a single decision by a county prosecutor that deprived an individual of his Fourth and Fourteenth Amendment rights satisfied *Monell*'s "official policy" standard. The prosecutor had given local sheriffs the go-ahead to break down plaintiff's office door and conduct a search. The Supreme Court reinstated plaintiff's section 1983 action for the allegedly unlawful search. Because state law authorized sheriffs to obtain instructions to search from local prosecutors, and because the sheriffs in the case at bar had followed the prosecutor's directive, the

---

*   States may not be sued directly in federal court because of the Eleventh Amendment, and hence even suits challenging statewide practices are against individual state officials. Edelman v. Jordan, 415 U.S. 651 (1974). A state or state agency is not considered a citizen or person for purposes of section 1983. Will v. Michigan Department of State Police, 491 U.S. 58 (1989). Even in suits against state officials, some forms of relief that implicate the public fisc are also barred by the Eleventh Amendment.

**   Regardless of whether a municipality is formally found liable, very frequently local government entities indemnify their employees for any liability to which they are subject under section 1983. See Schwartz, Should Juries be Informed that Municipality Will Indemnify Officer's § 1983 Liability for Constitutional Wrongdoing?, 86 Iowa L.Rev. 1209 (2001).

prosecutor effectively acted as the county's "final decisionmaker," thereby exposing the county to section 1983 liability.

Board of the County Commissioners of Bryan County, Oklahoma v. Brown, 520 U.S. 397 (1997), revealed the difficult factual issues that may arise from the policy or custom requirement of *Monell* for municipal liability. Plaintiff brought a section 1983 claim against the county based on a deputy's use of excessive force to remove her from her vehicle. The plaintiff claimed that the sheriff's decision to hire the deputy without performing an adequate background check on the new employee violated her federal rights. The deputy had a prior record of driving infractions, assault and battery, and other misdemeanors. The Court held that to establish a municipal policy necessary to give rise to liability, the plaintiff must show that deliberate conduct attributable to the municipality was the "moving force" behind the alleged injury. Specifically, the municipality must take the action with the requisite degree of culpability, and the plaintiff must establish a direct causal link between the municipal action and the deprivation of federal rights. The Court stated that a full review of the deputy's record would not necessarily have revealed that a reasonable policymaker should have concluded that the deputy's use of excessive force would be the "plainly obvious consequence" of the decision to hire the deputy.

A recurring issue before the Court has been whether a municipality's failure to provide adequate training to certain employees, most notably its police force, amounts to an official policy. In City of Canton v. Harris, 489 U.S. 378 (1989), plaintiff was arrested and brought to a police station where she twice slumped to the floor. The officers left plaintiff on the floor so she wouldn't fall again, but they never summoned medical assistance for her. After the police released plaintiff, she was taken to a hospital and diagnosed as suffering from various emotional ailments. Plaintiff brought a section 1983 action against the city for its deprivation of her right to receive necessary medical care while in custody. She pointed to the city policy that gave station shift commanders the sole discretion to determine when an arrestee required medical care and the city's failure to train specially its officers to recognize when to summon such care. The Court, in remanding for further proceedings, held that "[t]he inadequacy of police training may serve as a basis for section 1983 liability only where the failure to train amounts to deliberate indifference to the rights of persons with whom the police come into contact." Furthermore, the Court required that the asserted training deficiency must actually have caused the officers' indifference to plaintiff's medical needs.

What constitutes "deliberate indifference?" In Farmer v. Brennan, 511 U.S. 825 (1994), a transsexual prison inmate claimed violation of Eighth Amendment rights by prison officials who placed him in the general prison population, allegedly subjecting him to special risks of harm, which came to fruition. In response to plaintiff's claim of deliberate indifference, the court held that its objective standard under *Canton* was not the appropriate test for cruel and unusual punishment under the Eighth Amendment. Rather, a subjective test was called for:

> We hold instead that a prison official cannot be found liable under the Eighth Amendment for denying an inmate humane conditions of confinement unless the official knows of and disregards an excessive risk to inmate health and safety.

Would a letter to the prison superintendent in *Farmer*, explaining the facts and risk to the plaintiff when he was placed in the general prison population, have sufficed to satisfy the subjective standard adopted by the Court?

The Court also refined *Canton* by concluding that not every failure to train government employees amounts to a constitutional violation. In Collins v. City of Harker Heights, 503 U.S. 115 (1992), the Court rejected a claim involving the death of a city sanitation worker who was asphyxiated in a manhole while attempting to unplug a sewer line. The Court held that the city's inadequate training of the employee did not amount to a violation of due process.

"Acting under color of state law." In *Monroe*, the Court held that conduct under color of state law embraced conduct of a state official contrary to state law. This holding has been reaffirmed, and today the state action requirement under section 1983 is generally assumed to be identical to the threshold required by the Fourteenth Amendment. In Polk County v. Dodson, 454 U.S. 312 (1981), the Court interpreted "under color of state law" to require more than that a governmental employee was responsible for the deprivation. A public defender, appointed to represent plaintiff in a criminal proceeding, was held to be performing an essentially independent, private function in deciding how best to represent her client.

Private action may constitute "state action" if made possible only because of state support or acquiescence, as where a shopkeeper detains a suspected shoplifter pursuant to an agreement with the police. See Adickes v. S.H. Kress & Co., 398 U.S. 144 (1970). In Richardson v. McKnight, 521 U.S. 399 (1997), the Court held that prison guards who are employed by a private prison management firm are subject to section 1983 liability. In addition, the Court held that the prison guards were not entitled to qualified immunity from section 1983 suits because it could not identify a history or purpose of granting immunity to privately employed prison guards. And despite its nominally private character, a state athletic association's role in enforcing a rule restricting improper recruiting of high school athletes constituted state action because of the entanglement between the association and public schools, public officials, and financing from public sources. Brentwood Academy v. Tennessee Secondary School Athletic Ass'n, 531 U.S. 288 (2001). See generally Winter, The Meaning of "Under Color of" Law, 91 Mich.L.Rev. 323 (1992).

"Who subjects another or causes another to be subjected to." Section 1983 creates a cause of action only against a person who "subjects" another or "causes" another "to be subjected" to the deprivation of constitutional rights. A threshold issue was raised in DeShaney v. Winnebago County Department of Social Services, 489 U.S. 189 (1989), in which a child under the jurisdiction of defendant county department of social services was seriously injured by his father's sustained pattern of physical abuse. The section 1983 claim against defendant was for denial of a liberty interest protected by the Due Process Clause by failing to intervene and provide protection. In denying any affirmative obligation on the part of the governmental agency, the Court stated:

> [I]t is well to remember once again that the harm was inflicted not by the State of Wisconsin, but by [plaintiff's] father. The most that can be said of the state functionaries in this case is that they stood by and did nothing when suspicious circumstances dictated a more active role for them.

In Town of Castle Rock, Colorado v. Gonzales, p. 258 supra, the Court denied a plaintiff's claim that she had a *property interest* in the enforcement of a restraining order. The Court in *Castle Rock* explained that there is no federally imposed obligation on state or local officials to intervene to enforce a restraining order and protect an individual from other private actors.

Recall the discussion of *Riss v. City of New York* and the notes that follow, p. 227 supra. Are the considerations that were salient there the same as those that seem central in the section 1983 context? Is *Harper v. Herman*, p. 129 supra, a closer analogy?

The "subjects another or causes another to be subjected" language also raises problems when supervisory officials are sued. Occasionally, plaintiffs can show that the supervisory defendant directed, encouraged, or participated in the unlawful conduct of the subordinate officials. Often, however, the supervisor may have been unaware of the conduct until after the harm occurred. In the latter situation, suits against supervisory officials under section 1983 are usually brought under a theory of failure to train subordinates adequately, lack of adequate supervision, or some form of vicarious liability.

Most courts have construed this language in section 1983 to require some level of individual blameworthiness more serious than negligence and have held that superior officers may not be held liable under the doctrine of respondeat superior for the acts of subordinates. Williams v. Vincent, 508 F.2d 541 (2d Cir.1974). (Would a superior officer be subject to respondeat superior under common law principles?) In Rizzo v. Goode, 423 U.S. 362 (1976), citizens brought a section 1983 action against superior officers of the Philadelphia Police Department seeking relief because of the officers' failure to correct unconstitutional conduct by subordinates. After finding a "pattern of frequent police violations" of the rights of minorities, the trial court granted injunctive relief. The

Supreme Court reversed, finding insufficient evidence that the supervisory officials had implemented, or acquiesced in, an unconstitutional policy.

What qualifies a government officer's acts as a due process violation? In County of Sacramento v. Lewis, 523 U.S. 833 (1998), the Court determined that a police officer's decision to pursue a suspect in a high-speed chase did not violate the suspect's due process rights. To show a violation of due process in the context of a high-speed chase, the government actor's conduct must "shock the conscience." The Court also observed that conduct that may be a constitutional violation in one environment may be acceptable, lawful conduct in an alternative setting.

"Citizen of the United States or other person within the jurisdiction thereof." Section 1983 claims may be brought by all natural persons who are citizens as well as resident aliens. Graham v. Richardson, 403 U.S. 365 (1971). Corporations have uniformly been permitted to sue under section 1983. E.g., Discovery House, Inc. v. City of Indianapolis, 319 F.3d 277 (7th Cir.), cert. denied, 540 U.S. 879 (2003). However, in Inyo County, California v. Paiute-Shoshone Indians of The Bishop Community of the Bishop Colony, 538 U.S. 701 (2003), the Supreme Court held that a Native American tribe seeking to enforce its rights as a sovereign against the enforcement of a search warrant was not a "person" entitled to bring a section 1983 case.

"Rights . . . secured by the Constitution and laws." In 1980, the Court held that, since section 1983 speaks of rights "secured by the Constitution and laws" of the United States, an action lies under that section for purely statutory violations of federal law. Maine v. Thiboutot, 448 U.S. 1 (1980)(claim under section 1983 for deprivation of welfare benefits to which the plaintiffs claimed entitlement under the federal Social Security Act).

Section 1983 does not, however, provide a cause of action if 1) the statute in question does not create enforceable "rights" within the meaning of section 1983, or 2) Congress has foreclosed a section 1983 action in the enactment of the statute itself. Wright v. Roanoke Redevelopment & Housing Authority, 479 U.S. 418 (1987).

In Golden State Transit Corp. v. City of Los Angeles, 493 U.S. 103 (1989), the Court laid out a three-part test for determining whether a particular statute or constitutional provision creates an enforceable "right" under section 1983. First, the provision must create obligations binding on the governmental unit; second, the plaintiff's interest must not be so vague and amorphous as to be beyond the judiciary's competence to enforce; and third, the provision at issue must have been intended to benefit the plaintiff. Applying this test, the Court held that the Supremacy Clause, which gives superior force to federal constitutional and statutory provisions whenever they conflict with state law, does not create rights that are enforceable under section

1983. See also Gonzaga University v. Doe, 536 U.S. 273 (2002)(Family Educational Rights and Privacy Act, which provides a mechanism for maintaining confidentiality of student records, creates no personal right that can be enforced in section 1983 action). In contrast, the Court has held that suits for alleged violations of the Commerce Clause (which protects against state actions that impose a substantial burden on interstate commerce) may be brought under section 1983. Dennis v. Higgins, 498 U.S. 439 (1991).

With respect to a particular statutory enactment, Congress may foreclose a section 1983 action in one of two ways. First, Congress may include an express provision to that effect in the statute itself. Second, Congress may invest the statute with a remedial scheme that is sufficiently comprehensive to demonstrate an intent to preclude a judicial remedy via a section 1983 action. Wilder v. Virginia Hospital Ass'n, 496 U.S. 498 (1990). In Middlesex County Sewerage Authority v. National Sea Clammers Ass'n, 453 U.S. 1 (1981), the Court found that the extensive enforcement mechanisms in several federal environmental statutes demonstrated congressional intent to bar section 1983 actions for alleged state violations of those statutes. See Sunstein, Section 1983 and the Private Enforcement of Federal Law, 49 U.Chi.L.Rev. 394 (1982).

Issues may also arise in state criminal cases regarding the nature of the "rights" protected under section 1983. Heck v. Humphrey, 512 U.S. 477 (1994), held that no section 1983 action could be brought by a convicted defendant while his appeal from conviction was still pending. Such suits must wait until the state conviction has been "reversed on direct appeal, expunged by executive order, declared invalid by a state tribunal authorized to make such determination, or called into question by a federal court's issuance of a writ of habeas corpus." In Albright v. Oliver, 510 U.S. 266 (1994), an earlier prosecution had been dismissed on the grounds that it failed to state an offense under Illinois law. The section 1983 claim against the state officials was based on denial of due process in groundlessly prosecuting the plaintiff. The Court held that any such claim, if actionable at all, must be based on the Fourth Amendment rather than on substantive due process—and no Fourth Amendment claim was before the court.

The Prison Litigation Reform Act of 1995, 42 U.S.C. § 1997e(a), requires that prisoners pursue any administrative remedy that may be provided by the state or prison before they may bring a section 1983 suit. In Booth v. Churner, 532 U.S. 731 (2001), the Court held that exhaustion of such remedies is required, even if the administrative scheme cannot provide the remedy—money damages—that the plaintiff seeks for the alleged violations.

Attorney's Fees. Unlike the general "American rule," pursuant to which the parties bear their own attorney's fees, federal law permits a prevailing plaintiff in section 1983 litigation to recover attorney's fees.

42 U.S.C. § 1988(b). A substantial body of case law that addresses when a plaintiff has obtained sufficient relief to qualify as "prevailing" and recover fees, and the appropriate rules for determination of the amount of those fees has developed under this statute. See, e.g., Hensley v. Eckerhart, 461 U.S. 424 (1983). This provision affords a distinct advantage to section 1983 claims for plaintiffs when a common law tort claim is also available.

b.   IMMUNITIES

A major recurring problem has been the nature of defenses available under the statute. In reading the following notes, keep in mind the discussion of governmental liability at p. 226 supra. Do any common considerations underlie the issues raised?

Government immunity: The Wilson v. Layne *sequencing analysis.* In Wilson v. Layne, 526 U.S. 603 (1999), plaintiff Wilson sued police officers for allowing representatives of the media to accompany them while executing an arrest warrant in a private home. The Supreme Court held that this type of media ride-along violates the Fourth Amendment, but that because the state of the law was not clearly established at the time the search in this case took place, the officers are entitled to qualified immunity. *Id.* at 617. In the course of its opinion, the Court stated that the procedure courts should follow in future cases was to first determine if a constitutional right has been violated based on the plaintiff's allegation, and, only if there is such a violation, proceed to the issue of qualified immunity. See also Saucier v. Katz, 533 U.S. 194 (2001). Is such a sequence for analyzing section 1983 actions the most efficient scheme for resolving these claims? Pearson v. Callahan, 555 U.S. 223 (2009), modifies the requirement set out in *Wilson* and mandated in *Saucier* that the two-step process of deciding constitutional violation and then immunity be followed. While it is often beneficial, the Court recognizes—after reciting a litany of evils that can occur by rigidly imposing the *Saucier* two-step—that there are cases in which it is more sensible to proceed directly to the matter of qualified immunity and decide that matter initially.

Would the Wilsons be entitled to recover attorney's fees as prevailing plaintiffs under section 1988, above? In Hill v. McKinley, 311 F.3d 899 (8th Cir.2002), plaintiff, a female prisoner who was unruly and uncooperative, was restrained, naked, for hours in front of male guards. The court held that her constitutional right to privacy was violated but that the defendants were entitled to qualified immunity. Because qualified immunity prevented plaintiff from obtaining any relief, she was not a "prevailing party" entitled to fees. See also Hewitt v. Helms, 482 U.S. 755 (1987) (if qualified immunity prevents plaintiff from obtaining any judicial relief, attorney's fees are unavailable, even if suit serves as a "catalyst" for government to change practices).

Qualified immunity. Are there persuasive reasons for granting immunities to government officials despite the lack of explicit mention in section 1983? Should government actors be liable in damages only for the violation of "clearly established" statutory or constitutional rights? How does the Court define "clearly established" rights? Is that a satisfactory standard? What impact does it have on governmental action that is an abuse of authority?

Even when a government employee's actions do stray over the constitutional line, lack of clarity about the location of the line will often support qualified immunity. In Brosseau v. Haugen, 543 U.S. 194 (2004), a police officer shot a disturbed felon who was attempting to flee. The case law in the area was mixed and highly dependent on the factual context. The officer's action fell in the "hazy border between excessive and acceptable force," and he was therefore entitled to qualified immunity. Compare Hope v. Pelzer, 536 U.S. 730 (2002)(rejecting lower court's "materially similar" precedent and instead considering whether precedent has provided "fair warning" even in "novel factual circumstances"); Anderson v. Creighton, 483 U.S. 635 (1987)(that the precise issue has not been decided is not automatic assurance of qualified immunity). According to the Court, "[q]ualified immunity gives government officials breathing room to make reasonable but mistaken judgments," and "protects all but the plainly incompetent or those who knowingly violate the law." Stanton v. Sims, 134 S.Ct. 3 (2013)(granting qualified immunity to defendant police officer who had entered the plaintiff's yard without a warrant while in hot pursuit of a third party who had committed a misdemeanor, because when defendant "made his split-second decision to enter [plaintiff's yard,] courts across the country were either equivocal or sharply divided about whether a warrant was required in such circumstances, and so even if defendant had "been mistaken in believing his actions were justified, he was not plainly incompetent").

Qualified immunity does not mean that plaintiffs who establish a constitutional or statutory violation have no remedy. Courts may issue injunctive relief barring such behavior in the future if there is a risk of it being repeated by defendants. Presumably the precedential effect of such decisions also affects the behavior of other governmental officials who are not the subject of injunctive relief. And, as *Wilson* reveals, once the legal right has been established, qualified immunity will no longer be available for future violations.

Absolute immunity. Absolute immunities have traditionally been recognized for officials performing judicial and legislative functions. Can an absolute, as distinguished from a qualified, immunity be justified? Consider Mireles v. Waco, 502 U.S. 9 (1991), in which plaintiff attorney alleged that the defendant judge had ordered bailiffs to drag plaintiff from another courtroom in the building because he was late for the defendant's morning calendar call. The Court summarily decided that absolute immunity applied. The alleged act could not be a nonjudicial action because "a judge's direction to court officers to bring a person . . . before him is a function normally performed by a judge." The action was taken in the "very aid of the judge's jurisdiction over a matter before him," and thus could not be said to have been taken in the absence of jurisdiction. Is absolute immunity warranted here? Consider also Stump v. Sparkman, 435 U.S. 349 (1978), in which a woman sued Judge Harold D. Stump for granting her mother's petition to have a tubal ligation performed on her without her knowledge. In holding that Judge Stump's behavior was judicial and thus that he was entitled to absolute immunity, the Court held that the test to be used in evaluating whether a judge's behavior is a judicial act is whether the act is a function normally performed by a judge, and whether the parties dealt with the judge in his judicial capacity.

What are the limits of the judicial function? In Forrester v. White, 484 U.S. 219 (1988), the Court limited the scope of absolute immunity for judicial officers. The defendant, a state judge who was authorized to hire and fire probation officers, hired plaintiff to be an adult and juvenile probation officer. After promoting plaintiff to a supervisory position, defendant fired her. Plaintiff filed suit under section 1983 alleging sex discrimination in violation of the Fourteenth Amendment's Equal Protection Clause. The Supreme Court rejected defendant's claim that as a judicial officer, he was entitled to absolute immunity from a civil damages suit. Applying a "functional" approach, the Court reasoned that immunity for "truly judicial" acts was needed to protect "judicial independence by insulating judges from vexatious actions prosecuted by disgruntled litigants." In the instant case, plaintiff's allegations went to defendant's administrative responsibilities. The threat of vexatious lawsuits brought by fired employees was not sufficiently grave to justify absolute immunity. Would the Court's decision in Forrester extend to a federal judge who discriminated against women in hiring law clerks?

In Imbler v. Pachtman, 424 U.S. 409 (1976), the Court determined that state prosecutors enjoy absolute immunity from section 1983 for actions relating to their conduct "in initiating a prosecution and in presenting the State's case," insofar as that conduct is "intimately associated with the judicial phase of the criminal process[.]" In Kalina v. Fletcher, 522 U.S. 118 (1997), the Court held that absolute immunity shielded a prosecutor from section 1983 liability for allegedly making false statement in the preparation and filing of charging documents and an arrest warrant. The prosecutor, however, was protected by only qualified immunity for her conduct in executing a certification for determination of probable cause for the arrest. The Court reasoned that the absolute immunity of state prosecutors is limited to the performance of traditional functions of an advocate. The prosecutor's actions in serving as a complaining witness to establish probable cause for an arrest fell outside traditional advocate functions, and therefore, the prosecutor had only qualified immunity for such conduct.

In Buckley v. Fitzsimmons, 509 U.S. 259 (1993), the Court held that a prosecutor is entitled only to qualified immunity when engaging in investigatory, rather than prosecutorial functions. Thus the prosecutor could claim only qualified immunity when he allegedly engaged in misconduct while attempting to determine if a bootprint at the crime scene had been left by the suspect.

Where on the spectrum of prosecutorial functions does failing properly to train lawyers in the office about their obligations to provide impeachment material to defense counsel fall? In Van De Kamp v. Goldstein, 129 S.Ct. 855 (2009), involving information about concessions made to a jail-house informant for helpful information passed along to law enforcement officials, the Court held that the conduct fell on the "lawyer function" side, even though it looked like an administrative/supervisory task. The court reasoned that if the defendants had been accused of failing to provide impeachment material, they would be entitled to absolute immunity. That they are alleged to have failed to provide adequate training for other lawyers should not change that outcome. Preparing training materials of this sort requires legal knowledge and much the same analysis as would be required of a prosecutor directly confronting this issue.

Absolute immunity for legislators was established in Tenney v. Brandhove, 341 U.S. 367 (1951), in which the Court found that state legislators enjoy absolute immunity from liability for their legislative acts. Absolute immunity was extended to local legislators in Bogan v. Scott-Harris, 523 U.S. 44 (1998).

Immunity for government entities. As noted above, some government entities may be subject to section 1983 liability for employee conduct resulting from a government's policy or custom that causes a violation of an individual's constitutional or statutory rights. Unlike public employees, the government is not granted the protection of qualified or absolute immunity. In Owen v. City of Independence, 445 U.S. 622 (1980), the city was held liable for a section 1983 violation when government officials dismissed the police chief without proper notice or hearing. The Court rejected the city's argument that municipalities should receive qualified immunity for their "good-faith constitutional violations."

The Court concluded that the traditional rationales for sovereign immunity were not sufficient to overcome the legislative purpose or considerations of public policy in enacting section 1983. First, government entities were historically granted immunity to protect governmental functions from the challenge or threat of liability, which could stifle decisionmaking and the execution of the law. The Court rejected this justification for immunity because Congress enacted section 1983 with the purpose of making government entities amenable to suit. Second, government entities were granted immunity due to the discretionary nature of the legislative and executive processes. Sovereign immunity limited the ability of the courts to "substitut[e] their own judgment on matters within the lawful discretion of the municipality." In its rejection of this basis for immunity, the majority concluded that the violation of constitutional and statutory rights is not within the discretionary authority of the government, and therefore, section 1983 actions are necessary to prevent the misuse or abuse of government power.

In the absence of a right to qualified immunity, are government entities being held strictly liable for their employees' conduct? Is the underlying official misconduct in these cases likely to be "intentional" according to the traditional definition of intended harm? What are the strongest arguments for subjecting government entities to a type of vicarious liability in these cases?

Should it matter that the constitutional right relied on by plaintiff was declared after the contested dismissal occurred?

State immunity. In Quern v. Jordan, 440 U.S. 332 (1979), the Court, relying heavily on the Eleventh Amendment, held that states are immune from liability under section 1983. The plaintiff, however, successfully circumvented state immunity in Kentucky v. Graham, 473 U.S. 159 (1985), by seeking prospective injunctive relief against a state officer in her official capacity. Several Eleventh Amendment issues involving prospective versus retroactive relief and injunctive relief versus monetary damages remain unsettled.

c.   DAMAGES

What is the proper measure of damages for the deprivation of a constitutional right? In *Monroe,* Justice Harlan, concurring, had suggested that in enacting section 1983 Congress may have believed that:

> A deprivation of a constitutional right is significantly different from and more serious than a violation of a state right . . . even though the same act may constitute both a state tort and the deprivation of a constitutional right.

In Carey v. Piphus, 435 U.S. 247 (1978), the plaintiffs had been denied procedural due process by being suspended from high school without a hearing. The court of appeals had held: 1) that if the suspension was in fact justified and would have occurred even if a hearing had been held, the plaintiffs could recover no damages for the suspension, but 2) that they could recover substantial presumed damages for the violation of the constitutional right itself. The Supreme Court agreed with the first ruling but reversed the second ruling and held that the plaintiffs would have to present proof of actual injury arising from the violation of the right, which might include mental and emotional distress. The Court drew on its recent decisions in defamation law, particularly the *Gertz* case, reprinted at p. 1085 infra. Finally, the court held that even if the plaintiffs could not show actual injury they were entitled to nominal damages of one dollar because their constitutional rights had been violated.

Damages for personal injury in section 1983 may not always be identical to those recoverable under state tort law. Recall that only a few states permit recovery for loss of life in a case in which the defendant's tortious conduct deprived the decedent of years of life, p. 744 supra. In Bass v. Wallenstein, 769 F.2d 1173 (7th Cir.1985), plaintiff's decedent, a prison inmate, died as a result of an acute cardiorespiratory arrest. The prison physician, despite being called multiple times about the emergency, did not respond for 15 minutes. In the ensuing section 1983 claim, the court rejected adoption of Illinois law, which does not provide damages for loss of life, and held that, to further the deterrent purpose of section 1983, the estate could recover in a survival action for the loss of life.

In City of Newport v. Fact Concerts, Inc., 453 U.S. 247 (1981), the Court held that a municipality could not be held liable for punitive damages. Nothing in the legislative history suggested that Congress intended such liability. Moreover, public policy would not permit such liability. Punitive damages were likely to be a windfall to the plaintiff and to cause an "increase in taxes or a reduction of public services for the citizens footing the bill." Although a public official who maliciously and knowingly deprives others of their civil rights may become the "appropriate object of the community's vindictive sentiments," a municipality "can have no malice independent of the malice of its officials. Damages awarded for *punitive* purposes, therefore, are not sensibly assessed against the governmental entity itself."

Nor did the deterrence rationale warrant a different result. Even compensatory damages imposed on a municipality may induce the public to vote the wrongdoers out of office. Also, a punitive award against the specific official is a more likely source of deterrence than the indirect deterrent of imposing punitive damages on the municipality.

d.   SECTION 1985(3)

Another section of the Ku Klux Klan Act—now 42 U.S.C. § 1985(3)—creates a damage remedy for citizens deprived of constitutional rights by persons acting in a conspiracy. In Griffin v. Breckenridge, 403 U.S. 88 (1971), the Supreme Court held that section 1985(3) could be invoked to redress injuries inflicted by purely private conspiracies even though the participants lacked any state nexus. In *Griffin,* the four black Mississippi plaintiffs alleged that they were driving down the highway when the defendants, two white local residents, mistook the driver for a civil rights worker, stopped the car, and clubbed the occupants.

The Court held that in order to state a cause of action under this section a plaintiff must allege the existence of a conspiracy for the purpose of depriving someone of equal protection or privileges and immunities, acts in furtherance of the conspiracy, and injury to the person or his property or deprivation of his constitutional rights. The Court stressed that a conspiratorial deprivation would not be redressable under section 1985(3) without proof of "invidiously discriminatory animus." This "animus" involved a "racial or otherwise class-based" attempt to discriminate against a certain group. Without proof of such class-based animus, the asserted constitutional deprivation would not rise above the level of an ordinary "tortious injury."

Section 1985(3) seems unlikely to provide many plaintiffs with an effective remedy. Plaintiffs have generally encountered great difficulty in attempting to demonstrate the requisite class-based animus. See Harrison v. Brooks, 519 F.2d 1358 (1st Cir.1975); McNally v. Pulitzer Publishing Co., 532 F.2d 69 (8th Cir.1976). A second hurdle is that Congress may lack the constitutional authority to bypass the "state action" requirement of the Fourteenth Amendment as to most civil rights. See Cohen v. Illinois Institute of Technology, 524 F.2d 818 (7th Cir.1975). The Court in *Griffin* avoided this problem by finding congressional authority to reach the defendant's behavior under the congressional power to protect the right to travel and under the Thirteenth Amendment (relying here on Jones v. Alfred H. Mayer Co., 392 U.S. 409 (1968), which held that the Thirteenth Amendment authorized Congress to provide remedies for "racially discriminatory private action" aimed at depriving blacks "of the basic rights that the law secures to all free men").

Are the plaintiffs in *Griffin* better off than they would have been had they proceeded only under state law? Might the answer depend on factors other than the content of the applicable substantive law?

2. LIABILITY OF FEDERAL OFFICIALS

In Chapter III, we considered the availability of remedies against the United States under the Federal Tort Claims Act, p. 247 supra. As we have seen, liability for negligence may be available under the statute, although recovery on a strict liability basis is not permitted. Here, we consider the available remedies for citizens who sustain intentional injury at the hands of federal government employees.

The Federal Tort Claims Act addresses the problem of intentional torts in section 2680(h), which provides that the Act shall not apply to:

> (h) Any claim arising out of assault, battery, false imprisonment, false arrest, malicious prosecution, abuse of process, libel, slander, misrepresentation, deceit, or interference with contract rights: *Provided,* That, with regard

to acts or omissions of investigative or law enforcement officers of the United States Government, the provisions of this chapter and section 1346(b) of this title shall apply to any claim arising, on or after the date of the enactment of this proviso, out of assault, battery, false imprisonment, false arrest, abuse of process, or malicious prosecution. For the purpose of this subsection, "investigative or law enforcement officer" means any officer of the United States who is empowered by law to execute searches, to seize evidence, or to make arrests for violations of Federal law.

The part before the proviso was in the original Act. The proviso was added in 1974 largely as the result of several "no-knock" raids carried out by federal narcotics agents. An action against the agents was first recognized in Bivens v. Six Unknown Named Federal Narcotics Agents, 403 U.S. 388 (1971), which served as the basis for the claims against the federal officials in *Wilson v. Layne.* In amending the Federal Tort Claims Act, Congress observed that the individual officials who are the defendants in *Bivens* actions are unlikely to be solvent. Thus, the amendment, which provides for liability of the federal government, provides a solvent defendant. Yet today when federal officials are sued in a *Bivens* action, the government almost always pays for an attorney to represent the defendants and indemnifies those officials for any liability they incur. See Pillard, Taking Fiction Seriously: The Strange Results of Public Officials' Individual Liability Under *Bivens*, 88 Geo.L.J. 65 (1999). On the 1974 amendment, see Boger, Gitenstein & Verkuil, The Federal Tort Claims Act Intentional Torts Amendment: An Interpretative Analysis, 54 N.C.L.Rev. 497 (1976).

In *Bivens,* the plaintiff alleged that federal agents had ransacked his apartment during an illegal warrantless search. Although the only effective remedy was money damages, section 1983 was inapplicable because the wrongdoers were federal agents and therefore not acting under color of *state* law. Moreover, section 2680(h), prior to the 1974 amendment, excepted almost all intentional torts from the waiver of sovereign immunity contained in the Federal Tort Claims Act; thus the United States could not be sued. Nevertheless, the Supreme Court recognized a federal claim for damages against the federal officials, individually, based directly on the Fourth Amendment, despite the lack of a statutory remedy. Writing for the majority, Justice Brennan stated:

> "[I]t is . . . well settled that where legal rights have been invaded, and a federal statute provides for a general right to sue for such invasion, federal courts may use any available remedy to make good the wrong done." Bell v. Hood, 327 U.S. at 684 (footnote omitted). The present case involves no special factors counselling hesitation in the absence of affirmative action by Congress.

The Court offered little guidance on when it would be proper to imply the damage remedy to vindicate constitutional interests. The Government had argued that the Court should create remedies based on the Constitution only when "essential" to the protection of the right, reasoning that Congress may displace or modify a Court-created remedy for statutory violations but is powerless to modify a remedy that the Court has determined is required by the Constitution. Justice Brennan rejected the "essentiality" standard but offered no alternative.

Because the Constitution creates a number of federally protected interests, it seems clear that the *Bivens* rationale should apply to protect other rights guaranteed by the Constitution as well. Not surprisingly, therefore, claims have been recognized against federal officers for alleged deprivations of other constitutional rights.

In Carlson v. Green, 446 U.S. 14 (1980), the Court decided that the fact that plaintiff could sue under the Federal Tort Claims Act did not bar a suit under the *Bivens* doctrine. The two actions were not equivalent. Under *Bivens,* deterrence might be stronger when the action is brought against the individual defendants, and only *Bivens* authorizes punitive damages. Also, liability under the FTCA depends on whether a private person "would be liable to the claimant in accordance with the law of the place where the act or omission occurred." This creates a local focus in contrast to *Bivens,* which creates a unified system of substantive law.

A *Bivens* action is unavailable, however, where Congress has expressly created an alternative remedial scheme. See, e.g., Chappell v. Wallace, 462 U.S. 296 (1983)(redress against racial discrimination by a superior officer was available through the military justice system); Correctional Services Corp. v. Malesko, 534 U.S. 61 (2001)(relying, in part, on alternative remedies available to federal prisoner who sued a private company that operated a halfway house for the Bureau of Prisons to conclude no *Bivens* action was available against private entity); Schweiker v. Chilicky, 487 U.S. 412 (1988)(individuals who alleged that their Social Security benefits were improperly terminated had effective remedy through congressionally provided administrative appeal system). For a critical discussion of the Court's rationales for barring certain *Bivens* actions, see Nichol, *Bivens, Chilicky,* and Constitutional Damages Claims, 75 Va.L.Rev. 1117 (1989). Valerie Plame's suit against Vice-President Cheney, Scooter Libby, and others foundered on this "alternative remedy" doctrine. The Privacy Act supplied such an alternative scheme, even though it did not apply to Cheney and two other defendants. Wilson v. Libby, 535 F.3d 697 (D.C.Cir.2008).

In *Bivens* cases, as in cases under section 1983, the critical issues concern the role of defenses. In Butz v. Economou, 438 U.S. 478 (1978), plaintiff sued several officials in the Department of Agriculture after the Department brought an unsuccessful administrative proceeding against him. He sued under *Bivens* claiming that the officials (including the Secretary, Assistant Secretary, the administrative judge, the hearing examiner who recommended the proceeding, and the attorney who presented the case) had violated his constitutional rights in various ways. The Court, 5–4, held that when a plaintiff claims that officials of an executive department have violated constitutional rights, the defendants generally are entitled only to qualified immunity. Prior cases "have recognized that it is not unfair to hold liable the official who knows or should know he is acting outside the law, and that insisting on an awareness of clearly established constitutional limits will not unduly interfere with the exercise of official judgment." Federal officials "will not be liable for mere mistakes in judgment, whether the mistake is one of fact or one of law. But we see no substantial basis for holding, as the United States would have us do, that executive officers generally may with impunity discharge their duties in a way that is known to them to violate the United States Constitution or in a manner that they should know transgresses a clearly established constitutional rule." The majority believed that insubstantial suits "can be quickly terminated" at the pleading stage. (On this score, the Court later held that a plaintiff must "allege the violation of a clearly established constitutional right" to get beyond summary judgment on a defendant's qualified immunity claim. Siegert v. Gilley, 500 U.S. 226 (1991)).

The majority did recognize that there were "some officials whose special functions require a full exemption from liability." Specifically, the analogies to the judicial branch were so apt that they had to be followed. The reason for immunities in the judicial branch is not the officials' location within government, but the "special nature of their responsibilities." The case was remanded to determine how these principles should be applied to the various defendants before the court. Reconsider the discussion of judicial immunity under section 1983 at p. 989 supra.

Is qualified immunity based on the subjective belief of the defendant, or on an objective assessment of the state of the law? In Groh v. Ramirez, 540 U.S. 551 (2004), the officer executed a search warrant that was so patently invalid (it failed to identify the property to be seized) that the Court found it a nullity. The Court held that no reasonable law enforcement official could be unaware that a warrantless search of a residence violated the Fourth Amendment. Thus, the defendant had no qualified immunity. Two dissenting Justices thought that the invalidity of the warrant was the result of defendant's clerical error—neglecting to fill in the property to be seized—a mistake that a reasonable officer might make and which would lead to the unconstitutional search that occurred.

When a former president was sued for improperly arranging to discharge a government employee who "blew the whistle" on military cost overruns, the Court, 5–4, accorded absolute immunity. Nixon v.

Fitzgerald, 457 U.S. 731 (1982). The absolute immunity was "a functionally mandated incident of the President's unique office, rooted in the constitutional tradition of the separation of powers and supported by our history." The immunity extended to "damages liability predicated on his official acts."

Although absolute immunity accorded to other executive officials had been limited to the particular functions of the office, that limit would be inadequate here. The President "has discretionary responsibilities in a broad variety of areas, many of them highly sensitive. In many cases it would be difficult to determine which of the President's innumerable 'functions' encompassed a particular action." The absolute immunity would extend to acts within the "outer perimeter" of his official responsibility. The action alleged here fell within that broad sweep.

Such a result would not leave the country without sufficient protection against misconduct by its chief executive. Impeachment remained available as did "formal and informal checks" on Presidential action, including "constant scrutiny by the press," oversight by Congress, the desire for re-election, the need to maintain prestige as an element of Presidential influence, and the "President's traditional concern for his historical stature."

In Harlow v. Fitzgerald, 457 U.S. 800 (1982), the Court held that senior aides to the President did not automatically share his immunity for the firing of Fitzgerald. They would receive qualified or good faith immunity. If they claimed that absolute immunity was justified because they were entrusted with discretionary authority in a sensitive area like national security or foreign policy, the defendants had to establish the claim.

Empirical data on the frequency and success of both section 1983 and *Bivens* actions are discussed in Eisenberg & Schwab, The Reality of Constitutional Tort Litigation, 72 Cornell L.Rev. 641 (1987), and Schwab & Eisenberg, Explaining Constitutional Tort Litigation: The Influence of the Attorney Fees Statute and the Government as Defendant, 73 Cornell L.Rev. 719 (1988). See also Symposium on Section 1983, 15 Touro L.J. 1481–1650 (1999).

As to *Bivens* actions, see Pillard, Taking Fiction Seriously: The Strange Result of Public Officials' Individual Liability under *Bivens*, 88 Geo.L.J. 65 (1999), reporting that "out of approximately 12,000 *Bivens* claims filed between 1971 and 1985, *Bivens* plaintiffs actually obtained a judgment that was not reversed on appeal in only four cases." Although similar figures after 1985 are unavailable, the author reports that "both settlements and litigated judgments continue to be extraordinarily rare." See generally Jeffries, The Right-Remedy Gap in Constitutional Law, 109 Yale L.J. 87 (1999).

CHAPTER XIV

DEFAMATION

A. COMMON LAW BACKGROUND

1. WHAT IS DEFAMATORY?

As with other torts, defamation has evolved through common law developments as a matter of state law. A principal difference between defamation and other torts that we have considered so far is the interest protected; the core concern of defamation is protecting a person's reputation. Since the notion of reputation is at the core of the defamation action, we will begin our consideration with a look at that concept. Another difference from the torts previously considered is that defamation has been enormously influenced and reshaped by First Amendment considerations of freedom of speech and the press. Since 1964, the Supreme Court has become involved in continuing efforts to establish the boundaries between freedom of communication and protection of reputation.

In tracing the developments in this complex area, we begin with the common law regime. The constitutional developments have not created a totally new legal area; rather, they have altered or influenced some of the pre-existing state rules and left others in place. As a result, despite the major impact of the Supreme Court, state law retains great significance in suits for defamation. It is often possible, for example, for a case to be decided under the traditional state rules without any invocation of the First Amendment.

Defamation has a venerable and still influential history. Early in the sixteenth century the common law courts began to recognize a claim for defamation that had previously been within the exclusive jurisdiction of the ecclesiastical courts. Since the common law remedy was framed as an action on the case, with its traditional focus on damages rather than ecclesiastical sanctions, the common law action became extremely popular. In another development during the same period, the Star Chamber assumed jurisdiction over all aspects of the press, and printed defamation came to be treated as a crime. Attacks on officials were seditious libels, and libels against private persons contributed to breaches of the peace. After the Restoration, both concepts were preserved: the Star Chamber's view of libel as a crime and the antecedent common law view of slander as a tort.

Although the English defamation law crossed the Atlantic, it seems never to have been enforced in the United States as vigorously as it was in England. This was true long before any constitutional questions were raised explicitly. In Government and Mass Communications 106–07 (1947), Professor Zechariah Chafee speculated:

> [The difference] is probably due to the fact that English jurymen and judges live in a different intellectual climate from the fluid and migratory society of the United States. The Englishman is born into a definite status where he tends to stick for life. What he *is* has at least as much importance as what he *does* in an active career. A slur on his reputation, if not challenged, may cause him to drop several rungs down the social ladder. A man moves within a circle of friends and associates and feels bound to preserve his standing in their eyes. Consequently, *not* to sue for libel is taken as an admission of truth.
>
> An able American has too much else to do to waste time on an expensive libel suit. Most strangers will not read the article, most of his friends will not believe it, and his enemies, who will believe it of course, were against him before. Anyway, it is just one more blow in the rough-and-tumble of politics or business. . . . A libeled American prefers to vindicate himself by steadily pushing forward his career and not by hiring a lawyer to talk in a courtroom.

Even in the United States, however, certain slurs cannot be ignored, and lead to pursuit of legal recourse.

Romaine v. Kallinger
Supreme Court of New Jersey, 1988.
109 N.J. 282, 537 A.2d 284.

■ HANDLER, J.

[This case arose out of a nonfiction book, "The Shoemaker," written about a man who went on a criminal rampage. One of the episodes involved events at the Romaine house. Part of that description included the following:

> A militant women's libber, Maria Fasching was famous among her friends for her battles on behalf of the weak and downtrodden. She would always try to rescue someone a bully had attacked, and she could not tolerate racists.
>
> Maria thought of herself as a "free spirit." She resisted anything that she considered a restriction on her freedom. She cared for cats that had been hit by cars and for birds with broken wings.
>
> Today, Maria Fasching was on the four-to-midnight shift at Hackensack Hospital, and she wore her nurse's uniform under her coat. In the morning Maria's friend Randi Romaine, who lived in the stucco house, had called Maria and asked her

to drop over for coffee. The two women had not seen each other for a long time, for between hospital duties and preparations for her wedding, Maria's schedule was full.

At first Maria said that she couldn't visit because she had to go to a wake. This wake, however, was only for an acquaintance. Randi and her twin sister, Retta, had been Maria's friends since they were all in the first grade. Besides, Maria was eager for news from Randi about a junkie they both knew who was doing time in prison. Finally, Maria changed her mind. She didn't go to the wake, but drove her Volkswagen to the two-story tan stucco house at 124 Glenwood Avenue, the house of Mr. and Mrs. Dewitt Romaine.

During the ensuing episode Fasching was killed. Among the variety of claims pressed by several plaintiffs, we concern ourselves with Randi Romaine's libel claim against the publisher and author. The trial court granted defendants' motion for summary judgment and the Appellate Division affirmed.]

According to plaintiffs, one sentence in the passage falsely depicts the reason for Ms. Fasching's visit: "Besides, Maria was eager for news from Randi about a junkie they both knew who was doing time in prison." . . .

Plaintiff Randi Romaine asserts that the particular sentence is defamatory as a matter of law, or alternatively, that the statement's defamatory content was at least a question for the jury. She claims this sentence falsely accuses her of criminality or associations with criminals. Plaintiff also contends that the false accusation was particularly damaging because it injured Ms. Romaine's professional reputation as a drug counsellor and a social worker, interfering with her ability to obtain future employment.

A defamatory statement is one that is false and "injurious to the reputation of another" or exposes another person to "hatred, contempt or ridicule" or subjects another person to "a loss of the good will and confidence" in which he or she is held by others. [ ]; see also Restatement (Second) of Torts § 559 (1977)(a defamatory communication is one that "tends so to harm the reputation of another so as to lower him in the estimation of the community or to deter third persons from associating or dealing with him").

The threshold issue in any defamation case is whether the statement at issue is reasonably susceptible of a defamatory meaning. [ ] This question is one to be decided first by the court. [ ] In making this determination, the court must evaluate the language in question "according to the fair and natural meaning which will be given it by reasonable persons of ordinary intelligence." [ ] In assessing the language, the court must view the publication as a whole and consider particularly the context in which the statement appears. [ ]

If a published statement is susceptible of one meaning only, and that meaning is defamatory, the statement is libelous as a matter of law. [ ] Conversely, if the statement is susceptible of only a non-defamatory meaning, it cannot be considered libelous, justifying dismissal of the action. [ ] However, in cases where the statement is capable of being assigned more than one meaning, one of which is defamatory and another not, the question of whether its content is defamatory is one that must be resolved by the trier of fact. [ ]

Certain kinds of statements denote such defamatory meaning that they are considered defamatory as a matter of law. A prime example is the false attribution of criminality. [ ]; [ ] (statement that plaintiff might be charged with criminal conduct defamatory as a matter of law). Relying essentially on this example of defamation, plaintiff Randi Romaine contends in this case that the published offending statement must be considered libelous per se. According to Ms. Romaine, the sentence has only a defamatory meaning, in that it accuses her of having engaged in criminal conduct or having associated with criminals relating to drugs.

The trial court concluded, and the Appellate Division agreed, that only the most contorted reading of the offending language could lead to the conclusion that it accuses plaintiff of illegal drug use or criminal associations. We concur in the determinations of the courts below. "[A]ccording to the fair and natural meaning which will be given [this statement] by reasonable persons of ordinary intelligence," [ ] it does not attribute any kind of criminality to plaintiff. A reasonable and fair understanding of the statement simply does not yield an interpretation that the plaintiff was or had been in illegal possession of drugs or otherwise engaging in any illegal drug-related activity. See Valentine v. C.B.S., Inc., 698 F.2d 430, 432 (11th Cir.1983)("The Plaintiff's interpretation does not construe the words as the common mind would understand them but is tortured and extreme."); Forsher v. Bugliosi, 608 P.2d 716, 723 (Cal.1980)("the claimed defamatory nature of the book as it relates to appellant is so obscure and attenuated as to be beyond the realm of reasonableness").

At most, the sentence can be read to imply that plaintiff knew a junkie. Even if we assume that a commonly accepted and well-understood meaning of the term "junkie" is "a narcotics peddler or addict," Webster's Third New International Dictionary 1227 (1981), see also Dictionary of American Slang 300 (2d ed. 1975)(defining "junkie" as a "drug addict"), the statement still does not suggest either direct or indirect involvement by plaintiff herself in any criminal drug-related activities. Absent exceptional circumstances, the mere allegation that plaintiff knows a criminal is not defamatory as a matter of law. See, e.g., Gonzales v. Times Herald Printing Company, 513 S.W.2d 124 (Tex.Civ.App.1974)(statement that plaintiff's husband was engaged in the sale and importation of narcotics did not defame her); Rose v. Daily

Mirror, Inc., 31 N.E.2d 182 (N.Y.1940)(plaintiff not defamed by being mistakenly described as the widow of a mobster); cf. Bufalino v. Associated Press, 692 F.2d 266 (2d Cir.1982)(mere imputation of family relationship with Mafia leader not defamatory; characterization of plaintiff as a political contributor with alleged mob ties found to have a potentially defamatory meaning).

Beyond the language itself, we are satisfied that the statement in its contextual setting cannot fairly and reasonably be invested with any defamatory meaning. Maria Fasching, we note, is described in the chapter as a person who had compassion for others and who would care for less fortunate persons. The reasonable meaning of the critical sentence that is implied from this context is that Ms. Fasching's interest in the "junkie" stemmed from sympathy and compassion, not from any predilection toward or involvement in criminal drug activity. As extended to Randi Romaine, the only fair inference to be drawn from the larger context is that Ms. Romaine shared her friend's feelings, attitudes and interests, and that her own interest in the junkie was similar to that of Ms. Fasching's.

We note the further contention that this statement had a defamatory meaning because it implied that the only reason for Ms. Fasching's visit to the Romaine home was her "interest" in news about a "junkie." A review of the full text, however, indicates that there were several reasons for the visit, only one of which was Ms. Fasching's interest in the "junkie." The lower courts soundly rejected this contention.

We conclude that the statement is not defamatory as a matter of law and accordingly uphold the ruling of the lower court on this point.

. . .

[JUSTICE O'HERN dissented on this point, contending that the passage was ambiguous and "reasonably susceptible of a defamatory meaning" and thus presented a jury question.]

NOTES AND QUESTIONS

1. *Publication.* Since harm to reputation is at the core of this tort, it is crucial that someone other than the plaintiff receive the statement. This element, called "publication," has nothing to do with mass circulation or with putting a statement into print. It simply means that the message must reach at least one third party who understands a defamatory thrust from the statement. Thus, making a statement over the telephone to someone other than the plaintiff is a "publication" of that statement. But at common law the plaintiff has to show that the publication was either intentional or negligent; no liability exists if a third person unexpectedly overhears a private conversation between plaintiff and defendant.

In Staples v. Bangor Hydro-Electric Co., 629 A.2d 601 (Me.1993), plaintiff's supervisor told superiors within the company that he had reason to believe that plaintiff had "sabotaged" a company computer. Among the defenses was one asserting that there had been no "publication" of the charge. The court recognized that some states hold that when one agent talks to another agent, the corporation "is simply communicating with itself." The court preferred the other view because "damage to one's reputation within the corporate community may be as devastating as that outside; and that the defense of qualified privilege [discussed at p. 1034 infra] provides adequate protection." To hold otherwise "would be to ignore the nature of the right protected by the law of defamation."

Normally, sending a sealed letter that charges the addressee with a crime will not lead to a defamation action because the recipient will usually be responsible for showing the letter to others. Most states follow this approach even if the plaintiff is "compelled" to publish the defamation herself—as when she must show prospective future employers a termination letter from defendant after having been asked why she left that job. Consider White v. Blue Cross and Blue Shield of Massachusetts, Inc., 809 N.E.2d 1034 (Mass.2004). Plaintiff, a former employee, sued his employer for allegedly defamatory statements made to the employee by the employer during his employment and subsequently communicated by the employee to prospective employers. The court recognized "the conundrum faced by discharged employees who are required by prospective employers to explain the circumstances of their discharge." Still, the court concluded that such issues were better resolved under employment law rather than tort law and refused to recognize compelled self-publication as a basis for the employee's defamation action. But see Overcast v. Billings Mutual Insurance Co., 11 S.W.3d 62 (Mo.2000)(permitting defamation action where recipient of letter accusing plaintiff of arson could be expected to have shown it to other insurers, thereby permitting the inference of publication, when they asked if plaintiff had ever had a claim denied or been denied insurance).

Single publication rule. At common law, the sale of each individual copy of a publication could be considered a separate cause of action. Most states, either by case law or by adoption of the Uniform Single Publication Act, 13 U.L.A. 517, have developed the rule that the entire edition of a printed work is to be treated as a single publication and that all damages for this publication must be recovered in a single action. See Pippen v. NBCUniversal Media, LLC, 734 F.3d 610, 615–16, (7th Cir.2013)(holding that the single publication rule applies to publication over the Internet, and citing a unanimity among other state and federal courts that have considered the question).

As a consequence of this single publication rule, the statute of limitations on the claim begins to run with the first publication, when the claim first accrues. At first this was limited to one action in each state, but now it is recognized that all damages for the nationwide single publication may, and in some cases must, be resolved in a single action. If a new edition of the work is published, however, such as a paperback version of a hardcover book, it is considered a new and separate publication for which a separate cause of action arises.

An International Perspective: The Internet Era. In the Internet era, when one "hit" may be sufficient for a libel action and publication recognizes no national boundaries, so-called "libel tourism" became a well-known phenomenon—and something of a political embarrassment in nations, particularly England, where plaintiffs filed claims against foreign defendants relying on especially favorable defamation laws.

The Securing the Protection of our Enduring and Established Constitutional Heritage Act ("SPEECH Act"), 28 U.S.C. § 4101 et seq., was enacted in 2010. Designed to fight libel tourism, the Act provides that no foreign defamation judgment can be enforced in United States courts unless the rendering country "provided at least as much protection for freedom of speech and press in that case as would be provided by the first amendment to the Constitution of the United States and by the constitution and law of the state in which the domestic court is located." Alternatively, the judgment can be enforced if a domestic court, on the facts of the case, would not have been prevented from entering judgment for the enforcer based on state and federal constitutional restrictions. The burden is on the enforcer of the judgment to make this showing, which may require relitigating the foreign case. Moreover, the enforcer must show that personal jurisdiction over the defendant comported with due process standards. In addition, before judgments against Internet providers can be enforced, the law must have been consistent with the Communications Decency Act. For a court that found a foreign defamation judgment unenforceable under the SPEECH Act, see Trout Point Lodge, Ltd. v. Handshoe, 729 F.3d 481 (5th Cir.2013). David Anderson critiques the SPEECH Act in Anderson, Transnational Libel, 53 Va. J.Int'l L. 71 (2012).

The British adopted modest reform legislation designed to counter England's reputation as the forum of choice for libel actions and to restrict somewhat Britain's generous libel laws. The most important provision limits English courts to entertaining only those defamation actions that are most appropriately brought in England. See Lyall, *Libel Cases Now Harder to Bring in England*, N.Y. Times, Apr. 26, 2013, at A4. It also adopts a "serious harm" to reputation threshold that will result in most trials being resolved by the court rather than a jury. Finally, it also provides protection to passive website operators who do not provide the content that is posted on their website. Defamation Act 2013 to Improve Libel Laws, BBC News UK (Dec. 31, 2013), http://www.bbc.com/news/uk-25551640.

2. *What is defamatory?* Unless defendant says something as patent as "plaintiff murdered Smith," the determination of whether the statement is actionable usually involves two steps. The first is to determine whether the words can bear the "spin" that plaintiff is alleging. In *Romaine* this question is whether the words defendant actually used could reasonably be understood to accuse her of "criminality or associations with criminals." If the answer to that is negative, there is nothing further to do—plaintiff loses. If the answer is affirmative, the second question must be addressed: whether it is defamatory of someone to say that she engages in this sort of behavior or associates with criminals. Usually, the plaintiff will try to telescope these two questions into one by arguing that the words used by defendant can reasonably be understood to make a charge that reasonable recipients could consider defamatory.

The court noted that in determining the meaning of the passage in question, it must seek the "fair and natural meaning which will be given it by reasonable persons of ordinary intelligence." Why is that the standard— as opposed, say, to the "most impressionable" readers? Or the "most intelligent" readers?

3. *What do the words mean?* In interpreting statements, courts consider all of the accoutrements of language, such as punctuation and paragraphing. Thus, in Wildstein v. New York Post Corp., 243 N.Y.S.2d 386 (Sup.Ct.)(aff'd without opinion), 261 N.Y.S.2d 254 (App.Div.1965), the defendant wrote that the plaintiff was one of "several women described as 'associated' with" a slain executive. The judge observed that if the word "associated" had not been in quotation marks the statement would not have been defamatory; the quotation marks implied a euphemistic use of the word, suggesting an illicit relationship between plaintiff and the deceased.

a.   *Internal context.* The *Romaine* court also observed that it "must view the publication as a whole." Certainly, it would seem wrong to allow a libel to be based on one sentence of an article or book if the surrounding sentences make clear that the pinpointed sentence should be read innocently.

On the other hand, what if the first paragraph of a newspaper article is defamatory, but is totally explained away in the twentieth paragraph of the story? Should the court still view the article "as a whole"? What if a big headline conveys a defamatory meaning that is removed by the text? What if a caption under a photograph conveys a defamatory meaning but the text of the accompanying article removes it? In Gambuzza v. Time, Inc., 239 N.Y.S.2d 466 (App.Div.1963), the court, 3–2, concluded that a defamatory caption accompanying a photo spread had to be read together with the text that removed the sting. Generally, courts require that headlines must be read in context with the story. Some courts have held that sensational headlines may be interpreted separately from the text: "a person passing a newsstand . . . may be able to catch a glimpse of a headline without the opportunity or desire to read the accompanying article or may skim through the paper jumping from headline to headline." In *Gambuzza,* however, the caption and text were so close to each other that they had to be read together. The dissenters argued that the critical words in the caption were in bold capital letters and thus should be considered separately.

See also Kunst v. New York World Telegram Corp., 280 N.Y.S.2d 798 (App.Div.1967), in which the lead paragraph and a photo caption conveyed a defamatory implication. The majority upheld the complaint because the negation of the sting appeared only in a statement that a "persistent and careful reader would discover near the end of the reasonably lengthy article." A writing must be "construed, not with the high degree of precision expected of and used by lawyers and judges, but as it would be read and understood by an ordinary member of the public to whom it is directed." A dissenter responded that although the negating statement appeared near the end of the article, "the article is to be taken as a whole and read in its entirety."

b. *External context.* Although the point is not involved in *Romaine*, it is sometimes necessary for the plaintiff to allege facts beyond those asserted in the publication in order to show how the plaintiff was defamed by the publication. For example, suppose an article stated only that the plaintiff had often been seen at "123 Hay Road." What if some in the community knew that there was a brothel at that address? Plaintiff need not show that the defamation was contained solely in the published words. If the words alone do not clearly convey the defamatory thrust explicitly or by implication, the plaintiff must plead extrinsic facts that would explain how those who knew the unstated facts would take a defamatory meaning. Such an allegation—that neighbors and others know that 123 Hay Road is a brothel—is called the "inducement."

If, after putting the explicit statement and added extrinsic facts together, the thrust of the defamation is still not obvious, the plaintiff must allege the "meaning" that plaintiff thinks flows from the combination. This is called the "innuendo." The innuendo is not a fact; it is the plaintiff's assertion of how the passage would be understood by those who received the explicit statement and knew the extrinsic facts (inducement). In our example, it would be that those who know about 123 Hay Road understood the newspaper article to imply that plaintiff frequents a brothel. In most cases, when the explicit statements and the extrinsic facts are combined, the nature of the claimed defamation becomes clear.

c. *Roles of judge and jury.* The *Romaine* court observes that if the statement in question is clearly defamatory in its only reasonable reading (or in all of its reasonable readings), the court will declare it so. On the other hand, if it is clearly not defamatory in any reasonable reading, the court will dismiss the case. But if there are two or more reasonable meanings that might be attached to the statement (on its face or as expanded upon by external context), with at least one being defamatory and at least one not, the trier of fact is to decide which meaning would be taken. How is the trier to make this determination? What evidence should be admissible on this question?

Illinois takes an unusual approach to ambiguous statements, called the "innocent construction rule." This requires the court to dismiss a defamation case if a reasonable nondefamatory meaning can be ascribed to the statement—even if plaintiff could prove that most readers would have taken the defamatory reading. The situation is summarized in Barter v. Wilson, 512 N.E.2d 816 (Ill.App.1987), in which the court held that saying "the fix is in" on plaintiff developer's permit application did not defame the developer. The court used a definition of "fix" from a law dictionary: "determine, settle, make permanent." Thus, the statement could have meant no more than that "a decision had already been made."

4. *Is the ascribed meaning defamatory?* Recall that the *Romaine* court quoted two approaches to determining whether a statement is defamatory—that of the Restatement and that of Prosser & Keeton. How do they differ? Some states, including New York, tend to list a series of more specific criteria. Consider, for example, that of Nichols v. Item Publishers, Inc., 132 N.E.2d 860 (N.Y.1956): a statement that "tends to expose a person to hatred, contempt or aversion, or to induce an evil or unsavory opinion of him in the minds of a substantial number in the community." Does this formulation differ significantly from the ones quoted in *Romaine*? Consider the following passage from 1 R. Sack, Sack on Defamation: Libel, Slander, and Related Problems 2–18 (4th ed.2010):

> These variations among definitions of defamation have little apparent effect on the actual outcome of cases. If what is libelous in Mississippi is not libelous in New York, or vice versa, it is far more likely to reflect different social circumstances than the language adopted by particular courts to define the term "defamatory."

If that notion is correct, then what is the core that each of the differing formulations is trying to get at—if only for its own state? Apply these varying definitions in each of the following cases, assuming the statement to be false.

a.   A statement that the plaintiff has died. Decker v. Princeton Packet, Inc., 561 A.2d 1122 (N.J.1989)(an obituary "does not impugn reputation"). But see Ravnikar v. Bogojavlensky, 782 N.E.2d 508 (Mass.2003), in which the parties were competing physicians. Defendant told a patient that plaintiff was dying of cancer—that her condition was "terminal." In fact, plaintiff had breast cancer but was recovering. The defendant knew that plaintiff had cancer but admitted that he had no reason to think she was dying. After she learned about the behavior, plaintiff sued. The court held that the statement was defamatory because it would deter others from associating with plaintiff. Also, a prospective patient would think that the professional relationship would be brief and impaired.

b.   An assertion that plaintiff small town mayor was "manipulating" the press to keep it from reporting negative matters about the mayor. In West v. Thomson Newspapers, 872 P.2d 999 (Utah 1994), the court held that "[a]lthough a dictionary may define and give some content to allegedly defamatory words, it cannot be dispositive. A court simply cannot determine whether a statement is capable of sustaining a defamatory meaning by viewing individual words in isolation; rather it must carefully examine the context in which the statement was made, giving the words their most common and accepted meaning." Read this way, the use of "manipulating" was nothing more than a charge that a person in power, without running afoul of ethical or legal norms, was trying to use that power to get a favorable press. "While no politician would welcome such criticism—and indeed might find it personally offensive—this does not render it defamatory. 'A publication is not defamatory simply because it is nettlesome or embarrassing. . . .' [ ] West must establish that the statement is more than sharp criticism." The court concluded that no reasonable person could consider this charge damaging to reputation.

5. *Insults and name-calling.* At a meeting of about 100 condominium owners, plaintiff wife stood up to make comments supporting those just made by her husband. At this point, defendant, sitting nearby, jumped up and shouted: "Don't listen to these people. They don't like [or hate] Jews. She's a bitch." The court held that neither expression was actionable. Ward v. Zelikovsky, 643 A.2d 972 (N.J.1994). The court used the standard of defamation stated in *Romaine.*

Turning first to "content," the court relied largely on a passage from comment e to section 566 of the Second Restatement:

> There are some statements that ... cannot reasonably be understood to be meant literally and seriously and are obviously mere vituperation and abuse. A certain amount of vulgar name-calling is frequently resorted to by angry people without any real intent to make a defamatory assertion, and it is properly understood by reasonable listeners to amount to nothing more. This is true particularly when it is obvious that the speaker has lost his temper and is merely giving vent to insult. Thus when, in the course of an altercation, the defendant loudly and angrily calls the plaintiff a bastard in the presence of others, he is ordinarily not reasonably to be understood as asserting the fact that plaintiff is of illegitimate birth but only to be abusing him to his face.

Can you think of a situation where the use of "bastard" would be actionable? As to "context," the court stressed the face-to-face confrontation, distinguishing words uttered in that context from "words written after time for thought or published in a newspaper [that] may be taken to express the defamatory charge and to be intended to be taken seriously."

As to "bitch," as used here, a reasonable listener "would interpret the term to indicate merely that the speaker disliked Mrs. Ward and is otherwise inarticulate."

As to "dislikes [or hates] Jews," the court also found relevant a line of cases concluding that such political charges had become so common in recent years that they had lost content, citing Stevens v. Tillman, 855 F.2d 394 (7th Cir.1988)(charge of being a "racist" is not actionable because word has "been watered down by overuse, becoming common coin in political discourse"). A charge of bigotry might be defamatory if it alleged specific acts, such as making racist statements or denying employment to another because of race or religion, but there was no such charge or implication in these facts.

6. *Libel by implication.* What if each fact reported in an article is true but they are stated in such a way that the ordinary reader reaches a false, and defamatory, conclusion? In Healey v. New England Newspapers, Inc., 555 A.2d 321 (R.I.1989), defendant reported that Lampinski had been involved in a personnel dispute with the local YMCA and had had a heart attack and died while demonstrating about 200 yards from a YMCA board meeting. The story continued that his family was angry because they felt he "should have been given early attention by either a doctor or a paramedic at the board meeting." The next paragraph began "Dr. Paul J. Healey is Y president and was at the meeting when Lampinski collapsed." How are these two sentences to be read?

The court upheld a jury verdict and judgment for $302,000. Looking at the evidence in the most favorable light to plaintiff, the court thought a reader could understand that "plaintiff was asked and refused to help Lampinski and that there was enough time for plaintiff to render aid to Lampinski."

7. *Substantial and respectable minority of the community.* Ambiguity must be distinguished from the situation in which readers may understand a statement differently because of different backgrounds they bring to the material. Is there a difference between bringing expertise to a subject and simply knowing more about the facts than most readers? In Ben-Oliel v. Press Publishing Co., 167 N.E. 432 (N.Y.1929), the plaintiff, an expert on Palestinian art and customs, was falsely stated to have written an article on that subject that appeared in the defendant's Sunday newspaper. The article would have impressed virtually all of the newspaper's regular readers. Unfortunately, the article had several errors that would lead fellow experts to think the writer incompetent. The court held that a jury could find that plaintiff had been defamed in the eyes of the very small number of experts even though they were overwhelmed in number by the ordinary readers.

On this subject, the Second Restatement's section 559 comment e states that to be actionable the content of a statement must be of the sort that would hurt the plaintiff "in the eyes of a substantial and respectable minority" of the community. Was the minority substantial in the *Ben-Oliel* case? Should it have to be?

Jews For Jesus, Inc. v. Rapp, 997 So.2d 1098 (Fla.2008), provides a different context for determining the appropriate audience in whose eyes the plaintiff suffers reputational harm. "The gravamen of Rapp's claim is that Jews for Jesus [based on an article her stepson, an employee of defendant, wrote] falsely and without her permission stated that she had "joined Jews for Jesus, and/or [become] a believer in the tenets, the actions, and the philosophy of Jews for Jesus." The court adopted the standard in Restatement (Second) of Torts section 559 comment e, which requires only that the statement would prejudice the plaintiff with a "substantial and respectable minority."

In Grant v. Reader's Digest Ass'n, 151 F.2d 733 (2d Cir.1945), defendant published an article calling the plaintiff lawyer "a legislative representative for the Massachusetts Communist Party." Judge Learned Hand stated the question to be whether it was defamatory "to write of a lawyer that he has acted as agent of the Communist Party and is a believer in its aims and methods." Defendant argued that under New York law the question was whether "right thinking" persons would find the assertion defamatory. The court responded that a person "may value his reputation even among those who do not embrace the prevailing moral standards; and it would seem that the jury should be allowed to appraise how far he should be indemnified for the disesteem of such persons." It suffices "if there be some, as there certainly are," who would think ill of the plaintiff as the result of defendant's assertion "even though they would be 'wrong-thinking' people if they did."

8. Consider the following examples in terms of the nature of defamation and the role of minority attitudes:

a. A statement that the plaintiff is of illegitimate birth. Shelby v. Sun Printing & Publishing Ass'n, 38 Hun. 474 (1886), aff'd on the opinion below, 15 N.E. 895 (N.Y.1888). Has the notion of "illegitimacy" lost its power to defame?

b. A statement that a reputable physician illegally terminated life support services for a terminally ill patient who was in great pain and who had stated in writing several times that he wished to die. Might it be defamatory to say that the physician refused the patient's request to do so?

c. A statement that the plaintiff worked as a federal undercover agent. Agnant v. Shakur, 30 F.Supp.2d 420 (S.D.N.Y.1998).

d. A statement that erroneously accused a hit man of missing his target. See Note, The Community Segment in Defamation Actions: A Dissenting Essay, 58 Yale L.J. 1387 (1949).

9. As *Romaine* indicates, a defamatory statement is one based on a false statement of fact. The distinction between fact and opinion has long plagued the courts, and the issue remains central to the definition of a defamatory statement. In this regard, consider the following case.

Davis v. Boeheim

Court of Appeals of New York, 2015.
24 N.Y.3d 262, 22 N.E.3d 999, 998 N.Y.S.2d 131.

OPINION OF THE COURT

■ RIVERA, J.

On this appeal from a pre-answer dismissal of plaintiffs' defamation action, we conclude that the challenged statements are reasonably susceptible of a defamatory connotation, and not otherwise privileged nonactionable "pure opinion." Therefore, we reverse the Appellate Division.

I.

Plaintiffs Robert Davis and his stepbrother Michael Lang sued defendants Syracuse University and James Boeheim, the University's head basketball coach, for defamation based on statements by Boeheim made in response to Davis' and Lang's allegations of sexual molestation by Bernie Fine, Boeheim's longtime friend and the team's associate head coach. Plaintiffs claimed that Fine used his position and authority within the University's basketball program to gain access to and control over Davis and Lang for purposes of sexually molesting them.

According to plaintiffs, from the time Davis and Lang were children in the 1980s, Fine lured them with opportunities to attend the games and assist the team as "ball boys." For years the sexual abuse continued, on and off campus, on team trips away from the University, in Fine's car and in his home. Davis alleged that in his case the abuse continued for almost two decades, commencing when he was about 11 years old. Plaintiffs further alleged that Boeheim had observed Davis with Fine at practices, at games, and on trips with the team, including once in Fine's hotel room during the 1987 NCAA Final Four.

[Between 2002 and 2005, Davis made his claims known to the police, a local newspaper, and the University, none of whom took any action.]

Plaintiffs' claims became public in 2011 after unrelated allegations by other victims of sexual abuse surfaced against another coach at another well known university. In that year, similar claims surfaced of sexual abuse of multiple victims by former Penn State University assistant football coach Jerry Sandusky. As with the plaintiffs' claims against Fine, the Penn State sexual abuse scandal involved allegations that Sandusky had used the University's football program in order to gain access to underage victims. Penn State's head football coach, Joe Paterno, was alleged to have covered up the abuse.

The Penn State scandal renewed national and local media interest in plaintiffs' allegations. Within two weeks of the initial breaking news coverage of the Penn State story, and as the media focus on the Penn State allegations continued, ESPN issued a news report about the allegations against Fine. The story also relayed Davis' statement that Boeheim saw Davis lying on Fine's hotel room bed during the 1987 NCAA Final Four.

The day after the ESPN story, the University released a statement in which it described its 2005 four-month investigation into Davis' allegations. The University stated that it had interviewed persons named by Davis, but was unable to corroborate the claims. The University further stated that it would have acted had it found any evidence or corroboration of the allegations in 2005.

The same day the ESPN story broke, and before the University's statement went public, Boeheim issued a one-paragraph statement, released by the Syracuse University news service, in which he too announced that the University had investigated the allegations and had concluded they were unfounded. Boeheim further declared that "Bernie [Fine] has my full support," and that he had known Fine for over 40 years and had "never seen or witnessed anything to suggest that [Fine] would be involved in any of the activities alleged." Boeheim stated that if he had "seen or suspected anything, I would have taken action."

Boeheim made several other statements to reporters, which were quoted in the print and online versions of the New York Times, on the

Syracuse Post-Standard's website Syracuse.com, on SportingNews.com, and on ESPN.com. In these statements, Boeheim reasserted his support for Fine and his denial of any knowledge of the claimed events as described by Davis. He also called Davis and Lang liars, and stated that their allegations were financially motivated.

Davis and Lang commenced this action against Boeheim and the University for defamation, claiming that several of Boeheim's statements to ESPN, the Post-Standard, and the New York Times, were false and defamatory, and had caused them economic, emotional and reputational harm. The University and Boeheim filed a motion to dismiss . . . , on the grounds that the statements were not defamatory as a matter of law because they constituted nonactionable opinion, not facts. Supreme Court granted the motion concluding that a reasonable reader would conclude that Boeheim's statements were "a biased and personal opinion on the accusations against Bernie Fine, not fact."

The Appellate Division affirmed in a split 3–2 decision. The majority concluded that although Boeheim's statements that Davis fabricated allegations and was motivated by financial gain had certain factual elements, based on "the content of the communication as a whole, as well as its tone and apparent purpose," and "the over-all context in which the assertions were made," a reasonable reader would have believed that the challenged statements were conveying opinion and not facts [ ]. The dissent concluded that dismissal on a pre-answer motion to dismiss was error because Boeheim's statements that Davis was lying about Fine to get money, and that he had done so in the past, constituted opinion that implies a basis in facts not disclosed to the reader or listener, and thus constituted actionable "mixed opinion."

Davis and Lang contend that the Appellate Division erred because the complaint sufficiently pleads a cause of action for defamation against Boeheim and the University based on statements that are defamatory facts or, alternatively, mixed opinion. We agree the complaint is sufficient to survive the motion to dismiss, and reverse the Appellate Division.

II.

. . . In determining the sufficiency of a defamation pleading, we consider "whether the contested statements are reasonably susceptible of a defamatory connotation" [ ]. As we have previously stated, "[i]f, upon any reasonable view of the stated facts, plaintiff would be entitled to recovery for defamation, the complaint must be deemed to sufficiently state a cause of action" [ ]. We apply this liberal standard fully aware that permitting litigation to proceed to discovery carries the risk of potentially chilling free speech, but do so because, as we have previously stated, "we recognize as well a plaintiff's right to seek redress, and not have the courthouse doors closed at the very inception of an action, where the pleading meets [the] minimal standard necessary to resist dismissal of [the] complaint" [ ].

In order for the challenged statements to be susceptible of a defamatory connotation, they must come within the well established categories of actionable communications. Thus, a false statement "that tends to expose a person to public contempt, hatred, ridicule, aversion or disgrace constitutes defamation" [ ]. "Since falsity is a necessary element of a defamation cause of action and only 'facts' are capable of being proven false, ' . . . only statements alleging facts can properly be the subject of a defamation action' " [ ].

A defamatory statement of fact is in contrast to "pure opinion" which under our laws is not actionable because "[e]xpressions of opinion, as opposed to assertions of fact, are deemed privileged and, no matter how offensive, cannot be the subject of an action for defamation" [ ]. For, "[h]owever pernicious an opinion may seem, we depend for its correction not on the conscience of judges and juries but on the competition of other ideas" [ ]. A pure opinion may take one of two forms. It may be "a statement of opinion which is accompanied by a recitation of the facts upon which it is based," or it may be "[a]n opinion not accompanied by such a factual recitation" so long as "it does not imply that it is based upon undisclosed facts" [ ].

While a pure opinion cannot be the subject of a defamation claim, an opinion that "implies that it is based upon facts which justify the opinion but are unknown to those reading or hearing it, . . . is a 'mixed opinion' and is actionable" [ ]. This requirement that the facts upon which the opinion is based are known "ensure[s] that the reader has the opportunity to assess the basis upon which the opinion was reached in order to draw [the reader's] own conclusions concerning its validity" [ ]. What differentiates an actionable mixed opinion from a privileged, pure opinion is "the implication that the speaker knows certain facts, unknown to [the] audience, which support [the speaker's] opinion and are detrimental to the person" being discussed [ ].

Distinguishing between fact and opinion is a question of law for the courts, to be decided based on "what the average person hearing or reading the communication would take it to mean" [ ]. "The dispositive inquiry . . . is 'whether a reasonable [reader] could have concluded that [the statements were] conveying facts about the plaintiff' " [ ].

We apply three factors in determining whether a reasonable reader would consider the statement connotes fact or nonactionable opinion:

> "(1) whether the specific language in issue has a precise meaning which is readily understood; (2) whether the statements are capable of being proven true or false; and (3) whether either the full context of the communication in which the statement appears or the broader social context and surrounding circumstances are such as to signal . . . readers or listeners that what is being read or heard is likely to be opinion, not fact" [ ].

The third factor "lends both depth and difficulty to the analysis" [ ], and requires that the court consider the content of the communication as a whole, its tone and apparent purpose [ ]. Thus, we have adopted a holistic approach to this inquiry.

> "Rather than sifting through a communication for the purpose of isolating and identifying assertions of fact, the court should look to the over-all context in which the assertions were made and determine on that basis 'whether the reasonable reader would have believed that the challenged statements were conveying facts about the . . . plaintiff'" [ ].

III.

In their complaint, Davis and Lang alleged that Boeheim made defamatory statements that they were liars seeking money. In support of their claim, they identified quotes from Boeheim in which he stated:

1. "This is alleged to have occurred . . . what? Twenty years ago? Am I in the right neighborhood? . . . So we are supposed to do what? Stop the presses 26 years later? For a false allegation? For what I absolutely believe is a false allegation? I know [Davis is] lying about me seeing him in his hotel room. That's a lie. If he's going to tell one lie, I'm sure there's a few more of them."

2. "The Penn State thing came out and the kid behind this is trying to get money. He's tried before. And now he's trying again. . . . That's what this is about. Money."

3. "It is a bunch of a thousand lies that [Davis] has told. . . . He supplied four names to the university that would corroborate his story. None of them did . . . there is only one side to this story. He is lying." Boeheim continued, "I believe they saw what happened at Penn State, and they are using ESPN to get money. That is what I believe."

4. "You don't think it is a little funny that his cousin (relative) is coming forward?"

5. Boeheim stated that the timing of Lang's decision to speak out about his abuse seemed "a little suspicious."

Applying the aforementioned principles to this case, the first and second factors weigh in favor of finding that Boeheim's statements were factual assertions. With respect to the first factor, Boeheim used specific, easily understood language to communicate that Davis and Lang lied, their motive was financial gain, and Davis had made prior similar statements for the same reason. These are clear statements of the plaintiffs' actions and the driving force for their allegations against Fine. Consideration of the second factor similarly weighs in favor of treating Boeheim's statements as factual because the statements are capable of being proven true or false, as they concern whether plaintiffs made false sexual abuse allegations against Fine in order to get money, and whether Davis had made false statements in the past [ ]. Moreover, they were not "rhetorical hyperbole rather than objective fact" [ ]. Our inquiry, however, does not rest on these two factors because the third factor in the analysis "is often the key consideration in categorizing a statement as fact or opinion" [ ]. It is this third factor that the parties vigorously dispute, and which we conclude establishes the sufficiency of plaintiffs' complaint.

Defendants contend that the context in which the statements were made leads inexorably to the conclusion that Boeheim's statements are nonactionable pure opinion. They argue that a reader would consider Boeheim's statements as an obvious and transparent effort to defend his longtime close friend and colleague against allegations of sexual abuse, as well as an effort to defend against suggestions that Boeheim knew about the alleged abuse and did nothing. They further argue that he specifically denied any special knowledge when he stated, "I know nothing" and "I really don't have any facts."

Essentially, defendants argue that because a reader could interpret the statement as pure opinion, the statement is as a consequence, nonactionable and was properly dismissed. . . . However, on a motion to dismiss we consider whether any reading of the complaint supports the defamation claim. Thus, although "[i]t may well be that [the challenged statements] are subject to defendants' interpretation . . . the motion to dismiss must be denied if the communication at issue, taking the words in their ordinary meaning and in context, is also susceptible to a defamatory connotation" [ ]. We find this complaint to meet this minimum pleading requirement.

Here, Boeheim stated that Davis and Lang lied and did so for monetary gain, and that Davis had done so in the past. Boeheim's assertions that Davis previously made the same claims, for the same purpose, communicated that Boeheim was relying on undisclosed facts that would justify Boeheim's statements that Davis and Lang were neither credible nor victims of sexual abuse. That, as defendants argue, Boeheim denied knowledge of facts, or prefaced some statements by saying "I believe," is insufficient to transform his statements into nonactionable pure opinion, because in context, a reasonable reader could view his statements as supported by undisclosed facts despite these denials [ ].

The context further suggests to the reader that Boeheim spoke with authority, and that his statements were based on facts. Boeheim was a well respected, exalted member of the University and the Syracuse community-at-large, and as head coach of the team appeared well placed to have information about the charges. Boeheim's initial statement, which contained information about the University's investigation, was released on the school's website, confirming his status within the University. His statement contained information about Davis' allegations and the University's investigation, which a reader could understand was based on Boeheim's access to factual details unavailable to the public, facts which supported his assertions about Davis and his motive. That Boeheim's statement was issued prior to the University's first public statement about the investigation, further suggests that Boeheim had access to otherwise confidential information. Moreover, Boeheim worked with Fine for many years and claimed to "know" Davis from when Davis was a child assisting the team and serving as a babysitter, further suggesting that Boeheim had particular details upon which he relied in asserting that the allegations were untrue. In addition, Boeheim knowingly made these statements to reporters during the media investigation and coverage of the plaintiffs' allegations. Those statements were then published in news-related articles that described the allegations, comparing them to the Penn State victims' claims, and discussing the impact of the sexual abuse charges on the individuals involved. Although the placement of the articles is but one factor to be considered, because the articles cited by plaintiffs cannot be categorized as op-eds or letters to the editor, "the common expectations that apply to those more opinionated journalistic endeavors were inapplicable here [ ]. Thus, the circumstances under which these accusations were published 'encourag[ed] the reasonable reader to be less skeptical and more willing to conclude that [they] stat[ed] or impl[ied] facts' " [ ].

IV.

At this early stage of the litigation, on this pre-answer motion to dismiss and on the record before us, we cannot state as a matter of law that the statements are pure opinion. There is a reasonable view of the claims upon which Davis and Lang would be entitled to recover for defamation; therefore the complaint must be deemed to sufficiently state a cause of action [ ]. Accordingly, the Appellate Division order should be reversed, with costs, and the motion to dismiss the complaint denied.

■ CHIEF JUDGE LIPPMAN and JUDGES GRAFFEO, READ, SMITH and ABDUS-SALAAM concur; JUDGE PIGOTT taking no part.

NOTES AND QUESTIONS

1.   The court grounds its analysis of the fact/opinion issue in the requirement that an actionable defamatory statement be a false statement of fact. Why should falsity be a requisite to establishing reputational harm? Isn't it the case that truthful assertions about an individual's character can be equally damaging to her reputation?

2.   The court applies a three-factor test in determining whether a statement is fact or opinion: whether the language has a precise meaning; whether the statement is capable of being proven true or false; and whether the context in which the statement was made is suggestive of fact or opinion. Is the court convincing that these factors weigh in favor of a

preliminary finding of factual content in the five statements that it identifies as central to the plaintiffs' claims?

3. Does it seem sensible to give particular weight to context?

4. Can an opinion ever be false under the court's analysis? Suppose the defendant asserted that the plaintiff was an incompetent litigator, even though her track record was thirty successful trial efforts without a single defeat?

5. The fact/opinion issue has taken on constitutional dimensions, which are addressed at p. 1118 infra.

2. "OF AND CONCERNING" PLAINTIFF

Identification. In addition to showing the defamatory nature of the publication, the plaintiff must show that the statement was understood to refer to, although not necessarily aimed at, the plaintiff. This is not difficult if the plaintiff is named or clearly identified in the publication, but sometimes the requirement can raise serious questions. This element is often called "colloquium" and establishes that the plaintiff is the person (or among the persons) defamed.

Identification problems sometimes arise in works of fiction. See Muzikowski v. Paramount Pictures Corp., 322 F.3d 918 (7th Cir.2003), in which plaintiff, a Little League coach, alleged that he had been defamed by defendant's movie, "Hardball." He claimed that he resembled an unsavory coach in the movie, although there were also some differences between the two. The court, using Illinois law, held that calling a book or film "fiction" did not automatically protect the creator—even in a state like Illinois that follows the "innocent construction" rule. The issue was whether a "reasonable" reader or viewer would think it portrayed the plaintiff. The court reversed the dismissal because the plaintiff "might be able to produce evidence showing that there is in fact no *reasonable* interpretation of the movie that would support an innocent construction." For the special problems of identification of plaintiffs in works of fiction, see Symposium, Defamation in Fiction, 51 Brook.L.Rev. 223 (1985).

A common problem stems from the use of generic file photographs to illustrate a story in the print media. See, e.g., Clark v. American Broadcasting Cos., Inc., 684 F.2d 1208 (6th Cir.1982), involving a program about prostitution. The plaintiff, who had been photographed without her knowledge while walking on a city street, was shown on the screen while the narrator was describing the prevalence of prostitution in the neighborhood.

Corporations. It is clear that corporations may be defamation plaintiffs. Section 561 of the Second Restatement states that a for-profit corporation may sue if "the matter tends to prejudice it in the conduct of its business or to deter others from dealing with it." A corporation that is not for profit may sue if it "depends upon financial support from the public, and the matter tends to interfere with its activities by prejudicing it in public estimation."

A separate question involves the relationship between a corporation and its shareholders. If the corporation is large and its stock widely held, courts generally conclude that stockholders may not sue for the libel of the corporation. But in closely held corporations, courts have held that a libel of the corporation may be understood by the reasonable audience to be addressed as well to the controlling individuals, even if they are not mentioned in the story. This result is even clearer if the individual and the corporation have the same name. See discussion in Schiavone Construction Co. v. Time Inc., 619 F.Supp. 684 (D.N.J.1985).

Group libel. Different problems exist when the statement is about one or more members of a group of individuals. In such cases might one member be able to claim that the statement hurt his or her personal reputation? At the extreme, an attack on all lawyers in the United States or on all clergymen would be held to be such a general broadside that no individual lawyer or clergyman could sue. The same would be true of broadside attacks on racial, religious, or ethnic groups.

At the other extreme, it is generally accepted that a charge made against a small group may defame all members of that group. For example, a newspaper article may assert that "the officers" of a corporation have embezzled funds. There are only four officers of the corporation. Each of them may be found to have been defamed even though the statement was that "one of the officers of the corporation" had embezzled funds. The group is small enough so that all four officials are put under a shadow, and most states would permit all four to sue.

As the group grows larger, the impact of the statement may depend on the inclusiveness of the language as well as the size of the total group. In one case, a defamatory charge was made against one unidentified member of a 21-member police force. All 21 sued. The trial court's dismissal was affirmed. It was feared that allowing the action would permit a suit by an entire baseball team over a report that one member was disciplined for brawling. Such a result "would chill communication to the marrow." The court explained, "By no stretch of imagination can it be thought to suggest that the conduct of the one [described in the article] is typical of all. Noting the individual's membership in the group does not suggest a common determinant of character so much as simply a practical reference point." But suppose the charge had been against "all but one" of the members of that police force? Such a statement may reflect on each member of the force. Arcand v. Evening Call Publishing Co., 567 F.2d 1163 (1st Cir.1977).

One case presented three aspects of this problem. A book about Dallas stated that "some" Neiman-Marcus department store models were "call girls. . . . The salesgirls are good, too—pretty and often much cheaper. . . ." And "most of the [male] sales staff are fairies, too."

Suits were filed by all nine models, 30 of the 382 saleswomen, and 15 of the 25 salesmen. The defendants did not challenge the right of the nine models to sue. The other two groups were challenged as being too large.

The claim of "the salesgirls" was dismissed. The result would be the same even if the authors had explicitly referred to "all"—and even if all 382 had sued. The judge cited cases rejecting suits when the statements attacked all officials of a statewide union or all the taxicab drivers in Washington, D.C.

On the other hand, the salesmen's case was not dismissed. It was close to others involving members of a posse, or the 12 doctors on a hospital's residential staff. Neiman-Marcus v. Lait, 13 F.R.D. 311 (S.D.N.Y.1952). Would the result have been the same if the authors had referred to "some" or "a few" of the men?

Although defamation of large groups—ethnic, religious, professional—does not result in a cause of action in any state, some states have sought to develop criminal sanctions against such attacks. Even though these statutes were held not to violate the First Amendment, 5–4, in Beauharnais v. Illinois, 343 U.S. 250 (1952)(upholding statute barring portrayals of "depravity, criminality, unchastity, or lack of virtue of a class of citizens, of any race, color, creed, or religion" that subjected that group to "contempt, derision, or obloquy or which is productive of breach of the peace or riots"), they have been put in some doubt by R.A.V. v. City of St. Paul, 505 U.S. 377 (1992). In *R.A.V.*, the Court invalidated, on First Amendment grounds, a city ordinance that punished anyone who places on public or private property any "symbol, object, appellation, characterization or graffiti, including but not limited to, a burning cross or Nazi swastika, which one knows or has reasonable grounds to know arouses anger, alarm or resentment in others on the basis of race, color, creed, religions or gender."

3. STRICT LIABILITY

The common law often held a publisher strictly liable for defamatory statements. Thus, the case was established even if the offending statement appeared on its face to be either neutral or positive, but, when supplemented by other facts, unknown to defendant, turned out to be defamatory. Similarly, if a magazine carries what it believes to be fiction but readers reasonably (even if unaware) think the words refer to an identifiable plaintiff, a defamation may be found. These subjects are discussed at length in Smith, *Jones v. Hulton*: Three Conflicting Views as to Defamation, 60 U.Pa.L.Rev. 365, 461 (1912); Holdsworth, A Chapter of Accidents in the Law of Libel, 57 L.Q.Rev. 74

(1941). By contrast, the common law did not impose strict liability on what were viewed as disseminators of the finished product—newsstands, bookstores, and libraries. These institutions were held liable only if the plaintiff could establish that the defendant knew or had reason to know of the presence of the defamation in the work being sold or loaned.

Although, as we shall see shortly, the common law developed a few privileges that softened the rigors of strict liability on original publishers, strict liability has remained a fixture of the tort. Most of the constitutional developments to be discussed later are traceable to this feature.

4. DAMAGES: LIBEL AND SLANDER

Generally, tort plaintiffs are entitled to recover damages for harm they can prove they sustained. Defamation generally—but not always—permits plaintiffs to recover proven damages. These may include lost wages and similar losses, as well as proven damages for broad reputational loss. The first type, called "special damages," includes specific identifiable pecuniary losses that the plaintiff can prove he or she sustained and can trace to the defendant's defamatory statement.

The second type, "general damages," includes damages to reputation that the plaintiff has suffered in ways that do not straightforwardly translate into dollars and cents. This is usually a claim that the plaintiff has suffered general reputational harm in some community—whether it be a geographical community or one based on, say, religious, social, or professional relationships.

Defamation law has two aspects that are unlike tort law generally. One is that plaintiffs sometimes can recover "presumed" general damages—without proving that they have suffered any actual damage, whether special or general. In awarding damages for presumed general damages, the trier is to consider the words used, the medium used, and the predicted response of the community. The other unusual feature is that sometimes the plaintiff must prove the existence of special damages before being allowed to recover *any* general damages—even if plaintiff can prove harm of the sort compensated by general damages.

Under these two unusual damage rules, some plaintiffs may receive a substantial recovery without proof of any damages, while others may recover nothing at all because they were required, but were unable, to prove special damages. In this latter situation, they are barred from recovering any general damages whether provable or presumed, even in cases in which most people would recognize that the plaintiffs had been seriously harmed.

The determination of what damages plaintiffs must prove in defamation cases is largely rooted in history and requires the introduction of the terms "libel" and "slander." When the relevant damage rules evolved, slanders, generally oral defamations, were sued upon in the common law courts. Libels, generally written defamations, had become a major concern of the English government because of the recent development of printing. Libels were addressed in the Court of Star Chamber. After the Star Chamber was abolished, oral and written defamations were both redressed by the common law courts. Those courts, however, preserved some damage distinctions between the two types of defamation that have survived to our day.

As the court explains in Matherson v. Marchello, 473 N.Y.S.2d 998 (App.Div.1984):

A plaintiff suing in slander must plead special damages unless the defamation falls into any one of four per se categories [discussed in the next main case].

On the other hand, a plaintiff suing in libel need not plead or prove special damages. . . . Thus, unlike the law of slander, in the law of libel the existence of damage is conclusively presumed from the publication itself and a plaintiff may rely on general damages. . . .

. . .

Traditionally, the demarcation between libel and slander rested upon whether the words were written or spoken [ ]. Written defamations were considered far more serious because, at the time the distinction arose, few persons could read or write and, therefore, anything which was written would carry a louder ring of purported truth [ ]. In addition, a written defamation could be disseminated more widely and carried a degree of permanence.

Which of the justifications offered for the differing treatment of written and oral defamation is strongest? In addition to those offered by the court, consider the notion that a writing still may be given more weight because it requires more thought and planning than a spontaneous oral utterance, which might simply be tossed off.

Virtually all states classify defamation by radio or television as libel. California, by statute, is an outlier. Civil Code sections 46 and 48.5(4) treat defamations by radio and television as slander. The rise of the Internet has raised the question of whether Internet postings should be treated as slander or libel. In *Varian Med. Sys., Inc. v. Delfino*, a California court found that such postings were properly characterized as libel rather than slander. 6 Cal.Rptr.3d 325, 340–43 (Ct.App.2003); see also Mathis v. Cannon, 573 S.E.2d 376 (Ga.2002)(construing libel retraction statute to apply to Internet postings).

In some states, including New York, the answer to the special damages question is complete once the publication has been determined to be libel because in those states libel never requires special damages.

In a second group of states, however, even if the statement is classified as libel, special damages are required unless: (1) the defamatory sting is clear on its face; or (2) if not clear on its face, when fleshed out with extrinsic facts, the sting would be slander per se.

The terms "per se" and "per quod" have different meanings in libel and slander. Consider the following excerpt from 1 R. Sack, Sack on Defamation: Libel, Slander, and Related Problems 2–123–24 (4th ed. 2010):

> As a practical matter, words that, uttered orally, are slanderous per se, are *usually* also libelous per se when written. But the reason they are slanderous per se normally has little to do with the reason that they are libelous per se. To say of a woman that she is a whore or of a man that he robs his business associates blind is slanderous per se because it falls within one of the four categories. The same words when written are libelous per se, not because they fit within a slander category, but because they tend on their face to disgrace the person about whom they are written. Extrinsic facts are unnecessary to explain their defamatory meaning.
>
> But the converse is not true. Statements which are libelous per se when written often are not slanderous per se when spoken. However degrading a statement, however injurious to reputation, however outrageous, however plain the defamatory meaning on the face of the statement and therefore however clear that the statement when written is libelous per se, unless the defamatory charge falls within one of the four specific slander categories, it is not slanderous per se when merely spoken, and special damages must be pleaded and proved. To call someone a "coward," for example, is libelous per se but probably not slanderous per se.

The following case addresses the special slander categories referred to in the excerpts from *Matherson* and Sack.

Liberman v. Gelstein
Court of Appeals of New York, 1992.
80 N.Y.2d 429, 605 N.E.2d 344, 590 N.Y.S.2d 857.

■ KAYE, JUDGE.

[Plaintiff landlord sued a member of the tenants' board of governors for slander. This case involves the second and fifth causes of action. In the second, defendant is alleged to have had the following exchange with Kohler, a fellow member of the board of directors:

"Gelstein: Can you find out from your friend at the precinct which cop is on the take from Liberman?

"Kohler: What are you talking about?

"Gelstein: There is a cop on the take from Liberman. That's why none of the building's cars ever get tickets—they can park anywhere because Liberman's paid them off. He gives them a hundred or two hundred a week."

The fifth cause of action alleged that defendant made the following statement in the presence of employees of the building: "Liberman threw a punch at me. He screamed at my wife and daughter. He called my daughter a slut and threatened to kill me and my family."]

. . . After discovery, defendant sought summary judgment dismissing the complaint. On the second cause of action, defendant invoked the "common interest" qualified privilege, characterizing his conversation with Kohler, a colleague on the board of governors, as an inquiry designed to uncover wrongdoing by the landlord affecting tenants. At his deposition, defendant testified that several vehicles operated by the building's management regularly parked in front of the building beyond the legal limit but never received parking summonses. He further testified that he was told by two building employees, whom he identified, that Liberman was bribing the police to avoid parking tickets. Defendant admitted that he did not know whether the allegations were true, but testified that they "sounded truthful" to him. Accordingly, defendant testified that he approached Kohler—whose friend was captain of the local police precinct—in an effort to discover whether the allegations were true.

. . .

[On the fifth cause of action, defendant argued that the statements were either true, not defamatory, or never made. The lower court dismissed the second cause of action on the ground that it was qualifiedly privileged and that plaintiff had failed to raise triable issues on other grounds. The fifth cause of action was dismissed on the ground that the words could only have been understood by those who were familiar with the parties' history of conflict as rhetorical hyperbole. The Appellate Division affirmed.]

II.

Slander as a rule is not actionable unless the plaintiff suffers special damage. [ ] Special damages contemplate "the loss of something having economic or pecuniary value" (Restatement § 575, comment b; [ ]). Plaintiff has not alleged special damages, and thus his slander claims are not sustainable unless they fall within one of the exceptions to the rule.

The four established exceptions (collectively "slander per se") consist of statements (i) charging plaintiff with a serious crime; (ii) that tend to injure another in his or her trade, business or profession; (iii) that plaintiff has a loathsome disease; or (iv) imputing unchastity to a woman [ ]. When statements fall within one of these categories, the law presumes that damages will result, and they need not be alleged or proven.

Plaintiff claims that both sets of statements were slanderous per se inasmuch as they charged him with criminal conduct. Not every imputation of unlawful behavior, however, is slanderous per se. "With the extension of criminal punishment to many minor offenses, it was obviously necessary to make some distinction as to the character of the crime, since a charge of a traffic violation, for example, would not exclude a person from society, and today would do little, if any, harm to his [or her] reputation at all" [ ]. Thus, the law distinguishes between serious and relatively minor offenses, and only statements regarding the former are actionable without proof of damage (see, Restatement § 571, comment *g* [list of crimes actionable as per se slander includes murder, burglary, larceny, arson, rape, kidnapping]).

We agree with plaintiff that defendant's alleged statement that "[t]here is a cop on the take from Liberman" charges a serious crime— bribery (see, Penal Law § 200.00; [ ]). Accordingly, the statements constituting the second cause of action are actionable without the need to establish special harm, and absent any privilege would be sufficient to go to a jury.

We disagree, however, with plaintiff's contention that the statement "Liberman . . . threatened to kill me and my family" was slanderous per se. Plaintiff claims these words falsely attributed to him the commission of the crime of harassment (see, Penal Law § 240.25; [ ]). Harassment is a relatively minor offense in the New York Penal Law—not even a misdemeanor—and thus the harm to the reputation of a person falsely accused of committing harassment would be correspondingly insubstantial. Hence, even if we agreed with plaintiff that the statement would not have been construed by the listeners as rhetorical hyperbole, the cause of action must nevertheless be dismissed because it is not slanderous per se to claim that someone committed harassment.

Plaintiff alternatively argues that the statements in the fifth cause of action tended to harm him in his business as a property owner, and thus are actionable under the "trade, business or profession" exception. That exception, however, is "limited to defamation of a kind incompatible with the proper conduct of the business, trade, profession or office itself. The statement must be made with reference to a matter of significance and importance for that purpose, rather than a more general reflection upon the plaintiff's character or qualities" [ ]. Thus, "charges against a clergyman of drunkenness and other moral misconduct affect his fitness for the performance of the duties of his profession, although the same charges against a business man or tradesman do not so affect him" (Restatement § 573, comment *c*). The statements at issue are unrelated to plaintiff's status as a landlord, and therefore do not fall into the "trade, business or profession" exception [ ].

In sum, the second cause of action is on its face sustainable without special damages because it involves charges of serious crime, and the fifth cause of action was correctly dismissed.

[The court concluded that the plaintiff had not presented enough to overcome defendant's privilege as to the bribery charge. The dismissal of the second cause of action was affirmed. We return to this issue at p. 1034 infra.]

■ SIMONS, ACTING C.J., and TITONE, HANCOCK and BELLACOSA, JJ., concur with KAYE, J. [JUDGE SMITH dissented in part on an issue related to privilege, discussed infra].

NOTES AND QUESTIONS

1. Why does the second cause of action not require special damages? Why does the fifth cause of action require them? What kinds of special damages might a plaintiff in this situation be able to show?

2. In *Ward v. Zelikovsky*, note 5, p. 1009 supra, involving the statement at a meeting of condominium owners, the lower court had found the charge of bigotry was actionable and then decided that a showing of special damages was not required. The court reached that position by adding a fifth category to the slander per se list for imputations of racial or ethnic bigotry. In reversing on the ground that the statement was not actionable, the supreme court noted its refusal to add new categories to the four existing ones: the "trend of modern tort law is to focus on the injury not the wrong and the slander per se categories are a relic from tort law's previous age." It left for "another day" the question of whether to abolish the slander per se categories and require special damages for all slanders. On this issue, see Anderson, Reputation, Compensation, and Proof, 25 Wm. & Mary L.Rev. 747 (1984).

3. In the following case, the court revisits the slander per se categories in the context of dicta in earlier cases—including *Matherson*, p. 1022, supra—that would have recognized a fifth category, the false imputation of homosexuality. The opinion provides an opportunity to reflect on the relationship between the categories and evolving social values.

Yonaty v. Mincolla

New York Supreme Court, Appellate Division, 2012.
945 N.Y.S.2d 774.

■ MERCURE, J.P.

This appeal presents the issue of whether statements falsely describing a person as lesbian, gay or bisexual constitute slander per se. Given this state's well-defined public policy of protection and respect for the civil rights of people who are lesbian, gay or bisexual, we now overrule our prior case to the contrary and hold that such statements are not defamatory per se.

After a nonparty allegedly told defendant that plaintiff was gay or bisexual, defendant relayed that information to third-party defendant, a close family friend of plaintiff's long-time girlfriend, with the hope that the girlfriend would be told. Plaintiff maintains that defendant's actions caused the deterioration and ultimate termination of his relationship with his girlfriend. He commenced this action against defendant, alleging slander, intentional infliction of emotional distress and prima facie tort. Defendant then commenced the third-party action, seeking indemnification based upon the republication of the statements.

. . . As relevant here, the court concluded that it was bound to follow prior appellate case law holding that statements falsely imputing homosexuality constitute defamation per se and, thus, plaintiff's slander claim need not be dismissed despite his failure to allege special damages. The parties cross-appeal, and we now modify by dismissing the complaint and third-party complaint in their entirety.

Whether particular statements are susceptible of a defamatory meaning—and therefore actionable—presents a question of law [citations]. Only "[i]f the contested statements are reasonably susceptible of a defamatory connotation [does] it become [ ] the jury's function to say whether that was the sense in which the words were likely to be understood by the ordinary and average [person]" [ ]. A statement has defamatory connotations if it tends to expose a person to "public hatred, shame, obloquy, contumely, odium, contempt, ridicule, aversion, ostracism, degradation or disgrace, or to induce an evil opinion of [a person] in the minds of right-thinking persons" [ ]. Because the defamatory tendency of a statement depends "upon the temper of the times [and] the current of contemporary public opinion," a statement that is "harmless in one age . . . may be highly damaging to reputation at another time" [citation].

Generally, a plaintiff asserting a cause of action sounding in slander must allege special damages contemplating "the loss of something having economic or pecuniary value" (*Liberman v. Gelstein,* 80 N.Y.2d 429, 434–435, 590 N.Y.S.2d 857, 605 N.E.2d 344 [2003] [internal quotation marks and citation omitted]; [ ]. Plaintiff has not done so and, thus, he cannot maintain his slander claim unless the challenged statements constitute "slander per se"—those categories of statements that are commonly recognized as injurious by their nature, and so noxious that the law presumes that pecuniary damages will result (*see Liberman v. Gelstein,* 80 N.Y.2d at 435, 590 N.Y.S.2d 857, 605 N.E.2d 344). The four established "per se" categories recognized by the Court of Appeals are "statements (i) charging [a] plaintiff with a serious crime; (ii) that tend to injure another in his or her trade, business or profession; (iii) that [a] plaintiff has a loathsome disease; or (iv) imputing unchastity to a woman" (*id.*). As Supreme Court noted, the Appellate Division Departments, including this Court in dicta, have recognized statements falsely imputing homosexuality as a fifth per se category (*see* [ ]; *Matherson v. Marchello,* 100 A.D.2d 233, 241–242, 473 N.Y.S.2d 998 [2d Dept. 1984]; [ ]).

We agree with defendant and amici that these Appellate Division decisions are inconsistent with current public policy and should no longer be followed. Defamation "necessarily . . . involves the idea of disgrace" [ ]. Defendant and amici argue—correctly, in our view—that the prior cases categorizing statements that falsely impute homosexuality as defamatory per se are based upon the flawed premise that it is shameful and disgraceful to be described as lesbian, gay or bisexual. In fact, such a rule necessarily equates individuals who are lesbian, gay or bisexual with those who have committed a "serious crime"—one of the four established per se categories (*see Liberman v. Gelstein,* [ ].

That premise is inconsistent with the reasoning underlying the decision of the Supreme Court of the United States in *Lawrence v. Texas,* 539 U.S. 558, 123 S.Ct. 2472, 156 L.Ed.2d 508 (2003), in which the Court held that laws criminalizing homosexual conduct violate the Due Process Clause of the Fourteenth Amendment of the United States Constitution [ ]. The Court stated that people who are homosexual "*are entitled to respect for their private lives*" (*id.* [emphasis added]), but "[w]hen homosexual conduct is made criminal by the law of the State, that declaration in and of itself is an invitation to subject homosexual persons to discrimination in both the public and in the private spheres" [ ]. These statements of the Supreme Court simply cannot be reconciled with the prior line of Appellate Division cases concluding that being described as lesbian, gay or bisexual is so self-evidently injurious that the law will presume that pecuniary damages have resulted.

In regard to New York in particular, we locate "the public policy of [this] state in the law as expressed in statute and judicial decision and also [by] consider[ing] the prevailing attitudes of the community" [ ]. Rather than countenancing the view that homosexuality is disgraceful, the Human Rights Law, since 2002, has expressly prohibited discrimination based on sexual orientation in employment, public accommodations, credit, education and housing [ ]. Most revealing of the respect that the people of this state currently extend to lesbians, gays and bisexuals, the Legislature passed the Marriage Equality Act [ ], which was strongly supported by the Governor and gave same-sex couples the right to marry in New York, thereby granting them all the benefits of marriage, including "the symbolic benefit, or moral satisfaction, of seeing their relationships recognized by the State" [ ]. Even prior to the Marriage Equality Act, this Court had previously explained that "the public policy of our state protects same-sex couples in a myriad of ways"—including numerous statutory benefits and judicial decisions expressing a policy of acceptance [ ]. . . .

We note that the most recent Appellate Division decision considering the issue in depth was decided nearly 30 years ago (*Matherson v. Marchello,* 100 A.D.2d 233, 241–242, 473 N.Y.S.2d 998 [2d Dept. 1984], *supra*). In that case, the Second Department concluded that it was "constrained . . . *at this point in time* " to hold that a statement imputing homosexuality was defamatory per se in light of the then-existing "social opprobrium of homosexuality" and "[l]egal sanctions imposed upon homosexuals in areas ranging from immigration to military service" ([ ] [emphasis added]). Ultimately, the Court held that "the potential and probable harm of a false charge of homosexuality, in terms of social and economic impact, cannot be ignored" [ ]. In light of the tremendous evolution in social attitudes regarding homosexuality, the elimination of the legal sanctions that troubled the Second Department in 1984 and the considerable legal protection and respect that the law of this state now accords lesbians, gays and bisexuals, it cannot be said that current public opinion supports a rule that would equate statements imputing homosexuality with accusations of serious criminal conduct or insinuations that an individual has a loathsome disease [ ]. While lesbians, gays and bisexuals have historically faced discrimination and such prejudice has not been completely eradicated, "the fact of such prejudice on the part of some does not warrant a judicial holding that gays and lesbians [and bisexuals], merely because of their sexual orientation, belong in the same class as criminals" [ ].

In short, the disputed statements in this case are not slanderous per se and, thus, plaintiff's failure to allege special damages requires that the remaining cause of action for slander be dismissed. Inasmuch as the complaint did not adequately allege extreme and outrageous conduct sufficient to support plaintiff's claim of intentional infliction of emotional distress or special damages to support a prima facie tort claim [ ], Supreme Court properly dismissed those causes of action. Accordingly, the complaint and third-party complaint should be dismissed in their entirety.

NOTES AND QUESTIONS

1.   In Obergefell v. Hodges, 135 S.Ct. 2584 (2015), the Supreme Court held that the Fourteenth Amendment guarantees a right to same-sex marriage, further supporting the *Yonaty* court's view that false ascription of homosexuality is "inconsistent with public policy." Would you expect the same outcome in other states?

2.   In ruling that an assertion of homosexuality is not per se slanderous, has the court necessarily decided that such statements are no longer defamatory? Why might the court have limited its holding to rejection of slander per se categorization?

3.   Should deterring false assertions of this kind be relevant in assessing the court's view of public policy?

4. In addition to general and special damages, two other classifications loom large in defamation law: nominal damages and punitive damages. Although nominal damages are unimportant in most tort actions, they may be central in defamation cases. The award of a symbolic amount such as six cents usually shows that the jury found the attack to be false but also found the words not to have hurt. But was that because the speaker was not credible, or the plaintiff's strong reputation blunted the harm, or his reputation was so low that nothing could really hurt it? See Reynolds v. Pegler, 223 F.2d 429 (2d Cir.1955)(upholding a jury award of $1 in compensatory damages and $175,000 in punitive damages against the various defendants). Recall in this regard that any punitive damages award that exceeds the compensatory award by a factor of 10 or more is presumptively unconstitutional under a line of Supreme Court cases first decided in the 1990s. See p. 756, supra.

5. Several states at common law have rejected the concept of punitive damages in all tort cases; others have sharply limited the availability and amount of such damages. See p. 824 supra. Some states have decided to bar punitive damages only in defamation cases and other tort cases involving harm through speech. As we shall see shortly, recent federal and state constitutional developments also restrict the availability of such damages in libel cases.

6. For an extensive consideration of the nature of defamation and the interests it might vindicate, see Post, The Social Foundations of Defamation Law: Reputation and the Constitution, 74 Cal.L.Rev. 691 (1986).

5. DEFENSES

In this section we consider the variety of state common law or statutory defenses to the basic defamation claim. Although traditional tort defenses such as consent apply, our focus here is on those defenses unique to defamation law.

a. TRUTH

The most obvious defense, but one little relied upon in litigation, is to prove the essential truth of the defamatory statement. During the period when the English government rigorously used the law of criminal libel, truth was not a defense because unfavorable truths about government or officials were more likely to foment anti-government attitudes and actions than were falsehoods. But now truth is recognized as a complete defense to civil libel. Because the action is intended to compensate those whose reputations are damaged falsely, if the defendant has spoken the truth, the reputational harm is deemed to provide no basis for an action. (A minority of states purport to require the truth to have been spoken with "good motives" or for "justifiable ends" or both.)

The defendant need not prove literal truth but must establish the truth of the "sting" of the charge. Thus, if the defendant has charged the plaintiff with stealing $25,000 from a bank, truth will be established even if the actual amount was only $12,000. In Masson v. New Yorker Magazine, Inc., 501 U.S. 496 (1991), the Court captured the common law's spirit in observing that the common law of libel "overlooks minor inaccuracies and concentrates upon substantial truth." Thus, the test was whether what was published "would have had a different effect upon the mind of the reader from that which the pleaded truth would have produced." Compare Posadas v. City of Reno, 851 P.2d 438 (Nev.1993), holding actionable a claim based on defendant's false charge that plaintiff police officer had "admitted he lied under oath" (the crime of perjury), when in fact he had admitted to lying (not under oath) to two other officers who questioned him about the charges against him—apparently not a crime.

On the other hand, the false accusation must be close to the true facts. "A sexual deviant might have a worse reputation than an embezzler, but it would not be a defense to a charge of falsely accusing a person of being an embezzler that while he is not an embezzler, he is a sexual deviant, which is worse." Desnick v. American Broadcasting Companies, Inc., 44 F.3d 1345 (7th Cir.1995). Nonetheless, it may help mitigate damages to show that the plaintiff's reputation was already in low esteem for other reasons, and thus the plaintiff has suffered less harm than might otherwise have occurred.

The role of headlines needs special attention because of the difficulty of capturing the story in a few words. In Gunduz v. New York Post Co., 590 N.Y.S.2d 494 (App.Div.1992), the headline was "Public Enemy No.1" with a much smaller but adjacent sub-head, "City moves to yank license of Apple's 'worst taxi driver.'" The story, about New York City's efforts to revoke plaintiff's taxi license, reported that he had received more summonses and violations than any other cab driver in the city, and described incidents of overcharging and abusing customers. The court thought the big headline "was a fair index of the truthful matter contained in the related news article."

Expungement. In Bahr v. Statesman Journal Co., 624 P.2d 664 (Or.App.1981), a newspaper reported that plaintiff, a candidate for public office, in an interview had "refused to discuss a 1964 conviction on an embezzlement charge. . . . 'I have no record of convictions. My record is clean. I have never been convicted of embezzlement.' " In fact, the conviction had occurred and had later been expunged under state law. The expungement statute gave plaintiff the right to deny that he had ever been convicted. But it also provided that the expungement itself could not be relied upon in a civil action in which the truth of the conviction was an element of the lawsuit. Thus, the newspaper's defense of truth succeeded. What result if the statute had not provided explicitly for the contingency of a libel suit?

Truth is little used as a defense, although it would enable a decisive confrontation, perhaps because most statements sued upon are false. Even where the defendant still thinks the statement true, it may be very expensive to establish that truth. A defendant relying on truth usually bears the legal costs of a full-dress trial as well as the sometimes major expense of investigating the matter and gathering enough evidence to ensure the outcome. Particularly when the charge involved is vague and does not allege specific events, the defense of truth may be quite expensive. It can also be risky, because a failed attempt to show truth may only impress the jury with the defendant's intransigence.

Recent constitutional developments have sharply altered the role of truth. See particularly p. 1118 infra.

b. PRIVILEGES

Not only are there disadvantages to the defense of truth, there are attractive alternatives. Over the centuries the law of defamation has developed several privileges to protect those who make defamatory statements.

Absolute privileges. Some privileges are "absolute" in the sense that if the occasion gives rise to an absolute privilege, there will be no liability even if the speaker deliberately lied about the plaintiff. The most significant example of this narrow group is the federal and state constitutional privilege afforded legislators, who may not be sued for defamation for any statement made during debate. High executive officials, judges, and participants in judicial proceedings also have an absolute privilege to speak freely on matters relevant to their obligations. No matter how such a speaker abuses the privilege by lying, no tort liability is permitted. See Barr v. Matteo, 360 U.S. 564 (1959).

In Carradine v. State of Minnesota, 511 N.W.2d 733 (Minn.1994), the court considered immunity for an arresting officer's statements. The court noted that high-level executive officials—the state's commissioner of the department of public welfare, for example—had absolute privilege. But the test was not the defendant's level in the hierarchy; the rationale for extending such immunity was that "unless the officer in question is absolutely immune from suit, the officer will timorously, instead of fearlessly, perform the function in question and, as a result, government—that is, the public—will be the ultimate loser."

The court thought this standard justified extending such protection to the officer's arrest report. The report is an essential part of the officer's job; the report is also used by prosecutors in deciding whether to file charges and, if so, what charges; it plays a role in any trial in refreshing recollection and providing the basis for impeachment. The absence of immunity may well deter the honest officer from fearlessly and vigorously preparing a detailed, accurate report and increase the likelihood that the officer will hesitate to prepare anything more than a bland report that will be less useful within the department and in any subsequent prosecution and trial. To put it another way, instead of preparing a detailed report, the officer will be tempted to leave out certain details, saving those for trial, when any testimony by the officer is absolutely privileged under the judicial privilege.

This would lead to trial by surprise—something the state has been trying to avoid. On the other hand, statements by the arresting officer in response to press inquiries did not deserve such protection. It was not essential to the officer's duties to respond to the press. Such responses were "allowed" by the department but not required.

In Vultaggio v. Yasko, 572 N.W.2d 450 (Wis.1998), defendant attended a city council meeting at which she spoke about the changes in her neighborhood and, in the process, attacked the upkeep of several buildings belonging to plaintiff. In his suit, the court held, 4–3, that defendant should not be absolutely privileged. The majority cited other cases denying such a privilege to those "who supply voluntary testimony to a legislative body." Compare Hartman v. Keri, 883 N.E.2d 774 (Ind.2008), in which the court held that complaints by students about a faculty member violating University anti-harassment policy were absolutely privileged, relying on analogy to judicial proceedings privilege. What are the arguments each way in these cases?

In another important area, the courts split on whether a litigant has an absolute privilege to announce publicly and to the press that he has just filed a civil complaint. The act of filing the complaint is absolutely privileged in all states—the split is over the public announcement that summarizes the contents of the complaint. Attorneys who are privileged to speak freely in judicial proceedings may not claim that same level of protection when responding to reporters' questions. See Kennedy v. Zimmermann, 601 N.W.2d 61 (Iowa 1999).

The broadcast media are given an absolute privilege when they are required to grant candidates access to the airwaves. If a candidate commits defamation, the broadcaster is not liable. See Farmers Educational & Cooperative Union of America v. WDAY, Inc., 360 U.S. 525 (1959). Cucinotta v. Deloitte & Touche, L.L.P., 302 P.3d 1099 (Nev. 2013), reflects a broader privilege that encompasses the privilege recognized in *WDAY*. Defendant, a public auditor, disclosed information it had obtained from the FBI about illegal activity by a company and two members of its Board to the Board's Audit Committee. The Board members resigned and, after an investigation by outside counsel that exonerated them, sued the auditor for defamation. The court adopted section 592A of the Second Restatement of Torts, which provides an absolute privilege to those who are required by law to speak. This privilege is applicable to the auditor here, explained the court, because federal securities law requires an auditor who "becomes aware of information that an illegal act . . . has or may have occurred" to inform appropriate management.

Qualified or conditional privileges. The much more common type of privilege is "qualified" or "conditional," and is considered in the following case. (The terms "qualified" and "conditional" are synonymous.)

Liberman v. Gelstein

Court of Appeals of New York, 1992.
80 N.Y.2d 429, 605 N.E.2d 344, 590 N.Y.S.2d 857.

■ KAYE, JUDGE.

[The facts are reprinted at p. 1023 supra. After finding that the charge concerning bribery was actionable, the court turned to the next issue.]

We next consider whether the courts below properly concluded that defendant's conversation with Kohler was conditionally privileged and that plaintiff failed to raise an issue of fact on malice.

Courts have long recognized that the public interest is served by shielding certain communications, though possibly defamatory, from litigation, rather than risk stifling them altogether [ ]. When compelling public policy requires that the speaker be immune from suit, the law affords an absolute privilege, while statements fostering a lesser public interest are only conditionally privileged [ ].

One such conditional, or qualified, privilege extends to a "communication made by one person to another upon a subject in which both have an interest" [ ]. This "common interest" privilege (see, Restatement § 596) has been applied, for example, to employees of an organization [ ], members of a faculty tenure committee [ ], and constituent physicians of a health insurance plan [ ]. The rationale for applying the privilege in these circumstances is that so long as the privilege is not abused, the flow of information between persons sharing a common interest should not be impeded.

We thus agree . . . that defendant's conversation with Kohler was conditionally privileged (see, Restatement § 596, comment *d* ["Tenants in common . . . are included within the rule stated in this Section as being conditionally privileged to communicate among themselves matter defamatory of others which concerns their common interests"]). Gelstein and Kohler were members of the governing body of an association formed to protect the tenants' interests. If Liberman was in fact bribing the police so that his cars could occupy spaces in front of the building, that would be inimical to those interests. Thus, Gelstein had a qualified right to communicate his suspicions—though defamatory of Liberman—to Kohler.

The shield provided by a qualified privilege may be dissolved if plaintiff can demonstrate that defendant spoke with "malice" [ ]. Under common law, malice meant spite or ill will [ ]. In New York Times Co. v. Sullivan, 376 U.S. 254 (1964), however, the Supreme Court established an "actual malice" standard for certain cases governed by the First Amendment: "knowledge that [the statement] was false or . . . reckless disregard of whether it was false or not" [ ]. Consequently, the term "malice" has become somewhat confused [ ]. Indeed, as the Supreme Court itself recently acknowledged [Masson v. New Yorker Mag., 501 U.S. 496 (1991)]:

> Actual malice under the *New York Times* standard should not be confused with the concept of malice as an evil intent or a motive arising from spite or ill will. . . . We have used the term actual malice as a shorthand to describe the First Amendment protections for speech injurious to reputation and we continue to do so here. But the term can confuse as well as enlighten. In this respect, the phrase may be an unfortunate one.

Nevertheless, malice has now assumed a dual meaning, and we have recognized that the constitutional as well as the common-law standard will suffice to defeat a conditional privilege [ ].

Under the *Times* malice standard, the plaintiff must demonstrate that the "statements [were] made with [a] high degree of awareness of their probable falsity" [ ]. In other words, there "must be sufficient evidence to permit the conclusion that the defendant in fact entertained serious doubts as to the truth of [the] publication" [ ]; see also, Restatement § 600, comment *b*.

Applying these principles, we conclude that there is no triable malice issue under the *Times* standard. Although the dissenter below suggested that Gelstein's admission that he did not know whether the bribery charge was true raised a triable issue on malice, there is a critical difference between not knowing whether something is true and being highly aware that it is probably false. Only the latter establishes reckless disregard in a defamation action. Moreover, as the motion court correctly observed, plaintiff's mere characterization of Gelstein's informants as "disgruntled" is insufficient to raise a triable issue. Although plaintiff criticizes defendant for not producing affidavits from the informants—arguing that "it has never been factually established that Gelstein had any source"—it was plaintiff's burden to raise a factual issue on malice, and he did not seek to depose the employees either. In sum, this record is insufficient to raise a triable issue of fact under the *Times* standard of malice.

Similarly, there is insufficient evidence of malice under the common-law definition. A jury could undoubtedly find that, at the time

Gelstein discussed his bribery suspicions with Kohler, Gelstein harbored ill will toward Liberman. In this context, however, spite or ill will refers not to defendant's general feelings about plaintiff, but to the speaker's motivation for making the defamatory statements, [ ]. If the defendant's statements were made to further the interest protected by the privilege, it matters not that defendant also despised plaintiff. Thus, a triable issue is raised only if a jury could reasonably conclude that "malice was the one and only cause for the publication" [ ].

Plaintiff has not sustained that burden. Significantly, Gelstein did not make a public announcement of his suspicions—from which an inference could be drawn that his motive was to defame Liberman—but relayed them to a colleague who was in a position to investigate. As noted, the conversation was within the common interest of Gelstein and Kohler, and there is nothing in this record from which a reasonable jury could find that Gelstein was not seeking to advance that common interest.

Thus, the courts below properly concluded that defendant's conversation with Kohler was qualifiedly privileged, and plaintiff failed to raise a fact issue on malice.

Accordingly, the order of the Appellate Division should be affirmed, with costs.

■ SIMONS, ACTING C.J., and TITONE, HANCOCK and BELLACOSA, JJ., concur with KAYE, J.

[JUDGE SMITH dissented in part and would have reinstated the second cause of action. He thought the record indicated that plaintiff might be able to prove either kind of malice and thus overcome the privilege.]

NOTES AND QUESTIONS

1.   Why does this situation not deserve an absolute privilege? Why does it deserve a qualified privilege? What if defendant had told his suspicions to a tenant who was not on the board? To a social friend in a nearby building who has a friend on the police force?

2.   Consider the introductory note to Restatement section 592A, stating that a qualified privilege is based on the view "that it is essential that true information be given whenever it is reasonably necessary for the protection of one's own interests, the interests of third persons or certain interests of the public." Would that formulation apply to the tenant in *Liberman*?

3.   *Employer references.* One important area for qualified privilege protects responses from employers or former employers to inquiries from prospective employers about how an employee performed on the job. See Erickson v. Marsh & McLennan Co., Inc., 569 A.2d 793 (N.J.1990), using three criteria to determine that a qualified privilege was appropriate: "the appropriateness of the occasion on which the defamatory information is

published, the legitimacy of the interest thereby sought to be protected or promoted, and the pertinence of the receipt of that information by the recipient."

The immediate concern is to encourage this exchange of information without opening the door to dishonest attacks on the employee. Traditionally, most states have accorded a qualified privilege based on the "common interest" of the inquirer and the responder—a protection that may not apply when the former employer volunteers information. See Coclin v. Lane Press, Inc., 620 N.Y.S.2d 41 (App.Div.1994), finding a qualified privilege when an employer sent information on an employee to an outsider. The court quoted an earlier decision of the court of appeals:

> A communication made bona fide upon any subject matter in which the party communicating has an interest, or in reference to which he has a duty, is privileged if made to a person having a corresponding interest or duty, although it contained criminating matter which, without this privilege, would be slanderous and actionable, and this though the duty be not a legal one, but only a moral or social duty of imperfect obligation.

Employers assert that without an absolute privilege, they will be less inclined to respond to such inquiries or to state only the dates of employment. Initially, one might have thought that this terse reply itself might carry implied defamation. Today, however, it is such a common technique that it does not carry pejorative meaning. Rather, the concern is that the flow of information has been retarded by employer fears of lawsuits or vengeance.

Is this a problem? Should it be handled by changing the qualified privilege to an absolute privilege? By creating a duty to respond when asked about a former employee's record? Note that if the former employer writes a dishonest report that praises the worker as a way of easing the worker's departure that may come back to haunt the employer. Is there a duty to disclose an observed potential for violence in a former worker? Recall *Randi W.*, p. 141 supra. The issue of making a partial disclosure that may be a misleading half-truth is discussed in the context of deceit in Chapter XVI.

Some statutes may prevent employers from informing prospective employers about disciplinary actions taken against the worker—including true statements. See the discussion of the Illinois statute in Delloma v. Consolidation Coal Co., 996 F.2d 168 (7th Cir.1993). What might motivate this type of legislation?

4. *Credit reports.* Most states agree that a qualified privilege protects credit reporting services. E.g., Weir v. Equifax Services, Inc., 620 N.Y.S.2d 675 (App.Div.1994); Stationers Corp. v. Dun & Bradstreet, Inc., 398 P.2d 785 (Cal.1965). The common law in this area has, however, been largely replaced by the federal Fair Credit Reporting Act, 15 U.S.C. § 1681 et seq., granting subjects of credit reports certain protections. See, e.g., Guimond v. Trans Union Credit Information Co., 45 F.3d 1329 (9th Cir.1995); Henson v. CSC Credit Services, 29 F.3d 280 (7th Cir.1994).

5. Efforts to invoke a qualified privilege for general news reporting of matters important to the community have largely failed. Consider a California statute that might be thought to provide such protection: Civil Code section 47(c) provides a privilege for "a communication, without malice to a person interested therein, (1) by one who is also interested, or (2) by one who stands in such a relation to the person interested as to afford a reasonable ground for supposing the motive for the communication innocent, or (3) who is requested by the person interested to give the information."

Although some lower courts had applied this section to media reports of events of public interest in the community, that view was rejected in Brown v. Kelly Broadcasting Co., 771 P.2d 406 (Cal.1989). A consumer affairs segment of a daily television news show incorrectly attributed poor workmanship to plaintiff contractor. The court concluded that the legislature had not intended this section to apply to such media reports and that to find such coverage would mean that it "would apply to virtually every defamatory communication. Presumably, the news media generally publish and broadcast only matters that the media believe are of public interest, and the media defendant in every defamation action would therefore argue that the communication was a matter of public interest." Such a privilege would swallow the basic rule. (The court also noted that qualified privileges had developed during a period when strict liability was the rule in libel cases. Since, as we soon discuss, that is no longer the case, the court saw less need for extending them today.)

6. *Abuse.* After a situation warranting a qualified privilege is found, the next question is whether the privilege has been "abused." The criterion for abuse under common law was malice—which meant, as the court indicates, spite or ill will toward the plaintiff. This might be shown by evidence about the relationship, and sometimes might be inferred from defendant's behavior in making the statement to those who had no interest in learning it or not believing what was said. Recall the *Liberman* court's statement that defendant "did not make public announcement of his suspicions—from which an inference might be drawn that his motive was to defame Liberman," rather than to accomplish what he was seeking to accomplish.

7. The arrival of constitutional law has confused the question of abuse under common law. As the court notes, "actual malice" has now taken on the meaning of "knowledge that [the statement] was false or . . . reckless disregard of whether it was false or not." Although we will consider this phrase at length, beginning at p. 1062 infra, it is already clear that "actual" (or "constitutional" or "*N.Y Times*") malice focuses on the defendant's attitude toward the truth of the statement—not defendant's attitude toward the person attacked in the statement.

In light of the emergence of the constitutional standards, courts have adopted various stances. Some have adhered to the idea that abuse is shown by the defendant's ill will or spite toward the plaintiff. Others, such as New York in *Liberman*, and Maine in *Staples,* note 1, p. 1003 supra, have concluded that a plaintiff can overcome a qualified privilege by showing either type of malice. Still others, including New Jersey in *Erickson*, note 3, supra, have decided that to show abuse the plaintiff must establish "actual malice" in the constitutional sense. Although the intricacies of "actual malice" will be addressed later, it is important to realize here that the focus in "abuse" cases appears to be shifting from the defendant's attitude toward the plaintiff to defendant's attitude toward the truth.

8. *Fair comment.* Although most common law privileges primarily benefit nonmedia individuals, one is of special use to the media—fair comment.

Apparently this privilege entered English law in 1808 in Carr v. Hood, 1 Camp. 355, 170 Eng.Rep. 983. The defendant was charged with ridiculing the plaintiff author's talent so severely that sales of his book were discouraged and his reputation was destroyed. The plaintiff's attorney conceded that his client had exposed himself to literary criticism by making the book public, but insisted that the criticism should be "fair and liberal" and seek to enlighten the public about the book rather than to injure the author. The judge noted that ridicule may be an appropriate tool of criticism, but that criticism unrelated to the author as such would not be privileged. Any "attempt against free and liberal criticism" should be resisted "at the threshold." The result was a rule that criticism, regardless of its merit, was privileged if it was made honestly, with honesty being measured by the accuracy of the critic's descriptive observations. If a critic describing a literary, musical, or artistic endeavor gave the "facts" accurately and fairly, the critic's honest conclusions would be privileged as "fair comment."

American law recognized this privilege, and as long as it was applied in cases of literary and artistic criticism it caused little confusion. Classic cases discussing the privilege are Triggs v. Sun Printing & Publishing Ass'n, 71 N.E. 739 (N.Y.1904), Adolf Philipp Co. v. New Yorker Staats-Zeitung, 150 N.Y.S. 1044 (App.Div.1914), and Cherry v. Des Moines Leader, 86 N.W. 323 (Iowa 1901).

But at the end of the nineteenth century, cases arose in which the privilege of fair comment was claimed with regard to other matters of public interest, including the conduct of politicians. The privilege claimed would permit citizens to criticize and argue about the conduct of their officials, and these cases presented the problem of distinguishing between facts and opinion. In literary criticism the application of the privilege could depend upon the accuracy of the "facts" because they were usually readily apparent—in the book, on the stage, or in the restaurant. When dealing with politics, however, the "facts" were often elusive. This new problem created a judicial split.

In Post Publishing Co. v. Hallam, 59 F. 530 (6th Cir.1893), Judge Taft ruled that in order for criticism of officials to be privileged, it must be based upon true underlying facts. The newspaper asserted that it should be judged under the accepted rule that a former master responding to a request for information about a former servant would be privileged if the master stated some "facts" about the servant honestly but mistakenly. Judge Taft refused to apply this rule because in the servant case only the prospective master learned of the defamation, while here the entire public would hear of it. He continued:

> The existence and extent of privilege in communications are determined by balancing the needs and good of society against the right of an individual to enjoy a good reputation when he has done nothing which ought to injure it. The privilege should always cease where the sacrifice of the individual right becomes so great that the public good to be derived from it is outweighed. . . . But, if the privilege is to extend to cases like that at bar, then a man who offers himself as a candidate must submit uncomplainingly to the loss of his reputation, not with a single person or a small class of persons, but with every member of the public, whenever an untrue charge of disgraceful conduct is made against him, if only his accuser honestly believes the charge upon reasonable ground. We think that not only is such a sacrifice not required of everyone who consents to become a candidate for office, but that to sanction such a doctrine would do the public more harm than good.

> We are aware that public officers and candidates for public office are often corrupt, when it is impossible to make legal proof thereof, and of course it would be well if the public could be given to know, in such a case, what lies hidden by concealment and perjury from judicial investigation. But the danger that honorable and worthy men may be driven from politics and public service by allowing too great latitude in attacks upon their characters outweighs any benefit that might occasionally accrue to the public from charges of corruption that are true in fact, but are incapable of legal proof. The freedom of the press is not in danger from the enforcement of the rule we uphold. No one reading the newspaper of the present day can be impressed with the idea that statements of fact concerning public men, and charges against them, are unduly guarded or restricted; and yet the rule complained of is the law in many of the states of the Union and in England.

The privilege became more narrow as those courts following the *Hallam* view came to treat questions of motive—why the politician or official acted as he or she did—as "facts" that had to be true in order for subsequent comment to be privileged.

A contrasting position was taken in Coleman v. MacLennan, 98 P. 281 (Kan.1908), in which the court noted that "men of unimpeachable character from all political parties continually present themselves as candidates in sufficient numbers to fill the public offices and manage the public institutions" even though Kansas had long held that facts relating to matters of public interest are themselves privileged if they are honestly believed to be true; and, if the facts are privileged even if wrong, the comments based upon those facts are also privileged if they are honestly believed. *Coleman* adhered to the state's rejection of the *Hallam* distinction between fact and comment or opinion.

The fair comment privilege has become intertwined with constitutional developments that we discuss at p. 1061 infra.

Still another qualified privilege—fair and accurate report—is addressed in the next case.

Medico v. Time, Inc.

United States Court of Appeals, Third Circuit.
643 F.2d 134, cert. denied, 454 U.S. 836, 102 S.Ct. 139, 70 L.Ed.2d 116 (1981).

■ Before ADAMS, GARTH and SLOVITER, CIRCUIT JUDGES.

■ ADAMS, CIRCUIT JUDGE.

This appeal from a summary judgment in favor of the defendant presents an important question concerning the law of defamation. We must review the district court's determination that a news magazine enjoys a privilege, under the common law of Pennsylvania, to publish a summary of FBI documents identifying the plaintiff as a member of an organized crime "family." We affirm.

I.

In its March 6, 1978 issue, Time magazine published an article describing suspected criminal activities of then-Congressman Daniel J. Flood.

. . .

As an example of suspected misconduct, the Time article listed the following:

> Among the matters under scrutiny: Ties between Flood and Pennsylvania Rackets Boss Russell Bufalino. The suspected link: the Wilkes-Barre firm of Medico Industries, controlled by President Philip Medico and his brothers. The FBI discovered more than a decade ago that Flood steered Government business to the Medicos and traveled often on their company jet. Investigators say Bufalino frequently visited the Medico offices; agents tape-recorded Bufalino's description of Philip as a capo (chief) in his Mafia family. [Testimony by a former Flood aide] has sparked new investigative interest in the Flood-Medico-Bufalino triangle.

. . .

In January 1980, Time again moved for summary judgment based on the substantial truth of its publication. Time resubmitted the two FBI documents it had proffered to support its initial motion, supplemented with affidavits of two FBI agents. . . .

On this occasion the district court granted Time's motion for summary judgment, but not on the basis of the truth defense. . . .

After declining to hold for Time on the truth theory, the district court considered whether the Time article fell within the common law privilege accorded the press to report on official proceedings. The judge seemed troubled because Pennsylvania courts apparently had so far extended the privilege only to reports of proceedings open to the public, whereas Time had summarized reports which the FBI had kept secret and whose release to Time evidently had been unauthorized. But after an exhaustive analysis of Pennsylvania precedents, the court concluded that Pennsylvania courts, if presented with the question, would find summaries of non-public government reports within the privilege. The district judge then ascertained that the Time article represented a fair and accurate account of the FBI documents. Accordingly he held that the publication was privileged, and awarded summary judgment in favor of Time.

On appeal, Medico argues that the district court incorrectly determined that Time's publication was privileged under Pennsylvania law. Time counters that the district judge accurately construed the applicable state law on privilege, and contends further that the defense of truth applies and affords an alternate basis for affirming the district court. . . .

II.

The fair report privilege on which the district court relied developed as an exception to the common law rule that the republisher of a defamation was subject to liability similar to that risked by the original defamer. . . . The common law regime created special problems for the press. When a newspaper published a newsworthy account of one person's defamation of another, it was, by virtue of the republication rule, charged with publication of the underlying defamation. Thus, although the common law exonerated one who published a defamation as long as the statement was true, a newspaper in these circumstances traditionally could avail itself of the truth defense only if the truth of the underlying defamation were established.

To ameliorate the chilling effect on the reporting of newsworthy events occasioned by the combined effect of the republication rule and the truth defense, the law has long recognized a privilege for the press[9] to publish accounts of official proceedings or reports even when these contain defamatory statements. So long as the account presents a fair and accurate summary of the proceedings, the law abandons the assumption that the reporter adopts the defamatory remarks as his own.[11] The privilege thus permits a newspaper or other press defendant to relieve itself of liability without establishing the truth of the substance of the statement reported. The fair report privilege has a

---

[9]   There is some dispute whether the privilege is available to non-press defendants. The *Restatement* [covers] "any person who makes an oral, written or printed report" on an official proceeding should have access to the defense. . . .

[11]   Analytically, the fair report privilege is similar to the truth defense. Both make verity the issue, although requiring that a report be fair and accurate may allow the press a somewhat greater margin of error than requiring that its report be true. . . .

somewhat more limited scope than the truth defense, however. So long as the speaker establishes the truth of his statement, he is shielded from liability, regardless of his motives; the fair report privilege, on the other hand, can be defeated in most jurisdictions by a showing that the publisher acted for the sole purpose of harming the person defamed.

Unlike many states, Pennsylvania has never codified the fair report privilege. . . . We believe it appropriate to accept as the law of Pennsylvania the version of the fair report privilege embodied in the current *Restatement.*

Section 611 of Restatement (Second) provides:

Report of Official Proceeding or Public Meeting

The publication of defamatory matter concerning another in a report of an official action or proceeding or of a meeting open to the public that deals with a matter of public concern is privileged if the report is accurate and complete or a fair abridgement of the occurrence reported.

With respect to the present controversy, the basic inquiry is whether Time's summary of FBI documents concerning Philip Medico is "a report of an official action or proceeding."[17]

The district court examined and rejected the possibility that the FBI reports in question are not "official" because they are not generally available to the public. Medico does not challenge this reasoning on appeal, and we perceive no need to rehearse arguments that the district court has already canvassed. Medico contends before this Court that the FBI documents should not be deemed "official" because they express only tentative and preliminary conclusions that the FBI has never adopted as accurate. He points out that the title page to the FBI report on La Cosa Nostra bears the following legend: "This document contains neither recommendations nor conclusions of the FBI. It is the property of the FBI and is loaned to your agency; it and its contents are not to be distributed outside your agency."

Neither the text of Section 611 nor the accompanying comments dispose of the issue Medico raises. Section 611 itself speaks only of "official" action or proceedings, without elaborating on when a statement is made in an official capacity. [The court notes that two comments to that section point in different ways on whether the report is within the scope of the privilege. The case law also failed to resolve the issue. The closest case protected a news report that summarized a defamatory civil complaint that had formed the basis for a temporary

---

[17] Although the Time article did not explicitly credit the FBI Report on La Cosa Nostra or the FBI personal file card on Medico as the Magazine's sources of information, the statements about Medico, taken in context, may reasonably be understood to inform the reader that the story was based on FBI materials. . . .

restraining order. Hanish v. Westinghouse Broadcasting Co., 487 F.Supp. 397 (E.D.Pa.1980)].[21]

Assuming the court in *Hanish* correctly predicted Pennsylvania law, we think that decision supports application of the Section 611 privilege to the present case. FBI files seem at least as "official" as the pleadings in civil cases. Although civil complaints are instituted, for the most part, by private parties, the FBI documents concerning Medico were compiled by government agents acting in their official capacities. Moreover, the danger that a civil litigant will willfully insert defamatory assertions in his complaint generally would appear at least as great as the risk that a criminal investigatory agency will knowingly include false or malicious statements in its files. If Pennsylvania courts would grant the privilege to newspaper accounts of civil complaints on which a court has acted ex parte, we think it likely that they would grant the privilege to republication of defamatory items from the FBI materials on Medico.

III.

Three policies underlie the fair report privilege, and an examination of them provides further guidance for our decision today. Initially, an agency theory was offered to rationalize a privilege of fair report: one who reports what happens in a public, official proceeding acts as an agent for persons who had a right to attend, and informs them of what they might have seen for themselves. The agency rationale, however, cannot explain application of the privilege to proceedings or reports not open to public inspection.

A theory of public supervision also informs the fair report privilege. Justice Holmes, applying the privilege to accounts of courtroom proceedings, gave the classic formulation of this principle:

> [The privilege is justified by] the security which publicity gives for the proper administration of justice. . . . It is desirable that the trial of causes should take place under the public eye, not because the controversies of one citizen with another are of public concern, but because it is of the highest moment that those who administer justice should always act under the sense of public responsibility and that every citizen should be able to satisfy himself with his own eyes as to the mode in which a public duty is performed.

Cowley v. Pulsifer, 137 Mass. 392, 394 (1884). The supervisory rationale has been invoked in the context of executive action as well.

We believe the public supervision rationale applies to the present case. As public inspection of courtroom proceedings may further the just administration of the laws, public scrutiny of the proceedings and records of criminal investigatory agencies may often have the equally

---

[21] Considerable controversy surrounds republication of defamations contained in pleadings on which no official action has been taken. . . .

salutary effect of fostering among those who enforce the laws "the sense of public responsibility." For example, exposing the content of agency records may, in some cases, help ensure impartial enforcement of the laws.

[We need not] decide, however, whether the supervisory rationale is relevant to every republication of documents found in FBI files. For any general supervisory concern with respect to the FBI is heightened in the present case by the public's interest in examining the conduct of individuals it elects to positions of civic trust. Elected officials derive their authority from, and are answerable to, the public. If the citizenry is effectively and responsibly to discharge its obligation to monitor the conduct of its government, there can be no penalty for exposing to general view the possible wrongdoing of government officials. Because the alleged defamation of Medico occurred in an article analyzing the conduct of former Congressman Flood, we believe it implicates this aspect of the supervisory rationale. Moreover, even though Time's publication arguably may have tarnished the reputation of Medico, a private individual, as well as that of Representative Flood, the public has a lively interest in considering the relationships formed by elected officials.

A third rationale for the fair report privilege rests, somewhat tautologically, on the public's interest in learning of important matters.[27] While "mere curiosity in the private affairs of others is of insufficient importance to warrant granting the privilege," the present case does not involve such idle probing. The Time article discussed two topics of legitimate public interest. First, for the same reasons that support the supervisory rationale, examination of the affairs of elected officials is obviously a matter of legitimate public concern. In addition, as various federal courts have already recognized, there is significant public importance to reports on investigations of organized criminal activities, whether or not these implicate government officials.

Because the Time article focused on organized crime, we think the informational rationale is especially relevant. The district court in the case at hand commented on the difficulty of gathering information pertaining to organized criminal activity: "Due to the size, sophistication and secrecy of most organized criminal endeavors, only the largest and most sophisticated intelligence-gathering entities can monitor them effectively. In practice this task has been taken up primarily by the Justice Department of the federal government and, in particular, by the FBI." Indeed, the documents that Time summarized had been compiled by a government agency. In light of the difficulty in obtaining independent corroboration of FBI information, the press may

---

[27] ...

Some jurisdictions rely on the informational rationale to extend the privilege to accounts of the proceedings of public meetings of private, nongovernmental organizations, as long as the meeting deals with matters of concern to the public.

often have to rely on materials the government acquires if it is to report on organized crime at all. We believe Time's publication of FBI materials mentioning Medico served a legitimate public interest in learning about organized crime.

Care must be taken, of course, to ensure that the supervisory and informational rationales not expand into justifications for reporting any defamatory matter maintained in any government file. Personal interests in privacy are not to be taken lightly, and are not to be overborne by mere invocation of a public need to know.[30] But we believe that the public interest is involved when, as here, information compiled by an enforcement agency may help shed light on a Congressman's alleged criminal or unethical behavior.

. . .

V.

Once the libel defendant establishes the existence of a "privileged occasion" for the publication of a defamatory article, the burden returns to the plaintiff to prove that the defendant abused its privilege. [ ] Pennsylvania recognizes two forms of "abuse": the account of an official report may fail to be fair and accurate,[40] as when the publisher overly embellishes the account, [ ] or the defamatory material may be published for the sole purpose of causing harm to the person defamed. [ ] Inasmuch as Medico does not allege that Time published its article for the purpose of harming him, the sole issue with respect to abuse of privilege is whether the district court erred in concluding that there was no genuine question whether Time's publication fairly and accurately summarized the FBI materials concerning Medico.

We agree with the district court that nothing in the record suggests that the Time article unfairly or inaccurately reported on the FBI materials. . . .

. . . Time has accurately portrayed the FBI records as indicating that Medico has been identified as part of the Bufalino crime family.

. . .

The judgment of the district court granting Time's motion for summary judgment will be affirmed.

NOTES AND QUESTIONS

1. The court discusses three theories that have been asserted to support the fair report privilege. Which one appears most persuasive? Will one generally support a broader protective net than the others?

---

[30] The excesses of the McCarthy era, for example, prompted some commentators to point out the reputational injury the republication of official defamation can cause, and to advocate restricting the fair report privilege. [ ]

[40] Placement on the plaintiff of the burden of demonstrating that a privileged report was not fair and accurate traditionally distinguished the fair report privilege from the truth defense, in which defendant bore the burden of proving truth. . . .

2. *Coverage of the privilege.* The court understands state law not to require actual reliance on the official report or proceeding. Do the three theories differ on this? The Second Circuit disagreed with the *Medico* court on its reading of Pennsylvania law on the ground that the privilege could not be "divorced from its underlying policy of encouraging the broad dissemination of public records." Protecting a defendant who did not actually rely on an official report "does nothing to encourage the initial reporting of public records and proceedings. Certainly, § 611 should not be interpreted to protect unattributed, defamatory statements supported only after-the-fact through a frantic search of official records." Bufalino v. Associated Press, 692 F.2d 266 (2d Cir.1982).

3. In a footnote, the *Bufalino* court observed that "even where the reporter has actually relied on official records, the privilege can be lost through failure to make proper attribution." Would the *Medico* court agree? What do the theories have to say on this point?

4. The coverage varies greatly state by state. In some states, for example, as suggested in *Medico,* the privilege extends to the fact of an arrest and the charges but not to details of the alleged crime that an arresting officer provides.

Medico is rejected in Wynn v. Smith, 16 P.3d 424 (Nev.2001), involving an internal Scotland Yard report that was not accessible to the public: "Allowing the privilege to cover confidential reports would bring to light information that the government had no intention of releasing, and which could be used as a powerful tool for injury." The court thought that permitting the privilege here would "undermine the basis of the privilege itself."

5. In Rouch v. Enquirer & News of Battle Creek, Michigan, 398 N.W.2d 245 (Mich.1986), the newspaper reported oral statements made by the police in connection with the plaintiff's arrest for rape. After plaintiff, who was never charged, was exonerated, he sued the newspaper. The paper's reliance on the state's privilege for fair and accurate report of "any public and official proceeding" was rejected on the ground that an "arrest that amounts to no more than an apprehension" was not a "proceeding." The statute was not intended to create a "government action," "arrest record," or "public records" privilege.

The legislature reacted by amending the privilege statute, Mich.Comp.Laws § 600.2911, which extended protection to "a fair and true report of matters of public record, a public and official proceeding, or of a governmental notice, announcement, written or recorded report or record generally available to the public, or act or action of a public body." Should such a statute extend to open meetings of a local political party or the state bar association?

6. *Codification.* As noted in *Medico* and in the discussion of several cases in these notes, many states have adopted legislation to codify this privilege. One typical version is New York's Civil Rights Law section 74, which provides:

> A civil action cannot be maintained against [any defendant] for the publication of a fair and true report of any judicial proceeding, legislative proceeding or other official proceeding. . . .

> This section does not apply to a libel contained in any other matter added by any person concerned in the publication; or in the report of anything said or done at the time and place of such a proceeding which was not a part thereof.

Notice that this does not protect reports of public meetings held by nongovernmental organizations, such as medical associations or publicly held corporations, or remarks made by political, sports, or entertainment figures outside of official proceedings. Should it? Does it protect a report of remarks made by an audience member at a meeting of a city council?

7. *Losing the privilege.* Although the defendant must establish the conditions showing that the privilege applies to the situation in the first instance, the plaintiff may be able to establish that the privilege has been lost.

Courts have not required precise use of legal language in testing the accuracy of these reports. How accurate must the report be? See Holy Spirit Ass'n for the Unification of World Christianity v. New York Times Co., 399 N.E.2d 1185 (N.Y.1979):

> [N]ewspaper accounts of legislative or other official proceedings must be accorded some degree of liberality. When determining whether an article constitutes a "fair and true" report, the language used herein should not be dissected and analyzed with a lexicographer's precision. This is so because a newspaper article is, by its very nature, a condensed report of events which must, of necessity, reflect to some degree the subjective view of its author. Nor should a fair report which is not misleading, composed and phrased in good faith under the exigencies of a publication deadline, be thereafter parsed and dissected on the basis of precise denotative meanings which may literally, although not contextually, be ascribed to the words used.

Most courts adopt a view similar to that in the discussion earlier of "substantial truth." Thus, in Koniak v. Heritage Newspapers, Inc., 499 N.W.2d 346 (Mich.App.1993), the defendant reported that plaintiff had been charged with assaulting someone 30 to 55 times when in fact he had been charged with eight assaults. The court observed that "whether plaintiff assaulted his stepdaughter once, eight times or thirty times would have little effect on the reader."

Questions of fairness usually involve the condensation or summary of a report. Comment f to section 611 states that "although it is unnecessary that the report be exhaustive and complete, it is necessary that nothing be omitted or misplaced in such a manner as to convey an erroneous impression to those who hear or read it, as for example a report of the discreditable testimony in a judicial proceeding and a failure to publish the exculpatory evidence." If the incriminating evidence in a trial emerged on the first day of the trial and the exculpatory evidence on the second day, is the newspaper obligated to report the second day's events in order to be protected for the first day's events? What if a newspaper reports that defendant was convicted yesterday after a trial—but reversal of the conviction a year later is not reported?

Courts disagree over whether the question of fairness and accuracy are for the court in all cases or whether the jury should resolve close questions. The states are split over whether "malice" in the sense of spite or ill will deprives the defendant of the privilege. Why might the defendant's desire to harm the subject of the article be relevant here?

What if the defendant "knows" or "believes" that the report being published is false? In Rosenberg v. Helinski, 616 A.2d 866 (Md.1992), the court stated:

> Under the modern view, the privilege exists even if the reporter of defamatory statements made in court believes or knows them to be false; the privilege is abused only if the report fails the test of fairness and accuracy.

Is this consistent with the rationale for the privilege? This privilege is extensively discussed in D. Elder, The Fair Report Privilege (1988).

c.   RETRACTION AND OTHER DEFENSES

In this section we consider a variety of defenses that do not go directly to the merits of the claim. Some, if successful, are complete defenses to the libel claim. Others, even if successful, are at most partial defenses.

Burnett v. National Enquirer, Inc.

Court of Appeal of California, 1983.
144 Cal.App.3d 991, 193 Cal.Rptr. 206.

■ Before ROTH, P.J., GATES and BEACH, JJ.

■ ROTH, P.J.

On March 2, 1976, appellant caused to appear in its weekly publication, the National Enquirer, a "gossip column" headlined "Carol Burnett and Henry K. in Row," wherein a four-sentence item specified in its entirety that:

> In a Washington restaurant, a boisterous Carol Burnett had a loud argument with another diner, Henry Kissinger. Then she traipsed around the place offering everyone a bite of her dessert. But Carol really raised eyebrows when she accidentally knocked a glass of wine over one diner and started giggling instead of apologizing. The guy wasn't amused and "accidentally" spilled a glass of water over Carol's dress.

Maintaining the item was entirely false and libelous, an attorney for Ms. Burnett, by telegram the same day and by letter one week later, demanded its correction or retraction "within the time and in the manner provided for in Section 48(a) of the Civil Code of the State of California," failing which suit would be brought by his client [respondent herein], a well known actress, comedienne and show-business personality.

In response to the demand, appellant on April 6, 1976, published the following retraction, again in the National Enquirer's gossip column:

> An item in this column on March 2 erroneously reported that Carol Burnett had an argument with Henry Kissinger at a Washington restaurant and became boisterous, disturbing other guests. We understand these events did not occur and we are sorry for any embarrassment our report may have caused Miss Burnett.

On April 8, 1976, respondent, dissatisfied with this effort in mitigation, filed her complaint for libel in the Los Angeles Superior Court. [A jury trial resulted in an award of $300,000 compensatory damages and $1.3 million punitive damages. The trial judge reduced these to $50,000 and $750,000 respectively.] This appeal followed.

. . . [T]he principal issues here are whether the National Enquirer is excluded from the protection afforded by Civil Code section 48a, and whether the damage award and penalty specified in the judgment can stand.

[The court quoted the entire section 48a at this point. The major provisions are that in any action for libel against a "newspaper" or slander in a broadcast, the "plaintiff shall recover no more than special damages unless a correction be demanded and be not published or broadcast, as hereinafter provided." The demand must be written, specifying the "statements claimed to be libelous and demanding that the same be corrected. Said notice and demand must be served within 20 days after knowledge of the publication or broadcast of the statements claimed to be libelous." If the correction be demanded and "be not published or broadcast in substantially as conspicuous a manner in said newspaper or on said broadcasting station as were the statements claimed to be libelous, in a regular issue thereof published or broadcast within three weeks after such service, plaintiff . . . may recover general, special, and exemplary damages." The statute defines each type of damages in conventional terms. Exemplary (punitive) damages were recoverable only if plaintiff proved "actual malice" and then only at the discretion of the trier of fact. "Actual malice" was defined as "that state of mind arising from hatred or ill will toward the plaintiff; provided, however, that such a state of mind occasioned by a good faith belief on the part of the defendant in the truth of the libelous publication or broadcast shall not constitute actual malice."]

. . .

The National Enquirer is a publication whose masthead claims the "Largest Circulation Of Any Paper in America." It is a member of the American Newspaper Publishers Association. It subscribes to the Reuters News Service. Its staff call themselves newspaper reporters. It describes its business as "newspaper" in its filings with the Los Angeles County Assessor and in its applications for insurance. A State Revenue Department has ruled it qualifies as a newspaper and is thus exempt from sales and use tax. The United States Department of Labor describes it as "belonging to establishments primarily engaged in publishing or printing and publishing newspapers."

By the same token the National Enquirer is designated as a magazine or periodical in eight mass media directories and upon the request and written representation of its general manager in 1960 that "In view of the feature content and general appearance [of the publication], which differ markedly from those of a newspaper . . . ," its classification as a newspaper was changed to that of magazine by the Audit Bureau of Circulation. It does not subscribe to the Associated Press or United Press International news services. According to statements by its Senior Editor it is not a newspaper and its content is based on a consistent formula of "how to" stories, celebrity or medical or personal improvement stories, gossip items and TV column items, together with material from certain other subjects. It provides little or no current coverage of subjects such as politics, sports or crime, does not attribute content to wire services, and in general does not make reference to time. Normal "lead time" for its subject matter is one to three weeks. Its owner allowed it did not generate stories "day to day as a daily newspaper does."

[In addressing the issue whether the trial court erred in denying the Enquirer the benefits of section 48a, the court treated the question as one of law. The trial court had concluded that the statute's major rationale was to protect publications that are "not generally in a position adequately to guard against the publication of material which is untrue." This led the trial court to focus on the element of time and to conclude that the Enquirer's mode of operation did not come within the rationale for the protection.]

Appellant . . . maintains that the special classification approved in Werner v. Southern Cal. etc. Newspapers, [216 P.2d 825 (Cal.1950)], depended on the public's interest in the "free dissemination of news," without reference to questions of timeliness; [and that several cases constituted an "unbroken line" of authority consistent with that view. The court explored several earlier cases, including a few that applied the statute to magazines without ever addressing the question.]

[The court concluded that the question was still open.] We nevertheless are of the opinion that what emerges as the better view from the authorities discussed is the proposition that the protection afforded by the statute is limited "to those who engage in the immediate dissemination of news on the ground that the Legislature could reasonably conclude that such enterprises . . . cannot always check their sources for accuracy and their stories for inadvertent publication errors. . . . [ ]"

Seen in this light, the essential question is not then whether any publication is properly denominated a magazine or by some other designation, but simply whether it ought to be characterized as a newspaper or not within the contemplation of § 48a, a question which must be answered, as the trial court supposed, in terms which justify an expanded barrier against damages for libel in those instances, and those only, where the constraints of time as a function of the requirements associated with production of the publication dictate the result.

[The trial court, using the proper rationale,] correctly determined the National Enquirer should not be deemed a newspaper for the purposes of the instant litigation.

[The court then upheld liability but reduced the punitive damages to $150,000. A dissenter would have affirmed the full award.]

NOTES AND QUESTIONS

1.   Since special damages are hard to prove, p. 1021 supra, what is the justification behind the retraction statute? Why do retraction statutes focus on damages rather than liability?

2.   Under the court's analysis, what result if the defamation appears in a regular edition of a weekly news magazine? In the weekly news section of a Sunday "newspaper"? In a special edition of a weekly news magazine that is produced in response to a major news event?

3.   If the court had found the Enquirer eligible to invoke the statute, it would then have had to face the question of whether the defendant had in fact published a "correction." Could it be argued that the correction was inadequate? (In the damages part of its opinion, the court found the correction "evasive" and "incomplete," and considered this relevant in the award of punitive damages.)

4.   If the correction is adequate, there is the further question whether it was published in substantially as conspicuous a manner as the original story. If the story is published in the same place, as apparently occurred in *Burnett,* there is little problem on this score. What if the correction is published in a regular box on page 2 of the publication that is devoted to corrections, but whose headline "Day's Corrections" is smaller than the headline that accompanied the original story that appeared on page 5? Page 1?

Some retraction statutes state simply that the retraction may be taken into account in measuring damages. Even in states without retraction statutes, it is generally held that an early correction may be relevant at trial to reduce the plaintiff's damages.

5. Some statutes have been interpreted to apply even though the original defamation was intentional. The California statute was so interpreted and upheld in the *Werner* case (cited in *Burnett*), which was later settled.

About half the states have retraction statutes of some sort. A few states have declared such statutes unconstitutional. See Boswell v. Phoenix Newspapers, Inc., 730 P.2d 186 (Ariz.1986)(statute violated state constitutional provision that right of action "to recover damages for injuries shall never be abrogated"), and Madison v. Yunker, 589 P.2d 126 (Mont.1978)(statute violated state constitutional provision that courts be "open to every person, and speedy remedy afforded for every injury to person, property, or character").

6. Injunctions have never been available to prevent personal defamation. See Pound, Equitable Relief against Defamation and Injuries to Personality, 29 Harv.L.Rev. 640 (1916); Sedler, Injunctive Relief and Personal Integrity, 9 St. Louis L.J. 147 (1964).

7. *The libel-proof plaintiff.* Defendant may show that the plaintiff's reputation was already low either because of earlier publications of the charge in question or for other reasons. This might induce the jury to lower its estimate of the damage that defendant's defamation had caused plaintiff.

A few courts have moved beyond this mitigation defense and have begun to dismiss libel cases on the ground that the plaintiff's reputation is already so bad that there is no chance that plaintiff can obtain and keep any damage award.

Judge (later Justice) Scalia expressed great skepticism about the doctrine in Liberty Lobby v. Anderson, 746 F.2d 1563 (D.C.Cir.1984), vacated on other grounds, 477 U.S. 242 (1986). For the majority, he observed that reputation is not monolithic. The law "proceeds upon the optimistic assumption that there is a little good in all of us—or perhaps the pessimistic assumption that no matter how bad someone is, he can always be worse." He offered this analogy: "It is shameful that Benedict Arnold was a traitor; but he was not a shoplifter to boot, and one should not have been able to make that charge while knowing its falsity with impunity."

See also Simmons Ford, Inc. v. Consumers Union, 516 F.Supp. 742 (S.D.N.Y.1981), in which a plaintiff with a previously good reputation was found to have been rendered libel-proof by the unchallenged or true parts of the same article that was the basis for the defamation: "Given the abysmal performance and safety evaluations [of plaintiff's electrically powered car] detailed in the article, plaintiffs could not expect to gain more than nominal damages based on the addition to the article of the misstatement relating to federal safety standards." This issue is also addressed in Jewell v. NYP Holdings, Inc., 23 F.Supp.2d 348 (S.D.N.Y.1998)(refusing to apply the *Simmons Ford* approach to articles discussing the past of a former Olympic guard in Atlanta who was suspected in a bombing).

Can the *Simmons Ford* situation, which is often referred to as involving "incremental harm," be justified on the same basis as the "libel-proof plaintiff" doctrine? See Note, Libel-Proof Plaintiffs and the Question of Injury, 71 Tex.L.Rev. 401 (1992).

    8. *Internet service provider immunity.* As indicated earlier, disseminators of a defamatory work are not subject to common law strict liability; rather, they can only be held liable if they know or have reason to know of the defamatory statement. See p. 1021 supra. Although the common law might have developed a similar protection in cases involving computer bulletin boards, a congressional enactment immunizes Internet service providers for defamation distributed through their facilities.

Carafano v. Metrosplash.com, Inc.

United States Court of Appeals, Ninth Circuit, 2003.
339 F.3d 1119.

■ Before THOMAS, PAEZ, CIRCUIT JUDGES, and REED, DISTRICT JUDGE.

■ THOMAS, CIRCUIT JUDGE.

    This is a case involving a cruel and sadistic identity theft. In this appeal, we consider to what extent a computer match making service may be legally responsible for false content in a dating profile provided by someone posing as another person. Under the circumstances presented by this case, we conclude that the service is statutorily immune pursuant to 47 U.S.C. § 230(c)(1).

I

    Matchmaker.com is a commercial Internet dating service. For a fee, members of Matchmaker post anonymous profiles and may then view profiles of other members in their area, contacting them via electronic mail sent through the Matchmaker server. A typical profile contains one or more pictures of the subject, descriptive information such as age, appearance and interests, and answers to a variety of questions designed to evoke the subject's personality and reason for joining the service.

    Members are required to complete a detailed questionnaire containing both multiple-choice and essay questions. In the initial portion of the questionnaire, members select answers to more than fifty questions from menus providing between four and nineteen options. Some of the potential multiple choice answers are innocuous; some are sexually suggestive. In the subsequent essay section, participants answer up to eighteen additional questions, including "anything that the questionnaire didn't cover." Matchmaker policies prohibit members from posting last names, addresses, phone numbers or e-mail addresses within a profile. Matchmaker reviews photos for impropriety before posting them but does not review the profiles themselves, relying instead upon participants to adhere to the service guidelines.

    On October 23, 1999, an unknown person using a computer in Berlin posted a "trial" personal profile of Christianne Carafano in the

Los Angeles section of Matchmaker. (New members were permitted to post "trial" profiles for a few weeks without paying.) The posting was without the knowledge, consent or permission of Carafano. The profile was listed under the identifier "Chase529."

Carafano is a popular actress. Under the stage name of Chase Masterson, Carafano has appeared in numerous films and television shows, such as "Star Trek: Deep Space Nine," and "General Hospital." Pictures of the actress are widely available on the Internet, and the false Matchmaker profile "Chase529" contained several of these pictures. Along with fairly innocuous responses to questions about interests and appearance, the person posting the profile selected "Playboy/Playgirl" for "main source of current events" and "looking for a one-night stand" for "why did you call." In addition, the open-ended essay responses indicated that "Chase529" was looking for a "hard and dominant" man with "a strong sexual appetite" and that she "liked sort of being controlled by a man, in and out of bed." The profile text did not include a last name for "Chase" or indicate Carafano's real name, but it listed two of her movies (and, as mentioned, included pictures of the actress).

In response to a question about the "part of the LA area" in which she lived, the profile provided Carafano's home address. The profile included a contact e-mail address, cmla2000@yahoo.com, which, when contacted, produced an automatic e-mail reply stating, "You think you are the right one? Proof it!!" [sic], and providing Carafano's home address and telephone number.

Unaware of the improper posting, Carafano soon began to receive messages responding to the profile. Although she was traveling at the time, she checked her voicemail on October 31 and heard two sexually explicit messages. When she returned to her home on November 4, she found a highly threatening and sexually explicit fax that also threatened her son. Alarmed, she contacted the police the following day. As a result of the profile, she also received numerous phone calls, voicemail messages, written correspondence, and e-mail from fans through her professional e-mail account. Several men expressed concern that she had given out her address and phone number (but simultaneously expressed an interest in meeting her). Carafano felt unsafe in her home, and she and her son stayed in hotels or away from Los Angeles for several months.

Sometime around Saturday, November 6, Siouxzan Perry, who handled Carafano's professional website and much of her e-mail correspondence, first learned of the false profile through a message from "Jeff." Perry exchanged e-mails with Jeff, visited the Matchmaker site, and relayed information about the profile to Carafano. Acting on Carafano's instructions, Perry contacted Matchmaker and demanded that the profile be removed immediately. The Matchmaker employee indicated that she could not remove the profile immediately because

Perry herself had not posted it, but the company blocked the profile from public view on Monday morning, November 8. At 4:00 AM the following morning, Matchmaker deleted the profile.

Carafano filed a complaint in California state court against Matchmaker and its corporate successors, alleging [defamation and other claims]. The defendants removed the case to federal district court. The district court granted the defendants' motion for summary judgment in a published opinion. Carafano v. Metrosplash.com, Inc., 207 F.Supp.2d 1055 (C.D.Cal.2002). The court rejected Matchmaker's argument for immunity under 47 U.S.C. § 230(c)(1) after finding that the company provided part of the profile content. Id. at 1067–68. However, the court rejected Carafano's [claims on other grounds, affording constitutional protection to defendant on the defamation claim].

Carafano timely appealed. America Online, eBay, and two coalitions of online businesses intervened to challenge the district court's construction of § 230(c)(1). Several privacy advocacy groups and two organizations representing entertainers intervened in support of Carafano.

II

The dispositive question in this appeal is whether Carafano's claims are barred by 47 U.S.C. § 230(c)(1), which states that "[n]o provider or user of an interactive computer service shall be treated as the publisher or speaker of any information provided by another information content provider." Through this provision, Congress granted most Internet services immunity from liability for publishing false or defamatory material so long as the information was provided by another party. As a result, Internet publishers are treated differently from corresponding publishers in print, television and radio. See Batzel v. Smith, 333 F.3d 1018, 1026–27 (9th Cir.2003).

Congress enacted this provision as part of the Communications Decency Act of 1996 for two basic policy reasons: to promote the free exchange of information and ideas over the Internet and to encourage voluntary monitoring for offensive or obscene material. [ ] (recounting the legislative history and purposes of this section). Congress incorporated these ideas into the text of § 230 itself, expressly noting that "interactive computer services have flourished, to the benefit of all Americans, with a minimum of government regulation," and that "[i]ncreasingly Americans are relying on interactive media for a variety of political, educational, cultural, and entertainment services." 47 U.S.C. § 230(a)(4), (5). Congress declared it the "policy of the United States" to "promote the continued development of the Internet and other interactive computer services," "to preserve the vibrant and competitive free market that presently exists for the Internet and other interactive computer services," and to "remove disincentives for the development and utilization of blocking and filtering technologies." 47 U.S.C. § 230(b)(1), (2), (4).

In light of these concerns, reviewing courts have treated § 230(c) immunity as quite robust, adopting a relatively expansive definition of "interactive computer service" and a relatively restrictive definition of "information content provider." Under the statutory scheme, an "interactive computer service" qualifies for immunity so long as it does not also function as an "information content provider" for the portion of the statement or publication at issue.

We recently considered whether § 230(c) provided immunity to the operator of an electronic newsletter who selected and published an allegedly defamatory e-mail over the Internet. [*Batzel*]. We held that the online newsletter qualified as an "interactive computer service" under the statutory definition and that the selection for publication and editing of an e-mail did not constitute partial "creation or development" of that information within the definition of "information content provider." Although the case was ultimately remanded for determination of whether the original author intended to "provide" his e-mail for publication, [ ], the *Batzel* decision joined the consensus developing across other courts of appeals that § 230(c) provides broad immunity for publishing content provided primarily by third parties. [The court discussed Zeran v. America Online, Inc., 129 F.3d 327 (4th Cir.1997), cert. denied, 524 U.S. 937 (1998), at length and two other federal appellate cases.]

The fact that some of the content was formulated in response to Matchmaker's questionnaire does not alter this conclusion. Doubtless, the questionnaire facilitated the expression of information by individual users. However, the selection of the content was left exclusively to the user. The actual profile "information" consisted of the particular options chosen and the additional essay answers provided. Matchmaker was not responsible, even in part, for associating certain multiple choice responses with a set of physical characteristics, a group of essay answers, and a photograph. Matchmaker cannot be considered an "information content provider" under the statute because no profile has any content until a user actively creates it.

As such, Matchmaker's role is similar to that of the customer rating system at issue in Gentry v. eBay, Inc., [121 Cal.Rptr.2d 703 (App.2002)]. In that case, the plaintiffs alleged that eBay "was an information content provider in that it was responsible for the creation of information, or development of information, for the online auction it provided through the Internet." [ ] Specifically, the plaintiffs noted that eBay created a highly structured Feedback Forum, which categorized each response as a "Positive Feedback," a "Negative Feedback," or a "Neutral Feedback." [ ] In addition, eBay provided a color coded star symbol next to the user name of a seller who had achieved certain levels of "Positive Feedback" and offered a separate "Power Sellers" endorsement based on sales volume and Positive Feedback ratings. [ ] The court concluded that § 230 barred the claims:

> Appellants' negligence claim is based on the assertion that the information is false or misleading because it has been manipulated by the individual defendants or other co-conspiring parties. Based on these allegations, enforcing appellants' negligence claim would place liability on eBay for simply compiling false and/or misleading content created by the individual defendants and other coconspirators. We do not see such activities transforming eBay into an information content provider with respect to the representations targeted by appellants as it did not create or develop the underlying misinformation.

[ ] Similarly, the fact that Matchmaker classifies user characteristics into discrete categories and collects responses to specific essay questions does not transform Matchmaker into a "developer" of the "underlying misinformation."

We also note that, as with eBay, Matchmaker's decision to structure the information provided by users allows the company to offer additional features, such as "matching" profiles with similar characteristics or highly structured searches based on combinations of multiple choice questions. Without standardized, easily encoded answers, Matchmaker might not be able to offer these services and certainly not to the same degree. Arguably, this promotes the expressed Congressional policy "to promote the continued development of the Internet and other interactive computer services." 47 U.S.C. § 230(b)(1).

Carafano responds that Matchmaker contributes much more structure and content than eBay by asking 62 detailed questions and providing a menu of "pre-prepared responses." However, this is a distinction of degree rather than of kind, and Matchmaker still lacks responsibility for the "underlying misinformation."

Further, even assuming Matchmaker could be considered an information content provider, the statute precludes treatment as a publisher or speaker for "*any* information provided by *another* information content provider." 47 U.S.C. § 230(c)(1) (emphasis added). The statute would still bar Carafano's claims unless Matchmaker created or developed the particular information at issue. As the *Gentry* court noted,

> [T]he fact appellants allege eBay is an information content provider is irrelevant if eBay did not itself create or develop the content for which appellants seek to hold it liable. It is not inconsistent for eBay to be an interactive service provider and also an information content provider; the categories are not mutually exclusive. The critical issue is whether eBay acted as

an information content provider with respect to the information that appellants claim is false or misleading.

[ ]

In this case, critical information about Carafano's home address, movie credits, and the e-mail address that revealed her phone number were transmitted unaltered to profile viewers. Similarly, the profile directly reproduced the most sexually suggestive comments in the essay section, none of which bore more than a tenuous relationship to the actual questions asked. Thus Matchmaker did not play a significant role in creating, developing or "transforming" the relevant information. Thus, despite the serious and utterly deplorable consequences that occurred in this case, we conclude that Congress intended that service providers such as Matchmaker be afforded immunity from suit. Thus, we affirm the judgment of the district court, albeit on other grounds.

AFFIRMED.

NOTES AND QUESTIONS

1.   In *Zeran v. America Online, Inc.*, cited above, a few days after the bombing of the federal building in Oklahoma City, an AOL bulletin board carried what purported to be an advertisement for "Naughty Oklahoma T-Shirts" with offensive slogans. Interested buyers were given plaintiff's home phone number. Plaintiff, who had no connection with the product, was bombarded with scurrilous and threatening letters. The court relied heavily on section 230(c) in holding that defendant was immune from suit. According to the court, "lawsuits seeking to hold a service provider liable for its exercise of a publisher's traditional editorial functions—such as deciding whether to publish, withdraw, postpone or alter content—are barred." Does statutory immunity under the facts in *Carafano* follow as a matter of course from *Zeran*?

2.   Is the court persuasive in relying on the *Gentry* case for its reading of section 230(c)?

3.   What changes in the facts might have led the court to conclude that defendant fell outside the intent of section 230(c)?

4.   Five years following *Carafano*, the Ninth Circuit explained that the case should not be read to suggest that a dating website could never be liable under any circumstances. In Fair Hous. Council of San Fernando Valley v. Roommates.Com, LLC, 521 F.3d 1157 (9th Cir.2008), plaintiff claimed that defendant's online questions and customer profiles fostered illegal housing discrimination. Revisiting Carafano, the court averred that:

> We correctly held [in *Carafano*] that the website was immune, but incorrectly suggested that it could never be held liable because "no profile has any content until a user actively creates it." . . . [E]ven if the data are supplied by third parties, a website operator may still contribute to the content's illegality and thus be liable as a developer.[ ] Providing immunity every time a website uses data initially obtained from third parties

would eviscerate the exception to section 230 for "develop[ing]" unlawful content "in whole or in part." 47 U.S.C. § 230(f)(3).

5. Defendant, an alternative health proponent critical of conventional medicine, posted to newsgroups on the Internet an e-mail message she had received from a third person referring to one of the plaintiffs in vituperative terms:

> Dr. Barrett is arrogant, bizarre, closed-minded; [*sic*] emotionally disturbed, professionally incompetent, intellectually dishonest, a dishonest journalist, sleazy, unethical, a quack, a thug, a bully, a Nazi, a hired gun for vested interests, the leader of a subversive organization, and engaged in criminal activity (conspiracy, extortion, filing a false police report, and other unspecified acts).

Barrett brought suit against the alternative health proponent. The court held that the section 230(c) immunity applied to distributors of Internet communications and that the defendants qualified as "users" within the meaning of the Act. Thus, the only person subject to liability for the defamatory communication was its third-person originator. Barrett v. Rosenthal, 146 P.3d 510 (Cal. 2006).

6. Plaintiff's former boyfriend posted on a public Yahoo website nude photographs of plaintiff taken without her knowledge and soliciting sexual intercourse. Plaintiff was inundated in her office with emails, phone calls, and personal visits, all in the expectation of sex. Based on Yahoo policy, she applied multiple times to have the offending material removed, but Yahoo basically ignored her requests for months (until she filed suit), save for one occasion when a Yahoo employee contacted plaintiff, asked her to fax her prior communications, and promised to undertake removal. The employee didn't follow up on his promise. Plaintiff's tort claim was for negligent undertaking, rather than defamation, based on defendant's promise to remove the content. The court concluded that this undertaking claim involves precisely what publishers do and therefore could not be pursued because of the Communications Decency Act (CDA). But the court held that plaintiff's promissory estoppel claim—a derivative of contract law—was not barred by the CDA. Barnes v. Yahoo!, Inc., 570 F.3d 1096 (9th Cir.2009). See also, F.T.C. v. Accusearch, Inc., 570 F.3d 1187 (10th Cir.2009), in which defendant website operator—a seller of personal data, including phone records—was denied immunity under the CDA, as an information content provider. A concurring judge made the point that all section 230 says is that an ISP should not be treated as a publisher, not that it is immune from tort suits where being a publisher is not an element of the case.

Claims of "revenge porn," as in *Barnes*, frequently generate right of privacy claims, which are discussed at p. 1157 infra.

7. For coverage of a suit by two female Yale law students against AutoAdmit, a law school discussion board, and Google, based on reputation-maligning postings—again, raising issues of CDA immunity—see David Margolick, Slimed Online, Conde Nast Portfolio, March 2009, at 80.

B. CONSTITUTIONAL LIMITATIONS ON DEFAMATION

The First Amendment provides:

> Congress shall make no law respecting an establishment of religion, or prohibiting the free exercise thereof; or abridging the freedom of speech, or of the press; or the right of the people peaceably to assemble, and to petition the Government for a redress of grievances.

In Near v. Minnesota, 283 U.S. 697 (1931), in the process of invalidating what it saw as a prior restraint on the speech of the press, the majority observed:

> But it is recognized that punishment for the abuse of the liberty accorded to the press is essential to the protection of the public, and that the common-law rules that subject the libeler to responsibility for the public offense, as well as for the private injury, are not abolished by the protection extended in our Constitution.

In the late 1930s a syndicated columnist asserted that Congressman Sweeney was blocking the appointment of a federal judge because the prospective appointee was Jewish. Sweeney sued several newspapers, with varying results. Compare Sweeney v. Patterson, 128 F.2d 457 (App.D.C.1942)(holding the column privileged), with Sweeney v. Schenectady Union Publishing Co., 122 F.2d 288 (2d Cir.1941), aff'd by an equally divided court, 316 U.S. 642 (1942)(lower court had found no privilege). This Supreme Court split vote suggested the presence of a difficult constitutional question.

In Chaplinsky v. New Hampshire, 315 U.S. 568 (1942), however, libelous words, along with "fighting words" and obscenity, were said to be among the "well-defined and narrowly limited classes of speech, the prevention and punishment of which have never been thought to raise any Constitutional problem." The proposition that libelous utterances were not "within the area of constitutionally protected speech" was relied upon by Justice Frankfurter, writing for a 5–4 majority in *Beauharnais v. Illinois,* p. 1020 supra, to sustain a state criminal libel law.

This sequence set the stage for the following case from Alabama, a state that had long followed the narrow *Hallam* view, p. 1039 supra, for criticism of public officials.

1.   PUBLIC OFFICIALS

New York Times Co. v. Sullivan

Supreme Court of the United States, 1964.
376 U.S. 254, 84 S.Ct. 710, 11 L.Ed.2d 686.

■ MR. JUSTICE BRENNAN delivered the opinion of the Court.

[This action was based on a full-page advertisement in the New York Times on behalf of several individuals and groups protesting a "wave of terror" against blacks involved in nonviolent demonstrations in the South. Plaintiff, one of three elected commissioners of Montgomery, the capital of Alabama, was in charge of the police department. When he demanded a retraction, as state law required, the Times instead responded that it failed to see how he was defamed, even though it did subsequently publish a retraction at the request of the Alabama governor, whose complaint was similar to Sullivan's. Plaintiff then filed suit against the Times and four clergymen whose names appeared— although they denied having authorized this—in the ad. Plaintiff alleged that the third and the sixth paragraphs of the advertisement libelled him:

> "In Montgomery, Alabama, after students sang 'My Country, 'Tis of Thee' on the State Capitol steps, their leaders were expelled from school, and truckloads of police armed with shotguns and tear-gas ringed the Alabama State College Campus. When the entire student body protested to state authorities by refusing to re-register, their dining hall was padlocked in an attempt to starve them into submission."

> . . .

> "Again and again the Southern violators have answered Dr. King's peaceful protests with intimidation and violence. They have bombed his home almost killing his wife and child. They have assaulted his person. They have arrested him seven times—for 'speeding,' 'loitering' and similar 'offenses.' And now they have charged him with 'perjury'—a *felony* under which they could imprison him for *ten years*. . . ."

Plaintiff claimed that he was libelled in the third paragraph by the reference to the police, since his responsibilities included supervision of the Montgomery police. He asserted that the paragraph could be read as charging the police with ringing the campus and seeking to starve the students by padlocking the dining hall. As to the sixth paragraph, he contended that the word "they" referred to his department since arrests are usually made by the police and the paragraph could be read as accusing him of committing the acts charged. Several witnesses testified that they read the statements as referring to plaintiff in his capacity as commissioner.

The defendants admitted several inaccuracies in these two paragraphs: the students sang The Star Spangled Banner, not My Country, 'Tis of Thee; nine students were expelled, not for leading the demonstration, but for demanding service at a lunch counter in the county courthouse; the dining hall was never padlocked; police at no time ringed the campus though they were deployed nearby in large numbers; they were not called to the campus in connection with the demonstration; Dr. King had been arrested only four times; and officers disputed his account of the alleged assault. Plaintiff proved that he had not been commissioner when three of the four arrests occurred and that he had nothing to do with procuring the perjury indictment.

The trial judge charged that the statements were libel per se, that the jury should decide whether they were made "of and concerning" the plaintiff and, if so, general damages were to be presumed. Although noting that punitive damages required more than carelessness, he refused to charge that they required a finding of actual intent to harm or "gross negligence and recklessness." He also refused to order the jury to separate its award of general and punitive damages. The jury returned a verdict for $500,000—the full amount demanded. The Alabama Supreme Court affirmed, holding that malice could be found in several aspects of the Times's conduct.]

I.

We may dispose at the outset of two grounds asserted to insulate the judgment of the Alabama courts from constitutional scrutiny. The first is the proposition relied on by the State Supreme Court—that "The Fourteenth Amendment is directed against State action and not private action." That proposition has no application to this case. Although this is a civil lawsuit between private parties, the Alabama courts have applied a state rule of law which petitioners claim to impose invalid restrictions on their constitutional freedoms of speech and press. It matters not that that law has been applied in a civil action and that it is common law only, though supplemented by statute. [ ] The test is not the form in which state power has been applied but, whatever the form, whether such power has in fact been exercised. [ ]

The second contention is that the constitutional guarantees of freedom of speech and of the press are inapplicable here, at least so far as the Times is concerned, because the allegedly libelous statements were published as part of a paid, "commercial" advertisement. [The argument was rejected.]

II.

Under Alabama law as applied in this case, a publication is "libelous per se" if the words "tend to injure a person . . . in his reputation" or to "bring [him] into public contempt"; the trial court stated that the standard was met if the words are such as to "injure him in his public office, or impute misconduct to him in his office, or want of official integrity, or want of fidelity to a public trust. . . ." The jury must find that the words were published "of and concerning" the plaintiff, but where the plaintiff is a public official his place in the governmental hierarchy is sufficient evidence to support a finding that his reputation has been affected by statements that reflect upon the agency of which he is in charge. Once "libel per se" has been established, the defendant has no defense as to stated facts unless he can persuade the jury that they were true in all their particulars. [ ] His privilege of "fair comment" for expressions of opinion depends on the truth of the facts upon which the comment is based. [ ] Unless he can discharge the burden of proving truth, general damages are presumed, and may be awarded without proof of pecuniary injury. A showing of actual malice is apparently a prerequisite to recovery of punitive damages, and the defendant may in any event forestall a punitive award by a retraction meeting the statutory requirements. Good motives and belief in truth do not negate an inference of malice, but are relevant only in mitigation of punitive damages if the jury chooses to accord them weight. [ ]

The question before us is whether this rule of liability, as applied to an action brought by a public official against critics of his official conduct, abridges the freedom of speech and of the press that is guaranteed by the First and Fourteenth Amendments.

Respondent relies heavily, as did the Alabama courts, on statements of this Court to the effect that the Constitution does not protect libelous publications. Those statements do not foreclose our inquiry here. None of the cases sustained the use of libel laws to impose sanctions upon expression critical of the official conduct of public officials. . . . In deciding the question now, we are compelled by neither precedent nor policy to give any more weight to the epithet "libel" than we have to other "mere labels" of state law. NAACP v. Button, 371 U.S. 415, 429 (1963). Like insurrection, contempt, advocacy of unlawful acts, breach of the peace, obscenity, solicitation of legal business, and the various other formulae for the repression of expression that have been challenged in this Court, libel can claim no talismanic immunity from constitutional limitations. It must be measured by standards that satisfy the First Amendment.

The general proposition that freedom of expression upon public questions is secured by the First Amendment has long been settled by our decisions. . . . Mr. Justice Brandeis, in his concurring opinion in Whitney v. California, 274 U.S. 357, 375–376 (1927), gave the principle its classic formulation:

> Those who won our independence believed . . . that public discussion is a political duty; and that this should be a fundamental principle of the American government. . . . Believing in the power of reason as applied through public discussion, they eschewed silence coerced by law—the argument of force in its worst form. Recognizing the occasional

tyrannies of governing majorities, they amended the Constitution so that free speech and assembly should be guaranteed.

Thus we consider this case against the background of a profound national commitment to the principle that debate on public issues should be uninhibited, robust, and wide-open, and that it may well include vehement, caustic, and sometimes unpleasantly sharp attacks on government and public officials. See Terminiello v. Chicago, 337 U.S. 1, 4 (1949); De Jonge v. Oregon, 299 U.S. 353, 365 (1937). The present advertisement, as an expression of grievance and protest on one of the major public issues of our time, would seem clearly to qualify for the constitutional protection. The question is whether it forfeits that protection by the falsity of some of its factual statements and by its alleged defamation of respondent.

Authoritative interpretations of the First Amendment guarantees have consistently refused to recognize an exception for any test of truth—whether administered by judges, juries, or administrative officials—and especially one that puts the burden of proving truth on the speaker. Cf. Speiser v. Randall, 357 U.S. 513, 525–526 (1958). The constitutional protection does not turn upon "the truth, popularity, or social utility of the ideas and beliefs which are offered." NAACP v. Button, 371 U.S. 415, 445 (1963). As Madison said, "Some degree of abuse is inseparable from the proper use of every thing; and in no instance is this more true than in that of the press." 4 Elliot's Debates on the Federal Constitution (1876), p. 571. In Cantwell v. Connecticut, 310 U.S. 296, 310 (1940), the Court declared:

> In the realm of religious faith, and in that of political belief, sharp differences arise. In both fields the tenets of one man may seem the rankest error to his neighbor. To persuade others to his own point of view, the pleader, as we know, at times, resorts to exaggeration, to vilification of men who have been, or are, prominent in church or state, and even to false statement. But the people of this nation have ordained in the light of history, that, in spite of the probability of excesses and abuses, these liberties are, in the long view, essential to enlightened opinion and right conduct on the part of the citizens of a democracy.

That erroneous statement is inevitable in free debate, and that it must be protected if the freedoms of expression are to have the "breathing space" that they "need . . . to survive," NAACP v. Button, 371 U.S. 415, 433 (1963), was also recognized by the Court of Appeals for the District of Columbia Circuit in Sweeney v. Patterson, 128 F.2d 457, 458 (D.C.Cir.1942). Judge Edgerton spoke for a unanimous court which affirmed the dismissal of a Congressman's libel suit based upon a newspaper article charging him with anti-Semitism in opposing a judicial appointment. He said:

Cases which impose liability for erroneous reports of the political conduct of officials reflect the obsolete doctrine that the governed must not criticize their governors. . . . The interest of the public here outweighs the interest of appellant or any other individual. The protection of the public requires not merely discussion, but information. Political conduct and views which some respectable people approve, and others condemn, are constantly imputed to Congressmen. Errors of fact, particularly in regard to a man's mental states and processes, are inevitable. . . . Whatever is added to the field of libel is taken from the field of free debate.[13]

Injury to official reputation affords no more warrant for repressing speech that would otherwise be free than does factual error. Where judicial officers are involved, this Court has held that concern for the dignity and reputation of the courts does not justify the punishment as criminal contempt of criticism of the judge or his decision. Bridges v. California, 314 U.S. 252 (1941). This is true even though the utterance contains "half-truths" and "misinformation." Pennekamp v. Florida, 328 U.S. 331, 342, 343, n. 5, 345 (1946). . . . Criticism of their official conduct does not lose its constitutional protection merely because it is effective criticism and hence diminishes their official reputations.

If neither factual error nor defamatory content suffices to remove the constitutional shield from criticism of official conduct, the combination of the two elements is no less inadequate. This is the lesson to be drawn from the great controversy over the Sedition Act of 1798, 1 Stat. § 596, which first crystallized a national awareness of the central meaning of the First Amendment. . . .

Although the Sedition Act was never tested in this Court,[16] the attack upon its validity has carried the day in the court of history. Fines levied in its prosecution were repaid by Act of Congress on the ground that it was unconstitutional. . . . The invalidity of the Act has also been assumed by Justices of this Court. [ ] These views reflect a broad consensus that the Act, because of the restraint it imposed upon criticism of government and public officials, was inconsistent with the First Amendment.

There is no force in respondent's argument that the constitutional limitations implicit in the history of the Sedition Act apply only to Congress and not to the States. It is true that the First Amendment

---

[13] See also Mill, On Liberty (Oxford: Blackwell, 1947), at 47:

" * * * [T]o argue sophistically, to suppress facts or arguments, to misstate the elements of the case, or misrepresent the opposite opinion * * * all this, even to the most aggravated degree, is so continually done in perfect good faith, by persons who are not considered, and in many other respects may not deserve to be considered, ignorant or incompetent, that it is rarely possible, on adequate grounds, conscientiously to stamp the misrepresentation as morally culpable; and still less could law presume to interfere with this kind of controversial misconduct."

[16] The Act expired by its terms in 1801.

was originally addressed only to action by the Federal Government, and that Jefferson, for one, while denying the power of Congress "to controul the freedom of the press," recognized such a power in the States. [ ] But this distinction was eliminated with the adoption of the Fourteenth Amendment and the application to the States of the First Amendment's restrictions. [ ]

What a State may not constitutionally bring about by means of a criminal statute is likewise beyond the reach of its civil law of libel. The fear of damage awards under a rule such as that invoked by the Alabama courts here may be markedly more inhibiting than the fear of prosecution under a criminal statute. [ ] Alabama, for example, has a criminal libel law which subjects to prosecution "any person who speaks, writes, or prints of and concerning another any accusation falsely and maliciously importing the commission by such person of a felony, or any other indictable offense involving moral turpitude," and which allows as punishment upon conviction a fine not exceeding $500 and a prison sentence of six months. [ ] Presumably a person charged with violation of this statute enjoys ordinary criminal-law safeguards such as the requirements of an indictment and of proof beyond a reasonable doubt. These safeguards are not available to the defendant in a civil action. . . . And since there is no double-jeopardy limitation applicable to civil lawsuits, this is not the only judgment that may be awarded against petitioners for the same publication.[18] Whether or not a newspaper can survive a succession of such judgments, the pall of fear and timidity imposed upon those who would give voice to public criticism is an atmosphere in which the First Amendment freedoms cannot survive. Plainly the Alabama law of civil libel is "a form of regulation that creates hazards to protected freedoms markedly greater than those that attend reliance upon the criminal law." Bantam Books, Inc. v. Sullivan, 372 U.S. 58, 70 (1963).

The state rule of law is not saved by its allowance of the defense of truth. . . . Allowance of the defense of truth, with the burden of proving it on the defendant, does not mean that only false speech will be deterred.[19] Even courts accepting this defense as an adequate safeguard have recognized the difficulties of adducing legal proofs that the alleged libel was true in all its factual particulars. See, e.g., Post Publishing Co. v. Hallam, 59 F. 530, 540 (C.A.6th Cir.1893); see also Noel, Defamation of Public Officers and Candidates, 49 Col.L.Rev. 875, 892 (1949). Under such a rule, would-be critics of official conduct may be deterred from voicing their criticism, even though it is believed to be true and even

---

[18] The Times states that four other libel suits based on the advertisement have been filed against it by others who have served as Montgomery City Commissioners and by the Governor of Alabama; that another $500,000 verdict has been awarded in the only one of these cases that has yet gone to trial; and that the damages sought in the other three total $2,000,000.

[19] Even a false statement may be deemed to make a valuable contribution to public debate, since it brings about "the clearer perception and livelier impression of truth, produced by its collision with error." Mill, On Liberty (Oxford: Blackwell, 1947), at 15; see also Milton, Areopagitica, in Prose Works (Yale, 1959), Vol. II, at 561.

though it is in fact true, because of doubt whether it can be proved in court or fear of the expense of having to do so. They tend to make only statements which "steer far wider of the unlawful zone." [*Speiser v. Randall*]. The rule thus dampens the vigor and limits the variety of public debate. It is inconsistent with the First and Fourteenth Amendments.

The constitutional guarantees require, we think, a federal rule that prohibits a public official from recovering damages for a defamatory falsehood relating to his official conduct unless he proves that the statement was made with "actual malice"—that is, with knowledge that it was false or with reckless disregard of whether it was false or not. An oft-cited statement of a like rule, which has been adopted by a number of state courts, is found in the Kansas case of Coleman v. MacLennan, 98 P. 281 (Kan.1908). . . .

Such a privilege for criticism of official conduct is appropriately analogous to the protection accorded a public official when *he* is sued for libel by a private citizen. In Barr v. Matteo, 360 U.S. 564, 575 (1959), this Court held the utterance of a federal official to be absolutely privileged if made "within the outer perimeter" of his duties. The States accord the same immunity to statements of their highest officers, although some differentiate their lesser officials and qualify the privilege they enjoy. But all hold that all officials are protected unless actual malice can be proved. The reason for the official privilege is said to be that the threat of damage suits would otherwise "inhibit the fearless, vigorous, and effective administration of policies of government" and "dampen the ardor of all but the most resolute, or the most irresponsible, in the unflinching discharge of their duties." [*Barr v. Matteo*]. Analogous considerations support the privilege for the citizen-critic of government. It is as much his duty to criticize as it is the official's duty to administer. . . . As Madison said, [ ], "the censorial power is in the people over the Government, and not in the Government over the people." It would give public servants an unjustified preference over the public they serve, if critics of official conduct did not have a fair equivalent of the immunity granted to the officials themselves.

We conclude that such a privilege is required by the First and Fourteenth Amendments.

III.

We hold today that the Constitution delimits a State's power to award damages for libel in actions brought by public officials against critics of their official conduct. Since this is such an action, the rule requiring proof of actual malice is applicable. While Alabama law apparently requires proof of actual malice for an award of punitive damages, where general damages are concerned malice is "presumed." Such a presumption is inconsistent with the federal rule. . . . Since the trial judge did not instruct the jury to differentiate between general and punitive damages, it may be that the verdict was wholly an award of one or the other. But it is impossible to know, in view of the general verdict returned. Because of this uncertainty, the judgment must be reversed and the case remanded.

Since respondent may seek a new trial, we deem that considerations of effective judicial administration require us to review the evidence in the present record to determine whether it could constitutionally support a judgment for respondent. . . .

Applying these standards, we consider that the proof presented to show actual malice lacks the convincing clarity which the constitutional standard demands, and hence that it would not constitutionally sustain the judgment for respondent under the proper rule of law. The case of the individual petitioners requires little discussion. Even assuming that they could constitutionally be found to have authorized the use of their names on the advertisement, there was no evidence whatever that they were aware of any erroneous statements or were in any way reckless in that regard. The judgment against them is thus without constitutional support.

As to the Times, we similarly conclude that the facts do not support a finding of actual malice. [The testimony of the Secretary of the Times that he believed the advertisement to be "substantially correct" was "at least a reasonable [belief], and there was no evidence to impeach the witness' good faith in holding it." Nor was the later retraction for the governor evidence of actual malice toward plaintiff. Leaving open the question of whether failure to retract "may ever constitute such evidence," it could not suffice here because the letter showed reasonable doubt whether the ad referred to plaintiff at all, and also because the letter was not a final refusal. The Court responded to the claim that the Times published the ad without first checking news stories in its own files, by noting that the "mere presence" of such stories "does not, of course, establish that the Times' knew 'the advertisement was false', since the state of mind required for actual malice would have to be brought home to the persons in the Times' organization having responsibility for the publication of the advertisement." Those persons relied on the "good reputation of many of those whose names were listed as sponsors of the advertisement, and upon the letter from A. Philip Randolph, known to them as a responsible individual, certifying that the use of the names was authorized."]

We also think the evidence was constitutionally defective in another respect: it was incapable of supporting the jury's finding that the allegedly libelous statements were made "of and concerning" respondent. Respondent relies on the words of the advertisement and the testimony of six witnesses to establish a connection between it and himself. . . . There was no reference to respondent in the advertisement, either by name or official position. A number of the allegedly libelous statements—the charges that the dining hall was padlocked and that Dr. King's home was bombed, his person assaulted, and a perjury prosecution instituted against him—did not even concern the police; despite the ingenuity of the arguments which would attach this significance to the word "They," it is plain that these statements could not reasonably be read as accusing respondent of personal involvement in the acts in question. The statements upon which respondent principally relies as referring to him are the two allegations that did concern the police or police functions: that "truckloads of police * * * ringed the Alabama State College Campus" after the demonstration on the State Capitol steps, and that Dr. King had been "arrested * * * seven times." These statements were false only in that the police had been "deployed near" the campus but had not actually "ringed" it and had not gone there in connection with the State Capitol demonstration, and in that Dr. King had been arrested only four times. The ruling that these discrepancies between what was true and what was asserted were sufficient to injure respondent's reputation may itself raise constitutional problems, but we need not consider them here. Although the statements may be taken as referring to the police, they did not on their face make even an oblique reference to respondent as an individual. Support for the asserted reference must, therefore, be sought in the testimony of respondent's witnesses. But none of them suggested any basis for the belief that respondent himself was attacked in the advertisement beyond the bare fact that he was in overall charge of the Police Department and thus bore official responsibility for police conduct; to the extent that some of the witnesses thought respondent to have been charged with ordering or approving the conduct or otherwise being personally involved in it, they based this notion not on any statements in the advertisement, and not on any evidence that he had in fact been so involved, but solely on the unsupported assumption that, because of his official position, he must have been. This reliance on the bare fact of respondent's official position was made explicit by the Supreme Court of Alabama. . . .

This proposition has disquieting implications for criticism of governmental conduct. For good reason, "no court of last resort in this country has ever held, or even suggested, that prosecutions for libel on government have any place in the American system of jurisprudence." City of Chicago v. Tribune Co., [139 N.E. 86, 88 (Ill.1923)]. The present proposition would sidestep this obstacle by transmuting criticism of government, however impersonal it may seem on its face, into personal criticism, and hence potential libel, of the officials of whom the government is composed. There is no legal alchemy by which a State may thus create the cause of action that would otherwise be denied for a publication which, as respondent himself said of the advertisement, "reflects not only on me but on the other Commissioners and the community." Raising as it does the possibility that a good-faith critic of government will be penalized for his criticism, the proposition relied on by the Alabama courts strikes at the very center of the constitutionally protected area of free expression.[30] We hold that such a proposition may not constitutionally be utilized to establish that an otherwise impersonal attack on governmental operations was a libel of an official responsible for those operations. Since it was relied on exclusively here, and there was no other evidence to connect the statements with respondent, the evidence was constitutionally insufficient to support a finding that the statements referred to respondent.

The judgment of the Supreme Court of Alabama is reversed and the case is remanded to that court for further proceedings not inconsistent with this opinion.

Reversed and remanded.

■ MR. JUSTICE BLACK, with whom MR. JUSTICE DOUGLAS joins, concurring.

I concur in reversing this half-million-dollar judgment against the New York Times Company and the four individual defendants. In reversing the Court holds that "the Constitution delimits a State's power to award damages for libel in actions brought by public officials against critics of their official conduct." I base my vote to reverse on the belief that the First and Fourteenth Amendments not merely "delimit" a State's power to award damages to "public officials against critics of their official conduct" but completely prohibit a State from exercising such a power. The Court goes on to hold that a State can subject such critics to damages if "actual malice" can be proved against them. "Malice," even as defined by the Court, is an elusive, abstract concept, hard to prove and hard to disprove. The requirement that malice be proved provides at best an evanescent protection for the right critically to discuss public affairs and certainly does not measure up to the sturdy safeguard embodied in the First Amendment. Unlike the Court, therefore, I vote to reverse exclusively on the ground that the Times and the individual defendants had an absolute unconditional constitutional right to publish in the Times advertisement their criticisms of the Montgomery agencies and officials. . . .

The half-million-dollar verdict does give dramatic proof, however, that state libel laws threaten the very existence of an American press virile enough to publish unpopular views on public affairs and bold enough to criticize the conduct of public officials. . . . In fact, briefs before us show that in Alabama there are now pending eleven libel suits by local and state officials against the Times seeking $5,600,000 and five such suits against the Columbia Broadcasting System seeking

---

[30] Insofar as the proposition means only that the statements about police conduct libeled respondent by implicitly criticizing his ability to run the Police Department, recovery is also precluded in this case by the doctrine of fair comment. See American Law Institute, Restatement of Torts (1938), § 607. Since the Fourteenth Amendment requires recognition of the conditional privilege for honest misstatements of fact, it follows that a defense of fair comment must be afforded for honest expression of opinion based upon privileged, as well as true, statements of fact. Both defenses are of course defeasible if the public official proves actual malice, as was not done here.

$1,700,000. Moreover, this technique for harassing and punishing a free press—now that it has been shown to be possible—is by no means limited to cases with racial overtones; it can be used in other fields where public feelings may make local as well as out-of-state newspapers easy prey for libel verdict seekers. . . . This record certainly does not indicate that any different verdict would have been rendered here whatever the Court had charged the jury about "malice," "truth," "good motives," "justifiable ends," or any other legal formulas which in theory would protect the press. Nor does the record indicate that any of these legalistic words would have caused the courts below to set aside or to reduce the half-million-dollar verdict in any amount.

. . .

. . . An unconditional right to say what one pleases about public affairs is what I consider to be the minimum guarantee of the First Amendment.[6]

I regret that the Court has stopped short of this holding indispensable to preserve our free press from destruction.

■ MR. JUSTICE GOLDBERG, with whom MR. JUSTICE DOUGLAS joins, concurring in the result.

. . .

In my view, the First and Fourteenth Amendments to the Constitution afford to the citizen and to the press an absolute, unconditional privilege to criticize official conduct despite the harm which may flow from excesses and abuses. . . .

. . .

. . . It may be urged that deliberately and maliciously false statements have no conceivable value as free speech. That argument, however, is not responsive to the real issue presented by this case, which is whether that freedom of speech which all agree is constitutionally protected can be effectively safeguarded by a rule allowing the imposition of liability upon a jury's evaluation of the speaker's state of mind. If individual citizens may be held liable in damages for strong words, which a jury finds false and maliciously motivated, there can be little doubt that public debate and advocacy will be constrained. And if newspapers, publishing advertisements dealing with public issues, thereby risk liability, there can also be little doubt that the ability of minority groups to secure publication of their views on public affairs and to seek support for their causes will be greatly diminished. . . .

. . .

This is not to say that the Constitution protects defamatory statements directed against the private conduct of a public official or

---

[6]   Cf. Meiklejohn, Free Speech and Its Relation to Self-Government (1948).

private citizen. Freedom of press and of speech insures that government will respond to the will of the people and that changes may be obtained by peaceful means. Purely private defamation has little to do with the political ends of a self-governing society. The imposition of liability for private defamation does not abridge the freedom of public speech or any other freedom protected by the First Amendment.[4] . . .

. . .

NOTES AND QUESTIONS

1. What is the problem with strict liability? Would a negligence standard pose the same problems? Would absolute privilege be objectionable? How does the "actual malice" standard appear to differ from the *Hallam* standard, p. 1039 supra? The *Coleman* standard?

Do you consider either of the concurring opinions preferable to the majority approach?

2. Justice Brennan's concern lest speakers have to "steer far wider of the unlawful zone" than legally necessary has been articulated by others as the concern that fear of liability has the potential to "chill" speech. In the cited case of *Speiser v. Randall*, the Court invalidated a procedure under which veterans seeking a California tax exemption bore the burden of proving that they had not advocated the overthrow of the government. Justice Brennan, writing in that case, noted that where speech is close to the line between lawful and unlawful:

> [T]he possibility of mistaken factfinding—inherent in all litigation—will create the danger that the legitimate utterance will be penalized. The man who knows that he must bring forth proof and persuade another of the lawfulness of his conduct necessarily must steer far wider of the unlawful zone than if the state must bear these burdens.

How is this concern relevant to the problems raised by libel law?

3. Which single step seems more likely to prevent the "chilling" of speech: shifting the burden of proving falsity to plaintiffs or introducing "actual malice"? Although the Court might have made only one of these changes, lower courts took the Court's definition of "actual malice" to have subsumed the showing of falsity as well: proof that the statement was made with "knowledge that it was false or with reckless disregard of whether it was false or not." This is discussed further at p. 1077 infra.

4. How can the Court decide that there is insufficient evidence of malice in the record to support a verdict at retrial when the plaintiff, at the earlier trial, did not know of the malice requirement and the need to adduce proof about it?

---

[4] In most cases, as in the case at bar, there will be little difficulty in distinguishing defamatory speech relating to private conduct from that relating to official conduct. I recognize, of course, that there will be a gray area. The difficulties of applying a public-private standard are, however, certainly of a different genre from those attending the differentiation between a malicious and nonmalicious state of mind. . . .

5. Commenting after the *Times* case, Professor Kalven speculated on the case's future:

> The closing question, of course, is whether the treatment of seditious libel as the key concept for development of appropriate constitutional doctrine will prove germinal. It is not easy to predict what the Court will see in the *Times* opinion as the years roll by. It may regard the opinion as covering simply one pocket of cases, those dealing with libel of public officials, and not destructive of the earlier notions that are inconsistent only with the larger reading of the Court's action. But the invitation to follow a dialectic progression from public official to government policy to public policy to matters in the public domain, like art, seems to me to be overwhelming. If the Court accepts the invitation, it will slowly work out for itself the theory of free speech that Alexander Meiklejohn has been offering us for some fifteen years now.

Kalven, The *New York Times* Case: A Note on "The Central Meaning of the First Amendment," 1964 Sup.Ct.Rev. 191, 221. Does his prediction seem sound? Keep it in mind as we proceed. The story of the Supreme Court's deliberation in the *Sullivan* case is told in intriguing detail in A. Lewis, "Make No Law" (1991).

6. The majority in the *New York Times* case did not explicitly reject the concurring approaches. A few months later, in Garrison v. Louisiana, 379 U.S. 64 (1964), the Court, in an opinion by Justice Brennan, extended the *Times* rule to cases of criminal libel and also held that truth must be a defense in cases brought by public officials. The majority explained its refusal to protect deliberate falsity:

> Although honest utterance, even if inaccurate, may further the fruitful exercise of the right of free speech, it does not follow that the lie, knowingly and deliberately published about a public official, should enjoy a like immunity. At the time the First Amendment was adopted, as today, there were those unscrupulous enough and skillful enough to use the deliberate or reckless falsehood as an effective political tool to unseat the public servant or even topple an administration. [ ] That speech is used as a tool for political ends does not automatically bring it under the protective mantle of the Constitution. For the use of the known lie as a tool is at once at odds with the premises of democratic government and with the orderly manner in which economic, social, or political change is to be effected. Calculated falsehood falls into that class of utterances which "are no essential part of any exposition of ideas, and are of such slight social value as a step to truth that any benefit that may be derived from them is clearly outweighed by the social interest in order and morality. . . ." [*Chaplinsky*]. Hence the knowingly false statement and the false statement made with reckless disregard of the truth, do not enjoy constitutional protection.

In an explicit, but not entirely successful, effort to avoid confusion between common law malice and "actual malice," the Court observed that:

> Debate on public issues will not be uninhibited if the speaker must run the risk that it will be proved in court that he spoke out of hatred; even if he did speak out of hatred, utterances honestly believed contribute to the free interchange of ideas and the ascertainment of the truth.

2. PUBLIC FIGURES

Shortly after *New York Times*, the Court considered two cases together: Curtis Publishing Co. v. Butts, and Associated Press v. Walker, 388 U.S. 130 (1967).

In *Butts*, the defendant magazine had accused the plaintiff athletic director of disclosing his game plan to an opposing coach before their game. Although he was on the staff of a state university, Butts was paid by a private alumni organization. In *Walker,* the defendant news service reported that the plaintiff, a former United States Army general who resigned to engage in political activity, had personally led students in an attack on federal marshals who were enforcing a desegregation order at the University of Mississippi.

In both cases, lower courts affirmed substantial jury awards against the defendants and refused to apply the *Times* doctrine on the ground that public officials were not involved. The Supreme Court divided several ways, affirming *Butts,* 5–4, and reversing *Walker,* 9–0. Chief Justice Warren wrote the pivotal opinion in which he concluded that both men were "public figures" and that the standard developed in *New York Times* should apply to "public figures" as well:

> To me, differentiation between "public figures" and "public officials" and adoption of separate standards of proof for each has no basis in law, logic, or First Amendment policy. Increasingly in this country, the distinctions between governmental and private sectors are blurred. Since the depression of the 1930's and World War II there has been a rapid fusion of economic and political power, a merging of science, industry, and government, and a high degree of interaction between the intellectual, governmental, and business worlds. Depression, war, international tensions, national and international markets, and the surging growth of science and technology have precipitated national and international problems that demand national and international solutions. While these trends and events have occasioned a consolidation of governmental power, power has also become much more organized in what we have commonly considered to be the private sector. In many situations, policy determinations which traditionally were channeled through formal political institutions are now originated and

implemented through a complex array of boards, committees, commissions, corporations, and associations, some only loosely connected with the Government. This blending of positions and power has also occurred in the case of individuals so that many who do not hold public office at the moment are nevertheless intimately involved in the resolution of important public questions or, by reason of their fame, shape events in areas of concern to society at large.

Viewed in this context then, it is plain that although they are not subject to the restraints of the political process, "public figures," like "public officials," often play an influential role in ordering society. And surely as a class these "public figures" have as ready access as "public officials" to mass media of communication, both to influence policy and to counter criticism of their views and activities. Our citizenry has a legitimate and substantial interest in the conduct of such persons, and freedom of the press to engage in uninhibited debate about their involvement in public issues and events is as crucial as it is in the case of "public officials." The fact that they are not amenable to the restraints of the political process only underscores the legitimate and substantial nature of the interest, since it means that public opinion may be the only instrument by which society can attempt to influence their conduct.

Chief Justice Warren concluded that, on the merits, malice had not been shown in *Walker*. In *Butts*, he found that defendant's counsel had deliberately waived the *Times* doctrine, and he also found evidence establishing reckless behavior. He thus voted to reverse *Walker* and affirm *Butts*.

Justice Harlan, joined by three others, argued that something less than the *Times* standard should apply to public figures because criticism of government was not involved:

We consider and would hold that a "public figure" who is not a public official may also recover damages for a defamatory falsehood whose substance makes substantial danger to reputation apparent, on a showing of highly unreasonable conduct constituting an extreme departure from the standards of investigation and reporting ordinarily adhered to by responsible publishers.

Applying that standard, Justice Harlan concluded that Walker had failed to establish a case, but that Butts had shown that the Saturday Evening Post ignored elementary precautions in preparing a potentially damaging story. Together with the Chief Justice's vote, there were five votes to affirm *Butts*.

Although some courts seemed to regard Justice Harlan's opinion as the prevailing opinion, in part because it came first in the reports, it should have been clear that the same "actual malice" standard that applied in "public official" cases also applied in "public figure" cases. Should it? For an extended argument against identical standards for the two categories, see Schauer, Public Figures, 25 Wm. & Mary L.Rev. 905 (1984).

Later in this chapter, we will attempt to identify the critical features of the "public figure." In order to consider how those rules work, however, we only need to recognize that the identical "actual malice" rules apply to plaintiffs called "public officials" and to those called "public figures."

3. THE "ACTUAL MALICE" STANDARD

The Court's choice of the phrase "actual malice" in 1964 was the source of much confusion that would not have occurred if the Court had created some new term that had no link with traditional common law libel. The phrase "actual malice" did not clearly convey the shift in focus from the common law's attention to hatred, ill will, or spite toward the plaintiff to the new notion of looking at the defendant's attitude toward the truth of the defamatory statement. The Court has had several occasions to consider "actual malice" in detail. After considering substantive aspects of the doctrine, we turn to procedural issues.

a. SUBSTANTIVE ISSUES

In St. Amant v. Thompson, 390 U.S. 727 (1968), the defendant repeated false charges against plaintiff without having checked the charges or investigating the source's reputation for veracity. The Supreme Court concluded that "reckless disregard" had not been shown. It recognized that the term could receive no single "infallible definition" and that its outer limits would have to be developed in "case-to-case adjudication." The record must provide "sufficient evidence to permit the conclusion that the defendant in fact entertained serious doubts as to the truth of his publication" in order for recklessness to be found. Anticipating the argument that this position would encourage publishers not to verify their assertions, Justice White, for the Court, stated:

> The defendant in a defamation action brought by a public official cannot, however, automatically insure a favorable verdict by testifying that he published with a belief that the statements were true. The finder of fact must determine whether the publication was indeed made in good faith. Professions of good faith will be unlikely to prove persuasive, for example, where a story is fabricated by the defendant, is a product of his imagination, or is based wholly on an unverified anonymous telephone call. Nor will they be likely to prevail

when the publisher's allegations are so inherently improbable that only a reckless man would have put them in circulation. Likewise, recklessness may be found where there are obvious reasons to doubt the veracity of the informant or the accuracy of his reports.

How would the Court's test apply to an extreme partisan who would readily believe anything derogatory about his opponent?

In the second case, Herbert v. Lando, 441 U.S. 153 (1979), the plaintiff, Colonel Anthony Herbert, an admitted public figure, sued the producer and reporter of the television program "60 Minutes" and the CBS network for remarks on the program about his behavior while in military service in Vietnam. During his deposition, Lando, the producer, was generally responsive, but he refused to answer some questions about why he made certain investigations and not others; what he concluded about the honesty of certain people he interviewed for the program; and about conversations he had with Mike Wallace, the reporter, in the preparation of the program segment. Lando contended that these thought processes and internal editorial discussions were protected from disclosure by the First Amendment. The Supreme Court disagreed.

Justice White, writing for the Court, understood the defendants to be arguing that "the defendant's reckless disregard of truth, a critical element, could not be shown by direct evidence through inquiry into the thoughts, opinions and conclusions of the publisher but could be proved only by objective evidence from which the ultimate fact could be inferred." This was a barrier of some substance, "particularly when defendants themselves are prone to assert their good-faith belief in the truth of their publications, and libel plaintiffs are required to prove knowing or reckless falsehood with 'convincing clarity.'"

Although pretrial discovery techniques had led to "mushrooming litigation costs," this was happening in all areas of litigation. Until major changes in pretrial procedures were developed for all cases, the Court would rely on "what in fact and in law are ample powers of the district judge to prevent abuse."

Plaintiff also sued the Atlantic Monthly for a story written by Lando. The magazine "conducted no independent inquiry into the facts because that is not its practice. It maintains no research department." Since Lando, a freelance author, was "an apparently reasonable journalist" and the article was not "inherently implausible," the magazine had no obligation to investigate the facts and was not vicariously liable for Lando's statements. Herbert v. Lando, 596 F.Supp. 1178 (S.D.N.Y.1984), aff'd on other grounds, 781 F.2d 298 (2d Cir.1986).

Would there be First Amendment problems if a state were to conclude that "actual malice" on the part of an employee in the print shop or a dishonest reporter could subject the publisher to damages?

In Harte-Hanks Communications, Inc. v. Connaughton, 491 U.S. 657 (1989), the newspaper accused a judicial candidate of having used "dirty tricks" to smear his opponent, the incumbent. A unanimous Court upheld an award of $5,000 compensatory and $195,000 punitive damages.

The evidence of "dirty tricks" relied heavily on a source whose credibility had been seriously impugned by other witnesses and whose version of the episode was essentially unconfirmed. Reviewing the record extensively, the Court concluded that actual malice could be found from several uncontroverted findings: (1) the newspaper's failure to interview "the one witness that both [the plaintiff and the source] claimed would verify their conflicting accounts of the relevant events" was "utterly bewildering"; (2) the paper's failure to listen to a tape that the paper had been told exonerated plaintiff, which plaintiff had delivered to the paper at the paper's request; (3) an earlier article on the election that "could be taken to indicate that [the editor] had already decided to publish [the source's] allegations, regardless of how the evidence developed and regardless of whether or not [the source's] story was credible upon ultimate reflection"; and (4) that a crucial witness was not interviewed—or a variety of arguably inconsistent reasons offered by defendant's employees.

Accepting the jury's implicit determination that the newspaper's explanations for not interviewing the crucial witness and for not listening to the tape "were not credible, it is likely that the newspaper's inaction was a product of a deliberate decision not to acquire knowledge of facts that might confirm the probable falsity of [the source's] charges. Although failure to investigate will not alone support a finding of actual malice [*St. Amant*], the purposeful avoidance of the truth is in a different category."

Edited quotations: The Masson *case.* In Masson v. New Yorker Magazine, Inc., 501 U.S. 496 (1991), plaintiff alleged that an article in defendant magazine written by Janet Malcolm had attributed to plaintiff fabricated quotations that hurt his reputation. The lower courts had upheld summary judgment for the defendants. The Supreme Court reversed. First, the Court concluded that readers of nonfiction in a magazine that "at the relevant time seemed to enjoy a reputation for scrupulous factual accuracy," could take the accuracy of quotations "at face value. A defendant may be able to argue to the jury that quotations should be viewed by the reader as nonliteral or reconstructions, but we conclude that a trier of fact in this case could find that the reasonable reader would understand the quotations to be nearly verbatim reports of statements made by the subject."

The plaintiff then argued that "excepting corrections of grammar or syntax, publication of a quotation with knowledge that it does not contain the words the public figure used demonstrates actual malice." The Court was unwilling to go that far. Interviewers often must reconstruct interviews from notes. Use of language that the subject did not use does not amount to actual malice in that situation. Even if an interview is tape recorded, the "full and exact statement will be reported in only rare circumstances":

> We conclude that a deliberate alteration of the words uttered by a plaintiff does not equate with knowledge of falsity for purposes of [*Times*] unless the alteration results in a material change in the meaning conveyed by the statement. The use of quotation to attribute words not in fact spoken bears in a most important way on that inquiry, but it is not dispositive in every case.

In this case readers may have found the article "especially damning because so much of it appeared to be a self-portrait, told by the [plaintiff] in his own words." The Court doubted that "readers will assume that direct quotations are but a rational interpretation of the speaker's words, and we decline to adopt any such presumption in determining the permissible interpretations of the quotations in question here."

Applying these principles to the case, the Court reversed the summary judgment. It concluded that several passages could be read as more damning in the article than what the plaintiff alleges he in fact said and the record contained evidence that would support a jury determination that Malcolm "deliberately or recklessly altered the quotations."

In Air Wisconsin Airlines Corp. v. Hoeper, 134 S.Ct. 852 (2014), an airline pilot who failed a required test and knew that he was going to be terminated "responded angrily to this failure—raising his voice, tossing his headset, using profanity, and accusing the instructor of 'railroading the situation.'" The airline, which arranged a flight home for him, reported to TSA that as a pilot authorized to carry a weapon, he might be armed, that the airline was concerned that he was mentally unstable, and that he had been terminated that day. There were some minor inaccuracies in these statements, and the pilot sued for defamation in state court where he was successful. This case was decided in a narrow frame, namely the immunity provided in the Aviation and Transportation Security Act for statements to TSA relating to airline security. The Court concluded that the immunity provided in the statute was meant to be co-extensive with the *Times* standard. Reverting to *Masson* for the requirement that the statement must be materially false for actual malice to exist, *Air Wisconsin* reconfirms that the materially false standard that may exist at common law is a constitutional standard for which actual malice is required.

Actual malice in the lower courts. Some important questions about actual malice have been addressed by lower courts. A few follow.

1.   Is lack of fairness in the article probative? In Westmoreland v. CBS, Inc., 601 F.Supp. 66 (S.D.N.Y.1984), the court said no:

> The fairness of the broadcast is not at issue in the libel suit. Publishers and reporters do not commit a libel in a public figure case by publishing unfair one-sided attacks. . . . The fact that a commentary is one sided and sets forth categorical accusations has no tendency to prove that the publisher believed it to be false. The libel law does not require the publisher to grant his accused equal time or fair reply. . . . A publisher who honestly believes in the truth of his accusations . . . is under no obligation under the libel law to treat the subject of his accusations fairly or evenhandedly.

In Costello v. Ocean County Observer, 643 A.2d 1012 (N.J.1994), the court held that a "highly unfair" story did not show actual malice. The fact that the reporter was young and had been a reporter for only seven months was relevant in trying to determine whether his work was the result of actual malice or negligence. The defendants "narrowly escape liability, but they do not escape the loss of credibility that results from slipshod journalism."

2.   Is haste alone enough to show malice? In Meisler v. Gannett Co., 12 F.3d 1026 (11th Cir.), cert. denied, 512 U.S. 1222 (1994), the defendant carried an article based on an Associated Press wire service story marked "URGENT" even though AP indicated that "MORE" would be coming on this story. Although the second version arrived before the deadline, the author of the first version never saw it. Since the writer had no serious doubt about the article's accuracy at the time of publication, actual malice was not established.

3.   Can a journalist avoid trial by asserting that he honestly thought he saw something that did not in fact exist? The court said no in Currier v. Western Newspapers, Inc., 855 P.2d 1351 (Ariz.1993), in which plaintiff presented evidence that defendant repeated a defamatory statement after plaintiff had informed the newspapers of the falsity—a columnist's claim that he "believed [he] saw" a crucial signature on a document when it was not in fact there. The court denied summary judgment on the actual malice question: the columnist "either did not look at the public records at all or was careless in reading and recording what he saw."

4.   Is failure to investigate enough? In Sweeney v. Prisoners' Legal Services of New York, Inc., 647 N.E.2d 101 (N.Y.1995), the court reversed the determination of two lower courts that actual malice had been shown. Failure to investigate standing alone was not enough to establish actual malice. Evidence that defendants purposefully avoided the truth may support a finding of actual malice if supported by evidence that the inaction sprang from a desire not to know, citing *Harte-Hanks,* p. 1079 supra. In the absence of "some direct evidence that defendants in this case were aware that [the quoted source's

charge] was probably false, they cannot be found to have harbored an intent to avoid the truth."

b.   PROCEDURAL ISSUES

1.   *Convincing clarity.* Although the "actual malice" rule is the major substantive protection available to defendants being sued by public plaintiffs, an important procedural protection developed in *New York Times* requires public plaintiffs to prove their actual malice cases with "convincing clarity."

In Long v. Arcell, 618 F.2d 1145 (5th Cir.1980), after a jury finding for the public-figure plaintiff, the trial court granted the defendant newspaper a judgment notwithstanding the verdict. The trial court's ruling was affirmed on appeal. The only evidence for the jury involved conflicting accounts of conversations:

> If the applicable burden of proof had been a preponderance of the evidence, a jury verdict either way would have to stand. Similarly, if liability could be imposed on a clear and convincing showing of negligence, we would be hard pressed to disregard the jury's verdict. We repeat, however, that the plaintiff's burden was to prove actual malice by clear and convincing evidence. This record simply does not contain clear and convincing evidence that the defendants knew that their information was incorrect or had a "high degree of awareness of . . . [its] probable falsity." [*Garrison*].

Although not required to do so, some states have adopted this heightened burden of proof for some aspects of the state common law libel action.

2.   *Independent appellate review.* The requirement of clear and convincing evidence has been bolstered by a further explicit requirement that appellate courts must exercise "independent review" to assure that the required proof has been presented with the required clarity. In Bose Corp. v. Consumers Union, 466 U.S. 485 (1984), a federal judge sitting as trier found actual malice and entered judgment against defendant magazine. The court of appeals understood its obligation to be to "independently examin[e] the record to ensure that the district court has applied properly the governing constitutional law and that the plaintiff has indeed satisfied its burden of proof." Using that standard the court of appeals reversed.

The Court, 6–3, upheld the court of appeals. It analogized libel cases to those others in which the unprotected character of particular communications depends upon "judicial evaluation of special facts that have been deemed to have constitutional significance":

> The rule of independent appellate review . . . emerged from the exigency of deciding concrete cases; it is law in its purest form under our common law heritage. It reflects a

deeply held conviction that judges—and particularly members of this Court—must exercise such review in order to preserve the precious liberties established and ordained by the Constitution. The question whether the evidence in the record in a defamation case is of the convincing clarity required to strip the utterance of First Amendment protection is not merely a question for the trier of fact. Judges, as expositors of the Constitution, must independently decide whether the evidence in the record is sufficient to cross the constitutional threshold that bars the entry of any judgment that is not supported by clear and convincing proof of "actual malice."

For extended treatment, see the Court's discussion in the *Harte-Hanks* case, p. 1079 supra, upholding a determination of actual malice. Why, in this particular category of cases, does the Supreme Court feel special urgency to have independent appellate review? Reconsider, in that regard, *New York Times*, p. 1062 supra.

3. *The summary judgment standard.* In Anderson v. Liberty Lobby, Inc., 477 U.S. 242 (1986), the Court held, 6–3, that the standard for considering summary judgment motions under rule 56 of the Federal Rules of Civil Procedure must take into account the burden plaintiff will have to meet at trial. For public plaintiffs, then, on a summary judgment motion, the judge must decide "whether the evidence in the record could support a reasonable jury finding either that the plaintiff has shown actual malice by clear and convincing evidence or that the plaintiff has not." Using a preponderance standard was rejected because it "makes no sense to say that a jury could reasonably find for either party without some benchmark as to what standards govern its deliberations and within what boundaries its ultimate decision must fall, and these standards and boundaries are in fact provided by the applicable evidentiary standards."

The Court denied that its holding denigrated the role of the jury. "Credibility determinations, the weighing of the evidence, and the drawing of legitimate inferences from the facts are jury functions, not those of a judge, whether he is ruling on a motion for summary judgment or for a directed verdict."

4. *Confidential sources and proof of actual malice.* How can the plaintiff prove actual malice if the defendant journalist asserts reliance on a "confidential source" who is not identified? This important question, beyond the scope of this book, is explored in M. Franklin, D. Anderson & L. Lidsky, Cases and Materials: Mass Media Law (8th ed.2011).

5. *SLAPP suits.* In recent years, much concern has been expressed about defamation suits brought against persons making public statements in an apparent effort to dissuade them from participating in public discourse. Much of this involved suits against tenants' associations, environmental groups, and persons testifying at

city council meetings. See Pring, SLAPPs: Strategic Lawsuits Against Public Participation, 7 Pace Envtl.L.Rev. 3 (1989). The concern led to what have been called anti-SLAPP statutes, which do not alter the substantive law applicable to the case. Rather, they offer procedural devices by which to identify and dismiss at an early stage nonmeritorious suits that interfere with free speech rights. Those who believe that they are the victims of such a suit may prevail on an early "motion to strike, unless the court determines that the plaintiff has established that there is a probability that the plaintiff will prevail on the claim."

For the California version of the statute, see Cal. Code Civ.Proc. § 425.16. For a discussion of the philosophy behind the statute and how it operates, see Manufactured Home Communities, Inc. v. County of San Diego, 544 F.3d 959, 961 (9th Cir.2008). The statute has also been employed to dismiss cases brought against those posting anonymously to Internet message boards. See, e.g., Ampex v. Cargle, 27 Cal.Rptr.3d 863 (App.2005)(dismissing suit against former employee who disparaged the firm's business practices); Global Telemedia International, Inc. v. Doe 1, 132 F.Supp.2d 1261 (C.D.Cal.2001)(dismissing suit for comments questioning a software manufacturer's profitability on a discussion board for investors); see also Reder & O'Brien, Corporate Cybersmear: Employers File John Doe Defamation Lawsuits Seeking the Identity of Anonymous Employee Internet Posters, 8 Mich.Telecomm.Tech.L.Rev. 195 (2001).

4. PRIVATE PLAINTIFFS

Soon after deciding its first "public figure" cases, the Court confronted Rosenbloom v. Metromedia, Inc., 403 U.S. 29 (1971), involving a broadcaster's report that a magazine distributor sold obscene material and was arrested in a police raid. For a plurality, Justice Brennan, joined by Chief Justice Burger and Justice Blackmun, concluded that the *Times* standards should be extended to "all discussion and communication involving matters of public or general concern, without regard to whether the persons involved are famous or anonymous." The arrest and the distributor's subsequent claims against the police were thought to fit this category and the *Times* standard was applied. In reaching that position, Justice Brennan concluded that the focus on the plaintiff's status begun in the *Times* case bore "little relationship either to the values protected by the First Amendment or to the nature of our society.... Thus, the idea that certain 'public' figures have voluntarily exposed their entire lives to public inspection, while private individuals have kept theirs carefully shrouded from public view is, at best, a legal fiction." Discussion of a matter of public concern must be protected even when it involves an unknown person. If the states fear that private citizens will be unable to respond to adverse publicity, "the solution lies in the direction of ensuring their ability to respond, rather than in stifling public discussion of matters of public concern," a reference to possible use of the right of reply.

Justice White concurred on the narrow ground that the press is privileged to report "upon the official actions of public servants in full detail." Justice Black provided the fifth vote against liability, for the reasons stated in his earlier opinions. Justice Douglas did not participate in the case. Justices Harlan, Stewart and Marshall dissented on various grounds, but they agreed that the private plaintiff should be required to prove no more than negligence in this case. The dissenters also agreed that some limitations on damages should exist. Yet the dissenters disagreed with each other as well as with the plurality on major points. The area was ripe for rethinking.

Gertz v. Robert Welch, Inc.

Supreme Court of the United States, 1974.
418 U.S. 323, 94 S.Ct. 2997, 41 L.Ed.2d 789.

■ MR. JUSTICE POWELL delivered the opinion of the Court.

[Plaintiff, an attorney, was retained to represent the family of a youth killed by Nuccio, a Chicago policeman. In that capacity, plaintiff attended the coroner's inquest and filed an action for damages but played no part in a criminal proceeding in which Nuccio was convicted of second degree murder. Respondent published American Opinion, a monthly outlet for the views of the John Birch Society. As part of its efforts to alert the public to an alleged nationwide conspiracy to discredit local police, the magazine's editor engaged a regular contributor to write about the Nuccio episode. The article that appeared charged a frame-up against Nuccio and portrayed plaintiff as a "major architect" of the plot. It also falsely asserted that he had a long police record, was an official of the Marxist League for Industrial Democracy, and was a "Leninist" and a "Communist-fronter." The editor said he had no reason to doubt the charges and made no effort to verify them.

Gertz filed an action for libel in district court because of diversity of citizenship. The trial judge first ruled that Gertz was not a public official or public figure and that under Illinois law there was no defense. The jury awarded $50,000. On post-trial motion, the judge decided that since a matter of public concern was being discussed, the *Times* rule should apply, and he granted the defendant judgment notwithstanding the jury's verdict. He thus anticipated the plurality's approach in *Rosenbloom v. Metromedia, Inc.* The court of appeals, relying on the intervening decision in *Rosenbloom,* affirmed because of the absence of clear and convincing evidence of actual malice. According to *St. Amant v. Thompson*, p. 1077 supra, failure to investigate, without more, could not establish reckless disregard for truth. Gertz appealed.]

. . .

III.

We begin with the common ground. Under the First Amendment there is no such thing as a false idea. However pernicious an opinion may seem, we depend for its correction not on the conscience of judges and juries but on the competition of other ideas. But there is no constitutional value in false statements of fact. Neither the intentional lie nor the careless error materially advances society's interest in "uninhibited, robust, and wide-open" debate on public issues. . . .

Although the erroneous statement of fact is not worthy of constitutional protection, it is nevertheless inevitable in free debate. . . . And punishment of error runs the risk of inducing a cautious and restrictive exercise of the constitutionally guaranteed freedoms of speech and press. Our decisions recognize that a rule of strict liability that compels a publisher or broadcaster to guarantee the accuracy of his factual assertions may lead to intolerable self-censorship. Allowing the media to avoid liability only by proving the truth of all injurious statements does not accord adequate protection to First Amendment liberties. . . . The First Amendment requires that we protect some falsehood in order to protect speech that matters.

The need to avoid self-censorship by the news media is, however, not the only societal value at issue. If it were, this Court would have embraced long ago the view that publishers and broadcasters enjoy an unconditional and indefeasible immunity from liability for defamation. . . .

The legitimate state interest underlying the law of libel is the compensation of individuals for the harm inflicted on them by defamatory falsehood. We would not lightly require the State to abandon this purpose, for, as Mr. Justice Stewart has reminded us, the individual's right to the protection of his own good name

> "reflects no more than our basic concept of the essential dignity and worth of every human being—a concept at the root of any decent system of ordered liberty. The protection of private personality, like the protection of life itself, is left primarily to the individual States under the Ninth and Tenth Amendments. But this does not mean that the right is entitled to any less recognition by this Court as a basic of our constitutional system." Rosenblatt v. Baer [] (concurring opinion).

Some tension necessarily exists between the need for a vigorous and uninhibited press and the legitimate interest in redressing wrongful injury. . . .

The *New York Times* standard defines the level of constitutional protection appropriate to the context of defamation of a public person. Those who, by reason of the notoriety of their achievements or the vigor and success with which they seek the public's attention, are properly classed as public figures and those who hold governmental office may recover for injury to reputation only on clear and convincing proof that the defamatory falsehood was made with knowledge of its falsity or with reckless disregard for the truth. This standard administers an extremely powerful antidote to the inducement to media self-censorship of the common-law rule of strict liability for libel and slander. And it exacts a correspondingly high price from the victims of defamatory falsehood. Plainly many deserving plaintiffs, including some intentionally subjected to injury, will be unable to surmount the barrier of the *New York Times* test. Despite this substantial abridgment of the state law right to compensation for wrongful hurt to one's reputation, the Court has concluded that the protection of the *New York Times* privilege should be available to publishers and broadcasters of defamatory falsehood concerning public officials and public figures. [ ] We think that these decisions are correct, but we do not find their holdings justified solely by reference to the interest of the press and broadcast media in immunity from liability. Rather, we believe that the *New York Times* rule states an accommodation between this concern and the limited state interest present in the context of libel actions brought by public persons. For the reasons stated below, we conclude that the state interest in compensating injury to the reputation of private individuals requires that a different rule should obtain with respect to them.

Theoretically, of course, the balance between the needs of the press and the individual's claim to compensation for wrongful injury might be struck on a case-by-case basis. As Mr. Justice Harlan hypothesized, "it might seem, purely as an abstract matter, that the most utilitarian approach would be to scrutinize carefully every jury verdict in every libel case, in order to ascertain whether the final judgment leaves fully protected whatever First Amendment values transcend the legitimate state interest in protecting the particular plaintiff who prevailed." [*Rosenbloom*]. But this approach would lead to unpredictable results and uncertain expectations, and it could render our duty to supervise the lower courts unmanageable. Because an *ad hoc* resolution of the competing interests at stake in each particular case is not feasible, we must lay down broad rules of general application. Such rules necessarily treat alike various cases involving differences as well as similarities. Thus it is often true that not all of the considerations which justify adoption of a given rule will obtain in each particular case decided under its authority.

With that caveat we have no difficulty in distinguishing among defamation plaintiffs. The first remedy of any victim of defamation is self-help—using available opportunities to contradict the lie or correct the error and thereby to minimize its adverse impact on reputation. Public officials and public figures usually enjoy significantly greater access to the channels of effective communication and hence have a more realistic opportunity to counteract false statements than private individuals normally enjoy.[9] Private individuals are therefore more vulnerable to injury, and the state interest in protecting them is correspondingly greater.

More important than the likelihood that private individuals will lack effective opportunities for rebuttal, there is a compelling normative consideration underlying the distinction between public and private defamation plaintiffs. An individual who decides to seek governmental office must accept certain necessary consequences of that involvement in public affairs. He runs the risk of closer public scrutiny than might otherwise be the case. And society's interest in the officers of government is not strictly limited to the formal discharge of official duties. As the Court pointed out in [*Garrison v. Louisiana*], the public's interest extends to "anything which might touch on an official's fitness for office. . . . Few personal attributes are more germane to fitness for office than dishonesty, malfeasance, or improper motivation, even though these characteristics may also affect the official's private character."

Those classed as public figures stand in a similar position. Hypothetically, it may be possible for someone to become a public figure through no purposeful action of his own, but the instances of truly involuntary public figures must be exceedingly rare. For the most part those who attain this status have assumed roles of especial prominence in the affairs of society. Some occupy positions of such persuasive power and influence that they are deemed public figures for all purposes. More commonly, those classed as public figures have thrust themselves to the forefront of particular public controversies in order to influence the resolution of the issues involved. In either event, they invite attention and comment.

Even if the foregoing generalities do not obtain in every instance, the communications media are entitled to act on the assumption that public officials and public figures have voluntarily exposed themselves to increased risk of injury from defamatory falsehood concerning them. No such assumption is justified with respect to a private individual. He has not accepted public office or assumed an "influential role in ordering society." *Curtis Publishing Co. v. Butts*, [ ] (Warren, C.J., concurring in result). He has relinquished no part of his interest in the protection of his own good name, and consequently he has a more compelling call on the courts for redress of injury inflicted by defamatory falsehood. Thus, private individuals are not only more vulnerable to injury than public officials and public figures; they are also more deserving of recovery.

---

[9] Of course, an opportunity for rebuttal seldom suffices to undo harm of defamatory falsehood. Indeed, the law of defamation is rooted in our experience that the truth rarely catches up with a lie. But the fact that the self-help remedy of rebuttal, standing alone, is inadequate to its task does not mean that it is irrelevant to our inquiry.

For these reasons we conclude that the States should retain substantial latitude in their efforts to enforce a legal remedy for defamatory falsehood injurious to the reputation of a private individual. The extension of the *New York Times* test proposed by the *Rosenbloom* plurality would abridge this legitimate state interest to a degree that we find unacceptable. And it would occasion the additional difficulty of forcing state and federal judges to decide on an *ad hoc* basis which publications address issues of "general or public interest" and which do not—to determine, in the words of Mr. Justice Marshall, "what information is relevant to self-government." [*Rosenbloom*]. We doubt the wisdom of committing this task to the conscience of judges. Nor does the Constitution require us to draw so thin a line between the drastic alternatives of the *New York Times* privilege and the common law of strict liability for defamatory error. The "public or general interest" test for determining the applicability of the *New York Times* standard to private defamation actions inadequately serves both of the competing values at stake. On the one hand, a private individual whose reputation is injured by defamatory falsehood that does concern an issue of public or general interest has no recourse unless he can meet the rigorous requirements of *New York Times*. This is true despite the factors that distinguish the state interest in compensating private individuals from the analogous interest involved in the context of public persons. On the other hand, a publisher or broadcaster of a defamatory error which a court deems unrelated to an issue of public or general interest may be held liable in damages even if it took every reasonable precaution to ensure the accuracy of its assertions. And liability may far exceed compensation for any actual injury to the plaintiff, for the jury may be permitted to presume damages without proof of loss and even to award punitive damages.

We hold that, so long as they do not impose liability without fault, the States may define for themselves the appropriate standard of liability for a publisher or broadcaster of defamatory falsehood injurious to a private individual. This approach provides a more equitable boundary between the competing concerns involved here. It recognizes the strength of the legitimate state interest in compensating private individuals for wrongful injury to reputation, yet shields the press and broadcast media from the rigors of strict liability for defamation. At least this conclusion obtains where, as here, the substance of the defamatory statement "makes substantial danger to reputation apparent." [*Butts*] This phrase places in perspective the conclusion we announce today. Our inquiry would involve considerations somewhat different from those discussed above if a State purported to condition civil liability on a factual misstatement whose content did not warn a reasonably prudent editor or broadcaster of its defamatory potential. Cf. Time, Inc. v. Hill, 385 U.S. 374 (1967). Such a case is not now before us, and we intimate no view as to its proper resolution.

IV.

Our accommodation of the competing values at stake in defamation suits by private individuals allows the States to impose liability on the publisher or broadcaster of defamatory falsehood on a less demanding showing than that required by *New York Times*. This conclusion is not based on a belief that the considerations which prompted the adoption of the *New York Times* privilege for defamation of public officials and its extension to public figures are wholly inapplicable to the context of private individuals. Rather, we endorse this approach in recognition of the strong and legitimate state interest in compensating private individuals for injury to reputation. But this countervailing state interest extends no further than compensation for actual injury. For the reasons stated below, we hold that the States may not permit recovery of presumed or punitive damages, at least when liability is not based on a showing of knowledge of falsity or reckless disregard for the truth.

The common law of defamation is an oddity of tort law, for it allows recovery of purportedly compensatory damages without evidence of actual loss. Under the traditional rules pertaining to actions for libel, the existence of injury is presumed from the fact of publication. Juries may award substantial sums as compensation for supposed damage to reputation without any proof that such harm actually occurred. The largely uncontrolled discretion of juries to award damages where there is no loss unnecessarily compounds the potential of any system of liability for defamatory falsehood to inhibit the vigorous exercise of First Amendment freedoms. Additionally, the doctrine of presumed damages invites juries to punish unpopular opinion rather than to compensate individuals for injury sustained by the publication of a false fact. More to the point, the States have no substantial interest in securing for plaintiffs such as this petitioner gratuitous awards of money damages far in excess of any actual injury.

We would not, of course, invalidate state law simply because we doubt its wisdom, but here we are attempting to reconcile state law with a competing interest grounded in the constitutional command of the First Amendment. It is therefore appropriate to require that state remedies for defamatory falsehood reach no farther than is necessary to protect the legitimate interest involved. It is necessary to restrict defamation plaintiffs who do not prove knowledge of falsity or reckless disregard for the truth to compensation for actual injury. We need not define "actual injury," as trial courts have wide experience in framing appropriate jury instructions in tort actions. Suffice it to say that actual injury is not limited to out-of-pocket loss. Indeed, the more customary types of actual harm inflicted by defamatory falsehood include impairment of reputation and standing in the community, personal humiliation, and mental anguish and suffering. Of course, juries must be limited by appropriate instructions, and all awards must be supported by competent evidence concerning the injury, although there need be no evidence which assigns an actual dollar value to the injury.

We also find no justification for allowing awards of punitive damages against publishers and broadcasters held liable under state-defined standards of liability for defamation. In most jurisdictions jury discretion over the amounts awarded is limited only by the gentle rule that they not be excessive. Consequently, juries assess punitive damages in wholly unpredictable amounts bearing no necessary relation to the actual harm caused. And they remain free to use their discretion selectively to punish expressions of unpopular views. Like the doctrine of presumed damages, jury discretion to award punitive damages unnecessarily exacerbates the danger of media self-censorship, but, unlike the former rule, punitive damages are wholly irrelevant to the state interest that justifies a negligence standard for private defamation actions. They are not compensation for injury. Instead, they are private fines levied by civil juries to punish reprehensible conduct and to deter its future occurrence. In short, the private defamation plaintiff who establishes liability under a less demanding standard than that stated by *New York Times* may recover only such damages as are sufficient to compensate him for actual injury.

V.

Notwithstanding our refusal to extend the *New York Times* privilege to defamation of private individuals, respondent contends that we should affirm the judgment below on the ground that petitioner is either a public official or a public figure. There is little basis for the former assertion. Several years prior to the present incident, petitioner had served briefly on housing committees appointed by the mayor of Chicago, but at the time of publication he had never held any remunerative governmental position. Respondent admits this but argues that petitioner's appearance at the coroner's inquest rendered him a "de facto public official." Our cases recognize no such concept. Respondent's suggestion would sweep all lawyers under the *New York Times* rule as officers of the court and distort the plain meaning of the "public official" category beyond all recognition. We decline to follow it.

Respondent's characterization of petitioner as a public figure raises a different question. That designation may rest on either of two alternative bases. In some instances an individual may achieve such pervasive fame or notoriety that he becomes a public figure for all purposes and in all contexts. More commonly, an individual voluntarily injects himself or is drawn into a particular public controversy and thereby becomes a public figure for a limited range of issues. In either case such persons assume special prominence in the resolution of public questions.

Petitioner has long been active in community and professional affairs. He has served as an officer of local civic groups and of various professional organizations, and he has published several books and

articles on legal subjects. Although petitioner was consequently well
known in some circles, he had achieved no general fame or notoriety in
the community. None of the prospective jurors called at the trial had
ever heard of petitioner prior to this litigation, and respondent offered
no proof that this response was atypical of the local population. We
would not lightly assume that a citizen's participation in community
and professional affairs rendered him a public figure for all purposes.
Absent clear evidence of general fame or notoriety in the community,
and pervasive involvement in the affairs of society, an individual should
not be deemed a public personality for all aspects of his life. It is
preferable to reduce the public-figure question to a more meaningful
context by looking to the nature and extent of an individual's
participation in the particular controversy giving rise to the defamation.

In this context it is plain that petitioner was not a public figure. He
played a minimal role at the coroner's inquest, and his participation
related solely to his representation of a private client. He took no part
in the criminal prosecution of Officer Nuccio. Moreover, he never
discussed either the criminal or civil litigation with the press and was
never quoted as having done so. He plainly did not thrust himself into
the vortex of this public issue, nor did he engage the public's attention
in an attempt to influence its outcome. We are persuaded that the trial
court did not err in refusing to characterize petitioner as a public figure
for the purpose of this litigation.

We therefore conclude that the *New York Times* standard is
inapplicable to this case and that the trial court erred in entering
judgment for respondent. Because the jury was allowed to impose
liability without fault and was permitted to presume damages without
proof of injury, a new trial is necessary. We reverse and remand for
further proceedings in accord with this opinion.

It is so ordered.

■ MR. JUSTICE BLACKMUN, concurring.

[Although I joined the *Rosenbloom* plurality opinion,] I am willing
to join, and do join, the Court's opinion and its judgment for two
reasons:

1.   By removing the specters of presumed and punitive damages
in the absence of *New York Times* malice, the Court eliminates
significant and powerful motives for self-censorship that otherwise are
present in the traditional libel action. By so doing, the Court leaves
what should prove to be sufficient and adequate breathing space for a
vigorous press. What the Court has done, I believe, will have little, if
any, practical effect on the functioning of responsible journalism.

2.   The Court was sadly fractionated in *Rosenbloom*. A result of
that kind inevitably leads to uncertainty. I feel that it is of profound
importance for the Court to come to rest in the defamation area and to
have a clearly defined majority position that eliminates the unsureness

engendered by *Rosenbloom's* diversity. If my vote were not needed to create a majority, I would adhere to my prior view. A definitive ruling, however, is paramount. [ ]

For these reasons, I join the opinion and the judgment of the Court.

■ MR. CHIEF JUSTICE BURGER, dissenting.

. . .

Agreement or disagreement with the law as it has evolved to this time does not alter the fact that it has been orderly development with a consistent basic rationale. . . . I would prefer to allow this area of law to continue to evolve as it has up to now with respect to private citizens rather than embark on a new doctrinal theory which has no jurisprudential ancestry.

The petitioner here was performing a professional representative role as an advocate in the highest tradition of the law, and under that tradition the advocate is not to be invidiously identified with his client. The important public policy which underlies this tradition—the right to counsel—would be gravely jeopardized if every lawyer who takes an "unpopular" case, civil or criminal, would automatically become fair game for irresponsible reporters and editors who might, for example, describe the lawyer as a "mob mouthpiece" for representing a client with a serious prior criminal record, or as an "ambulance chaser" for representing a claimant in a personal injury action.

I would reverse the judgment of the Court of Appeals and remand for reinstatement of the verdict of the jury and the entry of an appropriate judgment on that verdict.

■ MR. JUSTICE DOUGLAS, dissenting.

. . .

. . . The standard announced today leaves the States free to "define for themselves the appropriate standard of liability for a publisher or broadcaster" in the circumstances of this case. This of course leaves the simple negligence standard as an option with the jury free to impose damages upon a finding that the publisher failed to act as "a reasonable man." With such continued erosion of First Amendment protection, I fear that it may well be the reasonable man who refrains from speaking.

Since in my view the First and Fourteenth Amendments prohibit the imposition of damages upon respondent for this discussion of public affairs, I would affirm the judgment below.

■ MR. JUSTICE BRENNAN, dissenting.

I agree with the conclusion, expressed in Part V of the Court's opinion, that, at the time of publication of respondent's article, petitioner could not properly have been viewed as either a "public official" or "public figure"; instead, respondent's article, dealing with an alleged conspiracy to discredit local police forces, concerned petitioner's purported involvement in "an event of public or general interest." . . .

. . .

Although acknowledging that First Amendment values are of no less significance when media reports concern private persons' involvement in matters of public concern, the Court refuses to provide, in such cases, the same level of constitutional protection that has been afforded the media in the context of defamation of public persons. The accommodation that this Court has established between free speech and libel laws in cases involving public officials and public figures—that defamatory falsehood be shown by clear and convincing evidence to have been published with knowledge of falsity or with reckless disregard of truth—is not apt, the Court holds, because the private individual does not have the same degree of access to the media to rebut defamatory comments as does the public person and he has not voluntarily exposed himself to public scrutiny.

While these arguments are forcefully and eloquently presented, I cannot accept them, for the reasons I stated in *Rosenbloom*:

> The *New York Times* standard was applied to libel of a public official or public figure to give effect to the [First] Amendment's function to encourage ventilation of public issues, not because the public official has any less interest in protecting his reputation than an individual in private life. While the argument that public figures need less protection because they can command media attention to counter criticism may be true for some very prominent people, even then it is the rare case where the denial overtakes the original charge. Denials, retractions, and corrections are not "hot" news, and rarely receive the prominence of the original story. When the public official or public figure is a minor functionary, or has left the position that put him in the public eye . . . , the argument loses all of its force. In the vast majority of libels involving public officials or public figures, the ability to respond through the media will depend on the same complex factor on which the ability of a private individual depends: the unpredictable event of the media's continuing interest in the story. Thus the unproved, and highly improbable, generalization that an as yet [not fully defined] class of "public figures" involved in matters of public concern will be better able to respond through the media than private individuals also involved in such matters seems too insubstantial a reed on which to rest a constitutional distinction. [ ]

. . .

. . . Under a reasonable-care regime, publishers and broadcasters will have to make pre-publication judgments about juror assessment of such diverse considerations as the size, operating procedures, and financial condition of the newsgathering system, as well as the relative costs and benefits of instituting less frequent and more costly reporting at a higher level of accuracy. [ ] Moreover, in contrast to proof by clear and convincing evidence required under the *Times* test, the burden of proof for reasonable care will doubtless be the preponderance of the evidence. . . .

The Court does not discount altogether the danger that jurors will punish for the expression of unpopular opinions. This probability accounts for the Court's limitation that "the States may not permit recovery of presumed or punitive damages, at least when liability is not based on a showing of knowledge of falsity or reckless disregard for the truth." [ ] But plainly a jury's latitude to impose liability for want of due care poses a far greater threat of suppressing unpopular views than does a possible recovery of presumed or punitive damages. Moreover, the Court's broad-ranging examples of "actual injury," including impairment of reputation and standing in the community, as well as personal humiliation, and mental anguish and suffering, inevitably allow a jury bent on punishing expression of unpopular views a formidable weapon for doing so. Finally, even a limitation of recovery to "actual injury"—however much it reduces the size or frequency of recoveries—will not provide the necessary elbowroom for First Amendment expression. . . .

On the other hand, the uncertainties which the media face under today's decision are largely avoided by the *Times* standard. I reject the argument that my *Rosenbloom* view improperly commits to judges the task of determining what is and what is not an issue of "general or public interest."[3] I noted in *Rosenbloom* that performance of this task would not always be easy. [ ] But surely the courts, the ultimate arbiters of all disputes concerning clashes of constitutional values, would only be performing one of their traditional functions in undertaking this duty. . . .

■ MR. JUSTICE WHITE, dissenting.

. . .

The impact of today's decision on the traditional law of libel is immediately obvious and indisputable. No longer will the plaintiff be able to rest his case with proof of a libel defamatory on its face or proof of a slander historically actionable *per se*. In addition, he must prove some further degree of culpable conduct on the part of the publisher . . .

---

[3]   . . .

Parenthetically, my Brother WHITE argues that the Court's view and mine will prevent a plaintiff—unable to demonstrate some degree of fault—from vindicating his reputation by securing a judgment that the publication was false. This argument overlooks the possible enactment of statutes, not requiring proof of fault, which provide for an action for retraction or for publication of a court's determination of falsity if the plaintiff is able to demonstrate that false statements have been published concerning his activities.

And if he succeeds in this respect, he faces still another obstacle: [denial of recovery for presumed damages]. The Court rejects the judgment of experience that some publications are so inherently capable of injury, and actual injury so difficult to prove, that the risk of falsehood should be borne by the publisher, not the victim. . . .

So too, the requirement of proving special injury to reputation before general damages may be awarded will clearly eliminate the prevailing rule, worked out over a very long period of time, that, in the case of defamations not actionable *per se,* the recovery of general damages for injury to reputation may also be had if some form of material or pecuniary loss is proved. Finally, an inflexible federal standard is imposed for the award of punitive damages. No longer will it be enough to prove ill will and an attempt to injure.

These are radical changes in the law and severe invasions of the prerogatives of the States. . . .

. . .

The Court evinces a deep-seated antipathy to "liability without fault." But this catch-phrase has no talismanic significance and is almost meaningless in this context where the Court appears to be addressing those libels and slanders that are defamatory on their face and where the publisher is no doubt aware from the nature of the material that it would be inherently damaging to reputation. He publishes notwithstanding, knowing that he will inflict injury. With this knowledge, he must intend to inflict that injury, his excuse being that he is privileged to do so—that he has published the truth. But as it turns out, what he has circulated to the public is a very damaging falsehood. Is he nevertheless "faultless"? Perhaps it can be said that the mistake about his defense was made in good faith, but the fact remains that it is he who launched the publication knowing that it could ruin a reputation.

In these circumstances, the law has heretofore put the risk of falsehood on the publisher where the victim is a private citizen and no grounds of special privilege are invoked. The Court would now shift this risk to the victim, even though he has done nothing to invite the calumny, is wholly innocent of fault, and is helpless to avoid his injury. . . . The press today is vigorous and robust. To me, it is quite incredible to suggest that threats of libel suits from private citizens are causing the press to refrain from publishing the truth. I know of no hard facts to support that proposition, and the Court furnishes none.

The communications industry has increasingly become concentrated in a few powerful hands operating very lucrative businesses reaching across the Nation and into almost every home. Neither the industry as a whole nor its individual components are easily intimidated, and we are fortunate that they are not. Requiring them to pay for the occasional damage they do to private reputation will play no substantial part in their future performance or their existence.

In any event, if the Court's principal concern is to protect the communications industry from large libel judgments, it would appear that its new requirements with respect to general and punitive damages would be ample protection. . . .

It is difficult for me to understand why the ordinary citizen should himself carry the risk of damage and suffer the injury in order to vindicate First Amendment values by protecting the press and others from liability for circulating false information. This is particularly true because such statements serve no purpose whatsoever in furthering the public interest or the search for truth but, on the contrary, may frustrate that search and at the same time inflict great injury on the defenseless individual. The owners of the press and the stockholders of the communications enterprises can much better bear the burden. And if they cannot, the public at large should somehow pay for what is essentially a public benefit derived at private expense.

. . .

For the foregoing reasons, I would reverse the judgment of the Court of Appeals and reinstate the jury's verdict.

NOTES AND QUESTIONS

1. Why did the majority adhere to the *Times* rule for public officials? For public figures?

2. Why does the majority in *Gertz* prefer its approach to the plurality's approach in *Rosenbloom*?

3. The *Gertz* retrial, which did not occur for several years, produced a jury verdict for plaintiff for $100,000 compensatory damages and $300,000 punitive damages. On appeal, the court of appeals affirmed. It concluded that the jury could find "actual malice" on the part of the editor of the magazine, who solicited a person with a "known and unreasonable propensity to label persons or organizations as Communist, to write the article; and after the article was submitted, made virtually no effort to check the validity of statements that were defamatory *per se* of Gertz, and in fact added further defamatory material based on [the writer's] 'facts.'" It also held that, contrary to most cases involving freelance writers, the conduct of the writer could be imputed to the magazine because of the "significant control" exercised by the editor over the content and focus of the article. An agency relationship had been created. Gertz v. Robert Welch, Inc., 680 F.2d 527 (7th Cir.1982), cert. denied, 459 U.S. 1226 (1983).

4. Even if constitutional law does not bar punitive damages in cases in which actual malice is shown, state law may impose a variety of impediments, such as barring punitive damages in all tort cases, or in cases involving speech. Many of the state tort reform statutes that limit punitive damages to a maximum amount or to a multiple of compensatory damages, although enacted primarily with personal injury in mind, apply also to defamation actions. Also, some states require a showing of some further element, such as animosity toward plaintiff, in addition to actual malice. Moreover, some states have demanded that the state law requirements for punitive damages be shown with convincing clarity.

5. *More protective state approaches.* Justice Powell phrased the permissible standard in private citizen cases negatively: states may use whatever standard they wish "so long as they do not impose liability without fault." It may be theoretically possible to develop a standard more protective of defendants than strict liability but less demanding of plaintiffs than negligence, but states have not made the attempt. Note that at the end of part IV, Justice Powell himself used "negligence" in a way that suggests that he considered that it is the next level above strict liability: "punitive damages are wholly irrelevant to the state interest that justifies a negligence standard for private defamation actions."

A very few states have adopted some version of the *Rosenbloom* plurality's approach. But by far the most important aberration has been New York, which has developed its own standard for private figure cases:

> [W]here the content of the article is arguably within the sphere of legitimate public concern, which is reasonably related to matters warranting public exposition, the party may recover; however, to warrant such recovery he must first establish, by a preponderance of the evidence, that the publisher acted in a grossly irresponsible manner without due consideration for the standards of information gathering and dissemination ordinarily followed by responsible parties.

Chapadeau v. Utica Observer-Dispatch, Inc., 341 N.E.2d 569 (N.Y.1975). Is this closer to *Gertz* or to *Rosenbloom*?

Much litigation has addressed the scope and effect of *Chapadeau*. In Huggins v. Moore, 726 N.E.2d 456 (N.Y.1999), defendant newspaper ran articles reporting charges by plaintiff's ex-wife that he had committed "economic spousal abuse" by cheating her out of her interest in an entertainment company they had built together. Holding the articles entitled to protection under *Chapadeau*, the court reviewed the situation:

> A publication's subject is not a matter of public concern when it falls "into the realm of mere gossip and prurient interest" [ ]. In addition, publications directed only to a limited, private audience are "matters of purely private concern" [ ]. Moreover, the fact that the article has been published in a newspaper is not conclusive that its subject matter warrants public exposition [ ].

> Yet we have stated repeatedly that the *Chapadeau* standard is deferential to professional journalistic judgments. Absent clear abuse, the courts will not second-guess editorial decisions as to what constitutes matters of genuine public concern [ ]. This applies equally to the determination whether any particular portion of the text is "reasonably related" to the subject of public concern in the article [ ]. There is no "abuse of editorial discretion"

[ ] so long as a published report can be "fairly considered as relating to any matter of political, social, or other concern of the community" [ ].

> In applying this standard, our cases establish that a matter may be of public concern even though it is a "human interest" portrayal of events in the lives of persons who are not themselves public figures, so long as some theme of legitimate public concern can reasonably be drawn from their experience. . . . Thus, the *Chapadeau* standard applies to statements about a "private legal dispute," so long as those statements, in the context of the entire publication, are illustrative of a larger subject of legitimate concern to the public at large.

In the case before it, the court rejected the lower court's emphasis on the fact that the case involved an acrimonious divorce:

> That the "core" of the dispute between Moore and plaintiff was a divorce is not conclusive. The articles also portrayed Moore's alleged victimization by her financial as well as marital partner to the point of economic and career ruination. It is this episode of human interest that reflected a matter of genuine social concern.

New Jersey has also been active in developing its own approach. In Dairy Stores, Inc. v. Sentinel Publishing Co., 516 A.2d 220 (N.J.1986), defendant newspapers, during a drought, reported that the water being bottled and sold at plaintiff's local store was not the pure spring water it purported to be. Although the lower court had denied defendants' motions for summary judgment on the ground that plaintiff was private and did not need to prove actual malice, the state's highest court thought that "the more appropriate principle is the common-law privilege of fair comment."

Although "constitutional considerations have dominated defamation law in recent years, the common law provides an alternative, and potentially more stable, framework for analyzing statements about matters of public interest." The safety of drinking water was a "paradigm of legitimate public concern." To overcome the state privilege, plaintiff would have to prove "actual malice" in the constitutional sense.

Even for ordinary, non-public interest, non-public figure speech, negligence is required for liability. In Senna v. Florimont, 958 A.2d 427 (N.J. 2008), the court decided that the extended protection for matters of public interest previously adopted was not applicable to the speech in this case: a competitor's bad-mouthing another boardwalk game operator, calling him a crook and dishonest and stating that he didn't redeem coupons won at his games. Thus, defendant was subject to a negligence, rather than actual malice standard. The court clearly laid out the development of common law privileges as the backdrop for *Sullivan*, the progeny of *Sullivan*, and state court developments more protective than the First Amendment.

What are the merits and demerits of the New York approach? The New Jersey approach?

6. Before we explore the nature of negligence and related operational aspects of the *Gertz* case, it is important to note how few cases truly present these questions. The vast majority of reported cases against media (and we would expect unreported cases as well) are litigated as "actual malice" cases and not as negligence cases for at least two reasons.

First, plaintiffs mentioned in the media are likely to be either admittedly public or found to be public. Second, even a plaintiff called "private" who wants to recover presumed or punitive damages must go the "actual malice" route from the start. If the jury finds that the plaintiff has succeeded in that effort, there is no occasion to focus on the meaning of "actual injury" damages. Similarly, in cases in which the plaintiff cannot establish "actual injury" damages—no matter what they are held to encompass—the litigation will likely go off on an attempt to prove "actual malice." (There is the further limitation that the Court's language in *Gertz* referred to "publishers" and "broadcasters," leaving doubt about what parts of the case might apply to nonmedia defendants.)

7. Justice White was particularly concerned about having private citizens bear the burden of defamation. If the media cannot bear the expense of the harm they cause, the public should "somehow pay for what is essentially a public benefit derived at private expense." For many years, it was widely observed that defamation law was running counter to trends in other areas of tort law. Thus, personal injury law appeared to be moving toward greater imposition of liability, through techniques that increased chances of recovery in negligence cases and through development of new doctrines that increased the imposition of strict liability, as in aspects of the law of defective products. Meanwhile, defamation law had been moving the other way—from strict liability to denying liability in many cases unless something substantially greater than negligence could be shown. To the extent this perception was (and remains) accurate, is this an even more appropriate occasion for strict liability than the defective products area?

For an extensive discussion of the cross-currents in strict liability, see Weiler, Defamation, Enterprise Liability, and Freedom of Speech, 17 U. Toronto L.J. 278 (1967); see also Kalven, The Reasonable Man and the First Amendment: *Hill, Butts,* and *Walker,* 1967 Sup.Ct.Rev. 267. But see Anderson, Libel and Press Self-Censorship, 53 Tex.L.Rev. 422, 432 n.52 (1975)(arguing that the analogy is flawed because the other enterprises "have no choice but to accept the additional risk of liability if they are to continue their profit-making activities, while most broadcasters and publishers can avoid liability, without discontinuing their activities or reducing their profits, by ceasing to carry material that creates the risk of liability—i.e., by increasing their self-censorship"). Can a sound argument be made for strict liability in this area? Note the lack of a first-party insurance device for potential libel victims that would operate along the lines of medical and income-protection insurance available to potential personal injury victims.

8. *How negligence operates.* Justice Powell spoke of the "reasonably prudent editor or broadcaster." The phrase "reasonably prudent" makes sense when applied to automobile drivers or airplane pilots or physicians.

But how is that phrase to be applied to a field in which the media vary from sedate, if not stodgy, journals at one extreme to racy tabloids and scandal sheets at the other; from those that treat public relations releases as news to those that disbelieve every statement made by government officials and engage in extensive investigative reporting? What about differences between editors at very well financed and profitable publications or broadcast stations and those at marginal media with small, or nonexistent, research staffs and budgets too tight to keep a libel lawyer on retainer?

The Restatement (Second) of Torts section 580B, comment h, suggests that the reasonableness of the investigation varies with the following factors: (1) The "time element"—investigations may be shorter for topical news than for a story that has no time pressure. (2) The "nature of the interest promoted by publication"—a story informing the public of matters important in a democracy may warrant quicker publication than a story involving "mere gossip." (3) "Potential damage to plaintiff if the communication proves to be false"—whether the statement is defamatory on its face; how many readers will understand the defamation; how harmful is the charge. Do these factors take into account "social harm" from publication of a false story?

One court has stated two other factors: the nature and reliability of the source of the information and the "reasonableness in checking the veracity of the information, considering its cost in terms of money, time, personnel, urgency of the publication, nature of the news and any other pertinent element." Torres-Silva v. El Mundo, 3 Med.L.Rptr. 1508 (P.R.1977). See generally Bloom, Proof of Fault in Media Defamation Litigation, 38 Vand.L.Rev. 247 (1985).

Some have questioned the emphasis on time pressure. In Schaefer, Defamation and the First Amendment, 52 Colo.L.Rev. 1 (1980), a former Chief Justice of Illinois said:

> It has been suggested that the press, television, and radio all operate under severe time constraints and that this consideration should excuse or justify defamatory statements. It should not be forgotten, however, that these time constraints are entirely self-imposed. Apparently the media people believe that for competitive reasons it is desirable to be first with a particular news story. My own impression is that the public is massively unconcerned about that question. But if my impression is wrong, deadline pressures afford no more justification for harm caused by negligent attacks upon reputation than for harm caused by a reporter's negligent driving in his haste to cover a story. Both negligent acts are and have been insurable.

Do you agree?

9. *The role of experts.* Another question is whether the standard should be stated in terms of professional negligence or ordinary due care. This may be significant both in formulating the standard and in requiring expert testimony to show the standard and the deviation. The few states that have addressed this question have split. In Gobin v. Globe Publishing

Co., 531 P.2d 76 (Kan.1975), the court stated the standard to be "the conduct of the reasonably careful publisher or broadcaster in the community or in similar communities under the existing circumstances." Troman v. Wood, 340 N.E.2d 292 (Ill.1975), rejected the professional negligence approach because "it would make the prevailing newspaper practices in a community controlling. In a community having only a single newspaper, the approach suggested would permit that paper to establish its own standards. And in any community it might tend, in 'Gresham's law' fashion, toward a progressive depreciation of the standard of care."

The Second Restatement section 580B, comment g, states that a professional disseminator of news "is held to the skill and experience normally possessed by members of that profession. Customs and practices within the profession are relevant in applying the negligence standard, which is, to a substantial degree, set by the profession itself, though a custom is not controlling."

10. *Plaintiffs must prove falsity—The* Hepps *case.* Although the Court's focus has been on the fault requirement, the role of falsity has also raised questions. In Philadelphia Newspapers, Inc. v. Hepps, 475 U.S. 767 (1986), the Court, 5–4, held that the plaintiff had the burden of proving falsity in cases brought by private plaintiffs, at least where the speech was of public concern. For the majority, Justice O'Connor concluded that to "ensure that true speech on matters of public concern is not deterred, we hold that the common-law presumption that defamatory speech is false cannot stand when a plaintiff seeks damages against a media defendant for speech of public concern." (Two of the five joining the majority opinion rejected the limitation to media defendants.) Even though this burden would "insulate from liability some speech that is false, but unprovably so," that result was essential to avoid the "chilling" effect that would otherwise accompany true speech on matters of public concern.

Justice Stevens, for the dissenters, thought the majority result "pernicious," positing a situation in which a defendant, knowing that the plaintiff could not prove the statement false, deliberately lied about the plaintiff. This situation might occur due to the passage of time, the loss of critical records, or the absence of an eyewitness. The majority's analysis was an "obvious blueprint for character assassination."

11. *Procedural issues.* Most courts refuse to apply independent appellate review in cases in which the negligence standard controls. See Levine v. CMP Publications, Inc., 738 F.2d 660 (5th Cir.1984). Most courts also refuse to require "clear and convincing" evidence of negligence. See Lansdowne v. Beacon Journal Publishing Co., 512 N.E.2d 979 (Ohio 1987).

12. *Actual injury.* As we have already seen, the subject of damages in defamation cases was complicated enough at common law. Whether a plaintiff needed to show "special" damages and, if so, what constituted "special" damages produced much litigation. The Supreme Court's introduction, in *Gertz,* of "actual injury damages" did not purport to track any pre-existing concept of damages. Indeed, the Court went out of its way to use examples that showed that the new term did not track "special" damages. The problem has fallen to the lower courts to give content to this term, drawing solely from the few sentences in *Gertz* that address the problem—and from the *Firestone* case.

In Time, Inc. v. Firestone, 424 U.S. 448 (1976), discussed p. 1106 infra, plaintiff withdrew her claim for reputational harm on the eve of trial. Defendant argued that this barred her from recovering under *Gertz*. The Court disagreed. If Florida permitted recoveries in defamation actions that did not claim harm to reputation, *Gertz* did not forbid it:

> In [*Gertz*] we made it clear that States could base awards on elements other than injury to reputation, specifically listing "personal humiliation, and mental anguish and suffering" as examples of injuries which might be compensated consistently with the Constitution upon a showing of fault.

In *Firestone*, the plaintiff had presented evidence from her minister, her attorney in the divorce proceedings, and several friends and neighbors. One of the latter was a physician who testified to "having to administer a sedative to respondent in an attempt to reduce discomfort wrought by her worrying about the article." Plaintiff also testified that she feared the effect that the false report of her adultery might have on her young son when he grew older. "The jury decided these injuries should be compensated by an award of $100,000. We have no warrant for re-examining this determination."

In addition to the reasons discussed earlier, fewer cases discuss actual injury than might be expected because: (1) the cases in New York and the few other states that have higher standards for liability produce fewer discussions of any damage issues than would occur under a negligence standard; and (2) the cases that are resolved on state issues—as when the defendant argues that plaintiff's proof does not satisfy a state rule requiring "special" damages or requiring certain types of proof for compensatory damages, or when defendant asserts that the damages are excessive under state law. The result of all these is that relatively few courts have been forced to decide the content of *Gertz* "actual injury" damages.

5. THE PUBLIC-PRIVATE DISTINCTION

Now that we have considered the two categories developed by the Supreme Court, we turn to the issue of deciding how to classify plaintiffs. We begin with the determination of whether plaintiff is a public official. We then turn to the more complex question of classifying nongovernmental plaintiffs.

a. IDENTIFYING A "PUBLIC OFFICIAL"

In Rosenblatt v. Baer, 383 U.S. 75 (1966), plaintiff Baer had been hired by the three elected county commissioners to supervise a public recreation facility owned by the county. When he sued over a newspaper attack on the management of the facility, Justice Brennan's majority opinion held that Baer might be a "public official" under the *Times* rule:

> Criticism of government is at the very center of the constitutionally protected area of free discussion. . . . It is clear . . . that the "public official" designation applies at the very least to those among the hierarchy of government employees who have, or appear to the public to have, substantial responsibility for or control over the conduct of government affairs.
>
> . . . Where a position in government has such apparent importance that the public has an independent interest in the qualifications and performance of the person who holds it, beyond the general public interest in the qualifications and performance of all government employees, both elements we identified in *New York Times* are present and the *New York Times* malice standards apply.[13]

Justice Stewart's separate concurrence in *Rosenblatt* sought to express the affirmative values to be found in a libel action:

> The right of a man to the protection of his own reputation from unjustified invasion and wrongful hurt reflects no more than our basic concept of the essential dignity and worth of every human being—a concept at the root of any decent system of ordered liberty.

From the social perspective, he warned of dangers associated with Senator Joseph McCarthy:

> Moreover, the preventive effect of liability for defamation serves an important public purpose. For the rights and values of private personality far transcend mere personal interests. Surely if the 1950's taught us anything, they taught us that the poisonous atmosphere of the easy lie can infect and degrade a whole society.

Candidates. In a pair of cases involving false charges made about a candidate for office, the Court unanimously extended the *Times* rationale to candidates because "it can hardly be doubted that the constitutional guarantee has its fullest and most urgent application precisely to the conduct of campaigns for political office." Monitor Patriot Co. v. Roy, 401 U.S. 265 (1971), and Ocala Star-Banner Co. v. Damron, 401 U.S. 295 (1971).

---

[13] It is suggested that this test might apply to a night watchman accused of stealing state secrets. But a conclusion that the *New York Times* malice standards apply could not be reached merely because a statement defamatory of some person in government employ catches the public's interest: that conclusion would virtually disregard society's interest in protecting reputation. The employee's position must be one which would invite public scrutiny and discussion of the person holding it, entirely apart from the scrutiny and discussion occasioned by the particular charges in controversy.

The three-legged stool. Perhaps the most extensive effort to grapple with the "public official" category occurred in Kassel v. Gannett Co., Inc., 875 F.2d 935 (1st Cir.1989), in which plaintiff staff psychologist for the Veterans Administration claimed that he was defamed by an article in defendant's newspaper mistakenly attributing to him a statement about the Vietnam war. The district court ruled that plaintiff was not a public official, and the jury found for the plaintiff. The court of appeals affirmed on the issue of plaintiff's status.

The court thought that the test rested on a "tripodal base." The first leg recognizes that discussion of issues of public importance must be "uninhibited, robust, and wide-open." Thus, "[p]olicymakers, upper-level administrators, and supervisors" are public officials because they "occupy niches of 'apparent importance' sufficient to give the public an independent interest in the qualifications and performances of the persons who hold them." If, as stated in the *Rosenblatt* footnote, "a night watchman accused of stealing state secrets" is not a public official, then the "inherent attributes of the position, not the occurrence of random events, must signify the line of demarcation."

The second leg entails the plaintiff's access to media to counteract the impact of false and injurious statements (building on *Gertz*). The court explained that "government workers who, by virtue of their employment, may easily defuse erroneous or misleading reports without judicial assistance should more likely be ranked as 'public officials' for libel law purposes. Conversely, those who work for the sovereign, but who enjoy little or no sway over, or 'special' access to, the news media are less likely to be trapped within the seine" of public officialdom.

The final leg, again drawing on *Gertz*, involves the degree to which the plaintiff has assumed the risk of exposure to criticism by the media: "[p]ersons who actively seek positions of influence in public life do so with the knowledge that, if successful in attaining their goals, diminished privacy will result." On the other hand, there are public employees who have not assumed an influential role in government and cannot be said to have "exposed themselves to increasing risk of injury from defamatory falsehood concerning them."

The court then applied its analysis to the facts of the case: (1) plaintiff held a lower level position at the VA that did not invite scrutiny independent of the controversy caused by the defendant's story and did not "govern" in any sense of the word. His job was "seeing patients and administering tests." (2) He did not have access to channels of communication that would enable him to counteract false and injurious statements. The plaintiff's position as staff psychologist "commanded no extraordinary media exposure" and his "duties did not involve answering press inquiries." To focus on the attention he attracted *after* the story was "bootstrapping of the most flagrant sort." (3) There was "no evidence that, by accepting employment as a staff psychologist in a VA hospital, Kassel assumed the risk of sensationalist media coverage."

Do the self-help and assumed risk analyses make sense in the context of public officials? Consider *Rosenblatt* and *Kassel* in the context of each of the following occupations.

Police officers. There is virtual unanimity that police officers are public officials for defamation purposes. See Rotkiewicz v. Sadowsky, 730 N.E.2d 282 (Mass.2000). See e.g. Jones v. Palmer Communications, Inc., 440 N.W.2d 884 (Iowa 1989).

Public school personnel. The courts are split over whether public school teachers are public officials. See Kelley v. Bonney, 606 A.2d 693 (Conn.1992)(citing cases on both sides of the question). Courts also disagree about public school principals. Compare Palmer v. Bennington School District, 615 A.2d 498 (Vt.1992)(public official), with Ellerbee v. Mills, 422 S.E.2d 539 (Ga.1992)(not public official).

Social workers. In the relatively few cases presenting the issue, social workers have been held to be public officials. See e.g. Kahn v. Bower, 284 Cal.Rptr. 244 (App.1991).

Former public officials. Former officials remain public officials for purposes of commentary on their past performance. In Crane v. The Arizona Republic, 972 F.2d 1511 (9th Cir.1992), a former head of the Justice Department's organized crime strike force was a public official when charged with having "avoided prosecuting certain organized crime figures." But he was a private person as to charges that, after leaving office, as an attorney he exploited personal contacts in the department to seek favorable treatment for his clients.

b. IDENTIFYING A "PUBLIC FIGURE"

After *Gertz*, the distinction between public and private plaintiffs became important. The Court addressed that topic in a series of cases that we now briefly summarize, and which are discussed again in the principal case that follows.

The Firestone *case.* In Time Inc. v. Firestone, 424 U.S. 448 (1976), a magazine incorrectly reported that a member of "one of America's wealthier industrial families" had obtained a divorce because of his wife's adultery. A five-member majority held plaintiff to be private: "Respondent did not assume any role of especial prominence in the affairs of society, other than perhaps Palm Beach society, and she did not thrust herself to the forefront of any particular public controversy in order to influence the resolution of the issues involved in it." The fact that the case may have been of great public interest did not make plaintiff a public figure. Moreover, the Court observed, plaintiff was compelled to go to court to seek relief in a marital dispute and her involvement was not voluntary. The fact that she held "a few" press conferences during the case did not change her otherwise private status. She did not attempt to use them to influence the outcome of the trial or to thrust herself into an unrelated dispute. (Defendant's added argument that the reporting of judicial proceedings should never be subject to liability for negligence was rejected as an attempt to resurrect the subject matter criterion, which *Gertz* had rejected.)

The Wolston *case.* In Wolston v. Reader's Digest Ass'n, 443 U.S. 157 (1979), defendant's 1974 book incorrectly listed plaintiff as one of a group "who were convicted of espionage or falsifying information or perjury and/or contempt charges following espionage indictments or who fled to the Soviet bloc to avoid prosecution." In fact, he had been indicted for and convicted of contempt of court for failing to appear before a grand jury.

During the six weeks in 1958 between his failure to appear and his sentencing, plaintiff's case was the subject of 15 stories in Washington and New York newspapers. "This flurry of publicity subsided" following the sentencing, and plaintiff "succeeded for the most part in returning to the private life he had led" prior to the subpoena. A six-member majority held plaintiff private because he had neither "voluntarily thrust" nor "injected" himself into the forefront of the controversy surrounding the investigation of Soviet espionage in the United States. Wolston had not "engaged the attention of the public in an attempt to influence the resolution of the issues involved. . . . He did not in any way seek to arouse public sentiment in his favor and against the investigation. Thus, this is not a case where a defendant invites a citation for contempt in order to use the contempt citation as a fulcrum to create public discussion about the methods being used in connection with an investigation or prosecution."

The Hutchinson *case.* In Hutchinson v. Proxmire, 443 U.S. 111 (1979), decided the same day as *Wolston,* defendant, a United States Senator, had criticized government grants to certain scientists, including plaintiff, on the grounds that the grants were examples of wasteful government spending on unjustifiable scientific research. (Absolute privilege did not apply because the claimed defamations were in press releases and newsletters.)

The eight-member majority held plaintiff to be private. Neither the fact that plaintiff had successfully applied for federal funds nor that he had access to media to respond to Senator Proxmire's charges, "demonstrates that Hutchinson was a public figure prior to the controversy." Rather, his "activities and public profile are much like those of countless members of his profession. His published writings reach a relatively small category of professionals concerned with research in human behavior." Those charged with defamation "cannot, by their own conduct, create their own defense by making the claimant a public figure. See [*Wolston*]." Nor had plaintiff "assumed any role of public prominence in the broad question of concern about expenditures."

The Court then left the lower courts to work out the distinction. The following case suggests the kind of inquiry that is required.

Wells v. Liddy

United States Court of Appeals, Fourth Circuit, 1999.
186 F.3d 505.

■ Before WILKINS and WILLIAMS, CIRCUIT JUDGES, and LEE, UNITED STATES DISTRICT JUDGE for the Eastern District of Virginia, sitting by designation.

■ WILLIAMS, CIRCUIT JUDGE.

[This case grew out of the Watergate break-in at the Democratic National Committee (DNC) in June 1972. The "majority or conventional" theory had been that the burglars were attempting to replace a malfunctioning listening device that had been installed in an earlier break-in. During the break-in period plaintiff Ida Maxine ("Maxie") Wells had worked as secretary to Spencer Oliver, the Executive Director of the Association of State Democratic Chairmen, whose phone was tapped. Wells often used Oliver's phone when he was not there, and her calls were also intercepted. A key to her desk was found in the burglars' possession when they were arrested. Wells was subpoenaed to testify before the grand jury and also (although not on television) before the Senate Select Committee that investigated the break-in.

Defendant Liddy at the time was counsel to the Committee to Reelect the President (Nixon). As a result of the break-in he was convicted on multiple counts, including burglary, conspiracy, and interception of wire and oral communications, and served 52 months in jail.

In 1984, the book *Secret Agenda* by Jim Hougan mentioned the possibility that the break-in was tied in some way to the arrest of an attorney named Phillip Mackin Bailley for Mann Act charges. Wells was identified as the person whose desk key was found on one of the burglars, but Wells was not mentioned in connection with prostitution. In 1991, Len Colodny and Robert Gettlin wrote a book called *Silent Coup: The Removal of a President*, which relied heavily on Bailley, and asserted that the break-in had been ordered by John Dean, legal counsel to President Nixon, to see whether the DNC was arranging call girls for visiting dignitaries. The book asserted that Dean wanted to learn whether Maureen Biner's name appeared on the list or in photographs that were said to be locked in a drawer in Wells's desk. Alfred Baldwin, who was operating the listening post and other surveillance, was said to have posed as a friend of Oliver's and obtained a visit to the DNC office to "case" it, during which he "somehow obtained a key from Wells or stole one."

By 1991, Liddy had concluded that the book's theory was correct and began repeating it in various forms in various contexts. This case involves suits over four such pronouncements: (1) a speech at James Madison University in Virginia; (2) during his talk on a cruise ship in the Mediterranean; (3) over a radio show heard nationwide; and (4) the website of an organization, Accuracy in Media.

The trial judge granted summary judgment on all four episodes. The court of appeals concluded that the statement in the JMU speech was defamatory under Virginia law because listeners could well have taken it to mean that "Wells was a participant in a scheme to procure prostitutes." The same analysis applied to the cruise ship. After reviewing the transcript of the radio show the court concluded that it could not be found defamatory. Nor could the court find any proof that Liddy had ever authorized Accuracy in Media to state his theory. The court then turned to the constitutional questions that remained in the two actions that survived state law requirements.]

. . .

IV.

Wells next appeals the district court's conclusion that for purposes of the public debate on Watergate she is an involuntary public figure, and therefore required to prove that Liddy acted with actual malice before she can recover compensatory damages for actual injury. Liddy argues that the district court's conclusion that Wells is an involuntary public figure is correct and asserts in the alternative that Wells's participation in Watergate-related dialogue is sufficient to qualify her as a voluntary limited-purpose public figure. Because the level of culpability the plaintiff must prove to recover compensatory damages under state law is dependent upon the plaintiff's public or private figure status, we must address this issue, which is a matter of law. [ ]

A.

[The court reviewed the constitutional developments from *New York Times* to *Gertz*—and noted that there was no claim that Wells was an "all-purpose public figure."], [W]e have interpreted *Gertz* as creating three distinct types of public figures:

> (1) "involuntary public figures," who become public figures through no purposeful action of their own; (2) "all-purpose public figures," who achieve such pervasive fame or notoriety that they become public figures for all purposes and in all contexts; and (3) "limited-purpose public figures," who voluntarily inject themselves into a particular public controversy and thereby become public figures for a limited range of issues.

Foretich v. Capital Cities/ABC, Inc., 37 F.3d 1541, 1551–52 (4th Cir.1994).

Since *Gertz*, it has been clear that the First Amendment sets limits on a public figure's ability to recover for defamation. A public figure "may recover for injury to reputation only on clear and convincing proof that the defamatory falsehood was made with knowledge of its falsity or with reckless disregard for the truth." [ ] After *Gertz*, however, the level of defendant's fault that must be proved by private figures to recover compensatory damages in defamation actions is left to the states even when the defamatory communication touches on matters of public concern, with the caveat that strict liability schemes run afoul of the First Amendment. [ ]

B.

The Court has revisited public figure status three times since it handed down its decision in *Gertz*. [The Court reviewed *Firestone, Wolston* and *Proxmire*.]

C.

Applying the foregoing Supreme Court precedents, this Circuit has developed a five-factor test to determine whether a plaintiff is a limited-purpose public figure. Liddy has asserted that Wells meets the test for limited-purpose public figure status. Because the jurisprudence regarding limited-purpose public figures is well-established in this Circuit, we address Liddy's contentions regarding the voluntary nature of Wells's participation in the Watergate controversy first, before weighing-in on the district court's ultimate conclusion that Wells qualifies as an involuntary public figure.

Before a plaintiff can be classified, as a matter of law, as a limited-purpose public figure, the defendant must prove that:

> (1) the plaintiff has access to channels of effective communication;

> (2) the plaintiff voluntarily assumed a role of special prominence in the public controversy;

> (3) the plaintiff sought to influence the resolution or outcome of the controversy;

> (4) the controversy existed prior to the publication of the defamatory statement; and

> (5) the plaintiff retained public-figure status at the time of the alleged defamation.

See Reuber v. Food Chemical News, Inc., 925 F.2d 703, 708–10 (4th Cir.1991) (en banc). In *Foretich*, we added an additional consideration to the limited-purpose public figure inquiry when we held that if the content of a defamatory statement touches upon an area that state law has traditionally considered to be defamatory per se, then the plaintiff cannot be categorized as a limited-purpose public figure solely because he makes reasonable public replies to the statement. [ ] In evaluating an individual's limited-purpose public figure status we look at "the nature and extent of an individual's participation in the particular controversy giving rise to the defamation." [*Gertz*]

In order to prevail on his assertion that Wells's participation in the Watergate controversy merits her classification as a limited-purpose public figure Liddy must establish each of the five elements recited above. See *Foretich*, [ ] (noting that the defendant bears the burden on all five elements). According to Liddy, Wells's voluntary injection into the Watergate controversy, an event of unprecedented historical interest and importance, is sufficient to satisfy the five-part test because she was interviewed by the FBI, mentioned in the newspaper, subpoenaed to testify before the grand jury, and called before the Senate in the early 1970s. Additionally, Liddy points to several media exposures Wells has had since the prostitution-oriented theory of the Watergate break-in emerged in 1984. Specifically, Liddy points out that Wells published a letter to the editor in the *New York Times* in 1985, spoke to a reporter on the twentieth anniversary of the Watergate break-in for an article that appeared in the *Washington Post* in 1992, spoke to the BBC in 1993, was named in an Arts & Entertainment Network broadcast entitled "The Key to Watergate" and a Geraldo Rivera documentary "Now it Can be Told," and spoke to historian James Rosen. Although Liddy has amply demonstrated that Wells has "access to channels of effective communication," we conclude that Liddy has failed to show that Wells has "voluntarily assumed [a role] of special prominence in the . . . public controversy."[24] Therefore, we cannot conclude that Wells is a limited-purpose public figure.

[The court concluded that *Gertz*, *Firestone*, and *Wolston* supported the view that limited-purpose public figure status requires that the plaintiff play an active role in a controversy.]

In light of the foregoing, viewing Wells's public exposures during and after the Watergate break-in collectively, we conclude that Wells has not "voluntarily assumed [a role] of special prominence in the . . . public controversy." *Foretich* [ ]. *Gertz*, *Firestone*, and *Wolston* establish conclusively that Wells was not a public figure during the immediate aftermath of the Watergate break-in in the 1970s. Like Wolston, Wells's involvement in the Watergate investigation was wholly involuntarily; she was "dragged unwillingly into the controversy," [ ], initially by the commission of a crime at her workplace and later by the governmental investigation that ensued. Wells's discussions with the FBI, response to the grand jury subpoena, and appearance before the Senate committee simply were not voluntary actions but rather were compelled by the force of law. [ ] Even if we assume *arguendo* that Wells was involved in criminal activity during her employment at the DNC, precedent

---

[24] We need not dwell on what is usually a preliminary question, whether the statements in question were made in connection with a public controversy. [ ] (indicating that the public controversy requirement is a preliminary inquiry). Watergate is perhaps the quintessential public controversy, an event that has evoked extensive political and historical interest and debate and has had effects felt well beyond the direct participants. . . .

counsels that activity likely to engender publicity, even criminal activity, does not equate to taking on a role of special prominence in a public controversy. See *Wolston*, [ ] ("reject[ing] the further contention . . . that any person who engages in criminal conduct automatically becomes a public figure for purposes of comment on a limited range of issues relating to his conviction."); *Gertz*, [ ] (holding that an attorney who took on a case linked to a public controversy but who did not speak to the press was not a public figure).

The question then arises whether Wells voluntarily has attained special prominence in the Watergate controversy as a result of the revelation of the prostitution-related theory of the break-in. For the most part, Wells's reported role in Watergate has remained unchanged after *Secret Agenda* [an earlier book on Watergate] and *Silent Coup*— Wells is named as Spencer Oliver's secretary and a woman whose phone calls were overheard on illegal wire taps. To the extent that Wells's role has expanded, it has done so because *Secret Agenda* and *Silent Coup* revealed that Watergate burglar Martinez possessed a key to her desk, exposed prostitution activities that purportedly were occurring at the DNC, and implied that Wells may have had some connection to those illicit activities. There is no proof that any of these disclosures were the result of Wells's voluntary interaction with the authors. Instead, it is clear, as the district court concluded, that the story was divulged by a sole source, Bailley. [ ] Because the disclosures of *Secret Agenda* and *Silent Coup* cannot be fairly attributed to Wells's voluntary participation, we cannot conclude that she sought a prominent role in the Watergate controversy as a result of being named therein.

Therefore, the question of whether Wells has "voluntarily assumed [a role] of special prominence in the . . . public controversy," *Foretich*, [ ], ultimately, on this record, revolves around four media contacts: (1) her letter-to-the-editor of the *New York Times*, published in 1985; (2) her 1992 interview with a *Washington Post* reporter on the twentieth anniversary of the Watergate break-in; (3) her interview with the BBC in 1993; and (4) her discussions with historian James Rosen. The letter-to-the-editor, made in response to a book review of *Secret Agenda* that named her as a figure involved in arranging dates with prostitutes, clearly falls within the category of self-help and reasonable response to reputation-injuring statements of the type that we approved in *Foretich*. [ ] Therefore, Wells's letter-to-the-editor should not contribute to the public figure analysis.

Regarding Wells's three other media contacts, *Firestone* makes clear that voluntary discussion of events with the press does not per se indicate that a defamation plaintiff has "thrust herself to the forefront of [a public] controversy." [ ] Rather, when an individual has had contact with the press, the proper questions are whether he has attempted to influence the merits of a controversy, or has "draw[n] attention to himself in order to invite public comment," *Wolston*, [ ], or "invited that degree of public attention and comment . . . essential to meet the public figure level," [*Hutchinson v. Proxmire*]. . . .

Twenty-seven years after the event, the still-controversial aspects of Watergate revolve around bigger issues such as why the break-in occurred, who was responsible, whether our Constitutional checks and balances are adequate, whether the American populace lost confidence in politicians as a result of the scandal, etc. Liddy has failed to point to evidence demonstrating that Wells has made any attempt to become a spokesperson on any of these types of matters. Therefore, we cannot conclude that Wells has voluntarily undertaken a position at the forefront of the Watergate controversy. The record establishes that Wells has conducted only a handful of interviews over the course of twenty-seven years and each one has been in response to inquiries from reporters requesting her eye-witness account. As a result, we conclude that Liddy has not met his burden of proving each of the five elements of this circuit's limited-purpose public figure test, and we must determine that Wells is not a limited-purpose public figure under our jurisprudence.

D.

The district court also concluded that Wells did not meet the five-part test governing limited-purpose public figure status. Rather, the district court concluded that Wells was an involuntary public figure. [ ] Wells appeals this ruling. We conclude that Wells was not an involuntary public figure and reverse.

The concept of an involuntary public figure has its origins in one sentence from *Gertz*: "Hypothetically, it may be possible for someone to become a public figure through no purposeful action of his own, but the instances of truly involuntary public figures must be exceedingly rare." [ ] So rarely have courts determined that an individual was an involuntary public figure that commentators have questioned the continuing existence of that category. [ ] Although we have acknowledged that involuntary public figures constitute one of the three classes of public figures categorized in *Gertz*, we have never explored the parameters of the involuntary branch of the public figure typography. [ ] Thus, Wells's challenge to the district court's conclusion that she is an involuntary public figure presents a novel question of law.

The district court ruled, applying Dameron v. Washington Magazine, Inc., 779 F.2d 736 (D.C.Cir.1985), that Wells was an involuntary public figure because she had the "misfortune" of being "drawn by a series of events into the Watergate controversy." [ ] Because we conclude that "misfortune" is but one aspect of the considerations that should be weighed before concluding that an individual is an involuntary public figure, we are not persuaded by the district court's analysis.

The *Dameron* case, the leading case on involuntary public figure status, involved an air-traffic controller who had been the sole controller on duty during a 1974 airline crash near Dulles Airport in Northern Virginia. [ ] In 1982, following the crash of Air Florida Flight 90 into the Potomac River on takeoff from National Airport in Washington, D.C., *Washingtonian* magazine published a story that listed, *inter alia*, plane crashes that had occurred in the Washington, D.C. metropolitan area and were attributable to controller error. [ ] The magazine article stated that controller error was partially to blame for the 1974 Dulles crash. [ ] As a result, the air traffic controller filed a defamation action. [ ]

The D.C. Circuit, recognizing that the air traffic controller had not voluntarily injected himself into a public controversy, and therefore could not satisfy the court's definition of a limited-purpose public figure, concluded that the air traffic controller could nevertheless be considered a public figure. [ ] The court applied two of the three parts of its *Waldbaum* test for limited-purpose public figures and evaluated whether there was a public controversy and whether the allegedly defamatory statements concerned the public controversy. [ ] (citing *Waldbaum v. Fairchild Publications, Inc.*, 627 F.2d 1287, 1296–98 (D.C.Cir.1980)). Instead of inquiring whether the air traffic controller had voluntarily entered the fray, however, the D.C. Circuit concluded that "[b]y sheer bad luck" the air traffic controller had become a prominent figure, central to the resolution of a public question. [ ] On that basis, the D.C. Circuit held that the air traffic controller was an involuntary public figure. [ ]

We are hesitant to rest involuntary public figure status upon "sheer bad luck." *Gertz* tells us that involuntary public figures "must be exceedingly rare," [ ], and, unfortunately, bad luck is relatively common. The *Dameron* definition of an involuntary public figure, someone who by bad luck is an important figure in a public controversy, runs the risk of returning us to the *Rosenbloom* plurality's conception of defamation law. Under *Rosenbloom*, all defamation plaintiffs were required to prove actual malice when the allegedly defamatory statements occurred during "discussion and communication involving matters of public or general concern, without regard to whether the persons involved are famous or anonymous." [ ] The Supreme Court expressly repudiated the "public interest" test in *Gertz*, [ ], and further disavowed it in *Wolston*, [ ] ("To accept such reasoning would in effect reestablish the doctrine advanced by the plurality opinion in *Rosenbloom* . . . which concluded that the *New York Times* standard should extend to defamatory falsehoods relating to private persons if the statements involved matters of public or general concern. We repudiated this approach in *Gertz* and in *Firestone*, however, and we reject it again today."). Because *Dameron* has not narrowly tailored the class of possible involuntary public figures, it has created a class of individuals who must prove actual malice that is equivalent to the class in *Rosenbloom*. Under either *Dameron* or *Rosenbloom* all individuals defamed during discourse on a matter of public concern must prove actual malice. In light of the Supreme Court's repeated rejection of *Rosenbloom*, we are unwilling to adopt an approach that returns us to an analysis that is indistinguishable. [ ]

In order to flesh out the boundaries of who may constitute an involuntary public figure, a return to *Gertz*, the only Supreme Court case to mention the concept, is in order. In *Gertz*, Justice Powell iterated two rationales for concluding that public figure status must be the determinative inquiry in the balance of interests between the plaintiff and the First Amendment in a defamation case. First, the public figure can take better advantage of the free press and has an easier time resorting to self-help because notoriety guarantees better access to the media and channels of communication. [ ] Second, the public figure has taken actions through which he has voluntarily assumed the risk of publicity. [ ] We conclude that in order to ensure that the balance between states' and individuals' interests in protection of reputation and First Amendment freedoms at the heart of Constitutional defamation law is maintained, any standard for determining who is an involuntary public figure must be mindful of both of these underpinnings. See Khawar v. Globe Int'l, Inc., [965 P.2d 696, 702 (Cal.1998), reprinted p. 1138 infra] (holding that the characterization of involuntary public figure must be reserved for those individuals who satisfy both of *Gertz*'s supporting grounds), cert. denied, 526 U.S. 1114 (1999). Yet, because the usual and natural conception of a public figure encompasses a sense of voluntary participation in public debate, and because to do otherwise would threaten a return to *Rosenbloom*, the class of involuntary public figures must be a narrow one, so as to encompass only "exceedingly rare" cases. [ ]

With *Gertz*'s two supporting rationales and the need for a narrow class of involuntary public figures in mind, we believe that the following considerations are warranted. First, to prove that a plaintiff is an involuntary public figure the defendant must demonstrate to the court that the plaintiff has become a central figure in a significant public controversy and that the allegedly defamatory statement has arisen in the course of discourse regarding the public matter. To prove that the plaintiff is a central figure in the controversy, the defendant must put forth evidence that the plaintiff has been the regular focus of media reports[26] on the controversy. A significant public controversy is one that

---

[26] The extent of media coverage required to prove that the plaintiff is a central figure will vary greatly depending upon the scope of the public controversy. For a controversy that is localized in a specific community, the defendant may rely on local media outlets such as the local newspaper and the local television news. In contrast, when the defendant seeks to show that the plaintiff is a central figure in a national or international controversy, the scope of media coverage must be significantly broader.

touches upon serious issues relating to, for example, community values, historical events, governmental or political activity, arts, education, or public safety. Second, although an involuntary public figure need not have sought to publicize her views on the relevant controversy, she must have nonetheless assumed the risk of publicity. Therefore, the defendant must demonstrate that the plaintiff has taken some action, or failed to act when action was required, in circumstances in which a reasonable person would understand that publicity would likely inhere. See Reuber v. Food Chemical News, Inc., 925 F.2d 703, 709 (4th Cir.1991) (en banc)("[E]ven involuntary participants can be public figures when they choose a course of conduct which invites public attention."). Unlike the limited-purpose public figure, an involuntary public figure need not have specifically taken action through which he has voluntarily sought a primary role in the controversy to influence the outcome of debate on the matter.

To summarize, an involuntary public figure has pursued a course of conduct from which it was reasonably foreseeable, at the time of the conduct, that public interest would arise. A public controversy must have actually arisen that is related to, although not necessarily causally linked, to the action. The involuntary public figure must be recognized as a central figure during debate over that matter. Further, we retain two elements of the five-part *Reuber* test, specifically: (1) the controversy existed prior to the publication of the defamatory statement; and (2) the plaintiff retained public-figure status at the time of the alleged defamation. [ ] Additionally, to the extent that an involuntary public figure attempts self-help, the *Foretich* rule must apply with equal strength. [ ]

We believe that the foregoing test captures that "exceedingly rare" individual who, although remaining mute during public discussion of the results of her action, nevertheless has become a principal in an important public matter. Further, this test excludes from the category of involuntary public figures those individuals who by happenstance have been mentioned peripherally in a matter of public interest or have merely been named in a press account. Also, the foregoing analysis avoids resurrecting *Rosenbloom* because this conception of the involuntary public figure does not cast too broad a net and encompass all individuals who become linked in the media to a matter of public concern. Every plaintiff who is allegedly defamed during discussion of a public controversy will not necessarily be required to prove actual malice to recover compensatory damages under this test.

Applying this formulation to Wells, we determine that she is not an involuntary public figure. Wells simply has not been a central figure in media reports on Watergate. Liddy has been able to point to very few published reports on Watergate even mentioning Wells by name. Prior to the revelation of the call-girl ring theory, Liddy has shown that Wells was mentioned by name only in an *International Herald Tribune* article noting that her conversations, and those of her boss Spencer Oliver, had been overheard on a listening device. Since the emergence of the call-girl ring theory, in those instances where the media has mentioned Wells, she has been a very minor figure in the discussion of the primary actors in the Watergate affair—the burglars, Dean, [E. Howard] Hunt, Liddy, and, of course, President Nixon. We cannot say that in any of the reports contained in the record Wells is portrayed as a central figure in the Watergate controversy. The focus has always been on the roles of other people.

. . .

E.

Based upon the preceding analysis, we must conclude that Wells is a private figure. She need not prove actual malice to recover compensatory damages under the applicable law. Therefore, this case must be remanded for the district court to reconsider Wells's claims under the lesser standard. . . .

. . .

VI.

In sum, two statements identified by Wells as potentially defamatory are capable of defamatory meaning: the JMU speech, governed by the substantive law of Virginia, and the cruise ship speech, governed by the maritime common law. Because Wells is a private figure, these two claims must be remanded for trial under the applicable negligence standards for Liddy's culpability. Finally, Wells has succeeded in raising a genuine issue of material fact on the issue of Liddy's actual malice. For these reasons we remand this case for further proceedings consistent with this opinion.

NOTES AND QUESTIONS

1.   What element was missing to make plaintiff a public figure?

2.   Who should have the burden of proof on these facts?

3.   The court notes how important it is to judge these matters by general standards so that others will know where they stand. What kind of guidance can be drawn from this case to advise others?

4.   On the remand of *Wells v. Liddy*, the trial court granted judgment as a matter of law on behalf of defendant after a hung jury. The court of appeals reversed and remanded, 37 Fed.Appx. 53 (4th Cir.2002)(unpublished), because the "evidence did not preclude Wells from proving that Liddy failed to take reasonable steps in assessing the veracity of his statements." On retrial, the jury found that Liddy's statements about plaintiff's association with call girls had not harmed her reputation. See Gibson, Jury Rejects Claim that Liddy Hurt Reputation, Balt. Sun, July 4, 2002, at 1A.

5. Thomas M. Cooley Law Sch. v. Kurzon Strauss, LLP, 759 F.3d 522, 529 (6th Cir.2014), involved a suit by a law school against the law firm that was representing graduates of the school in a putative class action. The graduates alleged misrepresentation of employment statistics by the law school that was defamatory in content. One issue confronted by the court was whether the law school is a limited-purpose public figure. The court concluded in the affirmative, based on the public controversies over whether law school is a good financial investment, whether law schools are being honest with their employment data, and the law school's participation in the debate by responding to reports and articles. Once the court concluded that actual malice was required, and that plaintiff law school had failed to introduce clear and convincing evidence of actual malice, the lower court's granting of summary judgment was affirmed.

6. *General public figures.* General public figures have been few and far between since *Gertz*. According to *Waldbaum*, cited in the principal case:

> [A] general public figure is a well-known "celebrity," his name a "household word." The public recognizes him and follows his words and deeds, either because it regards his ideas, conduct, or judgment as worthy of the attention or because he actively pursues that consideration.

Is that consistent with *Gertz*? Is it a useful way to approach the question? Which of the following might meet the *Waldbaum* standard: Sarah Palin? Tiger Woods? Bill O'Reilly? George Clooney? Oprah Winfrey? Is law-student familiarity or unfamiliarity with a name probative? Conclusive?

7. *Corporations as public figures.* The overwhelming majority of courts have concluded that the fact of incorporation alone does not make the plaintiff a public figure. See Schiavone Construction Co. v. Time, Inc., 619 F.Supp. 684 (D.N.J.1985); Bank of Oregon v. Independent News, Inc., 693 P.2d 35 (Or.1985). Contra Jadwin v. Minneapolis Star & Tribune Co., 367 N.W.2d 476 (Minn.1985).

6. THE DEFENDANT AS COMMENTATOR

Dictum in Justice Powell's *Gertz* opinion denying the concept of a "false idea" was once thought to suggest another constitutional defense. Many lower courts understood this concept to create a means by which defendants were able to win cases on "constitutional" grounds as early as the motion to dismiss the complaint. Of course, this "constitutional defense" required distinguishing between fact and opinion. The Court had already confronted this issue in a case involving a citizen's charge at a city council meeting that plaintiff was "blackmailing" the city in connection with pending real estate negotiations. Greenbelt Cooperative Publishing Ass'n v. Bresler, 398 U.S. 6 (1970). Although in some contexts a charge of "blackmail" might be understood as charging a specific crime, that was not true in this case. The word was "no more than rhetorical hyperbole, a vigorous epithet used by those who considered Bresler's vigorous negotiating position extremely unreasonable." Since no reasonable reader could have taken the report to charge a crime in context, the words were not actionable.

In Letter Carriers v. Austin, 418 U.S. 264 (1974), decided at the same time as *Gertz,* the defendant union had published Jack London's famous definition of a "scab" as a "traitor to his God, his country, his family and his class." The Court held that no one could reasonably understand this to be a charge of the crime of treason. The words were being used "in a loose, figurative sense . . . merely rhetorical hyperbole, a lusty and imaginative expression of the contempt felt by union members toward those who refuse to join them."

Lower courts extended the analysis to claims based on vague language, such as calling plaintiff a "fellow traveler" of the fascists or describing a magazine as an "openly fascist journal." One court called these "loosely definable, variously interpretable statements of opinion . . . made inextricably in the contest of political, social, or philosophical debate." But the same court declared actionable the following charge:

> Like Westbrook Pegler, who lied day after day in his column about Quentin Reynolds and goaded him into a lawsuit, Buckley could be taken to court by any one of several people who had enough money to hire competent legal counsel and nothing else to do.

Buckley v. Littell, 539 F.2d 882 (2d Cir.1976). Why the different treatments?

The "epithet" or "rhetorical hyperbole" analysis had been part of the common law long before the libel area first became constitutionalized. As one court summarized the reasons in rejecting an action by someone referred to as one of "those bastards":

> [I]t is perfectly apparent that [the words] were used as mere epithets, as terms of abuse and opprobrium. As such they had no real meaning except to indicate that the individual who used them was under a strong emotional feeling of dislike toward those about whom he used them. Not being intended or understood as statements of fact they are impossible of proof or disproof. Indeed such words of vituperation and abuse reflect more on the character of the user than they do on that of the individual to whom they are intended to refer.

Curtis Publishing Co. v. Birdsong, 360 F.2d 344 (5th Cir.1966). Do these reasons justify the common law rule? What if the speaker "intended" the words to be understood as statements of fact?

In the 1980s, a number of courts recognized a constitutional defense for "opinion." A good example is Ollman v. Evans, 750 F.2d 970 (D.C.Cir.1984)(en banc), cert. denied, 471 U.S. 1127 (1985). Briefly, syndicated columnists Evans and Novak argued against the proposed appointment of a Marxist political science professor to head the Department of Government and Politics at the University of Maryland.

Among other statements, the column quoted a political scientist who, refusing to be identified, was said to have asserted that "Ollman has no status within the profession, but is a pure and simple activist." The president of the University of Maryland rejected the appointment.

The trial judge's dismissal was affirmed by a split court that produced seven opinions. The lead opinion emphasized four factors for analysis: (1) "the common usage or meaning of the specific language of the challenged statements itself"; (2) "the statement's verifiability—is the statement capable of being objectively characterized as true or false?", (3) "the full context of the statement—the entire article or column"; and (4) "the broader context or setting in which the statement appears. Different types of writing have . . . widely varying social conventions which signal to the reader the likelihood of a statement's being either fact or opinion."

After lower courts spent some years arguing over the *Ollman* approach, the Supreme Court addressed the issue.

Milkovich v. Lorain Journal Co.

Supreme Court of the United States, 1990.
497 U.S. 1, 110 S.Ct. 2695, 111 L.Ed.2d 1.

■ CHIEF JUSTICE REHNQUIST delivered the opinion of the Court.

[Milkovich was coach of the Maple Heights High School wrestling team, which was involved in a brawl with a competing team. After a hearing, the Ohio High School Athletic Association (OHSAA) censured Milkovich and placed his team on probation. Parents of some of the team members sued to enjoin OHSAA from enforcing the probation, contending OHSAA's investigation and hearing violated due process. Milkovich and Scott, the superintendent, testifying at a judicial hearing on the suit, both denied that Milkovich had incited the brawl through his behavior toward the crowd and a meet official. The judge granted the restraining order sought by the parents. A sports columnist who had attended the meet, but not the judicial hearing, wrote about the hearing in a column published the next day in the defendant newspaper. The headline was "Maple beat the law with the 'big lie.'" The theme of the column was that at the judicial hearing Milkovich and Scott misrepresented Milkovich's role in the altercation and thereby prevented the team from receiving the punishment it deserved. The concluding paragraphs of the column were as follows:

> Anyone who attended the meet, whether he be from Maple Heights, Mentor [the opposing school] or impartial observer, knows in his heart that Milkovich and Scott lied at the hearing after each having given his solemn oath to tell the truth.

> But they got away with it.

Is that the kind of lesson we want our young people learning from their high school administrators and coaches?

I think not.

Milkovich and Scott both sued the newspaper, alleging that the column accused them of perjury and thus was libelous per se. After 15 years of litigation and several appeals, the Ohio Court of Appeals held in Milkovich's case that the column was constitutionally protected opinion and granted the newspaper's motion for summary judgment. The Supreme Court reversed.]

[The opinion reviewed the various constitutional limitations imposed on state libel law in the series of cases beginning with *New York Times v. Sullivan*. The Court also mentioned *Hepps*, note 10, p. 1102 supra, and its holding in *Hustler Magazine, Inc. v. Falwell*, p. 931 supra, that an ad parody "could not reasonably have been interpreted as stating actual facts about the public figure involved."]

. . .

Respondents would have us recognize, in addition to the established safeguards discussed above, still another First Amendment-based protection for defamatory statements which are categorized as "opinion" as opposed to "fact." For this proposition they rely principally on the following dictum from our opinion in *Gertz:*

> "Under the First Amendment there is no such thing as a false idea. However pernicious an opinion may seem, we depend for its correction not on the conscience of judges and juries but on the competition of other ideas. But there is no constitutional value in false statements of fact." [ ]

Judge Friendly appropriately observed that this passage "has become the opening salvo in all arguments for protection from defamation actions on the ground of opinion, even though the case did not remotely concern the question." [Cianci v. New Times Publishing Co., 639 F.2d 54 (2d Cir.1980)]. Read in context, though, the fair meaning of the passage is to equate the word "opinion" in the second sentence with the word "idea" in the first sentence. Under this view, the language was merely a reiteration of Justice Holmes' classic "marketplace of ideas" concept. [ ]

Thus we do not think this passage from *Gertz* was intended to create a wholesale defamation exemption for anything that might be labeled "opinion." Not only would such an interpretation be contrary to the tenor and the context of the passage, but it would also ignore the fact that expressions of "opinion" may often imply an assertion of objective fact.

If a speaker says, "In my opinion John Jones is a liar," he implies a knowledge of facts which lead to the conclusion that Jones told an untruth. Even if the speaker states the facts upon which he bases his opinion, if those facts are either incorrect or incomplete, or if his assessment of them is erroneous, the statement may still imply a false assertion of fact. Simply couching such statements in terms of opinion does not dispel these implications; and the statement, "In my opinion Jones is a liar," can cause as much damage to reputation as the statement, "Jones is a liar." As Judge Friendly aptly stated: "[It] would be destructive of the law of libel if a writer could escape liability for accusations of [defamatory conduct] simply by using, explicitly or implicitly, the words 'I think,' " see *Cianci* [ ]. It is worthy of note that at common law, even the privilege of fair comment did not extend to a "false statement of fact, whether it was expressly stated or implied from an expression of opinion." Restatement (Second) of Torts, supra, § 566 Comment *a*.

Apart from their reliance on the *Gertz* dictum, respondents do not really contend that a statement such as, "In my opinion John Jones is a liar," should be protected by a separate privilege for "opinion" under the First Amendment. But they do contend that in every defamation case the First Amendment mandates an inquiry into whether a statement is "opinion" or "fact," and that only the latter statements may be actionable. They propose that a number of factors developed by the lower courts (in what we hold was a mistaken reliance on the *Gertz* dictum) be considered in deciding which is which. But we think the " 'breathing space' " which " 'freedoms of expression require to survive' " [ ] is adequately secured by existing constitutional doctrine without the creation of an artificial dichotomy between "opinion" and fact.

Foremost, we think *Hepps* stands for the proposition that a statement on matters of public concern must be provable as false before there can be liability under state defamation law, at least in situations, like the present, where a media defendant is involved.[6] Thus, unlike the statement, "In my opinion Mayor Jones is a liar," the statement, "In my opinion Mayor Jones shows his abysmal ignorance by accepting the teachings of Marx and Lenin," would not be actionable. *Hepps* ensures that a statement of opinion relating to matters of public concern which does not contain a provably false factual connotation will receive full constitutional protection.

Next, the *Bresler-Letter Carriers-Falwell* line of cases provide protection for statements that cannot "reasonably [be] interpreted as stating actual facts" about an individual. [ ] This provides assurance that public debate will not suffer for lack of "imaginative expression" or the "rhetorical hyperbole" which has traditionally added much to the discourse of our nation. [ ]

The *New York Times-Butts* and *Gertz* culpability requirements further ensure that debate on public issues remains "uninhibited,

---

[6]   In *Hepps* the Court reserved judgment on cases involving nonmedia defendants, [ ] and accordingly we do the same. Prior to *Hepps,* of course, where public-official or public-figure plaintiffs were involved, the *New York Times* rule already required a showing of falsity before liability could result. [ ]

robust, and wide-open." [ ] Thus, where a statement of "opinion" on a matter of public concern reasonably implies false and defamatory facts regarding public figures or officials, those individuals must show that such statements were made with knowledge of their false implications or with reckless disregard of their truth. Similarly, where such a statement involves a private figure on a matter of public concern, a plaintiff must show that the false connotations were made with some level of fault as required by *Gertz*. Finally, the enhanced appellate review required by *Bose Corp.,* provides assurance that the foregoing determinations will be made in a manner so as not to "constitute a forbidden intrusion of the field of free expression." [ ]

We are not persuaded that, in addition to these protections, an additional separate constitutional privilege for "opinion" is required to ensure the freedom of expression guaranteed by the First Amendment. The dispositive question in the present case then becomes whether or not a reasonable factfinder could conclude that the statements [in the column] imply an assertion that petitioner Milkovich perjured himself in a judicial proceeding. We think this question must be answered in the affirmative. . . . This is not the sort of loose, figurative or hyperbolic language which would negate the impression that the writer was seriously maintaining petitioner committed the crime of perjury. Nor does the general tenor of the article negate this impression.

We also think the connotation that petitioner committed perjury is sufficiently factual to be susceptible of being proved true or false. A determination of whether petitioner lied in this instance can be made on a core of objective evidence by comparing, inter alia, petitioner's testimony before the trial court. As the [Ohio Supreme Court noted in the case of the superintendent] "[w]hether or not H. Don Scott did indeed perjure himself is certainly verifiable by a perjury action with evidence adduced from the transcripts and witnesses present at the hearing. Unlike a subjective assertion the averred defamatory language is an articulation of an objectively verifiable event." [ ] So too with petitioner Milkovich.

The numerous decisions discussed above establishing First Amendment protection for defendants in defamation actions surely demonstrate the Court's recognition of the Amendment's vital guarantee of free and uninhibited discussion of public issues. But there is also another side to the equation; we have regularly acknowledged the "important social values which underlie the law of defamation,". . . .

We believe our decision in the present case holds the balance true. The judgment of the Ohio Court of Appeals is reversed and the case remanded for further proceedings not inconsistent with this opinion.

[JUSTICE BRENNAN, joined by JUSTICE MARSHALL, dissented. He said the Court addressed the opinion issue "cogently and almost entirely correctly," and agreed that the lower courts had been under a "misimpression that there is a so-called opinion privilege wholly in addition to the protections we have already found to be guaranteed by the First Amendment." But he disagreed with the application of agreed principles to the facts: "I find that the challenged statements cannot reasonably be interpreted as either stating or implying defamatory facts about petitioner. Under the rule articulated in the majority opinion, therefore, the statements are due 'full constitutional protection.'"

He characterized the columnist's assumption that Milkovich lied as "patently conjecture" and asserted that conjecture is as important to the free flow of ideas and opinions as "imaginative expression" and "rhetorical hyperbole," which the majority agreed are protected. He offered several examples:

> Did NASA officials ignore sound warnings that the Challenger Space Shuttle would explode? Did Cuban-American leaders arrange for John Fitzgerald Kennedy's assassination? Was Kurt Waldheim a Nazi officer? Such questions are matters of public concern long before all the facts are unearthed, if they ever are. Conjecture is a means of fueling a national discourse on such questions and stimulating public pressure for answers from those who know more.

The dissent argued that the language of the column itself made clear to readers that the columnist was engaging in speculation, personal judgment, emotional rhetoric, and moral outrage. "No reasonable reader could understand [the columnist] to be impliedly asserting—as fact—that Milkovich had perjured himself."]

NOTES AND QUESTIONS

1.   Why does the Constitution require protection of rhetorical hyperbole but not opinion? Is rhetorical hyperbole less likely to damage reputation? Is it a more valuable form of speech?

2.   The majority says "the statement, 'In my opinion Mayor Jones shows his abysmal ignorance by accepting the teachings of Marx and Lenin,' would not be actionable." If the mayor does not accept the teachings of Marx and Lenin, might the statement be actionable? Does the Court mean only that the statement that the mayor is abysmally ignorant is not actionable if the rest of the statement is true?

3.   What should the trial judge do if persuaded that the lay readers of a mass-circulation publication took a statement as one of fact but that there is simply no way in which to try the truth or falsity of the statement? For example, what result if a survey showed that virtually all who read that statement concluded that it asserted a "fact"? Does that affect the verifiability issue?

4.   *Parody.* Addressing an issue similar to the one confronted in Hustler Magazine v. Falwell, p. 931 supra, albeit in the defamation context, is Farah v. Esquire Magazine, 736 F.3d 528 (D.C. Cir.2013). A birther book, "Where's the Birth Certificate? The Case that Barack Obama is not Eligible to Be President," was released with some extraordinary claims, including

"It's out! The book that proves Obama's ineligible." One day later, Esquire magazine had an article on its politics blog that was entitled "**BREAKING: Jerome Corsi's Birther Book Pulled from Shelves!**" (emphasis in original). It stated, in part: "In a stunning development one day after the release of [the Corsi book], [Farah (the publisher)] has announced plans to recall and pulp the entire 200,000 first printing run of the book, as well as announcing an offer to refund the purchase price to anyone who has already bought . . . the book." An hour and a half later, Esquire published a notice explaining to those "who didn't figure it out yet" that the article was satire.

The court was confronted with the question, based on the standard adopted in *Hustler*, whether Esquire's statements "could reasonably be understood as stating or implying actual facts about" plaintiffs. One might have thought that those who "didn't get it," some of whom contacted plaintiffs seeking a refund of their purchase, demonstrated that the Esquire article was understood as conveying facts. The Court of Appeals disagreed:

> Indeed, satire is effective as social commentary precisely because it is often grounded in truth. In a similar case involving a satirical news article, the Texas Supreme Court observed that satire works by "distort[ing] . . . the familiar with the pretense of reality in order to convey an underlying critical message." Here, too, Esquire's story conveyed its message by layering fiction upon fact. The test, however, is not whether some actual readers were misled, but whether the hypothetical reasonable reader could be (after time for reflection). And to the extent Farah and Corsi rely on Esquire's "update" to demonstrate reader confusion, Esquire can hardly be penalized for attempting to set the record straight and avoid confusion by those readers who did not at first "get" the satirical nature of Warren's article.

Would Esquire be "penalized" for updating its website to correct misimpressions or is its correction evidence that readers understood Esquire's article as conveying the fact of a recall?

5. The state and lower federal courts have struggled with the approach announced in *Milkovich*, as the following case suggests.

Flamm v. American Association of University Women

United States Court of Appeals, Second Circuit, 2000.
201 F.3d 144.

■ Before: Meskill, Miner and Parker, Circuit Judges.

■ Meskill, Circuit Judge.

. . .

Appellees American Association of University Women and the AAUW Legal Advocacy Fund (collectively "AAUW") are non-profit corporations dedicated to improving educational opportunities for women and girls. Among its other programs and services, the AAUW maintains a referral service of attorneys and other professionals who are willing to consult with women involved in higher education who have brought or are considering bringing gender discrimination actions. As part of this service, the AAUW compiles a directory of the participating attorneys and other professionals, listing names, contact information, and a short blurb about each person. In October 1997 the AAUW distributed copies of the directory, together with a cover letter, to the people listed in it, to members of the AAUW, and to any others requesting a copy.

Neither the cover letter nor the directory explained how the directory was compiled, although two of the directory entries included the notation "not reached in survey." Some of the entries appear to include statements made by the person listed. For example, Mr. K stated: "If they [cases] cannot be resolved early on, then I plan on being there for the long run, since these cases can take 5+ years to work up, try and handle appeals." However, of the approximately 275 entries in the directory, only Flamm's contained a negative comment. His directory entry appeared as follows:

> Leonard N. Flamm 880 Third Ave. New York, N.Y. 10022 B–212/752–3380 H–212/755–7867 Mr. Flamm handles sex discrimination cases in the area of pay equity, harassment, and promotion. *Note: At least one plaintiff has described Flamm as an "ambulance chaser" with interest only in "slam dunk cases."*

Flamm filed suit in state court, alleging that the description "an 'ambulance chaser' with interest only in 'slam dunk cases'" constitutes libel *per se*. He sought both compensatory and punitive damages. The AAUW removed the action to federal court and filed a motion to dismiss. The district court granted the motion because it determined that the statement challenged by Flamm could not reasonably be construed as a statement of objective fact. [ ]

We disagree. In light of the inclusion of the statement in an otherwise fact-laden directory, the description of Flamm as an "ambulance chaser" might imply to the reader of the directory that Flamm engages in the unethical solicitation of clients. Consequently, dismissal at this stage of the proceedings was improper.

DISCUSSION

The central issue on appeal is whether the statement challenged by Flamm is protected by either the United States Constitution or the New York Constitution. . . . The Court's opinion in *Gertz* was widely understood to extend an "absolute constitutional protection" to expressions of opinions. See, e.g., Steinhilber v. Alphonse, [501 N.E.2d 550, 553 (N.Y.1986)].

Subsequently, however, the Supreme Court disclaimed "an additional separate constitutional privilege for 'opinion'" under the First Amendment. [*Milkovich*]. . . .

In response, the Court of Appeals of New York grounded its pre-*Milkovich* protection for expressions of opinion in the New York Constitution. See Immuno AG. v. Moor-Jankowski, [567 N.E.2d 1270 (N.Y.1991)]. In its decision, the court reaffirmed that "the standard articulated and applied in *Steinhilber* furnishes the operative standard in this State for separating actionable fact from protected opinion." [ ] To resolve this appeal we must test the statement challenged by Flamm against the standards set by both the First Amendment and the New York Constitution. Although the analysis "does and is intended to differ," the dispositive inquiry here is the same: whether the challenged statement can reasonably be construed to be stating or implying facts about the defamation plaintiff. [ ]

I.   *The Federal Standard*

In defamation suits against media defendants, a statement that involves a matter of public concern must be provable as false before liability can be established. [ ] This follows directly from [*Hepps*], which requires defamation plaintiffs to bear the burden of proving falsity in suits against media defendants that involve matters of public concern. [ ] The *Milkovich* Court did not decide, however, whether the same rules apply in suits against nonmedia defendants. . . .

The distinctions found in the law of defamation—between matters of public and private concern, between media and nonmedia defendants, and between public officials or public figures and private plaintiffs— were enunciated in an attempt to balance "the State's interest in compensating private individuals for injury to their reputation against the First Amendment interest in protecting . . . expression." See, e.g., Dun & Bradstreet v. Greenmoss Builders, 472 U.S. 749, 757–61 (1985); [The court reviewed the *Rosenbloom-Gertz* sequence.]

The Court re-examined *Gertz* in *Dun & Bradstreet*. In *Dun & Bradstreet*, a defamation action against a credit-reporting agency, the jury awarded plaintiff presumed and punitive damages. The state trial court granted a new trial after the defendant challenged the award under *Gertz*. On appeal, the Vermont Supreme Court reversed. The court acknowledged that a distinction between media defendants and nonmedia defendants would not always be easy to draw, but nonetheless concluded that the constitutional protection of *New York Times* did not extend to nonmedia defendants such as Dun & Bradstreet.

The Supreme Court affirmed on different grounds. Although there was no opinion for the Court, a majority of justices agreed that the *Gertz* rule requiring a showing of actual malice to support recovery of presumed or punitive damages does not apply to cases involving matters of only private concern. The plurality opinion explained: "It is speech on 'matters of public concern' that is 'at the heart of the First Amendment's protection.' . . . In contrast, speech on matters of purely private concern is of less First Amendment concern." [ ]

Significantly, the plurality opinion and the concurring opinions declined to adopt the media/nonmedia distinction drawn by the state court, and that distinction was expressly rejected by the four dissenting justices and by Justice White [who concurred]: "Such a distinction is irreconcilable with the fundamental First Amendment principle that '[t]he inherent worth of . . . speech in terms of its capacity for informing the public does not depend upon the identity of its source, whether corporation, association, union, or individual.' First Amendment difficulties lurk in the definitional questions such an approach would generate. And the distinction would likely be born an anachronism." [ ]

We agree that a distinction drawn according to whether the defendant is a member of the media or not is untenable. However, we need not extend the constitutional safeguards of *Hepps* and *Milkovich*, which involved media defendants, to every defamation action involving a matter of public concern. Rather, in a suit by a private plaintiff involving a matter of public concern, we hold that allegedly defamatory statements must be provably false, and the plaintiff must bear the burden of proving falsity, at least in cases where the statements were directed towards a public audience with an interest in that concern. [ ]

This approach, akin to a "common interest" privilege for matters of public concern, balances the competing values at stake. On the one hand, the state interest in compensating private individuals for wrongful injury to reputation is significantly weaker "when the factfinding process [is] unable to resolve conclusively whether the speech is true or false; it is in those cases that the burden of proof is dispositive." [*Hepps*] On the other hand, the First Amendment interest in protecting free expression is advanced by requiring private plaintiffs to prove the falsity of allegedly defamatory statements involving matters of public concern, especially when the challenged statements are directed towards a public audience with an interest in that concern.

Turning to the case at bar, whether a publication addresses a matter of public concern "must be determined by the content, form, and context of a given statement, as revealed by the whole record." Connick v. Myers, 461 U.S. 138, 147–48 (1983); see also [*Dun & Bradstreet*]. Gender discrimination is a problem of constitutional dimension, and the efforts of the AAUW to combat it clearly relate to a matter of public concern. The purported allegation that Flamm, an attorney specializing in the field, engages in the unethical solicitation of victims of gender discrimination is also a matter for public concern, especially when brought to the public's attention by way of a publication with the imprimatur of the AAUW. See [Unelko Corp. v. Rooney, 912 F.2d 1049, 1056 (9th Cir.1990)] (holding statements about product effectiveness aired on "60 Minutes" to be matter of public concern). Indeed, the common law recognizes that publications commenting on "persons who present [ ] themselves or their services or goods to the public" are matters of public concern. [ ] The directory was also distributed to a public audience with an interest in issues of gender discrimination. It was mailed, at a minimum, to hundreds of Flamm's peers and fellow professionals nationwide. This mailing was clearly intended to, and can reasonably be viewed as an attempt to, influence public discourse and affect the public response to incidents of gender discrimination.

For the foregoing reasons we conclude that, to survive this motion to dismiss, Flamm must have shown that a reasonable person could find that the challenged statement alleges or implies a provably false fact. We conclude that he has.

[The court reviewed *Milkovich* at length.]

Flamm alleges in his complaint that his description in the AAUW directory as an "ambulance chaser" states that he "has engaged in improper activities to solicit and obtain clients." Following *Milkovich*, we must decide whether the description of Flamm as an "ambulance chaser" reasonably implies that he has engaged in unethical solicitation, and if so, whether the accusation of unethical solicitation is capable of being proven false. The second question, however, is conceded by the defendants. They admit that the term "ambulance chaser" is provable as true or false when understood literally to accuse a lawyer of the unethical or criminal behavior of solicitation.

We conclude that the statement challenged by Flamm reasonably implies that he has engaged in unethical solicitation. The directory in all other respects states facts: names, addresses and phone numbers; a note that Ms. R "will not be able to consult with anyone affiliated with the Florida State University system because of a conflict of interest"; the warning that Mr. A "charges a $50.00 initial consultation fee and does not discuss potential cases over the phone"; and so on. Furthermore, the directory has the stated purpose of providing referrals to qualified attorneys and professionals to assist victims of gender discrimination. A reader of the directory, seeing the only negative comment among several hundred entries, would likely turn elsewhere for assistance. Indeed, the note about Flamm is highlighted in italics, suggesting that it warrants special attention and consideration.

[The court held that *Letter Carriers*, p. 1119 supra, did not apply here because "scab" was used in a "loose, figurative sense." Similarly, the "use of the word 'traitor' could not reasonably imply that the plaintiffs were, in fact, being accused of treason."] See also Greenbelt Coop. Publ'g Ass'n v. Bresler, 398 U.S. 6, 14 (1970) (finding it "impossible to believe" that readers of a newspaper article reporting statements made at public hearings would understand "blackmail" to be charging plaintiff with a crime). Here, however, we do not think it would be "impossible to believe" that the description of Flamm as an "ambulance chaser" implies that he engages in unethical solicitation. More to the point, it would not be unreasonable to think so, even if "ambulance chaser" is a figurative way to describe it. Exaggerated rhetoric may be commonplace in labor disputes, but a reasonable reader would not expect similar hyperbole in a straightforward directory of attorneys and other professionals. Indeed, the opposite is true. A reasonable reader is more likely to treat as fact the description of Flamm as an "ambulance chaser" because there is nothing in the otherwise fact-laden directory to suggest otherwise.

Next, the AAUW contends that the phrase "with interest only in 'slam dunk cases'" indicates that the challenged statement cannot be read literally, because "slam dunk" is an imprecise term of slang suggesting that the entire statement amounts to a purely subjective judgment. There is little merit to this argument. Even if the "slam dunk" language might cause a reasonable reader to consider whether the entire statement was merely an informal complaint, we cannot say that it would be unreasonable to conclude otherwise. The description "an 'ambulance chaser' with interest only in 'slam dunk cases'" can reasonably be interpreted to mean an attorney who improperly solicits clients and then takes only easy cases. This reading, which separates to a degree the "ambulance chaser" characterization from the "slam dunk cases" language, is especially plausible because, in the challenged statement as printed, each of those phrases was separately enclosed in quotation marks. It would not be unreasonable to read the "ambulance chaser" excerpt literally, because it could have been unrelated to the "slam dunk cases" reference in whatever passage the AAUW was quoting.

. . .

The AAUW also argues that "ambulance chaser" cannot be read in the literal sense of a lawyer who "has engaged in improper activities to solicit and obtain clients" because dictionary definitions of "ambulance chaser" typically refer to solicitation of negligence or accident victims. [ ] This peculiar argument, challenging the alleged meaning of "ambulance chaser" as overly literal because not literal enough, is without merit. Although "rhetorical hyperbole" and "lusty and imaginative expression" may not be actionable, [*Letter Carriers*], there is at the same time no requirement that the defamatory meaning of a challenged statement correspond to its literal dictionary definition. It is sufficient, for the purpose of defeating this motion to dismiss, that the challenged statement reasonably implies the alleged defamatory meaning.

We therefore hold that the challenged statement is "reasonably susceptible to the defamatory meaning imputed to it." [ ] However, it remains for the jury to decide whether the challenged statement was likely to be understood by the reader in a defamatory sense. [ ]

In sum, the AAUW's contention that the term "ambulance chaser" was mere hyperbole falls short. Considering the "general tenor" of the publication—a directory for referrals put out by a national professional organization—it would not be unreasonable to think that the description of Flamm conveyed an assertion of fact. Thus, the challenged statement reasonably implies a defamatory fact capable of being proven false, and the AAUW is not entitled to dismissal under the First Amendment.

II. *The New York Standard*

In New York, the courts employ a flexible approach in distinguishing actionable fact from non-actionable opinion. Three factors are generally considered: "(1) whether the specific language in issue has a precise meaning which is readily understood; (2) whether the statements are capable of being proven true or false; and (3) whether either the full context of the communication in which the statement appears or the broader social context and surrounding circumstances are such as to 'signal . . . readers or listeners that what is being read or heard is likely to be opinion, not fact.' " [ ] (quoting *Steinhilber*). These criteria apply whether the defendant is a member of the media or not. [ ]

The Court of Appeals of New York has made clear, however, that a proper analysis should not consist of a mechanical enumeration of each factor adopted in *Steinhilber*. Instead, "the court should look to the over-all context in which the assertions were made and determine on that basis 'whether the reasonable reader would have believed that the challenged statements were conveying facts about the libel plaintiff.' " [ ]

Since *Steinhilber*, the Court of Appeals of New York has consistently focused its analysis on the overall context in which the complained-of assertions were made. See [ ] (statements published on op-ed page of newspaper); [ ] (accusation made in the course of a lengthy, copiously documented newspaper series); [*Immuno AG*] (letter to the editor of a scientific journal); see also [*Steinhilber*] (examining first "the content of the whole communication as well as its tone and its apparent purpose"). The *Immuno AG* court only subsequently analyzed the presence of specific language, e.g., the use of "appeared to be," "might well be," "could well happen," and "should be" to signal presumptions and predictions rather than facts. [ ]

In the present case, the challenged language appears in a national directory nearly seventy pages in length, compiled and distributed by a reputable professional organization with a 100 year history of supporting education. The directory purports to list "attorneys and other specialists" willing to consult with women involved in higher education who are seeking redress for sex-based discrimination. The directory provides names, addresses, phone numbers and, generally, a short statement of the person's area of interest or expertise. In such a fact-laden context, the reasonable reader would be "less skeptical and more willing to conclude that [the directory] stated or implied facts." [ ]

The cases cited by the AAUW are unavailing, involving situations (unlike the situation here) that suggest that the alleged defamations should not be understood to be stating facts. . . .

Finally, the district court held that the phrase "with interest only in 'slam dunk cases' " rendered the entire statement so informal as to lack a precise and readily understood meaning. Although acknowledging that " 'ambulance chaser' standing alone may have a precise meaning," and indeed, "does have a specific meaning, particularly among lawyers and professionals," the court focused on the "slam dunk" language. [ ] The court reasoned that "an 'ambulance chaser' is not someone who is interested only in 'slam dunk cases,' but rather, he is someone who is much less selective and who must 'chase' after cases." [ ] We do not agree. There is nothing inherently inconsistent about an "ambulance chaser" interested only in "slam dunk" cases. To accuse Flamm of improper solicitation—but only of easy cases—is still to accuse him of improper solicitation.

The AAUW's other arguments were considered previously and rejected in our discussion of First Amendment privilege. Consequently, the AAUW is not entitled to dismissal at this stage of the litigation.

. . .

NOTES AND QUESTIONS

1.   Note the statement that defendant published in its directory was that one plaintiff had reported that Flamm was an ambulance chaser. The reason that the truth of *that* statement—one plaintiff stated he was an ambulance chaser—was not a defense in the case is that even if one reports facts based on a named source, there is no common law privilege of repetition apart from the special circumstances discussed in the next section at p. 1138 infra.

2.   What should happen on remand of this case? Will the jury have a role?

3.   Why does the court conclude that the defendant is entitled to the protections accorded to the press? Is this conclusion consistent with *Dun & Bradstreet*?

4.   Why does the plaintiff have the burden of proof on the issue of falsity?

5.   How does the federal standard for determining whether a statement is actionable differ from the New York standard? Why is New York permitted to adopt a different standard? Is the court's analysis of the statement sound under both standards?

6.   Is the court's analysis consistent with *Letter Carriers*? With *Greenbelt*?

7. The "fact-opinion" line continues to perplex courts. See, e.g., Weyrich v. The New Republic, 235 F.3d 617 (D.C.Cir.2001)(accusation of "paranoia" not actionable); Horsley v. Rivera, 292 F.3d 695 (11th Cir.2002)(Geraldo Rivera's statement that plaintiff, who published a website with the names of abortion doctors, was an aider and abetter of the murder of a physician was protected by the First Amendment as "rhetorical hyperbole"); Moldea v. New York Times Co., 22 F.3d 310 (D.C.Cir.)(a book reviewer's assertion that the plaintiff's book on professional football contained "too much sloppy journalism to trust the bulk" of the book, was not actionable), cert. denied, 513 U.S. 875 (1994).

8. *State law.* As *Flamm* indicates, some states have asserted that the state's constitutional law applicable to comments may provide broader protection than *Milkovich* offers. New York has been a leader in this move. Compare *Flamm* with *Boeheim*, p. 1011 supra.

Private Plaintiffs and Matters of Public Interest

As noted in *Flamm*, the Supreme Court in *Greenmoss v. Dun & Bradstreet* addressed the category of private plaintiffs who are swept up in discussions of matters of public interest. In *Greenmoss,* Dun & Bradstreet, the credit reporting agency, whose business involves providing confidential information to subscribers about the credit ratings of businesses and others, sent a report to five subscribers stating that Greenmoss Builders, Inc. had filed a voluntary petition for bankruptcy. The report, prepared by a high school student employed by the defendant to review state bankruptcy proceedings, had incorrectly attributed to Greenmoss a bankruptcy petition filed by one of its former employees.

The trial judge permitted the jury to award presumed and punitive damages without finding actual malice. The jury awarded $50,000 in compensatory damages and $300,000 in punitive damages. The Vermont Supreme Court upheld the award on the ground that as a "matter of federal constitutional law, the media protections outlined in *Gertz* are inapplicable to nonmedia defamation actions." The Supreme Court affirmed, 5–4, but on grounds that did not involve the distinction between media and nonmedia defendants.

For a plurality of three, Justice Powell interpreted *Gertz* to apply only to cases in which the expression involved (variously) "a public issue," "public speech," or "an issue of public concern." Although no passages in *Gertz* drew this distinction, the "context of *Gertz*" was such that the opinion could have applied only to "cases involving public speech." Justice Powell asserted that in this case the First Amendment interest differed from that in *Gertz*:

> We have long recognized that not all speech is of equal First Amendment importance. It is speech on "matters of public concern" that is "at the heart of the First Amendment's protection. . . ." In contrast, speech on matters of purely private concern is of less First Amendment concern. . . .

While such speech is not totally unprotected by the First Amendment, [ ], its protections are less stringent. In *Gertz,* we found that the state interest in awarding presumed and punitive damages was not "substantial" in view of their effect on speech at the core of First Amendment concern. [ ] This interest, however, *is* "substantial" relative to the incidental effect these remedies may have on speech of significantly less constitutional interest. The rationale of the common law rules has been the experience and judgment of history that "proof of actual damage will be impossible in a great many cases where, from the character of the defamatory words and the circumstances of publication, it is all but certain that serious harm has resulted in fact." [ ] As a result, courts for centuries have allowed juries to presume that some damage occurred from many defamatory utterances and publications. [ ] This rule furthers the state interest in providing remedies for defamation by ensuring that those remedies are effective. In light of the reduced constitutional value of speech involving no matters of public concern, we hold that the state interest adequately supports awards of presumed and punitive damages—even absent a showing of "actual malice."

Justice Powell also replied to the dissenters:

If the dissent were the law, a woman of impeccable character who was branded a "whore" by a jealous neighbor would have no effective recourse unless she could prove "actual malice" by clear and convincing evidence. This is not malice in the ordinary sense, but in the more demanding sense of *New York Times.* The dissent, would, in effect, constitutionalize the entire common law of libel.

Finally, Justice Powell briefly explained why the speech in the case did not "involve a matter of public concern":

In a related context, we have held that "[w]hether . . . speech addressed a matter of public concern must be determined by [the expression's] content, form, and context . . . as revealed by the whole record." Connick v. Myers, 461 U.S. at 147–148 [district attorney's power to discipline an assistant depends in part on whether the assistant's speech that provoked the discipline involved a "matter of public interest"—Eds.]. These factors indicate that petitioner's credit report concerns no public issue. It was speech solely in the individual interest of the speaker and its specific business audience. [ ] This particular interest warrants no special protection when—as in this case—the speech is wholly false and clearly damaging to the victim's business reputation. [ ] Moreover, since the credit report was made available only to five subscribers, who, under the terms of the subscription agreement, could not disseminate it further, it cannot be said that the report involves any "strong interest in the free flow of commercial information." [ ] There is simply no credible argument that this type of credit reporting requires special protection to ensure that "debate on public issues [will] be uninhibited, robust and wide-open."

In addition, the speech here, like advertising, is hardy and unlikely to be deterred by incidental state regulation. [ ] It is solely motivated by the desire for profit, which, we have noted, is a force less likely to be deterred than others. [ ] Arguably, the reporting here was also more objectively verifiable than speech deserving of greater protection. [ ] In any case, the market provides a powerful incentive to a credit reporting agency to be accurate, since false credit reporting is of no use to creditors. Thus, any incremental "chilling" effect of libel suits would be of decreased significance.

Chief Justice Burger concurred in the judgment only because he felt bound by *Gertz* until it was overruled. He thought *Gertz* was limited to expressions that concern "a matter of general public importance, and that the expression in question here related to a matter of essentially private concern."

Justice White also concurred only in the judgment. He thought both *Times* and *Gertz* had been wrongly decided: He asserted that Justice Powell "declines to follow the *Gertz* approach," which Justice White thought "was intended to reach cases that involve any false statements of fact injurious to reputation, whether the statement is made privately or publicly and whether or not it implicates a matter of public importance."

Justice White agreed with the result in *Greenmoss* because: (1) he was still unreconciled to *Gertz* and (2) strict liability should be used for publications that do not deal with matters of public importance. (He also suggested alternative approaches that the Court might take in these cases—alternatives that we consider p. 1148 infra, as part of a more general look at possible reform.)

There were thus five votes for the recovery of presumed and punitive damages without a showing of actual malice.

Justice Brennan, joined by Justices Marshall, Blackmun and Stevens, dissented. Although protecting the speech in this case is admittedly not the "central meaning of the First Amendment," *Gertz* "makes clear that the First Amendment nonetheless requires restraints on presumed and punitive damages awards for this expression." Apart from unhappiness that the majority justices were "cut[ting] away the protective mantle of *Gertz*," Justice Brennan objected that "[w]ithout explaining what *is* a 'matter of public concern,' the plurality opinion proceeds to serve up a smorgasbord of reasons why the speech at issue here is not, [ ], and on this basis affirms" the award. Any standard that can be gleaned from the opinions is "impoverished" and "irreconcilable with First Amendment principles. The credit reporting at issue here surely involves a subject matter of sufficient public concern to require the comprehensive protections of *Gertz*."

Speech about "economic matters . . . is an important part of our public discourse." An "announcement of the bankruptcy of a local company is information of potentially great concern to residents of the community where the company is located; like the labor dispute at issue in *Thornhill,* such a bankruptcy 'in a single factory may have economic repercussions for a whole region.' "

The possibility that *Greenmoss* might lead to a distinction between media and nonmedia defendants has not been borne out. In this and other cases, a majority of the justices have rejected that distinction. Nonmedia defendants have not been stripped of *Gertz* protection solely because of their nonmedia status. See, e.g., Underwager v. Salter, 22 F.3d 730 (7th Cir.), cert. denied, 513 U.S. 943 (1994)(holding that Wisconsin law would require public figure to prove actual malice in suit against nonmedia defendant).

If the media-nonmedia distinction is not at work, why did the defendant lose in *Greenmoss*? Why was this information not a matter of public concern? Was it that only five persons received the information? Was it that the five could not disseminate it further? Most observers have thought that this limited circulation explains the case because it seems unlikely that news of a commercial bankruptcy would not qualify as a matter of public interest. Indeed it seems certain that *Gertz* would have applied if the erroneous report had appeared in the local newspaper.

Nor has *Greenmoss* been read as allowing public plaintiffs to recover without having to show "actual malice" See, e.g., Dworkin v. Hustler Magazine Inc., 867 F.2d 1188 (9th Cir.) ("we doubt that it is possible to have speech about a public figure but not of public concern"), cert. denied, 493 U.S. 812 (1989). Why should that be?

In Snead v. Redland Aggregates, Ltd., 998 F.2d 1325 (5th Cir.1993), one party sued over a press release issued (in connection with the filing of a complaint) by the other party after failed negotiations between the two. The court treated the case as one involving a private plaintiff and private content so as to come within the framework of *Greenmoss*. The court, concluding that five Justices there supported the use of "common law standards" for what it called "private-private" cases, held that presumed and punitive damages could be awarded without a showing of fault.

In Johnson v. Johnson, 654 A.2d 1212 (R.I.1995), defendant ex-husband called his ex-wife a "whore" in a restaurant. Although the trial judge concluded that the statement was true, he upheld a jury award of $5,000 compensatory and $20,000 punitive damages. Under the state's constitution, in civil and criminal actions for libel or slander "the truth, unless published or uttered from malicious motives, shall be sufficient defense to the person charged." The court upheld the finding that the words had been uttered with ill will sufficient to sustain the compensatory award. But the provocation of the situation was such that punitive damages were not permissible under state law. Although the court noted that the defendant had not preserved "federal constitutional issues," it nonetheless concluded that no federal rule prevented the recovery here. *Greenmoss* showed that *Gertz* did not apply since the statement was not of public concern. Nor did the *Garrison* case, note 6, p. 1074 supra, which "absolutely prohibits punishment of truthful criticisms of public officials," apply to *Johnson* "because we are not dealing with public officials, public figures, or even matters of public concern."

9. *Government officials as commentators.* In Nadel v. Regents of the University of California, 34 Cal.Rptr.2d 188 (App.1994), the court of appeal held that government officials were entitled to the protection of the *New York Times* doctrine in comments made about public figures. The court approved a passage from Shiffrin, Governmental Speech, 27 UCLA L.Rev. 565 (1980):

> Government has legitimate interests in informing, in educating, and in persuading. If government is to secure cooperation in implementing its programs, if it is to be able to maintain a dialogue with its citizens about their needs and the extent to which government can or should meet those needs, government must be able to communicate. An approach that would invalidate all controversial government speech would seriously impair the democratic process.

The court recognized that government has unique power in the war of words with citizens—and that "[e]vents of the past few decades have demonstrated that government is quite capable of misleading the public and defaming its citizens." But the extent of this concern had become "debatable in light of general post-Watergate skepticism about anything government has to say." Moreover, this "claim of plaintiff vulnerability could be made as to any 'big media' defendant." The court concluded that holding government officials subject to liability under the *New York Times* doctrine would reduce potential abuse of power since officials would know they could be held liable under *Times* or *Gertz*. Common law strict liability was thought inconsistent with the role government had to play in the public debate.

As a separate ground for its result, the court noted that in *New York Times,* the Court had suggested that since government officials were often protected for their speech, giving citizens a comparable protection would balance the power. That view suggested that in this case constitutional protection was needed to put the officials not otherwise protected in balance with the citizens.

————

Recall that the AAUW in *Flamm* did not make the statements on its own. Rather, it purported to quote an unidentified respondent. Should the analysis in the case have been different if the source of the statement had been identified in the directory? As noted earlier, the common law developed the fair report privilege to protect those who repeated certain kinds of defamatory statements. A situation not traditionally covered by that privilege is addressed in the following case.

7. THE PRESS AS REPEATER

Khawar v. Globe International, Inc.

Supreme Court of California, 1998.
19 Cal.4th 254, 965 P.2d 696, 79 Cal.Rptr.2d 178, cert. denied, 526 U.S. 1114, 119
S.Ct. 1760, 143 L.Ed.2d 791 (1999).

■ KENNARD, JUSTICE.

We granted review to decide certain issues concerning the federal Constitution's guarantees of freedom of speech and of the press insofar as they restrict a state's ability to impose tort liability for the publication of defamatory falsehoods. More specifically, we address the definition of a "public figure" for purposes of tort and First Amendment law, the existence in this state of a privilege for "neutral reportage," and the showings required to support awards of compensatory and punitive damages for the republication of a defamatory falsehood.

On these issues, we conclude: (1) A young journalist who was photographed near a nationally prominent politician moments before the politician's assassination, but who was never a suspect in the government's investigation of the assassination, whose views on the assassination were never publicized, and who never sought to influence public discussion about the assassination, was not a public figure in relation to a tabloid newspaper's article reporting a book's false accusation that the journalist assassinated the politician; (2) this state does not recognize a neutral reportage privilege for republication of a libel concerning a private figure (and we need not and do not decide here whether this state recognizes a neutral reportage privilege for republication of a libel concerning a public official or public figure); and (3) the evidence produced at the trial in this case supports the jury's findings of negligence and actual malice, which in turn support the awards of compensatory and punitive damages.

[In June 1968, when Senator Robert F. Kennedy was assassinated in Los Angeles, plaintiff was a freelance photographer working on assignment. He was photographed near Kennedy by a friend. Plaintiff did not follow Kennedy into the hall where he was shot. In 1988, a publisher, Roundtable Press, brought out a book by Robert Morrow entitled *The Senator Must Die: The Murder of Robert Kennedy* (the Morrow book), alleging that the Iranian Shah's secret police (SAVAK), working together with the Mafia, carried out the 1968 assassination. The book contended that Kennedy's assassin was not Sirhan Sirhan, who had been convicted of the murder, but a man named Ali Ahmand, whom the Morrow book described as a young Pakistani who, on the evening of the Kennedy assassination, wore a gold-colored sweater and carried what appeared to be a camera but was actually the gun with which Ahmand killed Kennedy. The Morrow book contained four photographs of a young man the book identified as Ali Ahmand standing in a group of people around Kennedy at the Ambassador Hotel in Los Angeles shortly before Kennedy was assassinated.]

Globe International, Inc., (Globe) publishes a weekly tabloid newspaper called Globe. Its issue of April 4, 1989, contained an article on page 9 under the headline: *Former CIA Agent Claims*: IRANIANS KILLED BOBBY KENNEDY FOR THE MAFIA (the Globe article). Another headline, appearing on the front page of the same issue, stated: *Iranian secret police killed Bobby Kennedy*. The Globe article, written by John Blackburn (a freelance reporter and former Globe staff reporter), gave an abbreviated, uncritical summary of the Morrow book's allegations. The Globe article included a photograph from the Morrow book showing a group of men standing near Kennedy; Globe enlarged the image of these individuals and added an arrow pointing to one of these men and identifying him as the assassin Ali Ahmand. [In fact, the arrow pointed to plaintiff.]

[Plaintiff and his father (Ali Ahmad—not Ahmand) sued for defamation.] Morrow defaulted, and Roundtable settled with both Khawar and Ahmad before trial. As part of the settlement, Roundtable executed a retraction disavowing "any and all statements, intimations, or references that Khalid Iqbal Khawar or Ali Ahmad were in any way associated with or committed the assassination of United States Senator Robert F. Kennedy." A jury trial ensued on the claims against Globe.

. . . After Khawar read the Globe article, he became very frightened for his own safety and that of his family. He received accusatory and threatening telephone calls about the article from as far away as Thailand, he and his children received death threats, and his home and his son's car were vandalized. A Bakersfield television station interviewed Khawar about the Globe article.

. . . As to Khawar, the jury returned, among others, these special verdicts: (1) the Globe article contained statements about Khawar that were false and defamatory; (2) Globe published the article negligently and with malice or oppression; (3) with respect to Kennedy's assassination, Khawar was a private rather than a public figure; and (4) the Globe article was a neutral and accurate report of the Morrow book. The parties had previously agreed that the jury's findings on the last two issues would be advisory only. The jury awarded Khawar $100,000 for injury to his reputation, $400,000 for emotional distress, $175,000 in presumed damages, and, after a separate punitive damages phase, $500,000 in punitive damages.

After the return of these special verdicts, the trial court reviewed those that were deemed advisory and determined as a matter of law that (1) the Globe article was *not* an accurate and neutral report of the statements and charges made in the Morrow book (thus disagreeing with and rejecting the jury's advisory special verdict); and (2) with respect to the events in question, Khawar was a private and not a public figure (thus agreeing with and adopting the jury's advisory special verdict). The trial court's finding that the Globe article was not an accurate and neutral report of the Morrow book was apparently based on the court's subsidiary finding that although Khawar could be identified from the photograph of him that appeared in the Globe article, which included an arrow pointing directly at Khawar, it was impossible to identify Khawar from the smaller, darker, and less distinct image of him, without an arrow, that appeared in the Morrow book. Based upon its findings that Khawar was not named in and could not be identified from the photographs in the Morrow book, the trial court vacated Morrow's default and ultimately entered judgment in his favor. The court granted judgment on the special verdicts for Khawar and against Globe in the amount of $1,175,000.

Globe appealed from the judgment. The Court of Appeal reached these conclusions: (1) Khawar was not a public figure; (2) California has not adopted a neutral reportage privilege for private figures; (3) in light of these conclusions, it was unnecessary to decide whether California has adopted a neutral reportage privilege for public figures or whether the Globe article was a neutral and accurate report of the Morrow book; and (4) the evidence supported the trial court's findings of negligence and actual malice. The Court of Appeal affirmed the judgment.

We granted Globe's petition for review raising these issues: (1) When a published book places a person at the center of a public controversy, is that person an involuntary public figure for the limited purpose of a media report about that book and that controversy? (2) Does the First Amendment to the federal Constitution mandate a privilege for a media defendant's publication of a neutral and accurate report about a controversial book's allegations regarding matters of public concern? (3) Does the evidence support the jury's special verdict finding of actual malice? (4) Does the evidence support the jury's special verdict finding of negligence? (5) Did the trial court usurp the jury's role and violate Globe's right to due process of law when it determined the Globe article to be an "original libel" without giving Globe the opportunity to be heard or present evidence on that issue?

II. PUBLIC FIGURE

We consider first Globe's contention that the trial court and the Court of Appeal erred in concluding that Khawar is a private rather than a public figure for purposes of this defamation action.

[The court first rejected the argument that plaintiff was an involuntary public figure. "[A]ssuming a person may ever be accurately characterized as an involuntary public figure, we infer from the logic of *Gertz* that the high court would reserve this characterization for an individual who, despite never having voluntarily engaged the public's attention in an attempt to influence the outcome of a public controversy, nonetheless has acquired such public prominence in relation to the controversy as to permit media access sufficient to effectively counter media-published defamatory statements." No evidence supported such a finding here.

The court also rejected arguments that plaintiff was a public figure based on his actions in having his photograph taken with Senator Kennedy before his speech. First the conduct occurred before the controversy arose. Second, any role in the political campaign was "trivial at best."]

III. NEUTRAL REPORTAGE PRIVILEGE

Globe contends that the trial court and the Court of Appeal erred in holding that the neutral reportage privilege does not apply to insulate from defamation liability its republication of the Morrow book's defamatory falsehoods.

A. Background

At common law, one who republishes a defamatory statement is deemed thereby to have adopted it and so may be held liable, together with the person who originated the statement, for resulting injury to the reputation of the defamation victim. [ ] California has adopted the common law in this regard [ ], although by statute the republication of defamatory statements is privileged in certain defined situations (see, e.g., Civ.Code, § 47).

In a 1977 decision, a federal appellate court held that, under certain circumstances, as an exception to the common law republication rule, the federal Constitution's First Amendment mandates an absolute privilege for the republication of defamatory statements. (Edwards v. National Audubon Society, Inc. (2d Cir.1977) 556 F.2d 113, cert. den. 434 U.S. 1002 (*Edwards*).) This privilege has since come to be known as the neutral reportage privilege. The *Edwards* court defined the privilege this way: "[W]hen a *responsible, prominent organization* . . . makes serious charges against a *public figure*, the First Amendment protects the *accurate and disinterested reporting* of those charges, regardless of the reporter's private views regarding their validity." ([ ], italics added.)[1]

The theory underlying the privilege is that the reporting of defamatory allegations relating to an existing public controversy has significant informational value for the public regardless of the truth of the allegations: If the allegations are true, their reporting provides

---

[1] The neutral reportage privilege to some extent resembles and overlaps the common law privilege of "fair report," which California has codified in Civil Code section 47, subdivisions (d) and (e) [ ] and also the "wire service defense," which has been adopted by some courts in other jurisdictions [ ] but has yet to be considered by any published decision of a court of this state. Globe does not argue that either the statutory fair report privilege or the wire service defense immunizes it from liability to Khawar for damages occasioned by publication of the Globe article. Accordingly, we have no occasion to consider application of Civil Code section 47 to the circumstances of this case.

Also, because Globe conceded at trial that the Globe article was not a book review, we have no occasion here to consider whether republication of a defamatory statement in the context of a book review would require a different analysis or result.

valuable information about the target of the accusation; if the allegations are false, their reporting reflects in a significant way on the character of the accuser. In either event, according to the theory, the very making of the defamatory allegations sheds valuable light on the character of the controversy (its intensity and perhaps viciousness). As we understand it, the theory also rests on a distinction between publication and republication. Applying this distinction, proponents of the neutral reportage privilege urge that the reporting of a false and defamatory accusation should be deemed neither defamatory nor false if the report accurately relates the accusation, makes it clear that the republisher does not espouse or concur in the accusation, and provides enough additional information (including, where practical, the response of the defamed person) to allow the readers to draw their own conclusions about the truth of the accusation.

The United States Supreme Court has not stated whether it agrees with this theory, and it has never held that the First Amendment mandates a neutral reportage privilege [ ]. Nor have we ever addressed the question whether the neutral reportage privilege will be recognized in this state.

. . .

B.   Analysis

Without deciding whether some form of the neutral reportage privilege should be recognized in this state, the Court of Appeal in this case declined to apply the neutral reportage privilege on the ground that Khawar is a private figure. Globe argues that this conclusion is erroneous either because Khawar is a public figure or because the neutral reportage privilege extends to defamatory falsehoods about private figures. In concluding that Khawar is a private figure, we have already rejected the first of these grounds. We now consider the second.

. . .

Some commentators have argued that the privilege should apply to a published report of an accusation that a public figure has made against a private figure because "the public has a greater interest in knowing what its public figures are saying than it does in protecting private figures from accusations by public figures." [ ] They reason like this: "Through an understanding of who is saying what, public figures may be analyzed more insightfully, their statements reflecting as much about themselves as they do about the target. Inevitably, the conflicting interests are considered in a balancing test. It is more important to refrain from chilling republication of speech made by public figures, often the political speech at the core of the first amendment, than to protect the reputations of private figure targets." Under this view, the neutral reportage privilege would protect the Globe article, even though it reported a false and defamatory accusation against a private figure (that is, Khawar), if the person who made the original accusation (that is, Morrow) was a public figure.

Because we do not accept this view of the neutral reportage privilege, we do not decide whether Morrow was a public figure. We find more persuasive the arguments of other commentators that republication of accusations made against private figures is never protected by the neutral reportage privilege, whether or not the person who made the original accusation was a public figure. These commentators explain that although the public has a legitimate interest in knowing that prominent individuals have made charges, perhaps unfounded, against a private figure, recognition of an absolute privilege for the republication of those charges would be inconsistent with the United States Supreme Court's insistence on the need for balancing the First Amendment interest in promoting the broad dissemination of information relevant to public controversies against the reputation interests of private figures: "If the scope of the privilege were to include defamations of private figures, a neutral reportage route out of liability could emasculate the *Gertz* distinction between private and public figure plaintiffs." [ ]

. . .

Because in this defamation action Khawar is a private figure plaintiff, he was required to prove only negligence, and not actual malice, to recover damages for actual injury to his reputation. But Khawar was required to prove actual malice to recover punitive or presumed damages for defamation involving the Kennedy assassination. Because Khawar sought punitive and presumed damages as well as damages for actual injury, the issues of both actual malice and negligence were submitted to the jury. The jury found that in publishing the Globe article Globe acted both negligently and with actual malice. Globe challenged both findings on appeal. In this court, Globe contends that the Court of Appeal erred in rejecting its challenges to these two findings.

We consider first the issue of actual malice. In doing so, we consider only actual malice as defined in decisions of the United States Supreme Court imposing constitutional restrictions on the right to recover damages for defamation. Because Globe has raised no issue concerning proof of malice as defined under state law (see, e.g., Civ.Code, § 48a, subd. 4(d)), we do not address what additional proof requirements, if any, state law may impose.

. . .

. . . When, as in this case, a finding of actual malice is based on the republication of a third party's defamatory falsehoods, "failure to investigate before publishing, even when a reasonably prudent person would have done so, is not sufficient." [ ] Nonetheless, the actual malice finding may be upheld " 'where there are obvious reasons to doubt the veracity of the informant or the accuracy of his reports' " [ ], and the republisher failed to interview obvious witnesses who could have confirmed or disproved the allegations [ ] or to consult relevant documentary sources ([*Harte-Hanks*] [failure to listen to tape]).

There were, to say the least, obvious reasons to doubt the accuracy of the Morrow book's accusation that Khawar killed Kennedy. The assassination of a nationally prominent politician, in the midst of his campaign for his party's nomination for the presidency, had been painstakingly and exhaustively investigated by both the FBI and state prosecutorial agencies. During this massive investigation, these agencies accumulated a vast quantity of evidence pointing to the guilt of Sirhan as the lone assassin. As a result, Sirhan alone was charged with Kennedy's murder. At Sirhan's trial, "it was undisputed that [Sirhan] fired the shot that killed Senator Kennedy" and "[t]he evidence also established conclusively that he shot the victims of the assault counts." (*People v. Sirhan*, [ ]) The jury returned a verdict finding beyond a reasonable doubt that Sirhan was guilty of first degree murder. On Sirhan's appeal from the resulting judgment of death, this court carefully reviewed the evidence and found it sufficient to sustain the first degree murder conviction. [ ] In asserting that Khawar, and not Sirhan, had killed Kennedy, the Morrow book was making the highly improbable claim that results of the official investigation, Sirhan's trial, and this court's decision on Sirhan's appeal, were all fundamentally mistaken.

Because there were obvious reasons to doubt the accuracy of the Morrow book's central claim, and because that claim was an inherently defamatory accusation against Khawar, the jury could properly conclude that Globe acted with actual malice in republishing that claim if it found also, as it impliedly did, that Globe failed to use readily available means to verify the accuracy of the claim by interviewing obvious witnesses who could have confirmed or disproved the allegations or by inspecting relevant documents or other evidence. [ ] The evidence at trial supports the jury's implied finding that neither Blackburn (who wrote the Globe article) nor Globe's editors made any such effort.

. . .

Having independently reviewed the record, we agree with the Court of Appeal that the evidence at trial strongly supports an inference that Globe purposefully avoided the truth and published the Globe article despite serious doubts regarding the truth of the accusation against Khawar. In short, we conclude that clear and convincing evidence supports the jury's finding that in republishing the Morrow book's false accusation against Khawar, Globe acted with actual malice—that is, with reckless disregard of whether the accusation was false or not.

. . .

The judgment of the Court of Appeal is affirmed.

■ GEORGE, C.J., and MOSK, BAXTER, WERDEGAR, CHIN and BROWN, JJ., concur.

NOTES AND QUESTIONS

1. How does the neutral report privilege discussed here differ from the common law privilege of fair and accurate report that we explored p. 1041 supra? How often are the two likely to overlap?

2. Is the court's determination that plaintiff is not a public figure sound? For neutral report purposes why should it matter whether the plaintiff is a public figure? Does a privilege exist for a newspaper to report accurately that a senator has claimed that his otherwise anonymous hometown neighbor is threatening the senator's family?

3. What are the justifications offered for the privilege? What are the arguments against it? Is the proposed privilege inconsistent with *Gertz*? More generally, is it "inconsistent with the United States Supreme Court's First Amendment jurisprudence"? In Norton v. Glenn, 860 A.2d 48 (Pa.2004), newspaper articles detailed comments made by borough council member Glenn accusing plaintiff council members of molesting children and engaging in homosexual behavior. Plaintiffs sued media defendants that reported the charges. The defendants asserted a neutral reportage privilege grounded in both the First Amendment and the state constitution that they said "immunized media defendants from defamation liability even where media have doubts about truth of the statements published." The court held that neither Supreme Court precedent, nor the Pennsylvania constitution, required either the abandonment of the "actual malice" standard or the adoption of the neutral reportage doctrine.

4. The court suggests that the source's insolvency is one argument against the privilege. Is that problem unique to this aspect of libel law? To libel law generally?

5. Context was relevant in the previous section. In footnote 1 in *Khawar*, the court suggests that if the discussion had occurred in a book review a different result might be warranted. Why might that be? What if the discussion occurred in a blog on the Internet?

6. *Edwards* summarized its privilege as follows: "Succinctly stated, when a responsible, prominent organization . . . makes serious charges against a public figure, the First Amendment protects the accurate and disinterested reporting of those charges, regardless of the reporter's private views of their validity." Consider each element in more detail.

"Responsible, prominent organization." What is there in the nature of this privilege that should require that the charge come from this type of source?

What if the source of the defamation is a rumor? In *Martin v. Wilson Publishing Co.*, discussed in *Khawar*, the defendant paper reported on the reactions of a very small community whose residents were concerned that plaintiff was acquiring much of the property in the community. Despite his announced good intentions for the community, plaintiff's actions made many residents apprehensive. The article stated: "some residents stretch available facts when they imagine Mr. Martin is connected with the 1974 rash of fires in the village." The court rejected any analogy to the common law fair report because the source was not identified: "To attempt to defend against a rumor is not unlike attempting to joust with a cloud. Publication of a rumor further fuels the continued repetition and does so in an especially egregious way by enshrining it in print." Nor would it adopt *Edwards* in this situation.

What if time is of the essence? Assume that there is a rumor in the community that a candidate in a forthcoming election is under investigation for having engaged in a massive fraud. The local paper runs an article before the election truthfully announcing that the rumor—which it repeats—is being widely discussed and then reporting that despite extensive efforts the paper found nothing to support the rumor. Might the candidate have an action? What if, in the above example, the newspaper in the course of normal election coverage truthfully reports the existence and content of the rumor but makes no effort to check its accuracy? See Schauer, Slightly Guilty, 1993 U.Chi.L. Forum 83.

Outside the election context, consider the example from 1 R. Sack, Sack on Defamation: Libel, Slander, and Related Problems 7–59 (4th ed. 2010): "Suppose a rumor surfaces that the chairman of a large publicly held brokerage firm is about to be indicted for securities fraud and, as a result, the stock of the company falls precipitously." Can a story explaining why the stock fell be reported without running the risk of liability for libel? Is this a stronger, or weaker, case for legal protection than the election situation? In a footnote to this example, Sack states: "The republisher may be expected to report that a rumor is no more than that and to state that the rumor is false if it is known to be." What does "known" mean here? Was the falsity "known" in *Martin*? Is this requirement consistent with the rationale of the privilege?

"Makes serious charges." Why must the charges be serious? Why is it not enough that charges are flying between two persons or groups? Beyond that, must the charges be "made" in public before the newspaper writes its story? *Edwards* arose in large part because the Audubon Society had its own media outlets and had published its own charges in the first instance that allegedly damaged plaintiffs' scientific reputations.

Suppose there is no accusation in circulation until the reporter elicits it? In McManus v. Doubleday & Co., Inc., 513 F.Supp. 1383 (S.D.N.Y.1981), defendant's book asserted about the plaintiff priest, who was national coordinator for some Irish-American groups, that his "Irish Embassy file bears the mention 'homicidal tendencies.'" The information was said to have come from an interview with an Embassy official that the author initiated. The court rejected the neutral report defense. The judge first quoted *Edwards* for the view that the privilege was to keep the public "fully informed about controversies that often rage around sensitive issues." Unlike the reporter in *Edwards*, "who simply reported an autonomous news event, albeit with certain factual embellishments, [the author here] was engaged in purely investigative reporting. Unlike *Edwards,* no controversy raged around the libelous statements before the reporter entered the scene. . . . Since there is no indication in the *Edwards* opinion that the neutral reportage privilege was meant to cover investigative reporting, and since including reports of such journalist-induced charges within the protection of the privilege is unnecessary for promoting the purposes of *Edwards,* the freer reporting of raging controversies," the court denied the privilege. Would the analysis differ if the official had come to the author and volunteered the information?

"Against a public figure." This element was discussed in *Khawar.*

"Accurate and disinterested reporting of those charges." It seems agreed (except possibly in the rumor situation) that the publication must take no position on where the truth lies in the dispute.

What if, after one side attacks publicly, the other side refuses to comment? How, if at all, is the local newspaper to report this situation? Can the newspaper preserve the privilege by including in the story the accurate statement that "repeated phone calls to [the plaintiff or an attorney] were not returned"?

What if the article is indeed written with scrupulous fairness by a writer who does not honestly believe one side? In *Stockton Newspapers v. Superior Court,* 254 Cal.Rptr. 389 (App.1988), for example, the reporter admitted having doubts about the truth of the youth's story. Some have argued that a neutral report is of little use to the public because in most situations readers cannot judge the credibility of the sources being quoted. "Where the reporter has knowledge of falsity or serious doubts about the truth of a charge, meeting the 'actual malice' test, the reporter should be under a duty to report that information. Where there is reason to know the falsity of a statement, the reporter must do more than merely print a refutation." Note, The Privilege of Neutral Reportage, 1978 Utah L.Rev. 347. What are the contrary considerations?

As noted, virtually every element of *Edwards* has been interpreted narrowly by some courts. These disagreements may induce courts to expand the common law privilege to avoid entering the *Edwards* controversy. In Chapin v. Knight-Ridder, Inc., 993 F.2d 1087 (4th Cir.1993), for example, the court concluded that the state's fair report privilege would cover a report of the unofficial remarks of a congressman, and noted that until "we face a case with a 'prominent, responsible' but nongovernmental speaker, we need not cast our lot one way or the other on the full *Edwards* fair reportage privilege."

Broadcasting. In print journalism, the editor is able to make a considered judgment about what outside submissions warrant publication, as with letters to the editor or syndicated material. See Franklin, Libel and Letters to the Editor: Toward an Open Forum, 57 Colo.L.Rev. 651 (1986). In the broadcast of live call-in shows, that element of reflection and the ability to identify the persons submitting views are missing. So far as defamation is concerned, it will be difficult to establish actual malice or negligence if the broadcaster had no opportunity to review the material for libel or falsity before it is broadcast. Could a court properly conclude that using a live call-in format was itself actionable because it gave irresponsible callers the opportunity to defame others over the airwaves? (The much-publicized delay buttons are much more suited to preventing vulgarity than to allowing the person in charge to prevent subtle defamations.) See, e.g., Pacella v. Milford Radio Corp., 462 N.E.2d 355 (Mass.App.1984)(radio talk show host not liable for failing to cut off anonymous speaker), aff'd by an equally divided court, 476 N.E.2d 595 (Mass.1985).

8. REFORM PROPOSALS

a. NEED FOR REFORM?

Plaintiffs, defendants, and the public have had occasion to rethink the current state of the law of defamation. The statistics reported below are from three reports from Media Law Resource Center, 2014 Report of Trials and Damages (based on data for 1980–2013), 2004 Motion to Dismiss Study (based on data for 1980–2003), and 2007 Summary Judgment Study (based on data for 1980–2006).

Plaintiffs. As the sections on doctrine suggest, plaintiffs have had a most difficult time winning cases under the "actual malice" rule. Their success rate, leaving aside a relatively small number of settlements, runs under 10%. Plaintiffs whose primary interest was in showing the falsity of the story rather than in obtaining dollars might have been satisfied if the system had offered them a chance to prove that falsity. But with about 75% of the cases resulting in summary judgments for the defendant, the issue of truth or falsity is rarely decided. A case that produces a jury verdict of falsity but without actual malice is a rarity.

Plaintiffs who can get past summary judgment succeed with juries well over 50% of the time. Defendants' likelihood to appeal losses has dropped over the past few decades, but overall through the early 2000s, damage awards dropped over 80% percent from the amount awarded at trial to the amount awarded after post-trial motions and appeals. Nonetheless, on the high end, there has been a significant rise in the number of compensatory awards at trial over $1,000,000; reaching 38% in the first decade of the 2000s.

Private plaintiffs who seek to recover only for actual injury fare somewhat better because they get to juries more often, win before juries at least as often, and are not likely to lose their awards on appeal for failure to prove negligence.

Defendants. As a group, defendants obviously cannot complain about their overall success rate in these cases. But they do contend that the constitutional protections should operate earlier in the litigation process; that pretrial discovery is expensive; and that appeals are necessary to obtain reversals of so many plaintiffs' trial judgments.

Larger media stress the high costs of successful defense and suggest that they are being diverted from the investigative reporting that they should be doing by the demands of litigation.

Smaller media claim concern about the very fact of being sued and having to spend money for legal defense. They assert that a judgment of tens of thousands of dollars, much less millions, might bankrupt them— and that insurance is expensive because of the large defense costs (but that may account for the low payouts). Smaller media, in particular, claim that insurance is not much protection for several reasons. First, libel insurance is frequently written with a "deductible" or retained exposure under which the insured bears the first several thousand dollars of expenses in the case. This amount is intended to cause the management to consider carefully the material it is about to run and whether it wants to engage in investigative reporting at all. Second, one of the few major libel insurers now requires that in addition to the "deductible," insureds bear 20% of the legal expenses throughout the case, whatever the outcome. Smaller media claim the problem with both these limits on coverage is that the publication may suffer uncovered losses whenever it is sued, even if it ultimately wins the case. Thus, smaller media say that they are more likely to stop doing investigative reporting or to avoid running stories that may antagonize litigious persons or groups in the community.

Public. If the defendants are likely to perceive the situation as "chilling" and to respond by reducing their coverage of important activities, the public may lose by learning less true information about how our government and society are functioning. Although occasional stories purport to document the "chilling effect," it is something that major media representatives do not like to talk about and often deny. Smaller media, on the other hand, do assert that this is affecting their coverage.

But note that, to the extent the public now benefits from the constitutional protections we have been considering, these benefits are being financed by the victims of the defamations who cannot recover for the harm they have suffered. Should the public be paying in some way for the harms individual victims are suffering so that the public can get its "uninhibited, robust, and wide-open" debate? Recall Justice White's comments, p. 1095 supra. For a discussion of this line of thought with exploration of various funding mechanisms, see Schauer, Uncoupling Free Speech, 92 Colum.L.Rev. 1321 (1992).

Claims data. The amount of litigation is tiny compared to the physical harm area. According to the Media Law Resource Center study cited above, from 1980–2013, 611 defamation cases were tried by jury to a verdict. Data suggest that about 3 in 4 cases that are started do not get to the trial stage because motions to dismiss (generally state law privileges) or summary judgments (constitutional privileges) derail them.

Recall that not all plaintiffs who prove actual malice will recover punitive damages. Some states bar punitive damages in all cases; a few bar them in cases involving communications. In others, including the important state of New York, plaintiffs seeking punitive damages must prove, in addition to actual malice, some further element, such as spite or ill will—something difficult to show in most media cases.

Taking the broad picture, it seems clear that if the defendant cannot prevail before trial, at least one appeal may lie ahead. It is also clear that the awards of jury (and judge as well) are unlikely to survive that appeal. Much expensive legal effort has been exerted by all concerned to reach a result that often produces no award or requires a retrial. The vast bulk of libel insurance is not paid to plaintiffs but is absorbed in defense and legal expenses. And reputations have not been retrieved, even in cases of clear falsity.

From the standpoint of the individual newspaper or broadcaster, one might focus on the variance in the awards between the median and the average, which reflects the possibility that an "outlier" award may occur. The award need bear no relationship to any obvious anchors, such as the medical bills and lost earnings found in physical injury cases. It is thus no surprise that once a case is begun, little expense is spared in defending it. It is little solace that "most" awards are reduced or overturned on appeal. In an individual case an award may be affirmed on appeal that may seriously impede the defendant's continued viability.

b. PROPOSED REFORMS

By and large, proposals for change have focused on two main avenues: constitutional change at the doctrinal level and statutory or common law changes that seek to work within the existing constitutional framework. (A third approach is already in existence with some courts trying interstitial changes such as channeling discovery to a single issue that might be dispositive or assessing legal fees against parties who are not proceeding in good faith.)

Changes in case law. In the first category are the suggestions of either overruling *New York Times* and/or *Gertz* or cutting back on their scope or level of protection. This is usually tied to some proposed change in damage rules. In the *Greenmoss* case, p. 1133 supra, Justice White observed that the law had evolved in an unsatisfactory way:

> The *New York Times* rule thus countenances two evils: first, the stream of information about public officials and public affairs is polluted and often remains polluted by false information; and second, the reputation and professional life of the defeated plaintiff may be destroyed by falsehoods that might have been avoided with a reasonable effort to investigate the facts. In terms of the First Amendment and

reputational interest at stake, these seem grossly perverse results.

He noted that there was "much talk" about "liability without fault and the unfairness of presuming damages." But if the goal was to protect the press "from intimidating damages liability that might lead to excessive timidity, . . . it is evident that the Court engaged in severe overkill" in both *New York Times* and *Gertz*.

Justice White then suggested that the Court might better have (1) barred or limited punitive damages; or (2) barred or limited presumed damages. In such a situation strict liability could have been retained and the defamed public official "upon proving falsity, could at least have had a judgment to that effect. . . . He might have also recovered a modest amount, enough perhaps to pay his litigation expenses."

He doubted that defendants would be "unduly chilled by having to pay for the actual damages caused to those they defame." Other "commercial enterprises in this country not in the business of disseminating information must pay for the damage they cause as a cost of doing business, and it is difficult to argue that the United States did not have a free and vigorous press before the rule in *New York Times* was announced. In any event, the *New York Times* standard was formulated to protect the press from the chilling danger of numerous large damage awards. Nothing in the central rationale behind *New York Times* demands an absolute immunity from suits to establish the falsity of a defamatory misstatement about a public figure where the plaintiff cannot make out a jury case of actual malice."

As for *Gertz*, Justice White observed:

> . . . I doubt that the decision in that case has made any measurable contribution to First Amendment or reputational values since its announcement. Nor am I sure that it has saved the press a great deal of money. . . . I suspect the press would be no worse off financially if the common-law rules were to apply and if the judiciary were careful to insist that damages awards be kept within bounds. A legislative solution to the damages problem would also be appropriate. Moreover, since libel plaintiffs are very likely more interested in clearing their names than in damages, I doubt that limiting recoveries would deter or be unfair to them. In any event, I cannot assume that the press, as successful and powerful as it is, will be intimidated into withholding news that by decent journalistic standards it believes to be true.

Is there any reason why judicial control over damages should be more difficult here than in tort law generally? Justice White posits a "successful and powerful" press that can withstand the intimidation of large damage awards. Is that premise supportable in the current scene of falling circulation and mass closures of once widely-read newspapers and magazines?

For other suggestions that the focus be on control of damages rather than changing the rules of liability, see, e.g., Epstein, Was *New York Times v. Sullivan* Wrong? 53 U.Chi.L.Rev. 782 (1986); Anderson, Reputation, Compensation and Proof, 25 Wm. & Mary L.Rev. 747 (1984).

Proposals within existing law. The second type of change is the statutory approach within existing constitutional lines. Aside from damage limitation plans, these have tended to fall into one of two groups. One centers on a type of declaratory judgment action that permits an adjudication of the truth or falsity of the defamatory charge without addressing questions of fault. In this first group, critics have disagreed over whether the shift from a damage action to a declaratory judgment action should occur at the plaintiff's behest or whether the defendant should control the choice. Compare Franklin, A Declaratory Judgment Alternative to Current Libel Law, 74 Cal.L.Rev. 809 (1986)(proposing that plaintiff control that decision) with Barrett, Declaratory Judgment for Libel: A Better Alternative, 74 Cal.L.Rev. 847 (1986)(proposing that the choice be given to defendants).

Judge Pierre Leval, who presided over the famous libel case brought by General William Westmoreland against CBS, argued afterwards that a plaintiff could get around the constitutional strictures of the *New York Times* case by bringing an action for declaratory judgment and explicitly stating that no damages were being sought. Of course, that alone would not suffice unless state law permitted such an action. Leval, The No-Money, No-Fault Libel Suit: Keeping *Sullivan* in Its Proper Place, 101 Harv.L.Rev. 1287 (1988). The article also discusses negotiated agreements in which the parties might agree to dispense with the actual malice rule but litigate the issue of falsity.

The second approach centers on retraction and reply as ways to reduce or eliminate the harm done, working with the common law remedies discussed at p. 1049 supra. See Ackerman, Bringing Coherence to Defamation Law through Uniform Legislation: The Search for an Elegant Solution, 72 N.C.L.Rev. 291 (1994). For an elaborate empirical study of libel litigation and a proposal that libel cases be removed from the litigation and damages context and placed in the setting of some alternative mode of dispute resolution, see R. Bezanson, G. Cranberg & J. Soloski, Libel Law and the Press: Myth and Reality (1987).

Proposals introduced in several state legislatures to implement libel reform have rarely gotten out of committee. See generally Bezanson, The Libel Tort Today, 45 Wash. & Lee L.Rev. 535 (1988), and LeBel, Reforming the Tort of Defamation: An Accommodation of the Competing Interests within the Current Constitutional Framework, 66 Neb.L.Rev. 249 (1987).

Most commentators and critics have concluded that reform must come from the legislative branch. For a differing view, see Anderson, Is Libel Law Worth Reforming?, 140 U.Pa.L.Rev. 487 (1991), agreeing that the "present law of libel is a failure," and then suggesting that the Supreme Court itself should be "the principal reformer of libel law:"

> The Court would prescribe new accommodations of speech and reputational interests as a matter of constitutional law. It might decree, for example, that the Constitution requires no showing of fault if the remedy sought is only a declaration of falsity. It might announce new limitations of damages, with corresponding reductions in plaintiff's burdens. The Court might devise a more sophisticated accommodation, one that addresses the dynamics and costs of libel litigation as well as questions of fault and remedies. It might explicitly authorize trial judges to decide at the outset whether the challenged statement was sufficiently factual, harmful, and remote from truth to be justifiably burdened by further litigation. Acknowledging that effective protection of speech requires a diminished role for juries, it might authorize even more aggressive use of summary judgment and judicial review. The Court might even take the assessment of damages out of the jury's hands.

> Comprehensive law reform is not a familiar task for the Supreme Court. It is not accustomed to reviewing systems of law rather than specific rules. Case-by-case adjudication of specific constitutional issues does not invite advocacy on the redesign of an entire branch of tort law. Those are weighty objections, but they come too late. Over the past quarter century, case by case and bit by bit, the Court has thoroughly revised the common law of libel. It has created not merely a few constitutional limitations on state tort rules, but a matrix of substantive principles, evidentiary rules, and de facto innovations in judge-jury roles and other procedural matters. These are all constitutionally based and can only be changed by those who have the power to change constitutional rules. Having created the system that is the source of so much dissatisfaction, the Court cannot now demur on the ground that law reform is not its business.

Are you persuaded that wholesale reworking of *New York Times* and its progeny is warranted?

CHAPTER XV

PROTECTING PRIVACY

Privacy is a relatively new legal concept with many facets. Yet today, privacy concerns are quite broad and include protections related to government and private data banks, government surveillance, unreasonable searches and seizures, and identity theft, as well as family law issues. The types of protections accorded to privacy and the nature of the interests privileged differ in the constitutional and tort law contexts. A federal constitutional right of privacy has been found in the Due Process Clause of the Fourteenth Amendment. That jurisprudence has developed primarily in the area of family law, in which a woman's right to make decisions about contraception and abortion has been deemed fundamental. See, e.g., Planned Parenthood v. Casey, 510 U.S. 1309 (1994). A parent's capacity to make decisions about the care, custody, and control of his or her children has also been protected. See, e.g., Troxel v. Granville, 530 U.S. 57 (2000). Tort liability for invasion of privacy may be imposed in a much broader range of cases. Likewise, although the constitutional right of privacy can be enforced only against government action, privacy claims can be pursued under tort law wherever a duty is found. The remedies are also likely to be different. Tort law provides damages to those whose privacy has been invaded. The primary remedy for constitutional violations is an injunction barring enforcement of the offending statute. Privacy torts are one among many pathways to securing protection for recognized privacy interests.

We focus first on liability for disclosure of true statements that an individual would rather not have publicly disseminated. This is sometimes called the tort of "public disclosure of private facts." We then turn to liability for statements that present the plaintiff in a "false light," a tort that recalls defamation. We turn next to the "intrusion" aspect of privacy to ask how far others may go to obtain information from unwilling sources. We conclude with a section in which, although the word "privacy" is used, it appears that the plaintiffs are relying more upon a notion of controlling "publicity" than of privacy.

The idea that privacy should be legally protected is traceable to a law review article by Louis D. Brandeis and his law partner, Samuel D. Warren, entitled The Right to Privacy, 4 Harv.L.Rev. 193 (1890). The authors, reacting to the editorial practices of Boston newspapers, particularly a report about a family gathering that the Warrens had thought was private, made clear their concerns:

> The press is overstepping in every direction the obvious bounds
> of propriety and of decency. Gossip is no longer the resource of
> the idle and of the vicious, but has become a trade, which is

pursued with industry as well as effrontery. To satisfy a prurient taste the details of sexual relations are spread broadcast in the columns of the daily papers. To occupy the indolent, column upon column is filled with idle gossip, which can only be procured by intrusion upon the domestic circle. . . . When personal gossip attains the dignity of print, and crowds the space available for matters of real interest to the community, what wonder that the ignorant and thoughtless mistake its relative importance. Easy of comprehension, appealing to that weak side of human nature which is never wholly cast down by the misfortunes and frailties of our neighbors, no one can be surprised that it usurps the place of interest in brains capable of other things. Triviality destroys at once robustness of thought and delicacy of feelings. No enthusiasm can flourish, no generous impulse can survive under its blighting influence.

Working with a variety of rather remote precedents from other areas of law, the authors developed an argument that courts should recognize an action for invasion of privacy by media publication.

The theory was rejected in the first major case to consider it. In Roberson v. Rochester Folding Box Co., 64 N.E. 442 (N.Y.1902), the defendants, a flour company and a box company, obtained a good likeness of the plaintiff and reproduced it on their advertising posters. Plaintiff said she was humiliated and suffered great distress. The court, 4–3, rejected a common law privacy action on grounds that suggested concern about innovating after so many centuries; an inability to see how the doctrine, once accepted, could be judicially limited to appropriate situations; and skepticism about finding liability for an action that might actually please some potential "victims." The Warren and Brandeis article was discussed at length, but the court concluded that the precedents relied upon were too remote to sustain the proposed right.

The outcry was immediate. At its next session, the New York legislature created a statutory right of privacy (New York Civil Rights Law §§ 50 and 51). The basic provision was that "a person, firm or corporation that uses for advertising purposes, or the purposes of trade, the name, portrait or picture of any living person without having first obtained the written consent of such person, or if a minor of his or her parent or guardian, is guilty of a misdemeanor." The other section provided for an injunction and created an action for compensatory and punitive damages.

The unique New York development. Since New York is such an important state in law generally and tort law in particular, it is important to note at the outset that the New York experience has been substantially different from that of the vast majority of states, which developed a common law jurisprudence. New York's highest court still adheres to positions that deny the opportunity for common law development in the privacy area—and looks almost exclusively to the statute to resolve most of the tort claims that we explore in this chapter. For example, in Freihofer v. Hearst Corp., 480 N.E.2d 349 (N.Y.1985), plaintiff husband in a divorce action sued defendant newspaper for stories relating to the action. The stories were based upon the reporter's access to some court documents that, by statute, were to be kept confidential by court officials. Since the reporter did not violate the confidentiality statute for court records, the court held that the only basis for liability would be the privacy statute. The articles were not published for "advertising purposes" and were not for "purposes of trade," even though they were published to help the paper make a profit. The critical factor under the controlling privacy statute "is the content of the published article in terms of whether it is newsworthy, which is a question of law, and not the defendant's motive to increase circulation."

In Messenger v. Gruner & Jahr Printing & Publishing, 727 N.E.2d 549 (N.Y.2000), a 14-year-old aspiring model brought suit after the magazine YM (Young and Modern) used pictures it had taken of her on a photo shoot to illustrate its "Love Crisis" column. The pictures of plaintiff were captioned so as to correspond to events recounted in a letter from another 14-year-old, identified only as "Mortified," who claimed that she had sex with two of her boyfriend's friends as well as her boyfriend after getting drunk at a party. Although plaintiff had allowed her picture to be taken, no consent form had been signed by a parent or guardian.

The court held that plaintiff "may not recover under the Civil Rights Law, regardless of any false implication that might be reasonably drawn from the use of her photographs to illustrate the article." Otherwise liability under Civil Rights Law section 51 would "become indistinguishable from the common-law tort of false light invasion of privacy," a tort not recognized in New York because of the statute.

To avoid the complications of the New York statute, this chapter will focus on common law developments. We turn now to the type of privacy invasion that lay at the core of the Warren and Brandeis article.

A. PUBLIC DISCLOSURE OF PRIVATE FACTS

1. STATE TORT ANALYSIS

In the early twentieth century, other states, perhaps learning from the New York experience, slowly began to develop a common law right to privacy that was neither influenced by statutory language nor limited to advertising invasions. In addition to an action for commercial use of one's name (discussed later in this chapter), the courts also developed an action for truthful use of plaintiff's name in situations that were thought to be outside the areas of legitimate public concern. The action for invasion of privacy by publication of true editorial material began to take hold during the 1920s and early 1930s.

Beginning in the late 1930s, however, courts became more attentive to the Supreme Court's expanding protection of expression through the First Amendment. Operating on a common law level, the state courts tended to broaden protection for the media by taking a narrow view of what were legitimately private areas. This "newsworthiness" defense expanded because courts were reluctant to impose normative standards of what should be newsworthy. Instead, they leaned toward a descriptive definition that protected whatever an editor had decided would interest his or her readers. By the 1960s, it was unclear whether this branch of the action for invasion of privacy had any remaining vitality. See Kalven, Privacy in Tort Law—Were Warren and Brandeis Wrong?, 31 Law & Contemp.Probs. 326 (1966); Bloustein, Privacy, Tort Law, and the Constitution: Is Warren and Brandeis' Tort Petty and Unconstitutional As Well?, 46 Tex.L.Rev. 611 (1968). Also, by the 1960s, the Supreme Court was beginning to apply First Amendment protection in tort cases, beginning with *New York Times Co. v. Sullivan*, p. 1062 supra.

Yet, also during the late 1960s and early 1970s, society began sensing that privacy as a general social value was being threatened in different ways by the encroachment of computers, data banks, and electronic devices, as well as the media. Other aspects of privacy were also protected in Supreme Court cases dealing with birth control, abortion, and other personal issues—although these involved claims seeking to protect areas of privacy from government interference.

We begin our consideration with an exploration of state law that is developing in the so-called "public disclosure" tort. We will then turn to the constitutional developments in this area.

Haynes v. Alfred A. Knopf, Inc.

United States Court of Appeals, Seventh Circuit, 1993.
8 F.3d 1222.

■ Before POSNER, CHIEF JUDGE, and MANION and WOOD, CIRCUIT JUDGES.

■ POSNER, CHIEF JUDGE.

[The book, The Promised Land: The Great Black Migration and How It Changed America, by Nicholas Lemann, used the life of Ruby Lee Daniels to illustrate its themes about the social, political, and economic effects of the movement of blacks from the rural South to the cities of the North between 1940 and 1970. The author switched between general discussion of that migration and discussion of the migration's personal dimensions as reflected in Daniels's descriptions of her life and experiences, beginning when she was a sharecropper in

Mississippi and progressing through her move to Chicago and her life there over the next 40 years. Among the things she discussed was her relationship with her ex-husband, Luther Haynes. She depicted him as a man who drank heavily, who neglected his children, could not keep a job, was unfaithful, and eventually left her for another woman. The court quoted one excerpt:

> It got to the point where [Luther] would go out on Friday evenings after picking up his paycheck and Ruby would hope he wouldn't come home, because she knew he would be drunk. On the Friday evenings when he did come home—over the years Ruby developed a devastating imitation of Luther, and could re-create the scene quite vividly—he would walk into the apartment, put on a record and turn up the volume, and saunter into their bedroom, a bottle in one hand and a cigarette in the other, in the mood for love. On one such night, Ruby's last child, Kevin, was conceived. Kevin always had something wrong with him—he was very moody, he was scrawny, and he had a severe speech impediment. Ruby was never able to find out exactly what the problem was, but she blamed it on Luther; all that alcohol must have gotten into his sperm, she said.

Haynes admitted many of the incidents in the book, but alleged that they had all occurred 25 years earlier and that since then he had reformed, remarried, and lived an exemplary life. He and his present wife, Dorothy, sued the author and publisher for libel and invasion of privacy. The trial court granted summary judgment for the defendants. The court first held that the plaintiffs had no libel claim because the defamatory statements about them were substantially true. It then turned to the privacy claim.]

The major claim in the complaint, and the focus of the appeal, is . . . invasion of the right of privacy. In tort law the term "right of privacy" covers several distinct wrongs. Using a celebrity's (or other person's) name or picture in advertising without his consent. [ ] Tapping someone's phone, or otherwise invading a person's private space. [ ] Harassing a celebrity by following her too closely, albeit on a public street. [ ] Casting a person in a false light by publicizing details of the person's life that while true are so selected or highlighted as to convey a misleading impression of the person's character. [ ] Publicizing personal facts that while true and not misleading are so intimate that their disclosure to the public is deeply embarrassing to the person thus exposed and is perceived as gratuitous by the community. [ ] The last, the publicizing of personal facts, is the aspect of the invasion of privacy charged by the Hayneses.

Even people who have nothing rationally to be ashamed of can be mortified by the publication of intimate details of their life. Most people in no way deformed or disfigured would nevertheless be deeply upset if nude photographs of themselves were published in a newspaper or a book. They feel the same way about photographs of their sexual activities, however "normal," or about a narrative of those activities, or about having their medical records publicized. Although it is well known that every human being defecates, no adult human being in our society wants a newspaper to show a picture of him defecating. The desire for privacy illustrated by these examples is a mysterious but deep fact about human personality. It deserves and in our society receives legal protection. The nature of the injury shows, by the way, that the defendants are wrong to argue that this branch of the right of privacy requires proof of special damages. [ ]

But this is not the character of the depictions of the Hayneses in *The Promised Land*. Although the plaintiffs claim that the book depicts their "sex life" and "ridicules" Luther Haynes's lovemaking (the reference is to the passage we quoted in which the author refers to Ruby's "devastating imitation" of Luther's manner when he would come home Friday nights in an amorous mood), these characterizations are misleading. No sexual act is described in the book. No intimate details are revealed. Entering one's bedroom with a bottle in one hand and a cigarette in the other is not foreplay. Ruby's speculation that Kevin's problems may have been due to Luther's having been a heavy drinker is not the narration of a sexual act.

    . . .

[The branch of privacy law in this case] is concerned with the propriety of stripping away the veil of privacy with which we cover the embarrassing, the shameful, the tabooed, truths about us. [ ] The revelations in the book are not about the intimate details of the Hayneses' life. They are about misconduct, in particular Luther's. (There is very little about Dorothy in the book, apart from the fact that she had an affair with Luther while he was still married to Ruby and that they eventually became and have remained lawfully married.) The revelations are about his heavy drinking, his unstable employment, his adultery, his irresponsible and neglectful behavior toward his wife and children. So we must consider cases in which the right of privacy has been invoked as a shield against the revelation of previous misconduct.

Two early cases illustrate the range of judicial thinking. In Melvin v. Reid, 297 Pac. 91 (Cal.App.1931), the plaintiff was a former prostitute, who had been prosecuted but acquitted of murder. She later had married and (she alleged) for seven years had lived a blameless respectable life in a community in which her lurid past was unknown—when all was revealed in a movie about the murder case which used her maiden name. The court held that these allegations stated a claim for invasion of privacy. The Hayneses' claim is similar although less dramatic. They have been a respectable married couple for two decades. Luther's alcohol problem is behind him. He has steady employment as a doorman. His wife is a nurse, and in 1990 he told Lemann that the couple's combined income was $60,000 a year. He is not in trouble with the domestic relations court. He is a deacon of his church. He has come a long way from sharecropping in Mississippi and public housing in Chicago and he and his wife want to bury their past just as Mrs. Melvin wanted to do and in *Melvin v. Reid* was held entitled to do. [ ] In Luther Haynes's own words, from his deposition, "I know I haven't been no angel, but since almost 30 years ago I have turned my life completely around. I stopped the drinking and all this bad habits and stuff like that, which I deny, some of [it] I didn't deny, because I have changed my life. It take me almost 30 years to change it and I am deeply in my church. I look good in the eyes of my church members and my community. Now, what is going to happen now when this public reads this garbage which I didn't tell Mr. Lemann to write? Then all this is going to go down the drain. And I worked like a son of a gun to build myself up in a good reputation and he has torn it down."

But with *Melvin v. Reid* compare *Sidis v. F-R Publishing Corp.*, 113 F.2d 806 (2d Cir.1940), another old case but one more consonant with modern thinking about the proper balance between the right of privacy and the freedom of the press. A child prodigy had flamed out; he was now an eccentric recluse. The New Yorker ran a "where is he now" article about him. The article, entitled "April Fool," did not reveal any misconduct by Sidis but it depicted him in mocking tones as a comical failure, in much the same way that the report of Ruby's "devastating imitation" of the amorous Luther Haynes could be thought to have depicted him as a comical failure, albeit with sinister consequences absent from Sidis's case. The invasion of Sidis's privacy was palpable. But the publisher won. No intimate physical details of Sidis's life had been revealed; and on the other side was the undoubted newsworthiness of a child prodigy, as of a woman prosecuted for murder. Sidis, unlike Mrs. Melvin, was not permitted to bury his past.

. . .

. . . People who do not desire the limelight and do not deliberately choose a way of life or course of conduct calculated to thrust them into it nevertheless have no legal right to extinguish it if the experiences that have befallen them are newsworthy, even if they would prefer that those experiences be kept private. The possibility of an involuntary loss of privacy is recognized in the modern formulations of this branch of the privacy tort, which require not only that the private facts publicized be such as would make a reasonable person deeply offended by such publicity but also that they be facts in which the public has no legitimate interest. [ ]

The two criteria, offensiveness and newsworthiness, are related. An individual, and more pertinently perhaps the community, is most offended by the publication of intimate personal facts when the community has no interest in them beyond the voyeuristic thrill of penetrating the wall of privacy that surrounds a stranger. The reader of

a book about the black migration to the North would have no legitimate interest in the details of Luther Haynes's sex life; but no such details are disclosed. Such a reader does have a legitimate interest in the aspects of Luther's conduct that the book reveals. For one of Lemann's major themes is the transposition virtually intact of a sharecropper morality characterized by a family structure "matriarchal and elastic" and by an "extremely unstable" marriage bond to the slums of the northern cities, and the interaction, largely random and sometimes perverse, of that morality with governmental programs to alleviate poverty. Public aid policies discouraged Ruby and Luther from living together, public housing policies precipitated a marriage doomed to fail. No detail in the book claimed to invade the Hayneses' privacy is not germane to the story that the author wanted to tell, a story not only of legitimate but of transcendent public interest.

The Hayneses question whether the linkage between the author's theme and their private life really is organic. They point out that many social histories do not mention individuals at all, let alone by name. That is true. Much of social science, including social history, proceeds by abstraction, aggregation, and quantification rather than by case studies. . . . But it would be absurd to suggest that cliometric or other aggregative, impersonal methods of doing social history are the only proper way to go about it and presumptuous to claim even that they are the best way. Lemann's book has been praised to the skies by distinguished scholars, among them black scholars covering a large portion of the ideological spectrum—Henry Louis Gates, Jr., William Julius Wilson, and Patricia Williams. Lemann's methodology places the individual case history at center stage. If he cannot tell the story of Ruby Daniels without waivers from every person who she thinks did her wrong, he cannot write this book.

Well, argue the Hayneses, at least Lemann could have changed their names. But the use of pseudonyms would not have gotten Lemann and Knopf off the legal hook. The details of the Hayneses' lives recounted in the book would identify them unmistakably to anyone who has known the Hayneses well for a long time (members of their families, for example), or who knew them before they got married; and no more is required. . . . Lemann would have had to change some, perhaps many, of the details. But then he would no longer have been writing history. He would have been writing fiction. The nonquantitative study of living persons would be abolished as a category of scholarship, to be replaced by the sociological novel. That is a genre with a distinguished history punctuated by famous names, such as Dickens, Zola, Stowe, Dreiser, Sinclair, Steinbeck, and Wolfe, but we do not think that the law of privacy makes it (or that the First Amendment would permit the law of privacy to make it) the exclusive format for a social history of living persons that tells their story rather than treating them as data points in a statistical study. Reporting the true facts about real people is necessary to "obviate any impression that the problems raised in the [book] are remote or hypothetical." [ ] And surely a composite portrait of ghetto residents would be attacked as racial stereotyping.

The Promised Land does not afford the reader a titillating glimpse of tabooed activities. The tone is decorous and restrained. Painful though it is for the Hayneses to see a past they would rather forget brought into the public view, the public needs the information conveyed by the book, including the information about Luther and Dorothy Haynes, in order to evaluate the profound social and political questions that the book raises. Given the *Cox* decision [discussed below], moreover, all the discreditable facts about the Hayneses that are contained in judicial records are beyond the power of tort law to conceal; and the disclosure of those facts alone would strip away the Hayneses' privacy as effectively as *The Promised Land* has done. (This case, it could be argued, has stripped them of their privacy, since their story is now part of a judicial record—the record of this case.) We do not think it is an answer that Lemann got his facts from Ruby Daniels rather than from judicial records. The courts got the facts from Ruby. We cannot see what difference it makes that Lemann went to the source.

Ordinarily the evaluation and comparison of offensiveness and newsworthiness would be, like other questions of the application of a legal standard to the facts of a particular case, matters for a jury, not for a judge on a motion for summary judgment. But summary judgment is properly granted to a defendant when on the basis of the evidence obtained in pretrial discovery no reasonable jury could render a verdict for the plaintiff, [ ], and that is the situation here. . . .

Illinois has been a follower rather than a leader in recognizing claims of invasion of privacy. [ ] The plaintiffs are asking us to innovate boldly in the name of the Illinois courts, and such a request is better addressed to those courts than to a federal court. . . .

Does it follow, as the Hayneses' lawyer asked us rhetorically at oral argument, that a journalist who wanted to write a book about contemporary sexual practices could include the intimate details of named living persons' sexual acts without the persons' consent? Not necessarily, although the revelation of such details in the memoirs of former spouses and lovers is common enough and rarely provokes a lawsuit even when the former spouse or lover is still alive. The core of the branch of privacy law with which we deal in this case is the protection of those intimate physical details the publicizing of which would be not merely embarrassing and painful but deeply shocking to the average person subjected to such exposure. The public has a legitimate interest in sexuality, but that interest may be outweighed in such a case by the injury to the sensibilities of the person made use of by the author in such a way. [ ] At least the balance would be sufficiently close to preclude summary judgment for the author and publisher. [ ]

The judgment for the defendants is affirmed.

NOTES AND QUESTIONS

1.   Compare *Melvin v. Reid* with *Sidis v. F-R Publishing Corp.* Are the cases distinguishable or are they in conflict?

2.   Does the plaintiff in *Haynes* lose because the material was not sufficiently offensive? Because although it was offensive, it was nonetheless "newsworthy" or "of legitimate concern to the public"? Are the two factors related? Compare the approach of the Second Restatement in section 652D:

> One who gives publicity to a matter concerning the private life of another is subject to liability to the other for invasion of his privacy, if the matter publicized is of a kind that
>
> (a) would be highly offensive to a reasonable person, and
>
> (b) is not of legitimate concern to the public.

Does this formulation suggest any interaction between the two elements?

3.   It should not be surprising that those who seek the public limelight are thought to have a lesser claim to privacy protection than those brought into the glare of publicity simply because they are either the unfortunate victims of an accident or crime or are otherwise swept up in an event. But involuntary subjects may not be that much different. As comment f to section 652D puts it:

> These persons are regarded as properly subject to the public interest, and publishers are permitted to satisfy the curiosity of the public as to its heroes, leaders, villains and victims, and those who are closely associated with them. As in the case of the voluntary public figure, the authorized publicity is not limited to the event that itself arouses the public interest, and to some extent includes publicity given to facts about the individual that would otherwise be purely private.

Comment h adds:

> Permissible publicity to information concerning either voluntary or involuntary public figures is not limited to the particular events that arouse the interest of the public. That interest, once aroused by the event, may legitimately extend, to some reasonable degree, to further information concerning the individual and to facts about him, which are not public and which, in the case of one who had not become a public figure, would be regarded as an invasion of his purely private life. Thus the life history of one accused of murder, together with such heretofore private facts as may throw some light upon what kind of person he is, his possible guilt or innocence, or his reasons for committing the crime, are a matter of legitimate public interest. . . . On the same basis the home life and daily habits of a motion picture

actress may be of legitimate and reasonable interest to the public that sees her on the screen.

The extent of the authority to make public private facts is not, however, unlimited. There may be some intimate details of her life, such as sexual relations, which even the actress is entitled to keep to herself. In determining what is a matter of legitimate public interest, account must be taken of the customs and conventions of the community; and in the last analysis what is proper becomes a matter of the community mores. The line is to be drawn when the publicity ceases to be the giving of information to which the public is entitled, and becomes a morbid and sensational prying into private lives for its own sake, with which a reasonable member of the public, with decent standards, would say that he had no concern.

4.   What is the justification for using plaintiff's name in *Haynes*? Is the court's reasoning persuasive? In some privacy cases, the event is important, and the question is whether to name some participant in the event who happened to have something embarrassing happen to him or her. Should a rape victim who is not independently newsworthy be identified? Should a local resident on whom a load of manure was accidentally dumped be named?

On the other hand, some stories are newsworthy because they involve newsworthy people. Of all the people each day who get parking citations, the newspapers are likely to be interested in very few—but probably would be eager to learn that the mayor's spouse picked up 10 parking violations in three days. Or the paper might find irony if a recently released felon assaulted the daughter of a parent who has been active in urging early release for violent felons.

How different are these two types of situations? What fact pattern is involved in *Haynes*?

Ross v. Midwest Communications, Inc., 870 F.2d 271 (5th Cir.1989), involved the identification of a rape victim. Defendant's investigative reporting team came to the conclusion that a man convicted in two rape cases had been wrongfully accused. In its broadcast to that effect, defendant presented facts about the two rapes, including the identities of the victims and a photograph of the house in which plaintiff had lived at the time.

The court of appeals affirmed summary judgment for the defendant. Although plaintiff claimed that all the facts about the rape were private, her major claim was that defendant should not have identified her as the victim. The court, relying on an earlier case, stated that the name and the photograph "strengthen the impact and credibility of the article. They obviate any impression that the problems raised in the article are remote or hypothetical." The court noted that the "infamous Janet Cooke controversy (about the fabricated, Pulitzer-Prize-winning Washington Post series on the child-addict, Jimmy) suggests the legitimate ground for doubts that may arise about the accuracy of a documentary that uses only pseudonyms." Since the program sought to persuade the public and the authorities that an innocent man had been convicted, it was especially important to use real names.

The court did leave open the possibility of recovery where "the details of the rape victim's experience are not so uniquely crucial to the story as they are in this case, or when the publisher's 'public concern' goes to a general, sociological issue."

5. In Virgil v. Time, Inc., 527 F.2d 1122 (9th Cir.1975), a prominent surfer sued about a report that he dove head first down a flight of stairs, ate "spiders and other insects," had never learned to read, and was thought "abnormal" by other surfers. All these were thought to have some bearing on plaintiff's "reckless disregard for his own safety" in body surfing. The appellate court framed the issue as whether the revelations were of "legitimate public concern" and remanded to the trial court for a determination of whether the article might be found "morbid and sensational prying," which bore on whether plaintiff could maintain his privacy claim.

On remand, the trial judge granted the magazine summary judgment. Although the facts were "generally unflattering and perhaps embarrassing," they did not approach being highly offensive. Even if offensiveness were found, the magazine was entitled to summary judgment because the parties "agree that body surfing at the Wedge is a matter of legitimate public interest, and it cannot be doubted that Mike Virgil's unique prowess at the same is also of legitimate public interest. Any reasonable person . . . would have to conclude that the personal facts concerning Mike Virgil were included as a legitimate journalistic attempt to explain Virgil's extremely daring and dangerous style of body surfing at the Wedge. There is no possibility that a juror could conclude that the personal facts were included for any inherent morbid, sensational, or curiosity appeal they might have." Virgil v. Sports Illustrated, 424 F.Supp. 1286 (S.D.Cal.1976).

During an assassination attempt on President Ford in San Francisco, Oliver Sipple knocked the arm of the assailant, Sara Jane Moore, as she sought to aim a second shot at the President. Sipple was the object of extensive media attention, including stories that he was gay. Sipple, asserting that relatives who lived in the Midwest did not know of his sexual orientation, sued the San Francisco Chronicle. The newspaper defended in part on the argument that privacy was not involved because Sipple had marched in gay parades and had acknowledged that at least 100 to 500 people in San Francisco knew he was gay.

Summary judgment was affirmed on appeal. First, the facts were not private. Second, they were newsworthy. The article was prompted by "legitimate political considerations, i.e., to dispel the false public opinion that gays were timid, weak and unheroic figures and to raise the equally important political question whether the President of the United States [who failed promptly to thank Sipple] entertained a discriminatory attitude or bias against a minority group such as homosexuals." Sipple v. Chronicle Publishing Co., 201 Cal.Rptr. 665 (App.1984).

6. Must the editor's judgment concerning the relationship of the plaintiff's name or photograph to a story be reasonable as well as honest? What does "reasonable" mean in this context? What if the court thinks that the editor honestly saw a connection between two events but that most people would not see it the same way? Most editors?

7. Might the context of the publication be relevant? Could a daily newspaper in plaintiff's hometown identify a rape victim—while a distant paper could not? Vice versa?

What if the disclosure in *Haynes* had been made in a tabloid newspaper or on a television talk show? What missing element might that context supply?

8. In defamation, the source of the statement is relevant and often crucial to the decision. Here, the court says that the source is not important. What is the difference?

9. Although "public disclosure" claims usually arise in a media context, they also emerge in other settings as well. One of the questions that must be answered in the absence of mass publication is what constitutes public disclosure. In Robert C. Ozer, P.C. v. Borquez, 940 P.2d 371 (Colo.1997), the court explored the nature of "publicity." During his employment with the law firm Ozer & Mullin, plaintiff associate, who had not disclosed his homosexuality to his colleagues, discovered that his partner had AIDS. Plaintiff concluded that because of his distress at this situation and his anxiety about his own future, he should find substitutes for, or reschedule, a deposition and arbitration hearing. He decided to disclose the situation, requesting confidentiality, to Robert Ozer, president of the firm. Ozer, however, disseminated the information to several others, and soon everyone in the firm knew. Plaintiff was subsequently fired, and brought claims of wrongful discharge and publication of private facts. A judgment for plaintiff was reversed on appeal for instructional error.

In analyzing the "public disclosure" element, the court observed that the "requirement of public disclosure connotes publicity, which requires communication to the public in general or to a large number of persons, as distinguished from one individual or a few." Yet, even if "the disclosure must be made to the general public or to a large number of persons, there is no threshold number." Each case was fact-specific. Furthermore, the defendant may "merely initiate the process whereby the information is eventually disclosed to a large number of persons." The trial judge had instructed the jury that the disclosure requirement would be met if Ozer had revealed the information to one other person. This instruction misstated the law, since defendant's publication to a single other person would be insufficient, and a new trial was ordered. Would disclosure to two people be considered "public"? Three? What if those three people were known to gossip assiduously? If they were the only three partners of the firm?

10. *Breach of confidence.* In McCormick v. England, 494 S.E.2d 431 (S.C.App.1997), the court recognized a cause of action against a physician who breached his duty of confidentiality by revealing his diagnosis of plaintiff's depression and alcoholism in a letter to the court during her divorce proceeding. The court distinguished between publication of private facts and breach of confidence. First, the standard applied in the former type of case—that the conduct must be "highly offensive" and "likely to cause serious mental injury"—is inappropriate for a breach of confidence case "because it focuses on the content, rather than the source of the information." Likewise, whereas "[p]ublicity involves disclosure to the public, not just an individual or a small group," breach of confidence may occur even in the case of disclosure to one person—for example, a spouse.

According to *McCormick*, most states faced with the issue, as of 1997, had "recognized a cause of action against a physician for the unauthorized disclosure of confidential information unless the disclosure is compelled by law or is in the patient's interest or the public interest" [citing cases from 13 states]. Courts continue to have difficulties with the tort, however, primarily concerning the kinds of confidential relationships that should be recognized and the issue of what constitutes a privileged disclosure. For scholarship on this area, see Richards & Solove, Privacy's Other Past: Recovering the Law of Confidentiality, 96 Geo.L.J. 123 (2007), and Gilles, Promises Betrayed: Breach of Confidence as Remedy for Invasions of Privacy, 43 Buff.L.Rev. 1 (1995).

Might plaintiff in *Ozer* have prevailed on a breach of confidence theory?

11. *Privacy and the Internet.* The concept of privacy has taken on new meaning in the digital age. See Schwartz, From Victorian Secrets to Cyberspace Shaming, 76 U.Chi.L.Rev. 1407 (2009)(reviewing D. Solove, The Future of Reputation: Gossips, Rumor, and Privacy on the Internet (2007)). Among other contentious issues, consider the following:

a.   *The right to be forgotten.* In 2014, the European Court of Justice issued a landmark decision on the right of individuals to have search results about themselves removed by search engines. The court affirmed a Spanish tribunal's order that Google eliminate from its search results a 10-year-old report on an auction of property of a Spanish lawyer to pay his debts. The court adopted a balancing test for determining whether search engines must remove information, requiring balancing the privacy interests of the individual requesting omission with the public interest in obtaining access to the information. The court also said links should be removed if they are "inadequate, irrelevant or no longer relevant." There is general agreement that the First Amendment would prevent any analogous right being recognized in the United States. For exploration of the divergent cultural views between the United States and Europe that are underscored by this decision, see Toobin, The Solace of Oblivion, The New Yorker, Sept. 29, 2014 at 26. By early November 2015, almost 18 months after the decision, Google had received 337,676 requests to remove 1,201,555 URLs, and had removed 58.1% of the URLs. http://www.google.com/transparency report/removals/europeprivacy/?hl=en. (last visited, Nov. 4, 2015).

b.   *Revenge porn.* "Revenge porn sites feature explicit photos posted by ex-boyfriends, ex-husbands, and ex-lovers, often accompanied by disparaging descriptions and identifying details, like where the women live and work, as well as links to Facebook pages." Goode, *Victims Push Laws to End Online Revenge Posts*, N.Y. Times, Sept. 24, 2013 at A11. Images posted on these sites have led to civil claims ranging from privacy to copyright violations. A growing number of states have enacted criminal provisions characterizing the activity as harassment and hate crimes. See Citron and Franks, Criminalizing Revenge Porn, 49 Wake Forest L.Rev. 345 (2014).

————

In *Haynes*, Judge Posner observed that facts contained in "judicial records are beyond the power of tort law to conceal." He also mentioned that in certain situations the First Amendment would not permit privacy law to recognize a tort. We turn now to cases that explore the range of constitutional limits on the public disclosure privacy tort.

2.   CONSTITUTIONAL PRIVILEGE

In 1975, the Supreme Court decided its first "true facts" privacy case. In Cox Broadcasting Corp. v. Cohn, 420 U.S. 469 (1975), a 17-year-old had been raped in Georgia and did not survive. A Georgia criminal statute made it a misdemeanor for "any news media or any other person to print and publish, broadcast, televise or disseminate through any other medium of public discussion . . . the name or identity of any female who may have been raped." During a recess in a criminal hearing in the case, a television reporter was allowed to inspect the indictment, which named the victim. Cox Broadcasting used the victim's name in reporting on the case that night.

The victim's father brought a tort action for revelation of his daughter's name. The state supreme court held that the complaint stated a common law action for damages. A First Amendment defense was rejected on the ground that the statute was an authoritative declaration that Georgia considered a rape victim's name not to be a matter of public concern. The court could discern "no public interest or general concern about the identity of the victim of such a crime as will make the right to disclose the identity of the victim rise to the level of First Amendment protection."

The Supreme Court reversed. Cox Broadcasting argued for a "broad holding that the press may not be made criminally or civilly liable for publishing information that is neither false nor misleading but absolutely accurate, however damaging it may be to reputation or individual sensibilities." Justice White's majority opinion avoided the broad ground by addressing the narrower question of "whether the State may impose sanctions on the accurate publication of the name of a rape victim obtained from public records—more specifically, from judicial records which are maintained in connection with a public prosecution and which themselves are open to public inspection. We are convinced that the State may not do so."

Justice White noted that the public relies on the press to provide in convenient form the facts about the operation of government. Without such information "most of us and many of our representatives would be unable to vote intelligently or to register opinions on the administration of government generally." The "commission of crime, prosecutions resulting from it, and judicial proceedings arising from the prosecutions . . . are without question events of legitimate concern to the public and consequently fall within the responsibility of the press to report the operations of government."

Justice White noted that the developing law of privacy afforded the press a privilege to report the events of judicial proceedings. "By placing the information in the public domain on official court records, the State must be presumed to have concluded that the public interest was thereby being served. Public records by their very nature are of interest to those concerned with the administration of government, and a public benefit is performed by the reporting of the true contents of the records by the media." Freedom to publish material released by government is of "critical importance to our type of government in which the citizenry is the final judge of the proper conduct of public business." In such situations, "the States may not impose sanctions on the publication of truthful information contained in official court records open to public inspection."

The Court was "reluctant to embark on a course that would make public records generally available to the media but forbid their publication if offensive to the sensibilities of the supposed reasonable man. Such a rule would make it very difficult for the media to inform citizens about the public business and yet stay within the law. The rule would invite timidity and self-censorship and very likely lead to the suppression of many items that would otherwise be published and that should be made available to the public."

————

To appreciate fully the significance of the next case, it is necessary to be familiar with the major features of a few Supreme Court cases in which the press disclosed information despite a judge's order or a statute to the contrary. Oklahoma Publishing Co. v. District Court, 430 U.S. 308 (1977), struck down a judge's order barring the identification of juveniles when the judge had held an open proceeding that allowed those present to learn the identities by observation. Landmark Communications, Inc. v. Virginia, 435 U.S. 829 (1978), struck down a state bar against the publication of truthful news reports that a sitting judge was under investigation by a state commission. Smith v. Daily Mail Publishing Co., 443 U.S. 97 (1979), barred criminal prosecution against a newspaper that, in violation of a statute against such conduct, had identified a juvenile suspect based on interviews with eyewitnesses to the event.

These three cases, decided after *Cox Broadcasting,* came into play as the Court decided another case involving the identification of rape victims. At the time, Florida was one of a handful of states that sought to prevent such publications by criminal statute. That criminal statute was the basis for the following civil suit.

The Florida Star v. B.J.F.

Supreme Court of the United States, 1989.
491 U.S. 524, 109 S.Ct. 2603, 105 L.Ed.2d 443.

■ JUSTICE MARSHALL delivered the opinion of the Court.

Florida Stat. section 794.03 (1987) makes it unlawful to "print, publish, or broadcast . . . in any instrument of mass communication" the name of the victim of a sexual offense. Pursuant to this statute, appellant The Florida Star was found civilly liable for publishing the name of a rape victim which it had obtained from a publicly released police report. The issue presented here is whether this result comports with the First Amendment. We hold that it does not.

I

The Florida Star is a weekly newspaper which serves the community of Jacksonville, Florida, and which has an average circulation of approximately 18,000 copies. A regular feature of the newspaper is its "Police Reports" section. The section, typically two to three pages in length, contains brief articles describing local criminal incidents under police investigation.

On October 20, 1983, appellee B.J.F. reported to the Duval County, Florida, Sheriff's Department (the Department) that she had been robbed and sexually assaulted by an unknown assailant. The Department prepared a report on the incident which identified B.J.F. by her full name. The Department then placed the report in its press room. The Department does not restrict access either to the press room or to the reports made available therein.

A Florida Star reporter-trainee sent to the press room copied the police report verbatim, including B.J.F.'s full name, on a blank duplicate of the Department's forms. A Florida Star reporter then prepared a one-paragraph article about the crime, derived entirely from the trainee's copy of the police report. The article included B.J.F.'s full name. It appeared in the "Robberies" subsection of the "Police Reports" section on October 29, 1983, one of fifty-four police blotter stories in that day's edition. The article read:

"[B.J.F.] reported on Thursday, October 20, she was crossing Brentwood Park, which is in the 500 block of Golfair

Boulevard, enroute to her bus stop, when an unknown black man ran up behind the lady and placed a knife to her neck and told her not to yell. The suspect then undressed the lady and had sexual intercourse with her before fleeing the scene with her 60 cents, Timex watch and gold necklace. Patrol efforts have been suspended concerning this incident because of lack of evidence."

In printing B.J.F.'s full name, The Florida Star violated its internal policy of not publishing the names of sexual offense victims.

[B.J.F. sued both the newspaper and the Sheriff's Department. The latter settled for $2,500. The Star's motion to dismiss was denied.]

At the ensuing day-long trial, B.J.F. testified that she had suffered emotional distress from the publication of her name. She stated that she had heard about the article from fellow workers and acquaintances; that her mother had received several threatening phone calls from a man who stated that he would rape B.J.F. again; and that these events had forced B.J.F. to change her phone number and residence, to seek police protection, and to obtain mental health counseling. In defense, The Florida Star put forth evidence indicating that the newspaper had learned B.J.F.'s name from the incident report released by the Department, and that the newspaper's violation of its internal rule against publishing the names of sexual offense victims was inadvertent.

At the close of B.J.F.'s case, and again at the close of its defense, The Florida Star moved for a directed verdict. On both occasions, the trial judge denied these motions. He ruled from the bench that section 794.03 was constitutional because it reflected a proper balance between the First Amendment and privacy rights, as it applied only to a narrow set of "rather sensitive . . . criminal offenses." [ ] At the close of the newspaper's defense, the judge granted B.J.F.'s motion for a directed verdict on the issue of negligence, finding the newspaper per se negligent based upon its violation of section 794.03. [ ] This ruling left the jury to consider only the questions of causation and damages. The judge instructed the jury that it could award B.J.F. punitive damages if it found that the newspaper had "acted with reckless indifference to the rights of others." [ ] The jury awarded B.J.F. $75,000 in compensatory damages and $25,000 in punitive damages. Against the actual damage award, the judge set off B.J.F.'s settlement with the Department.

The First District Court of Appeal affirmed in a three-paragraph per curiam opinion. . . . The Supreme Court of Florida denied discretionary review.

The Florida Star appealed to this Court. We noted probable jurisdiction, [ ], and now reverse.

II

The tension between the right which the First Amendment accords to a free press, on the one hand, and the protections which various statutes and common-law doctrines accord to personal privacy against the publication of truthful information, on the other, is a subject we have addressed several times in recent years. Our decisions in cases involving government attempts to sanction the accurate dissemination of information as invasive of privacy, have not, however, exhaustively considered this conflict. On the contrary, although our decisions have without exception upheld the press' right to publish, we have emphasized each time that we were resolving this conflict only as it arose in a discrete factual context.

The parties to this case frame their contentions in light of a trilogy of cases which have presented, in different contexts, the conflict between truthful reporting and state-protected privacy interests. [The Court briefly reviewed *Cox Broadcasting, Oklahoma Publishing,* and *Daily Mail.*]

Appellant takes the position that this case is indistinguishable from *Cox Broadcasting.* [ ] Alternatively, it urges that our decisions in the above trilogy, and in other cases in which we have held that the right of the press to publish truth overcame asserted interests other than personal privacy, can be distilled to yield a broader First Amendment principle that the press may never be punished, civilly or criminally, for publishing the truth. [ ] Appellee counters that the privacy trilogy is inapposite, because in each case the private information already appeared on a "public record," [ ] and because the privacy interests at stake were far less profound than in the present case. [ ] In the alternative, appellee urges that *Cox Broadcasting* be overruled and replaced with a categorical rule that publication of the name of a rape victim never enjoys constitutional protection. [ ]

We conclude that imposing damages on appellant for publishing B.J.F.'s name violates the First Amendment, although not for either of the reasons appellant urges. Despite the strong resemblance this case bears to *Cox Broadcasting,* that case cannot fairly be read as controlling here. The name of the rape victim in that case was obtained from courthouse records that were open to public inspection, a fact which Justice White's opinion for the Court repeatedly noted, [ ] (noting "special protected nature of accurate reports of *judicial* proceedings") (emphasis added); [ ]. Significantly, one of the reasons we gave in *Cox Broadcasting* for invalidating the challenged damages award was the important role the press plays in subjecting trials to public scrutiny and thereby helping guarantee their fairness. [ ] That role is not directly compromised where, as here, the information in question comes from a police report prepared and disseminated at a time at which not only had no adversarial criminal proceedings begun, but no suspect had been identified.

Nor need we accept appellant's invitation to hold broadly that truthful publication may never be punished consistent with the First Amendment. Our cases have carefully eschewed reaching this ultimate question, mindful that the future may bring scenarios which prudence counsels our not resolving anticipatorily. See, e.g., *Near v. Minnesota* [ ] (hypothesizing "publication of the sailing dates of transports or the number and location of troops"); see also *Garrison v. Louisiana,* [ ] (endorsing absolute defense of truth "where discussion of public affairs is concerned," but leaving unsettled the constitutional implications of truthfulness "in the discrete area of purely private libels"); Landmark Communications, Inc. v. Virginia, 435 U.S. 829, 838 (1978); Time, Inc. v. Hill, 385 U.S. 374, 383, n. 7 (1967). Indeed, in *Cox Broadcasting,* we pointedly refused to answer even the less sweeping question "whether truthful publications may ever be subjected to civil or criminal liability" for invading "an area of privacy" defined by the State. [ ] Respecting the fact that press freedom and privacy rights are both "plainly rooted in the traditions and significant concerns of our society," we instead focused on the less sweeping issue of "whether the State may impose sanctions on the accurate publication of the name of a rape victim obtained from public records—more specifically, from judicial records which are maintained in connection with a public prosecution and which themselves are open to public inspection." [ ] We continue to believe that the sensitivity and significance of the interests presented in clashes between First Amendment and privacy rights counsel relying on limited principles that sweep no more broadly than the appropriate context of the instant case.

In our view, this case is appropriately analyzed with reference to such a limited First Amendment principle. It is the one, in fact, which we articulated in *Daily Mail* in our synthesis of prior cases involving attempts to punish truthful publication: "[I]f a newspaper lawfully obtains truthful information about a matter of public significance then state officials may not constitutionally punish publication of the information, absent a need to further a state interest of the highest order." [ ] According the press the ample protection provided by that principle is supported by at least three separate considerations, in addition to, of course, the overarching "public interest, secured by the Constitution, in the dissemination of truth." [ ] The cases on which the *Daily Mail* synthesis relied demonstrate these considerations.

First, because the *Daily Mail* formulation only protects the publication of information which a newspaper has "lawfully obtain[ed]," [ ], the government retains ample means of safeguarding significant interests upon which publication may impinge, including protecting a rape victim's anonymity. To the extent sensitive information rests in private hands, the government may under some circumstances forbid its nonconsensual acquisition, thereby bringing outside of the *Daily Mail* principle the publication of any information so acquired. To the extent sensitive information is in the government's custody, it has even greater power to forestall or mitigate the injury caused by its release. The government may classify certain information, establish and enforce procedures ensuring its redacted release, and extend a damages remedy against the government or its officials where the government's mishandling of sensitive information leads to its dissemination. Where information is entrusted to the government, a less drastic means than punishing truthful publication almost always exists for guarding against the dissemination of private facts. See, e.g., [*Landmark Communications*] ("much of the risk [from disclosure of sensitive information regarding judicial disciplinary proceedings] can be eliminated through careful internal procedures to protect the confidentiality of Commission proceedings"); [*Oklahoma Publishing*] (noting trial judge's failure to avail himself of the opportunity, provided by a state statute, to close juvenile hearing to the public, including members of the press, who later broadcast juvenile defendant's name); [*Cox Broadcasting*] ("If there are privacy interests to be protected in judicial proceedings, the States must respond by means which avoid public documentation or other exposure of private information").[8]

A second consideration undergirding the *Daily Mail* principle is the fact that punishing the press for its dissemination of information which is already publicly available is relatively unlikely to advance the interests in the service of which the State seeks to act. It is not, of course, always the case that information lawfully acquired by the press is known, or accessible, to others. But where the government has made certain information publicly available, it is highly anomalous to sanction persons other than the source of its release. We noted this anomaly in *Cox Broadcasting:* "By placing the information in the public domain on official court records, the State must be presumed to have concluded that the public interest was thereby being served." [ ] The *Daily Mail* formulation reflects the fact that it is a limited set of cases indeed where, despite the accessibility of the public to certain information, a meaningful public interest is served by restricting its further release by other entities, like the press. As *Daily Mail* observed in its summary of *Oklahoma Publishing,* "once the truthful information was 'publicly revealed' or 'in the public domain' the court could not constitutionally restrain its dissemination." [ ]

A third and final consideration is the "timidity and self-censorship" which may result from allowing the media to be punished for publishing certain truthful information. [ ] *Cox Broadcasting* noted this concern with overdeterrence in the context of information made public through official court records, but the fear of excessive media self-suppression is applicable as well to other information released without qualification, by the government. A contrary rule, [denying] protection to those who rely on the government's implied representations of the lawfulness of

---

[8]   The *Daily Mail* principle does not settle the issue of whether, in cases where information has been acquired *unlawfully* by a newspaper or by a source, government may ever punish not only the unlawful acquisition, but the ensuing publication as well. This issue was raised but not definitively resolved in New York Times Co. v. United States, 403 U.S. 713 (1971), and reserved in [*Landmark Communications*]. We have no occasion to address it here.

dissemination, would force upon the media the onerous obligation of sifting through government press releases, reports, and pronouncements to prune out material arguably unlawful for publication. This situation could inhere even where the newspaper's sole object was to reproduce, with no substantial change, the government's rendition of the event in question.

Applied to the instant case, the *Daily Mail* principle clearly commands reversal. The first inquiry is whether the newspaper "lawfully obtain[ed] truthful information about a matter of public significance." [ ] It is undisputed that the news article describing the assault on B.J.F. was accurate. In addition, appellant lawfully obtained B.J.F.'s name. Appellee's argument to the contrary is based on the fact that under Florida law, police reports which reveal the identity of the victim of a sexual offense are not among the matters of "public record" which the public, by law, is entitled to inspect. [ ] But the fact that the state officials are not required to disclose such reports does not make it unlawful for a newspaper to receive them when furnished by the government. Nor does the fact that the Department apparently failed to fulfill its obligation under section 794.03 not to "cause or allow to be . . . published" the name of a sexual offense victim make the newspaper's ensuing receipt of this information unlawful. Even assuming the Constitution permitted a State to proscribe *receipt* of information, Florida has not taken this step. It is clear, furthermore, that the news article concerned "a matter of public significance," [ ] in the sense in which the *Daily Mail* synthesis of prior cases used that term. That is, the article generally, as opposed to the specific identity contained within it, involved a matter of paramount public import: the commission, and investigation, of a violent crime which had been reported to authorities. See *Cox Broadcasting* (article identifying victim of rape-murder); [*Oklahoma Publishing*] (article identifying juvenile alleged to have committed murder); [*Daily Mail*] (same); cf. [*Landmark Communications*] (article identifying judges whose conduct was being investigated).

The second inquiry is whether imposing liability on appellant pursuant to section 794.03 serves "a need to further a state interest of the highest order." [*Daily Mail*] Appellee argues that a rule punishing publication furthers three closely related interests: the privacy of victims of sexual offenses; the physical safety of such victims, who may be targeted for retaliation if their names become known to their assailants; and the goal of encouraging victims of such crimes to report these offenses without fear of exposure. [ ]

At a time in which we are daily reminded of the tragic reality of rape, it is undeniable that these are highly significant interests, a fact underscored by the Florida Legislature's explicit attempt to protect these interests by enacting a criminal statute prohibiting such dissemination of victim identities. We accordingly do not rule out the possibility that, in a proper case, imposing civil sanctions for publication of the name of a rape victim might be so overwhelmingly necessary to advance these interests as to satisfy the *Daily Mail* standard. For three independent reasons, however, imposing liability for publication under the circumstances of this case is too precipitous a means of advancing these interests to convince us that there is a "need" within the meaning of the *Daily Mail* formulation for Florida to take this extreme step. Cf. *Landmark Communications* (invalidating penalty on publication despite State's expressed interest in nondissemination, reflected in statute prohibiting unauthorized divulging of names of judges under investigation).

First is the manner in which appellant obtained the identifying information in question. As we have noted, where the government itself provides information to the media, it is most appropriate to assume that the government had, but failed to utilize, far more limited means of guarding against dissemination than the extreme step of punishing truthful speech. That assumption is richly borne out in this case. B.J.F.'s identity would never have come to light were it not for the erroneous, if inadvertent, inclusion by the Department of her full name in an accident report made available in a press room open to the public. Florida's policy against disclosure of rape victims' identities, reflected in section 794.03, was undercut by the Department's failure to abide by this policy. Where, as here, the government has failed to police itself in disseminating information, it is clear under *Cox Broadcasting, Oklahoma Publishing,* and *Landmark Communications* that the imposition of damages against the press for its subsequent publication can hardly be said to be a narrowly tailored means of safeguarding anonymity. [ ] Once the government has placed such information in the public domain, "reliance must rest upon the judgment of those who decide what to publish or broadcast," [*Cox Broadcasting*] and hopes for restitution must rest upon the willingness of the government to compensate victims for their loss of privacy, and to protect them from the other consequences of its mishandling of the information which these victims provided in confidence.

That appellant gained access to the information in question through a government news release makes it especially likely that, if liability were to be imposed, self-censorship would result. Reliance on a news release is a paradigmatically "routine newspaper reporting techniqu[e]." [*Daily Mail*] The government's issuance of such a release, without qualification, can only convey to recipients that the government considered dissemination lawful, and indeed expected the recipients to disseminate the information further. Had appellant merely reproduced the news release prepared and released by the Department, imposing civil damages would surely violate the First Amendment. The fact that appellant converted the police report into a news story by adding the linguistic connecting tissue necessary to transform the report's facts into full sentences cannot change this result.

A second problem with Florida's imposition of liability for publication is the broad sweep of the negligence per se standard applied under the civil cause of action implied from section 794.03. Unlike claims based on the common law tort of invasion of privacy, [ ], civil actions based on section 794.03 require no case-by-case findings that the disclosure of a fact about a person's private life was one that a reasonable person would find highly offensive. On the contrary, under the per se theory of negligence adopted by the courts below, liability follows automatically from publication. This is so regardless of whether the identity of the victim is already known throughout the community; whether the victim has voluntarily called public attention to the offense; or whether the identity of the victim has otherwise become a reasonable subject of public concern—because, perhaps, questions have arisen whether the victim fabricated an assault by a particular person. Nor is there a scienter requirement of any kind under section 794.03, engendering the perverse result that truthful publications challenged pursuant to this cause of action are less protected by the First Amendment than even the least protected defamatory falsehoods: those involving purely private figures, where liability is evaluated under a standard, usually applied by a jury, of ordinary negligence. See *Gertz v. Robert Welch, Inc.* [ ]. We have previously noted the impermissibility of categorical prohibitions upon media access where important First Amendment interests are at stake. See Globe Newspaper Co. v. Superior Court, 457 U.S. 596, 608 (1982) (invalidating state statute providing for the categorical exclusion of the public from trials of sexual offenses involving juvenile victims.) More individualized adjudication is no less indispensable where the State, seeking to safeguard the anonymity of crime victims, sets its face against publication of their names.

Third, and finally, the facial under-inclusiveness of section 794.03 raises serious doubts about whether Florida is, in fact, serving, with this statute, the significant interests which appellee invokes in support of affirmance. Section 794.03 prohibits the publication of identifying information only if this information appears in an "instrument of mass communication," a term the statute does not define. Section 794.03 does not prohibit the spread by other means of the identities of victims of sexual offenses. An individual who maliciously spreads word of the identity of a rape victim is thus not covered, despite the fact that the communication of such information to persons who live near, or work with, the victim may have consequences equally devastating as the exposure of her name to large numbers of strangers. [ ]

When a State attempts the extraordinary measure of punishing truthful publication in the name of privacy, it must demonstrate its commitment to advancing this interest by applying its prohibition evenhandedly, to the small time disseminator as well as the media giant. Where important First Amendment interests are at stake, the mass scope of disclosure is not an acceptable surrogate for injury. A ban on disclosures effected by "instrument[s] of mass communication" simply cannot be defended on the ground that partial prohibitions may effect partial relief. See [*Daily Mail*] (statute is insufficiently tailored to interest in protecting anonymity where it restricted only newspapers, not the electronic media or other forms of publication, from identifying juvenile defendants); *id.,* at 110 (Rehnquist, J., concurring in judgment) (same); cf. Arkansas Writers' Project, Inc. v. Ragland, 481 U.S. 221, 229 (1987); Minneapolis Star & Tribune Co. v. Minnesota Comm'r of Revenue, 460 U.S. 575, 585 (1983). Without more careful and inclusive precautions against alternative forms of dissemination, we cannot conclude that Florida's selective ban on publication by the mass media satisfactorily accomplishes its stated purpose.

III

Our holding today is limited. We do not hold that truthful publication is automatically constitutionally protected, or that there is no zone of personal privacy within which the State may protect the individual from intrusion by the press, or even that a State may never punish publication of the name of a victim of a sexual offense. We hold only that where a newspaper publishes truthful information which it has lawfully obtained, punishment may lawfully be imposed, if at all, only when narrowly tailored to a state interest of the highest order, and that no such interest is satisfactorily served by imposing liability ... under the facts of this case. The decision below is therefore reversed.

■ JUSTICE SCALIA, concurring in part and concurring in the judgment.

I think it sufficient to decide this case to rely upon the third ground set forth in the Court's opinion [ ]: that a law cannot be regarded as protecting an interest "of the highest order" [ ], and thus as justifying a restriction upon truthful speech, when it leaves appreciable damage to that supposedly vital interest unprohibited. I would anticipate that the rape victim's discomfort at the dissemination of news of her misfortune among friends and acquaintances would be at least as great as her discomfort at its publication by the media to people to whom she is only a name. Yet the law in question does not prohibit the former in either oral or written form. Nor is it clear, as I think it must be to validate this statute, that Florida's general privacy law would prohibit such gossip. Nor, finally, is it credible that the interest meant to be served by the statute is the protection of the victim against a rapist still at large—an interest that arguably would extend only to mass publication. There would be little reason to limit a statute with that objective to rape alone; or to extend it to all rapes, whether or not the felon has been apprehended and confined. In any case, the instructions here did not require the jury to find that the rapist was at large.

This law has every appearance of a prohibition that society is prepared to impose upon the press but not upon itself. Such a prohibition does not protect an interest "of the highest order." For that reason, I agree that the judgment of the court below must be reversed.

[JUSTICE WHITE, joined by CHIEF JUSTICE REHNQUIST and JUSTICE O'CONNOR, dissented. He distinguished the three cases on which the Court relied (but noted that *Oklahoma Publishing* was much less relied upon than the other two). The "State-law scheme [in *Cox Broadcasting*] made public disclosure of the victim's name almost inevitable; here, Florida law forbids such disclosure." "By amending its public records statute to exempt rape victims' names from disclosure [ ], and forbidding its officials from releasing such information, [ ], the State has taken virtually every step imaginable to prevent what happened here." *Cox Broadcasting* bars the state only from making the press "its first line of defense in withholding private information from the public—it cannot ask the press to secrete private facts that the State makes no effort to safeguard in the first place."

Justice White distinguished *Daily Mail* on the ground that it involved revelation of the name of the perpetrator of a murder and this case involved a victim: "whatever rights alleged criminals have to maintain their anonymity pending an adjudication of guilt—the rights of crime victims must be infinitely more substantial." Also, *Daily Mail* noted that the case involved "no issue of privacy." "But in this case, there is an issue of privacy—indeed, this is the principal issue—and therefore, this case falls outside of [*Daily Mail*]."

Justice White then turned to the Court's "independent" reasons for deciding *Florida Star*. First, the government's release of the information was "inadvertent." When the state makes a mistake in its efforts to protect privacy "it is not too much to ask the press, in instances such as this, to respect simple standards of decency and refrain from publishing a victim's name, address, and/or phone number." In a footnote at this point, Justice White noted that the Court's proper concern for a free press should "be balanced against rival interests in a civilized and humane society. An absolutist view of the former leads to insensitivity as to the latter."

Second, the Court's concern about strict liability was unavailable on this record because the jury found the Star reckless. In any event, it was permissible for the standard of care to be set by the legislature rather than the courts.

As to the third point—under-inclusiveness—Justice White was willing to accept the apparent legislative conclusion that "neighborhood gossips do not pose the danger and intrusion to rape victims that 'instrument[s] of mass communication' do. Simply put: Florida wanted to prevent the widespread distribution of rape victims' names, and therefore enacted a statute tailored almost as precisely as possible to achieving that end." Moreover, it was entirely possible that Florida's common law of privacy might apply against neighborhood gossips in an appropriate case.

Justice White then turned to "more general principles at issue here to see if they recommend the Court's result." He feared that the result would "obliterate one of the most noteworthy legal inventions of the twentieth century: the tort of the publication of private facts." If the plaintiff here could not prevail it was hard to imagine who could win such a case. There was no public interest in identifying the plaintiff here and "no public interest in immunizing the press from liability in the rare cases where a State's efforts to protect a victim's privacy have failed."]

NOTES AND QUESTIONS

1. Why is the Star's defense not precisely covered by *Cox Broadcasting?* By *Daily Mail?*

2. How might the Star's defense have been analyzed in a state that had no statute?

3. How might the Star's defense have been analyzed if the Star had learned about the name from an eyewitness rather than as the result of a mistake in the sheriff's office?

4. What might change if it turned out that the Star got the name from a sheriff's deputy who violated a statute in revealing the name?

5. A California case prior to *Cox* had provided relief to a former criminal whose identity was revealed. In Briscoe v. Reader's Digest Ass'n, 483 P.2d 34 (Cal.1971), a magazine article on the chanciness of truck hijacking reported that 11 years earlier the plaintiff and another had hijacked a truck in Kentucky, only to find that it contained four bowling pin spotting machines. The article was published in 1967, by which time plaintiff alleged that he had served his time, had become rehabilitated, and was living in California with family and friends who did not know about his past. The court stated: "Ideally, his neighbors should recognize his present worth and forget his past life of shame. But men are not so divine as to forgive the past trespasses of others, and plaintiff therefore endeavored to reveal as little as possible of his past life." The court concluded that it was for the trier of fact to decide whether plaintiff had been rehabilitated, whether "identifying him as a former criminal would be highly offensive and injurious to the reasonable man," whether defendant published the information "with a reckless disregard for its offensiveness," and whether any independent justification existed for printing plaintiff's identity.

The court reconsidered *Briscoe* in Gates v. Discovery Communications Inc., 101 P.3d 552 (Cal.2004). A rehabilitated criminal sued a television company that produced a documentary about a murder-for-hire case in which plaintiff had been involved many years earlier. The court rejected the claim despite the law-abiding and private life that the plaintiff had lived since serving his sentence. The court overruled *Briscoe*, in view of the Supreme Court holdings in this area. The First Amendment precluded holding the news media liable for the publication of truthful information contained in official court records open to the public.

Does it follow from the *Cox Broadcasting-Florida Star* line of cases that *Briscoe* could not survive the First Amendment limitations imposed on the privacy tort?

6. Is the privilege of *Cox Broadcasting* and *Florida Star* so broad that it bars exceptions such as one that would facilitate the rehabilitation of criminals? Do these cases suggest that the use of expungement may be legally suspect?

———

The problem for editors. In *Virgil*, note 5, p. 1166 supra, the publisher initially argued that the First Amendment protected all true statements from liability. The court rejected that claim, suggesting that at least some private facts could be protected notwithstanding the First Amendment. The publisher then made a different argument:

> A press which must depend upon a governmental determination as to what facts are of "public interest" in order to avoid liability for their truthful publication is not free at all. . . . A constitutional rule can be fashioned which protects all the interests involved. This goal is achieved by providing a privilege for truthful publications which is defeasible only when the court concludes as a matter of law that the truthful publication complained of constitutes a clear abuse of the editor's constitutional discretion to publish and discuss subjects and facts which in his judgment are matters of public interest.

Again the court disagreed. In libel and obscenity cases juries utilize community standards, and the court thought they should do so here, too, "subject to close judicial scrutiny to ensure that the jury resolutions comport with First Amendment principles." What is the difference between defendant's position and that adopted by the court?

Courts have tended to resolve these issues on a case-by-case basis, and editors complain that such an approach breeds intolerable uncertainty. An editor must decide today based on a prediction of what might happen in court several years later—and the standards are said to be vague. Who can predict what will be found "highly offensive to a reasonable person," or to violate "community standards and mores"? Juries given these questions may punish unpopular publishers or broadcasters.

Compare this situation with that confronting an editor in the defamation area. There, the editor, with advice from lawyers, must decide whether the *Times* or *Gertz* rule applies and then determine whether the publication's conduct meets that standard. And truth is always a defense. Do you see a sharp difference between the editor's position in defamation and in privacy? See Ingber, Rethinking Intangible Injuries: A Focus on Remedy, 73 Cal.L.Rev. 772 (1985).

Successful plaintiffs. During the 1960s and 1970s, it began to look as though the public disclosure tort was interesting academically but not achieving success in the courts. The 1980s began to show signs of change.

In Diaz v. Oakland Tribune, Inc., 188 Cal.Rptr. 762 (App.1983), a columnist wrote of plaintiff:

> More education stuff: The students at the College of Alameda will be surprised to learn that their student body president, Toni Diaz, is no lady, but is in fact a man whose real name is Antonio.
>
> Now I realize that in these times, such a matter is no big deal, but I suspect his female classmates in P.E. 97 may wish to make other showering arrangements.

The plaintiff had had transsexual surgery. A judgment for $775,000 (of which $250,000 was compensatory) was reversed on appeal for trial errors but the court went out of its way to say that recovery was permitted on these facts and that the size of the recovery might not be a problem. The author knew the result would be "devastating" but never sought to contact plaintiff beforehand. His attempt to be "flip" and what the jury could find to be his "callous and conscious disregard for Diaz's privacy interests" justified the punitive award. The case was then settled.

A plaintiff won—and kept—a privacy award of $1,500 compensatory and $25,000 punitive damages in Hawkins v. Multimedia, Inc., 344 S.E.2d 145 (S.C.), cert. denied, 479 U.S. 1012 (1986)(Brennan, J., dissenting). In a sidebar article to a story on teenage pregnancies, defendant's newspaper identified plaintiff as the teenage father of an illegitimate child. Most of the article focused on the teenage mother. After the mother identified plaintiff as the father, the reporter called plaintiff twice to obtain comments. The reporter first spoke with plaintiff's mother. The second time she spoke with the reluctant plaintiff for three or four minutes. "In neither call did the reporter request permission to identify or quote [plaintiff]."

Over defendant's objection, the trial judge charged that a minor cannot consent to an invasion of privacy. The appellate court did not reach the issue because it found that defendant had failed to establish consent in the first place. Although plaintiff did not hang up immediately, he was "very shy." He never agreed to the use of his name.

The court rejected defense arguments that the article was of "general interest" because that defense requires "legitimate" public interest. "Public or general interest does not mean mere curiosity, and newsworthiness is not necessarily the test." This issue was properly submitted to the jury.

In Doe v. Mills, 536 N.W.2d 824 (Mich.App.1995), defendants searched the trash bin at an abortion clinic and obtained the names of two women who were scheduled to have abortions the following day. When the women arrived defendants raised large signs listing the plaintiffs' real names that implored them, among other things, not to "kill their babies." Summary judgment dismissing plaintiffs' public disclosure of private facts claims was reversed; the court also upheld an action for intentional infliction of emotional distress.

B. FALSE LIGHT PRIVACY

The conventional idea of invasion of privacy as conceived by Warren and Brandeis involved true statements about aspects of plaintiff's life that others had no business knowing. But along the way, a few cases surfaced that placed the plaintiff in a false light but did not do harm to "reputation" so as to permit an action for defamation. For example, a group used plaintiff's name without authorization on a petition to the governor to veto a bill. Although falsely stating that plaintiff had signed the petition would not have been defamatory, the court found the situation actionable because it cast plaintiff in a false light. Hinish v. Meier & Frank Co., 113 P.2d 438 (Or.1941).

This type of case tested the line between defamation and privacy. The distinction between the false light cause of action and the "true" privacy case, however, also became blurred after Time, Inc. v. Hill, 385 U.S. 374 (1967). In 1952, James Hill and his family were held hostage in their home for 19 hours by three escaped convicts who apparently treated them decently. The incident received extensive nationwide coverage. Thereafter the Hills moved to another state, sought seclusion, and refused to make public appearances. A novel modeled in general on the event was published the following year. In 1955, Life magazine, in a very short article, announced that a play and a motion picture were being made from the novel, which it said was "inspired" by the Hill episode. The play, "a heart-stopping account of how a family rose to heroism in a crisis," would enable the public to see the Hill story "re-enacted." Photographs in the magazine showed actors performing scenes from the play at the house at which the original events had occurred. The Hills claimed that the story was inaccurate because the novel and the play showed the convicts committing violence on the father and uttering a "verbal sexual insult" at the daughter.

Suit was brought under the New York statute that required plaintiff to show that the article was being used for advertising purposes or for purposes of trade. A claim based on a truthful article, no matter how offensive and unpleasant for the Hills, would have failed. On the other hand, a few state courts had previously indicated that falsity would show that the article was really for purposes of trade and not for public enlightenment. (Recall that this hint has since been rejected in *Messenger*, p. 1157 supra.) The state courts allowed the Hills a recovery after lengthy litigation.

The Supreme Court, by a very fragile majority, decided that the privilege to comment on matters of public interest had constitutional protection and could not be lost by the introduction of falsity unless the falsity was either deliberate or reckless. The Court used the defamation analogy that was then being developed in the wake of *New York Times* and applied it to this privacy case that involved falsity, ignoring the fact that the falsity was relatively trivial. Was the false report any more harmful than an absolutely true one would have been? If not, why does the falsity matter? The Court had not yet considered defamation actions by private citizens.

Cantrell v. Forest City Publishing Co.

Supreme Court of the United States, 1974.
419 U.S. 245, 95 S.Ct. 465, 42 L.Ed.2d 419.

■ MR. JUSTICE STEWART delivered the opinion of the Court.

Margaret Cantrell and four of her minor children brought this diversity action in a Federal District Court for invasion of privacy against the Forest City Publishing Co., publisher of a Cleveland newspaper, the Plain Dealer, and against Joseph Eszterhas, a reporter formerly employed by the Plain Dealer, and Richard Conway, a Plain Dealer photographer. The Cantrells alleged that an article published in the Plain Dealer Sunday Magazine unreasonably placed their family in a false light before the public through its many inaccuracies and untruths. The District Judge struck the claims relating to punitive damages as to all the plaintiffs and dismissed the actions of three of the Cantrell children in their entirety, but allowed the case to go to the jury as to Mrs. Cantrell and her oldest son, William. The jury returned a verdict for $60,000 against all three of the respondents for compensatory money damages in favor of these two plaintiffs.

The Court of Appeals for the Sixth Circuit reversed, holding that, in the light of the First and Fourteenth Amendments, the District Judge should have granted the respondents' motion for a directed verdict as to all the Cantrells' claims. . . .

I.

On December 1967, Margaret Cantrell's husband Melvin was killed along with 43 other people when the Silver Bridge across the Ohio River at Point Pleasant, West Virginia, collapsed. The respondent Eszterhas was assigned by the Plain Dealer to cover the story of the disaster. He wrote a "news feature" story focusing on the funeral of Melvin Cantrell and the impact of his death on the Cantrell family.

Five months later, after conferring with the Sunday Magazine editor of the Plain Dealer, Eszterhas and photographer Conway returned to the Point Pleasant area to write a follow-up feature. The two men went to the Cantrell residence, where Eszterhas talked with the children and Conway took 50 pictures. Mrs. Cantrell was not at home at any time during the 60 to 90 minutes that the men were at the Cantrell residence.

Eszterhas' story appeared as the lead feature in the August 4, 1968, edition of the Plain Dealer Sunday Magazine. The article stressed the family's abject poverty; the children's old, ill-fitting clothes and the deteriorating condition of their home were detailed in both the text and accompanying photographs. As he had done in his original, prize-winning article on the Silver Bridge disaster, Eszterhas used the Cantrell family to illustrate the impact of the bridge collapse on the lives of the people in the Point Pleasant area.

It is conceded that the story contained a number of inaccuracies and false statements. Most conspicuously, although Mrs. Cantrell was not present at any time during the reporter's visit to her home, Eszterhas wrote, "Margaret Cantrell will talk neither about what happened nor about how they are doing. She wears the same mask of non-expression she wore at the funeral. She is a proud woman. Her world has changed. She says that after it happened, the people in town offered to help them out with money and they refused to take it." Other significant misrepresentations were contained in details of Eszterhas' descriptions of the poverty in which the Cantrells were living and the dirty and dilapidated conditions of the Cantrell home.

The case went to the jury on a so-called "false light" theory of invasion of privacy. In essence, the theory of the case was that by publishing the false feature story about the Cantrells and thereby making them the objects of pity and ridicule, the respondents damaged Mrs. Cantrell and her son William by causing them to suffer outrage, mental distress, shame, and humiliation.[2]

II.

In [*Hill*], the Court considered a similar false-light, invasion-of-privacy action. The New York Court of Appeals had interpreted New York Civil Rights Law §§ 50–51 to give a "newsworthy person" a right of action when his or her name, picture or portrait was the subject of a "fictitious" report or article. Material and substantial falsification was the test for recovery. [ ] Under this doctrine the New York courts awarded the plaintiff James Hill compensatory damages based on his complaint that Life Magazine had falsely reported that a new Broadway play portrayed the Hill family's experience in being held hostage by

---

[2] Although this is a diversity action based on state tort law, there is remarkably little discussion of the relevant Ohio or West Virginia law by the District Court, the Court of Appeals, and counsel for the parties. It is clear, however, that both Ohio and West Virginia recognize a legally protected interest in privacy. [ ] Publicity that places the plaintiff in a false light in the public eye is generally recognized as one of the several distinct kinds of invasions actionable under the privacy rubric. [ ]

three escaped convicts. This Court, guided by its decision in *New York Times Co. v. Sullivan,* [ ], which recognized constitutional limits on a State's power to award damages for libel in actions brought by public officials, held that the constitutional protections for speech and press precluded the application of the New York statute to allow recovery for "false reports of matters of public interest in the absence of proof that the defendant published the report with knowledge of its falsity or in reckless disregard of the truth." [ ] Although the jury could have reasonably concluded from the evidence in the *Hill* case that Life had engaged in knowing falsehood or had recklessly disregarded the truth in stating in the article that "the story re-enacted" the Hill family's experience, the Court concluded that the trial judge's instructions had not confined the jury to such a finding as a predicate for liability as required by the Constitution. [ ]

The District Judge in the case before us, in contrast to the trial judge in *Time Inc. v. Hill,* did instruct the jury that liability could be imposed only if it concluded that the false statements in the Sunday Magazine feature article on the Cantrells had been made with knowledge of their falsity or in reckless disregard of the truth. No objection was made by any of the parties to this knowing-or-reckless-falsehood instruction. Consequently, this case presents no occasion to consider whether a State may constitutionally apply a more relaxed standard of liability for a publisher or broadcaster of false statements injurious to a private individual under a false-light theory of invasion of privacy, or whether the constitutional standard announced in *Time Inc. v. Hill* applies to all false-light cases. Cf. [*Gertz*]. Rather, the sole question that we need decide is whether the Court of Appeals erred in setting aside the jury's verdict.

III.

At the close of the petitioners' case-in-chief, the District Judge struck the demand for punitive damages. He found that Mrs. Cantrell had failed to present any evidence to support the charges that the invasion of privacy "was done maliciously within the legal definition of that term." The Court of Appeals interpreted this finding to be a determination by the District Judge that there was no evidence of knowing falsity or reckless disregard of the truth introduced at the trial. Having made such a determination, the Court of Appeals held that the District Judge should have granted the motion for a directed verdict for respondents as to all the Cantrells' claims. [ ]

. . .

Although the verbal record of the District Court proceedings is not entirely unambiguous, the conclusion is inescapable that the District Judge was referring to the common-law standard of malice rather than to the *New York Times* "actual malice" standard when he dismissed the punitive damages claims. . . .

Moreover, the District Judge was clearly correct in believing that the evidence introduced at trial was sufficient to support a jury finding that the respondents Joseph Eszterhas and Forest City Publishing Co. had published knowing or reckless falsehoods about the Cantrells.[5] There was no dispute during the trial that Eszterhas, who did not testify, must have known that a number of the statements in the feature story were untrue. In particular, his article plainly implied that Mrs. Cantrell had been present during his visit to her home and that Eszterhas had observed her "wear[ing] the same mask of non-expression she wore [at her husband's] funeral." These were "calculated falsehoods," and the jury was plainly justified in finding that Eszterhas had portrayed the Cantrells in a false light through knowing or reckless untruth.

The Court of Appeals concluded that there was no evidence that Forest City Publishing Co. had knowledge of any of the inaccuracies contained in Eszterhas' article. However, there was sufficient evidence for the jury to find that Eszterhas' writing of the feature was within the scope of his employment at the Plain Dealer and that Forest City Publishing Co. was therefore liable under traditional doctrines of *respondeat superior*. . . .

For the foregoing reasons, the judgment of the Court of Appeals is reversed and the case is remanded to that court with directions to enter a judgment affirming the judgment of the District Court as to the respondents Forest City Publishing Co. and Joseph Eszterhas.

It is so ordered.

■ MR. JUSTICE DOUGLAS, dissenting.

. . .

A bridge accident catapulted the Cantrells into the public eye and their disaster became newsworthy. To make the First Amendment freedom to report the news turn on subtle differences between common-law malice and actual malice is to stand the Amendment on its head. Those who write the current news seldom have the objective, dispassionate point of view—or the time—of scientific analysts. They deal in fast-moving events and the need for "spot" reporting. The jury under today's formula sits as a censor with broad powers—not to impose a prior restraint, but to lay heavy damages on the press. The press is "free" only if the jury is sufficiently disenchanted with the Cantrells to let the press be free of this damages claim. That regime is thought by some to be a way of supervising the press which is better than not supervising it at all. But the installation of the Court's regime would require a constitutional amendment. Whatever might be the

---

[5] Although we conclude that the jury verdicts should have been sustained as to Eszterhas and Forest City Publishing Co., we agree with the Court of Appeals' conclusion that there was insufficient evidence to support the jury's verdict against the photographer Conway. . . .

ultimate reach of the doctrine Mr. Justice Black and I have embraced, it seems clear that in matters of public import such as the present news reporting, there must be freedom from damages lest the press be frightened into playing a more ignoble role than the Framers visualized.

I would affirm the judgment of the Court of Appeals.

NOTES AND QUESTIONS

1.   How would you analyze a defamation action brought by the Cantrells?

2.   Justice Stewart analyzes this case as involving the "false light" category of privacy. Might it also be analyzed as a public disclosure privacy case in which the media claimed the defense of newsworthiness but lost because the defense is not available when the material reported is deliberately or recklessly false? What are the differences between the two analyses?

A few years after *Cantrell,* in *Zacchini v. Scripps-Howard Broadcasting Co.,* p. 1236 infra, the Court approvingly quoted Dean Prosser's statement that the interest protected in false light actions "is clearly that of reputation, with the same overtones of mental distress as in defamation." Under this view, why might a state permit liability for errors that do not harm reputation?

3.   What is this tort getting at? A few states have doubted its utility and have rejected it. See, e.g., Renwick v. The News and Observer Publishing Co., 312 S.E.2d 405 (N.C.1984), in which the court noted that in states that recognize the action: "[T]he false light need not necessarily be a defamatory light. [ ] In many if not most cases, however, the false light is defamatory and an action for libel or slander will also lie." The court stated that it would "create a grave risk of serious impairment of the indispensable service of a free press in a free society if we [were to] saddle the press with the impossible burden of verifying to a certainty the facts associated in news articles with a person's name, picture or portrait, particularly as related to nondefamatory matter." The court thought the action "constitutionally suspect" and thought it "would not differ significantly" from the existing defamation action.

In Lake v. Wal-Mart Stores, Inc., 582 N.W.2d 231 (Minn.1998), photos of two plaintiff women showering nude together were developed at defendant's store and disseminated by defendant's employee. The court held that plaintiffs stated claims for intrusion and public disclosure of private facts—but in dictum declined to recognize the tort of false light publicity. Observing that "[f]alse light is the most widely criticized of the four privacy torts and has been rejected by several jurisdictions," the court relied most heavily on the observation that the false light tort overlaps significantly with defamation, and, thus, there are hardly any pure false light claims: "The primary difference between defamation and false light is that defamation addresses harm to reputation in the external world, while false light protects harm to one's inner self. . . . [B]ecause of the overlap . . . a case has rarely succeeded squarely on a false light claim."

For differing perspectives on the need for a false light tort, compare Schwartz, Explaining and Justifying a Limited Tort of False Light Invasion of Privacy, 41 Case W.Res.L.Rev. 885 (1991), with Zimmerman, False Light Invasion of Privacy: The Light That Failed, 64 N.Y.U.L.Rev. 364 (1989).

4. *Actual malice or negligence?* In a footnote to his concurring opinion in *Cox Broadcasting,* p. 1169 supra, Justice Powell observed:

> . . . The Court's abandonment of the "matter of general or public interest" standard as the determinative factor for deciding whether to apply the *New York Times* malice standard to defamation litigation brought by private individuals, [ ], calls into question the conceptual basis of *Time, Inc. v. Hill.* In neither *Gertz* nor our more recent decision in [*Cantrell*], however, have we been called upon to determine whether a State may constitutionally apply a more relaxed standard of liability under a false-light theory of invasion of privacy. [ ]

The question of actual malice or negligence in false light cases has persisted. The situation is summarized in Lovgren v. Citizens First National Bank of Princeton, 534 N.E.2d 987 (Ill.1989), in which the court upheld such a claim in favor of a plaintiff whose property was advertised without his consent as being up for sale at a forthcoming public auction. After summarizing the *Hill-Cantrell* sequence, the court concluded that it would, as a matter of state law, insist on "actual malice." It quoted from the Prosser & Keeton treatise:

> It is suggested that virtually all actionable invasions of privacy have been intentional invasions or invasions of a kind that defendant knew or had reason to know would not only be offensive but rightly so and are therefore examples of outrageous conduct that was committed with knowledge or with reason to know that it would cause severe mental stress. Recovery for an invasion of privacy on the ground that the plaintiff was depicted in a false light makes sense only when the account, if true, would not have been actionable as an invasion of privacy. In other words, the outrageous character of the publicity comes about in part by virtue of the fact that some part of the matter reported was false and deliberately so.

Is the rationale that most cases fit this pattern, or is it that deliberate falsity should be the minimum for this type of tort for some other reason? If the falsity is the key notion, then why shouldn't the state use the same standards that it has developed for libel? Is there something "weaker" or "less important" about the false light action than about libel? (In the *Lovgren* case, the "highly offensive" element was satisfied by "the allegation that the unauthorized advertisement made it practically impossible for plaintiff to obtain refinancing of his mortgage loan. A trier of fact could conclude that the defendants knew that the publication of this false fact would prove highly offensive to the plaintiff.")

In discussing the requirement that the publication be "highly offensive to a reasonable person," the *Lovgren* court cautioned that "minor mistakes in reporting, even if made deliberately, or false facts that offend a hypersensitive individual, will not satisfy this element." What might motivate the court to protect deliberately false reporting?

5. Do these cases suggest that the combination of serious fault and highly offensive falsity is essential to persuade states to adopt this tort? Compare Restatement section 652E, addressing the false light privacy tort, providing for liability if "(a) the false light in which the other was placed would be highly offensive to a reasonable person, and (b) the actor had knowledge of or acted in reckless disregard as to the falsity of the publicized matter and the false light in which the other would be placed."

6. How are compensatory damages to be measured in *Cantrell*? Is the falsity relevant in that calculation?

7. In Dempsey v. National Enquirer, 702 F.Supp. 934 (D.Me.1989), plaintiff, an experienced pilot, had fallen out of a small airplane in flight but clung to the open boarding ladder on the side and survived his co-pilot's emergency landing with only a few scratches. Defendant Star magazine carried a story about the episode. The article was prefaced by a short third-person narrative that concluded: "Here, Dempsey . . . tells in his own words how he found himself suddenly thrust into the ultimate dare-devil stunt." The by-line said "by Henry Dempsey" and the article was a dramatic first person narrative that included quoted statements purporting to be Dempsey's reactions. Plaintiff alleged that he had never been interviewed by Star, had not given them information, and had not written the article in question. Defendant moved to dismiss plaintiff's false light claim.

The court denied the motion. Although the article was essentially a true account of what had happened to plaintiff, it "unequivocally attributed authorship to the plaintiff." This falsity could be found by a jury to portray plaintiff as "otherwise than as he is," and to be highly offensive to a reasonable person.

Recall the *Masson* case, p. 1079 supra, involving the claim of fabricated quotations. Might plaintiff have relied also on a false light theory?

8. *False light by association?* A few cases have permitted a false light recovery to persons whose photographs have appeared in certain magazines without their consent. One involved a model whose nude photographs appeared in Hustler magazine. Douglass v. Hustler Magazine, Inc., 769 F.2d 1128 (7th Cir.1985). After the court described the magazine's contents, it concluded that a jury could reasonably find that the magazine was offensive and that "to be depicted as voluntarily associated with [Hustler] . . . is unquestionably degrading to a normal person, especially if the depiction is erotic." For other reasons, plaintiff's judgment was reversed and a new trial ordered.

In Braun v. Flynt, 726 F.2d 245 (5th Cir.1984), plaintiff was employed at an amusement park. Part of her job included working in a novelty act with "Ralph, the Diving Pig." "Treading water in a pool, plaintiff would hold out a bottle of milk with a nipple on it. Ralph would dive into the pool and feed from the bottle." Publicity photographs of the act were used without authorization in Chic Magazine in a section entitled "Chic Thrills," a collection of vignettes, most of which "either concerned sex overtly or were accompanied by a photograph or cartoon of an overtly sexual nature." According to the court, the "particular issue of the magazine with which the case is involved contained numerous explicit photographs of female genitalia. Suffice it to say that *Chic* is a glossy, oversized, hard-core men's magazine."

From that base, the court concluded that the jury had implicitly found that "the ordinary reader automatically will form an unfavorable opinion about the character of a woman whose picture appears in *Chic* magazine." Even if no reader thought plaintiff unchaste, the jury "might have found that the publication implied Mrs. Braun's approval of the opinions expressed in *Chic* or that it implied Mrs. Braun had consented to having her picture in *Chic*. Either of these findings would support the jury verdict that the publication placed Mrs. Braun in a false light highly offensive to a reasonable person." The court upheld an award of $15,000 compensatory and $50,000 punitive damages as not excessive for the false light claim.

In Faloona v. Hustler Magazine, Inc., 799 F.2d 1000 (5th Cir.1986), plaintiffs had consented to be photographed nude for two books on human sexuality. Hustler published an excerpt from one book and a review of the other. Photographs of plaintiffs accompanied both publications. Their false light theory was rejected on the ground that "no reasonable person could consider the photographs as indicating plaintiffs' approval of *Hustler,* or that they were willing to pose nude for *Hustler*. It is obvious that the photographs were reproductions from the books being reviewed or excerpted. No tie to *Hustler* is claimed or suggested. It is this sharp definition of context which distinguishes this case from" *Douglass* and *Braun*.

In the absence of the clear context in *Faloona,* why might readers in the *Douglass* and *Braun* cases think that persons whose names and photographs appear in a publication have had any control over that use?

9. States that have adopted the false light action must determine the relation between false light and defamation, including whether the array of common law and statutory limitations on defamation, such as retraction statutes, special damage requirements, and statutes of limitations, apply as well to false light privacy.

In Fellows v. National Enquirer, Inc., 721 P.2d 97 (Cal.1986), defendant's article asserted that "Gorgeous Angie Dickinson's all smiles about the new man in her life—TV producer Arthur Fellows. Angie's steady-dating Fellows all over TinselTown, and happily posed for photographers with him as they exited the swanky Spago restaurant in Beverly Hills." Accompanying the article was a photograph of Dickinson and Fellows over the caption stating that Dickinson was "Dating a Producer."

Fellows demanded a retraction under California Civil Code section 48a, asserting that plaintiff "has never dated Miss Dickinson, is not 'the new man in her life,' and has been married to Phyllis Fellows for the last 18 years." Defendant refused retraction and plaintiff sued for libel and false light privacy. Plaintiff withdrew his libel claim and proceeded solely on a false light claim with no allegation of special damages.

Under California law, libel that relies on extrinsic facts has to be supported by special damages. Civil Code § 45a. Plaintiff's privacy claim asserted that he had been falsely portrayed as the "new man" in Dickinson's life and as "steady-dating" her. The trial judge dismissed the privacy claim for lack of special damages and was affirmed on appeal.

The clear purpose of section 45a was to provide additional protection to libel defendants. Since "virtually every published defamation would support an action for false light invasion of privacy, exempting such actions from the requirement of proving special damages would render the statute a nullity." Under this rationale, is there any state requirement that protects libel defendants that would not also be applied to plaintiffs who sue on a false light theory? What should happen if a false light claim is based on language that does not rise to the level of being defamatory? The court went out of its way to announce that its ruling did not apply to false light claims "that would be actionable as a public disclosure of private facts had the representation made in the publication been true."

C. INTRUSION

In this section we consider efforts to gather information about or from an unwilling source. Intrusion may also involve efforts to impart information or "noise" to an unwilling recipient.

Nader v. General Motors Corp.

Court of Appeals of New York, 1970.
25 N.Y.2d 560, 255 N.E.2d 765, 307 N.Y.S.2d 647.

■ CHIEF JUDGE FULD.

[Plaintiff Ralph Nader, at the time a famous author and lecturer on consumer safety, had been a severe critic of defendant for several years. Nader alleged that the defendant, learning that he was about to publish a book that was highly critical of one of defendant's cars, "Unsafe at Any Speed," initiated a series of efforts to intimidate him and suppress his criticism. These included inquiring into his political, social, racial, and religious views, his integrity, and his sexual behavior; casting aspersions on his character; keeping him under lengthy surveillance in public places; having "girls" accost him to entrap him into illicit relationships; making threatening, harassing, and obnoxious telephone calls to him; tapping his telephone and eavesdropping mechanically and electronically on his private conversations; and conducting a continuing and harassing investigation of him. The parties agreed that the law of the District of Columbia controlled the litigation. The trial court denied defendant's motion to dismiss the privacy claims in the case and the appellate division affirmed.]

. . .

Turning, then, to the law of the District of Columbia, it appears that its courts have not only recognized a common-law action for invasion of privacy but have broadened the scope of that tort beyond its traditional limits. (See Pearson v. Dodd, 410 F.2d 701 [D.C.Cir.1969]; Afro-American Pub. Co. v. Jaffe, 366 F.2d 649 [D.C.Cir.1966]; [ ].) Thus, in the most recent of its cases on the subject, [*Pearson*], the Federal Court of Appeals for the District of Columbia declared:

> "We approve the extension of the tort of invasion of privacy to instances of *intrusion,* whether by physical trespass or not, into spheres from which an ordinary man in a plaintiff's position could reasonably expect that the particular defendant should be excluded." (Italics supplied.)

It is this form of invasion of privacy—initially termed "intrusion" by Dean Prosser in 1960 (Privacy, 48 Cal.L.Rev. 383, 389 et seq.; [ ])—on which the two challenged causes of action are predicated.

Quite obviously, some intrusions into one's private sphere are inevitable concomitants of life in an industrial and densely populated society, which the law does not seek to proscribe even if it were possible to do so. "The law does not provide a remedy for every annoyance that occurs in everyday life." [ ] However, the District of Columbia courts have held that the law should and does protect against certain types of intrusive conduct, and we must, therefore, determine whether the plaintiff's allegations are actionable as violations of the right to privacy under the law of that jurisdiction. To do so, we must, in effect, predict what the judges of that jurisdiction's highest court would hold if this case were presented to them. [ ] In other words, what would the Court of Appeals for the District of Columbia hold is the character of the "privacy" sought to be protected? More specifically, would that court accord an individual a right, as the plaintiff before us insists, to be protected against any interference whatsoever with his personal seclusion and solitude? Or would it adopt a more restrictive view of the right as the appellant urges, merely protecting the individual from intrusion into "something secret," from snooping and prying into his private affairs?

The classic article by Warren and Brandeis [ ]—to which [*Pearson*] referred as the source of the District's common-law action for invasion of privacy [ ]—was premised, to a large extent, on principles originally developed in the field of copyright law. The authors thus based their thesis on a right granted by the common law to "each individual . . . of determining, ordinarily, to what extent his thoughts, sentiments and emotions shall be communicated to others" [ ]. Their principal concern appeared to be not with a broad "right to be let alone" [ ] but, rather, with the right to protect oneself from having one's private affairs known to others and to keep secret or intimate facts about oneself from the prying eyes or ears of others.

In recognizing the existence of a common-law cause of action for invasion of privacy in the District of Columbia, the Court of Appeals has expressly adopted this latter formulation of the nature of the right. [ ] Quoting from the Restatement, Torts (§ 867), the court in the *Jaffe* case [ ] has declared that "[l]iability attaches to a person who 'unreasonably and seriously interferes with another's interest in *not having his affairs known to others.*'" (Emphasis supplied.) And, in *Pearson,* where the court extended the tort of invasion of privacy to instances of "intrusion," it again indicated, contrary to the plaintiff's submission, that the interest protected was one's right to keep knowledge about oneself from exposure to others, the right to prevent *"the obtaining of the information* by improperly intrusive means" ([ ]; emphasis supplied). In other jurisdictions, too, the cases which have recognized a remedy for invasion of privacy founded upon intrusive conduct have generally involved the gathering of private facts or information through improper means. [ ]

It should be emphasized that the mere gathering of information about a particular individual does not give rise to a cause of action under this theory. Privacy is invaded only if the information sought is of a confidential nature and the defendant's conduct was unreasonably intrusive. Just as a common-law copyright is lost when material is published, so, too, there can be no invasion of privacy where the information sought is open to public view or has been voluntarily revealed to others. [ ] In order to sustain a cause of action for invasion of privacy, therefore, the plaintiff must show that the appellant's conduct was truly "intrusive" and that it was designed to elicit information which would not be available through normal inquiry or observation.

The majority of the Appellate Division in the present case stated that *all of "[t]he activities complained of"* in the first two counts constituted actionable invasions of privacy under the law of the District of Columbia [ ]. We do not agree with that sweeping determination. At most, only two of the activities charged to the appellant are, in our view, actionable as invasions of privacy under the law of the District of Columbia. However, since the first two counts include allegations which are sufficient to state a cause of action, we could—as the concurring opinion notes—merely affirm the order before us without further elaboration. To do so, though, would be a disservice both to the judge who will be called upon to try this case and to the litigants themselves. In other words, we deem it desirable, nay essential, that we go further and, for the guidance of the trial court and counsel, indicate the extent to which the plaintiff is entitled to rely on the various allegations in support of his privacy claim.

. . .

Turning, then, to the particular acts charged in the complaint, we cannot find any basis for a claim of invasion of privacy, under District of Columbia law, in the allegations that the appellant, through its agents or employees, interviewed many persons who knew the plaintiff, asking questions about him and casting aspersions on his character. Although those inquiries may have uncovered information of a personal nature, it is difficult to see how they may be said to have invaded the plaintiff's privacy. Information about the plaintiff which was already known to others could hardly be regarded as private to the plaintiff. Presumably, the plaintiff had previously revealed the information to such other persons, and he would necessarily assume the risk that a friend or acquaintance in whom he had confided might breach the confidence. If, as alleged, the question tended to disparage the plaintiff's character, his remedy would seem to be by way of an action for defamation not for breach of his right to privacy. [ ]

Nor can we find any actionable invasion of privacy in the allegations that the appellant caused the plaintiff to be accosted by girls with illicit proposals, or that it was responsible for the making of a large number of threatening and harassing telephone calls to the plaintiff's home at odd hours. Neither of these activities, howsoever offensive and disturbing, involved intrusion for the purpose of gathering information of a private and confidential nature.

As already indicated, it is manifestly neither practical nor desirable for the law to provide a remedy against any and all activity which an individual might find annoying. On the other hand, where severe mental pain or anguish is inflicted through a deliberate and malicious campaign of harassment or intimidation, a remedy is available in the form of an action for the intentional infliction of emotional distress—the theory underlying the plaintiff's third cause of action. But the elements of such an action are decidedly different from those governing the tort of invasion of privacy, and just as we have carefully guarded against the use of the prima facie tort doctrine to circumvent the limitations relating to other established tort remedies [ ], we should be wary of any attempt to rely on the tort of invasion of privacy as a means of avoiding the more stringent pleading and proof requirements for an action for infliction of emotional distress. (See, e.g., Clark v. Associated Retail Credit Men, 105 F.2d 62, 65 [D.C.Cir.1939].)

Apart, however, from the foregoing allegations which we find inadequate to spell out a cause of action for invasion of privacy under District of Columbia law, the complaint contains allegations concerning other activities by the appellant or its agents which do satisfy the requirements for such a cause of action. The one which most clearly meets those requirements is the charge that the appellant and its codefendants engaged in unauthorized wiretapping and eavesdropping by mechanical and electronic means. [*Pearson*] expressly recognized that such conduct constitutes a tortious intrusion [ ], and other jurisdictions have reached a similar conclusion. [ ] In point of fact, the appellant does not dispute this, acknowledging that, to the extent the two challenged counts charge it with wiretapping and eavesdropping, an actionable invasion of privacy has been stated.

There are additional allegations that the appellant hired people to shadow the plaintiff and keep him under surveillance. In particular, he claims that, on one occasion, one of its agents followed him into a bank, getting sufficiently close to him to see the denomination of the bills he was withdrawing from his account. From what we have already said, it is manifest that the mere observation of the plaintiff in a public place does not amount to an invasion of his privacy. But, under certain circumstances, surveillance may be so "overzealous" as to render it actionable. (See [*Pearson*]; [ ].) Whether or not the surveillance in the present case falls into this latter category will depend on the nature of the proof. A person does not automatically make public everything he does merely by being in a public place, and the mere fact that Nader was in a bank did not give anyone the right to try to discover the amount of money he was withdrawing. On the other hand, if the plaintiff acted in such a way as to reveal that fact to any casual observer, then, it may not be said that the appellant intruded into his private sphere. In any event, though, it is enough for present purposes to say that the surveillance allegation is not insufficient as a matter of law.

. . .

We would but add that the allegations concerning the interviewing of third persons, the accosting by girls and the annoying and threatening telephone calls, though insufficient to support a cause of action for invasion of privacy, are pertinent to the plaintiff's third cause of action—in which those allegations are reiterated—charging the intentional infliction of emotional distress. However, as already noted, it will be necessary for the plaintiff to meet the additional requirements prescribed by the law of the District of Columbia for the maintenance of a cause of action under that theory.

The order appealed from should be affirmed, with costs. . . .

■ BREITEL, J. (concurring in result).

There is no doubt that the first and second causes of action are sufficient in alleging an invasion of privacy under what appears to be the applicable law in the District of Columbia [ ]. This should be the end of this court's proper concern with the pleadings, the only matter before the court being a motion to dismiss specified causes of action for insufficiency.

Thus it is not proper, it is submitted, for the court directly or indirectly to analyze particular allegations in the pleadings, once the causes of action are found sufficient, in order to determine whether they would alternatively sustain one cause of action or another, or whether evidence offered in support of the allegations is relevant only as to one rather than to another cause of action. Particularly, it is inappropriate to decide that several of the allegations as they now appear are referable only to the more restricted tort of intentional infliction of mental distress rather than to the common-law right of privacy upon which the first and second causes of action depend. The third cause of action is quite restricted. Thus many of the quite offensive acts charged will not be actionable unless plaintiff succeeds in the very difficult, if not impossible, task of showing that defendants' activities were designed, actually or virtually, to make plaintiff unhappy and not to uncover disgraceful information about him. The real issue in the volatile and developing law of privacy is whether a private person is entitled to be free of certain grave offensive intrusions unsupported by palpable social or economic excuse or justification.

True, scholars, in trying to define the elusive concept of the right of privacy, have, as of the present, subdivided the common law right into separate classifications, most significantly distinguishing between unreasonable intrusion and unreasonable publicity. [ ] This does not mean, however, that the classifications are either frozen or exhausted or that several of the classifications may not overlap.

Concretely applied to this case, it is suggested, for example, that it is premature to hold that the attempted entrapment of plaintiff in a public place by seemingly promiscuous ladies is no invasion of any of the categories of the right to privacy and is restricted to a much more limited cause of action for intentional infliction of mental distress. Moreover, it does not strain credulity or imagination to conceive of the systematic "public" surveillance of another as being the implementation of a plan to intrude on the privacy of another. Although acts performed in "public," especially if taken singly or in small numbers, may not be confidential, at least arguably a right to privacy may nevertheless be invaded through extensive or exhaustive monitoring and cataloguing of acts normally disconnected and anonymous.

These are but illustrations of the problems raised in attempting to determine issues of relevancy and allocability of evidence in advance of a trial record. The other allegations so treated involve harassing telephone calls, and investigatory interviews. It is just as important that while allegations treated singly may not constitute a cause of action, they may do so in combination, or serve to enhance other violations of the right to privacy.

It is not unimportant that plaintiff contends that a giant corporation had allegedly sought by surreptitious and unusual methods to silence an unusually effective critic. If there was such a plan, and only a trial would show that, it is unduly restrictive of the future trial to allocate the evidence beforehand based only on a pleader's specification of overt acts on the bold assumption that they are not connected causally or do not bear on intent and motive.

It should be observed, too, that the right to privacy, even as thus far developed, does not always refer to that which is not known to the public or is confidential. Indeed, the statutory right of privacy in this State and perhaps the most traditional right of privacy in the "common law sense" relates to the commercialized publicity of one's face or name, perhaps the two most public aspects of an individual. [ ]

. . .

The broad statements in the opinion of the Appellate Division can be met, as this court has done so often, by declaring that they are not necessarily adopted in concluding that a cause or causes of action have been stated.

Accordingly, because of the prematurity of ruling on any other question but the sufficiency of the causes of action, I concur in result only.

■ JUDGES SCILEPPI, BERGAN and GIBSON concur with CHIEF JUDGE FULD; JUDGE BREITEL concurs in result in an opinion in which JUDGES BURKE and JASEN concur.

NOTES AND QUESTIONS

1.   As a matter of judicial craft, who has the better of the argument about how far the appellate opinion should go at this time? Is your view affected by the fact that a few months later General Motors, denying any wrongdoing, settled with Nader for $425,000? Actions against two detective agencies were also dropped as part of the settlement. N.Y. Times, Aug. 14, 1970, at 1.

2.   This case, in addition to presenting a range of asserted invasions by means of intrusion into plaintiff's privacy, also indicates the close relationship between the privacy tort and other tort areas. The alleged surveillance provides a good example. Can you suggest facts that would make surveillance an invasion of privacy? An intentional infliction of emotional distress? A defamation? Are these categories mutually exclusive or might the same surveillance situation be actionable under two or more categories?

3.   Is there a given degree of surveillance that must be shown before there can be any action at all? Under any theory, what is the minimum that Nader must show about the bank episode? Might you be liable for looking over the shoulder of the person in line ahead of you at the bank?

In Koeppel v. Speirs, 808 N.W.2d 177 (Iowa 2011), an employee who discovered a hidden video camera in the workplace bathroom brought an invasion of privacy action against her employer as did the other female employee in the office. The employer had installed the camera allegedly because he believed one of the two female employees was engaged in misconduct, perhaps involving the use of illegal drugs. However, the camera was never functional, and the employer was never able to view or record either employee. Employer moved for summary judgment on the invasion of privacy claim on this ground. The employees claimed that the tort was completed when the employer placed the camera in the bathroom with the intent to view either of them and the camera was operable. The trial court granted the motion.

The Supreme Court reasoned that invasion of privacy is about the specific method employed to obtain private information, not the content or use. The court surveyed how other courts ruled on this question:

> Courts across the nation are divided on the question whether a person can intrude without actually viewing or recording the victim. . . . The point of disagreement among courts across the nation essentially boils down to whether the harm sought to be remedied by the tort is caused by accessing information from the plaintiff in a private place or by placing mechanisms in a private place that are capable of doing so at the hand of the defendant.

Based on the offensiveness of even placing a surveillance device to capture private acts and an inference from the language in the Second Restatement, the court decided in favor of the first approach provided the equipment was capable of recording, regardless of whether it was ever actually being operated. On the court's view, why should the camera being operative be required?

4.   Even if such surveillance is shown, what justifications might be available to the defense? A common instance is insurance companies' efforts to ascertain whether workers' compensation claimants are hurt as seriously as they allege. Should this behavior be permitted at all? If so, what limits should be placed upon it?

Similarly, creditors are given leeway to attempt to reach the debtor and to recover what is claimed to be owing. See Montgomery Ward v. Shope, 286 N.W.2d 806 (S.D.1979).

Surveillance may also be employed during the course of an action for divorce or a custody battle. Plaxico v. Michael, 735 So.2d 1036 (Miss.1999), arose after a mother's former husband, Michael, took photographs of the mother's lesbian partner sitting in bed nude from the waist up during the course of investigations he undertook to obtain custody of their child. He showed the pictures only to his lawyer, who then disclosed them to the former wife during pretrial discovery. Plaxico, the wife's companion, sued the husband for intrusion after he was awarded custody of the daughter. On appeal, a divided court affirmed a judgment for defendant, stating that, although "Plaxico was in a state of solitude or seclusion in the privacy of her bedroom where she had an expectation of privacy," "a reasonable person would not feel Michael's interference with Plaxico's seclusion was a substantial one that would rise to the level of gross offensiveness as required to prove . . . intentional intrusion upon seclusion or solitude." According to the majority, the husband's attempt to obtain verification of the rumors he had heard about his ex-wife's relationship was justifiable. Since Michael was concerned about the welfare of his daughter, and "believed that he took these pictures for the sole purpose to protect his minor child," his actions could not be construed as highly offensive to a reasonable person. If the rumors had been groundless, would the court's result have been the same? What if they had been disseminated by someone that the husband knew held a grudge against the wife?

The dissenters protested that Michael's goal of ensuring the best interest of his child should not justify the means he took to obtain it. "Neither rumors concerning an ex-wife's lifestyle nor a parent's justifiable concern over the best interests of his child . . . gave Michael a license to spy on a person's bedroom, take photographs of her in a semi-nude state and have those photographs developed by third parties and delivered to his attorney thereby exposing them to others." The publication of the photographs to others was significant only in demonstrating the offensiveness of Michael's act.

Are the divorced parent and the injured employee situations comparable?

5. In Taus v. Loftus, 151 P.3d 1185 (Cal. 2007), plaintiff was the subject of an article on recovery of repressed memory of childhood sexual abuse. Defendants, two critics of repressed memory recovery theory, published an article criticizing the original article, in the course of which the family background of and personal details about the subject, but not her identity, were revealed. The court rejected plaintiff's claim of intrusion based on information about her that was gleaned from public records. However, based on allegations that one of the defendants made misrepresentations (hotly denied by defendant Loftus) about her working with the author of the first article (whom the family trusted) to family members of the subject in the course of interviewing them, the court held that such improper and deceitful conduct could support a claim for intrusion.

6. The *Nader* majority emphasizes that not every annoyance in life has a legal remedy. Compare Vernars v. Young, 539 F.2d 966 (3d Cir.1976), in which the court upheld a complaint alleging that the principal officer of a small corporation opened and, without consent, read mail that was addressed to plaintiff. Plaintiff was another officer of the corporation, but the mail was "addressed to her and marked personal." The court relied on the Restatement (Second) section 652B, providing that "One who intentionally intrudes . . . upon the solitude or seclusion of another, or his private affairs or concerns, is subject to liability . . . if the intrusion would be highly offensive to a reasonable person."

7. Should it be an invasion of privacy to ask neighbors about Nader's views, interests, and sexual habits? Can you add facts that might convert this inquiry into an intentional infliction of emotional distress? A defamation? If you find an action under any of these theories, would you permit the defendant the same justifications discussed in note 4 that are allowed for surveillance?

8. Nader alleged that the invasions were all intentional. Should that be a necessary element in this type of invasion of privacy? What does intent mean in the intrusion context? Reconsider the basic definition of "intent" in the Torts Restatements, p. 899 supra:

> A person intrudes by thrusting himself or herself in without invitation, permission, or welcome. A person acts intentionally when he or she either desires to cause the consequence of an act or believes that the consequence is substantially certain to result from the act. By definition, then, an actor commits an intentional intrusion if the actor either desires to cause an unauthorized intrusion or believes that an unauthorized intrusion is substantially certain to result from committing the invasive act in question.

Would this differ from the approach to intent taken in *Nader*?

Galella v. Onassis

United States Court of Appeals, Second Circuit, 1973.
487 F.2d 986.

■ Before SMITH, HAYS and TIMBERS, CIRCUIT JUDGES.

■ J. JOSEPH SMITH, CIRCUIT JUDGE.

[Photographer Ron Galella sued Jacqueline Kennedy Onassis for false arrest and malicious prosecution after he had been arrested by Secret Service agents who were protecting Mrs. Onassis's children, John and Caroline. Mrs. Onassis denied the charges and counterclaimed for injunctive relief against Galella's continuous efforts to photograph her and her children. The court of appeals affirmed the dismissal of Galella's claim. The portion of the opinion that follows deals with the propriety of the District Court's grant of injunctive relief to Mrs. Onassis and to the government, which had intervened in its capacity as protector of the children's safety.]

Galella fancies himself as a "paparazzo" (literally a kind of annoying insect, perhaps roughly equivalent to the English "gadfly"). Paparazzi make themselves as visible to the public and obnoxious to their photographic subjects as possible to aid in the advertisement and wide sale of their works.

Some examples of Galella's conduct brought out at trial are illustrative. Galella took pictures of John Kennedy riding his bicycle in Central Park across the way from his home. He jumped out into the boy's path, causing the agents concern for John's safety. The agents' reaction and interrogation of Galella led to Galella's arrest and his action against the agents; Galella on other occasions interrupted Caroline at tennis, and invaded the children's private schools. At one time he came uncomfortably close in a power boat to Mrs. Onassis swimming. He often jumped and postured around while taking pictures of her party notably at a theater opening but also on numerous other occasions. He followed a practice of bribing apartment house, restaurant and nightclub doormen as well as romancing a family servant to keep him advised of the movements of the family.

. . .

After a six-week trial the court dismissed Galella's claim and granted relief to both the defendant and the intervenor. Galella was enjoined from (1) keeping the defendant and her children under surveillance or following any of them; (2) approaching within 100 yards of the home of defendant or her children, or within 100 yards of either child's school or within 75 yards of either child or 50 yards of defendant; (3) using the name, portrait or picture of defendant or her children for advertising; (4) attempting to communicate with defendant or her children except through her attorney.

. . .

Discrediting all of Galella's testimony[10] the court found the photographer guilty of harassment, intentional infliction of emotional distress, assault and battery, commercial exploitation of defendant's personality, and invasion of privacy. Fully crediting defendant's testimony, the court found no liability on Galella's claim. Evidence offered by the defense showed that Galella had on occasion intentionally physically touched Mrs. Onassis and her daughter, caused fear of physical contact in his frenzied attempts to get their pictures, followed defendant and her children too closely in an automobile, endangered the safety of the children while they were swimming, water skiing and horseback riding. Galella cannot successfully challenge the court's finding of tortious conduct.[11]

Finding that Galella had "insinuated himself into the very fabric of Mrs. Onassis' life . . ." the court framed its relief in part on the need to prevent further invasion of the defendant's privacy. Whether or not this accords with present New York law, there is no doubt that it is sustainable under New York's proscription of harassment.

Of course legitimate countervailing social needs may warrant some intrusion despite an individual's reasonable expectation of privacy and freedom from harassment. However the interference allowed may be no greater than that necessary to protect the overriding public interest. Mrs. Onassis was properly found to be a public figure and thus subject to news coverage. [ ] Nonetheless, Galella's action went far beyond the reasonable bounds of news gathering. When weighed against the *de*

---

[10] The court's findings on credibility are indeed broad, but they are supported in the record. Galella demonstrated a galling lack of respect for the truth and gave no indication of any consciousness of the meaning of the oath he had taken. Not only did he admit blatantly lying in his testimony, he admitted attempting to have other witnesses lie for him.

[11] Harassment is a criminal offense [in New York] when with intent to harass a person follows another in a public place, inflicts physical contact or engages in any annoying conduct without legitimate cause. Galella was found to have engaged in this proscribed conduct. Conduct sufficient to invoke criminal liability for harassment may be the basis for private action. [ ]

minimis public importance of the daily activities of the defendant, Galella's constant surveillance, his obtrusive and intruding presence, was unwarranted and unreasonable. If there were any doubt in our minds, Galella's inexcusable conduct toward defendant's minor children would resolve it.

Galella does not seriously dispute the court's finding of tortious conduct. Rather, he sets up the First Amendment as a wall of immunity protecting newsmen from any liability for their conduct while gathering news. There is no such scope to the First Amendment right. Crimes and torts committed in news gathering are not protected. [ ] There is no threat to a free press in requiring its agents to act within the law.

> . . .

Injunctive relief is appropriate. Galella has stated his intention to continue his coverage of defendant so long as she is newsworthy, and his continued harassment even while the temporary restraining orders were in effect indicate that no voluntary change in this technique can be expected. New York courts have found similar conduct sufficient to support a claim for injunctive relief. [ ]

The injunction, however, is broader than is required to protect the defendant. Relief must be tailored to protect Mrs. Onassis from the "paparazzo" attack which distinguishes Galella's behavior from that of other photographers; it should not unnecessarily infringe on reasonable efforts to "cover" defendant. Therefore, we modify the court's order to prohibit only (1) any approach within twenty-five (25) feet of defendant or any touching of the person of the defendant Jacqueline Onassis; (2) any blocking of her movement in public places and thoroughfares; (3) any act foreseeably or reasonably calculated to place the life and safety of defendant in jeopardy; and (4) any conduct which would reasonably be foreseen to harass, alarm, or frighten the defendant.

Any further restriction on Galella's taking and selling pictures of defendant for news coverage is, however, improper and unwarranted by the evidence. [ ]

Likewise, we affirm the grant of injunctive relief to the government modified to prohibit any action interfering with Secret Service agents' protective duties. Galella thus may be enjoined from (a) entering the children's schools or play areas; (b) engaging in action calculated or reasonably foreseen to place the children's safety or well being in jeopardy, or which would threaten or create physical injury; (c) taking any action which could reasonably be foreseen to harass, alarm, or frighten the children; and (d) from approaching within thirty (30) feet of the children.

As modified, the relief granted fully allows Galella the opportunity to photograph and report on Mrs. Onassis' public activities. Any prior restraint on news gathering is minuscule and fully supported by the findings.

. . .

■ TIMBERS, CIRCUIT JUDGE [dissented from the reduction of the distance limits imposed by the trial judge].

. . .

NOTES AND QUESTIONS

1. In 1982, Galella was found guilty of 12 violations of the earlier order for taking photographs within 25 feet of Mrs. Onassis. The judge suspended a fine of $120,000 when Galella agreed to pay the $10,000 in legal fees incurred by Onassis and agreed never again to photograph her. Galella was told that if he should renege, the judge would revive the fine or impose a six-month jail sentence for each violation. N.Y.L.J., Mar. 25, 1982, at 1. See Galella v. Onassis, 533 F.Supp. 1076 (S.D.N.Y.1982).

2. The court's analysis was affected by the fact that New York law controlled, and the New York privacy statute made it difficult to press a direct privacy claim. But the court in an omitted footnote suggested that the New York courts would not read the statute to preclude the judicial development of an action that treated unjustified intrusion into one's solitude as an actionable tort. The court thought the statute was directed only to liability for publishing as opposed to gathering activities. Nonetheless, the court did not need to reach the question since it found liability on clearer grounds.

3. Might section 652B of the Second Restatement, note 6, p. 1201 supra, apply to Galella's actions?

4. The court observed that Onassis was a "public figure." What is the significance of that fact in this type of case? What if Onassis had been an ordinary citizen whose appearance attracted Galella—and the publications that purchased his photographs?

5. In California v. Greenwood, 486 U.S. 35 (1988), the Court rejected a claim, based on the Fourth Amendment proscription of unreasonable searches and seizures, that criminal defendants had a reasonable expectation of privacy with respect to trash that was searched by police after the defendants had placed it on the street for collection. Writing for a six-member majority, Justice White said, "It is common knowledge that plastic garbage bags left on or at the side of a public street are readily accessible to animals, children, scavengers, snoops, and other members of the public. . . . Accordingly, having deposited their garbage in an area particularly suited for public inspection and . . . for the express purpose of having strangers take it, [ ] respondents could have had no reasonable expectation of privacy in the inculpatory items that they discarded."

6. *Stalking.* Courts and legislatures have begun developing sanctions against "stalking." In addition to criminal sanctions, some states have developed civil remedies. California Civil Code section 1708.7 requires the plaintiff to show that the defendant: (1) engaged in a "pattern of conduct the intent of which was to follow, alarm, place under surveillance, or harass" the plaintiff, (2) as a result of which the plaintiff "reasonably feared for his or her safety, or the safety of an immediate family member." The defendant as part of the "pattern of conduct" must have made a "credible threat with either (i) the intent to place the plaintiff in reasonable fear for his or her safety, or the safety of an immediate family member, or (ii) reckless disregard for the safety of the plaintiff or that of an immediate family member. In addition, the plaintiff must have, on at least one occasion, clearly and definitively demanded that the defendant cease and abate the pattern of conduct and that the defendant persisted in his or her pattern of conduct unless exigent circumstances make the plaintiff's communication of the demand impractical or unsafe." Damages and an injunction are available. Would this have been useful to the plaintiff in *Galella v. Onassis*? For common law liability for stalking, see Summers v. Bailey, 55 F.3d 1564 (11th Cir.1995)(seller of store liable under Florida law for stalking buyer in an attempt to regain the store).

Desnick v. American Broadcasting Companies, Inc.

United States Court of Appeals, Seventh Circuit, 1995.
44 F.3d 1345.

■ Before POSNER, CHIEF JUDGE, and COFFEY and MANION, CIRCUIT JUDGES.

■ POSNER, CHIEF JUDGE.

[The plaintiffs, the ophthalmic clinic known as the "Desnick Eye Center" and two doctors who worked there, appeal from the dismissal of their suit against the ABC television network, a producer of the ABC program PrimeTime Live named Entine, and the program's main reporter, Donaldson. The complaint alleged that Entine told Dr. Desnick, the clinic's owner—who is not a plaintiff in this case—that he wanted to do a segment on cataract practice; that it would not involve "ambush" interviews or "undercover" surveillance, and that it would be "fair and balanced." Plaintiff permitted an ABC crew to film a "live" operation and to interview personnel in the Chicago office. Plaintiff clinic alleged that unbeknownst to it, Entine dispatched persons who posed as patients with concealed cameras to other Desnick eye centers in Indiana and Wisconsin where the individual doctors worked. Plaintiffs asserted claims for defamation and a second related series of claims, arising from filming conducted at the clinic, including invasion of privacy and trespass.]

The program aired on June 10. Donaldson introduces the segment by saying, "We begin tonight with the story of a so called 'big cutter,' Dr. James Desnick. . . . [I]n our undercover investigation of the big cutter you'll meet tonight, we turned up evidence that he may also be a big charger, doing unnecessary cataract surgery for the money." . . . Donaldson tells the viewer that PrimeTime Live has hired a professor of ophthalmology to examine the test patients who had been told they needed cataract surgery, and the professor tells the viewer that they didn't need it. With regard to one, he says, "I think it would be near malpractice to do surgery on him." Later in the segment he denies that this could just be an honest difference of opinion between professionals.

An ophthalmic surgeon is interviewed who had turned down a job at the Desnick Eye Center because he would not have been "able to screen who I was going to operate on." He claims to have been told by one of the doctors at the Center (not [the two plaintiff doctors]) that "as soon as I reject them [i.e., turn down a patient for cataract surgery], they're going in the next room to get surgery." A former marketing executive for the Center says Desnick took advantage of "people who had Alzheimer's, people who did not know what planet they were on, people whose quality of life wouldn't change one iota by having cataract surgery done." . . . A former employee tells the viewer that Dr. Desnick alters patients' medical records to show they need cataract surgery . . . and that he instructs all members of his staff to use pens of the same color in order to facilitate the alteration of patients' records.

One symptom of cataracts is that lights of normal brightness produce glare. [One plaintiff doctor is shown telling a patient], "You know, you're getting glare. I would say we could do significantly better [with an operation]." And [the other plaintiff physician] is shown asking two patients, "Do you ever notice any glare or blurriness when you're driving, or difficulty with the signs?" Both say no, and immediately Donaldson tells the viewer that "the Desnick Center uses a very interesting machine, called an auto-refractor, to determine whether there are glare problems." Donaldson demonstrates the machine, then says that "Paddy Kalish is an optometrist who says that when he worked at the Desnick clinic from 1987 to 1990, the machine was regularly rigged. . . ." Kalish gives a demonstration, adding, "This happened routinely for all the older patients that came in for the eye exams." Donaldson reveals that Dr. Desnick has obtained a judgment against Kalish for defamation, but adds that "Kalish is not the only one to tell us the machine may have been rigged. PrimeTime talked to four other former Desnick employees who say almost everyone failed the glare test."

. . . Donaldson accosts Desnick at O'Hare Airport and cries, "Is it true, Doctor, that you changed medical records to show less vision than your patients actually have? We've been told, Doctor, that you've changed the glare machine so we have a different reading. Is that correct? Doctor, why won't you respond to the questions?"

The second class of claims in this case concerns, as we said, the methods that the defendants used to create the broadcast segment. There are four such claims: that the defendants committed a trespass in insinuating the test patients into the Wisconsin and Indiana offices of the Desnick Eye Center, that they invaded the right of privacy of the Center and its doctors at those offices (specifically [the two plaintiff doctors]), that they violated federal and state statutes regulating electronic surveillance, and that they committed fraud by gaining access to the Chicago office by means of a false promise that they would present a "fair and balanced" picture of the Center's operations and would not use "ambush" interviews or undercover surveillance.

To enter upon another's land without consent is a trespass. The force of this rule has, it is true, been diluted somewhat by concepts of privilege and of implied consent. But there is no journalists' privilege to trespass. [ ]; Le Mistral, Inc. v. Columbia Broadcasting System, 402 N.Y.S.2d 815 (App.Div.1978). And there can be no implied consent in any nonfictitious sense of the term when express consent is procured by a misrepresentation or a misleading omission. The Desnick Eye Center would not have agreed to the entry of the test patients into its offices had it known they wanted eye examinations only in order to gather material for a television expose of the Center and that they were going to make secret videotapes of the examinations. Yet some cases, illustrated by Martin v. Fidelity & Casualty Co., 421 So.2d 109, 111 (Ala.1982), deem consent effective even though it was procured by fraud. There must be something to this surprising result. Without it a restaurant critic could not conceal his identity when he ordered a meal, or a browser pretend to be interested in merchandise that he could not afford to buy. Dinner guests would be trespassers if they were false friends who never would have been invited had the host known their true character, and a consumer who in an effort to bargain down an automobile dealer falsely claimed to be able to buy the same car elsewhere at a lower price would be a trespasser in the dealer's showroom. Some of these might be classified as privileged trespasses, designed to promote competition. Others might be thought justified by some kind of implied consent—the restaurant critic for example might point by way of analogy to the use of the "fair use" defense by book reviewers charged with copyright infringement and argue that the restaurant industry as a whole would be injured if restaurants could exclude critics. But most such efforts at rationalization would be little better than evasions. The fact is that consent to an entry is often given legal effect even though the entrant has intentions that if known to the owner of the property would cause him for perfectly understandable and generally ethical or at least lawful reasons to revoke his consent.

The law's willingness to give effect to consent procured by fraud is not limited to the tort of trespass. The Restatement gives the example of a man who obtains consent to sexual intercourse by promising a woman $100, yet (unbeknownst to her, of course) he pays her with a counterfeit bill and intended to do so from the start. The man is not guilty of battery, even though unconsented to sexual intercourse is a battery. Restatement (Second) of Torts § 892B, illustration 9, pp. 373–74 (1979). Yet we know that to conceal the fact that one has a venereal disease transforms "consensual" intercourse into battery. [ ] Seduction, standardly effected by false promises of love, is not rape, [ ]; intercourse under the pretense of rendering medical or psychiatric treatment is, at least in most states. [ ] It certainly is battery. [ ] Trespass presents close parallels. If a homeowner opens his door to a purported meter reader who is in fact nothing of the sort—just a busybody curious about the interior of the home—the homeowner's consent to his entry is not a defense to a suit for trespass. [ ] And likewise if a competitor gained entry to a business firm's premises posing as a customer but in fact hoping to steal the firm's trade secrets. [ ]

How to distinguish the two classes of cases—the seducer from the medical impersonator, the restaurant critic from the meter reader impersonator? The answer can have nothing to do with fraud; there is fraud in all the cases. It has to do with the interest that the torts in question, battery and trespass, protect. The one protects the inviolability of the person, the other the inviolability of the person's property. The woman who is seduced wants to have sex with her seducer, and the restaurant owner wants to have customers. The woman who is victimized by the medical impersonator has no desire to have sex with her doctor; she wants medical treatment. And the homeowner victimized by the phony meter reader does not want strangers in his house unless they have authorized service functions. The dealer's objection to the customer who claims falsely to have a lower price from a competing dealer is not to the physical presence of the customer, but to the fraud that he is trying to perpetuate. The lines are not bright—they are not even inevitable. They are the traces of the old forms of action, which have resulted in a multitude of artificial distinctions in modern law. But that is nothing new.

There was no invasion in the present case of any of the specific interests that the tort of trespass seeks to protect. The test patients entered offices that were open to anyone expressing a desire for ophthalmic services and videotaped physicians engaged in professional, not personal, communications with strangers (the testers themselves). The activities of the offices were not disrupted, as in [ ], another case of gaining entry by false pretenses. See also *Le Mistral, Inc. v. Columbia Broadcasting System*, [ ]. Nor was there any "inva[sion of] a person's private space," [ ], as in our hypothetical meter reader case, as in the famous case of De May v. Roberts, 9 N.W. 146 (Mich.1881) (where a doctor, called to the plaintiff's home to deliver her baby, brought along with him a friend who was curious to see a birth but was not a medical doctor, and represented the friend to be his medical assistant), as in one of its numerous modern counterparts, Miller v. National Broadcasting Co., 232 Cal.Rptr. 668, 679 (App.1986), and as in Dietemann v. Time, Inc., 449 F.2d 245 (9th Cir.1971), on which the plaintiffs in our case rely. *Dietemann* involved a home. True, the portion invaded was an office, where the plaintiff performed quack healing of nonexistent ailments. The parallel to this case is plain enough, but there is a difference. Dietemann was not in business, and did not advertise his services or charge for them. His quackery was private.

No embarrassingly intimate details of anybody's life were publicized in the present case. There was no eavesdropping on a private conversation; the testers recorded their own conversations with the Desnick Eye Center's physicians. There was no violation of the doctor patient privilege. There was no theft, or intent to steal, trade secrets; no disruption of decorum, of peace and quiet; no noisy or distracting demonstrations. Had the testers been undercover FBI agents, there would have been no violation of the Fourth Amendment, because there would have been no invasion of a legally protected interest in property or privacy. [ ] "Testers" who pose as prospective home buyers in order to gather evidence of housing discrimination are not trespassers even if they are private persons not acting under color of law. [ ] The situation of the defendants' "testers" is analogous. Like testers seeking evidence of violation of antidiscrimination laws, the defendants' test patients gained entry into the plaintiffs' premises by misrepresenting their purposes (more precisely by a misleading omission to disclose those purposes). But the entry was not invasive in the sense of infringing the kind of interest of the plaintiffs that the law of trespass protects; it was not an interference with the ownership or possession of land. We need not consider what if any difference it would make if the plaintiffs had festooned the premises with signs forbidding the entry of testers or other snoops. Perhaps none, [ ], but that is an issue for another day.

What we have said largely disposes of two other claims: infringement of the right of privacy, and illegal wiretapping. The right of privacy embraces several distinct interests, but the only ones conceivably involved here are the closely related interests in concealing intimate personal facts and in preventing intrusion into legitimately private activities, such as phone conversations. [ ] As we have said already, no intimate personal facts concerning the two individual plaintiffs (remember that Dr. Desnick himself is not a plaintiff) were revealed; and the only conversations that were recorded were conversations with the testers themselves. [ ]

The federal and state wiretapping statutes that the plaintiffs invoke allow one party to a conversation to record the conversation unless his purpose in doing so is to commit a crime or a tort or (in the case of the state, but not the federal, law) to do "other injurious acts." 18 U.S.C. § 2511(2)(d); [ ]. The defendants did not order the camera armed testers into the Desnick Eye Center's premises in order to commit a crime or tort. Maybe the program as it was eventually broadcast was tortious, for we have said that the defamation count was dismissed prematurely. But there is no suggestion that the defendants sent the testers into the Wisconsin and Indiana offices for the purpose of defaming the plaintiffs by charging tampering with the glare machine. The purpose, by the plaintiffs' own account, was to see whether the Center's physicians would recommend cataract surgery on the testers. By the same token it was not to injure the Desnick Eye Center, unless the public exposure of misconduct is an "injurious act" within the meaning of the Wisconsin statute. Telling the world the truth about a Medicare fraud is hardly what the framers of the statute could have had in mind in forbidding a person to record his own conversations if he was trying to commit an "injurious act." [ ]

Last is the charge of fraud in the defendants' gaining entry to the Chicago office and being permitted while there to interview staff and film a cataract operation, and in their obtaining the Desnick Eye Center's informational videotape. [The court held that under the unusual law of Illinois, promissory fraud was not actionable unless it was part of a scheme to defraud. Since that did not exist here there was no basis for liability. Nor did harm flow from the alleged fraud.]

One further point about the claims concerning the making of the program segment, as distinct from the content of the segment itself, needs to be made. The Supreme Court in the name of the First Amendment has hedged about defamation suits, even when not brought by public figures, with many safeguards designed to protect a vigorous market in ideas and opinions. Today's "tabloid" style investigative television reportage, conducted by networks desperate for viewers in an increasingly competitive television market [ ], constitutes—although it is often shrill, one sided, and offensive, and sometimes defamatory—an important part of that market. It is entitled to all the safeguards with which the Supreme Court has surrounded liability for defamation. And it is entitled to them regardless of the name of the tort, see, e.g., Hustler Magazine, Inc. v. Falwell, 485 U.S. 46 (1988), and, we add, regardless of whether the tort suit is aimed at the content of the broadcast or the production of the broadcast. If the broadcast itself does not contain actionable defamation, and no established rights are invaded in the process of creating it (for the media have no general immunity from tort or contract liability, [ ]), then the target has no legal remedy even if the investigatory tactics used by the network are surreptitious, confrontational, unscrupulous, and ungentlemanly. In this case, there may have been—it is too early to tell—an actionable defamation, and if so the plaintiffs have a remedy. But none of their established rights under either state law or the federal wiretapping law was infringed by the making, as opposed to the dissemination, of the broadcast segment of which they complain, with the possible and possibly abandoned exception of contract law.

Affirmed in Part, Reversed in Part, and Remanded.

NOTES AND QUESTIONS

1. *Trespass.* We have explored the notion of trespass in the context of actions brought by landowners for invasions of their possessory interests, p. 940 supra. How does the trespass claim in this case differ?

2. In the cited *Le Mistral* case, employees of CBS-TV were ordered to take a camera crew to visit restaurants that had been cited for health code

violations. Defendants entered plaintiff's restaurant at lunch time "with cameras rolling" and used bright lights that were necessary to get the pictures. The jury could find that the crew entered "in a noisy and obtrusive fashion and following the loud commands of the reporter, Rich, to photograph the patrons dining." Some patrons left without paying their bills. Others "hid their faces behind napkins or table cloths or hid themselves beneath tables." This was held an actionable trespass. When Rich claimed that the restaurant was a place of public accommodation, the court responded that defendants admitted that the crew "did not seek to avail themselves of the plaintiff's 'accommodation'; they had no intention of purchasing food or drink."

How does this case fit into the *Desnick* court's analysis?

3. In the cited *Dietemann* case, a reporter and photographer went to the entrance of plaintiff's home and falsely stated that one of them needed advice and that they had been referred by someone. After being admitted to plaintiff's home and taken into his den, the defendants secretly taped and photographed as the plaintiff waved a wand over the "patient" and advised her that she had a lump in her breast because she had eaten rancid butter 11 years, 9 months, and 7 days earlier. Photos and a story appeared in defendant's magazine.

The court stated that the initial entry was not actionable because "one who invites another to his home or office takes a risk that the visitor may not be what he seems, and that the visitor may repeat all he hears and observes when he leaves." But the surreptitious use of tape recorders and cameras was actionable. One "does not and should not be required to take the risk that what is heard and seen will be transmitted by photograph or recording, or in our modern world, in full living color and hi-fi to the public at large or to any segment of it that the visitor may select. A different rule could have a most pernicious effect upon the dignity of man and it would surely lead to guarded conversations and conduct where candor is most valued, e.g., in the case of doctors and lawyers."

How does this case fit into the *Desnick* court's analysis? Is there a difference between a tape recorder, which preserves the words actually spoken, and a camera, which creates and preserves visual images that the reporters could have described afterward only verbally and only from memory?

4. Should it be relevant that *Le Mistral* was brought on a trespass theory and that *Dietemann* was brought on a privacy theory?

5. Restatement (Second) of Torts section 892B provides that consent to the conduct of another is effective "for all consequences of the conduct and for the invasion of any interests resulting from it" unless within the limitation of subsection (2):

> If the person consenting to the conduct of another is induced to consent by a substantial mistake concerning the nature of the invasion of his interests or the extent of the harm to be expected from it and the mistake is known to the other or is induced by the

other's misrepresentation, the consent is not effective for the unexpected invasion or harm.

Is this relevant in *Desnick*? To Dietemann's misunderstanding about who sent the visitors and why they were there?

6. *Wiretapping.* Why does the wiretapping claim fail in *Desnick*? The federal statute is less protective than some state provisions because it exempts from the ban any conversation in which one party records the contents or in which one party authorizes a third party to record it.

Florida made it criminal for any "person not acting under color of law" to intercept a wire or oral communication unless all parties to the communication had given prior consent. Reporters and others challenged the statute, claiming that the use of concealed recording equipment was essential to investigative reporting for three reasons: it aided accuracy of reporting; persons being interviewed would not be candid if they knew they were being recorded; and the recording provided corroboration in case of suit for defamation.

The Florida Supreme Court upheld the statute's constitutionality. The statute allows "each party to a conversation to have an expectation of privacy from interception by another party to the conversation. It does not exclude any source from the press, intrude upon the activities of the news media in contacting sources, prevent the parties to the communication from consenting to the recording, or restrict the publication of any information gained from the communication. First Amendment rights do not include a constitutional right to corroborate news gathering activities when the legislature has statutorily recognized the private rights of individuals."

The court quoted *Dietemann*'s concern about the effect on the "dignity of man." In response to the argument that secret recording may be the only way to get credible information about crime, the court stated that protection against intrusion might extend even to a person "reasonably suspected of committing a crime." Shevin v. Sunbeam Television Corp., 351 So.2d 723 (Fla.1977), appeal dismissed, 6–3, for want of a substantial federal question, 435 U.S. 920 (1978).

7. In Ribas v. Clark, 696 P.2d 637 (Cal.1985), a wife asked the defendant to listen in on an extension phone as she talked to her estranged husband. The husband learned about the episode when the defendant testified in an arbitration hearing about matters she overheard. He then sued for violation of California Penal Code section 631(a), which provides in relevant part for punishment of any person "who . . . intentionally taps, or makes any unauthorized connection . . . with any . . . telephone wire, line, cable or instrument, . . . or who willfully and without the consent of all parties to the communication, or in any unauthorized manner, reads, or attempts to read, or to learn the contents or meaning of any message . . . while the same is in transit . . . , or is being sent from, or received at any place within this state. . . ."

Section 637.2 provided a civil action against violators for the greater of $3,000 or trebled actual damages. The court upheld the complaint. The statute was read broadly to bar "far more than illicit wiretapping," including the recording of a conversation without the other's consent:

> While one who imparts private information risks the betrayal of his confidence by the other party, a substantial distinction has been recognized between the secondhand repetition of the contents of a conversation and its simultaneous dissemination to an unannounced second auditor, whether that auditor be a person or mechanical device. [ ]

> As one commentator has noted, such secret monitoring denies the speaker an important aspect of privacy of communication— the right to control the nature and extent of the firsthand dissemination of his statement. [ ] Partly because of this factor, the Privacy Act has been read to require the assent of all parties to a communication before another may listen.

Shulman v. Group W Productions, Inc.

Supreme Court of California, 1998.
18 Cal.4th 200, 955 P.2d 469, 74 Cal.Rptr.2d 843.

■ WERDEGAR, JUSTICE.

[Plaintiffs, mother and son, were injured when a car in which they and other family members were riding, overturned, tumbled down an embankment and came to rest upside down in a ditch on state-owned property. Ruth, the mother, was pinned in the wreckage. A Mercy Air rescue helicopter was dispatched to the scene by county officials. On board were nurse Carnahan, the pilot, a medic, and Joel Cooke. A video cameraman employed by defendant Group W., Cooke was recording the events for later broadcast. Carnahan was wearing a wireless microphone that picked up conversations with the victims and other rescue personnel. A nine-minute tape was broadcast on a segment on rescue operations. After Carnahan steps from the helicopter, she can be seen and heard speaking about the situation with various rescue workers. A firefighter assures her they will hose down the area to prevent any fire from the wrecked car. Only a glimpse is shown of the son, Wayne, and his voice is never heard. "Ruth is shown several times, either by brief shots of a limb or her torso, or with her features blocked by others or obscured by an oxygen mask. She is also heard speaking several times. Carnahan calls her 'Ruth' and her last name is not mentioned on the broadcast."]

While Ruth is still trapped under the car, Carnahan asks Ruth's age. Ruth responds, "I'm old." On further questioning, Ruth reveals she is 47, and Carnahan observes that "it's all relative. You're not that old." During her extrication from the car, Ruth asks at least twice if she is dreaming. At one point she asks Carnahan, who has told her she will be taken to the hospital in a helicopter: "Are you teasing?" At another point she says: "This is terrible. Am I dreaming?" She also asks what happened and where the rest of her family is, repeating the questions even after being told she was in an accident and the other family members are being cared for. While being loaded into the helicopter on a stretcher, Ruth says: "I just want to die." Carnahan reassures her that she is "going to do real well," but Ruth repeats: "I just want to die. I don't want to go through this."

Ruth and Wayne are placed in the helicopter, and its door is closed. The narrator states: "Once airborne, Laura and [the flight medic] will update their patients' vital signs and establish communications with the waiting trauma teams at Loma Linda." Carnahan, speaking into what appears to be a radio microphone, transmits some of Ruth's vital signs and states that Ruth cannot move her feet and has no sensation. The video footage during the helicopter ride includes a few seconds of Ruth's face, covered by an oxygen mask. Wayne is neither shown nor heard.

The helicopter lands on the hospital roof. With the door open, Ruth states while being taken out: "My upper back hurts." Carnahan replies: "Your upper back hurts." "That's what you were saying up there." Ruth states: "I don't feel that great." Carnahan responds: "You probably don't."

Finally, Ruth is shown being moved from the helicopter into the hospital. The narrator concludes by stating: "Once inside both patients will be further evaluated and moved into emergency surgery if need be. Thanks to the efforts of the crew of Mercy Air, the firefighters, medics and police who responded, patients' lives were saved." As the segment ends, a brief, written epilogue appears on the screen, stating: "Laura's patient spent months in the hospital. She suffered severe back injuries. The others were all released much sooner."

[Ruth, who was left paraplegic, saw the program in her hospital room when her son called to tell her it was on. She testified that she was "shocked, so to speak, that this would be run and I would be exploited, have my privacy invaded, which is what I felt had happened."] She did not know her rescue had been recorded in this manner and had never consented to the recording or broadcast. Ruth had the impression from the broadcast "that I was kind of talking non-stop, and I remember hearing some of the things I said, which were not very pleasant." Asked at deposition what part of the broadcast material she considered private, Ruth explained: "I think the whole scene was pretty private. It was pretty gruesome, the parts that I saw, my knee sticking out of the car. I certainly did not look my best, and I don't feel it's for the public to see. I was not at my best in what I was thinking and what I was saying and what was being shown, and it's not for the public to see this trauma that I was going through."

[The plaintiff sued for both intrusion and public disclosure of private facts. Plaintiffs stipulated that Mercy Air was sent based on an agreement with the county, and "that auto accidents on public highways and publicly provided emergency rescue and medical services were both matters of public interest that constituted public affairs." The trial court granted defendants summary judgment.]

[The court, 5–2, affirmed the dismissal of the private facts part of both claims. The court then turned to the intrusion claims.]

As to intrusion, the Court of Appeal correctly found triable issues exist as to whether defendants invaded plaintiffs' privacy by accompanying plaintiffs in the helicopter. Contrary to the holding below, we also hold triable issues exist as to whether defendants tortiously intruded by listening to Ruth's confidential conversations with Nurse Carnahan at the rescue scene without Ruth's consent. Moreover, we hold defendants had no constitutional privilege so as to intrude on plaintiffs' seclusion and private communications.

. . .

II.   Intrusion

Of the four privacy torts identified by Prosser, the tort of intrusion into private places, conversations or matter is perhaps the one that best captures the common understanding of an "invasion of privacy." It encompasses unconsented-to physical intrusion into the home, hospital room or other place the privacy of which is legally recognized, as well as unwarranted sensory intrusions such as eavesdropping, wiretapping, and visual or photographic spying. [ ] It is in the intrusion cases that invasion of privacy is most clearly seen as an affront to individual dignity. "[A] measure of personal isolation and personal control over the conditions of its abandonment is of the very essence of personal freedom and dignity, is part of what our culture means by these concepts. A man whose home may be entered at the will of another, whose conversations may be overheard at the will of another, whose marital and familial intimacies may be overseen at the will of another, is less of a man, has less human dignity, on that account. He who may intrude upon another at will is the master of the other and, in fact, intrusion is a primary weapon of the tyrant." [ ]

Despite its conceptual centrality, the intrusion tort has received less judicial attention than the private facts tort, and its parameters are less clearly defined. The leading California decision is Miller v. National Broadcasting Co., [232 Cal.Rptr. 668 (App.1986)] (*Miller*). *Miller*, which like the present case involved a news organization's videotaping the work of emergency medical personnel, adopted the Restatement's formulation of the cause of action: "One who intentionally intrudes, physically or otherwise, upon the solitude or seclusion of another or his private affairs or concerns, is subject to liability to the other for invasion of his privacy, if the intrusion would be highly offensive to a reasonable person." [ ]

As stated in *Miller* and the Restatement, therefore, the action for intrusion has two elements: (1) intrusion into a private place, conversation or matter, (2) in a manner highly offensive to a reasonable person. We consider the elements in that order.

We ask first whether defendants "intentionally intrude[d], physically or otherwise, upon the solitude or seclusion of another," that is, into a place or conversation private to Wayne or Ruth. [ ] "[T]here is no liability for the examination of a public record concerning the plaintiff. . . . [Or] for observing him or even taking his photograph while he is walking on the public highway. . . ." (Rest.2d Torts, § 652B, com. *c.*); see, e.g., Aisenson v. American Broadcasting Co., [269 Cal.Rptr. 379 (App.1990)] (where judge who was subject of news story was filmed from public street as he walked from his home to his car, any invasion of privacy was "extremely de minimis"); [ ]. To prove actionable intrusion, the plaintiff must show the defendant penetrated some zone of physical or sensory privacy surrounding, or obtained unwanted access to data about, the plaintiff. The tort is proven only if the plaintiff had an objectively reasonable expectation of seclusion or solitude in the place, conversation or data source. [ ]

Cameraman Cooke's mere presence at the accident scene and filming of the events occurring there cannot be deemed either a physical or sensory intrusion on plaintiffs' seclusion. Plaintiffs had no right of ownership or possession of the property where the rescue took place, nor any actual control of the premises. Nor could they have had a reasonable expectation that members of the media would be excluded or prevented from photographing the scene; for journalists to attend and record the scenes of accidents and rescues is in no way unusual or unexpected. (Cf. Pen.Code, §§ 409.5, subd. (d), 409.6, subd. (d) [exempting press representatives from certain emergency closure orders].)

Two aspects of defendants' conduct, however, raise triable issues of intrusion on seclusion. First, a triable issue exists as to whether both plaintiffs had an objectively reasonable expectation of privacy in the interior of the rescue helicopter, which served as an ambulance. Although the attendance of reporters and photographers at the scene of an accident is to be expected, we are aware of no law or custom permitting the press to ride in ambulances or enter hospital rooms during treatment without the patient's consent. [ ] Other than the two patients and Cooke, only three people were present in the helicopter, all Mercy Air staff. As the Court of Appeal observed, "[i]t is neither the custom nor the habit of our society that any member of the public at large or its media representatives may hitch a ride in an ambulance and ogle as paramedics care for an injured stranger." [ ]

Second, Ruth was entitled to a degree of privacy in her conversations with Carnahan and other medical rescuers at the accident scene, and in Carnahan's conversations conveying medical information regarding Ruth to the hospital base. Cooke, perhaps, did not intrude into that zone of privacy merely by being present at a place where he could hear such conversations with unaided ears. But by placing a microphone on Carnahan's person, amplifying and recording what she said and heard, defendants may have listened in on conversations the parties could reasonably have expected to be private.

The Court of Appeal held plaintiffs had no reasonable expectation of privacy at the accident scene itself because the scene was within the sight and hearing of members of the public. The summary judgment record, however, does not support the Court of Appeal's conclusion; instead, it reflects, at the least, the existence of triable issues as to the privacy of certain conversations at the accident scene, as in the helicopter. The videotapes (broadcast and raw footage) show the rescue did not take place "on a heavily traveled highway," as the Court of Appeal stated, but in a ditch many yards from and below the rural superhighway, which is raised somewhat at that point to bridge a nearby crossroad. From the tapes it appears unlikely the plaintiffs' extrication from their car and medical treatment at the scene could have been observed by any persons who, in the lower court's words, "passed by" on the roadway. Even more unlikely is that any passersby on the road could have heard Ruth's conversation with Nurse Carnahan or the other rescuers.

Whether Ruth expected her conversations with Nurse Carnahan or the other rescuers to remain private and whether any such expectation was reasonable are, on the state of the record before us, questions for the jury. We note, however, that several existing legal protections for communications could support the conclusion that Ruth possessed a reasonable expectation of privacy in her conversations with Nurse Carnahan and the other rescuers. A patient's conversation with a provider of medical care in the course of treatment including emergency treatment, carries a traditional and legally well-established expectation of privacy. . . .

. . .

We turn to the second element of the intrusion tort, offensiveness of the intrusion. In a widely followed passage, the *Miller* court explained that determining offensiveness requires consideration of all the circumstances of the intrusion, including its degree and setting and the intruder's "motives and objectives." [ ] The *Miller* court concluded that reasonable people could regard the camera crew's conduct in filming a man's emergency medical treatment in his home, without seeking or obtaining his or his wife's consent, as showing "a cavalier disregard for ordinary citizens' rights of privacy" and, hence, as highly offensive. [ ]

We agree with the *Miller* court that all the circumstances of an intrusion, including the motives or justification of the intruder, are pertinent to the offensiveness element. Motivation or justification becomes particularly important when the intrusion is by a member of the print or broadcast press in the pursuit of news material. Although, as will be discussed more fully later, the First Amendment does not immunize the press from liability for torts or crimes committed in an effort to gather news [ ], the constitutional protection of the press does reflect the strong societal interest in effective and complete reporting of events, an interest that may—as a matter of tort law—justify an intrusion that would otherwise be considered offensive. . . .

In deciding, therefore, whether a reporter's alleged intrusion into private matters (i.e., physical space, conversation or data) is "offensive" and hence actionable as an invasion of privacy, courts must consider the extent to which the intrusion was, under the circumstances, justified by the legitimate motive of gathering the news. Information collecting techniques that may be highly offensive when done for socially unprotected reasons—for purposes of harassment, blackmail or prurient curiosity, for example—may not be offensive to a reasonable person when employed by journalists in pursuit of a socially or politically important story. Thus, for example, "a continuous surveillance which is tortious when practiced by a creditor upon a debtor may not be tortious when practiced by media representatives in a situation where there is significant public interest [in discovery of the information sought]." [ ]

The mere fact the intruder was in pursuit of a "story" does not, however, generally justify an otherwise offensive intrusion; offensiveness depends as well on the particular method of investigation used. At one extreme, " 'routine . . . reporting techniques,' " such as asking questions of people with information ("including those with confidential or restricted information") could rarely, if ever, be deemed an actionable intrusion. [ ] At the other extreme, violation of well-established legal areas of physical or sensory privacy—trespass into a home or tapping a personal telephone line, for example—could rarely, if ever, be justified by a reporter's need to get the story. Such acts would be deemed highly offensive even if the information sought was of weighty public concern; they would also be outside any protection the Constitution provides to newsgathering. [ ]

Between these extremes lie difficult cases, many involving the use of photographic and electronic recording equipment. Equipment such as hidden cameras and miniature cordless and directional microphones are powerful investigative tools for newsgathering, but may also be used in ways that severely threaten personal privacy. California tort law provides no bright line on this question; each case must be taken on its facts.

On this summary judgment record, we believe a jury could find defendants' recording of Ruth's communications to Carnahan and other rescuers, and filming in the air ambulance, to be "highly offensive to a reasonable person." [ ] With regard to the depth of the intrusion [ ], a reasonable jury could find highly offensive the placement of a microphone on a medical rescuer in order to intercept what would otherwise be private conversations with an injured patient. In that setting, as defendants could and should have foreseen, the patient would not know her words were being recorded and would not have occasion to ask about, and object or consent to, recording. Defendants, it could reasonably be said, took calculated advantage of the patient's "vulnerability and confusion." [ ] Arguably, the last thing an injured accident victim should have to worry about while being pried from her wrecked car is that a television producer may be recording everything she says to medical personnel for the possible edification and entertainment of casual television viewers.

For much the same reason, a jury could reasonably regard entering and riding in an ambulance—whether on the ground or in the air—with two seriously injured patients to be an egregious intrusion on a place of expected seclusion. Again, the patients, at least in this case, were hardly in a position to keep careful watch on who was riding with them, or to inquire as to everyone's business and consent or object to their presence. A jury could reasonably believe that fundamental respect for human dignity requires the patients' anxious journey be taken only with those whose care is solely for them and out of sight of the prying eyes (or cameras) of others.

Nor can we say as a matter of law that defendants' motive—to gather usable material for a potentially newsworthy story—necessarily privileged their intrusive conduct as a matter of common law tort liability. A reasonable jury could conclude the producers' desire to get footage that would convey the "feel" of the event—the real sights and sounds of a difficult rescue—did not justify either placing a microphone on Nurse Carnahan or filming inside the rescue helicopter. Although defendants' purposes could scarcely be regarded as evil or malicious (in the colloquial sense), their behavior could, even in light of their motives, be thought to show a highly offensive lack of sensitivity and respect for plaintiffs' privacy. [ ] A reasonable jury could find that defendants, in placing a microphone on an emergency treatment nurse and recording her conversation with a distressed, disoriented and severely injured patient, without the patient's knowledge or consent, acted with highly offensive disrespect for the patient's personal privacy comparable to, if not quite as extreme as, the disrespect and insensitivity demonstrated in *Miller*.

Turning to the question of constitutional protection for newsgathering, one finds the decisional law reflects a general rule of *nonprotection*: the press in its newsgathering activities enjoys no immunity or exemption from generally applicable laws. [The court, after reviewing several Supreme Court decisions, concluded that] defendants enjoyed no constitutional privilege, merely by virtue of their status as members of the news media, to eavesdrop in violation of section 632 [the state's wiretapping and eavesdropping statute—Eds.] or otherwise to intrude tortiously on private places, conversations or information.

Courts have impliedly recognized that a generally applicable law might, under some circumstances, impose an "impermissible burden" on newsgathering [ ]; such a burden might be found in a law that, as applied to the press, would result in "a significant constriction of the flow of news to the public" and thus "eviscerate[ ]" the freedom of the press. [ ] No basis exists, however, for concluding that either section 632 or the intrusion tort places such a burden on the press, either in general or under the circumstances of this case. The conduct of journalism does not depend, as a general matter, on the use of secret devices to record private conversations. (Accord, [*Dietemann*]; [ ]). More specifically, nothing in the record or briefing here suggests that reporting on automobile accidents and medical rescue activities depends on secretly recording accident victims' conversations with rescue personnel or on filming inside an occupied ambulance. Thus, if any exception exists to the general rule that "the First Amendment does not guarantee the press a constitutional right of special access to information not available to the public generally" [ ], such exception is inapplicable here.[18]

As should be apparent from the above discussion, the constitutional protection accorded newsgathering, if any, is far narrower than the protection surrounding the publication of truthful material; consequently, the fact that a reporter may be seeking "newsworthy" material does not in itself privilege the investigatory activity. The reason for the difference is simple: the intrusion tort, unlike that for publication of private facts, does not subject the press to liability for the contents of its publications. Newsworthiness, as we stated earlier, is a complete bar to liability for publication of private facts and is evaluated with a high degree of deference to editorial judgment. The same deference is not due, however, when the issue is not the media's right to publish or broadcast what they choose, but their right to intrude into secluded areas or conversations in pursuit of publishable material. . . .

Defendants urge a rule more protective of press investigative activity. Specifically, they seek a holding that "when intrusion claims are brought in the context of newsgathering conduct, that conduct be deemed protected so long as (1) the information being gathered is about a matter of legitimate concern to the public and (2) the underlying conduct is lawful (i.e., was undertaken without fraud, trespass, etc.)." Neither tort law nor constitutional precedent and policy supports such a broad privilege. [*Miller, Dietemann*] and [ ] were all cases in which the reporters and photographers were acting in pursuit of newsworthy material, but were held to have tortiously intruded on the plaintiffs' privacy because their conduct was highly offensive to a reasonable

---

[18] Defendants urge us to hold that any damages for intrusion do not include compensation for injury resulting from the publication of material gathered through intrusion. The only intrusion case defendants cite on this point is against them. [*Dietemann*] [allowing publication damages in intrusion case]; [ ]. We do not reach the question, as the measure of plaintiffs' damages is not before us on this appeal from summary judgment in favor of the defense.

person, not because they had committed any independent crime or
tort.[19] [ ]

. . .

[N]o constitutional precedent or principle of which we are aware
gives a reporter general license to intrude in an objectively offensive
manner into private places, conversations or matters merely because
the reporter thinks he or she may thereby find something that will
warrant publication or broadcast.

. . .

In short, the state may not intrude into the proper sphere of the
news media to dictate what they should publish and broadcast, but
neither may the media play tyrant to the people by unlawfully spying
on them in the name of newsgathering. Summary judgment for the
defense was . . . improper as to the cause of action for invasion of
privacy by intrusion. . . .

The judgment of the Court of Appeal is affirmed except insofar as
the Court of Appeal reversed and remanded for further proceedings on
Ruth Shulman's cause of action for publication of private facts.

■ GEORGE, C.J., and KENNARD, J., concur.

■ KENNARD, JUSTICE, concurring.

[This concurrence, joined by Justice Mosk, focused on the private
facts part of the case.]

■ CHIN, JUSTICE, concurring [in the private facts part of the case] and
dissenting [in the intrusion part on the grounds that defendants'
conduct did not meet the standard of "highly offensive to a reasonable
person."].

■ MOSK, J., concurs.

■ [JUSTICE BROWN, joined by JUSTICE BAXTER, agreed with the
resolution of the intrusion part of the case but dissented from the
dismissal of the private facts part.]

NOTES AND QUESTIONS

1. Can the court's decision be reconciled with *Desnick* and
Dietemann? Is there a consistent theme running through these cases?

---

[19] In *Miller* the camera crew's entry into the Miller home was also deemed a trespass [ ],
but the court's discussion of the intrusion tort does not depend on this fact. [ ]

In *Dietemann* [ ], reporters for Life Magazine gained consensual access to the home office
of a quack doctor, where they secretly photographed him and recorded his remarks as he
purportedly diagnosed a medical condition of one of the reporters. [ ] The federal court,
applying California law, concluded the facts showed an invasion of privacy. [ ] Presumably
because a peaceable entry by consent does not constitute trespass under California law [ ], no
question of liability for trespass arose in *Dietemann*.

2. Note that the opinion suggests that asking questions of one with confidential or restricted information is not actionable intrusion. Is that consistent with *Nader*?

3. Does the court suggest that the weight to be given to newsworthiness should be different in public disclosure cases from what it is in intrusion cases? Would that make sense?

4. Does the use of technology contribute to the offensiveness of an intrusion? In Sanders v. American Broadcasting Companies, Inc., 978 P.2d 67 (Cal.1999), a newsgatherer obtained employment with a telepsychic marketing company and covertly obtained videotaped statements from plaintiff employee during discussions in the office. The unanimous court decided that the plaintiff, although having limited privacy rights against coworkers who might repeat his statements, had a privacy right against covert photography, recalling the *Dietemann* case, discussed note 3, p. 1212 supra.

5. *Damages.* For purposes of damages, should publication of private facts and intrusion be considered one tort or two? In *Shulman, Dietemann*, and other cases, the issue of the connection between the two arises and may be critical on the issue of damages. In footnote 18, the *Shulman* court raises the question of whether damages for an actionable intrusion can include those from a publication that would itself not be actionable under the public disclosure doctrine. How should this be resolved? Would restricting damages recoverable for intrusion provide an alternative way of protecting the First Amendment issues that concerned the *Shulman* court?

6. In Food Lion, Inc. v. Capital Cities/ABC, Inc., 194 F.3d 505 (4th Cir.1999), the Food Lion chain sued ABC and two ABC television employees who had used false resumes to procure jobs at Food Lion stores and secretly videotape "unwholesome" food handling practices—including repackaging and re-dating meat that had passed its expiration date, grinding old beef with new, and applying barbeque sauce to chicken to mask its rancid odor. On appeal, the court considered whether the employees of ABC had breached their duty of loyalty to Food Lion and committed a trespass, and whether Food Lion should, on First Amendment grounds, be prevented from proving publication damages as the result of the intrusion.

On the trespass claim, the court held—citing *Desnick,* p. 1206 supra— that the two employees could not be considered trespassers on the basis of their resume misrepresentations, since these did not completely negate the fact that Food Lion had consented to their employment: " 'Consent to an entry is often given legal effect'; even though it was obtained by misrepresentation or concealed intentions." The ABC reporters were, however, liable for breach of their duty of loyalty to Food Lion. Since "[t]he interests of the employer (ABC) to whom Dale and Barnett gave complete loyalty were adverse to the interests of Food Lion, the employer to whom they were unfaithful," the two had committed "a wrongful act in excess of Dale and Barnett's authority to enter Food Lion's premises as employees."

Despite this fact, Food Lion could not recover damages for publication. Although the district court had denied these damages on the basis of proximate cause, the Fourth Circuit determined instead that First Amendment concerns would prohibit Food Lion from recovering them. According to the court, "What Food Lion sought to do . . . was to recover defamation-type damages under non-reputational tort claims, without satisfying the stricter (First Amendment) standards of a defamation claim." Does this limitation on damages seem justified?

7. *Constitutional protection.* One theme in the *Shulman* opinion is the distinction between newsgathering and news publication in the protection afforded to the media. At one point, the court remarks that the protection afforded to newsgathering, "if any, is far narrower, than the protection surrounding the publication of truthful material." On the relationship among newsgathering, news publication, and the intrusion tort from a constitutional perspective, consider the following case.

Bartnicki v. Vopper

Supreme Court of the United States, 2001.
532 U.S. 514, 121 S.Ct. 1753, 149 L.Ed.2d 787.

■ JUSTICE STEVENS delivered the opinion of the Court.

These cases raise an important question concerning what degree of protection, if any, the First Amendment provides to speech that discloses the contents of an illegally intercepted communication. That question is both novel and narrow. Despite the fact that federal law has prohibited such disclosures since 1934, this is the first time that we have confronted such an issue.

The suit at hand involves the repeated intentional disclosure of an illegally intercepted cellular telephone conversation about a public issue. The persons who made the disclosures did not participate in the interception, but they did know—or at least had reason to know—that the interception was unlawful. Accordingly, these cases present a conflict between interests of the highest order—on the one hand, the interest in the full and free dissemination of information concerning public issues, and, on the other hand, the interest in individual privacy and, more specifically, in fostering private speech. The Framers of the First Amendment surely did not foresee the advances in science that produced the conversation, the interception, or the conflict that gave rise to this action. It is therefore not surprising that Circuit judges, as well as the Members of this Court, have come to differing conclusions about the First Amendment's application to this issue. Nevertheless, having considered the interests at stake, we are firmly convinced that the disclosures made by respondents in this suit are protected by the First Amendment.

I

During 1992 and most of 1993, the Pennsylvania State Education Association, a union representing the teachers at the Wyoming Valley West High School, engaged in collective-bargaining negotiations with the school board. Petitioner Kane, then the president of the local union, testified that the negotiations were " 'contentious' " and received "a lot of media attention." [ ] In May 1993, petitioner Bartnicki, who was acting as the union's "chief negotiator," used the cellular phone in her car to call Kane and engage in a lengthy conversation about the status of the negotiations. An unidentified person intercepted and recorded that call.

In their conversation, Kane and Bartnicki discussed the timing of a proposed strike, [ ], difficulties created by public comment on the negotiations, [ ], and the need for a dramatic response to the board's intransigence. At one point, Kane said: " 'If they're not gonna move for three percent, we're gonna have to go to their, their homes . . . To blow off their front porches, we'll have to do some work on some of those guys. (PAUSES). Really, uh, really and truthfully because this is, you know, this is bad news. (UNDECIPHERABLE).' " [ ]

In the early fall of 1993, the parties accepted a non-binding arbitration proposal that was generally favorable to the teachers. In connection with news reports about the settlement, respondent Vopper, a radio commentator who had been critical of the union in the past, played a tape of the intercepted conversation on his public affairs talk show. Another station also broadcast the tape, and local newspapers published its contents. After filing suit against Vopper and other representatives of the media, Bartnicki and Kane (hereinafter petitioners) learned through discovery that Vopper had obtained the tape from Jack Yocum, the head of a local taxpayers' organization that had opposed the union's demands throughout the negotiations. Yocum, who was added as a defendant, testified that he had found the tape in his mailbox shortly after the interception and recognized the voices of Bartnicki and Kane. Yocum played the tape for some members of the school board, and later delivered the tape itself to Vopper.

II

In their amended complaint, petitioners alleged that their telephone conversation had been surreptitiously intercepted by an unknown person using an electronic device, that Yocum had obtained a tape of that conversation, and that he intentionally disclosed it to Vopper, as well as other individuals and media representatives. Thereafter, Vopper and other members of the media repeatedly published the contents of that conversation. The amended complaint alleged that each of the defendants "knew or had reason to know" that the recording of the private telephone conversation had been obtained by means of an illegal interception. Relying on both federal and

Pennsylvania statutory provisions, petitioners sought actual damages, statutory damages, punitive damages, and attorney's fees and costs.

After the parties completed their discovery, they filed cross-motions for summary judgment. Respondents contended that they had not violated the statute because (a) they had nothing to do with the interception, and (b) in any event, their actions were not unlawful since the conversation might have been intercepted inadvertently. Moreover, even if they had violated the statute by disclosing the intercepted conversation, respondents argued, those disclosures were protected by the First Amendment. The District Court rejected the first statutory argument because, under the plain statutory language, an individual violates the federal Act by intentionally disclosing the contents of an electronic communication when he or she "know[s] or ha[s] reason to know that the information was obtained" through an illegal interception.[3] [ ] Accordingly, actual involvement in the illegal interception is not necessary in order to establish a violation of that statute. With respect to the second statutory argument, the District Court agreed that petitioners had to prove that the interception in question was intentional, but concluded that the text of the interception raised a genuine issue of material fact with respect to intent. That issue of fact was also the basis for the District Court's denial of petitioners' motion. Finally, the District Court rejected respondents' First Amendment defense because the statutes were content-neutral laws of general applicability that contained "no indicia of prior restraint or the chilling of free speech."

Thereafter, the District Court granted a motion for an interlocutory appeal, pursuant to 28 U.S.C. § 1292(b). It certified as controlling questions of law: "(1) whether the imposition of liability on the media Defendants under the [wiretapping statutes] solely for broadcasting the newsworthy tape on the Defendant [Vopper's] radio/public affairs program, when the tape was illegally intercepted and recorded by unknown persons who were not agents of [the] Defendants, violates the First Amendment; and (2) whether imposition of liability under the aforesaid [wiretapping] statutes on Defendant Jack Yocum solely for providing the anonymously intercepted and recorded tape to the media Defendants violates the First Amendment." [ ] The Court of Appeals accepted the appeal, and the United States, also a petitioner, intervened pursuant to 28 U.S.C. § 2403 in order to defend the constitutionality of the federal statute.

All three members of the panel agreed with petitioners and the Government that the federal and Pennsylvania wiretapping statutes are "content neutral" and therefore subject to "intermediate scrutiny."

---

[3]   Title 18 U.S.C. § 2511(1)(c) provides that any person who "intentionally discloses, or endeavors to disclose, to any other person the contents of any wire, oral, or electronic communication, knowing or having reason to know that the information was obtained through the interception of a wire, oral, or electronic communication in violation of this subsection; . . . shall be punished. . . ." The Pennsylvania Act contains a similar provision.

[ ] Applying that standard, the majority concluded that the statutes were invalid because they deterred significantly more speech than necessary to protect the privacy interests at stake. The court remanded the case with instructions to enter summary judgment for respondents. In dissent, Senior Judge Pollak expressed the view that the prohibition against disclosures was necessary in order to remove the incentive for illegal interceptions and to preclude compounding the harm caused by such interceptions through wider dissemination. . . .

. . .

IV

The constitutional question before us concerns the validity of the statutes as applied to the specific facts of this case. Because of the procedural posture of the case, it is appropriate to make certain important assumptions about those facts. We accept petitioners' submission that the interception was intentional, and therefore unlawful, and that, at a minimum, respondents "had reason to know" that it was unlawful. Accordingly, the disclosure of the contents of the intercepted conversation by Yocum to school board members and to representatives of the media, as well as the subsequent disclosures by the media defendants to the public, violated the federal and state statutes. Under the provisions of the federal statute, as well as its Pennsylvania analog, petitioners are thus entitled to recover damages from each of the respondents. The only question is whether the application of these statutes in such circumstances violates the First Amendment.[8]

In answering that question, we accept respondents' submission on three factual matters that serve to distinguish most of the cases that have arisen under § 2511. First, respondents played no part in the illegal interception. Rather, they found out about the interception only after it occurred, and in fact never learned the identity of the person or persons who made the interception. Second, their access to the information on the tapes was obtained lawfully, even though the information itself was intercepted unlawfully by someone else. Cf. *Florida Star v. B.J.F.,* [p. 1171 supra] ("Even assuming the Constitution permitted a State to proscribe *receipt* of information, Florida has not taken this step"). Third, the subject matter of the conversation was a matter of public concern. If the statements about the labor negotiations had been made in a public arena—during a bargaining session, for example—they would have been newsworthy. This would also be true if a third party had inadvertently overheard Bartnicki making the same statements to Kane when the two thought they were alone.

---

[8] In answering this question, we draw no distinction between the media respondents and Yocum. [ ]

V

We agree with petitioners that § 2511(1)(c), as well as its Pennsylvania analog, is in fact a content-neutral law of general applicability. "Deciding whether a particular regulation is content based or content neutral is not always a simple task. . . . As a general rule, laws that by their terms distinguish favored speech from disfavored speech on the basis of the ideas or views expressed are content based." Turner Broadcasting System, Inc. v. FCC, 512 U.S. 622, 642–643 (1994). In determining whether a regulation is content based or content neutral, we look to the purpose behind the regulation; typically, "[g]overnment regulation of expressive activity is content neutral so long as it is *justified* without reference to the content of the regulated speech.'" Ward v. Rock Against Racism, 491 U.S. 781, 791 (1989).

In this case, the basic purpose of the statute at issue is to [protect the privacy of wire, electronic, and oral communications.] The statute does not distinguish based on the content of the intercepted conversations, nor is it justified by reference to the content of those conversations. Rather, the communications at issue are singled out by virtue of the fact that they were illegally intercepted—by virtue of the source, rather than the subject matter.

On the other hand, the naked prohibition against disclosures is fairly characterized as a regulation of pure speech. Unlike the prohibition against the "use" of the contents of an illegal interception in § 2511(1) (d), subsection (c) is not a regulation of conduct. It is true that the delivery of a tape recording might be regarded as conduct, but given that the purpose of such a delivery is to provide the recipient with the text of recorded statements, it is like the delivery of a handbill or a pamphlet, and as such, it is the kind of "speech" that the First Amendment protects. As the majority below put it, "[i]f the acts of 'disclosing' and 'publishing' information do not constitute speech, it is hard to imagine what does fall within that category, as distinct from the category of expressive conduct."

VI

As a general matter, "state action to punish the publication of truthful information seldom can satisfy constitutional standards." Smith v. Daily Mail Publishing Co., 443 U.S. 97, 102 (1979). More specifically, this Court has repeatedly held that "if a newspaper lawfully obtains truthful information about a matter of public significance then state officials may not constitutionally punish publication of the information, absent a need . . . of the highest order." *Id.,* at 103; see also [*Florida Star v. B.J.F*]; Landmark Communications, Inc. v. Virginia, 435 U.S. 829 (1978).

Accordingly, in New York Times Co. v. United States, 403 U.S. 713 (1971) (*per curiam*), the Court upheld the right of the press to publish information of great public concern obtained from documents stolen by a third party. In so doing, that decision resolved a conflict between the basic rule against prior restraints on publication and the interest in preserving the secrecy of information that, if disclosed, might seriously impair the security of the Nation. In resolving that conflict, the attention of every Member of this Court was focused on the character of the stolen documents' contents and the consequences of public disclosure. Although the undisputed fact that the newspaper intended to publish information obtained from stolen documents was noted in Justice Harlan's dissent, [ ], neither the majority nor the dissenters placed any weight on that fact.

However, *New York Times v. United States* raised, but did not resolve the question "whether, in cases where information has been acquired *unlawfully* by a newspaper or by a source, government may ever punish not only the unlawful acquisition, but the ensuing publication as well." [ ] The question here, however, is a narrower version of that still-open question. Simply put, the issue here is this: "Where the punished publisher of information has obtained the information in question in a manner lawful in itself but from a source who has obtained it unlawfully, may the government punish the ensuing publication of that information based on the defect in a chain?" [ ]

Our refusal to construe the issue presented more broadly is consistent with this Court's repeated refusal to answer categorically whether truthful publication may ever be punished consistent with the First Amendment. . . .

The Government identifies two interests served by the statute— first, the interest in removing an incentive for parties to intercept private conversations, and second, the interest in minimizing the harm to persons whose conversations have been illegally intercepted. We assume that those interests adequately justify the prohibition in § 2511(1)(d) against the interceptor's own use of information that he or she acquired by violating § 2511(1)(a), but it by no means follows that punishing disclosures of lawfully obtained information of public interest by one not involved in the initial illegality is an acceptable means of serving those ends.

The normal method of deterring unlawful conduct is to impose an appropriate punishment on the person who engages in it. If the sanctions that presently attach to a violation of § 2511(1)(a) do not provide sufficient deterrence, perhaps those sanctions should be made more severe. But it would be quite remarkable to hold that speech by a law-abiding possessor of information can be suppressed in order to deter conduct by a non-law-abiding third party. . . .

With only a handful of exceptions, the violations of § 2511(1)(a) that have been described in litigated cases have been motivated by either financial gain or domestic disputes. In virtually all of those cases, the identity of the person or persons intercepting the communication has been known. Moreover, petitioners cite no evidence that Congress viewed the prohibition against disclosures as a response to the difficulty of identifying persons making improper use of scanners and other surveillance devices and accordingly of deterring such conduct, and there is no empirical evidence to support the assumption that the prohibition against disclosures reduces the number of illegal interceptions.

Although this case demonstrates that there may be an occasional situation in which an anonymous scanner will risk criminal prosecution by passing on information without any expectation of financial reward or public praise, surely this is the exceptional case. Moreover, there is no basis for assuming that imposing sanctions upon respondents will deter the unidentified scanner from continuing to engage in surreptitious interceptions. Unusual cases fall far short of a showing that there is a "need of the highest order" for a rule supplementing the traditional means of deterring antisocial conduct. The justification for any such novel burden on expression must be "far stronger than mere speculation about serious harms." [ ] Accordingly, the Government's first suggested justification for applying § 2511(1)(c) to an otherwise innocent disclosure of public information is plainly insufficient.[19]

The Government's second argument, however, is considerably stronger. Privacy of communication is an important interest, Harper & Row, Publishers, Inc. v. Nation Enterprises, 471 U.S. 539, 559 and Title III's restrictions are intended to protect that interest, thereby "encouraging the uninhibited exchange of ideas and information among private parties. . . ." Brief for United States 27. Moreover, the fear of public disclosure of private conversations might well have a chilling effect on private speech.

> "In a democratic society privacy of communication is essential if citizens are to think and act creatively and constructively. Fear or suspicion that one's speech is being monitored by a stranger, even without the reality of such activity, can have a seriously inhibiting effect upon the willingness to voice critical and constructive ideas." President's Commission on Law Enforcement and Administration of Justice, The Challenge of Crime in a Free Society 202 (1967).

Accordingly, it seems to us that there are important interests to be considered on *both* sides of the constitutional calculus. In considering that balance, we acknowledge that some intrusions on privacy are more

---

[19] Our holding, of course, does not apply to punishing parties for obtaining the relevant information unlawfully. "It would be frivolous to assert—and no one does in these cases—that the First Amendment, in the interest of securing news or otherwise, confers a license on either the reporter or his news sources to violate valid criminal laws. Although stealing documents or private wiretapping could provide newsworthy information, neither reporter nor source is immune from conviction for such conduct, whatever the impact on the flow of news." Branzburg v. Hayes, 408 U.S. 665, 691 (1972).

offensive than others, and that the disclosure of the contents of a private conversation can be an even greater intrusion on privacy than the interception itself. As a result, there is a valid independent justification for prohibiting such disclosures by persons who lawfully obtained access to the contents of an illegally intercepted message, even if that prohibition does not play a significant role in preventing such interceptions from occurring in the first place.

We need not decide whether that interest is strong enough to justify the application of § 2511(c) to disclosures of trade secrets or domestic gossip or other information of purely private concern. Cf. *Time, Inc. v. Hill,* [ ] (reserving the question whether truthful publication of private matters unrelated to public affairs can be constitutionally proscribed). In other words, the outcome of the case does not turn on whether § 2511(1)(c) may be enforced with respect to most violations of the statute without offending the First Amendment. The enforcement of that provision in this case, however, implicates the core purposes of the First Amendment because it imposes sanctions on the publication of truthful information of public concern.

In this case, privacy concerns give way when balanced against the interest in publishing matters of public importance. . . .

Our opinion in *New York Times Co. v. Sullivan,* [ ], reviewed many of the decisions that settled the "general proposition that freedom of expression upon public questions is secured by the First Amendment." [ ] Those cases all relied on our "profound national commitment to the principle that debate on public issues should be uninhibited, robust and wide-open," [ ]. It was the overriding importance of that commitment that supported our holding that neither factual error nor defamatory content, nor a combination of the two, sufficed to remove the First Amendment shield from criticism of official conduct. [ ]

We think it clear that parallel reasoning requires the conclusion that a stranger's illegal conduct does not suffice to remove the First Amendment shield from speech about a matter of public concern. The months of negotiations over the proper level of compensation for teachers at the Wyoming Valley West High School were unquestionably a matter of public concern, and respondents were clearly engaged in debate about that concern. That debate may be more mundane than the Communist rhetoric that inspired Justice Brandeis' classic opinion in Whitney v. California, [274 U.S. 357, 372 (1927)], but it is no less worthy of constitutional protection.

The judgment is affirmed.

■ JUSTICE BREYER, with whom JUSTICE O'CONNOR joins, concurring.

I join the Court's opinion because I agree with its "narrow" holding, [ ], limited to the special circumstances present here: (1) the radio broadcasters acted lawfully (up to the time of final public disclosure); and (2) the information publicized involved a matter of unusual public concern, namely a threat of potential physical harm to others. I write separately to explain why, in my view, the Court's holding does not imply a significantly broader constitutional immunity for the media.

. . .

I would ask whether the statutes strike a reasonable balance between their speech-restricting and speech-enhancing consequences. Or do they instead impose restrictions on speech that are disproportionate when measured against their corresponding privacy and speech-related benefits, taking into account the kind, the importance, and the extent of these benefits, as well as the need for the restrictions in order to secure those benefits? What this Court has called "strict scrutiny"—with its strong presumption against constitutionality—is normally out of place where, as here, important competing constitutional interests are implicated. [ ]

The statutory restrictions before us directly enhance private speech. . . . The statutes ensure the privacy of telephone conversations much as a trespass statute ensures privacy within the home. That assurance of privacy helps to overcome our natural reluctance to discuss private matters when we fear that our private conversations may become public. And the statutory restrictions consequently encourage conversations that otherwise might not take place.

At the same time, these statutes restrict public speech directly, deliberately, and of necessity. They include media publication within their scope not simply as a means, say, to deter interception, but also as an end. Media dissemination of an intimate conversation to an entire community will often cause the speakers serious harm over and above the harm caused by an initial disclosure to the person who intercepted the phone call. . . .

As a general matter, despite the statutes' direct restrictions on speech, the Federal Constitution must tolerate laws of this kind because of the importance of these privacy and speech-related objectives. . . .

Nonetheless, looked at more specifically, the statutes, as applied in these circumstances, do not reasonably reconcile the competing constitutional objectives. Rather, they disproportionately interfere with media freedom. For one thing, the broadcasters here engaged in no unlawful activity other than the ultimate publication of the information another had previously obtained. They "neither encouraged nor participated directly or indirectly in the interception." . . .

For another thing, the speakers had little or no *legitimate* interest in maintaining the privacy of the particular conversation. . . .

Further, the speakers themselves, the president of a teacher's union and the union's chief negotiator, were "limited public figures," for they voluntarily engaged in a public controversy. They thereby subjected themselves to somewhat greater public scrutiny and had a lesser interest in privacy than an individual engaged in purely private affairs. [ ]

This is not to say that the Constitution requires anyone, including public figures, to give up entirely the right to private communication, *i.e.,* communication free from telephone taps or interceptions. But the subject matter of the conversation at issue here is far removed from that in situations where the media publicizes truly private matters. [ ]

Thus, in finding a constitutional privilege to publish unlawfully intercepted conversations of the kind here at issue, the Court does not create a "public interest" exception that swallows up the statutes' privacy-protecting general rule. Rather, it finds constitutional protection for publication of intercepted information of a special kind. Here, the speakers' legitimate privacy expectations are unusually low, and the public interest in defeating those expectations is unusually high. Given these circumstances, along with the lawful nature of respondents' behavior, the statutes' enforcement would disproportionately harm media freedom.

. . .

■ CHIEF JUSTICE REHNQUIST, with whom JUSTICE SCALIA and JUSTICE THOMAS join, dissenting.

Technology now permits millions of important and confidential conversations to occur through a vast system of electronic networks. These advances, however, raise significant privacy concerns. We are placed in the uncomfortable position of not knowing who might have access to our personal and business e-mails, our medical and financial records, or our cordless and cellular telephone conversations. In an attempt to prevent some of the most egregious violations of privacy, the United States, the District of Columbia, and 40 States have enacted laws prohibiting the intentional interception and knowing disclosure of electronic communications. The Court holds that all of these statutes violate the First Amendment insofar as the illegally intercepted conversation touches upon a matter of "public concern," an amorphous concept that the Court does not even attempt to define. But the Court's decision diminishes, rather than enhances, the purposes of the First Amendment: chilling the speech of the millions of Americans who rely upon electronic technology to communicate each day.

. . .

[T]he Court places an inordinate amount of weight upon the fact that the receipt of an illegally intercepted communication has not been criminalized. [ ] But this hardly renders those who knowingly receive and disclose such communications "law-abiding," [ ], and it certainly does not bring them under the *Daily Mail* principle. The transmission of the intercepted communication from the eavesdropper to the third party is itself illegal; and where, as here, the third party then knowingly discloses that communication, another illegal act has been committed.

The third party in this situation cannot be likened to the reporters in the *Daily Mail* cases, who lawfully obtained their information through consensual interviews or public documents.

. . .

The "dry up the market" theory, which posits that it is possible to deter an illegal act that is difficult to police by preventing the wrongdoer from enjoying the fruits of the crime, is neither novel nor implausible. It is a time-tested theory that undergirds numerous laws, such as the prohibition of the knowing possession of stolen goods. . . .

The same logic applies here and demonstrates that the incidental restriction on alleged First Amendment freedoms is no greater than essential to further the interest of protecting the privacy of individual communications. Were there no prohibition on disclosure, an unlawful eavesdropper who wanted to disclose the conversation could anonymously launder the interception through a third party and thereby avoid detection. Indeed, demand for illegally obtained private information would only increase if it could be disclosed without repercussion. The law against interceptions, which the Court agrees is valid, would be utterly ineffectual without these antidisclosure provisions.

. . .

Surely "the interest in individual privacy," [ ], at its narrowest must embrace the right to be free from surreptitious eavesdropping on, and involuntary broadcast of, our cellular telephone conversations. The Court subordinates that right, not to the claims of those who themselves wish to speak, but to the claims of those who wish to publish the intercepted conversations of others. Congress' effort to balance the above claim to privacy against a marginal claim to speak freely is thereby set at naught.

NOTES AND QUESTIONS

1.   Which opinion is most persuasive on the argument that affording First Amendment protection to the disseminator, under the circumstances of *Bartnicki*, is likely to have a significant impact on the deterrent effect of the statutes?

2.   Which opinion is most persuasive on the balance between deterring private communications facilitated through electronic means and encouraging public dissemination of newsworthy information?

3.   Is the plurality resurrecting the *Rosenbloom* "public concern" standard that was earlier abandoned as a limitation on defamation claims in *Gertz*, see p. 1085 supra? In this regard, is Justice Breyer's concurrence convincing in reading the plurality opinion to apply only to "information of a special kind" as he construes it? Would his "special kind" approach provide a workable limitation on the circumstances in which dissemination of illegally intercepted information would be protected?

4. Is *Bartnicki* a logical progression from the *Cox-Florida Star* line of cases considered earlier? See p. 1169 supra.

5. Boehner v. McDermott, 484 F.3d 573 (D.C.Cir.2007), addresses an aspect of *Bartnicki*: the means by which the publisher obtains the illegally obtained communication, and perhaps more importantly, whether the context of the acquisition imposes limitations on the recipient's use of it. Defendant, a member of the House of Representatives, obtained a recording of an illegally intercepted telephone conversation among several Republican politicians, including Newt Gingrich, about how to handle an ethics violation. Defendant obtained the tape from the couple who had made it and who became concerned about their having violated the law. They brought it to Washington and gave it to defendant, concerned about their potential liability, after being advised that they should turn it over to the House Ethics Committee, of which defendant was a member. After playing the tape, defendant turned it over to two journalists who then wrote articles about it. The court held that, despite *Bartnicki*, defendant did not have a First Amendment right to disseminate the communication, because he breached House rules mandating confidentiality for evidence obtained by the Committee in making public information that he received as an agent of the House Ethics Committee.

D. APPROPRIATION

"Appropriation" claims involve the attempts of celebrities to control the exploitation of their names, likenesses, and fame and any pecuniary value resulting therefrom. The claim was explicitly recognized for the first time in Haelan Laboratories v. Topps Chewing Gum, Inc., 202 F.2d 866 (2d Cir.1953), in which the court spoke of the need to protect the proprietary interest of celebrities in the use of their names and likenesses. Since *Haelan,* similar claims about the improper use of names and likenesses have been widely recognized. Although some states have adopted the action as a separate common law remedy, most have developed it as an offshoot of either the common law right of privacy or of a privacy statute.

Is the claim a type of privacy, or should it properly be conceptualized as a distinct tort? One inherent difference between it and the more traditional privacy rights is that privacy protects against undesired public intrusion into one's personal life, while the right of publicity is usually invoked to protect against persons who would profit by taking, without compensation, something the celebrity would prefer to sell. For example, a famous person may not generally object to commercial exploitation of his or her name or other feature but may want to be compensated for it. But some cases appear to go beyond the desire for compensation. See, e.g., Martin Luther King, Jr., Center for Social Change, Inc. v. American Heritage Products, Inc., 296 S.E.2d 697 (Ga.1982), in which plaintiff successfully stopped defendant from making plastic busts of the late Dr. King. Could plaintiff have stopped a "recognized" painter from painting a portrait of Dr. King? A street fair painter?

Whether or not the claim for appropriation is considered as a subset of privacy rights has important implications for its judicial development. For example, it is unclear whether it survives the death of the celebrity in whom the right is based; that is, whether a celebrity's heirs or assigns can profit from any such right after the famous person has died. Courts that have held the right to be descendible have analogized it to an ordinary property right or a copyright, both of which are inheritable. Courts that have rejected a descendible right have emphasized the personal nature of the claim, the analogy to rights of privacy, which are not inheritable, and the line-drawing difficulties inherent in any development of a right that survives the death of the celebrity.

Zacchini v. Scripps-Howard Broadcasting Co.

Supreme Court of the United States, 1977.
433 U.S. 562, 97 S.Ct. 2849, 53 L.Ed.2d 965.

■ MR. JUSTICE WHITE delivered the opinion of the Court.

Petitioner, Hugo Zacchini, is an entertainer. He performs a "human cannonball" act in which he is shot from a cannon into a net some 200 feet away. Each performance occupies some 15 seconds. In August and September 1972, petitioner was engaged to perform his act on a regular basis at the Geauga County Fair in Burton, Ohio. He performed in a fenced area, surrounded by grandstands, at the fair grounds. Members of the public attending the fair were not charged a separate admission fee to observe his act.

On August 30, a freelance reporter for Scripps-Howard Broadcasting Co., the operator of a television broadcasting station and respondent in this case, attended the fair. He carried a small movie camera. Petitioner noticed the reporter and asked him not to film the performance. The reporter did not do so on that day; but on the instructions of the producer of respondent's daily newscast, he returned the following day and videotaped the entire act. This film clip, approximately 15 seconds in length, was shown on the 11 o'clock news program that night, together with favorable commentary.[1]

Petitioner then brought this action for damages, alleging that he is "engaged in the entertainment business," that the act he performs is one "invented by his father and . . . performed only by his family for the

---

[1] The script of the commentary accompanying the film clip read as follows:

"This . . . now . . . is the story of a *true spectator* sport . . . the sport of human cannonballing . . . in fact, the great *Zacchini* is about the only human cannonball around, these days . . . just happens that, *where* he is, is the Great Geauga County Fair, in Burton . . . and believe me, although it's not a *long* act, it's a thriller . . . and you really need to see it *in person* . . . to appreciate it. . . ." (Emphasis in original.) [ ]

last fifty years," that respondent "showed and commercialized the film of his act without his consent," and that such conduct was an "unlawful appropriation of plaintiff's professional property." [ ] Respondent answered and moved for summary judgment, which was granted by the trial court.

. . .

. . . Insofar as the Ohio Supreme Court held that the First and Fourteenth Amendments of the United States Constitution required judgment for respondent, we reverse the judgment of that court.

. . .

Even if the judgment in favor of respondent must nevertheless be understood as ultimately resting on Ohio law, it appears that at the very least the Ohio court felt compelled by what it understood to be federal constitutional considerations to construe and apply its own law in the manner it did. In this event, we have jurisdiction and should decide the federal issue; for if the state court erred in its understanding of our cases and of the First and Fourteenth Amendments we should so declare, leaving the state court free to decide the privilege issue solely as a matter of Ohio law. [ ] If the Supreme Court of Ohio "held as it did because it felt under compulsion of federal law as enunciated by this Court so to hold, it should be relieved of that compulsion. It should be freed to decide . . . these suits according to its own local law." [ ]

The Ohio Supreme Court relied heavily on *Time, Inc. v. Hill*, [ ], but that case does not mandate a media privilege to televise a performer's entire act without his consent. Involved in *Time, Inc. v. Hill* was a claim under the New York "Right of Privacy" statute that Life Magazine, in the course of reviewing a new play, had connected the play with a long-past incident involving petitioner and his family and had falsely described their experience and conduct at that time. The complaint sought damages for humiliation and suffering flowing from these nondefamatory falsehoods that allegedly invaded Hill's privacy. The Court held, however, that the opening of a new play linked to an actual incident was a matter of public interest and that Hill could not recover without showing that the Life report was knowingly false or was published with reckless disregard for the truth—the same rigorous standard that had been applied in [*New York Times Co. v. Sullivan*].

Time, Inc. v. Hill, which was hotly contested and decided by a divided Court, involved an entirely different tort from the "right of publicity" recognized by the Ohio Supreme Court. . . .

The differences between these two torts are important. First, the State's interests in providing a cause of action in each instance are different. "The interest protected" in permitting recovery for placing the plaintiff in a false light "is clearly that of reputation, with the same overtones of mental distress as in defamation." Prosser, [Privacy, 48 Cal.L.Rev. 383, 400 (1960)]. By contrast, the State's interest in permitting a "right of publicity" is in protecting the proprietary interest of the individual in his act in part to encourage such entertainment. As we later note, the State's interest is closely analogous to the goals of patent and copyright law, focusing on the right of the individual to reap the reward of his endeavors and having little to do with protecting feelings or reputation. Second, the two torts differ in the degree to which they intrude on dissemination of information to the public. In "false light" cases the only way to protect the interests involved is to attempt to minimize publication of the damaging matter, while in "right of publicity" cases the only question is who gets to do the publishing. An entertainer such as petitioner usually has no objection to the widespread publication of his act as long as he gets the commercial benefit of such publication. Indeed, in the present case petitioner did not seek to enjoin the broadcast of his act; he simply sought compensation for the broadcast in the form of damages.

Nor does it appear that our later cases such as [*Rosenbloom; Gertz; and Firestone*] require or furnish substantial support for the Ohio court's privilege ruling. These cases, like *New York Times,* emphasize the protection extended to the press by the First Amendment in defamation cases, particularly when suit is brought by a public official or a public figure. None of them involve an alleged appropriation by the press of a right of publicity existing under state law.

Moreover, *Time, Inc. v. Hill*, *New York Times*, [*Rosenbloom*], *Gertz,* and *Firestone* all involved the reporting of events; in none of them was there an attempt to broadcast or publish an entire act for which the performer ordinarily gets paid. It is evident, and there is no claim here to the contrary, that petitioner's state-law right of publicity would not serve to prevent respondent from reporting the newsworthy facts about petitioner's act. Wherever the line in particular situations is to be drawn between media reports that are protected and those that are not, we are quite sure that the First and Fourteenth Amendments do not immunize the media when they broadcast a performer's entire act without his consent. The Constitution no more prevents a State from requiring respondent to compensate petitioner for broadcasting his act on television than it would privilege respondent to film and broadcast a copyrighted dramatic work without liability to the copyright owner, [ ], or to film and broadcast a prize fight, [ ], or a baseball game, [ ], where the promoters or the participants had other plans for publicizing the event. There are ample reasons for reaching this conclusion.

The broadcast of a film of petitioner's entire act poses a substantial threat to the economic value of that performance. As the Ohio court recognized, this act is the product of petitioner's own talents and energy, the end result of much time, effort, and expense. Much of its economic value lies in the "right of exclusive control over the publicity given to his performance"; if the public can see the act free on television, it will be less willing to pay to see it at the fair.[12] The effect of a public broadcast of the performance is similar to preventing petitioner from charging an admission fee. . . . Moreover, the broadcast of petitioner's entire performance, unlike the unauthorized use of another's name for purposes of trade or the incidental use of a name or picture by the press, goes to the heart of petitioner's ability to earn a living as an entertainer. Thus, in this case, Ohio has recognized what may be the strongest case for a "right of publicity"—involving, not the appropriation of an entertainer's reputation to enhance the attractiveness of a commercial product, but the appropriation of the very activity by which the entertainer acquired his reputation in the first place.

Of course, Ohio's decision to protect petitioner's right of publicity here rests on more than a desire to compensate the performer for the time and effort invested in his act; the protection provides an economic incentive for him to make the investment required to produce a performance of interest to the public. This same consideration underlies the patent and copyright laws long enforced by this Court. . . .

There is no doubt that entertainment, as well as news, enjoys First Amendment protection. It is also true that entertainment itself can be important news. *Time, Inc. v. Hill*. But it is important to note that neither the public nor respondent will be deprived of the benefit of petitioner's performance as long as his commercial stake in his act is appropriately recognized. Petitioner does not seek to enjoin the broadcast of his performance; he simply wants to be paid for it. Nor do we think that a state-law damages remedy against respondent would represent a species of liability without fault contrary to the letter or spirit of [*Gertz v. Robert Welch, Inc.*]. Respondent knew exactly that petitioner objected to televising his act but nevertheless displayed the entire film.

We conclude that although the State of Ohio may as a matter of its own law privilege the press in the circumstances of this case, the First and Fourteenth Amendments do not require it to do so.

Reversed.

■ MR. JUSTICE POWELL, with whom MR. JUSTICE BRENNAN and MR. JUSTICE MARSHALL join, dissenting.

Disclaiming any attempt to do more than decide the narrow case before us, the Court reverses the decision of the Supreme Court of Ohio based on repeated incantation of a single formula: "a performer's entire act." The holding today is summed up in one sentence:

---

[12] It is possible, of course, that respondent's news broadcast increased the value of petitioner's performance by stimulating the public's interest in seeing the act live. In these circumstances, petitioner would not be able to prove damages and thus would not recover. But petitioner has alleged that the broadcast injured him to the extent of $25,000. App. 5, and we think the State should be allowed to authorize compensation of this injury if proved.

"Wherever the line in particular situations is to be drawn between media reports that are protected and those that are not, we are quite sure that the First and Fourteenth Amendments do not immunize the media when they broadcast a performer's entire act without his consent."

I doubt that this formula provides a standard clear enough even for resolution of this case.[1] In any event, I am not persuaded that the Court's opinion is appropriately sensitive to the First Amendment values at stake, and I therefore dissent.

Although the Court would draw no distinction, [ ], I do not view respondent's action as comparable to unauthorized commercial broadcasts of sporting events, theatrical performances, and the like where the broadcaster keeps the profits. There is no suggestion here that respondent made any such use of the film. Instead, it simply reported on what petitioner concedes to be a newsworthy event, in a way hardly surprising for a television station—by means of film coverage. The report was part of an ordinary daily news program, consuming a total of 15 seconds. It is a routine example of the press fulfilling the informing function so vital to our system.

The Court's holding that the station's ordinary news report may give rise to substantial liability has disturbing implications, for the decision could lead to a degree of media self-censorship. [ ] Hereafter whenever a television news editor is unsure whether certain film footage received from a camera crew might be held to portray an "entire act," he may decline coverage—even of clearly newsworthy events—or confine the broadcast to watered-down verbal reporting, perhaps with an occasional still picture. The public is then the loser. This is hardly the kind of news reportage that the First Amendment is meant to foster. [ ]

In my view the First Amendment commands a different analytical starting point from the one selected by the Court. Rather than begin with a quantitative analysis of the performer's behavior—is this or is this not his entire act?—we should direct initial attention to the actions of the news media: what use did the station make of the film footage? When a film is used, as here, for a routine portion of a regular news program, I would hold that the First Amendment protects the station from a "right of publicity" or "appropriation" suit, absent a strong

---

[1]   Although the record is not explicit, it is unlikely that the "act" commenced abruptly with the explosion that launched petitioner on his way, ending with the landing in the net a few seconds later. One may assume that the actual firing was preceded by some fanfare, possibly stretching over several minutes, to heighten the audience's anticipation: introduction of the performer, description of the uniqueness and danger, last-minute checking of the apparatus, and entry into the cannon, all accompanied by suitably ominous commentary from the master of ceremonies. If this is found to be the case on remand, then respondent could not be said to have appropriated the "entire act" in its 15-second news-clip—and the Court's opinion then would afford no guidance for resolution of the case. Moreover, in future cases involving different performances, similar difficulties in determining just what constitutes the "entire act" are inevitable.

showing by the plaintiff that the news broadcast was a subterfuge or cover for private or commercial exploitation.[4]

. . . In a suit like the one before us, however, the plaintiff does not complain about the fact of exposure to the public, but rather about its timing or manner. He welcomes some publicity, but seeks to retain control over means and manner as a way to maximize for himself the monetary benefits that flow from such publication. But having made the matter public—having chosen, in essence, to make it newsworthy— he cannot, consistent with the First Amendment, complain of routine news reportage. Cf. *Gertz v. Robert Welch, Inc.*, [ ] (clarifying the different liability standards appropriate in defamation suits, depending on whether or not the plaintiff is a public figure).

Since the film clip here was undeniably treated as news and since there is no claim that the use was subterfuge, respondent's actions were constitutionally privileged. I would affirm.

[Mr. Justice Stevens dissented on the ground that he could not tell whether the Ohio Supreme Court had relied on federal constitutional issues in deciding the case. He would have remanded the case to that court "for clarification of its holding before deciding the federal constitutional issue."]

NOTES AND QUESTIONS

1. On remand, the Ohio Supreme Court took advantage of the opportunity afforded by the majority opinion and decided that nothing in the Ohio Constitution protected the behavior of the media defendant. The case was remanded for trial and for assessment of damages if liability was established. Zacchini v. Scripps-Howard Broadcasting Co., 376 N.E.2d 582 (Ohio 1978).

2. How important is it that the majority treats the 15 seconds as the "entire act"? In a case involving the televising of a figure skating championship, a telecaster argued that a short newscast drawn from hours of film would not be an "entire" act under *Zacchini*. The judge, however, said it was "conceivable that a two-minute broadcast, focused solely on the top performer of the day, would embody the essence of the commercially valuable performance, and thus could possibly be a broadcast of the 'entire' act." The case was decided on other issues. Post Newsweek Stations-Connecticut, Inc. v. Travelers Insurance Co., 510 F.Supp. 81 (D.Conn.1981).

3. Does *Zacchini* involve an aspect of "privacy"? Of "publicity"? Why did the defendant in *Cox Broadcasting* not have to pay for using the name of the rape victim, or the defendant in *Haynes* not have to pay anyone who

---

[4] This case requires no detailed specification of the standards for identifying a subterfuge, since there is no claim here that respondent's news use was anything but bona fide. [ ] I would point out, however, that selling time during a news broadcast to advertisers in the customary fashion does not make for "commercial exploitation" in the sense intended here. [ ]

appeared in the book although the defendant in *Zacchini* may have to pay for what it did?

4. After *Zacchini,* what would happen in a case in which a street artist who survives on contributions from passersby—a mime, an accordionist, a dancer—is taped by the local television station and shown in a story about summer diversions on the streets of the city? Is the street artist's claim as strong as Zacchini's?

5. Promoters of entertainment and sports events normally protect their rights by controlling access to the event. Terms of admission often prohibit use of cameras or tape recorders. Broadcasting rights are protected by allowing only those who have contracted with the promoters to set up their broadcasting equipment. Performers, in turn, protect their interests through their contracts with the promoters; whether the promoter has a right to authorize a live broadcast of a concert, for example, is usually determined by the terms of the contract between the performer and the promoter.

If Zacchini did not protect his rights contractually, why should the courts provide him a remedy through tort law? The television station was permitted—probably even encouraged—by the fair officials to broadcast film of various events at the fair. Should the station be entitled to rely on that invitation without inquiring into the officials' authority to extend it?

6. Plaintiffs generally have been unsuccessful when they have tried to invoke *Zacchini* to create a cause of action not otherwise provided by the law of copyright or the tort of commercial exploitation of name or likeness. Ginger Rogers, who often performed with dancer Fred Astaire, relied on *Zacchini* in an attempt to prevent Federico Fellini from using the title "Ginger and Fred" for his 1986 movie about an Italian dancing couple. The district court characterized *Zacchini* as a "narrowly drawn opinion effectively limited to its facts," and distinguished it on the ground that "Ginger and Fred" did not threaten Rogers's economic viability. Rogers v. Grimaldi, 695 F.Supp. 112 (S.D.N.Y.1988), aff'd, 875 F.2d 994 (2d Cir.1989).

Winter v. DC Comics

Supreme Court of California, 2003.
30 Cal.4th 881, 69 P.3d 473, 134 Cal.Rptr.2d 634.

■ CHIN, J.

Celebrities have a statutory right of publicity by which they can prohibit others from using their likeness. (*Civ. Code, § 3344.*) An obvious tension exists between this right of publicity and the First Amendment to the United States Constitution. (Comedy III Productions, Inc. v. Gary Saderup, Inc., [21 P.3d 797 (Cal.2001)] (*Comedy III*).) In *Comedy III*, we considered when constitutional free speech rights may trump the statutory right of publicity. We formulated "what is essentially a balancing test between the First Amendment and the right of publicity based on whether the work in question adds significant creative elements so as to be transformed into something more than a mere celebrity likeness or imitation." [ ]. In that case, we concluded that lithographs and T-shirts bearing the likeness of The Three Stooges were not sufficiently transformative to receive First Amendment protection.

In this case, we apply the same balancing test to comic books containing characters that evoke musician brothers Johnny and Edgar Winter. We conclude that, in contrast to a drawing of The Three Stooges, the comic books do contain significant creative elements that transform them into something more than mere celebrity likenesses. Accordingly, the comic books are entitled to First Amendment protection.

I.   FACTS AND PROCEDURAL HISTORY

In the 1990's, DC Comics published a five-volume comic miniseries featuring "Jonah Hex," a fictional comic book "anti-hero." The series contains an outlandish plot, involving giant worm-like creatures, singing cowboys, and the "Wilde West Ranch and Music and Culture Emporium," named for and patterned after the life of Oscar Wilde. The third volume ends with a reference to two new characters, the "Autumn brothers," and the teaser, "NEXT: The Autumns of Our Discontent." The cover of volume 4 depicts the Autumn brother characters, with pale faces and long white hair. [ ] One brother wears a stovepipe hat and red sunglasses, and holds a rifle. The second has red eyes and holds a pistol. This volume is entitled Autumns of Our Discontent, and features brothers Johnny and Edgar Autumn, depicted as villainous half-worm, half-human offspring born from the rape of their mother by a supernatural worm creature that had escaped from a hole in the ground. At the end of volume 5, Jonah Hex and his companions shoot and kill the Autumn brothers in an underground gun battle.

Plaintiffs, Johnny and Edgar Winter, well-known performing and recording musicians originally from Texas, sued DC Comics and others alleging several causes of action including, as relevant here, appropriation of their names and likenesses under Civil Code section 3344. They alleged that the defendants selected the names Johnny and Edgar Autumn to signal readers the Winter brothers were being portrayed; that the Autumn brothers were drawn with long white hair and albino features similar to plaintiffs'; that the Johnny Autumn character was depicted as wearing a tall black top hat similar to the one Johnny Winter often wore; and that the title of volume 4, Autumns of Our Discontent, refers to the famous Shakespearean phrase, "the winter of our discontent." They also alleged that the comics falsely portrayed them as "vile, depraved, stupid, cowardly, subhuman individuals who engage in wanton acts of violence, murder and bestiality for pleasure and who should be killed."

Defendants moved for summary judgment, partly relying on the First Amendment. The trial court granted summary judgment on all causes of action and entered judgment in defendants' favor. The Court of Appeal originally affirmed the judgment. We granted review and held the matter pending our decision in *Comedy III* [ ]. Later, we remanded the matter for the Court of Appeal to reconsider its decision in light of *Comedy III*. This time, the Court of Appeal affirmed the summary adjudication of all causes of action other than the one for misappropriation of likeness. On the misappropriation cause of action, the court concluded that triable issues of fact exist whether or not the comic books are entitled to protection under the test adopted in *Comedy III*. It reversed the judgment and remanded for further proceedings on that cause of action.

We granted the defendants' petition for review to decide whether the comic books are protected under the *Comedy III* transformative test.

II. DISCUSSION

Civil Code section 3344 provides as relevant: "(a) Any person who knowingly uses another's name, voice, signature, photograph, or likeness, in any manner, on or in products, merchandise, or goods, or for purposes of advertising or selling, or soliciting purchases of, products, merchandise, goods or services, without such person's prior consent . . . shall be liable for any damages sustained by the person or persons injured as a result thereof."

In *Comedy III*, [ ], the registered owner of all rights to the former comedy act known as The Three Stooges sued an artist who, without permission, sold lithographs and T-shirts bearing a likeness of The Three Stooges reproduced from a charcoal drawing the artist had made. We noted that the right of publicity threatens two purposes of the First Amendment: (1) preserving an uninhibited marketplace of ideas; and (2) furthering the individual right of self-expression. "Because celebrities take on public meaning, the appropriation of their likenesses may have important uses in uninhibited debate on public issues, particularly debates about culture and values. And because celebrities take on personal meanings to many individuals in the society, the creative appropriation of celebrity images can be an important avenue of individual expression." (*Comedy III*, [ ].) "[T]he very importance of celebrities in society means that the right of publicity has the potential of censoring significant expression by suppressing alternative versions of celebrity images that are iconoclastic, irreverent, or otherwise attempt to redefine the celebrity's meaning. [Citations.] . . . 'The right of publicity derived from public prominence does not confer a shield to ward off caricature, parody and satire. Rather, prominence invites creative comment.' " (*Ibid.*, quoting with approval [ ].)

Accordingly, we held that some, although not all, uses of celebrity likenesses are entitled to First Amendment protection. "When artistic expression takes the form of a literal depiction or imitation of a celebrity for commercial gain, directly trespassing on the right of publicity without adding significant expression beyond that trespass, the state law interest in protecting the fruits of artistic labor outweighs the expressive interests of the imitative artist." (*Comedy III*, [ ].) Thus, "depictions of celebrities amounting to little more than the appropriation of the celebrity's economic value are not protected expression under the First Amendment." [ ] "The right-of-publicity holder [may still] enforce the right to monopolize the production of conventional, more or less fungible, images of the celebrity." [ ] "On the other hand, when a work contains significant transformative elements, it is not only especially worthy of First Amendment protection, but it is also less likely to interfere with the economic interest protected by the right of publicity. . . . [W]orks of parody or other distortions of the celebrity figure are not, from the celebrity fan's viewpoint, good substitutes for conventional depictions of the celebrity and therefore do not generally threaten markets for celebrity memorabilia that the right of publicity is designed to protect." [ ]

We developed a test to determine whether a work merely appropriates a celebrity's economic value, and thus is not entitled to First Amendment protection, or has been transformed into a creative product that the First Amendment protects. The "inquiry is whether the celebrity likeness is one of the 'raw materials' from which an original work is synthesized, or whether the depiction or imitation of the celebrity is the very sum and substance of the work in question. We ask, in other words, whether a product containing a celebrity's likeness is so transformed that it has become primarily the defendant's own expression rather than the celebrity's likeness. And when we use the word 'expression,' we mean expression of something other than the likeness of the celebrity." (*Comedy III*, [ ].) These "transformative elements or creative contributions that require First Amendment protection are not confined to parody and can take many forms, from factual reporting [citation] to fictionalized portrayal [citations], from heavyhanded lampooning [citation] to subtle social criticism [citation]." (*Ibid.*) "[A]n artist depicting a celebrity must contribute something more than a 'merely trivial' variation, [but must create] something recognizably 'his own' [citation], in order to qualify for legal protection." (*Id.* at [ ].) "[W]hen an artist's skill and talent is manifestly subordinated to the overall goal of creating a conventional portrait of a celebrity so as to commercially exploit his or her fame, then the artist's right of free expression is outweighed by the right of publicity." (*Ibid.*)

We made two important cautionary observations. First, "the right of publicity cannot, consistent with the First Amendment, be a right to control the celebrity's image by censoring disagreeable portrayals. Once the celebrity thrusts himself or herself forward into the limelight, the First Amendment dictates that the right to comment on, parody, lampoon, and make other expressive uses of the celebrity image must be given broad scope. The necessary implication of this observation is that the right of publicity is essentially an economic right. What the right of publicity holder possesses is not a right of censorship, but a right to prevent others from misappropriating the economic value generated by the celebrity's fame through the merchandising of the 'name, voice, signature, photograph, or likeness' of the celebrity. [Citation.]" (*Comedy III*, [ ].) Second, "in determining whether the work is transformative, courts are not to be concerned with the quality of the artistic contribution—vulgar forms of expression fully qualify for First Amendment protection. [Citations.] On the other hand, a literal depiction of a celebrity, even if accomplished with great skill, may still be subject to a right of publicity challenge. The inquiry is in a sense more quantitative than qualitative, asking whether the literal and imitative or the creative elements predominate in the work." (*Id. at* [ ].)

We also cautioned against "wholesale importation of the fair use doctrine [of copyright law] into right of publicity law," although it provides some guidance. (*Comedy III*, [ ].) We explained that one factor of the fair use test, " 'the effect of the use upon the potential market for or value of the copyrighted work' (17 U.S.C. § 107(4)) . . . bears directly on this question. We do not believe, however, that consideration of this factor would usefully supplement the test articulated here. If it is determined that a work is worthy of First Amendment protection because added creative elements significantly transform the celebrity depiction, then independent inquiry into whether or not that work is cutting into the market for the celebrity's images . . . appears to be irrelevant." [ ]. . . .

We then summarized the rule. "In sum, when an artist is faced with a right of publicity challenge to his or her work, he or she may raise as [an] affirmative defense that the work is protected by the First Amendment inasmuch as it contains significant transformative elements or that the value of the work does not derive primarily from the celebrity's fame." (*Comedy III*, [ ].)

In applying this test in *Comedy III* itself, we viewed the work in question and concluded that the right of publicity prevailed. We could "discern no significant transformative or creative contribution. [The artist's] undeniable skill is manifestly subordinated to the overall goal of creating literal, conventional depictions of The Three Stooges so as to exploit their fame. Indeed, were we to decide that [the artist's] depictions were protected by the First Amendment, we cannot perceive how the right of publicity would remain a viable right other than in cases of falsified celebrity endorsements. Moreover, the marketability and economic value of [the artist's] work derives primarily from the fame of the celebrities depicted. While that fact alone does not necessarily mean the work receives no First Amendment protection, we can perceive no transformative elements in [the] works that would require such protection." (*Comedy III*, [ ].)

Application of the test to this case is not difficult. We have reviewed the comic books. . . . We can readily ascertain that they are not just conventional depictions of plaintiffs but contain significant expressive content other than plaintiffs' mere likenesses. Although the fictional characters Johnny and Edgar Autumn are less-than-subtle evocations of Johnny and Edgar Winter, the books do not depict plaintiffs literally. Instead, plaintiffs are merely part of the raw materials from which the comic books were synthesized. To the extent the drawings of the Autumn brothers resemble plaintiffs at all, they are distorted for purposes of lampoon, parody, or caricature. And the Autumn brothers are but cartoon characters—half-human and half-worm—in a larger story, which is itself quite expressive. The characters and their portrayals do not greatly threaten plaintiffs' right of publicity. Plaintiffs' fans who want to purchase pictures of them would find the drawings of the Autumn brothers unsatisfactory as a substitute for conventional depictions. The comic books are similar to the trading cards caricaturing and parodying prominent baseball players that have received First Amendment protection. (Cardtoons v. Major League Baseball Players, [95 F.3d 959 (10th Cir.1996)] discussed in *Comedy III*, [ ].) Like the trading cards, the comic books " 'are no less protected because they provide humorous rather than serious commentary.' " (*Comedy III*, [ ], quoting *Cardtoons*, [ ].)

. . .

Plaintiffs also argue, and the Court of Appeal found, that the record contains evidence that defendants were trading on plaintiffs' likenesses and reputations to generate interest in the comic book series and increase sales. This, too, is irrelevant to whether the comic books are constitutionally protected. The question is whether the work is transformative, not how it is marketed. If the work is sufficiently transformative to receive legal protection, "it is of no moment that the advertisements may have increased the profitability of the [work]." [ ] If the challenged work is transformative, the way it is advertised cannot somehow make it nontransformative. Here, as we have explained, the comic books are transformative and entitled to First Amendment protection.

Accordingly, we conclude that the Court of Appeal erred in finding the existence of triable issues of fact. . . .

III. CONCLUSION

The artist in *Comedy III*, [ ] essentially sold, and devoted fans bought, pictures of The Three Stooges, not transformed expressive works by the artist. Here, by contrast, defendants essentially sold, and the buyers purchased, DC Comics depicting fanciful, creative characters, not pictures of the Winter brothers. This makes all the difference. The comic books here are entitled to First Amendment protection.

Accordingly, we reverse the judgment of the Court of Appeal and remand the matter for further proceedings consistent with our opinion.

■ GEORGE, C.J., KENNARD, J., BAXTER, J., WERDEGAR, J., BROWN, J., and MORENO, J., concurred.

NOTES AND QUESTIONS

1. As the court states, *Comedy III*, decided just two years earlier, was similarly decided under the California right of publicity statute, section 3344. But in that case, the court upheld the claimed violation of publicity rights based on the likeness of a charcoal drawing of The Three Stooges comedy team that was sold in lithographs and on T-shirts. Suppose the T-shirts had borne a recognizable caricature of The Three Stooges. Would plaintiff still have stated a claim under the approach adhered to in *Winter*? What is the underlying rationale for the "significant transformative elements" test?

2. Is the test, as the court suggests, a "balancing test"? What is being balanced? If the comic book series in *Winter* has creative elements to it, what could plaintiff show that would tip the balance in its favor?

3. In re NCAA Student-Athlete Name & Likeness Licensing Litigation, 724 F.3d 1268 (9th Cir.2013) involved claims under the California right of publicity statute and on common law privacy grounds against a video game producer that simulated college football playing conditions and relied on avatars that were likenesses of plaintiff and fellow team members. Relying in part on the transformative use test in *Winter*, the court (2–1) dismissed all defense claims. The dissenting judge argued that the focus on likeness to team players was excessively narrow, and that the gamers' ability to manipulate the avatars, as well as the accompanying simulated crowd ambience, satisfied the *Winter* test. In accord with the majority is Hart v. Electronic Arts, Inc., 717 F.3d 141 (3d Cir.2013).

4. In White v. Samsung Electronics America, Inc., 971 F.2d 1395 (9th Cir.1992), reh'g denied, 989 F.2d 1512 (1993)(en banc), defendant's television commercial—one of a series promoting the idea that its product will still be popular in the next century—used a robot that suggested TV personality Vanna White in her role of turning letters on the program "Wheel of Fortune." After holding that White had no action under the California publicity statute because the robot was not a "likeness" within the statute, the majority held that her common-law right of publicity had been violated. It was "not important how the defendant has appropriated the plaintiff's identity, but whether the defendant has done so":

> Viewed separately, the individual aspects of the advertisement in the present case say little. Viewed together, they leave little doubt about the celebrity the ad is meant to depict. The female-shaped robot is wearing a long gown, blond wig, and large jewelry. Vanna White dresses exactly like this at times, but so do many other women. The robot is in the process of turning a block letter on a game-board. Vanna White dresses like this while turning letters on a game-board but perhaps similarly attired Scrabble-playing women do this as well. The robot is standing on what looks to be the Wheel of Fortune game show set. Vanna

White dresses like this, turns letters, and does this on the Wheel of Fortune game show. She is the only one. Indeed, defendants themselves referred to their ad as the "Vanna White" ad. We are not surprised.

Television and other media create marketable celebrity identity value. Considerable energy and ingenuity are expended by those who have achieved celebrity value to exploit it for profit. The law protects the celebrity's sole right to exploit this value whether the celebrity has achieved her fame out of rare ability, dumb luck, or a combination thereof. We decline [defendants'] invitation to permit the evisceration of the common law right of publicity through means as facile as those in this case. Because White has alleged facts showing that [defendants] had appropriated her identity, the district court erred by rejecting, on summary judgment, White's common law right of publicity claim.

When defendant argued that the ad was constitutionally protected, the majority responded:

In defense, defendants cite a number of cases for the proposition that their robot ad constituted protected speech. The only cases they cite which are even remotely relevant to this case are [*Hustler Magazine v. Falwell,* p. 931 supra] and L.L. Bean, Inc. v. Drake Publishers, Inc., 811 F.2d 26 (1st Cir.1987). Those cases involved parodies of advertisements run for the purpose of poking fun at Jerry Falwell and L.L. Bean, respectively. This case involves a true advertisement run for the purpose of selling Samsung VCRs. The ad's spoof of Vanna White and Wheel of Fortune is subservient and only tangentially related to the ad's primary message: "buy Samsung VCRs." Defendants' parody arguments are better addressed to non-commercial parodies. The difference between a "parody" and a "knock-off" is the difference between fun and profit.

How would the *Winter* court have decided *White v. Samsung*? Are the two cases distinguishable?

White v. Samsung evoked a sharp dissent by Judge Kozinski from the order rejecting an en banc hearing. The flavor of that extended dissent—asserting incompatibility with the Copyright Act, the Copyright Clause, and the First Amendment—may be gauged from the following excerpts:

KOZINSKI, CIRCUIT JUDGE, with whom CIRCUIT JUDGES O'SCANNLAIN and KLEINFELD join, dissenting from the order rejecting the suggestion for rehearing en banc.

I

Saddam Hussein wants to keep advertisers from using his picture in unflattering contexts. Clint Eastwood doesn't want tabloids to write about him. Rudolf Valentino's heirs want to control his film biography. The Girl Scouts don't want their image soiled by association with certain activities. George Lucas wants to keep Strategic Defense Initiative fans from calling it "Star Wars." Pepsico doesn't want singers to use the word "Pepsi" in their songs. Guy Lombardo wants an exclusive property right to ads that show big bands playing on New Year's Eve. Uri Geller thinks he should be paid for ads showing psychics bending metal through telekinesis. Paul Prudhomme, that household name, thinks the same about ads featuring corpulent bearded chefs. And scads of copyright holders see purple when their creations are made fun of. [The opinion cites references for each example.]

Something very dangerous is going on here. Private property, including intellectual property, is essential to our way of life. It provides an incentive for investment and innovation; it stimulates the flourishing of our culture; it protects the moral entitlements of people to the fruits of their labors. But reducing too much to private property can be bad medicine. Private land, for instance, is far more useful if separated from other private land by public streets, roads and highways. Public parks, utility rights-of-way and sewers reduce the amount of land in private hands, but vastly enhance the value of the property that remains.

So too it is with intellectual property. Overprotecting intellectual property is as harmful as underprotecting it. Creativity is impossible without a rich public domain. Nothing today, likely nothing since we tamed fire, is genuinely new: Culture, like science and technology, grows by accretion, each new creator building on the works of those who came before. Overprotection stifles the very creative forces it's supposed to nurture. [ ]

The panel's opinion is a classic case of overprotection. Concerned about what it sees as a wrong done to Vanna White, the panel majority erects a property right of remarkable and dangerous breadth: Under the majority's opinion, it's now a tort for advertisers to remind the public of a celebrity. Not to use a celebrity's name, voice, signature or likeness; not to imply the celebrity endorses a product; but simply to evoke the celebrity's image in the public's mind. This Orwellian notion withdraws far more from the public domain than prudence and common sense allow. It conflicts with the Copyright Act and the Copyright Clause. It raises serious First Amendment problems. It's bad law, and it deserves a long, hard second look.

II

. . .

The ad that spawned this litigation starred a robot dressed in a wig, gown and jewelry reminiscent of Vanna White's hair and dress; the robot was posed next to a Wheel-of-Fortune-like game board. [ ] The caption read "Longest-running game show. 2012 A.D." The gag here, I take it, was that Samsung would still be around when White had been replaced by a robot.

Perhaps failing to see the humor, White sued, alleging Samsung infringed her right of publicity by "appropriating" her "identity." Under California law, White has the exclusive right to use her name, likeness, signature and voice for commercial purposes. [ ] But Samsung didn't use her name, voice or signature, and it certainly didn't use her likeness. The ad just wouldn't have been funny had it depicted White or someone who resembled her—the whole joke was that the game show host(ess) was a robot, not a real person. No one seeing the ad could have thought this was supposed to be White in 2012.

. . .

VI

. . .

The majority dismisses the First Amendment issue out of hand because Samsung's ad was commercial speech. [ ] So what? Commercial speech may be less protected by the First Amendment than noncommercial speech, but less protected means protected nonetheless. . . .

In our pop culture, where salesmanship must be entertaining and entertainment must sell, the line between the commercial and noncommercial has not merely blurred; it has disappeared. Is the Samsung parody any different from a parody on Saturday Night Live or in Spy Magazine? Both are equally profit-motivated. Both use a celebrity's identity to sell things—one to sell VCRs, the other to sell advertising. Both mock their subjects. Both try to make people laugh. Both add something, perhaps something worthwhile and memorable, perhaps not, to our culture. Both are things that the people being portrayed might dearly want to suppress. [ ]

. . .

VII

For better or worse, we are the Court of Appeals for the Hollywood Circuit. Millions of people toil in the shadow of the law we make, and much of their livelihood is made possible by the existence of intellectual property rights. But much of their livelihood—and much of the vibrancy of our culture—also depends on the existence of other intangible rights: The right to draw ideas from a rich and varied public domain, and the right to mock, for profit as well as fun, the cultural icons of our time.

In the name of avoiding the "evisceration" of a celebrity's rights in her image, the majority diminishes the rights of copyright holders and the public at large. In the name of fostering creativity, the majority suppresses it. Vanna White and those like her have been given something they never had before, and they've been given it at our expense. I cannot agree.

———

What limitation on recovery for a right of publicity is Judge Kozinski suggesting? Does it correspond to the approach taken by the court in *Winter*?

5. Jordan v. Jewel Food Stores, Inc., 743 F.3d 509 (7th Cir.2014) (Illinois law), involved a full page ad congratulating Michael Jordan on his induction into the Basketball Hall of Fame. The ad was placed in a special issue of Sports Illustrated devoted to Jordan. Jordan sued for, among other claims, invasion of privacy, and defendant Jewel countered that its noncommercial speech was entitled to full First Amendment protection.

The text of the ad (it also contained a picture of basketball sneakers with Jordan's number 23 displayed on them) read:

A Shoe In!

> After six NBA championships, scores of rewritten record books and numerous buzzer beaters, Michael Jordan's elevation in the Basketball Hall of Fame was never in doubt! Jewel-Osco salutes # 23 on his many accomplishments as we honor a fellow Chicagoan who was "just around the corner" for so many years.

Discussing Supreme Court precedent on the issue of distinguishing commercial from noncommercial speech, the court brushed aside the fact that the ad did not propose a commercial transaction. In context, the ad did attempt to promote Jewel's supermarkets and to do so through the connection to Jordan. Concluding the effort was a "form of image advertising," the court held that the First Amendment, while providing protection available for commercial speech, did not bar Jordan's claims.

Would Judge Kozinski afford recovery to Jordan? Would the *Winter* court?

6. *Advertising prior work.* New York has decided that a medium's use of an earlier story to advertise its own product does not come within "advertising purposes" under the statute. In Booth v. Curtis Publishing Co., 223 N.Y.S.2d 737 (App.Div.), aff'd without opinion, 182 N.E.2d 812 (N.Y.1962), Holiday magazine published a photograph of actress Shirley Booth in a story about a prominent resort. The color photograph was "a very striking one, show[ing] Miss Booth in the water up to her neck, but wearing a brimmed, high-crowned, street hat of straw." Several months after the story appeared, Holiday took out full-page advertisements in the New Yorker and Advertising Age magazines. Both reprinted the Booth photograph as a sample of the content of Holiday magazine. "Because of the photograph's striking qualities it would be quite effective in drawing attention to the advertisements; but it was also a sample of magazine content."

The court found the use of the photograph to be an "incidental" mentioning of plaintiff in the course of advertising itself. "It stands to reason that a publication can best prove its worth and illustrate its content by submission of complete copies of or extraction from past editions. . . . And, of course, it is true that the publisher must advertise in other public media, just as it must by poster, circular, cover, or soliciting letter. This is a practical necessity which the law may not ignore in giving effect to the purposes of the statute."

Although the court recognized that "realistically" the use of the photograph attracted the attention of the reader, that use was outweighed by the magazine's need to demonstrate its content. Finally, nothing in the advertisement suggested that plaintiff endorsed defendant's magazine.

See also Montana v. San Jose Mercury News, Inc., 40 Cal.Rptr.2d 639 (App.1995)(denying claim by former football star for defendant newspaper's sale of poster reproductions of its newspaper pages that showed plaintiff's photograph).

7. *Docudramas.* How should one analyze the technique of "docudramas," in which the program mixes truth and fiction? When ABC announced in 1982 that it was planning a docudrama on the life of Elizabeth Taylor, the actress responded by seeking an injunction. Her first theory was that "I am my own commodity. I am my own industry." Someday "I will write my autobiography, and perhaps film it, but that will be my choice. By doing this, ABC is taking away from my income." What if she had tried to enjoin an unauthorized biography?

Taylor's second theory was false light invasion of privacy. "They plan to use my name throughout the show, to hire an actress who supposedly resembles me and to have her speak lines which they want the public to believe I used in numerous personal and private conversations."

Taylor's lawyer contended: "The docudrama is a fairly new form of expression. It's not biography, it's not a documentary and it's not her story. It's a drama. We're talking about a live actress who is entitled not to have lies told about her. When you mix fact and fiction and say this is a life story, no matter how flattering you are, you're showing the subject in a false light, and creating a wrong image."

Later, ABC announced that it had dropped its plans, for "creative reasons." This account of the dispute is taken mainly from Tamar Lewin, *Whose Life Is It Anyway? Legally, It's Hard to Tell*, N.Y. Times, Nov. 21, 1982, § II, at 1. See Manson, The Television Docudrama and the Right of Publicity, in Comm. & the Law, Feb. 1985, at 41, concluding that since the docudrama is "neither fiction nor straight documentary" it does not fall within the protection accorded "biographies and documentaries; it does not provide a dissemination of information. Furthermore, the docudrama does not come under the first amendment protection of drama; it is not evident to the public that the events depicted in the docudrama are fictitious." By its "very nature, the docudrama tends to confuse the viewer, making it difficult to discern when true events in the life of the public figure portrayed merge and blend with purely fanciful fabrications. To confuse the viewer is a disservice to the public—to society. Further, confusion also diminishes and thereby damages the value of the public figure's 'name, likeness and persona.' "

NBC also pursued the development of a mini-series based on Taylor's life story. She was unsuccessful in attempting to enjoin production and broadcast of the mini-series, which was eventually completed in 1996. Taylor v. National Broadcasting Co., 1994 WL 780690 (Cal.Super.1994).

In a later case, Ruffin-Steinback v. dePasse, 82 F.Supp.2d 723 (E.D.Mich.2000), former members of the Motown group the "Temptations" sued several defendants involved in producing a mini-series docudrama based on the group's story. The court granted summary judgment for the defendants, holding that the depiction of one's life story, "particularly where some of the events are fictionalized," does not violate the right of publicity under Michigan law. It further observed that, "Plaintiffs have failed to cite caselaw from any jurisdiction supporting their claim that the right of publicity may be extended to preclude depiction of one's life-story."

Which is the easier case for the plaintiff—complaining about a work that is characterized as fiction or a docudrama?

8.   *Nonfamous plaintiffs.* A teenager was filmed at an accident site by a TV news crew. She had gone to the site of a car accident in the mistaken belief that her boyfriend's sister might have been killed. The news photographer sold the footage to a film producer. That footage later found its way into a movie called *Faces of Death,* which has been banned in 46 countries because of its grisly content. In the movie, the footage of the teenager was edited to make it appear that she was reacting to seeing the bloody body of a bicyclist killed by a semitrailer truck. What harm, if any, has the teenager suffered? Should she have an action for false light privacy? For commercial appropriation of her face? Recall the *Shulman* case, p. 1214 supra. The teenager sued the photographer, the film's producer, and its distributor, seeking royalties, damages, and an injunction barring exhibition until deletion of the scene. Editor & Publisher, Jan. 28, 1989, at 26. How would you measure her damages on each claim?

In Staruski v. Continental Telephone Co., 581 A.2d 266 (Vt.1990), plaintiff's employer, without consent, ran her name, photo, and a purported statement about what work she did and how she enjoyed her work. Although plaintiff was not a famous person she was entitled to sue for the appropriation of her name and likeness for commercial purposes. Although there may be "incidental" uses, as in crowd scenes in commercials, there was "nothing incidental about plaintiff's appearance in the ad."

Recall that the *Roberson* case itself, p. 1156 supra, involved a nonfamous person whose face was used for an advertisement.

CHAPTER XVI

INTENTIONAL ECONOMIC HARM

We turn now to a group of claims based on economic loss. By "economic loss," we mean pecuniary harm that does not result from personal injury or property damage. Thus, for example, street vendors in the Gulf Coast who lost sales because tourists stayed away following the BP oil spill suffered economic loss. These issues are not being raised for the first time. Recall, for example, that we have already considered questions of the duty owed by attorneys and accountants to non-clients, p. 299 supra—the harm suffered in such cases is economic loss. The question there was one of whether there is negligence liability for pure economic loss. Here we address intentionally caused economic harm and begin by considering liability for intentional misrepresentation. We continue with an examination of intentional efforts to interfere with the contract rights or expected economic advantage of others. Again, recall that we considered the scope of liability for negligent interference with these interests at p. 319 supra.

A. MISREPRESENTATION

1. INTRODUCTION

Although we have been concerned primarily with physical acts that have caused harm, we have also had occasion to consider situations in which words have caused harm. Recall the misleading reference letter that may have led to assault, p. 141 supra, problems of product labels and instructions, p. 608 supra, and the incorrect accounting reports and legal advice that caused harm to others, p. 299 supra. In this section we explore the problem of intentional misrepresentation, emphasizing the cases in which the parties are dealing directly with one another. The fear of unlimited liability, which played such a large role earlier, recedes—to be replaced by problems of determining the boundary between contract and tort, and the role of negotiations preliminary to entering into contracts. Although we have addressed the tort-contract line earlier, e.g., in connection with the line between the Uniform Commercial Code and tort law, p. 672 supra, our focus here is on the use of words that are designed to mislead and result in economic harm to the relying party.

Sometimes it is clear that only one cause of action, if any, is available. Thus, when the only problem is a failure to fulfill a contractual obligation, usually no tort remedy is available. But consider Channel Master Corp. v. Aluminum Ltd. Sales, Inc., 151 N.E.2d 833

(N.Y.1958), in which defendant orally expressed willingness to supply 400,000 pounds of aluminum ingot per month to plaintiff for five months. After the defendant failed to supply the ingots, any contract action would have been barred by the statute of frauds. But the court held that a tort action might still lie:

> The present action is in tort, not contract, depending not upon agreement between the parties, but rather upon deliberate misrepresentation of fact, relied on by the plaintiff to his detriment. . . . If the proof of a promise or contract, void under the statute of frauds, is essential to maintain the action, there may be no recovery, but, on the other hand, one who fraudulently misrepresents himself as intending to perform an agreement is subject to liability *in tort* whether the agreement is enforceable or not. [ ] The policy of the statute of frauds is "not directed at cases of dishonesty in making" a promise [ ]; never intended as an instrument to immunize fraudulent conduct, the statute may not be so employed.

Can you articulate what was deliberately misleading in the defendant's oral agreement to supply aluminum ingot?

In The Common Law Tradition: Deciding Appeals 473 (1960), Professor Karl Llewellyn attacked the holding in *Channel Master*:

> The situation is one in which the torts theorists (Restatement, Harper and James, Prosser, all gathered and cited) have launched as unconsidered a jamboree as ever has been suggested in the books: in the instant "application" of the idea, word-of-mouth negotiations for a contract which have led to no acceptance, which need not have led even to an offer, and which would in an action on an actually completed contract be incapable of submission to the jury for lack of a signed writing—these become admissible in the teeth of the statute against frauds and perjuries, admissible moreover, in such fashion as to allow damages of a range and extent which would be dubious of procurement in any action based on an agreement fully closed, formally authenticated, and unambiguously relied on. All of this by virtue of merely adjusting the pleadings and the evidence to run down an alley which is rather easier to travel with persuasiveness than is the alley of contract-closing. . . .

Later courts have recognized the tension between the two views and have reconciled them "through a rule, widely adopted by the state and federal courts, pursuant to which a false promise can support a claim of fraud only where that promise was 'collateral or extraneous' to the terms of an enforceable agreement in place between the parties." GBJ Corp. v. Eastern Ohio Paving Co., 139 F.3d 1080 (6th Cir.1998).

Questions about allowing tort remedies in these cases may arise when consideration fails, when the statutes of limitations between tort and contract differ, or when the contract itself asserts that neither party is relying on oral statements that are not reflected in the written contract. States disagree about the viability of tort in each situation. When both tort and contract actions are available, the plaintiff's preference will depend upon such factors as the applicable measure of compensatory damages, the availability of punitive damages, and the impact of the statute of limitations. Of course, proof of wrongdoing is more likely to play a role in tort law. Although the remedy of rescission does not require a showing of fault, Seneca Wire & Mfg. Co. v. A. B. Leach & Co., 159 N.E. 700 (N.Y.1928), the plaintiff may not be in a position to undo the transaction after learning about the misrepresentation. The parties may have engaged in further deals or actions that make it impossible to rescind. See, e.g., Mertens v. Wolfeboro National Bank, 402 A.2d 1335 (N.H.1979).

2. DECEIT

The tort actions arising from misrepresentations first became clearly identified in cases involving deliberate misstatements. Actions for this type of misrepresentation became known as actions for "deceit" or "fraud."

Scienter. In the leading English case, Derry v. Peek, 14 A.C. 337 (H.L. 1889), Lord Herschell stated that:

> [F]raud is proved when it is shown that a false representation has been made (1) knowingly, or (2) without belief in its truth, or (3) recklessly, careless whether it be true or false. Although I have treated the second and third as distinct cases, I think the third is but an instance of the second, for one who makes a statement under such circumstances can have no real belief in the truth of what he states. To prevent a false statement being fraudulent, there must, I think, always be an honest belief in its truth.

As a corollary he noted that "making a false statement through want of care falls far short of, and is a very different thing from fraud, and the same may be said of a false representation honestly believed though on insufficient grounds." On the matter of belief he stated:

> I quite admit that the statements of witnesses as to their belief are by no means to be accepted blindfolded. The probabilities must be considered. Whenever it is necessary to arrive at a conclusion as to the state of mind of another person, and to determine whether his belief under given circumstances was such as he alleges, we can only do so by applying the standard of conduct which our own experience of the ways of men has enabled us to form; by asking ourselves whether a

reasonable man situated as the defendants were, with their knowledge and means of knowledge, might well believe what they state they did believe, and consider that the representations made were substantially true.

How does this compare with the notion of "actual malice" developed in libel cases? What is the apparent role of honest, but unreasonable, belief?

In Chatham Furnace Co. v. Moffatt, 18 N.E. 168 (Mass.1888), the court stated:

[T]he charge of fraudulent intent, in an action for deceit, may be maintained by proof of a statement made as of the party's own knowledge, which is false; provided the thing stated is not merely a matter of opinion, estimate or judgment, but is susceptible of actual knowledge; and in such case it is not necessary to make any further proof of an actual intent to deceive. The fraud consists in stating that the party knows the thing to exist when he does not know it to exist; and, if he does not know it to exist, he must ordinarily be deemed to know that he does not. Forgetfulness of its existence after a former knowledge, or a mere belief of its existence, will not warrant or excuse a statement of actual knowledge.

The types of conduct discussed in *Derry v. Peek* are grouped under the Latin term "scienter." The elements of the action for deceit were stated by the court in *Channel Master* to be "[mis]representation of a material existing fact, falsity, *scienter*, deception and injury."

In Greycas, Inc. v. Proud, 826 F.2d 1560 (7th Cir.1987), an attorney incorrectly asserted that no liens existed on a client's property. The court noted that although the plaintiff was suing for negligent misrepresentation, the case appeared to be one of fraud:

No doubt Proud was negligent in failing to conduct a search, but we are not clear why the misrepresentation is alleged to be negligent rather than deliberate and hence fraudulent. . . . Proud did not merely say, "There are no liens"; he said, "I have conducted a U.C.C., tax, and judgment search"; and not only is this statement, too, a false one, but its falsehood cannot have been inadvertent, for Proud knew he had not conducted such a search.

The court then speculated about the plaintiff's choice of theory:

It may have feared that Proud's insurance policy for professional malpractice excluded deliberate wrongdoing from its coverage, or may not have wanted to bear the higher burden of proving fraud, or may have feared that an accusation of fraud would make it harder to settle the case—for most cases, of course, are settled, though this one has not been.

The passage about the "the higher burden of proving fraud" refers to the fact that in civil fraud cases, most state courts have stated that plaintiffs must prove their case with "clear and convincing evidence." The explanation has generally been based on the close relationship between civil and criminal fraud or on the ease with which plaintiff may claim that the defendant has made a specific statement at a time when no one else was present. This position has been rejected in a few states on the ground that there is no reason to reject the usual preponderance of the evidence standard in civil cases involving fraud. See the discussion in Liodas v. Sahadi, 562 P.2d 316 (Cal.1977).

Ambit of liability. Even when courts find the requisite scienter to justify a deceit action, they generally restrict the persons eligible to recover damages by permitting recovery only by those to whom the misrepresentations were made. If a prospective victim declined to act on the representation but told a friend about the opportunity, early courts denied the friend an action.

The ambit has been expanding. See, e.g., Geernaert v. Mitchell, 37 Cal.Rptr.2d 483 (App.1995)(extending a fraudulent seller's liability to a buyer several steps down the chain where each successive seller— perhaps innocently—repeated the misrepresentation). Nonetheless, it still appears that the scope of liability for misrepresentation is narrower for both intentional and negligent tortfeasors than it is for those who commit intentional or negligent acts resulting in physical injury or damage to property. This, of course, recalls the reservations courts expressed about extending liability for economic harm caused by negligence, in Chapter IV.

Material existing fact. Problems of scienter aside, the greatest difficulty has surrounded the efforts to identify a "material existing fact." Why should a fact have to be "material" if it is deliberately false and achieves its purpose of deceiving the plaintiff to his detriment? Does the requirement help in determining whether the defendant should have foreseen or did foresee the plaintiff's reliance on the misrepresentation? The Third Restatement of Torts provides that a fact is material if "a reasonable person would give weight to it in deciding whether to enter into the relevant transaction, or if the defendant knew that the plaintiff would give it weight (whether reasonably or not)." Restatement (Third) of Torts: Liability for Economic Harm § 9 cmt. d (Tent. Draft No. 2, 2014).

The term "existing fact" has a broad sweep. Courts generally consider a statement of intention to be a statement of fact sufficient to support a fraud claim, id. § 15, because a person's intent is capable of ascertainment, although almost always only through circumstantial evidence.

In California Conserving Co. v. D'Avanzo, 62 F.2d 528 (2d Cir.1933), defendant, when he was in dire financial straits, bought goods from the plaintiff on credit. He went bankrupt and was unable to pay for the goods. The plaintiff sought to reclaim the goods for fraud. If successful, he would not have to share pro rata with other creditors. In discussing the alleged fraud, Judge Learned Hand observed:

> He may mean to pay if he survives, though he knows that he is extremely unlikely to do so. If his promise declares only that he intends to pay, it would be hard in such a case to say that he has deceived the seller; and the doctrine presupposes some deceit. But promises, like other utterances, must be read with their usual implications. True, they are predictions and no one can foretell the future; the seller knows this as well as the buyer. However, a man's affairs may reach such a pass that ordinarily honest persons would no longer buy, if they had no greater chance to pay; and the seller is entitled to rely upon that implication. He may assume that the buyer would not promise if the odds were so heavy against him. He may read the promise as more than the declaration of a conditional intent, as affirming that that intent had reasonable hope of fruition. In that event, if the buyer knows that it has no such hope, he deceives the seller, as much as though he intended not to pay at all. This duty does not indeed depend upon what reasonable persons would think of his chances.

Another aspect of defining "fact" involves the distinction between "fact" and "opinion." Consider the statement of Judge Learned Hand in Vulcan Metals Co. v. Simmons Mfg. Co., 248 F. 853 (2d Cir.1918), involving claims made concerning a vacuum cleaner. To induce the buyer to take over its vacuum cleaner manufacturing business, Simmons made a number of representations about the product. These included commendations of the cleanliness, economy, and efficiency of the machine; that it was absolutely perfect in even the smallest detail; that water power, by which it worked, marked the most economical means of operating a vacuum cleaner with the greatest efficiency; that the cleaning was more thoroughly done than by beating or brushing; that, having been perfected, it was a necessity which everyone could afford; that it was so simple that a child of six could use it; that it worked completely and thoroughly; that it was simple, long-lived, easily operated, and effective; that it was the only sanitary portable cleaner on the market; that perfect satisfaction would result from its use; that it would last a lifetime; that it was the only practical jet machine on the market; and that perfect satisfaction would result from its use, if properly adjusted. Speaking of these claims, Judge Hand observed:

> An opinion is a fact, and it may be a very relevant fact; the expression of an opinion is the assertion of a belief, and any rule which condones the expression of a consciously false opinion condones a consciously false statement of fact. When the parties are so situated that the buyer may reasonably rely upon the expression of the seller's opinion, it is no excuse to

give a false one. [ ] And so it makes much difference whether the parties stand "on an equality." For example, we should treat very differently the expressed opinion of a chemist to a layman about the properties of a composition from the same opinion between chemist and chemist, when the buyer had full opportunity to examine. The reason of the rule lies, we think, in this: There are some kinds of talk which no sensible man takes seriously, and if he does he suffers from his credulity. If we were all scrupulously honest, it would not be so; but, as it is, neither party usually believes what the seller says about his own opinions, and each knows it. Such statements, like the claims of campaign managers before election, are rather designed to allay the suspicion which would attend their absence than to be understood as having any relation to objective truth. It is quite true that they induce a compliant temper in the buyer, but it is by a much more subtle process than through the acceptance of his claims for his wares.

. . .

In the case at bar, since the buyer was allowed full opportunity to examine the cleaner and to test it out, we put the parties upon an equality. It seems to us that general statements as to what the cleaner would do, even though consciously false, were not of a kind to be taken literally by the buyer. As between manufacturer and customer, it may not be so; but this was the case of taking over a business, after ample chance to investigate. Such a buyer, who the seller rightly expects will undertake an independent and adequate inquiry into the actual merits of what he gets, has no right to treat as material in his determination statements like these. The standard of honesty permitted by the rule may not be the best; but, as Holmes, J., says in Deming v. Darling, 20 N.E. 107 [Mass.1889], the chance that the higgling preparatory to a bargain may be afterwards translated into assurances of quality may perhaps be a set-off to the actual wrong allowed by the rule as it stands. We therefore think that the District Court was right in disregarding all these misrepresentations.

Thus, even opinions can be the basis for a fraud claim. How to distinguish between those that are actionable and those that, like the ones in *Vulcan* appear to be the sort of "puffing" that a buyer should view skeptically and verify before relying on?

Consider Powell v. Flechter, 18 N.Y.S. 451 (N.Y.Com.Pl.1892), in which defendant vendor knowingly misrepresented to plaintiff purchaser, "a woman utterly ignorant of violins and their value," that a violin was made by Gaspard di Dniffoprugear [sic] and was worth at least $1,000. The trial record showed that plaintiff did not rely on the representation of make but did rely on the representation of value. On defendant's appeal from a judgment for plaintiff, the court stated that an intentionally false statement as to value is actionable "where one in purchasing goods, the value of which can only be known to experts, relies upon the vendor, who is a dealer in such goods, to give him accurate information concerning them."

In Banner v. Lyon & Healy, Inc., 293 N.Y.S. 236 (App.Div.1937), aff'd without opinion, 13 N.E.2d 774 (N.Y.1938), defendant sold plaintiff a violin represented as having been made by Stradivarius. There was evidence that it was made by another violin maker. The court considered the statement to be one of opinion:

> When the sale took place in 1919, Stradivarius had been dead for some 200 years, a fact known to the whole world and to the parties concerned. Plaintiff himself was a noted violinist, generally familiar with violins and of those made by Stradivarius. In these circumstances, he must have understood that the defendant Freeman, in any representations made, was but expressing his opinion and honest belief that the instrument was in all respects genuine.

Would a different result follow if the purchaser were the plaintiff in *Powell*? Do consumers generally expect honesty in all types of transactions? Do merchants expect honesty from each other? Should the law attempt to craft the rules to what typical parties actually expect, or should it attempt to mold expectations?

The Third Restatement addresses the matter of false opinions:

A false statement of opinion may result in liability only if

> (a) the parties are in a fiduciary or confidential relationship, or
>
> (b) the defendant claims to have expertise or other knowledge not accessible to the plaintiff, and offers the opinion to provide a basis for reliance by the plaintiff.

Restatement (Third) of Torts: Liability for Economic Harm § 14 (Tent. Draft No. 2, 2014). Does section 14 capture the considerations reflected in the cases discussed above?

Not all misrepresentations are made with words. One important cluster of cases involves acts of active concealment—cases in which defendants paint over leaking surfaces to hide them from a prospective buyer. These cases have presented no problems for the courts and have been analyzed as though the defendant had made a deliberate misrepresentation. See Herzog v. Capital Co., 164 P.2d 8 (Cal.1945). A situation that still presents serious problems is that of nondisclosure, discussed in the following case.

Ollerman v. O'Rourke Co., Inc.

Supreme Court of Wisconsin, 1980.
94 Wis.2d 17, 288 N.W.2d 95.

■ ABRAHAMSON, JUSTICE.

This appeal is from an order overruling the motion of O'Rourke Co., Inc., the seller, . . . to dismiss Roy Ollerman's, the buyer's, amended complaint for failing to state a claim upon which relief can be granted. We conclude that the complaint states a claim, and we affirm the order of the circuit court.

[The buyer alleged that he bought a vacant lot in order to build a house, and that while excavating for the house a well was uncapped and water was released.]

The complaint further alleges that the seller is a corporation engaged in the business of developing and selling real estate; that it is experienced in matters of real estate; that it had owned and subdivided the area of real estate in which the subject lot is located; that it was offering the subject lot and other lots in the same area for public sale; that it is familiar with the particular area of real estate in which the lot is located; that the area is zoned residential and that the seller knew it was zoned residential.

The complaint further states that the buyer "was a stranger to the area"; that he was inexperienced in matters of real estate transactions; that he purchased the lot to construct a house; that he did not know of the existence of a well under the land surface hidden from view; that if he had known of the well, he either would not have purchased the property or would have purchased it at a lower price; that the well constituted a defective condition of the lot; that the well made the property worth less for residential purposes than he had been led to believe; that the well made the property unsuitable for building without added expense; and that the seller's failure to disclose the existence of the well was relied upon by the buyer and he was thereby induced to buy this lot in ignorance of the well.

. . .

Additional allegations applicable to what is labeled in the complaint as the "first cause of action" are that the seller, through its agents, knew of the existence of the underground well and, in order to induce buyer to buy the land, "falsely and with intent to defraud," failed to disclose this fact which it had a duty to disclose and which would have had a material bearing on the construction of a residence on the property.

[A "second cause of action" alleged that defendant knew or should have known about the well, and had a duty to ascertain and disclose such information.]

. . .

This court has recognized that misrepresentation is a generic concept separable into the three familiar tort classifications: intent (sometimes called fraudulent misrepresentation, deceit or intentional deceit), negligence and strict responsibility.

. . .

II.

We discuss first whether the complaint states a claim for intentional misrepresentation. Initially we observe, as did the seller, that the complaint does not allege the first two elements of the tort of intentional misrepresentation, namely that the seller made a representation of fact and that the representation was untrue. The gravamen of the wrong is the nature of the false words used and the reliance which they may reasonably induce. In lieu of these allegations of false words, the complaint recites that the seller failed to disclose a fact, the existence of the well. The general rule is that silence, a failure to disclose a fact, is not an intentional misrepresentation unless the seller has a duty to disclose.[7] If there is a duty to disclose a fact, failure to disclose that fact is treated in the law as equivalent to a representation of the nonexistence of the fact. . . .

The question thus presented in the case at bar is whether the seller had a duty to disclose to the buyer the existence of the well. If there is a duty to disclose, the seller incurs tort liability for intentional misrepresentation (i.e., the representation of the non-existence of the fact), if the elements of the tort of intentional misrepresentation are proved. [ ]

The question of legal duty presents an issue of law. . . .

We recognize that the traditional rule in Wisconsin is that in an action for intentional misrepresentation the seller of real estate, dealing at arm's length with the buyer, has no duty to disclose information to the buyer and therefore has no liability in an action for intentional misrepresentation for failure to disclose.

The traditional legal rule that there is no duty to disclose in an arm's-length transaction is part of the common law doctrine of caveat emptor which is traced to the attitude of rugged individualism reflected in the business economy and the law of the 19th century. The law of misrepresentation has traditionally been closely aligned with mores of the commercial world because the type of interest protected by the law of misrepresentation in business transactions is the interest in formulating business judgments without being misled by others that is, an interest in not being cheated.

---

[7]   3 Restatement (Second) of Torts, sec. 551, Comment *b* (1977) states:

". . . In the absence of a duty of disclosure . . . one who is negotiating a business transaction is not liable in deceit because of his failure to disclose a fact that he knows his adversary would regard as material. . . ." [ ]

Under the doctrine of caveat emptor no person was required to tell all that he or she knew in a business transaction, for in a free market the diligent should not be deprived of the fruits of superior skill and knowledge lawfully acquired. The business world, and the law reflecting business mores and morals, required the parties to a transaction to use their faculties and exercise ordinary business sense, and not to call on the law to stand in loco parentis to protect them in their ordinary dealings with other business people.

The picture in sales and in land deals is, in the beginning, that of a community whose trade is simple and face to face and whose traders are neighbors. The goods and the land were there to be seen during the negotiation and particularly in the case of land, everybody knew everybody's land; if not, trade was an arm's length proposition with wits matched against skill. Of course caveat emptor would be the rule in such a society. But caveat emptor was more than a rule of no liability; it was a philosophy that left each individual to his own devices with a minimum of public imposition of standards of fair practice. In the beginning the common law did grant relief from fraud and did recognize that if the seller made an express promise as to his product at the time of the sale he remained liable after the sale on this "collateral" promise. Indeed covenants for title in the deed were such collateral promises which survived the sale. [ ]

Over the years society's attitudes toward good faith and fair dealing in business transactions have undergone significant change, and this change has been reflected in the law. Courts have departed from or relaxed the "no duty to disclose" rule by carving out exceptions to the rule and by refusing to adhere to the rule when it works an injustice. Thus courts have held that the rule does not apply where the seller actively conceals a defect or where he prevents investigation;[13] where the seller has told a half-truth or has made an ambiguous statement if the seller's intent is to create a false impression and he does so; where there is a fiduciary relationship between the parties; or where the facts are peculiarly and exclusively within the knowledge of one party to the transaction and the other party is not in a position to discover the facts for himself.

On the basis of the complaint, the case at bar does not appear to fall into one of these well-recognized exceptions to the "no duty to disclose" rule. However, Dean Prosser has found a "rather amorphous tendency on the part of most courts toward finding a duty of disclosure

---

[13] 3 Restatement (Second) of Torts, sec. 550 (1977) states:

"One party to a transaction who by concealment or other action intentionally prevents the other from acquiring material information is subject to the same liability to the other, for pecuniary loss as though he had stated the nonexistence of the matter that the other was thus prevented from discovering." [ ]

in cases where the defendant has special knowledge or means of knowledge not open to the plaintiff and is aware that the plaintiff is acting under a misapprehension as to facts which could be of importance to him, and would probably affect his decision."

Dean Keeton [in Fraud Concealment and Nondisclosure, 15 Tex.L.Rev. 1, 31 (1936)], described these cases abandoning the "no duty to disclose" rule as follows:

In the present stage of the law, the decisions show a drawing away from this idea (that nondisclosure is not actionable), and there can be seen an attempt by many courts to reach a just result in so far as possible, but yet maintaining the degree of certainty which the law must have. The statement may often be found that if either party to a contract of sale conceals or suppresses a material fact which he is in good faith bound to disclose then his silence is fraudulent.

The attitude of the courts toward nondisclosure is undergoing a change and . . . it would seem that the object of the law in these cases should be to impose on parties to the transaction a duty to speak whenever justice, equity, and fair dealing demand it. This statement is made only with reference to instances where the party to be charged is an actor in the transaction. This duty to speak does not result from an implied representation by silence, but exists because a refusal to speak constitutes unfair conduct.

The test Dean Keeton derives from the cases to determine when the rule of nondisclosure should be abandoned—that is "whenever justice, equity and fair dealing demand it"—presents, as one writer states, "a somewhat nebulous standard, praiseworthy as looking toward more stringent business ethics, but possibly difficult of practical application." [ ]

. . .

The draftsmen of the most recent Restatement of Torts (Second) (1977) have attempted to formulate a rule embodying this trend in the cases toward a more frequent recognition of a duty to disclose. Sec. 551(1) of the Restatement sets forth the traditional rule that one who fails to disclose a fact that he knows may induce reliance in a business transaction is subject to the same liability as if he had represented the nonexistence of the matter that he failed to disclose if, and only if, he is under a duty to exercise reasonable care to disclose the matter in question.[17] Subsection (2) of sec. 551 then sets forth the conditions

---

[17] Sec. 551 Liability for Nondisclosure

"(1) One who fails to disclose to another a fact that he knows may justifiably induce the other to act or refrain from acting in a business transaction is subject to the same liability to the other as though he had represented the nonexistence of the matter that he has failed to disclose, if, but only if, he is under a duty to the other to exercise reasonable care to disclose the matter in question."

under which the seller has a duty to use reasonable care to disclose certain information.[18] Sec. 551(2)(e) is the "catch-all" provision setting forth conditions under which a duty to disclose exists; it states that a party to a transaction is under a duty to exercise reasonable care to disclose to the other "facts basic to the transaction, if he knows that the other is about to enter into it under a mistake as to them, and that the other, because of the relationship between them, the customs of the trade or other objective circumstances, would reasonably expect a disclosure of those facts." Comment *l* to sec. 551 recognizes the difficulty of specifying the factors that give rise to a reasonable expectation of disclosure:

> *l.* The continuing development of modern business ethics has, however, limited to some extent this privilege to take advantage of ignorance. There are situations in which the defendant not only knows that his bargaining adversary is acting under a mistake basic to the transaction, but also knows that the adversary, by reason of the relation between them, the customs of the trade or other objective circumstances, is reasonably relying upon a disclosure of the unrevealed fact if it exists. In this type of case good faith and fair dealing may require a disclosure.
>
> It is extremely difficult to be specific as to the factors that give rise to this known, and reasonable, expectation of disclosure. In general, the cases in which the rule stated in Clause (e) has been applied have been those in which the advantage taken of the plaintiff's ignorance is so shocking to the ethical sense of the community, and is so extreme and unfair, as to amount to a form of swindling, in which the plaintiff is led by appearances into a bargain that is a trap, of whose essence and substance he is unaware. In such a case, even in a tort action for deceit, the plaintiff is entitled to be compensated for the loss that he has sustained.

---

[18] Sec. 551

"(2) One party to a business transaction is under a duty to exercise reasonable care to disclose to the other before the transaction is consummated,

(a) matters known to him that the other is entitled to know because of a fiduciary or other similar relation of trust and confidence between them; and

(b) matters known to him that he knows to be necessary to prevent his partial or ambiguous statement of the facts from being misleading; and

(c) subsequently acquired information that he knows will make untrue or misleading a previous representation that when made was true or believed to be so; and

(d) the falsity of a representation not made with the expectation that it would be acted upon, if he subsequently learns that the other is about to act in reliance upon it in a transaction with him; and

(e) facts basic to the transaction, if he knows that the other is about to enter into it under a mistake as to them, and that the other, because of the relationship between them, the customs of the trade or other objective circumstances, would reasonably expect a disclosure of those facts."

Section 551(2)(e) of the Restatement (Second) of Torts limits the duty to disclose to disclosure of those "facts basic" to the transaction. Comment *j* to sec. 551 differentiates between basic facts and material facts as follows: "A basic fact is a fact that is assumed by the parties as a basis for the transaction itself. It is a fact that goes to the basis, or essence, of the transaction, and is an important part of the substance of what is bargained for or dealt with. Other facts may serve as important and persuasive inducements to enter into the transaction, but not go to its essence. These facts may be material, but they are not basic."

However, the draftsmen of the Restatement recognized that the law was developing to expand the duty to disclosure beyond the duty described in [comment *l* to] sec. 551:

> There are indications, also, that with changing ethical attitudes in many fields of modern business, the concept of facts basic to the transaction may be expanding and the duty to use reasonable care to disclose the facts may be increasing somewhat. This Subsection is not intended to impede that development.

This court has moved away from the rule of caveat emptor in real estate transactions, as have courts in other states.

. . .

An analysis of the cases of this jurisdiction and others indicates that the presence of the following elements is significant to persuade a court of the fairness and equity of imposing a duty on a vendor of real estate to disclose known facts: the condition is "latent" and not readily observable by the purchaser; the purchaser acts upon the reasonable assumption that the condition does (or does not) exist; the vendor has special knowledge or means of knowledge not available to the purchaser; and the existence of the condition is material to the transaction, that is, it influences whether the transaction is concluded at all or at the same price.

The seller argues that public policy demands that we not abandon the traditional rule that no action lies against the seller of real estate for failure to disclose in an arm's-length transaction. The seller contends, in its brief, that if this court affirms the circuit court's order overruling the motion to dismiss and allows the buyer to proceed to trial, the court is adopting "what really amounts to a strict policy of 'let the seller beware.'" The seller goes on to state, "Woe indeed to anyone who sells a home, a vacant lot or other piece of real estate and fails to itemize with particularity or give written notice to each prospective buyer of every conceivable condition in and around the property, regardless of whether such a condition is dangerous, defective or could become so by the negligence or recklessness of others. A seller of real estate is not and should not be made an insurer or guarantor of the competence of those with whom the purchaser may later contract."

The seller's position is that imposing a duty to disclose on a vendor of real estate dealing at arm's length with a purchaser would result in an element of uncertainty pervading real estate transactions; that there would be chaos if a vendor were subject to liability after parting with ownership and control of the property; that a rash of litigation would ensue; and that a purchaser could protect himself or herself by inspection and inquiry and by demanding warranties.

The seller's arguments are not persuasive in light of the facts alleged in the complaint and our narrow holding in this case.

Where the vendor is in the real estate business and is skilled and knowledgeable and the purchaser is not, the purchaser is in a poor position to discover a condition which is not readily discernible, and the purchaser may justifiably rely on the knowledge and skill of the vendor. Thus, in this instant case a strong argument for imposing a duty on the seller to disclose material facts is this "reliance factor." The buyer portrayed in this complaint had a reasonable expectation of honesty in the marketplace, that is, that the vendor would disclose material facts which it knew and which were not readily discernible. Under these circumstances the law should impose a duty of honesty on the seller.

In order to determine whether the complaint states a claim for intentional misrepresentation we hold that a subdivider-vendor of a residential lot has a duty to a "non-commercial" purchaser to disclose facts which are known to the vendor, which are material to the transaction, and which are not readily discernible to the purchaser. A fact is known to the vendor if the vendor has actual knowledge of the fact or if the vendor acted in reckless disregard as to the existence of the fact. This usage of the word "know" is the same as in an action for intentional misrepresentation based on a false statement. [ ] A fact is material if a reasonable purchaser would attach importance to its existence or nonexistence in determining the choice of action in the transaction in question; or if the vendor knows or has reason to know that the purchaser regards or is likely to regard the matter as important in determining the choice of action, although a reasonable purchaser would not so regard it. See 3 Restatement (Second) of Torts, sec. 538 (1977). Whether the fact is or is not readily discernible will depend on the nature of the fact, the relation of the vendor and purchaser and the nature of the transaction.

The seller's brief asserts that the well is not a material fact because it does not constitute a defective condition; that the existence of the well was well known in the community; and that the buyer should have made inquiry about the lot. These are matters to be raised at trial, not on a motion to dismiss. The buyer must prove at trial that the existence of the well was a material fact and that his reliance was justifiable.

. . .

For the reasons set forth, we hold that the allegations of the complaint state a claim upon which relief can be granted and that the motion to dismiss the complaint was properly overruled.

[Three concurring justices agreed that the complaint set forth a claim on which relief could be granted. They disagreed with the majority's extended discussion of the law when only an amended complaint was before it. "There is no necessity for expounding on various legal principles relating to the theories of recovery advanced by the plaintiff at the pleading stage. In most instances, attempting to decide the law of the case when the case has not been tried and the facts are not before the court is an appellate practice to be avoided."]

NOTES AND QUESTIONS

1.   The complaint asserts that the seller "falsely and with intent to defraud" failed to disclose the well's existence. How can silence ever be "false"? How might it be found false in this case?

2.   The court lists several categories of cases in which courts had already decided that silence was actionable, but notes that plaintiff's case "does not appear to fall into" any of them. Why not? What is the basis on which this complaint is upheld?

3.   When the court lists the elements that it finds working toward a duty to disclose in this case, one of them is that "the vendor has special knowledge or means of knowledge not available to the purchaser." Won't that always be the case?

4.   *Limits on fraudulent misrepresentation.* In Doe v. Dilling, 888 N.E.2d 24 (Ill.2008), plaintiff brought an action against the parents of her deceased fiancé. The fiancé had been ill, and the parents told plaintiff that their son suffered from heavy-metal poisoning and Lyme disease. In fact, he was HIV-positive and had been diagnosed with AIDS. Plaintiff alleged fraudulent misrepresentation against the parents, which allegedly resulted in her delaying HIV testing and treatment. In overturning a $2 million verdict for plaintiff, the court held that fraudulent misrepresentation is limited to the commercial and transactional context and economic harm. While other torts may be available when a victim suffers personal injury or emotional harm, the court found none was available under these circumstances to impose a duty on the parents with regard to their representations to plaintiff. Alternatively, the court found that any reliance by plaintiff was not justifiable. See note 8 infra. To similar effect is Tolliver v. Visiting Nurse Ass'n of Midlands, 771 N.W.2d 908 (Neb.2009), in which the court held that the estate of decedent could not recover for pain and suffering decedent experienced as a result of misrepresentation by defendants about the care provided at defendant hospice. But see Nelson v. Progressive Corp., 976 P.2d 859 (Alaska 1999)(permitting recovery for emotional harm in bad faith, misrepresentation claim against insurer so long as consequent harm is severe).

5. *Negligent misrepresentation.* In an omitted portion of the *Ollerman* opinion, the court addressed plaintiff's negligent misrepresentation claim, observing that imposing a duty of due care for representations that cause economic harm is a more difficult issue than when the misrepresentation involves deceit. Courts have been more reluctant to permit recovery for negligently misrepresentations that cause economic harm than for those causing physical injury, and a narrower scope of liability that for fraud is justified by the lesser culpability of one who unknowingly but carelessly makes a false statement. This subject is addressed in detail in Chapter IV-B, p. 299 supra.

6. *Partial disclosure.* In Junius Const. Corp. v. Cohen, 178 N.E. 672 (N.Y.1931), plaintiff was to buy land from defendant, who informed plaintiff that the final maps of the local governing body showed two roads that, if opened, would modify the plot's boundaries to minor extents. Defendant did not tell plaintiff about a third street that, if opened, would cut the plot in half. Judge Cardozo stated:

> Misrepresentation, if there was any, as to a risk so vital was something that went to the very essence of the bargain. We do not say that the seller was under a duty to mention the projected streets at all. That question is not here. What we say is merely this, that having undertaken or professed to mention them, he could not fairly stop half way, listing those that were unimportant and keeping silent as to the other. The enumeration of two streets, described as unopened but projected, was a tacit representation that the land to be conveyed was subject to no others, and certainly subject to no others materially affecting the value of the purchase.

Does the rationale apply only to other roads or would it extend to sewer lines? How about a forthcoming tax increase? Are there any limits?

7. *Falsity.* Although the element of "falsity" has presented little legal difficulty, it produces many controverted questions of fact. Courts have concluded that although statements might literally be accurate, they might be found to be false if they would mislead recipients. In Remeikis v. Boss & Phelps, Inc., 419 A.2d 986 (D.C.App.1980), for example, a termite report stated that there was "no visible evidence of present termite activity." Although literally true, it might be actionable if "made to create a false impression" as with extensive "invisible" damage or visible evidence of "past" activity. The court relied on an earlier case in which the seller of a rooming house was held liable for a statement that accurately told the level of present rentals but that left the incorrect impression that those rental charges were legally permissible.

8. *Reliance.* What is the role of reliance in *Ollerman*? The element of reliance is a composite of several different ideas. The first is "actual" reliance, which corresponds to the factual cause requirement in other torts. If the plaintiff has not relied on the defendant's misrepresentation, then the critical connection between misconduct and damages is missing. In Nader v. Allegheny Airlines, Inc., 626 F.2d 1031 (D.C.Cir.1980), the plaintiff was "bumped" from a plane because by the time he arrived other confirmed passengers on the overbooked flight had already been seated. As a result he missed a rally at which he was to deliver a speech. He asserted that the airline had misrepresented its policy concerning "confirmed" reservations by not informing passengers that it engaged in overbooking. Among the reasons for dismissing the case, the court noted that Nader "was an extraordinarily knowledgeable passenger, an able lawyer and a famous and distinguished advocate of consumer rights, including the rights of airline passengers." In fact, he had been bumped twice before in similar situations, the second time only two days before he reserved his seat for the Allegheny flight. It "cannot be said that Nader relied on his confirmed reservation with Allegheny as a guarantee of passage."

A scope of liability aspect of reliance requires that plaintiff's harm must result from reliance on the misrepresented fact. Assume that D misrepresents several facts about a company's financial health in order to induce P to buy that company's stock. D is not liable if the stock suddenly falls in value solely because of the unexpected death of the company's chief operating officer—even though P would not have bought the stock had D not misrepresented. See Restatement (Third) of Torts: Liability for Economic Harm § 12 (Tent. Draft No. 2, 2014).

The reliance must also be "justifiable." The Third Restatement in comment d to section 11 explains:

> Justifiable reliance amounts to freedom from recklessness: plaintiffs who close their eyes to a known or obvious danger that a statement is fraudulent cannot recover losses they suffer from reliance on it. [ ] The rules also differ because reasonableness is measured against community standards of behavior. Justifiable reliance has a personalized character. It is measured by reference to the plaintiff's capabilities and knowledge; a plaintiff's sophistication may affect a court's judgments about what dangers were fairly considered obvious. Compare Illustrations 7 and 8. Finally, the justifiable reliance required by this Section does not call for a comparison of the fault attributable to the plaintiff and defendant. It is a threshold requirement; if it is satisfied, incremental doubts about the plaintiff's degree of care will not reduce the resulting recovery from the intentional tortfeasor.

> Requiring justifiable reliance creates some tension with the usual rule that contributory negligence is no defense to an intentional-tort claim. The requirement serves partly to bolster the element of actual reliance; if a plaintiff claims to have relied on the defendant's statements in the face of obvious indications that the statements were false, one may doubt that the plaintiff meaningfully relied at all. [ ] The requirement does not impose a duty of active investigation on a plaintiff, and does not entitle a defendant to exploit a plaintiff's foolishness with impunity; if the defendant has deliberately preyed on the plaintiff's inattention, that inattention should not be considered an instance of unjustifiable reliance.

Does this discussion of reliance clarify its role on remand in *Ollerman*?

Can reliance be found in inaction? See Small v. Fritz Companies, Inc., 65 P.3d 1255 (Cal.2003), recognizing generally a misrepresentation action for shareholders who, relying on alleged misrepresentations, hold their stock instead of selling it, but imposing a heightened pleading burden on plaintiffs for reliance. Another complex aspect of reliance that applies to the securities world involves whether a plaintiff can recover for what is called "fraud on the market." This theory excuses plaintiffs from showing individual reliance where a public misrepresentation affects the price of a security and rests on the idea that purchasers of publicly traded securities may rely on the integrity of the stock market and its pricing of stocks. See the extended discussion in Kaufman v. i-Stat Corp., 754 A.2d 1188 (N.J.2000).

9. *Defenses.* As stated in the Restatement excerpt in note 8, courts generally agree that contributory negligence is no defense whatever to intentional misrepresentation. See Florenzano v. Olson, 387 N.W.2d 168 (Minn.1986). There is some disagreement, though, over whether comparative negligence should be used when the defendant has negligently misrepresented. The court in *Florenzano* concluded that the reasons that warranted using comparative negligence in personal injury cases applied as well to cases of economic harm. See also *Greycas, Inc. v. Proud,* p. 1258 supra (asserting that plaintiff's negligence "is as much a defense to negligent misrepresentation as to any other tort of negligence").

10. *Merger and "as is" clauses.* Courts increasingly conclude that the existence of an "as is" provision in the contract or a statement that the buyer is relying only on a personal inspection will not prevent consumer or other unsophisticated plaintiffs from showing that fraud occurred. See, e.g., Cirillo v. Slomin's Inc., 768 N.Y.S.2d 759, 767 (Sup.Ct.2003) (distinguishing earlier precedent that upheld no-reliance clauses because they involved "transactions between sophisticated business people, negotiated at arm's length"). Compare Extra Equipamentos E Exportacao Ltda. v. Case Corp., 541 F.3d 719, 724 (7th Cir.2008)(enforcing a no-reliance clause against plaintiff corporation that was represented by counsel in the negotiations that resulted in the contract containing the no-release clause). As the court colorfully put it:

> In the trade, no-reliance clauses are called "big boy" clauses (as in "we're big boys and can look after ourselves"). But if someone who is *not* a big boy—indeed is not even represented by counsel—signs a big-boy clause, there can be a problem, and this has led some courts to require, before such a clause can be enforced, an inquiry into the circumstances of its negotiation, to make sure that the signatory knew what he was doing.

Because plaintiff was a "big boy," no further inquiry was required. Id. at 725.

11. *Measure of damages.* A plaintiff who surmounts these difficulties is entitled to damages. There is disagreement over the proper measure of compensatory damages. The tort standard would appear to be the cost of the property plaintiff bought less the actual value of that property. This is the usual out-of-pocket rule. But some states use the difference between what the value would have been if the representations had been true and the actual value—the usual contract measure, often called the benefit-of-the-bargain rule. Some states follow one or the other exclusively. Others use one or the other depending on the specific facts. See, e.g., American Family Service Corp. v. Michelfelder, 968 F.2d 667 (8th Cir.1992)(prospective buyer entitled to benefit-of-the-bargain damages where seller misrepresented intent to sell). Which measure would you prefer if you were the victim of a sham art dealer who assured you that the painting he was selling you at a favorable price was a genuine Rembrandt?

B. Interference with Contract

Earlier we had occasion to consider questions arising when the defendant's negligence interfered with the contractual relations of others. Those defendants had no desire to interfere with anyone's contracts, and the cases tested how far courts thought it appropriate to extend liability for economic harm.

Now we consider cases in which defendants, knowing of the existence of a contract between the plaintiff and a third party, deliberately undertake to interfere with that contractual relationship.

Imperial Ice Co. v. Rossier

Supreme Court of California, 1941.
18 Cal.2d 33, 112 P.2d 631.

■ Traynor, J.

The California Consumers Company purchased from S.L. Coker an ice distributing business, inclusive of good will, located in territory comprising the city of Santa Monica and the former city of Sawtelle. In the purchase agreement Coker contracted as follows: "I do further agree in consideration of said purchase and in connection therewith, that I will not engage in the business of selling and or distributing ice, either directly or indirectly, in the above described territory so long as the purchasers, or anyone deriving title to the good will of said business from said purchasers, shall be engaged in a like business therein." Plaintiff, the Imperial Ice Company, acquired from the successor in interest of the California Consumers Company full title to this ice distributing business, including the right to enforce the covenant not to compete. Coker subsequently began selling in the same territory, in violation of the contract, ice supplied to him by a company owned by W. Rossier, J.A. Matheson, and Fred Matheson. Plaintiff thereupon brought this action in the superior court for an injunction to restrain Coker from violating the contract and to restrain Rossier and the Mathesons from inducing Coker to violate the contract. The complaint alleges that Rossier and the Mathesons induced Coker to violate his contract so that they might sell ice to him at a profit. The trial court sustained without leave to amend a demurrer to the complaint of the defendants Rossier and the Mathesons and gave judgment for those defendants. Plaintiff has appealed from the judgment on the sole ground that the complaint stated a cause of action against the defendants Rossier and the Mathesons for inducing the breach of contract.

The question thus presented to this court is under what circumstances may an action be maintained against a defendant who has induced a third party to violate a contract with the plaintiff.

It is universally recognized that an action will lie for inducing breach of contract by a resort to means in themselves unlawful such as libel, slander, fraud, physical violence, or threats of such action. [ ] Most jurisdictions also hold that an action will lie for inducing a breach of contract by the use of moral, social, or economic pressures, in themselves lawful, unless there is sufficient justification for such inducement. [ ]

Such justification exists when a person induces a breach of contract to protect an interest that has greater social value than insuring the stability of the contract. (Rest., Torts, sec. 767.) Thus, a person is justified in inducing the breach of a contract the enforcement of which would be injurious to health, safety, or good morals. (Brimelow v. Casson, (1924) 1 Ch. 302; [ ].) The interest of labor in improving working conditions is of sufficient social importance to justify peaceful labor tactics otherwise lawful, though they have the effect of inducing breaches of contracts between employer and employee or employer and customer. [ ] In numerous other situations justification exists (see Rest., Torts, secs. 766 to 774) depending upon the importance of the interest protected. The presence or absence of ill-will, sometimes referred to as "malice," is immaterial, except as it indicates whether or not an interest is actually being protected. (Boyson v. Thorn, 98 Cal. 578 [1893].)

It is well established, however, that a person is not justified in inducing a breach of contract simply because he is in competition with one of the parties to the contract and seeks to further his own economic advantage at the expense of the other. [ ] Whatever interest society has in encouraging free and open competition by means not in themselves unlawful, contractual stability is generally accepted as of greater importance than competitive freedom. Competitive freedom, however, is of sufficient importance to justify one competitor in inducing a third party to forsake another competitor if no contractual relationship exists between the latter two. [ ] A person is likewise free to carry on his business, including reduction of prices, advertising, and solicitation in the usual lawful manner although some third party may be induced thereby to breach his contract with a competitor in favor of dealing with the advertiser. [ ] Again, if two parties have separate contracts with a third, each may resort to any legitimate means at his disposal to secure performance of his contract even though the necessary result will be to cause a breach of the other contract. [ ] A party may not, however, under the guise of competition actively and affirmatively induce the breach of a competitor's contract in order to secure an economic advantage over that competitor. The act of inducing the breach must be an intentional one. If the actor had no knowledge of the existence of the contract or his actions were not intended to induce a breach, he cannot be held liable though an actual breach results from his lawful and proper acts. [ ]

In California the case of *Boyson v. Thorn*, supra, has been considered by many as establishing the proposition that no action will lie in this state for inducing breach of contract by means which are not otherwise unlawful. In that case the manager of a hotel induced the owner of the hotel to evict plaintiffs in violation of a contract. The complaint expressly alleged the existence of malicious motives on the part of the manager. This court affirmed a judgment entered on an order which sustained a demurrer without leave to amend, stating that an act otherwise lawful was not rendered unlawful by the existence of "malice." It is clear that the confidential relationship that existed between the manager of the hotel and the owner justified the manager in advising the owner to violate his contract with plaintiffs. His conduct thus being justified, it was lawful despite the existence of ill-will or malice on his part. The statements to the effect that no interference with contractual relations is actionable if the means employed are otherwise lawful were not necessary to the decision and should be disregarded. . . .

The complaint in the present case alleges that defendants actively induced Coker to violate his contract with plaintiffs so that they might sell ice to him. The contract gave to plaintiff the right to sell ice in the stated territory free from the competition of Coker. The defendants, by virtue of their interest in the sale of ice in that territory, were in effect competing with plaintiff. By inducing Coker to violate his contract, as alleged in the complaint, they sought to further their own economic advantage at plaintiff's expense. Such conduct is not justified. Had defendants merely sold ice to Coker without actively inducing him to violate his contract, his distribution of the ice in the forbidden territory in violation of his contract would not then have rendered defendants liable. They may carry on their business of selling ice as usual without incurring liability for breaches of contract by their customers. It is necessary to prove that they intentionally and actively induced the breach. Since the complaint alleges that they did so and asks for an injunction on the grounds that damages would be inadequate, it states a cause of action, and the demurrer should therefore have been overruled.

The judgment is reversed.

■ EDMONDS, J., SHENK, J., and GIBSON, C.J., concurred. CURTIS, J., concurred in the judgment.

NOTES AND QUESTIONS

1. The tortious interference with contract claim originated in Lumley v. Gye, 118 Eng.Rep. 749 (Q.B.1853). Lumley, who was lessee and manager of Queen's Theatre, hired Johanna Wagner, a world-famous singer, to perform at Queen's. Gye, who was Lumley's competitor, offered Wagner more money, apparently inducing her to breach her contract. Lumley then brought an action to enforce a covenant in his contract with Wagner that prohibited her from performing for anyone else during the term of her contract without Lumley's consent. That injunction was granted in Lumley v. Wagner, 42 Eng.Rep. 687 (Ch.1852), but apparently Wagner decided to sing for no one and did not return to the plaintiff's theatre. (Why didn't Lumley seek specific performance of his contract? Is enforcement of the covenant uncomfortably close to ordering performance?) When the first action did not bring Wagner back, Lumley brought his second action—against Gye for inducing breach of contract. Although a statute had been passed in 1349, in the wake of the Black Death, designed to deter scarce workers from changing their jobs, it had been limited to master-servant relations. In *Lumley*, such meddling was barred in personal service contracts as well. The doctrine has since been extended to protect contracts generally from intentional interference. Do Lumley and Imperial Ice Co. need tort actions in addition to their contract actions?

2. For a discussion of whether plaintiff must prove "improper" motive as an element of a prima facie case or the defendant has the burden of justifying the behavior as an affirmative defense, see United Truck Leasing Corp. v. Geltman, 551 N.E.2d 20 (Mass.1990).

3. *Mixed motive.* Generally, if the defendant has a legitimate economic justification for interfering with the plaintiff's contract, additional improper motives will not defeat the privilege. E.g., Trepanier v. Getting Organized, Inc., 583 A.2d 583 (Vt.1990). Some courts, however, when confronted with both proper and improper motives, have sought the "dominant" one. In such cases the defendant has the burden of proving that the predominant motive justified the interference. See Crandall Corp. v. Navistar International Transportation Corp., 395 S.E.2d 179 (S.C.1990). Since evidence in cases involving multiple motives is usually conflicting, virtually all of these cases go to a jury. Suppose that the predominant motive justified the interference but an unjustified non-dominant motive would have resulted in the defendant taking the same interfering activity? Recall the discussion of multiple sufficient causes p. 346 supra (two negligently set fires, each independently sufficient to burn down plaintiff's house). Fikes v. Furst, 81 P.3d 545 (N.M.2003), arose out of a "bitter feud" between two academic anthropologists that began when the junior anthropologist, Fikes, criticized some of the seminal work by the senior anthropologist, Furst:

Dr. Furst made statements that Dr. Fikes was "a lousy anthropologist," "beset by devils," and was "pursuing a half-assed fantasy." Dr. Fikes, for his part, wrote a book that chronicled his disagreement with Dr. Furst's conclusions . . . that was entitled *Carlos Castaneda: Academic Opportunism and the Psychedelic Sixties.* The manuscript contained statements, referring to Dr. Furst's work with the Huichol Indians, such as, "I discovered what may be the most complicated and fascinating anthropological hoax of the 20th century."

Fikes had a contract to publish the manuscript. Furst wrote a letter to the publisher stating his intention to sue if the book were published. The publisher broke the contract, and Fikes sued Furst for interference with the contractual relationship. The court held that Furst's interest in self-protection—his academic reputation—was a legitimate motive for the letter. While animus toward his critic, Fikes, may also have played a role, the court held, contrary to *Crandall*, that plaintiff had the burden to demonstrate that the desire to harm was the dominant purpose for the letter. Fikes's failure to proffer such evidence in response to Furst's motion for summary judgment justified granting the motion. What might a trial have provided that the summary judgment proceeding did not?

4. Why does *Imperial Ice* say that contractual stability is "generally accepted as of greater importance than competitive freedom"? In Perlman, Interference with Contract and Other Economic Expectancies: A Clash of Tort and Contract Theory, 49 U.Chi.L.Rev. 61 (1982), the author suggests that the notion of "efficient breach" in contract law should lead to the encouragement of breaches that serve the social interest in putting limited resources to higher-valued uses unless the means are unlawful: "In [the] case of other lawful acts, tort liability works at cross-purposes with contract policies. Contract remedies seem to promote efficiency, whereas the addition of inducer liability inhibits efficient outcomes." Is there a persuasive response to this argument?

5. As *Imperial Ice* provides, a defendant may justify an otherwise unpermitted interference with the contract relations of others. It is clear that one cannot interfere with a contract for a finite term on the ground of economic self-interest. Bank of New York v. Berisford International, 594 N.Y.S.2d 152 (App.Div.1993). Beyond that, deciding whether the interest that the defendant is seeking to protect has greater social value than that of insuring the stability of contract is a difficult and often unpredictable task.

Competitors generally may talk with plaintiff's dissatisfied customers but not attempt to enlist satisfied customers who are under contract with the plaintiff. See Kendall/Hunt Publishing Co. v. Rowe, 424 N.W.2d 235 (Iowa 1988).

One of the most important justifications has been the claim of labor organizations referred to in *Imperial Ice*. So long as violent and other tortious means are not involved, the states' power to impose liability for such action has been preempted by federal legislation regulating labor-management relations. UAW-CIO v. Russell, 356 U.S. 634 (1958). To the extent traditional torts are involved, state law is still applicable. Concerted refusals to deal that seek to gain competitive advantage are now regulated extensively by antitrust legislation at both the federal and state levels. This is explored in courses on Antitrust Law, Labor Law, and Unfair Competition.

6. On occasion, the defendant's interference does not take the form of inducing the promisor to breach, but rather involves efforts to make it more difficult for the promisor to perform. For example, in McNary v. Chamberlain, 34 Conn. 384 (1867), plaintiff alleged that the defendant, knowing that the town was paying plaintiff a flat rate to keep a particular road in good repair, dumped stones and rubbish on the road and clogged a drain to flood the road. The court held that a claim had been stated because defendant "knew that the plaintiff had made such a contract, and took advantage of its existence to injure him in the manner described." See also Wilspec Technologies, Inc. v. DunAn Holding Group, Co., Ltd., 204 P.3d 69 (Okla.2009)(recognizing intentional interference with promisor's performance of contract as provided in Restatement (Second) of Torts section 766A and that, unlike intentional interference with a contract, this tort does not require breach of the contractual relationship—plaintiff may recover for additional expenses incurred in performing).

7. *Consultants.* Consultants hired by a business to advise it cannot be liable when they suggest that the business breach its contract with the plaintiff so long as the consultant was asked for advice and gave it honestly and in good faith. See *Trepanier*, note 3 supra.

C. INTERFERENCE WITH PROSPECTIVE ECONOMIC ADVANTAGE

We have just examined instances in which defendants were found liable for damages resulting from intentional interference with existing contractual relationships. The question of how far that action might extend beyond contracts in place has been the subject of much discussion and confusion. The following case addresses the issue—and at the same time reappraises *Imperial Ice v. Rossier*.

Della Penna v. Toyota Motor Sales, U.S.A., Inc.

Supreme Court of California, 1995.
11 Cal.4th 376, 902 P.2d 740, 45 Cal.Rptr.2d 436.

■ ARABIAN, J.

We granted review to reexamine, in light of divergent rulings from the Court of Appeal and a doctrinal evolution among other state high courts, the elements of the tort variously known as interference with "prospective economic advantage," "prospective contractual relations," or "prospective economic relations," and the allocation of the burdens of proof between the parties to such an action. . . .

[Toyota was trying to prevent Lexus autos exported to other countries from being re-exported to Japan and took several steps to prevent that from happening. When it became apparent that, despite its efforts, re-exporting was still occurring, defendant compiled a list of "offenders" and warned its dealers that those who did business with such offenders faced possible sanctions. Plaintiff did a profitable business as a wholesaler buying Lexus cars from retailers at near retail prices and re-exporting them to Japan for resale. As a result of defendant's efforts, plaintiff's supply of cars dried up.

When its tort claim for interference with prospective economic advantage was tried to a jury, the judge decided, over objection, to charge that the plaintiff had the burden of showing that the defendant's interference was "wrongful." After losing that objection, plaintiff framed a definition of "wrongful" that the judge read to the jury that included conduct "outside the realm of legitimate business transactions. . . . Wrongfulness may lie in the method used or by virtue of an improper motive." The jury returned a defense verdict. The court of appeal reversed on the ground that the judge erred by putting the burden of proof on the plaintiff.]

II

A

[The court began by noting that *Lumley v. Gye*, p. 1277 supra, was generally thought to be the origin of the "two torts—interference with contract and its sibling, interference with prospective economic relations—in the form in which they have come down to us."]

The opinion in *Lumley* dealt, of course, with conduct intended to induce the breach of an existing contract, not conduct intended to prevent or persuade others not to contract with the plaintiff. That such an interference with prospective economic relations might itself be tortious was confirmed by the Queen's Bench over the next 40 years. [The court discussed Temperton v. Russell (1893) 1 Q.B. 715, in which a labor union in a dispute with builders demanded that the builders' suppliers cease furnishing materials to the builder. If a supplier failed to comply the union would bring pressure on those who supplied that supplier to cease doing so. In a suit by one supplier against the union, the court recognized a tort action on the ground that "in the words of Lord Esher, the Master of the Rolls, 'the distinction . . . between the claim for inducing persons to break contracts already entered into . . . and . . . inducing persons not to enter into contracts . . . can [not] prevail.' "]

"There was the same wrongful intent in both cases, wrongful because malicious," Lord Esher wrote. "There was the same kind of injury to the plaintiff. It seems rather a fine distinction to say that, where a defendant maliciously induces a person not to carry out a contract already made with the plaintiff and so injures the plaintiff, it is actionable, but where he injures the plaintiff by maliciously preventing a person from entering into a contract with the plaintiff, which he otherwise would have entered into, it is not actionable." [*Temperton*].

As a number of courts and commentators have observed, the keystone of the liability imposed in [*Lumley* and *Temperton*] to judge from the opinions of the justices, appears to have been the "malicious" intent of a defendant in enticing an employee to breach her contract with the plaintiff, and damaging the business of one who refused to cooperate with the union in achieving its bargaining aims. While some have doubted whether the use of the word "malicious" amounted to anything more than an intent to commit an act, knowing it would harm the plaintiff (see, e.g., Dobbs, Tortious Interference with Contractual Relationships (1980) 34 Ark. L.Rev. 335, 347, fn. 37), Dean Keeton, assessing the state of the tort as late as 1984, remarked that "[w]ith intent to interfere as the usual basis of the action, the cases have turned almost entirely upon the defendant's motive or purpose and the means by which he has sought to accomplish it. As in the cases of interference with contract, any manner of intentional invasion of the plaintiff's interests may be sufficient if the purpose is not a proper one." [ ]

. . .

[Historically] the plaintiff need only allege a so-called "prima facie tort" by showing the defendant's awareness of the economic relation, a deliberate interference with it, and the plaintiff's resulting injury. [ ] By this account of the matter—the traditional view of the torts and the one adopted by the first Restatement of Torts—the burden then passed to the defendant to demonstrate that its conduct was privileged, that is, "justified" by a recognized defense such as the protection of others or, more likely in this context, the defendant's own competitive business interests. [ ]

These and related features of the economic relations tort and the requirements surrounding its proof and defense led, however, to calls for a reexamination and reform as early as the 1920's. . . . The nature of the wrong itself seemed to many unduly vague, inviting suit and hampering the presentation of coherent defenses. More critically in the view of others, the procedural effects of applying the prima facie tort principle to what is essentially a business context led to even more untoward consequences.

. . .

Calls for a reformulation of both the elements and the means of establishing the economic relations tort reached a height around the time the Restatement Second of Torts was being prepared for publication and are reflected in its departures from its predecessor's version. Acknowledging criticism, the American Law Institute discarded the prima facie tort requirement of the first Restatement. A new provision, section 766B, required that the defendant's conduct be "improper," and adopted a multifactor "balancing" approach, identifying seven factors for the trier of fact to weigh in determining a defendant's liability. The Restatement Second of Torts, however, declined to take a position on the issue of which of the parties bore the burden of proof, relying on the "considerable disagreement on who has the burden of pleading and proving certain matters" and the observation that "the law in this area has not fully congealed but is still in a formative stage" [ ]. In addition, the Restatement Second provided that a defendant might escape liability by showing that his conduct was justifiable and did not include the use of "wrongful means." [ ]

B

In the meantime, however, an increasing number of state high courts had traveled well beyond the Second Restatement's reforms by redefining and otherwise recasting the elements of the economic relations tort and the burdens surrounding its proof and defenses. In Top Service Body Shop, Inc. v. Allstate Ins. Co. (Ore. 1978) 582 P.2d 1365 (*Top Service*), the Oregon Supreme Court, assessing this "most fluid and rapidly growing tort," noted that "efforts to consolidate both recognized and unsettled lines of development into a general theory of 'tortious interference' have brought to the surface the difficulties of defining the elements of so general a tort without sweeping within its terms a wide variety of socially very different conduct." [ ]

Recognizing the force of these criticisms, the court went on to hold in *Top Service* [ ], that a claim of interference with economic relations "is made out when interference resulting in injury to another *is wrongful by some measure beyond the fact of the interference itself.* Defendant's liability may arise from improper motives or from the use of improper means. They may be wrongful by reason of a statute or other regulation, or a recognized rule of common law, or perhaps an established standard of a trade or profession. No question of privilege arises unless the interference would be wrongful but for the privilege; it becomes an issue only if the acts charged would be tortious on the part of an unprivileged defendant." [ ]; (italics added).

[The court reviewed similar developments in other courts, concluding that "[o]ver the past decade or so, close to a majority of the high courts of American jurisdictions have imported into the economic relations tort variations on the *Top Service* line of reasoning, explicitly approving a rule that requires the plaintiff in such a suit to plead and prove the alleged interference was either 'wrongful,' 'improper,' 'illegal,' 'independently tortious' or some variant on these formulations."]

III

In California, the development of the economic relations tort has paralleled its evolution in other jurisdictions. For many years this court declined to adopt the holding of [*Lumley*] on the ground that, as we reasoned in Boyson v. Thorn (1893) 98 Cal. 578, "[i]t is a truism of the law that an act which does not amount to a legal injury cannot be actionable because it is done with a bad intent. . . . If it is right, and the means used to procure the breach are right, the motive cannot make it a wrong. . . ." [ ]. In [*Imperial Ice Co.*], however, a unanimous court, speaking through Justice Traynor, pronounced these statements in *Boyson* "not necessary to the decision" and directed that they be "disregarded." [ ] California thus joined the majority of jurisdictions in adopting the view of the first Restatement of Torts by stating that "an action will lie for *unjustifiably* inducing a breach of contract." [ ]; (italics added).

[The court traced its own thinking in this area at length. It then noted that developments in the courts of appeal had, "if anything, outdistanced our own formulations of the elements of the tort and the allocation of the burden of proof in at least two respects." The first was that plaintiff was being given the burden of proving "wrongful" conduct. The second was that defendant could "defeat liability by showing that its conduct was not independently 'wrongful.'"]

IV

In searching for a means to recast the elements of the economic relations tort and allocate the associated burdens of proof, we are guided by an overmastering concern articulated by high courts of other jurisdictions and legal commentators: The need to draw and enforce a sharpened distinction between claims for the tortious disruption of an existing contract and claims that a prospective contractual or economic relationship has been interfered with by the defendant. Many of the cases do in fact acknowledge a greater array of justificatory defenses against claims of interference with prospective relations. Still, in our view and that of several other courts and commentators, the notion that the two torts are analytically unitary and derive from a common principle sacrifices practical wisdom to theoretical insight, promoting the idea that the interests invaded are of nearly equal dignity. They are not.

The courts provide a damage remedy against third party conduct intended to disrupt an existing contract precisely because the exchange of promises resulting in such a formally cemented economic relationship is deemed worthy of protection from interference by a stranger to the agreement. Economic relationships short of contractual, however, should stand on a different legal footing as far as the potential for tort liability is reckoned. Because ours is a culture firmly wedded to the social rewards of commercial contests, the law usually takes care to draw lines of legal liability in a way that maximizes areas of competition free of legal penalties.

. . . Our courts should, in short, firmly distinguish the two kinds of business contexts, bringing a greater solicitude to those relationships that have ripened into agreements, while recognizing that relationships short of that subsist in a zone where the rewards and risks of competition are dominant.

Beyond that, we need not tread today. It is sufficient to dispose of the issue before us in this case by holding that a plaintiff seeking to recover for alleged interference with prospective economic relations has the burden of pleading and proving that the defendant's interference was wrongful "by some measure beyond the fact of the interference itself." [ ] It follows that the trial court did not commit error when it [required] the jury to find that defendant's interference was "wrongful." And because the instruction defining "wrongful conduct" given the jury by the trial court was offered by plaintiff himself, we have no occasion to review its sufficiency in this case. The question of whether additional refinements to the plaintiff's pleading and proof burdens merit adoption by California courts—questions embracing the precise scope of "wrongfulness," or whether a "disinterested malevolence," in Justice Holmes's words (American Bank & Trust Co. v. Federal Reserve Bank (1921) 256 U.S. 350, 358) is an actionable interference in itself, or whether the underlying policy justification for the tort, the efficient allocation of social resources, justifies including as actionable conduct that is recognized as anticompetitive under established state and federal positive law [ ]—are matters that can await another day and a more appropriate case.

. . . The judgment of the Court of Appeal is reversed and the cause is remanded with directions to affirm the judgment of the trial court.

■ LUCAS, C.J., and KENNARD, BAXTER, GEORGE and WERDEGAR, JJ., concur.

■ Concurring opinion by MOSK, J.

. . .

Like the majority, I would reverse the Court of Appeal's judgment in this regard. As I shall explain, I believe that any instructional error was not prejudicial.

I

With the dissonance caused by such terms as "malice," "justification," and "privilege" [ ], the common law on the tort of intentional interference with prospective economic advantage, both in American jurisdictions generally and in California specifically, is fast approaching incoherence. [ ]

. . .

A

One reason for the common law's near-incoherence on the tort of intentional interference with prospective economic advantage may be discovered in its doctrinal basis.

During the second half of the 19th century and the first half of the 20th, as the times pressed hard on both law and society, common law courts, first in England and then in the United States, developed what has become known as the "prima facie tort doctrine." [ ] The traditional source was the old action on the case. [ ] The analytical object was a framework "capable of assisting comprehension and guiding an internal systematic development of the subject matter" [ ] to the end that "principle rather than precedent" might govern [ ].

In Mogul Steamship Company v. McGregor, Gow, & Co. (1889) 23 Q.B.D. 598, 613, affirmed [1891] A.C. 25, Lord Justice Bowen in the Court of Appeal made the famous statement of the prima facie tort doctrine: "[I]ntentionally to do that which is calculated in the ordinary course of events to damage, and which does, in fact, damage another in that person's property or trade, is actionable if done without just cause or excuse."

In Aikens v. Wisconsin (1904) 195 U.S. 194, 204, Justice Holmes, who "was in large measure responsible for the introduction of the [prima facie tort] doctrine in this country" [ ], made the equally famous statement: "It has been considered that, prima facie, the intentional infliction of temporal damage is a cause of action, which, as a matter of substantive law, whatever may be the form of pleading, requires a justification if the defendant is to escape."

In the middle of this century, Dean Pound made the following restatement: "One who intentionally does anything which on its face is injurious to another is liable to repair the resulting damage unless he can establish a liberty or privilege by identifying his claim to act as he did with some recognized public or social interest." (3 Pound, Jurisprudence (1959) p. 9.)

. . .

The prima facie tort doctrine exhibits a general deficiency. Perhaps it has resulted in a kind of "internal systematic development of the subject matter." [ ] But if it has, it has done so by sacrificing an external connection to society. "The idea is that 'intentional infliction of harm' is, prima facie, a tort. The problem is that almost any legitimate act can cause 'intentional' harm. . . ." [Dobbs, Tortious Interference with Contractual Relationships, 34 Ark.L.Rev. 335 (1980)]. Therefore, "[i]t must be understood that intentional infliction of harm . . . covers a multitude of desirable acts as well as a multitude of sins." [ ] "The prima facie tort rule, then, is not a rule about wrongdoing at all. It seems to be a philosophical effort to state all"—or at least much—of "tort law in a single sentence rather than an effort to state a meaningful principle." [Dobbs]: "[P]rinciple rather than precedent" may indeed govern. [ ] But it is a principle that is peculiarly empty.

. . .

B

A second reason for the common law's near-incoherence on the tort of intentional interference with prospective economic advantage may be discovered within the law itself.

To borrow words from Brennan v. United Hatters, [65 A. 165 (N.J.L.1906)], the premise of the tort seems to be that, "[i]n a civilized community which recognizes the right of private property among its institutions, the notion is intolerable that a man should be protected by the law in the enjoyment of property once it is acquired, but left unprotected by the law in his efforts to acquire it."

The tort's "protectionist" premise, however, is at war with itself. For the person who deserves protection in the acquisition of property is not only the interfered-with party but also the interfering party. . . .

Further, liability under the tort may threaten values of greater breadth and higher dignity than those of the tort itself.

One is the common law's policy of freedom of competition. "The policy of the common law has always been in favor of free competition, which proverbially is the life of trade. So long as the plaintiff's contractual relations are merely contemplated or potential, it is considered to be in the interest of the public that any competitor should be free to divert them to himself by all fair and reasonable means. . . . In short, it is no tort to beat a business rival to prospective customers. Thus, in the absence of prohibition by statute, illegitimate means, or some other unlawful element, a defendant seeking to increase his own business may cut rates or prices, allow discounts or rebates, enter into secret negotiations behind the plaintiff's back, refuse to deal with him or threaten to discharge employees who do, or even refuse to deal with third parties unless they cease dealing with the plaintiff, all without incurring liability." [ ]

. . .

C

A third reason for the common law's near-incoherence on the tort of intentional interference with prospective economic advantage may be discovered in its focus on the interfering party's motive, that is, why he seeks whatever it is that he seeks through his interference, and on his moral character as revealed thereby.

[In an extended discussion of *Boyson v. Thorn,* Justice Mosk approvingly quoted its language that "the existence of a bad motive, in the case of an act which is not in itself illegal, will not convert that act into a civil wrong for which reparation is due." He concluded that *Imperial Ice* had erred when it rejected *Boyson*'s assertion that motive was irrelevant.]

The untoward results of the focus on the interfering party's motive may present themselves in individual cases in the form of arbitrary and capricious outcomes. [ ] In matters in which the trier of fact believes it has discerned good motive or at least persuades itself it has, an interfering party who has both engaged in objectively bad conduct and produced objectively bad consequences may evade liability for injury. By contrast, in matters in which it adopts a contrary view, an interfering party who has neither engaged in such conduct nor produced such consequences may be made to pay for what is simply damnum absque injuria. In a word, much may depend on mere appearances and perceptions and on nothing more.

     . . .

II

With all this said, we are put to the question: What are we to do about the tort of intentional interference with prospective economic advantage?

It would be unreasonable to choose to do nothing. As stated, in this regard the common law is approaching incoherence. It is not about to turn to consistency of its own accord.

It would also be unreasonable to choose abolition. Such a course commands little support among courts or commentators. That is unsurprising. Most agree that the interfering party should not be granted general immunity, but should be exposed to liability under at least some circumstances. [ ] For just as "[i]t cannot be . . . a theorem of justice that liability is always just" [ ], neither can it be a principle of law that immunity is invariably proper.

In view of the foregoing, the only reasonable choice is reformulation. . . .

It follows that the tort may be satisfied by intentional interference with prospective economic advantage by independently tortious means. [ ]

     ...

[In an extended discussion, Justice Mosk develops bases for recovery in this situation. Although the harm is generally directed at the plaintiff, that is not required—as in cases in which the defendant makes misrepresentations to third parties to persuade them not to deal with plaintiff. The tort also may be satisfied by a showing of "restraint of trade, including monopolization." The common "independently tortious means" including "assault and battery, defamation, and fraud and deceit, are well defined and long settled." Such an approach would remove the tort's "protectionist" premise, leaving plaintiffs subject only to defendant's use of "independently tortious means or restraints of trade." He then turned to the case at bar.]

Under the tort as reformulated, it is plain that the Court of Appeal erred. To be sure, the instructions appear erroneous. They did not expressly require objective, and unlawful, conduct or consequences.

Neither, it seems, did they do so impliedly. Any error, however, was not prejudicial. The reason is manifest. To the extent that they were satisfied by mere "wrongfulness"—which, at Della Penna's request, was defined under a kind of " 'business ethics' standard" as behavior "outside the realm of legitimate business transactions" because of "method" or "motive"—they were satisfied by far too little. For to that extent they did not demand the use of independently tortious means or restraints of trade. It is true that their focus on motive— "[w]rongfulness may lie . . . by virtue of an improper motive"—might threaten an arbitrary and capricious outcome in a given case. The same is true of their use of the term "wrongful" and its cognates, which are inherently ambiguous [ ]. But, in spite of the foregoing, there is simply no basis to conclude that the outcome here was either arbitrary or capricious.

IV

It is evident in the analysis presented above that, on many points, I agree with the majority's discussion of the tort of intentional interference with prospective economic advantage and Della Penna's claim against Toyota asserting such a cause of action.

On two major points, however, I am compelled to state my disagreement.

First, I would not adopt the "standard" of "wrongfulness." As I have noted, the term and its cognates are inherently ambiguous. They should probably be avoided. They should surely not be embraced. . . .

Second, if I were to adopt such a "standard," I would not allow it to remain undefined. Otherwise, our effort . . . to rationalize the governing principles would be undermined. Formerly, the interfering party as defendant was left "knowing he was entitled to some defense, but not knowing what defenses would be accounted sufficient." . . . Any definition of the "standard," of course, should avoid suggesting that the interfering party's motive might be material for present purposes. As I have explained, the focus on this issue is inappropriate. [ ] A position of this sort, one must acknowledge, would result in the imposition of no liability on a person who is purely, but merely, "malicious"—who acts, to quote Justice Holmes, with "disinterested malevolence" (Amer. Bank & Trust Co. v. Federal Bank (1921) 256 U.S. 350, 358). Although such a person might be held responsible in conscience, he should not be made answerable in tort. To reiterate: "The law has no roving commission to root out bad people or people whose minds may harbor bad thoughts."
. . .

  . . .

NOTES AND QUESTIONS

1. What error did the court of appeal find in the trial judge's conduct in this case? Why did the supreme court reject that determination?

2. What are the consequences of the majority's decision? Should plaintiff's case ever have gone to trial?

3. With regard to which party should shoulder the burden of proof, consider the observation of Justice Mosk that "it must be understood that intentional infliction of harm . . . covers a multitude of desirable acts as well as a multitude of sins" (quoting Dobbs, cited in *Della Penna*). Would it be helpful in assigning the burden of proof to know the relative frequency of desirable acts and sins? What else might inform appropriate placement of the burden of proof?

4. If the underlying facts are not in dispute, what does it mean to say that a party bears the burden of proof on wrongfulness?

5. How did the first and second Restatements differ? Did the court adopt the approach of either one? Section 767 of the Second Restatement lists the seven factors referred to by the court that determine whether or not an intentional interference with either a contractual or prospective contractual relation is improper:

(a) the nature of the actor's conduct,

(b) the actor's motive,

(c) the interests of the other with which the actor's conduct interferes,

(d) the interests sought to be advanced by the actor,

(e) the social interests in protecting the freedom of action of the actor and the contractual interests of the other,

(f) the proximity or remoteness of the actor's conduct to the interference, and

(g) the relations between the parties.

How might these factors have affected *Imperial Ice*? *Della Penna*? How might Justice Mosk react to these factors?

6. Does the majority reject the result of *Imperial Ice*? The analysis? What is the concurring opinion's stance concerning that case? What differences between interference with contract and interference with prospective economic advantage are important?

7. *Unlawful means.* Justice Mosk identifies several independently tortious means of inflicting harm. In the business context, other types of conduct have also been important. We briefly review a few of these, which are covered more extensively in courses on Unfair Competition and Copyright.

a. *False statements about a competitor's product.* The action of "slander of title" or "trade libel" or "disparagement" has evolved to cover false statements concerning ownership of goods and was further extended to untrue statements dealing with the quality of goods as well as the title to them. See, e.g., System Operations, Inc. v. Scientific Games Development Corp., 555 F.2d 1131 (3d Cir.1977), listing the elements of disparagement as: "(1) publication (2) with malice (3) of false allegations concerning plaintiff's property or product (4) causing special damages, i.e., pecuniary harm." As might be expected, "malice" is a subject of confusion. Some attacks on product quality may impugn management and be actionable as defamations. See Harwood Pharmacal Co. v. National Broadcasting Co., 174 N.E.2d 602 (N.Y.1961).

State law has flatly barred injunctions in defamation cases. Since disparagement occurs in the context of competition, some courts have been willing to view the disparagement as the basis of a tort for unfair competition or intentional interference with economic advantage and have permitted injunctive relief on those bases. The Supreme Court has accorded commercial speech at least some First Amendment protection. Central Hudson Gas & Electric Corp. v. Public Service Commission of New York, 447 U.S. 557 (1980), provides the doctrinal framework.

In Proctor & Gamble Co. v. Haugen, 222 F.3d 1262 (10th Cir.2000), competitors of plaintiff and their distributors spread a rumor that plaintiff's president had told a television show that a "large portion of the profits from [P & G] products go to support his satanic church." When asked whether announcing this would hurt his business he was said to have responded "[t]here are not enough Christians in the United States to make a difference." The court held that a state tort claim was available for interference with prospective economic advantage. A jury could find that the defendants intended to interfere with plaintiff's business relationships with "anti-satanic consumers and distributors."

b.   *False statements about a firm's own product.* Tort actions may be harder to ground where the falsity is in the puffing of the speaker's own product rather than the disparagement of a competitor's product. It has been harder to show that plaintiff suffered from the statement—and how much.

In Mosler Safe Co. v. Ely-Norris Safe Company, 273 U.S. 132 (1927), Mosler falsely advertised that its safes had explosion-proof chambers. The Supreme Court refused to allow a suit by a company whose safes did have such a device. What if plaintiff were the only manufacturer of explosion-proof safes? The unavailability of a tort action led to the creation of statutory remedies to deter false advertising.

c.   *Conscious imitation of a product's appearance.* A statutory or common law action for trademark infringement or an action for unfair competition will lie when a competitor "passes off" its own product as that of another competitor by the use of intentionally similar and potentially confusing trademarks or trade dress. See Harold F. Ritchie, Inc. v. Chesebrough-Pond's, Inc., 281 F.2d 755 (2d Cir.1960), in which defendant was found liable for infringement of plaintiff's registered trademark "Brylcreem" by the marketing of its hair care product, "Valcream."

d.   *Misappropriation of patents, copyrights and trade secrets.* Patents and copyrights provide specific protection for products and writings that meet certain statutory requirements. Infringement of a patent or copyright gives rise to an action for damages and injunction under federal statutes.

Trade secrets do not enjoy the same type or level of protection accorded to patents. While an inventor has a monopoly on a patented invention for a statutory period of time, competitors can make use of a company's trade secret so long as the information was obtained in a legitimate manner— reverse engineering, independent research, or disclosure by the firm itself, for example. But improper methods used by a competitor to acquire another's trade secrets will lead to a common law tort action.

The tortious methods may be unlawful in themselves, such as fraud, theft, wiretapping, or other acts of industrial espionage. Liability may also be based on inducing others to divulge secret business information told them in confidence. Kewanee Oil v. Bicron Corp., 416 U.S. 470 (1974); see also Note, A Balanced Approach to Employer-Employee Trade Secrets Disputes in California, 31 Hastings L.J. 671 (1980).

e.   *Violating professional ethical standards.* In Nostrame v. Santiago, 61 A.3d 893 (N.J.2013), a malpractice attorney who was discharged by his client brought suit against the successor attorney for tortious interference. First, the court decided that because a client has an unfettered right to select or change attorneys, this case should be analyzed as one involving interference with an expectancy of a prospective relationship. Second, violation of rules of professional conduct in soliciting a client away from another attorney would constitute "wrongful means" to support such a claim, but because plaintiff's complaint contained insufficient allegations of such, the complaint should be dismissed.

8.   *Beyond competition.* Some important cases of economic harm arise from situations in which the parties are not in competition. For example, in Auvil v. CBS "60 Minutes," 67 F.3d 816 (9th Cir.1995), defendant in 1989 reported that "[t]he most potent cancer-causing agent in our food supply is a substance sprayed on apples to keep them on the trees longer and make them look better" and that those most at risk were children. Following the broadcast, "consumer demand for apples and apple products decreased dramatically." A disparagement action was allowed to proceed and then dismissed for failure to prove falsity. As a result of the broadcast, several states adopted statutes creating civil actions on behalf of producers of perishable products for "willful or malicious" dissemination of "false information" that a food product is not safe for human consumption. "False information" is defined as "not based on reliable, scientific facts and reliable scientific data which the disseminator knows or should have known to be false." See Fla.Stat.Ann. § 865.065.

When boycotts or other concerted actions do not involve labor disputes or economic conflicts, they tend to have political, social, or religious ramifications. Some examples follow:

a.   In Watch Tower Bible & Tract Society v. Dougherty, 11 A.2d 147 (Pa.1940), the defendants Roman Catholic Archbishop of Philadelphia and a priest were sued by the plaintiff religious society. For ten years the plaintiff had conducted a series of radio programs on a Philadelphia station owned indirectly by a department store. The priest objected that the plaintiff "attacks the Catholic Church, misrepresents her teachings and foments religious hatred and bigotry," and threatened to cancel his charge account at the store if it renewed the plaintiff's contract to broadcast. The plaintiff also alleged that the defendants urged their parishioners to inundate the store with similar messages. The store refused to renew plaintiff's contract. The trial court's dismissal of the complaint was affirmed in one paragraph:

> The order of the court below was proper. No valid cause of action was pleaded. The defendants are leaders of their church. They cannot be mulcted in damages for protesting against the utterances of one who they believe attacks their church and misrepresents its teachings nor for inducing their adherents to make similar protests. A right of action does not arise merely because a group withdraws its patronage or threatens to do so and induces others to do likewise where the objects sought to be obtained are legitimate.

What if defendants' threat to withdraw patronage had been made during the term of plaintiff's contract? What if plaintiff's claims were true? Or consisted of honestly held opinions?

b.   In Missouri v. National Organization for Women, Inc., 620 F.2d 1301 (8th Cir.1980), the State of Missouri brought a suit to enjoin NOW's campaign discouraging groups from scheduling conventions in states that had not ratified the proposed Equal Rights Amendment. The district court's denial of relief was affirmed. Because NOW's concerted action was an effort to exercise its First Amendment right to petition the government and to seek to influence the legislature's actions, the Sherman Antitrust Act did not apply and liability for tortious interference with an advantageous relationship did not lie. "[T]he right to petition is of such importance that it is not an improper interference even when exercised by way of a boycott."

Would the case be different if NOW sought to persuade groups that had already signed agreements to hold their conventions in Missouri to cancel those plans?

c.   In NAACP v. Claiborne Hardware Co., 458 U.S. 886 (1982), the NAACP organized a boycott of white merchants in Claiborne County, Mississippi, to gain acceptance of "a lengthy list of demands for equality and racial justice." Some violence occurred during the boycott. Merchants who had suffered economic losses during the extended boycott sued the NAACP for damages for the concerted conduct. The state courts found that violence and the fear of reprisal had been influential in causing some blacks to withhold patronage from the white merchants. This led to the conclusion that the NAACP was liable for all the damages resulting from the boycott, a total of more than one million dollars.

The Supreme Court unanimously reversed. The boycott "clearly involved constitutionally protected activity":

> . . . Through speech, assembly, and petition—rather than through riot or revolution—petitioners sought to change a social order that had consistently treated them as second-class citizens.

> The presence of protected activity, however, does not end the relevant constitutional inquiry. Governmental regulation that has an incidental effect on First Amendment freedoms may be

justified in certain narrowly defined instances. [ ] A nonviolent and totally voluntary boycott may have a disruptive effect on local economic conditions. This Court has recognized the strong governmental interest in certain forms of economic regulation, even though such regulation may have an incidental effect on rights of speech and association. [ ] The right of business entities to "associate" to suppress competition may be curtailed. [ ] Unfair trade practices may be restricted. Secondary boycotts and picketing by labor unions may be prohibited, as part of "Congress' striking of the delicate balance between union freedom of expression and the ability of neutral employers, employees, and consumers to remain free from coerced participation in industrial strife." [ ]

While states have broad power to regulate economic activity, we do not find a comparable right to prohibit peaceful political activity such as that found in the boycott in this case. . . .

. . .

The First Amendment does not protect violence. "Certainly violence has no sanctuary in the First Amendment, and the use of weapons, gunpowder, and gasoline may not constitutionally masquerade under the guise of 'advocacy.' " [ ] Although the extent and significance of the violence in this case is vigorously disputed by the parties, there is no question that acts of violence occurred. No federal rule of law restricts a State from imposing tort liability for business losses that are caused by violence and by threats of violence. When such conduct occurs in the context of constitutionally protected activity, however, "precision of regulation" is demanded. [ ] Specifically, the presence of activity protected by the First Amendment imposes restraints on the grounds that may give rise to damages liability and on the persons who may be held accountable for those damages. . . .

. . . While the State legitimately may impose damages for the consequences of violent conduct, it may not award compensation for the consequences of nonviolent, protected activity. Only those losses proximately caused by unlawful conduct may be recovered.

. . .

The taint of violence colored the conduct of some of the petitioners. They, of course, may be held liable for the consequences of their violent deeds. The burden of demonstrating that it colored the entire collective effort, however, is not satisfied by evidence that violence occurred or even that violence contributed to the success of the boycott. A massive and prolonged effort to change the social, political, and economic structure of a local environment cannot be characterized as a violent conspiracy simply by reference to the ephemeral consequences of relatively few violent acts.

Questions about the legality of various "means" have not been common.

9. *"Disinterested malevolence."* How does Justice Mosk's position concurring in *Della Penna* differ from that of the majority on the question of "disinterested malevolence"? Consider Tuttle v. Buck, 119 N.W. 946 (Minn.1909). Plaintiff, a village barber, alleged that a local businessman was trying to destroy plaintiff's business by, among other things, employing a series of barbers to operate a competing shop. Plaintiff also alleged that the defendant's sole purpose was to destroy the plaintiff's business and not to serve "any legitimate interest of his own." The trial judge denied a motion to dismiss the complaint and in affirming the lower court, the supreme court stated:

> To divert to one's self the customers of a business rival by the offer of goods at lower prices is in general a legitimate mode of serving one's own interest, and justifiable as fair competition. But when a man starts an opposition place of business, not for the sake of profit to himself, but regardless of loss to himself, and for the sole purpose of driving his competitor out of business, and with the intention of himself retiring upon the accomplishment of his malevolent purpose, he is guilty of a wanton wrong and an actionable tort. In such a case he would not be exercising his legal right, or doing an act which can be judged separately from the motive which actuated him. To call such conduct competition is a perversion of terms. It is simply the application of force without legal justification, which in its moral quality may be no better than highway robbery.

Notwithstanding the moral high ground of *Tuttle*, the Utah Supreme Court more recently rejected improper purpose as a ground for a tortious interference claim, instead limiting the tort to defendant's use of wrongful means. Concerns about the vagueness of what constitutes improper purpose, the difficulty of determining the predominant purpose when other legitimate purposes exist, deterrence of legitimate competitive activity, along with a trend among other state courts to restrict improper-purpose claims led to the court's overruling prior precedent recognizing such claims. Eldridge v. Johndrow, 345 P.3d 553 (Utah 2015).

D. CONTRACT AND TORT IN THE ECONOMIC SPHERE

We have considered the interrelationship between contract and tort at several points in the course. Some, as in the section on the economic loss rule, p. 299 supra, and the discussion of economic loss caused by defective products, p. 672 supra, have been explicit. Others, as when we considered medical malpractice, have been implicit. In this section, we reconsider the appropriate role of tort and contract law in claims that arise between parties to a contract.

All-Tech Telecom, Inc. v. Amway Corp.
United States Court of Appeals, Seventh Circuit, 1999.
174 F.3d 862.

■ Before POSNER, CHIEF JUDGE, and BAUER and MANION, CIRCUIT JUDGES.

■ POSNER, CHIEF JUDGE.

A disappointed plaintiff, All-Tech Telecom, appeals from the district court's grant of summary judgment to the defendant, Amway, on All-Tech's claims of intentional and negligent misrepresentation and promissory estoppel. All-Tech was allowed to get to the jury on claims of breach of warranty, and the jury found a breach but awarded no damages. There is no challenge to the jury's verdict, only to the grant of summary judgment on the other claims. The basis of federal jurisdiction is diversity of citizenship, and the parties agree that the substantive issues are governed by Wisconsin law.

In 1987, Amway had offered distributors a new product (really a product plus a service), the "TeleCharge" phone. The phone was intended for the use of customers of hotels and restaurants. The customer would use a credit card or telephone calling card to pay for a long-distance call. The hotel or restaurant, along with the distributor, Amway, and the long-distance phone companies involved in the calls, would divide the line charges. Beginning in 1988, All-Tech, which was created for the very purpose of being an Amway distributor of TeleCharge phones and the associated telephone service, bought a large number of the phones. For a variety of reasons beyond All-Tech's control, including equipment problems, regulatory impediments to the provision of the TeleCharge program, and finally the obsolescence of the phones, which caused Amway to withdraw the product from the market in 1992, TeleCharge was a flop. All-Tech claims to have been lured into and kept in this losing venture by a series of misrepresentations, such as that Amway had done extensive research before offering the service, that the service would be the "best" in the nation, that any business telephone line could be used with the TeleCharge phone, that the service had been approved in all 50 states and did not require the approval of any telephone company, that each phone could be expected to generate an annual revenue for the distributor of $750, that the carrier retained by Amway to handle the calls and billings for the TeleCharge phones (International TeleCharge, Inc. (ITI)) was the largest company of its kind in the nation, and that the purchaser of a TeleCharge phone would have to deal with ITI—the phone could not be reprogrammed to work with any other carrier.

The district court threw out All-Tech's claims of misrepresentation on the basis of the "economic loss" doctrine of the common law. Originally this doctrine was merely a limitation on who could bring a tort suit for the consequences of a personal injury or damage to property: only the injured person himself, or the owner of the damaged property himself, and not also persons having commercial links to the owner, such as employees or suppliers of a merchant whose store was burned down as a result of the negligence of a third party, the tort defendant. [ ] Since damage to property and even to person is a real cost and hence "economic," the doctrine would be better named the "commercial loss" doctrine. [ ]

One explanation for it is that a tort may have indirect consequences that are beneficial—in the example just given, to competitors of the burned-down store—as well as harmful, and since the tortfeasor is not entitled to sue for the benefits, neither should he have to pay for the losses. [ ] Another and less esoteric explanation is the desirability of confining remedies for contract-type losses to contract law. Suppliers injured in their pocketbook because of a fire at the shop of a retailer who buys and distributes their goods sustain the kind of purely business loss familiarly encountered in contract law, rather than the physical harm, whether to person or to property, with which tort law is centrally concerned. These suppliers can protect themselves from the loss caused them by the fire by buying business-loss insurance, by charging a higher price, or by including in their contract with the retailer a requirement that he buy a minimum quantity of goods from the supplier, regardless. The suppliers thus don't need a tort remedy. [ ]

This point has implications for commercial fraud as well as for business losses that are secondary to physical harms to person or property. Where there are well-developed contractual remedies, such as the remedies that the Uniform Commercial Code (in force in all U.S. states) provides for breach of warranty of the quality, fitness, or specifications of goods, there is no need to provide tort remedies for misrepresentation. The tort remedies would duplicate the contract remedies, adding unnecessary complexity to the law. Worse, the provision of these duplicative tort remedies would undermine contract law. That law has been shaped by a tension between a policy of making the jury the normal body for resolving factual disputes and the desire of parties to contracts to be able to rely on the written word and not be exposed to the unpredictable reactions of lay factfinders to witnesses who testify that the contract means something different from what it says. Many doctrines of contract law, such as the parol evidence and "four corners" rules, are designed to limit the scope of jury trial of contract disputes (another example is the statute of frauds). Tort law does not have these screens against the vagaries of the jury. In recognition of this omission, the "economic loss" doctrine in the form invoked by the district judge in this case on the authority of a growing body of case law illustrated by [ ], forbids commercial contracting parties (as distinct from consumers, and other individuals not engaged in business) to escalate their contract dispute into a charge of tortious misrepresentation if they could easily have protected themselves from the misrepresentation of which they now complain. The principle is well illustrated by Tatge v. Chambers & Owen, Inc., [579 N.W.2d 217 (Wis.1998)], a suit by a former employee claiming that the employer had misrepresented the employment contract to be terminable only for cause, rather than at will. The bearing of those representations could be fully considered in a suit for breach of contract.

The function of the economic-loss doctrine in confining contract parties to their contractual remedies is particularly well illustrated by cases involving product warranties, [ ]. If the seller makes an oral representation that is important to the buyer, the latter has only to insist that the seller embody that representation in a written warranty. The warranty will protect the buyer, who will have an adequate remedy under the Uniform Commercial Code if the seller reneges. To allow him to use tort law in effect to enforce an oral warranty would unsettle contracts by exposing sellers to the risk of being held liable by a jury on the basis of self-interested oral testimony and perhaps made to pay punitive as well as compensatory damages. This menace is averted by channeling disputes into warranty (contract) law, where oral warranties can be expressly disclaimed, or extinguished by operation of the parol evidence rule. UCC §§ 2–202, 2–316(1) and comment 2; 1 James J. White & Robert S. Summers, Uniform Commercial Code, § 12–4 (3d ed. 1988). It is true that, in principle, the cheapest way to prevent fraud is to punish the fraudfeasor; but in practice, owing to the ever-present possibility of legal error, the really cheapest way in some cases may be to place a burden of taking precautions on the potential victim. Cf. Alon Harel, "Efficiency and Fairness in Criminal Law: The Case for a Criminal Law Principle of Comparative Fault," 82 Calif. L. Rev. 1181 (1994).

Some of our cases describe the economic-loss doctrine in words that might seem to imply the abolition of the tort of misrepresentation (including deliberate fraud) in all cases in which the plaintiff and the defendant are business firms having a preexisting contractual relationship that had given rise to the fraud or other misrepresentation. [ ] But it is a disservice to courts, as well as a common source of erroneous predictions concerning the scope and direction of the law, to treat a judicial opinion as if it were a statute, every clause of which was Law. It is difficult to write a judicial opinion without making some general statements by way of background and explanation. But in a system of case law such statements can be misleading if carelessly lifted from the case-specific contexts in which they were originally uttered. That is why courts in assessing the binding effect of previous decisions distinguish between the dicta, which are the inessential parts of the opinion, and the holding.

If commercial fraud is to go completely by the boards, as a literal reading of some of the economic-loss cases might suggest, then prospective parties to contracts will be able to obtain legal protection against fraud only by insisting that the other party to the contract reduce all representations to writing, and so there will be additional contractual negotiations, contracts will be longer, and, in short, transaction costs will be higher. And the additional costs will be incurred in the making of every commercial contract, not just the tiny fraction that end up in litigation. Granted, there are costs of uncertainty from the possibility of falsely charging fraud when a contractual relationship sours, as it did in this case. But the fraud tort comes with safeguards against false claims, such as the requirement of pleading fraud with particularity and (in many though not all jurisdictions) a heightened burden of proof—clear and convincing evidence versus a bare preponderance of the evidence, the standard civil burden. [ ]

But the representations challenged in this case do not press against the boundaries of the economic-loss doctrine. For they are in the nature of warranties (remember that the plaintiff made warranty claims, which the judge sent to the jury), and we cannot think of a reason why the fact that the "product" warranted was a hybrid of a product and a service should affect the application of the doctrine. A genuine stumbling block to affirming on its basis, however, is the fact that its application to cases of intentional misrepresentation [in Wisconsin] is uncertain. . . . We need not choose. Amway has a solid alternative ground for affirmance: All-Tech failed to present any evidence of actionable misrepresentation. Some of the alleged misrepresentations were corrected before All-Tech bought its first TeleCharge phone, such as the misrepresentations that the phone could be installed on any business line and that regulatory approval of the service had been obtained in all 50 states. The victim of a misrepresentation about a product who learns the truth before he buys, but decides to buy the product anyway, cannot complain about the misrepresentation. [ ] Whatever he has relied on, it is not that.

Some of the representations were made not by Amway but by one of its distributors, at a trade meeting attended by All-Tech's principals. Amway distributors are independent contractors, [ ], rather than employees whose representations might bind their employer by force of the doctrine of respondeat superior. The distributor in question was describing his own experience in selling TeleCharge phones, and there is no evidence that he was speaking with Amway's actual or apparent authority or that Amway ratified and by ratifying adopted his remarks. In these circumstances, Amway was not legally responsible for them. [ ] An agent "cannot just bootstrap himself into a position where he can bind his principal." [ ] It would be absurd to hold a supplier to every representation made by distributors or dealers in its products— distributors or dealers who in the case of some suppliers, such as Amway, number in the thousands.

Many of Amway's alleged misrepresentations were either pure puffing (such as TeleCharge is "the best")—which is to say, empty superlatives on which no reasonable person would rely, [ ]—or meaningless sales patter, such as that Amway had put the same effort into developing this product as it did with its other products. Amway sells a vast array of products, and obviously doesn't expend the same absolute or proportional amount of money on the development of each one; no one could believe such a thing, as pointed out in [ ]. "There are some kinds of talk which no sensible man takes seriously, and if he does he suffers from his credulity." Vulcan Metals Co. v. Simmons Mfg. Co., 248 F. 853, 856 (2d Cir.1918)(L. Hand, J.). All-Tech doesn't claim to be run by the sort of naifs who got suckered into raising Chinchillas in the 1950s.

The TeleCharge service was new, and like many new services it ran into unexpected, and ultimately fatal, problems. As these problems surfaced, Amway would notify its distributors, including All-Tech. Despite a barrage of bad news, All-Tech continued buying TeleCharge phones. It could not have been relying on the alleged misrepresentations. All of them had either been corrected before All-Tech bought the phones or would not have misled a commercial purchaser. Or were not material, such as ITI's size—whether or not it was the largest company of its kind, the kind the parties call "alternative operator service," it was not a fly-by-night outfit incapable of providing the service for which Amway had contracted with it. Or were hypothetical: "If you charge the one dollar maximum access fee, with an average of only three billable long-distance calls a day, five days per week, 50 weeks per year, you may generate up to $750 a year from just one phone"—impeccable arithmetic, given the premises, which Amway did not warrant. Or were predictions that either were too vague to ground reasonable reliance or were not falsified. Or were not made at all, such as the representation that the phone could not be reprogrammed to work with another operator service besides ITI. There were, in short, no actionable misrepresentations.

All-Tech's alternative claim is promissory estoppel. The doctrine of promissory estoppel provides an alternative basis to consideration for treating a promise as a contractual undertaking. When applicable, which is to say when the promise is definite enough to induce a reasonable person to rely, [ ], the doctrine makes the promise enforceable.

Promises are usually forward-looking; one promises to do something, necessarily in the future. The promise that All-Tech stresses as the basis for its claim of promissory estoppel—that Amway had thoroughly researched the TeleCharge program before offering it to distributors—is not of that character. It warrants a past or existing condition rather than committing to some future action and is thus more precisely described as a warranty than as a promise. [ ] But a warranty is a type of promise—in this case a promise by Amway to pay for the consequences should the research that went into the development of TeleCharge not have been thorough after all. Metropolitan Coal Co. v. Howard, 155 F.2d 780, 784 (2d Cir.1946)(L. Hand, J.)(a warranty "amounts to a promise to indemnify the promisee for any loss if the fact warranted proves untrue, for obviously the promisor cannot control what is already in the past"); [ ].

Since a warranty can induce reasonable reliance, its breach can be the basis for a claim of promissory estoppel. [ ] But only in limited circumstances. A promisee cannot be permitted to use the doctrine to do an end run around the rule that puffing is not actionable as misrepresentation or around the parol evidence rule. [ ] That rule is as applicable to a suit on an oral warranty as to a suit on any other oral promise. The Uniform Commercial Code is explicit about this. UCC § 2–316(1) and comment 2; [ ].

The objections to AllTech's claim of promissory estoppel are related to our earlier point that the economic-loss doctrine serves to protect contract doctrines and to prevent the piling on of duplicative remedies. Promissory estoppel is meant for cases in which a promise, not being supported by consideration, would be unenforceable under conventional principles of contract law. When there is an express contract governing the relationship out of which the promise emerged, and no issue of consideration, there is no gap in the remedial system for promissory estoppel to fill. [ ] To allow it to be invoked becomes in those circumstances gratuitous duplication or, worse, circumvention of carefully designed rules of contract law. In our case the parties had a contract covering the relationship in the course and within the scope of which the alleged warranty of thorough research was made. This either was one of the warranties of the contract or it was not (by virtue of disclaimer, the puffing exemption, or the parol evidence rule). If it was not (and it was not), we cannot think of any reason for using the doctrine of promissory estoppel to resuscitate it. "Promissory estoppel is not a doctrine designed to give a party . . . a second bite at the apple in the event it fails to prove a breach of contract." [ ]

Affirmed.

NOTES AND QUESTIONS

1.   Does the distinction between "economic loss" and "commercial loss" help clarify the nature of the underlying doctrine that bars tort claims? Recall the discussion of the *Rardin* case, p. 682 supra. Which of the justifications for the doctrine presented here seem the strongest?

2.   Should the doctrine apply as well to cases of "commercial fraud" as to the area of secondary harms? Recall *Channel Master*, p. 1255 supra.

3.   At one point the court suggests that contract law has many more "screens" than tort law. Do you agree? Later, the opinion observes that the

tort law surrounding fraud claims has more screens than other tort claims. Is that sound?

4. The court expresses concern about the role of "legal error" in adjudication. How does that apply in this case?

5. How are the distinctions between promises and warranties relevant to the discussion? Is the distinction between statements of past or existing conditions and those relating to future conditions important? Are all of these statements by the court dicta?

6. Toward the end of the opinion the court suggests that a dispute over whether a contract was at will or for a term can be resolved in an action for breach of contract. There is, however, one significant contract area in which tort claims play a role.

A few courts have applied the tort of breach of the implied covenant of good faith and fair dealing in the employment context. At the outset, it is crucial to distinguish the tort of bad faith breach from the tort of wrongful discharge. The latter is an action that an employee may bring if he or she has been dismissed for refusing to participate in an immoral or illegal act or for asserting constitutional or statutory rights, as in Nees v. Hocks, 536 P.2d 512 (Or.1975)(employee fired for refusing to seek exemption from jury duty). Some states have adopted legislation to protect the jobs of "whistleblowers" and others. E.g., Fleming v. Correctional Healthcare Solutions, Inc., 751 A.2d 1035 (N.J.2000), protecting an employee under the state's Conscientious Employee Protective Act. In most states, as these cases suggest, the issue is not the reason for the firing but rather whether the action should be recognized at all. Underlying that concern may be the unease created by difficult cases like Gardner v. Loomis Armored Inc., 913 P.2d 377 (Wash.1996). Gardner was the driver of one of defendant's armored cars. One of the company's "fundamental" rules was that the driver must not leave the truck unattended. The rule was so strong that even if a police officer pulled the truck over, the driver was to show a sign saying that he would not exit the vehicle but would follow the officer to a police station. On the day in question, plaintiff's partner left the vehicle to make a scheduled stop at a bank. While alone, plaintiff observed a man with a knife chasing a woman he knew. The plaintiff left the truck, saved the woman, helped apprehend the man—and was fired for violating the company's rule. The court held that, although the rule was defensible and quite important, the discharge violated the state's policy. That policy was based on encouraging citizens to render aid to those facing life-threatening situations. Defendant argued that plaintiff could have used his radio or his horn to help. The court responded that the reasons for leaving the truck must be considered—such as a fire. By focusing on "the narrow public policy encouraging citizens to save human lives from life-threatening situations, we continue to protect employers from frivolous lawsuits."

Three concurrers observed that although the rule was normally sensible and reasonable for plaintiff's own safety and that of his partner, it "defies what I believe is true about human nature that anyone would be willing to watch a person die in order to comply with a company safety rule." A dissenter accepted the defendant's argument that its rule "actually serves the interests of society, is consistent with public policy and therefore cannot be the basis of a claim for wrongful termination in violation of public policy." He also observed that the rule will now be drawn into question in all future cases: What if the driver leaves the truck in the reasonable, but mistaken, belief that another is in mortal danger or if there is a danger but it is not life-threatening? What if the belief is honest but not reasonable? Do the dissenter's concerns suggest doubt about the majority's analysis?

INDEX

References are to Pages

Nuclear power plant operations, Price-
    Anderson Act, 884
Private nuisance, 695
Public utilities, power failure liabilities
    Economic harm, 324
    Personal injuries, 166
Standard of care, 44, 47
Stray voltage, 695

ELECTRONIC RECORDS
See Computer Records, this index

EMERGENCIES
    See also Rescuers, this index
Good Samaritan laws, 70, 165
Intentional torts, private necessity
    defense, 968
911 services, 233

**EMERGENCY MEDICAL
    TREATMENT AND ACTIVE
    LABOR ACT**
Generally, 165

EMOTIONAL DISTRESS
Intentional Infliction of Emotional
    Distress, this index
Negligent infliction. See Emotional Harm,
    this index

EMOTIONAL HARM
    Generally, 261 et seq.
Airline cases, 267
Airline crash v. automobile crash fears,
    266
Asbestos cases, 269
Attorney malpractice, 308
Bodily injury or sickness distinguished,
    265
Bystander claims
        Generally, 293
        Childbirth incidents, 284
        Parental anguish, 282, 286
        Pet cases, 285
        Relationship to victim, 291
        Severity, 290
        Zone of danger, 292
Cancer, this index
Child sexual abuse, 293
Closeness of relationship to accident
    victim, 288
Consortium, negligent interference with,
    294
Corpse mistreatment, 284
Culpability of defendants conduct, 275
Damages, 261
Death, emotional distress preceding, 267
Defamation, this index
Direct and indirect harms, 284
Direct v. bystander claims
        Generally, 293
        Bystander claims, above
Duty
        Generally, 268
        Physical symptomology, emotional
            harm without, 266, 271
Economic harm compared, 299

Fear of cancer, 269, 275
Fear of harm
        Generally, 261
        Reasonable fear, 265, 280
Federal Employers' Liability Act, 269
Fright, 261
HIV fear, 275, 279
Impact rule, 261, 266, 269
Kidnapped infant, 281
Negligent infliction of emotional distress
        Generally, 261 et seq.
        See also Intentional Infliction
            of Emotional Distress,
            this index
        Intentional infliction compared, 922
        Municipal and state liability, 235
        Severity, 276, 278
Negligent interference with consortium,
    294
Observance of accident, 287
Parental anguish
        Generally, 282
        Kidnapped baby, 281
        Switched babies, 284
Pet cases, 285
Physical impact rule, 261, 266, 269
Physical manifestation requirements, 280
Physical proximity to accident, 287
Pregnancy
        Generally, 266, 275
        Injury to child during delivery, 284
Pre-impact fright, 268
Products liability emotional distress
    claims, 574
Property losses, emotional distress claims
    based on, 284, 323
Proximate cause, 262, 399
Reasonable person standard, 285
Reasonableness of fear, 265, 280
Relationship to victim
        Generally, 287
        Bystander claims, 291
        Unmarried couples, 293
Sensory perception requirement, 290
Serious mental distress, 278
Severity
        Bystander claims, 291
        Negligent infliction, 276, 278
Special relationship analysis of duty, 279
Strict liability emotional distress claims,
    533
Switched babies, 284
Toxic exposures, 269
Unmarried couples, 293
Window of concern, HIV exposure, 275
Wrongful birth, 334
Wrongful death, 267
Zone of danger
        Generally, 270, 274
        Bystander claims, 292

EMPLOYERS
        See also Civil Rights
            Torts, this index
        Generally, 647